Also by Robert M. Parker, Jr.

BORDEAUX: THE DEFINITIVE GUIDE FOR THE WINES
PRODUCED SINCE 1961

THE WINES OF THE RHÔNE VALLEY AND PROVENCE

PARKER'S WINE BUYER'S GUIDE

BURGUNDY

A COMPREHENSIVE GUIDE
TO THE PRODUCERS,
APPELLATIONS, AND WINES

ROBERT M. PARKER, JR.
Author and Publisher of *The Wine Advocate*

Maps by
JEANYEE WONG
Drawings by
CHRISTOPHER WORMELL

Simon and Schuster
New York London Toronto Sydney Tokyo Singapore

Simon and Schuster
Simon & Schuster Building
Rockefeller Center
1230 Avenue of the Americas
New York, New York 10020

Designed by Levavi & Levavi, Inc.
Manufactured in the United States of America

1   3   5   7   9   10   8   6   4   2

Library of Congress Cataloging-in-Publication Data
Parker, Robert M.
Burgundy: a comprehensive guide to the producers, appellations,
and wines/Robert M. Parker, Jr.; drawings by Christopher Wormell.
p.   cm.
Includes bibliographical references and index.
1. Wine and wine making—France—Burgundy.   I. Title.
TP553.P373   1990
641.2'2'09444—dc20   90-38342
                                                                          CIP
ISBN 0-671-63378-3

This book is dedicated to Pat, Maia, Sarah, Cece,
Bubba, and to my dear friend, Bob Lescher.

ACKNOWLEDGMENTS

I would like to express my gratitude to the following people whose assistance, cooperation, and support have been immensely appreciated.

Jacques d'Angerville, Jim Arsenault, Eve Auchincloss, Bruce Bassin, Ruth Bassin, Michel Bettane, Lalou Bize-Leroy, Christopher Cannan, Jeanne-Marie de Champs, Louis-Marc Chevignard, Bob Cline, Geoffrey Connor, Alain Corcia, Jane Crawford, Bill Deutsch, Sherwood Deutsch, Michael Dresser, Robert Drouhin, Stanley Dry, Georges Duboeuf, Hubrecht Duijker, Paul Evans, Anne Faiveley, François Faiveley, Bob Fiore, Joel Fleischman, Michael Franklin, André Gagey, Pierre-Henri Gagey, Steve Gilbertson, Bernard Godec, Michael Goldstein, Madame J. Gros, Daniel Haas, Robert Haas, Josué Harari, Alexandra Harding, Brenda Hayes, Thomas Hoving, Tom Hurst, Henri Jayer, Ed Jonna, Alain Junguenet, Robert Kacher, Allen Krasner, Carole Lalli, Jacques Lardière, Philippe Leclerc, Vincent Leflaive, Susan Lescher, Eliot Mackey, Eve Metz, Frank Metz, Jay Miller, M. Mongeard, Sidney Moore, the late Dr. Georges Mugneret, Mitchell Nathanson, Jill Norman, Bob Orenstein, Miranda Page-Wood, Joan Passman, Allen Peacock, Frank Polk, Martha Reddington, Neal Rosenthal, Christophe Roumier, Jean-Marie Roumier, Charles Rousseau, Tom Ryder, Ed Sands, the Sangoy family, Martine Saunier, Bob Schindler, Jacques Seysses, Ernie Singer, Elliott Staren, Jean Trapet, Peter Vezan, Aubert de Villaine, Jean-Claude Vrinat, Steve Wallace, Becky Wasserman, Karen Weinstock, Joseph Weinstock, Larry Wiggins, Jeanyee Wong, and Gérard Yvernault.

CONTENTS

PART ONE: THE GROWERS AND PRODUCERS OF BURGUNDY   61

Domaine Bertrand Ambroise • Bernard Amiot • Pierre Amiot et Fils • Amiot-Bonfils • Domaine Robert Ampeau • Domaine Pierre André • Domaine Marquis d'Angerville • Domaine Arlaud Père et Fils • Domaine de l'Arlot • Domaine Comte Armand • Domaine Arnoux Père et Fils • Domaine Robert Arnoux • Auvigue-Burrier-Revel • Domaine Bernard Bachelet et Fils • Domaine Denis Bachelet • Domaine Jean-Claude Bachelet • Domaine Bachelet-Ramonet • Château Bader-Mimeur • Domaine Raymond Ballot-Millot et Fils • Domaine André Bart • Domaine Gaston Barthod-Noëllat • Domaine L. Bassy • Château du Basty • Domaine Philippe Batacchi • Domaine Charles et Paul Bavard • Paul Beaudet • Château de Beauregard • Domaine Adrien Belland • Domaine Joseph Belland • Domaine Gérard Berger • Domaine Bernard • Domaine Alain Bernillon • Domaine Pierre Bernollin • Domaine René Berrod-Les Roches du Vivier • Domaine Bersan et Fils • Domaine Bertagna • Domaine Denis Berthaut • Domaine Pierre Bertheau • Domaine Besancenot-Mathouillet • Domaine André Besson • Albert Bichot • Domaine Léon Bienvenu • Domaine Billard-Gonnet • Domaine Billaud-Simon • Domaine Bitouzet-Prieur

CONTENTS

A List of the Maps of Burgundy

Strawberry, cherry, raspberry, and plum predominate in the young wine, but as it ages, the cherry becomes more scented, the plums turn to prunes, chocolate and woodsmoke and figs mingle with truffles and over-hung game and the decayed stink of old vegetables.

—*Oz Clarke*
Sainsbury's Regional Wine Guide

Fine, mature burgundy is velvety, usually quite alcoholic, often heady. And even young, immature burgundy does not have the swingeingly tannic dryness, the astringency of red bordeaux.

—*Michael Broadbent*
The Great Vintage Wine Book

Burgundy has great genius. It does wonders within its period; it does all except to keep up in the race; it is short-lived.

—*George Meredith*
The Egoist

Great burgundy smells of shit. It is most surprising, but the French recognized long ago, "ça sent la merde" and "ça sent le purin" being common expressions of the Côte.

—*Anthony Hanson*
Burgundy

Burgundy has the advantage—to which a young palate is particularly sensitive—of a clear, direct appeal, immediately pleasing and easy to comprehend on a primary level. . . . Burgundy is a lovely thing when you can get anybody to buy it for you.

—*A. J. Liebling*
Between Meals

Burgundy is an easier wine to taste, judge, and understand than bordeaux.

—*Hugh Johnson*
Modern Encyclopedia of Wine

I rejoiced in Burgundy. How can I describe it. For centuries every language has been strained to define its beauty, and has produced only wild conceits or the stock epithets of the trade.

—*Evelyn Waugh*
Brideshead Revisited

INTRODUCTION

The legendary wine-producing area in eastern France known as Burgundy encompasses five basic regions. The most renowned and prestigious wines emerge from either Chablis or the Côte d'Or, which encompasses the two famous golden slopes called the Côte de Beaune and Côte de Nuits. Immediately south of the Côte d'Or are the potentially promising, largely unexplored Côte Chalonnaise and the vast, well-known and exploited Mâconnais area, both of which are within the geographic department the French call Saône-et-Loire. Lastly, there is Beaujolais, the most southern viticultural region, ironically located within the Department of the Rhône, but historically considered part of Burgundy.

The continental climate of Burgundy is significantly different from the maritime climate of Bordeaux, which is located on the Atlantic Ocean in western France. While the microclimates of Bordeaux are shaped by the ocean to the west and the giant Gironde River that divides the region in half, there are no rivers in Burgundy that significantly affect the climate. Burgundy, as a result, suffers more than Bordeaux from the significant rainfall that is often carried on the prevailing west winds that buffet the area. There are also devastating hailstorms. While such storms are not uncommon in Bordeaux, in Burgundy they can reach catastrophic proportions, particularly when triggered by the high heat and humidity of August. The hailstones cause the vines to shed their foliage, scar the grape skins, and promote the growth of rot. These hailstorms are particularly common in the northern half of the Côte d'Or, particularly in the Côte de Nuits. Balancing these negative weather factors is the northerly latitude of Burgundy, which provides for longer hours of daylight than Bordeaux. Anyone who has spent a summer evening in Burgundy will undoubtedly remember the 10:00–10:30 P.M. sunset. As a result, Burgundy receives almost as much sunlight as Bordeaux, located hundreds of miles to the southwest with an undoubtedly hotter, more stable maritime climate. Burgundy, in order to attain a top vintage, must have dry, sunny (not necessarily torrid) days from the beginning of September onward. Historically, Burgundy's finest vintages have been those when July and August were dry and warm, and September spectacular. While windy, cold, damp weather in June often reduces the size of the crop (Chablis has notoriously unpredictable weather in late spring and is particularly vulnerable), poor weather early will have no bearing on the vintage's quality if July, August, and September are generally dry and warm. Of these three months, September is the most important because cold or wet weather during this month will dilute the grapes, lower acidities and sugar, and promote the growth of rot. No wonder the vignerons in Burgundy say, *"Juin fait la quantité et septembre fait la qualité,"* meaning June makes the quantity and September makes the quality.

When Mother Nature cooperates, the Pinot Noir and Chardonnay grapes excel in such a frosty northerly latitude due to the kimmeridge clay/limestone soil. In Chablis, this soil and its cousin, the portlandian limestone, are ideal for Chardonnay. The famed Côte d'Or, which for many connoisseurs of Burgundy is that region's beginning and end, is essentially a limestone ridge representing the eastern edge of a calcareous plateau that empties into the Saône River basin. The northern half, the Côte de Nuits, has an easterly orientation that gradually shifts toward a more southeasterly exposure. This ridge runs for about 31 miles between Marsannay and Santenay. In the Côte Chalonnaise, the limestone ridge begins to break up into a chain of small hills that have limestone subsoils with clay/sand topsoils that are occasionally enriched with iron deposits. However, the underlying limestone strata are still present and continue not only through the Côte Chalonnaise but also through the pastoral, rolling hills of the neighboring Mâconnais region, giving way finally to the granite-based soils of the Beaujolais region.

Each of Burgundy's five major wine-producing regions possesses an identity and character that I have attempted to capture in this book. With a production of nearly 1,200,000 cases of Chardonnay a year, Chablis, the most northern of Burgundy's famed wine regions, perplexingly remains a mystery wine. No doubt the multitude of styles of wine produced, in addition to the fact that the name Chablis has been reprehensibly bastardized throughout the world, have combined to cause many consumers to turn their noses at the mention of Chablis. Nevertheless, there are seven Grands Crus of Chablis that are capable of producing hauntingly intense wines with extraordinary precision and clarity to their flavors. There are also more than two dozen principal Premiers Crus, several meriting Grand Cru status, and a number undeserving of their Premier Cru status. All of this translates into confusion—making Chablis the most enigmatic wine region of Burgundy.

The Côte d'Or, or golden slope (so named not because the wines produced there are worth their weight in gold, but because of the deep golden brown color of the vineyards in autumn), is surely the most thoroughly scrutinized and inspected stretch of real estate in the world. Historically, the monks of the Abbey of Cîteaux first exploited these hills. But over the last 150 years, the French government has examined every field, valley, crevice, and outcropping, and determined that only 31 vineyards in a 31-mile stretch of limestone are capable of producing Grand Cru red and white burgundy. Just over 300 of these fields were deemed suitable enough to produce Premier Cru red and white burgundies. If the French government had not chosen to painstakingly inspect and classify the tens of thousands of fields that make up this golden slope, and if the vast estates of the church and wealthy landowners had not been dismantled during France's 1789 revolution, today's fragmented world of Burgundy might resemble Bordeaux, with its huge châteaux and giant vineyards.

Why Burgundy, and in particular the Côte d'Or, is so excruciatingly difficult to comprehend is best illustrated by the complexity of one of the golden slope's most hallowed Grand Cru vineyards, Clos Vougeot. This 124-acre vineyard has 77 different proprietors. Some of them sell their wines to large brokers to be blended with Clos Vougeot from other producers. At least three dozen growers estate-bottle their production. In short, the consumer is confronted with nearly four dozen different versions of Clos Vougeot. All of it is entitled to Grand Cru status, all of it is frighteningly expensive, yet only a small percentage of the wines could ever be described as sublime or celestial. Imagine, if you can, 77 different growers/producers making wine at the famous 125-acre Château Ducru-Beaucaillou, or the 120-acre Château Latour in Bordeaux. Clos Vougeot is the Côte d'Or's most distressingly chaotic vineyard to fathom, but its fragmented ownership and enormous range of wine quality typify Burgundy.

South of the Côte d'Or is the Côte Chalonnaise, today's best source for reasonably priced, well-made red and white burgundies. In the nineties consumers will need to take advantage of this viticultural region if they are intent on drinking affordable French red or white burgundy. Two-thirds of the vineyards are planted with Pinot Noir, a grape that has demonstrated a fondness for the clay subsoils of the area. The top Chardonnay vineyards are planted in chalky, limestone soils. This is an exciting area to watch as evidenced by the significant investments made in the Côte Chalonnaise by several of the Côte d'Or's leading producers.

The Mâconnais region lies to the south of the Côte Chalonnaise. It is a pastoral landscape with small ridges broken up by tree-topped hillsides. It is primarily white wine country as the chalky, limestone soil there is ideal for producing fresh, exuberant whites from the Chardonnay grape. Red wine is also made in the Mâconnais, but it is generally insipid and feeble.

When the hillsides of the Mâconnais turn into small mountains, blanketed with vineyards and ranging in height from 2,300 to 3,500 feet, you are in Beaujolais. The landscape is not the only major change in evidence here; the red wine grape also changes from Pinot Noir to Gamay. In the sandy, stony, schistous soil of these hillsides, the world's fruitiest, freshest, and most exuberant red wine is produced in oceanic quantities, and is generally drunk within hours of purchase. I have never been able to comprehend why Beaujolais is considered part of Burgundy (officially it is within France's Department of the Rhône), but historically it is.

The grapes of Burgundy are well known. The great reds are the result of only one grape—the Pinot Noir, the most fickle and difficult grape from which to cultivate and produce wine. While it buds and ripens early, its thin, fragile skin makes it highly vulnerable to rot and mildew. Although it likes warmth, it will shed much of its aromatic character, flavor, dimension, and precision when it is grown in too hot a climate. It is a grape that can offer an astoundingly complex bouquet and flavor, but rarely provides great color. To those weaned on Bordeaux or California Cabernet, red burgundy must indeed look suspiciously feeble. However, new techniques, including the controversial extended cold maceration prior to fermentation, seem to suggest that the Pinot Noir can produce deeply colored wines under certain circumstances.

In Burgundy, if the Pinot Noir fails, the red wine producers have no recourse to other grapes. Contrast that with the situation in Bordeaux where four major red grape varietals may be employed in a number of different proportions. If the Merlot crop is diluted because of rain, the percentage of Cabernet Sauvignon can be increased, or other grapes, such as Cabernet Franc or Petit Verdot, can be used to augment the blend. In short, intelligent blending can still produce a very fine wine if one varietal fails. In Burgundy, however, the grower lives or dies with the Pinot Noir.

The only other red wine grape to be found in Burgundy is the Gamay. It is widely planted in the Mâconnais area and generally produces vapid wines. However, it is responsible for the delicious, crunchy, fruity, exuberant red wines of Beaujolais. It is not capable of producing long-lived wines, although a handful of producers who possess old vines and discourage high yields can make Beaujolais, particularly from the cru Moulin-à-Vent, that can last up to a decade. For the majority of producers, however, the Gamay's strengths are its prolific yields, and its ability, when fermented via the carbonic maceration method, to routinely turn out extremely fresh, profitable wines that can be drunk within months of the grape harvest.

As for Burgundy's white wine grapes, the Chardonnay is king. The great white burgundies are the standard-bearers for the rest of the world. The tiny fields of Corton-Charlemagne, Puligny-Montrachet, Chassagne-Montrachet, and Meursault produce wines that are emulated by many, equalled by few, surpassed by none. The Chardonnay grape thrives in Burgundy's limestone soil and, unlike the Pinot Noir, seems capable of producing decent wine even during exceptionally wet harvest months. All of the growers and producers acknowledge that it is easy to make good Chardonnay, but exceedingly rare to produce compelling, great Chardonnay.

The white wine grape Aligoté is also found in Burgundy. At its worst, it is lean, mean, acidic, and nasty. At its best, Aligoté represents an excellent value and delicious wine at a budget price. Pinot Blanc is occasionally planted. It often tends to be too heavy, but there are some good examples, particularly in the Côte de Nuits. There is also Pinot Gris, frequently called Pinot Beurot. Personally, I would like to see more Pinot Gris made in Burgundy since the examples I have tasted are fascinating.

A BRIEF HISTORY
OF BURGUNDY

Geologists believe the limestone shelf now called the Côte d'Or was formed over 150 million years ago, well before man appeared on the scene. During what is called the Jurassic Period (between 135 and 195 million years ago), the geological face of Burgundy began to take shape. Formed during this epoch were the petrified remains of sea life, compressed over time with a calcareous mudstone, as well as the rock that resulted from the precipitation of lime from the seawater that then covered Burgundy. The limestone rocks sprinkled with marlstone comprise the backbone of the various hillsides and most renowned vineyard sites of not only the Côte d'Or, but also the slopes of Chablis, the Côte Chalonnaise, and the Maconnais.

Viticulture is believed to have been launched in Burgundy by either the Greeks or the Romans. There was a thriving Greek settlement at Marseilles around 600 B.C., leading some observers to surmise that the Greeks, travelling through the Rhône Valley, were responsible for the vineyards planted along the hillsides of the Rhône River as well as those further north in Burgundy. Other observers claim that viticulture was brought to Burgundy by the Romans, whose influence can be seen in the architectural ruins that archaeologists have unearthed. In 52 B.C. Julius Caesar destroyed the 250,000-man army of Gaul led by Vercingetorix, thus consolidating Roman rule. Along with Caesar's legions and his conquest of Gaul came a degree of stability and civilization that provided the necessary economy to foster the production of wine. It would be unlikely that the Romans, who adored wine, would not encourage vineyard development and wine production in a territory so far from their home vineyards. However, the absence of any hard evidence makes such theories conjectural.

While the Greeks or Romans probably planted the first vineyards in Burgundy, it was the advent of Christianity and the flourishing of the church that brought Burgundy to its ascendency. The Benedictine order of Cluny in the Mâconnais, founded in the tenth century by the Duc d'Aquitaine, was the dominant monastic order of Burgundy. Historians have long wondered whether the Duc d'Aquitaine's gift to the Benedictine monks of Cluny was inspired by bad-faith power politics, or was simply a charitable donation. Clearly the Duc realized that the Benedictines controlled more than 1,500 monasteries throughout Europe and were as powerful an entity as any government of the time. Until the French Revolution at the end of the eighteenth century, the Abbey of Cluny was one of the greatest religious centers in Europe as well as an immense political and economic power.

In 1098 A.D., another Benedictine order, the Cistercians, was established at the Abbey of Cîteaux in a desolate area just to the east of the village of Nuits St.-Georges. This village, and its wine, was to be unwaveringly tied to the influence and prosperity of the church until the French Revolution of 1789.

The new abbey at Cîteaux was governed according to the fundamental teachings of St. Benedict. The monks' religious enthusiasm and work ethic were renowned. They believed in a spartan lifestyle and physically exhausting hard labor. This philosophy apparently led to the Cistercians' decision to cultivate the poor, infertile, rocky soil of what today is known as the Côte d'Or. This stretch of limestone hillsides had long proved unsuitable for crops, but the Cistercians, with their commitment to back-breaking labor, believed the vine could be cultivated and quality wine produced. While it may have been just good fortune, it seems more likely that the shrewd monks realized all too well that the production of quality wine, and its presence on the finest tables of Europe, was of greater influence than their most articulate and persuasive diplomat.

The expansion and empire building of the ecclesiastic orders in Burgundy was impressive, even by today's standards. In 1141 A.D. the nuns of the Cistercian Abbey of Notre Dame du Tart purchased a vineyard in Morey St.-Denis which became known as the Clos de Tart. It remained under their control until the French Revolution. The Cistercians also launched a branch of their order at the Clos de Vougeot. They had no way of knowing that hundreds of years later that particular vineyard would become part of an elaborate appellation system imposed on all of the best winemaking regions of France. France's appellation system, inaugurated in the twentieth century, established guidelines for the production of wine, a qualitative hierarchy based on a vineyard's potential, as well as the price for which the wine would sell. It was considered a revolutionary concept, but in hindsight, hardly original. For example, the monks had their own notions about the quality of wine from their vineyards at Clos de Vougeot. The wine from the lower slopes of the Clos de Vougeot was called the Cuvées des Moines (the cuvée for the monks). The wine from the superior middle slopes was called Cuvées des Rois (or cuvée for the kings), and the wine from the top slopes (the finest parcels) of the Clos de Vougeot (which now abut the neighboring Grands Crus of Musigny and Grands Echézeaux) was called the Cuvée des Papes (cuvée for the popes). One of the most frequently heard arguments today is that the lower, flat ground of the Clos de Vougeot should not be entitled to Grand Cru status as it is incapable of making wine as profound as that from the top slopes. The monks, with their three separate cuvées of Clos Vougeot, apparently realized this eight centuries ago.

These religious orders controlled much of the wine that was shipped to the government in Paris, principally because France's other renowned viticultural region, Bordeaux, was at that time controlled by the English. The market for claret was in London, not Paris.

The height of Burgundy's power, historically referred to as the Golden Age, was from the middle of the fourteenth century to the middle of the fifteenth century. During this era, the great dukes of Burgundy controlled not only Burgundy, but also the majority of northern France and large portions of what is now Belgium, the Netherlands, and Luxembourg. This period witnessed an extraordinary flourishing of art, architecture, and music. The reputation the dukes of Burgundy had for enjoying all things fine and expensive has been largely unsurpassed, even by the most materialistic, excessive dictators of the twentieth century. Under the dukes, the huge monastic orders prospered. They were the beneficiaries of large land grants, and were encouraged by the dukes to build great abbeys and cathedrals. To no one's surprise, the church's chief worldly export, wine, prospered as well.

There were four great dukes during this one-hundred-year "eat, drink, and be merry" reign of good fortune. Philip the Bold (1364–1404), the first of these powerful dukes, obviously possessed a fine palate because in 1395 he ordered the Gamay grape to be pulled up and replaced by Pinot Noir. Philip was followed by his son, John the Fearless (1404–1419), who was assassinated by his political opponents. He was succeeded by Philip the Good (1419–1467). Primarily known as the duke who turned over France's greatest heroine, Joan of Arc, to the English, Philip was a staunch defender and aggressive promoter of the wines of Burgundy. In 1441, he declared that the flat, poorly drained fields surrounding Dijon were legally off limits for planting Pinot Noir. He was also reputed to have frequently claimed that Burgundy was far superior to its rival to the southwest, Bordeaux. Philip the Good named Nicolas Rolin as his Chancellor. When Rolin died in 1443, he had amassed a considerable estate, which he bequeathed to the Hôtel Dieu in Beaune. Today, this building, part of the Hospices de Beaune, is a hospital that survives on money from the sale of wine produced from donated vineyards. Burgundy's power and influence reached its zenith under the last of the great dukes, Charles the Bold (1467–1477). Charles' undoing was his unending belligerence. When he was killed in battle in 1477 and his army destroyed, the era in which the dukes of Burgundy had enjoyed such great wealth, power, and independence came to an end.

I suspect modern-day Burgundy bears little resemblance to the Burgundy of the great dukes. The French Revolution of 1789 fundamentally altered the landscape of Burgundy, tearing apart most of the gigantic wine estates owned by the wealthy and the monastic orders. Subsequently, the Napoleonic-Sallic Code increased the fragmentation of Burgundy's vineyards. This code required that upon the death of a parent, the land be divided equally among all sons. With each new generation, Burgundy's lands became more and more fragmented, each parcel of land owned by a different person. Today's Burgundy is, therefore, distressingly difficult to grasp and comprehend. This multiple ownership of the same vineyard reaches its preposterous, dizzyingly frustrating absurdity with the great vineyard of Clos Vougeot, which possesses 124 acres and 77-plus landowners. One hardly needs to be reminded of the infinite number of variations in quality that can occur from the same vineyard when the wine is made by as many as six dozen different producers.

In the late nineteenth century, Burgundy was ravaged by the phylloxera epidemic that devastated all of Europe's vineyards. While Burgundy did escape serious damage during World War I, the area was occupied by Germany during World War II. In late 1944 and early 1945, there were some small but fierce battles between the Allied forces and the retreating Germans, particularly in the Côte de Beaune. An endearing story of a French commander has emerged from the skirmishes of the last years of World War II. The commander apparently delayed his attack on the retreating Germans for fear of damaging the best Premier Cru and Grand Cru vineyards of Chassagne-Montrachet, Puligny-Montrachet, and Meursault. When he was subsequently apprised that the Germans were occupying only the lower slopes, or those vineyards not entitled to Premier Cru or Grand Cru status, he immediately ordered his soldiers to attack the German positions.

HOW TO USE
THIS BOOK

In order to facilitate the reader's understanding of the world's most complicated wine region, I have divided the balance and heart of this book into three closely related parts. The first and most important part of this trilogy is an alphabetical listing of the major as well as many minor producers, the wines they produce, and an overview of the quality and style of wine that emerge from their cellars. One thing I have irrefutably learned in the years of research that went into this book is that it is the grower/producer who makes all the difference in Burgundy. Without a thorough understanding of who are the better producers, there is absolutely no possibility of finding the best bottles of Santenay, Mâcon-Villages, Moulin-à-Vent, Chambertin, etc.

The second part of the book addresses the different appellations of Burgundy, starting in the north with Chablis and working south through the Côte d'Or, Côte Chalonnaise, the Mâconnais, and concluding with Beaujolais. I have tried to highlight the most salient features of each Villages or appellation, pointing out those producers who merit the most

attention for their exemplary efforts. At the same time, I have chosen
not to ignore many famous producers whose commitment to quality
leaves a great deal to be desired. I have also been cognizant of the
need, where possible, to point out the best values. At least in the Côte
d'Or, burgundy is not a wine that one associates with the word "bargain." However, certain Villages do satisfy both the palate and the
purse. The sketches of the different Villages and appellations supple-
ment the information about the specific growers. These village portraits
are designed to give the reader a basic understanding of what to expect
from each area's wines. I have not ignored the region's best restaurants
and hotels, because Burgundy is one of the most fascinating and rewarding areas of the world to visit. It has as many art treasures and
architectural wonders as any part of France. It is also France's gastronomic center, and possesses what I consider the best cooking available
in a country known the world over for its exacting culinary standards. I
believe the restaurants and hotels add a dimension to the book that
allows the visitor to share some of the same wonderful experiences my
wife and I have enjoyed over the years.

The third section of this trilogy is the assessment of vintages from
1945 through 1989. Specific tasting notes are provided for the wines
from the vintages of 1988, 1987, 1986, 1985, and 1983. In a real sense,
only the tasting notes for 1988, 1987, 1986, and 1985 are of any practical
use since the wines from the other vintages have, for all intents and
purposes, long disappeared from the marketplace. Lamentably, I think
that most of the best 1985s have disappeared as well. It is important to
share these tasting notes in order to demonstrate to the reader how I
thought the wines were showing, what they tasted like, and how they
fared vis-à-vis their peer group. There are also summaries of the other
vintages, including the most prominent and most disappointing wines.

EVALUATING WINES

How I evaluate wines has been well documented in my other writings,
but it is important that it be restated.

It goes without saying that in evaluating wines professionally, proper
glasses and correct serving temperature of the wine must be prerequi-
sites to any objective and meaningful tasting. Traditionally, the best
glasses for critical tasting have been those approved by the International Standards Organization. Called the ISO glass, it is tulip shaped
and has been designed for tasting. However, in my office I have begun
to use new glasses developed in France several years ago. Called "Les
Impitoyables" (the pitiless), they are without question the finest tasting

glasses ever designed. Much larger than the ISO glass, the Impitoyables glasses exaggerate the wine's bouquet, making flaws or defects much easier to spot. They are not good glasses to drink from because their opening is so narrow, but for critical evaluation, they have no equals. As for the temperature of the wine, 60°–62° F is best for red and white burgundies. If the temperature is too warm, the bouquet becomes diffuse and the taste muddled and flat. If the temperature is too cold, there is no discernible bouquet and the flavors are completely locked in by the chilling effect on the wine.

When I examine a wine critically, there is both a visual and physical examination. Against a white background the wine is first given a visual exam for its brilliance, richness, and intensity of color. For red burgundies color is significantly less important than it is for Bordeaux, Rhônes, or California Cabernets. However, all the great vintages of red burgundy, when young, traditionally share a rich, medium ruby color, whereas the poorer vintages often have weaker, less intense ruby colors due to poor weather and rain. Certainly, in 1978, 1985, and 1988 the general color of the red wines was moderately dark. In 1982, 1984, and 1986 it was medium to light ruby.

In looking at an older wine, the rim of the wine next to the glass should be examined for amber, orange, rusty, and brown colors. These are signs of maturity and are normal. When they appear in a good vintage of a serious red burgundy under 3 or 4 years old something is awry. For example, young wines that have been sloppily made and exposed to unclean barrels or air will mature at an accelerated rate and take on the look of old wines when young. Grey rot, a common problem in Burgundy, particularly in vintages such as 1983 and 1986, will cause a 3- or 4-year-old burgundy to rapidly lose its color and take on a brownish orange hue. The rot eats away at the coloring matter, and the more rampant it is in a wine, the quicker the wine will lose its color.

In addition to looking at the color of the wines, I examine the "legs" of the wine, which are the tears or residue of the wine that run down the inside of the glass. Rich vintages tend to have "good legs" because the grapes are rich in glycerols and alcohol-producing sugar, giving the wine a viscosity that causes this "tearing" effect. Examples of vintages that produced wines with good to excellent "legs" would be 1978, 1985, 1988, and 1989.

After the visual examination is completed, the actual physical examination of the wine takes place. The physical exam is composed of two parts: the smell of the wine, which depends on the olfactory senses, and the taste of the wine, which is tested on the palate. After swirling a wine, the nose must be placed into the glass (not the wine) to smell the aromas that the wine is exuding. This is an extremely critical step because the aroma of the wine will tell the examiner the ripeness and richness of the underlying fruit, the state of maturity, and whether there is anything unclean or suspicious about the wine. No responsible professional taster understates the significance of a wine's aromas. Émile Peynaud, in his classic book on wine tasting, *Le Gout du Vin* (Bordas, 1983), states that there are nine principal categories of wine aromas. They are:

1. animal odors: smells of game, beef, venison;
2. balsamic odors: smells of pine trees, resin, vanilla;
3. woody odors: smells of new wood of oak barrels;
4. chemical odors: smells of acetone, mercaptan, yeasts, hydrogen sulfide, lactic and fermentation odor;
5. spicy odors: smells of pepper, cloves, cinnamon, nutmeg, ginger, truffles, anise, mint;
6. empyreumatic odors: smells of crème brulée, smoke, toast, leather, coffee;
7. floral odors: smells of flowers, violets, roses, lilacs, jasmine;
8. fruity odors: smells of blackcurrants, raspberries, cherries, plums, apricots, peaches, figs;
9. vegetable odors: smells of herbs, tea, mushrooms, vegetables.

The presence or absence of any of these aromas, their intensity, their complexity, their persistence, all serve to create the bouquet or nose of a wine that can be said to be distinguished and interesting, or flawed and simple.

Once the wine's aroma has been examined thoroughly, the wine is simultaneously tasted and inhaled to release the aromas. The weight, richness, depth, balance, and length of a wine are apparent from the tactile impression the wine leaves on the palate. Sweetness is experienced on the tip of the tongue, saltiness just behind the tongue's tip, acidity on the sides, and bitterness at the back. Most professional tasters will spit the wine out, although some wine is swallowed in the process. The finish or length of a wine, its ability to give off aromas and flavors even though it is no longer on the palate, is the major difference between a good young wine and a great young wine. When the flavor and the aroma of the wine seem to last and last on the palate, it is usually a great, rich wine that has just been tasted. The compelling wines from great vintages are always characterized by a purity, opulence, richness, depth, and ripeness of grapes. When such wines also have sufficient tannin and acidity, a good balance is struck. It is these characteristics that separate many a great 1985 or 1978 from a good 1987 or 1980.

RATING THE PRODUCERS AND GROWERS

Who's who in the world of wine becomes readily apparent after years of tasting and visiting the vineyards and wine cellars of the world's producers and growers. Great producers are, unfortunately, still quite rare, but with new technology and increased knowledge, good wine is being produced more frequently than before. All the producers in this book are evaluated using a five-star system, five stars and an "outstanding" rating to those producers deemed to be the very best, four stars to those who are "excellent," three stars to "good" producers, and two stars or one star to "average" and "below average" producers. Since the aim of the book is to provide you with the names of the very best producers, the content is dominated by the top producers rather than the less successful ones.

Those few growers and producers who have received five-star ratings make the world's finest wines. They have been selected for this rating because of two reasons: They make the greatest wines, and they are remarkably consistent and reliable even in mediocre and poor vintages. Ratings, whether they be specific numerical ratings of individual wines or classifications of growers, are always likely to create controversy among both the growers and wine tasters. But such ratings can be reliable and powerfully informative if done impartially, with a global viewpoint, and with firsthand, on-premises *(sur place)* knowledge of the wines, the producers, and the type and quality of the winemaking. The important thing for readers to remember is that the growers/producers who receive either a four-star or five-star rating are the ones to search out; I suspect few consumers will ever be disappointed with one of their wines. The three-star rated growers/producers are less consistent, but can be expected to make fine wines in the very good to excellent vintages. Their weaknesses stem from either the fact that their vineyards are not so strategically placed, or because they are unable to make the severe selections necessary to make only the finest quality wine. In short, purchasing their wine in a less than spectacular vintage is fraught with risk.

Rating the growers and producers is one of this book's most significant features and its importance cannot be underestimated. Years of wine tasting have taught me many things, but the more one tastes and assimilates knowledge, the more one begins to isolate the handful of truly world-class growers and producers who seem to rise above the crowd in great as well as mediocre vintages. I always admonish consumers against blind faith in one grower or producer, or one specific vintage, but the producers and growers rated "outstanding" and "excellent" are as close to a guarantee of high quality as you are likely to find.

THE STAR RATINGS

***** A grower or producer who consistently produces the finest wines of the appellation and whose goals are totally governed by quality. These are producers who spare no expense in time, labor, or materials to come as close to perfection as Mother Nature will permit.

**** An excellent to outstanding grower or producer who produces brilliant wines in most years, but can lack consistency in difficult years.

*** A good, sound grower or producer who can be expected to produce above-average quality wines in the best vintages.

** A grower or producer who turns out standard quality, unexciting wine.

* A grower or producer whose wines generally lack character and quality.

TASTING NOTES AND WINE RATINGS

All of my tastings were done in peer-group, single-blind conditions, when possible (meaning that the same types of wines are tasted against each other and the producers' names are not known), either in my tasting room or in the cellars of the producers. The ratings reflect an independent, critical look at the wines. Neither price nor the reputation of the producer or grower affect the rating in any manner. I spend three months of every year tasting in vineyards. During the other nine months of the year, six- and sometimes seven-day workweeks are devoted solely to tasting and writing. I do not participate in wine judgings or trade tastings for many reasons, but principal among these are the following: (1) I prefer to taste from an entire bottle of wine, (2) I find it essential to have properly sized and cleaned professional tasting glasses, (3) the temperatures of the wine must be correct, and (4) I alone wish to determine the time allocated to the number of wines to be critiqued.

The numeral rating given is a guide to what I think of the wine vis-à-vis its peer group. Certainly, wines rated above 85 are very good to excellent, and any wine rated 90 or above will be outstanding for its particular type. While some have suggested that scoring is not well suited to a beverage that has been romantically extolled for centuries, wine is no different from any consumer product. There are specific standards of quality that full-time wine professionals recognize, and there are benchmark wines against which all others can be judged. I know of no one with three or four different glasses of wine in front of him or her, regardless of how good or bad the wines might be, who cannot say "I prefer this one to that one." Scoring wines is simply taking a professional's opinion and applying some sort of numerical system to it on a consistent basis. Scoring permits rapid communication of information to expert and novice alike.

The rating system I employ in my wine journal, *The Wine Advocate*, is the one I have utilized in this book. It is a 50–100 point scale, the most repugnant of all wines meriting 50 since that is the starting point of the scale, and the most glorious gustatory experience commanding 100. I prefer my system to the more widely quoted 20-point scale called the Davis Scale, of the University of California at Davis, because it permits much more flexibility in scoring. It is also easier to understand because it corresponds to the American grading system, and it avoids the compression of scores from which the Davis Scale suffers. It is not without its own problems, though, because readers will often wonder what the difference is between an 86 and 87, both very good wines. The only answer I can give is a simple one: When tasted side by side, I thought the 87-point wine slightly better than the 86-point wine.

The score given for a specific wine reflects the quality of the wine at its best. I often tell people that evaluating a wine and assigning a score to a beverage that will change and evolve in many instances for up to 10 or more years is analogous to taking a photograph of a marathon runner. Much can be ascertained at that instant but, like the moving object, the wine will also evolve and change. Wines from obviously badly corked or defective bottles are retried, since a wine from such a single bad bottle does not indicate an entirely spoiled batch. Many of the wines reviewed here have been tasted many times, and the score represents a cumulative average of the wine's performance in tastings to date. Scores, however, do not tell the entire story about a wine. The written commentary that accompanies the ratings is often a better source of information regarding the wine's style and personality, its relative quality level vis-à-vis its peers, and its relative value and aging potential than any score could ever indicate.

Here then is a general guide to interpreting the numerical ratings:

90–100 is equivalent to an *A* and is given only for an outstanding or special effort. Wines in this category are the very best produced of their type and, like a three-star Michelin restaurant, merit the trouble to find and taste. There is a taste difference between a 90 and a 99, but both are top marks. As you will note throughout the text, there are few wines that actually make it into this top category simply because there just are not many truly great wines.

80–89 is equivalent to a *B* in school and such a wine, particularly in the 85–89 range, is very, very good; many of the wines that fall into this range often are great values as well. I would not hesitate to have any of these wines in my own personal collection.

70–79 represents a *C*, or average mark, but obviously 79 is a much more desirable score than 70. Wines that receive scores between 75 and 79 are generally pleasant, straightforward wines that simply lack complexity, character, or depth. If inexpensive, they may be ideal for uncritical quaffing.

Below 70 is a *D* or *F*, depending on where you went to school; for wine, too, it is a sign of an imbalanced, flawed, or terribly dull or diluted wine that will be of little interest to the smart wine consumer.

In terms of awarding points, my scoring system gives every wine a base of 50 points. The wine's general color and appearance merit up to 5 points. Since most wines today are well made, thanks to modern technology and the increased use of professional oenologists, they tend to receive at least 4, often 5 points. The aroma and bouquet merit up to 15 points, depending on the intensity level and extract of the aroma and bouquet as well as the cleanliness of the wine. The flavor and finish merit up to 20 points, and again, intensity of flavor, balance, cleanliness, and depth and length on the palate are all important considerations when giving out points. Finally, the overall quality level or potential for further evolution and improvement—aging—merits up to 10 points.

Scores are important for the reader to gauge a professional critic's overall qualitative placement of a wine vis-à-vis its peers. However, it is also vital to consider the description of the wine's style, personality, and potential. No scoring system is perfect, but a system that provides for flexibility in scores, if applied without prejudice, can quantify different levels of wine quality and provide the reader with a professional's judgment. However, there can never be any substitute for your own palate nor any better education than tasting the wine yourself.

ONE FURTHER CAVEAT

In dealing with the typical Burgundian grower/producer, one becomes acutely aware of *size*. The microsizes of Burgundy producers' holdings must be conveyed to the reader since size impacts dramatically on not only a reader's ability to find a given wine, but the price that must ultimately be paid for it.

In this book, I have converted everything from hectares to acres since the latter unit of measurement is employed in America. (For the record, 1 hectare equals 2.47 acres.) Holdings have been rounded off, either to the nearest tenth or hundredth of an acre. I have tried to verify the acreage claimed by each producer, but my figures cannot always be guaranteed, nor can the list of wines the producer claims to make. Years of experience and contradictory facts given to me by the producers have caused me to write down their information with my tongue pressed firmly against my cheek. Most of the facts given to me are extremely accurate, but growers have a tendency to understate their production while overstating their vineyard holdings, often including acreage they lease, not own. I trust readers who may be more intimately aware of a producer's holdings will promptly advise me should my numbers be in error.

TWENTY
QUESTIONS
ABOUT
BURGUNDY

Is it possible to describe the attributes of a great red burgundy?
It is doubtful that anyone will ever satisfactorily describe these qualities
that make a great red burgundy. It is easier to agree upon these key
factors that frequently result in great red burgundy. In order of importance they are: (1) the soil and exposition of the vineyard, (2) low yields,
(3) a hospitable growing season, and (4) superior winemaking, which
includes exacting sanitary conditions as well as vigilant concern over
the wine's upbringing, with minimal intervention save for the occasional
racking (transfer of the wine from one barrel to another barrel). All the
greatest red burgundies, at the very least, are the product of these
factors. But red burgundy at its most sublime is the most difficult wine
on earth to describe. Is it because truly profound burgundy is so rarely
encountered, or because the Pinot Noir grape possesses an unfathomable mystery that yields no telltale, discernible signature like Cabernet
Sauvignon or Chardonnay?

The greatest examples of mature red burgundy I have ever tasted—whether it was the 1959, 1978, or 1980 La Tâche, the 1966 or 1978 Richebourg (all from the Domaine de la Romanée-Conti), the 1949 Pommard Les Rugiens from Pothier-Rieusset, the 1945 or 1947 Clos des Lambrays, the 1949 or 1955 Chambertin from the Maison Leroy, the 1969 Chambertin from Armand Rousseau, the 1947 or 1980 Ponsot Clos de la Roche, the 1964 Domaine de la Pousse d'Or's Volnay La Bousse d'Or, or the 1947, 1969, 1972 Comte de Vogüé's Musigny Vieilles Vignes—all shared the following characteristics. First, they had penetrating and compelling bouquets that exhibited a decadent, even raunchy, almost decaying or aged-beef sort of smell, combined with an intense and exhilarating aroma of oriental spices and dried herbs. Second, they had layers and layers of black and red fruits that virtually exploded on the palate with a cascade of increasingly expanding textural sensations. And third, they were relatively high in alcohol, with a lusciousness and silky finish that lasted several minutes. Drinking these wines was an experience akin to eating candy because of the extraordinary sweetness they conveyed.

Are these the characteristics of great red burgundy? I am not certain, but all these wines, coming from different vineyards, vintages, and winemakers, possessed these same intrinsic qualities.

Is it possible to describe what constitutes great white burgundy?
Everyone who drinks wine no doubt has a strong idea of what the finest Chardonnays, particularly those from the new world, offer in terms of smell and taste. But how many of you have drunk truly profound white burgundy? Actually, comparing a great white burgundy with a new world Chardonnay is almost unfair. The preponderant number of new world Chardonnays must be consumed within 2–3 years after the vintage. As enjoyable as they are, they often have all their components playing against one another rather than in complete harmony. Perhaps it is because most new world Chardonnays must be acidified, but when one tastes them, the overall perception is one of separate but equal building blocks of acid, structure, fruit, and wood. On the other hand, great white burgundies incorporate all these components, resulting in a blend where no one element has the upper hand. The greatest examples combine an extraordinary perfume of apples, honey, vanilla, wet stones, and sometimes lemons with flavors that range from a smoky, buttery, and nutty taste to oranges, occasionally peaches, and in the more opulent, ripe examples, to tropical fruits such as bananas, mangos, and pineapples. Of course, what makes them so compelling is their precision and balance, with all of these marvelously complex compo-

nents unfolding in the glass and on the palate. I should also note that some white burgundies have the added advantage that in certain vintages they can last for as many as 10 to 20 years in the bottle, improving and developing more nuances as they age.

The greatest producers of white burgundy, among them Michel Niellon and André Ramonet in Chassagne-Montrachet, Étienne Sauzet and the Domaine Leflaive in Puligny-Montrachet, Jean-Marie Raveneau in Chablis, Château Fuissé in Pouilly-Fuissé, the exquisite Corton-Charlemagnes of the Maison Louis Latour and Faiveley in Corton-Charlemagne, or the unfiltered, compelling Meursaults of Jean-François Coche-Dury and Comte Lafon, all seem to share these characteristics in various proportions, depending on the quality of the vintage.

Great white burgundy is indeed rare and expensive, but one of the things I have learned over the years of tasting wine is that I would rather buy one bottle of truly profound white burgundy than five or six bottles of new world Chardonnay.

Is burgundy as good a candidate for cellaring and aging as Bordeaux?
The answer to this question is a resounding "no." While some oldtimers lament that burgundy is not made the way it once was, they seem to have forgotten that burgundy never has been capable of aging extremely well. There is no doubt that one can point to a handful of rare examples, as I have in this book, of truly exciting burgundies that lasted two, three, sometimes four or more decades, retaining their fruit and developing greater nuances and subtleties, but those cases are a distinct minority. This applies equally to red and white burgundy.

Of course, one has a tendency to recall, perhaps even to embellish, the memory of a glorious 1949 Pommard Les Rugiens or a 1962 Corton-Charlemagne, but anyone who broadly advises you to lay away burgundies for a decade clearly does not have your best interests at heart. Most modern-day red burgundies, even from the best vintages, should generally be consumed within 10 years of the vintage. This rule is even more restrictive for white burgundies. The window of drinking opportunity is normally within 7 to 8 years of the vintage for white burgundies.

The reasons for this are quite simple. Red burgundies, made from the Pinot Noir grape, simply do not have the tannin levels or general depth and concentration to sustain them beyond a decade of life. Additionally, one of the Pinot Noir grape's most distinct pleasures is its bouquet, which tends to be the first aspect of a wine to crack up and decay. Even the finest red burgundies, while they may last two or more decades, are generally more enjoyable to drink in their first decade of life. Anyone who loves great red burgundy should only buy enough to drink within the immediate future. Red burgundy's suspect aging capabilities have always been a problem and are not due to any modern-day winemaking techniques, although the high yields now being practiced have further diminished red burgundy's ability to age gracefully beyond a decade.

I have come to the realization that if you are buying burgundy for drinking in 15 or 20 years, you should be restricting your purchases to the wines from no more than a half dozen or so producers. In particular, the Maison Leroy, the two old-line *négociants*, Bourée in Gevrey-Chambertin or Doudet-Naudin in Savigny-Lès-Beaune, and small producers such as Hubert de Montille and Comte Lafon still produce wines that last well beyond 10 years, and sometimes 20 years. Even Burgundy's most expensive and frequently greatest wines, those of superlative producers such as the Domaine de la Romanée-Conti, Henri Jayer, Domaine Dujac, Philippe Leclerc, and Jean Gros, are usually at their best between 8 and 15 years of age, rarely improving or holding well beyond that.

Are the best wines of Burgundy viable candidates for investment?
While investment in wine has become more popular given the luxury prices demanded for the top châteaux of Bordeaux, burgundy has never represented as good an investment as Bordeaux. While personally I abhor the practice of investing in wine for financial profit, it is done regularly, at least with the first growths and super second châteaux of Bordeaux, as well as a handful of the limited production Pomerols and St.-Émilions. But there is a great deal of difference between buying Bordeaux and buying burgundy. For starters, in the spring following the vintage, Bordeaux is offered as a wine future at what is called an "opening" or entry-level price. If the vintage is widely acclaimed and of great quality, the price is propelled in only one direction—upward. For example, the 1982 Bordeaux prices escalated by 400% to 600% within only 5 or 6 years. Burgundy is not sold as a wine future, although certain merchants regrettably, and in my opinion irresponsibly, offer to sell burgundy to their customers on a prearrival basis. Today, most burgundies from current vintages sell at prices higher than do the older vintages of the same wine. A review of any of the auction catalogues from Christie's, Sotheby's, or the Chicago Wine Company precisely illustrates this. Vintages from the forties, fifties, and sixties of some of the greatest burgundies sell at prices that are often less than the 1985, 1988, or 1989. The reasons for this are: (1) consumers lack confidence in burgundy, (2) smart buyers recognize burgundy's fragility and du-

bious aging potential, and (3) merchants can ask and receive astronomical prices for the wines upon their release because of the limited production. But rarely do these same wines appreciate in value after release. In fact, in most cases they will drop in value. Of course there are exceptions, such as some limited production Montrachets and the Romanée-Conti and La Tâche of the Domaine de la Romanée-Conti. All in all, burgundy is a notoriously bad investment.

Why are the best burgundies prohibitively expensive?
The pricing of burgundy can be explained entirely by the rules of supply and demand. Burgundy has the unique and enviable situation of having far more admirers and prospective purchasers than available wine. In addition, great burgundy alone among the finest French wines has no competition from within the borders of France, or in the world at large. The problem at the Premier Cru and Grand Cru levels is exacerbated by the truly microscopic quantities of wine offered by the best producers. Some specific case production figures demonstrate the point dramatically. For example, the most expensive red burgundies are those of the Domaine de la Romanée-Conti. In an abundant year, the production of their Romanée-Conti ranges from 300 to 500 cases. Their exclusively owned *monopole* vineyard, La Tâche, produces between 900 and 1,800 cases a year. One of Burgundy's most sought-after winemakers, Henri Jayer, usually produces, in a prolific year, 50 cases of Richebourg and 125 cases of Echézeaux. The coproprietor of the Domaine de la Romanée-Conti, Lalou Bize-Leroy, at her new Domaine Leroy in Vosne-Romanée, turns out extraordinarily sublime wines, but only 25 cases of her two Grands Crus of Musigny and Chambertin were made in 1988. The Domaine Roumier is one of the most revered names in Burgundy, and their Bonnes Mares Cuvée Vieilles Vignes is considered to be a heroic wine. However, only 100 cases were made in the plentiful vintage of 1988. Everyone who loves great burgundy considers Hubert Lignier's Clos de la Roche to be one of the top dozen or so red wines made in Burgundy, yet he rarely makes more than 300 cases.

These are not isolated examples, Louis Jadot's production of the excellent Beaune-Clos des Ursules is considered massive by Burgundy standards, but only 1,100 cases are made in a hugely abundant year. Jadot sells his wines to every civilized country in the world. How much of this lovely wine will make it to the shelves of the finest wine merchants in Omaha, Nebraska, or Edinburgh, Scotland? Perhaps a case or two? In Bordeaux a production of 1,000 cases is considered minuscule. Château Pétrus, which makes Bordeaux's rarest and most expensive red wine, produces 4,500 cases in a good year.

This frustrating situation (at least for buyers) is similar for white burgundies. There are usually no more than 150 cases made of Faiveley's superb Corton-Charlemagne. Louis Jadot, who makes sublime Corton-Charlemagne, can, in an abundant year, produce 1,200 cases, but that must be spread around not only to the restaurants of France, but to Jadot's clients throughout the world. Even worse is the situation with the Domaine Ramonet's celestial Montrachet. A whopping 50 cases are made in an abundant vintage!

Most of the finest Grand Cru and Premier Cru red and white burgundies could be sold exclusively to France's top restaurants, should the producers so desire. Of course, that is not their intention, and they try to ensure an equitable distribution to their suppliers throughout the world. But it is because of these tiny quantities that the prices for burgundy are so astronomically high. As more and more wine connoisseurs from a growing number of countries demand fine wine, the most recent good vintage will probably fetch exorbitant prices.

Why are the finest burgundies so difficult to find in the American marketplace?
The answer again relates to the tiny quantities of top wines that are produced. America is an extremely important purchaser of top quality burgundies, particularly white burgundies. Once the small quantities sold to the best producers' importers are allocated to the 10 or 12 best wine markets in the United States, however, a top merchant may only end up with a case or 2 of Leflaive Chevalier-Montrachet, and 6 bottles of a Domaine de la Romanée-Conti Montrachet. This situation is no different in the United States than it is in Switzerland, the United Kingdom, Belgium, or Japan. It is immensely frustrating for buyers who cherish these wines. Certainly I have been discouraged when I find a superb producer only to learn that just 10 or 15 cases will be allocated to the American market. These are the realities when dealing with burgundy, and seemingly only add to its mystique.

Are estate-bottled burgundies superior to those from the négociants?
The overall quality of winemaking, and therefore of the wines of Burgundy, has soared dramatically since the early eighties. This growing commitment to higher quality has been particularly apparent at the *négociant* level. *"Négociant"* is the French word for a wine broker. *Négociants* include firms that do not own any vineyards. They rely totally on purchases of finished wines from growers, which they then sell under their own names. *Négociants* can also be firms that own vineyards. Several—for example, Faiveley and Bouchard Père et Fils

—are among the largest vineyard owners in Burgundy. *Négociants* have long controlled the Burgundy wine business, as the movement of growers to estate-bottle their wines has been a relatively recent phenomenon. The fact that many of the most insipid and vapid burgundies have consistently been produced by several of the largest and most prominent firms has been the principal reason for the negative image many consumers have of a Burgundy *négociant*. *Négociants* have also been maligned by growers and importers who argue that the most authentic and individualistic burgundies can only emerge from individual domaines. The better *négociants* have responded in a positive manner to this criticism. Since the mid-eighties, they have significantly upgraded the quality of their wines, with the best of them challenging and often surpassing those produced by the finest growers.

This trend of estate-bottled burgundies, started by the late founder of *La Revue du Vin de France*, Raymond Baudoin, and subsequently encouraged by the great American importer, the late Frank Schoonmaker, has still not reached its zenith. The *négociants*, faced with losing many of their sources for wine thanks to growers who decided to become free-lancers and estate-bottle their own production, not only tried to sign up certain growers to exclusivity contracts, but recognized the need to improve the quality of their wines. Many *négociants* have long made fine wines, particularly Louis Latour, Joseph Drouhin, Faiveley, Leroy, Louis Jadot, and Bourée Père et Fils. In fact, little has changed at these firms, which continue to set standards every bit as high as the most meticulous and conscientiously run estate bottlers. Some might even argue that the greatest wines from Bourée and Lalou Bize-Leroy not only rival but surpass most of the estate-bottled burgundies. Even the firm of Faiveley, which actually owns most of its vineyards but in the minds of the public is still a *négociant*, produces compellingly elegant wines that are often benchmarks for their type. And who can dispute the quality of the white wines from Louis Latour whose Corton-Charlemagne is among the greatest white burgundies made? In addition, the wine of Joseph Drouhin has increased in quality since the late seventies and the firm is now a pacesetter for both graceful white wines and very charming, elegant, classy red wines.

There are, however, *négociants* that continue to lag behind in quality. Among the most notable of these is the huge firm of Jean-Claude Boisset, the firms of Patriarche, Bouchard Père et Fils, Albert Bichot (except for their exquisite wines from the Domaine de Clos Frantin and Domaine Long-Depaquit), and the highly promoted, often mediocre wines of La Reine Pedauque. Today, you are not likely to get a bad wine from these firms, but rather a sound, commercial one with no soul or personality. Admittedly, there must be a vast market for such wines as these firms are among the wealthiest and most successful in France.

It is ridiculous today to suggest that estate-bottled wines are always better than *négociant* wines. My blind tastings have conclusively proven that the top wines from the best *négociants* are certainly as fine as those from the best individual domaines.

One argument frequently offered is that the wines of the *négociants* have the same taste. To me that seems irrelevant. The top *négociants*, while they respect the individual vineyard's terroir, obviously employ the same philosophy in making all of their wines, and try to keep the identity of the vineyard and appellation unto itself. The wines of Leroy, Faiveley, or Bourée all share a similar signature, but then so do the wines of domaines such as Roumier, Ponsot, Roty, Jean Gros, or the Domaine de la Romanée-Conti. At the most meticulously run estate-bottled operation the same philosophy is employed for making each wine. The wines from the great domaine of Armand Rousseau in Gevrey-Chambertin will have a certain similarity because the wine-making, the *élevage*, the overall philosophy is precisely the same for each wine. Nevertheless, Rousseau's Chambertin will taste different from a Gevrey-Chambertin-Clos St.-Jacques or Clos de la Roche from neighboring Morey St.-Denis. The signature is just as prominent in a grower's cellar as it is in a *négociant*'s. The argument that small estates turn out more authentic and better wines than the finest *négociants* is a sham, at least when applied to *négociants* such as Joseph Drouhin, Leroy, Bourée Père et Fils, Joseph Faiveley, Louis Jadot, and Louis Latour.

What is the most important information to know in order to purchase top-quality red and white burgundy?
The French frequently utilize the following expression when they discuss burgundy, *"c'est l'homme qui fait la différence,"* meaning, it is man who makes the difference. This simplistic expression actually encompasses all one needs to know when it comes to buying red or white burgundy. While the quality of the vintage is an extremely important fact to know when buying burgundy, it is more vital to recognize the quality of the producer. This is important because a superb grower or *négociant* will make a better wine in an off year than a mediocre or incompetent producer or *négociant* will make in a great year. If you desire to have the odds in your favor when purchasing burgundy, it is essential that you learn the names of the best producers for each of the Burgundy appellations. Of course, their styles of wine may not always be to your liking, but at least you should be aware of the names of the

most committed and highly motivated winemakers. Simply memorizing a top vintage year in Burgundy and then buying blindly is a practice that assures disaster.

Is there anywhere else in the world that has demonstrated the ability to produce compelling wine from the Pinot Noir grape?

One of the most frustrating aspects of buying burgundy is the realization that there is really no competition from anywhere else in the world. Yes, one can point to the exquisite Pinot Noirs made by the tiny Calera winery (its single vineyard Pinot Noirs from vintages such as 1985 and 1987 rival the best Premiers Crus from the Côte de Nuits), and to the progress made by up-and-coming California Pinot Noir specialists such as Au Bon Climat, Saintsbury, Kalin, and Robert Mondavi, as well as Oregon's top producers, Ponzi and Eyrie, but collectively, the annual total production of their finest Pinot Noirs adds up to only about 5,000 cases. Furthermore, the future looks dismal, as there are just too few people mentally, physically, and financially committed to making wine from the world's most fickle grape. Even those who are successful must, because of the unattractive economics of producing majestic Pinot Noir, charge relatively high prices for their wines. For whatever reason, Burgundy's golden slopes seem to be the only place in the world where Pinot Noir can be consistently produced successfully.

Are the wines of Burgundy as good today as they were 20 or 40 years ago?

Not only are the wines of Burgundy as good today as they were in the past, they are significantly better. First, there is no longer any evidence of adulterating red burgundies. The illegal practice of blending inferior, more alcoholic and more deeply colored wine from southern France and northern Africa, in wide practice until the early seventies, has been stopped.

Second, many producers recognized the folly of planting clones of Pinot Noir (such as the Pinot Droit which emphasized prolific yields rather than quality), and have begun, encouraged and supported by the oenology departments of the leading universities, to replant with lower yielding Pinot Noir clones, such as the Pinots Fins called 113, 114, and 115.

A third and possibly even more important quality factor has been the strong movement, started in the mid-eighties, to move away from the excessive fining and filtration of Pinot Noir and Chardonnay for fear of eviscerating the wine and removing its flavor. With the advent of modern technology in the mid-seventies, many growers learned how to bottle their wines as quickly as possible, aided immeasurably by German micropore filters and centrifuges that could clarify (and eviscerate) a wine with a push of a button. This eliminated the need for the cumbersome and labor-intensive racking. It also allowed the growers to be paid for their wines more quickly, since the wines could be rushed into the bottle. The results, all too often, were wonderfully brilliant, polished, attractive-looking wines that had little character or flavor. The excessive fining (clarifying) and filtration of wines continues to be a major problem in Burgundy. However, the best producers are not filtering, and influential people are becoming more and more concerned about the ramifications of filtration. Even Professor Feuillat, the head of the Department of Oenology at the University of Dijon, issued a position paper that recommended not filtering Premiers Crus and Grands Crus of Burgundy if the wine was otherwise biologically stable and clear. However, too many of those brokers and importers responsible for purchasing burgundy have encouraged their producers to use a filter, rather than assume responsibility for shipping the wine in temperature-controlled containers, and guaranteeing it be distributed in a healthy condition. Two of the most influential burgundy purchasers, American Rebecca Wasserman and Englishman Tim Marshall, have refused to discourage the use of filtration by their growers. There are, however, a growing number of American burgundy importers who not only insist that their wines be minimally fined and filtered, but who also ship their wines in temperature-controlled containers. Martine Saunier of Martine's Wines in San Rafael, California, Neal Rosenthal of Select Vineyards in New York, Robert Kacher of Robert Kacher Selections in Washington, D.C., Robert Chadderdon in New York, Wine Imports in San Francisco, Pacific Vine Co. in San Francisco, and Kermit Lynch in Berkeley, California are the most prominent importers of high quality burgundy who do indeed care.

These factors, combined with lower yields, the use of higher quality barrels, and improved sanitary conditions in the cellars, have resulted in better wines being produced today than twenty years ago. In addition, there is a new generation of young, highly motivated winemakers who are taking quality more seriously than ever. Inspired by such people as the Domaine Dujac's Jacques Seysses, Burgundy's new *jeune équipe* (young team) of François Faiveley, Étienne Grivot, Patrick Bize, Christophe Roumier, Dominique Lafon, Jean-François Coche-Dury, Bruno Clair, Laurent Ponsot, Jean-Pierre De Smet (of the Domaine de L'Arlot), and Jean-Marc Bouley are pushing themselves as well as their peers to produce as fine quality burgundies as is possible.

In addition, more and more producers and *négociants* are branding the corks used in the bottle with both the vintage and the vineyard name, packaging the wines in wooden cases, and using heavier and better bottles for their wines. In the last decade, the use of excessive fertilization and other chemical soil enhancers was reduced dramatically. Some producers, such as Lalou Bize at her Domaine Leroy, have even decided to produce wines organically, using no herbicides or pesticides whatsoever.

There are a great many positive trends in Burgundy and, as a result, optimism runs high. However, I do not want to suggest that all is well. There remain many underachievers, some with historically revered names, who are turning out wines that are thin, vapid, denuded, and pleasureless. These producers are as integral a part of Burgundy's modern-day history as is the new generation of producers dedicated to high quality.

What are the significant differences in the wines of the Côte de Beaune and Côte de Nuits?
The Côte d'Or, or Burgundy's Golden Slope, as it is sometimes called, is where the most awesomely concentrated, profound wines from all of Burgundy are produced. However, there are significant differences between the two hillsides that make up the Côte d'Or. The Côte de Nuits, which starts just south of Dijon and runs south of Nuits St.-Georges, produces almost exclusively red wine, while the Côte de Beaune, which starts just north of Beaune and extends to Santenay south of Beaune, produces superlative red and white wines.

The red wines of the Côte de Nuits tend to be fuller, slightly more tannic, and are characterized by a more earthy, black fruit and exotic character than those from the Côte de Beaune. Of course, these are generalizations, but the red wines from the Côte de Beaune tend to offer slightly less body, less tannin, and seem to be filled with aromas and flavors of red fruits. In addition, they seem less earthy, less exotic, and in most cases less ageworthy, although there are exceptions. One could correctly assert that a big, rich, generous, virile Pommard or Corton from the Côte de Beaune is a larger-scaled, fuller wine than anything produced from Chambolle-Musigny in the Côte de Nuits.

While the Côte de Nuits produces only a handful of white wines, of which a few are superlative, the Côte de Beaune produces the world's greatest white wines from the Chardonnay grape. Whether it is the extraordinarily long-lived, rich, precisely defined white wines of Corton-Charlemagne; the nutty, luscious, lusty, easy-to-drink Meursaults; the elegant, steely Puligny-Montrachets; or the opulent, fleshy Chassagne-Montrachets the Côte de Beaune is known for both elegant, stylish reds, and extraordinary whites.

Are burgundy wines sold as wine futures?
For over two decades the Bordeaux châteaux have offered their wines on a prearrival futures basis at an opening price in the spring following the vintage. Burgundy is not sold in this manner, although trade members who have dealt with growers and *négociants* are allowed and even expected to make their reservations, and haggle over their allocations as early as possible. In general, most burgundy producers do not require payment from their clients until just before they are ready to bottle the wine. However, a disturbing trend has occurred among wine merchants over the last several years: They have begun to offer burgundy wines to consumers prior to delivery on a prearrival price basis. This is largely done to help finance the merchant's purchase of burgundy. Of course, the consumer is required to lay out 100% of the cost in advance. Not only are consumers unaware of whether the wine will be to their liking, but they are dealing with a notoriously irregular product. I am not sure whether this practice is here to stay. I recognize that the merchant who deals in Burgundy wines must have access to vast sums of money in order to finance the huge expenses involved in buying burgundy. By offering it on a prearrival basis, he can raise the necessary capital for those wines in demand. But must the consumer always fund these purchases?

In general, burgundy should not be purchased as futures. If you must buy on a prearrival basis, you should do as much fact gathering as you can to ascertain exactly what you are getting. In addition, you should have a firm agreement with the merchant as to how many months or years your money will be tied up.

Is the significance of the soil and vineyard designations as important as the Burgundians would have everyone believe?
The fundamental concept behind the *appellation controlée* system is the integrity and individualistic qualities of the soils that characterize the Premier and Grand Cru vineyards. The French argue that the grapes grown in these unique parcels of earth produce wines vastly superior to wines from vineyards not entitled to such exalted status.

I have always wondered whether it is the vineyard or the producer that ultimately controls the quality of the wine. I am not sure anyone will ever know the answer to this question. For example, suppose it could be arranged for the Domaine de la Romanée-Conti to begin making the wines from the famed La Grande Rue Premier Cru vineyard in

Vosne-Romanée, or the nearby Les Gaudichots vineyard, whose wines are now made respectively by Henri Lamarche and the Forey family. Would we see a striking difference in the quality and character of these wines? I believe we would, for many reasons. The owners of the Domaine de la Romanée-Conti routinely restrict their yields to 20–25 hectoliters per hectare. This is half of the yields produced by Monsieur Lamarche or the Forey family. Additionally, the domaine utilizes 100% new oak and does not filter. All of these factors would dramatically alter the character and quality of the wines from vineyards such as La Grand Rue and Les Gaudichots if the Domaine de la Romanée-Conti produced the wines. Is the quality of these wines dictated by the soil or the winemaker?

The Domaine Leroy in Vosne-Romanée is the most dramatic example of how one person's zealous passion for quality can totally lift the quality of wines from mediocre to sublime. No one can argue with the fact that Madame Lalou Bize, the coproprietor of the Domaine de la Romanée-Conti and owner of her own *négociant* business in Auxey-Duresses, makes burgundy that not only stands the test of time, but also reflects the wine's appellation, providing as much flavor and character as any wine in the Côte d'Or. Recently, she acquired the Domaine Noëllat in Vosne-Romanée, and produced her first vintage in 1988. The wines she produced from that vintage were of such high quality that they may rival those of her beloved Domaine de la Romanée-Conti. A review of the wines made by the Noëllat family before 1988 reveals wines that were often oxidized, dirty, and watery, even though the raw materials came from such spectacular vineyards as Les Boudots and Les Vignes Rondes in Nuits St.-Georges, Aux Brûlées and Les Beaux Monts in Vosne-Romanée, and Grand Cru vineyards such as Clos Vougeot, Romanée St.-Vivant, and Richebourg. The quality level of the 1988s was spectacular because: (1) Madame Lalou Bize-Leroy kept her yields to an average of 20–22 hectoliters per hectare; (2) she insured that the wines were made under sanitary conditions and that the barrels used were clean; (3) she employed as her cellarmaster the famed André Porcheret who had made the wines of the Hospices de Beaune for almost a decade; and (4) she refused to filter her wines. The soil, in this case, certainly did not change, while the commitment to quality by the producer did.

While the French do, of course, know what they are doing, and the vineyards are extremely important, are they the most important factor? Perhaps. But it seems to me that since so many mediocre wines come from great vineyards, the vineyard alone cannot be considered reason enough to purchase a wine, or to create excitement. Growers and producers are, at the minimum, equally as important. Their commitment to the quality of the wine must be unwavering. There can be no compromises if one is to extract the highest quality from Burgundy's most renowned vineyard parcels. This book has sufficient examples of producers who own great vineyards but are content with mediocrity. It is also replete with examples of growers who, while they do not own Premiers Crus, or own less well-placed Premiers Crus, make wines that are sometimes of Grand Cru quality because of their low yields and enormous talent in the wine cellar.

I do not think the French, particularly in Burgundy, are wrong with respect to their classifications of Premiers Crus and Grands Crus, because these parcels do represent the very best vineyard sites. However, a Premier Cru or Grand Cru status does not in itself guarantee high quality. Rather, the quality depends on whether or not the producer is committed to making the best wine of which he or she is capable.

How is great red burgundy made?
Most burgundy growers will tell you only so much, but from what I have been able to glean after years of research, the three most important components that contribute to great red burgundy are: (1) the excellence of the vineyard, (2) low yields, and (3) the competence of the winemaker. If all three of these exist, the end result is likely to be quite compelling and exciting.

How all the different growers and *négociants* vinify and handle their wines differs far more in Burgundy than it does in Bordeaux. In Bordeaux, the basic winemaking and upbringing of the wine are essentially similar at all the major properties. In Burgundy, there are many different ways of making top-class red wine.

One of the most popular techniques today at the top level is for partial destemming of the grapes. Destemming is the process whereby the stems are removed from the grape bunches. Many producers feel the stems impart a vegetal flavor to the wine, as well as more astringent tannins. For that reason, some producers, most notably the great Master, Henri Jayer, believe in 100% destemming in certain vintages. Other producers believe a certain percentage of stems adds structure and more character to the wine. In a healthy vintage, this technique uses no more than 30%–50% of the stems, a 2- to 3-day maceration of the grapes prior to the actual start of the fermentation, and a *cuvaison* and maceration period that extends for 2–3 weeks. This procedure is believed to achieve excellent aromatic complexity and purity, and good ripeness and richness. Most of the producers who follow this method tend to use between 50% and 100% new oak for their top Premiers Crus and Grands Crus. The proponents of this school of winemaking include the likes of Jacques Seysses of the Domaine Dujac, Jean-Pierre de Smet of Domaine L'Arlot, François Faiveley of the Maison Faiveley, Domaine Mongeard-Mugneret, and the Domaine Roumier.

Most modern-day burgundy producers routinely destem for fear of making wines with too much tannin and structure. Proponents of no destemming (such as the Domaine de la Romanée-Conti and Philippe Leclerc) believe this practice adds character, structure, and longevity to the wine. Interestingly, all the growers mentioned so far are also adamantly against any filtration of their wines. Philippe Leclerc neither fines nor filters, preferring to keep his Pinot Noir in cask for nearly three years and then bottle it by hand unfiltered. Faiveley also bottles his Premiers Crus and Grands Crus by hand, but he does fine them, as does Jacques Seysses. Henri Jayer bottles by hand and fines, but never filters.

But even these talented winemakers disagree on certain principles. Henri Jayer, the Domaine de la Romanée-Conti, and the Domaine Ponsot believe the wine is made in the vineyard as much as it is in the cellars. They feel the search for high quality obligates the grower to prune back the vineyard, if conditions warrant, by cutting off grape bunches. To these producers, high yields are the undoing of the wine, regardless of how talented the winemaker is, or what wizardry can be accomplished within the cellar. On the other hand, Jacques Seysses argues that large yields are acceptable, and that concentration can still be obtained by the process of bleeding off the excess juice (a process the French call *saigner*). This technique increases the proportion of skins and stems to the remaining juice and therefore, according to its proponents, increases the concentration. Henri Jayer claims this is nothing but a gimmick whose shortcomings become apparent after the wine spends 5 or 6 years in the bottle.

Another area where these irrefutably great winemakers disagree concerns the percentage of new oak used. Henri Jayer believes in 100% new oak, the firms of Bourée and Faiveley significantly less, and the Domaine Ponsot abhors it altogether. However, it should be noted that the trend for Premiers Crus and Grands Crus in Burgundy is toward increased percentages of new oak.

Another school of winemaking embraces the technique of an extremely long period of cold maceration prior to fermentation. It is practiced by a group of winemakers who have employed the controversial Nuits St.-Georges oenologist, Guy Accad, to look after their winemaking. This practice has been condemned by many in Burgundy for producing wines that have more in common with Côte Rôtie than Pinot

Noir. However, it is still too early to know whether Accad's extreme techniques will stand the test of time. They do indeed produce irrefutably impressive, almost black-colored wines that are explosively rich and aromatic when young. But do they reflect their appellations as well as some of the less extreme methods of fermentation? Accad does not believe in destemming, and allows the grape bunches to macerate chilled for ten days or more before any fermentation starts. To his credit, he does not believe in rushing anything into the bottle. He counsels his clients against fining and filtration, and advises them not to bottle their wines until they are fully ready. His producers, who include the likes of Jacky Confuron in Vosne-Romanée, Étienne Grivot in Vosne-Romanée, Georges Chicotot in Nuits St.-Georges, Daniel Senard in Aloxe-Corton, and the Château de la Clos Vougeot in Vougeot, to name a few of the most prominent, all seem to produce intensely colored, rich, aromatic, concentrated wines that are impressive young. Unfortunately, I do not know how well these wines stand the test of time, as I was unable to taste any of the wines from Jacky Confuron made in the late seventies with Accad's techniques, and I could not find any to purchase in the marketplace. But giving him the benefit of the doubt, they are immensely impressive wines when young. It is too soon to know if Accad is Burgundy's new winemaking wizard. Much of the criticism aimed at Accad and his clients borders on the paranoid, and may be the result of jealousy and envy rather than anything scientifically based—at least for now.

The other schools of thought for making top-quality red burgundy basically eschew any of the techniques of cold maceration prior to fermentation. They believe in crushing and fermenting at warm temperatures in order to extract color, body, and tannin via a more traditional method. They disagree with those who argue that great aromatic Pinot Noir can only be obtained by a cool fermentation or cold maceration prior to fermentation. Some of the best examples of this school of thought include the Maison Louis Jadot and Bourée Père et Fils, whose red wines are macerated for a long time, fermented at extremely high temperatures, yet still retain their aromatic purity and last and last in the bottle. Philippe Leclerc, the Domaine Ponsot, and the Domaine Georges Mugneret are three other superlative producers who think cold maceration prior to fermentation is nonsense.

Of course, the big question is what does the Domaine de la Romanée-Conti do? Unquestionably, they, along with the Domaine Leroy, consistently produce not only the most expensive, but frequently the greatest wines of Burgundy. The one common denominator between these two properties is that their yields are half, sometimes one-third that of the other domaines. That in itself is probably the reason their wines attain such great concentration. Both average 20–25 hectoliters per hectare as opposed to the 45–65 obtained elsewhere. There is no destemming and neither producer admits to any cold maceration prior to fermentation. Given the aromatic complexity of their wines, however, I wonder about this. There is quite a long *cuvaison* of over three weeks, and the wines spend nearly 18 months in 100% new Allier oak casks. While they are lightly fined, they are never filtered. If these techniques are an accurate portrait of their winemaking, then they fall into the more conventional school followed by such excellent producers as Louis Jadot, the Bourée firm, the Domaine Ponsot, and the Domaine Georges Mugneret.

As all of this indicates, there are a multitude of methods employed that can result in great wines. All of the producers I have mentioned are capable of producing some of the finest wines in Burgundy. Those people who tend to turn out neutral, vapid, mediocre red burgundies seem to also possess certain things in common: (1) their crop sizes are far above average, (2) they bottle early, and (3) they both fine and filter their wines in order to get the wine in the bottle as quickly as possible, and receive their payment. As a result, most of the wines are pale imitations of what great and original red burgundy should and can taste like.

After all my research for this book, I am convinced that overproduction and excessive fining and/or filtration are the undoing of most Pinot Noirs. In support of this, I would point to examples of domaines that at one time made profound and compelling unfiltered wines, such as the Domaine Trapet before 1971, the Domaine Gouges before 1971, and the Domaine du Comte de Vogüé before 1973. While these three properties have historically produced some of the greatest wines in Burgundy, overproduction and filtration have caused their reputations to sag enormously.

How is great white burgundy made?
White burgundy seems remarkably easy to produce and the techniques relatively similar when compared to the numerous variations used to make red burgundy.

While the generic white burgundies and wines from the Mâconnais and Chalonnais regions ferment in stainless steel and are bottled early, the great white burgundies of the Côte d'Or are all barrel fermented, generally kept in contact with their lees for 10–12 months, and racked as little as possible. At the same time, it should be pointed out that those producers who keep their yields under control produce white burgundies with the greatest levels of concentration and depth. I am speaking of producers such as the Comte Lafon, Jean-François Coche-Dury, Domaine Leflaive, Domaine Ramonet, and Domaine Michel Niellon. While there are others, these producers all have low yields, long lees (sediment) contact, and a reluctance to intervene or interfere with the natural evolution of the wine in the cask unless there is an emergency. For the Comte Lafon and Coche-Dury there is the almost unheard of idea of bottling their white wines without filtration, a particularly risky and dangerous operation because if there is any bacteria or yeast left in the wine, exposure of the bottle to heat could trigger a secondary fermentation. However, the Comte Lafon's cellars are so cold and the wines kept in cask so long that their wines are totally stable by the time they are bottled. The techniques employed by Jean-François Coche-Dury are similar.

As great as these wines are, this is not to say that filtration, if done lightly, harms white burgundy. Anyone who has tasted the wines of Domaine Leflaive or Domaine Ramonet knows how extraordinary white burgundy can be, and yet these wines are lightly filtered.

Today, most white burgundies at the Premier Cru and Grand Cru levels see about 50% to 100% new oak casks, usually Allier but it can be a blend of different oaks. They are normally bottled after 12 to 14 months. But again, the vineyard site, the competence of the winemaker, and the attention to keeping yields conservative are the three major factors that result in great white burgundies.

Does burgundy have to be handled or served differently from Bordeaux? The most striking thing to anyone who has eaten in a restaurant in Burgundy or in the home of one of the region's producers is the revelation that rarely does a Burgundian decant a bottle of red burgundy, even an old one with a great deal of sediment. In contrast to Bordeaux, where even young vintages are routinely decanted, the practice in Burgundy is simply to pull the cork and serve the wine directly from the bottle. This has intrigued me for a number of years and I have often wondered why there was such a dramatic difference in wine service between these two regions. Was it based on the fact that Bordeaux actually improved with decantation and burgundy did not? Or were there other reasons, based more on history?

Some Burgundians have suggested that Burgundy, being principally a land of farmers and small growers, never tolerated the sort of haute service and rigidity that one experiences in Bordeaux, which for centuries was dominated by the British, long known for their emphasis on formality. This is apparent in the way of life of both these regions today.

It is quite unusual to find anyone in the wine trade or any professional taster travelling around Bordeaux without a suit and tie. On the other hand, I do not think I have ever seen a grower in Burgundy in a suit and tie. Casual dress is not only tolerated, but it is accepted form when visiting the growers. Does this extend also to the table where a decanter clearly seems to imply a more pompous sort of service? Certainly the large English glassworks built in the eighteenth and nineteenth centuries promoted the use of decanters for claret, which has always seemed to have a heavier sediment than the lighter, finer sediment often found in burgundies. Is this why it became routine to decant Bordeaux and not burgundy? Perhaps, but many growers in Burgundy have told me that decanters were looked upon as an extravagance and therefore to be eschewed.

It has been my experience that much of a great burgundy's character comes from its immense aromatic complexity. Bottle bouquet, particularly a highly nuanced one, can be very ephemeral and begin to break apart if exposed to air. Decanting a tight, young, austere Bordeaux can often make it seem more open after 5 or 10 minutes in a decanter. However, I have found, with only a handful of exceptions, that excessive airing of burgundy by decanting often causes it to totally lose its bouquet and become flaccid and formless. No doubt there are exceptions. Many of the *négociants* who have old stocks claim that certain ancient wines require a good one to two hours of breathing as well as decantation prior to being consumed. My feelings on this matter are at odds with this position. It seems that most of the old burgundies I have tasted were at their very best when the cork was pulled and they were poured, regardless of how much sediment was at the bottom of the bottle. I say all this because I personally never decant red burgundy, although I have on occasion decanted some of the great white burgundies simply because I think they are pretty in a decanter. I have noticed that wines such as the Meursaults of the Comte Lafon, and the Chassagne-Montrachets and Montrachets of the Domaine Ramonet often improve significantly with 15 to 20 minutes of airing.

Another major difference between Burgundy and Bordeaux is the stemware in which burgundy is often served. In Bordeaux, the standard tulip-shaped glass or the famous INAO glass is preferred. In Burgundy, a balloon-shaped, cognac-styled, fat, squat glass with a short stem can be found not only in the growers' cellars and *négociants'* offices, but even in Burgundy's restaurants. It is believed that these broader glasses tend to accentuate the big, intense, heady Burgundian perfume. Some restaurants carry this to the extreme and offer their clients an oversized, 24-ounce glass. This glass is so large the wine can actually get lost, and the bouquet disappears so quickly the patron never has a chance to smell it. The small balloon-shaped, cognac-styled glasses are excellent for burgundy as are the INAO and tulip-shaped glasses used for Bordeaux. In general, all the fuss made over the stemware for Bordeaux and burgundy is nonsense. A good INAO glass is just as useful for Bordeaux as it is for burgundy, and works just as well for red wine as it does for white.

It is extremely important that burgundy be served cooler than Bordeaux, preferably at 58°–62°F, no warmer. Red burgundy, given its relatively high alcohol content and perfume, is best served at a slightly chilled temperature where the precision of its flavors and the purity and delineation of all the complex nuances in its bouquet can be deciphered. To prove my point, all you have to do is serve the same wine at 65°–70°F and see how soupy, muddled, and alcoholic the wine tastes. Beaujolais should be served even colder, 53°–56°F, and good white burgundy at 58°–60°F. A great Montrachet or Meursault should be served slightly warmer, at 60°–62°F. It is foolish to spend the money for a compelling, complex white burgundy and then over-chill it, ushering its bouquet and flavors into hibernation.

In conclusion, there are two things to remember when serving and handling burgundy as opposed to Bordeaux. First, burgundy can be damaged severely by excessive aeration, whereas Bordeaux is rarely hurt by this, although it is debatable as to how much it improves with decanting. Second, burgundy must be served slightly chilled to be at its very best, but Bordeaux can be served at 64°–66°F, a good 4° to 6° warmer than burgundy.

What is the optimum age of red and white burgundy for drinking?
To try to predict when most burgundies will reach maturity is a particularly dangerous game to play, given the variation in winemaking techniques and philosophies employed by the growers and negociants in Burgundy.

However, the majority of the wines of Chablis should be consumed in their first 5 or 6 years of life, as only a handful of Chablis producers (i.e., Raveneau) make wines that last or improve after 6 years in the bottle.

In terms of the wines of Beaujolais and Mâconnais, while one can always point to a 10-year-old Beaujolais or an extraordinary Pouilly-Fuissé that lasted 10 or 20 years, these are indeed rare wines. Ninety-five percent of the wines of Beaujolais and Mâconnais should be drunk before they attain three years of age. Once past 3 years the odds are stacked against the consumer.

As for the big red and white wines of Burgundy's Côte d'Or, while it is a matter of taste, if you are buying burgundy and not drinking it within its first 10 years of life, I am convinced that you will be disappointed by most bottles you open after that time. Even the most rugged, concentrated, intense red and white burgundies seem to shed their tannins surprisingly fast and reach a plateau of maturity 5 to 6 years after the vintage. At that point they begin to lose their freshness and decay sets in after 10 to 12 years. Obviously the vintage itself can make a great deal of difference. Those who purchased 1982 red burgundies should consume them well before they reach the age of 10, but those who purchased 1983s may feel that the wait will only make these brawny, tannic, often rot-afflicted, controversial wines better. A good rule of thumb is to drink your red burgundy within 10 years of the vintage, realizing there are certain vintages, such as 1983, 1976, and 1972 for red burgundy, which may, for the finest examples, take more than 10 years to reach full maturity. But these are the exceptions, even for wines from those vintages.

The window of opportunity for drinking red and white burgundy is also one of the smallest of any great wine in the world. One of the great attributes of Bordeaux and a reason, no doubt, why it commands the prices and international following it does, is the broad span of years over which it can be drunk. When a bottle of Bordeaux reaches its plateau of maturity, it can frequently remain there for 10, 15, sometimes 20 years before it begins a very slow process of decline. I have seen burgundies reach their plateau of maturity in 5 years and unceremoniously begin to fade after another 6 or 7 months. The optimum drinking window for most red and white burgundies is small, and closes quickly. This is not an unusual phenomenon. Collectors who have cellared and drunk burgundy relate similar experiences, many of them sad. While Bordeaux has a broad, generous period over which it can be consumed, connoisseurs of burgundy should pay fastidious attention to the development of their burgundies, or suffer the unsavory consequences. Most burgundies can literally peak and begin their decline, which is often frightfully rapid, within 6 to 9 months after having attained full maturity. This is distressing, but it is a reality of buying and cellaring both red and white burgundies.

Will the prices for burgundy wines ever moderate?
Unfortunately, the answer to this question is no. There is always the chance that an international financial crisis could precipitate a worldwide depression that would affect a luxury item such as fine wine. However, given the international demand for the top-quality wines of

this region, the general trend for prices in Burgundy can only be upward. While the huge quantities of wines produced in Mâconnais, Beaujolais, and Chablis may show more variation in prices, the economic prognosis for the Premiers Crus and Grands Crus from Burgundy's famed Côte d'Or is for frighteningly higher prices. When one considers the fact that there are only 30 Grands Crus, producing barely 1% of the total wine of Burgundy, the unmistakable message conveyed is that prices can only escalate. Given the tiny quantity of potentially great burgundy and the growing number of purchasers, it is not unlikely that by the turn of the century prices for Grands Crus will be double what they are today. Presently, there are more purchasers of fine wine than ever before.

The wine market has become even more competitive in the last five years with the aggressive purchasing of the Japanese. Their strong currency and yearning thirst to discover what the best French wine is all about have created an entirely new pricing structure for Premier Cru and Grand Cru burgundies. History has proven that it is the wealthiest countries that drink the world's finest wines. If the Japanese are prepared to pay the premium prices, why shouldn't they enjoy the best?

The same can be said for the awakening interest in great wines in France itself. While France has traditionally consumed oceans of wine, it has never developed much of an appreciation for its own great wines. Increasing interest from Switzerland, Germany, Belgium, Sweden, and Denmark, all with strong economies and a thirst for fine wine, has further strained the supplies of good burgundies. The traditional markets of England and America will have to adjust to higher and higher prices or be isolated from the Burgundy marketplace. Eastern Europe, now that the walls of communism have been torn down, offers an entirely new market. Its countries have rich traditions that frequently involve the consumption of fine wine. For nearly four decades their hedonistic desires have been suppressed. When their economies strengthen and a middle class arises, what additional pressures will they put on the available supplies of red and white burgundy?

As for the generic appellation wines, they certainly will not appreciate to the extent that the Premiers Crus and Grands Crus will. However, Burgundy, much like Bordeaux, has become somewhat of a caste system for wine producers. The greatest wines from the greatest producers are able to fetch astronomical prices because there is no shortage of wealthy clients prepared to buy them. While the prices exclude most consumers and students of wine, it does encourage them to look for values in the more obscure appellations, such as Saint-Aubin, Saint-Romain, and of course, the up-and-coming appellations of the Côte

Chalonnaise. While none of these wines will ever approach the magnificent qualities of a Grand Cru such as Musigny of Chambertin-Clos de Bèze, they still have enough burgundy character to satisfy a great majority of even the most demanding palates.

The situation with the great white burgundies is even more exacerbated by excessive demand. When one considers that great Grands Crus such as Montrachet and Chevalier-Montrachet consist of only 19.7 and 18.1 acres, respectively, it seems inevitable that prices will double or even triple over the next decade.

Today's connoisseur of burgundy must be prepared either to pay a high price, or to search elsewhere for great Pinot Noir and Chardonnay.

What are the most notable trends in Burgundy today?
There are many positive things happening in Burgundy. I have already alluded to the increasing quality of all the wines of Burgundy that started in the late seventies. In addition, growers and *négociants* are paying far greater attention to the type of root stocks used, to the proper, higher quality clones of Pinot Noir being planted, and to the care and sanitary conditions in which the wines are made. The wines that result are more interesting and of higher quality. A new generation of producers and growers is also emerging, producing fine wines from what were once the obscure appellations. Saint-Aubin, Saint-Romain, Auxey-Duresses, and the appellations of the Côte Chalonnais such as Mercurey, Montagny, Givry, Rully, and Bouzeron are names that will be increasingly significant in the nineties.

Burgundy may well be experiencing a new golden age, starting with the superb 1985 vintage. In 1986 there was a superb white wine vintage but a variable yet sometimes good red wine vintage, in 1987 a terribly underrated, delicious red wine vintage, and in 1988 another excellent vintage. As for 1989, it should prove to be at least very good, and in some cases superb. It is certainly the finest white wine vintage in more than a decade. There is a lot of fine burgundy in the marketplace, but it is expensive. However, the overall quality level has never been higher.

At the *négociant* level, with a few major exceptions, there has been a recognition of the importance of either acquiring vineyards to insure a source of grapes for their wines, or signing exclusivity contracts with growers to produce and market the wines of certain domaines. This is a trend that I believe will continue, and lead to not only greater competition in the Burgundy marketplace, but also to higher and higher quality wine. The *négociants* have the financial means to produce superb wines; it is just a question of whether or not they have the proper philosophical commitment to do so. Many do. Perhaps it is wishful thinking to believe that those *négociants* who continue to lag behind in the production of high quality wine will find themselves left out in the cold. However, in today's wine world of intense competition, overbearing scrutiny from writers and wine merchants, and the relentless demand by consumers for better products, it is quality that sells best.

The growth of estate-bottled burgundies is a relatively recent phenomenon. Who do we have to thank for that development?
Raymond Baudoin was the man responsible for encouraging some of Burgundy's best small growers, such as Ponsot in Morey St.-Denis, Rousseau in Gevrey-Chambertin, Roumier in Chambolle-Musigny, Gouges in Nuits St.-Georges, Ramonet in Cassagne-Montrachet, and d'Angerville in Volnay to estate-bottle their wines. In the 1920s Baudoin founded *La Revue du Vin de France*, which to this day remains the leading French wine publication. Baudoin had lamented the fact that the great burgundies of the Côte d'Or would be sold to *négociants*, and then lose their individual identities by being blended with a large quantity of inferior wine. He began to purchase barrels of wine directly from the growers, who would estate-bottle them for him. In turn, he would sell them privately to clients and restaurants in Paris. Baudoin, who died in 1953, is the father of the estate-bottling movement in Burgundy.

However, it was Frank Schoonmaker, the American importer, who deserves recognition for being the first to see the potential and quality of these estate-bottled burgundies, and to expose the American market to them. Frank Schoonmaker died in 1976, and most wine neophytes, unfortunately, are probably not familiar with the significance of his contributions. For these wine consumers, I highly recommend *The Frank Schoonmaker Encyclopedia of Wine*, a classic that was first published in 1964 and most recently updated by the well-known New York wine writer, Alexis Bespaloff, in 1988. This encyclopedia is only one of the legacies Frank Schoonmaker left wine enthusiasts. Schoonmaker, a Renaissance man born in the town of Spearfish, South Dakota, came from a family that stressed education and enlightenment. His father taught at Columbia University and his mother was a leading feminist of the times. After graduating from college in the mid-twenties, Schoonmaker went to Europe. There, he had his first exposure to wine. In 1927, at age 21 he wrote the book, *Through Europe on $2 a Day*. Although it appeared just before the Depression, the book was a success, and led to Schoonmaker's collaboration with Lowell Thomas on two additional travel books: *Come with Me Through France* and *Come with Me Through Spain*. These in turn resulted in several magazine articles about wine in *The New Yorker*, commissioned by shrewd editors who realized the potential for interest in wine when Prohibition ended in 1933.

My research has never been able to reveal the exact date that Schoonmaker met Raymond Baudoin, but the Marquis d'Angerville was able to establish that it was over a wine tasting and meal at a restaurant called Le Roy Gourmet sometime in the late twenties or early thirties. At this meeting Schoonmaker and Baudoin discussed the possibility of Schoonmaker's purchasing wine from Baudoin, or alternatively, directly from the growers who were estate-bottling their wines for Baudoin to sell in France.

In 1935 Schoonmaker and some other investors formed the importing firm of Bates and Schoonmaker. At the same time men like Freddy Wildman and Julian Street were starting merchant businesses dedicated to the sale of fine French wine and estate-bottled burgundies. The Marquis d'Angerville shared with me a copy of his first wine order from Bates and Schoonmaker. It came on April 30, 1935 when Schoonmaker ordered 10 cases of Volany-Clos des Fremiets 1929, costing a total of 1,680 francs. Other producers, such as the Tollots in Chorey-Lès-Beaune, as well as Rousseau and Gouges, remember selling wine directly to Schoonmaker's firm in New York City at about the same time.

Schoonmaker's heir apparents include Robert Haas, who founded one of America's leading companies dedicated to estate-bottled burgundies, and the late Alexis Lichine, who, in the 1960s, developed the idea of purchasing wine directly from the growers, commercializing it under his own name, but also indicating the name of the grower on the label.

These gentlemen were the cornerstones of the estate-bottled burgundy movement. The Schoonmaker selections are represented today by Château and Estates. Frederick Wildman and Company is still a thriving import firm in New York City, as is Vineyard Brands, the company started by Robert Haas in Chester, Vermont. Alexis Lichine sold his wine company to the English firm of Bass-Charrington and concentrated on his beloved château in Margaux, Prieuré-Lichine, which he purchased in 1951.

As more and more growers begin to domaine-bottle their wines, the recognition and promotion of estate-bottled burgundies has never been stronger. In addition to Château and Estates, Frederick Wildman and Company, and Robert Haas, the American importers of estate-bottled burgundy include the idiosyncratic, outspoken Berkeley importer, Kermit Lynch, Neal Rosenthal of Select Vineyards in New York City, Alain Blanchon of Blanchon Cellars, Fort Washington, Pennsylvania, Robert Kacher Selections in Washington, D.C., Martine Saunier Selections in

San Rafael, California, and a handful of American and French special-ists living and working in France. These include the Paris-based Peter Vezan, a transplanted American who is one of the most knowledgeable people I have ever talked to about burgundy. He has ferreted out many top growers, whose wine he sells to importers in America, the United Kingdom, and Europe. Becky Wasserman, an American woman who set up shop in the tranquil countryside west of Savigny-Lès-Beaune, represents small Burgundy estates and sells their wines to American importers. Another young woman, Jeanne-Marie de Champs, primarily known as a Beaune broker, has put together an extensive portfolio of top quality small growers whose wine she sells throughout the world.

A Beaune resident named Alain Corcia finances the purchase of barrels, and persuades growers who had been selling their crops to *négociants* that they would benefit from signing an exclusivity contract with him. Corcia provides the capital necessary for buying barrels, corks, labels, and bottles, and then represents the growers' wines in-ternationally. As one might expect, Corcia has few friends among *né-gociants*. However, he has put together a strong lineup of quality producers.

AN AFTERTHOUGHT

If most of the responses to these twenty questions distressingly suggest that the wines of Burgundy are too expensive, too variable in quality, too quick to fall apart, too difficult and troublesome to find, then why are they so cherished? Are the only people who buy these wines wealthy masochists? Is it because burgundy, of all the wines in the world, defies definition, defies systemization, and resists standardization? It would appear that no matter how much time, effort, and money is spent trying to understand the wines of Burgundy, to a large extent they remain an unfathomable mystery. Given the perplexing, fragmented nature of Burgundy's vineyards, the notorious inconsistency in wine quality, its hideously high, even appalling prices, and the relatively short life span most burgundies possess, the answer can only be that when Burgundy is at its greatest, it irrefutably provides the world's most majestic, glorious, and hedonistic red and white wine.

PART I

THE GROWERS AND PRODUCERS OF BURGUNDY

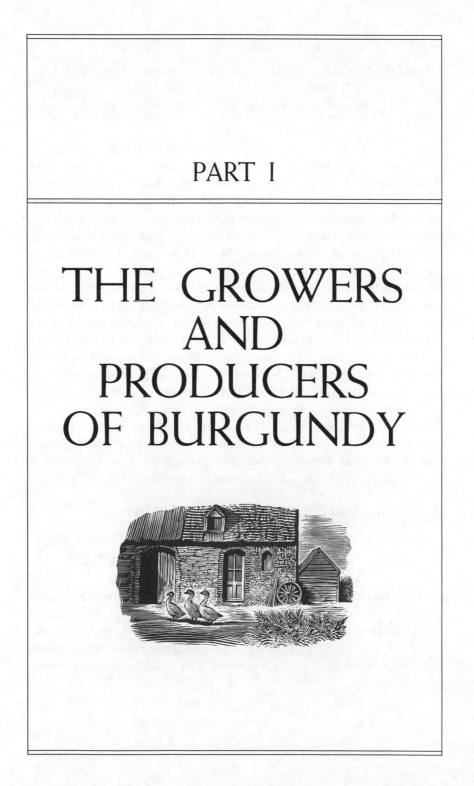

DOMAINE BERTRAND AMBROISE (PRÉMEAUX)****

> Wines Produced: Bourgogne Blanc, Corton-Rognet, Côte de Nuits-Villages, Nuits St.-Georges, Nuits St.-Georges Rue de Chaux, Nuits St.-Georges Les Vaucrains.

I was happy to discover the small domaine of Bertrand Ambroise on one of my recent trips to Burgundy. Ambroise, a young protégé of Daniel Chopin of the Domaine Chopin-Groffier, has his cellars in Prémeaux. I have only followed his wines since 1987, but in the two vintages I have tasted, the wines were remarkable for their outstanding color, their faithfulness to their appellations, and their exceptional richness and purity. Ambroise usually believes in 100% destemming, although in healthy vintages, such as 1988 and 1989, as much as one-quarter of the stems are left in to give the wines more structure and tannin. Like Daniel Chopin, Ambroise believes in a cold prefermentation maceration to extract color and perfume from the grapes. Fifty percent new oak is employed for both his Grand Cru Corton-Rognet and his Premiers Crus. The wines spend 18 months in small casks and are bottled with very little fining, and as light a filtration as possible. Judging from the vintages I have tasted, Ambroise makes three staggering wines from his small domaine: the Nuits St.-Georges Rue de Chaux, the Nuits St.-Georges Les Vaucrains, and his spectacular Corton-Rognet. These wines will catapault the name Bertrand Ambroise into the limelight in the nineties. His wines give every indication of being capable of aging gracefully for up to a decade.

BERNARD AMIOT (CHAMBOLLE-MUSIGNY)**

> Wines Produced: Chambolle-Musigny, Chambolle-Musigny Les Charmes, Chambolle-Musigny Les Chatelots.

This is a tiny domaine of 14.8 acres that makes elegant, relatively light wines from the sleepy village of Chambolle-Musigny. I have only tasted a few vintages from Bernard Amiot. His 1985s, 1987s, and 1988s are sound, although they were all wines that required consumption within 5–6 years of the vintage. Lower yields and a lighter filtration would improve quality.

PIERRE AMIOT ET FILS (MOREY ST.-DENIS)***

> Wines Produced: Bourgogne Rouge, Chambolle-Musigny Les Baudes, Charmes-Chambertin, Clos de la Roche, Clos St.-Denis, Gevrey-Chambertin, Gevrey-Chambertin Les Combottes, Morey St.-Denis, Morey St.-Denis aux Charmes, Morey St.-Denis Les Millandes.

Pierre Amiot, from a different family and village than Bernard Amiot, is one of the best known and most well liked of the small Burgundy growers. A man whose girth is almost equal to his height, he produces wonderfully fruity, elegant wines that drink extremely well young. They are never particularly tannic or powerful, but if it is finesse and pure charm you want, then Amiot's wines are sure to please. His domaine includes 24 acres of prestigious vineyards spread throughout three different Côte de Nuits appellations. His principal holdings include a 3.7-acre parcel of Clos de la Roche, a 2.1-acre parcel of Morey St.-Denis Les Millandes, and 6.2 acres of Morey St.-Denis. He also has tiny half-acre parcels of Clos St.-Denis and Charmes-Chambertin, as well as a 1.6-acre parcel of Gevrey-Chambertin Les Combottes, and smaller parcels of Gevrey-Chambertin Villages and Chambolle-Musigny Les Baudes. Amiot's wines spend 15–20 months in oak casks, of which 10% are new, except for his Grands Crus, which are aged in nearly 100% new oak. His recent vintages, such as 1985, 1987, and 1988, have been successful. Buyers of Pierre Amiot wines should make a mental note to be sure and drink them up within 5–7 years of the vintage as they are not long-distance runners.

AMIOT-BONFILS (CHASSAGNE-MONTRACHET)****

> Wines Produced: Bourgogne Aligoté, Chassagne-Montrachet Les Caillerets, Chassagne-Montrachet Les Champains, Chassagne-Montrachet Clos St.-Jean, Chassagne-Montrachet Les Macherelles, Chassagne-Montrachet La Maltroie, Chassagne-Montrachet Rouge, Chassagne-Montrachet Les Vergers, Le Montrachet, Puligny-Montrachet Les Demoiselles.

Note: This firm also sells its wine under the label of Pierre Amiot.

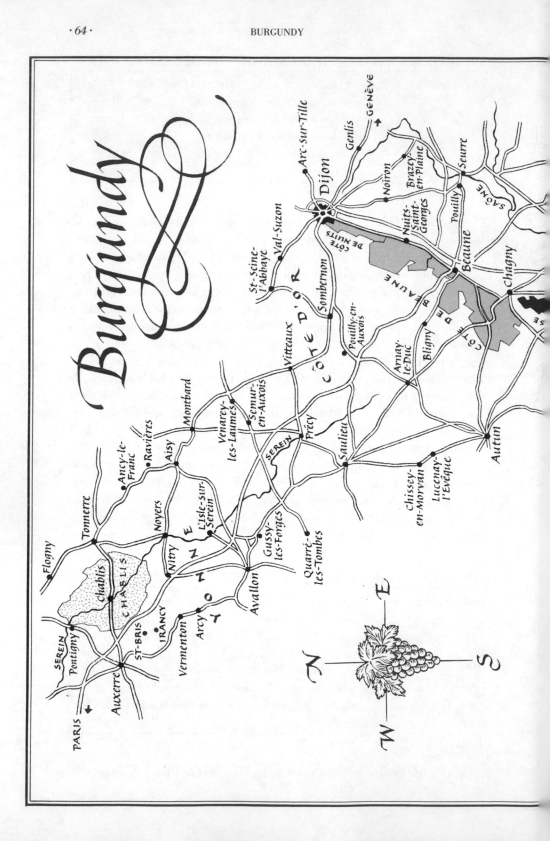

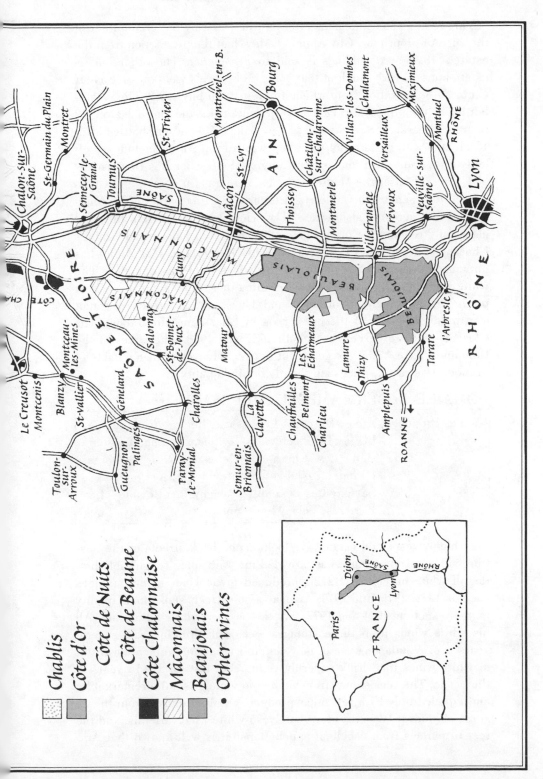

Chablis
Côte d'Or
Côte de Nuits
Côte de Beaune
Côte Chalonnaise
Mâconnais
Beaujolais
• Other wines

This estate was established after World War I by the grandfather of the current proprietor, Guy Amiot. Today, half the production from the estate's 18.96-acre holdings is sold to *négociants*. The other half is estate-bottled, with much of that going to France's well-known Savour Club, an organization from which amateurs can buy wine. The estate-bottled white wines are aged in 50% new oak, and bottled after 12 months in cask. The reds see less new oak, 25%, and are bottled after 15 months with no filtration. The top wines from Amiot include excellent wines from the Premier Cru Puligny-Montrachet Les Demoiselles (.74 acres), Chassagne-Montrachet Les Vergers (1.6 acres), and Chassagne-Montrachet Les Caillerets (1.6 acres). A tiny parcel of Le Montrachet (.24 acres) is also owned. The wines tend to be rich, full, and classically rendered. Curiously, in 1986 and 1988 I preferred Amiot's Chassagne-Montrachet Les Vergers to his Montrachet. Guy Amiot has immensely improved the quality of the wines from this domaine. The white wines may be on the verge of rivaling those from some of the best producers in Puligny-Montrachet and Chassagne-Montrachet. Amiot also produces some of the finest reds in Chassagne-Montrachet. His Clos St.-Jean was excellent in both 1987 and 1988. The wines of the Domaine Pierre Amiot are good, but not terribly well known outside of France. As a result, prices lag slightly behind quality.

DOMAINE ROBERT AMPEAU (MEURSAULT)****

Wines Produced: Auxey-Duresses-Eccussaux, Beaune Clos du Roi, Blagny-La Pièce Sous le Bois, Meursault, Meursault Les Charmes, Meursault Les Perrières, Pommard, Puligny-Montrachet Les Combettes, Savigny-Lès-Beaune, Savigny-Lès-Beaune Les Lavières, Volnay Santenots.

This highly respected estate, overlooking the back streets of the bustling village of Meursault, has provided me with some remarkable bottles of white burgundy. Having produced great wines in top vintages such as 1973, 1978, and 1979, Ampeau also extracts sensational quality in years such as 1974 and 1977, and this is particularly admirable. All his white wines from these vintages were still drinking well several years ago. A judicious use of new oak and a careful vinification result in white wines that drink superbly young, but last for 10–15 years in the bottle. The consistency from vintage to vintage is quite remarkable, and equaled only by a few other producers in Burgundy. From the 25 acres of vineyards, 13 are, fortunately, in white wine varietals, and the rest in parcels from excellent appellations. It is well known that Ampeau's magical tough with white wines rarely extends to his red wine-making. His best reds tend to be his Volnay Santenots and Beaune Clos du Roi, which are good, but simply not as sublime or as complex as his Meursaults and Puligny-Montrachet Les Combettes. Ampeau, a fierce negotiator when it comes to selling his wines, often makes purchasers take several bottles of red wine for every bottle of white they buy. He is also one of the last producers to sell a given vintage, frequently holding his wines for 4–7 years before releasing them. This may explain why much of his wine is not seen in the export markets.

DOMAINE PIERRE ANDRÉ (ALOXE-CORTON)***

Wines Produced: Clos Vougeot, Corton-Charlemagne, Corton-Clos du Roi, Corton Les Rénardes, Savigny-Lès-Beaune-Clos des Guettes, Savigny-Lès-Beaune-Clos des Langres.

Pierre André is the founder and principal owner of the large commercial *négociant* in Beaune called La Reine Pédauque. This enterprise is known largely for its range of dull, commercial burgundies, wines that are highly promoted but rarely ever inspiring. However, André has a line of wines from his own 55-acre estate, which includes superb vineyard parcels in Corton-Charlemagne, Corton-Clos du Roi, Clos Vougeot, and the unheralded but extremely good Savigny-Lès-Beaune-Clos des Guettes. The wines that appear under the Domaine Pierre André label are significantly better than those from La Reine Pédauque, although one suspects that with a little less filtration and commercial compromise they could be superior. Nevertheless, they are well made, clean, sound wines that reflect their appellations and can be cellared for 8–10 years in the top vintages.

DOMAINE MARQUIS D'ANGERVILLE (VOLNAY)***

Wines Produced: Bourgogne Rouge, Meursault-Santenots, Pommard, Volnay, Volnay Les Caillerets, Volnay Champans, Volnay-Clos des Ducs, Volnay Fremiets, Volnay Taillepieds.

This beautiful estate on the hillside in the village of Volnay has had great historical significance. The current proprietor, the Marquis Jacques d'Angerville, saw his father ostracized by other winemakers because of his attempts to combat dishonest practices in the thirties and forties in Burgundy. This commitment to the appellation laws and the planting of only the finest clones of Pinot Noir has been continued by Jacques d'Angerville, an erudite man who remains one of the most knowledgeable men concerning the wines of Burgundy. His estate now includes 34.5 acres of vineyards, with his two top parcels being his *monopole* vineyard, the Volnay-Clos des Ducs and his Volnay Champans. (N.B.:I have also had good luck with his Volnay Taillepieds.) His wines are made in a rather light, delicate style. While in certain vintages this has left me desiring a bit more richness and flesh, I must admit I have a minority point of view on the subject. The Marquis believes in 100% destemming and the use of 25% new wood, but I believe his decision to filter his wines strips them of some of their essence and richness. In most recent vintages his wines have aged well for 6–10 years.

DOMAINE ARLAUD PÈRE ET FILS
(NUITS ST.-GEORGES)**

Wines Produced: Bonnes Mares, Bourgogne Rouge, Chambolle-Musigny, Charmes-Chambertin, Clos de la Roche, Clos St.-Denis, Gevrey-Chambertin, Gevrey-Chambertin Les Combottes, Morey St.-Denis, Nuits St.-Georges.

Hervé Arlaud runs this sizable estate with plenty of well-placed vineyards. His cellars are located in Nuits St.-Georges. The vintages I have tasted have hardly been classic red burgundies. Many of the wines exhibit a sweet taste as a result of sugar, as this is an estate that clearly believes in the maximum use of *chaptalization*. Nevertheless many of the wines of Domaine Arlaud have a lush, sweetish seductive appeal. The estate is highly morselated, the biggest parcels consisting of 2.79 acres of the Grand Cru Charmes-Chambertin (usually the domaine's best wine), and 5.4 acres of Morey St.-Denis. All of the remaining holdings are less than one hectare, with the exception of the 15.3-acre parcel that Arlaud uses to produce his Bourgogne Rouge. These are wines to drink young when they are straightforward, gushing with fruit, and easy to understand. They are not classic red burgundies by any means, nor do they age particularly well. For uncomplicated drinking, however, they have their following.

DOMAINE DE L'ARLOT (PRÉMEAUX)****

Wines Produced: Nuits St.-Georges Blanc, Nuits St.-Georges-Clos
de l'Arlot, Nuits St.-Georges-Clos des Forêts St.-
Georges.

In Burgundy, where time is measured over centuries, new domaines
are rare. One of the most encouraging developments in the last several
years has been the formation of the Domaine de l'Arlot. The domaine
was made from vineyards previously owned by the *négociant* Jules Belin
and acquired by one of France's large insurance companies. Jean-
Pierre de Smet, a former apprentice of Jacques Seysses of the Domaine
Dujac, is in charge, and he has transferred virtually all of the Domaine
Dujac winemaking techniques to this new 31.2-acre estate. The results
are excellent 1987s and stunning 1988s. There is no destemming. A
prefermentation maceration of the grape bunches for 3–5 days is done,
followed by a relatively long maceration of three weeks or more. Fifty
percent new oak barrels are used, very few rackings, and bottling of
the wine is done after 15–18 months in barrel, with no filtration. As
mentioned, the quality of the first two vintages is impeccable, with the
wines showing very fragrant, aromatic personalities, and stylish, beautiful layers of Pinot fruit in abundance. Domain de l'Arlot is one of the
up-and-coming stars of Nuits St.-Georges, and is capable of challenging
some of the best producers of this appellation.

DOMAINE COMTE ARMAND (POMMARD)****

Wines Produced: Pommard-Clos des Epeneaux.

This is an unusual domaine in the sense that only one wine is produced.
From 13.04 acres of the vineyard Clos des Epeneaux, an enclosed portion of the larger Les Epenots vineyard, comes a full-bodied, rich, big,
oaky, plummy Pommard with a great deal of character. The young
Canadian *régisseur*, Pascal Marchand, oversees the making and upbringing of this wine, which is aged in 50%–60% new oak casks where
it spends 18–22 months. If conditions are right, a filtration is avoided,
but in some vintages there may be a light filtration before bottling. This
is one of the best wines of Pommard; the 1985 and 1988 were stunning.
Occasionally, tiny quantities of a Cuvée Vieilles Vignes are also produced, but I have never seen a bottle available commercially.

DOMAINE ROBERT ARNOUX (VOSNE-ROMANÉE)****

> Wines Produced: Bourgogne Rouge, Clos Vougeot, Echézeaux, Nuits St.-Georges des Corvées-Paget, Nuits St.-Georges Les Poirets, Nuits St.-Georges Les Procès, Romanée St.-Vivant, Vosne-Romanée Les Chaumes, Vosne-Romanée Maiziers, Vosne-Romanée Les Suchots.

The tall, robust Robert Arnoux can produce exceptional Pinot Noir. His 1978s, now beginning to fade, were among the great wines of that vintage. He also turned in other superb performances in 1980 and 1985. In vintages with large yields, his wines can be a bit risky, but when Arnoux is on target his wines are among the most seductive and complex wines in all of Burgundy, with a character not unlike downsized versions of the wines of the Domaine de la Romanée-Conti. The estate consists of 27.17 acres with some very important Premier Cru holdings in Vosne-Romanée and Nuits St.-Georges. There are three Grand Cru holdings in Clos Vougeot, Echézeaux, and Romanée St.-Vivant. Arnoux's best wines are usually his Vosne-Romanée Les Suchots, Clos Vougeot, and Romanée St.-Vivant. For whatever reason I never find his Premiers Crus from Nuits St.-Georges to be as good, but they certainly represent the appellation. Arnoux uses 30% new oak with a higher percentage for his Grands Crus, and keeps his wines 15–18 months in oak casks. The wines are bottled without any filtration if possible, although in recent vintages he has been inclined to employ a light filtering at the time of bottling. When Arnoux gets everything right, his domaine is a satisfying source of excellent red burgundy that is sold at a reasonable price. Arnoux's wines, even in the best vintages, should be drunk within their first 7–8 years of life.

DOMAINE ARNOUX PÈRE ET FILS (CHOREY-LÈS-BEAUNE)**

> Wines Produced: Aloxe-Corton, Beaune, Beaune en Genet, Bourgogne Aligoté, Bourgogne Passe-Tout-Grains, Bourgogne Rouge, Chorey-Lès-Beaune, Corton Rognet, Savigny-Lès-Beaune, Savigny-Lès-Beaune aux Guettes.

Standard-quality wines are produced by Michel and Remi Arnoux from their 55.2 acres of vineyards. Their most significant holdings are 24.7 acres of Chorey-Lès-Beaune and 13.3 acres of Savigny-Lès-Beaune. The wines see 10% new oak and after 14 months are filtered and then bottled. The style of winemaking seems to produce somewhat coarse, straightforward wines that lack complexity and bouquet, and finish with a bit too much tannin. Perhaps they improve with extended aging, but my guess is that they just don't have enough fruit for the amount of tannin.

AUVIGUE-BURRIER-REVEL (CHARNAY-LES-MÂCON)***

> Wines Produced: Mâcon-Villages, Pouilly-Fuissé, Pouilly-Fuissé-Les Chailloux, Pouilly-Fuissé-Solutré, Saint-Véran.

This small firm, established in 1946, is one of the most respected specialists in the wines of Pouilly-Fuissé and Saint-Véran. Their production is small, but the quality is of the highest level. Their wines from the Pouilly-Fuissé appellation are among the top half-dozen wines produced in that region. In addition, their Saint-Véran often has a great deal more depth and richness than other examples of that wine. The winemaking is very traditional, with aging in wooden casks rather than stainless steel vats. The wines are usually bottled after 8–10 months. The wines from this domaine are favorites of such great restaurants in France as La Mere Blanc in Vonnas, as well as Lasserre and Maxim's in Paris.

DOMAINE BERNARD BACHELET ET FILS (DEZIZE-LES-MARANGES)**

> Wines Produced: Bourgogne Aligoté, Bourgogne Blanc, Bourgogne Rouge, Chassagne-Montrachet Morgeot Blanc, Chassagne-Montrachet Rouge, Côte de Beaune-Villages, Gevrey-Chambertin, Meursault, Meursault Le Cromin, Meursault Les Narvaux, Meursault Les Vireuils, Monthélie, Pommard, Pommard Les Chanlins, Puligny-Montrachet, Santenay.

Working with 16 appellations, Bernard Bachelet and his sons have a considerable domaine of 73.02 acres. They sell about half their production to *négociants* and estate-bottle the rest. The wines have a certain following, but in the vintages I have tasted, 1983 (too much rot), 1984 (too much acidity), 1985 (no problems), and 1986 (too prolific a crop), I have wondered why this domaine has such a good reputation. The red wines are too frequently meagerly endowed, and show entirely too much tannin for their shallow fruitiness. I have had a number of disappointing bottles, including their Côte de Beaune-Villages (27.5 acres) and a number of flawed Santenays (6.67 acres). Their best wine is usually the Pommard Les Chanlins (1.9 acres). The red wines see 15% new oak and are bottled after 14–18 months in cask; the white wines see 20%–25% new oak and are bottled after 12 months. The domaine has some important holdings in Meursault, including 1.8 acres in Meursault Les Narvaux, 1.85 acres in Meursault Les Vireuils, and 1.23 acres in Meursault Le Cromin. Overall, these are wines I would approach with a great deal of caution given the inconsistencies I have noticed.

DOMAINE DENIS BACHELET
(GEVREY-CHAMBERTIN)****

Wines Produced: Bourgogne Rouge, Charmes-Chambertin, Gevrey-Chambertin, Gevrey-Chambertin Les Corbeaux, Gevrey-Chambertin Vieilles Vignes.

This minuscule domaine of 5.14 acres has been run by Denis Bachelet since 1983. He has a lot of talent, and a good touch for allowing the fruit of the wine to come through in a pure, unfettered manner. Although his property is tiny, he has a great many vines 35 years or older. He makes a Gevrey-Chambertin Vieilles Vignes from a 2.47-acre parcel, as well as a Gevrey-Chambertin Les Corbeaux from relatively old vines on a tiny parcel of .74 acre. He has one section of Grand Cru vineyard, a 1.23-acre tract in Charmes-Chambertin. If one goes by the example of his 1985, 1986, and 1987, this is clearly his best wine, although at quadruple the price of his Gevrey-Chambertin Vieilles Vignes, it's not his best value. Bachelet also has just less than one acre of vines outside the appellation of Gevrey-Chambertin that is entitled only to Bourgogne Rouge status. Denis Bachelet is an excellent producer who has shown in his brief career that he can do well in top vintages, such as 1985, as well as in mediocre years, such as 1986.

DOMAINE JEAN-CLAUDE BACHELET
(SAINT-AUBIN)****

Wines Produced: Bienvenues-Bâtard-Montrachet, Bourgogne Aligoté, Bourgogne Rouge, Chassagne-Montrachet, Chassagne-Montrachet-Blanchot-Dessus, Chassagne-Montrachet Les Boudriottes, Chassagne-Montrachet Les Encegnières, Chassagne-Montrachet Les Encegnières Blanc, Chassagne-Montrachet Rouge, Puligny-Montrachet Les Aubues, Puligny-Montrachet Sous les Puits, Saint-Aubin Les Champlots, Saint-Aubin-Derrière la Tour.

For years Jean-Claude Bachelet sold half his crop to *négociants*, but in the last several years he has estate-bottled nearly all his wine. His 18.5 acres of vineyards are spread out through the villages of Chassagne-Montrachet, Puligny-Montrachet, and Saint-Aubin. He is an excellent winemaker, producing wines with great finesse and elegance. His top wine is his only Grand Cru, the Bienvenues-Bâtard-Montrachet. Unfortunately, he owns only .22 acre of this vineyard, which he planted in 1971. His largest parcels are his Puligny-Montrachet-Les Aubues, Chassagne-Montrachet Rouge, and his excellent stylish, cherry-scented red wine, the Saint-Aubin-Derrière la Tour. The red wines are bottled after 18 months, following a very light filtration, and the whites see 5–10% new oak casks and are bottled after 12–14 months. In most vintages, the wines of Jean-Claude Bachelet should be consumed within 7–8 years of the vintage.

DOMAINE BACHELET-RAMONET
(CHASSAGNE-MONTRACHET)**–***

Wines Produced: Bâtard-Montrachet, Bienvenues-Bâtard-Montrachet, Chassagne-Montrachet Les Caillerets, Chassagne-Montrachet-Clos de la Boudriotte, Chassagne-Montrachet-Clos St.-Jean, Chassagne-Montrachet La Grande Montagne, Chassagne-Montrachet Morgeot, Chassagne-Montrachet La Romanée, Chassagne-Montrachet Les Ruchottes.

Most white burgundy enthusiasts operate under the assumption that the famous name Ramonet on a label of white burgundy guarantees ecstasy in the bottle. Caveat emptor—particularly with the wines from Bachelet-Ramonet. I have encountered many oxidized bottles of wine from this grower, especially from the 1982 and 1983 vintages, and a look at the dreary, unkempt cellar hardly inspires confidence. That being said, this important estate of 25 acres has choice parcels in some of the best vineyards in Chassagne-Montrachet, and the raw materials produced from these vineyards are superb. The problem appears to be the lack of attention the wine receives in the cellar. Fortunately, Bachelet's 1986s showed better in cask; hopefully this high quality will be evident in the bottle as well. This estate also makes two rather simple but pleasant red wines from the Clos St.-Jean and Clos de la Boudriotte vineyards in Chassagne-Montrachet.

CHÂTEAU BADER-MIMEUR
(CHASSAGNE-MONTRACHET)**

Wines Produced: Chassagne-Montrachet-Clos du Château Blanc, Chassagne-Montrachet-Clos du Château Rouge, St.-Aubin-en Remilly.

Pierre Bader runs this 14.37-acre estate and produces rather straight-forward, average quality wine. Most of the production is in a rather dull Chassagne-Montrachet Rouge, and perhaps the best wine is the least expensive one, the white St.-Aubin. The red wines see 12–18 months in cask, are filtered and then bottled, while the white wines spend 12–14 months in cask. One hundred percent of the production is estate-bottled, and no new oak is presently used.

DOMAINE RAYMOND BALLOT-MILLOT ET FILS
(MEURSAULT)****

Wines Produced: Beaune, Beaune-Les Epenottes, Bourgogne Aligoté, Bourgogne Rouge, Chassagne-Montrachet Morgeot, Chassagne-Montrachet La Romanée, Chassagne-Montrachet Rouge, Meursault Blanc, Meursault Les Charmes, Meursault Les Criots, Meursault Les Genevrières, Meursault Les Perrières, Meursault Rouge, Pommard, Pommard Les Pézerolles, Pommard Les Rugiens, Volnay Santenots, Volnay Taillepieds.

Philippe Ballot and his family run this moderately large estate (by Burgundian standards) of 34.9 acres with a great deal of care and commitment to quality. The logistical nightmare of having to make wine from 19 separate appellations must certainly cause many a sleepless night during the harvest, but very often the results justify all the work. This is an estate that can excel in both red and white wines. I have tasted some superb Pommard Les Pézerolles (1.48 acres), as well as some nearly top-notch Pommard Les Rugiens (1.06 acres), and Volnay Taillepieds (.88 acre) from this outstanding producer. Ballot uses 33% new oak for his red wines and bottles them without filtration after 14–18 months in cask. As for the white wines, Ballot's four top whites are the Meursault Les Perrières, Chassagne-Montrachet La Romanée, Meursault Les Genevrières, and Meursault Les Charmes. However, there is also very good straight Meursault Blanc, and for collectors, even a tiny quantity of the rarely encountered Meursault Rouge. The white wines see 25% new oak and are bottled after 10–12 months in cask. Most of the production of Ballot-Millot is sold in Europe, but increasing quantities are being seen outside of the Common Market. The same wines also appear under the labels Dancer-Lochardet and Ballot et Dancer.

DOMAINE ANDRÉ BART (MARSANNAY)**

> Wines Produced: Bonnes Mares, Bourgogne Rouge, Chambertin, Fixin, Fixin Les Hervelets, Marsannay Blanc, Marsannay Rosé, Marsannay Rouge, Santenay.

This unheralded domaine has 32.1 acres of vineyards with just over half in generic Bourgogne and the rest sprawled over appellations from Fixin to Santenay. André, the father, and Martin, the son, also own 1 acre of Chambertin-Clos de Bèze and 1.2 acres of Bonnes Mares. The wines are solid and soundly made with the Grands Crus seeing 40% new oak for 14–15 months. The 1986s, 1987s, and 1988s are not exciting enough to justify much enthusiasm.

DOMAINE GASTON BARTHOD-NOËLLAT (CHAMBOLLE-MUSIGNY)****

> Wines Produced: Bourgogne Rouge, Chambolle-Musigny, Chambolle-Musigny aux Beaux Bruns, Chambolle-Musigny Les Charmes, Chambolle-Musigny Les Cras, Chambolle-Musigny Les Varoilles.

Like many small Burgundy growers, the elderly, wise Gaston Barthod is a one-man show. He plows and prunes his vineyards, and brings up the wines with the help of his wife and daughter. Barthod speaks only after much reflection, preferring to let his wines do all the talking for him. They are handcrafted, unfiltered wines that are rarely profound but are richly satisfying. His entire domaine consists of 12.47 acres, with his biggest parcel a 6.24-acre, well-placed vineyard of the village Chambolle-Musigny. He does have 3 Premiers Crus, including Chambolle-Musigny Les Cras (1.3 acres), an excellently placed Premier Cru vineyard near the Grand Cru Bonnes Mares. The wines here are aged in 20%–40% new oak casks for 15–18 months. In 1988 he began to produce a Chambolle-Musigny Les Varoilles from a parcel of vines further up the hill above Bonnes Mares. I have found the wines of Barthod-Noëllat to be very elegant and stylish, and they usually age nicely for 7–8 years. His best recent vintage is 1988, followed by the 1985 vintage.

DOMAINE L. BASSY (ODENAS)***

> Wine Produced: Côte de Brouilly.

Monsieur Bassy is one of the best small growers in the appellation of Côte de Brouilly, making wonderfully lush, luxuriously fruity, perfumed, expansively flavored wines. They are absolutely irresistible young, and age well for 2–3 years.

CHÂTEAU DU BASTY (LANTIGNIE)***

> Wines Produced: Beaujolais Lantignié, Beaujolais Régnié.

Proprietor Maurice Perroud runs this modestly sized 37-acre estate primarily known for its smooth, supple Beaujolais Lantignié. A supple, fragrant Beaujolais Régnié is also made here. The property has been in the same family for over 15 generations.

DOMAINE PHILIPPE BATACCHI
(GEVREY-CHAMBERTIN)**

> Wines Produced: Clos de la Roche, Côte de Nuits-Villages, Gevrey-Chambertin, Morey St.-Denis, Morey St.-Denis-Premier Cru.

Batacchi is an adequate, if somewhat irregular producer, with a modestly sized domaine of 13.04 acres. The biggest parcels are in appellation Gevrey-Chambertin Controlée (5.67 acres), Côte de Nuits-Villages (3.40 acres), and in the village Morey St.-Denis (2.47 acres). In addition, he has just over 1 acre of Morey St.-Denis Premier Cru, and .49 of an acre of the famous Grand Cru of Morey St.-Denis, Clos de la Roche. His wines tend to be rather light, and are meant to be drunk within their first 5–6 years of life.

DOMAINE CHARLES ET PAUL BAVARD
(PULIGNY-MONTRACHET)****

> Wines Produced: Bâtard-Montrachet.

In the sixties, it was possible to find estate-bottled Bâtard-Montrachet from the Domaine Bavard. In fact, one of the most memorable white burgundies I ever had was the 1966 Bavard Bâtard-Montrachet. When tasted in 1988, it was an utterly mind-blowing wine, and amazingly fresh for its age. Today, the sons of Joseph Bavard, Charles and Paul, own 1.63 acres of this great Grand Cru. Their entire production is sold to the *négociant* firm of Antonin Rodet in Mercurey. This may partially explain why, in recent vintages, Rodet's Bâtard-Montrachet has tasted so concentrated and intense.

PAUL BEAUDET (PONTENEVAUX)***

> Wines Produced: An entire range of Beaujolais and Mâconnais wines are produced by this firm.

The firm of Paul Beaudet is now in the hands of the fourth generation, Jean Beaudet, who seems firmly convinced that the wines of his firm can compete with the best in Beaujolais. This is one of the better sources for richly fruity, reliable, consistently well-made Beaujolais. The Beaudet firm has 32.1 acres spread out in the Beaujolais region, their most important domaine being Chénas-Château des Vignes. The wines can be recommended without hesitation, as they are consistently quite good. Much of the 100,000-case production is exported or sold to restaurants in foreign markets.

CHÂTEAU DE BEAUREGARD (FUISSÉ)***

> Wines Produced: Pouilly-Fuissé, Saint-Véran.

While not in the very top class of the Pouilly-Fuissés, the Château de Beauregard, run by Jacques Burier, is still a very capable, high-quality producer of relatively lush, ripe, soft, and perfumed Pouilly-Fuissé and Saint-Véran. I am not sure if the difference in price between the more expensive Pouilly-Fuissé and the Saint-Véran, at less than half the price, is reflected by the quality, but this is a very good domaine producing quite a bit of wine from 64.2 acres of vines. Both these wines see 10% new oak and are bottled after 6 months of aging in cask and tank.

DOMAINE ADRIEN BELLAND (SANTENAY)****

> Wines Produced: Aloxe-Corton, Bourgogne Rouge, Chambertin, Chassagne-Montrachet Morgeot-Clos Charreau, Corton-Charlemagne, Corton-Clos de la Vigne Saint, Côte de Beaune-Villages, Puligny-Montrachet, Santenay, Santenay-Clos Genêt, Santenay-Clos des Gravières, Santenay La Comme.

Adrien Belland, a robust man with a full head of grey hair, operates from a wine cellar that requires a great deal of kneeling if anyone over 5'10" is intent on tasting from cask. Given how many wines he makes, and the fact that I see him only every several years, a visit there often requires 2–3 hours, during which one can never stand up straight. His top wines include an excellent Chambertin from a 1.01-acre parcel. In fact, his Chambertin is a much greater, more complex wine than those from such legendary and overrated producers as Trapet, Damoy, and Camus. He also does an excellent job making full-flavored, tannic, long-lived wines from Corton and his three Premiers Crus of Santenay, of which he owns 8.76 acres. There is a tiny quantity of Corton-Charlemagne made here as well, which is quite superb. Belland's wines have a reputation for being quite tannic and forbidding in their youth, but I have not found this to be the case, except for his 1983s. He uses 25% new oak for his red wines, and bottles them after 18–24 months in cask. Very little fining or filtration is done here as Belland is a stickler for hand-crafted wines. The red wines can easily last for 10–15 years.

His white wines see 12–15 months in oak casks, 50% of which are new, giving them, in my opinion, just the right amount of spicy, toasty, vanillin flavors.

DOMAINE JOSEPH BELLAND (SANTENAY)***

Wines Produced: Chassagne-Montrachet-Clos Pitois, Côte de Beaune-Villages, Criots-Bâtard-Montrachet, Pommard Les Cras, Puligny-Montrachet Les Champs Gains, Santenay, Santenay-Clos de Beauregard, Santenay La Comme, Santenay Les Gravières.

Two more members of the Belland family, Joseph and Roger Belland, have 51 acres of vines that generally produce quite supple, charming, and more commercially oriented wines than Adrien Belland. All of their Santenays, including their excellent Santenay La Comme and Santenay Les Gravières, exhibit less tannin, but still reflect the spicy, earthy terroir. There is also a good Pommard Les Cras, and two very good white wines, Criots-Bâtard-Montrachet and Puligny-Montrachet Les Champs Gains. These are wines that require drinking within the first 5–6 years of their lives, and are usually modestly priced for their pedigrees.

DOMAINE GÉRARD BERGER
(CHEILLY-LES-MARANGES)***

> Wines Produced: Bourgogne Aligoté, Bourgogne Rosé, Bourgogne
> Rouge, Crémant de Bourgogne, Mercurey Châ-
> teaubeau Rouge, Rully Blanc, Rully Rouge.

Gérard Berger and his son Xavier have 44.31 acres and produce stylish,
crisp, fresh, modern-style fruity wines that offer considerable value.
There is a good Rully Blanc, an acceptable Rully Rouge, a decent
Crémant de Bourgogne, and a stylish Bourgogne Aligoté made without
excessive acidity. Two-thirds of the production is sold to *négociants*,
but the rest is estate-bottled and sold primarily to private clients in
Europe. These are wines to be consumed in their youth.

DOMAINE BERNARD (FLEURIE)***

> Wines Produced: Fleurie.

Much of the wine of this small producer is sold to *négociants*, with the
balance being imported to Switzerland. The estate consists of 22.7
acres in Fleurie, and the wine is reputed to be very fruity and lively.

DOMAINE ALAIN BERNILLON (SAINT-LAGER)**

> Wines Produced: Côte de Brouilly.

This producer turns out solid Côte de Brouilly although it often has a
bit too much tannin. Nevertheless, it is a spicy, sturdy wine made from
the grower's 17.29-acre vineyard. The wines spend 6–12 months in oak
foudres prior to bottling.

DOMAINE PIERRE BERNOLLIN (JULLY-LES-BUXY)***

> Wines Produced: Bourgogne Aligoté, Bourgogne Passe-Tout-Grains,
> Bourgogne Rouge, Crémant de Bourgogne, Mon-
> tagny Premier Cru.

Pierre Bernollin makes quite acceptable, and occasionally delicious,
wines from his 17.29-acre domaine. All of the production is estate-
bottled, and the red wines see 12–18 months of cask aging. There is a
surprisingly good Crémant de Bourgogne made here, but virtually the

entire production is sold to private clients. His Montagny Premier Cru
is also an extremely well-made wine.

DOMAINE RENÉ BERROD-LES ROCHES DU VIVIER (FLEURIE)****

Wines Produced: Beaujolais-Villages, Fleurie, Moulin-à-Vent.

René Berrod has one of the best reputations in all of Beaujolais for his
explosively fruity, rich, velvety Fleurie, and more powerful, spicy Moulin-à-Vent. However, one should not overlook the best value in his
portfolio, the ripe cherry and banana-scented Beaujolais-Villages. Berrod is a magician when it comes to wine, and even his Beaujolais from
less successful years seems to be imbued with a roundness and fragrance that transcends the wines of his competitors. He has 17.29 acres
of vineyards and keeps his red wines in *foudres* for 6–8 months prior to
bottling. His Moulin-à-Vent is bottled unfiltered and can last for 4–6
years. This is Beaujolais at its very best, and it gets my highest recom-
mendations.

DOMAINE BERSAN ET FILS (SAINT-BRIS-LE-VINEUX)**

Wines Produced: Bourgogne Aligoté, Bourgogne Blanc, Bourgogne
Irancy Rouge, Bourgogne Passe-Tout-Grains,
Bourgogne Rouge, Sauvignon de St.-Bris Chablis.

This relatively large family domaine of 59.28 acres is best known for its
stylish, herbaceous-scented Sauvignon de St.-Bris. The wines are all
made to be consumed within 2–3 years of the vintage.

DOMAINE BERTAGNA (VOUGEOT)***

Wines Produced: Chambertin, Chambolle-Musigny-Clos St.-Denis,
Chambolle-Musigny Les Plantes, Clos Vougeot,
Nuits St.-Georges Les Murgers, Vosne-Romanée
Les Beaux Monts, Vougeot-Clos de la Perrière,
Vougeot Premier Cru.

The Bertagna estate has 28.8 acres of important holdings including the
monopole vineyard, Vougeot-Clos de la Perrière, which sits to the right
of the road leading up to the château of Clos Vougeot. Not surprisingly,
this vineyard produces Bertagna's most interesting and complex wine.
Although they do have some Clos Vougeot, Chambertin, and Clos St.-

Denis, none of these wines seem to reach the heights of the Premier Cru, Clos de la Perrière. The Bertagna estate is one of the few in Burgundy owned by a German winemaking family from the Mosel. The Reh family, who also control the Von Kesselstatt estate, has committed much of its resources to improving the image and quality of the wines produced at Bertagna. In the last 20 years, the Bertagna wines have steadily improved, but the Rehs are still not in the top class of Burgundy producers. The wines are made from grapes that are completely destemmed, vinified in stainless-steel tanks, and put in small oak casks of which 50% are new each year. Following a rather intense filtration and fining, they're bottled after 12–14 months in cask. Perhaps a little less emphasis on commercial clarity and stability would result in more flavor in some of the wines. These are wines that should be drunk within their first 7–8 years of life.

DOMAINE DENIS BERTHAUT (FIXIN)***

> Wines Produced: Côte de Nuits-Villages, Fixin, Fixin Les Arvelets, Fixin Les Clos, Fixin Les Crais, Gevrey-Chambertin, Gevrey-Chambertin-Clos Chezeaux, Gevrey-Chambertin Premier Cru.

Denis Berthaut, a young, friendly, handsome, and open-minded man, has 28.8 acres of vineyards from which he produces a range of rather robust, tannic, old-style wines. His vinification is quite traditional, with a fairly hot fermentation temperature, 100% destemming, and 15–18 months of aging in different sized wood barrels and *foudres*. He only has a handful of new oak barrels in his tiny cellars in Fixin. The value of his wines lies in the reasonable prices he charges. His best wines are consistently his Fixin Les Arvelets and Gevrey-Chambertin-Clos Chezeaux. Berthaut's wines are for those who like plenty of tannin, muscle, and robustness in their red burgundy, as they frequently border on being coarse. His wines do indeed age well, and most can be safely drunk over a 10- to 12-year period. Recent vintages have been successful except for the 1983s, which exhibited varying degrees of rot.

DOMAINE PIERRE BERTHEAU (CHAMBOLLE-MUSIGNY)****

> Wines Produced: Bonnes Mares, Chambolle-Musigny, Chambolle-Musigny Les Amoureuses, Chambolle-Musigny Les Charmes.

I have only had a few vintages of this producer's wines (1982, 1983, 1984, 1985, 1986, and 1987), so I hardly know them well. Yet, I continue to be impressed with what I have seen to date. Pierre Bertheau, a diminutive, enthusiastic, middle-aged man, is the most underrated producer of Chambolle-Musigny. He believes in a warm fermentation of 32° C, ages his wines for 18 months in oak barrels, only a tiny percentage of which are new, and does neither a filtration nor fining prior to bottling. In large-quantity vintages, such as 1982 and 1986, over 50% of his production is sold to *négociants*. His top wines are his extraordinary Bonnes Mares, one of the best made from this Grand Cru, as well as his Chambolle-Musigny Les Amoureuses. But don't ignore his Chambolle-Musigny Les Charmes or his Chambolle-Musigny, which have been consistently impressive in flavor and complexity and sell for one-third the price of his Grands Crus. This is an unheralded, meticulously run estate that is worthy of the most serious Burgundy connoisseurs' attention. Bertheau's wines appear to be capable of lasting a decade in most vintages.

DOMAINE BESANCENOT-MATHOUILLET (BEAUNE)****

Wines Produced: Aloxe-Corton, Beaune Les Bressandes, Beaune Les Cent Vignes, Beaune Clos du Roi, Beaune Les Grèves, Beaune Les Teurons, Beaune Les Toussaints, Bourgogne Aligoté, Bourgogne Rouge, Corton-Charlemagne, Pernand-Vergelesses Blanc, Pernand-Vergelesses Rouge.

This domaine is an excellent, occasionally outstanding source for Beaune wines that reveal a wonderful respect for the different vineyards owned by Bernard Besancenot, a relatively young, enthusiastic winemaker. On his small estate of 24.7 acres, located just outside the gates of Beaune on the road to Dijon, there have been some stunning successes over recent vintages, including wonderful wines in 1980, 1985, 1987, and 1988. It is hard to say which wine is best here, but the biggest vineyard in Besancenot's stable is his 7.41 acres of Beaune Les Cent Vignes. Most of his other holdings range from 1.23 acres for such vineyards as Beaune Les Toussaints, Beaune Les Grèves, and Beaune Clos du Roi, to 3.7 acres for Beaune Les Teurons. There is even a tiny quantity (from a .74-acre parcel) of an outstanding Corton-Charlemagne. The wines see 12% new oak casks where they stay for 24 months. There is very little filtration practiced at the Domaine Besancenot-Mathouillet. Most of the wines, except in a vintage like 1983, can be drunk young, but have the ability to last for well over a decade.

DOMAINE ANDRÉ BESSON (SOLUTRE-POUILLY)***

Wines Produced: Pouilly-Fuissé, Saint-Véran.

The Pouilly-Fuissé and Saint-Véran, made by André and Tony Besson from their 20-acre vineyard, are reliably good, but not complex. The wines are aged in tank and cask for 6 months without any new oak being used. Most of the production is in Pouilly-Fuissé.

ALBERT BICHOT (BEAUNE)*–****

Domaine Wines Produced: Clos Frantin Chambertin, Clos Frantin Clos Vougeot, Clos Frantin Corton, Clos Frantin Corton-Charlemagne, Clos Frantin Echézeaux, Clos Frantin Gevrey-Chambertin, Clos Frantin Grands Echézeaux, Clos Frantin Nuits St.-Georges, Clos Frantin Vosne-Romanée Les Malconsorts, Long Depaquit Chablis, Long Depaquit Chablis les Beugnons, Long Depaquit Chablis Blanchots, Long Depaquit Chablis Les Clos, Long Depaquit Chablis Les Epinottes, Long Depaquit Chablis Les Lys, Long Depaquit Chablis Moutonne, Long Depaquit Chablis les Preuses, Long Depaquit Chablis Vaillons, Long Depaquit Chablis les Vaudesirs, Lupé-Cholet Bourgogne Rouge-Clos de Lupé, Lupé-Cholet Château de Divières Chablis, Lupé-Cholet Château Gris Nuits St.-Georges.

Note: The firm of Albert Bichot also produces an enormous range of wines under its *négociant* label, A. Bichot, and under any of the following names: Jean Bouchard, Paul Bouchard, Bauchot-Ludot, Maurice Dart, Charles Drapier, Lupé-Cholet, Fortier-Picard, Remy Gauthier, Leon Rigault, Caves Syndicales de Bourgogne.

The family Bichot, with its holdings of nearly 223 acres, is among the largest producers of Burgundy wine. The firm was founded in 1831. While the firm produces an ocean of insipid, dull wine under their own name and under the many secondary labels listed above, the two major estates owned by the Bichot firm, the 33.83-acre estate of Clos Frantin in the Côte d'Or, and the 96.33-acre estate of the Domaine Long Depaquit in Chablis, produce wines that are often quite stunning, dazzling, rich, and complex. For example, I still have some bottles of 1971 Clos Frantin Vosne-Romanée Les Malconsorts and Clos Vougeot in my cellar that have outlived and aged better than most other 1971s. Recent vintages such as 1983, 1985, and 1987 have also produced memorable wines. The Long Depaquit produced extraordinary Chablis in 1978, 1983, 1985, and 1986. How Bichot can lavish so much attention and care on these two estates, yet ignore the bulk of its production, is one of the great mysteries of Burgundy. With sales of over one million cases, and with the Clos Frantin and Long Depaquit representing a microportion of the firm's business, one wonders if anyone at Bichot is willing to address the issue, particularly in view of the fact that they claim to be the largest exporter of burgundy in the Côte d'Or. The Clos Frantin wines can easily last for 10–15 years, and the Long Depaquit Chablis, particularly the Premiers Crus and Grands Crus, are capable of lasting 8–10 years. Of the other wines, most of which are vapid and should be ignored, the best wine is the Lupé-Cholet Château Gris Nuits St.-Georges.

DOMAINE LEON BIENVENU (IRANCY)✱✱

Wines Produced: Bourgogne Irancy Rosé, Bourgogne Irancy Rouge, Bourgogne Passe-Tout-Grains.

Leon Bienvenu, president of the local syndicate of growers, has 30.9 acres of vines from which he produces one of the more serious, ageworthy red wines of Irancy. It is aged in large oak *foudres* for 10 months, and tends to be a robust wine that can be drunk or cellared for 5–6 years.

DOMAINE BILLARD-GONNET (POMMARD)✱✱

Wines Produced: Beaune, Beaune-Clos des Mouches, Beaune Les Montrevenots, Bourgogne Rouge, Pommard, Pommard Les Poutures, Pommard Les Charmots, Pommard-Clos des Vergers, Pommard Les Pézerolles, Pommard Les Rugiens.

I have never quite been able to understand the Billard family's wines. Grape growers in Pommard since 1766, they began to estate-bottle most of their production with the 1966 vintage. While I've been told that the wines age extremely well, I wonder how much true pleasure they provide. The problem is that the wines are unforgivably hard, lean, and tough, seemingly regardless of vintage conditions, suggesting to me that they need years of cellaring before they are drinkable. The estate cannot be accused of producing overcommercialized wines, as the average yield for the last five vintages has been less than 34 hectolitres per hectare, far below the excessive yields normally seen in Pommard. Billard-Gonnet is a small yet important estate of 19.9 acres, and Monsieur Billard believes in a 12-day maceration of the destemmed grapes with the juice. All the aging is done in oak barrels of which one-fourth are new. The wines are egg-white fined and lightly filtered prior to bottling. The best wines I have tasted have consistently been the Pommard Les Rugiens and Pommard-Clos des Vergers, but these rarely show the sumptuous or opulent fruit seen in other top Pommards. Those collectors who like rare wines should look for some of the minuscule quantities of Beaune-Clos des Mouches produced from Billard's .33-acre vineyard. On the positive side, the 1987s and 1988s that were tasted appeared to suggest Pierre Billard was trying to get more fruit, finesse, and charm in his wines.

DOMAINE BILLAUD-SIMON(CHABLIS)**

Wines Produced: Chablis, Chablis Blanchot, Chablis Les Clos, Chablis Mont de Milieu, Chablis Montée de Tonnerre, Chablis Les Preuses, Chablis Les Vaillons, Chablis Vaudésir.

With over 55 acres of vineyard, one should see quite a bit of wine from the Domaine Billaud-Simon. However, at least one-half of Jean Billaud's production is sold to *négociants*, and the rest is estate-bottled after spending a year in vat. Only a handful of his wines spend time in old barrels, and then only because there is no room in his enamel-lined vats. I've never been terribly impressed with the wines from this estate. They are often a bit musty and unclean, and even good examples seem to lack the concentration and nervosity of other producers. Billaud-Simon wines should be drunk within the first 5–6 years of life.

DOMAINE PIERRE BITOUZET
(SAVIGNY-LÈS-BEAUNE)****

Wines Produced: Corton-Charlemagne, Savigny-Lès-Beaune Les Goudelettes.

Pierre Bitouzet, a well-dressed, impeccably groomed manager and winemaker is renowned for the elegant red wines of the Prince de

Mérode estate. However, he also produces approximately 250 cases of an extraordinary Corton-Charlemagne and small quantities of a white Savigny-Lès-Beaune Les Goudelettes from his own estate. Bitouzet believes in a lot of new oak, barrel fermentation, and is not shy when it comes to putting flavor and character in his wines. They are among the best white wines made, and the Savigny-Lès-Beaune Les Goudelettes is an exceptional bargain for the quality. However, it is almost always a difficult wine to find in the marketplace.

DOMAINE BITOUZET-PRIEUR (VOLNAY)***

Wines Produced: Bourgogne Rouge, Meursault-Clos du Cromin, Meursault Les Perrières, Volnay, Volnay Les Aussy, Volnay Clos des Chênes, Volnay Pitures, Volnay Taillepieds.

The village of Volnay has many well-known and reliably, good winemakers. One of the best and surprisingly least known is Vincent Bitouzet. He has 23.46 acres of vineyards and seems to be equally talented with his superb white wines and excellent, stylish, velvety red wines. His two Meursaults, the Meursault-Clos du Cromin (4.32 acres) and his exceptional Meursault Les Perrières (1.85 acres), are beautifully made wines that show plenty of smoky, toasty oak, and a great deal of richness. Aged in 100% new oak, his whites are bottled after 12 months with only minimal filtration. His best red is the Volnay Taillepieds (7.45 acres), especially the vintages of 1985, 1987, and 1988. This wine sees 15%–20% new oak, and is bottled after 16–18 months aging. All of his red wines are filtered via the Kisselguhr system prior to bottling, although his American importer does bring in specific barrels that are neither fined nor filtered. Bitouzet's wines are best drunk within 7–8 years of the vintage.

DOMAINE SIMON BIZE ET FILS (SAVIGNY-LÈS-BEAUNE)****

Wines Produced: Bourgogne Les Perrières, Savigny-Lès-Beaune, Savigny-Lès-Beaune aux Guettes, Savigny-Lès-Beaune Les Marconnets, Savigny-Lès-Beaune Les Vergelesses.

While Simon Bize and his son Patrick (one of the most respected and talented of the young generation of vignerons in Burgundy) do not have any glamorous or famous vineyards, shrewd connoisseurs of Burgundy know that a Simon Bize Savigny-Lès-Beaune is a wine of high quality. The wonderful juicy, strawberry, cherry fruit is brilliantly and vibrantly displayed in the wines from their vineyards in Savigny. This is an old estate of 34.6 acres that has been passed through the Bize family for nearly 160 years. The wines have a delicacy and lightness, yet are full-flavored—a rare combination. The secret seems to be little manipulation of the wine, a moderately long *cuvaison*, a prefermentation cold maceration, 14–18 months in oak barrels, of which one-third are new, and little or no filtration. The wines from Savigny-Lès-Beaune can last longer than most people claim and the wines of Bize can certainly remain 7–10 years in the bottle. If you are looking for Burgundy that represents a high rapport in quality/price, then consider this producer.

DOMAINE DE BLAGNY (BLAGNY)**

> Wines Produced: Blagny-La Pièce Sous le Dos d'Ane, Meursault-Blagny, Puligny-Montrachet Les Chalumeaux.

A 14.07-acre domaine administered by the Comtesse de Montlivant, the Domaine de Blagny specializes in its Meursault-Blagny, a chunky, robust, nutty-flavored white wine made from the estate's 7.41-acre vineyard. The wine is good, but rarely deserving of its high price. The other wines tend to be straightforward, rather commercial examples of white burgundy.

DOMAINE BLAIN-GAGNARD (CHASSAGNE-MONTRACHET)****

> Wines Produced: Bâtard-Montrachet, Chassagne-Montrachet Blanc, Chassagne-Montrachet La Boudriotte Blanc, Chassagne-Montrachet Les Caillerets, Chassagne-Montrachet-Clos St.-Jean, Chassagne-Montrachet Morgeot, Chassagne-Montrachet Rouge, Criots-Bâtard-Montrachet, Pommard.

Thirty-five percent of the production of Jean-Marc and Claudine Blain's 13.73-acre estate is sold to *négociants*. The balance of white wine is put in one-third new oak and bottled after 14–16 months in cask. The red wines also see one-third new oak, but are bottled after 18 months of cask aging. The top wines include the Bâtard-Montrachet (.83 acre) and the Chassagne-Montrachet Morgeot (1.5 acres). A tiny quantity of

Criots-Bâtard-Montrachet (.51 acres) is also made, but I have never tasted it. Those white wines I have tried from Blain-Gagnard are very intense and clearly the product of low yields. They are lusty burgundies for those who like rich and intense wines. It is a shame there are not more of this producer's wines in the marketplace.

DOMAINE BLONDEAU-DANNE (MEURSAULT)**

Wines Produced: Chassagne-Montrachet,   Criots-Bâtard-Montrachet, Meursault, Puligny-Montrachet La Garenne, Saint-Aubin, Volnay.

Proprietor Denis Blondeau-Danne resides in the beautiful Château de Saint-Aubin in the commune of Meursault. This domaine's most famous wine is the Criots-Bâtard-Montrachet, made from several rows of vines that were replanted in 1979. Less than two barrels of this wine are made in an abundant vintage, so the likelihood of encountering any is remote. I have tasted only one vintage, the 1986, and it was disappointing. The other wines seem to lack freshness and have a heavy, coarse personality, suggesting improvements need to be made.

DOMAINE GUY BOCARD (MEURSAULT)**

Wines Produced: Bourgogne Blanc, Meursault Les Charmes, Meursault-Les Grands Charons, Meursault Le Limozin, Meursault Les Narvaux, Meursault-Sous la Velle.

The young Monsieur Bocard seems to be enjoying increased recognition and prosperity after selling his excellent 1985s in America and Europe. However, the more recent vintages, of 1986, 1987, and 1988, all displayed a rather processed, watery, and sculptured character with little intensity. He has a good-sized domaine of 19.76 acres, but given the high quality of the 1985s, he must be stretching the production of his vineyard in more recent vintages. At present, one-third new oak is used, and the wines stay in oak 8–12 months before they are bottled after a relatively intense filtration.

DOMAINE MARCEL BOCQUENET
(NUITS ST.-GEORGES)***

Wines Produced: Echézeaux, Nuits St.-Georges, Vosne-Romanée.

This tiny domaine of 9.8 acres includes two village wines, a good Vosne-Romanée and solid, robust Nuits St.-Georges, and 1.23 acres of the Grand Cru Echézeaux. Thirty percent new oak is used; the wine spends 18 months in cask, and there is no filtration. I have had very limited experience with the wines of Marcel Bocquenet, but those I have tasted displayed excellent winemaking and quite a bit of depth and character. This could be a producer well worth following more closely, and my star rating may be conservative.

DOMAINE HENRI BOILLOT (POMMARD)***

Wines Produced: Beaune Clos du Roi, Beaune-Les Epenottes, Meursault, Meursault Les Genevrières, Nuits St.-Georges Les Cailles, Pommard, Pommard Les Fremiers, Pommard Les Jarolières, Pommard Les Rugiens, Puligny-Montrachet, Puligny-Montrachet-Clos de la Mouchère, Puligny-Montrachet Les Pucelles, Savigny-Lès-Beaune Les Lavières, Savigny-Lès-Beaune Les Vergelesses, Volnay, Volnay Les Caillerets, Volnay-Chevrets, Volnay Fremiets.

Jean Boillot and his son Henri run this complicated and large 54.8-acre estate. It is spread out over a whopping 18 different appellations. While it is difficult to produce such a variety of wines, the quality level here ranges from average to very good. Many of the red wines are aged in 100% new oak casks and bottled after 12–14 months aging with only a light filtration. The white wines see 60%–100% new oak and are bottled after 6–7 months. Clearly the Boillots believe in getting the wine in the bottle as quickly as possible in order to conserve its fruitiness. I have rarely had a chance to taste the entire range produced by Boillot, but the top wines include the excellent whites—the Meursault Les Genevrières and Puligny-Montrachet Les Pucelles. Among the red wines the Pommard Les Rugiens, Pommard Les Jarolières, and Volnay Les Caillerets are consistently at the top of the Boillot stable. Somewhat confusing is the fact that the wines appear under the name of Henri Boillot as well as under the name of the father, Jean Boillot. Most wines from Henri Boillot require drinking within the first 7–8 years of life.

JEAN-MARC BOILLOT (POMMARD)**

Wines Produced: Beaune Les Montrevenots, Pommard, Pommard Les Saussilles.

I have tasted only one vintage of Jean-Marc Boillot, the son of André Boillot, the winemaker for Olivier Leflaive. I felt his 1987s were light, elegant, medium-bodied wines that seemed pleasant, but commercially oriented and lacking depth and character. Given the family background, I suspect my star rating is conservative.

DOMAINE LUCIEN BOILLOT ET FILS
(GEVREY-CHAMBERTIN) ***

> Wines Produced: Bourgogne Rouge, Côte de Nuits-Villages, Fixin, Gevrey-Chambertin, Gevrey-Chambertin Les Cherbaudes, Gevrey-Chambertin Les Corbeaux, Nuits St.-Georges Les Pruliers, Pommard, Volnay Les Angles.

Lucien Boillot has rarely impressed me as one of Burgundy's best producers. His 1983s were dominated by rot and excessively astringent tannins. His 1985 wines, while cleanly made, tended to be coarse and tannic, and often suggested they were aged in rather old, musty barrels. The 1986s were thin and charmless. Both his 1987s and 1988s looked to be much improved. Coincidentally, he stopped filtering his wines with the 1987 vintage. This is an important estate of 20 acres, with the biggest parcel (11.13 acres) in Gevrey-Chambertin. Boillot does have some Premiers Crus, 2.81 acres in Volnay Les Angles, 1.30 acres in Nuits St.-Georges Les Pruliers, and tiny parcels in Gevrey-Chambertin Les Corbeaux and Gevrey-Chambertin Les Cherbaudes. Boillot's other wines are Villages wines from Pommard and Fixin, generic wines from two parcels he owns in the Côte de Nuits-Villages, and one parcel entitled to only a Bourgogne Rouge appellation. Quality appears to be on the upswing if the 1987s and 1988s are valid indications of Boillot's direction.

DOMAINE PIERRE BOILLOT (MEURSAULT) ****

> Wines Produced: Bourgogne Aligoté, Bourgogne Rouge, Meursault Blanc, Meursault Les Charmes, Meursault Les Gouttes d'Or, Meursault Rouge, Pommard, Volnay Santenots.

This small 13.58-acre estate is highly regarded for its splendid oaky, toasty, full-bodied Meursault Les Charmes. Unfortunately, Pierre Boillot only has a 1.23-acre parcel of this outstanding vineyard in Meursault. His other top white wine is his Meursault Les Gouttes d'Or, from an even smaller parcel of .61 acre. His best white wines remain in 33% new oak for at least 12 months. Filtration is as light as possible; as a result, in top vintages such as 1985 and 1986, one sees dazzling flavor levels in most of Boillot's white wines. It should be mentioned that he is one producer who believes in limiting the yield of Chardonnay to less than 45 hectoliters per hectare. His red wines are good, but do not match the top quality level of his white wines. Boillot's best red wine, not surprisingly, is his Volnay Santenots, which often needs 4–5 years in the bottle to show its true character.

DOMAINE DE BOISCHAMPT (JULLIÉ)**

Wines Produced: Juliénas.

Straightforward, uninspiring Beaujolais comes from this estate of 14.1 acres. The proprietors, the Dupond family, also own Domaine de la Renjardière in the Côtes de Rhône.

CHÂTEAU DE BOISFRANC (JARNIOUX)**

Wines Produced: Beaujolais, Beaujolais Blanc.

A sizeable domaine of 42 acres, this domaine is known primarily for its Beaujolais Supéricur, and the fact that the vineyard is cultivated by organic principles. The wines are straightforward and relatively light, but quite decent.

JEAN-CLAUDE BOISSET (NUITS ST.-GEORGES)*

Domaine Wines Produced: Aloxe-Corton, Gevrey-Chambertin, Montagny, Nuits St.-Georges-Clos des Corvées, Nuits St.-Georges Les Damodes, Vosne-Romanée Domaine de Château de Vosne-Romanée. The wines of the Domaine Claudine Deschamps are represented by this firm.

Note: This firm also produces a vast quantity of wine as a *négociant.*

Jean-Claude Boisset is one of the most successful and wealthiest firms in Burgundy. They own 28.2 acres of vineyards, but most of their vast production comes from purchased wine. The quality of the wine tends to be mediocre, with the wines rarely showing much character, nor reflecting their appellations. Serena Sutcliffe, in her excellent book, *Pocket Guide to the Wines of Burgundy*, put it more diplomatically, stating, "I am afraid these burgundies give me absolutely no lift at all." Nevertheless, there are apparently plenty of people willing to buy Boisset wines. The firm recently acquired such other *négociant* Burgundy houses as Charles Vienot, Lionel J. Bruck, and Thomas-Bassot. Most Boisset wines should be drunk within 5–7 years of the vintage.

DOMAINE BOISSON-VADOT (MEURSAULT)***

Wines Produced: Bourgogne Rouge, Meursault, Meursault Les Chevalières, Meursault Les Genevrières, Meursault Rouge, Puligny-Montrachet Les Folatières.

This 17.29-acre estate is run by Bernard Boisson, a rotund, straight-talking man in his late thirties. His wines are not terribly well known, but they are certainly good, and even very good in the instance of his excellent Meursault Les Genevrières and Puligny-Montrachet Les Folatières. Twenty-five to thirty percent new oak casks are used, and there is a lot of lees contact here prior to bottling. The wines have a great deal of flavor. Monsieur Boisson feels that not only the lees contact, but also the vineyard's high percentage of old vines result in rich, age-worthy wines. This is a house worth looking at a bit more closely.

DOMAINE DE LA BOITTIÈRE (JULIÉNAS)**

Wines Produced: Beaujolais-Villages, Juliénas, Morgon, Moulin-à-Vent.

The Domain de la Boittière can trace its history back to 1601. However, the wines seem to be simple, somewhat insipid, and not equal to the potential of the estate.

DOMAINE ANDRÉ BONHOMME (VIRÉ)****

Wines Produced: Mâcon-Viré.

The Domaine André Bonhomme is a tiny, top-notch vineyard that produces only one wine, a Mâcon-Viré from 14.82 acres of vines. Many local growers consider Bonhomme's Mâcon-Viré to be the best of that village. All of his production is estate-bottled, and the wine is aged in 25% new oak for 6 months. A taste of this wine shows how good a

Mâcon can be when handled with care and given impeccable treatment in the cellar. Bonhomme's Mâcons, unlike most from this vast viticultural region, can last for 4–6 years.

DOMAINE BONNEAU DU MARTRAY (PERNAND-VERGELESSES)****

Wines Produced: Aloxe-Corton, Le Corton, Corton-Charlemagne, Pernand-Vergelesses.

High up on the hillside of the quaint village of Pernand-Vergelesses are the cellars of the Domaine Bonneau du Martray. This estate produces four wines, its superstar being its exquisite, ageworthy Corton-Charlemagne. The red wines are good, but have nowhere near the sheer style and magnificence of the Martray Corton-Charlemagne. With its 27 acres of vineyards in Corton-Charlemagne producing 3500 cases of wine, this is one domaine in Burgundy where large quantities of fine wine can often be found. A visit to most of the top 2- and 3-star restaurants in France will reveal that the Martray Corton-Charlemagne is on the wine list. However, the domaine is proud of the fact that it sells its wines to more than two dozen foreign countries. The current owner, Comte Jean le Bault de la Morinière, believes in using one-third new oak for this extraordinary wine. It is interesting to compare his Corton-Charlemagne with the famous Hospices de Beaune Corton-Charlemagne. The Cuvée François de Salins is often the most expensive white wine of the Hospices, because it is aged in 100% new oak and comes from a parcel of vineyards adjacent to Martray's vineyard in Corton-Charlemagne. The two wines could not be more different. Great vintages of the Corton-Charlemagne, which include the 1983, 1985, 1986, and 1988, age and improve in the bottle for at least 10 years, but can be drunk after 20 with great pleasure. Ironically, this is one estate whose white wine outlives the aging capacity of its red wine.

CHÂTEAU BONNET (LA CHAPELLE-DE-GUINCHAY)***

Wines Produced: Chénas, Juliénas, Moulin-à-Vent.

Proprietor Pierre Perrachon has 29.4 acres spread among Moulin-à-Vent, Juliénas, and Chénas. His best wines come from his Chénas vineyard and are fruity, with a fragrant bouquet and a silky, long finish. I doubt if they age well, but for drinking within 2–3 years of the vintage, one can hardly go wrong.

DOMAINE BONNOT-LAMBLOT
(SAVIGNY-LÈS-BEAUNE)***

> Wines Produced: Aloxe-Corton Valozières, Bourgogne Aligoté, Sa-
> vigny-Lès-Beaune Blanc, Savigny-Lès-Beaune
> Rouge, Savigny-Lès-Beaune La Dominode, Sa-
> vigny-Lès-Beaune Les Vergelesses.

Roger Bonnot runs this tiny estate of 14.32 acres, which specializes
primarily in the wines of Savigny-Lès-Beaune. As a result, their La
Dominode, from a 1.08-acre parcel, is the estate's best wine. The style
of the winemaking here tends to emphasize a lot of muscle and body,
with perhaps less charm than certain producers, such as Simon Bize or
Capron-Manieux. However, the wines age well, and a good bottle of
Savigny-Lès-Beaune La Dominode or Aloxe-Corton Valozières will
drink well for up to a decade. The winemaking technique stresses 10%–
15% new oak and the wines are bottled after 12 months aging in both
cask and vat. Given the muscular, full-bodied style sought by Roger
Bonnot, perhaps a bit more new oak might be helpful.

DOMAINE BORDEAUX-MONTRIEUX (MERCUREY)***

> Wines Produced: Mercurey, Mercurey-Clos Fortoul.

Jacques Bordeaux-Montrieux has a tiny estate of 17.04 acres from
which he makes only two wines, an excellent Mercurey-Clos Fortoul
and an acceptable Mercurey Villages. He is also the director of the
well-known Domaine Thenard in Givry. Fifty percent new oak is used
and bottling takes place after 12–14 months in cask. The wines tend to
be very full and rich, with a smell of raspberries and spicy oak. Unfortunately, little of Bordeaux-Montrieux's wine is exported as private
clients purchase the bulk of the production.

DOMAINE RENÉ BORGEON (JAMBLES)**

> Wines Produced: Bourgogne Aligoté, Bourgogne Blanc, Bourgogne
> Passe-Tout-Grains, Bourgogne Rouge, Givry.

René Borgeon produces straightforward red and white burgundies from
his modest estate of 20.95 acres. The red wines see 20% new oak and
are bottled after 18–24 months in cask. His Bourgogne Blanc and Bourgogne Aligoté are aged in tank and bottled after 5–6 months of aging.

These are wines to be appreciated for their simple, direct, commercial style.

BOUCHARD PÈRE ET FILS (BEAUNE)**–***

Domaine Wines Produced: Beaune-du-Château Blanche, Beaune-Clos de la Mousse, Beaune-Clos St.-Landry, Beaune Les Grèves-Vignes de l'Enfant Jésus, Beaune-Marconnets, Beaune Les Teurons, Bourgogne Aligoté, Bourgogne Aligoté Bouzeron-Domaine Carnot, Bourgogne La Vignée, Chambertin, Chambolle-Musigny, Chevalier-Montrachet, Le Corton, Corton-Charlemagne, Hautes-Côtes de Beaune, Ladoix-Clos Royer, Meursault Les Genevrières, Montrachet, Nuits St.-Georges-Clos St.-Marc, Pouilly-Vinzelles, La Romanée, Savigny-Lès-Beaune Les Lavières, Volnay Les Caillerets, Volnay Fremiets-Clos-de-la-Rougeotte, Volnay Taillepieds, Vosne-Romanée aux Reignots.

Note: This gigantic firm also produces an entire range of nondomaine wines that they sell throughout the world. They tend to purchase grapes rather than juice from the growers to ensure better control over the fermentation.

This is one of the most famous Burgundy houses, as well as largest and greatest. The Bouchard family owns an amazing 234.65 acres of vineyards in the Côte d'Or, with 175.37 of these acres consisting of Premiers Crus and Grands Crus. The cellars, which are in the ramparts of the Château de Beaune, have an existing stock of four million bottles, with vintages going back as far as 1830. Nine generations of fathers and sons have carried on the Bouchard firm, originally founded in 1731. The current father and son combination is Claude Bouchard, and his son Jean-François. While the cellars are not open to the public, the underground caves are among the most remarkable ones in France.

Although there are some remarkable Cortons from the late forties and fifties, most of the wines made in the seventies and early to mid-eighties are of standard quality, often lacking depth; they seem almost to be the product of a high-tech winemaking style. Some wines (the 1981 Montrachet, for example) were simply lacking fruit, and could have easily been mistaken for a Mâcon-Villages. The Bouchards seem to have realized their wines were no longer competitive with those of the better *négociants*, and in 1986 they constructed an entirely new facility with state-of-the-art equipment. Bouchard also decided to buy grapes rather than wine from the growers he uses for selling his wines under his *négociant* business.

This vast estate, which includes potentially spectacular wines such as the Corton, the La Romanée from Château de Vosne-Romanée of the Belair-Lignier family, the Beaune Les Grèves-Vignes de l'Enfant Jésus, and an assortment of Premier Cru Beaunes and Volnays has increased the quality of their wines dramatically since the 1986 vintage. The 1987 and 1988 vintages look as if they will be the strongest portfolio of Bouchard wines in decades.

The white wines start off life surprisingly stern and backward, but do improve and age well. However, they are far from my favorite style of white Burgundy, being too austere and often lacking charm and depth. For their top red wines, nearly 100% new oak is used, and all the top wines are aged in Allier oak, racked three times, and bottled after 14–16 months aging. My suspicion is that they have been fined and filtered too much in the past. While I think there is entirely too much fining and filtration today, the Bouchards must ship their wines throughout the world 12 months a year and feel that no risk is warranted. The Bouchards eschew the taste of oak in their white wines, and consequently ferment their wines in stainless steel and then transfer them to oak for aging. The wines do not always develop as much complexity and profoundness as the Bouchards claim.

This proud estate has a fabulous wealth of vineyards. Some of their top vineyard sites include 9.04 acres in Corton, 7.41 acres in Corton-Charlemagne, 9.88 acres in Savigny-Lès-Beaune Les Lavières, 8.32 acres in Beaune Les Teurons, and 9.88 acres in Beaune Les Grèves-Vignes de l'Enfant Jésus. The Bouchards are also significant holders of some great Grands Crus in Burgundy, including the largest holding of Chevalier-Montrachet (they own 6.17 acres) and 3.7 acres of Le Montrachet itself.

BOUCHARD-AINÉ ET FILS (BEAUNE) **–***

Domaine Wines Produced: Chambertin-Clos de Bèze (Domaine Marion), Fixin-Clos du Chapitre, Mercurey Blanc, Mercurey-Clos du Chapitre, Mercurey-Clos la Marche.

Note: This firm also produces a line of *négociant* wines from purchased grapes, as well as juice.

This old-line *négociant*, which seems to keep a relatively low profile, was established in 1750 by the family that separated from the larger and more famous Beaune firm of Bouchard Père et Fils. While Bouchard-Ainé is located in Beaune, 96% of their vineyards are in the Mercurey appellation. Their 57-acre domaine in Mercurey produces very good, traditionally made wines. They are fermented at high temperatures in open wood *cuves*, aged for 14–18 months in cask, of which one-third of the wood is new, and given a light filtration prior to bottling. The wines are textbook examples of old-style, interesting, ageworthy, complex white and red wines from the Côte Chalonnaise. Other estate wines come from Chambertin-Clos de Bèze and Fixin-Clos du Chapitre where Bouchard-Ainé buys the grapes from the 7.85 acre Domaine Marion. These wines tend to be more variable in quality, but certainly can be well above average. In contrast, their *négociant* wines tend to be dull, lifeless, and mediocre.

DOMAINE BOUILLARD (CHIROUBLES)***

> Wines Produced: Chiroubles.

René Bouillard produces textbook Chiroubles—light in color but marvelously perfumed, deliciously fruity, and altogether captivating. He has 19.76 acres and bottles his wine after 6–8 months of aging in *foudres*. While I would recommend the Bouillard wines in very good years such as 1985 and 1988, I was disappointed in the 1986.

DOMAINE JEAN-MARC BOULEY (VOLNAY)****

> Wines Produced: Beaune Les Reversées, Bourgogne Aligoté, Bourgogne Blanc, Bourgogne Rouge, Pommard, Pommard Les Fremières, Pommard Les Pézerolles, Pommard Les Rugiens, Volnay, Volnay Les Caillerets, Volnay Les Carelles, Volnay Clos des Chênes.

Volnay is a village with a reputation for consistently high-quality wines. However, some of the best-known names are no longer making wines at the quality level one might expect. For years the benchmark producers were Domaine de la Pousse d'Or and the Marquis d'Angerville (an immensely important estate in terms of estate-bottling and commitment to authenticity). Unfortunately, both the Pousse d'Or and d'Angerville wines, at least the cuvées that make it to the American market, seem overly processed and shallow. Luckily, there is a new hot star in Volnay by the name of Jean-Marc Bouley. Although he is young, in his mid-thirties, and his first vintage was only 1984, he is from a family who has long been producing wine. I doubt the quality has ever been more impressive than it is now. Sprinkled over 13 different appellations, the Bouley estate is 32.11 acres. I first visited Jean-Marc when his superb 1985s were just being bottled. While 1985 was easy to vinify and handle, Bouley also made good 1986s and striking wines in 1987 and 1988. His policy is to use 50% new oak for all his wines, except for the Premiers Crus, which are aged in 75% new oak for 14 to 16 months. There is generally a light filtration done and I would not be surprised, given Bouley's commitment to quality, to see him eliminate that clarification technique. Even in highly abundant vintages such as 1986, yields are kept to 35 hectoliters per hectare. The results are extremely concentrated, harmonious, balanced wines bursting with fruit and character. Bouley has some superb vineyards and has produced outstanding wines from Les Caillerets and Clos des Chênes in Volnay, and from Les Rugiens and Les Pézerolles in Pommard. Perhaps the sleeper wine in Bouley's portfolio is his excellent Beaune Les Reversées which can normally be found for half the price of his Premiers Crus from Volnay and Pommard. Jean-Marc Bouley is producing a style of burgundy that reflects the appellation; it shows gorgeous up-front, forward fruit, but has the structure and character to last for up to a decade.

DOMAINE GEORGES BOULON (CHIROUBLES)***

Wines Produced: Beaujolais-Villages-Domaine des Côtes de Fonta-bon, Chiroubles-Domaine de Clos Verdy, Fleurie-Domaine des Côtes de Fontabon.

Georges Boulon produces typically delicate, fragrant, soft, and elegant Chiroubles. His Chiroubles vineyard is his largest holding among the 40.5 acres he owns, but he also has a domaine in Fleurie. There he produces straightforward, fruity wine, and a small amount of Beaujolais-Villages. He keeps his wine in large oak *foudres* for 5–6 months prior to bottling.

BOURÉE PÈRE ET FILS (GEVREY-CHAMBERTIN)****

> Wines Produced: Beaune-Les Epenottes, Beaune Premier Cru, Bonnes Mares, Chambertin, Chambolle-Musigny, Chambolle-Musigny Les Amoureuses, Chambolle-Musigny Les Charmes, Charmes-Chambertin, Clos de la Roche, Côte de Beaune-Villages, Côte de Nuits-Villages, Gevrey-Chambertin Les Cazetiers, Gevrey-Chambertin Clos de la Justice, Gevrey-Chambertin Lavaux St.-Jacques, Morey St.-Denis, Nuits St.-Georges, Nuits St.-Georges Les Vaucrains, Santenay Les Gravières, Vosne-Romanée.

Note: The above range of wines may vary with each vintage, contingent upon what this firm purchases from the Burgundy growers.

The Bourée firm is a small *négociant* business located right on the main thoroughfare (Route Nationale 74) in Gevrey-Chambertin. Founded in 1864 it now sells a modest 10,000 to 20,000 cases of wine per year. (The fluctuations are due to the size of the crop in Burgundy.) For some years, this quality enterprise has been run by M. Vallet, nephew of the late Pierre Bourée. The wines are made in the *ancienne méthode:* no destemming, an extremely long *cuvaison* of 18–24 days, high temperature fermentation of 34°C, sometimes 38°C, the least possible racking (usually only two are done), never any filtration, and bottling of the wine directly from the barrel. The wines rarely see any time in new oak barrels (although I did notice some 1988 Chambertin aging in new oak on my last visit), and spend at least 24–30 months in ancient oak casks. While a large part of the business is as *négociants*, with the wines listed above produced in good vintages, Bourée's firm does own 4.94 acres of a walled vineyard called Clos de la Justice. This vineyard, located on the east side of N 74, frequently produces wines of at least Premier Cru quality, but is only entitled to the appellation Gevrey-Chambertin. The firm also owns a tiny 2.84-acre parcel of Grand Cru Charmes-Chambertin vineyards and just over one-half acre of Beaune-Les Epenottes. All the rest of the wines are made from purchased grapes, not the grape juice, and, as Monsieur Vallet says, "doing our own traditional vinification" in the cellar. The wines here tend to be excellent, even outstanding, and possess a lot of color, extract, and tannin. They generally need 7–8 years to be at their best in the top vintages, and can be surprisingly sturdy and robust in lightweight vintages. M. Vallet, who's been running the shop since 1970, believes that many Burgundy producers have become "victims of modern technology," and have begun bottling their wines too early. As Vallet says, everyone here now wants to "get their money as quickly as possible." Of the top wines here, the aforementioned Clos de la Justice is consistently very good to excellent, and the great majority of the Premiers Crus and Grands Crus from the Côte de Nuits are among the better wines produced in a given vintage. Two of Bourée's best, yet unknown, stars are his Beaune-Les Epenottes and Santenay Les Gravières. (England is the largest market for the wines of Bourée, followed by the United States.) These wines age very well.

DOMAINE DENIS BOUSSEY (MONTHÉLIE)***

> Wines Produced: Bourgogne Rouge, Meursault, Meursault Les Charmes, Monthélie, Monthélie Les Champs Fulliots Blanc, Monthélie Les Champs Fulliots Rouge, Pommard, Savigny-Lès-Beaune, Volnay, Volnay Premier Cru.

Denis Boussey competently administers 23.93 acres of vineyards. He makes both delicious white wines from the appellation of Meursault and one of Monthélie's finest whites, his Monthélie Les Champs Fulliots Blanc (from a .49-acre vineyard). He also produces a rather stylish (if that is the correct word for the robust, muscular wines of Monthélie) Monthélie Les Champs Fulliots Rouge from 1.43 acres. While a healthy percentage of his production is sold to *négociants*, two-thirds is estate-bottled. Boussey believes in using 15% new oak barrels where the wine rests for 15–19 months. These are wines that can be drunk young or aged for 5–7 years.

DOMAINE XAVIER BOUZERAND (MONTHÉLIE)**

> Wines Produced: Auxey-Duresses Blanc, Bourgogne Passe-Tout-Grains, Meursault, Monthélie Blanc, Monthélie Les Champs Fulliots Rouge, Monthélie Rouge.

All the production from Xavier Bouzerand's 16 acres is estate-bottled. His biggest production is in generic Monthélie Rouge, but he does own 2.47 acres of the Premier Cru, Monthélie Les Champs Fulliots. His wines spend 15 months in cask, and see very little new oak aging. A small amount of white wine is made from Auxey-Duresses, Meursault, and Monthélie Blanc that is fresh and exuberant, but uncomplex. The wines from Bouzerand represent fair values in the scheme of Burgundy pricing.

DOMAINE MICHEL BOUZEREAU (MEURSAULT)**

> Wines Produced: Beaune Les Vignes-Franches, Blagny, Bourgogne Aligoté, Meursault, Meursault Les Genevrières, Pommard, Puligny-Montrachet, Volnay.

Not one of my favorite estates, Domaine Michel Bouzereau seems inconsistent in the quality of its wines which often have a rather musty, unclean smell and taste. Seventy percent of the production is estate-bottled and the rest is sold to *négociants*. Bouzereau's best market for the wines from his 17.04-acre domaine is in Europe. His strongest wine should be his Meursault-Genevrières, but three vintages tasted showed rather excessive acidity, and not terribly well-focused or clean Chardonnay fruit.

DOMAINE HUBERT BOUZEREAU-GRUÈRE (MEURSAULT)**

> Wines Produced: Bourgogne Aligoté, Bourgogne Blanc, Chassagne-Montrachet, Chassagne-Montrachet Blanc, Chassagne-Montrachet Les Chaumées, Corton Les Bressandes, Meursault, Meursault Les Charmes, Meursault Les Genevrières, Meursault Le Limozin, Meursault Rouge, Meursault Les Tillets, Puligny-Montrachet, Santenay, Saint-Aubin Le Charmois.

Hubert Bouzereau has a very important domaine of 25.81 acres, but I find virtually all his wines boring and not terribly pleasant to taste. In his wines, he clearly aims for very high acidity and a tart, lean personality. The wines do seem to have aging potential, and often the Bouzereau Meursault will still taste very alive and vibrant after 4–5 years, but to describe any of his wines as providing a great deal of pleasure would be overstating the case. Some of Bouzereau's wines have such a green, oaky character and hard, rigid framework that they seem unforgivably reticent and lacking charm. I did think his 1988s and 1986s showed more character than the 1985s. There is no doubt that his best two wines are the Meursault Les Genevrières (.49 acre) and the Meursault Les Charmes (2.9 acres). I found his white wines from Chassagne-Montrachet, including what should be an excellent Chassagne-Montrachet Les Chaumées, to be mediocre.

DOMAINE BOYER-MARTENOT (MEURSAULT)***

> Wines Produced: Meursault, Meursault Les Charmes, Meursault Les Genevrières, Meursault Les Narvaux, Meursault en l'Ormeau, Meursault Les Perrières, Puligny-Montrachet.

The aim of this small cellar is to produce a full-flavored wine that will age well. Proprietor Yves Boyer has 19.76 acres of well-placed vineyards in Meursault, and in addition is responsible for looking after the viticultural aspect of several of the Meursault vineyards owned by the Hospices de Beaune. He believes in prolonging the malolactic fermentation, and letting the wine rest on its lees as long as is prudent. There is only a light filtration and very little racking done in order to promote as much flavor and complexity in the wines as possible. Unfortunately, I have only seen Boyer's 1988s, but I was remarkably impressed by his Meursault Les Perrières, Meursault Les Genevrières, and Meursault Les Charmes. The wines see 33% new oak casks and are bottled after 12–15 months in cask. This cellar could be a star of the nineties.

DOMAINE GUY BRAILLON (CHÉNAS)****

> Wines Produced: Chénas.

Braillon has always been one of my favorite producers of Chénas and I have enjoyed numerous vintages of his rich, plummy, blackberry- and raspberry-scented wines. While he will tell you they should be drunk within 3–4 years of the vintage, I have had 6- and 7-year-old bottles that have shown remarkable youth and vibrance. This is a fairly big style Chénas with a considerable wallop of alcohol.

DOMAINE JEAN-CLAUDE BRELIÈRE (RULLY)***

> Wines Produced: Rully-Les-Margotey Blanc, Rully-le-Pria.

This tiny yet excellent domaine of 12.3 acres run by Jean-Claude Brelière produces only two wines, a Rully Premier Cru blanc and a Rully Premier Cru rouge. Both wines see one-third new oak and are bottled after 12 months. The white wine reveals a stylish, floral character, good acidity, plenty of fruit, and is capable of lasting for 4–5 years. The red has a pleasantly straightforward, light, strawberry fruitiness with 3–4 years of staying power. Brelière's most famous client is Jacques Lameloise, the owner of the famous three-star Michelin restaurant in Chagny.

DOMAINE BRESSAND (POUILLY-FUISSÉ)***

Wines Produced: Pouilly-Fuissé, Pouilly-Fuissé Les Crays.

This is a relatively new estate run by a transplanted Bordelaise, Madame Galley. She is beginning to use more new oak, and her top cuvée, the Pouilly-Fuissé Les Crays, exhibits elegance and good ripeness. Given the commitment of Madame Galley, this could be an estate worth watching.

DOMAINE MICHEL BRIDAY (RULLY)***

Wines Produced: Mercurey Rouge, Rully-Le-Bergerie Blanc, Rully-Les-Chailloux, Rully-Champcloux, Rully-Grésigny Premier Cru Blanc, Rully-La-Pucelle Blanc, Rully Rouge.

Michel Briday, an up-and-coming serious producer in Rully, makes elegant and stylish wines. Until the mid-eighties, I found his whites a bit lean and austere, but today his wines appear to have more fruit and flavor. Perhaps this is because of the higher-quality vintages, or because of the increased usage of new oak and slightly cooler vinification. For whatever reason, his fine Rully-Grésigny and Rully-La-Pucelle have a whiff of hazelnuts, good crisp acidity, and a touch of toasty oak in vintages such as 1985 and 1988. He uses 33% new oak for his whites and bottles after 12 months. The red wines are on the lighter side, but drink well young and show a strawberry and cherry fruitiness married nicely with spicy, toasty oak. They are bottled after 14 months, aging in 25%–33% new oak. His finest red, made by organic methods since 1988, is the Rully-Champcloux. Briday's domaine is small, only 24.7 acres, but the quality is on the ascent. These wines should generally be consumed within 4–6 years of the vintage.

DOMAINE LUC BRINTET ET FRÉDÉRIC CHARLES (MERCUREY)**

Wines Produced: Bourgogne Blanc, Bourgogne Rouge, Mercurey Blanc, Mercurey-Champillot, Mercurey-La Charmée, Mercurey-La Corvée, Mercurey-La Levrière, Mercurey-Les Ormeaux, Mercurey-Les Vignes d'Orge.

Founded only in 1984, this new estate specializes primarily in the wines of Mercurey. The red wines see 10% new oak and are bottled after 18–

24 months in cask. The white wines are kept in large *foudres* and bottled after 12–18 months. It is too soon to get an accurate picture of what the quality of these wines will be, but the 1986 and 1987 vintages produced rather straightforward one-dimensional wines of no great interest or character.

DOMAINE MARC BROCOT (MARSANNAY)**

Wines Produced: Gevrey-Chambertin, Marsannay Blanc, Marsannay Rouge.

I found little to get excited about in the wines from the 12.35 acres of Marc Brocot except for his rather amazing Marsannay Rouge. Made from 30-year-old vines, it has more character and flavor than his Gevrey-Chambertin, and should be highly sought after by those buyers of Burgundy who are looking for a great value. It is a very full-bodied, robust, rich wine that is capable of lasting for 7–10 years in the bottle.

DOMAINE DES BRUREAUX (CHÉNAS)****

Wines Produced: Chénas.

If you are looking for serious, smoky, raspberry-scented, old-style Beaujolais with great body, richness, and a powerful long finish, then look no further than Daniel Robin's 19.76-acre vineyard in Chénas. It is the only wine he makes, and it is an explosively rich wine that in a blind tasting could easily be confused with a Premier Cru red burgundy from the Côte d'Or. This is sensational wine, and one only wishes that more than 25% of his production could make it into the export market. If you are in southern Burgundy, the wines of the Domaine des Brureaux are available at the famous restaurant Greuze in Tournus, and also at Daniel Robin's own excellent eating establishment in Chénas.

DOMAINE DE LA BRUYÈRE (ROMANÈCHE-THORINS)**

Wines Produced: Moulin-à-Vent.

Raymond and Michel Siffert produce a medium- to full-bodied, concentrated, chunky Moulin-à-Vent from their 17.29-acre vineyards. The wine is aged in *foudres* for 7–12 months prior to bottling. It is a reliable wine, but not one of my favorites as it often seems to have too much tannin for its own good.

DOMAINE GEORGES BRYCZEK (MOREY ST.-DENIS)****

Wines Produced: Chambolle-Musigny, Gevrey-Chambertin, Morey St.-Denis, Morey St.-Denis-Cuvée du Pape, Morey St.-Denis Clos Sorbès.

The eccentric Georges Bryczek, of Polish descent and a sculptor as well, produces rich, textbook red burgundies from his two parcels in Morey St.-Denis. He offended certain people with his production of a Morey St.-Denis that he called Cuvée du Pape, but for him it was a way to pay homage and respect to a religion to which he is deeply committed. The wines here are the product of classic vinification and a high percentage of old vines, and can age for several decades, even at the "Villages" level. The 1969 Morey St.-Denis from my cellar was still alive and drinking well in 1989. The Domaine Georges Bryczek is an extremely fine source for ageworthy, rich, heady red burgundies, but the production from his 10-acre domaine is minuscule.

DOMAINE A. BUISSON-BATTAULT (MEURSAULT)***

Wines Produced: Beaune-Les Epenottes, Bourgogne Blanc, Bourgogne Rouge, Meursault, Meursault Les Charmes, Meursault Les Genevrières, Meursault Les Gouttes d'Or, Meursault Le Poruzot, Pommard, Puligny-Montrachet.

My only encounters with the wines of André Buisson have been in Europe and they have been encouraging. It is a shame more of his production is not exported. He has 19.21 acres of superbly situated vines, with important parcels in Meursault Le Poruzot (1 acre), Meursault Les Genevrières (1.5 acres), Meursault Les Charmes (.98 acres), and Meursault Les Gouttes d'Or (3.9 acres). All of these wines can be recommended. Buisson's basic philosophy requires a relatively cool fermentation for his whites, 30% new oak, and aging of the wines for 14 to 18 months in wood. He also makes a delicious Bourgogne Blanc. His Bourgogne Aligoté can be drunk on its own merits without adding crème de cassis to cut its sharp acidity. The red wines from Buisson-Battault are somewhat less successful. They appear to be aged too long in barrels, as they often have a rather dry, slightly oxidized character. All things considered, the white wines of Buisson-Battault should be sought out and the red wines approached with a degree of caution.

ALAIN BURGUET (GEVREY-CHAMBERTIN)****

> Wines Produced: Gevrey-Chambertin, Gevrey-Chambertin Champeaux, Gevrey-Chambertin Vieilles Vignes.

It is a shame that Alain Burguet does not own any Grand Cru vineyards in Gevrey-Chambertin. Fortunately, his newly acquired parcel of Premier Cru Champeaux will add a more prestigious vineyard to his portfolio. Until 1988, his vineyards included only a Villages Gevrey-Chambertin, and a quite exceptional Gevrey-Chambertin Vieilles Vignes. Burguet obtains an extract, richness, and complexity in his wines that is quite sensational. In a blind tasting it would be easy to confuse his village Gevrey-Chambertin Vieilles Vignes for many producers' Premiers Crus, or even some Gevrey-Chambertin Grands Crus. His wines are reasonably priced and are largely undiscovered. Based on the vintages in the eighties, Burguet's top years have been 1985, 1986, and 1987, and his wines are all capable of lasting at least a decade in the bottle.

CHÂTEAU DE BYONNE (CHARNAY-LES-MÂCON)**

> Wines Produced: Crémant de Bourgogne, Mâcon-Rouge, Mâcon-Villages.

This 7.5-acre estate produces primarily white wine, with some adequate red made also. The wines are marketed exclusively by the firm of Chevalier et Fils in Mâcon. While his white wines tend to be rather high in acidity, they are fresh and lively, yet more highstrung and austere than other examples of Mâconnais.

DOMAINE JACQUES CACHEUX-BLÉE ET FILS (VOSNE-ROMANÉE)****

> Wines Produced: Bourgogne Aligoté, Bourgogne Rouge, Echézeaux, Nuits St.-Georges, Vosne-Romanée, Vosne-Romanée Les Suchots.

While this is a tiny estate (10 acres), those lucky enough to run across a bottle of Jacques and Patrice Cacheux's Vosne-Romanée Les Suchots or Echézeaux will be treated to quite an exceptional burgundy. Their old-style wines are rich, concentrated, and powerful, spend 18–22 months in oak casks, are neither fined nor filtered, and see 10%–20% new oak. Unfortunately, most of the production is sold to private customers and in Western Europe (particularly Switzerland, Holland, and Belgium), so little makes it off the continent. Cacheux's biggest holding is in Bourgogne Rouge. He also has an important 1.48-acre, well-situated parcel of old vines of Vosne-Romanée Les Suchots and a 1.23-acre parcel of Grand Cru Echézeaux with vines planted in 1934 and 1945. These are wines that can last 10–12 years, and should be sought out by any conscientious lover of Burgundy. Cacheux made brilliant wines in 1985 and 1988, very good wines in 1987, 1986, and even 1982.

ROGER CAILLOT ET FILS (MEURSAULT)****

Wines Produced: Bâtard-Montrachet, Bourgogne Aligoté, Bourgogne Blanc, Bourgogne Rouge, Meursault Le Cromin, Monthélie, Puligny-Montrachet Les Folatières.

Roger Caillot farms 20.99 acres of vines. His best wine is shared under a *métayage* agreement with Jacqueline Vaudiaux-Poirier. These agreements, which are common in Burgundy, allow for the individual who cultivates and controls the harvest (in this case Roger Caillot) to retain one-half the fruit. The rest is given to the proprietor (in this case Madame Vaudiaux-Poirier). She sells her half of the grapes from the 1.67-acre parcel of Bâtard-Montrachet to the *négociant* Louis Jadot, while Caillot estate-bottles his half. These arrangements generally run for years on verbal agreements. Caillot, who has two sons, Dominique and Michel, both in their late twenties, is a highly talented winemaker, making not only fabulous Bâtard-Montrachet, but also excellent Puligny-Montrachet Les Folatières and good, straightforward Bourgogne Blanc. He uses 25%–35% new oak casks and bottles after 12 months in oak. His wines are consistently very good, and have the potential, in the case of the Bâtard-Montrachet or the Premier Cru Puligny-Montrachet, to age for 10–12 years. His red wines are less impressive than his whites.

CHÂTEAU CAMBON (SAINT-JEAN-D'ARDIÈRES)*

Wines Produced: Beaujolais Supérieur.

All the Beaujolais Supérieur of Château Cambon is aged in large oak vats for 5–6 months prior to bottling. The entire domaine, consisting of 22.23 acres, produces a Beaujolais that is inconsistent at best.

DOMAINE CAMUS (GEVREY-CHAMBERTIN) ***

> **Wines Produced:** Bourgogne Rouge, Chambertin, Charmes-Chambertin, Gevrey-Chambertin, Latricières-Chambertin, Mazis-Chambertin, Mazoyères-Chambertin.

With 42.5 acres of some of the most extraordinary vineyards in all Gevrey-Chambertin (4 acres of Chambertin and 16 of Charmes-Chambertin), no domaine is in a better position to offer great wines than the Domaine Camus. However, I have never been able to understand the wines of Camus. The estate was founded in 1830 by the Camus family, and one gets the impression that little has changed since then. Twenty-five percent new wood is used for all the wines, and after a long, 3-week *cuvaison* and a light filtration, the wines are put directly into barrel. There is another filtration at bottling, which is done after the wines have spent 30 months in cask. Raoul Camus, father, and Hubert, son, run the estate, although Raoul's role, at age 80, seems to be to give visiting tourists and journalists a history lesson in Gevrey-Chambertin and the Domaine Camus. The last time I visited Camus there was no tasting in their drab cellars, but rather in a dimly lit "bureau" where a strong smell of cat urine dominated the olfactory senses. The wines here are believed by many to be quite long lived, given the long maceration and 30 months aging in oak, but I often find them a bit too woody and dried out upon release. I have never drunk a great bottle of Camus wine. Both Hubert and Raoul think 1988 is the best vintage since 1959 and 1961, and I must agree that, when tasted from cask, those wines did have impressive color, richness, and length. I would like to see them bottled without filtration after 20 rather than 30 months of cask aging. The 1987s are also successful, the 1986s tasted very hard and malnourished, and the 1985s are certainly good, but not exceptional for the vintage. This is a domaine that could, with a few changes, produce some of the finest wines in the Côte d'Or. Do they have the courage and/or commitment to make a change?

DOMAINE LUC CAMUS
(SAVIGNY-LÈS-BEAUNE) ***–****

> **Wines Produced:** Bourgogne Blanc, Savigny-Lès-Beaune, Savigny-Lès-Beaune Les Gravains, Savigny-Lès-Beaune Les Lavières, Savigny-Lès-Beaune Les Narbantons, Savigny-Lès-Beaune Vieilles Vignes.

Luc Camus would appear to be an up-and-coming star of the nineties. I think it will be just a matter of time before his wines become better known in the international marketplace. He owns just over 16 acres, with a very high proportion of old vines. In fact, his Savigny-Lès-Beaune Vieilles Vignes, from a 77-year-old parcel of vines, is sold exclusively in England through Bibendum Wines Ltd. It is reputed to be as good as his Premiers Crus. Camus' winemaking techniques are traditional, although he has increased his percentage of new oak to 33%. His wines are bottled after 12–15 months in cask with minimal clarification. Most of his Savignys are drinkable young, although I would have no reservations about cellaring his Cuvée Vieilles Vignes and his Premiers Crus from the top vintages for 7–9 years.

DOMAINE BERNARD CANTIN (IRANCY)*

Wines Produced: Bourgogne Irancy Rouge, Bourgogne Passe-Tout-Grains, Bourgogne Rosé, Bourgogne Rouge, Gamay-Cuvée du Moutier.

The domaine is comprised of 19.76 acres with its best wine coming from 10 acres of Bourgogne Irancy Rouge. This wine is aged 15–18 months in cask and tends to be relatively tannic and lacking in charm and finesse.

DOMAINE CAPITAIN-GAGNEROT
(LADOIX-SERRIGNY)***

Wines Produced: Aloxe-Corton, Aloxe-Corton-Les Moutottes, Bourgogne Rouge, Chorey-Lès-Beaune, Clos Vougeot, Corton-Charlemagne, Corton-Grandes Lollières, Corton Les Rénardes, Côte de Nuits-Villages, Ladoix Blanc, Ladoix La Micaude, Ladoix Rouge, Pernand-Vergelesses.

Roger Capitain's domaine of 29.8 acres is not as well known as it deserves to be because much of his wine comes from little known appellations. With parcels spread out over 13 different appellations in Burgundy, his most famous wines come from a .86-acre parcel of Corton-Charlemagne, a .81-acre parcel of the Grand Cru Corton Les Rénardes, and a tiny, beautifully situated, upper-slope, .44-acre parcel of Clos Vougeot. Most of the latter wine is sold directly to clients and is made from a relatively young vineyard replanted in 1975. The winemaking style here utilizes 20% new oak, with higher percentages being used for the Grands Crus. The wine is aged for 18–24 months in cask, and very little filtration is done as Capitain wants his wines to be full of the vineyard flavor. Several of his best values include an excellent Ladoix La Micaude and Aloxe-Corton-Les Moutottes. Both these wines are bursting with vivid cherry and berry fruit. Les Moutottes is made from vines that were planted in the 1930s, and despite being a Premier Cru, it can rival many of the Grands Crus from other producers. This is an underrated producer whose wines sell at very realistic prices. Generally, the wines of Capitain-Gagnerot should be drunk within the first 7–8 years of the vintage. A visit here is sure to be exciting given Roger Capitain's animated character and enthusiasm for his wines.

DOMAINE CAPRON-MANIEUX
(SAVIGNY-LÈS-BEAUNE)***

Wines Produced: Bourgogne Aligoté, Savigny-Lès-Beaune Blanc, Savigny-Lès-Beaune Rouge, Savigny-Lès-Beaune Les Lavières, Savigny-Lès-Beaune Les Peuillets.

This is a tiny 7.16-acre domaine producing extremely elegant, supple velvety wines that are meant to be drunk within the first 5–7 years of life. The Savigny-Lès-Beaune Les Lavières is consistently their best wine (the 1985, 1987, and 1988 are wonderful). Small quantities of a straightforward, compact Savigny-Lès-Beaune Blanc and a decent Bourgogne Aligoté are also produced. Ten percent new oak is used, and the wine is bottled after 18–20 months in cask.

DOMAINE LOUIS CARILLON
(PULIGNY-MONTRACHET)***

Wines Produced: Bienvenues-Bâtard-Montrachet, Bourgogne Rouge, Chassagne-Montrachet, Côte de Beaune-Villages, Puligny-Montrachet, Puligny-Montrachet Champ Canet, Puligny-Montrachet Les Combettes, Puligny-Montrachet Les Perrières.

This important domaine in Puligny-Montrachet has been part of the Carillon family for over 350 years. The estate consists of 54 acres of vineyards, a vast amount in the morseled world of Burgundy. The wines, aged one year in 10%–25% new oak casks, are reliably good. In each vintage at least half the crop is sold to *négociants* with the best kept for the Carillon family. The wine produced by the black-haired, round-faced Louis Carillon is elegant, graceful, and supple. The three best recent vintages have been the 1988, 1986 (probably the best recent vintage), and 1985. My favorite is, of course, the Grand Cru, the Bienvenues-Bâtard-Montrachet, but the Puligny-Montrachet Les Combettes is often every bit as good, as is the Puligny-Montrachet Les Perrières. Carillon is not one of the best-known white burgundy producers in the export markets, but the quality here is extremely high. Given the precocious style of the white wines of Carillon, they should be drunk within their first 5–6 years of life.

DOMAINE DENIS CARRÉ (MELOISEY)**

Wines Produced: Auxey-Duresses-Le-Bas-Des-Duresses, Bourgogne Aligoté, Bourgogne Blanc, Bourgogne Hautes-Côtes de Nuits Rouge, Meursault Les Tillets, Pommard Les Charmots, Saint-Romain Rouge.

The wines produced by Denis Carré from his 16.91-acre domaine tend to be rather straightforward, correct, and reflective of their appellation's character. However, they lack complexity, depth, and individuality. His best wine is the Pommard Les Charmots. His *cuvaison* is relatively short and he ages his red wines in 15%–20% new oak, bottling them after 12–15 months. The whites see 10%–15% new oak and are bottled after 8–10 months. The wines from Carré are perhaps a bit too filtered, which may account for their lack of extra flesh, bouquet, and character.

DOMAINE GUY CASTAGNIER (MOREY ST.-DENIS)****

Wines Produced: Bonnes Mares, Bourgogne Rouge, Chambolle-Musigny, Clos de la Roche, Clos St.-Denis, Latricières-Chambertin, Morey St.-Denis.

The wines of Guy Castagnier also appear under the label of Vadey-Castagnier. A very consistent yet surprisingly unknown domaine, Castagnier produces wines in a very expansive, ripe, opulent, generous style with loads of fruit and flavor. I have had no experience with any vintages older than 1982, but certainly the top wines in recent vintages have consistently been their Grands Crus and Chambolle-Musigny. The wines exhibit a judicious use of toasty new oak casks and have wonderfully ripe, satiny-textured fruit. These would not appear to be wines for the long term, as they frequently lack acidity and structure. It is probably best to consume them within 7–8 years of the vintage.

DOMAINE CATHIARD-MOLINIER (VOSNE-ROMANÉE)****

> Wines Produced: Clos Vougeot, Nuits St.-Georges Les Murgers, Romanée St.-Vivant, Vosne-Romanée, Vosne-Romanée Les Malconsorts.

The wines of this small domaine are rarely seen, except on some of the finest wine lists in Europe (Taillevent in Paris and the l'Enoteca Pinchiorri in Florence). The quality is of the highest class as Cathiard's wines are fragrant, rich, concentrated, and potentially long lived. Old vines, an extended *cuvaison* with stems (no cool prefermentation maceration here), one-third new oak barrels, and minimal clarification of their wines result in full-bodied, intensely flavored, compelling red burgundies. I remain perplexed as to why this domaine is not better known.

CAVES DE BAILLY (SAINT-BRIS-LE-VINEUX)**

> Wines Produced: This enterprise produces sparkling white and rosé Crémant de Bourgogne wines by the Méthode Champenoise.

Located in the heart of the Auxerre district, eight miles from the village of Chablis, is the large Caves de Bailly. The firm has been extremely successful in producing sparkling wines from over 691 acres of vineyards and have Pinot Noir, Aligoté, Chardonnay, and Gamay planted. They utilize a huge twelfth-century quarry for making and storing their product. The wines tend to be rather neutral and straightforward, but are quite acceptable when reasonably priced. They are not to be confused with Champagne, but then their prices are totally in line with their quality.

CAVES DES VIGNERONS DE BUXY (BUXY)***

Wines Produced: This huge cooperative produces an entire range of wines, mostly from modest appellations such as Bourgogne Rouge, Bourgogne Blanc, and Bourgogne Aligoté, but there are special cuvées of Montagny Cuvée Speciale and Montagny Premier Cru.

This high-tech cooperative, which includes many of the small growers from Buxy and Montagny, was founded in 1931 and vinifies the wines from over 1,976 acres of vines (primarily those of generic appellations). The cooperative was completely modernized in the last decade and now has temperature-controlled, stainless-steel tanks for all of its wines. The wines are bottled early to preserve their freshness. They are light, refreshing, crisp, technically correct, and a good value. The best cuvées are those marked Cuvée Speciale.

DOMAINE CECI (VOUGEOT)***

Wines Produced: Chambolle-Musigny Les Echanges, Clos Vougeot, Gevrey-Chambertin, Morey St.-Denis.

From what I have tasted, this tiny 10-acre estate appears committed to turning out very fine wines. All the wines are aged in 50% new oak except for the Clos Vougeot, which is put in 100% new French oak barrels. Founded 20 years ago, Domaine Ceci is under joint French-Belgium ownership and seems intent on turning out rather obviously oaky wines with a lot of soft, precocious, berry fruit in them. The top wine (and also the most expensive) from each of the recent vintages has been the Clos Vougeot. Given the forward, fruity style of these wines, they should be consumed within 5–6 years of the vintage.

CELLIER DES SAMSONS (QUINCIÉ)**

Wines Produced: An entire range of Beaujolais wines are produced by this association of cooperatives.

This group of ten regional cooperatives produces adequate, yet somewhat uninspirational Beaujolais that tastes high in alcohol and is not as fresh and fruity as one might wish. Prices tend to be low.

CHÂTEAU DE LA CHAIZE (ODENAS) **

> Wines Produced: Brouilly.

This vast and extraordinarily impressive château produces an ocean of Brouilly from its 237.12 acres of vineyards. For years, Brouilly was considered to produce the textbook wine of Beaujolais. Perplexingly, I have found the wine tastes much better when drunk in France than in the United States. One wonders if the wines sent to the United States are pasteurized or sterile filtered, and those sold in France are less processed. Whatever the reason, I have found bottles of Château de la Chaize drunk in France to be enormously fruity, elegant, and all that a Brouilly should be. When drunk in the United States, they often taste dull, oxidized, and lacking in character. The wines are aged in *foudres* for 3–5 months and the château claims there is no distinction made in the cuvées for different markets. This is a wine that should be consumed within 2 years of the vintage.

DOMAINE YVES CHALEY (CURTIL-VERGY) ***

> Wines Produced: Bourgogne Aligoté, Bourgogne Hautes-Côtes de Nuits Blanc, Bourgogne Hautes-Côtes de Nuits Rouge, Bourgogne Passe-Tout-Grains.

This modestly sized estate of 22.7 acres has built a solid reputation for the quality of its Bourgogne Hautes-Côtes de Nuits Rouge. Chaley is a serious winemaker who uses 25% new oak and bottles his wine with minimal clarification after 8–12 months cask aging. He even puts his tiny quantities of Bourgogne Aligoté and Bourgogne Hautes-Côtes de Nuits Blanc in casks. The red wines here show a lot of berry fruit and give every indication of being capable of lasting for 5–7 years. The prices asked make this an excellent domain to consider for both quality and value.

CHÂTEAU DE CHAMBOLLE-MUSIGNY
(CHAMBOLLE-MUSIGNY) ****

> Wines Produced: Bonnes Mares, Chambolle-Musigny Les Amoureuses, Chambolle-Musigny Les Fuées, Le Musigny Vieilles Vignes.

This is a relatively new domaine run by the young, enthusiastic Jacques-Frederic Mugnier. Mugnier, who apprenticed under Bruno

Clair when he launched the domaine in 1978, is now in full control, and apparently has given up his career as an engineer. At present, the domaine consists of only 10 acres, but the well-known Clos de la Maréchale vineyard in Nuits St.-Georges will come back into the Mugnier family in 2002, when the lease now held by the Faiveley firm runs out. The wines of Château de Chambolle-Musigny are marked by a great deal of toasty, vanilla-scented, new oak, as the domaine believes 100% new oak is appropriate for their wines. To date, the top vintages have been the 1985, 1987, and 1988. These highly scented wines have proven to be remarkably seductive and intense, with gobs of sweet fruit, and plenty of toasty oak. Their flavor suggests that they should be drunk within 4–6 years of the vintage rather than cellared for their long-term potential.

DOMAINE DU CHÂTEAU DE CHAMILLY (CHAMILLY)**

Wines Produced: Bourgogne Aligoté, Bourgogne Passe-Tout-Grains, Bourgogne Rouge, Mercurey Blanc, Mercurey Rouge.

The Desfontaine family that runs this domaine does not own any Premiers Crus. They produce acceptable, commercially viable, generic Mercurey and Bourgogne Rouge and Blanc from their 32.48 acres of vineyards. One hundred percent of the domaine's production is estate-bottled, and both the red and white wines spend 6–8 months in vats and small casks before bottling.

DOMAINE CHAMPAGNON (CHÉNAS)****

Wines Produced: Chénas, Fleurie, Moulin-à-Vent.

The Domaine Champagnon is a very serious estate that makes traditional Beaujolais aged in cask for 6–10 months. It has even begun to employ 10% new oak casks for the Moulin-à-Vent. The entire domaine consists of 17 acres and one cannot go wrong here trying the powerful, age-worthy Moulin-à-Vent; the plummy, explosively rich, and powerful Chénas; or the lighter, more delicate Fleurie.

DOMAINE BERNARD CHAMPIER (ODENAS)**

Wines Produced: Côte de Brouilly.

Bernard Champier's wines are a bit too tannic and robust for me, but he has his admirers in France. He is a small grower with only 7.41 acres, all dedicated to producing Côte de Brouilly.

CHAMPY PÈRE (BEAUNE)***

> Wines Produced: Beaune Les Avaux, Beaune-Le Clos des Mouches, Clos Vougeot, Pommard, Savigny-Lès-Beaune Les Dominaudes. (Plus a range of wines under their *négociant* label.)

Note: In December, 1989, this firm and its vineyard holdings were acquired by the large American-owned Beaune *négociant*, Louis Jadot. The following information should be read with this in mind.

A strong argument can be made that the Champy firm is one of the most traditionally run winemaking domaines in all of Burgundy. While they own 15.6 acres of vineyards from which they make the wines listed above, they also produce a range of wines as a *négociant*. The wine-making techniques used in their 1891 *cuverie* include no new oak barrels, no filtration, and hand-bottling the wine directly from each cask. All the red wine grapes are totally destemmed, given a fairly hot 33° C fermentation, and a 3-week *cuvaison*. The wines then spend 12–24 months in ancient barrels.

Created in 1720, the Champy firm had the distinction of being the oldest Burgundy firm still in the same family. While I have never clearly understood these wines, with experience I've come to respect them. The red wines are all rather deeply colored, chunky, muscular wines, with a robust, forceful texture, and plenty of tannin and extract. They often lack the finesse of the top wines of Burgundy, but they do deliver flavor, and certainly are capable of lasting in the bottle for 10–15 years. The best wines are the estate wines, which come with a very old-fashioned, bluish/purple label. Although the *négociant* wines are correct, sound, and clearly representative of their appellations, they seem too straightforward to deserve the highest marks. The best three wines from Champy are consistently the Clos Vougeot, from a 6-acre parcel on the lower slope of the Clos, the Les Dominaudes from a 5-acre vineyard in Savigny-Lès-Beaune, and the Beaune Les Avaux, a rich, fleshy, rather structured wine with a good bit of character.

DOMAINE DE LA CHANAISE (VILLIÉ MORGON)****

> Wines Produced: Beaujolais, Morgon.

Pierre and Dominique Piron run this excellent domaine of 31.93 acres. Pierre Piron has long been the president of the local wine growers association, and makes one of the most exuberantly fruity, vibrant, and vivacious Morgons of the appellation. He has 31.93 acres of vineyards, and bottles his wines after 5–6 months aging in vats. They are not among the most long-lived wines of Morgon and should be drunk up within 2–3 years of the vintage.

DOMAINE ÉMILE CHANDESAIS (FONTAINES)***

> Wines Produced: Beaujolais-Villages-Château de Néty, Bourgogne Aligoté-Domaine Gouffier, Bourgogne Rouge, Bourgogne Rouge-Clos de la Fortune, Mercurey.

Note: This is also a *négociant* business, producing a broad range of wines, primarily from the Côte Chalonnaise.

Manager Émile Chandesais looks after this small 15.4-acre estate. He makes modern-style, fruity, soft white and red wines meant for immediate consumption. The wines are rarely encountered outside of Europe, but for those who might encounter the Bourgogne Rouge-Clos de la Fortune or the stylish Beaujolais-Villages-Château de Néty, they are two reliable wines.

DOMAINE CHANDON DE BRIAILLES
(SAVIGNY-LÉS-BEAUNE)****

> Wines Produced: Corton Blanc, Corton Les Bressandes, Corton-Clos du Roi, Corton Les Marechaudes, Pernand Île de Vergelesses, Pernand-Vergelesses, Savigny-Lès-Beaune, Savigny-Lès-Beaune Les Lavières.

Domain Chandon de Briailles, a seriously run estate with 31.2 acres of vineyards, should be better known. I have had people tell me that the quality was somewhat spotty in the seventies, but certainly since the mid-eighties, the wines produced at this domaine have been excellent. The property is run by the Comte Aymard-Claude de Nicolay, who is related to the Chandons of the Champagne region. The winemaking technique is quite traditional, with no destemming (probably a mistake in years such as 1983), a 3-week *cuvason*, and a fairly warm fermentation temperature of 30°–32° C. The wines are filtered after malolactic fermentation and then again with the Kisselguhr System prior to bottling. The normal amount of time the red wines spend in oak barrels (50% new) is 15 months.

I have found the 1985s superb, and the 1986s good, considering that the Côte de Beaune was the least favored area that year. Consumers will have a lot to look forward to with the gloriously fruity 1987s, and the superb 1988s should finally bring the Domaine Chandon de Briailles the recognition that it merits. Tiny quantities (less than 200 cases) of a 100% Chardonnay called Corton Blanc are also made. It is quite an exotic wine with a smoky, intense, lavishly rich character that seems to win as many admirers as it does critics. As for the red wines, for those with the patience to wait for them to mature, the Corton-Clos du Roi is profound. It is aged in 100% new oak and made from 25-year-old vines. The Corton Les Bressandes is equally superb. Made from even older vines (average age 35 years), in recent vintages it has shown more precocious fruit and charm than the Clos du Roi. For value, the Pernand Île de Vergelesses and Corton Les Marechaudes should be considered. These are all serious wines, although I would like to see the estate do away with the filtration after the malolactic fermentation as this seems to take something from the wine. Despite these criticisms, there is no doubting the quality of recent vintages from the Domaine Chandon de Briailles.

DOMAINE CHANSON PÈRE ET FILS (BEAUNE)***

Wines Produced: Beaune Les Bressandes, Beaune-Clos des Fèves, Beaune-Clos des Mouches, Beaune Clos du Roi, Beaune Les Grèves, Beaune Les Teurons, Beaune-Clos des Marconnets, Beaune-Champimonts, Bourgogne Blanc, Bourgogne Rouge, Chablis Mont de Milieu, Chambertin-Clos de Bèze, Pernand-Vergelesses Blanc, Savigny La Dominode, Savigny Les Marconnets.

Note: Additionally, the Chanson family produces wines under its négociant label. The range of selections varies from year to year, depending on what they purchase.

This is a sizeable Beaune négociant and vineyard holder that sells a quarter-million cases of burgundy wine each year. They own 110 acres, much of it in well-placed Premiers Crus. Some of their largest parcels include 9.21 acres of Beaune-Clos des Fèves, 5.43 acres of Beaune Les Grèves, 10.69 acres of Beaune-Clos des Mouches, 9.38 acres of Savigny Les Marconnets, 6.57 acres of Beaune Clos du Roi, 9.38 acres of Beaune Les Teurons, and 4.36 acres of Savigny La Dominode. The wines from Chanson Père et Fils, while not among the most brilliant examples of red or white burgundy, are extremely reliable. They are made in a very soft, velvety, expansive style and possess plenty of fruit and spicy, earthy flavors. Perhaps less time in cask and a higher percentage of new oak would give the wines a bit more structure and definition. However, they are certainly good examples of red burgundy. The major portion of Chanson's production is red wine. However, some white wine is made. It tends to be dull and heavy, and is rarely impressive. Most of the wines of Chanson should be consumed within the first 7–8 years of life.

The wines made under their *négociant* labels seem significantly less impressive than their domaine wines (frequently the case for many Burgundy *négociants*).

CHANUT FRÈRES (ROMANÈCHE-THORINS)****

> Wines Produced: An entire range of Beaujolais is produced by this firm.

By the standards of Beaujolais, this is a relatively small firm with production and sales between 150,000 and 180,000 cases. Both their nouveau Beaujolais and their Crus are deliciously rich, ripe, and fruity. They are, along with Georges Duboeuf and Pierre Ferraud, my favorite *négociant* in Beaujolais. The firm was founded in 1910 and is currently run by Madame F. Roux-Chanut. Some of its best wines are its wonderfully rich, concentrated Moulin-à-Vent-Domaine de la Teppe, Morgon-Croix de Chèvre, Saint-Amour-Château de Saint-Amour, and its wonderful Saint-Véran-Domaine des Dîmes. It is a shame that Chanut Frères wines are not better represented in America.

DOMAINE CHANZY FRÈRES-DOMAINE DE L'HERMITAGE (BOUZERON)**

> Wines Produced: Bourgogne Aligoté Bouzeron Clos de la Fortune, Bourgogne Blanc-Clos de la Fortune, Bourgogne Rouge-Clos de la Fortune, Mercurey Les Carabys, Mercurey-Clos du Roi, Rully Blanc, Rully Rouge.

This large, aggressive firm owns 66.81 acres and is being run with increasing attention to detail by Daniel Chanzy. In the past there were many rather mediocre bottles of Chanzy Frères wine, but since the mid-eighties the quality has improved. This is a big firm with a large production, and consumers should be aware that good vintages, such as 1985, 1987, and 1988, are better gambles than years such as 1984 and 1986. Their best wines are their Bourgogne Rouge and Bourgogne Blanc from Clos de la Fortune. They also make a very fine Bourgogne Aligoté from Bourzeron, the village that is considered to have the best soil for making a flavorful Aligoté wine. Their wines from Mercurey tend to lag far behind in quality.

DOMAINE MAURICE CHAPUIS (ALOXE-CORTON)***

Wines Produced: Aloxe-Corton, Aloxe-Corton Les Perrières, Aloxe-Corton Premier Cru, Bourgogne Blanc, Corton Charlemagne, Corton Les Languettes.

This 25-acre domaine, with its cellars located in the tiny village of Aloxe-Corton, is run by the warm, red-faced Maurice Chapuis and his son. The white wines from the estate, the Bourgogne Blanc made from young vines in Corton-Charlemagne and the extraordinary Corton-Charlemagne, are two of the better white wines made in the Côte d'Or. The Corton Les Languettes, which is planted in Pinot Noir, would qualify as a Corton-Charlemagne if it were planted in Chardonnay. Perhaps they should consider replanting. Ironically, 90% of the production here is in red wine, which ranges from insipid to barely above average in quality.

If you must be adventurous and try one of the red wines, make it the Aloxe-Corton Les Perrières, which is made from vines planted in 1948. It tends to be the most concentrated and complex of the Chapuis red wines. One caveat is that both the white and red wines should be drunk within the first 5–6 years of the vintage. The style of their Corton-Charlemagne is for drinking early.

DOMAINE FRANÇOIS CHARLES (NANTOUX)***

Wines Produced: Beaune-Les Epenottes, Bourgogne Aligoté, Bourgogne Hautes-Côtes de Beaune Rouge, Meursault, Pommard, Volnay, Volnay Fremiets.

Of the two vintages I have tasted from the 25.66-acre domaine of François Charles, the wines have been delicious. I was impressed by an excellent 1985 Beaune-Les Epenottes (1.6 acres), and a very stylish, expansively flavored, perfumed Volnay Fremiets (.98 acres). Even a Bourgogne Hautes-Côtes de Beaune Rouge, which represents Charles's largest production, exhibited supple, silky cherry fruit and a nice touch of spicy oak. The red wines are aged in 10% new oak casks for 18–24 months. The white wines see no new oak and are bottled after 10 months. This would appear to be a domaine worth closer examination.

DOMAINE MAURICE CHARLEUX
(DEZIZE-LES-MARANGES)**

> Wines Produced: Bourgogne Rouge, Côte de Beaune-Villages, Santenay.

Correct, spicy, robust red wines are traditionally made by this estate of 19.63 acres. Maurice Charleux believes in producing red wines that can age for up to 5 years. The estate bottles 20% of its production, with the rest being sold to *négociants*. The wines are kept in large oak *foudres* and small oak barrels for up to 24 months.

DOMAINE PHILIPPE CHARLOPIN-PARIZOT
(MARSANNAY)***

> Wines Produced: Charmes-Chambertin, Clos St.-Denis, Gevrey-Chambertin, Marsannay, Morey St.-Denis.

My first introduction to a wine made by the youthful Philippe Charlopin was a 1980 Charmes-Chambertin that in a blind tasting surpassed every wine but the 1980 Domaine de la Romanée Conti La Tache. I bought several cases of that wine for my cellar, and still have some bottles left which are drinking splendidly. Unfortunately, this 25-acre domaine, which became hot in the early eighties, now seems to be bottling its wines as quickly as possible, and there has not been a wine since the 1980 Charmes-Chambertin that has displayed the same richness, concentration, and character. Why? It would appear that Monsieur Charlopin is stretching the production of his vineyards to the maximum, and the intensity exhibited in some of his wines from the 1980 vintage has been missing in more recent harvests. At present, most of the wine is sold directly to private customers, and the vinification is quite classic, with a *cuvaison* of three weeks, and the use of one-third new oak. There is a lot of potential here, but has M. Charlopin's early success gone to his head?

DOMAINE JEAN-MARC CHARMET (LE BREUIL)***

> Wines Produced: Beaujolais, Beaujolais Blanc.

There are a number of different cuvées produced by this proprietor of straight Beaujolais. Most of his wine is allocated to the Nouveau market and sold within several months of the vintage. It is a charming, fruity wine that represents one of the better examples of Beaujolais on the market.

CHÂTEAU DE LA CHARRIÈRE (SANTENAY)****

> Wines Produced: Santenay, Santenay-Clos Rousseau, Santenay La Comme, Santenay Les Gravières, Santenay La Maladière.

The gnarled and weather-beaten Jean Girardin resembles one of the old vines in his vineyards. His estate of 31.7 acres in the hills of Santenay produces some of the best bargains in red burgundy. All of M. Girardin's vines average 30 years of age, and he meticulously limits the yield to no more than 45 hectolitres per hectare. His wines are all fermented in both tanks and wooden vats, and aged 14–16 months in both *foudre* and smaller oak casks. Over 50% of Girardin's production each year is sold to *négociants;* he skims off the rest for his own production. Girardin's red wines are often well-colored, very robust, rich, full-bodied wines that age surprisingly well. I have fond memories of his 1978s, which are just entering their plateau of maturity after a decade of aging. His best wines clearly come from his Premiers Crus vineyards, particularly his Clos Rousseau, La Comme, and Les Gravières. When consumers begin to put pleasure before prestige, wines of high quality such as the Château de la Charrière's Santenays will become more and more popular. The top recent vintages here have been 1988, 1987, and 1985.

DOMAINE JEAN CHARTRON
(PULIGNY-MONTRACHET)****

> Wines Produced: Chevalier-Montrachet, Puligny-Montrachet-Clos de Cailleret Blanc, Puligny-Montrachet-Clos de Cailleret Rouge, Puligny-Montrachet-Clos de la Pucelle, Puligny-Montrachet Les Folatières.

The wines of Jean-René Chartron, a balding, round-faced, enthusiastic vigneron, are commercialized by the *négociant* firm of Charton et Trébuchet. This domaine has 23.96 acres of outstanding vineyards, including a large 2.37-acre parcel of Chevalier-Montrachet, 2.86 acres of Puligny-Montrachet-Clos de la Pucelle, 2.86 acres of Puligny-Montrachet Les Folatières, and 3.97 acres of Puligny-Montrachet-Clos de Cailleret. The wines are excellent, and the Chevalier-Montrachet is one of the top wines of that superb appellation.

CHARTRON ET TRÉBUCHET
(PULIGNY-MONTRACHET)***

Wines Produced: Bâtard-Montrachet, Beaune, Chassagne-Montrachet, Chassagne-Montrachet Morgeot, Chevalier-Montrachet, Corton-Charlemagne, Mercurey, Meursault, Meursault Les Charmes, Le Montrachet, Pernand-Vergelesses, Pouilly-Fuissé, Puligny-Montrachet, Puligny-Montrachet-Clos des Pucelles, Puligny-Montrachet Les Folatières, Puligny-Montrachet Les Garennes, Puligny-Montrachet Les Referts, Rully Chaume, Saint-Aubin, Saint-Aubin La Chatenière, Santenay-Sous la Fée.

This enterprise was formed in 1984 by two energetic Burgundians, Jean-René Chartron, who also has his own domaine of 23.96 acres, and Louis Trébuchet, who worked for ten years for the Beaune *négociant* Jaffelin. Dedicated to producing very stylish, elegant, fresh white burgundies of delicacy and finesse, Chartron et Trébuchet set up a modern installation in Puligny-Montrachet. Their wines are bottled early, usually within 10–12 months of the vintage. All the vintages to date have exhibited a light, fresh style and average character. They are not blockbuster, muscular white burgundies and they could benefit from additional concentration and character. For value, one should search out the Chartron et Trébuchet wines from Saint-Aubin and Rully, which are excellent. Among the other wines, their Premiers Crus from Puligny-Montrachet and Chassagne-Montrachet are clearly their best. At the very top level, I preferred their Chevalier-Montrachet to their other Grands Crus such as the Montrachet, Bâtard-Montrachet, or Corton-Charlemagne. These wines are not meant to last for more than 6–7 years in the bottle; they are ultra-refined and ideal for drinking young. The wines of the Domaine Jean Chartron, which are marketed by Chartron et Trébuchet, are generally deeper, riper, fuller wines than those that appear under the *négociant* label.

CHÂTEAU DE CHASSAGNE-MONTRACHET
(CHASSAGNE-MONTRACHET)***

> Wines Produced: Chassagne-Montrachet Blanc, Chassagne-Montrachet-Clos du Château Rouge.

This tiny 14.37-acre estate is run by Pierre Bader. I have tasted only two vintages: a delicious Chassagne-Montrachet Blanc aged in 100% new Allier oak, and a stylish, elegant, very fruity red. There is not much wine from this estate, but what I have tasted is very good and should be consumed within 5–6 years of the vintage. The wines also appear under the name Château Bader-Mimeur.

CHÂTEAU DU CHASSELAS (CHASSELAS)**

> Wines Produced: Saint-Véran.

This is a tiny estate of 5.28 acres run by Georges Remé, well respected by local growers. I find his wines fresh and fruity, but rather simple.

F. CHAUVENET (NUITS ST.-GEORGES)***

> Wines Produced: An entire range of both white and red burgundies are produced by this large *négociant*.

This firm's wines also appear under the name Poulet Père et Fils, Marc Chevillot, as well as Guy Leblanc and Louis Max. Founded in 1853, F. Chauvenet is now one of the largest firms in Burgundy. Much of their success and cash flow comes from their rather insipid sparkling burgundy that is sold throughout the world. Their wines from the decade of the 1980s have been very good, as Chauvenet manages to employ a modern, technical approach to winemaking without sacrificing the quality of its products. The firm is an active buyer of many of the excellent Hospices de Beaune wines. All things considered, both the white wines and the red wines, while clearly being products of the modern, high-tech, impeccably clean, ready-to-drink school of winemaking, are, nevertheless, well made and generally fairly priced.

DOMAINE JEAN CHAUVENET
(NUITS ST.-GEORGES)****

Wines Produced: Bourgogne Passe-Tout-Grains, Nuits St.-Georges, Nuits St.-Georges Les Bousselots, Nuits St.-Georges Les Perrières, Nuits St.-Georges Les Vaucrains, Vosne-Romanée.

Jean Chauvenet, a small grower with 15.16 acres of vineyards, produces some of the most elegant, stylish wines in Nuits St.-Georges. In most vintages he bottles his wines without any fining or filtration. Fifteen to twenty percent new oak is used, and the wines are aged for 16–22 months in cask. His two best wines are consistently his Nuits St.-Georges Les Vaucrains (6.98 acres), and his Nuits St.-Georges Les Bousselots (1.35 acres). However, I usually prefer the Villages Vosne-Romanée to his Villages Nuits St.-Georges because of its greater depth of fruit. In most vintages the wines of Jean Chauvenet should be drunk within the first 8–10 years of life. His only weakness would appear to be those years where there is an unusually abundant burgundy crop (i.e., 1986, 1982).

DOMAINE ANNE-MARIE CHAVY
(PULIGNY-MONTRACHET)***

Wines Produced: Bâtard-Montrachet, Bourgogne Aligoté, Bourgogne Blanc, Bourgogne Passe-Tout-Grains, Bourgogne Rouge, Puligny-Montrachet Les Referts.

The Chavy family is one of the oldest in Puligny-Montrachet. For a long period the wines were made by Christian Chavy. He passed away in 1982, and his wife, Anne-Marie, took over the management of the domaine's 14.8 acres of vines. She is assisted by her three daughters. All of the red wine production is sold directly to *négociants*. Some of the white wine is estate-bottled and the rest sold to Bouchard Père et Fils in Beaune. The two best wines from Chavy have always been their Premier Cru Puligny-Montrachet Les Referts and their very good Bâtard-Montrachet, made from a .34-acre parcel of vines.

DOMAINE DES CHAZELLES (VIRÉ)****

Wines Produced: Mâcon-Villages.

The Chaland family owns this tiny 4.94-acre estate. Those consumers looking for one of the richest, most concentrated and honeyed styles of

Mâcon-Villages, akin to some of the wines of Chassagne-Montrachet, should try this lovely, elegant, surprisingly compelling Mâcon-Villages. It competes with white burgundies selling for three times the price. Unfortunately, little of it is seen in the export markets.

DOMAINE DE CHERVIN (BURGY)**

> Wines Produced: Mâcon-Burgy Blanc, Mâcon-Rouge, Mâcon-Villages.

This small estate of 15.3 acres is run by Albert Goyard and all of its production is sold to private clients in Europe. The wines are bottled after 7–8 months aging in both tank and large *foudres*. His reds tend to be straightforward and agreeable, but undistinguished. The whites are pleasant, floral, and light, but no better than most cuvées from the larger, dominant cooperatives of the Mâconnaise region.

DOMAINE CHEVALIER PÈRE ET FILS (BUISSON)**

> Wines Produced: Aloxe-Corton, Bourgogne Aligoté, Bourgogne Passe-Tout-Grains, Corton-Charlemagne, Corton Rognet, Côte de Nuits-Village, Ladoix Blanc, Ladoix Premier Cru, Ladoix Rouge.

Georges and Claude Chevalier operate this 24.57-acre estate. They make standard-quality wines from nine different appellations. Their biggest holdings include 8.64 acres of Ladoix and an important 3.7-acre parcel of the Grand Cru Corton Rognet. They also hold a small but highly prized .61-acre parcel of Corton-Charlemagne (which happens to be the best wine produced by the Chevaliers, in my opinion). Most of the production is red wine, which is aged in one-third new oak for 14–18 months. The wines tend to have a certain compactness and sternness that bodes well for their aging potential, but I have never had a red wine from this estate that I found terribly profound or exciting. The same cannot be said of their excellent Corton-Charlemagne.

DOMAINE THOMAS LA CHEVALIÈRE (BEAUJEU)**

> Wines Produced: An entire range of Beaujolais, as well as some Beaujolais Blanc, is produced here.

Founded in 1851, this firm makes straightforward, average-quality wines. The current manager is Jean-Louis Thomas and their sales represent nearly 175,000 cases per year.

DOMAINE GEORGES ET MICHEL CHEVILLON
(NUITS ST.-GEORGES)****

Wines Produced: Nuits St.-Georges, Nuits St.-Georges aux Champs Perdrix, Nuits St.-Georges Les Poirets, Nuits St.-Georges Premier Cru, Nuits St.-Georges Les Saint-Georges.

The label employed by Georges and Michel Chevillon is strikingly similar to that of their renowned cousin, Robert Chevillon. Such confusion for consumers is common in the fragmented world of Burgundy. The difference in quality between the wines of Robert Chevillon and his cousins, Georges and Michel, is small. These are excellent wines that are sold primarily in England. They resemble those of Robert in their stylish, elegant personalities, and ripe, rich fruitiness. Their two best wines are consistently their Nuits St.-Georges Les Saint-Georges and Nuits St.-Georges aux Champs Perdrix, the latter from a vineyard which is planted in very old vines. If the wines differ at all from those of Robert Chevillon, they are more forward and less structured, suggesting that they should be drunk within their first 6–7 years of life. Twenty-five to thirty percent new oak is used, and the wine is bottled after 14–15 months in cask. A light filtration is done.

ROBERT CHEVILLON (NUITS ST.-GEORGES)****

Wines Produced: Bourgogne Passe-Tout-Grains, Nuits St.-Georges, Nuits St.-Georges Les Cailles, Nuits St.-Georges Les Perrières, Nuits St.-Georges Les Roncières, Nuits St.-Georges Les Saint-Georges, Nuits St.-Georges Les Vaucrains.

It is hard not to like both the handsome, friendly Robert Chevillon and his wines. His track record is exemplary in the 1980s, particularly his wines from 1981, 1982, and 1983, three difficult years. Not surprisingly, his 1985s, 1987s, and 1988s are of exceptional quality, and 1986s pleasant. Chevillon owns 20.74 acres of vines, and believes in using one-third new oak, and bottling his wines after they have aged in cask for 18 months. A light filtration is the rule here rather than the exception.

His two most gorgeous wines are his Nuits St.-Georges Les Saint-Georges (1.55 acres) and his Nuits St.-Georges Les Vaucrains (4.02 acres). Among his other Premiers Crus, I have generally liked his Nuits St.-Georges Les Cailles (2.91 acres) and his Nuits St.-Georges Les Perrières (1.08 acres). His wines are extremely flattering to taste young, but also age beautifully for 8–10 years. One sees significant differences among each of the Premiers Crus, as there is really no house style that blurs distinctions between vineyards or vintages. Robert Chevillon is a shining example of one of the most talented and consistent winemakers in the Côte d'Or.

DOMAINE PAUL CHEVROT
(CHEILLY-LES-MARANGES)***

Wines Produced: Bourgogne Aligoté, Bourgogne Hautes-Côtes de Beaune, Bourgogne Rouge, Cheilly-Les-Maranges, Crémant de Bourgogne, Santenay-Clos Rousseau.

The husband and wife team of Fernand and Catherine Chevrot carefully farm the 21.98 acres of this domaine. The estate is primarily known for its good Côte de Beaune-Villages and richly fruity, soft, velvety Santenay-Clos Rousseau, (the Chevrots have 4.07 acres). Not so well known, but one of the best examples of its type, is their Crémant de Bourgogne, which is made from 100% Pinot Noir. The Chevrot wines are bottled early to preserve their freshness as Chevrot has no pretensions to making anything grander than the appellations he has inherited from his family. Consequently, all the wines in this stable should be consumed within 5–6 years of the vintage.

DOMAINE CHEYSSON-LES-FARGUES (CHIROUBLES)***

Wines Produced: Chiroubles.

This is one of the largest estates in Chiroubles, covering over 37.05 acres. The wines are extremely delicate, and are bottled very soon after harvest. Proprietor Émil Cheysson believes wines should spend no more than 3–4 months in *foudres* or vats prior to bottling. Cheysson makes one of the lightest wines of Chiroubles and in all of France. It has somewhat of a cult following.

DOMAINE GEORGES CHICOTOT
(NUITS ST.-GEORGES)****

Wines Produced: Nuits St.-Georges, Nuits St.-Georges Les Pruliers, Nuits St.-Georges Les Saint-Georges, Nuits St.-Georges Les Vaucrains.

Georges Chicotot, a small, wiry, intense, and pushy man, has just over 15 acres of vineyards. He has long been one of the disciples of the controversial oenologist, Guy Accad. Accad counsels all his clients to follow an extensive cold maceration of the grapes prior to fermentation in order to extract as much color and fruit as possible. Critics claim that this extended maceration of cold grapes prior to the fermentation results in wines that blur distinctions between the appellations and the vintages. These same critics also claim that the Accad style of wines are unstable and short lived. Chicotot's wines make a strong case for the Accad method. He does not believe in any fining or filtration, producing explosively rich, powerful wines that should last for at least a decade. While I have never seen an old vintage of Chicotot's wines, he claims to have been practicing the cold maceration since the 1975 vintage. The powerful, sensationally concentrated style of Chicotot's wines is in keeping with his belief in a month-long *cuvaison*, perhaps one of the longest maceration periods employed by any winemaker in Burgundy. The results in recent vintages, particularly 1987 and 1988, have been stunning. His best wines are consistently his Nuits St.-Georges Les Vaucrains (he owns .8 of an acre) and his Nuits St.-Georges Les Saint-Georges (he owns nearly 3 acres). His vines are fairly old, averaging between 25 and 55 years of age. Chicotot also produces a minuscule quantity of white Nuits St.-Georges, but I have never seen a bottle of this wine. He claims his best markets are in Switzerland and Belgium. Chicotot's wines are well worth obtaining, and represent some of the finest examples of the Accad style of vinification.

DOMAINE MICHEL CHIGNARD (FLEURIE)****

Wines Produced: Fleurie Les Moriers.

Chignard is a superlative producer of Fleurie. His wines have a wonderful exuberant raspberry, curranty fruitiness, a luscious velvety texture, and plenty of length. I have had many memorable bottles of his 1985, 1987, and 1988 Fleurie Les Moriers, and would recommend his wines to anyone wanting an idea of what a textbook Fleurie should taste like. He has 17.29 acres in Fleurie and bottles his wine after 6 months aging in oak *foudres*.

DOMAINE JEAN CHOFFLET (RUSSILLY)***

> Wines Produced: Bourgogne Passe-Tout-Grains, Givry Rouge.

Five generations of Chofflets have toiled at this tiny 12.35-acre estate located close to Givry. The current proprietor, Jean Chofflet, produces good, richly fruity, stylish wines that are meant to be consumed upon release. He uses 33% new oak for his red wines and bottles after 12 months aging in concrete vats and oak casks. There is partial destemming when the grapes are picked, a moderate *cuvaison*, and a slight filtration at bottling. Chofflet's best recent vintages include a wonderful 1985 and a very elegant 1988. Overall, his reds are better than his whites.

DOMAINE ANDRÉ CHOPIN ET FILS
(COMBLANCHIEN)***

> Wines Produced: Bourgogne Passe-Tout-Grains, Bourgogne Rouge, Chambolle-Musigny, Côte de Nuits-Villages, Nuits St.-Georges, Nuits St.-Georges Les Murgers.

This relatively unknown producer has 27.9 acres. Most of Chopin's production is in a surprisingly good, sturdy, deeply colored Côte de Nuits-Villages, of which he owns 17.78 acres of well-placed vineyards. His best wine, however, is from his only Premier Cru vineyard, the Nuits St.-Georges Les Murgers. The style of winemaking here emphasizes 25% new oak casks and 12–16 months barrel aging. The wines are bottled after a light filtration and have the capacity to age well for 5–7 years.

DOMAINE DANIEL CHOPIN-GROFFIER
(PRÉMEAUX)****

> Wines Produced: Chambolle-Musigny, Clos Vougeot, Côte de Nuits-Villages, Nuits St.-Georges, Nuits St.-Georges Les Chaignots, Vougeot.

One of the great discoveries I made during my years of research was this 25-acre estate tucked into an alley in the tiny village of Prémeaux.

Daniel Chopin, a middle-aged enthusiastic grower, had never sold any of his wine to America but was highly recommended to me by François Faiveley. The first time I visited him I left his tiny cellar ecstatic over the quality of his wines, which showed brilliance even in tough vintages such as 1986. He uses 50% new oak and follows the Henri Jayer principle of 3–4 days of cold maceration of his grape bunches prior to starting the fermentation. His wines are imbued with a wonderful purity of fruit and yet they have structure. Chopin keeps his wines 18 months in oak barrels and destems 70%. In vintages where there is some rot he will destem everything. His *cuvaison* is a fairly long three-week period. There is a high percentage of very old wines at this domaine, and the top wines, the Clos Vougeot and Vougeot, are made from 50- to 60-year-old vines. There are also 50-year-old vines in his parcel of Chambolle-Musigny. Not surprisingly, this wine could compete with most Chambolle Premiers Crus. Other wines include a well-made Côte de Nuits-Villages, ideal for drinking in its first 5 years of life, and a harder, more structured, rich Nuits St.-Georges Les Chaignots. Having tasted five consecutive vintages of Daniel Chopin's wines, he would certainly get my vote as one of the top producers in Burgundy. It's a shame we don't see more of his wine in the commercial marketplace.

DOMAINE CHOUET-CLIVET (MEURSAULT)**

> Wines Produced: Meursault-Chevalière, Meursault Les Cras, Meursault Les Perrières, Meursault Les Tillets.

Daniel Chouet's 14.82 acres include both his property and some that he has under a *métayage* agreement. He sells between 25%–35% of his production each year to *négociants*. His top wines are his Meursault Les Perrières and Meursault Les Cras. Twenty percent new oak is used and, while the wines are perhaps filtered more than they should be, this is certainly an average quality domaine making sound Meursaults.

DOMAINE BRUNO CLAIR (MARSANNAY)****

> Wines Produced: Chambertin-Clos de Bèze, Fixin La Croix Blanche, Gevrey-Chambertin Les Cazetiers, Gevrey-Chambertin-Clos de Fonteny, Gevrey-Chambertin-Clos St.-Jacques, Marsannay Blanc, Marsannay-Vaudenelles, Marsannay Les Longeroies, Morey St.-Denis, Rosé de Marsannay, Savigny-Lès-Beaune Les Dominaudes, Vosne-Romanée Les Champs Perdrix.

Young Bruno Clair reveals increasing talent in directing the affairs of this large, 42-acre domaine. The estate's cellars are located in the tiny village of Marsannay. Each vintage is somewhat of a logistical nightmare for Clair given the number of different wines he produces. This domaine is the source of Burgundy's finest Rosé de Marsannay, but little of it makes it into the export market. The local restaurants take virtually all of the 2,000 cases Clair makes of this dry, flavorful wine. Clair is doing more than any other producer in the Côte de Nuits to improve the image of the white wines from Marsannay and Fixin. He has experimented with blends of Chardonnay, Pinot Blanc, and Pinot Gris, and the results have been encouraging. Clair claims that one of his long-term goals is to augment his production of white wine from the northern part of the Côte de Nuits. He employs 20% new oak casks for aging his white wine.

While his rosé and white wines are quick cash-flow wines, Clair knows that his reputation must ultimately rest on the quality of his red wines. This estate has significant holdings in some of the finest vineyards in Gevrey-Chambertin, the largest being a 2.5-acre parcel of Gevrey-Chambertin-Clos St.-Jacques, and nearly 2 acres of the famed Grand Cru, Chambertin-Clos de Bèze. Clair also has approximately 2 acres of the great Premier Cru Gevrey-Chambertin Les Cazetiers. While most of his customers clamor for his top wines from Gevrey-Chambertin, Clair is one of the finest producers of red wines from Marsannay. He has increasingly moved to vineyard-designating his best Marsannays, and is now producing serious, ageworthy red Marsannays from vineyards called La Casse Tête (from 30-year-old vines), Longeroies (from 50-year-old vines), and Vaudenelles from 20-year-old vines. The best-kept secret of the entire Clair cellar is the explosively rich, full-bodied, and ageworthy Savigny-Lès-Beaune Les Dominaudes, from a parcel of vines averaging 50 years in age.

Clair's philosophy of winemaking reflects a healthy respect for the traditional methods. There is no cold prefermentation maceration; instead, a vigorous and lengthy hot fermentation is performed with the temperature rising as high as 34° C. After a 14- to 16-day *cuvaison*, the red wines are moved directly into casks, of which 20%–30% are new. Bottling usually takes place after 16–18 months in cask. Clair reluctantly acknowledges that in 1985 he overly filtered his wines. Since then, he has switched from an intense filtration to a more gentle style of handling the wines at bottling. The results have been obvious, with finer wines produced in 1987 and 1988 than in 1985.

Given the commitment to excellence at this domaine, I fully expect that in the nineties, the Domaine Bruno Clair will restore the credibility and reputation for great quality that the Clair family enjoyed in the fifties and sixties.

DOMAINE MICHEL CLAIR (SANTENAY)***

> Wines Produced: Bourgogne Aligoté, Bourgogne Rouge, Santenay Blanc, Santenay-Clos de la Comme, Santenay-Clos de Tavenne, Santenay Les Gravières, Santenay Rouge.

Like many vignerons from Santenay, Michel Clair sells much of his wine to private clients who like the price and the quality they find in his small, cramped, damp cellars. Clair is a competent winemaker who turns out a surprisingly good Santenay Rouge from his 16.79 acres (over two-thirds of his entire domaine of 23.34 acres). He has some attractive Premier Cru Santenays, such as Clos de la Comme and Les Gravières. However, it is rare to see these wines in the commercial market, since most of the production is sold either to *négociants* (45%) or directly to private clients. He bottles his red wine after 12–15 months in cask and his white wines after 6–8 months. Michel Clair makes a pleasant Santenay Blanc, but only a handful of barrels are produced in a good vintage. Clair's wines are not as tannic and robust as some wines from Santenay, and therefore should be drunk before they are 7–8 years old.

DOMAINE HENRI CLERC ET FILS (PULIGNY-MONTRACHET)***

> Wines Produced: Bâtard-Montrachet, Beaune-Chaume Gaufriot, Bienvenues-Bâtard-Montrachet, Blagny-La Pièce Sous le Dos d'Ane, Bourgogne Aligoté, Bourgogne Blanc, Bourgogne Rouge, Chevalier-Montrachet, Clos Vougeot, Puligny-Montrachet Blanc, Puligny-Montrachet Les Combettes, Puligny-Montrachet Les Folatières, Puligny-Montrachet Rouge.

Bernard Clerc, an enthusiastic grower in Puligny-Montrachet, has 53.37 acres of excellent vineyards throughout the Côte de Beaune. He even owns a tiny .74 acre-parcel of Grand Cru Clos Vougeot, although it is at the very bottom of the slope, adjacent to route N 74. While this has always been a cellar with great potential, the results have frequently been very spotty. Clerc sells approximately one-third of his production to Beaune *négociants*, reserving the rest to estate-bottle on the premises. His three most famous wines are his Grands Crus: Chevalier-Montrachet, of which he has two parcels of vines, 5 and 17 years old, Bâtard-Montrachet, which are his oldest vines, averaging nearly 33 years in age, and the Bienvenues-Bâtard-Montrachet, with vines averaging 13 and 15 years old. All of these wines are good rather than dazzling. Older vintages can be a bit patchy, tasting as if the *élévage* was not always as impeccable as it should have been. Clerc, who runs the cellars with his son Laurent, now in his early twenties, also makes two excellent Premier Cru Puligny-Montrachets, Les Folatières (3.68 acres) and Les Combettes (1.53 acres). These wines, while not rivaling the flavor intensity of his Grand Cru white burgundies, are still representative, particularly in later vintages. Clerc believes in one-third new oak (although I saw much more than that on my last visit to his cellars in 1988, and bottles his wines after 12 months aging in cask. In most cases, the wines of Henri Clerc et Fils should be drunk within their first 5–7 years.

DOMAINE GEORGES CLERGET (VOUGEOT)***

> **Wines Produced:** Bourgogne Rouge, Chambolle-Musigny Les Charmes, Echézeaux, Morey St.-Denis, Vosne-Romanée Les Violettes, Vougeot Premier Cru.

Georges Clerget's small estate of 9.01 acres includes an important 1.97 parcel of Echézeaux; the remainder of his holdings are only between 1 and 1.3 acres each. The Echézeaux is his best wine, followed by his Vosne-Romanée Les Violettes. The wines see 50% new oak and are bottled after 20–22 months of cask aging. The performance of Georges Clerget's wines has been inconsistent over the last ten years. However, starting in the mid-eighties, increased attention to detail, as well as a longer maceration period, have resulted in better wines. Vintages prior to that should be approached with caution.

DOMAINE MICHEL CLERGET (VOUGEOT)***

> **Wines Produced:** Chambolle-Musigny, Chambolle-Musigny Les Charmes, Echézeaux.

Michel Clerget, whose wines appear under a label identical to his brother George's, has a small estate of 4.69 acres. His biggest parcel of vines is nearly 1.5 acres of Chambolle-Musigny Les Charmes. Like his brother, he keeps his wines in oak casks for 20–22 months, but he uses less new oak, preferring to use only 33% for his red burgundies. His wines have begun to improve in quality after a mediocre period in the late seventies and early eighties.

DOMAINE RAOUL CLERGET (SAINT-AUBIN)**–***

> Wines Produced: Chassagne-Montrachet Blanc, Chassagne-Montrachet Les Chaumées, Chassagne-Montrachet Rouge, Saint-Aubin Le Charmois Blanc, Saint-Aubin Les Frionnes Blanc, Saint-Aubin Les Frionnes Rouge.

The dominant family of Saint-Aubin has long been the Clergets with their 40.75 acres and cellars at the Domaine du Pimont. They also produce wines under their name as a *négociant*. The quality of wines from Raoul Clerget has not always been to my liking. Whether a result of poor storage or shipment conditions, I have often found their wines to be too woody, dull, and slightly oxidized. Curiously, when tasted in France the wines seemed to have more of a smoky character and better freshness than when tasted in the United States. The principal wines are their good Saint-Aubin Le Charmois Blanc and tasty, yet relatively woody Saint-Aubin Les Frionnes Blanc and Rouge. The woody taste can often be overwhelming in wines of this pedigree. Maurice Clerget is in charge of this estate, and one hopes he will begin to try to balance the fruit with the wood.

DOMAINE YVON CLERGET (VOLNAY)***

> Wines Produced: Bourgogne Rouge, Meursault Les Chevalières, Pommard Les Rugiens, Volnay, Volnay Les Caillerets, Volnay Carelle Sous La Chapelle, Volnay-Clos du Verseuil, Volnay Premier Cru, Volnay Santenots.

The handsome, tall Yvon Clerget appears to keep a low profile, but this domaine produces excellent wine and deserves a far greater following. While the size of the estate, 13.58 acres, unfortunately precludes great popularity, there is no doubting that wines such as the Pommard Les Rugiens (from 2.34 acres), Volnay Les Caillerets (.79 acre), and Volnay-Clos du Verseuil (1.67 acres) faithfully represent their appellations. They are elegant and supple with good red fruit and excellent balance. Clerget believes in using 20% new oak and bottling his red wines after

18 months in cask. The white wine is bottled after 12 months in 20% new oak casks.

DOMAINE DU CLOS DES LAMBRAYS
(MOREY ST.-DENIS)**

Wines Produced: Clos des Lambrays, Morey St.-Denis.

I suppose it's time to examine what is occurring at this superbly located Morey St.-Denis vineyard of 21 acres. Purchased in 1979 by Louis and Fabien Saier, this *monopole* vineyard was partially replanted and elevated from Premier to Grand Cru status in 1981. The track record for the last decade has been dismal, as the wines have shown a diluted quality that can only be caused by an overly prodigious crop and a failure to regulate yields. There has been extensive replanting of the vineyard in the eighties, so perhaps as the vines get older, the quality will improve. I remember extraordinarily great wines from Clos des Lambrays in the thirties and forties, particularly the 1945, 1947, 1948, and 1949. Unfortunately, in the last 15 years there has not been a wine that one could even call excellent. Clos des Lambrays remains one of the most renowned underachievers of the Côte d'Or.

DOMAINE MICHEL CLUNY ET FILS (BROCHON)**

Wines Produced: Bourgogne Rouge, Chambolle-Musigny Les-Charmes, Chambolle-Musigny Les Noirots, Côte de Nuits-Villages, Gevrey-Chambertin, Gevrey-Chambertin Premier Cru, Gevrey-Chambertin Les Champeaux.

This 15.78-acre domaine makes relatively light, elegant wines that show a good deal of supple fruit, and are clearly meant to be drunk in their youth. The practice of using 20% new oak and aging the wine for up to two years in cask tends to soften it quite a bit. The best wines are the Premiers Crus of Gevrey-Chambertin and Chambolle-Musigny. Cluny's largest holdings are in Gevrey-Chambertin.

DOMAINE JULIEN COCHE-DEBORD (MEURSAULT)***

Wines Produced: Auxey-Duresses, Meursault, Meursault Les Charmes, Meursault Les Chevaliers, Meursault Les Gouttes d'Or, Meursault Les Limozins, Meursault-Lupré, Meursault en L'Ormeau, Monthélie.

Alain Coche, whose techniques in winemaking are extremely similar to those of the Comte Lafon, runs this small 9.8-acre domaine. Coche is

one of the few growers making white burgundy who ferments every bit
of his wine in small casks (50% new oak), with the wines remaining in
contact with the lees until bottling, nearly 24 months later. The wines
are always extremely ageworthy, and a chat with Alain Coche reveals
his unsympathetic posture toward those winemakers who produce
wines that he calls "too low in acidity with soft, commercial appeal."
He also criticizes growers who tear their vines out before they reach
the age of 50–60 years. With this attitude, his percentage of old vines,
and winemaking techniques that mirror those of the Comte Lafon, one
would suspect brilliant quality here. In fact, some of Coche's wines
such as his Meursault Les Chevaliers and Meursault Les Charmes, are
indeed superb and very long lived. However, in recent vintages such as
1985 and 1986, while his wines have all been very good, only the
Charmes and Chevaliers were consistently superb. Since I have had no
experience with any Coche wines more than five or six years old, perhaps they will reveal even more with aging. The red wines, once shockingly mediocre, are now too oaky and overbearing. Nevertheless, this
is a very good to excellent domain and is not well known by many
customers searching out high quality white Burgundy. The exact same
cuvées also appear under the name of Coche-Bizouard.

DOMAINE J. F. COCHE-DURY (MEURSAULT)*****

> Wines Produced: Auxey-Duresses, Bourgogne Blanc, Corton-Char-
> lemagne, Côte de Beaune-Villages, Meursault,
> Meuersault Les-Casse-Têtes, Meursault Les Che-
> valièrs, Meursault Les Perrières, Monthélie, Vol-
> nay.

J. F. Coche-Dury is universally regarded as one of the five or six best
white-wine makers in Burgundy. The tall, thin, bespectacled, young
Jean-François Coche-Dury is a follower of the unfiltered style of winemaking practiced by the Comte Lafon family. He has built his micro-
sized domaine up to 17.3 acres, including a tiny bit of Corton-Charlemagne. His secret to making great wine is 33%–50% new Allier oak for
his white wines, two rackings of the wine, 18–22 months in oak, and
absolutely no filtration, a fact proudly displayed on the labels of his
wine bottles. Coche had a mind-boggling succession of excellent vintages in the 1980s, with extraordinary wines in 1981, 1982, 1983, 1985,
1986, and 1988. It's really hard to pick a favorite because his Villages
Meursault is as good as most people's Premiers Crus, and his Meursault
Les Perrières (fewer than 250 cases produced) is better than many
Montrachets. The tiny quantities of Corton-Charlemagne (usually fewer

than 100 cases produced) are sublime examples of white burgundy at its purest. For this writer, Coche-Dury is one of the three greatest wine producers in Burgundy, André Ramonet and the Comte Lafon being the other two. While lavish attention is paid to his white wines, Coche-Dury is also a super red-wine producer. Although he does not own any famous vineyards, his Auxey-Duresses and Volnay can frequently embarrass many Premiers Crus. His wines, which drink extraordinarily well young, are capable of lasting up to a decade in the bottle.

DOMAINE FERNAND COFFINET (CHASSAGNE-MONTRACHET)****

> Wines Produced: Bâtard-Montrachet, Chassagne-Montrachet, Chassagne-Montrachet La Romanée, Chassagne-Montrachet Rouge.

This minuscule domaine estate-bottles half of its production (which is then sold to private clients) and sells the other half to *négociants*. Their most famous wine, an outstanding Bâtard-Montrachet, is made from a parcel of .64 acre. It has been excellent in recent vintages. Their other wines are also extremely well made, and show a great deal of confidence and competence in the cellars. This is a relatively unknown estate that merits serious consideration.

DOMAINE MARC COLIN (CHASSAGNE-MONTRACHET)****

> Wines Produced: Bourgogne Aligoté, Bourgogne Rouge, Chassagne-Montrachet, Chassagne-Montrachet Les Caillerets, Chassagne-Montrachet Les Champs Gains, Chassagne-Montrachet Rouge, Montrachet, Saint-Aubin La Chatenière, Saint-Aubin Rouge, Santenay.

Marc Colin is the fourth generation of winemakers, and is one of the most talented proprietors in the Côte d'Or. His low-key, modest, and humble personality conceals his enormous talents until one tastes his wines. With his wife Michele and their four children, he exploits 20.4 acres of vineyards, including the famous .42-acre Grand Cru Montrachet. His Montrachet does justice to the appellation, but the wines frequently require 8–10 years of aging to reach their peak. He also makes excellent Chassagne-Montrachet Les Champs Gains and Chassagne-Montrachet Les Caillerets (the latter wine is more structured and longer-lived). His Saint-Aubin La Chatenière is a super white-wine bargain. However, far too many private clients already know of the wine and consequently little is seen in commercial channels. He uses 20% new oak for all his wines (except his Montrachet, which is kept in 100% new oak), and bottles after 10–12 months. A little bit of red wine is made here; the Chassagne-Montrachet Rouge and Saint-Aubin Rouge are elegant and stylish, but usually not as long lived as his whites.

DOMAINE MICHEL COLIN
(CHASSAGNE-MONTRACHET)****

> Wines Produced: Chassagne-Montrachet,　Chassagne-Montrachet Les Chaumées, Chassagne-Montrachet Morgeot, Chassagne-Montrachet en Remilly, Chassagne-Montrachet Les Vergers, Puligny-Montrachet Les Demoiselles.

Michel Colin is from the well-known Colin family of Chassagne-Montrachet. He is a good-looking man who is now approaching fifty, and he produces distinguished wines with a great deal of fruit and complexity. The best parcels of his 22.2 acres are the Premiers Crus of Chassagne-Montrachet. They include the outstanding honeyed, rich, concentrated Puligny-Montrachet Les Demoiselles, a minuscule 1.4-acre parcel bordering the two Grands Crus, Chevalier-Montrachet and Le Montrachet. His parcel has vines that average 48 years of age, and the resulting wine has more in common with a Grand Cru than with a Premier Cru. In the four vintages I have tasted, 1981, 1983, 1985, and 1986, the wine was stunning. Additionally, there is very fine Chassagne-Montrachet Les Vergers, and a more elegant, deep Chassagne-Montrachet Morgeot. Michel Colin believes in extended lees contact, 25% new oak, and bottling after 12–14 months. His wines give every indication of lasting up to a decade. This is one of the best small domaines in the village.

DOMAINE ROBERT COLINOT (IRANCY)**

> Wines Produced: Bourgogne Les Cailles Rouge, Bourgogne Irancy Rosé, Bourgogne Irancy Rouge, Bourgogne Palotte Rouge.

A small 9.9-acre estate known for its solid, straightforward red wines and sound rosé, Robert Colinot bottles his red wine after 6–12 months in cask and vat. The wines are quite acceptable and cleanly made.

DOMAINE JEAN COLLET (CHABLIS)****

> Wines Produced: Chablis, Chablis Blanchot, Chablis Mont de Milieu, Chablis Montée de Tonnerre, Chablis Montmains, Chablis Vaillons, Chablis Valmur.

Jean Collet, a reclusive individual who seems to shy away from publicity, has quite a cult following in Chablis. There are those who would argue that his Vaillons and Valmur are the finest in all of Chablis. He is one of only a handful of growers who continue to ferment in oak *foudres*. He then ages his wine 7–12 months prior to bottling. Filtration, widely employed elsewhere in Chablis, is rarely used by Collet. As a result, his wines are imbued with an extraordinary amount of flavor and the famous mineral, flinty smell that makes Chablis distinctive. I have had bad bottles marked by excessive amounts of sulphur dioxide, but I've also had truly superb examples that rival Chablis made by top growers such as René Dauvissat and François and Jean-Marie Raveneau. Much of Collet's production is sold to top restaurants in Paris, and to Michelin three-star restaurants such as La Côte St.-Jacques in Joigny, but he still produces a good amount of wine to sell to consumers from his 49.91-acre estate. His two biggest holdings are Chablis Montmains (4.82 acres) and Chablis Vaillons (17.29 acres).

DOMAINE LES COLOMBIERS (SAINT-VÉRAN)***

> Wines Produced: Mâcon-Villages, Saint-Véran.

This large estate of 88 acres includes the Domaine Les Colombiers in Saint-Véran and the Domaine de la Batie. The Janin family, who are gregarious and anxious to receive visitors, produce a very fresh, tasty Saint-Véran that should be drunk within 2–3 years of the vintage.

DOMAINE DE LA COMBE AU LOUP (CHIROUBLES)***

> Wines Produced: Chiroubles, Morgon, Régnié.

Gérard-Roger Meziat makes aromatic, rather full, heady wines in three of the Beaujolais crus, Chiroubles, Morgon, and Régnié. He is proudest of his Chiroubles, as he claims it has more finesse and elegance than either his Morgon or Régnié. The Domaine de la Combe au Loup wines are aged in wood *foudres* and cement vats for 6 months prior to bottling.

DOMAINE DE LA CONDEMINE (MÂCON-VILLAGES/PIERRE JANNY)***

Wines Produced: Mâcon-Villages.

This is a competent estate-bottled Mâcon-Villages that enjoys a high reputation in France.

DOMAINE JEAN-JACQUES CONFURON (PREMEAUX)***

Wines Produced: Bonnes Mares, Bourgogne Rouge, Clos Vougeot, Nuits St.-Georges, Nuits St.-Georges Les Chaboufs, Nuits St.-Georges Les Vaucrains.

Jean-Jacques Confuron seems to have a growing reputation in Burgundy, which I cannot understand. His wines all have an underlying vegetal, coarse characteristic. Even his top wines, such as the Grand Cru Clos Vougeot and Bonnes Mares, share this trait. His parcel of Clos Vougeot is superbly situated at the very top of the Clos, and should produce extraordinary wines. I usually prefer Confuron's wines from Nuits St.-Georges as they show more of an earthy, spicy *terroir* character (particularly the Nuits St.-Georges Les Vaucrains made from his half-acre parcel). Much of his wine is sold to clients in Europe and France. It does possess the constitution and depth to age nicely for up to a decade. However the vegetal, weedy character is annoying and probably the result of the use of too many stems.

DOMAINE J. CONFURON-COTETIDOT (VOSNE-ROMANÉE)****

Wines Produced: Chambolle-Musigny, Clos Vougeot, Echézeaux, Gevrey-Chambertin, Nuits St.-Georges, Nuits St.-Georges Premier Cru, Vosne-Romanée, Vosne-Romanée Les Suchots.

For several years, the tough-minded, hardworking Jackey Confuron and his wife Bernadette have had a cult following among European connoisseurs. Their domaine is quite small, consisting of 17.15 acres spread among the appellations listed above. Confuron recently added a tiny parcel of old vines in Gevrey-Chambertin and in 1988 purchased a small plot in Chambolle-Musigny. The style of winemaking here produces wines shockingly deep in color with an extraordinary amount of perfume. They perform extremely well young and my only query would be about their aging potential given their seductive, precocious charm early in life. Confuron, a stocky man, was one of the first winemakers to employ the winemaking philosophy of the increasingly famous oenologist, Guy Accad. Accad believes in extremely long cold macerations of the uncrushed grape bunches prior to starting the fermentation. Confuron himself will often keep these grapes (which are never destemmed) macerated under a bed of sulphur dioxide for a week. It is believed that this cold maceration extracts an extraordinary perfume from the grapes and results in wines with much deeper color. Confuron's best wines have consistently been his Vosne-Romanée Les Suchots and Echézeaux. I only started tasting his wines in 1981. The quality looks to be splendid, so I find it hard to justify the criticism, often bordering on paranoia, of this man's wines. He made excellent rot-free 1983s and surprisingly good 1984s. His 1985s, 1987s, and 1988s possess remarkable richness, intense color as well as outstanding potential. These wines spend up to 3 years in cask, and are neither fined nor filtered. Oenologist Guy Accad has an ever growing following among Burgundy's better producers, but Jackey Confuron was one of his earliest disciples, first utilizing Accad's techniques in 1977. It will be interesting to see how the wines from vintages such as 1985, 1986, and 1987 age.

DOMAINE EVON ET CHANTAL CONTAT-GRANGÉ (CHEILLY-LÈS-MARANGES)**

Wines Produced: Bourgogne Hautes-Côtes de Beaune Rouge, Bourgogne Rouge, Cheilly-Lès-Maranges, Santenay St.-Jean de Narosse.

This is a relatively new domaine that produces straightforward, compact wines, the best being their Cheilly-Lès-Maranges. The entire domaine consists of 19.31 acres and 33% of the production is estate-bottled. The red wines spend 8–10 months in 20% new oak and are bottled early after a moderate filtration.

COOPERATIVE LA CHABLISIENNE (CHABLIS)***

Wines Produced: An entire range of Chablis from the members of this cooperative is produced, including virtually all of the Premiers Crus and Grands Crus, as well as Petit-Chablis and Chablis-Villages.

La Chablisienne is the biggest cooperative of Chablis and accounts for over one-third of the area's production. It boasts 250 members and exploits over 1,500 acres of vines, including all the Grands Crus except Valmur, and all the Premiers Crus. There are mixed feelings both in Chablis and outside the district as to the omnipotence of this gigantic cooperative. First, only 20% of the cooperative's production is actually bottled by the coop and sold to the public. Even those sales are considered somewhat controversial because of the cooperative's practice of occasionally using growers' names on labels. This implies the wine is estate-bottled, when in fact it has come from a blend of wine from that particular vineyard of Chablis. The rest of the production is sold either in bulk (about 20%) or sold back to *négociants* in Beaune (60%–70%) to be bottled under that *négociant*'s name. While this cooperative clearly sets the pricing for Chablis in every vintage, and has the power to influence the quality image of a given vintage, the wines that emerge from the cooperative are usually good. In this decade, small oak casks have been used for certain Grands Crus, and the wines have been carefully made. This Chablis will not rival the best from winemakers such as Raveneau, Jean Collet, or René and Vincent Dauvissat, but the overall quality is impressive for a cooperative.

COOPERATIVE CHARNAY-LES-MÂCON (CHARNAY-LES-MÂCON)**

Wines Produced: An entire range of Mâcon wines are produced, plus Saint-Véran.

This is a relatively old but modernly equipped cooperative, founded in 1929, with 70 members. Of its 158 acres of vines, the best wine is its Saint-Véran. Much of the wine is sold in bulk for private labeling.

COOPERATIVE CLESSÉ-LA-VIGNE-BLANCHE (CLESSÉ)***

Wines Produced: An entire range of Mâcon-Villages wines with different cuvées available to prospective purchasers, priced according to quality.

Cooperatives dominate the Mâconnais region more than any other wine region of France. The Cooperative Clessé cultivates over 296 acres of vines and has 80 members. The wines are the product of stainless-steel fermentation and early bottling. As in all the cooperatives, there is a range of cuvées that prospective purchasers may select from, paying a few francs more for those cuvées deemed to be slightly fuller and deeper. As a general rule, the white wines from virtually all the cooperatives of the Mâconnais region should be consumed within 2 years of the vintage.

COOPERATIVE IGÉ-LES-VIGNERONS D'IGÉ (IGÉ)***

Wines Produced: An entire range of Mâcon wines, with their top cuvées called Mâcon-Igé.

This cooperative, founded in 1927, has 102 members and cultivates over 617 acres of vines. They make an entire range of Mâconnais wines, including some Crémant de Bourgogne, the rather dull sparkling wine produced in this region, and lower-end cuvées such as Mâcon-Superior. The wines of the Cooperative Igé tend to be among the top three or four in quality of wines produced cooperatively.

COOPERATIVE LUGNY (LUGNY)***

Wines Produced: An entire range of Mâcon wines, with their top cuvée being their Mâcon-Lugny-Les-Charmes.

The largest of the Mâconnais cooperatives, Cooperative Lugny has 930 members and cultivates 2,297 acres of vines. It was founded in 1927, but began to flourish in the seventies and eighties as a result of its reasonably priced, and extremely well-made wines. The wines are clean, fresh and floral. Seventy percent of the cooperative's production is exported to the United States, the United Kingdom, Southeast Asia, and the Benelux countries. Their best wine is the Cuvée Mâcon-Lugny-Les-Charmes, a textbook Mâcon with its flowery, fruity nose, its dry, crisp flavors, and its medium body. Other wines from this cooperative, such as the Mâcon Supérieur Red and Rosé, as well as the Crémant de Bourgogne, leave a lot to be desired.

COOPERATIVE MANCEY (MANCEY)**

Wines Produced: An entire range of Mâcon wines.

This cooperative, founded in 1929, exploits 321 acres and has 180 members. The quality of the wines produced is less than exciting, as most of the wines tend to be rather dull, formless, and lacking a degree of freshness and crispness.

COOPERATIVE PRISSÉ (PRISSÉ)***

> Wines Produced: An entire range of Mâcon wines including Mâcon-Villages, Bourgogne Aligoté, and Saint-Véran.

This cooperative enjoys a very fine reputation for its stylish, fresh, flowery white wines. Founded in 1928, the cooperative has 240 members who cultivate 864 acres. There is an entire range of cuvées produced here. All the wines are fermented in stainless steel and bottled directly from tank, although a handful of cuvées are given a small amount of aging in wood.

COOPERATIVE VIRÉ (VIRÉ)***

> Wines Produced: An entire range of Mâcon-Villages wines, including Crémant de Bourgogne.

The Cooperative Viré has a very good reputation for its Mâcon-Villages wines and prides itself on being a specialist in making only white wine. The cooperative of 691 acres of vines is owned by 248 separate growers. As with the other cooperatives in the Mâconnais region, there are many different cuvées available for sale, but the best one is a Mâcon-Viré. It is fermented in stainless-steel vats and aged in oak casks for 5 months prior to bottling. The wines of Viré tend to be among the fruitiest of all the cooperatives, with more body and staying power than most.

DOMAINE COQUARD-LOISON-FLEUROT (FLAGEY-ECHÉZEAUX)***

> Wines Produced: Bourgogne Rouge, Chambolle-Musigny, Charmes-Chambertin, Clos de la Roche, Clos St.-Denis, Clos Vougeot, Echézeaux, Gevrey-Chambertin, Grands Echézeaux, Morey St.-Denis, Vosne-Romanée.

This moderately sized domaine of 17.26 acres, owned by Raymond Coquard, has six holdings in Grand Cru vineyards in the Côte de Nuits, including a 2.79-acre parcel of Clos de la Roche and a 3.03-acre parcel of Echézeaux. In addition, Coquard has parcels of Clos Vougeot (from the lower, southern end of the slope), and tiny parcels of the Grand Cru vineyards Clos St.-Denis, Grands Echézeaux, and Charmes-Chambertin. The wines of this vineyard are well made, tannic, ripe, and rich, but are sold primarily to private clients and *négociants;* few are seen in the major export marketplaces. Perhaps Monsieur Coquard will eventually estate-bottle more of his production, since nearly two-thirds of it is sold off to *négociants* in Beaune. The wine that is bottled is kept in oak casks (⅙ are new) for 24 months.

CHÂTEAU DE CORCELLES
(CORCELLES-EN-BEAUJOLAIS)**

Wines Produced: Beaujolais, Beaujolais Rosé, Beaujolais-Villages, Brouilly.

Château de Corcelles is an impeccably manicured estate with a real château. This domaine produces rather light, elegant, flowery Beaujolais that is put into a distinctive bottle. Given its delicate structure, it is one Beaujolais that must be drunk within 1–2 years of the vintage.

DOMAINE ROGER CORDIER (FUISSÉ)***

Wines Produced: Pouilly-Fuissé.

Roger Cordier is now aging all his Pouilly-Fuissé in oak casks. The results are relatively brawny, full-bodied, big wines with a lot of character and perfume. While they are not quite in the same league as those of Château Fuissé or Madame Ferret, there has been significant improvement over the last several years. Cordier's wines generally keep relatively well for Pouilly-Fuissé, lasting 3 to 5 years.

CHÂTEAU DE COREAUX (LEYNES)***

Wines Produced: Saint-Véran.

This lovely estate of 19.2 acre is run by the Bernard family. It produces several different cuvées of Saint-Véran, all of which show excellent fruit, depth, and freshness. No wood is used and the wines are bottled early in order to preserve their freshness.

DOMAINE CLAUDE CORNU (MAGNY-LES-VILLERS)**

Wines Produced: Bourgogne Aligoté, Bourgogne Hautes-Côtes de Beaune Blanc, Bourgogne Hautes-Côtes de Nuits Blanc, Bourgogne Hautes-Côtes de Nuits Rouge, Bourgogne Passe-Tout-Grains, Le Corton, Côte de Nuits-Villages, Ladoix Rouge.

Claude Cornu is a very traditional winemaker, producing rustic, old-style white and red burgundies. His wines spend a lot of time in old casks with the exception of his Grand Cru Corton (1.5 acres), which is aged for nearly 18 months in 100% new oak casks. The rest of his wines are the products of relatively warm fermentations, long *cuvaisons,* and exhibit plenty of hard tannins and robust body. They often lack finesse and charm, but I am told they can last for 10 or more years and do mellow as they age. I have never tasted anything older than three years and do not know if such praise is warranted. Most of what Cornu produces is Bourgogne Hautes-Côtes de Nuits Rouge. This wine had a lot of power and muscle in vintages such as 1985 and 1988, but seemed overly tannic and thin in 1986, and lacked charm in 1987.

DOMAINE EDMOND CORNU (LADOIX-SERRIGNY)***

Wines Produced: Aloxe-Corton, Aloxe-Corton Les Moutottes, Bourgogne Aligoté, Bourgogne Rouge, Chorey-Lès-Beaune Blanc, Chorey-Lès-Beaune Rouge, Corton Les Bressandes, Ladoix Rouge, Savigny-Lès-Beaune.

The tall, deep-voiced wiry Edmond Cornu is a very talented and meticulous winemaker who probably would be much better known if he were not situated in the small village of Ladoix. Cornu's prices are hard to beat, particularly in view of the quality of his wines in vintages such as 1985 and 1988. However, he is not a producer to follow in years where the grape yield is overly abundant (i.e., 1979 and 1986). I should note that the cuvées of wine sold to his American importer are superior to those sold elsewhere because they are all neither fined or filtered. The estate now encompasses 21.4 acres, and the wines spend 12–14 months in oak casks with only a tiny 5%–10% new each year. However, nearly 100% new oak is used for the Corton Les Bressandes. The best wines of Edmond Cornu include an often astonishing Corton Les Bressandes from his 1.35-acre parcel of his Grand Cru, as well as his Aloxe-Corton Les Moutottes, a Premier Cru vineyard. Most of Cornu's wines should be drunk within 5–6 years of the vintage, although those cuvées sold to America represent richer and fuller wines.

CORON PÈRE ET FILS (BEAUNE)***

Domaine Wines Produced: Beaune Les Cent Vignes, Beaune Les Champs Pimonts, Beaune Le Clos des Mouches, Beaune Clos du Roi, Beaune Les Grèves.

Note: A range of *négociant* wines is also produced under the Coron label.

This small firm was founded in 1864 by Claude Coron and has continued to make some very good red and white burgundies with very little fanfare. The estate wines, which come from 25.93 acres of vines, are excellent examples of Premier Cru red burgundies, with delicious concentrated fruit, good body and structure, and the capacity to last for 10 or more years. Coron's *négociant* wines are less consistent, but I have tasted some fine examples of those as well. It is curious that this firm does not receive more publicity and attention for its wines. The red wines see 20%–30% new oak and are bottled after 14–16 months in cask. They are delicious young, and therefore are best drunk within their first 5–6 years of life.

DOMAINE CORSIN (POUILLY-FUISSÉ)**

Wines Produced: Mâcon-Blanc,   Mâcon-Rouge,   Pouilly-Fuissé, Saint-Véran.

Unexciting but consistently acceptable, straightforward wines are made by Joseph Corsin. He owns 15.3 acres and bottles both his white and red wines after 5–7 months of aging in 10%–15% new oak casks.

DOMAINE GUY COTTON (ODENAS)***

Wines Produced: Brouilly, Côte de Brouilly.

This is an excellent producer with a very high reputation. He makes some of the best Brouilly and Côte de Brouilly of both appellations. His wines spend 6–7 months in oak *foudres* and are bottled following a very light filtration. Unfortunately, Cotton's entire production is sold out within six to seven months after the vintage, as he owns only 11.5 acres.

DOMAINE DE MADAME DE COURCEL (POMMARD)****

Wines Produced: Bourgogne Rouge, Pommard Les Croix Noires, Pommard Les Fremiers, Pommard Grands Clos des Epenots, Pommard Les Rugiens.

Many connoisseurs in search of a great Pommard have found relief with a bottle from the Domaine de Madame de Courcel. Its two superb wines are Pommard Grands Clos des Epenots and Pommard Les Rugiens, from its important 12.35-acre holding in Les Epenots and 2.64 acres in Les Rugiens. The domaine's other red wines are often blended together or sold off in bulk to *négociants*, but the two aforementioned wines can be quite staggeringly rich, with tremendous extraction of fruit and flavor. A 1976 and 1978 I tasted recently were still not ready to drink, but showed so much potential that it will be worth waiting until the turn of the century to drink them. A 1962 drunk in 1988 was stupendous. The Domaine de Courcel, run by Yves Tavant and owned by Gilles de Courcel, believes in partial destemming of the grapes, but is flexible enough to destem completely in years where rot is a problem. After a relatively warm fermentation designed to extract as much color, flavor, and tannin as possible, the wine spends at least three weeks macerating. There is a great deal of punching down the cap at Courcel, with two to three *pigeages* a day. The wine is then put in one-third new oak barrels and bottled after 15 months. The wines are filtered very lightly for fear of removing body and potential for bouquet development. The Domaine de Courcel Pommards are among the sturdiest made of the appellation, vying with those from Hubert de Montille as perhaps the longest-lived red wines of the Côte de Beaune.

DOMAINE DES COURTIS (MILLY)**

Wines Produced: Chablis, Petit-Chablis.

Over half of the production from this small 26.79-acre domaine, run by Frederic Prain, is sold to Burgundy *négociants*. The estate-bottled wine is kept 10–12 months in tank and filtered prior to bottling. The wines are rather straightforward, simple, austere Chablis, with perhaps the best value being the modestly priced Petit-Chablis from the 9.8-acre vineyard. These relatively innocuous Chablis require drinking within 3–5 years of the vintage.

DOMAINE GÉRARD CREUSEFOND
(AUXEY-DURESSES)**

Wines Produced: Auxey-Duresses Le Val, Meursault Le Poruzot, Volnay.

Monsieur Creusefond's moderately small 20-acre domaine turns out standard quality, sound wines that must be drunk within 4–5 years of the vintage. The two vintages of his Meursault I tasted were disappointing; perhaps he has a better touch with his red wines than his white wines.

DOMAINE LOUIS CURVEUX (FUISSÉ)***

> Wines Produced: Pouilly-Fuissé, Pouilly-Fuissé Les Menestrières, Pouilly-Fuissé Les Vignes Blanches.

At this small estate of 13.8 acres, proprietor Louis Curveux uses 10% new oak and bottles his wines after 8 months of aging in small oak casks. His best cuvées are his Pouilly-Fuissé Les Menestrières, from one of the best *lieux-dits* of the appellation of Pouilly-Fuissé, and his Cuvée Vieilles Vignes (not produced in every vintage). Curveux's wines are buttery and spicy with a lot of fruit, and should be drunk within 3–4 years of the vintage.

DOMAINE DALICIEUX (LAVERNETTE)****

> Wines Produced: Beaujolais Blanc, Beaujolais-Villages, Mâcon-Villages Blanc.

This excellent small estate has begun to experiment with a cuvée aged in new oak that resembles Côte Rôtie rather than Beaujolais. The wines of the Domaine Dalicieux, run with great care by Bernard Dalicieux, are among my favorites from the Beaujolais-Villages appellation. This serious estate was founded only in 1975. The Beaujolais-Villages-Clos de la Jacarde-Vieilles Vignes is sensational.

DOMAINE PIERRE DAMOY (GEVREY-CHAMBERTIN)**

> Wines Produced: Chambertin, Chambertin-Clos de Bèze, Chapelle-Chambertin, Gevrey-Chambertin-Clos du Tamisot *(monopole)*.

This 23.46-acre domaine, run by Jacques Damoy, has the most important holding of Chambertin-Clos de Bèze (13.23 acres), as well as a 1.25-acre parcel of Chambertin. There is great potential for extraordinary wines, but the domaine has been run without a great deal of attention to detail. The results have been wines that turned brown at an early age and lacked concentration, structure, and character. There were encouraging signs in the mid- to late-eighties indicating that the Domaine Damoy had begun to turn things around, but to date this remains an estate that owns some of the most treasured vineyards in the appellation of Gevrey-Chambertin, but does not exploit their potential quality.

DOMAINE DARNAT (MEURSAULT)**–***

> **Wines Produced:** Bourgogne Blanc, Meursault, Meursault-Clos Richemont Les Cras, Meursault Les Gouttes d'Or.

This family domaine, run by four brothers and sisters, is renowned for its excellent, sometimes outstanding Meursault-Clos Richemont Les Cras from a 1.4-acre, highly praised vineyard. The wine sees less than 10% new oak, and is bottled after 14–15 months of cask aging. I have also seen this selection sold by the house of Jean Germain from purchased grapes, so the Darnats do sell some of the crop. Their other wines are not nearly as distinguished. The entire domaine is tiny, consisting of only 8.91 acres.

DOMAINE JEAN DAUVISSAT (CHABLIS)***

> **Wines Produced:** Chablis Chatain, Chablis L'Homme Mort, Chablis Mont de Milieu, Chablis Les Preuses, Chablis Vaulorent.

Jean Dauvissat produces elegant, crisp, medium-bodied, fresh, graceful wines of Chablis. I have seen only a few vintages of his wines, and therefore have been conservative with regard to his star rating. They require drinking within 5–6 years of the vintage.

DOMAINE RENÉ & VINCENT DAUVISSAT
(CHABLIS)*****

> **Wines Produced:** Chablis Les Clos, Chablis Le Forêt, Chablis Les Preuses, Chablis Sechet, Chablis Les Vaillons.

René Dauvissat, a bald, soft-spoken, extremely friendly man, makes some of the greatest wines from Chablis. There are no secrets to his vinification or *élevage*. The wines are barrel-fermented at 20°–22° C, and aged in cask for 10 months. He does not use any new oak for his Premiers Crus, but for Grands Crus like Les Preuses and Les Clos, he used 20%–40% new oak. All of the Dauvissat barrels are Allier wood. His Chablis stand out because they keep for an extraordinarily long time (15 years is not unusual for his top wines), yet drink extremely well young. They exhibit a marriage of fruit and spicy vanilla oak that is glorious to experience. The top two wines are consistently Les Preuses and Les Clos, but for value consumers should seek out the Chablis Le

Forêt, which is almost as good in top years such as 1985, 1986, and 1988. Dauvissat is a star of Chablis.

DAVID ET FOILLARD (ST.-GEORGES-DE-RENEINS)**

> Wines Produced: An entire range of Beaujolais and Rhône wines are produced by this firm.

This firm frequently enters the Beaujolais market, bottling wines that tend to be rather chunky and too alcoholic to merit much enthusiasm. The Rhône wine selections are more on target, as they are both better wines and better wine values.

DOMAINE JEAN DEFAIX (MILLY)***

> Wines Produced: Chablis, Chablis Beugnons, Chablis Chatain, Chablis-Côte de Lechet, Chablis Les Lys.

This estate of 39.52 acres produces Chablis that is fermented in stainless steel, centrifuged, and then kept in contact with its lees for one year prior to bottling. No oak casks are used. The straightforward, flowery, crisp wines drink well young, and have the ability to age well for 5–8 years. The firm's best wines are the Premiers Crus, particularly Chablis Les Lys, and the Chablis-Côte de Lechet. The domaine is also in the process of planting a section of the Grand Cru Blanchots vineyard, but it will not be in production for several more years.

DOMAINE ROBERT ET PHILIPPE DEFRANCE (ST.-BRIS-LE-VINEUX)**

> Wines Produced: Bourgogne Aligoté, Bourgogne Blanc, Bourgogne Rouge, Sauvignon de St.-Bris.

This 31.3-acre estate is prized for its crisp, tank-fermented, herbaceous Sauvignon de St.-Bris. The other wines include a light yet stylish, soft, fruity Bourgogne Rouge.

DOMAINE AMÉDÉE DEGRANGE (CHÉNAS)**

> Wines Produced: Chénas, Moulin-à-Vent.

A sound, rather rustic, chunky Moulin-à-Vent is Degrange's best wine. He keeps it in old oak *foudres* for six months prior to bottling. The entire estate consists of 16.32 acres.

DOMAINE ROGER DELALOGE (IRANCY)**

> Wines Produced: Bourgogne Irancy, Bourgogne Irancy Rosé, Cré-
> mant de Bourgogne.

The best wine from this 12.35-acre estate is its delicate, elegant, effusively fruity, dry rosé, which is bottled quickly for freshness. It is
comparable to some of the best rosés of Marsannay, but sells for half
the price.

DOMAINE MARIUS DELARCHE
(PERNAND-VERGELESSES)***

> Wines Produced: Corton-Charlemagne, Corton Le Corton, Corton
> 　　　　　　　Les Rénardes, Pernand-Vergelesses, Pernand-
> 　　　　　　　Vergelesses Les Vergelesses, Pernand-Verge-
> 　　　　　　　lesses Île des Vergelesses.

The cellars of Marius Delarche sit high up on the hillside in Pernand-
Vergelesses, just across the street from those of Bonneau du Martray,
the renowned producer of Corton-Charlemagne. This father and son
team tends to excel in years when there is excellent ripeness (much like
the other growers in Pernand-Vergelesses). However, in cold or wet
years their wines, from some of the less desirable slopes in Pernand-
Vergelesses, tend to lack body and intensity. I remember a superb 1985
Corton Le Corton that was as good as any of the top wines in that
vintage. Delarche is also capable of turning out some superb Corton-
Charlemagne from his 3.2-acre parcel. The entire Delarche domaine
consists of 19.3 acres, most in red wine varietals. Delarche's method of
winemaking calls for 100% destemming and a warm fermentation, followed by a 7- to 10-day *cuvaison*. The *cuvaison* period seems surprisingly short, but Delarche is fearful of extracting too much tannin from
his wines. Perhaps that is why his 1985s were brilliant while his 1987s
were disappointing. The red wines see 50% new oak. While this can be
a bit overwhelming in lighter-styled vintages, it can work in years like
1985 or 1988. Delarche's Corton-Charlemagne starts off life quite tight
and closed, but seems to be a good candidate for 10–15 years of aging
potential. I have given high marks to his 1985 and 1986, although the
1987 (only 600 cases were made) seemed light, excessively high in
acidity, and watery. All things considered, Delarche is a spotty per-
former, but in the good vintages this can be a cellar with some excellent
wines.

DOMAINE GEORGES DELÉGER
(CHASSAGNE-MONTRACHET)****

Wines Produced: Bourgogne Aligoté, Chassagne-Montrachet, Chassagne-Montrachet   Maltroie,   Chassagne-Montrachet Morgeot, Chassagne-Montrachet Rouge,
Chassagne-Montrachet Les Vergers, Chevalier-
Montrachet.

This tiny estate of 10 acres is primarily known for the exquisite white
wine made from its .39-acre holding in the Grand Cru vineyard of
Chevalier-Montrachet. However, Deléger also makes excellent Chassagne-Montrachet Morgeot, Vergers, and Maltroie, and a rather fleshy
yet elegant, berry-scented Chassagne-Montrachet Rouge. Much of his
red wine production is sold off to *négociants*, whereas his white wine
production is all estate-bottled. His white wines are fermented in small
oak barrels, one-third is aged in new oak, one-third is aged in 2-year-
old barrels, and the rest in a melange of barrels that range in age from
2 to 10 years old. A portion of the crop is also aged in tanks and all of
this is then blended together prior to bottling. It's incontestable that
Deléger's greatest wine is the Chevalier-Montrachet (it was fantastic in
1985, 1986, and 1988). Unfortunately, with a production of less than 100
cases, few consumers ever have a chance to try it. Both his white and
red wines should be drunk within 5–6 years of the vintage.

DOMAINE DENIS PÈRE ET FILS
(PERNAND-VERGELESSES)**

Wines Produced: Bourgogne Aligoté, Bourgogne Passe-Tout-Grains,
Bourgogne Rouge, Savigny-Lès-Beaune, Pernand-
Vergelesses.

This modestly sized estate of 18.77 acres has no Premier Cru or Grand
Cru vineyards, but makes competent, palatable wines from less renowned appellations. For pure value, the straight Pernand-Vergelesses
and Bourgogne Rouge are worthy of consideration. The Denis family
utilizes 10%–20% new oak, and bottles their wines after one year.
These are wines to be drunk within the first 4–5 years of life.

DOMAINE JACQUES DEPAGNEUX
(VILLEFRANCHE-SUR-SAÔNE)****

Wines Produced: Beaujolais-Villages-Château de Lacarelle, Côte de Brouilly, Mâcon-Viré-Clos du Chapitre, Morgon Les Versauds, Moulin-à-Vent-Domaine de la Tour du Bief.

Jacques Depagneux is an excellent source of Beaujolais, as well as a vineyard holder (he owns the 7.5-acre estate at Mâcon-Viré-Clos du Chapitre). He buys wines from some of the best domaines, Domaine de la Tour du Bief and Domaine Les Versauds (from which Georges Duboeuf also buys wine). The wines are aged in cask and are consistently well made as he is one of the top eight or nine producers of Beaujolais.

DOMAINE ANDRÉ DEPARDON (LEYNES)***

Wines Produced: Mâcon-Villages, Saint-Véran.

André Depardon produces straightforward and meticulous, crisp, apple-scented wines. They have a reputation for aging better than other Mâconnais wines. However, I have seen no old bottles, so I cannot form a first-hand opinion.

DOMAINE DESPLACES FRÈRES (RÉGNIÉ-DURETTE)**

Wines Produced: Beaujolais Régnié, Chiroubles.

I have not been overly impressed with the wines from this small estate of 15.3 acres run by René and Louis Desplace. The Chiroubles has lacked fruit and concentration, and the Beaujolais Régnié has been a bit diluted and insipid.

VINS DESSALLE (SAINT-JEAN-D'ARDIÈRES)**–***

Wines Produced: Beaujolais-Villages Cuvée Pierre Soitel, Brouilly-Domaine des Samsons, Fleurie-Cuvée Métrat, Juliénas-Cuvée Michel Tête, Moulin-à-Vent Cuvée Ernest Lafond, Saint-Amour Cuvée Pierre Patissier, Saint-Véran-Prissé.

The wines of this modestly sized firm (sales average 100,000 cases per year) can be found in the United States under the names Sylvain

Fessy. The name Héleǹe Maisonneuve is also used in other markets. The firm was founded in 1978 and immediately won rave reviews for its early releases. They exhibited delicious rich fruit in modern-style Beaujolais and were neither too alcoholic nor tannic. For whatever reasons, the quality of the wines has deteriorated since the late seventies and early eighties. Nevertheless, this serious *négociant* is capable of producing very fine Beaujolais.

DOMAINE LOUIS CLAUDE DESVIGNES (VILLIÉ-MORGON) ***

> Wines Produced: Morgon-Côte du Py, Morgon-Javernières.

This old family estate can trace its history back to 1712. It has remained a tiny (10.08 acres) estate, but the quality of the wines made here ranges from good to excellent. They are full, rich wines that need 6–12 months in vats to show their best.

DOMAINE DES DEUX ROCHES (DAVAYÉ) ****

> Wines Produced: Saint-Véran.

Jean-Claude Vrinat, of the world famous restaurant in Taillevent, and Georges Duboeuf, of Beaujolais fame, feel this well-known estate produces one of the finest Saint-Véran wines. The 29 acres of vines are adjacent to the famous Roche de Solutré and are meticulously cared for by Jean-Luc Terrier, Henri Collovray, and his son Christian. While the vinification techniques are modern, new wood barrels can be found on the estate. The wine is rich enough to handle the taste and vanilla aroma of new oak. A serious estate, Domaine des Deux Roches makes outstanding Saint-Véran, with part of the crop commercialized under the Georges Duboeuf label. Nearly half of the production is sold to Germany, where the proprietors, Mr. Collovray and Mr. Terrier, have cultivated virtually all their export business. This is a wine that can be aged for 4–5 years.

DOMAINE JEAN-PIERRE DICONNE (AUXEY-DURESSES) ***

> Wines Produced: Auxey-Duresses Blanc, Auxey-Duresses Les Duresses Rouge, Bourgogne Blanc, Bourgogne Passe-Tout-Grains, Bourgogne Rouge, Meursault.

The Domaine Jean-Pierre Diconne is one of the best small estates in Auxey-Duresses. It produces one of the two or three best red wines of the appellation, the Auxey-Duresses Les Duresses Rouge, from a tiny 1.6-acre parcel of old vines. Jean-Pierre Diconne also makes a very tasty Auxey-Duresses Blanc from 2.19 acres that is frequently better, as well as less expensive, than his Meursault. The entire estate consists of only 12.39 acres and the approach to winemaking is very artisanal. Less than 10% new oak is used for both the red and white wines, and they are bottled after 18 months of cask aging. The results are always stylish wines with good fruit and balance. They are never blockbusters, but are certainly quite satisfying and capable of aging for 5–7 years.

DOMAINE DIOCHON (ROMANÈCHE-THORINS)****

Wines Produced: Moulin-à-Vent.

Diochon produces one of the top Moulin-à-Vents year after year. It is a fragrant, highly extracted, concentrated, personality-filled wine. It seems best when drunk between 3–5 years of age, although given its proportions, it can no doubt last a great deal longer.

DOMAINE GÉRARD DOREAU (MONTHÉLIE)**

Wines Produced: Bourgogne Aligoté, Meursault, Monthélie, Monthélie Les Champs Fulliots, Monthélie Premier Cru, Saint-Romain Blanc.

Doreau's red wines are typical of wines from Monthélie. They have a rustic, robust heavyweight texture. There are 16.4 acres under vine.

DOMAINE DOUDET-NAUDIN (SAVIGNY-LÈS-BEAUNE)***

Wines Produced: Aloxe-Corton Les Boutières, Beaune Clos du Roi, Corton Le Corton, Corton Les Marechaudes, Ladoix La Marechaud, Pernand-Vergelesses Les Fichots, Savigny-Lès-Beaune aux Guettes, Savigny-Lès-Beaune-Redrescut Blanc.

Note: This firm also produces a small range of other wines under their *négociant* label.

This old domaine was founded in 1849. I had heard that the wines were dusty, old style, dried out and impossible to taste. The wines are made to last twenty to thirty years, and in tasting the 1987s one could easily see that these wines are impenetrable when young, very hard, very tannic, yet concentrated, full and rich. These wines are not meant to be seductive young, so I asked if it would be possible to taste some of the older vintages from both mediocre and good years, and the results were impressive. Judging by the old vintages, these are wines that keep and keep. Of course, they are not for everybody, and those who want to drink their burgundy within the first decade of life might as well stop reading this section. I am sure Doudet-Naudin considers it to be infanticide to open one of their wines before it is at least ten years old, for when I asked to taste a 1979, which was a relatively light, fast-maturing vintage, they thought the wine way too young. In fact, it turned out to be in great shape and would probably last another fifteen or twenty years. It seems that their decision to filter is their only acknowledgment of the advances of modern technology. Given how the wines are otherwise made, this concession does not make any sense. Nevertheless, they do filter, although they still seem to get plenty of extract and character in the wines. Most of this firm's small production is sold in England and Switzerland. This is an interesting, relatively small *négociant* business that produces less than 1,800 cases of wine each year. They also have extensive stocks of old vintages for sale. For those merchants and importers looking for some interesting, well-made wines from old vintages, this is a firm to visit. One of the most unique wines of Doudet-Naudet is their extremely long-lived white wine from the Redrescut vineyard in Savigny.

DOMAINE JEAN-PAUL DROIN (CHABLIS)***

> Wines Produced: Chablis-Brocs de Biques, Chablis Les Clos, Chablis Fourchaume, Chablis Grenouilles, Chablis Montée de Tonnerre, Chablis Montmains, Chablis Les Vaillons, Chablis Valmur, Chablis Vaudésir, Chablis Vosgros.

This modestly sized estate of 32.85 acres includes significant Grand Cru holdings in parts of Grenouilles, as well as some important Premiers Crus. Droin ferments all his wines in vat, but only his Grands Crus go into barrel for 6–12 months. His Premiers Crus spend about 9 months in vat and are bottled after a sterile filtration. One hundred percent new oak is used for the best Premiers Crus and Grands Crus. His wines are floral, elegant, fresh, and lively without great depth or complexity. They are consistently good, but rarely exhilarating. Both the Premiers Crus and Grands Crus should be drunk within 6 to 7 years of the vintage.

JOSEPH DROUHIN (BEAUNE)****

Domaine Wines Produced: Beaune-Clos des Mouches Blanc, Beaune-Clos des Mouches Rouge, Bonnes Mares, Chablis Les Clos, Chablis Premier Cru, Chablis Vaudésir, Chambolle-Musigny Les Amoureuses, Chambolle-Musigny Premier Cru, Clos Vougeot, Corton, Echézeaux, Grands Echézeaux, Griotte-Chambertin, Musigny, Volnay Clos des Chênes.

Note: The firm of Joseph Drouhin also produces an enormous range of wine as a *négociant*, and has the rights to produce and market the wines produced from the 5.08 acres of the Grand Cru vineyard Le Montrachet, owned by the Marquis de Laguiche.

Founded in 1756 and purchased by Joseph Drouhin in 1880, this famed house has built a reputation for wines that are among the very best of the modern style of red and white burgundies. Much of the credit must go to the tall, angular Robert Drouhin who has been in charge of the firm since 1957. The estate consists of 148.2 acres, of which 88.92 are in Chablis and the rest in the Côte d'Or. While the quality of the wines was somewhat shaky in the 60s, the wines grew increasingly better in the 70s. In the 80s, numerous outstanding wines were produced.

Robert Drouhin, one of Burgundy's most visible spokespeople, has expanded his operation to the new world, purchasing nearly 100 acres of plantable acreage in Oregon's Willamette Valley. There, he hopes to produce top quality Pinot Noir. Drouhin is a stickler for authenticity in burgundy and is one *négociant* who does not produce wines from any other region outside of Burgundy.

The white wines from this house are perhaps even greater successes than the reds. Drouhin seems to have a magic formula for producing wines of great finesse, elegance, and class, while maintaining richness and flavor. Having followed most of his white wines over the last decade and a half, the top wines are consistently his Montrachet-Marquis de Laguiche (which was absolutely sensational in 1985), his Bâtard-Montrachet, his Beaune-Clos des Mouches (a house specialty and sometimes equivalent to a Grand Cru in quality), his Chablis Les Clos, and his Corton-Charlemagne. Almost as good are his two Premier Cru Puligny-Montrachets where he buys the juice, the Puligny-Montrachet Les Folatières, and the Puligny-Montrachet Les Pucelles. I have never been a great admirer of Drouhin's Meursaults or his wines from Chassagne-Montrachet, but he does a very good job with appellations such as Saint-Romain, Saint-Aubin, and Rully, offering excellent wines at good prices. For consumers on a tight budget, his Bourgogne Blanc called Laforêt is a model generic white burgundy. For the white wines, he vinifies all the Grands Crus in new oak casks and ages them there for up to a year before they are bottled. The Premiers Crus are vinified in wood casks, of which none are new. However, skillful blending results in these Premiers Crus seeing some new oak prior to bottling. The other white wines are vinified in stainless-steel tanks and bottled quickly to preserve their freshness.

The proud Robert Drouhin would be the first to admit that his outstanding white wines could not be such without the impeccable advice of his top oenologist, Laurence Jobard, and his daughter Veronique, also an oenologist. Veronique is scheduled to look after the winemaking at the Domaine Drouhin in Oregon.

The red wines are aged in 66%–100% new oak casks for up to 16–18 months. Drouhin, like *négociants* such as Faiveley and Bouchard Père et Fils, now buys grapes rather than wine so he has total control over the winemaking procedure. His red wines tend to be very fruity, impeccably clean, and certainly have a house style. I have talked at length with Robert Drouhin about whether it is appropriate to filter wines, particularly the Premiers and Grands Crus, but have had no success in convincing him that filtration may not be necessary. His best red wines include all of his Grands Crus, but particularly his Musigny, Griotte-Chambertin, Grands Echézeaux, Echézeaux, Charmes-Chambertin, and Clos Vougeot. He owns two parcels of Clos Vougeot. The larger parcel of 1.53 acres is beautifully situated about two-thirds of the way up the hillside on the northern side of Clos Vougeot, whereas the smaller parcel, .71-acre, is poorly situated at the very bottom of the slope next to Route N 74. Among his Premiers Crus, Drouhin normally does an excellent job with wines such as Vosne-Romanée Les Suchots, Volnay Clos des Chênes, Gevrey-Chambertin Lavaux St.-Jacques, and Chambolle-Musigny Les Amoureuses. I have not been as impressed with some of his wines from Clos de la Roche, or his straight Villages wines. The Villages wines tend to be straightforward and simple, and not as good as those from *négociants* such as Louis Jadot or Faiveley. Nevertheless, the wines from Joseph Drouhin are impeccably made, and both the top level red and white wines are certainly capable of lasting for 10–15 years.

DOMAINE DROUHIN-LAROSE
(GEVREY-CHAMBERTIN)***—****

Wines Produced: Bonnes Mares, Chambertin-Clos de Bèze, Chapelle-Chambertin, Clos Vougeot, Gevrey-Chambertin, Gevrey-Chambertin Premier Cru, Latricières-Chambertin, Mazis-Chambertin.

This is an extremely wealthy domaine of 31.2 acres in the village of
Gevrey-Chambertin. Drouhin-Larose boasts impressively sized and situated parcels in Chambertin-Clos de Bèze, Bonnes Mares, and an extraordinary parcel of 3 acres in one of the finest sections of Clos
Vougeot. My tasting notes reveal some wonderful wines from this domaine in vintages such as 1959, 1966, 1969, 1971, 1972, 1978, and 1980.
However, it seems as if his wines, which were always known for their
highly perfumed, aromatic, supple character, have become significantly
lighter in the 1980s. Whether this is the result of excessive yields or a
change in winemaking techniques is hard to tell, but Bernard Drouhin
and his son Philippe deny that their production is any different. In any
event, the last several vintages, particularly 1986, 1987, and 1988,
hardly produced profound wines. According to the Drouhins (who are
not related to Robert Drouhin in Beaune), the grapes are destemmed,
macerated for only 7–10 days, and then put in oak barrels, of which a
very high percentage is new. For the Grands Crus, such as Bonnes
Mares, Latricières-Chambertin, Clos Vougeot, and Chambertin-Clos
de Bèze, 100% new oak is used. Given the style of the wines today, the
wines of Drouhin-Larose should be drunk within the first 7–8 years of
the vintage.

GEORGES DUBOEUF (ROMANÈCHE-THORINS)****

Wines Produced: While Georges Duboeuf possesses several tiny estates, he is best known as a *négociant* who makes
his own Beaujolais selections and bottles them
under his famous flower label. Additionally, he
represents numerous domaines in both Beaujolais
and Mâconnais, and has the wines bottled for the
estate, with not only the domaine's name, but his
name on the label as well. In 1989, he released a
special twenty-fifth anniversary cuvée for most of
the Beaujolais crus.

Beaujolais's most famous and frequently best producer is Georges Duboeuf, a wiry, bushy-haired, self-proclaimed workaholic. No person dominates any wine region of France as completely as Georges Duboeuf does Beaujolais, where he is called "le Grand Roi de Beaujolais." He started his company in 1964, and because of his fair prices, consistently high quality, and total commitment to authentic wines of each appellation, Duboeuf has single-handedly made the civilized world aware of the glorious, hedonistic, yet simple pleasures of a bottle of Beaujolais. His sales now account for almost 10% of the total production from the appellation, and many of the finest domaines have chosen Duboeuf to bottle their wines to sell them under both their own names and his. His first major break came when the two famous restaurant critics, Henri Gault and Christian Millau, visited him in 1968. It was, as they said, "love at first taste." Their critical acclaim led to Duboeuf's burgeoning business in Beaujolais. His remarkable success has led to many imitators and also to intense jealousy from competitors. Nevertheless, Duboeuf has prevailed because of the high quality of his wine. He has revolutionized the entire Beaujolais business with his bright, flowery labels, and has achieved top quality without sacrificing his wines by flash pasteurization or sterile filtration, as so many of his competitors have done. The results are remarkably fresh, lively, vibrant wines of Beaujolais.

Duboeuf's best domaines are listed below, and while there are other outstanding small growers in Beaujolais, each of these domaines is about as fine a representative of its village as exists. His entire range of 1989s tasted in March 1990, after they were bottled, were the finest Beaujolais I have ever tasted.

DUBOEUF'S BEST SINGLE GROWERS

Beaujolais Régnié (du Potet)
Beaujolais-Villages (Grand Grange)
Beaujolais-Villages (Granit-Bleu)
Brouilly (de Nervers)
Brouilly (du Prieuré)
Chiroubles (de Javernand)
Chiroubles (de Raousset)
Chiroubles (Desmeures)
Chénas (La Combe Remont)
Chénas (Manoir des Journets)
Fleurie (Quatre Vents)
Fleurie (Les Déduits)
Fleurie (Bachelard)

Juliénas (des Mouilles)
Juliénas (des Vignes)
Morgon (des Versauds)
Morgon (Princesse Lieven)
Morgon (Jean Descombes)
Moulin-à-Vent (des Caves)
Moulin-à-Vent (Charvet)
Moulin-à-Vent (La Tour du Brief)
Moulin-à-Vent Heritiers Tagent
Régnié (des Buyats)
Saint-Amour (du Paradis)
Saint-Amour (des Pins)

DOMAINE ROGER DUBOEUF ET FILS (CHAINTRÉ)***

> Wines Produced: Beaujolais Blanc, Mâcon-Chaintré Blanc, Pouilly-Fuissé, Pouilly-Fuissé Les Plessis.

Roger Duboeuf and his son, members of the famous Duboeuf family, produce small quantities of good Pouilly-Fuissé Les Plessis from their 5-acre vineyard. In addition, one should not miss their light, vibrant, remarkably fresh Beaujolais Blanc. The entire domaine consists of 12.35 acres and the wines are bottled after 7 months aging in small casks, of which 10% are new.

DOMAINE P. DUBREUIL-FONTAINE ET FILS (PERNAND-VERGELESSES)****

> Wines Produced: Aloxe-Corton, Bourgogne Aligoté, Corton Les Bressandes, Corton-Charlemagne, Corton-Clos du Roi, Corton Les Perrières, Pernand-Vergelesses, Pernand-Vergelesses Blanc, Pernand-Vergelesses Clos Berthet, Pernand-Vergelesses Clos Berthet Blanc, Pernand-Vergelesses Île des Vergelesses, Savigny-Lès-Beaune Les Vergelesses.

Bernard Dubreuil produces some of the most elegant wines in the Côte de Beaune from his multitude (12 different appellations) of vineyards. His cellars, tucked away on a hillside in the tiny village of Pernand-Vergelesses, are impeccably kept, and on my two visits were always filled with admiring visitors. The wines are never blockbusters, but are rather deliciously supple, elegant, velvety wines meant to be drunk young. I would question their aging potential beyond 6–7 years, but there is no denying their beautiful fruit and precocious charm. Dubreuil's top wines include the only *monopole* vineyard of Pernand-Vergelesses, the Clos Berthet, from which both white and red wines are made. He also produces two outstanding Cortons, Corton-Clos du Roi (2.47 acres) and a slightly smaller amount of wine from Corton Les Bressandes. These wines are frequently imbued with a wonderful cherry, strawberry fruitiness, and show an intelligent use of 20% new oak casks. The Corton-Charlemagne here, from a 1.17-acre parcel, is excellent rather than outstanding, and the Pernand-Vergelesses Blanc or the aforementioned Pernand-Vergelesses Clos Berthet Blanc are probably a better value. In summary, this is an excellent estate of 37.17 acres, producing very high quality red and white wines. If there is a criticism, it is that they perhaps lack staying power, but for consumers and restaurants desiring immediately drinkable wines, there is no denying the appeal of Bernard Dubreuil.

DOMAINE DUCHET (BEAUNE)***

Wines Produced: Beaune Blanches Fleurs, Beaune Blanchisserie, Beaune Les Bressandes, Beaune Les Cent Vignes, Beaune Les Grèves, Beaune-Pertuisots, Beaune Les Teurons, Beaune Les Tuvilains, Corton-Charlemagne, Pommard, Savigny-Lès-Beaune Les Peuillets.

The Duchet family put together this fragmented domaine of 12.2 acres by purchasing vineyards between 1941 and 1946. The late Monsieur Duchet, at one time the mayor of Beaune, began to estate-bottle about half his production in the early sixties, with the intention of selling his wine directly to clients. However, his political career kept him so busy that the wines were left in the cellar, bottled, but never sold. In the early eighties the American importer, Robert Haas, discovered the estate and reached an agreement to sell the old vintages, 1969, 1971, 1972, at great prices. For a while, there were some delicious, fully mature red burgundies available for sale. Currently, the wines are made by M. Duchet's son, who believes in fermentation in wooden vats with a *cuvaison* of 10–15 days. There is partial destemming and the wines are aged in 10%–15% new oak barrels. They are not fined, but are given a polishing filtration prior to bottling. My experience with all the red wines from this estate (particularly the Beaune Les Bressandes and Beaune Les Grèves) has been very positive. The wines are rich in fruit, well structured, and have plenty of character and complexity. I've never tasted any of the tiny quantities of the Corton-Charlemagne or the Pommard that are made. Domaine Duchet, while not terribly well known, has to date offered very good wines at fair prices, and the buyer should make an effort to find their products. The red wines from Beaune have given every indication of being able to age well for 10–12 years in good vintages.

DOMAINE DES DUCS (SAINT-AMOUR-BELLEVUE)***

Wines Produced: Beaujolais-Villages, Saint-Amour.

An historic estate founded in the twelfth century, the Domaine des Ducs is run by Marie, Joe, Jacques, and Claude Duc. Seventy percent of their production is exported, and the quality of their Saint-Amour leaves little to be desired. It is a rich, ripe, very traditionally made Beaujolais aged in large oak *foudres*, and is frequently quite deep in color, with a full, raspberry, plummy fruitiness.

DUFOULEUR PÈRE ET FILS (NUITS ST.-GEORGES)***

Wines Produced: Clos Vougeot, Côte de Nuits-Villages, Mercurey, Mercurey-Champs Martin, Mercurey-Clos L'Évêque, Santenay-Clos Genêts, Nuits St.-Georges Les Poulettes, Nuits St.-Georges Les Perrières, Nuits St.-Georges Les Chaines Carteaux

Note: An entire range of wines is produced by this firm as a *négociant*. The Domaine Dufouleur Père et Fils owns only 44.4 acres, but it produces a good Santenay-Clos Genêts and Nuits St.-Georges Les Perrières. The other wines are rarely exciting, solidly made, rustic, full-bodied burgundies that would appear to have the constitution to age well. Most of the production is sold within Europe.

DOMAINE PIERRE DUGAT (GEVREY-CHAMBERTIN)*****

Wines Produced: Charmes-Chambertin, Gevrey-Chambertin Champeaux, Gevrey-Chambertin Vieilles Vignes.

Pierre Dugat, a self-assured, middle-aged grower with only 12.35 acres in his domaine, keeps his impressive wines very much a secret. He sells some of his extraordinary Charmes-Chambertin to the Maison Leroy and the rest of it (including his exceptional Gevrey-Chambertin Champeaux and Gevrey-Chambertin Vieilles Vignes) to private clients in France and Switzerland. When I saw him in late 1988 he had no clients outside of the continent. Perhaps with a bit of persuasion he will begin to sell to the United States and Canada, as these are compelling and exceptional wines of great richness and complexity. Dugat believes in 100% destemming, tiny yields, old vines, a very high fermentation temperature of 34° C, and a 3–4 week *cuvaison*. The wines are aged for 16–18 months in oak casks, of which about 50% are new, and are bottled unfiltered. As one might suspect, his wines have remarkable color and extract. However, I left his cellar feeling that it is really the high concentration of old vines and his impeccable winemaking that are responsible for some of Burgundy's best kept secrets. Another reason to visit Dugat's cellar is that his *cave* was actually the cellar of a thirteenth-century abbey. Domaine Dugat is a name for connoisseurs of Burgundy wines to remember.

DOMAINE DUJAC (MOREY ST.-DENIS)*****

> Wines Produced: Bonnes Mares, Chambolle-Musigny Premier Cru, Charmes-Chambertin, Clos de la Roche, Clos St.-Denis, Echézeaux, Gevrey-Chambertin aux Combottes, Morey St.-Denis.

Note: This estate has begun to produce several other wines, including a Meursault-Limozin, under the name Druid Wines.

Domaine Dujac is one of the very finest estates in Burgundy. Proprietor Jacques Seysses is one of the most influential and innovative winemakers in the Côte d'Or, and his wines are always among its most elegant, complex, and flavorful. His Grands Crus receive 100% new wood aging, the Premiers Crus 50%, and there is no filtration. If the grapes are ripe and healthy, there is no destemming. A cold prefermentation of 3–5 days is done because Seysses believes this adds to the aromatic complexity of the Pinot Noir. While Seysses does believe in a 16- to 20-day *cuvaison* for his Pinot Noir, he does not allow the temperature of his fermentation to rise above 30° C. He also insists on bottling his wines after 14–15 months in oak barrels.

He has enlarged his domaine to 28 acres, which includes very important holdings in Clos de la Roche (4.5 acres) and Clos St.-Denis (4 acres). Seysses has also begun to produce tiny quantities of a Morey St.-Denis white wine, and makes a very fine rosé from excess production in bountiful crop years such as 1986 and 1982. One cannot go wrong with the wines of the Domaine Dujac as they are wonderfully perfumed, rich, extremely ripe, aromatic wines that not only drink well young but can age for 10–15 years. The top vintages for this domaine have been 1969, 1971, 1976, 1978, 1985, 1987, and 1988. It's hard picking a favorite, but for extended cellaring either the Bonnes Mares, the Clos de la Roche, or the Clos St.-Denis should be one's choice. The Echézeaux, made from relatively young vines, tends to be the lightest of the Pinot Noirs from Domaine Dujac. Perhaps the most underrated wine from this cellar is the Gevrey-Chambertin aux Combottes, which drinks extremely well young but can also age. Even more important than the commitment to quality here has been the inspiration that Jacques Seysses has been to many of the younger generation of Burgundy winemakers. An outspoken critic of oenologists who, he claims, "push for too much intervention in the winemaking process and seek only security and stability, not quality," Seysses has consistently been against filtration and over-manipulation of Pinot Noir. The number of Seysses' disciples who value quality over quantity is growing.

DOMAINE DUPERON (CHASSELAS)***

> Wines Produced: Saint-Véran.

This fine estate run by Nichol and Marcel Rivet produces one of the better Saint-Vérans of the appellation. It has a very floral, richly fruity bouquet, and good length and depth on the palate. The 1988 is delicious.

DOMAINE MARCEL DUPLESSIS (CHABLIS)**

> Wines Produced: Chablis Les Clos, Chablis Fourchaume, Chablis Montmains, Chablis Montée de Tonnerre, Chablis Les Vaillons.

Duplessis has a tiny estate of only 12 acres, and his wines are difficult to find outside of a few commercial marketplaces. His winemaking practice is to ferment the wine in tank and then transfer it to wood for 6–12 months. Following a rather severe filtration, it is bottled. My tasting experience here has been limited to only several wines from a few vintages, so it's hard to make any sort of objective assessment. However, what I have tasted has been of average to above-average quality, and I would guess the wines should be drunk within 4–5 years of the vintage.

DOMAINE GUILLEMARD DUPONT ET FILS (MELOISEY)**–***

> Wines Produced: Auxey-Duresses Blanc, Auxey-Duresses Rouge, Beaune, Beaune Les Avaux, Beaune-Clos des Avaux, Beaune-Clos des Coucherias, Beaune Les Grèves, Beaune Les Perrières, Beaune Les Teurons, Bourgogne Hautes-Côtes de Beaune Blanc, Bourgogne Hautes-Côtes de Beaune Rouge, Bourgogne Passe-Tout-Grains, Meursault Les Narvaux, Pommard.

This is quite an important estate of 57.87 acres. It is probably a logistical nightmare to operate, as the vineyards are spread out over 14 different appellations. The strength of the domaine is its Beaune Premiers Crus, of which their Clos des Avaux, Beaune Les Grèves, and Beaune Teurons are the best wines. There are also 22.6 acres of Bourgogne Hautes-Côtes de Beaune Rouge. The wine from these vineyards tends to be rather straightforward and simple, although certainly priced fairly. The white wines seem to lack vibrancy, and taste dull and a bit oxidized. All of the wines from Guillemard Dupont are aged in small oak casks for 16–24 months and are bottled after a filtration. If one stays with the Premiers Crus of Beaune, one is unlikely to be disappointed; in other wines consistency in quality and individuality in character are problems.

DOMAINE MICHEL DUPONT-FAHN (MEURSAULT)**

Wines Produced: Auxey-Duresses, Meursault, Monthélie-Premier Cru.

Michel Dupont makes straightforward, technically correct, but uninteresting wines. The estate consists of 8.64 acres with the largest holdings being a 5-acre parcel in Auxey-Duresses.

DOMAINE DUPONT-TISSERANDOT
(GEVREY-CHAMBERTIN)**

Wines Produced: Chambertin, Charmes-Chambertin, Gevrey-Chambertin.

The wines from this small domaine tend to be uneven in quality and rarely merit their reputation (particularly the Chambertin). It is possible that overproduction is a problem.

DOMAINE RAYMOND DUPUIS
(COULANGES-LA-VINEUSE)***

Wines Produced: Bourgogne Coulanges-la-Vineuse Rouge.

Dupuis is a highly regarded producer who owns only 14.82 acres. He is dedicated to producing a generic red Bourgogne which is very popular with the local producers. His wine is aged in vats and bottled after 6–8 months.

DOMAINE JEAN ET YVES DURAND (RÉGNIÉ-DURETTE)***

Wines Produced: Beaujolais Régnié, Brouilly, Brouilly-Pisse-Vieille.

The Durand family makes stylish, very light yet fruity, well-focused wines with good concentration from their 32.11-acre estate. Over half their production is sold to *négociants,* but the best cuvées are kept to be estate-bottled and are then sold directly to private clients. As with most wines from this appellation, they should be drunk within 2–3 years of the vintage. The 1989 Régnié was one of the great stars of that super vintage.

DOMAINE RENÉ DURAND (COMBLANCHIEN)**–***

Wines Produced: Corton, Côte de Nuits-Villages, Ladoix.

René Durand has built a local, almost frenzied following for his splendid Corton. He purchased less than one acre of Corton from the domaine of Charles Vienot when that estate was sold in 1984. The parcel is all in old vines, and the quality of Durand's wine is stunning. Unfortunately, the production is so tiny it is primarily sold to friends and private clients. His other wines include a mediocre Ladoix and straightforward Côte de Nuits-Villages.

DOMAINE JACQUES DURAND-ROBLOT (FIXIN)**

Wines Produced: Bourgogne Aligoté, Fixin, Gevrey-Chambertin.

This 17.29-acre domaine is not very well known. While the wines are never terribly elegant or filled with finesse, they are rustic and competent. The biggest holding of Jacques Durand is in Fixin where he has 12.35 acres.

DOMAINE DUREUIL-JANTHIAL (RULLY)***

Wines Produced: Mercurey Rouge, Puligny-Montrachet Premier Cru, Rully Blanc, Rully Rouge.

Raymond Dureuil is the third generation of his family to farm this 22.23-acre estate. The red wines are aged for several years in old oak casks before being bottled. The whites are matured in vats and bottled after

7–9 months of aging. Much of Dureuil's business is in sales to private clients. I have found the wines to have a great deal of color, power, and richness, but no underlying finesse or complexity. Perhaps refinement comes with aging. When young, the wines are certainly concentrated and full-bodied, obviously the result of a long time spent in vat and low yields. This is a serious, old-style domaine whose wines merit attention, and they appear to be extremely long lived.

DOMAINE G. DUVERNAY (RULLY)**

Wines Produced: Rully Les Cloux, Rully en Rebourcé.

This is a tiny father and son operation producing straightforward, competent wines from Rully. Their white wines, from the two excellent Premiers Crus, Les Cloux and en Rebourcé, represent a decent value, but should be drunk within their first several years of life.

DOMAINE MAURICE ECARD ET FILS (SAVIGNY-LÈS-BEAUNE)****

Wines Produced: Savigny-Lès-Beaune, Savigny-Lès-Beaune Les Hauts Jarrons (Blanc), Savigny-Lès-Beaune Les Narbantons, Savigny-Lès-Beaune Les Peuillats, Savigny-Lès-Beaune Premier Cru, Savigny-Lès-Beaune Les Serpentières.

My experience with Maurice Ecard's Savigny-Lès-Beaune Les Serpentières has been consistently excellent, and may well be the very best wine made in this appellation year after year. Ecard owns 5.68 acres of this superb Premier Cru of Savigny-Lès-Beaune. The wine is aged in 25% new oak and bottled after 14–18 months of cask aging. Usually, Ecard, who looks very much like the famous Bordeaux proprietor, Jean-Michel Cazes of Lynch-Bages, does not destem. One of the rarities of this estate is the excellent Savigny-Lès-Beaune Les Hauts Jarrons, made from the Pinot Blanc grape. What makes these wines special are low yields, attention to detail in the vineyard, and a wonderfully pure, fresh cherry fruitiness. Ecard's wines drink well young, but age well for 10–12 years. It is a shame more people don't recognize the high quality of this domaine which totals 26 acres in size.

DOMAINE DE L'EGLANTIÈRE (MALIGNY)***

Wines Produced: Chablis, Chablis Fourchaume, Chablis Montée de
Tonnerre, Chablis Montmains, Chablis-Vau-de-
Vey, Petit-Chablis.

Jean Durup, an imposing man with a full beard and confident manner,
is a member of a family that has owned vineyards in the Chablis area
since the fifteenth century. His estate of 247 acres is one of the largest
in the region. His holdings have been greatly enlarged by the extension
of the appellation's boundaries and his desire to increase his landholdings in Chablis. Durup does not own any Grands Crus, but he has a
very large holding of 39.52 acres which produce his best wine, the
Premier Cru, Chablis Fourchaume. Durup ferments his wines in fiber-
glass-lined cement vats and bottles them after 8–10 months. They are
relatively light, but impeccably clean, stylish, and always a pleasure to
drink. They rarely provide the degree of complexity or profound concentrated flavors of producers such as René and Vincent Dauvissat, or
the Domaine Raveneau. However, the wines from Domaine de l'Eglantière do last, and several 1978s drunk at the age of 10 were still crisp,
lively wines that had certainly stood the test of time. This vast estate
produces wines under a bevy of labels including the Domaine de
l'Eglantière, Château de Maligny, a fabulous château that has been
restored by Jean Durup, Domaine des Valéry, Domaine de Paulière,
and under the name of Jean Durup himself. All these wines are exactly
the same cuvées.

DOMAINE RENÉ ENGEL (VOSNE-ROMANÉE)****

Wines Produced: Clos Vougeot, Echézeaux, Grands Echézeaux,
Vosne-Romanée, Vosne-Romanée Les Brûlées.

Philippe Engel, one of the young, enthusiastic new generation of wine-
makers/grape growers in Burgundy, has revamped his family's estate
and turned around a property that had slipped badly in quality. He is
now producing some of the better wines in Vosne-Romanée. The estate,
while not large, does have 17.5 acres of vineyards in the above mentioned appellations with an important 3.75 well-placed acres in Clos
Vougeot. Under Philippe Engel, the winemaking since 1985 has improved greatly. All of the grapes are destemmed, and after an 18- to 25-
day *cuvaison* the wines are put directly into oak barrels, 70% of which
are new for the Grands Crus (such as Grands Echézeaux and Clos
Vougeot), and 30% for the Premiers Crus. Yet, this is a flexible estate,

as the percentage of new wood varies according to the year. The best wines have consistently been the Grands Echézeaux (of which there are usually less than 150 cases made) and the Clos Vougeot. The Vosne-Romanée Les Brûlées is usually Engel's most disappointing wine because his parcel of the vineyard is in young vines. The 1988s are the best wines I have tasted since Philippe began running this property, followed by the 1987s and 1985s. These are rather classic examples of wines from the Côte de Nuits, and it's encouraging to see the enthusiasm of young Philippe Engel.

DOMAINE M. FRÉDÉRIC ESMONIN
(GEVREY-CHAMBERTIN)****

> Wines Produced: Griotte-Chambertin, Mazis-Chambertin, Gevrey-Chambertin-Lavaux St.-Jacques, Gevery-Chambertin Estournelles St.-Jacques.

Frédéric Esmonin, another of the up-and-coming Esmonins in Gevrey-Chambertin, is one of the best winemakers in that appellation. Until 1987, Esmonin sold most of his production to *négociants*, primarily Louis Jadot and Leroy. He has now begun to estate-bottle his tiny production. His top wine is from a parcel of Griotte-Chambertin, the great Grand Cru that faces the more celebrated and often more expensive Chambertin-Clos de Bèze. His wines first came to my attention when I tasted the 1986 (a vintage I am not enamored of) and found it bursting with the smell of rich red fruits with a wonderfully subtle touch of spicy new oak. Esmonin followed that wine with elegant, stylish 1987s, and blockbuster 1988s. His wines are made from 100% de-stemmed grapes that are vinified at very high temperatures (up to 35° centigrade), and macerated for nearly 3 weeks. Afterward, they are aged in 50% new oak and are bottled without filtration after aging in cask for 14 to 17 months. Another member of Frédéric's family, Michel Esmonin, produces the superb Gevrey-Chambertin-Clos St.-Jacques, so the Esmonin family should have a highly successful 1990s.

DOMAINE MICHEL ESMONIN
(GEVREY-CHAMBERTIN)****

> Wines Produced: Gevrey-Chambertin,   Gevrey-Chambertin-Clos St.-Jacques.

Tucked in back of the village of Gevrey-Chambertin just below the famous hillside vineyard of Clos St.-Jacques is the minuscule cellar of Michel Esmonin. Esmonin has an important parcel (3.5 acres) of the 15-acre Clos St.-Jacques Vineyard. He began to estate-bottle his wine in

1985 after having sold it in bulk to *négociants*, primarily Madame Lalou Bize-Leroy. An impressive winemaker, Esmonin keeps his wine for 15–24 months in 50% new oak casks. He does no filtration unless the wine does not fall brilliant naturally. I was impressed by his extraordinary 1985 as well as the 1987 and 1988. Despite the tiny quantities of wine produced and the fact that there is only one variety of wine this is a gem of a cellar.

JOSEPH FAIVELEY (NUITS ST.-GEORGES)*****

Domaine Wines Produced: Bourgogne Blanc, Bourgogne Rouge, Chambertin-Clos de Bèze, Chambolle-Musigny, Chambolle-Musigny Premier Cru, Clos Vougeot, Corton-Charlemagne, Corton-Clos des Cortons, Echézeaux, Gevrey-Chambertin, Gevrey-Chambertin Les Cazetiers, Gevrey-Chambertin Combe aux Moines, Latricières-Chambertin, Mazis-Chambertin, Mercurey-Clos des Myglands, Mercurey-Clos Rochette, Mercurey-Clos du Roy, Mercurey Les Mauvarennes, Musigny, Nuits St.-Georges, Nuits St.-Georges Clos de la Maréchale, Nuits St.-Georges Les Porets St.-Georges, Nuits St.-Georges Les Saint-Georges, Rully Blanc, Rully Rouge.

Note: A number of wines are also produced by this firm as a *négociant*.

The low-profile family firm of Faiveley, now run by the young, bushy-haired François Faiveley, is one of Burgundy's greatest sources for top-quality wines. Additionally, the firm is also one of the very largest vineyard holders in all of Burgundy. The Faiveleys own 247 acres of vineyards that provide 85% of the wine produced by this firm. In short, only 15% of their production qualifies as the wine of a *négociant*. Faiveley wines have always been very good to excellent, but since François took over the winemaking in 1978, their quality has soared to the very top. Today, only a handful of domaines (Domaine de la Romanée-Conti and Domaine Leroy) make finer wines than those of Faiveley.

With respect to the actual winemaking here, all the wines since 1983 have benefitted from a 2- to 4-day cold maceration prior to the actual fermentation. François Faiveley believes this heightens the aromatic complexity of the wine and also extracts more color. Additionally, there is an 18- to 22-day *cuvaison*, and of course all the grapes are destemmed before any of this process begins. In vintages such as 1982 and 1986, Faiveley practiced a *saigner* (or bleeding of the *cuves*) of at least 15%–20% of the juice in order to give the wines more concentration. All of the Faiveley wines generally spend between 14–18 months in oak barrels, of which 15%–25% are new, except for certain Grands Crus, which receive 100% new oak. Since 1985, all of the Grands Crus and many of the Premiers Crus of the Faiveley firm are both bottled by hand and unfiltered.

Another trend at this firm is the aggressive action they have taken in the appellation of Mercurey in the Côte Chalonnaise. The Faiveleys, along with the Rodet family, are great believers in the potential of Mercurey and have become the leading winemakers in this appellation.

Equal care is given to the Faiveley's *négociant* wines. Since the early eighties the Faiveley firm has increasingly moved to purchase grapes rather than wine from growers. This allows the Faiveleys to exert as much quality control as possible. In the mid-eighties an expensive table of triage was constructed and every incoming grape is now hand sorted and discarded if not in excellent condition. François Faiveley's wines have moved increasingly toward a more elegant, graceful, well-balanced style, away from his father Guy's more muscular, alcohol-intense style.

Perhaps the best kept secret of the Faiveley firm is the outstanding quality of their white wines. While very little white wine is produced, their Mercurey-Clos Rochette, a 100% Chardonnay wine from their own estate, and their Rully Blanc are brilliant wines and very good values. Their Corton-Charlemagne rivals that of Louis Latour and J. F. Coche-Dury as one of the three finest wines of that appellation. Yet few people outside of the Faiveley family ever see it as the production is usually less than 150 cases (or six barrels) of wine.

Although I have followed the Faiveley wines for years, it is hard to pick any favorites as there is great consistency throughout the entire portfolio. However, there is no doubting that among the Grands Crus, the Chambertin-Clos de Bèze, Mazis-Chambertin, Charmes-Chambertin, Corton-Clos des Cortons, and Latricières-Chambertin are usually the best wines. In many vintages the Premiers Crus made by the Faiveley firm from Nuits St.-Georges, such as the Saint-Georges, Les Damodes, and those cuvées they purchase at the Hospices de Nuits auction are of Grand Cru quality. For value, there are wines such as the exceptional Mercurey-Clos du Roy, Mercurey-Clos des Myglands, or the Nuits St.-Georges-Clos de la Maréchale. Even wines such as their generic burgundy called Cuvée Joseph Faiveley are exceptionally well made and represent outstanding bargains.

All things considered, this is one of the most impeccably run firms in all of Burgundy, and under the inspired leadership of the young François Faiveley the wines now rival the best made in Burgundy. They are not inexpensive, but then there are no compromises permitted in making them. Most of the Premiers Crus and Grands Crus of the Faiveley firm can age well for 10–20 years.

DOMAINE JEAN FAUROIS
(VOSNE-ROMANÉE)****–*****

> Wines Produced: Clos Vougeot, Vosne-Romanée Les Chaumes.

The wiry, highly competent Jean Faurois is one of those growers who knows exactly how to get the most from his tiny 10 acres of vineyards. Fortunately, he has two outstanding parcels in Les Chaumes and Clos du Vougeot. He made superb wines in both 1987 and 1988, with his wines showing less differences between the two vintages than one might expect. Faurois is clearly of the minimal interventionist theory of winemaking as he neither fines nor filters his wines, preferring to let them rest undisturbed except for an occasional racking. They are bottled after 18–24 months in cask, of which 50% are new. Unfortunately, only tiny quantities of Faurois's wines are available outside of France. This is one of the great, relatively unknown sources of superb Clos Vougeot and Premier Cru Vosne-Romanée from the Les Chaumes vineyard. Faurois claims his parcel of Clos Vougeot, which is leased from the Domaine Méo-Camuzet and located next to the Château Clos Vougeot, has vines that were planted in 1920.

DOMAINE PIERRE FERRAUD ET FILS
(BELLEVILLE)****

> Wines Produced: Beaujolais-Cuvée des Montagnards, Beaujolais-Villages, Brouilly-Domaine Rolland, Chénas-Domaine Côte de Remont, Chénas-Cuvée Jean-Michel, Chiroubles-Domaine de la Chapelle des Bois, Côte de Brouilly-Domaine du Grand Cuvage, Côte de Brouilly-Domaine des Paves Bleus, Côte de Brouilly-Domaine Rolland, Fleurie-Château de Grand Pré, Juliénas-Cuvée Georges Manin, Juliénas-Domaine du Treve, Morgon-Domaine de l'Évêque, Moulin-à-Vent-G.F.A. des Marquisats, Régnié-Cuvée Antoine Ferraud, St.-Amour-Château du Chapitre.

Note: In addition to these wines, the firm of Pierre Ferraud et Fils makes all the Beaujolais crus that are designated under the name of the cru without a domaine designation. Ferraud also produces an entire range of white wines from Pouilly-Fuissé, Pouilly-Vinzelles, Saint-Véran, Beaujolais Blanc, Mâcon-Villages, and small quantities of Beaujolais Rosé.

While this medium-sized Beaujolais firm does have nearly 28 acres of vineyards, its fame comes from its *négociant* line of wines, which are among the very best Beaujolais made. In fact, after selections of Georges Duboeuf, my favorite Beaujolais are consistently those of Pierre Ferraud. The firm, founded in 1882 and family owned since, represents about 2% of the entire Beaujolais production. All the top wines are aged in large oak *foudres* and stainless-steel vats prior to bottling. The wines tend to be slightly less powerful than those of Duboeuf, have a mellowed, aged character, and are perhaps slightly less exuberant and crisp. This is not said pejoratively, as it is simply a different style. These are excellent Beaujolais, and they consistently get high marks in my tastings.

Of the domaine wines, I have been especially impressed with their Fleurie-Château de Grand Pré, Juliénas-Cuvée Georges Manin, Régnié-Cuvée Antonin Ferraud, Côte de Brouilly-Domaine de Grand Cuvage, and the Chénas-Domaine Côte de Remont.

This is one of the most consistently reliable, excellent producers of Beaujolais.

DOMAINE J. A. FERRET (FUISSÉ) *****

> Wines Produced: Pouilly-Fuissé, Pouilly-Fuissé Les Menestrières, Pouilly-Fuissé Les Perrières, Pouilly-Fuissé-Hors Classé, Pouilly-Fuissé-Tête de Cru.

The youthful, exuberant 82-year-old Madame Jeanne Ferret doubles as one of France's greatest winemakers and personalities. Her domaine was founded in 1762. One is likely to spark strong arguments as to whether Madame Ferret or Marcel and Jean-Jacques Vincent of the Château Fuissé produce the finest wine of the appellation. Both certainly produce the richest, most concentrated and most expensive wines of Pouilly-Fuissé. The wines of Madame Ferret, as well as those of Château Fuissé, usually last for 5–10 years, and are more akin to a good Premier Cru from Chassagne-Montrachet than anything else.

When Madame Ferret's husband died in 1974, the talk of the town was that she would be incapable of carrying on a tradition that had lasted for over two hundred years. Not only has she carried on, she has excelled in recent vintages, making a wine that is the Montrachet of Pouilly-Fuissé. Her secret is low yields, long aging in cask, minimal intervention by the winemaker, and some superb vineyard sites in the choicest hillside locations of Pouilly-Fuissé. The quality of her recent vintages is mind boggling, and while one might be shocked at the price of $30 a bottle for Pouilly-Fuissé, when one considers that her wines are better than the great majority of Premiers Crus of Puligny-Montracht, Chassagne-Montrachet, and even many of the Grands Crus, her price seems more sensible. When I last saw Madame Ferret in September, 1989, many of the other domaines had begun picking, but she intended to wait, because, as she said, "when it is hot; harvest early, when it is cold; harvest anytime you want." She said that she was expecting a great crop in 1989 to celebrate "the 200th anniversary of the French Revolution." In 1987 she made no Hors Classé, her top cuvée, preferring to put everything in her Tête de Cru. It is an outstanding Chardonnay with unctuous, rich, buttery fruit, a nutty scent, and an amazingly long, crisp finish. Her two 1986s are magnificent. I felt the 1986 Les Menestrières-Hors Classé (or top cuvée) was even richer and longer than the dazzling 1986 Pouilly-Fuissé-Tête de Cru. These are both fabulously concentrated, deep, rich, old-style wines with layers of fruit and a persistence on the palate that is rarely encountered given today's gigantic crops and early-to-bottle wineries. These are sensational wines that demonstrate how great Pouilly-Fuissé can be. One has to wonder why other growers do not aspire to produce something this extraordinary. If you have never tasted a great Pouilly-Fuissé, run, don't walk, to a shop that carries these magnificent selections.

Madame Ferret's wines are consistently superb, but are released very late into the market as she believes in giving them plenty of bottle age. Her cuvées will generally not appear in the market until 1–2 years after other producers have released theirs. Her secret is low yields and old vines. She uses only about 5%–10% new oak and bottles after about 7–8 months aging in tank and cask. The wines produced from her 32.21-acre domaine are truly superb, and glorious, hedonistic examples of Pouilly-Fuissé at its best.

VINS FESSY (SAINT-JEAN-D'ARDIÈRES)**–***

> Wines Produced: Beaujolais Régnié-Domaine des Braves, Beaujolais Régnié-Domaine des Vergers, Beaujolais-Villages-Domaine de la Comte Arnoux, Brouilly, Morgon, Moulin-à-Vent.

Georges Fessy runs the Fessy enterprise and markets his wines under the name Vins Fessy or Henri Fessy. Fessy is not only a *négociant*, but also a vineyard owner of 24.2 acres. I have had mixed results in my tastings of these wines, but some of the cuvées, particularly those mentioned above, have shown well. Others have been a little dull and insipid, but the firm does have a good reputation in Western Europe.

DOMAINE BERNARD FÈVRE (SAINT-ROMAIN)***

Wines Produced: Auxey-Duresses, Beaune-Les Epenottes, Beaune Les Montrevenots, Beaune Les Teurons, Pommard, Pommard Les Epenots, Pommard Premier Cru, Saint-Romain (white), Saint-Romain (red), Savigny-Lès-Beaune.

This could well be another estate that emerges in the nineties as a top-quality source for red and white burgundy. Fèvre is the brother of Regis Rossignol, the well-known wine producer in Volnay, and is married to the daughter of Monsieur Trapet, the owner of the famous estate by the same name in Gevrey-Chambertin. All the wines see a great deal of new oak, benefit from an extended *cuvaison*, and show surprising richness and fruit. Until 1988 Fèvre's wines were vinified and cellared by André Mussy at his domaine in Pommard. The only difference between the wines of Fèvre and those of Mussy is that Fèvre bottles his wines 3–4 months sooner than did Mussy. One of the great stars of this house is the Auxey-Duresses Rouge, which is not a Premier Cru, but a wine made from vines that are an average of 80 years in age. Both the 1987 and 1988 exhibited tremendous richness and body, and the ability to improve for 5–8 years. The wine is certainly less expensive than Fèvre's Beaune-Les Epenottes or Pommard Les Epenots yet competes with them. The three best wines of this estate in order of preference are the Pommard Les Epenots, Beaune-Les Epenottes, and Auxey-Duresses, followed by an excellent Saint-Romain blanc that is barrel-fermented, given lees contact, and bottled within 10–12 months of the vintage. Both the 1987 and 1988 were elegant, crisp, lighter-styled, and delicious white burgundies that should be drunk in their first 2–3 years of life.

DOMAINE WILLIAM FÈVRE (CHABLIS)✱✱✱
DOMAINE DE LA MALADIÈRE (CHABLIS)
ANCIEN DOMAINE AUFFRAY (CHABLIS)

> Wines Produced: Chablis Beauroy, Chablis Bougros, Chablis Les Clos, Chablis Fourchaume, Chablis Grenouilles, Chablis Les Lys, Chablis Montmains, Chablis Les Preuses, Chablis Les Vaillons, Chablis Valmur, Chablis Vaudésir.

William Fèvre, a staunch defender of the wines of Chablis, and president of the Syndicate de la Défence de l'Appellation de Chablis, is outspoken in his belief that limits in the appellation should be restricted to only those areas that have proven successful for growing Chardonnay. He has spoken out bitterly on the rampant expansion of Chablis into areas he believes are unsuitable for the production of top-quality wine.

 Fèvre has a large estate of 122.26 acres, of which 40 are in Grands Crus such as Les Clos (10 acres), Bougros (15 acres), Les Preuses (7 acres), Valmur (3 acres), Vaudésir (3 acres), and Grenouilles (1.5 acres). The rest of the estate is all in Premiers Crus except for a small vineyard of Chablis "simple." Fèvre knows the value of selling all his wine, so in addition to seeing bottles of Chablis from Domaine William Fèvre, one will see the exact same wines under the names Domaine de la Maladière and Ancien Domaine Auffray. The Premiers Crus and Grands Crus all spend up to a year in new oak barrels, as Fèvre feels the new oak adds complexity and gives the wines more structure. I have always liked the wines of Fèvre, but in certain vintages have found the oak too excessive, and the wines lacking a bit of concentration. It appears that he's stretching the production of his vineyards to the maximum. This is a good source of Chablis, but remains somewhat of an underachiever in the Chablis firmament.

DOMAINE FICHET (VOLNAY)✱✱✱

> Wines Produced: Bourgogne Aligoté, Meursault, Meursault Les Perrières, Volnay, Volnay Champans.

I have tasted only two vintages from the young Monsieur Fichet. It is perhaps too early to get excited, but he seems to have an excellent touch with both Pinot Noir and Chardonnay. His Meursault Les Perrières in 1988 was quite rich and concentrated in a year when many producers' yields were excessive. Fichet's Bourgogne Aligoté was also well above average for wines from that varietal. His Volnays show the classic character of the appellation: fruit, elegance, and character. This could be an unknown name to search out given the quality I have seen in the vintages of 1987 and 1988. My star rating may, therefore, be conservative.

DOMAINE RENÉ FLEUROT-LAROSE
(SANTENAY)***—****

> Wines Produced: Bâtard-Montrachet, Chassagne-Montrachet Morgeot, Chassagne-Montrachet Blanc, Chassagne-Montrachet Rouge, Le Montrachet, Santenay-Clos du Passe Temps.

René Fleurot, along with his son Nicolas, exploits 27.17 acres of vines. They are primarily known for their holdings in Montrachet (.39 acres) and Bâtard-Montrachet (.14 acre). Their holdings include tiny parcels, which Fleurot farms on behalf of his sister, Jacqueline Gaye. The production from Le Montrachet vineyard is estate-bottled, whereas production from the Bâtard-Montrachet vineyard is sold to the famous Beaune *négociant* and vineyard owner, Joseph Drouhin. The cellars, located in a beautiful property called Château du Passe Temps in Santenay, are extremely damp and cool. Fleurot believes in using virtually 100% new oak for his two Grands Crus of white wine, but his red wine is aged in older oak casks. Given the high quality of the red and white wines from René Fleurot, one wonders why more is not seen in the major export markets.

DOMAINE DE LA FOLIE (RULLY)***—****

> Wines Produced: Bourgogne Aligoté, Rully Blanc, Rully Chaponnière Rouge, Rully-Clos de Bellecroix Blanc, Rully-Clos de Bellecroix Rouge, Rully-Clos Roch Blanc, Rully-Clos St.-Jacques Blanc, Rully-Les St.-Jacques Blanc, Rully Rouge.

This well-known and highly respected property produces what many observers feel is the best white wine of the Rully appellation, Rully-Clos St.-Jacques. In abundant vintages, nearly 4,000 cases of this wine are produced. The wine has surprising flavor depth and richness, and the owner, Xavier Noël-Bouton, employs approximately 40%–50% new oak barrels in most vintages. The other white wines are also of very high quality. The red wine has never thrilled me as much as the white, but it is a pleasant, lighter-style Pinot Noir made to be drunk within the first 5–6 years of its life. The Domaine de la Folie has nearly 67 acres of well-situated vineyards in Rully.

DOMAINE FONTAINE-GAGNARD
(CHASSAGNE-MONTRACHET)****

Wines Produced: Bâtard-Montrachet, Chassagne-Montrachet, Chassagne-Montrachet Les Caillerets, Chassagne-Montrachet Maltroie, Chassagne-Montrachet Morgeot, Chassagne-Montrachet Les Vergers, Criots-Bâtard-Montrachet, Pommard Les Rugiens, Volnay Clos des Chênes.

This is a 12.35-acre estate run by Richard Fontaine, the son-in-law of Jacques Gagnard of the Domaine Gagnard-Delarange and brother-in-law of Jean-Marc Blain of the Domaine Blain-Gagnard. Richard Fontaine, a tall man in his late thirties who looks younger than his years, has a number of superb vineyards for both red and white wine. This is a serious estate, using 20%–25% new oak for both the red and white. The white wines tend to show excellent richness, medium to full body, and plenty of sweet, expansive Chardonnay fruit. The red wines taste a bit more straightforward and less exciting, but perhaps they need more time in the bottle. Bottling of the white wines takes place after 14–16 months of cask aging; for the red wines bottling is done after 18 months. The estate made very good 1987s and even better 1988s. The style of the wines suggest they should be drunk within their first 7–8 years of life.

DOMAINE ANDRÉ FOREST (VERGISSON)***

Wines Produced: Pouilly-Fuissé, Pouilly-Fuissé Les Crays.

André and Michel Forest produce very good to excellent Pouilly-Fuissé that is just a notch below the Pouilly-Fuissés made by Madame Ferret and Château Fuissé. The entire estate consists of only 8.57 acres. The wines are matured in small oak casks and bottled after 10 months. There is very little fining or filtration done here for fear of removing the flavor and character of the wine. Recent vintages have included a very good 1986 and an excellent 1988. Forest wines are very popular in Paris and can be found at such glamorous restaurants as the Ritz and Joel Robuchon's Jamin. Both these Pouilly-Fuissés can last for 5–7 years. There is also a Cuvée Vieilles Vignes produced.

DOMAINE FOREY PÈRE ET FILS
(VOSNE-ROMANÉE)***

> Wines Produced: Bourgogne Rouge, Echézeaux, Nuits St.-Georges, Nuits St.-Georges Les Perrières, Vosne-Romanée, Vosne-Romanée Les Gaudichots.

Jean and Regis Forey have their cellars adjacent to those of the Domaine de la Romanée-Conti in the rear of the village of Vosne-Rommanée. This is a low-profile producer who owns only 10.02 acres, but has a very high reputation for quality. Their most famous vineyard is the .22-acre Premier Cru Vosne-Romanée Les Gaudichots. It is said to have the same soil and root stock as the adjacent vineyard of La Tache, which of course, is a Grand Cru. Unfortunately, this wine is virtually impossible to find in the market given the microproduction. Forey Père et Fils also produces an excellent Echézeaux, and a very good Nuits St.-Georges Les Perrières. The wines spend 16–18 months in 15%-20% new oak casks. However, a much higher percentage of new oak is used for their Grand Cru Echézeaux. The firm is also responsible for making the famous La Romanée from a vineyard owned by the Liger-Belair family. This particular wine is made by Jean and Regis Forey and then sold in barrels to the famous Beaune *négociant*, Bouchard Père et Fils. When I was last at Forey cellars they were having doubts about the light filtration they give their wines, and were contemplating bottling their wines unfiltered. I hope they choose to do so. Forey Père et Fils is a consistently good domaine that made excellent wines in 1985, 1987, and 1988.

DOMAINE GABRIEL FOURNIER (MEURSAULT)**

> Wines Produced: Beaune, Bourgogne Aligoté, Bourgogne Rouge, Meursault, Meursault Les Chevalières, Pommard.

Over two-thirds of the production from Gabriel Fournier is sold to *négociants;* the rest is estate-bottled. The wines are acceptable, but unexciting. His best wine is his Meursault Les Chevalières, but unfortunately he only owns a .49-acre parcel of Chevalières.

DOMAINE JEAN-CLAUDE FOURRIER
(GEVREY-CHAMBERTIN)**

Wines Produced: Chambolle-Musigny, Gevrey-Chambertin, Gevrey-Chambertin-Clos St.-Jacques, Gevrey-Chambertin Combe aux Moine, Gevrey-Chambertin Premier Cru, Griotte-Chambertin, Morey St.-Denis, Vougeot Premier Cru.

Under current proprietor Jean-Claude Fourrier's great uncle, Fernand Pernot, this estate produced a succession of truly extraordinary wines in the sixties and early seventies (especially the 1966, the 1969, and 1971 vintages). In fact, much of the estate's reputation was derived from these extraordinary wines. The estate's name has changed from Pernot-Fourrier to Jean-Claude Fourrier, and while the domaine is packed with 20 acres of excellent vineyards, the quality of the wines is no longer outstanding. Monsieur Fourrier's efforts to produce the maximum amount of wine from his vineyards have resulted in a succession of mediocre wines in the decade of the eighties. At present, there are .65 of an acre in Griotte-Chambertin, 2.22 acres in Clos St.-Jacques, .87 of an acre in Combe aux Moine, 2.5 acres in Premier Cru vineyards, .85 of an acre in Vougeot Premier Cru, 9.27 acres of Gevrey-Chambertin-Villages, 1.69 acres of Chambolle-Musigny, and 1.6 acres of Morey St.-Denis. Even more impressive, the average age of the vines is now approaching 50 years. The wines are filtered lightly prior to bottling, but never fined, and are vinified in old open wood vats. The *cuvaison* period lasts 12–15 days, and Fourrier practices total destemming.

Fourrier's problems arise from excess production and an uninspired and sloppy *élevage* in some of the dampest, dirtiest cellars in all of Burgundy. Despite these conditions, the estate has great potential, as he owns a myriad of well-placed vineyards. Fourrier need only pay meticulous attention to production levels as well as the quality and condition of the barrels in his damp cellar to produce great wine. Someone should sit down and have a heart-to-heart talk with Jean-Claude Fourrier.

DOMAINE MARCEL ET BERNARD FRIBOURG
(VILLERS-LA-FAYE)**

Wines Produced: Bourgogne Aligoté, Bourgogne Hautes-Côtes de Nuits Blanc, Bourgogne Hautes-Côtes de Nuits Rouge, Bourgogne Passe-Tout-Grains, Côte de Nuits-Villages.

This 38.7-acre estate produces straightforward, rather one-dimensional wines. Their biggest production is in Bourgogne Hautes-Côtes de Nuits Rouge. Like the other red wines here, it is aged in large oak *foudres* for 8–10 months prior to bottling. The wines represent an adequate value, but lacks style and character.

CHÂTEAU FUISSÉ (FUISSÉ) *****

> **Wines Produced:** Juliénas, Morgon-Charmes, Pouilly-Fuissé, Pouilly Fuissé-Domaine de l'Arrilière, Pouilly-Fuissé Les Vieilles Vignes, Saint-Véran.

There is no domaine in all of southern Burgundy that has more of a legendary reputation than this extraordinary estate of 106.21 acres. The wines of Mme. Ferret and occasionally those of Giles Noblet can rival Château Fuissé's in taste, but not in fame. This family enterprise was established in 1850 and is now run with great care by Marcel Vincent and his son. The Château Fuissé Pouilly-Fuissé is the most expensive Pouilly-Fuissé in the world, and is on virtually all the wine lists of Michelin two- and three-star restaurants in France. One may question why their Cuvée Vieilles Vignes Pouilly-Fuissé can fetch $35–$40 a bottle in wine merchant shops and nearly twice that at a restaurant. However, in vintages such as 1985, 1986, and 1988, the Château Fuissé is reminiscent of the best wines of Chassagne-Montrachet or Meursault. It is an extraordinarily rich, ripe, concentrated wine oozing with buttery, popcorn-scented Chardonnay fruit.

Like the other white wines from this excellent domaine, the Pouilly-Fuissé is aged in 25%–35% new oak casks and bottled after 8–10 months. The regular cuvée of Pouilly-Fuissé is slightly less concentrated, but still a textbook example of what a good Pouilly-Fuissé can be. For value, consumers should look for the Saint-Véran, as it usually sells at one-third the price of the Cuvée Vieilles Vignes. This particular cuvée can last for 7–8 years in the bottle, with certain vintages evolving and improving over an even longer period of time. The estate also makes very good Beaujolais, but their Beaujolais have never quite attained the high reputation of this firm's white wines.

DOMAINE G.A.E.C. DE CHANTEMERLE (LA CHAPELLE-VAUPELTEIGNE) ***

> **Wines Produced:** Chablis, Chablis Fourchaume, Chablis L'Homme Mort, Petit-Chablis.

This firm owes its creation and success to the extension of the appellation area in Chablis. The proprietors, the enthusiastic Adhémar Boudin and his son, Francis, have created a domaine of 29 acres producing one of the best Petit-Chablis of the entire appellation from 75-year-old vines. While some people feel Petit-Chablis is always too acidic and sour, this wine is an example of the high quality of this appellation's better wines. The other wines include Boudin's Premier Cru Chablis Fourchaume and his tiny portion of Premier Cru Fourchaume bottled under the name L'Homme Mort (which morbidly translates to "the dead man"). This is a very modern operation that believes in the use of a centrifuge, but not in aging in oak. The wines are fermented in stainless steel, bottled after 7–9 months in tank, and rushed to the market. Although this is not normally the style of Chablis that I find the most interesting, my experience with the wines of Adhémar Boudin has been positive, as they are fresh, crisp, and fruity. Boudin's wines should be consumed within 5–6 years of the vintage.

DOMAINE G.A.E.C. DU CLOS DU ROI (COULANGES-LA-VINEUSE)*

Wines Produced: Bourgogne Coulanges-La-Vineuse.

While his wines are highly respected by the local producers, my experience with Michel Bernard's 19.76-acre estate has been unsatisfactory. The wines I have tasted from three relatively good vintages have appeared to be rather dull and watery.

DOMAINE G.A.E.C. DU COLOMBIER (FONTENAY)**

Wines Produced: Chablis, Chablis-Bougros, Chablis Fourchaume, Chablis-Vaucoupin, Petit-Chablis.

This family estate of 41.6 acres is run by Guy, Jean-Louis, and Thierry Mothe. Their wines are made in the modern style, as the wines are fermented and aged in stainless-steel tanks. They are bottled after 9 months and are fresh, straightforward, rather uncomplex wines that must be consumed young. The Mothe family estate-bottles only one-third of its total production, selling the rest to *négociants* in Beaune. Their two best wines are their Chablis Fourchaume and Chablis-Bougros. One immediate way to improve the quality of their wines would be to eliminate the hiring of a mobile bottling plant. This plant sterile-filters the wine prior to bottling, often denuding it of much of its character.

DOMAINE G.F.A. DE COMBIATY
(SAINT-ÉTIENNE LA VARENNE)***

Wines Produced: Brouilly.

Dominique Peron (also involved with the Domaine de la Chanaise in Morgon) makes deliciously fruity, ripe, and occasionally sumptuous Brouilly from a tiny 12.35-acre vineyard. Peron is one of my favorite producers of the appellation, but his wines are extremely difficult to find outside of France.

DOMAINE JEAN-NOËL GAGNARD
(CHASSAGNE-MONTRACHET)****

Wines Produced: Bâtard-Montrachet, Bourgogne Aligoté, Chassagne-Montrachet Blanc, Chassagne-Montrachet Les Caillerets, Chassagne-Montrachet Clos de la Maltroye, Chassagne-Montrachet-Clos St.-Jean, Chassagne-Montrachet Morgeot, Chassagne-Montrachet Rouge, Chassagne-Montrachet Premier Cru, Santenay-Clos de Tavannes.

Jean-Noël Gagnard, one of the Côte de Beaune's most meticulous winemakers, often makes some inspirational white wines from this 20.99-acre estate. He made fabulous 1983s (a problematic vintage), good 1984s, great 1985s, very good 1986s, somewhat light but tasty 1987s, and seemingly excellent 1988s. He also produces very stylish, vibrant, rich, easy-to-drink red wines from vineyards such as Chassagne-Montrachet Clos de la Maltroye, Chassagne-Montrachet Morgeot, and Chassagne-Montrachet-Clos St.-Jean. He even has a tiny parcel of Santenay-Clos de Tavannes. However, the glories of this house are their white wines, which reveal wonderfully rich apple-butter and toasty flavors, good acidity, and plenty of aging potential. Those consumers lucky enough to taste his Chassagne-Montrachet Les Caillerets or his Bâtard-Montrachet (.88 acre) are not likely to forget Domaine Jean-Noël Gagnard. His red wines normally drink well upon bottling, but can keep for 5–7 years. The white wines have the same longevity, except for the Bâtard-Montrachet, which is capable of lasting 10 or more years.

DOMAINE GAGNARD-DELAGRANGE
(CHASSAGNE-MONTRACHET)***–****

Wines Produced: Bâtard-Montrachet, Chassagne-Montrachet Blanc, Chassagne-Montrachet La Boudriotte Blanc, Chassagne-Montrachet-Clos St.-Jean, Chassagne-Montrachet Morgeot Blanc, Chassagne-Montrachet Morgeot Rouge, Chassagne-Montrachet Rouge, Le Montrachet, Volnay Champans.

This domaine is run by Jacques Gagnard. He owns 11.78 acres of vines, including a .19-acre parcel of Le Montrachet and a .66-acre parcel of Bâtard-Montrachet. For years, Jacques Gagnard sold much of his production to *négociants*, but today 65% of it is estate-bottled and the rest sold off to Beaune *négociants*. Gagnard believes in using 15% new oak casks for his white wines, with bottling taking place after 15 months. The same formula is employed for the red wines. The best wines are the two white Grands Crus, Bâtard-Montrachet and Le Montrachet. He made excellent 1982s, somewhat spotty 1983s, and strong 1985s and 1986s. His wines should be drunk within 5–7 years of the vintage.

DOMAINE MICHEL GAIDON
(ROMANÈCHE-THORINS)***

Wines Produced: Beaujolais Blanc, Beaujolais Supérieur, Chiroubles-Château Portier, Fleurie Les Moriers, Meursault, Moulin-à-Vent-Château Portier.

Michel Gaidon makes rather loosely knit, big, alcoholic, fat wines at the Château Portier. His Moulin-à-Vent spends 6 months in oak casks, of which 10% are new. The entire domaine consists of 120.5 acres, including 25 acres in Moulin-à-Vent, 14.8 in Chiroubles, and 17.23 in Fleurie. The balance of the wines is primarily in Beaujolais, but Gaidon also produces a Meursault and tiny quantities of an elegant Beaujolais Blanc.

DOMAINE JEAN GARAUDET (POMMARD)****

Wines Produced: Beaune-Clos des Mouches, Monthélie, Pommard, Pommard Les Charmots.

The wines of Jean Garaudet are the best-kept secret of Pommard. Unfortunately, that can hardly last much longer. Few Burgundy enthusiasts are likely to get the chance to taste the wines from Garaudet's tiny, impeccably run 12-acre estate. His elegant wines, imbued with lavish amounts of ripe fruit and harmonious, mouthfilling, satisfying flavors, offer formidable evidence of the positive effects of low yields and old vines. Garaudet, a tiny man, almost seems to be making excuses for his excellent Beaune-Clos des Mouches when he says it is made from "only 15-year-old vines." No excuses are necessary. The 1988 is one of the best wines I tasted from the southern Côte de Beaune yet. Garaudet's Beaune is his least distinguished wine. His Pommard is as good as a generic wine from this village can be. Made from 70-year-old vines, it has proven itself consistently to be a fat, ripe, concentrated wine that embarrasses most of the dull, alcoholic Pommards produced. Garaudet's Pommard has real class and style. His top wine, the Pommard Les Charmots, is made from a vineyard planted in 1902. In abundant vintages less than 100 cases of this hedonistic Pommard are produced. Normally, Garaudet prefers to use 50% new oak, rack his wines three times, and bottle them with little or no filtration after 18 months in cask. In 1988 his Les Charmots was so concentrated and intense that he decided to use 100% new oak. The result was a stunningly good wine. One of the overlooked wines in his cellar is the Monthélie. Most wines from that appellation tend to turn out coarse, but Garaudet's is beautifully pure and elegant.

DOMAINE DU GARDIN-CLOS SALOMON (GIVRY)***

Wines Produced: Givry Rouge.

Madame Jacqueline du Gardin, a member of the Salomon family, is the current owner of this famous 17-acre vineyard. Her family has controlled this vineyard for over 3 centuries. For many years the wine was bottled after nearly 36 months in cask. This process resulted in wines that were not fresh. Since 1982, and the appointment of a new *régisseur*, Hervé de la Salle, the winemaking procedure has changed completely. The wine now sees 10% new oak and is bottled after 18 months. This seems to make more sense and is certainly more pleasing to modern-day tastes. Whether Clos Salomon will remain one of the benchmark estates of Givry has yet to be seen, but the wines certainly have improved. Top vintages, such as 1988 and 1985, have good aging potential and should keep for 8–10 years.

DOMAINE MICHEL GAUNOUX (POMMARD)****

Wines Produced: Beaune Les Beaux Fougets, Beaune Les Bons Feuves, Beaune Les Boucherottes, Beaune-Les Epenottes, Beaune Les Prévoles, Bourgogne Rouge, Corton Les Rénardes, Pommard Les Arvelets, Pommard Les Charmots, Pommard Les Combes, Pommard Les Grands Epenots, Pommard Les Rugiens.

This has always been one of my favorite Côte de Beaune domaines. The late Michel Gaunoux (who died in 1984) did everything by the ancient methods. He even used people to tread the wine's chapeau. Men and women were hired to jump in and wade around in the old wooden *cuves*. A long, 3-week *cuvaison*, followed by aging in one-third new oak casks for 24 months, refusing to ever filter the wine, and in many vintages, barely fining it, created wines that were explosively full, rich, and capable of aging for 20–30 years. A 1962 drunk at the famous Taillevent Restaurant in 1988 was still as vibrant as many 5- or 6-year-old modern-style red burgundies. None of this should change under his widow, who now runs the estate.

The 23.93 acres are virtually all in top vineyard sites, with a large 7.21-acre parcel of Pommard-Grands Epenots, and a much smaller 1.7-acre parcel of Pommard-Rugiens. Most wine connoisseurs would agree that these are Gaunoux's best wines, both splendidly rich, deep, and ageworthy. However, Gaunoux also produces some other outstanding Premiers Crus from Pommard such as the Les Charmots and several top-notch Beaune Premiers Crus. In particular, the Beaune-Les Epenottes is excellent. For those lucky enough to find any, the Gaunoux family, makes a profound wine from their 3 acres of the Grand Cru Corton Les Rénardes. Unfortunately, little of Gaunoux's wine is exported as their traditional clientele is France's best restaurants. This is an outstanding estate still run with great attention to detail by the widow of Michel Gaunoux.

DOMAINE PAUL GAUTHIER (BLACÉ)**

Wines Produced: Beaujolais, Beaujolais-Villages.

Paul Gauthier is a tiny producer known for the excellent Beaujolais Nouveau and good, solid Beaujolais-Villages made from his 14.82-acre domaine.

DOMAINE GAY PÈRE ET FILS
(CHOREY-LÈS-BEAUNE)***

> Wines Produced: Aloxe-Corton, Beaune-Clos des Perrières, Beaune Les Toussaints, Bourgogne Aligoté, Bourgogne Rouge, Chorey-Lès-Beaune, Corton Les Rénardes, Savigny-Lès-Beaune, Savigny-Lès-Beaune Les Serpentières, Savigny-Lès-Beaune Les Vergeleses.

Over two-thirds of the wine from the Gay family's 32.11 acres of vineyards is sold in bulk to *négociants*. The high quality of the domaine-bottled wine makes me wonder why these wines are not more renowned in Burgundy circles. Ten percent new oak is used and the wine is bottled after 18–24 months in cask. The best wines produced at this estate include an excellent Savigny-Lès-Beaune Les Serpentières from a 2.47-acre parcel, and a delicious Corton Les Rénardes from 1.23 acres. Their best value is the Chorey-Lès-Beaune (13.46 acres) with its good strawberry and cherry fruit. These are wines that require drinking within their first 6–7 months of life.

DOMAINE GEANTET-PANSIOT
(GEVREY-CHAMBERTIN)***

> Wines Produced: Charmes-Chambertin, Gevrey-Chambertin, Gevrey-Chambertin Poissenot.

This small 9.50-acre domaine run by Edmund Geantet consistently produces wines that exhibit good color, a spicy, robust, meaty fruitiness, and competent winemaking. The top wine is no surprise: It's the Charmes-Chambertin produced from a 1.1-acre parcel of this Grand Cru vineyard. Most wines from Geantet-Pansiot should be drunk within the first 6–7 years of life.

DOMAINE GEISWEILER ET FILS
(NUITS ST.-GEORGES)**

> Domaine-Produced Wines: Bourgogne Hautes-Côtes de Nuits Blanc, Bourgogne Hautes-Côtes de Nuits Rouge.

This large producer of standard-quality burgundy is owned by the Grands Metropolitan Hôtels chain. Their specialty is Bourgogne

Hautes-Côtes de Nuits, both red and white, of which they own 173 acres. Among their other important acreage is some generic Nuits St.-Georges and some property in the Pouilly-Vinzelles area. Given the enormous production here, one should not expect high quality. While the general level of their Hautes-Côtes de Nuits is sound and correct, the wine is never particularly inspiring or complex. All the wines from this firm should be drunk within 4–5 years of the vintage.

DOMAINE PIERRE GELIN (FIXIN)****

Wines Produced: Bourgogne Aligoté, Chambertin-Clos de Bèze, Fixin, Fixin-Clos de Chapitre, Fixin-Clos Napoleon, Fixin Les Hervelets, Gevrey-Chambertin, Mazis-Chambertin.

The Domaine Pierre Gelin, now run by Stephen Gelin and André Molin, consists of 32.85 acres. The wines produced here tend to be big, beefy, and medium bodied with a lot of color and depth, plenty of flavor, and often excellent aging potential. Gelin and Molin's most important holding is the 11.8-acre parcel of Fixin-Clos de Chapitre; it is one of the best-situated Premiers Crus of this underrated appellation. In addition, there is a 4.52-acre parcel of Fixin-Clos Napoleon, and a 1.4-acre parcel of Fixin Les Hervelets. Gelin produces tiny quantities of Mazis-Chambertin from a .93-acre parcel, and Chambertin-Clos de Bèze from a 1.48-acre parcel.

In terms of quality and value, the three Premier Cru Fixins are Gelin's best wines. Gelin makes other wines, such as the Côte de Nuits-Villages and Villages Gevrey-Chambertin, but they are much less interesting than his Premiers Crus Fixins and his Grands Crus. He uses about one-third new oak for the Premiers Crus and about two-thirds for the Grands Crus. These are wines with a great deal of weight and richness, and they often take a good decade to reach maturity. For example, most of Gelin's 1976s had not yet reached their plateau of maturity in early 1989.

DOMAINE LOUIS GENILLON (VILLIÉ-MORGON)**

Wines Produced: Morgon.

Louis Genillon makes delicate yet adequate Morgon from his modestly sized estate. He believes in bottling his wines after 4–6 months of aging in vats.

CHÂTEAU GÉNOT-BOULANGER (MEURSAULT)***

Wines Produced: Beaune Les Grèves, Chassagne-Montrachet Premier Cru Blanc, Mercurey Blanc, Mercurey Rouge, Mercurey Saumonts, Mercurey Les Sazenay, Meursault-Clos du Cromin, Pommard, Pommard Le Clos Blanc, Volnay, Volnay Les Aussy.

This is an important estate of 47.41 acres with significant holdings in the appellations of Mercurey and Pommard (especially the outstanding vineyard called Pommard Le Clos Blanc), and a wonderful parcel of Premier Cru Beaune called Beaune Les Grèves (2.96 acres). The proprietors, Charles and Henri Génot, sell over three-fourths of the production to *négociants*, preferring to estate-bottle only 20% of their wine. The red wines see 20% new oak and are bottled after 12–14 months of cask aging. The white wines see the same amount of new oak and are bottled after eight months. The Génots employ very traditional techniques to make ageworthy wines capable of lasting, in the case of red wines, 8–10 years. Their best white wine is the Meursault-Clos du Cromin. The best way to obtain any of these wines is to buy them directly from the proprietors, since very little is exported.

DOMAINE ALAIN GEOFFROY (BEINES)***

Wines Produced: Chablis, Chablis Beauroy, Chablis Fourchaume, Chablis Vaulignot.

This domaine was originally created in 1850 but has been augmented by the recent extension of the Chablis appellation. Proprietor Alain Geoffroy, the mayor of the village of Beines, was one of the strongest proponents of what he calls the "revised" appellation. (Critics call it the "extension" or "augmentation" of the appellation.) The estate consists of 62.91 acres, its most important holding being a 15.9-acre parcel of Chablis Premier Cru, Beauroy. The approach to winemaking here is relatively typical of the majority of the domaines of Chablis. The wines are fermented and aged in vats, but occasionally older oak casks are used for certain wines for 6–8 months. Bottling takes place after a slight filtration. Geoffroy claims to want to taste the fruit and the character of the vineyard, rather than that of new oak, and is adamantly against and critical of those producers who use new oak for fermenting and/or aging their Chablis. The wines from this estate should be consumed within 4–6 years of the vintage.

DOMAINE LUCIEN GEOFFROY
(GEVREY-CHAMBERTIN)***

> Wines Produced: Gevrey-Chambertin Les Champeaux, Gevrey-Chambertin Clos Prieur, Gevrey-Chambertin Les Escorvées, Gevrey-Chambertin Les Perrières, Mazis-Chambertin.

Geoffroy makes a style of Burgundy that I am not sure I am capable of fully appreciating. I have visited his cellars twice and have tasted all his vintages since 1985. Geoffroy's wines have a remarkable black/ruby color and generous (and to my taste, excessive) amounts of toasty new oak. There is no doubting their concentration. These wines will appeal more to those who like their burgundy powerful, obvious, oaky, and alcoholic. As impressively colored and intensely flavored as they are, they always strike me as a bit awkward. I am told by those who follow Geoffroy's wines that their muscular, robust character becomes tamer after 7–8 years in the bottle. Certainly the wines exhibit enough evidence to suggest they will last. But will they ever develop complexity, finesse, and harmony?

DOMAINE DE LA GÉRARDE (RÉGNIÉ-DURETTE)***

> Wines Produced: Beaujolais Régnié.

Roland Magrin runs this tiny 14.82-acre estate. The Domaine de la Gérarde is dedicated to producing very stylish, elegant, richly fruity wines from Beaujolais' newest cru, Régnié. They are among the best of the appellation and should be drunk within 3–4 years of the vintage.

DOMAINE FRANÇOIS GERBET (VOSNE-ROMANÉE)***

> Wines Produced: Bourgogne Hautes-Côtes de Nuits, Clos Vougeot, Echézeaux, Vosne-Romanée, Vosne-Romanée Les Petits Monts, Vosne-Romanée aux Réas.

Two sisters, one blond, one brunette, Marie-Andrée and Chantal Gerbet, run this sizeable estate of 37.05 acres. They have some extremely well-placed vineyards, including Grand Cru acreage in Clos Vougeot (their vines were planted in 1956 and are located on the lower slope near route N74), and a tiny parcel of Echézeaux. Their two specialties are the Vosne-Romanée Les Petits Monts and Vosne-Romanée aux Réas. There is also a solid, pleasant, realistically priced wine from the

Hautes-Côtes de Nuits. While these wines are never dazzling, they are consistently good, showing fine ripeness, elegance, and the potential to last for 5–10 years. The current practice is to use 15%–20% new oak casks and keep all the wines 22–24 months in barrel. The Hautes-Côtes de Nuits is an exception, as it spends 10–12 months in cask.

DOMAINE HENRI GERMAIN (MEURSAULT)***

Wines Produced: Beaune Les Bressandes, Chassagne-Montrachet Morgeot Blanc, Chassagne-Montrachet Rouge, Meursault, Meursault Les Charmes.

This small 7.41-acre domaine estate-bottles three-fourths of its production, and sells the balance to *négociants*. The top wines include an excellent Meursault Les Charmes from a .64-acre parcel and a very fine Chassagne-Montrachet Morgeot Blanc from 1.4 acres. The best red wine is the firm's Beaune Les Bressandes. Ten percent new oak is used in each vintage, and both the white and red wines are bottled after 14–16 months in cask.

DOMAINE JACQUES GERMAIN
(CHOREY-LÈS-BEAUNE)****

Wines Produced: Beaune Les Boucherottes, Beaune Les Cent Vignes, Beaune Les Crais, Beaune Les Teurons, Beaune Les Vignes-Franches, Bourgogne Rouge, Chorey-Lès-Beaune-Château de Chorey, Pernand-Vergelesses Blanc.

The Germain wines are extremely silky, elegant, authentic red burgundies that display a judicious use of toasty new oak, beautifully seductive cherry fruit, and a medium-bodied, harmonious format. These are wines that are not only delicious in vintages such as 1985 and 1988, but also in difficult vintages such as 1986. In 1986 the Côte de Beaune suffered more rain and rot than the Côte de Nuits. The best wines tend to be Jacques Germain's excellent Beaune Teurons (5.6 acres), Beaune Les Vignes-Franches (2.43 acres), Beaune Les Cent Vignes (1.43 acres), Beaune Boucherottes (2.46 acres), and an excellent, reasonably priced Chorey-Lès-Beaune-Château de Chorey (10.49 acres). Another good value is the Pernand-Vergelesses Blanc. At present, the Domaine Jacques Germain consists of 39.32 acres spread among eight appellations. Germain believes in using 30% new oak and keeping his red wines in cask for 20–24 months. The white wines are bottled after spending 12 months in 15% new oak casks. In the high-priced world of red and white burgundy, the high-quality wines of the Domaine Jacques Germain have remained excellent bargains.

MAISON JEAN GERMAIN (MEURSAULT)***

Wines Produced: Bourgogne-Clos de la Fortune, Meursault, Meursault Les Meix Chavaux, Puligny-Montrachet Cuvée des Vignes, Puligny-Montrachet Les Grands Champs, Saint-Romain Clos Sous le Château.

This small *négociant* (he also owns 3.9 acres of vines) is tucked away on a back street of Meursault, adjacent to the Comte Lafon vineyard of Clos de la Barre. Jean Germain, a small, enthusiastic man, and Tim Marshall, an Englishman and Burgundy wine broker, operate this enterprise. Together they produce a bevy of high quality wines (the whites are clearly superior to the reds). These are some superb values to be plucked from this small operation, including one of the best generic Bourgogne Blancs made in the region, and a superb Saint-Romain that is vinified and aged in new oak. As one might expect, the Meursaults and Puligny-Montrachets are classy, and certainly very representative of their appellations. For a long period of time Jean Germain was Meursault's Bernard Michelot's (of Meursault fame) chief winemaking assistant. As Germain says, the key here is an extended lees contact. The juice produces wines of more flavor and finesse.

DOMAINE MAURICE AND JEAN-MICHEL GIBOULOT (SAVIGNY-LÈS-BEAUNE)**

Wines Produced: Savigny-Lès-Beaune Blanc, Savigny-Lès-Beaune aux Fourneaux, Savigny-Lès-Beaune Rouge, Savigny-Lès-Beaune Les Serpentières.

Maurice and Jean-Michel Giboulot own 19.88 acres and produce four straightforward, somewhat one-dimensional burgundies. Even their best parcel of vineyard, a 2.47-acre piece of Savigny-Lès-Beaune Les Serpentières, seems to render wines that are a bit hard and charmless. No new oak is used, and the wines are bottled after 10–14 months of cask aging.

DOMAINE EMILIAN GILLET (MÂCON)∗∗∗

> Wines Produced: Mâcon-Clessé, Mâcon-Viré.

This producer has been assisted by one of the greatest winemakers in the Mâconnais region, Jean Thevenet. The first two vintages I tasted of Gillet's Mâcon-Clessé and Mâcon-Viré, showed wonderfully balanced fruit, impeccable winemaking, and real flavor. This is a domaine worth watching.

DOMAINE ARMAND GIRARDIN (POMMARD)∗∗∗∗

> Wines Produced: Beaune-Clos des Mouches, Pommard, Pommard Les Charmots, Pommard Les Epenots, Pommard Les Rugiens.

Armand Girardin, the mayor of Pommard, produces tiny quantities of wine from his 9.88 acres of vineyards. His 1985 vintage was among the blackest-colored Pinot Noirs I have ever seen. The wines were succulent, sweet, unctuous, and chocolatey, and showed tremendous aging potential. His 1986s seemed extremely odd and unusual, but the 1987s and 1988s again looked to be special—massive, old-style, chewy, intense wines with 8–12 years of further evolution. Currently, Armand's daughter, Aleth, is responsible for the winemaking and what the Girardins don't estate-bottle is sold to *négociants*. Their best wines are their Rugiens and Epenots, with the latter wine coming from a parcel of vines averaging 80 years in age. This seems to be a domaine with some fabulous potential. I note they are increasing the percentage of new oak, a good sign given the huge extract of these wines.

DOMAINE GIRARD-VOLLOT ET FILS
(SAVIGNY-LÈS-BEAUNE)∗∗

> Wines Produced: Aloxe-Corton, Bourgogne Blanc, Bourgogne Rouge, Pernand-Vergelesses, Savigny-Lès-Beaune Les Peuillets.

My notes show that Girard-Vollot made a tasty 1985, 1986, and 1987 Savigny-Lès-Beaune Les Peuillets, but I have notes from other vintages that reveal wines that were rustic, lacking in fruit, and had overly coarse tannins. Perhaps the Girard family, who own 29.64 acres, is now producing wines with more charm and muscle—I hope so. The red wines spend 16–18 months in cask, but see no new oak. It would seem prudent to drink the wines of this estate within 5–6 years of the vintage.

DOMAINE BERNARD GLANTENAY (VOLNAY)***

Wines Produced: Bourgogne Passe-Tout-Grains, Pommard, Pommard Les Rugiens, Volnay, Volnay Clos des Chênes, Volnay Santenots.

In most recent years this estate sells at least half of its production to *négociants*. Bernard Glantenay, whose father, Louis, was a long-time mayor of the tiny village of Volnay, follows a long line of family producers. Although the entire domaine consists of only 19.76 acres, the Glantenays have some excellent vineyards. The top three wines include their Pommard Les Rugiens, Volnay Santenots (their largest holding at 1.67 acres), and Volnay Clos des Chênes (1.21 acres). The wines are aged in less than 5% new oak casks and bottled after 18 months. Most of the estate-bottled production is sold to private clients in Europe. The Glantenays feel their wines show best after four years in the bottle.

GOBET (BLACERET)***

Wines Produced: Beaujolais-Domaine des Grands Tours, Beaujolais-Villages-Les Quatre Clochers, Brouilly-Pisse-Vieille, Chiroubles, Côte de Brouilly-La Chapelle du Mont, Fleurie, Morgon, Moulin-à-Vent, Saint-Amour.

Note: As with most of the other Beaujolais *négociant* firms, this producer sells an entire range of Beaujolais and Mâconnais wines.

The wines of the firm of Gobet often appear in the United States under the name Jean Bedin. I have had some deliciously fruity, heady, and alcoholic wines from Gobet. I remember surprisingly delicious wines in 1983, and less successful wines in 1985. This is a good, middle-of-the-road producer with some decent wines, but cannot be put in the same category as Georges Duboeuf or Pierre Ferraud.

DOMAINE LAURENT GOILLOT (BERNOLLIN)***

Wines Produced: Bourgogne Rouge, Gevrey-Chambertin.

Domaine Laurent Goillot, a tiny estate of 11.1 acres, specializes in a robust, unmanipulated Villages wine from Gevrey-Chambertin. Aged in 10% new oak, the wine has plenty of personality, and can often compete with the best Villages wines of the appellation. It has the potential to last 7–10 years in most vintages.

DOMAINE RENÉ GONON (JULIÉNAS) ***

Wines Produced: Juliénas.

This small estate run by René Gonon produces some of the best wine of the appellation. It has plenty of body and backbone, and oozes with rich, plummy, raspberry fruit. I have had no experience with these wines after four or five years in the bottle, but for pure hedonistic pleasure look for the Juliénas from Domaine Gonon when released.

DOMAINE MICHEL GOUBARD (SAINT-DESERT) ***

Wines Produced: Bourgogne Aligoté, Bourgogne Blanc, Bourgogne
                Passe-Tout-Grains, Bourgogne Rouge, Bourgogne
                Rouge-Mont Avril.

Michel Goubard has won many hearts with his delicious Bourgogne Rouge-Mont Avril. In fact, this wine represents nearly two-thirds of his production from his 29.64 acres of vines. In top vintages such as 1985 or 1988, Goubard's Mont Avril Bourgogne Rouge can easily be as good as many of the village wines from the Côte d'Or. It is delicious—earthy and loaded with berry fruit. He also makes a stylish Bourgogne Blanc and Bourgogne Aligoté, but I have found his Bourgogne Passe-Tout-Grains to be a bit acidic and light. His red wines see 5%–15% new oak casks and are bottled after 18–24 months. Goubard performs little or no filtration for fear of removing flavor from his wines.

DOMAINE HENRI GOUGES (NUITS ST.-GEORGES) **

Wines Produced: Nuits St.-Georges Les Chaignots, Nuits St.-
                Georges Clos des Porrets, Nuits St.-Georges Les
                Perrières (Blanc), Nuits St.-Georges Les Pruliers,
                Nuits St.-Georges Les Saint-Georges, Nuits St.-
                Georges Les Vaucrains.

Henri Gouges' wines are among my earliest reference points for red burgundy. In the 1920s and 1930s, Henri Gouges, along with the Marquis d'Angerville, was instrumental in combatting the rampant fraud and illegal blending of inferior wines with burgundy. The father, Henri Gouges, championed low-yielding clones of Pinot Noir and for decades stood for all that was right about Burgundy. On my first visit to the estate in 1975, I was shown the entire range of 1966s and 1969s from their cellars. The wines reflected both their appellation and individual vineyard site and were definitions of exquisite red Burgundy. Since that time, the estate, for unknown reasons, has never produced another great vintage of red burgundy. Perhaps lack of supervision and attention to detail resulted in over-production. It could also be a result of the estate's decision to filter its wines. The results, from 1970 onward, have been a series of mediocre vintages. The 1971s that I bought early were round and completely dissipated by the mid-seventies. While rumors continue to emerge that this estate is coming back under the young Christian Gouges, the results in the eighties were not encouraging. The domaine still has 24 acres of vineyards in Nuits St.-Georges, with 2.69 acres of the famous vineyard of Les Saint-Georges and 2.44 acres of the famous Premier Cru Les Vaucrains. Additionally, Gouges has a relatively large holding of 4.64 acres of Nuits St.-Georges Clos des Porrets, and nearly one acre of Nuits St.-Georges Les Perrières. The Les Perrieres produces a delicious white wine from a mutation of the Pinot Noir grape. The best recent vintage has been the 1985, but in the context of that vintage the wines were light and slightly diluted. Given the great historic significance of the Domaine Henri Gouges, it is sad to see the quality of the current wines.

DOMAINE BERTRAND DE GRAMONT
(NUITS ST.-GEORGES)****

Wines Produced: Nuits St.-Georges Les Allots, Nuits St.-Georges Les Hauts Pruliers, Vosne-Romanée aux Réas.

The estate of Domaine Bertrand de Gramont emerged in 1985 after a division of the family's domaine. Bertrand's brother, Aymar de Gramont, kept most of the appellations and vineyards, and Bertrand ended up with only 7.4 acres of vines. However, despite the tiny size of the domaine, these wines should not be overlooked. Bertrand de Gramont, a good-looking man with a jovial personality, makes exquisitely rich, deep, chewy, ageworthy wine from his parcel of old vines in Nuits St.-Georges Les Hauts Pruliers. His Nuits St.-Georges Les Allots and Vosne-Romanée are also very good. His 1986s were certainly very successful, and his 1988s look to be the best wines he's yet produced individually. These appear to be wines that will last for 10–12 years, and in fact, often require cellaring for 4–5 years in order to shed their tannins.

MACHARD DE GRAMONT (NUITS ST.-GEORGES)****

Wines Produced: Aloxe-Corton Les Morais, Beaune Les Chou-acheux, Beaune-Les Epenottes, Bourgogne La Vierge Romaine, Chambolle-Musigny, Chorey-Lès-Beaune Les Beaumonts, Nuits St.-Georges Les Damodes, Nuits St.-Georges Les Hauts Poir-ets, Nuits St.-Georges en La Perrière Noblot, Nuits St.-Georges Les Vallerots, Pommard Le Clos Blanc, Puligny-Montrachet, Savigny-Lès-Beaune Les Guettes, Savigny-Lès-Beaune Les Vergelesses Blanc.

In top vintages this 50-acre estate produces a bevy of wines that are among the most undervalued of Burgundy. The producer, the bull-doggish Aymar Gramont, is a very forthright individual and is quick to let a visitor know what he likes and dislikes. For example, he detests the 1983 red burgundies, yet adores the 1985s and 1988s. He is not terribly keen on his 1986s, feeling they are too hard and tannic without enough supporting fruit. Such openness, especially in Burgundy, is indeed rare. As for the wines, their personality trademarks are excel-lent color, plenty of body and tannin, and superb depth of fruit and richness. They are wines that can easily last 10–15 years in the bottle, and often take a few years to open up. The wines are normally aged for 16–18 months in 30%–50% new oak barrels. Gramont believes in a lengthy maceration period of at least 21 days, and racks the wines two or three times prior to bottling. A visit to his cellars shows how pressed he is for space as the barrels are crammed in every corner as well as stacked up to the ceiling. Gramont is not a believer in Burgundy's new rage of cold maceration of grape bunches prior to fermentation, as he feels this procedure makes wines that show well young but do not age well. He believes in crushing and letting his fermentation temperature go rather high, to 33°–34° C. The results are, of course, wines that are exceptionally rich, full, and tannic. While all Gramont's wines are good, his best are consistently his selections from Nuits St.-Georges, partic-ularly the Perrière Noblot, Les Vallerots, and Les Damodes. He also produces a superb Savigny-Lès-Beaune Les Guettes and an exceptional Pommard from Le Clos Blanc. All things considered, Gramont is one of the most reliable names to search out in Burgundy. His prices are also among the most realistic given the very high quality of the wines.

DOMAINE DE LA GRAND COUR (FLEURIE)**

Wines Produced: Brouilly-Domaine des Côteaux de Vuril, Fleurie.

This 20.7-acre estate produces correct, straightforward wines that sell for too high a price. No doubt the great demand for the wines of Fleurie allows proprietor Jean-Louis Dutraive to ask a high price.

CHÂTEAU DU GRAND VERNAY (CHARENTAY)***

Wines Produced: Beaujolais, Beaujolais-Villages, Côte de Brouilly.

This estate has a good reputation in Paris for its fruity, rich Beaujolais-Villages. The wine is matured in large oak *foudres* for 4–8 months prior to bottling. The entire estate consists of 29.64 acres and is run by Claude Geoffray.

DOMAINE DES GRANDES BRUYÈRES (SAINT-ÉTIENNE-DES-OULLIÈRES)***

Wines Produced: Beaujolais-Villages, Mâcon-Villages.

This estate produces good quality Beaujolais-Villages. René Teissèdre, the proprietor, recently planted nearly 30 acres of vines in the Mâcon-Villages appellation.

DOMAINE DES GRANGES (CHAINTRÉ)***

Wines Produced: Beaujolais Blanc, Mâcon-Chaintré, Pouilly-Fuissé.

Proprietor Jean-François Cognard owns 17.29 acres of vines. He produces very stylish, tank-fermented white wines, including a deliciously vibrant, exuberant Beaujolais Blanc. This Beaujolais is probably his best value and the most underrated wine of his portfolio. The wines are all well made and are good examples of the potential quality of wines from small producers.

DOMAINE ALAIN GRAS (SAINT-ROMAIN)***

> Wines Produced: Auxey-Duresses Rouge, Bourgogne Passe-Tout-Grains, Saint-Romain Blanc, Saint-Romain Rouge.

This small, enthusiastic, impeccable winemaker frequently produces the best wines from the appellation of Saint-Romain. Alain Gras has only 12.35 acres, but obtains an elegance and character in his wines that make them all outstanding values for their quality. My favorite Gras wine is his lovely, floral, stylish Saint-Romain Blanc from a 2.47-acre parcel. He ages this wine in one-third new oak and bottles it after six months of cask aging. He also makes a lovely Saint-Romain Rouge filled with the scent of strawberries and cherries. This wine is a delight to drink within its first 5–6 years of life. Gras' other wines are certainly good, but he is most famous for these two wines.

CHÂTEAU DE LA GREFFIÈRE
(LA ROCHE VINEUSE)****

> Wines Produced: Mâcon-Villages.

Château de la Greffière, another tiny estate in the Mâconnais region, produces just over 1,000 cases of wine. The estate consists of 14.82 acres of vines averaging 35 to 45 years of age. Small yields result in intensely concentrated, rich Mâcon-Villages. This wine puts to shame many of the Mâconnais' industrially made, vapid, diluted wines. The owners, Henri and Vincent Greuzard, export very little wine.

DOMAINE HENRI-LUCIUS GRÉGOIRE (DAVAYÉ)***

> Wines Produced: Bourgogne Passe-Tout-Grains, Crémant de Bourgogne, Mâcon-Davayé Rouge, Mâcon-Rosé, Pouilly-Fuissé, Saint-Véran Les Cras, Saint-Véran Les Poncettys.

Engineer turned wine grower, Henri-Lucius Grégoire has a small 8.2-acre domaine. He produces very good, sometimes excellent Saint-Véran from two vineyard sites called Les Poncettys and Les Cras, and a very good Pouilly-Fuissé. I have not tasted either his red wines or his tiny quantity of sparkling Crémant de Bourgogne. Virtually all of Grégoire's wine is sold directly to private clients and is not exported. The white wines see 12 months of aging in large wood *foudres* prior to bottling.

DOMAINE ALBERT GRIVAULT (MEURSAULT)****

> Wines Produced: Meursault, Meursault-Clos des Perrières, Meursault Les Perrières, Pommard Le Clos Blanc.

The Meursault-Clos des Perrières (2.35 acres) of this estate has the ability to be a white Burgundy of absolutely extraordinary flavor dimension and dazzling complexity. It lived up to this potential in vintages such as 1979, 1985, 1986, and 1988. While some of the vintages in the early eighties lacked attention to detail, more recent vintages seem to be excellent. The Domaine Albert Grivault also makes an exceptional Meursault Les Perrières (3.82 acres), and a very good Villages Meursault. Madame Vardet-Grivault, ancient but still vibrant, is not known for her flexibility in winemaking, but she has a splendid estate of 11.95 acres. She also produces tiny quantities of Pommard Le Clos Blanc. The first and only vintage I tasted of this wine was the 1988, and it was supple, well colored, and attractive. Both wines from the Perrières vineyard, while drinkable young, can easily last for up to a decade in vintages with sufficient acidity.

DOMAINE JEAN GRIVOT (VOSNE-ROMANÉE)****

> Wines Produced: Bourgogne Rouge, Chambolle-Musigny La Combe d'Orveaux, Clos Vougeot, Nuits St.-Georges Les Boudots, Nuits St.-Georges Les Charmoix, Nuits St.-Georges Les Lavières, Nuits St.-Georges Les Pruliers, Nuits St.-Georges Les Roncières, Richebourg, Vosne-Romanée, Vosne-Romanée Les Beaumonts, Vosne-Romanée Les Brûlées, Vosne-Romanée Les Charmes, Vosne-Romanée Les Suchots.

I have always thought this outstanding producer of classic red burgundy had as difficult a job turning out such good wines as anybody. While his entire estate consists of only 25.4 acres, it is spread over fifteen different appellations. The wines produced by the scholarly looking Jean Grivot and his son Étienne range from very good to exhilarating. Since 1980, his wines have consistently been among the best made in Burgundy. In 1987, Grivot began to follow the advice of oenologist Guy Accad, and he now practices a prefermentation maceration, a relatively warm fermentation temperature of 30° C or more, and the use of 25% to as much as 100% new oak for Grands Crus. The wines spend 18–24 months in oak and are filtered very lightly or not at all. The top wines are usually the firm's outstanding Richebourg (unfortunately the Grivots own only .79 acre), the exceptional Clos Vougeot (4.61 acres, all at the bottom of the slope), the Nuits St.-Georges Les Boudots (2.09 acres), their Vosne-Romanée Les Beaumonts (2.47 acres), and their Vosne-Romanée Les Brûlées (.49 acre). Their other wines are also very good, particularly their Chambolle-Musigny La Combe d'Orveaux. This village wine does not qualify as a Premier Cru, but comes from a well-placed vineyard in a valley above Clos Vougeot. The Grivot wines consistently drink well young, but also have the cunning ability to age extremely well; the top Premiers and Grands Crus should last 8–12 years.

DOMAINE ROBERT GROFFIER (MOREY ST.-DENIS)****

Wines Produced: Bonnes Mares, Bourgogne Rouge, Chambertin-Clos de Bèze, Chambolle-Musigny Les Amoureuses, Chambolle-Musigny Les Hauts-Doix, Chambolle-Musigny Les Sentiers, Gevrey-Chambertin.

Robert Groffier's 17.3-acre domaine is never a model of consistency, but he often produces some of the most lush and seductive red burgundies in the Côte de Nuits. A curious producer to follow, he made better wines in 1986 than 1985, and has a tendency to fall on his face in certain years (i.e., 1985 and 1979). He may still be in the process of learning his trade as, prior to 1972, he sold all of his wine to the huge *négociant*, Piat. Nevertheless, there is a lot here to get excited about, particularly in recent vintages like 1988. Groffier's style aims at oodles of up-front, delicious berry fruit wrapped up in plenty of toasty, smoky new oak. His wines rest in cask for 18–24 months, and his Grands Crus see nearly 100% new oak in all vintages. Prices for Groffier's wines tend to be on the high side, but few expenses are spared in making the wine. While Groffier does produce some straightforward Bourgogne Rouge, the glories of this small estate are his parcels in Grand Cru vineyards such as Bonnes Mares (2.42 acres), Chambolle-Musigny Les Sentiers (2.64 acres), Chambertin-Clos de Bèze (1 acre), and in Premier Cru vineyards such as Chambolle-Musigny Les Amoureuses (2.64 acres). Most Groffier wines should be consumed within 5–7 years of the vintage.

DOMAINE ANNE-FRANÇOISE GROS
(VOSNE-ROMANÉE)**

> Wines Produced: Chambolle-Musigny, Clos Vougeot, Richebourg.

If Burgundy is not confusing enough, one must also contend with the number of domaines that have similar names. The Domaine Anne-Françoise Gros is the third domaine in Vosne-Romanée owned by members of the Gros family. The wines here are made by the sister of both Bernard Gros, who runs the Domaine Gros Frère et Soeur, and Michel Gros, who makes wines at the Domaine Jean Gros. There are 7.41 acres, most of them in Chambolle-Musigny, with tiny parcels in Clos Vougeot and Richebourg. The wines to date have not shown either the remarkable class of the Domaine Jean Gros wines, or the exotic opulence and richness of the wines of Gros Frère et Soeur. However, the vineyards are capable of producing something excellent, and one suspects that higher quality will ultimately emerge from this micro-estate with cellars in Vosne-Romanée.

DOMAINE JEAN GROS (VOSNE-ROMANÉE)*****

> Wines Produced: Bourgogne Hautes-Côtes de Nuits, Bourgogne Rouge, Clos Vougeot, Nuits St.-Georges, Richebourg, Vosne-Romanée, Vosne-Romanée-Clos des Réas.

The Domaine Jean Gros, run by the widowed Madame Gros and her son Michel, now in his mid-thirties, is one of the most serious and impeccably run domaines in Burgundy. A woman of uncommon elegance, Madame Gros is a strong political force (she has been the Mayor of Vosne-Romanée for a number of years). The wines from her 29.91-acre domaine are exquisite red burgundies, ranging from a celestial Richebourg (1.4 acres), to the *monopole* vineyard of Vosne-Romanée-Clos des Réas (5.23 acres). Even her Bourgogne Hautes-Côtes de Nuits (12.35 acres) is a classic example of its type. These are wines with excellent color, wonderful richness and depth, and aging potential of 10 to as much as 15 years. This domaine stresses high fermentation temperatures in order to extract as much color as possible, and prolong fermentation and maceration to extract fruit and tannin. A great deal of new oak is used, with the Grands Crus seeing 100% and the rest 60%–75%. The wines are given a very light filtration at the time of bottling. This estate also owns one of the most prized portions (.51 acre) of the upper slope of Clos Vougeot, but unfortunately, after the 1985 vintage the old vines were pulled out and the entire parcel replanted. It will be several more years before the Domaine Jean Gros Clos Vougeot returns to its previous exquisite form.

DOMAINE GROS FRÈRE ET SOEUR
(VOSNE-ROMANÉE)****

> Wines Produced: Bourgogne Rouge, Clos Vougeot, Grands Echézeaux, Richebourg, Vosne-Romanée.

Although Bernard Gros, the son of Madame Gros, is sometimes gruff and brusque, his wines are among the most extraordinarily exotic, hedonistic wines produced in all of Burgundy. His domaine of 20.62 acres includes 2.57 acres of Richebourg, .86 acre of Grands-Echézeaux, and the most prized and prestigious parcel of the entire Clos Vougeot. This 3.7-acre parcel is wedged in the northern corner, on the upper slope of the Clos, and is adjacent to Musigny in neighboring Chambolle-Musigny. Additionally, Bernard Gros owns 8.64 acres of generic Vosne-Romanée, and produces a Bourgogne Rouge from nearly 6 acres of vines. The wines that emanate from this producer are sweet, with an incredible level of fruit extract, displaying a cascade of cassis, apricot, and raspberry aromas and flavors. Gros believes in a prefermentation, cool maceration period, refuses to let the temperature of his fermentation get too intense, and does not employ any press wine. He uses 66% to 75% new oak casks, in which he keeps his wine 22 to 30 months. The Gros Frère et Soeur wines are in great demand throughout the world, and much of the production is sold to private clients who visit the cellars. A friend of mine who buys wines from Bernard Gros says Gros actually warms up after about a dozen visits to his cellars. All things considered, this is a source of some exceptionally interesting and staggeringly exotic red burgundies. I often wonder what miracles occur in his cellars to produce wines with such incredible bouquets of oranges, raspberries, and apricots. It is almost as if someone blended a *trockenbeerenauslese* with a great bottle of Pétrus. The wines of the Domaine Gros Frère et Soeur normally should be drunk within the first decade of their lives.

GROUPEMENT DE PRODUCTEURS DE PRISSÉ
(PRISSÉ)***

Wines Produced: Mâcon-Villages, Saint-Véran.

This cooperative of 220 growers collectively owns 3000 acres of vines. It was created over 60 years ago to coordinate the growers' resources, forming a winery where all their wines could be produced under textbook conditions, blended together for consistency, and sold under a trade name. There are different cuvées available to buyers, but most of the wines are among the better Saint-Vérans and are from the very modern school of stainless-steel fermentation and early bottling. The wines are always technically correct and have good fruit, but should be drunk very young.

DOMAINE CLAUDIUS GUERIN (ODENAS)**

Wines Produced: Côte de Brouilly.

Claudius Guerin's reputation for Côte de Brouilly is quite good. I have found his wines rather stern, perhaps a bit too alcoholic, but certainly acceptable. His wines are aged for six months in oak *foudres* prior to bottling.

DOMAINE RENÉ GUERIN (VERGISSON)**

Wines Produced: Pouilly-Fuissé La Roche, Saint-Véran.

René Guerin makes rather straightforward, acceptable wines from his 11.1-acre estate. He believes in 10% new oak, ages his wines in cask for 6–8 months, and finally bottles them after a moderate filtration. The wines seem to lack real class and individuality, but are certainly acceptable and satisfying.

DOMAINE GUFFENS-HEYNEN (VERGISSON)****

Wines Produced: Mâcon-Pierreclos Blanc, Mâcon-Pierreclos Rouge, Pouilly-Fuissé La Roche.

This micro-estate of 5.9 acres is run by an eccentric and exuberant young Belgian. It produces one of the two or three best Pouilly-Fuissés made in Burgundy, and perhaps the very finest example of a Mâcon. The wines are remarkably rich and full, and have more in common with a Premier Cru from Chassagne-Montrachet than most wines produced in the Mâconnais region. Even the red wine, made from vines averaging 45 years in age, seems to have a structure, richness, unctuosity, and fatness like the wines of the Côte d'Or. Consumers may wonder why the prices for Guffens-Heynen's Mâcon-Pierreclos and Pouilly-Fuissé are so high, but the quality is superb. Impeccable and absolutely brilliant wines were produced in 1983, 1985, 1986, and 1988. This is a tiny gem of a domaine worth every effort to find.

DOMAINE PIERRE GUILLEMOT (SAVIGNY-LÈS-BEAUNE)***

Wines Produced: Savigny-Lès-Beaune Blanc, Savigny-Lès-Beaune des Golardes, Savigny-Lès-Beaune Les Grands Picotins, Savigny Lès Jarrons, Savigny-Lès-Beaune Planchots de la Champagne, Savigny-Lès-Beaune Rouge, Savigny Les Serpentières.

The Gillemot family has an excellent reputation among the other vignerons of Savigny-Lès-Beaune. They only have 14.27 acres, but the plots are well placed (particularly the 2.98-acre parcel of Savigny Les Serpentières and Savigny Lès Jarrons). The red wines see 18 months in cask, 33% of which are new. Anne-Marie Guillemot looks after the winemaking and *élevage*. Interestingly, the white wine is made from Pinot Blanc, not Chardonnay, and tends to have a rather lean, yet flowery character. The best recent vintage for Guillemot was 1985.

DOMAINE GUILLOT (MÂCON)**

Wines Produced: Bourgogne Blanc, Bourgogne Rouge, Mâcon-Rouge.

Domaine Guillot is one of an increasing number of estates that are beginning to make organic wines. Essentially, this means no insecticides, herbicides, or sulphur are used in the production of the wine. The first vintages of these organic wines are sound but uninspiring.

DOMAINE JEAN GUITTON (BLIGNY-LÈS-BEAUNE)**

Wines Produced: Aloxe-Corton, Beaune Les Sizies, Bourgogne Aligoté, Ladoix La Corvée, Savigny-Lès-Beaune, Savigny-Lès-Beaune Les Haut Jarrons, Savigny-Lès-Beaune Les Peuillets.

Jean Guitton is a young, bright-eyed, extremely pleasant producer who has 25 acres of vineyards spread throughout the Côte de Beaune. When I first visited him I was struck by the quality of his 1986s. However, I was disappointed by his 1987s, and found the 1988s to be less successful than I would have expected. A lot of new oak is employed at this estate, and I think 50% new wood for wines such as Savigny Les Beaune and Ladoix may be excessive, obliterating what charm and fruit the wines possess. Consistently his best wine, Guitton's Beaune Les Sizies was excellent in 1987 and 1988. I admire the enthusiasm of Jean Guitton, but I wish I could be more impressed with the quality of the wines I have seen in the bottle.

DOMAINE ANTONIN GUYON (SAVIGNY-LÈS-BEAUNE)**

> Wines Produced: Aloxe-Corton Les Fournières, Beaune, Bourgogne Aligoté, Bourgogne Hautes-Côtes de Nuits, Bourgogne Rouge, Chambolle-Musigny, Charmes-Chambertin, Chorey-Lès-Beaune, Corton, Corton Les Bressandes, Corton-Charlemagne, Corton Clos du Roi, Corton Les Rénardes, Gevrey-Chambertin, Meursault Les Charmes, Pernand-Vergelesses Premier Cru Blanc, Volnay Clos des Chênes.

In 1970 the very successful Dijon wine shop, Guyon, acquired the Domaine Thevenot. The size of the domaine has since expanded because of the acquisition of 56.81 acres in the Bourgogne Hautes-Côte de Nuits appellation. At present this is an extensive domaine of 119.7 acres, spread out over 18 different appellations. Wine is made from vineyards as far south as the Premier Cru Meursault Les Charmes and as far north as Charmes-Chambertin. I have never found the wines of Domaine Antonin Guyon to be anything more than standard. Despite marvelous vineyards in Meursault Les Charmes, Corton-Charlemagne, Volnay Clos des Chênes, Charmes-Chambertin, Corton, and the three wonderful Grands Crus of Corton—Clos du Roi, Bressandes, and Rénardes—the style of winemaking here tends to produce rather clipped, compact red and white burgundies that lack complexity and charm. The red wines are aged in 40% new oak and are bottled after 18 months in cask. The white wines are aged in 50% new oak and are bottled after 12 months. The wines from this estate also appear under the Domaine Dominique Guyon label. Most of the Guyon wines can age for up to 7–10 years, but I am not sure they always improve during that time.

DOMAINE HUBERT GUYOT-VERPIOT (RULLY)**

Wines Produced: Bourgogne Aligoté, Crémant de Bourgogne, Rully
Blanc, Rully Rouge.

Hubert Guyot runs this family-owned vineyard of 15.9 acres. The domaine was established in 1973. Like other top Rully vineyards, its
Chardonnay and Pinot Noir are planted on chalky clay soil with a south-
easterly exposure. This estate does not use any new oak, preferring to
age its wines in vats and in small, older casks for 12 months prior to
bottling. While I have been disappointed with their Crémant de Bourgogne, which I found to be slightly dirty, the other wines are competently made. They include a straightforward, light yet technically
correct Rully Blanc and a rustic, spicy Rully Rouge. Perhaps a small
percentage of new oak would give the red wines more focus and character.

DOMAINE HAEGELEN-JAYER (VOSNE-ROMANÉE)****

Wines Produced: Chambolle-Musigny, Clos Vougeot, Echézeaux.

This is a tiny estate, but the wines are consistently excellent, displaying
fragrant, intense bouquets, and rich, concentrated flavors. Proprietor
Alfred Haegelen has excelled in vintages such as 1985 and 1988, and
succeeded admirably in years such as 1986 and 1987. A long *cuvaison*,
low yields, and old vines are the ingredients for success. This is a highly
recommended source for top-notch red burgundy.

CHÂTEAU PHILIPPE LE HARDI (SANTENAY)**

Wines Produced: Mercurey.

This producer has 185.25 acres of vineyards in Mercurey, and makes
nearly 450,000 bottles of wine a year. The quality is acceptable, but
uninspirational. Perhaps lower yields would result in a more concentrated and interesting wine. This wine should be drunk within the first
4–5 years of life.

DOMAINE DES HAUTES-CORNIÈRES (SANTENAY)**

Wines Produced: Aloxe-Corton, Bourgogne Rouge, Chassagne-Mon-
trachet Blanc, Chassagne-Montrachet Rouge,
Côte de Beaune-Villages, Santenay Les Commes,
Santenay Les Gravières, Santenay Rouge.

This relatively large estate of 44.46 acres is run by Roger Chapelle. For years the wines here lacked substance and seemed extremely light and a bit diluted. More recently the Chapelle family has given more attention to detail and has extended the maceration time for their Pinot Noir. The results are correct, straightforward wines that are not disappointing, but not memorable enough to merit the purchase of a second bottle. The best wine is the Santenay Les Gravières, followed by the Santenay Les Commes. I have never tasted a bottle of his Chassagne-Montrachet Blanc.

DOMAINE HERESZTYN (GEVREY-CHAMBERTIN)***

Wines Produced: Bourgogne Rouge, Clos St.-Denis, Gevrey-Chambertin, Gevrey-Chambertin Les Champonnets, Gevrey-Chambertin Les Corbeaux, Gevrey-Chambertin Les Goulots, Gevrey-Chambertin La Perrière.

This is an interesting domaine with some important holdings in Gevrey-Chambertin as well as a well-situated parcel of the Grand Cru Clos St.-Denis. The property is run by two brothers, Stanislas and Bernard Heresztyn, and their sister Régine. They own 22.6 acres. While their wines are extremely impressive in cask, they seem to come out of the bottle much lighter and overly polished and processed, suggesting that the fining and filtration is done too heavy handedly. This is sad, because the raw materials and the care in the élevage of the wine is, otherwise, quite impeccable.

The vineyards average between 20 and 50 years old. They generally destem about 50%, and believe in a warm, hot fermentation to extract plenty of color. Maceration usually lasts about three weeks. The wines spend 14 to 18 months in Limousin oak barrels from the Vosges. The family is committed to high quality so I suspect they may cut back or even completely eliminate filtration. Domaine Heresztyn made very good 1987s and 1988s. In my opinion, their two best wines are their Gevrey-Chambertin Les Champonnets and Gevrey-Chambertin Les Corbeaux, both of which seem better than their Grand Cru Clos St.-Denis.

DOMAINE ANDRÉ L'HERITIER (CHAGNY)**

Wines Produced: Bourgogne Aligoté-Bouzeron, Bourgogne Blanc-Clos de la Carbonnade, Bourgogne Rouge-Clos de la Carbonnade, Rully-Clos Roche Blanc, Rully-Clos Roche Rouge.

This tiny 10.18-acre domaine produces wines that are decent and correct, but unexciting. The red wines spend 16–24 months in cask and the whites 6–12 months. No new oak is used. One hundred percent of the wines are estate-bottled. The best is the Rully-Clos Roche Rouge, as it tends to have more depth and concentration than the other cuvées. L'Heritier generally produces fresh, fruity wines that require drinking within 2–4 years of the vintage.

DOMAINE L'HERITIER-GUYOT (DIJON)**

Wines Produced: Clos Blanc de Vougeot, Clos Vougeot, Vougeot Premier Cru Les Cras.

This domaine of 27.6 acres is owned by the Maison l'Heritier-Guyot, a domaine that was founded in Dijon in 1945 and is probably better known for its cassis liqueur. A rather standard quality Clos Vougeot and Vougeot Premier Cru Les Cras is produced. However, this estate controls the only white wine made at Clos Vougeot. The domaine produces approximately 9000 bottles of the white wine from a blend of 90% Chardonnay and 10% Pinot Blanc. The wines come from several of the best-situated parcels (5.2 acres) in the entire Clos Vougeot. On the north the vines, originally planted by the Cistercians, touch the famous Grand Cru vineyard of Les Amoureuses in Chambolle-Musigny and abut the Grand Cru Musigny. The Clos Blanc de Vougeot is one of those rare white wines with tremendous power and richness, and excellent aging potential. It should be (given its price), and usually is, the finest white wine made in the Côte de Nuits. The 1983, 1985, 1986, and 1988 are the most recent top vintages.

DOMAINE HOSPICES DE BEAUNE (BEAUNE)****–*****

On August 4, 1443, Nicholas Rolin (one of the chancellors of Philip the Good), passed away and decreed that all of his worldly possessions be sold and the money used to build a hospital to provide care for the poor. What became known as the Hôtel Dieu was completed in 1451 and provided care and housing for the area's sick, elderly, and impoverished. Over the centuries, the Hôtel Dieu and its surrounding buildings, now collectively called the Hospices de Beaune, have been the beneficiaries of a number of landowners who donated their vineyards to the Hospices. The profits earned from the sale of these wines serve to finance the Hospices' operation. There have been a great number of benefactors and the Hospices de Beaune now owns a total of 143 acres. All of the land is in the Côte de Beaune, with the exception of a tiny parcel, donated in 1977, of 3.7 acres of Mazis-Chambertin in the Côte de Nuits. The wine from all of these plots is sold at a charity auction on the third Sunday of November. The entire weekend has become one giant festival in celebration of Burgundy, and, in particular, of the Hospices de Beaune. The sale has become the leading barometer of both the trade's perception of the newest vintage, and the prices that those burgundies will demand.

The Hospices wines have been impeccably made since 1977, when Monsieur André Porcheret was hired to look after the fermentation and bringing up of the wines in preparation for their sale. In addition to rigorous pruning of the vineyards to keep the production levels modest, the amount of fertilizer and pesticides was strictly controlled. The Hospices also began to use 100% new oak and prolong its maceration period to three weeks or more so as to extract as much flavor and intensity from the wines as possible. At present, about 25%–32% of the stems are added in, depending on the quality of the vintage and the degree of rot in the grapes.

Porcheret left in 1987 to look after the wines of the Domaine Leroy and was replaced by Monsieur Bruley. It's not expected that the style of the Hospices wines will change, but there is no doubt that the quality of the Hospices wines is controlled by the individual in charge of the vinification and *élevage*. Monsieur Bruley is widely considered to be less talented than Porcheret. Before 1977 many of the Hospices de Beaune wines were poorly made, and were often a bad reflection of their vineyards. The wines are sold in barrel several months after the vintage, and then transferred to the buyer's cellar (usually some of Burgundy's major *négociants*). This has complicated the quest for quality, as some *négociants* are much more careful with their wines than others. Yet, few people have had reason to complain about the quality of the wines since 1977, and much of the criticism leveled at the Hospices wines, particularly in Anthony Hanson's 1982 book called *Burgundy*, can no longer be justified. However, I do have to question the use of 100% new oak in lightweight vintages such as 1984, as this can often obliterate and mask the character of the vineyard.

The Hospices de Beaune has made exceptional wines in most of the 1980s vintages, and was very careful in 1983 to destem 100% to avoid the taste of rot. Consequently, many of their wines turned out to be extremely successful in that frequently catastrophic vintage. While it's difficult to see all the wines after they've been sold at the Hospices, there is no question that the highest prices paid for the red wines are generally for the Cuvée Charlotte Dumay, the Cuvée Docteur Peste from Corton, the Beaune Nicholas Rolin and the Pommard Dames de la Charité. Over recent years, the top price asked for a red wine has been from the only parcel the Hospices owns on the Côte de Nuits, the Mazis-Chambertin Madeleine Collignon. With respect to the white wines, the Corton-Charlemagne Françoise de Salins has consistently brought the highest price.

Following is a list of the different cuvées and the total acreage for each of the vineyards.

Red Wines

Cuvée Madeleine Collignon: 3.7 acres in Mazis-Chambertin

Cuvée Boillot: 1.85 acres in Auxey-Duresses Les Duresses

Cuvée Lebelin: 2.16 acres in Monthélie Les Duresses

Cuvée Gauvain: 4.6 acres primarily in Volnay Santenots, with a small parcel of Volnay Les Pitures

Cuvée Jehan de Massol: 3.7 acres in Volnay Santenots

Cuvée General Muteau: 4.27 acres in Volnay le Village, plus tiny parcels of Volnay Les Caillerets, Volnay Fremiets, Volnay Taillepieds

Cuvée Blondeau: 4.21 acres, with a sizeable portion of Volnay Champans and Volnay Taillepieds

Cuvée Billardet: 4.6 acres, with parcels in Pommard Les Epenots, Pommard Les Noizons, Pommard Les Arvelets, and Pommard Les Rugiens

Cuvée Dames de la Charité: 3.95 acres, with parcels in Pommard Les Epenots, Pommard Les Rugiens, Pommard Les Noizons, Pommard La Refène, and Pommard Les Combes Dessus

Cuvée Dames Hospitalières: 6.1 acres, with parcels in Beaune Les Bressandes, Beaune La Mignotte, Beaune Les Teurons, and Beaune Les Grèves

Cuvée Rousseau-Deslandes: 5.9 acres, with parcels in Beaune Les Cent Vignes, Beaune Les Montrevenots, Beaune La Mignotte, and Beaune Les Avaux

Cuvée Hugues et Louis Bétault: 5.1 acres, with parcels in Beaune Les Grèves, Beaune La Mignotte, Beaune Les Aigrots, Beaune Les Sizies, and Beaune Les Vignes Franches

Cuvée Maurice Drouhin: 6.07 acres, with parcels in Beaune Les Avaux, Beaune Les Boucherottes, Beaune Les Champs Pimont, and Beaune Les Grèves

Cuvée Brunet: 5.86 acres, with parcels in Beaune Teurons, Beaune Les Bressandes, Beaune La Mignotte, and Beaune Les Cents Vignes

Cuvée Clos des Avaux: 4.94 acres in Beaune Les Avaux

Cuvée Guigone de Salins: 5.4 acres, with parcels in Beaune Les Bressandes, Beaune en Senrey, and Beaune Les Champs Pimonts

Cuvée Nicolas Rolin: 5.4 acres, with parcels in Beaune Les Cents Vignes, Beaune Les Grèves, and Beaune en Genêt

Cuvée Arthur Girard: 4.4 acres, with parcels in Savigny-Lès-Peuillets and Savigny-Lès-Marconnets

Cuvée Fouquerand: 5.2 acres, with parcels in Savigny Basses Vergelesses, Savigny Lès Talmettes, Savigny aux Gravains, and Savigny aux Serpentières

Cuvée Fourneret: 4.1 acres, with parcels in Savigny Lès Vergelesses and Savigny aux Gravains

Cuvée Rameau-Lamarosse: 1.63 acres in Pernand-Vergelesses Les Basses Vergelesses

Cuvée Docteur Peste: 7.41 acres, with parcels in Corton Les Bressandes, Corton Chaumes et

Voirosses, Corton Clos du Roi,
Corton Fiètre, and Corton Les Grèves
Cuvée Charlotte Dumay: 8.65 acres, with parcels in Corton Les
Rénardes, Corton Les Bressandes,
and Corton Clos du Roi

White Wines

Cuvée Françoise de Salins: .61 of an acre in Corton-Charlemagne
Cuvée Baudot: 3.48 acres in Meursault Les Genevrières
Cuvée Philippe le Bon: 1.48 acres in Meursault Les Genevrières
Cuvée de Bahèzre de Lanlay: 2.2 acres in Meursault Les Charmes
Cuvée Albert-Grivault: 1.23 acres in Meursault Les Charmes
Cuvée Jehan Humblot: 1.72 acres in Meursault Le Poruzot and
Meursault Les Grands Charrons
Cuvée Loppin: 1.48 acres in Meursault Les Criots
Cuvée Goureau: 2.12 acres, with parcels in Meursault Le
Poruzot, Meursault Les Pitures, and
Meursault Les Cras
Cuvée Paul Chanson: .61 of an acre in Corton-Vergennes

As the acreage figures indicate, the minuscule quantities of available Hospices wines, combined with their celebrated status, and, since 1978, their high quality, have guaranteed intense buying for them in top vintages such as 1985, 1988, and 1989. Since 1969, the Hospices de Beaune has provided its own labels to insure the authenticity of their wines. It is more important that the consumer buy only those wines whose labels reflect that the wine has been "raised" by a conscientious *négociant*. Nevertheless, the overall quality of the Hospices de Beaune wines today is quite exemplary, and certainly promotes a positive image of Burgundy.

DOMAINE HOSPICES DE NUITS
(NUITS ST.-GEORGES) ****

Wines Produced: Nuits St.-Georges Les Boudots, Nuits St.-Georges Bourgogne Rouge, Nuits St.-Georges Les Corvées-Pagets, Nuits St.-Georges Les Didiers, Nuits St.-Georges Les Murgers, Nuits St.-Georges Les Porrets, Nuits St.-Georges Rue de Chaux, Nuits St.-Georges Les Saint-Georges, Nuits St.-Georges Les Vignes Rondes.

The Hospices de Nuits is the sister charity to the Hospices de Beaune, although it receives far less publicity. Its wine sale, which benefits the local hospital, is held the Sunday before Palm Sunday and dates from 1692. As with the Hospices de Beaune, all of the wines are made from vineyards that have been donated for charity. At present, their acreage totals 23.3 acres and is almost entirely in top Premier Cru vineyards. The three largest Premier Cru holdings are a 6.05-acre parcel of Nuits St.-Georges Les Didiers, a 2.47-acre parcel of Nuits St.-Georges Les Vignes Rondes, and a 2.34-acre parcel of Nuits St.-Georges Les Saint-Georges. All of the cuvées are aged in 100% new oak and are sold at the auction, after which the buyer has the option of continuing to age the wine in new oak or transferring it to 1- or 2-year-old oak barrels. The cuvées include the Cuvée Georges Faiveley, Cuvée Cabet, Cuvée Jacques Duret, and Cuvée des Sires de Vergy, all of which come from the Premier Cru vineyard of Les Saint-Georges. There is also the Cuvée Camille Rodier from the Premier Cru Rue de Chaux, the Cuvée Mesny de Boisseaux from the Premier Cru Les Boudots, the Cuvée Antide Midan from the Premier Cru Les Porrets, and the Cuvée Guyard de Changey from the Premier Cru Les Murgers. Additionally, there are other cuvées from lesser-known parcels including the Cuvée Claude Poyen, Cuvée Guillaume Labye, Cuvée Soeurs Hospitaliers, Cuvée Grands Grangier, and Cuvée Mignotte. As with the wines from the Hospices de Beaune, all the wines of the Hospices de Nuits get impeccable care and are quite well made. One might debate whether certain vintages, such as 1984 or 1986, need 100% new oak, but there is no doubting that these wines are generally as good examples of Nuits St.-Georges as one is likely to find. Some of the more active buyers include the house of Faiveley, who frequently buys the Cuvée Georges Faiveley as well as the Cuvée Les Didiers, the Burgundy *négociant* Remoissenet, and a handful of other *négociants*. Most of the wines from the Hospices de Nuits are capable of lasting 5–10 years.

DOMAINE ALAIN HUDELOT-NOËLLAT
(VOUGEOT)***–****

> Wines Produced: Chambolle-Musigny,   Chambolle-Musigny Les
> Charmes, Clos Vougeot, Nuits St.-Georges Les
> Murgers,   Richebourg,   Romanée   St.-Vivant,
> Vosne-Romanée Les Malconsorts, Vosne-Roma-
> née Les Suchots.

A sizeable domaine by Burgundy's Côte de Nuits standards, this estate of 29.6 acres produces extremely seductive, creamy wines that have a vivid, well-focused, rich fruitiness, and good body. They normally should be drunk within their first 7–10 years of life. The proprietor, Alain Hudelot, has an impeccable winemaking technique, destalking at least two-thirds of the crop, vinifying the wine in large stainless-steel vats at a moderate temperature, and macerating the skins and the grape juice for at least three weeks or longer if possible. There's plenty of new oak used, with the Grands Crus such as Clos Vougeot, Richebourg, and Romanée St.-Vivant receiving 100% new oak aging for 16–18 months, and the top Premiers Crus, 40%–50%. The wines are frequently over-filtered, which seems a particular tragedy here given the stunning quality in the top vintages. Hudelot has many private clients in Europe and Great Britain, and little of his wine seems to appear at the wine merchant level. But, these are clearly wines worth the effort to search out. The top wines from this domaine are usually the Richebourg and the Clos Vougeot. The tiny parcel of Clos Vougeot is actually two morsels, one at the very bottom of the slope next to the Route N 74 and the other morsel at the very top of the Clos Vougeot. Hudelot has had quite a run of good vintages recently, with superb wines in 1985 and 1988.

DOMAINE BERNARD HUDELOT-VERDEL
(VILLARS-FONTAINE)***

> Wines Produced: Bourgogne Aligoté, Bourgogne Hautes-Côtes de
> Nuits Blanc, Bourgogne Hautes-Côtes de Nuits
> Rouge, Bourgogne Passe-Tout-Grains.

This is one of the better estates of the Hautes-Côtes de Nuits. It produces very stylish, richly fruity, well-made wines that drink well young, but can age for 6–7 years. Bernard Hudelot, one of the pioneers in planting vineyards in the Hautes-Côtes de Nuits, produces an excellent Bourgogne Hautes-Côtes de Nuits Rouge that is aged in 33%–50% new oak casks for 14 to 24 months. Little or no filtration takes place here as

Hudelot does not want to remove any flavor or character. The tiny quantity of Bourgogne Aligoté, one of the best in the Hautes-Côtes de Nuits, are to be recommended, as is the stylish, spicy, sometimes a bit too oaky Bourgogne Hautes-Côtes de Nuits Blanc.

DOMAINE HUGUENOT PÈRE ET FILS (MARSANNAY)**

> Wines Produced: Bourgogne Aligoté, Charmes-Chambertin, Côte de Nuits-Village, Fixin, Gevrey-Chambertin, Marsannay Rosé, Marsannay Rouge.

This is a large family business of 41.61 acres. Over half of the domaine (23.46 acres) is in Marsannay Rouge, and the rest is primarily in Fixin (7.65 acres), and in appellations such as Marsannay Rosé and Bourgogne Aligoté. Huguenot does have a tiny .74-acre parcel of Charmes-Chambertin, and 3.45 acres of Village Gevrey-Chambertin. The wines tend to be straightforward and representative, but rarely excellent.

DOMAINE FREDERICK HUMBERT (GEVREY-CHAMBERTIN)**

> Wines Produced: Bourgogne Rouge, Charmes-Chambertin, Gevrey-Chambertin, Gevrey-Chambertin Champonnet, Gevrey-Chambertin Crapillot, Gevrey-Chambertin Estournelles St.-Jacques, Gevrey-Chambertin-Lavaux-St.-Jacques, Gevrey-Chambertin Poissenot.

Most of the production of Frederick Humbert is sold directly to buyers who pass through the village of Gevrey-Chambertin. The 12.94-acre domaine is highly fragmented, but Humbert does produce a number of Premiers Crus, of which the best are his Estournelles St.-Jacques and Lavaux-St.-Jacques. A tiny quantity of Charmes-Chambertin is also made. Twenty percent new oak barrels are used, and the wine generally is aged 18 months prior to bottling. Most of the wines of Humbert should be drunk within the first 5–6 years of their lives. Humbert sells nearly half his crop to *négociants*.

JABOULET-VERCHERRE (BEAUNE)**–***

> Domaine Wines Produced: Beaune-Clos de L'Écu, Corton Les Bressandes, Pommard-Clos de la Commaraine, Volnay Caillerets.

Note: This large firm produces nearly 750,000 cases of wine under its *négociant* label.

This old-line firm, established in the Rhône Valley in 1824, spread its operation to Burgundy with the opening of its cellars in Beaune in 1920. I agree with Europe's most famous and prolific wine writer, Dutchman Hubrecht Duijker, that because of their Rhône origins, this firm's wines tend to be impressively colored, alcoholic, and full, but often lack the character of their appellations. Jaboulet-Vercherre has over 30 acres of vines. The firm's best wines, their well-known Pommard-Clos de la Commaraine and Beaune-Clos de L'Écu, offer relatively rich, intense flavors, full body, and plenty of heady alcohol. They are not classic examples of their appellations, but are interesting and satisfying wines. As for the *négociant* wines, I have noted some dramatic improvements in the most recent vintages, especially with the lower-level generic wines. In several tastings, their Bourgogne Rouge and Bourgogne Blanc actually came out ahead of many wines from some of the best growers and *négociants*. Perhaps this is a sign they have decided to upgrade the quality of their wines. The Jaboulet-Vercherre wines are widely marketed. They are also seen under the name Louis Lesanglier.

DOMAINE LUCIEN JACOB (ÉCHEVRONNE) ***

Wines Produced: Aloxe-Corton, Bourgogne Hautes-Côtes de Beaune, Pernand-Vergelesses, Savigny-Lès-Beaune, Savigny-Vergelesses Premier Cru Blanc, Savigny-Vergelesses Premier Cru Rouge.

Lucien Jacob is well known in Burgundy as one of the people most concerned about the quality of the clones of Pinot Noir planted in the vineyards. In his own 49.4-acre vineyard he has planted a number of experimental clones and is very active in the INAO. His vineyard produces stylish, well-made, elegant wines that show a lot of fruit and intelligent winemaking. His red wines are bottled after 12–18 months of aging in small casks, and his whites after 8–10 months. His biggest vineyard is his 25-acre vineyard in Bourgogne Hautes-Côtes de Beaune and, not surprisingly, it is one of the best examples of a rather modern-style but delicious, supple, round, fruity wine. In addition, it is fairly priced. Jacob also produces some of the best crème de cassis in all of Burgundy, although it is not easy to find in the export markets.

CHÂTEAU DES JACQUES
(ROMANÈCHE-THORINS) ***–****

> Wines Produced: Beaujolais Blanc-Grand Clos de Loyse, Moulin-à-Vent Grand Carquelin, Moulin-à-Vent Grand Clos de Rochegrés.

This splendid estate of just over 100 acres in Moulin-à-Vent has, on occasion, made remarkable Beaujolais. I remember drinking vast quantities of the 1969 and 1971 Château des Jacques Moulin-à-Vent "Grand Carquelin" (from one of the domaine's most promising vineyards) while in law school. They also have 25 acres that produce a crisp, stylish, fruity Beaujolais Blanc called Grand Clos de Loyse. These wines age well and improve for 7–8 years rather than 2–3 as most Beaujolais seem to do. The quality declined in the late seventies and early eighties, but now Château des Jacques is making a comeback under the current proprietor, Jean-Paul Thorin of the Maison Thorin (also a *négociant*). Old-timers in Beaujolais reminisce ecstatically over the 1964, 1962, 1957, and 1947 Château des Jacques Moulin-à-Vents, so there is something to be said for this extraordinary domaine. The wines are aged in oak casks (10%–20% of which are new) for a year after they are fermented in temperature-controlled stainless-steel tanks. The maceration period of 10–14 days is surprisingly long for Beaujolais, and the grapes are harvested as late as possible in order to obtain *sur maturité* (or wanted intensity) in the wines. The wines of Château des Jacques are capable of lasting for at least 6–10 years in the bottle.

PAUL ET HENRI JACQUESON (RULLY) ***

> Wines Produced: Bourgogne Aligoté, Bourgogne Passe-Tout-Grains, Mercurey, Mercurey Les Naugues Premier Cru, Rully, Rully Les Cloux Premier Cru Rouge, Rully Les Chaponnières Premier Cru Rouge, Rully-Grésigny Premier Cru Blanc.

Many enthusiasts of the wines of Rully strongly argue that the best domaine is that of the father and son team of Henri and Paul Jacqueson. Their domaine is only 16.5 acres, and while they export 60% of their wines, they have great admirers in restaurants such as the famous Taillevent, Lameloise, Leon de Lyon, and La Tour d'Argent, as well as the fashionable Paris wine bar called Willi's. The secret here is a very traditional approach to winemaking. There is no destemming, an extremely long 3½-week *cuvaison*, plenty of pumping over, and aging of the red wines in 30% new oak and the white wines in 5%–10%. The red wines seem to burst with rich, berry-like fruit, have great finesse, and provide all the pleasure one could ask from a modestly priced wine. The handful of white wines the estate makes are not quite as exciting, but are still competent. They lack the supple, explosive fruitiness of the reds. Jacqueson's wines drink so well young that few people have the patience to wait for them. However, a 1978 Rully Premier Cru Rouge drunk in 1987 was still going strong and could easily have been mistaken for a good Premier Cru from Beaune. This is a very serious estate that made superb 1985s, delicious, elegant 1987s, and very rich and well-balanced 1988s.

LOUIS JADOT (BEAUNE)****–*****

Domaine Wines Produced: Beaune Les Avaux, Beaune Les Boucherottes, Beaune-Clos des Ursules, Beaune Teurons, Bonnes-Mares, Chambertin-Clos de Bèze, Chambolle-Musigny Les Amoureuses, Chapelle-Chambertin, Chevalier-Montrachet Les Demoiselles, Clos Vougeot, Corton-Charlemagne, Corton-Pougets, Gevrey-Chambertin-Clos St.-Jacques, Gevrey-Chambertin Estournelles St.-Jacques, Puligny-Montrachet Les Folatières, Savigny-Lès-Beaune Les Dominaudes.

Note: This house also produces a wide range of wines under its *négociant* label from purchased grapes and purchased juice.

The firm of Louis Jadot, a *négociant* as well as vineyard owner, is turning out some of the finest wines in Burgundy. In addition, Jadot recently made two acquisitions that can only improve the quality of the wines. In 1985, the firm bought the impressive Clair-Dau vineyards (42 acres) and in December 1989 they purchased the cellars and vineyards (15.6 acres) of the Maison Champy. The house of Louis Jadot was founded in 1858 and the entire domaine presently consists of 114.4 acres. Owning top vineyards does not in itself guarantee high-quality wine, but Louis Jadot is run with painstaking care by André Gagey, one of the great gentlemen and conscientious protectors of Burgundy.

The red wines of Jadot are made traditionally, and are generally full-bodied wines, rich in color and tannin, with plenty of depth and length.

Their quality is due to an extremely high fermentation temperature of 35°–36° C, 100% destemming, and an extremely long 21- to 28-day *cuvaison*. Additionally, in vintages such as 1986 André Gagey makes sure that all of the cuvées are *saignée*, (a technique in which excess juice in overly prolific years is drained off of the cuvées to increase the percentage of skin to juice). All the red wines are aged in 33% new oak casks for up to two years. The wines are bottled with as light a filtration as possible, as André Gagey understands the dangers of an overly vigorous filtering process. The top wines include a fabulous Gevrey-Chambertin-Clos St.-Jacques (this firm is now the largest producer of Gevrey-Chambertin-Clos St.-Jacques), Bonnes Mares, Chambertin-Clos de Bèze, Ruchottes-Chambertin, Chapelle-Chambertin, Clos Vougeot, Nuits St.-Georges-Clos des Corvées, Gevrey-Chambertin Estournelles St.-Jacques, Corton-Pougets, Chambolle-Musigny Les Amoureuses, Beaune-Clos des Ursules, Beaune-Clos des Couchereaux, and, of course, any of the cuvées that this firm buys from the Hospices de Beaune. They are consistent purchasers of the Cuvée Nicolas Rolin and the Cuvée Hospitalières. There have been outstanding successes at this firm over the years—great 1978s, delicious 1980s, some of the best 1982s in the entire Côte d'Or, rot- and trouble-free 1983s, superb 1985s, generally good 1986s, brilliant 1987s, and superb 1988s. Most of the red wines from Louis Jadot need 3–4 years in the bottle to round out, but can age for up to 15–20 years, depending on the particular cuvée.

The white wines are no less brilliant than the reds. This is a superb *négociant*, making powerful, rich, concentrated white wines that are probably the best of any *négociant* in Burgundy. Of course, the most famous wines of Jadot are the Montrachet, their exquisite Corton-Charlemagne (4.94 acres), an outstanding Chevalier-Montrachet Les Demoiselles (2.47 acres) and the sublime Puligny-Montrachet Les Folatières (.74 acre). André Gagey also produces quite beautiful Meursault Genevrières and Puligny-Montrachet Les Combettes. The wines from the Domaine Duc de Magenta are now made and marketed by the Maison Louis Jadot under the joint names of both Magenta and Jadot. This means there is usually an excellent Puligny-Montrachet Clos de la Garenne. The white wines from Jadot are loaded with the flavors of hazelnuts and buttery popcorn, and age extremely well. Gagey, an amazingly flexible winemaker, carefully regulates the malolactic fermentation in a year when the acidity is too low, blocking it before it is completely finished, as he did in 1983. The results were perhaps the best white burgundies of that vintage, and were followed by superb white burgundies in 1985 and 1986.

This is an extraordinary house where quality is the highest priority.

This is particularly good news since the firm is owned by its American importer, Kobrand Corporation of New York City.

JAFFELIN (BEAUNE)***

> Wines Produced: An entire line of wines are produced as *négociants*, but the following are the principal products of Jaffelin. A range of Beaujolais, Beaune Les Champimonts, Bourgogne Blanc, Chambolle-Musigny, Charmes-Chambertin, Chassagne-Montrachet Les Caillerets, Gevrey-Chambertin, Puligny-Montrachet Les Folatières, Rully, Vosne-Romanée. The only estate wines are Beaune Les Avaux, Beaune Les Bressandes, and Clos Vougeot.

This firm was purchased by Robert Drouhin in 1969, and the wines are made under his watchful eye. The wines that result are perhaps a bit less complex and profound than those from the firm of Joseph Drouhin, but they are well made, clean, commercial wines that reflect their appellations and show good fruit and immediate accessibility. They are not meant for long-term aging and should be drunk within the first 5–6 years of life. The Domaine Jaffelin's parcel of Clos Vougeot is well located midway up the northern side of the slope. They also have 5 acres of Premier Cru Beaune Les Bressandes and 1.23 acres of Beaune Les Avaux.

DOMAINE JACKY JANODET
(ROMANÈCHE-THORINS)****

> Wines Produced: Beaujolais Blanc, Beaujolais-Villages, Morgon, Moulin-à-Vent.

I have had some sensational bottles of incredibly rich, crunchy, concentrated, lush and velvety Moulin-à-Vent from Jacky Janodet's vineyard. He owns 17.21 acres, which have a high percentage of very old vines. I am not sure how well the wines age, but certainly if they are drunk within the first 5–6 years of life, these are splendid Beaujolais of the highest quality. The red wines are aged in large *foudres* and cement tanks for 6–12 months prior to bottling.

DOMAINE PATRICK JAVILLIER (MEURSAULT)**

> Wines Produced: Bourgogne Blanc, Meursault-Clos du Cromin, Meursault Les Tillets.

Javillier has 11.1 acres of vines from which he produces only white wines. They are good examples of the modern school of tank fermentation, minimal aging in oak barrels, and early bottling. They are crisp, clean, and very pleasant, but often lack depth and flavor dimension. Nevertheless, there is a market for such wines, and many consumers prefer this lighter, fresher style to those with more body and depth.

DOMAINE GEORGES JAYER (VOSNE-ROMANÉE)***-****

> Wines Produced: Echézeaux, Nuits St.-Georges.

The above rating is based on the opinion of others as I have never tasted the wines produced by Georges Jayer. Georges is Henri Jayer's brother, and until 1988 Henri tended the vineyard and produced the wines. Since then, Henri's nephew, Emmanuel Rouget, has assumed control. However, the minuscule quantities of wine produced (approximately 25 cases of Nuits St.-Georges and 125 cases of Echézeaux) will still bear Georges Jayer's label and will be sold exclusively in England by Bibendum Wines Ltd. The winemaking approach here is similar to Henri Jayer's, but there are significant differences. Like Henri, Georges believes in a cool prefermentation maceration of 4–5 days, but he then ages the wine in 1-year-old oak casks, rather than new oak, for 12–15 months. The wines are bottled unfiltered.

DOMAINE HENRI JAYER (VOSNE-ROMANÉE)*****

> Wines Produced: Bourgogne Rouge, Echézeaux, Nuits St.-Georges, Nuits St.-Georges Les Murgers, Richebourg, Vosne-Romanée, Vosne-Romanée Les Beaux Monts, Vosne-Romanée Les Brûlées, Vosne-Romanée Cros Parentoux.

The motto of Henri Jayer is "quality before everything else." As a result, there are several certainties regarding his wines: They are brilliantly made, they are expensive, and they are difficult to find. Jayer is a winemaker's winemaker. Everything in his cellar is spotless, and tasting there is always a great treat. Jayer, who looks a good 15 years younger than his 67 years of age (in 1990), has begun his retirement, and is now turning over the winemaking to his nephew, Emmanuel Rouget. Jayer continues to oversee things at his estate, while also consulting on the making of the wines for the Domaine Méo-Camuzet. He claims, "I only make wines in a style I like," and for many knowledgeable connoisseurs of Burgundy, that means wines without equal. His basic winemaking technique, increasingly emulated throughout the Côte de Nuits, is to destem and do a 5- to 7-day prefermentation *maceration à la froid*. The grapes are crushed and the wines macerated in the skins for as long as a month. The wine is then put in 100% new Allier and troncais oak, racked three times, kept 17–18 months in barrel, fined with egg whites, and bottled by hand with no filtration. Modern oenologists would no doubt be horrified by much of the winemaking process and the great risks that Jayer takes in making his wines, but I have never tasted a volatile or oxidized bottle of wine from Jayer. In fact, I have rarely tasted anything less than a superb bottle, as these wines are all quite profound, deeply colored, packed with fruit, and have the ability to last and improve for 8–12 years. There have been some extraordinary successes here, including 1978, 1980, 1985, 1986, and 1987. I hope that the magic of Henri Jayer will translate into even greater wines from the Domaine Méo-Camuzet.

DOMAINE JACQUELINE JAYER (VOSNE-ROMANÉE)***

> Wines Produced: Bourgogne Rouge, Echézeaux, Nuits St.-Georges, Vosne-Romanée, Vosne-Romanée Les Reignots, Vosne-Romanée Les Rouges.

Jacqueline Jayer produces two excellent wines from her tiny estate of 8.64 acres with the winemaking skills and consulting help of Jean and Étienne Grivot. The wines include the wonderful Vosne-Romanée Les Rouges, a small vineyard lying above the Premier Cru vineyard Les Beaux Monts, and, of course, the Grand Cru Echézeaux (only 1.53 acres). Jayer's other wines are solid and reliable, but uninspiring. Since the Domaine Jean Grivot is responsible for making Jayer's wine, the winemaking styles are identical. There is a prefermentation maceration and the use of at least one-third to one-half new oak barrels for up to 18 months. The wines are filtered as lightly as possible, or preferably not at all. In vintages such as 1985 and 1987, most of the wines of Jacqueline Jayer drink beautifully young, but also give every indication of being capable of lasting 6–8 years.

DOMAINE ROBERT JAYER-GILLES
(MAGNY LES VILLERS)****–*****

> Wines Produced: Bourgogne Aligoté, Côte de Nuits-Villages, Eché-
> zeaux, Hautes-Côtes de Beaune, Hautes-Côtes de
> Nuits, Hautes-Côtes de Nuits Blanc, Nuits St.-
> Georges Les Damodes.

From his 23.4 acres of vineyards and impeccable cellar in the hills behind Nuits St.-Georges, Robert Jayer, a cousin of Henri Jayer, produces impressive, expensive wines that are aged in 100% new Allier oak barrels. Jayer does not practice fining, and he does only a very light Kisselguhr filtration prior to bottling. Jayer, a tall man with a flamboyant black mustache, is a highly talented winemaker, and, to my way of thinking, makes probably the best wines from the Hautes-Côtes de Nuits appellation. He also produces a white Hautes-Côtes de Beaune from 100% Pinot Blanc. It is aged in 50% new oak and is a crisp, steely wine with a good deal of character. His red wines all have marvelous plummy and berry fruit, are well marked by vanilla and smoke from toasty new oak barrels, and promise 5–7 years of aging potential. His top two wines are the celestial Nuits St.-Georges Les Damodes (usually of Grand Cru quality), of which he usually produces less than 100 cases, and his extraordinary Echézeaux. The Echézeaux is from a 1.23-acre parcel of vines averaging 35 years in age. It can be sensational in years like 1985 and 1988, but has also been one of the best Grands Crus made in Burgundy in years such as 1986 and 1987. It is a wine that can last a good 15–20 years. These are frequently brilliant wines, and Jayer prices them accordingly. Jayer also recently completed what is certainly the most spectacular underground cellar in Burgundy's Côte d'Or. He justifies this extravagance by saying, "I have never taken a vacation."

DOMAINE JEANNIN-NALTET PÈRE ET FILS
(MERCUREY)***

> Wines Produced: Mercurey Blanc, Mercurey-Clos des Grands Voy-
> ens, Mercurey Rouge.

Thierry Jeannin-Naltet is president of the local syndicate of the wine growers of Mercurey and sets a good example with his wines. He has only 17.04 acres of vines. Over half of his estate (9.6 acres) is his excellent Mercurey-Clos des Grands Voyens, one of the best vineyards of the appellation. The wine here tends to be robust, with an earthy, mineral character and plenty of berry fruit. His formula of using 10%–20% new oak and bottling after 18 months seems to work best with his red wine. It has a great deal more character and complexity than his rather straightforward, neutral Mercurey Blanc. The top wine, the Clos des Grand Voyens, drinks well young but is capable of aging for 7–10 years in vintages such as 1988, 1985, and 1983.

DOMAINE JESSIAUME PÈRE ET FILS (SANTENAY)**

Wines Produced: Beaune Les Cent Vignes, Bourgogne Aligoté, Santenay, Santenay Les Gravières, Santenay Les Gravières Blanc, Volnay Les Brouillards.

Bernard Jessiaume produces wines of inconsistent quality from his 24.1 acres of vineyards. His most important holding is his 12.36 acres of Santenay Les Gravières. I have had good examples of the Santenay, the 1985 being the most recent, but too often the wine seems musty, with a pronounced smell of wet dog. He also makes tiny quantities of a rather hard, stony, not always clean Santenay Les Gravières Blanc, and a sharp, acidic Bourgogne Aligoté. There seems to be potential here, but some improvements need to be made.

The red wines see 10% new oak and are bottled after 18 months. The white wines see 50% new oak and are bottled after 12 months.

DOMAINE FRANÇOIS JOBARD (MEURSAULT)****

Wines Produced: Blagny-La Pièce Sous le Bois, Bourgogne Blanc, Meursault, Meursault-Blagny, Meursault Les Charmes, Meursault Les Genevrières, Meursault Le Poruzot.

François Jobard quietly and meticulously produces textbook, stylish Meursaults loaded with both flavor and finesse. This is a domaine of 11.1 acres with impeccably high standards. In Jobard's cold cellars, he utilizes between 10%–33% new oak and bottles his wines after 18–24 months of aging in cask. The wine sees a lot of lees contact and very little filtration. In 1987 he decided, largely because of the prodding of his American importer, Kermit Lynch, to abandon filtration. His 1987s were, coincidentally, superb. Jobard's wines in many respects are among the most elegant and stylish wines of Meursault, and often seem more like a Puligny-Montrachet than a fatter, nuttier Meursault. The wines age extremely well for up to 7–8 years. A tiny bit of red wine from Blagny is also produced, but I have never seen a bottle outside the cellars of Monsieur Jobard.

DOMAINE GEORGES JOBERT (MÂCON)***

> Wines Produced: Saint-Véran.

Georges Jobert's Saint-Véran is one of those wonderfully fruity, concentrated, delicious, and reasonably priced Chardonnays that frequently gets overlooked. Jobert has proven to be a very consistent winemaker is years of high yields, as well as in years when excessive sunshine and the potential for too much alcohol can prove to be a wine's undoing. His Saint-Véran should be consumed within 2–3 years of the vintage.

DOMAINE JOBLOT (GIVRY)****

> Wines Produced: Givry-Clos du Bois Chevaux, Givry-Clos du Cellier aux Moines, Givry-Clos de la Servoisine.

Jean-Marc Joblot, a young, intense man, is quickly emerging as one of the stars of the appellation of Givry. He is keen to taste the wines of all the top producers in Burgundy. Over the last few years he has moved toward utilizing a cooler and longer maceration period in order to extract as much fruit as possible. Ten percent of the stems are included in his fermentation, and in big, concentrated vintages such as 1985 and 1988 he has begun to employ 100% new Allier oak. In lighter years, such as 1986 and 1987, he utilizes 75% new oak. No filtration is done here for fear of removing any extract or flavor. The wines of Joblot are imbued with a wonderful rich, raspberry, cassis fruitiness and show a judicious use of new oak and toasty, vanillin aromas. While they drink well young, they also show every sign of being able to last for 6–8 years. Prices are remarkably fair for wines of this quality. The entire domaine of Joblot consists of 17.29 acres. His finest wine has always been the Givry-Clos du Celliers aux Moines, but in 1988 he introduced a splendid Givry-Clos de la Servoisine.

DOMAINE JEAN-LUC JOILLOT-PORCHERAY
(POMMARD)**

> Wines Produced: Beaune, Bourgogne Aligoté, Bourgogne-Hautes Côtes de Beaune, Bourgogne Rouge, Pommard, Pommard Les Epenots.

Although this domaine's label looks surprisingly like that of the Domaine Parent, the wines could not be more different. The wines of

Joillot-Porcheray are more delicate and very aromatic. If Domaine Parent's wines sometimes err in favor of an excess of body and alcohol, the Joillot-Porcheray wines tend to be a bit too light, tasting as if too many grapes were taken from the vineyard (15.98 acres). Fifty percent of the production is sold to *négociants*, and the rest is bottled after 18–24 months in cask. No new oak is employed. Jean-Luc Joillot's best vineyard is his .8-acre parcel of Pommard Les Epenots.

DOMAINE PHILIPPE JOLIET (FIXIN)****

Wines Produced: Fixin-Clos de la Perrière.

Philippe Joliet produces only one wine from his 12.79-acre parcel: the Premier Cru, Fixin-Clos de la Perrière. The wine spends 18–24 months in oak casks, of which 50%–65% are new. The wine from this *monopole* vineyard can be extremely good in a rich, full-bodied, meaty style, and tends to age very well. It will usually last at least 10–12 years in a top vintage.

DOMAINE JEAN JOLIOT ET FILS (NANTOUX)***

Wines Produced: Beaune Les Boucherottes Premier Cru, Bourgogne Aligoté, Bourgogne Hautes-Côtes de Beaune Rouge, Bourgogne Passe-Tout-Grains, Meursault, Pommard.

I have had some interesting wines from this small 24.5-acre domaine. Run by the Joliot family, this estate is adamant about not filtering its wines and about making sure each of its wines reflects the *terroir* of its vineyard. They make a delicious, rich, chewy, yet elegant Beaune Les Boucherottes, and a surprisingly flavorful Bourgogne Aligoté. However, the domaine's success rests on its strawberry and cherry-scented, supple, velvety Bourgogne Hautes-Côtes de Beaune Rouge. The red wines are aged in 25% new oak and are bottled after 18–24 months. The white wines see 20% new oak and are bottled after 12–18 months. There is no doubting that the new oak gives their Bourgogne Aligoté more character than most. This is a domaine whose prices seem remarkably modest given the quality of the wines that emerge from their cellars.

DOMAINE PIERRE JOMARD
(FLEURIEUX-SUR-L'ARBRESLE)**

Wines Produced: Beaujolais, Côteaux du Lyonnais.

Agreeable, straightforward Beaujolais are made at this 25.9-acre domaine. The Côteaux du Lyonnais is an especially good bargain.

DOMAINE MICHEL JUILLOT (MERCUREY) ***–****

> Wines Produced: Bourgogne Blanc, Bourgogne Rouge, Corton-Charlemagne, Corton Les Perrières, Mercurey, Mercurey Les Champs, Mercurey-Clos des Barraults, Mercurey-Clos Tonnerre.

Many observers rate Michel Juillot's supple and explosively fruity red Mercurey (especially his Mercurey-Clos des Barraults, Mercurey Les Champs, and his occasionally produced Mercurey Vieilles Vignes) among the top two or three wines made in that appellation. He uses one-third new oak, practices a fairly lengthy fermentation, and rarely filters his wine, thereby preserving all of its flavor and character. He made superb 1985s and 1988s, and has recently added a small parcel of Corton Les Perrières, which has the potential to be his top red wine. He also produces small quantities of a superb Corton-Charlemagne, fresh Bourgogne Blanc, and lean Mercurey Blanc from 5 acres of Chardonnay. The rest of the estate consists of 62 acres of Pinot Noir.

CHÂTEAU DE JULIÉNAS (JULIÉNAS) ***

> Wines Produced: Juliénas.

Proprietor François Condemine produces excellent wines from this significant 123.5-acre estate. He ages his big, rich, full-bodied Juliénas in oak *foudres* for eight months before bottling. However, the wines often take 1–2 years after bottling to shed their dumbness and reveal their immense depth and structure. If there is one Juliénas to hold for 5–6 years in a top Beaujolais vintage, it is the Château de Juliénas.

LABOURÉ-ROI (NUITS ST.-GEORGES) ***

Note: This *négociant* produces a broad range of wines. The following are some of the selections generally offered in each vintage.

This reliable *négociant* located in Nuits St.-Georges is run by the Cottin brothers. A third brother is the director of the late Baron Philippe de Rothschild's properties in Pauillac. This *négociant* produces 250,000 cases and its major markets are the United Kingdom, France, and the United States. In America Labouré-Roi does not have a national importer, but sells directly to each individual state. They think of themselves as a white wine house, specializing in good generic Chablis and white burgundy. The overall quality of the wine is quite acceptable but rarely thrilling. Labouré-Roi has increasingly sought exclusivities in order to control the production and marketing of certain domaines, the most prominent being the Domaine Chantal Lescure.

This *négociant*'s white wines all showed clean, correct winemaking, decent amounts of fruit, and good balance. Those that consistently stand out include an attractive Pouilly-Fuissé, a good, generic Bourgogne Blanc from the Domaine Manuel, and of course their top-of-the-line whites, the Meursault-Clos de Bouches Chères, a rich, full-bodied, spicy, toasty, buttery wine, and their Puligny-Montrachet-Clos de Vieux Château from the Domaine Maroslavac. The latter wine usually has excellent depth, richness, and plenty of spicy oak. I found their 1987 Corton-Charlemagne disappointing. The Bâtard-Montrachet, while not a great wine, is frequently well made, richly fruity and spicy with a nice touch of oak.

With respect to the red wines, there are some bargains at the lower end of the quality hierarchy. The Côte de Nuits-Villages Belle Marguerite is an excellent and inexpensive wine. It is a relatively full-bodied, spicy, muscular wine with a good deal of fruit and character. I also enjoyed the fine Gevrey-Chambertin-Domaine Jacqueson, which could easily have been a Premier Cru given its depth, richness, robust fruitiness, and interesting, complex bouquet.

Their top 1987 red wines include their Nuits St.-Georges Les Damodes-Domaine Chantal Lescure. This wine displayed a big, earthy, spicy, smoky bouquet, medium- to full-bodied flavors, and adequate acidity and tannin. It can be drunk young or aged until 1996–1997. The Echézeaux was more tannic and oaky. While good, it did not have the depth of the Nuits St.-Georges Les Damodes. Their Clos Vougeot seemed richer and more concentrated than the Echézeaux, but was also quite backward, spicy, and tannic. While this *négociant*'s wines do not match the quality of the neighboring house of Faiveley, or of Louis Jadot and Joseph Drouhin in Beaune, Labouré-Roi is a reliable house that makes a good range of wines.

CHÂTEAU DES LABOURONS (FLEURIE)**

> Wines Produced: Fleurie.

The Château des Labourons produces fruity, charming, supple, round, and easy-to-drink wines from their large 61.75-acre estate in Fleurie.

Half of the crop is sold to *négociants*, but the best is kept for the estate to bottle. The wines are aged for 4–6 months in oak *foudres* prior to bottling. This is a sound Fleurie, but somewhat overpriced given the low demand for wines from this Beaujolais village.

DOMAINE ANDRÉ ET BERNARD LABRY (MÉLIN)**

Wines Produced: Auxey-Duresses, Bourgogne Aligoté, Bourgogne Hautes-Côtes de Beaune Blanc, Bourgogne Hautes-Côtes de Beaune Rouge, Bourgogne Passe-Tout-Grains, Meursault, Monthélie.

The wines from this 25.1-acre estate tend to be straightforward and technically correct, but generally uninteresting; they should be drunk within the first 3–4 years of life. The domaine's largest acreage (11.1 acres) is in Auxey-Duresses. The Labry family uses twelve to fifteen percent new oak and the remainder of the reds are aged in 2- to 4-year-old casks.

CHÂTEAU DE LACARELLE (SAINT-ÉTIENNE-DES-OULLIÈRES)**

Wines Produced: Beaujolais-Villages.

This estate, the largest producer of Beaujolais-Villages, has been in the same family for over 200 years. The current proprietor, Comte Louis Durieu de Lacarelle, overlooks 334.45 acres of vineyards, and produces wine that is well made, fruity, round, and aromatic. His wine is a favorite of the famous Belle Époque restaurant Le Train Bleu in Paris' Gare de Lyon.

DOMAINE HENRI LAFARGE (BRAY)**

Wines Produced: Bourgogne Rouge, Mâcon-Blanc, Mâcon-Bray Rouge.

This small grower's wines are seen in certain European markets as he has a good reputation for his Mâcon-Blanc and Bourgogne Rouge. The Bourgogne Rouge is aged for 6–12 months in cask, of which 33% is new. Domaine Henri Lafarge is a reliable source of correct Mâconnais wines, with his best wine probably being the Bourgogne Rouge.

DOMAINE MICHEL LAFARGE (VOLNAY)***

> Wines Produced: Beaune Les Grèves, Bourgogne Aligoté, Bourgogne Rouge, Meursault, Volnay, Volnay Clos des Chênes, Volnay-Clos du Château des Ducs, Volnay Premier Cru.

Michel Lafarge, a modest and intelligent man, makes it a point to taste not only his neighbors' wines, but also as many of the wines of the world as possible. He can in certain vintages (1981, 1987, and 1988) produce some of the most stylish, finesse-filled wines of the entire village of Volnay. While I love his wines when they are very good, Lafarge can be a distressingly inconsistent winemaker. His uninspiring 1983s and 1986s are a case in point. He believes in using between one-third and one-half new oak barrels, and bottling his wines after 16–18 months of cask aging. He makes a little bit of white wine from the appellation of Meursault and Bourgogne Aligoté, but his top wines are his gorgeous Volnay Clos des Chênes, Beaune Les Grèves, and his newest vineyard, Volnay-Clos du Château des Ducs. These are wines that are often bursting with cherry fruit, and despite being seductively appealing young, have the ability to age well. At present, the estate consists of 19.76 acres, with the most important holdings being a 2.47-acre parcel of Volnay Clos des Chênes and a 1.23-acre parcel of Beaune Les Grèves. The largest total holding is Lafarge's 5.8-acre parcel of Volnay Villages.

DOMAINE COMTE LAFON (MEURSAULT)*****

> Wines Produced: Meursault Les Charmes, Meursault-Clos de la Barre, Meursault Les Genevrières, Meursault Les Désirées, Meursault Les Gouttes d'Or, Meursault Les Perrières, Monthélie, Montrachet, Volnay Champans, Volnay Clos des Chênes, Volnay Santenots.

Some of the finest, most elegant, and ageworthy white burgundies emerge from the very cold, damp cellars of the Comte Lafon. This 32.1-acre estate, with its handsome château-like building and cellars in the village of Meursault, is considered the standard-bearer of Meursault wines. The Lafon family now consists of René Lafon, the father, and his two sons, Dominique and Bruno. The splendid wines made at this meticulously run domaine are exceptional and unique in almost every way. The Lafons never rack or filter their white wines, preferring to let the wine sit undisturbed on its lees for almost two years until bottling. This procedure would horrify today's safety-conscious oenologists. However, the Lafons are blessed with what many feel is the most frigid cellar in Burgundy, so there is little evaporation, and the problems of bacterial spoilage are nonexistent. The Lafons' belief in no filtering (although the wine is given a slight egg-white fining) and in minimum yields (less than 40 hectoliters per hectare) helps to create these splendidly concentrated, rich, intense wines capable of lasting 15–20 years. The Lafons, though, are not perfect, and their decision to pick their grapes as late as possible has resulted in some prominent failures. Most recently, in 1983, their Chardonnay grapes developed extraordinary amounts of botrytis and rot, and the resulting wines seemed grotesquely alcoholic and unbalanced. Yet, when the weather cooperates, the Lafons often make the most spectacular white burgundies of all, as anyone who has tasted their 1978, 1979, 1982, 1985, 1986, and 1988 would attest.

With respect to the individual wines, everyone clamors to buy their Montrachet, which often needs a decade to open up, and their extraordinary Meursault Les Perrières. Their Montrachet is less opulent, flashy, and flamboyant than that of the Domaine Ramonet, but it ages magnificently. They make 1200 bottles of Montrachet a year from their tiny parcel. The wine I find to be their best is the other-worldly Meursault Les Perrières; it tastes as rich and ageworthy as most producers' Montrachets. Do not overlook the fabulous Meursault Les Charmes, produced from 65-year-old vines, or the exceptional Meursault-Clos de la Barre from their home *monopole* vineyard. The Lafons prefer Vosges oak barrels (20%–40% are new) for their white wines, and Allier oak barrels for their red wines from Volnay and Monthélie. The traditional practice of no destemming is followed for the red wines. The wines, of course, are not filtered, and are aged for almost two years in the casks.

The Lafon family has also played a major part in the colorful history of Burgundy. The Count Lafon, one of the most flamboyant personalities of all Burgundy, created the famous Paulée de Meursault in the mid-1920s as a festive way to conclude the Trois Glorieuses in Burgundy. This luncheon, held the Monday after the Hospices de Beaune sale, is attended by all of the growers and producers of Meursault and their favorite or most influential clients. The tradition of bringing the best bottles of wine gets more competitive each year. It is a luncheon and party not to be missed by anyone who enjoys a lot of eating and drinking. All things considered, this domaine produces quite extraordinary white wines, and amazingly good red wines that often are ignored in all the excitement over their white wines.

DOMAINE LAFOUGE (AUXEY-DURESSES)***

> Wines Produced: Auxey-Duresses Rouge, Auxey-Duresses Blanc, Auxey-Duresses La Chapelle.

The first several vintages I tasted from the Domaine Lafouge, 1986, 1987, and 1988, showed impressive winemaking for both Chardonnay and Pinot Noir. The firm is using between one-third and one-half new oak for both the red and white wines. There seems to be meticulous attention to detail throughout the winemaking process: they use only the ripest, healthiest grapes, practice a careful vinification, and watch the wine evolve in barrel. This could be an excellent estate from which to seek out values in Auxey-Duresses.

DOMAINE LAHAYE PÈRE ET FILS (POMMARD)**

> Wines Produced: Bourgogne Aligoté, Bourgogne Passe-Tout-Grains, Bourgogne Rouge, Côte de Beaune, Meursault Les Grands Charrons, Pommard, Pommard Les Arvelets, Pommard Premier Cru, Pommard Les Trois Follots, Pommard Les Vignots.

This domaine has a spotty performance record, although their white wine, the Meursault Les Grands Charrons, and their top wine, the Pommard Les Arvelets, are often excellent. The estate includes 22.4 acres of vineyards, and nearly 100% of the production is estate-bottled. The winemaking practice is to destem, use 10% new oak, and bottle the wine after 22–24 months in cask and a filtration. Perhaps a smaller yield from the vineyards and a shorter time in cask would result in wines that are a bit more charming and seductive. Most wines of the Domaine Lahaye should be drunk within the first 5–6 years of life.

DOMAINE LALEURE-PIOT
(PERNAND-VERGELESSES)***–****

> Wines Produced: Bourgogne Aligoté, Chorey-Lès-Beaune, Corton Les Bressandes, Corton-Charlemagne, Corton Rognet, Côte de Nuits-Villages, Pernand-Vergelesses Île des Vergelesses, Pernand-Vergelesses Premier Cru Rouge, Pernand-Vergelessess Les Vergelesses, Savigny-Lès-Beaune, Savigny-Lès-Beaune Les Vergelesses.

For years, this 20.62-acre domaine was known more for its white wines than its reds. Yet, after tasting of the recent vintages of Laleure-Piot, it would be hard to deny the quality of their earthy, rich, spicy red wines. They are not as precocious or as charming in their youth as some of the other Pernand-Vergelesses wines, but after 2–3 years of aging they seem capable of shedding their youthful cloaks of tannin and revealing plenty of spicy, berry fruit. The white wines remain extremely well made, particularly the Corton-Charlemagne and Pernand-Vergelesses Premier Cru Blanc. For those consumers searching for value, this is one of the few estates in Burgundy that does a very good job with Bourgogne Aligoté, producing a wine that is not too acidic. At present, the red wines see one-third new oak casks, in which they remain for 18 months prior to bottling. The white wines receive the same amount of new oak but are bottled after 12 months. The current proprietor is Jean-Marie Laleure.

DOMAINE LAMARCHE (VOSNE-ROMANÉE)***

Wines Produced: Clos Vougeot, Echézeaux, Grands Echézeaux, Vosne-Romanée, Vosne-Romanée La Grande Rue, Vosne-Romanée Les Malconsorts, Vosne-Romanée Les Suchots.

In the fifties and early sixties, the Domaine Lamarche had one of the best reputations in Burgundy. Sadly, the quality of its wines declined throughout the seventies and early eighties. The current proprietor, François Lamarche, took control after his father, Henri, passed away. Although the domaine consists of only 20 acres, it has many superb parcels in the Côte de Nuits, including its *monopole* vineyard, the gorgeously situated La Grande Rue (surrounded by vineyards such as La Tâche, La Romanée, Romanée-Conti). Le Grande Rue may well become Burgundy's next Grand Cru. The Lamarche style of winemaking has always been one that emphasized perfumed, lighter-styled red burgundies. The wines were never terribly deep in color, but demanded attention because of their sheer seductive power. When they became watery and thin, the reputation of the estate declined significantly. François Lamarche hopes to rebuild the prestige of this important Vosne-Romanée domaine. Lamariche uses 40% new oak and the wines spend 16 months in wood, after which they receive a polishing filtration and are then bottled. His recent successes have included the 1987s and 1988s, both better vintages than the 1985. The top wine should be La Grande Rue, given the splendid situation of this vineyard. However, as good at it usually is, I think it could be better. The Echézeaux and Vosne-Romanée Les Malconsorts are quite fine, and the Clos Vougeot and Grands Echézeaux are clearly the larger-framed and more tannic wines. Much of La Grande Rue vineyard was replanted, the most recent parcel in 1982. Perhaps the lightness of this wine over recent vintages has more to do with the youthfulness of the vineyard than winemaking techniques. This is one domaine that still merits a visit if you can get an appointment. The labyrinth of wine cellars is a treat to visit, and the tiny tasting room resembles a minuscule chapel hidden in the depths of Lamarche's underground wine cellars.

DOMAINE DE LA CAVE LAMARTINE (SAINT-AMOUR-BELLEVUE)***

Wines Produced: Juliénas, Saint-Amour-Clos du Chapitre, Saint-Amour-Clos de la Cure Blanc, Saint-Amour-Clos Vers-l'Église.

Charming, aromatic, intensely fruity wines are made by this 33.3-acre estate run by Paul Spay. The wines are very popular in the restaurants of Lyon and in Beaujolais' best restaurant, the Auberge de Cep in Fleurie. Fifty percent of the production is now exported.

LAMBLIN ET FILS (MALIGNY)**

Wines Produced: Chablis Blanchot, Chablis Mont de Milieu, Chablis Valmur, Petit-Chablis.

Note: In addition to its wide range of Chablis wines, this firm produces a line of generic *négociant* wines made from juice.

While the firm of Lamblin et Fils has 25.95 acres of Premiers Crus and Grand Crus, they are best known for their *négociant* line of wines (which includes several generic table wines that are sold in bulk) and a variety of wines sold under their *sous marques* or other labels, such as Paul Favey, Jacques Arnoul, Bernard Mille, Charles Montserat, Jacques de la Ferté, Paul Jarry, and Paul Ferrand. While the family can trace its origins in Chablis back to 1712, the quality of the current wines leaves much to be desired. The wines are often the products of high technology. Stripped by too much centrifuging at the beginning of life, put through a cold stabilization and several filtrations, including a sterile one, they seem to be lacking not only individuality and character, but flavor and satisfaction as well.

DOMAINE HUBERT LAMY (SAINT-AUBIN)***

> Wines Produced: Bourgogne Aligoté, Bourgogne Rouge, Chassagne-Montrachet Rouge, Criots-Bâtard-Montrachet, Puligny-Montrachet, Saint-Aubin Les Castets, Saint-Aubin Les Frionnes Blanc, Saint-Aubin Rouge.

This is a very serious domaine of 29.14 acres in Saint-Aubin. I have never tasted their only Grand Cru, the Criots-Bâtard-Montrachet (they own only .1 of an acre), but their Saint-Aubin Les Frionnes Blanc is a stylish, floral-scented, and toasty wine. It happens to be one of my three or four favorite white wines of the appellation. Like the other white wines, it is aged in one-third new oak and bottled after 8–12 months of cask aging. The best red wine from the Domaine Hubert Lamy is the Saint-Aubin Les Castets (4 acres). It shows delicious cherry and strawberry fruit married nicely with toasty oak from aging in 33% new oak casks. Bottling takes place after 14–16 months. The wines of Hubert Lamy should be drunk within the first 4–6 years of life.

DOMAINE LAMY-PILLOT (SANTENAY)**

> Wines Produced: Bâtard-Montrachet, Blagny-La Pièce Sous le Bois, Bourgogne, Bourgogne Aligoté, Chassagne-Montrachet, Chasssagne-Montrachet Boudriotte, Chassagne-Montrachet-Clos St.-Jean, Chassagne-Montrachet Morgeot, Côte de Beaune-Villages, Meursault, Santenay, Santenay Les Charrons, Saint-Aubin, Saint-Aubin Les Argillières, Saint-Aubin Les Castets, Saint-Aubin Les Pucelles.

This Côte de Beaune estate has a large following for both its red and white wines in France and other European countries. The domaine, which now consists of 42 acres, is run by René Lamy and does an effective job of promoting its wines. I have often found the vintages of Lamy-Pillot's red wines to have an unclear fecal aroma. As for the white wines, they tend to be made with a heavy hand, and lack finesse and elegance. I cannot muster much enthusiasm for the current wines from the Domaine Lamy-Pillot.

DOMAINE EDMUND LANEYRIE (SOLUTRÉ-FUISSÉ)***

Wines Produced: Pouilly-Fuissé.

This microproducer turns out wonderfully rich, full-bodied Pouilly-Fuissé. While not quite in the same league as the Château Fuissé or Madame Ferret, it is still a delicious wine and an excellent example of the appellation.

DOMAINE HUBERT LAPIERRE
(LA CHAPELLE DE GUICHAY)***

Wines Produced: Chénas, Moulin-à-Vent.

Lapierre makes big, spicy, powerful wines from his vineyards in Chénas and Moulin-à-Vent. He owns 18.1 acres, and while he sells nearly half his production to *négociants*, his estate-bottled wines are well worth trying to find.

DOMAINE LAROCHE (CHABLIS)***

Wines Produced: Chablis, Chablis Beauroy, Chablis Blanchot, Chablis Bougros, Chablis Les Clos, Chablis Fourchaume, Chablis Montée de Tonnerre, Chablis Montmains, Chablis Les Vaillons, Chablis Vau-de-Vey, Petit-Chablis.

Note: This firm also produces an entire line of Chablis under its *négociant* label, Bacheroy-Josselin.

Today's Domaine Laroche is run with enthusiasm and great business savior faire by Michel Laroche. It is one of the most successful companies in Chablis with estate holdings of 210.66 acres and a highly profitable *négociant* business under the name of Bacheroy-Josselin. It is a very active, aggressive company whose wines can be found in most of the markets in the world: Hong Kong, Tokyo, Amsterdam, Montreal, Hamburg, London, and the United States. Laroche's winemaking technique seems to synthesize the high-tech, modern style and the traditional small cask-aged oak style preferred by purists. All of the Grands Crus and some of the Premiers Crus see 2–4 months of aging in new oak casks, but are fermented in stainless steel and then put back in vats prior to bottling. Every aspect of the fermentation is temperature controlled and carried out under pristine sanitary conditions. For the lesser Premiers Crus, as well as their Petit-Chablis and Chablis, the wines are fermented in stainless steel and bottled early to preserve freshness and cleanliness. The results are wines that are far from being blockbusters, but are stylish, elegant, and usually very satisfying. They may not be as profound or complex as some wines from the small growers, but they exhibit plenty of fruit, represent their respective vineyards, and are not unreasonably priced. The wines under the Bacheroy-Josselin label, and the other *négociant* label called Château de Puligny-Montrachet (primarily used for white wines from the Côte d'Or), have less complexity and character than the estate wines under the Domaine Laroche label.

My favorite wines have consistently been their Chablis Blanchot (11.28 acres), which seems to be even better than their excellent Chablis Les Clos (2.76 acres). Among the Premiers Crus, their Chablis Fourchaume and Chablis Les Vaillons seem to have more character than their Chablis Vau-de-Vey. The Domaine Laroche also has a multitude of second labels, including names such as Henri Josset, Alain Combard, Paul Dupressoir, Ferdinand Bacherey, Jacques Millar, Roland Foucard, and Jean Baulat. This is clearly a domaine that stresses marketing, as evidenced by its sales figures. Eighty percent of its sales are to the export markets, with the rest being sold in France. They claim to sell wine to 200 restaurants that have earned from one to three stars in the Guide Michelin.

DOMAINE LARUE (SAINT-AUBIN)**

> Wines Produced: Bourgogne Aligoté, Bourgogne Rouge, Chassagne-Montrachet Rouge, Puligny-Montrachet, Puligny-Montrachet Les Garennes, Saint-Aubin Premier Cru, Saint-Aubin Rouge.

Almost 70% of this estate's production is sold to *négociants*. The remaining wines from the 25.93-acre estate include a lightish, straightforward Saint-Aubin Blanc, an adequate Puligny-Montrachet Les Garennes, and a somewhat spicy, peppery Saint-Aubin Rouge. The Larue family believes in using 20% new oak casks for both the red and white wines, with bottling for the reds taking place after 18 months, and for the whites after 8 months. Perhaps lower yields and less filtration at bottling would produce wines with a bit more fruit and charm.

DOMAINE ROGER LASSARAT (VERGISSON)***

> Wines Produced: Pouilly-Fuissé, Saint-Véran.

Roger Lassarat tends to make a ripe, rich, honeyed style of Pouilly-Fuissé from his vineyard (Clos de France). Little of the wine is produced, but it is good to excellent in quality, and quite consistent from vintage to vintage. Recent vintages seem to suggest that he is using more new oak. For the difference in price, I actually prefer Lassarat's Saint-Véran made from extremely old vines planted in a 5.6-acre parcel. It is usually one-half to one-third the price of his Pouilly-Fuissé, and seems, at least to this taster, to be every bit as good.

DOMAINE JEAN LATHUILIÈRE (CERCIÉ)****

Wines Produced: Brouilly-Pisse-Vieille, Côte de Brouilly, Morgon.

Jean Lathuilière wins more prizes for his Brouilly-Pisse-Vieille than any other vigneron of the appellation. His wines are stunningly fruity, and capable of lasting 3–4 years after the vintage. All of his wines are matured in large oak *foudres* for six months prior to bottling. He makes a tiny quantity of equally splendid Morgon, but all of it is sold directly to private clients.

DOMAINE HENRI LATOUR (AUXEY-DURESSES)**–***

Wines Produced: Auxey-Duresses, Auxey-Duresses Premier Cru, Bourgogne Hautes-Côtes de Beaune Rouge, Crémant de Bourgogne, St.-Romain Blanc.

Henri Latour produces very modern-style wines that show pleasing fruit, good clean winemaking, and about 10%–20% new oak from his 22.2-acre domaine. The biggest percentage of the production here is the Bourgogne Hautes-Côtes de Beaune Rouge, which is a straightforward, reasonably priced red wine. The two best wines from this house are the Auxey-Duresses Premier Cru and the St.-Romain Blanc.

LOUIS LATOUR (BEAUNE)***–*****

Domaine Wines Produced: Aloxe-Corton, Beaune Les Vignes-Franches, Chambertin, Chevalier-Montrachet Les Demoiselles, Corton-Charlemagne, Corton-Clos de la Vigne au Saint, Corton-Grancey, Givry, Pernand-Vergelesses Île des Vergelesses, Pommard Les Epenots, Romanée St.-Vivant.

Note: This large *négociant* firm also produces an entire range of wines from the Côte d'Or where they purchase juice and grapes.

Louis Latour, a handsome man at least 6'4", cuts an imposing figure in Beaune. This famous firm has an excellent reputation as a *négociant*, but is also an important vineyard owner (123.5 acres). The approach to winemaking here is extremely traditional, with all of the red wines destemmed 100%, fermented in wood *cuves*, and put in oak casks for 16–18 months. The percentage of new oak used is at least 33%, with the Grands Crus getting 100%. There is no fining and very little filtration, but much has been made of Louis Latour's pasteurization process. At the beginning of the century, the firm began to pasteurize its red wines for seven seconds at 70° C (158° F). While one might wonder if this is necessary, Louis Latour would suggest that the wines have to be manipulated less following this instantaneous exposure to high heat. In any event, the controversy continues to rage on, but in reality, the entire issue is equal to a tempest in a teapot. The overfining and filtration in evidence at other cellars is in many respects much more dangerous to the ultimate quality of the wine than this flash pasteurization. Latour's best red wines are the outstanding Corton-Grancey and the Corton-Clos de la Vigne au Saint. However, the Romanée St.-Vivant is also top notch, as is the firm's Pommard Les Epenots and Beaune Les Vignes-Franches. Many of the other red wine cuvées seem to taste a bit too much alike, but those I have recommended are excellent. In recent vintages such as 1985, 1987, and 1988 they would certainly stand out against all but the very elite of red burgundy. The red wines from Latour also last extremely well: The top Premiers and Grands Crus will age for 10–15 years.

However, even Louis Latour would admit that it is his white wines which have brought this firm most of its fame and good fortune. Latour claims to control 10% of the white wine production of the Côte d'Or. His firm must be the largest producer of Corton-Charlemagne, as they produce an average of 6,000 cases a year of truly remarkable Corton-Charlemagne from their 22.23-acre parcel. This is a wine that does indeed live up to its Grand Cru status, and older bottles such as the 1959 and 1962, drunk in 1987 and 1988 respectively, were absolutely staggering white burgundies. More recent vintages have included a stunning 1979, great 1983, and superb 1986 Corton-Charlemagne. The firm's Chevalier-Montrachet Les Demoiselles from their 1.23-acre parcel is also a wonderful wine, and usually one of the top dozen or so great white burgundies in any vintage. The firm makes Le Montrachet from juice purchased from the Comte Beaucaron, a small grower who owns nearly 2.47 acres of Le Montrachet vineyard. This domaine is also an excellent source for Mâcon-Lugny. Louis Latour produces nearly 50% of the crop from this famous village in the Mâconnais area. The Montagny from the Côte Chalonnaise is another intelligent wine made by Latour.

However, Louis Latour is not content with the limited amount of white wine he makes in Burgundy. He also has a 741-acre vineyard dedicated to Chardonnay in the hot, arid Ardeche section of France. He produces 45,000–55,000 cases of relatively inexpensive Chardonnay from this land. The wine will never be confused with his good Mâcon-Lugny, but it does represent a straightforward Chardonnay made in a modern, stainless-steel style. As for his serious white wines, they are all fermented and aged in oak casks for 12–14 months, and given very minimal clarification. They can be exhilarating wines, particularly the Corton-Charlemagne and Chevalier-Montrachet. The Corton-Charlemagne is capable of lasting for up to 20 years.

The firm of Louis Latour has its critics, but when chosen well, the best red wines are competitive in quality with Burgundy's finest, and the white wines here are as good as one is likely to find.

CHÂTEAU DE LATOUR-BOURDON (RÉGNIÉ-DURETTE)***

Wines Produced: Beaujolais Régnié, Beaujolais-Villages.

Michel and Jean-Paul Rampon run this newly established estate (1981). All their wines are matured in concrete vats for 4–6 months and then bottled. The wines tend to be round, richly fruity, and surprisingly alcoholic, often reaching 13.5% alcohol. These are delicious, rather heady, perfumed Beaujolais to be drunk within 2–3 years of the vintage.

DOMAINE LATOUR-GIRAUD (MEURSAULT)***

Wines Produced: Bourgogne Blanc, Côte de Beaune-Villages, Meursault, Meursault Les Caillerets Rouge, Meursault Les Charmes, Meursault Les Genevrières, Meursault Les Perrières, Pommard La Refène, Puligny-Montrachet Champ Canet, Volnay Clos des Chênes.

I have consistently enjoyed both the red and white wines of the Domaine Latour-Giraud. The domaine, a modestly sized estate of 20.15 acres, is run by Pierre and Jean-Pierre Latour. In 1982, they decided to stop selling their production to *négociants*. Their top white wines include the three Premier Cru vineyards of Meursault Les Charmes (.54 acre), Perrières (.37 acre), and Genevrières (5.9 acres), and their Puligny-Montrachet Champ Canet (.84 acre). The wines reveal intelligent winemaking and a judicious use of oak barrels. The style is somewhere between the rich, buttery, nutty style of a proprietor like Albert Grivault, and the stainless-steel fermented, crisp, lean style of a proprietor such as Patrick Javillier. The red wines are light, and while they are not at the same level of quality as the whites, there is a good Volnay Clos des Chênes and an interesting Meursault Les Caillerets Rouge. For value, the Côte de Beaune-Villages Rouge should be sought out. Most of the wines of the Domaine Latour-Giraud should be drunk within their first 5–7 years of life.

DOMAINE ROLAND LAVANTUREUX (LIGNORELLES)***

> Wines Produced: Chablis, Petit-Chablis.

While Roland Lavantureux owns no Premiers Crus or Grands Crus, he produces a competent, satisfying wine from his 27 acres. His domaine is primarily in Villages Chablis and Petit-Chablis. The Petit-Chablis is the better value as there is little difference in taste between the two wines, but a large difference in price. Lavantureux's wines should be drunk within the 4–5 years of the vintage.

DOMAINE PHILIPPE LECLERC
(GEVREY-CHAMBERTIN)*****

> Wines Produced: Bourgogne Rouge, Gevrey-Chambertin Les Caze-
> tiers, Gevrey-Chambertin Combe aux Moine, Gev-
> rey-Chambertin Les Platières.

While Philippe Leclerc's visual appearance could well qualify him as a senior member of the notorious Hell's Angels motorcycle gang, there's no doubting that inside his wild, crazy exterior there lurks a great winemaker. There is a fearful intensity to Leclerc that is translated to his wines. While his brother, René, also makes excellent wines, Philippe's are usually more intense and concentrated. He has only 12 acres of vineyards and believes in using 100% new oak barrels (50% Allier and 50% Limozin). He macerates his wine with the grape skins for at least one month, after allowing the fermentation temperature to reach an exceptionally high 33°–35° C. His wine spends over two years in the new oak barrels in his tiny, immaculate cellar, and is then bottled without any fining or filtration. His winemaking skills have become increasingly evident with each new vintage. Leclerc started making wine in 1979, and has proven that he can deal successfully with over-production (1982 and 1986), underripeness (1980 and 1984), superb, healthy grapes (1985, 1987, and 1988), and rot (1983 and 1986). His wines perform so well out of barrel and when young that I have often wondered how well they would age. A recent tasting of his first vintage, 1979, proved they are true thoroughbreds, and actually gain in complexity and breadth of flavor with cellaring. This is one of the top small growers in Gevrey-Chambertin, and his wines are worth the special effort it takes to find and drink them. Normally, one could expect the best vintages of Cazetiers and Combe aux Moine to last 10–12 years.

DOMAINE RENÉ LECLERC (GEVREY-CHAMBERTIN)****

Wines Produced: Bourgogne Rouge, Gevrey-Chambertin, Gevrey-Chambertin Clos Prieur, Gevrey-Chambertin Combe aux Moine, Gevrey-Chambertin Lavaux St.-Jacques.

René Leclerc is one of the well-known Leclerc brothers in Gevrey-Chambertin (the other being the wild Philippe Leclerc), and he usually produces good wines. Like his brother, he believes in aging his wines for 30 months in oak casks, and never filters the wine prior to bottling. Unlike his brother (who uses 100% new oak), René uses only one-fourth to one-third new oak casks. René's entire estate consists of 19.76 acres, most of which is in Gevrey-Chambertin. A 1.25-acre parcel consistently produces his top wine, the Premier Cru Gevrey-Chambertin Combe aux Moine. It can often be a blockbuster wine, with extraordinary deep color and a marvelous richness of fruit. His 1978, 1980, 1983, and 1985 were all wonderful wines. Most wines from this domaine can be drunk at a young age, but have a wonderful ability to last for 10 years.

DOMAINE LEFLAIVE (PULIGNY-MONTRACHET)*****

Wines Produced: Bâtard-Montrachet, Bienvenues-Bâtard-Montrachet, Blagny Rouge, Bourgogne Blanc, Chevalier-Montrachet, Puligny-Montrachet, Puligny-Montrachet Les Chalumeaux, Puligny-Montrachet Clavaillon, Puligny-Montrachet Les Combettes, Puligny-Montrachet Les Folatières, Puligny-Montrachet Les Pucelles.

What should a wine enthusiast in search of a classic white burgundy sample? From my perspective, the best introduction would be a tasting of the wines from the 52-acre Domaine Leflaive. This rich estate, with its air-conditioned, impeccably clean wine cellars, has as much respect internationally as any domaine producing red or white wine in Burgundy. The wines are remarkably consistent and simply never disappoint. They are often exhilarating in their gorgeous display of power and elegance. A visit to the cellars with the aristocratic Vincent Leflaive will quickly reveal that he is maniacal about cleanliness. There are water hoses everywhere to eliminate potential bacteria and off odors. All the white wines are fermented at 16°–18° C, and spend 16–18 months in stainless-steel tanks and small oak barrels (25%–33% new) before bottling. Leflaive uses Allier wood, although he has a few barrels from the Vosges.

Leflaive's best wines are, as one might expect, the Chevalier-Montrachet and Bâtard-Montrachet. He has 5-acre parcels of each of these Grands Crus. The Bâtard can be drunk at a younger age than the Chevalier, as the Chevalier often requires 6–7 years to unleash its remarkable richness and strength. His Bienvenues-Bâtard-Montrachet seems no better than either his Puligny-Montrachet Les Pucelles, of which he owns 7.5 acres, or his best-kept secret, his 2-acre parcel of Puligny-Montrachet Les Combettes. He makes the least amount of Puligny-Montrachet Les Combettes, but it can often rival his Grands Crus, and sells at Premier Cru prices. His lightest wine is the generic Puligny-Montrachet, where he has 9 acres. His Clavaillon, where he has 10 acres of vines, is never quite up to the quality of the Les Pucelles or Les Combettes. In most vintages Leflaive also produces about 1,200 cases of a Bourgogne Blanc from young vines. This wine is often one of the best buys in white burgundy. In 1989 he acquired two tiny parcels of Premiers Crus in Puligny, Les Folatières, and Les Chalumeaux.

Leflaive has always made excellent wine, but one could certainly argue with some degree of conviction that his greatest vintages have been in the last 15 years, including extraordinary wines in 1978, 1979, 1983, 1985, 1986, and 1988. Even in rainy years such as 1984 and 1987, Leflaive produced several superb wines, including his Chevalier-Montrachet. Despite their high prices and scarcity, these wines deserve to be tasted by anyone who is interested in the reference points of white burgundy. If they are to be criticized at all, it is because they rarely age well once they have passed 8 or 9 years of age.

OLIVIER LEFLAIVE FRÈRES
(PULIGNY-MONTRACHET) ***

> Wines Produced: Auxey-Duresses, Bâtard-Montrachet, Chassagne-Montrachet, Chassagne-Montrachet Morgeot, Chasssagne-Montrachet La Romanée, Meursault, Meursault Les Charmes, Meursault Les Genevrières, Meursault Les Gouttes d'Or, Meursault Les Perrières, Montagny Premier Cru, Puligny-Montrachet, Puligny-Montrachet Les Champs Gains, Puligny-Montrachet Les Garennes, Puligny-Montrachet Les Perrières, Rully Mont Palais, Rully Raclot, Saint-Aubin en Remilly, St.-Romain.

Olivier Leflaive, the young, enthusiastic nephew of Vincent Leflaive, started this *négociant* business in 1984. He has gradually increased the number of wines he sells each year, and is now one of the most successful *négociants* in the Côte de Beaune. His cellars have total temperature control (like his uncle's) yet he believes in producing shy and understated wines. The wines are certainly good, but often lack excitement. Proponents would argue that his wines discreetly balance power, fruit, and personality, but critics would say they are often too light, austere, and simple for their lofty price tags. Nevertheless, these are still good wines, made in a very fresh, modern, commercial style. They rarely ever show much new oak, although some is certainly utilized. The best values are from Rully, Saint-Aubin, and St.-Romain. I find the Premiers Crus of Puligny-Montrachet and Meursault, as well as the Grands Crus, to be a bit understated and simple for their appellations. These are wines that should be drunk in their first 5–6 years of life.

DOMAINE FRANÇOIS LEGROS
(NUITS ST.-GEORGES) ****

> Wines Produced: Bourgogne Rouge, Chambolle-Musigny Les Noirots, Morey St.-Denis-Clos Sorbés, Nuits St.-Georges Les Bousselots, Nuits St.-Georges La Perrière, Nuits St.-Georges La Roncière, Nuits St.-Georges Rue de Chaux, Vougeot Les Cras.

This newcomer produced his first vintage in 1988, so it is a bit premature to judge the quality of his wines. However, François Legros, a young, dark-haired, highly motivated winemaker, has some gorgeous parcels on the Côte de Nuits, including four Premiers Crus from Nuits St.-Georges. He destems 100%, ferments in old, traditional, open wood *cuves*, extends the maceration for up to 15 days, fines but does not filter, and bottles his wines after 18 months. The top wines of Legros' 1988 vintage revealed excellent winemaking skills. His respect for low yields and attention to the dangers of excessive fining and filtration resulted in firm, rich wines. This vineyard could be one of the up-and-coming stars of Nuits St.-Georges.

DOMAINE LEJEUNE (POMMARD)***

Wines Produced: Bourgogne Passe-Tout-Grains, Bourgogne Rouge, Pommard Les Argillières, Pommard Les Poutures, Pommard Les Rugiens.

The Domaine Lejeune is one of the few winemaking estates in Burgundy that is actually owned by a family from Pomerol, near Bordeaux. The Julian family owns this estate of 11.23 acres and their son, François, runs it with great enthusiasm. It is a tiny domaine, and its best vineyards are a .61-acre parcel of Pommard Les Rugiens, and a 3.3-acre parcel of Pommard Les Argillières. The wines tend to be very fruity, and are marked by a great deal of new oak (50%–100% new oak is used in most vintages). Some of the cuvées are vinified by the carbonic maceration method, a method rarely used in Burgundy. While the wines do have charm and character, they should be drunk within their first 5–6 years of life.

DOMAINE LEQUIN-ROUSSOT (SANTENAY)***

Wines Produced: Bâtard-Montrachet, Bourgogne Blanc, Bourgogne Rouge, Chassagne-Montrachet, Chassagne-Montrachet Les Caillerets, Chassagne-Montrachet Morgeot, Chassagne-Montrachet Les Vergers, Corton Les Languettes, Nuits St.-Georges, Pommard, Santenay, Santenay-Clos du Haut Village, Santenay-Clos Rousseau, Santenay la Comme, Santenay Passe Temps.

The Domaine Lequin-Roussot was founded by the Lequin family in 1869. An important estate of 39.25 acres, it stretches from the southern tip of the Côte de Beaune to the Nuits St.-Georges. The firm has been

estate-bottling at least 70% of its production since 1969. The best wines
are the white Bâtard-Montrachet, Chassagne-Montrachet Les Caillerets, Chassagne-Montrachet Morgeot, Chassagne-Montrachet Les Vergers, and the Santenay-Clos Rousseau (made from Pinot Blanc). These
remarkably rich wines are among the longest-lived white burgundies.
They are barrel-fermented, and aged in 25% new oak casks, with the
Bâtard-Montrachet seeing at least one-half new oak. However, they also
make an inferior line of red wines. Their red wines are often quite
mediocre in lightweight vintages (like 1986) and in vintages with difficulties (such as the rot in 1983). In top vintages such as 1985, their red
wines can be elegant expressions of a lighter-styled Pinot Noir. These
criticisms notwithstanding, the 1988 vintage represents their best effort
yet. The estate is now run by a Mutt and Jeff team of two brothers:
René Lequin, who handles the commercial end of the business, and
Louis Lequin, who manages the vineyard and is in charge of the winemaking. The Lequin-Roussot wines, in particular the splendid whites,
are also a good value.

DOMAINE LEROY (VOSNE-ROMANÉE)*****

Wines Produced: Auxey-Duresses, Chambertin, Clos Vougeot, Latricières-Chambertin, Musigny, Nuits St.-
Georges, Nuits St.-Georges Les Allots, Nuits St.-
Georges Les Boudots, Nuits St.-Georges Les Lavières, Nuits St.-Georges Les Vignes Rondes, Pommard Les Vignots, Puligny-Montrachet Les Folatières, Richebourg, Romanée St.-Vivant, Savigny-
Lès-Beaune Les Narbantons, Vosne-Romanée,
Vosne-Romanée Les Beaux Monts, Vosne-Romanée Les Brûlées, Vosne-Romanée Les Genevrières.

LEROY-NÉGOCIANT (AUXEY-DURESSES)****–*****

Wines Produced: They vary from year to year, depending on what is
purchased from individual growers.

At present, the wines produced by the remarkable and formidable Madame Lalou Bize-Leroy include those of the Domaine Leroy. Leroy
acquired the 32.2-acre Domaine Charles Noëllat in Vosne-Romanée in
1988, thereby expanding her holdings from 12.35 acres to 44.5 acres.
Soon after this coup, she hired the extraordinarily talented winemaker

of the Hospices de Beaune, André Porcheret, to look after her wines at
the new Domaine Leroy. Madame Bize-Leroy also acts as a *négociant*
in her home village of Auxey-Duresses, buying wines made to her spec-
ifications and bottling them at her cellars. In vintages such as 1985,
1986, and 1987 she was an active buyer and had several dozen selections available for sale. With her acquisition of the Domaine Noëllat,
she may now be content with the production of her 44.5-acre holdings.
She is also the coproprietor of Burgundy's most famous estate, the
Domaine de la Romanée-Conti.

The new Domaine Leroy includes extraordinary holdings, with 1.9
acres in Richebourg, 3.68 acres in Romanée St.-Vivant, 7.16 acres in
Vosne-Romanée Les Beaux Monts, 3.68 acres in Nuits St.-Georges Les
Boudots, and a large 4.19-acre holding (I should say two holdings) in
Clos Vougeot. The Clos Vougeot parcels were planted in 1955. The first
is located at the very top of the slope and the second from the middle
slope down to the Route Nationale. Additionally, tiny quantities of
Chambertin, Musigny, and Pommard Les Vignots are made from what
Madame Bize-Leroy owned previously. In 1989 she acquired over one
acre of Puligny-Montrachet Les Folatières and the Domaine Remy in
Gevrey-Chambertin. The Domaine Remy includes small but impressive
holdings in Latricières-Chambertin and Chambertin itself.

While Madame Lalou Bize-Leroy's prices are astronomically high,
her wines are the product of a perfectionist and a vociferous defender
of Burgundy. You simply will never get a disappointing bottle of wine
from Bize-Leroy. Her wines not only reflect their appellations, but are
Burgundy's reference points. In the new cellars, looked after by the
husky, bearded, dark-haired André Porcheret, the wines are vinified in
wooden *cuves* and put in 50% new oak barrels. As is the practice here,
the wines are bottled barrel by barrel with absolutely no filtration. The
1988s were the first wines produced in the new cellars. They are indeed
superb, but lamentably priced in the stratosphere. However, this remarkable woman also turns out the two best generic red and white
burgundies made. These wines, called Bourgogne d'Auvenay, make a
wonderful introduction to the Lalou Bize-Leroy style of winemaking.

Most wines from the Domaine Leroy are capable of lasting 20–30 or
more years in the bottle, an unusually long time for modern-day red
burgundy. In fact, I think it can be safely said that these are today's
only Burgundy wines that possess such aging potential.

DOMAINE THIERRY LESPINASSE (GIVRY)***

Wines Produced: Givry en Choué.

I have tasted only two vintages of Thierry Lespinasse's Givry, but in both 1987 and 1988 the wine was quite impressive, suggesting this is probably a high-quality source for reasonably priced red burgundy. Curiously, Lespinasse believes in fermenting his wines in large *foudres* and moving them to small oak casks after the malolactic fermentation. They remain in casks for six months, after which they are bottled with minimal fining and filtration. Perhaps this is why the wines seem imbued with gorgeous amounts of rich, red fruit, and have such a smoky, toasty character. These wines should be consumed within their first 4– 5 years of life.

DOMAINE DU LEVANT
(SAINT-ÉTIENNE-LA VARENNE)**

Wines Produced: Brouilly.

The Domaine du Levant makes commendable, yet somewhat unexciting Brouilly from its 19.26 acres of vineyards. Robert Farjat, the proprietor, estate-bottles most of his production. The majority of his top clients are private consumers and buyers in Europe.

DOMAINE GEORGES LIGNIER
(MOREY ST.-DENIS)***–****

Wines Produced: Bourgogne Aligoté, Bonnes Mares, Bourgogne Passe-Tout-Grains, Bourgogne Rouge, Chambolle-Musigny, Charmes-Chambertin, Clos de la Roche, Clos St.-Denis, Gevrey-Chambertin, Gevrey-Chambertin Les Combottes, Morey St.-Denis, Morey St.-Denis-Clos des Ormes, Morey St.-Denis Premier Cru.

The wine cellars of several outstanding small growers can be found on the main road leading into Morey St.-Denis from N 74 (the major artery between Dijon and Beaune). Entering the village of Morey St.-Denis, one sees the Domaine Dujac on the left and the cellars of Hubert Lignier, Pierre Amiot, Bernard Serveau, and Georges Lignier on the right. Young Georges Lignier, who must work in one of the most damp and moldy cellars in Burgundy, is not as consistent a winemaker as some of his peers, but in the top Burgundy vintages he is capable of turning out beautifully rich, lush, powerful wines with a great deal of character. In his mid-thirties, Lignier is a shy, reticent man with piercing blue-green eyes. He believes in a relatively hot fermentation, 18 months aging in cask, and only 15% new oak (except for his Grands Crus, which receive 100% new oak). His estate of 32 acres is very fragmented and includes fabulous Grands Crus like Clos St.-Denis (3.8 acres), Clos de la Roche (2.55 acres), Charmes-Chambertin (2.04 acres), and Bonnes Mares (.69 acre). He has an outstanding Premier Cru holding of 4.6 acres called Morey St.-Denis-Clos des Ormes. In addition, Lignier has an assemblage of Premiers Crus that he calls Morey St.-Denis Premier Cru, and an excellent Premier Cru, Gevrey-Chambertin Les Combottes. Villages wines are also made in Morey St.-Denis and Gevrey-Chambertin. As mentioned, the wines in the top vintages, such as 1978 and 1985, are rich, powerful, and have expansive, deep flavors. Young Lignier has yet to master winemaking techniques in problematic years and should stop using a filter. Most Lignier wines age extremely well. They are almost always at their prime in 5–7 years, but are capable of lasting for 8–10 years.

HUBERT LIGNIER (MOREY ST.-DENIS) *****

> Wines Produced: Bourgogne Rouge, Chambolle-Musigny Premier Cru, Charmes-Chambertin, Clos de la Roche, Gevrey-Chambertin Premier Cru, Morey St.-Denis Premier Cru.

Hubert Lignier is a sure-handed winemaker who produces excellent wines in both great and mediocre vintages. He is primarily known for his extraordinary Clos de la Roche (1.9 acres) and his Morey St.-Denis Premier Cru (7.41 acres). He also has micro parcels of other vineyards: one-quarter of an acre of Grand Cru Charmes-Chambertin, and one-acre holdings in Gevrey-Chambertin Premier Cru and Chambolle-Musigny Premier Cru. Unfortunately, these wines are impossible to find. Lignier's entire domaine consists of 18.3 acres. He keeps his wine in oak casks for 20–24 months (longer in powerful vintages such as 1985 and 1988). His Grands Crus see 100% new oak and the rest of his wines between 24%–33% new oak barrels. Lignier does not filter his wines unless they fail to fall brilliant in the cask. This is one place where the smell of raspberries in the wine is more than just an olfactory flight of fancy. His Clos de la Roche and Morey St.-Denis Premier Cru have stunning bouquets of raspberries and an opulence of fruit that make them undeniably seductive young. Vintages such as 1978, 1985, and

1986 also promise to age magnificently. Hubert Lignier is a brilliant winemaker.

DOMAINE A. LONG-DEPAQUIT (CHABLIS) *****–*****

Wines Produced: Chablis, Chablis Beugnons, Chablis Les Blanchots, Chablis Les Clos, Chablis Les Lys, Chablis La Moutonne, Chablis Les Preuses, Chablis Les Vaillons, Chablis Vaudésir.

This is an exceptional firm that makes some of the best Premier Cru and Grand Cru Chablis in the appellation. The 105-acre estate includes 47 acres of "simple" Chablis, 30 acres of Premiers Crus, and 25 acres of Grands Crus. It has important holdings in Vaudésir, Les Clos, Les Preuses, and the entire 5.6-acre parcel of Les Preuses and Vaudésir called La Moutonne. La Moutonne was named after the famous abbey of Pontigny where legend has it the monks skipped about like young sheep (moutons) after drinking the local wine. The wines of Long-Depaquit can have superb richness and depth when made from the Premier Cru and Grand Cru vineyards. Some of the finest Chablis I tasted from the 1978, 1983, 1986, and 1988 vintages was from Long-Depaquit. I would advise consumers to search out the La Moutonne, Les Preuses, Les Clos, and Vaudésir, as these are consistently their most successful wines. They are also wines that will keep for 10–12 years. This domaine is owned by the hugh Beaune *négociant*, Albert Bichot.

LORON ET FILS (PONTANEVAUX) ***

Domaine Wines Produced: Beaujolais-Villages Cuvée de Fondateur, Chiroubles-Domaine du Moulin, Fleurie-Château de Fleurie, Juliénas-Domaine de la Vieille Église, Mâcon-Villages-Château de Mirande, Moulin-à-Vent-Château Lemonon, Saint-Amour-Domaine des Billards, Saint-Véran-Château des Correaux.

Note: This large *négociant*, in addition to representing the above domaines on an exclusive basis, produces an entire line of *négociant* wines under its own name.

Founded in 1821, the Loron firm is best known for its blends of Beaujolais, which it sells to a number of French supermarket chains, and its rather gutsy, alcoholic Vins de Table. The firm's best wines are the domaine wines. They tend to be heady with a great deal of muscle and alcohol, but lack the finesse, charm, and appellation character of Georges Duboeuf's and Pierre Ferraud's wines.

DOMAINE LUMPP FRÈRES (GIVRY)**–***

> Wines Produced: Bourgogne Aligoté, Bourgogne Passe-Tout-Grains, Givry Blanc, Givry-Clos du Cras Long Rouge, Givry Rouge.

Vincent and François Lumpp established the Domaine Lumpp Frères in 1977, after finishing their studies at the Lycée Viticole in Beaune. This family-owned estate produces stylish, elegant, light- to medium-bodied red and white wines that are technically correct and fruity, but lack depth and individuality. The red wines, particularly the Givry-Clos du Cras Long, are better than the whites. The red wines see 20%–30% new oak casks and are bottled after 11–18 months. The white wines are fermented in stainless-steel tanks and are aged 6–8 months in oak casks (10% new). The enthusiastic proprietors of this firm aspire to produce reasonably priced, stylish wine. The prices are realistic, and the general quality of the wine is average to good. The best recent vintages have been 1985 and 1988.

LUPÉ-CHOLET (NUITS ST.-GEORGES)**

> Wines Produced: The estate wines, the Château Gris Nuits St.-Georges, are now produced under the auspices of the huge Bichot firm of Beaune.

Note: There is also a *négociant* line of wines made from purchased grape juice.

This *négociant* firm suffered greatly when it was taken over by the huge firm of F. Chauvenet. However, Chauvenet sold the firm to Moillard, who in turn sold it to Bichot in Beaune. Lupé-Cholet still has two *monopole* 7.4-acre vineyards, the most famous of which is the Nuits St.-Georges-Château Gris, a parcel of vines in the Premier Cru Nuits St.-Georges called Aux Crots. There have been some excellent wines from this parcel over the years, and the Bichots are vigorously trying to upgrade its quality. They are now using new oak barrels and a longer maceration period. They also own a 7.41-acre parcel of generic Bourgogne (another *monopole* vineyard) called Clos de Lupé, which has produced rather light, somewhat disappointing wines over recent years.

DOMAINE ROGER LUQUET (FUISSÉ) ***—****

> Wines Produced: Mâcon-Blanc-Clos de Condemine, Mâcon Fuissé Blanc, Pouilly-Fuissé, Pouilly-Fuissé en Chantenet, Pouilly-Fuissé-Clos du Bourg, Saint-Véran en Faux, Saint-Véran Les Grandes Bruyères.

Roger Luquet eschews any aging in cask, preferring to keep the Chardonnay from his Mâcon, Saint-Véran, and Pouilly-Fuissé vineyards in contact with the lees in stainless-steel casks until bottling takes place in the spring following the vintage. The results are some of the better examples of pure stainless-steel fermented and aged white wines. The star of this house, however, is the Pouilly-Fuissé-Clos du Bourg. It comes from a wonderful chalky, southerly exposed 1.65-acre vineyard, which many consider to be one of the top Pouilly-Fuissé sites in the appellation. Luquet's wines are very well balanced, and show a rather stony, mineral character, which is slightly different than some of the more lush, fuller-bodied, muscular wines of this region. Although I have never tasted an older wine, my inclination is that the wines should be drunk young.

LYCÉE AGRICOLE ET VITICOLE (BEAUNE) ***

> Wines Produced: Beaune Les Bressandes, Beaune Les Champs Pimonts, Beaune Montée Rouge, Beaune Les Perrières, Beaune Premier Cru, Bourgogne Aligoté, Bourgogne Blanc, Bourgogne Rouge, Côte de Beaune Blanc, Côte de Beaune Rouge, Puligny-Montrachet.

The Lycée Agricole was founded in 1884 and has educated many of the children of Burgundy's most famous proprietors. Appropriately, this institution produces good, stylish, straightforward wines with no defects. However, they often lack a bit of character. The wines are meant to be drunk young, and for that reason offer charm and surprising value. The school owns 44.87 acres of vineyards, with some very fine parcels in Premier Cru Beaunes. Their most famous wine is the Beaune Champimonts, produced from a 6-acre parcel. However, they make good straightforward, juicy, lush Beaune Les Perrières, Beaune Les Bressandes, and Beaune Montée Rouge. These wines should not be put in the cellar and forgotten for 7–8 years, as they are meant to be drunk within their first 5–6 years of life. They represent a fair value.

Virtually all the wine is sold via mail order in France, with some exported to Belgium and Switzerland.

DOMAINE DU DUC DE MAGENTA
(CHASSAGNE-MONTRACHET)****

Wines Produced: Auxey-Duresses Blanc, Auxey-Duresses Rouge, Bourgogne Blanc, Chassagne-Montrachet-Clos de la Chapelle, Meursault Les Meix Chavaux, Puligny-Montrachet-Clos de la Garenne.

This famous estate, which owns some historic monastic vineyards, had a track record of inconsistency in the sixties, seventies, and early eighties under proprietor Marquis Philippe de Mac Mahon. Recently, however, the domaine began to sell its grapes to the Beaune firm of Louis Jadot. The brilliant staff of Louis Jadot now makes and markets all the wine from the Domaine du Duc de Magenta and, as a result, the quality has never been better. The domaine's holdings include a superb Puligny-Montrachet-Clos de la Garenne parcel (5.68 acres) and an historic 10.62-acre parcel of Chassagne-Montrachet-Clos de la Chapelle. There is also some very good Meursault Les Meix Chavaux and an adequate Auxey-Duresses Blanc. Under the supervision of the staff of Louis Jadot, the red wines, such as Chassagne-Montrachet and Auxey-Duresses, should improve significantly. Jadot uses 25%–35% new oak, and the wines are bottled after 12–15 months' cask aging. When buying a wine from the Duc de Magenta, the label will indicate the name Louis Jadot, but will also indicate that it is from the Domaine du Duc de Magenta.

DOMAINE HENRI MAGNIEN (GEVREY-CHAMBERTIN)**

Wines Produced: Gevrey-Chambertin, Gevrey-Chambertin Les Cazetiers, Gevrey-Chambertin Estournelles St.-Jacques, Gevrey-Chambertin Lavaux St.-Jacques, Ruchottes-Chambertin.

Henri Magnien has only 5.5 acres of vineyards, but his style of winemaking produces elegant, supple, stylish wines. His wines can be deceptively light in color, yet are still imbued with a wonderful strawberry and cherry fruitiness. He promotes the fruit rather than the oak, and the results, in a vintage such as 1985, are wines filled with charm and finesse. However, they must be drunk within their first 5–7 years of life. The quality since 1986 has dipped significantly. I found the 1986s, 1987s, and 1988s to be watery and insipid.

DOMAINE MICHEL MAGNIEN (MOREY ST.-DENIS)***

Wines Produced: Bourgogne Passe-Tout-Grains, Bourgogne Rouge, Chambolle-Musigny, Clos de la Roche, Clos St.-Denis, Gevrey-Chambertin, Gevrey-Chambertin Les Cazetiers, Morey St.-Denis.

This is a reliable and sound producer of Burgundy. I wish that I knew his wines better, but those I have tasted possess a good deal of charm and character. The domaine consists of 16.6 acres, with tiny but important parcels in Gevrey-Chambertin Les Cazetiers, Morey St.-Denis, Clos de la Roche, and Clos St.-Denis. Domaine Michel Magnien is also a good source for straight Chambolle-Musigny. Most of the wines seem to be at their best 3–7 years after the vintage.

DOMAINE MAILLARD PÈRE ET FILS (CHOREY-LÈS-BEAUNE)***

Wines Produced: Aloxe-Corton, Beaune, Beaune Les Grèves, Bourgogne Rouge, Chorey-Lès-Beaune, Corton, Corton Les Rénardes, Côte de Beaune-Villages, Ladoix Rouge, Savigny-Lès-Beaune.

They produce a simple yet deliciously supple Chorey-Lès-Beaune (9.13 acres), a velvety, spicy Beaune Grèves (.91 acre), and a wonderful red wine, the Corton Les Rénardes (3.45 acres). They also own .46 of an acre of Grand Cru Corton, but I have never seen a bottle of this wine. Just over 50% of the wines from this 35.71-acre estate are sold to *négociants*. The rest are put in one-third new oak casks and bottled after 24 months.

DOMAINE LA MAISON (LEYNES)***

Wines Produced: Beaujolais-Villages, Saint-Véran.

Georges Chagny makes delicious, effusively fruity, stylish and graceful Saint-Véran from his 25-acre domaine. The production is split equally between the Saint-Véran and a well-made, fruity Beaujolais-Villages. He ages his white wine in vats and small casks, all old, for 6–8 months prior to bottling.

DOMAINE DES MALANDES (CHABLIS)**

> Wines Produced: Chablis, Chablis-Côte de Léchet, Chablis Four-
> chaume, Chablis Montmains, Chablis Vaudésir,
> Chablis Vaux de Vey.

Established in 1972, this estate now consists of 43.29 acres. It has some important small holdings in the excellent Premiers Crus of Fourchaume and Montmains, and a small parcel in the Grand Cru Vaudésir. The wines are fermented and aged in stainless-steel tanks and bottled after 6–8 months. The wines are clean and correct, but seem to lack a bit in concentration. Curiously, I find it difficult to tell the Grand Cru Vaudésir from the Premier Cru Montmains. The wines are best when consumed within 5–6 years of the vintage.

DOMAINE MICHEL MALLARD ET FILS
(LADOIX-SERRIGNY)***

> Wines Produced: Aloxe-Corton, Bourgogne Blanc, Bourgogne
> Rouge, Corton, Côte de Nuits-Villages, Ladoix,
> Ladoix Blanc, Ladoix Les Joyeuses, Savigny-Lès-
> Beaune.

The firm of Michel and Patrick Mallard exploits 37.91 acres of vineyard, and is one of the largest small growers in the Ladoix-Serrigny area. Their wines tend to show a lot of ripe, soft, velvety, sweet berry fruit married intelligently with the use of 25% new oak. In most cases, the bottling here takes place after 15–18 months. These are competent winemakers who know what it takes to provide a good glass of red burgundy. One of their best values is their Ladoix Les Joyeuses, made from a 3.21-acre Premier Cru vineyard; in the hands of the Mallards, this wine seems appropriately named. Additionally, they make a solid Ladoix Rouge from an 11.1-acre parcel, which does not have the stern, tannic, and tough texture of many other wines from Ladoix. If one is lucky enough to find it, their Grand Cru Corton, from a 2.96-acre parcel, can be all that Corton is meant to be, a wine with explosive richness and a long finish. The Domaine Michel Mallard et Fils, like many of the better domaines of Ladoix-Serrigny, is underestimated and the wines are often a good value in view of the stratospheric prices of Burgundy.

DOMAINE MALDANT (CHOREY-LÈS-BEAUNE) ✳✳–✳✳✳

Wines Produced: Aloxe-Corton, Aloxe-Corton Premier Cru, Bourgogne Aligoté, Bourgogne Blanc, Bourgogne Rouge, Chorey-Lès-Beaune, Corton-Charlemagne, Corton Les Grèves, Corton Les Rénardes, Ladoix, Savigny-Lès-Beaune Premier Cru.

The Domaine Maldant owns an impressive 25 acres of vineyards, spread over eleven different appellations. The winemaking is done by Sylvan Pitot, son-in-law of the famous Pierre Poupon. His philosophy of winemaking is to produce cleanly made and stylish wines that exhibit adequate quantities of pure berry fruit, and have the ability to age for 5–7 years. About one-third of the production is estate-bottled, and the remaining two-thirds is sold to *négociants*. My only criticism of the wines of the Domaine Maldant is that they are overly fined and filtered, and therefore lack personality and character. The white wines spend 12–18 months in small casks, of which a tiny percentage is new. I found the Corton-Charlemagne to be surprisingly good, but only several barrels are produced. The red wines all spend two years in cask prior to bottling, and, not surprisingly, the top red wine is the excellent Corton Les Rénardes. The other reds taste lean and attenuated. I have only tasted the 1987 and 1988 vintages.

CHÂTEAU DE LA MALTROYE
(CHASSAGNE-MONTRACHET) ✳✳✳✳

Wines Produced: Bâtard-Montrachet, Bourgogne Aligoté, Bourgogne Blanc, Bourgogne Rouge, Chassagne-Montrachet Les Chenevottes, Chassagne-Montrachet-Clos de la Maltroye, Chassagne-Montrachet-Clos St.-Jean, Chassagne-Montrachet Les Crets, Chassagne-Montrachet Les Grands Ruchottes, Chassagne-Montrachet Morgeot, Chassagne-Montrachet Morgeot-Vigne Blanche, Chassagne-Montrachet La Romanée, Santenay Blanc.

This large estate, beautifully situated in Chassagne-Montrachet, consists of 41.99 acres with numerous appellations. The property is run by the elderly Monsieur Cornut. He sensed that the winemaking in the late seventies and early eighties was a bit spotty, and put Jean-Luc Parent in full charge of the wines. Most of the production is in white wine.

Parent uses only 40% new oak for the majority of the wines, but uses 100% for the Morgeot-Vigne Blanche and Bâtard-Montrachet. While the white wines were patchy in the late seventies, they are very well made today, and are increasingly competitive with the wines of some of Chassagne's best producers. Since 1985, the vintages have been excellent. As for the red wines, the 1985s, 1987s, and 1988s were charming and delicious with gobs of berry fruit, and light tannins. They are wines that should be drunk in their first 7–8 years of life. The overall quality of winemaking from this beautiful estate leaves little to be desired.

DOMAINE MANCIAT-PONCET
(CHARNAY LES MÂCON)****

Wines Produced: Mâcon Charnay Blanc, Pouilly-Fuissé.

This is one of the top small domaines producing Pouilly-Fuissé and Mâcon Charnay Blanc. Claude Manciat oversees the winemaking process. The wines are made in stainless-steel vats and are then moved to oak casks for 7–8 months of aging. Manciat believes in using 15%–20% new oak for aging both his white wines. His entire domaine consists of 21.8 acres, and his Mâcon Charnay Blanc is one of the richest and most intense wines of the region. The Pouilly-Fuissé is also among the appellation's top 7–8 wines. The Domaine Manciat-Poncet gets high marks from virtually everybody, and its wines can last for 4–6 years.

DOMAINE MANIÈRE-NOIROT (VOSNE-ROMANÉE)****

Wines Produced: Bourgogne Rouge, Echézeaux, Nuits St.-Georges Les Boudots, Nuits St.-Georges Les Damodes, Vosne-Romanée, Vosne-Romanée Les Suchots.

This is a very good, sometimes excellent producer of ageworthy, concentrated, rich burgundies. These wines deserve far greater attention from serious wine consumers than they have received to date. The estate is moderately sized at 24.7 acres. Its proprietors, Marc and Thérèse Manière, use 25%–35% new oak, and believe in bottling their wines (after 18–20 months in cask) with either no filtration or as light a filtration as possible. The estate's two most important holdings are a 3.95-acre parcel of the excellent Premier Cru of Vosne-Romanée called Les Suchots, and a 3.5-acre parcel of the exceptional Premier Cru of Nuits St.-Georges called Les Damodes. Most of the wines from Domaine Manière-Noirot tend to have excellent color, plenty of body and tannin, and are capable of lasting for 10–15 years in a good vintage.

DOMAINE YVES MARCEAU
DOMAINE DE LA CROIX GAULT (MERCUREY)***

> Wines Produced: Bourgogne Aligoté, Bourgogne Blanc, Bourgogne Rosé, Bourgogne Rouge, Givry le Pied du Clou, Mercurey Rouge, Rully Rabourcé Blanc.

Another underrated, serious winemaking estate in Mercurey, this domaine deserves attention for its excellent Mercurey Rouge (not a Premier Cru), its very good Givry le Pied du Clou, and its white Rully Rabourcé. Proprietor Yves Marceau has 23.83 acres. He now uses 33% new oak for his red wines and bottles after 12 months. His white wines see less new oak and are bottled after 6–8 months. The wines show a lot of fruit, are supple, and are meant to be drunk within their first 5–6 years of life. Marceau is able to produce wines that are complex and filled with finesse without sacrificing richness or character.

DOMAINE MARCHAND-GRILLOT ET FILS
(GEVREY-CHAMBERTIN)***

> Wines Produced: Chambolle-Musigny, Gevrey-Chambertin, Gevrey-Chambertin Petite Chapelle, Morey St.-Denis, Ruchottes-Chambertin.

This 23.81-acre domaine has begun to acquire a following as the proprietor, Jacques Marchand, has assumed more control over the running of the estate. The wines tend to be deliciously supple, expansively flavored, and ready to drink upon release, although his Premier Cru, Gevrey-Chambertin Petite Chapelle, and Grand Cru, Ruchottes-Chambertin, are capable of lasting up to 10 years. Marchand uses about 30% new oak in good vintages. The most important holding here is a 16.79-acre parcel of Gevrey-Chambertin, but Marchand also has nearly 2 acres in both the Grand Cru Ruchottes-Chambertin and in the Premier Cru Gevrey-Chambertin Petite Chapelle. The latter wine is often this producer's best. Marchand's critics claim his wines lack backbone and grip.

P. DE MARCILLY FRÈRES (BEAUNE)***

> Wines Produced: Beaune, Bourgogne Marcilly Premier, Bourgogne Marcilly Réserve, Côte de Beaune-Villages.

Founded in 1849, the Domaine P. De Marcilly Frères takes its production from 37 acres of vineyards. This unusual producer blends its own wine with other purchased wines to make Marcilly Réserve and Marcilly Premier. They tend to be concentrated, full bodied, alcoholic, and quite good. The strategy of taking excellent wine from Beaune and blending it into a greater mass of purchased wine from lesser vineyards is questionable. However, the de Marcilly family has practiced this method most of the twentieth century and claims it has no reason to change. These wines are interesting, but expensive for generic wines.

DOMAINE JEAN MARECHAL (MERCUREY)****

Wines Produced: Bourgogne Rouge Les Gouletts, Mercurey Les Champs-Martins, Mercurey-Clos Barrault, Mercurey-Clos Barrault Blanc, Mercurey-Clos l'Évêque, Mercurey Les Naugues.

This small 21.39-acre estate is steeped in tradition. The current proprietor, Jean Marechal, is an opinionated man, proud of the fact that this domaine was established by his family in 1570. The estate is fortunate to have vineyards in the sections of Mercurey where the soil is a heavy, chalky clay with a perfect south/southeast exposure. The red wines see 25% new oak and are bottled after 12–15 months. Hand harvesting, partial destemming, and a long maceration period, produce wines that are rich, concentrated, and very fragrant with intense smells of cherries and raspberries. The white wines, which see 25% new oak and are bottled after 12 months, are also to be recommended. This estate produces some of the most long-lived wines of the Mercurey appellation. They made sublime wines in 1985, 1987, and 1988. Most of their sales are in France, with only a tiny percentage being exported to Switzerland, Belgium, Germany, the United Kingdom, and Denmark. The Domaine Jean Marechal is clearly one of the best in Mercurey for those who like traditional, long-lived, rich, concentrated, complex red and white burgundies. Furthermore, the prices are a bargain when one considers the quality of the wine.

DOMAINE DES MARONNIERS (PRÉHY)***

Wines Produced: Chablis, Chablis Montmains.

Established in 1976, this small domaine of 24.7 acres was founded by Bernard Légland. He owns land in only two appellations of Chablis. Seventy percent of his production comes from generic vineyards, and the rest is made from the excellent Premier Cru Chablis Montmains. Légland has evolved as a winemaker. He eschewed new oak when he started, but is now moving toward 50% new oak casks and bottling after 6 months for his Premier Cru Montmains. His Chablis sees no new oak and is a product of cold stabilization and early bottling. This process gives it a rather flowery, straightforward character. Légland, who has rather devilish good looks and an enormous amount of energy and enthusiasm for the wines of Chablis, seems like a small grower intent on establishing a name for quality.

DOMAINE MAROSLAVAC-LEGER
(CHASSAGNE-MONTRACHET) ** — ***

Wines Produced: Auxey-Duresses Les Breetterins, Auxey-Duresses Rouge, Bourgogne Aligoté, Bourgogne Blanc, Meursault, Puligny-Montrachet, Puligny-Montrachet Les Champs Gains, Puligny-Montrachet Les Combettes, Puligny-Montrachet Les Folatières, Saint-Aubin Les Murgers des Dents de Chien.

The Domaine Maroslavac-Leger sells some of its production to the well-known *négociant* Labouré-Roi in Nuits St.-Georges. Those wines appear under the domaine name, Maroslavac, but are commercialized by Labouré-Roi. The domaine also estate-bottles its own production, selling it directly under the Domaine Maroslavac-Leger label. The white wines here are significantly better than the reds, revealing an old-style, plump, toasty, rich, somewhat chunky, and heavy character with plenty of fruit. The red wines tend to be tannic, lean, and hard. The producers have not managed to capture all the possible fruit and charm available in their grapes.

DOMAINE TIM MARSHALL (NUITS ST.-GEORGES) ***

Wines Produced: Chambolle-Musigny, Nuits St.-Georges Les Argillières, Nuits St.-Georges Les Perrières, Volnay.

This minuscule domaine is owned by Tim Marshall, an Englishman who now lives in Burgundy. Marshall also runs a successful business repre-

senting some of the best small growers in the Côte d'Or and has a
financial interest in the firm of Jean Germain in Meursault. His own
tiny vineyard in Nuits St.-Georges produces a small amount of well-
made wine. About the only chance one has of finding Marshall's wine
is on the wine lists of some of the better restaurants in Nuits St.-
Georges. In 1989, Marshall added two new vineyards in Chambolle-
Musigny and Volnay to his portfolio.

DOMAINE MAURICE MARTIN (DAVAYÉ)***

Wines Produced: Mâcon-Rosé, Mâcon-Rouge, Saint-Véran.

This is an example of a very fruity, medium-bodied Saint-Véran that
benefits from 6 months aging in 10% new small oak casks. Maurice
Martin and his son own 22.97 acres. The bulk of their production is in
Saint-Véran and the balance is in a rather dull Mâcon-Rouge and competent Mâcon-Rosé. These are good wines, but almost impossible to
find in the export market. Martin has developed a significant following
in Europe and sells most of his production to private clients there.

DOMAINE RENÉ MARTIN
(CHEILLY-LÈS-MARANGES)***

Wines Produced: Bourgogne Aligoté, Bourgogne Blanc, Bourgogne
              Hautes-Côtes de Beaune Rouge, Bourgogne
              Rouge, Sampigny-Lès-Maranges.

If one is a shrewd shopper for wine values, then domaines like René
Martin's small estate of 17.41 acres merits attention. There are no
famous appellations here, only straight generic Bourgogne and a little
bit of Côte de Beaune-Villages from a tiny 1.23-acre parcel in Sampigny-Lès-Maranges. The wines offer a lot of rich, toasty new oak and
are supple and easy to drink young. This well-run estate aims to produce good hardy red and white burgundies with no pretensions. The
red wines see 25% new oak and are bottled after 14–16 months of cask
aging. The white wines see 25% new oak and are bottled after 12
months. Half the production is sold to *négociants* and the balance is
estate-bottled.

LES VINS MATHELIN (CHÂTILLON-D'AZERGUES) ***

Wines Produced: Beaujolais Coupe Paradis, Beaujolais Blanc-Domaine de Sandar, Beaujolais Rosé, Brouilly-Cuvée C. V. Geoffray, Juliénas Cuvée Bouchy, Morgon-Château Gaillard, Moulin-à-Vent-Domaine du Moulin-à-Vent.

Note: This firm also produces an entire range of Beaujolais under its name as a *négociant.*

Founded in 1972, this domaine is a respectable source for fruity, elegant, fresh and satisfying Beaujolais. If the wines are not in the very top league of quality, they are certainly in the second tier of producers.

DOMAINE MATHIAS (CHAINTRÉ) **

Wines Produced: Beaujolais-Villages, Mâcon Chaintré Blanc, Mâcon-Loche Blanc, Pouilly-Fuissé, Pouilly-Vinzelles.

Jean Mathias has a good reputation, but my experience with his wines has not been good. I have often noticed excessive amounts of sulphur in the nose, but I have friends in France who tell me they have never experienced such problems. Mathias makes relatively full-bodied, fruity wines from his 16.7 acres of vineyard. The wines are fermented in vats and then put in oak casks for 6 months. He prefers to use 5%–10% new oak in each vintage.

DOMAINE JOSEPH MATROT (MEURSAULT) ***

Wines Produced: Auxey-Duresses, Blagny-La Pièce Sous le Bois, Bourgogne, Bourgogne Aligoté, Meursault, Meursault-Blagny, Meursault Les Charmes, Puligny-Montrachet Les Chalumeaux, Volnay Santenots.

Domaine Matrot has been estate-bottling its wines for over 30 years, and is one of the largest and most significant vineyard holders in Meursault. The tall, blond Thierry Matrot, who sports an earring in his right ear, looks after the vineyards and makes the wines. While most of this estate's wines are white, with modest yields of no more than 40 hectoliters per hectare, one of the best red wines made in the Côte de Beaune is Matrot's Blagny-La Pièce Sous le Bois. Matrot makes a deliciously supple, richly fruity, smooth, and velvety red burgundy from this 5.85-acre parcel. His other top wines are his Meursault Les Charmes and Puligny-Montrachet Les Chalumeaux. For value, his Auxey-Duresses can be very good in vintages such as 1985 and 1988. The estate now consists of 30.75 acres, with its major parcels being the aforementioned Blagny, a 2.3-acre parcel in Meursault Les Charmes, a 2.45-acre parcel in Meursault-Blagny, and a 7.87-acre parcel in Meursault. The estate also owns 2.25 acres in Volnay-Santenots, 4.3 acres of Bourgogne Aligoté, 2 acres of Bourgogne, and 1.43 acres of Auxey-Duresses.

DOMAINE MAUME (GEVREY-CHAMBERTIN)****

Wines Produced: Charmes-Chambertin, Gevrey-Chambertin, Gevrey-Chambertin Les Champeaux, Gevrey-Chambertin Lavaux St.-Jacques, Gevrey-Chambertin en Pallud, Mazis-Chambertin.

Bernard Maume, the current proprietor, is a professor in biochemistry at the University of Dijon and commutes regularly to the family's domaine. This is a small 8.89-acre estate with superbly situated parcels of very old vines in both Premiers Crus and Grands Crus. The wines are often among the most concentrated and darkest colored wines made in Burgundy, and frequently need at least 8–10 years to shed their cloak of tannin. They are bottled unfiltered. The most famous wine of the Domaine Maume is their extraordinary Mazis-Chambertin. The wine is made from extremely old vines from a 1.72-acre parcel of land. Other top wines include the Charmes-Chambertin and an excellent Gevrey-Chambertin Lavaux St.-Jacques from a 1.7-acre parcel. These wines have quite a following of Burgundy connoisseurs as they have tremendous keeping qualities, often lasting for 10–20 years. At present, Bernard Maume is using 30% new oak, and keeps his wine 18 months in cask before bottling.

DOMAINE MAZILLY PÈRE ET FILS (MELOISEY)**

Wines Produced: Beaune Les Montrevenots, Beaune Les Vignes-Franches, Bourgogne Hautes-Côtes de Beaune Rouge, Bourgogne Passe-Tout-Grains, Bourgogne Rosé, Meursault, Pommard, Pommard Les Poutures.

Perhaps I have been unlucky, but the wines I have tasted from Pierre Mazilly's estate of 29.14 acres have always been overly tannic, muscular wines lacking freshness, charm, and supple fruit. My experience only covers the 1983, 1984, and 1985 vintages, but the wines seem too compact and hard. However, they may open and blossom with cellaring. The red wines are aged in small oak casks (15% are new) for 8–18 months, and are filtered prior to bottling.

DOMAINE MEIX FOULOT (MERCUREY)***–****

Wines Produced: Mercurey Blanc, Mercurey-Clos de Château Montaigu, Mercurey Cuvée Speciale, Mercurey Meix Foulot, Mercurey Veleys.

Yves De Launay meticulously runs this splendidly situated, 38-acre domaine in Mercurey. Most of the production (93%) is in red wine, but De Launay also makes tiny quantities of a rather lean, tart, austere white Mercurey. The red wines are among the best of Mercurey, and De Launay produces three separate cuvées. In ascending order of quality, there is the Mercurey Veleys, the Mercurey Meix Foulot, and his top wine, the Mercurey-Clos de Château Montaigu. All of the wines see 14–18 months aging in oak barrels (25% are new). The Clos de Château Montaigu is made from old vines planted in 1948 and 1946. I have tasted Mercureys from De Launay as far back as 1971 and found them to still be in superb condition. The winemaking technique here is quite traditional, and De Launay's yields per hectare are often well below those of his neighbors. His red wines are usually bottled with no filtration, always a sign of a committed and serious winemaker.

DOMAINE LOUIS MENAND PÈRE ET FILS (MERCUREY)**

Wines Produced: Bourgogne Aligoté, Mercurey Blanc, Mercurey-Clos des Combins, Mercurey Rouge.

This tiny, family-owned domaine founded in 1850 sells over 90% of its wine in France and exports to only a handful of countries (primarily Belgium, Switzerland, Germany, and the Netherlands). The wines are not exciting, but are competently made and straightforward, with the reds having more character and individuality than the whites. The red wines see 10% new oak, and are aged in small oak casks for 18–22 months. Both the Mercurey Blanc and the Bourgogne Aligoté see 10%

new oak and are bottled after 12 months. Filtration is kept to a minimum, and proprietor Georges-Claude Menand believes his wines are best when consumed within 5–6 years of the vintage.

DOMAINE MÉO-CAMUZET
(VOSNE-ROMANÉE)****–*****

> Wines Produced: Bourgogne Rouge, Clos Vougeot, Corton, Nuits St.-Georges, Nuits St.-Georges aux Boudots, Nuits St.-Georges aux Murgers, Richebourg, Vosne-Romanée, Vosne-Romanée aux Brûlées, Vosne-Romanée Les Charmes.

The elegant, gray-haired Jean Méo owns 27.17 acres of well-placed vineyards. Curiously, this estate sold its entire production in bulk to *négociants* prior to 1983, but has since estate-bottled its wines. They have enjoyed a rapidly growing reputation in France, no doubt because the brilliant Henri Jayer was brought in as a consultant. Jayer's techniques are in evidence—a 3- to 5-day prefermentation maceration, 100% new oak barrels, 100% destemming, a 15- to 20-day *cuvaison*, and aging of the wine for 18–24 months in cask prior to bottling. Against the advice of Jayer, Jean Méo for a time filtered the wine, but he discontinued this practice in 1988. This estate has some extremely old vines. The oldest, averaging about 30 years of age, are in his 4.98-acre parcel of Premier Cru Les Charmes in Vosne-Romanée. Méo's most important holding is his 7.5 acres of the fabulously situated vineyard on the upper slope of the Clos de Vougeot. This property, which was acquired in 1920, represents almost 6% of the entire surface area of this Grand Cru, and is considered to be one of the top three or four sites of the Clos de Vougeot. While some might argue that Méo's Clos Vougeot is his best wine, others feel his Richebourg, from a .86-acre parcel, and his fabulous Corton, from a 1.2-acre parcel in the Côte de Beaune, are even better. This is quite a serious domaine that made superb 1985s, somewhat variable 1986s, good 1987s, and magnificent 1988s. Most Méo-Camuzet wines can be drunk after 2–3 years in the bottle, but have the ability to age well for 10–12 years. I have found them to be very exotic, intensely aromatic, sumptuous red burgundies.

CHÂTEAU DE MERCEY (CHEILLY-LÈS-MARANGES)**

> Wines Produced: Bourgogne Aligoté, Bourgogne Hautes-Côtes de Beaune Blanc, Bourgogne Hautes-Côtes de Beaune Rouge, Mercurey Blanc, Mercurey Rouge, Santenay.

This is one of the most important Côte de Beaune-Villages domaines. It consists of 104.2 acres, which includes a significant vineyard in Bourgogne Hautes-Côtes de Beaune (56.81 acres). The wines tend to be a bit insipid and watery. Perhaps a tighter rein on the viticultural practices would result in lower yields and more concentrated wines. The red wines see 25% new oak and are bottled after 8–12 months. The white wines see the same amount of new oak and are bottled after 6 months. There is something to be said for bottling wines from these appellations early. The lack of flavor complexity can be accepted at the reasonable prices, but the lack of depth and shortness is a problem. This estate is managed by Jacques Berger, who claims there is entirely too much demand for the estate's production.

DOMAINE PRINCE FLORENT DE MÉRODE
(LADOIX-SERRIGNY)***

> Wines Produced: Aloxe-Corton Premier Cru, Corton Les Bressandes, Corton-Clos du Roi, Corton Les Maréchaudes, Corton Les Rénardes, Ladoix Les Chaillots, Pommard-Clos de la Platière.

There is a lot of history attached to this famous domaine, owned by the Mérode family since the mid-seventeenth century. The Domaine Prince Florent de Mérode somehow escaped the anger and destruction of the peasants during the French Revolution. The estate even sold wine to the powerful Ducs de Bourgogne. Today, it has an excellent reputation that is not always justified. The current domaine of 28.5 acres, large by Burgundy standards, consists of 7.9 acres in Ladoix, 9.33 acres in Pommard-Clos de la Platière, 3.83 acres in Corton Les Maréchaudes, 3 acres in Corton Les Bressandes, 1.7 acres in Aloxe-Corton, 1.43 acres in Corton-Clos du Roi, and 1.27 in Corton Les Rénardes.

The wines that emerge from these choice vineyards possess a very modern, clean, correct style with straightforward cherry fruit. They are also touched by vanilla scents from aging in 40% new oak barrels. The domaine believes in destemming at least 75% of incoming grape bunches, even in healthy years, and in a *cuvaison* of 7–10 days. The *cuvaison* seems a bit short and may account for the wines being somewhat light and less than profound on the palate. The wines used to be both fined and filtered prior to bottling, but in 1989, the policy of filtration was deemed harmful and therefore discontinued. Over the last decade, most of the wines have been ready to drink upon release and have shown little improvement after five or six years in the bottle. The 1978s, which are still drinkable, have neither improved nor declined after five years of age. The best wines usually are the Corton Les Bressandes, the Pommard-Clos de la Platière, and the Corton-Clos du Roi. This remains a well-known estate with high visibility in the export markets. However, its high standing seems suspicious in view of the quality of the wines produced.

DOMAINE MESTRE PÈRE ET FILS (SANTENAY)**–***

> Wines Produced: Aloxe-Corton,   Chassagne-Montrachet,   Chassagne-Montrachet Blanc, Chassagne-Montrachet Morgeot, Chassagne-Montrachet Rouge, Cheilly-Lès-Maranges, Corton, Ladoix, Ladoix Rouge, Morgeot, Santenay Beaurepaire, Santenay Blanc, Santenay la Comme, Santenay-Clos Faubard, Santenay-Clos de Tavannes, Santenay Les Gravières, Santenay Passe Temps.

This is a famous and highly regarded domaine in Santenay. The current generation of Mestres, Philippe, Gérard, Michel, and Gilbert is the fifth one to carry on the winemaking of this 44.63-acre domaine. The estate has some attractive Premiers Crus in Santenay, and some good parcels in Aloxe-Corton (especially a 1.23-acre parcel of Grand Cru Corton). The red wines tend to be very tannic, somewhat oxidized, and lacking freshness and charm. However, such criticism will draw a statement from the Mestres that they are not making Beaujolais, and that their wines all reflect their vineyards. Perhaps aging in cask for two or more years dries these wines out. Nevertheless, in vintages such as 1985 and 1988, the Mestres' Corton, their Premier Cru Santenay Les Gravières, and their Santenay la Comme are still impressive. In other vintages where the fruit is not in perfect condition, these wines are often too dry, and tend to reveal a great deal of brown at a shockingly early age. The white wines are often slightly musty as a result of the use of old barrels. The red wines see only 5% new oak, and are bottled after 24 months in cask. The white wines see 5% new oak and are bottled after

8 months. The Mestres sell over 50% of their production each year to *négociants* and estate-bottle the rest.

CHÂTEAU DE MEURSAULT (MEURSAULT)***–****

Wines Produced: Aloxe-Corton, Beaune Les Cent Vignes, Beaune Les Grèves, Bourgogne Blanc, Bourgogne Rouge, Meursault, Meursault-Château de Meursault, Pommard, Pommard Les Epenots, Savigny-Lès-Beaune, Savigny-Lès-Beaune Premier Cru, Volnay Clos des Chênes.

It is quite unusual to find magnificent châteaux in Burgundy, but the Château de Meursault is one of the most extraordinary buildings and properties in all of the Côte d'Or. Originally constructed in the fourteenth century, this impressive property and its cellars are one of the major tourist attractions in Burgundy. The current owner, André Boisseaux of Patriarche, the large *négociant* firm in Beaune, purchased this vast estate in 1973 from the Comte de Moucheron. While most people associate this château with its 22 acres of well-placed vineyards in Meursault, the estate also includes 54 acres of prestigious vineyards in the Côte de Beaune. For example, the Meursault, which is not listed as a Premier Cru, is made from a blend of grapes from four parcels—two are Meursault Villages parcels, the largest is a Premier Cru, Charmes, and the fourth is the top vineyard of Meursault, Les Perrières. The Charmes parcel is made up of 11 acres, whereas the Perrières parcel is 2.5 acres. The most significant red wineholding is in Savigny-Lès-Beaune and is followed by almost 9 acres in the Premier Cru vineyard Pommard Les Epenots.

The wines are made in a very modern style. Eighty percent of the white wine is fermented in stainless-steel tanks and the remaining 20% in new oak casks. The wine is then aged in 40% new oak casks from Allier, Nevers, and the Vosges Mountains. The wine stays in cask for 12–14 months, is racked once, and is bottled after a fining and a filtration. The production of Meursault has varied from just over 2,000 cases in 1983 to well over 4,500 cases in 1986. I've always preferred the white wine here, with certain vintages such as the 1981, 1983, 1985, and 1986 showing wonderful fruit, richness, and elegance. They're certainly as good as most of the top Premiers Crus made in Meursault. The white wines from top vintages should be drunk within 5–7 years. As for the red wines, they are also fermented in stainless-steel tanks and are then moved to oak barrels, a percentage of which are new. They have been generally sound and quite acceptable, but are too commercially correct for my taste. Nevertheless, they have their admirers. The red wines should be drunk within the first decade of the vintage, although vintages such as 1983 and 1988 will certainly last beyond 10 years.

DOMAINE BERNARD MEZIAT (CHIROUBLES)***

Wines Produced: Chiroubles.

This small estate of 14.82 acres is well respected in the appellation for its stylish, fragrant, delicate wine. Bottled after six months aging in tanks, it should be drunk within 2–3 years of the vintage.

DOMAINE BERNARD MICHEL (SAINT-VALLERIN)***

Wines Produced: Bourgogne Aligoté, Bourgogne Passe-Tout-Grains, Bourgogne Rouge, Montagny Les Coeres Premier Cru, Montagny Premier Cru.

The Domaine Bernard Michel is a very good estate that produces both red and white wine from its 21.8 acres of vineyards. Michel believes in 25% new oak for his reds and 10%–25% for his white wines. The wines have a good stony fruitiness. His best wine is his Montagny Les Coeres (1.23 acres).

DOMAINE LOUIS MICHEL (CHABLIS)****
DOMAINE DE LA TOUR VAUBOURG (CHABLIS)

Wines Produced: Chablis, Chablis Les Clos, Chablis Grenouilles, Chablis Montée de Tonnerre, Chablis Montmains, Chablis Les Vaillons, Chablis Vaudésir.

Louis Michel's 40-acre estate, which includes 34 acres of Premiers Crus and 6 acres of Grands Crus, produces what most observers would agree is the finest Chablis made with no oak aging. Some connoisseurs stridently argue that all Chablis must be aged in oak barrels and barrel fermented. Others claim the character of Chablis is best expressed when it never sees oak and is fermented and aged in stainless steel. Personally, I adore the barrel-fermented, lavishly rich, and oaky style of a René Dauvissat and François Raveneau, but I also enjoy and admire the Chablis of Louis Michel. His wines have an extraordinary amount of fruit and mineral-scented austerity that make them a delight to drink. The wines are fermented at cool temperatures in stainless-steel vats, and aged there for 6–9 months prior to bottling. Filtration is as light as possible and there is very little manipulation of the wine, as Michel believes the more man intervenes, the more the wine suffers.

Virtually any of the wines from Michel are well worth trying, although certainly the Grands Crus offer more intensity and flavor than the Premiers Crus. Among the Premiers Crus, one can hardly go wrong with the Montmains or Montée de Tonnerre. For commercial purposes, Michel also sells his wines under the Domaine de la Tour Vaubourg label. These wines keep surprisingly well, but I prefer them when they are young and crisp.

DOMAINE RENÉ MICHEL (CLESSÉ)****

Wines Produced: Mâcon-Villages.

This is a producer of excellent to outstanding Mâcon-Villages. The wine is made from extremely old vines planted in a 9.88-acre parcel at Clessé. Domaine René Michel makes intensely concentrated Chardonnay that has the potential to age well for 4–6 years, an unusual and rare quality for a Mâcon-Villages. Most of the production from this domaine is sold privately.

DOMAINE ALAIN MICHELOT
(NUITS ST.-GEORGES)****

Wines Produced: Nuits St.-Georges, Nuits St.-Georges Les Cailles, Nuits St.-Georges Les Chaignots, Nuits St.-Georges Les Champs Perdrix, Nuits St.-Georges Les Porrets St.-Georges, Nuits St.-Georges La Richemone, Nuits St.-Georges Les Vaucrains.

A large-framed man with red hair and a red beard, Alain Michelot looks as if he were an Irish wrestler rather than a French vigneron. He is one of the two or three finest growers and winemakers in Nuits St.-Georges. He has an impeccably run estate of 18.24 acres and his winemaking technique is similar to Henri Jayer's. He believes in a prefermentation cold maceration of the grape bunches, of which 80% are destemmed. This usually lasts for four to six days. Then there is a long, 3-week maceration of the grape skins with the juice, 16–20 months in oak barrels of which 50% are new, one racking, and a filtration prior to bottling. The wines tend to be gorgeously perfumed, pure, elegant, and precocious to taste. Michelot's best wines year in and year out are his

Les Champs Perdrix (since some of his oldest vines are here), as well as his Les Vaucrains and La Richemone. In 1989 his Nuits St.-Georges Les Porrets St.-Georges was replanted, and the vines are still relatively young. Michelot is not modest when judging his own wines, but he gives high marks to Robert Chevillon and the Machard de Gramont, two winemakers he admires greatly in Nuits St.-Georges. All of Michelot's wines are sold with corks branded with the vintage and vineyard, another sign of high quality. These are wines to drink within 7–8 years of the vintage.

DOMAINE JEAN MICHELOT (POMMARD) ***

Wines Produced: Bourgogne Hautes-Côtes de Beaune, Bourgogne Passe-Tout-Grains, Bourgogne Rouge, Meursault, Pommard.

Jean Michelot is now in his early fifties and has been making wine since the age of 15. His family has been in Pommard since the late 1600s. All of the Michelot domaine's 21.29 acres of vineyards are in Villages or generic wines. It is a shame they have never been able to obtain any Premier Cru vineyards, for a taste of a Michelot Pommard reveals the touch of a true winemaker. His 7.4 acres of Pommard turn out a wine that is stylish and elegant, yet always faithful to the robust richness and earthiness of a top-notch Pommard. Michelot believes in prolonging his *cuvaison* for two weeks or more, and keeps his red wines for 18–24 months in oak casks (one-third are new). Michelot's Meursault is often as good as many producer's Premiers Crus. He uses one-third new oak and bottles the wine after 12–18 months. This is a small but important domaine that produces elegant, stylish wines that should be consumed in the first 5–6 years of their youth.

DOMAINE MICHELOT-BUISSON (MEURSAULT) ****

Wines Produced: Bourgogne Blanc, Meursault, Meursault Les Charmes, Meursault-Clos St.-Felix, Meursault Les Genevrières, Meursault Le Limozin, Meursault Les Narvaux, Meursault Les Perrières, Meursault Les Tillets, Puligny-Montrachet.

Bernard Michelot, a diminutive yet remarkably energetic and dynamic man, runs this significant 49-acre domaine with Hollywood-like showmanship. A short, animated, ruddy-faced man, Michelot is a person who talks as fast as he thinks. A trip to his cellars is an unforgettable experience, as he takes tasters through all the different vineyards of Meursault. The vinification technique here stresses barrel fermentation, 25%–35% new oak barrels, 12 months in oak, and 12 months of lees contact. Finally, the wines are racked and given a light filtration prior to bottling. The results are wines that offer up sumptuous levels of buttery fruit and a healthy portion of toasty oak. In lighter years such as 1984 and 1981, the oak can get a little out of hand. But in years where the Chardonnay grapes are rich and ripe, as in 1985, 1986, and 1988, his mixture and winemaking techniques seem flawless.

Michelot makes a great deal of Meursault, and a visit here reinforces the image that he, not the vineyard, makes the wine. His best wines tend to be the Meursault Le Limozin, Meursault Les Narvaux, Meursault Les Charmes, and Meursault Les Genevrières. His Meursault Les Perrières should be his finest, but he had to tear up his tiny .5-acre parcel of Les Perrières in 1983, and the vines have not yet begun to produce wine of top quality.

If Michelot's wines have a weakness, it's the fact that they all should be drunk within 5–6 years of the vintage. Otherwise, they tend to lose their fruit, revealing a skeleton of oak, alcohol, and acid. Keeping that in mind, these are wines that offer sumptuous, full throttle, hazelnut, buttery flavors, and opulent textures that express Michelot's personality as much as they do Meursault's. They are rarely ever disappointing when drunk young.

DOMAINE M. MILLET (MONTAGNY)**

Wines Produced: Montagny Premier Cru Blanc.

This tiny estate in Montagny produces rather straightforward, cleanly made white wine. It should be consumed within several years of the vintage.

DOMAINE RAYMOND MILLOT ET FILS
(MEURSAULT)**

Wines Produced: Bourgogne Aligoté, Bourgogne Blanc, Bourgogne Passe-Tout-Grains, Bourgogne Rouge, Meursault Blanc, Meursault Les Gouttes d'Or, Meursault Rouge, Puligny-Montrachet.

Raymond Millot makes straightforward, competent, pleasant wines from his 14.96 acres of vineyards. The whites see 10% new oak and are bottled after 12–16 months in cask. Millot also produces small amounts of red wine, including an interesting but somewhat light Meursault Rouge. These are wines that should be drunk within the first 4–5 years of life.

DOMAINE PIERRE MILLOT-BATTAULT
(MEURSAULT)***

> Wines Produced: Beaune-Les Epenottes, Bourgogne Aligoté, Bourgogne Blanc, Bourgogne Passe-Tout-Grains, Bourgogne Rouge, Meursault, Meursault Les Charmes, Pommard Les Rugiens, Volnay Santenots.

Pierre Millot believes in robust, full-bodied white wines showing a lot of buttery, vanilla aromas of toasty oak. His wines are aged in 25%–35% new oak and are bottled after 12 months. His best wine is the fat, luscious Meursault Les Charmes, but he also makes small amounts of some good red wines, such as the Pommard Les Rugiens and Volnay Santenots. The red wines are aged in 50% new oak and are bottled after 15 months. Although not terribly well known, this is a very good estate that sells 25% of its production to *négociants*. The entire domaine consists of 18.94 acres, and the biggest parcels of Premier Cru vineyards are Millot's Meursault Les Charmes (2.8 acres), Meursault Villages (6.57 acres), and his Bourgogne Aligoté (1.97 acres). These are wines that will certainly keep well for up to a decade.

DOMAINE RENÉ ET CHRISTIAN MIOLANE
(SALLES-EN-BEAUJOLAIS)***

> Wines Produced: Beaujolais-Villages, Beaujolais-Villages Cuvée de la Cotabras.

This vineyard has existed for over 300 years, but was recently acquired by the Miolane family in 1977. Their Beaujolais-Villages is highly regarded for its ripe, raspberry, curranty fruitiness, and velvety texture. The estate consists of 38.2 acres and the best cuvée is the Cuvée de la Cotabras.

P. MISSEREY (NUITS ST.-GEORGES) ** — ***

> Wines Produced: Beaune, Bourgogne Hautes-Côtes de Nuits, Chab-
> lis, Côte de Beaune-Villages, Côte de Nuits-Vil-
> lages, Gevrey-Chambertin, Mercurey, Meursault,
> Nuits St.-Georges Les Cailles, Nuits St.-Georges-
> Clos de l'Arlot, Nuits St.-Georges-Clos des Forêts
> St.-Georges, Nuits St.-Georges Premier Cru,
> Nuits St.-Georges Les Vaucrains, Pouilly Fuissé,
> Santenay, Vosne-Romanée.

This *négociant* firm was founded in 1860 and has kept a relatively low
profile in Burgundy and the export markets. The firm specializes in
wines from Nuits St.-Georges, but as the above list demonstrates, it
purchases both grapes and wine from many appellations in Burgundy.
All the top red wines spend 12–15 months in oak casks of which one-
third are new. The wines are quite soundly made, but are rarely exceptional. In my experience, the best wines have been those from the Nuits
St.-Georges appellation. Most Misserey wines show good body and tannin, and in the top vintages can be cellared for at least a decade.

MOILLARD (NUITS ST.-GEORGES) *** — ****

> Domaine Wines Produced: Beaune Les Grèves, Bonnes Mares,
> Chambertin, Chambertin-Clos de Bèze,
> Clos Vougeot, Corton-Charlemagne,
> Corton-Clos du Roi, Echézeaux, Nuits
> St.-Georges-Clos des Grandes Vignes,
> Nuits St.-Georges-Clos de Torey, Nuits
> St.-Georges Les Murgers, Nuits St.-
> Georges Les Porets, Nuits St.-Georges
> La Richemone, Romanée St.-Vivant,
> Vosne-Romanée Les Beaux Monts,
> Vosne-Romanée Les Malconsorts.

Note: Moillard also produces an extensive line of wines under their
négociant label from the Côte de Nuits, Côte de Beaune, Chablis, Côte
du Rhône, Beaujolais, Mâconnais, and the Côte Chalonnaise.

This is an interesting firm to examine. Founded in 1850, Moillard is
not old by the standards of Burgundy, but is quite a large establishment
exporting to 45 countries. Moillard has a separate high-tech, modern
installation for the lower-level wines. In this facility, the wines see a

flash pasteurization, cold stabilization, and there are centrifuges and filter machines everywhere. This state-of-the-art winemaking technology produces technically perfect, often flavorless wines. Moillard uses a separate facility and employs much more traditional winemaking techniques for all their estate-bottled wines, as well as top Premiers Crus and Grands Crus made from purchased juice. In the 1980s the firm has experienced one of the greatest leaps in quality of any firm in Burgundy. The Thomas family who owns Moillard believes consumers like supple, round, velvety, dark-colored wines.

Despite some disappointing 1986s, this firm made excellent, often outstanding, 1985s, good 1987s, and excellent 1988s. Their white wines, made in a very full-bodied, lush, toasty style, are also recommended in top vintages where the fruit can stand up to the oaky style. There is no expense spared when it comes to new oak; the Grands Crus see 100% new oak and many of the Premiers Crus at least 40%–50%. I have found the best wines from Domaine Moillard to be their Bonnes Mares, Nuits St.-Georges La Richemone, Vosne-Romanée Les Beaux Monts, Vosne-Romanée Les Malconsorts, Corton-Clos du Roi, Romanée St.-Vivant, and Chambertin-Clos de Bèze. They also produce an excellent Echézeaux, Beaune Les Grèves, and Nuits St.-Georges-Clos de Torey (from their own vineyard). In most cases, the wines of Moillard can be drunk after 2–3 years in the bottle, and certainly demonstrate the ability to improve for 10–12 years.

DOMAINE DANIEL MOINE-HUDELOT
(CHAMBOLLE-MUSIGNY)***–****

> Wines Produced: Bonnes Mares, Chambolle-Musigny, Chambolle-Musigny Les Amoureuses, Chambolle-Musigny Premier Cru, Clos Vougeot, Musigny.

Daniel Moine makes very seductive, open-knit, richly fruity wines from some very well-placed vineyards in the Côte de Nuits. His best wines are the two Grands Crus of Chambolle-Musignys: Bonnes Mares and the Musigny. Moine uses two-thirds new oak barrels, and bottles his wine after 16 months of aging and a light filtration. The filtration is lamentably done by a mobile bottling firm that has on occasion eviscerated his wines (i.e., 1986 and 1987). These are wines that require drinking within 5–7 years of the vintage, although the Bonnes Mares and Musigny can last several years longer. The entire domaine covers only 17.3 acres, and his .34-acre parcel of Clos Vougeot is smaller than any other vineyard owner's. It is not one of the best situated either, as it is at the very bottom of the slope on the southern side of the Clos.

DOMAINE DE LA MONETTE (MERCUREY)★★★★

Wines Produced: Mercurey Rouge.

Paul-Jean Granger produces only one wine from his 24.4-acre estate. His Mercurey Rouge is often one of the wines to win the prestigious Tastevinage Award or the Chanteflute Award, given to the best wines of Mercurey. He uses 20%–25% new oak, ages his wine for 18–24 months in cask, and keeps fining and filtration to a minimum. The resulting wine, one of the best from the appellation of Mercurey Villages, is often bursting with blackcurrant and raspberry-scented fruit. It has a supple, silky texture, and a good finish. In vintages such as 1985, 1987, and 1988, it could easily be confused with a Côte de Beaune Premier Cru. This is a wine meant to be drunk within the first 5–6 years of the vintage.

DOMAINE MONGEARD-MUGNERET (VOSNE-ROMANÉE)★★★★–★★★★★

Wines Produced: Bourgogne Rouge, Clos Vougeot, Echézeaux, Fixin, Grands Echézeaux, Nuits St.-Georges Les Boudots, Richebourg, Savigny-Lès-Beaune Les Narbantons, Vosne-Romanée, Vosne-Romanée Les Suchots.

Jean Mongeard, a large, playful man with a wry smile, is a superb winemaker. He had been expanding his domaine over the last few years and it now totals 50 acres. While I was apprehensive about his ambitions, the quality of his wine has not slipped. This is clearly a source for excellent, sometimes stunning and exotic, red burgundy. At present, his estate includes 2.2 acres of Bourgogne Blanc, 5 acres of Bourgogne Rouge, 7.4 acres of Vosne-Romanée Villages, 3.7 acres of Vosne-Romanée Les Suchots, 2.5 acres of Fixin, 11.1 acres of Echézeaux, 4 acres of Grands Echézeaux, 1.4 acres of Nuits St.-Georges Les Boudots, 2.5 acres of Clos Vougeot, 1.25 acres of Vougeot, 3.75 acres of Savigny-Lès-Beaune, and less than one acre of Richebourg. Mongeard practices a 48-hour prefermentation cold maceration and vinifies all of his grape bunches (50% are destemmed in healthy years) in enamel-coated metal vats. He practices a relatively long *cuvaison* of 18–21 days, and puts his wines directly into oak barrels, of which 50% are new for the Premiers Crus and 100% new for the Grands Crus. The wines stay in oak for 20–24 months. They are fined lightly, and since

1978 have been given a minimal polishing filtration at bottling. The wines of Mongeard-Mugneret always seem to have a deep, dark ruby color, and are extremely fragrant and loaded with fruit. In the case of the Richebourg, Grands Echézeaux, Echézeaux, and Clos Vougeot, they seem to have an exotic bouquet that offers up plenty of smoky, bacon fat–scented, plummy fruit. These are lush, opulent wines with a great deal of personality and character. The Grands Crus certainly can last 10–12 years in the bottle, and the Premiers Crus, 5–7 years. Year in and year out Jean Mongeard's top wines tend to be his Grands Echézeaux, followed by his Clos Vougeot, Richebourg, Echézeaux, and Nuits St.-Georges Les Boudots. His best value is usually his Fixin, from that underrated appellation adjacent to Gevrey-Chambertin.

DOMAINE JEAN MONNIER ET FILS (MEURSAULT)****

Wines Produced: Beaune Les Montrevenots, Bourgogne Aligoté, Bourgogne Blanc, Bourgogne Rouge, Meursault, Meursalt Les Charmes, Meursault Les Genevrières, Pommard Les Argillières, Pommard Les Epenots-Clos de Cîteaux, Pommard Les Fremières, Puligny-Montrachet Corvées des Vignes.

The wines of this 39.34-acre estate are impeccably made by Jean and Jean-Claude Monnier. Unfortunately, they sell very little in the export markets, as the bulk of the production (70%) is sold either to restaurants in France or to private customers who buy directly from the domaine. This is certainly beneficial for the estate, but it is not a positive thing for lovers of fine white burgundy. Jean Monnier makes beautifully proportioned, elegant, stylish wines that are never overwhelming, but are pleasing in their precision and balance. Their Meursault Les Charmes (1.6 acres) is a textbook white burgundy, showing not only the lusciousness of the Charmes vineyard, but a wonderful hazelnut, ripe, and well-balanced palate. Even their lower level wines, such as their Bourgogne Blanc, are extremely well made and see some time in small oak casks.

The estate also owns the historic Pommard Les Epenots-Clos de Cîteaux (7.41 acres). This parcel was first planted in 1207 by the monks of Cîteaux, and was acquired by the Monniers in 1950. Today, they produce beautifully elegant wines that exhibit the spicy, earthy, *terroir* bouquet of a top-notch Pommard and an elegant, berry fruitiness that clearly defines the Jean Monnier style. They believe in 33% new oak for their red wines, and bottling after 18 months. They use between 25%–33% new oak for the white wines, and the bottling takes place

‌

after 10 months. The Monnier wines are cunningly delicious and supple young, but age (no doubt because of their superb balance) for up to 7–8 years. This is an estate whose wines I recommend with much enthusiasm.

DOMAINE RENÉ MONNIER (MEURSAULT)**–***

Wines Produced: Beaune Les Cent Vignes, Beaune Les Toussaints, Bourgogne Aligoté, Bourgogne Blanc, Bourgogne Rouge, Côte de Beaune-Villages, Meursault Les Charmes, Meursault Les Chevalières, Meursault Les Limozins, Pommard, Puligny-Montrachet, Puligny-Montrachet Les Folatières, Santenay, Volnay Clos des Chênes.

This has been a reliable and consistent producer of both white and red burgundy, although the whites are more interesting than the reds. I was disappointed by the 1987s and 1988s I tasted, and hope they do not signal a decline in quality. This is a large estate by Burgundy standards, totaling 44.26 acres. The Domaine René Monnier is jointly controlled by the Monnier family and an Englishman, Kenneth Ingleton, who oversees the running of the estate. Their best white wines include their Meursault Les Charmes (less fat and rich than many other Meursault-Charmes, but fruity and stylish), the Meursault Les Chevalières (at 7.41 acres, their biggest holding), and their sound Puligny-Montrachet Les Folatières and Meursault Les Limozins. The red wines from René Monnier tend to be light, but in ripe, rich vintages such as 1985, I have had good examples of the Volnay Clos des Chênes and Beaune Les Cent Vignes. The white wines are aged in 32% new oak casks for 7–12 months. The red wines see the same percentage of new oak but are bottled slightly later, after aging 16–18 months. Most of the wines from this firm seem to merit drinking at a young age.

DOMAINE JEAN-PIERRE MONNOT
(PULIGNY-MONTRACHET)****

Wines Produced: Bâtard-Montrachet,   Bienvenues-Bâtard-Montrachet, Puligny-Montrachet Les Folatières, Puligny-Montrachet Les Referts.

This 13.5-acre domaine is an excellent source of concentrated, intensely flavored white burgundy from the two grands Crus vineyards of

Bâtard-Montrachet and Bienvenues-Bâtard-Montrachet. Proprietor Jean-Pierre Monnot also makes small quantities of excellent white burgundy from Puligny-Montrachet Les Folatières and Puligny-Montrachet Les Referts. After Monnot has completed the malolactic fermentation, the wine is sold to the Beaune *négociant*, Louis Latour, where it is blended and sold under the name of this firm.

DOMAINE DE MONTBELLET (LUGNY)**

> Wines Produced: Mâcon-Villages.

The Baron Patrice de l'Épine produces very stylish, fruity, medium-bodied Mâcon-Villages wines from his 46.93-acre domaine (the Château de Mirande). The wines are aged for 9 months in large oak *foudres*. These are good, solid, simple Mâconnais wines that perhaps should be bottled a bit sooner to preserve some of their freshness.

CHÂTEAU DE MONTHÉLIE (MONTHÉLIE)***

> Wines Produced: Monthélie-Château de Monthélie, Rully, Rully Premier Cru Blanc.

For years, this 17.6-acre domaine of the Suremain family had some of the oldest vines in Burgundy. However, at present only 7.41 acres remain in old vines. The other parcels were replanted because of dwindling production attributed to the age of the vineyards. The wines are among the most formidable of Monthélie, and are imbued with a great deal of tannin, peppery spices, and a robust, muscular texture. Suremain uses 10% new oak, and bottles his wines after 18–24 months in cask. There is a small amount of Rully Premier Cru Blanc, which is quite well made and reasonably priced. To Suremain's credit, he ages it for about 12 months in oak casks. The best Monthélie is his Château de Monthélie Premier Cru made from an 11.1-acre parcel. Potential buyers should not rush judgment on this particular wine as it often needs 7–8 years in the bottle to shed its cloak of tannin.

DOMAINE MONTHÉLIE-DOUHAIRET (MONTHÉLIE)**–***

> Wines Produced: Monthélie, Monthélie-Premier Cru, Pommard Les Chanlins, Volnay Les Champans.

In 1988 I finally had a chance to meet Madame Douhairet, an enthusiastic and energetic octogenarian. She seems to be the unofficial spokesperson for the wines of Monthélie, but I must confess I found her remarkable exuberance and love of life more interesting than her wines. Diplomacy would lead me to say that these wines represent what red burgundy must have tasted like seventy or eighty years ago. There is a certain cheesy, musty quality to her wines that borders on being a flaw, but the big, deep flavors and gobs of tannin suggest that perhaps all of this will blow off and dissipate with 8–10 years of bottle age. These are full tilt, intense wines with plenty of tannin, and an odd-smelling type of oak that somewhat reminded me of damp, moldy chestnuts.

DOMAINE HUBERT DE MONTILLE (VOLNAY)****

> Wines Produced: Bourgogne Rouge, Pommard Les Epenots, Pommard Les Pezerolles, Pommard Les Rugiens, Volnay Champans, Volnay Mitan, Volnay Premier Cru, Volnay Taillepieds.

This impeccably run estate of 17.2 acres is the pride and joy of the Montille family. The current proprietor, Hubert de Montille, continues to practice law in Dijon, returning to the estate only on weekends. He is a winemaker's winemaker, and believes in letting the wine make itself. Consequently, he produces wines that need a good 4–5 years in the bottle before they begin to show their true breed. His best wines tend to be his Pommard Les Rugiens, Pommard Les Pezerolles, and Pommard Les Epenots, but I have found they need an additional 3–4 years more than other Pommards to reach maturity. They are often the least impressive wines when young. Hubert de Montille, a tough-looking man with closely cropped hair, ferments his wines with a high percentage of the stalks included, and allows the maceration to proceed for as long as 3–4 weeks. The wines spend 18 months in oak casks, of which 20%–35% are new. He never filters his wines, but he does believe in refining the tannins in the wine through a light egg-white fining. These are real *vin de garde* wines that can last 15–20 years. For example, his 1978s and 1980s are still not fully mature.

DOMAINE HENRI MORCONI
(PULIGNY-MONTRACHET)**–***

> Wines Produced: Bâtard-Montrachet, Bourgogne Aligoté, Bourgogne Blanc, Bourgogne Passe-Tout-Grains, Puligny-Montrachet Blanc, Puligny-Montrachet Les Perrières, Puligny-Montrachet Les Pucelles, Puligny-Montrachet Les Referts, Puligny-Montrachet Rouge.

Madame Jacqueline Jomain runs this domaine for the proprietor, Madame Henri Jacquin. Much of the production is sold to *négociants*, but the estate-bottled wine is distinguished by the excellent Puligny-Montrachet Les Pucelles (1.08 acres), and the Bâtard-Montrachet (a .79-acre parcel with vines planted in 1950). Mme Jomain uses 20% new oak and the wines are bottled after 12 months. The whites are occasionally heavy handed and oxidized, but the last few vintages have seen some excellent wines from the two aforementioned vineyards. These are wines to be drunk within their first 5–6 years of life.

DOMAINE BERNARD MOREAU
(CHASSAGNE-MONTRACHET)**

> Wines Produced: Bourgogne Aligoté, Bourgogne Rouge, Chassagne-Montrachet Blanc, Chassagne-Montrachet Les Chenevottes, Chassagne-Montrachet Les Grandes Ruchottes, Chassagne-Montrachet La Maltroye, Chassagne-Montrachet Morgeot, Chassagne-Montrachet Morgeot La Cardeuse, Chassagne-Montrachet Rouge, Saint-Aubin en Remilly.

I have had mixed results from the wines of this 18.37-acre domaine. Bernard Moreau uses 33% new oak and bottles his white wines after 12 months in cask. He utilizes 20% new oak and bottles his red wines after 16–18 months. The reds have always seemed overcropped and a bit light to me. As for the white wines, I have had far too many bottles that were a little musty and watery. However, on occasion I have seen excellent Chassagne-Montrachet Les Grandes Ruchottes and Chassagne-Montrachet La Maltroye. These probably would be the two Bernard Moreau wines to try should you run across them.

DOMAINE JEAN MOREAU (SANTENAY)**

> Wines Produced: Bourgogne Rouge, Côte de Beaune-Villages, Santenay Blanc, Santenay-Clos des Mouches, Santenay-Clos Rousseau, Santenay Rouge.

Jean Moreau produces very traditional wines from his 16.62 acres of vineyards. The red wines spend two or more years in cask, and the results are often not a success. The wines tend to be very tannic, robust, and do not always smell of totally clean, crisp fruit. Nevertheless, the *négociants* are big buyers, taking nearly two-thirds of whatever Moreau cannot sell. His best wine is the Santenay-Clos Rousseau, and there is also a decent Santenay Blanc made. As Jean Moreau laments, it is a shame so many people underestimate the white wines of this most southern village of the Côte d'Or. The name Domaine de la Buissière also appears on the label of Moreau's wines.

J. MOREAU ET FILS (CHABLIS)**–***

> Wines Produced: Chablis-Domaine de Biéville, Chablis Blanchot, Chablis Les Clos, Chablis-Clos des Hospices, Chablis-Domaine de Montée de Viviers, Chablis Les Vaillons, Chablis Valmur, Chablis Vaudésir.

Note: This firm also produces an entire range of wines as a *négociant*, including its most famous generic wine: Moreau Blanc.

In America, the best-known firm from the Chablis region is undoubtedly that of J. Moreau. This huge enterprise exploits 186.97 acres of vineyards in Chablis, and also sells wines under its name as a *négociant*. Additionally, there is the huge business of Moreau Blanc, a wine that is a blend of nonappellation French *vins de pays*. Many people think Moreau Blanc is a blend of declassified wines from the Chablis appellation or a production from younger vines, but in fact, it does not have a single drop of Chablis in it. The label's similarity to this firm's estate-bottled Chablis has added to the miscomprehension of this generic wine.

The firm itself was founded in 1814 and has a treasure trove of vineyards. They own 18.5 acres of the great Grand Cru vineyard called Les Clos, including the famous 5-acre parcel of Chablis-Clos des Hospices (formerly a parcel belonging to the hospital in Chablis), 5 acres of the Grand Cru Valmur, 2.5 acres of the Grand Cru Vaudésir, and 25 acres of the excellent Premier Cru Vaillons. The domaine wines are the product of a very modern approach to Chablis production. They are centrifuged when young, cold fermented, and kept in concrete and stainless-steel vats until the bottling takes place 6–8 months after the vintage. While many people criticize this huge enterprise for its wines' lack of individuality, the top wines from their Grand Cru vineyards are certainly good to very good, and capable of lasting for 5–7 years.

The wines that Moreau produces as a *négociant* and under its second labels (such as Alexandre de Ghislain, Philibert Ducard, Paul Vollereau, Les Petits Fils de Guenier, and Adolphe Hélie) often leave a great deal to be desired, and should usually be consumed within 2–3 years of the vintage. Nevertheless, no firm other than the huge cooperative, La Chablisienne, has more influence on the price of Chablis and the public's perception of its quality than J. Moreau et Fils. The company, now run by Jean-Jacques Moreau, was established in 1814 and is both the largest and oldest in Chablis. Fifty percent of the Moreau firm is now owned by the giant Canadian whiskey corporation, Hiram Walker.

DOMAINE BERNARD MOREY
(CHASSAGNE-MONTRACHET)****

> Wines Produced: Bâtard-Montrachet, Beaune Les Grèves, Chassagne-Montrachet Les Baudines, Chassagne-Montrachet Les Caillerets, Chassagne-Montrachet Les Embrazées, Chassagne-Montrachet Morgeot, Saint-Aubin, Santenay-Grand Clos Rousseau.

Bernard Morey, a scarlet-faced young man who sports the pompadour haircut popular in the late fifties, is one of my favorite growers. He has 21.6 acres of vineyards in Chassagne-Montrachet, and his wines, aged in 25% new Allier oak, are always lush, ripe, rich, hedonistic examples of white burgundy. He rarely had a failure in the eighties. Even his 1984s and 1987s were excellent. I would be happy to drink any wine from this domaine, but the three best wines are usually the exotic, opulent Les Embrazées, the more structured, ageworthy Les Caillerets, and the tiny quantities (less than 100 cases in most years) of Bâtard-Montrachet. Morey's wines should not be cellared for more than 7–8 years, but for drinking in their youth, they are hard to surpass.

DOMAINE JEAN-MARC MOREY
(CHASSAGNE-MONTRACHET)****

> Wines Produced: Beaune Les Grèves, Chassagne-Montrachet Blanc, Chassagne-Montrachet Les Caillerets, Chassagne-Montrachet Les Champs Gains, Chassagne-Montrachet Les Chaumées, Chassagne-Montrachet Rouge, Santenay-Grand Clos Rousseau, Saint-Aubin Les Charmois.

Jean-Marc, the brother of Bernard Morey, has a 13.04-acre estate, and produces white burgundies that are similar in style to those of his brother. They are ripe, lush, concentrated, full-bodied wines with a great deal of unctuous, buttery, and tropical Chardonnay fruit. His best whites are his Chassagne-Montrachet Les Chaumées, Chassagne-Montrachet Les Caillerets, and Chassagne-Montrachet Les Champs Gains. These are clearly wines to be drunk in their youth, while waiting for some of the more structured white burgundies from other producers to attain maturity.

DOMAINE MARC MOREY
(CHASSAGNE-MONTRACHET)***—****

> Wines Produced: Bâtard-Montrachet, Beaune, Chassagne-Montrachet Blanc, Chassagne-Montrachet Les Caillerets, Chassagne-Montrachet Les Chenevottes, Chassagne-Montrachet Rouge, Puligny-Montrachet Les Pucelles, Saint-Aubin Blanc.

Marc Morey is another member of the ubiquitous Morey family that has cellars throughout the village of Chassagne-Montrachet. Like the rest of the family, he produces very good, sometimes excellent white wines. However, I do not find them at quite the same quality level as the wines from Bernard Morey or Jean-Marc Morey. His best wines are his Bâtard-Montrachet (.2 acre) and Chassagne-Montrachet Les Caillerets. They are aged in one-third new oak for 15 months, and consequently show rich, spicy, smoky aromas. One of the best-kept secrets of this house is its fine Saint-Aubin Blanc. Morey makes a small amount of red wine, the best of which is his rustic, game-like Chassagne-Montrachet Rouge. This is a very good, sometimes excellent producer, particularly if you can find some of the splendid Bâtard-Montrachet. His wines are best if consumed within 4–6 years of the vintage.

DOMAINE PIERRE MOREY (MEURSAULT)****

> Wines Produced: Bâtard-Montrachet, Bourgogne Aligoté, Bour-
> gogne Blanc, Bourgogne Rouge, Meursault, Meur-
> salt Les Charmes, Meursalt Les Genevrières,
> Meursault Les Perrières, Meursault Rouge, Meur-
> sault Les Tessons, Monthélie Rouge, Montrachet,
> Pommard Les Epenots.

Pierre Morey's style of winemaking emphasizes power, muscle, and great depth and concentration. He makes stunning Meursault Les Per-rières, Genevrières, and Charmes, as well as a good village Meursault called Meursault Les Tessons. His Bâtard-Montrachet is one of the best of that appellation, and his Montrachet is excellent (from a .79-acre parcel) for those who can afford it. Morey uses 33% new oak, with higher percentages for his Grand Cru Montrachet and Bâtard-Mon-trachet, and bottles after 18 months. There is no filtration practiced unless the wines are not stable or clear. This is an estate whose wines are consistently superb, but they are not shy; they rely more on pure power and great concentration than on finesse or elegance. In 1989, Pierre Morey became the *régisseur* of the Domaine Leflaive, largely because many of his vineyard holdings, the result of the popular *mé-tayage* (or lease) arrangements, had terminated and reverted back to their owners.

DOMAINE ALBERT MOROT (BEAUNE)****

> Wines Produced: Beaune Les Bressandes, Beaune Les Cent Vignes,
> Beaune Les Grèves, Beaune Les Marconnets,
> Beaune Les Teurons, Beaune Les Toussaints, Sa-
> vigny-Lès-Beaune, Savigny Vergelesses-Clos la
> Bataillère.

This surprisingly unknown property, run with great enthusiasm by Ma-demoiselle Françoise Choppin, has 17.29 acres of vineyards. The aver-age age of the vineyards is well over 35 years, as this is an estate that believes in very old vines, small yields, and traditional vinification and élevage. In addition, the house of Albert Morot does business as a *négociant* under the Choppin label. This is a top-notch source for find-ing authentic Beaune wines from Premier Cru vineyards. The wines are all quite different, yet well made. I have often felt that a trip to visit Mademoiselle Choppin and taste her Premier Cru Beaunes is one of the best ways to get an education in the differences between the many Beaune vineyards.

The wines are made in a very traditional manner and the grapes are 100% destemmed. There is a fermentation in open wood vats, a lengthy *cuvaison* of three weeks, barrel aging of the wine for at least 14–20 months, and generally there is no filtration. If the wines do not fall brilliant, a light filtering is done. The percentage of new oak has been increased from zero to 33% for the 1986s, and 50% new oak for the 1987s and 1988s. The wines all have excellent richness and length, and are among the few authentic Beaune wines capable of lasting and improving in the bottle for 10–15 years. There have been some superb vintages here, including extraordinary 1971s and 1972s, excellent 1978s, some of the best 1979s made in the Côte de Beaune, gorgeous 1985s and 1987s, and spectacular 1988s. The Beaune Les Cent Vignes and Beaune Les Grèves tend to be more openly fruity and opulent than the Beaune Les Toussaints, Beaune Les Marconnets, and Beaune Les Teurons. The Beaune Les Bressandes is a transitional wine and is often the biggest and richest wine.

I can't applaud the quality of the wines at this estate enough, and they are generally sold at extremely reasonable prices.

DOMAINE DENIS MORTET (GEVREY-CHAMBERTIN)***

> Wines Produced: Bourgogne Rouge, Chambertin, Chambolle-Musigny aux Beaux Bruns, Clos Vougeot, Gevrey-Chambertin, Gevrey-Chambertin Champeaux, Gevrey-Chambertin-Clos Prieur.

Mortet, one of the young, up-and-coming stars from Gevrey-Chambertin, owns cellars that are located on the hillside above the village. Mortet's most famous wine, his Chambertin, is rarely his best. Insiders recognize that his two best wines are consistently the Gevrey-Chambertin Champeaux and Clos Vougeot. He recently added a very good Chambolle-Musigny aux Beaux Bruns to his portfolio. For whatever reason, Mortet's Chambertin is surprisingly light and thin (or *liquide*, as the French say) when compared to his other wines. Fifty percent new oak is used for all the wines, except for the Bourgogne Rouge. Mortet's style of wine emphasizes elegance, freshness, and softness, suggesting that these medium-bodied wines are potentially short lived. I would recommend drinking Mortet's wines before they turn 7–8 years old.

DOMAINE JEAN MORTET (ROMANÈCHE-THORINS)**

> Wines Produced: Beaujolais-Villages, Beaujolais-Villages-Clos de Romanèche, Moulin-à-Vent, Moulin-à-Vent Les Bois-Combes, Moulin-à-Vent Les Rouchaux.

The Domaine Jean Mortet is a good source for Moulin-à-Vent, but it is surpassed by at least a half-dozen other estates. The Moulin-à-Vent cuvées are aged in large oak *foudres* from 8 to 15 months, and the other wines are aged in cement vats for 6–7 months. The wines tend to be somewhat straightforward and chunky without much perfume and ripe velvety fruit.

DOMAINE MOSNIER (CHABLIS)**

> Wines Produced: Chablis, Chablis Premier Cru.

This small domaine, founded in 1978, makes straightforward, crisp, clean, yet relatively innocuous wines. Chablis produced here should be consumed within 4–5 years of the vintage.

CHÂTEAU DU MOULIN-À-VENT
(ROMANÈCHE-THORINS)****

> Wines Produced: Moulin-à-Vent.

Jean-Pierre Bloud is the current proprietor of this large, impressive estate with 74 acres of vines dedicated to producing Moulin-à-Vent. The wine sees 6–8 months of aging in oak casks, and the result is a large-scaled, muscular Moulin-à-Vent with plenty of power, alcohol, and depth. It usually needs 12–18 months after bottling to reveal its full character. For those who have the patience and don't mind laying down a Moulin-à-Vent for two or three years, this is a reliable choice.

DOMAINE GÉRARD MOUTON (PONCEY)***

> Wines Produced: Bourgogne Aligoté, Bourgogne Passe-Tout-Grains, Givry Blanc, Givry Rouge.

The Domaine Gérard Mouton is one of the best small estates of the Givry appellation. Founded in 1967, Gérard Mouton owns and runs this estate of 11.97 acres. Givry's best white wine and one of its top reds are made here. The white wine sees 25% new oak and is bottled after

8–12 months. The red wine sees the same percentage of new oak casks and is bottled after a full 12 months of aging. The wines are clean with a great deal of fruit complexity, and the earthy, spicy character associated with Givry. Mouton made excellent 1988s, good 1987s, and very fine 1985s. The only recent vintage I found lacking in character was the 1986.

DOMAINE GÉRARD ET RENÉ MUGNERET
(VOSNE-ROMANÉE)***

> Wines Produced: Bourgogne Rouge, Echézeaux, Gevrey-Chambertin, Nuits St.-Georges Les Boudots, Nuits St.-Georges Les Chaignots, Vosne-Romanée Les Suchots.

This 17.6-acre estate, tucked away on the back streets of Vosne-Romanée, produces solid, rustic, reliable red wines that are rarely complex. The best vineyards include the outstanding Premiers Crus of Nuits St.-Georges Les Boudots and Vosne-Romanée Les Suchots. Gérard and René Mugneret also own nearly 2 acres of the Grand Cru Echézeaux. The wines here see 25% new oak, and are bottled after 18 months in cask and a light filtration. In most cases they should be drunk within 7–8 years of the vintage.

DOMAINE MUGNERET-GIBOURG
(VOSNE-ROMANÉE)*****

> Wines Produced: Bourgogne Rouge, Chambolle-Musigny Les Feusselottes, Clos Vougeot, Echézeaux, Nuits St.-Georges Les Chaignots, Ruchottes-Chambertin, Vosne-Romanée.

The late Dr. Georges Mugneret was not only a man full of life but also a talented winemaker. When he died in late 1988, Burgundy lost one of its most articulate spokesmen and generous individuals. I usually try to maintain business relationships with producers, because blunt criticism is difficult once a friendship develops. Nevertheless, I found it hard not to like and respect Dr. Mugneret, and was profoundly touched by his death. He will be missed by everyone who ever came in contact with him, for he was a man who adored life. The estate is now run by his daughter, who was well trained by her father, and a niece. They continue to make wine in Mugneret's style. The domaine includes 21.6 acres with particularly superb vineyards in Ruchottes-Chambertin and

Echézeaux. They also have an extraordinarily well-placed parcel on the upper slope of Clos Vougeot. Mugneret fermented his wines at fairly warm temperatures, rarely destemmed more than 20% of the grapes, and macerated the wines for at least three weeks. While the use of new oak depended on the richness of the fruit and quality of the vintage, 50% new wood was used quite regularly for top vintages such as 1983, 1985, 1987, and 1988.

The Mugneret wines have the potential to age extremely well, and the Ruchottes-Chambertin, Clos Vougeot, and Echézeaux are easily capable of lasting 20–25 years in the bottle. In fact, bottles of the 1953s and 1966s drunk in the late eighties were spectacular in their well-focused, vibrant, intense fruit and grape complexity. This will continue to be one of the top domaines for finding high-quality burgundies, and if you see any of the spectacular 1985s or 1988s still on the marketplace, don't hesitate to buy them.

DOMAINE GUY MUGNIER-LA-P'TIOTE CAVE
(CHASSEY-LE CAMP)***

> Wines Produced: Bourgogne Passe-Tout-Grains, Bourgogne Rosé, Bourgogne Rouge, Chorey-Lès-Beaune, Mercurey-Champs Martin Blanc, Mercurey-Clos du Hays, Meursault Les Bouchères, Meursault Les Dressoles, Meursault Les Narvaux, Rully Les Chênes Blanc, Rully Montagne de Remenot Rouge.

Guy Mugnier is a wonderfully refreshing and disarming Burgundian. His answers to my questions were surprisingly honest. When asked about his 1988, his response was "it is still in cask, so I don't yet have a good feeling for its future." With respect to the 1987s he said, "certainly better than 1986," for 1986, "the wines lack balance and are too tannic, but no one else in the village will tell you that," and for 1985, "I made an excellent wine, as did most of my friends, but I don't believe the wine will meet my expectations after it has had a few years of aging, as I am concerned about its balance." There are very few winemakers who would be as critical of their wines as Monsieur Mugnier. He produces a bevy of wines from his 15.93 acres of vines, including some excellent Meursaults. He practices very traditional winemaking; both the white and red wines are aged in 20% new oak casks for 12 months. Mugnier still sells about 20% of his production to négociants, but is estate-bottling more and more of his wine. His best wines include his excellent Mercureys, both white and red, and his Rully Les Chênes

Blanc. However, none of these wines compared to his three Meursaults. The wines of Mugnier appear to have the potential to age well for 4–6 years. If you run into Guy Mugnier and he tells you that his 1986 Meursaults are "not bad at all," you should realize that he is a man gifted in the art of understatement.

DOMAINE GABRIEL MUSKOVAC (PERNAND-VERGELESSES)**

Wines Produced: Bourgogne Aligoté, Bourgogne Rouge, Corton-Charlemagne, Pernand-Vergelesses, Pernand-Vergelesses Blanc, Pernand-Vergelesses Premier Cru.

The most diplomatic thing I can say about this small estate of 7 acres is that the wines are correct and of standard quality. They lack complexity, seem compact, and are simply too straightforward to elicit much enthusiasm. The estate believes in 10% new oak for the red wines and in bottling after 16–18 months. The white wines receive 20% new oak and are bottled after one year.

DOMAINE ANDRÉ MUSSY (POMMARD)****

Wines Produced: Beaune-Les Epenottes, Beaune Les Montrevenots, Bourgogne Rouge, Pommard Les Epenots, Pommard Premier Cru, Volnay.

The ebullient André Mussy, a youthful 76 years old, has a cellar worthy of the most demanding connoisseur of Burgundy. His dynamic personality far exceeds his 5'6", thin frame, and makes a visit to his domaine mandatory. Mussy may look the part of the classic French winemaker —born, raised, and restricted to the vineyards—but his winemaking philosophy is one of great flexibility. He firmly believes in letting the vintage and the vineyard make the wine. Mussy says that if the grapes are "clean," he destems one-third of the bunches, but if there is some rot in the vineyards (as in 1983 and 1986), he destems completely. He keeps his production quite low by modern-day Burgundy standards. The wine spends 14–18 months in wood barrels of which only 10% are new. There is no filtration prior to bottling unless it is absolutely essential. M. Mussy's wines are often explosively ripe, rich, and rewarding both to drink and to cellar. It is remarkable how Monsieur Mussy can achieve such opulence in years when other producers sharing many of the same vineyards are turning out lean, hard, undernourished wines.

This is a cellar that routinely produces super wines regardless of the vintage conditions. Some of the best 1986s from the Côte de Beaune were from Mussy's cellar, and his 1987s and 1988s (particularly the 1988s) will be sensational. Mussy's wines drink extremely well young. They should be consumed within the first decade of life, although the Pommard Les Epenots has the potential to last longer.

PHILIPPE NADDEF (COUCHEY)***–****

Wines Produced: Bourgogne Rouge, Gevrey-Chambertin, Gevrey-Chambertin Cazetiers, Gevrey-Chambertin Champeaux, Marsannay Blanc, Marsannay Rouge, Mazis-Chambertin.

Philippe Naddef, a young, bushy-haired, bearded winemaker, has been making wine at his family's estate since 1983. He has already garnered a reputation as one of the best young growers/winemakers in Gevrey-Chambertin. The estate has only 11.25 acres and produces a range of 1,000–1,500 cases of wine, making Naddef's wines hard to find in the marketplace. He works from six different appellations. He produces a neutral white wine and a light, fruity red wine from Marsannay; to my taste, the red wine is better than his Bourgogne Rouge. In Gevrey-Chambertin his two best wines tend to be the Gevrey-Chambertin Les Cazetiers and the Mazis-Chambertin. The Mazis-Chambertin can be quite exquisite, as it is in 1985 and 1988, but his Cazetiers is frequently superior. Naddef destems all the grapes and ferments at a fairly high temperature of 33°C. All the wines from Gevrey-Chambertin spend 14–16 months in oak barrels, of which three-fourths are new. He has a lot of old vines in Gevrey-Chambertin (particularly in his Premiers Crus of Champeaux and Cazetiers), so the red wines have a good deal of flavor as well as elegance. His wines give every indication of lasting for 7–9 years. It is worth keeping an eye out for the wines of producer Philippe Naddef.

DOMAINE HENRI NAUDIN-FERRAND (MAGNY-LES-VILLERS)**

Wines Produced: Bourgogne Aligoté, Bourgogne Hautes-Côtes de Beaune Rouge, Bourgogne Hautes-Côtes de Nuits Blanc, Bourgogne Hautes-Côtes de Nuits Rouge, Bourgogne Passe-Tout-Grains, Côte de Nuits-Villages.

Henri Naudin makes straightforward red wines. His specialty is his fine Bourgogne Aligoté, which is sold at a very reasonable price considering its degree of flavor and character. It is one Bourgogne Aligoté that can be drunk on its own and is not marred by excessive acidity. The red wines from his 35.39-acre estate and his Bourgogne Aligoté are aged in small casks for 12–18 months. A few new oak barrels are used, but they are generally eschewed here.

DOMAINE NEWMAN (MOREY ST.-DENIS)**

Wines Produced: Bonnes Mares, Latricières-Chambertin, Mazis-Chambertin.

This tiny 3-acre domaine, owned by the Newman family of New Orleans, Louisiana, produces solid and uninspiring wines from its three Grand Cru vineyards. The vineyards are still young, so perhaps as they mature the concentration and depth of the wines will improve. The Bonnes Mares is the best wine in most vintages. It seems to have more depth than the Latricières-Chambertin (produced from very young wines) or the Mazis-Chambertin (which tends to be a rather tannic, harder-styled wine, lacking charm and grace). Domaine Newman wines are normally capable of aging and evolving in the bottle for 5–8 years.

DOMAINE MICHEL NIELLON (CHASSAGNE-MONTRACHET)*****

Wines Produced: Bâtard-Montrachet, Chassagne-Montrachet Les Chenevottes, Chassagne-Montrachet-Clos Saint-Jean, Chassagne-Montrachet La Maltroie, Chassagne-Montrachet Les Vergers, Chevalier-Montrachet.

Michel Niellon has only 10 acres of vines, but there is no doubting that his brilliant Chevalier-Montrachet, his awesome Bâtard-Montrachet (made from a parcel only .24 of an acre in size that was planted in 1927), and his Chassagne-Montrachet Les Vergers, are three extraordinary white burgundies. While one has to pay luxury prices for the honeyed richness of the Chevalier-Montrachet and the Bâtard-Montrachet, the Premier Cru Les Vergers is often nearly as good and sells at a fraction of the price. Niellon, a serious, handsome man, also makes tiny amounts of red wine from the Clos Saint-Jean vineyard, and tiny quantities of several other Chassagne-Montrachets such as La Maltroie and

Les Chenevottes. He ages his wine in less than 25% new Allier oak barrels, and keeps it in wood for only 12 months. The secret here is small yields and impeccable winemaking. This is one of the best small estates in Burgundy, but the wines are exceedingly difficult to find.

DOMAINE P. M. NINOT-CELLIER-MEIX-GUILLAUME (RULLY)***

Wines Produced: Mercurey Rouge, Mercurey Rouge La Crée, Rully-Grésigny Premier Cru Blanc.

While I have had bottles of this beautiful Rully-Grésigny Premier Cru Blanc with entirely too much sulphur in them, I have also had some marvelous ones. A very cold fermentation is done, followed by an *élevage* in 20%–30% new oak casks. In vintages such as 1985, 1986, and 1987, the resulting wine has plenty of power, richness, and an expansive bouquet and flavor. The red wines of the Ninot family are the products of manual harvesting, partial destemming, and a very traditional vinification in open wood vats. The wines are aged in 10%–20% new oak casks for 14–18 months before bottling. The best red wine is usually the Mercurey La Crée, the 1985 and 1987 vintages were delicious and capable of lasting for 5–7 years.

DOMAINE GILLES NOBLET (FUISSÉ)****

Wines Produced: Pouilly-Fuissé.

This superb small producer of Pouilly-Fuissé makes very concentrated, rich, powerful wines that can age well for 5–7 years. In many vintages, the wines of Gilles Noblet are nearly as good as those from the highly reputed domaine of Château Fuissé and those of Madame Ferret. However, Noblet's tiny estate consists of only 11.8 acres, and most of his wine is sold to private clients in France. He uses 20%–25% new oak and bottles after 6–7 months of cask aging. These are wines that show every indication of being able to age well for 5–7 years.

DOMAINE MICHEL NOËLLAT (VOSNE-ROMANÉE)***

Wines Produced: Chambolle-Musigny, Clos Vougeot, Nuits St.-Georges aux Boudots, Vosne-Romanée Les Beaux Monts, Vosne-Romanée Les Suchots.

Michel Noëllat runs this 25-acre estate with great enthusiasm. For years Noëllat sold most of the production to *négociants*, but in the last decade the trend has been to estate-bottle. The wines are traditionally made and capable of lasting for a decade. Noëllat's best wines are his rich, fragrant Vosne-Romanée Les Suchots, followed by the Vosne-Romanée Les Beaux Monts and Clos Vougeot. This could be a name to watch in the nineties.

DOMAINE ANDRÉ NUDANT ET FILS (LADOIX-SERRIGNY)***

> Wines Produced: Aloxe-Corton, Aloxe-Corton Premier Cru, Bourgogne Aligoté, Bourgogne Passe-Tout-Grains, Bourgogne Rouge, Chorey-Lès-Beaune, Corton Les Bressandes, Corton-Charlemagne, Ladoix Les Grechons, Ladoix Premier Cru, Ladoix Rouge.

The Domaine André Nudant et Fils sells much of its production directly to tourists travelling through the region, as its cellars are on the main road. The Nudant family owns an important domaine of 33.54 acres that produces wines from eleven different appellations. The holdings include 10.2 acres of Ladoix Rouge and a modestly sized 1.5-acre parcel of Corton Les Bressandes. Perhaps the best value is the Aloxe-Corton Premier Cru, nearly 2.4 acres in size, and the Chorey-Lès-Beaune. Monsieur Nudant, also reputed to be one of the better authorities on clones and vines, produces minuscule quantities of Corton-Charlemagne from a .37-acre parcel at the very top of the vineyard. The red wines are aged in 20% new oak and are bottled after 18 months, following a moderately intense filtration. The white wines see 25% new oak and are bottled after 8 months.

DOMAINE PARENT (POMMARD)***

> Wines Produced: Beaune-Les Boucherottes, Beaune-Les Epenottes, Bourgogne Rouge, Corton, Corton Les Rénardes, Côte de Beaune-Villages, Ladoix, Monthélic, Pommard, Pommard Le Clos Micault, Pommard Les Epenots, Pommard Les Rugiens.

At one time this historic domaine was the standard-bearer for the wines of Pommard. In fact, there is documentation that establishes that Domaine Parent provided wines for Thomas Jefferson. Today, there are

62 acres in production, including vineyards they have under lease. In the late sixties, I cut my teeth on many a Pommard Les Epenots and Rugiens from the wonderful 1964 and 1966 vintages. They were an introduction to Burgundy at its finest and Pommard at its best. Today, Jacques and François Parent make their wines in a monolithic style that offers plenty of color, body, and alcohol, but not a great deal of finesse or elegance. A tasting of 1985s, 1986s, and 1987s at their cellar revealed wines with very similar characters, and a lack of respect in the winemaking for the different *terroirs*, or vineyards of the grapes. Nevertheless, it is hard to be too critical about wines this tasty and heady. The top wines continue to be their substantially sized, alcoholic Pommard Les Epenots and Pommard Les Rugiens, but I do not think many consumers would be able to tell the difference between the two. In addition their Corton and Corton Les Rénardes are excellent, and for pure value, they make a sturdy, rustic, full-flavored Monthélie from 4.94 acres of vineyard. The other important holdings are 17.29 acres of Pommard Premiers Crus, 1.7 acres of both Corton and Corton Les Rénardes, and 5.9 acres of Beaune Premiers Crus. Most wines of the Domaine Parent can be drunk very young, but given their alcoholic content and size, they generally keep well for 8–10 years.

DOMAINE PARIGOT PÈRE ET FILS (MELOISEY)***

Wines Produced: Beaune-Les Epenottes, Beaune Les Grèves, Bourgogne Aligoté, Bourgogne Hautes-Côtes de Beaune Blanc, Bourgogne Hautes-Côtes de Beaune Rouge, Bourgogne Passe-Tout-Grains, Meursault Les Vireuils, Pommard, Pommard Les Charmots, Pommard Les Vignots.

This fine estate produces deliciously fruity, round, expansively flavored wines that reflect their appellation and are capable of aging for 5–7 years. I have had excellent success with Parigot's Beaune Les Grèves, Pommard Les Vignots, Pommard Les Charmots, and Beaune-Les Epenottes. Even their Bourgogne Hautes-Côtes de Beaune Rouge showed a surprising degree of fruit, character, and charm, well above the standard for the appellation. While the red wines are clearly the highlight of the Parigot portfolio, the Meursault Les Vireuils is delicious, and the Bourgogne Aligoté is sound. The estate consists of 26.62 acres. The red wines are aged in 25% new oak casks and bottled after 12–14 months. The Parigots clearly believe in putting their wines in the bottle while they are stil fresh, exuberant, and effusively fruity. The

Meursault sees 20% new oak and is bottled after 12 months. The Bourgogne Aligoté and Bourgogne Hautes-Côtes de Beaune Blanc see 1–2 months in new oak casks. They are then put in older oak and bottled after 8–10 months. Prices for the Parigot wines are quite modest considering the level of quality.

DOMAINE JEAN PASCAL ET FILS
(PULIGNY-MONTRACHET)**

Wines Produced: Bourgogne Blanc, Pommard, Puligny-Montrachet Blanc, Puligny-Montrachet Les Chalumaux, Puligny-Montrachet Les Champs Gains, Puligny-Montrachet Les Folatières, Puligny-Montrachet Hameau de Blagny, Puligny-Montrachet Rouge, Volnay, Volnay Les Caillerets.

Jean and Jean-Luc Pascal run this domaine of 21.24 acres. Over recent vintages (1985, 1986, 1987) I have found their wines to be somewhat dull and one-dimensional, with the exception of their Puligny-Montrachet Les Champs Gains and the Puligny-Montrachet Les Folatières. The wines are aged in 25%–33% new oak casks and bottled after 12 months. They simply lack complexity and character. and do not merit their high price tag. They should be drunk within the first 5–6 years of life.

PASQUIER-DESVIGNES (SAINT-LAGER)**

Wines Produced: An entire range of Beaujolais is produced by this large *négociant*. They do own 32 acres in the Beaujolais region that includes the Château de Fouilloux and Château de Corval.

The Pasquier-Desvignes family has been making wine since their family firm opened in 1420. As one of my colleagues has said, "with over 500 years of experience, one would think they would have learned how to make better wines." In any event, they have been successful, particularly with their well-known Beaujolais Le Marquisat. This wine comes in a bottle shaped like a Côte de Rhône bottle. Unfortunately, the wines are dull, too alcoholic, and rarely ever reflect their appellations of origin. This enterprise certainly has the money and the technical expertise to produce more interesting wine.

DOMAINE ALAIN PASSOT (CHIROUBLES)****

> Wines Produced: Chiroubles.

If one visits the cellars of Alain Passot in the spring following the vintage, chances are the only wine to be found will be the private collection of the Passot family. Passot's wines are so popular that the entire production is always reserved and sold out within six months of the harvest. It is extremely delicate, yet intensely fruity, light, wine, fascinating in its ability to please. Unfortunately, Passot owns only 14 acres of vines. His wine is bottled after 4–6 months of aging in oak *foudres*.

PATRIARCHE PÈRE ET FILS (BEAUNE)**

This gigantic operation in Burgundy has markets all over the world for its sparkling Burgundy (Kriter) and its range of *négociant* wines. These wines include most of the major vineyards and appellations of Burgundy. Patriarche does have some significant property holdings, including 98 acres of assorted vineyards in the Côte de Beaune and the extraordinary Château de Meursault. The Château de Mersault property consists of nearly 100 acres of vineyards, magnificent cellars, and a château. The proprietor and owner, Monsieur André Boisseaux, is an active buyer at the Hospices de Beaune sale. With few exceptions, he consistently buys the first lot. While the Château de Meursault wines and the estate-bottled wines from Patriarche are quite good, the *négociant* wines are bland and one-dimensional. However, there is no doubting the huge commercial success of Patriarche as bus loads of tourists wait in line to taste at their impressive cellars in Beaune.

BARON PATRICK (CHABLIS)**–***

> Wines Produced: This *négociant* firm produces various wines under both Chablis Premier Cru and Chablis Grand Cru appellations. Depending on the vintage and what is purchased, the range of wines varies according to the vintage. Also see A. Régnard et Fils.

This firm was started in 1979 by Baron Patrick de Ladoucette, the Loire Valley's most famous personality, and one of the great white wine specialists of Pouilly-Fumé, Sancerre, and Vouvray. Ladoucette attempted to purchase land in Chablis, but was blocked by local growers. Therefore, he operates as a *négociant*, purchasing wine from the growers and bottling at his firm in Chablis. The wines are clearly the product of modern-day style, as they are fresh, lively, generally well made, but lacking great individuality. They show good stony fruitiness and crisp, zesty acidity. They do not yet appear to be of the same quality level that Ladoucette aspires to in Pouilly-Fumé and Sancerre.

DOMAINE PAVELOT (PERNAND-VERGELESSES)**

Wines Produced: Bourgogne Aligoté, Corton, Corton-Charlemagne, Pernand-Vergelesses Blanc, Pernand-Vergelesses Encaradeux, Pernand-Vergelesses Les Fichots, Pernand-Vergelesses Île des Vergelesses, Pernand-Vergelesses Rouge, Pernand-Vergelesses Les Vergelesses.

Régis Pavelot, the proprietor, produces standard unexciting wines from his 15.48 acres of vineyards. The red wines tend to be spicy, straightforward, and simple, and the white wines a little lean and undernourished. Certainly he has some impressive holdings, including 1.45 acres of Corton-Charlemagne, but perhaps the production is too excessive to render wines that merit interest.

DOMAINE PAVELOT-GLANTENAY (SAVIGNY-LÈS-BEAUNE)***

Wines Produced: Bourgogne Aligoté, Pernand-Vergelesses Les Vergelesses, Savigny-Lès-Beaune Blanc, Savigny-Lès-Beaune Les Dominodes, Savigny-Lès-Beaune Les Guettes, Savigny-Lès-Beaune Les Narbantons, Savigny-Lès-Beaune Les Peuillets, Savigny-Lès-Beaune Rouge.

Jean-Marc Pavelot runs this 23-acre estate that includes some excellent Premiers Crus in Savigny-Lès-Beaune. The wines have a good deal of charm, a lovely cherry and strawberry fruitiness, and a healthy percentage of old vines (in vineyards such as Les Guettes and Les Dominodes). For years a good one-third of Pavelot's production was sold to Beaune *négociants*, but most of the wine is estate-bottled today. The wines are kept in 10%–20% new oak (the percentage is increased for the Les Dominodes), and bottled after 12–15 months. There is little or no filtration done here, as Jean-Marc Pavelot is afraid to strip the wines of their intrinsic character and quality. This is a serious domaine that makes good, intense, harmonious burgundies that can age for 7–8 years. The reds appear superior to the whites.

DOMAINE PAVILLON DE CHAVANNES (QUINCIÉ)**

Wines Produced: Côte de Brouilly.

This estate of 29.64 acres produces stylish, modern-styled, fruity, clean, correct Côte de Brouilly. Perhaps there is too much emphasis on technology and cleanliness, as the wines often lack a bit of individuality and character. They are bottled after four months aging in vats and should be consumed within 2–3 years of the vintage.

DOMAINE JOSEPH PELLERIN
(SAINT-GEORGES DE RENEINS)**–***

Wines Produced: This domaine makes an entire range of Beaujolais, but their most important wine is the Juliénas-Château des Capitans and the Fleurie-Clos des Moriers.

This old-line firm located outside of Lyon was founded in 1912. It produces average-quality, straightforward Beaujolais from all the different villages. The two best wines mentioned above can compete with the very best made in the region. It is a shame that the other wines are not of the same quality as the Juliénas-Château des Capitans and the Fleurie-Clos des Moriers.

DOMAINE ANDRÉ PELLETIER (JULIÉNAS)***

Wines Produced: Juliénas.

This is a top-quality producer making sturdy, ageworthy (no more than 4–5 years would be considered prudent bottle age), rather full-bodied, powerful Julienas.

DOMAINE DES PERDRIX (PRÉMEAUX-PRISSEY)***

Wines Produced: Bourgogne Rouge, Echézeaux, Nuits St.-Georges, Nuits St.-Georges-Clos du Bois Picot (both red and white), Nuits St.-Georges Les Perdrix, Vosne-Romanée.

Bernard Mugneret runs this good, solid, consistent estate. Its cellars are located just south of the village of Nuits St.-Georges in Prémeaux-Prissey. The percentage of new oak varies from one-third to two-thirds, with the Grand Cru Echézeaux getting the highest percentage. The wines rest in casks for up to 14–16 months, and then receives a light filtration prior to bottling. Mugneret also makes a tiny quantity of white wine, but it is rarely seen in the marketplace. Mugneret's largest holding is his 8.64 acres of Nuits St.-Georges Les Perdrix. The wines tend to need 1–2 years to round out as they often have a good deal of tannin. However, they are capable of lasting 7–8 years. While they are never spectacularly complex or profound, they are consistently good and satisfying.

DOMAINE PERNIN-ROSSIN (VOSNE-ROMANÉE)****

Wines Produced: Clos de la Roche, Morey St.-Denis Les Mont Luisants, Nuits St.-Georges, Nuits St.-Georges La Richemone, Vosne-Romanée, Vosne-Romanée Les Beaux Monts, Vosne-Romanée Les Reignots.

This minuscule domaine of 15.6 acres spread over the Côte de Nuits has a cult following in France. Its wines are produced from very old vines, tiny yields, and a long maceration of at least 21–30 days. In addition, André Pernin, the diminutive producer, increases his following by proudly announcing on his bottles that his wine is nonfiltered. Pernin is a disciple of the Lebanese oenologist, Guy Accad, and believes in at least one week of cold maceration of the grape bunches prior to the fermentation. The working conditions in the tiny garage attached to his home are deplorable, but the quality, the sensational color, and the fabulous perfume of his wines, such as his Morey St.-Denis Les Mont Luisants (he makes a whopping total of 25 cases a year), and his Nuits St.-Georges La Richemone present strong arguments in favor of his winemaking practices. Interestingly, one of the great Nuits St.-Georges La Richemone bottled and sold by the famous Madame Lalou Bize-Leroy (the 1985) was made from André Pernin's wine.

Pernin is not without his critics. They claim his wines lack stability, and disturbingly lose their color within 3–4 years of the vintage. Such charges merit çaution. I remember vividly how his 1982s and 1983s collapsed after several years in the bottle. The 1987s and 1988s made by Pernin looked sensational, so it will be interesting to see how they evolve.

DOMAINE PAUL PERNOT
(PULIGNY-MONTRACHET)****

> Wines Produced: Bâtard-Montrachet, Beaune, Beaune Les Teurons, Bienvenues-Bâtard-Montrachet, Meursault-Blagny, Puligny-Montrachet, Puligny-Montrachet Les Chalumeaux, Puligny-Montrachet-Clos de la Garenne, Puligny-Montrachet Les Folatières, Puligny-Montrachet Les Pucelles, Santenay.

The Domaine Pernot makes some exquisite white wines, especially their Puligny-Montrachet Les Folatières, Puligny-Montrachet Les Pucelles, Bienvenues-Bâtard-Montrachet, and Bâtard-Montrachet. However, few people are aware of just how stunning these wines can be. The estate has 29.64 acres spread out over a number of different appellations, and sells three-fourths of its wine to *négociants* in Beaune. The Domaine Pernot's philosophy of keeping its vineyard yields modest, barrel fermenting the top wines, and giving them at least 14–15 months in a hefty percentage of new oak barrels before bottling has resulted in some marvelous examples of white burgundy (such as 1985 and 1986). Paul Pernot and his two sons, who are in their mid-twenties, make a highly competent team. I would like to see more of their wines in the export market and fewer sold off to *négociants* to be blended with other white burgundies. Although my experience has been limited to the 1985, 1986, 1987, and 1988 vintages, the top Premiers Crus and Grands Crus from the Domaine Paul Pernot give every sign of aging for at least a decade in vintages such as 1985 and 1986. Their 1986 Bâtard-Montrachet was one of the greatest white burgundies I have ever tasted.

DOMAINE LES PERRIÈRES
(GEVREY-CHAMBERTIN)***–****

> Wines Produced: Bourgogne Rouge, Gevrey-Chambertin, Gevrey-Chambertin Petite Chapelle.

It is a shame that this small 12.4-acre estate is not better known, as its wines are consistently good to very good. Before taking over the winemaking in 1979, Proprietor François Perrot studied at the Lycée Viticole in Beaune. Perrot only produces three wines, and most of the production is in a muscular and meaty Villages Gevrey-Chambertin. This wine's bouquet of new leather and ground beef is very typical of a good Gevrey-Chambertin. The estate's best wine is its Premier Cru

Petite Chapelle, made from a 2.77-acre parcel. The 1978 and 1980 vintages of this particular wine were still drinking beautifully in 1989. The wines of the Domaine Les Perrières spend 12–18 months in oak barrels, and receive a light filtration prior to bottling. Most vintages of the Premier Cru can age nicely for 8–12 years, but the Bourgogne Rouge and Gevrey-Chambertin should be drunk within their first 5–6 years of life. This is an underrated source of fine wine.

DOMAINE NOËL PERRIN (CULLES-LES-ROCHES)**

Wines Produced: Bourgogne Blanc, Bourgogne Rouge-Clos des Chenoves, Clos des Chenoves, Mâcon-Supérieur Rouge (Gamay).

Half the production from this small domaine of 12.4 acres is sold to Moillard, the famous producer, vigneron, and *négociant* in Nuits St.-Georges. The rest is estate-bottled. The resulting wines are straightforward, correct, and fruity, and must be drunk early. They show a healthy dosage of new oak casks, as Perrin believes in 25% new oak and bottling both the red and white wines after 12 months of aging.

DOMAINE PERRIN-PONSOT (MEURSAULT)***

Wines Produced: Bourgogne, Bourgogne Aligoté, Bourgogne Rouge, Meursault, Meursault Les Charmes, Meursault Les Perrières, Pommard, Volnay, Volnay Santenots.

This small domaine of 15.7 acres produces two top-quality white wines: its Meursault Les Perrières and Meursault Les Charmes. The other wines are not as interesting and receive less attention. The white wines see 10% new oak and are bottled after 12 months. The red wines receive the same amount of new oak but stay in cask for 18 months. This domaine has a somewhat spotty performance record, but their top two wines, Meursault Les Perrières and Meursault Les Charmes, are rarely disappointing. Recent vintages indicate they should be drunk within their first 5–6 years of life.

DOMAINE HENRI PERROT-MINOT
(MOREY ST.-DENIS)**–***

> Wines Produced: Chambolle-Musigny, Chambolle-Musigny Premier
> Cru, Charmes-Chambertin, Gevrey-Chambertin,
> Morey St.-Denis La Riotte, Morey St.-Denis en La
> Rue de Vergy.

In the better vintages, Henri Perrot produces good wines from his 17-acre domaine. In troublesome years such as 1986, 1984, and 1982 there are domaines better managed and equipped to deal with problems of less than perfect vintages. Henri Perrot owns only one Grand Cru—a 3.7-acre parcel of Charmes-Chambertin, but he has some attractive Premiers Crus in Morey St.-Denis and Chambolle-Musigny. His wines spend 15–24 months in oak casks, of which 20% are new. He uses a higher percentage for the Charmes-Chambertin. Most wines from this estate should be drunk within 4–6 years of the vintage.

DOMAINE ANDRÉ PHILIPPON (FLEYS)****

> Wines Produced: Chablis, Chablis Mont de Milieu.

It is unfortunate that André Philippon only has 14.82 acres of vines, and that he sells half of his crop to local *négociants*. This is a serious proprietor who has an excellent 9.88-acre parcel of the Premier Cru Mont de Milieu, as well as 5 acres in Chablis Villages. He comes from a family of vignerons, and has a modern, intelligent, and flexible approach to making Chablis. He believes in cleanliness and therefore ferments his Chablis in stainless-steel vats. He feels the wine is enhanced by spending 7–8 months in oak casks, of which a small percentage is new. He practices minimal clarification and no cold stabilization other than that caused by winter's chill. The results are wines that exhibit a wonderfully steely, mineral, crisp fruitiness, and good flavor definition, depth, and complexity, qualities rarely found in most of the modern-day, commercially made Chablis. Little of Philippon's wine is seen in the export markets, as his entire estate-bottled production is sold directly to private clients in Europe.

PIAT PÈRE ET FILS (LA CHAPELLE DE GUICHAY)**

> Wines Produced: An entire range of purchased wine, primarily from
> the Beaujolais and Mâconnais regions, is produced
> at Piat.

This huge enterprise, founded in 1849 and now owned by International Distillers and Vintners, produces an enormous quantity (1.2 million cases) of straightforward, standard quality Beaujolais and Mâconnais wines. The one distinguishing feature of these wines is their bottle: a special Piat bottle, which is based on the traditional 50 centiliter Beaujolais *pot*. The Piat wines seem compact, clipped, and relatively devoid of character. It is hard to find much enthusiasm for them, although they are consistent and correct.

DOMAINE DES PIERRES BLANCHES (BEAUNE)***

Wines Produced: Aloxe-Corton, Côte de Beaune Blanc, Côte de Beaune Rouge.

This domaine, established in 1950, produces straightforward and supple wine with a good deal of fruit and spicy oak. They are not complex, yet I have always found them satisfying and reasonably priced. The top wines are their excellent Côte de Beaune Rouge and Aloxe-Corton. They are aged for 12 months in 33% new oak casks and are bottled without any filtration. Very little of this producer's wines is exported, as 70% of their production is sold in France.

DOMAINE DES PIERRES ROUGES (CHASSELAS)***

Wines Produced: Beaujolais, Mâcon-Fuissé Blanc, Pouilly-Fuissé, Saint-Véran.

Although I have never tasted their Beaujolais, this estate is well known for its richly fruity supple, floral-scented Saint-Véran. The Saint-Véran comprises over half of the 28.97-acre estate's production. Robert Marcel, the proprietor, ages this wine for six months in large vats prior to bottling. It is a wine that must be drunk within the first 2–3 years of life.

CHÂTEAU DE PIERREUX (ODENAS)**

Wines Produced: Brouilly.

The wines from this important 79-acre estate are kept in oak *foudres* for 6–8 months and then bottled. The quality of the wines is somewhat inconsistent, but in good years, such as 1985 and 1988, they exhibit a good raspberry and banana fruitiness, fine balance, and the ability to age well for 2–3 years.

DOMAINE DES PILLETS (VILLIÉ-MORGON)***

> Wines Produced: Morgon.

The Brisson family runs this large estate of 85.45 acres. The wines tend to be ripe, loaded with fruit, and delicious if drunk within 3–4 years of the vintage. They are among the more alcoholic wines of the appellation, often reaching 13%–13.5%. The firm employs a percentage of new oak. While this practice is unusual in Beaujolais, most of the wine is still aged in large oak *foudres* for 6–8 months prior to bottling. This is top-quality Morgon that is rarely ever disappointing.

DOMAINE FERNAND PILLOT
(CHASSAGNE-MONTRACHET)**

> Wines Produced: Chassagne-Montrachet Blanc, Chassagne-Montrachet Les Caillerets, Chassagne-Montrachet Morgeot Blanc, Chassagne-Montrachet Les Grandes Ruchottes, Chassagne-Montrachet Morgeot Rouge, Chassagne-Montrachet Rouge.

At one time this 19.73-acre estate was jointly run by two brothers, Jean and Fernand Pillot. Today, Fernand makes wine under his own name. Ten percent new oak is used and the wines are bottled after 15 months. Although less intense and complex than those of Paul Pillot, they are good, straightforward, commercial white burgundies that should be drunk within their first 5–6 years of life. The red wines tend to be light and lack character and charm.

DOMAINE PAUL PILLOT
(CHASSAGNE-MONTRACHET)***

> Wines Produced: Bourgogne Aligoté, Bourgogne Rouge, Chassagne-Montrachet Blanc, Chassagne-Montrachet Les Caillerets, Chassagne-Montrachet-Clos St.-Jean, Chassagne-Montrachet Les Grandes Ruchottes, Chassagne-Montrachet La Romanée, Chassagne-Montrachet Rouge.

At last count there were three separate Pillots, all related, in Chassagne-Montrachet. This 24.2-acre domain, run by Paul Pillot, produces the best wine of any of the Pillot family estates. The white wines see 25% new oak and are bottled after 12–16 months. There is very little racking and extended lees contact. The resulting wines are full bodied, lush, rich in fruit, and very ageworthy. The top wines include a beautiful Chassagne-Montrachet La Romanée, Chassagne-Montrachet Les Caillerets, and Chassagne-Montrachet Les Grandes Ruchottes. The red wines are a bit more patchy, but I have had delicious bottles of the Chassagne-Montrachet-Clos St.-Jean Rouge in 1985, 1982, and 1978. Twenty-five percent new oak is used for the red wines and bottling takes place after 18 months.

LOUIS PINSON (CHABLIS)***

Wines Produced: Chablis Les Clos, Chablis Les Forêts, Chablis Montmains, Chablis Montée de Tonnerre.

The Pinsons, some of the friendliest growers in Chablis, have been around for a long time. They make very traditional, ageworthy wines that are fermented in tanks and then aged 6–12 months in old oak barrels. The wines lack the dazzling personalities of Dauvissat or Raveneau Chablis, but are consistently very good, and can age well for 7–8 years.

DOMAINE PITOISET-URENA (MEURSAULT)****

Wines Produced: Bourgogne Blanc, Meursault Les Genevrières, Meursault Les Pellans, Meursault Le Poruzot, Puligny-Montrachet Les Chalumeaux.

This tiny estate, tucked away on the back streets of Meursault, consists of only 7.41 acres, but the quality of its wines ranges from very good to superb. Both Marie-Louis Urena and Georges Pitoiset look after the tiny estate-bottled production. All the white wines, from their good Bourgogne Blanc to their superb Meursault Les Genevrières (the estate's best wine), possess tremendous richness, elegance, and an intense perfumed character. They use 15% new oak and bottle their whites, with very little clarification, after 12 months of cask aging. I have not drunk any old vintages, so I do not have firsthand knowledge of how these wines evolve, but they should last for 5–7 years.

CHÂTEAU DE PIZAY (SAINT-JEAN-D'ARDIÈRES)***

Wines Produced: Beaujolais Blanc, Beaujolais Rosé, Beaujolais Rouge, Morgon.

This is a very important estate of 72.8 acres known primarily for its delicious Morgon. This wine is aged in one-third new oak casks. The estate also produces tiny quantities of zesty Beaujolais Blanc made from the Chardonnay grape, and a rosé, one of Beaujolais' rarest wines. The quality here is very good.

DOMAINE JEAN PODOR (IRANCY)***

> Wines Produced: Bourgogne Irancy Les Mazelot, Bourgogne Irancy Rosé, Bourgogne Irancy Rouge, Bourgogne Palotte Rouge.

Jean Podor owns the finest vineyard in all of Irancy, Les Mazelot. The wines from this vineyard have surprising depth and richness. However, his entire production is sold locally, and so little of this wine can be found in the export market. His red wines are kept 12–18 months in oak casks of which a small percentage, 10%–20%, are new. He owns only 7.78 acres, and his red wine is probably the best of the appellation. His stylish rosé is also to be recommended.

CHÂTEAU DE POMMARD (POMMARD)***

> Wines Produced: Pommard.

This impressive château and enclosed vineyard of nearly 50 acres is one of the major tourist attractions of Burgundy. Dr. Louis Laplanche, a famous professor at the Sorbonne, passionately runs the estate. The wine is aged in 100% new oak casks for nearly two years, and is then placed in specially designed, heavy, expensive bottles. Although the location of this enclosed vineyard is nothing more than Pommard "Villages," Laplanche's meticulous attention to detail results in a chunky, long-lived, deeply colored, firm, and tannic wine that can last 15 or more years. The two best recent vintages have been the 1985 and 1988. This impeccably maintained property and cellar are well worth a visit. Founded in 1726, it is one of the few châteaux in Burgundy.

DOMAINE PONSOT (MOREY ST.-DENIS)****-*****

> Wines Produced: Chambertin, Chambolle-Musigny Les Charmes, Chapelle-Chambertin, Clos de la Roche, Clos de la Roche-Vieilles Vignes, Clos St.-Denis, Griotte-Chambertin, Latricières-Chambertin, Morey St.-Denis Monts Luisants.

The Ponsot Domaine has been estate-bottling wine for over 50 years. The founder, Hippolyte Ponsot, was succeeded by his very popular and gifted son, Jean-Marie, who has been the mayor of Morey St.-Denis for a number of years. Jean-Marie's son, Laurent, now has control of this 25-acre estate. The average yields of the 35-year-old vines are, along with those of the Domaine de la Romanée-Conti and Domaine Leroy, the smallest in Burgundy. Everything here is done quite traditionally. The vinification takes place in old wooden vats and the maceration period lasts at least three weeks. There is no destemming when the grapes are healthy, but in years where rot is a problem, 100% destemming occurs. The wines are then placed directly into oak barrels and kept there for up to two years. The Ponsots abhor new oak. The wines are fined with egg whites, but are never filtered prior to bottling. Additionally, no sulphur dioxide is ever used in the winemaking.

The Domaine Ponsot, which was one of the earliest estates in Burgundy to domaine-bottle its wines (in 1934), has built a remarkable reputation for the extraordinary quality of its top wines such as the Clos de la Roche, Griotte-Chambertin, Clos St.-Denis, Chambertin, and Latricières-Chambertin. In fact, some of the greatest red burgundies I have ever drunk were the 1947s, 1949s, 1972s, 1978s, 1980s, 1983s, and 1985s from the Ponsot estate. The wines have a breadth, flavor, and depth that is simply extraordinary. While I am very fond of Ponsot's wines, the estate does have a disturbing tendency to produce poor wines in years with large yields, such as 1982, 1984, and 1986. All three of these vintages produced wines at Ponsot that lacked color, and, surprisingly, revealed amber/orange rims at a very young age. Nevertheless, this can be a source for some of the most remarkable wines in all of Burgundy. Ponsot also produces the Morey St.-Denis Monts Luisants, a rare white wine. Made from 80% Pinot Blanc and 20% Chardonnay, it tends to be a curious, heavy wine. It ages well for 15–20 years.

The estate is spread out with very important parcels of old vines in Clos de le Roche (6.8 acres), and others in Morey St.-Denis (3.13 acres), Griotte-Chambertin (1.65 acres), Latricières-Chambertin (1.52 acres), Chambolle-Musigny Les Charmes (1.45 acres). Gevrey-Chambertin (1.27 acres), Chapelle-Chambertin (1 acre), Clos St.-Denis (1 acre), and Chambertin (.4 acre). In the great vintages a Ponsot wine will improve in the bottle 15–25 years. Why the property does not succeed in vintages of large yields remains a mystery to me. Readers should know that several of Ponsot's wines also appear on the market under the name Domaine Chézeaux. The Ponsot's lease land from this estate. Under the terms of their agreement, the Domaine Chezeaux receives 50% of the grapes, which the Ponsots vinify and bottle for them.

DOMAINE POTHIER-RIEUSSET (POMMARD)****

> Wines Produced: Beaune Les Boucherottes, Bourgogne Aligoté,
> Bourgogne Blanc, Bourgogne Rouge, Meursault
> Les Caillerets, Pommard, Pommard Les Char-
> mots, Pommard-Clos de Vergers, Pommard Les
> Epenots, Pommard Les Rugiens, Volnay.

If I had to pick one grower in Burgundy who epitomizes the public's perception of a French winemaker, it would be Virgile Pothier. Very short, red-faced, bright-eyed, talkative, and, of course, philosophical, Virgile Pothier is a winemaker of considerable talent. His 1947 and 1949 Pommard Les Rugiens were two of the greatest wines from the Côte de Beaune that I have ever tasted. I tasted them in the 1980s and can still remember their flavor today. Pothier's wines are often remarkable to taste from the barrel, but once bottled they are extremely slow to evolve. his 1969s and 1972s are just now opening up. His 1985s, which looked so soft in cask, have slowed down in development and should be among the most structured and long-lived of the vintage.

Pothier's entire domain consists of 19.01 acres of vineyards, and his winemaking technique is quite traditional. He employs a lengthy *cuvaison*, one-third new oak casks, and 18–24 months of aging. In 1983 his importer apparently persuaded him to filter his wines, as they were so thick and tannic. The results were a botched group of wines that turned out to be less profound in the bottle than they were in cask. The 1986s and 1987s were disappointing. However, Pothier appears to have bounced back with a strong line-up of 1988s. Virgile Pothier is close to retirement, and there is no doubt that his niece is being groomed to take over the winery. Let's hope that nothing changes at this pace-setting Pommard estate.

This estate's best wines are consistently those from the 1.35-acre parcel of Pommard Les Rugiens and the 1.85 parcel of Pommard-Clos de Vergers. However, in most vintages these wines should not be touched for at least 6–8 years after the vintage. Ideally, they need a decade of cellaring. Even in lighter vintages, such as 1979, Pothier's wines need 7–10 years to reach maturity. They can remain at this level for another 15–20 years. He also makes outstanding Pommard Les Epenots from a tiny .37-acre parcel, and in certain vintages a good Bourgogne Rouge and Beaune Les Boucherottes. However, one of his best-kept secrets is the Meursault Les Caillerets, which ages like a red wine. This domaine can be one of the top sources for great Pommard, but its wines require patience.

DOMAINE MICHEL POUHIN-SEURRE (MEURSAULT)**

Wines Produced: Meursault Limozin, Meursault Le Poruzot, Meursault Rouge.

This tiny estate of 7.7 acres includes 6.5 acres of Meursault Villages, .6 of an acre of Meursault Le Poruzot, and .6 of an acre of Meursault Rouge. I've seen the wines over four different vintages and have yet to be impressed. There is nothing technically wrong with the wines but they lack excitement and personality. Both the red and whites should be drunk within 5–6 years of the vintage.

DOMAINE DE LA POULETTE (CORGOLOIN)***

Wines Produced: Bourgogne Rouge, Côte de Nuits-Villages (Rouge and Blanc), Nuits St.-Georges Les Brûlées, Nuits St.-Georges Les Chaboeufs, Nuits St.-Georges Les Poulettes, Nuits St.-Georges Les Saint-Georges, Nuits St.-Georges Les Vallerots, Nuits St.-Georges Les Vaucrains, Vosne-Romanée Les Suchots.

This estate sells most of its production exclusively within Europe as the owners, the Audidier-Maitrot family, have resisted the temptation to export beyond Western Europe. It is a modest-sized estate of 35.8 acres, with some excellent Premiers Crus in Nuits St.-Georges such as Les Vaucrains, Les Saint-Georges, Les Poulettes, and a tiny parcel of outstanding Premier Cru in Vosne-Romanée, Les Suchots. The greatest part of this estate's production is in Côte de Nuits-Villages Rouge and Blanc. Very little new oak is used, but the entire production is estate-bottled after having spent 18–24 months in cask. There is a light filtration prior to bottling. I have seen only a handful of Domaine de la Poulette wines, but those I have tasted exhibited good winemaking and respect for both the vintage and the vineyard.

DOMAINE DE LA POUSSE D'OR (VOLNAY)****

Wines Produced: Pommard Les Jarolières, Santenay-Clos Tavannes, Santenay Les Gravières, Volnay Les Caillerets, Volnay Les Caillerets-Clos des 60 Ouvrées, Volnay-Clos d'Audignac, Volnay-Clos de la Bousse d'Or.

For many years, one of the highlights of my trips to the Côte de Beaune was a stop at the Domaine de la Pousse d'Or and a tasting and discussion of recent vintages with the erudite proprietor, Gérard Potel. For my tastes, the 1964, 1966, 1978, 1979, 1980, and 1985 wines from this domaine defined what elegant, seductive, round, and immensely charming red burgundy should be all about. The domaine's flexible approach to winemaking no doubt accounts for its success in many different types of vintages. The Domaine de la Pousse d'Or 1976s are superb wines made in a very difficult vintage. The domaine again produced beautiful wines in the overly abundant year of 1979.

In principle, Potel does not destem, although in years when there is a chance of rot, he is flexible enough to destem most or all of his crop. The *cuvaison* is moderate in length, and the fermentation temperature is pushed to very high limits and then pulled back so that the aromatic complexity of the wines is not lost. The estate now consists of 31.04 acres of vineyards, many of which surround the domaine and cellars. From the terrace above the cellars there is a splendid view overlooking the village, and on a clear day one can see the Alps. The top wines emanate from the 5.28-acre parcel of Volnay-Clos de la Bousse d'Or, the Volnay Les Caillerets-Clos des 60 Ouvrées (5.9 acres), and the Pommard Les Jarolières (2.59 acres). However, those wanting to taste Santenay at its best certainly should try the excellent Santenay-Clos Tavannes (5.18 acres) or Santenay Les Gravières (4.52 acres).

All of the production here is estate-bottled, and about 30% new oak is preferred. The wines are bottled after 14–18 months of cask aging, and since 1980, Potel has practiced filtration. I am not sure this style of wine is helped by a filtration. Of the more recent vintages there have been light 1987s and excellent 1988s, but the 1986s were emaciated, and perhaps the most disappointing vintage for Gérard Potel this decade. In most vintages the wines of the Domaine de la Pousse d'Or drink surprisingly well young, but are capable of lasting for 10 to 15 years. If only Potel would throw away his filters!

DOMAINE JACQUES PRIEUR (MEURSAULT)**–***

Wines Produced: Beaune-Clos de la Féguine, Bourgogne Blanc, Bourgogne Rouge, Chambertin, Chambertin-Clos de Bèze, Chevalier-Montrachet, Clos Vougeot, Meursault-Clos de Mazeray Blanc, Meursault-Clos de Mazeray Rouge, Meursault Les Perrières, Montrachet, Musigny, Puligny-Montrachet Les Combettes, Volnay-Champans, Volnay-Clos des Santenots.

This famous domaine's wines are seen in many foreign markets, as over 85% of the production is exported. The wines not only appear under the name Jacques Prieur, but also under the label Château des Herbeaux. The estate has considerable treasures, including 1.43 acres in Montrachet, a tiny parcel of .32 acre in Chevalier-Montrachet, 3.68 acres in Puligny-Montrachet Les Combettes, .66 acre in Meursault Les Perrières, .32 acre of Chambertin-Clos de Bèze, 2.05 acres of Chambertin, and 2.05 acres of Musigny. The domaine also has 3.16 acres of Clos Vougeot on the very low end of the slope, which in any other Côte de Nuits appellation would only be a Villages wine. The domaine also includes parcels in Volnay-Santenots, and a large 7.9-acre parcel of Meursault-Clos de Mazeray that produces both white and red wine. The children of Jacques Prieur now manage this family-owned company. The two directly in charge are Jean Prieur and Pierre Poupon (the famous author who has written much about Burgundy).

While the wines have a relatively good reputation, I have been disappointed by them for many years. They are acceptable and well made, but they are not as concentrated, profound, or complex as they should be, given the Domaine Prieur's vineyards. The winemaking style seems to be too high tech, and perhaps the wines are too filtered and eviscerated in an effort to clean them up for early bottling. Both the red and white wines see 20%–25% new oak and are bottled after 12 months. The domaine maintains that their wines age extremely well. I do not doubt this, but there are many finer examples of these great appellations than the wines of the Domaine Jacques Prieur. In 1989, the Côte Chalonnaise firm of Antonin Rodet purchased the right to distribute Jacques Prieur's wines. Rodet's commitment to high quality may have a salutary influence on the Domaine Jacques Prieur.

DOMAINE MAURICE PRIEUR
(SAMPIGY-LÈS-MARANGES)***

Wines Produced: Bourgogne Aligoté, Bourgogne Hautes-Côtes de Beaune Rouge, Bourgogne Rouge, Côte de Beaune-Villages.

This tiny estate of 11.48 acres sells half of its production to *négociants* and estate-bottles the other half, selling most of it directly from their cellar. It is a shame there are not more of this property's wines available because the ones I have tasted have shown finesse considering their meager appellations. In addition, they reflect the hand of a winemaker who knows how to balance fruit and acidity. Producer Maurice Prieur also makes a lively, fresh, floral-scented Bourgogne Aligoté.

DOMAINE PRIEUR-BRUNET (SANTENAY)****

> Wines Produced: Bâtard-Montrachet, Beaune-Clos du Roi, Bourgogne Rouge, Chassagne-Montrachet Les Embazées, Chassagne-Montrachet Morgeot, Meursault, Meursault Les Charmes, Meursault Les Chevalières, Meursault Les Forges Blanc, Meursault Les Forges Rouge, Pommard La Platière, Santenay, Santenay-Clos Rousseau Blanc, Santenay La Comme, Santenay-Foulot, Santenay La Maladière, Volnay Santenots.

Founded in 1804 by the Prieur family, this is one of the oldest domaines in the Côte d'Or. The estate consists of 45.81 acres and all of the production is estate-bottled. I have had many fine wines from this underrated producer in Santenay, including some of the most delicious bottles of Santenay La Maladière I have ever tasted. The Domaine Prieur also produces small amounts of excellent wine from Santenay La Comme, Volnay Santenots, and Beaune-Clos du Roi. They do a splendid job with their white wine, including an outstanding Bâtard-Montrachet, Chassagne-Montrachet Les Embazées, and a delicious Santenay-Clos Rousseau. The Santenay-Clos Rousseau is also a stupendous bargain. The red wines see 10% new oak and are bottled after 18–24 months in cask. The white wines see 10%–25% new oak and are bottled after 12 months. This is a very reliable, consistent producer that handles great vintages such as 1985 without any problem, and manages to turn out very reliable, authentic, red and white burgundies that reflect their appellations in difficult years such as 1984 and 1983. The red wines should be drunk within their first decade of life, and the whites in their first 6–7 years.

DOMAINE DU PRIEURÉ (LUGNY)***

> Wines Produced: Mâcon-Villages.

This picturesque 25-acre estate, which takes its name from the ancient fifteenth-century priory and lovely Roman chapel, makes extremely elegant and flavorful Mâcon-Villages. It produces about 7,000 cases, but unfortunately, not much of that is available in the export marketplace.

DOMAINE DU PRIEURÉ (RULLY)***

Wines Produced: Bourgogne Aligoté, Bourgogne Rouge, Mercurey, Rully-Chapitre Rouge, Rully-Chaume Rouge, Rully-Grésigny Premier Cru Blanc, Rully-en-Pelleret Blanc, Rully-Preau Premier Cru Rouge, Rully-Le Rully Rouges, Rully-Sous-Mont-Palais Premier Cru Blanc, Rully-Sous-Mont-Palais Premier Cru Rouge.

Armand Monassier, formerly a restaurateur in Paris, owns and runs this 21.8-acre estate best known for its excellent red wines of Rully. They are aged in 25% new oak and bottled after 12–14 months. Having been a restaurateur, Monassier is sympathetic to those consumers who want stylish, supple, velvety wines for drinking immediately. I have had little experience with the white wines from this estate, except for a tasty, satisfying, spicy, oaky bottle of the 1986 Rully-Grésigny Blanc. The entire production from this domaine is estate-bottled, and the quality of the wines is consistently good to very good over recent vintages.

DOMAINE DU PRIEURÉ (SAVIGNY-LÈS-BEAUNE)**

Wines Produced: Bourgogne Aligoté, Bourgogne Hautes-Côtes de Beaune, Bourgogne Rouge, Savigny-Lès-Beaune, Savigny-Lès-Beaune Blanc, Savigny-Lès-Beaune Les Hauts Jarrons, Savigny-Lès-Beaune Les Lavières.

Proprietor Jean-Michel Maurice estate-bottles most of his production. He keeps the wines in 25% new oak and bottles them after 14–16 months. His best wine is the Savigny-Lès-Beaune Les Lavières, an elegant, stylish wine that lacks depth in vintages such as 1982 and 1986. However, when the vineyard (2.17 acres) gets plenty of sunshine and heat, this is an excellent wine. The white wines tend to be simple, lean, and often have too much acidity.

DOMAINE PROPRIETE DES VIGNES (PONCEY)**

Wines Produced: Bourgogne Aligoté, Bourgogne Passe-Tout-Grains, Givry Blanc, Givry-Clos du Vernoy, Givry Rouge.

One-third of this 22.17-acre estate's production is sold to *négociants* and the rest is estate-bottled. The best wine is their small quantity of

Givry-Clos du Vernoy, which sees 5%–10% new oak and is bottled after 12 months. The white wines tend to be rather dull and insipid.

PROSPER-MAUFOUX (SANTENAY)***

This *négociant* produces an entire range of wines from Beaujolais, Burgundy, and the Mâconnais region. To the firm's credit, all the important wines from the Côte d'Or are aged in oak casks for 12–18 months. The wines also appear under the name of Marcel Amance. Although the white wines tend to be a bit more satisfying and interesting than the red wines, the red wines are technically very well made, clean, and provide both value and consistency. They lack individuality, but not every producer prizes such character. The best wines include the Santenay Domaine St.-Michel, Volnay-Clos des Angles, Santenay-Clos des Gravières Blanc, and Château de Viré in the Mâcon-Villages area. Given the style of these fresh, delicate, fruity wines, they should be consumed within 5–7 years of the vintage.

DOMAINE MAURICE PROTHEAU ET FILS (MERCUREY)**

> Wines Produced: Mercurey Blanc, Mercurey-Clos des Corvées, Mercurey-Clos l'Évêque, Mercurey La Fauconnière, Mercurey Rouge.

The Domaine Maurice Protheau et fils is one of the largest estates of the appellation, consisting of 110 acres, with important vineyards in Clos l'Évêque, La Fauconnière, and Clos des Corvées. This estate, founded in 1720, produces rustic, spicy wines that often have an excess of tannin considering the amount of fruit. The wines are marketed by the family *négociant*, François Protheau. I have also seen a range of mediocre Beaujolais under this label. Overall, the wine quality is standard at best.

DOMAINE HENRI PRUDHON (SAINT-AUBIN)***

> Wines Produced: Bourgogne Aligoté, Bourgogne Blanc, Chassagne-Montrachet Rouge, Saint-Aubin, Saint-Aubin Les Frionnes, Saint-Aubin Les Sentières.

The young Gérard Prudhon, son of Henri, is one of the bright, shining stars of the up-and-coming appellation of Saint-Aubin. He makes ex-

cellent white wine that is aged in oak barrels (20% new), and very fine
red wine. His Saint-Aubin Les Frionnes is as good as many of the red
wines from more prestigious appellations in Beaune. Prudhon, a diminutive 5'5" with a long pointed nose well-suited to the smelling of wine,
believes Saint-Aubin has as much potential as Chassagne-Montrachet,
particularly for white wines. This remains one of the undiscovered
appellations of the Côte d'Or, and the quality of the winemaking in the
entire village is very high. It is curious that this tiny appellation and
village, only a three-minute drive from Chassagne-Montrachet, has remained such a secret to all but a handful of shrewd consumers.

DOMAINE MICHEL PRUNIER (AUXEY-DURESSES) ***

> **Wines Produced:** Auxey-Duresses Blanc, Auxey-Duresses-Clos du
> Val, Auxey-Duresses Rouge, Beaune Les Sizies,
> Volnay Les Caillerets.

When searching for well-made, rich, expressive red and white burgundies that offer good value, remember the name of Michel Prunier. He
has done little wrong in the eighties (the only vintages I am familiar
with). He seems to get a tremendous amount of fat and fruit in his
wines, in addition to a great deal of complexity and enough acidity for
balance. His top wines include his Auxey-Duresses-Clos du Val, beautifully made from very old vines, as well as his seductive, velvety
Beaune Les Sizies. Although he only has 11.85 acres, he is a talented
winemaker whose wines are remarkably consistent from vintage to vintage. He believes in 25% new oak for his red and 15% new oak for his
white wines. Prunier bottles after 18 months and practices a very light
filtration. His top wines, such as the Beaune Les Sizies, the more
tannic-structured Volnay Les Caillerets, and his Auxey-Duresses-Clos
du Val, are easily capable of lasting for 8–10 years in top vintages.

DOMAINE ROGER PRUNIER (AUXEY-DURESSES) **

> **Wines Produced:** Auxey-Duresses Blanc, Auxey-Duresses-Clos du
> Val, Auxey-Duresses Rouge, Pommard.

Roger Prunier, Michel Prunier's brother, manages a very modern installation, and produces wine from 9.13 acres in four different appellations. His most important holding is in Auxey-Duresses Rouge,
including 1.23 acres of Auxey-Duresses-Clos du Val. His wines seem to
be less intense and concentrated, and much more rustic than his

brother Michel's. They should be drunk young, usually within 5–7 years of the vintage.

DOMAINE MAX QUENOT FILS ET MEUNEVEAUX
(ALOXE-CORTON)**

Wines Produced: Aloxe-Corton, Corton Les Bressandes, Corton-Chaumes, Corton Les Perrières.

The Quenot and Meuneveaux families make reliable if unspectacular wines from their 10.92-acre domaine. The wines see 20% new oak and are aged for 18 months prior to receiving a light filtration. This estate has some important holdings, particular a 2.47-acre parcel of Corton Les Bressandes, and 1.23 acres of Corton Les Perrières. These are the domaine's best two wines. Most of the wines from this estate should be drunk within 5–7 years of the vintage.

DOMAINE CHARLES QUILLARDET
(GEVREY-CHAMBERTIN)**

Wines Produced: Bourgogne Rouge Le Montre Cul, Chambertin, Côte de Nuits-Villages, Fixin, Gevrey-Chambertin, Gevrey-Chambertin Les Champeaux, Gevrey-Chambertin Premier Cru, Marsannay, Marsannay Rosé.

The large, bear-like, fun-loving Charles Quillardet produces deeply colored wines that are often clumsy and coarse. They tend to have a lot of fruit, but rarely seem to reflect their appellations. His cellars, located on the famed Route Nationale 74 in Gevrey-Chambertin, are always full of visitors anxious to purchase cases of his wines. He is one of the most successful commercial names of Gevrey-Chambertin, selling nearly 10,000 cases from his domaine each year. While I think his wines lack complexity and charm, they have their admirers for their overbearing, unusual style. The vinification is quite traditional, making me question why Quillardet's wines do not show more character and finesse. Even his great Grand Cru, Chambertin, frequently tastes muddled, soupy, and straightforward. His most controversial, and in many ways most successful wine, is his Bourgogne Rouge Le Montre Cul, which sports a tasteless label of a woman bending over on the slopes of the vineyard with her derrière in full view.

QUINSON (FLEURIE)**–***

> Wines Produced: An entire range of Beaujolais is made by this large
> negociant.

The Quinson firm, founded in 1924, is now run by Maurice Quinson.
His style of winemaking tends to produce straightforward and fruity,
yet correct and clean wines. Quinson's best wines are from his own
48.1 acres in Beaujolais. The wines I would recommend are their Fleurie-Château de l'Abbaye St. Laurent d'Arpayé and Moulin-à-Vent-Château de la Bruyère.

DOMAINE RAGOT (PONCEY)**

> Wines Produced: Bourgogne Aligoté, Bourgogne Passe-Tout-Grains,
> Givry Blanc, Givry Rouge.

Jean-Pierre Ragot is a member of the fifth generation of Ragots who
have owned and farmed this 18.52-acre vineyard. The best wines here
are the Givry Blanc and Bourgogne Aligoté, both of which show a stony,
hazelnut fragrance and good depth of flavor. The white wines are fermented in stainless-steel casks and then aged in 10% new oak casks for
12–14 months. The red wines are traditionally made and straightforward, but often seem to have too much tannin for the amount of fruit
present. Ragot's wines should be drunk within 4–5 years of the vintage.

DOMAINE RAMONET (CHASSAGNE-MONTRACHET)*****

> Wines Produced: Bâtard-Montrachet,   Bienvenues-Bâtard-Mon-
> trachet, Bourgogne Aligoté, Bourgogne Blanc,
> Bourgogne Rouge, Chassagne-Montrachet Blanc,
> Chassagne-Montrachet Les Caillerets, Chas-
> sagne-Montrachet Les Chaumées, Chassagne-
> Montrachet-Clos de la Boudriotte Rouge, Chas-
> sagne-Montrachet-Clos St.-Jean Rouge, Chas-
> sagne-Montrachet Morgeot, Chassagne-Mon-
> trachet Morgeot Rouge, Chassagne-Montrachet
> Les Ruchottes, Chassagne-Montrachet Les Ver-
> gers, Le Montrachet.

This 44-acre domaine is considered by many to produce the world's
greatest bottles of Chardonnay. As a result, the family Ramonet—

grandfather Pierre, father André, and sons Noël and Jean-Claude—
have a book of press clippings as big as a Hollywood superstar's. Their
wines are in such demand they must decline sales to many famous
restaurants and governments. It is no secret that their Montrachet from
a .61-acre parcel of 62-year-old vines, their Bâtard-Montrachet from a
.32-acre parcel, their Bienvenues-Bâtard-Montrachet from a .3-acre
parcel, their Chassagne-Montrachet Les Ruchottes from a 2.42-acre
parcel (planted with 40-year-old vines), and their Chassagne-Montrachet Les Caillerets or Les Vergers are Chardonnays about as profound and long lived as one is likely to find.

In Burgundy, growers talk about those producers who have been
successful and made a name for themselves. For them, the Domaine
Ramonet has become an historical monument. The legend probably
began in 1938 when Raymond Baudoin, one of the founders of France's
famed *Revue du Vin de France*, and the de facto father of estate-bottled
burgundies, encountered Pierre Ramonet at an exposition for small
growers in Beaune. Upon tasting the 1934 Chassagne-Montrachet Les
Ruchottes, Baudoin was apparently spellbound. Six months later, Baudoin, accompanied by a young American by the name of Frank Schoonmaker, returned to Chassagne-Montrachet to look up Pierre Ramonet.
Schoonmaker was so impressed with the wines that he bought 200 cases
for the United States.

Vinification in the Ramonet cellars appears to be fairly standard.
Twenty-five to thirty-five percent new oak casks are used, and the
wines are bottled after 18–20 months. The domaine practices a light
filtration, but it does not seem to have any effect on the wine's quality;
no other Chardonnay has the flavor dimension and depth of a Ramonet
Chardonnay. Everyone who loves wine has passed through these cellars, including the late Fernand Point and today's modern wine and
food gurus—Jean-Claude Vrinat, Paul Bocuse, Alain Chapel, and
Pierre Troisgros—all of whom carry Ramonet's wines proudly on their
wine lists.

Somehow Ramonet has resisted the temptation to increase his yields.
He has had so many great vintages (the 1979, 1981, 1982, 1983, 1985,
and 1986), that I sometimes wonder how much longer the magic can
continue. It was fashionable in the late seventies to say there was too
much bottle variation, and, I remember tasting several Bienvenues-
Bâtard-Montrachet 1978s that were oxidized, suggesting a problem at
bottling. However, since that time I have had Ramonet wines that were
the greatest white burgundies I have ever tasted in my life. I am referring to the 1986, 1982, and 1979 Montrachets. White burgundy does not
get any better than it does at this estate. If you are lucky enough to run

across a bottle of the Domaine Ramonet's wine, do yourself a favor and give it 4–5 years in the bottle to develop, rather than opening it before its time.

CHÂTEAU DE RAOUSSET (CHIROUBLES)***

> Wines Produced: Beaujolais Blanc, Chiroubles, Fleurie, Fleurie-Vigneronnage de Grille-Midi, Morgon.

The lovely Château de Raousset has been family-owned since 1850. While the estate has an important 25-acre vineyard in Fleurie and a slightly larger vineyard in Morgon, its pride and joy is its Chiroubles, made from the domaine's 104.7-acre holdings in Beaujolais. Georges Duboeuf buys a cuvée from Château de Raousset and bottles it under both his name and the domaine's name. However, thirty percent of the production is estate-bottled, and it is as good as the Georges Duboeuf Cuvée. The Chiroubles can be beautifully rich, perfumed, stylish wine, although it is somewhat inconsistent. I thought both the 1988 Duboeuf cuvée and the estate-bottled cuvée were truly stunning. The wines are kept in old oak *foudres* for 4–7 months prior to bottling. This tends to be one of the richer and more ageworthy wines of Chiroubles.

DOMAINE RAPET PÈRE ET FILS (PERNAND-VERGELESSES)***

> Wines Produced: Aloxe-Corton, Beaune, Bourgogne Aligoté, Bourgogne en Bully, Corton, Corton-Charlemagne, Pernand-Vergelesses, Pernand-Vergelesses Sous la Vierge Blanc, Pernand-Vergelesses Les Vergelesses, Savigny-Lès-Beaune.

Robert Rapet and his son Roland have run this serious estate for many years. The estate includes 31.3 acres of vines, with some impressive holdings in Corton-Charlemagne and Corton. The Corton-Charlemagne can be outstanding, but needs years to reach its apogee. The Corton is also impressive, but is more elegant and stylish than the blockbuster, muscular Cortons of some producers. Other good wines from Rapet include the domaine's Savigny-Lès-Beaune and Pernand-Vergelesses Les Vergelesses. The Rapets have always believed in early bottling in order to preserve the fruit in their wines. Therefore the red wines, which see 25% new oak, are bottled after 12 months, and the white wines, which see the same amount of new oak, are bottled after 9–10 months. These are wines to drink in their first 7–8 years of life.

DOMAINE GASTON ET PIERRE RAVAUT
(LADOIX-SERRIGNY)***

Wines Produced: Aloxe-Corton, Bourgogne Rouge, Corton Les Bressandes, Corton-Charlemagne, Corton Hautes Mourottes, Côte de Nuits-Villages, Ladoix Blanc, Ladoix Les Corvées, Ladoix Premier Cru, Ladoix Rouge.

Although the Domaine Ravaut wines are not exhilarating, they are full-bodied, often tannic wines that can handle aging well. It is debatable whether they ultimately provide as much pleasure as their prices suggest. Gaston and Pierre Ravaut use very little new oak (10%), and bottle their wines after 14–18 months of cask aging. The white wines receive 8–12 months cask aging. Like several other producers of Ladoix, this domaine's problem appears to be an excess of tannin for the amount of fruit. However, the Ravauts have made some excellent wines from their Grand Cru .69-acre parcel in Corton Les Bressandes and their excellently situated 1.43-acre parcel of Corton Hautes Mourottes. Their top red wines can easily last 10–12 years, but they never seem to provide as much pleasure as might be expected.

DOMAINE FRANÇOIS ET JEAN-MARIE RAVENEAU
(CHABLIS)*****

Wines Produced: Chablis Blanchots, Chablis Butteaux, Chablis Chapelot, Chablis Les Clos, Chablis Forêts, Chablis Montée de Tonnerre, Chablis Valmur, Chablis Les Vaillons.

Many people feel the most quintessential examples of Premier Cru and Grand Cru Chablis come from François Raveneau and his son Jean-Marie's 16.8 acres of vineyards. The Raveneaus do not use any new oak; instead they age their wine in rather old barrels for at least 12–15 months. The introspective François Raveneau produces wines with great flavor depth, length, and dimension, which also have the austerity and mineral scents that make Chablis unique. It's hard to go wrong here with either the Premiers Crus or the Grands Crus. Even in lighter vintages, Raveneau's wines will last 10–15, even 20 years. He thought his 1964s were not fully mature until the late seventies, and feels his 1969s are just now beginning to drink well. His 1978s, after only a decade, are not yet fully mature, but for those lucky enough to taste one, they are indeed spectacular. Raveneau's recent great vintages are 1983, 1986, and 1989. Fame has its price, and Raveneau's wines are the most expensive of the appellation.

DOMAINE REBOUGEON-MURE (POMMARD)**

Wines Produced: Beaune-Les Epenottes, Beaune Les Vignes-Franches, Bourgogne Rouge, Pommard, Pommard Les Grands Epenots, Volnay, Volnay Santenots.

The wines from the Domaine Rebougeon-Mure are standard-quality, one-dimensional, uninteresting wines. This estate's winemaking technique is certainly not unusual. Twenty percent new oak is used and the wines spend 18–20 months in cask prior to bottling. The domaine includes 13.58 acres, and its most impressive parcels are a .66 of an acre parcel of Pommard Les Grands Epenots and a .64 of an acre parcel of Volnay Santenots. Most of the wines from this estate should be consumed within 5–6 years of the vintage.

DOMAINE HENRI REBOURSEAU
(GEVREY-CHAMBERTIN)**

Wines Produced: Chambertin, Chambertin-Clos de Bèze, Charmes-Chambertin, Clos Vougeot, Gevrey-Chambertin, Gevrey-Chambertin Le Fontenys, Mazis-Chambertin.

This splendidly situated domaine, located behind a large wall in the village of Gevrey-Chambertin, is now run by the grandson of the late Henri Rebourseau, Jean de Surrel. The estate has 33 acres of superb vineyards, including such illustrious Grands Crus as Chambertin-Clos de Bèze, Charmes-Chambertin, Mazis-Chambertin, Clos Vougeot, and Chambertin. The wines from these cellars should be excellent, given the percentage of new oak barrels used, the 32° C fermentation temperature, and the *cuvaison* of two weeks. However, what one tastes in the bottle is confusing, as the wines are light, over-cropped, and not always the cleanest examples of fine winemaking. The 1983s were catastrophic, the 1985s were pleasant but lighter than they should have been given the vintage, and the 1986s and 1987s were lightweight wines with little depth or length. All of this is mystifying given the superb potential of this domaine, and the apparent serious commitment by Jean de Surrel.

A. REGNARD ET FILS (CHABLIS)**–***

> **Wines Produced:** This *négociant* owns no vineyards in Chablis, but produces an entire range of Premier Crus, Grand Crus, Chablis Villages, and Petit-Chablis from purchased grape juice.

An historic company founded in 1860, A. Regnard et Fils is the only *négociant* in Chablis that does not own any vineyards. Despite this drawback, the company has always turned out competent examples of the modern style of Chablis. The wine is fermented in stainless steel, with the Premiers Crus and Grands Crus seeing 2–3 months of aging in new oak casks to give them greater complexity. The balance of the production is bottled relatively early in order to preserve its freshness and fruitiness. The firm was sold in 1985 to Patrick de Ladoucette who is expected to increase the level of quality. The wines of A. Regnard et Fils appear in many export markets under the names of Albert Pic et Fils, and Michel Remon (the dynamic, enthusiastic individual who has managed this company for the last several decades). The best wines from this firm have consistently been their Grands Crus, such as Les Clos and Vaudésir, but the Premier Cru Fourchaume is also a success. Most of these wines should be drunk within the first 5–7 years of the vintage.

LA REINE PEDAUQUE (ALOXE-CORTON)**–***

> **Wines Produced:** Aloxe-Corton, Clos Vougeot, Corton-Charlemagne, Corton-Clos des Langres, Corton-Clos du Roi, Corton Les Pougets, Corton de la Reine, Côte de Nuits-Villages, Ladoix-Clos Les Chaignots, Pommard, Savigny-Lès-Beaune, Savigny-Lès-Beaune Les Guettes, Savigny-Lès-Beaune Les Peuillets.

Note: This firm also produces an entire range of *négociant* wines.

After decades of producing mediocre, often inferior red and white burgundies, this firm is finally producing higher quality wines. It appears to have enormous potential, given the vineyard holdings and the amount of money available for investment in winemaking barrels and expertise. While the domaine's cellars are located in Aloxe-Corton, anyone traveling south on Route N 74 entering Beaune cannot miss the huge, well-located visitor's center run by Pedauque. The estate's specialties are the wines of Aloxe-Corton and Savigny-Lès-Beaune. They claim to control the production of nearly 40% of Savigny's wines.

Since 1985 the quality has gotten increasingly better. The wines I have tasted under the Pierre André label (he runs the estate) are superior to those under the firm's other labels, including its own La Reine Pedauque house label. The vast estate of 148.2 acres includes 17.29 acres of Grand Cru Corton, 2.47 acres of Clos Vougeot (all from the upper slope with vines planted in 1936, 1961, and 1980), 37.05 acres in Savigny-Lès-Beaune Premier Cru, and 6.17 acres in Corton-Charlemagne. Additionally, the firm owns a domaine of 44.5 acres in Mâcon called Domaine Viticole des Charmes, and a *monopole* vineyard of 17.29 acres of Ladoix-Clos Les Chagnots. With all these landholdings, it is reassuring to see the firm committed to higher quality wines. However, at best, the wines of La Reine Pedauque are still only above average to good in quality.

REMOISSENET PERE ET FILS (BEAUNE)***

Domaine Wines Produced: Beaune Les Grèves, Beaune Les Marconnets, Beaune Les Toussaints.

Note: Remoissenet produces an entire range of wines as a *négociant*, including the following (usually only offered in good vintages, such as 1978, 1983, and 1985): Aloxe-Corton, Beaune Les Grèves, Beaune Mares, Bourgogne Rouge, Chambolle-Musigny Les Charmes, Charmes-Chambertin, Clos Vougeot, Gevrey-Chambertin, Grands Echézeaux, Mercurey-Clos Fourtoul, Nuits St.-Georges, Nuits St.-Georges Les Argillets, Pommard Les Epenots, Richebourg, Santenay-Clos de Tavennes, Santenay La Comme, Santenay Les Gravières, Savigny-Lès-Beaune, Savigny-Lès-Beaune Les Gravains, Savigny-Lès-Beaune Les Guettes, Savigny-Lès-Beaune Les Serpentières, Volnay, Vosne-Romanée, Vosne-Romanée Les Chaumes, Vosne-Romanée Les Suchots.

Roland Remoissenet is one of the most dashing figures in Burgundy. Handsome, enthusiastic, extroverted, and warm, he always makes a visit to his cellars interesting and pleasant. He oversees an amazingly wealthy domaine that sits just within the walls of Beaune with remarkable underground cellars. Following a light filtration, his red wines are bottled after 18–24 months in cask. Unlike *négociants* such as Drouhin, Jadot, and Faiveley, Remoissenet is content to purchase the wine rather than the grapes. However, he is extremely selective and will often refuse to buy in years such as 1986 or 1984. The firm was founded in 1877, and it produces over 600,000 bottles in a good, abundant vintage.

The red wines from Remoissenet are generally soundly made and correct. Although Remoissenet represents many different appellations, his wines rarely show much variety in personality and character. These wines usually have good color, noticeable alcohol levels, and good tannins. They are meant to age well, and do often retain their freshness for 10–12 years. Old stocks have fills right to the cork and do not have a speck of sediment. This is remarkable for wines so old.

The white wines tend to exhibit more character and complexity. They are also extremely long lived. The best wines are his excellent Corton-Charlemagne Diamond Jubilee, his selections from Meursault, such as Genevrières, and his Puligny-Montrachet Premiers Crus Les Folatières and Les Combettes. Remoissenet's whites are generally equivalent to Joseph Drouhin and Louis Jadot's excellent whites.

The Remoissenet firm also exclusively markets the wines of Baron Thenard, who owns 4.52 acres of the famed Le Montrachet vineyard. Additionally, Baron Thenard owns and Remoissenet produces an excellent, reasonably priced Givry.

All things considered, this is a good, sometimes excellent source of white burgundy, and a consistent and competent source of red burgundy. I would personally like to see more individuality and complexity in the red wines. I also do not understand why the old, rare vintages possess such remarkable fills and have no sediment. However, the wines are certainly well made and never defective or unacceptable.

DOMAINE HENRI REMORIQUET
(NUITS ST.-GEORGES)***

> Wines Produced: Bourgogne Hautes-Côtes de Nuits, Nuits St.-Georges, Nuits St.-Georges Les Allots, Nuits St.-Georges Les Bousselots, Nuits St.-Georges Les Damodes, Nuits St.-Georges Rue de Chaux, Nuits St.-Georges Les Saint-Georges.

This small but important estate of nearly 19 acres produces a range of wines, primarily from the Nuits St.-Georges appellation. The proprietor, a youthful, thirtyish Gilles Remoriquet, follows a very traditional fermentation: He destems his grapes, ferments at fairly warm temperatures, practices a 3-week maceration in, as he says, "healthy years," and then puts the wine in one-third new oak casks for 18 months. There is also a light filtration prior to bottling. His Nuits St.-Georges Les Damodes is his best wine, but his Bourgogne Hautes-Côtes de Nuits, from a well-positioned 2-acre parcel should not be ignored. This wine can be as good as some of his other selections from Nuits St.-Georges. Remoriquet made very good 1985s and 1988s, but was less successful in 1986 and 1987. The wines here are best drunk within their first 6–7 years of life.

DOMAINE DES REMPARTS (SAINT-BRIS-LE-VINEUX)***

Wines Produced: Bourgogne Aligoté, Bourgogne Blanc, Bourgogne Rouge, Sauvignon de St.-Bris.

The Domaine Des Remparts dedicates 15 of its 41.2 acres of vines to producing Bourgogne Aligoté. As a result, many of the local cognoscenti feel it is the best Bourgogne Aligoté made in this part of France. It is fragrant and flowery, and has none of the harsh acidity that plagues so many wines made from this grape. The Domaine des Remparts' other wines include a tasty, elegant Sauvignon de St.-Bris, and a straightforward Bourgogne Rouge.

DOMAINE LOUIS REMY (GEVREY-CHAMBERTIN)**

Wines Produced: Chambertin, Chambolle-Musigny, Chambolle-Musigny Premier Cru, Clos de la Roche, Latricières-Chambertin, Morey St.-Denis.

Although this estate enjoys a considerable reputation in certain wine circles, I have never been overly impressed with their wines. The Domaine Louis Remy is a very traditionally run family domaine of 6.2 acres. Some of the parcels, including an acre of Grand Cru Chambertin, 1.6 acres of Clos de la Roche, and 1.4 acres of Latricières-Chambertin, are indeed prestigious. Nevertheless, the wines seem to lack freshness, depth, and charm. This would appear to be an estate that has lived off its reputation far too long. In 1989, all of the vineyards were sold to the Domaine Leroy in Vosne-Romanée.

DOMAINE DE LA RENARDE (RULLY)***

Wines Produced: Bourgogne Aligoté Bouzeron, Givry-Clos du Cellier aux Moines Rouge, Mercurey Rouge, Rully Blanc, Rully Premier Cru Blanc, Rully Premier Cru Rouge, Rully Rouge, Rully Varot.

Note: The proprietor, Jean-François Delorme, also produces an entire line of wines under the name of Domaine André Delorme. This line includes a range of Crémant de Bourgogne, in particular a sparkling Blanc de Blancs, Blanc de Noirs, and Rosé.

The Delorme family has enjoyed remarkable success by concentrating on reasonably priced, well-made wines from appellations such as Rully, Bourgogne Aligoté, Mercurey, and Givry. They have built their domaine up to 143.52 acres, and consistently turn out stylish wines that please both neophytes and connoisseurs. Eighty percent of their production is sold in Europe and the rest is exported. All of these wines are carefully vinified in stainless steel, and are bottled quickly in order to retain their freshness. Both white and red wines see 10% new oak; the whites are bottled after 8–9 months and the reds after 10–12 months. Delorme's best wine is his Rully Varot, made from a 44-acre vineyard. It is an austere, almost chalky-scented, crisp white wine that seems to develop hazelnut nuances as it ages. The red wines offer supple strawberry and cherry fruit, are very soft, and are made to be drunk within 3–5 years of the vintage. This estate's prices are reasonable and the quality of the wine is consistently good. Delorme will undoubtedly add to his holdings since demand for these wines is extremely high.

DOMAINE HENRI RICHARD (GEVREY-CHAMBERTIN)***

> Wines Produced: Charmes-Chambertin, Gevrey-Chambertin, Mazoyères-Chambertin.

The cellars of the Domaine Henri Richard can be found in the last house on the right as one leaves Gevrey-Chambertin heading south to Morey St.-Denis. This is a very traditional estate of 7.5 acres. The wines spend 2–2½ years in oak casks of which 40%–50% are replenished each year. The wines are very good, offering power and richness as well as plenty of tannin, body, and oak. The best recent vintages are 1988 and 1985, although this estate managed to make some pleasant 1986s. The wines appear capable of lasting 8–10 years.

DOMAINE RIGER-BRISET (PULIGNY-MONTRACHET)**

> Wines Produced: Bourgogne Aligoté, Meursault Les Genevrières, Pommard, Puligny-Montrachet, Saint-Aubin, Saint-Aubin Rouge.

The young, thin, handsome Monsieur Riger owns 12.35 acres of vineyards spread throughout seven different appellations in southern Burgundy. His best wines are his Saint-Aubin and Meursault Les Genevrières. His red wines, the Saint-Aubin Rouge and Pommard, are rather light, mediocre wines of no great style or character. Fortunately, two-thirds of his production is white wine. Riger keeps his white wine for one year in wood barrels, of which 25% is new, and his red wine 12–14 months in barrel, of which 33% is new.

DOMAINE BERNARD RION PÈRE ET FILS
(VOSNE-ROMANÉE)****

> Wines Produced: Bourgogne Rouge, Chambolle-Musigny Eché-zeaux, Clos Vougeot, Nuits St.-Georges, Nuits St.-Georges Les Chaignots, Nuits St.-Georges Les Murgers, Vosne-Romanée, Vosne-Romanée Les Chaumes.

Bernard Rion has totally changed the winemaking style of his father's estate. For years, Rion's wines had an impressive potential for longevity, but lacked charm and finesse. The wines were dense, and often loaded with coarse tannins and huge body. While they were capable of lasting, they never developed into anything interesting. Bernard Rion, a chunky young man in his mid-thirties, has 15 acres of vineyards, most of which are in top Premiers Crus. He believes in using at least 50% new oak (although 100% is employed for his Grand Cru Clos Vougeot) a long, hot *cuvaison*, 18 months in barrels, and a light filtration prior to bottling. He made good 1985s, attractive 1986s, superb 1987s (among the top wines of the vintage) and top-notch 1988s. The style of his wines is one of high concentration and deep colors with much more charm and fruit than his father's wines. Consequently, Rion has developed into a top producer. He is an undiscovered star of such appellations as Clos Vougeot, Nuits St.-Georges Les Murgers, and Vosne-Romanée Les Chaumes. He made outstanding wines from these vineyards in 1987 and 1988. Even his Bourgogne Rouge is one of the better examples of its class.

DOMAINE DANIEL RION (NUITS ST.-GEORGES)****

> Wines Produced: Bourgogne Aligoté, Bourgogne Passe-Tout-Grains, Chambolle-Musigny aux Beaux Bruns, Clos Vougeot, Côte de Nuits-Villages, Nuits St.-Georges, Nuits St.-Georges-Clos des Argillières, Nuits St.-Georges Les Hauts Pruliers, Nuits St.-Georges Les Vignes Rondes, Vosne-Romanée, Vosne-Romanée Les Beaux Monts, Vosne-Romanée Les Chaumes.

Daniel Rion and his three sons, Olivier, Christophe, and Patrice, own 36 acres of vines spread over 13 different appellations. The wines have steadily improved in the 1980s. Their personalities are marked by large quantities of gorgeous, sumptuous fruit in a very forward, seductive style. The spokesman for the domaine, Patrice Rion, indicates they have successfully practiced a prefermentation maceration of the grape bunches to extract aromas and color. The results have been a series of delicious wines, even in lesser vintages such as 1986 and 1980. The very top wines of the estate include the Vosne-Romanée Les Chaumes, Nuits St.-Georges Les Hauts Pruliers, Vosne-Romanée Les Beaux Monts, and Nuits St.-Georges-Clos des Argillières. These are not wines for long aging and should be consumed in their first 7–8 years.

DOMAINE DE ROALLY (VIRÉ)***

> Wines Produced: Mâcon-Viré Blanc.

This is an excellent source for full-flavored, crisp, fruity, and relatively powerful Mâcon-Viré Blanc. The proprietor, Henry Goyard, has only 7.41 acres, but estate-bottles his entire production. He produces one of the fullest and richest of the tank-fermented Mâcon-Villages wines. It should be drunk within 2–3 years of the vintage.

DOMAINE GUY ROBIN (CHABLIS)***

> Wines Produced: Chablis Blanchot, Chablis Butteaux, Chablis Montée de Tonnerre, Chablis Les Vaillons, Chablis Valmur, Chablis Vaudésir.

Guy Robin and his son Jean-Pierre produce essentially the same wine under two different names, Guy Robin and Jean-Pierre Robin. This is a very traditional estate of 28.8 acres with the majority of vineyards in

Premiers Crus such as Butteaux, Vaillons, and Montée de Tonnerre. The Robins have a small quantity of Grands Crus in Valmur and Vaudésir as well as Blanchot. The Grands Crus are fermented in oak barrels and then aged in cask for 6-12 months. The Premiers Crus are fermented in vats and bottled after 6 months. This can be a very good source for Chablis, but my tasting notes show the wines are amazingly inconsistent and often have elevated levels of sulphur dioxide. The estate's best wines tend to be the Butteaux and Vaudésir.

DOMAINE DE LA ROCHE (SAINT-VÉRAN)**

Wines Produced: Saint-Véran.

I have only tasted two vintages from this estate of 17 acres, and neither wine left a positive impression for its cleanliness or its quality.

DOMAINE ANDRÉ LA ROCHETTE (CHANES)**

Wines Produced: Beaujolais Blanc, Beaujolais-Villages, Saint-Véran.

This estate makes a solidly built, fruity Saint-Véran, but is better known for its Beaujolais.

DOMAINE JOEL ROCHETTE (RÉGNIÉ-DURETTE)***

Wines Produced: Beaujolais Régnié, Beaujolais-Villages, Brouilly-Pisse-Vieille.

Although Joel Rochette's wines are deceptively light and shallow in color, they are imbued with rich banana and raspberry fruitiness, and have excellent length, ripeness, and balance. His Beaujolais-Villages is one of the best of the appellation, and his Régnié is a textbook wine. He keeps his wines for 4–6 months in *foudres* prior to bottling. The entire estate consists of 15.68 acres, and the bulk of the production is in Beaujolais-Villages. His 1989s were stunning, particularly the Brouilly-Pisse-Vieille.

ANTONIN RODET (MERCUREY)***—****

> Wines Produced: Beaune-Clos de la Féguine, Chambertin, Chambertin-Clos de Bèze, Château de Chamirey Mercureys, Chevalier-Montrachet, Clos Vougeot, Meursault-Clos de Mazerey, Meursault Les Perrières, Montrachet, Musigny, Puligny-Montrachet Les Combettes, Château de Rully, Volnay Champans, Volnay-Clos de Santenots, Volnay Santenots.

This well-known Mercurey domaine has recently emerged as an important producer of wines from the Côte Chalonnaise. Its wines from Rully and Mercurey are especially good. In addition, the Rodet firm has important vineyard holdings in some of the most prestigious appellations of the Côte d'Or. Although the quality of the wines in the sixties and seventies was uninspired, it has significantly improved over the last decade. Today, one is generally safe purchasing any of the Rodet whites, as they tend to be fleshy, well-oaked, interesting wines. The red wines have also improved and are now soft, fruity, and easy to drink. In 1988 the Rodet firm acquired the right to distribute all of the wines from the important Domaine Jacques Prieur in commercial outlets, giving Rodet greater visibility. It is worth looking for some of Rodet's less expensive offerings, since both its white and red wines from Rully and Mercurey, particularly the Château de Chamirey Mercureys and Château de Rully wines, are extremely well made and excellent bargains. They are widely available because Rodet produces over 10,000 cases of wine from its 66-acre vineyard in Mercurey. Rodet is also an important *négociant*, purchasing and distributing wine under its own name. In the nineties, I fully expect this aggressive firm to become known as one of the finest sources for white and red burgundies.

DOMAINE MAURICE ROLLIN PÈRE ET FILS (PERNAND-VERGELESSES)**

> Wines Produced: Bourgogne Aligoté, Pernand-Vergelesses, Pernand-Vergelesses-Île des Vergelesses, Savigny-Lès-Beaune.

Having twice visited Monsieur Rollins' cellars, and having tasted all of his vintages since 1985, I have come to the conclusion that I like the man and his family more than his relatively thin, acidic, undernourished wines. Perhaps the location of his vineyards and the age of his vines prevent him from obtaining much charm and character in his wines. Despite their fair prices, these wines are mediocre.

DOMAINE DE LA ROMANÉE-CONTI
(VOSNE-ROMANÉE)*****

> Wines Produced: Bâtard-Montrachet, Echézeaux, Grands Eché-
> zeaux, Montrachet, Richebourg, Romanée-Conti,
> Romanée St.-Vivant, La Tâche, Vosne-Romanée.

No estate in Burgundy, perhaps even in France, is more famous than the Domaine de la Romanée-Conti, coowned by Aubert de Villaine and Lalou Bize-Leroy. Bottles of its wine sell at astronomically high prices. The demand for this estate's red burgundy far exceeds the tiny production from its 74 acres of vineyards (including the two *monopole* vineyards of La Tâche and Romanée-Conti). The wines have always been famous, but their quality is not always consistent. Although the 1959, 1962, and 1966 vintages were extraordinary, the wines made between 1967 and 1977, as good as many of them were, seemed overly alcoholic and loosely structured, and turned brown at a surprisingly early age. Since 1978, however, this estate has had an impeccable record of brilliant successes, with extraordinary wines produced in 1978, 1979, 1980, 1982, 1983, 1985, 1986, 1987, and 1988.

In addition to the domaine's preference to harvest very late in order to obtain a supermaturity in their vineyards, there is also their conservative philosophy regarding grape yields. No property in all of Burgundy has a more restricted yield than the 20–25 hectoliters per hectare that the Domaine de la Romanée-Conti routinely gets from its vineyards. Once the grapes arrive there is no destemming, the wines are fermented at moderately warm temperatures, and the *cuvaison* lasts up to one month, depending on the vintage. After the *cuvaison*, the wines are left in 100% new Allier and Vosges oak barrels for 18 months, are racked once, and are then bottled without ever being filtered. Since 1978, the domaine has shown a certain flexibility with respect to the number of rackings. For example, the 1980s were not racked at all. In 1985, they changed their bottling practices. They now assemble the barrels of each vineyard's wine in a tank and bottle directly from a master blend of the various barrels. The previous practice of bottling directly from the barrel had been controversial, and was frequently criticized because it resulted in excessive bottle variation. To ensure the quality of the oak used in the barrels, the Domaine routinely buys its wood and air-dries it for three years before the barrels are made.

The wines of the Domaine de la Romanée-Conti are irrefutably the greatest expression of red burgundy, and can only be challenged by the wines of the Domaine Leroy and a handful of other estates. While each of these wines is remarkably different from the others, they share certain personality traits in the top vintages: surreal and celestial aromas of oriental spices, flowers, masses of sweet, ripe fruit, scents of truffles, dazzling concentration, tremendous breadth, flavor, exquisite length, and 10–15 years of aging potential. In short, they can be show-stopping wines. However, extremely limited quantities of Domaine de la Romanée-Conti wines are produced. For example, the average production of Romanée-Conti (4.32 acres) is between 6,500–7,500 bottles, the average production of La Tâche (14.4 acres), between 13,000–26,000 bottles, the average production of Richebourg (8.6 acres), 13,500–14,500 bottles, the average production of Grands Echézeaux (8.6 acres), between 13,500–14,500 bottles, the average production of Echézeaux (11.4 acres), between 19,000–20,000 bottles, Romanée St.-Vivant (12.96 acres), between 21,000–23,000 bottles, and the average production of Montrachet (1.65 acres), 2,700 bottles. They also produce a small quantity of Bâtard-Montrachet and Vosne-Romanée that they claim are sold to *négociants*.

These wines are often referred to as the most expensive wines in the world. While that is undoubtedly true, the quality over the last decade has been brilliant. The wines from the Domaine de la Romanée-Conti are often used as standards against which all other burgundy wines are judged. Although the longevity of the domaine's wines is subject to speculation, the wines are clearly made for a very long life. I agree with those who claim that the wines from vintages such as 1978, 1979, 1980, 1983, 1985, 1986, 1987, and 1988 can last, as well as improve in the bottle, for 10–15 years.

ROPITEAU FRÈRES (MEURSAULT)***

> Wines Produced: Beaune Les Grèves, Bourgogne Blanc, Chambolle-Musigny, Clos Vougeot, Echézeaux, Meursault Les Bouchères, Meursault Les Charmes, Meursault Les Genevrières, Meursault Les Gouttes d'Or, Meursault Les Perrières, Meursault Le Poruzot, Monthélie, Pommard, Rully Blanc.

This domaine produces its own estate wines and a line of *négociant* wines. The *négociant* wines are purchased by Ropiteau and brought up in the firm's own modern cellars outside Meursault. Recently, it has been fashionable to find fault with the Ropiteau wines, but in tasting their Meursaults, the criticism does not appear to be justified. The white wines range from very good to excellent, and exhibit a great deal of toasty oak along with dramatic, bold, apple and popcorn-scented Chardonnay fruit. Although they are not on the same level as the wines of the top small growers and finest *négociants*, these white wines are certainly good to very good. On the other hand, the red wines tend to be a bit unfocused and unimpressive. Ropiteau's wines are meant to be drunk within 4–5 years of the vintage.

DOMAINE MICHEL ROSSIGNOL (VOLNAY)***

Wines Produced: Beaune Premier Cru, Beaune Les Teurons, Bourgogne Rouge, Côte de Beaune-Villages, Savigny-Lès-Beaune, Volnay, Volnay Pitures.

In my two visits to Michel Rossignol's domaine, I have found this enthusiastic, middle-aged winemaker dressed in a red jumpsuit and running shoes, dashing around his cramped cellar like a pixie. Rossignol makes very stylish, elegant red wines that are prized for their finesse and elegance rather than their power and structure. His best wines are his Beaune Les Teurons and Volnay Pitures. He was also hired to look after some of the vineyards for the Hospices de Beaune because of his fine reputation as an excellent viticulturist.

DOMAINE PHILIPPE ROSSIGNOL (GEVREY-CHAMBERTIN)***

Wines Produced: Bourgogne Rouge, Côte de Nuits-Villages, Gevrey-Chambertin

Young Philippe Rossignol, who is married to the sister of Joseph Roty, has been looking after his family's vineyard since 1975. This tiny domaine of 8.64 acres does not have any Premiers Crus or Grands Crus. However, Rossignol manages to produce textbook examples of excellent generic Bourgogne Rouge and Côte de Nuits-Villages from his modest appellations. His approach to winemaking is extremely serious, and he uses 25%–30% new oak. Where Rossignol feels it is necessary (for example, in vintages such as 1986), a *saigner* (bleeding of the *cuves*) is performed. His Gevrey-Chambertin is as good as many producers' Premiers Crus, and his Côte de Nuits-Villages is as good as many Gevrey-Chambertins. This is an estate that made serious 1985s, 1987s, and 1988s. As with most of the top domaines, there is little manipulation of the wine, and as light a filtration as possible.

DOMAINE RÉGIS ROSSIGNOL-CHANGARNIER
(VOLNAY)***

Wines Produced: Beaune Les Teurons, Bourgogne Aligoté, Bour-
gogne Rouge, Meursault, Pommard, Savigny-Lès-
Beaune Les Bas Liards, Volnay, Volnay Les
Brouillards, Volnay Premier Cru.

Régis Rossignol is an enthusiastic and dedicated winemaker, although
most of his wines come from appellations that are less glamorous than
many of his competitors'. He has 15.98 acres and estate-bottles his
entire production. He uses one-fourth new oak and his red wines spend
18 months in cask before they are bottled. The style is correct, pleasant, and straightforward, but is not exciting or profound. The Rossignol-
Changarnier wines should be drunk young.

DOMAINE JOSEPH ROTY (GEVREY-CHAMBERTIN)****

Wines Produced: Charmes-Chambertin, Gevrey-Chambertin Les
Champchenys, Gevrey-Chambertin Les Fontenys,
Gevrey-Chambertin Clos Prieur, Griottes-Cham-
bertin, Marsannay, Mazis-Chambertin, Pinot Noir
Les Pressonièrs.

Joseph Roty rarely lets visitors leave his cellar before several hours
have passed tasting the different barrels and looking at his most recent
harvest photographs in the family album. On occasion, he produces
some of the most exquisite wines of Burgundy. The loquacious Roty
made ethereal wines in 1978, 1980, 1985, and 1988. Given his enormous
talents, it is curious that other vintages, such as the 1983, 1986, and
1987 are not better. The domaine has a total of 17.29 acres and frequently uses 100% new *troncais* oak barrels in which the wine is kept
for 16 or more months. In vintages such as 1985 the wines are bottled
unfiltered by a mobile bottler. The Charmes-Chambertin and Mazis-
Chambertin are the estate's top two wines and can be virtually perfect
in top years. The Mazis is more savage than the elegant, supple, seductive Charmes, but both are aged in 100% new oak for 15–16 months,
and, if possible, bottled unfined and unfiltered. This domaine's other
wines can be very good in vintages such as 1985 and 1988, but should
be avoided when the crop size is enormous, as in 1982 and 1986, or in
years of excessive rot, as in 1983. Roty has one of the largest cult
followings of any of the small growers, but like many small growers, his

wines are not a model of consistency. As a result, I would recommend Roty only in the top vintages. His wines keep extremely well, usually lasting for 8–15 years.

DOMAINE ROUGEOT (MEURSAULT)***

> **Wines Produced:** Bourgogne Aligoté, Bourgogne Blanc Les Grandes Gouttes, Bourgogne Passe-Tout-Grains, Bourgogne Rouge, Ladoix, Meursault aux Village, Meursault Les Charmes, Meursault-Monatine, Meursault Sous la Velle, Pommard, Volnay Santenots.

This consistently good producer makes very ageworthy wines; their Meursault Les Charmes, in particular, can last 15–20 years in the bottle. The domaine includes 42 acres, the bulk of which is in appellations such as Bourgogne Rouge, Ladoix, and Bourgogne Blanc. Their Bourgogne Blanc is called Les Grandes Gouttes, and is a very good value. However, their best wines are the Meursault-Charmes, from a 1.23-acre parcel, and the Meursault-Monatine. The white wines see 40% new oak and are bottled after 12–16 months in cask. The red wines see 10% new oak and are bottled after 14–20 months aging in cask. Their best red wine is the Volnay Santenots, but very little of it is exported, as the Rougeot family owns only 2.47 acres of this vineyard.

DOMAINE EMANUEL ROUGET (NUITS ST.-GEORGES)***

> **Wines Produced:** Echézeaux, Nuits St.-Georges, Vosne-Romanée, Vosne-Romanée Les Beaux Monts.

Emanuel Rouget, the young nephew of Henri Jayer, has had the best possible teacher in Burgundy, so let us hope his winemaking efforts will improve. His wines are good, but they lack the great breadth and flavor dimension of his uncle's. His two best wines are his Vosne-Romanée Les Beaux Monts and his excellent Echézeaux, which is truly of Grand Cru quality. The winemaking style of Emanuel Rouget is, not surprisingly, identical to that of Henri Jayer.

DOMAINE GUY ROULOT (MEURSAULT)****

> Wines Produced: Bourgogne Blanc, Meursault Les Charmes, Meursault Les Luchets, Meursault Les Meix Chavaux, Meursault Les Perrières, Meursault Les Tessons, Meursault Les Tillets, Meursault Les Vireuils.

The 31-acre Roulot domaine has always been one of the most popular sources of top quality Meursault. Sadly, Guy Roulot, a much loved man in Burgundy, died following the harvest in 1982. His wife and nephew, Frank Greux, a tiny-boned, articulate young man, now run these wine cellars. An American, Ted Lemon, did an apprenticeship at the Domaine Roulot. He is now in charge of winemaking for the Château Woltner on Napa Valley's Howell Mountain. The wines are fermented in oak barrels at low temperatures of 18°–19° C, aged in Allier oak, of which 25% is new each year, and bottled after 10–12 months of aging. They are impeccably clean, well-balanced wines that have gobs of buttery and nut-scented fruit.

The Meursault Villages wines, with names like Les Luchets, Les Meix Chavaux, Les Vireuils, Les Tillets, and Les Tessons, are among the very best Villages wines made in Meursault. In particular, Les Meix Chavaux and Les Tessons are quite delicious, fleshy, sexy Chardonnays with a great deal of personality and character. The tiny quantities of Les Charmes and Les Perrières are among the very best in Burgundy. Roulot's wines are prized for their hazelnut and pineapple-scented fruitiness, and are best drunk within their first decade of life. They rarely age well beyond that except in a handful of vintages such as 1978. Recent outstanding vintages have included 1985, 1986, and 1989.

DOMAINE GEORGES ROUMIER
(CHAMBOLLE-MUSIGNY)*****

> Wines Produced: Bonnes Mares, Bonnes Mares Vieilles Vignes, Chambolle-Musigny, Chambolle-Musigny Les Amoureuses, Charmes-Chambertin, Clos Vougeot, Corton-Charlemagne, Morey St.-Denis-Clos de le Bussière, Musigny, Ruchottes-Chambertin.

The 40-acre Domaine Georges Roumier is undoubtedly one of the finest sources of classic, long-lived red burgundies. The American importer Frank Schoonmaker exported this estate's wines to the United States in the mid-thirties and late forties. The domaine began producing wine in 1924, and is now directed by the diminutive but enthusiastic Jean-Marie Roumier and his talented son, Christophe.

All aspects of this estate's winemaking are completely traditional. The Roumiers practice a very warm, 18-day maceration, no destemming in vintages such as 1985 and 1988, the use of 25% new wood (the percentage is increased for the Grands Crus), an egg-white fining, and a light filtration via gravity prior to bottling. Only the last step, which was introduced in the late seventies to appease the American market, could be considered a compromise of their high standards. Not surprisingly, the Roumiers decided to stop filtering in 1988. Two other modifications were also introduced in 1988: The entire cellar was air-conditioned and the Roumiers began to practice a 4–5 day prefermentation maceration of their grapes. The wines often need a good 4–5 years to show their best, but there have been many great vintages here including superlative 1966s, 1969s, 1971s, 1972s, 1976s, 1978s, 1983s, 1985s, and 1988s. It is hard to pick a favorite when tasting in the honeycomb cellars of Roumier, but their Musigny, Bonnes Mares, Clos Vougeot, Chambolle-Musigny Les Amoureuses, and their *monopole* vineyard Morey St.-Denis-Clos de la Bussière are superb. The longest-lived wine is the Ruchottes-Chambertin, which tends to be a splendidly rich wine that can last for up to 20 years. The Domaine also produces 125 cases of Corton-Charlemagne from a 1.5-acre parcel they bought in 1975. Even the village Chambolle-Musigny can be excellent in top years. All in all, this domaine makes a fasincating array of wines.

DOMAINE HERVÉ ROUMIER (CHAMBOLLE-MUSIGNY)**

Wines Produced: Bonnes Mares, Bourgogne Rouge, Chambolle-Musigny Les Amoureuses, Clos Vougeot, Echézeaux.

Hervé Roumier is the son of Alain Roumier and the cousin of Jean-Marie Roumier of the more famous Domaine Georges Roumier. He began bottling the wines of his 19.83-acre estate in 1978. Roumier's two largest holdings are his 8.64 acres of Bourgogne Rouge and 7.41 acres of Chambolle-Musigny. In addition, he owns some tiny parcels of Grands Crus, including 1.23 acres of Clos Vougeot, 1.23 acres of Bonnes Mares, and a very small parcel of Echézeaux. The wines to date have generally been straightforward burgundies with no great character or complexity. They spend 15–18 months in 10% new oak casks.

DOMAINE MICHEL DU ROURE (DAVAYÉ)**

Wines Produced: Saint-Véran.

Michel du Roure produces tiny quantities of a highly processed Saint-Véran. This wine tastes too much like a product of modern technology.

DOMAINE ARMAND ROUSSEAU (GEVREY-CHAMBERTIN)****

Wines Produced: Chambertin, Chambertin-Clos de Bèze, Charmes-Chambertin, Clos de la Roche, Gevrey-Chambertin, Gevrey-Chambertin Cazetieres, Gevrey-Chambertin-Clos St.-Jacques, Mazis-Chambertin, Ruchottes-Chambertin-Clos des Ruchottes.

Historically, the Rousseau domaine is one of Burgundy's most important. This domaine was among the first to estate-bottle its wine in the 1930s at the request of the late Raymond Baudoin, owners of the respected *Revue du Vin de France*. Today the estate is run by the meticulous Charles Rousseau who assumed control in 1959 when his father was tragically killed in an automobile accident. After a slump in the late seventies attributed to a fungal infection in his wine cellar, he has produced a succession of beautiful wines. This remarkable domaine has 35 acres of superb vineyards, of which only about one-quarter are in Premiers Crus and Villages wines. The rest are in Grands Crus and include important holdings in Chambertin, Chambertin-Clos de Bèze, and the extraordinary *monopole*, the Gevrey-Chambertin-Clos St.-Jacques.

The wines are made in a very traditional style. There is a 1- to 2-day cold maceration prior to fermentation, vinification in open stainless-steel vats at a rather high temperature of 30°–32° C to extract color, and a *cuvaison* of 15–18 days. Rousseau, who destems 100%, is not adverse to adding back 25% stems to the fermentation when the grapes are totally healthy. After the maceration the wines go into oak casks (25%–35% are new), except for the Chambertin and Chambertin-Clos de Bèze, which are aged in 100% new oak. The wines spend 18 months in cask and are then bottled after a light plaque filtration. Rousseau is adamantly against the new Kisselguhr filtration used by many growers since he feels this type of system strips the wines of body. Rousseau is a very modest man and refuses to promote any of his recent vintages over another. This is unusual in Burgundy, as growers usually praise the wine they have to sell. However, Rousseau will say that his 1949 and 1969 were two of the greatest vintages in his cellar. He has high hopes that his 1989 will turn out to be as good. The top wine here is the Chambertin, made from 50-year-old vines. Unfortunately, there are less than 300 cases made in an abundant year. Close in quality, and often more precocious, supple, and flattering to taste young, is the Chambertin-Clos de Bèze, 300 cases of which are produced in years such as 1985 and 1988. His Gevrey-Chambertin-Clos St.-Jacques, while not technically a Grand Cru, is produced from 61-year-old vines and can be a sensational wine in vintages such as 1985, 1987, and 1988. His Clos des Ruchottes, Clos de la Roche and Charmes-Chambertin are also excellent. In vintages such as 1985 and 1988, the wines of Domaine Rousseau can age gracefully for at least 8–15 years.

DOMAINE ROUX PÈRE ET FILS (SAINT-AUBIN) ***

> Wines Produced: Bourgogne Aligoté, Bourgogne Les Grands Charmeaux Rouge, Bourgogne Passe-Tout-Grains, Chassagne-Montrachet Blanc, Chassagne-Montrachet-Clos St.-Jean Rouge, Chassagne-Montrachet Rouge, Crémant de Bourgogne, Meursault-Clos des Poruzots, Puligny-Montrachet Les Enseignères, Santenay, Saint-Aubin La Chatenière, Saint-Aubin La Pucelle, Saint-Aubin Rouge.

This is the largest domaine operating in Saint-Aubin, producing wines from 13 different appellations in Burgundy. The proprietor, Marcel Roux, believes in 50% new oak for his white wines and bottles them after 8 months. He uses 30% new oak for the red wines and bottles them after 10 months. The estate's approach to winemaking and élevage is very modern, and as a result, the wines are crisp, fresh, flowery, and should to be drunk immediately upon release. They are never wines with a great deal of depth or richness. The wines are marketed in attractive, heavy bottles and have a large audience. The domaine sells many of its wines to restaurants, as restaurants prefer lighter-styled burgundies. I have had extremely good luck with the Saint-Aubin La Pucelle and the Saint-Aubin La Chatenière. For their price, they are better than some of the more prestigious white burgundies made by Domaine Roux from their vineyards in Puligny-Montrachet, Chassagne-Montrachet, and Meursault. As for the red wines, they tend to lack concentration, and often have an excess of tannin for the amount of fruit. The entire domaine consists of 47.74 acres, including 3.7 acres of

Crémant de Bourgogne (one of the best examples of this wine to be found). The wines of Marcel Roux should be drunk within their first 5–6 years of life.

DOMAINE ROY FRÈRES (AUXEY-DURESSES) **

> Wines Produced: Auxey-Duresses Blanc, Auxey-Duresses Les Duresses, Auxey-Duresses Rouge, Auxey-Duresses Le Val, Bourgogne Rouge, Volnay Santenots.

Bernard Roy, now assisted by his sons Vincent and Dominique, produces wines that tend to be rather rustic and imbued with a great deal of tannin. They are full-bodied, muscular wines that need some time in the bottle. However, the expectation that the hardness will melt away to reveal velvety fruit is not always realized. My favorite recent vintage is 1985, but the wines of that vintage had soft tannins. Roy's best wine tends to be his Auxey-Duresses Le Val, as it usually has more suppleness and texture than his Auxey-Duresses Les Duresses. The two vintages of Volnay Santenots I tasted were extremely hard, tannic, lean, and lacking charm and finesse. Bernard Roy owns 26.84 acres of vines, and utilizes 20% new oak for aging his red wines.

DOMAINE ROY PÈRE ET FILS
(GEVREY-CHAMBERTIN) **

> Wines Produced: Gevrey-Chambertin, Gevrey-Chambertin Clos Prieur.

The cellars of this tiny domaine of 10 acres are located in Gevrey-Chambertin. Proprietor Marc Roy produces wines from a fairly standard vinification and *élevage*. One-third new oak is employed and the wines are given a light polishing filtration prior to being bottled. The 1988s appeared to be the best recent vintage, with the 1985s a close second. The 1987s tasted light and the 1986s were lean, hard, and unmemorable.

DOMAINE RUET (CERCIÉ) ****

> Wines Produced: Beaujolais-Villages, Brouilly, Morgon.

Jean-Paul Ruet's Brouilly and his tiny quantities of Morgon define for me what Brouilly and Morgon are all about. They are fragrant wines with plenty of crunchy, supple berry fruit, soft tannins, and a heady, long finish. His wines are best consumed within 2–3 years of the vintage. Ruet owns 27.7 acres, with the bulk of his production in Brouilly.

CHÂTEAU DE RULLY (RULLY)***

> Wines Produced: Rully Les Bressandes du Château, Ruly Molesme Premier Cru Rouge.

This tiny 2.47-acre (1 hectare) estate, founded in 1629, makes excellent wines from very old vines. Twenty-five percent new oak is used for the red wines and 33% for the whites. The red wines are made in a very concentrated, rich, powerful style, and are bottled after 30 months of cask aging. The whites are bottled after 24 months. The firm of Antonin Rodet is responsible for the commercialization of the wines of Château de Rully. Some afficionados believe they are among the best of the appellation. They are marked by the smell of toasty new oak. There is no question that the muscular, powerful style of wine produced by the Comte C. d'Aviau de Ternay (the owner and proprietor) requires long aging in bottle to reach its peak.

DOMAINE DE RULLY SAINT-MICHEL (RULLY)****

> Wines Produced: Rully Champs Cloux Rouge, Rully-Clos de Pellerey, Rully Les Cloux, Rully Rabourcé.

One of the oldest estates in southern Burgundy, the Domaine de Rully Saint-Michel has been in the same family for six generations. Today, the property is looked after by Madame de Bodard de la Jacopière. She is a direct descendent of the treasurer for Napoleon III, who founded this estate. The red wines are supple, deliciously fruity, medium- to full-bodied, and represent outstanding values in vintages such as 1985, 1987, and 1988. Only the 1986, which was too tannic for correct balance, seemed problematical. As for the white wines, the Rully Rabourcé Blanc is one of the best wines of the appellation. It can easily compete with some of the Premiers Crus from more glamorous appellations such as Chassagne-Montrachet and Puligny-Montrachet. The Japanese Airlines, JAL, serves this white burgundy. In addition, it is one of the featured Rullys on sale at the famous Cave Taillevent, one of Paris's leading wine shops. I have not had any experience with the older wines from this estate, but I see no reason why they should not last 4–5 years given their good balance.

DOMAINE DE RUYÈRE (VILLIÉ-MORGON)**

Wines Produced: Beaujolais-Villages, Morgon.

The Domaine de Ruyère makes a rather straightforward Morgon. In my tastings it has never fared as well as the Morgons of some of the other small producers or *négociants* of the appellation. Proprietor Paul Collonge has 28.4 acres and bottles his wines after 6–7 months in large *foudres*.

DOMAINE FABIAN ET LOUIS SAIER (MERCUREY)**

Wines Produced: Mercurey Blanc, Mercurey Champs Martin, Mercurey Les Chenelots, Mercurey Rouge.

This sizeable 43.7-acre estate has the potential to be one of the best in Mercurey, given its excellent Premier Cru vineyard sites of 9.07 acres in Champs Martin and 4.94 acres in Chenelots. The domaine practices a traditional vinification, with a lengthy *cuvaison* of 3 weeks, and frequent pumping over of the wine during the vinification. All small oak barrels are used, of which a percentage is new, and the estate seems determined not to filter unless unavoidable. However, with the exception of the 1985s and 1988s, the wines have not been as impressive as could be expected. In good vintages, the wines should be drunk within 5–7 years of the harvest.

DOMAINE FRANCIS SAILLANT (SAINT-AMOUR)***

Wines Produced: Saint-Amour.

The exuberant, enthusiastic Francis Saillant owns only 9.88 acres, but he makes an explosively fruity, agreeable Saint-Amour bursting with blackberry and raspberry fruit. This wine is kept in oak casks and *foudres* for 5–6 months prior to bottling. Saillant's wines are difficult to find, but worth the effort.

DOMAINE SAINTE-CLAIRE (PRÉHY)***

Wines Produced: Bourgogne Aligoté, Bourgogne Blanc, Bourgogne Rouge, Chablis, Sauvignon de St.-Bris.

The Domaine Sainte-Claire is run by Jean-Marc Brocard. The modern cellars, built in 1980, are located in the center of his vineyard in the village of Préhy. His entire domaine consists of 92 acres, of which 61.75 are in Chablis Villages. The rest of his vineyards include some Sauvignon Blanc de St.-Bris, Bourgogne Aligoté, Bourgogne Rouge, and Bourgogne Blanc. Brocard believes in mechanical harvesting. He ferments his wine in stainless steel tanks, ages 10% in oak casks, and then blends the cuvées together. The result is a modern yet well-made, fruity, stylish wine that should be drunk within 4–5 years of the vintage. While I have never tasted it, Brocard has a good reputation for his Bourgogne Rouge, which he ages one year in cask prior to bottling.

DOMAINE JEAN-LOUIS SANTÉ (LA CHAPELLE DEGUINCHAY)****

Wines Produced: Chénas, Juliénas, Moulin-à-Vent.

Jean-Louis and Bernard Santé own 19.76 acres of vineyards. While they make a good Moulin-à-Vent and Juliénas, their pride and joy is their Chénas. They feel it has the most complex perfume and is typical of Beaujolais. The wines of Santé are wonderfully well focused and elegant Beaujolais that should be drunk within 2–3 years of the vintage.

PAUL SAPIN (LANCIÉ)**

Wines Produced: This moderately sized *négociant* produces an entire line of Beaujolais and Mâconnais wines.

Madame Paul Sapin is the latest Sapin to run this old family firm. I remember having some good Sapin wines in the late seventies, but the recent quality has left much to be desired. The wines are not defective or undrinkable; they are simply straightforward, technically correct, and dull.

ROBERT SARRAU-CAVES DE L'ARDIÈRES (BELLEVILLE)***

Wines Produced: Chénas-Domaine des Pins, Côte de Brouilly-Domaine de la Berthaudière, Fleurie Grand Pré, Juliénas-Château des Capitans, Morgon-Château Gaillard.

Note: This large firm also produces an entire *négociant* line of Beaujolais and Mâconnais wines under its own name.

The Sarrau family founded this enterprise in 1963. They own 56.81 acres primarily in excellent Beaujolais crus such as Juliénas, Fleurie, and Morgon. Their sales have reached almost 700,000 cases, of which a significant percentage (65%) is exported. The wines are very well made, and not far behind the high-quality wines of Georges Duboeuf and Pierre Ferraud. The Sarrau wines are characterized by good, ripe fruit, show respect for each of the villages of the Beaujolais and Mâconnais regions, and can be consistently recommended.

CHÂTEAU DE LA SAULE (MONTAGNY)****

> Wines Produced: Bourgogne Aligoté, Bourgogne Passe-Tout-Grains, Montagny, Montagny Premier Cru.

The Chateau de la Saule produces the best white wines I have tasted from the appellation of Montagny. This 28.03-acre estate is run with great attention to detail by Alain Roy-Thevenin. He uses 10% new oak for aging his white wine, and bottles after 8 months. These delicious medium- to full-bodied whites have retained their exuberance and complexity, and have gobs of fresh fruit. The red wines tend to be light, but elegant and tasty. All things considered, this is probably the best small estate of the Montagny appellation. The prices are extremely reasonable for wines of this quality level.

DOMAINE ÉTIENNE SAUZET
(PULIGNY-MONTRACHET)*****

> Wines Produced: Bâtard-Montrachet, Bienvenues-Bâtard-Montrachet, Chassagne-Montrachet-Villages, Puligny-Montrachet, Puligny-Montrachet Champ Canet, Puligny-Montrachet Les Combettes, Puligny-Montrachet Les Perrières, Puligny-Montrachet Les Referts, Puligny-Montrachet La Truffière.

This is one of the most serious white winemaking estates in Burgundy. Unfortunately, they are not easy to find, as much of the production is either allocated to restaurants in France or the export markets. The wines, now made by Sauzet's son-in-law, Gérard Boudot, are kept on their lees for 10–12 months, aged in 25%–33% new Allier oak, and then bottled after a coarse Kisselguhr filtration. They are elegant and well-balanced, textbook white burgundies, brimming with flavor. The 26-acre estate has important holdings spread among the following vineyards: 1.25 acres in Bâtard and Bienvenues-Bâtard-Montrachet, 3.75 in Puligny-Montrachet Les Combettes, 4 acres in Puligny-Montrachet

Champs Canet, 3.6 acres in Puligny-Montrachet Les Referts, 1.25 acres in Puligny-Montrachet Les Perrières, .6 of an acre in Puligny-Montrachet La Truffière, 10 acres of generic Puligny-Montrachet, and 1.6 acres of Chassagne-Montrachet. The average age of the vines is 33 years. The best wines here consistently are the Grands Crus Bâtard and Bienvenues-Bâtard-Montrachet, but virtually as good in many vintages are the Puligny-Montrachet Les Combettes and the Puligny-Montrachet La Truffière. The latter wine is quite hard to find, but is a favorite of many of France's top restaurants such as Taillevent, Jamin, La Marée, Lameloise, Pic, Boyer, Auberge d l'Ill, Georges Blanc, Alain Chapel, Paul Bocuse, and l'Espérance. Sauzet's wines drink extremely well young, but are capable of lasting for 10–12 years in the bottle.

DOMAINE SAVOYE (VILLIÉ-MORGON)****

> Wines Produced: Beaujolais, Beaujolais Rosé, Morgon, Morgon-Côte du Py.

Pierre Savoye is the son-in-law of Jean Descombes, the finest grower and winemaker in Morgon. Descombes' wines are bottled under both his name and that of *négociant* Georges Duboeuf. Pierre Savoye has adopted many of his father-in-law's winemaking techniques. As a result, he produces a wonderfully hedonistic, exuberant, rich, lush Morgon that has explosive fruitiness and plenty of body and length. The wines from his 33.74-acre domaine can last for 4–5 years, and are among the most highly prized of the village.

DOMAINE RENÉ SAVOYE (CHIROUBLES)***

> Wines Produced: Chiroubles.

This highly respected estate in Chiroubles produces deliciously fruity, vivacious, vibrant wines. They should be drunk within 3–4 years of the vintage.

DOMAINE DANIEL SENARD (ALOXE-CORTON)***–****

> Wines Produced: Aloxe-Corton Blanc, Aloxe-Corton Premier Cru, Aloxe-Corton Rouge, Beaune Premier Cru, Chorey-Lès-Beaune, Le Corton, Corton Les Bressandes, Corton-Clos des Meix, Corton-Clos du Roi.

This impressive domaine, located in the tiny village of Aloxe-Corton, has always made good wines. However, Philippe Senard's decision to hire Guy Accad, the famous Lebanese oenologist, has resulted in some especially remarkable wines in 1987 and 1988. The current domaine includes 22.2 acres spread throughout the appellation of Aloxe-Corton; an impressive 13.6 of these acres are in Grands Crus in Aloxe-Corton. Senard also has a small parcel of vines in Chorey-Lès-Beaune. The estate makes a tiny amount of a very rich, fleshy, fat Aloxe-Corton Blanc from the Pinot Gris grape. If you can find a bottle, this wine is excellent and worth buying.

The Senard wines are fermented in wooden, open *cuves* and steel vats. The estate believes in using at least 25% new oak, and the percentage is increased for its Grands Crus. The quality of the wines has never been better than it is today, and the 1987 and 1988 vintages should provide strikingly rich, aromatic wines.

DOMAINE CHRISTIAN SERAFIN
(GEVREY-CHAMBERTIN)****

> Wines Produced: Charmes-Chambertin, Gevrey-Chambertin, Gevrey-Chambertin Cazetieres, Gevrey-Chambertin Le Fonteny, Gevrey-Chambertin Vieilles Vignes.

Christian Serafin's cellars sit on the hillside behind the actual village of Gevrey-Chambertin. Although his domaine is tiny, only 10.8 acres, his wines have been consistently excellent throughout the 1980s. For years he sold most of his wine to private clients in Switzerland, but he has recently shown some interest in selling it outside Europe. His wines not only offer great power, but also reveal tremendous style and complexity. He believes in destemming 66% of his grape bunches, a very hot fermentation of 33°–34° C (he feels the heat gives the wine more structure and intensity), a three-and-one-half-week maceration, and 20 months of aging in 40% new oak (his Grand Cru, the Charmes-Chambertin, sees 100% new oak). The wines are given a very light filtration prior to bottling. His top wine is his Premier Cru, Gevrey-Chambertin Cazetieres, made from 38-year-old vines. It is a splendidly rich, exceptionally concentrated wine, even in lighter vintages such as 1986. These are very much the wines of a young perfectionist, and if you want to taste a lush, titillating burgundy filled with finesse and gorgeous amounts of berry fruit, then Serafin is your type of producer. Most of his wines appear to have the potential to age gracefully for at least a decade. For value, don't dare miss Serafin's Gevrey-Chambertin Vieilles Vignes.

DOMAINE BERNARD SERVEAU
(MOREY ST.-DENIS)***–****

> Wines Produced: Bourgogne Rouge, Chambolle-Musigny Les Amoureuses, Chambolle-Musigny Les Chabiots, Morey St.-Denis Les Sorbès, Nuits St.-Georges Les Chaines Carteaux.

This tiny, damp cellar, located on the main road into Morey St.-Denis from N 74, produces graceful examples of red burgundy, particularly in good vintages such as 1985, 1987, and 1988. While they are never blockbuster wines, they are juicy, round, aromatic, and extremely elegant. Bernard Serveau, the gracious, ruddy-faced father, and his son, one of the premier singers at the extravagant feasts of the Château de Clos Vougeot, own 16.8 acres. The land is divided evenly between generic Bourgogne and Premiers Crus and Grands Crus. This estate's winemaking would appear overly analytical and technical, based on a conversation with Serveau, but the wines come out as unprocessed, handcrafted expressions of Pinot Noir. Only 10%–15% new oak barrels are used, there is 100% destemming, and the top wine is consistently the Chambolle-Musigny Les Amoureuses. Unfortunately, only 5 barrels or less (or 125 cases) of this wine are made, even in abundant vintages. As for the other wines, I almost always prefer either the Chambolle-Musigny Les Chabiots or the Morey St.-Denis Les Sorbès to the rather lean, hard, compact Nuits St.-Georges Les Chaines Carteaux. The Bourgogne Rouge frequently displays excellent depth and loads of berry fruit, and in the world of high-priced burgundy, it is a real bargain. Most of Serveau's wines should be drunk within their first 5–7 years, although the Chambolle-Musigny Les Amoureuses can last for 8–12 years in top vintages.

DOMAINE SERVELLE-TACHOT
(CHAMBOLLE-MUSIGNY)***

> Wines Produced: Chambolle-Musigny, Chambolle-Musigny Les Amoureuses, Chambolle-Musigny Les Charmes.

The micro estate of Jean Servelle produces delicate, silky, supple red burgundies that drink extremely well young. In vintages with enormous yields (i.e., 1982 and 1986) the wines here can be a bit diluted, but in the better vintages these wines are full of finesse, charm, and elegance. This is not an estate where you will find blockbuster wines of power and intensity. Servelle-Tachot's best wine is the Chambolle-Musigny Les Amoureuses, of which Servelle has just over one acre of vineyards. He also makes a good Premier Cru from the Les Charmes vineyard of Chambolle-Musigny, and a harmonious, elegant, lighter-styled Chambolle-Musigny from his largest vineyard of 4.94 acres. Servelle ages his wines in 25% new oak for 18–24 months and then bottles them with as light a filtration as possible.

DOMAINE MAURICE ET HERVÉ SIGAUT (CHAMBOLLE-MUSIGNY)**

Wines Produced: Chambolle-Musigny Les Fuées, Chambolle-Musigny Les Sentières, Morey St.-Denis Les Charrières.

The 16-acre Sigaut estate has some important vineyards in Chambolle-Musigny and Morey St.-Denis. Although I have tasted only a few vintages, the wines appear to be sound, but not exceptional. The Sigaut family practices 100% destemming, a 2–3 week *cuvaison*, and fining and filtration after 15–17 months of aging in oak barrels, of which 50% are new. From what I have tasted, the wines appear to offer immediate gratification, and are best when consumed within 5–6 years of the vintage.

DOMAINE SIMON FILS (MAREY-LES-FUSSEY)**

Wines Produced: Bourgogne Aligoté, Bourgogne Blanc, Bourgogne Hautes-Côtes de Nuits Rouge, Bourgogne Passe-Tout-Grains, Bourgogne Rouge.

The Simon family's best wine is usually its Bourgogne Rouge. The wine tends to be supple, fruity, and ideal for consumption within the first 2–3 years of the vintage. The other wines often lack depth and charm. The 26.75-acre estate ages its wines in both cask and tank for 12–24 months prior to bottling. Perhaps earlier bottling would result in more freshness and fruit in these wines.

SIMONNET-FEBVRE (CHABLIS)**

Wines Produced: Chablis Mont de Milieu, Chablis Les Preuses.

Note: This firm also operates as a *négociant,* supplementing its limited production with significant purchases from growers. The firm produces an entire range of wines from Chablis, including Premiers Crus, Grands Crus, and Crémant de Bourgogne.

This 10.5-acre estate produces very modern-style Chablis under the *négociant* label of Simonnet-Febvre. The firm, founded in 1840, ferments and ages its wines in stainless steel and bottles after 5–8 months. The present-day proprietors, Jean-Claude and Jean-Pierre Simonnet believe the customer should be responsible for aging the wine. I find the quality of the wines here to be straightforward and insipid.

DOMAINE ROBERT SIRUGUE (VOSNE-ROMANÉE)***

> Wines Produced: Bourgogne Rouge, Chambolle-Musigny, Grands Echézeaux, Vosne-Romanée, Vosne-Romanée Les Petits Monts.

Robert Sirugue's face always seems to be friendly and animated, especially when he suspects a sale is imminent. He is a very commercially oriented grower, but the quality of his wines is high. Over half of his 24.2 acres are in generic Bourgogne Rouge. He also has 1.23 acres of old vines in the well-situated Vosne-Romanée Les Petits Monts, a tiny vineyard near Romanée-Conti and Richebourg. This wine can be an excellent value, although it is not as well known as some of the more highly publicized Premier Cru vineyards of Vosne-Romanée. Sirugue's best wine, however, is a sensational Grands Echézeaux from a .32-acre parcel. He only makes a few barrels of this wine, but it is quite remarkable and can rival the best made in Burgundy. Wines from the Domaine Robert Sirugue are consistently well made and Sirugue seems to handle mediocre vintages as well as he does top vintages. He uses 20%–35% new oak and bottles his wines after 18–20 months in cask. Sirugue bottles certain cuvées with no filtration, a practice that always signals a highly conscientious winemaker. These wines should be drunk within 6–7 years of the vintage.

DOMAINE DE LA SORBIÈRE (QUINCIÉ)**

> Wines Produced: Beaujolais-Villages.

Jean Charles Pivot runs this 34.58-acre estate. The domaine sells most of its wine in bulk to *négociants,* but does produce a straightforward, and commercial Beaujolais-Villages under its own name.

DOMAINE LUC SORIN (SAINT-BRIS-LE-VINEUX)***

> Wines Produced: Bourgogne Aligoté, Bourgogne Blanc, Bourgogne Irancy Rouge, Bourgogne Rouge, Sauvignon de St.-Bris.

Luc Sorin is one of the best growers of the Yonne area of France. Everything at the Domaine Luc Sorin is done after contemplation and careful consideration. Sorin makes a good Bourgogne Aligoté, which spends 6–9 months in tank prior to bottling; a crisp, herbaceous, flinty Sauvignon de St.-Bris, and a surprisingly serious Bourgogne Irancy Rouge. The Bourgogne Rouge spends 9–12 months in cask and is bottled with minimal fining and filtration. Sorin has begun to receive a great deal of publicity for his realistically priced wines. In 1981 he was exporting only 5% of his production, but by 1988 he was selling over half of his wines outside of France. There is a large foreign demand for reasonably priced white and red burgundies. All of his wines should be consumed with 2–3 years of the vintage.

DOMAINE ALBERT SOTHIER (SAINT-ÉTIENNE-LA-VARENNE)**

> Wines Produced: Beaujolais-Villages, Brouilly.

This small domaine of 16 acres makes straightforward, one-dimensional Brouilly and Beaujolais-Villages. The wines should be consumed within one year of the vintage.

DOMAINE SUREMAIN (MERCUREY)**

> Wines Produced: Mercurey Blanc, Mercurey-Bondue, Mercurey-Clos l'Évêque, Mercurey-Clos Voyen, Mercurey Les Crets, Mercurey Rouge, Mercurey Sazenay.

In my experience, Hugues and his son Yves Suremain do not always live up to their reputation for high-quality wines. The wines often reveal a musty, sometimes oxidized and overly rustic character that contradicts this estate's prestige. It is a large 50.01-acre estate with impressive holdings in some of the best vineyards of Mercurey, such as Clos l'Évêque and the Clos Voyen. The wines age well, and bottles of 10- to 15-year-old Mercurey Clos l'Évêque or Clos Voyen can provide satisfying if unexhilarating drinking. The red wines see 8% new oak and are bottled after 18–24 months in cask. The white wines see no new oak and are bottled from 6 to 15 months in oak. This time in oak seems excessive for a white wine from this appellation.

DOMAINE TALMARD (UCHIZY) ***

> Wines Produced: Bourgogne Rouge, Mâcon-Rouge, Mâcon-Uchizy, Mâcon-Villages.

While I have never been a great admirer of Paul and Philibert Talmard's red wines, their two white wines, the Mâcon-Villages and the Mâcon-Uchizy, are excellent examples of the potential of a Mâcon wine. They are aged in large oak *foudres* and smaller casks for 5–6 months before bottling. The red wines benefit from about 20% new oak casks. However, one should look for this estate's white wines. These brothers own 54.34 acres of well-placed vineyards in the Mâconnais area. Their 1988 Mâcon-Villages placed first in a blind tasting I did of the 1988 Mâcons. Their wines can last for 2–3 years.

DOMAINE JEAN TARDY (VOSNE-ROMANÉE) ****

> Wines Produced: Chambolle-Musigny, Clos Vougeot, Nuits St.-Georges Les Boudots, Vosne-Romanée Les Chaumes.

Jean Tardy is an accomplished winemaker. He keeps the best of his production from his 11.5 acres of vineyards for his own estate-bottled wines. The excess is sold to the famous Beaune *négociants*, Louis Jadot and Joseph Drouhin. His acreage includes a wonderfully situated parcel high up on the hill in Clos Vougeot. This is often his best wine, and in years such as 1986 and 1988 he did a *saigner* (bleeding the *cuves* of excess juice) to make a rosé of Clos Vougeot. Under Burgundy regulations, this wine is only entitled to a generic appellation. Tardy's other top wines include his smoky, rich Nuits St.-Georges Les Boudots, and his Vosne-Romanée Les Chaumes. Tardy, who keeps his wines in his heavily toasted new oak casks for up to 16 months, has proven to be an uncommonly consistent winemaker, making some of the most concentrated wines of the 1986 vintage, prevailing again in 1987, and making beautifully intense, concentrated wines in 1988. Most of the wines from the Domaine Jean Tardy are capable of lasting for up to a decade.

DOMAINE J. TAUPENOT-MERME
(MOREY ST.-DENIS)***

Wines Produced: Bourgogne Passe-Tout-Grains, Chambolle-Musigny, Charmes-Chambertin, Gevrey-Chambertin, Morey St.-Denis.

Jean Taupenot, who runs this 22.23-acre estate, claims 65% of their production is estate-bottled, although that increases to almost 100% for their 3.7-acre parcel of the grand cru vineyard, Charmes-Chambertin. The wines see a generous amount of new oak (approximately 50%), and are bottled after 15 months of cask aging. In the three vintages I have tasted, I found Taupenot's wines to be richly fruity, surprisingly herbaceous, and less focused and defined than some purists might require. Yet they are tasty, fat, commercial wines that are ideal for drinking in their first 5–7 years of life. The Charmes-Chambertin is Taupenot's finest wine, followed by his Villages Morey St.-Denis and Gevrey-Chambertin.

DOMAINE PHILIPPE TESTUT (CHABLIS)****

Wines Produced: Chablis, Chablis Les Grenouilles, Chablis Premier Cru.

Philippe Testut produces excellent Chablis from a tiny parcel of vines in the Grand Cru Les Grenouilles. Unfortunately, most of the family holding of Les Grenouilles was sold in the 1970s due to internal squabbles, and it is now run by the giant Chablis cooperative, La Chablisienne. Philippe Testut still retains a tiny parcel in addition to his Premier Cru Chablis and Chablis Villages. Testut ferments his wine in stainless-steel tanks and cement vats, and ages it in a percentage of new oak for 6–9 months. The quality of his Premiers Crus, and particularly of his Grand Cru Les Grenouilles is excellent. The wines are among the very best of the region and offer great style and concentration. They never sacrifice their richness and depth, and remain extremely well balanced and filled with finesse. If Testut's name sounds familiar to Rhône wine enthusiasts, it is because he is also the proprietor of a moderately sized vineyard in Lirac.

DOMAINE RAYMOND ET MICHEL TÊTE (JULIÉNAS)***

Wines Produced: Juliénas, Saint-Amour.

This excellent Juliénas domaine produces well-balanced wines that can be drunk young, but will stand up well to 3–4 years of aging. They are aged in oak *foudres* and concrete vats for 4–6 months prior to bottling. These wines also appear under the name of Clos du Fief.

DOMAINE THENARD (GIVRY)***

> Wines Produced: Chassagne-Montrachet-Clos St.-Jean, Corton-Clos du Roi, Givry Blanc, Givry Les Bons Chevaux Rouge, Givry Cellier aux Moines, Givry-Clos St.-Pierre, Grands Echézeaux, Le Montrachet, Pernand-Vergelesses Île des Vergelesses.

This famous old estate lived off its reputation for years producing only mediocre wines. It has been in the same family for over 200 years, and is finally beginning to get serious about the quality of its wines. Jacques Bordeaux-Montrieux is the director of the estate, and for the last decade the quality of his wines has been very good to excellent. The domaine is known for its large holding of the famous white-wine vineyard, Le Montrachet. The Thenards own 4.52 acres, making them the second largest landholder of this great Grand Cru vineyard. Additionally, they have 1.23 acres of Grands Echézeaux, 2.4 acres of Corton-Clos du Roi, and 18 acres of the excellent Givry Cellier aux Moines. The red wines enjoy 20% new oak and are bottled after 16–24 months of cask aging. The white wines see 100% new oak and are bottled after 12–18 months. The production of the Domaine Thenard is marketed by the famous Beaune *négociant*, Remoissenet. While there is still room for improvement in quality, the wines made at the Domaine Thenard have improved significantly during the last decade.

DOMAINE JEAN THEVENET (QUINTAINE-CLESSÉ)****

> Wines Produced: Mâcon-Clessé Blanc, Mâcon-Clessé Rouge.

Jean Thevenet makes very stylish yet highly concentrated, fruity, floral, and consistently superb white wines from his 18.27-acre Domaine de la Bongrand. The whites are fermented in stainless steel and then see 8–12 months in cask. These are wines to be consumed within 4–6 years of the vintage. In my opinion, they are the finest wines of the Mâconnais region. Thevenet has been known to produce a sweet Mâcon when his grapes are attacked by botrytis.

DOMAINE RENÉ THÉVENIN-MONTHÉLIE ET FILS
(SAINT-ROMAIN)**

> Wines Produced: Auxey-Duresses Rouge, Beaune, Bourgogne Rouge, Monthélie, Savigny-Lès-Beaune, Savigny-Lès-Beaune Les Peuillets, Saint-Romain Blanc, Saint-Romain Rouge, Volnay Clos des Chênes.

The Thévenin family has one of the largest domaines in Saint-Romain. It consists of 38.4 acres and is spread out over nine different appellations. Their biggest landholdings are in Saint-Romain Blanc and Saint-Romain Rouge. The Saint-Romain Blanc tends to be a light, stylish wine that lacks the depth or character of that made by Saint-Romain's best winemaker, Alain Gras. The Saint-Romain Rouge is a decent, rather rustic, but adequate example of this wine. They also produce a good, muscular, somewhat tannic Monthélie from a 6.6-acre vineyard. The red wines can last and evolve, but are often too tannic and hard for twentieth-century palates.

DOMAINE THEVENOT-LE-BRUN ET FILS
(MAREY LÈS FUSSEY)***

> Wines Produced: Bourgogne Aligoté, Bourgogne Hautes-Côtes de Nuits Blanc, Bourgogne Hautes-Côtes de Nuits-Clos du Vignon Blanc, Bourgogne Hautes-Côtes de Nuits-Clos du Vignon Rouge, Bourgogne Hautes-Côtes de Nuits Rouge, Bourgogne Passe-Tout-Grains, Bourgogne Rosé, Bourgogne Rouge.

One of the very finest domaines in the Hautes-Côtes de Nuits appellation, the domaine Thevenot-Le-Brun produces very stylish, flavorful wines that show a great deal of care in their winemaking and upbringing. The Thevenot family exploits 54.83 acres of vines and produces two white wines. One, called the Clos du Vignon Blanc, is a blend of Chardonnay and Pinot Gris (called Pinot Beurot in Burgundy). The other called Bourgogne Hautes-Côtes de Nuits Blanc, is made from the Pinot Blanc grape. The white wines are aged in small oak casks, of which a very high percentage (normally 50%–75%) is new. The results are lovely, toasty, vanillin wines with a rich fruity character and good structure, ideal for drinking in their first 3–4 years of life. The red wines are also to be recommended, particularly their excellent Hautes-Côtes de Nuits-Clos du Vignon Rouge. This wine has perhaps as much character and complexity as any wine from the Hautes-Côtes de Nuits region. I had the 1985 vintage in a blind tasting against several Premiers Crus from estates like Henri Gouges and came away feeling the Thevenot wine was the best. The red wines see 20% new oak and are bottled after 9–12 months of aging in casks. Thevenot-Le-Brun et Fils also makes a good Bourgogne Aligoté and tiny quantities of an austere, dry, crisp rosé.

CHÂTEAU THIVIN (ODENAS)**

Wines Produced: Brouilly, Côte de Brouilly.

This famous estate is probably the best-known producer of Côte de Brouilly in the export markets, particularly in the United States. Claude-Vincent Geoffray has owned the domaine for many years, and the 37.05-acre vineyard is primarily in Côte de Brouilly, although 7.5 acres are in Brouilly. The wines enjoyed a marvelous reputation in the fifties, sixties, and early seventies, but I have not had a good wine from this estate since the 1978 vintage. The 1980s wines have been watery and washed out in flavor and color, and frequently lack concentration and freshness. The Château Thivin needs to be shaken up and the quality of its wines improved.

DOMAINE GÉRARD THOMAS (SAINT-AUBIN)**

Wines Produced: Bourgogne Blanc, Bourgogne Passe-Tout-Grains, Bourgogne Rouge, Meursault-Blagny, Puligny-Montrachet La Garenne, Saint-Aubin Les Frionnes Rouge, Saint-Aubin Murger des Dents de Chien Blanc.

Along with Marc Colin, Jean-Claude Bachelet, and Henri Prudhon, Gérard Thomas is one of the top producers in the village of Saint-Aubin. His domaine is very small, only 15.7 acres, and most of it is in generic wine. He makes excellent stylish, floral white wines that see 8%–10% new oak and are bottled after 12 months. In addition to the Saint-Aubins, one should look for his Puligny-Montrachet La Garenne with its stony, mineral-scented fruit, and the more buttery, toasty Meursault-Blagny. His red wine tends to be somewhat light and straightforward. Gérard Thomas's wines should be drunk within their first 5–6 years of life.

DOMAINE TOLLOT-BEAUT ET FILS
(CHOREY-LÈS-BEAUNE)****

> Wines Produced: Aloxe-Corton, Beaune Les Blanches Fleurs, Beaune Clos du Roi, Beaune Les Grèves, Bourgogne Aligoté, Bourgogne Blanc, Bourgogne Rouge, Chorey-Lès-Beaune, Corton, Corton Les Bressandes, Corton-Charlemagne, Savigny-Lès-Beaune, Savigny-Lès-Beaune Les Lavières, Savigny Champs Chevrey.

This venerable estate was singled out earlier in this century by Frank Schoonmaker, the first American importer to realize the potential demand for estate-bottled, authentic burgundies. Consequently, Tollot-Beaut has been estate-bottling for much of this century. It is a domaine that has maintained a family tradition of winemaking since the vineyards were first planted in the late nineteenth century. The quality of the estate's wines ranges from very good to brilliant. The uncompromising winemaking of Tollot-Beaut renders wines that are bursting with cherry fruit, have just the right amount of spicy, toasty, vanilla-scented new oak, and are capable of aging for 7–15 years. The vinification of the wines from this 54-acre estate is still carried out in open wood *cuves*, with constant punching down of the wine's chapeau, or cap. There is 40%–50% destemming. The red wines stay in barrels (of which 40% are new) for 14–16 months, and are fined and filtered lightly prior to bottling. One of this house's rarities is the extraordinary Corton-Charlemagne. The Tollot-Beaut's tiny .61-acre vineyard produces less than 120 cases in a good vintage.

With respect to the red wines, you can never go wrong with the top-of-the-line Corton Les Bressandes, Corton, or the excellent Premiers Crus from Beaune (such as the Beaune Les Grèves and Beaune Clos du Roi). However, the *monopole* vineyard, the Savigny Champs Chevrey, and Chorey-Lès-Beaune are frequently the domaine's best values. This is an outstanding estate with a very high percentage of old vines.

DOMAINE FRANCIS TOMATIS ET FILS
(CHIROUBLES)**

> Wines Produced: Chiroubles.

This family domaine, run by a father and son, estate-bottles 100% of its production. The Tomatis own 17.29 acres of vineyards in Chiroubles.

The wines are lively, light, and very attractive, but must be drunk within two years of the vintage.

DOMAINE TORTOCHOT
(GEVREY-CHAMBERTIN)***–****

> **Wines Produced:** Clos Vougeot, Chambertin, Charmes-Chambertin, Gevrey-Chambertin, Gevrey-Chambertin Les Champeaux, Gevrey-Chambertin Lavaux St.-Jacques, Mazis-Chambertin, Morey St.-Denis.

Gabriel Tortochot is capable of making some of the best wines of Gevrey-Chambertin. He has been especially successful in the late seventies and early eighties. He continues to sell one-third to one-half of his production directly to *négociants*, and most of his estate-bottled wine is sold directly to private clients. Tortochot believes in less than 20% new oak barrels, 100% destemming, and a moderately long *cuvaison* of 12–14 days. I found his wines to be rather sweet, and perhaps overly chaptalized in many vintages, but enjoyable. These wines should be drunk within their first 5–7 years of life. Tortochot has an important 1-acre holding of the Grand Cru Chambertin, and .6 of an acre of Clos Vougeot at the bottom of the hill near route N 74.

CHÂTEAU DE LA TOUR (VOUGEOT)****

> **Wines Produced:** Beaune, Beaune Coucherias, Clos Vougeot.

This property has the potential to become one of Burgundy's most famous domaines. The estate boasts the largest holding in the famous Grand Cru, Clos Vougeot (13.2 acres, or nearly 11% of the entire Clos Vougeot). The proprietors of Château de la Tour, the Labet and Déchelette families, have only just begun to produce wines that merit the title of Grand Cru. For much of the seventies and early eighties, the wines produced were simple, commercial wines of no great interest or complexity. However, the young, attractive Françoise Labet has come under the spell of the fashionable guru and oenologist of Burgundy, Guy Accad. Accad has persuaded her to utilize a 5- to 7-day cold maceration of the grape bunches prior to fermentation. The results have been very good 1986s, and splendid 1987s and 1988s, bursting with rich berry fruit. The wines have great depth of flavor and the potential for 8–10 years of development. This is all encouraging since Château de la Tour's parcels are among the best placed in the entire Clos Vougeot. They use 100% new oak for their Clos Vougeot. The other wines produced here include a generic Beaune and Beaune Premier Cru, which are good, but are not of the same quality as the Clos Vougeot. This is clearly a property whose reputation will rise fast. Connoisseurs should know that in certain vintages tiny quantities of a Clos Vougeot Cuvée Vieilles Vignes is produced. The 1988 was staggering.

DOMAINE DE LA TOUR BAJOLE
(SAINT-MAURICE LES COUCHES)**

> Wines Produced: Bourgogne Aligoté, Bourgogne Blanc, Bourgogne Rosé, Bourgogne Rouge.

This moderately sized domaine of 21.3 acres is run by Roger Dessendre and his son Jean-Claude. The bulk of the estate's production is in Bourgogne Rouge, a rustic, tannic, full, earthy wine that is kept in large oak *foudres* and bottled after 28–30 months of aging. The vintages I have seen have shown a surprising tendency to age well. The other wines of the Domaine de la Tour Bajole include an insipid Bourgogne Blanc and a fresh, lively Bourgogne Aligoté.

CHÂTEAU DES TOURS
(SAINT-ÉTIENNE LA VARENNE)**

> Wines Produced: Brouilly.

This large estate of 118.56 acres has had a good reputation for many years but the quality of the wines has suffered recently. At present, excessive production precludes the production of high-quality wine. The results are wines that are relatively light and insipid, lacking the charm and fruit of a fine Brouilly.

DOMAINE LOUIS TRAPET (GEVREY-CHAMBERTIN)**

> Wines Produced: Chambertin, Chambertin Vieille Vignes, Chapelle-Chambertin, Gevrey-Chambertin, Gevrey-Chambertin Premier Cru, Latricières Chambertin.

The Domaine Trapet has estate-bottled virtually all of its production since the early fifties. The estate has 42.5 acres of vineyards in Gevrey-Chambertin. Many would argue that the Domaine Trapet is one of the most prominent names in all of Burgundy, yet the quality has enjoyed a roller-coaster existence since the late sixties. The last great vintage was vinified and bottled up by the father, Louis Trapet. I vividly remember M. Trapet's spectacular 1969s. Currently, his son Jean, a delightful, gregarious, and hospitable man, makes the wines.

In the 1970s, there were numerous disappointments, including 1978s that were not only watery and thin, but turned brown and were undrinkable by the time they were 5 years old. In the 1980s, the wine when tasted from the cask never seemed to possess the same qualities after it was bottled. The 1983s, which looked marvelous from cask, quickly turned brown and took on the taste of rot. The 1985 appeared rich and opulent in the cask, only to taste much lighter from the bottle. The 1986s are washed-out wines. The Chambertin did not taste like Napoleon's "king of wines," and was actually more for the "king of fools." There is no doubt that Trapet's obsession with excessive fining and filtration eviscerated many of his wines. Whether he's flexible enough to change remains a matter of conjecture.

At present, Trapet's vinification technique is to ferment in his new stainless-steel tanks with a system of automatic punching down for 12–15 days, filter the wine after it has gone through malolactic fermentation, and put it directly into oak barrels for 15–18 months. Most of the Grands Crus see 100% new oak, but the Premiers Crus and Villages wines receive significantly less oak aging. In certain vintages Trapet has produced a Chambertin Cuvée Vieilles Vignes from a parcel of 69-year-old vines in his 8.75 acres of Grand Cru Chambertin. Outrageously expensive, it has been great from cask, but uninspiring out of bottle. The most recent vintages of this wine have been the 1988, 1985, and 1983 (the latter vintage is now undrinkable because of rot and dilution). Other important holdings include 3.7 acres in Latricières-Chambertin, 3 acres in Chapelle-Chambertin, 5.75 acres in Gevrey-Chambertin Premiers Crus such as Petite Chapelle, Clos Prieur, Les Combettes, and Les Corbeaux, and 17.5 acres in Gevrey-Chambertin. Modest quantities of Bourgogne and Bourgogne Passe-Tout-Grains are also produced from nearly 7.5 acres of vineyards. This estate maintains a great reputation unwarranted by the quality of the wines. Improvements appear warranted.

DOMAINE GÉRARD TREMBLAY-DOMAINE DES ÎLES (POINCHY)***

Wines Produced: Chablis, Chablis Beauroy, Chablis-Côte de Lechet, Chablis Fourchaume, Chablis Montmains, Chablis Valmur, Petit-Chablis.

This modernly equipped 75.3-acre estate has some important holdings in the Grand Cru Valmur (4.94 acres), Premier Cru Fourchaume (13.58

acres), and an extensive holding in generic Chablis (34.58 acres). It produces intensely fruity, medium-bodied wines that are fermented as well as aged in stainless steel, and bottled after 7–8 months of aging. Gérard Tremblay, a young, open-minded individual, has experimented with small oak casks for his Grand Cru Valmur and his Premier Cru Fourchaume. He is not yet convinced that oak is the secret to making Chablis. The wines here are consistently well made, even in vintages where the fruit is less ripe. They are best drunk within their first 4–5 years. This is a consistent domaine that should be sought out by those who want a modern, fruity, nonoak-aged style of Chablis.

TRENEL ET FILS (CHARNAY-LES-MÂCON)***–****

> Wines Produced: This *négociant* produces an entire range of Beaujolais and Mâconnais wines, as well as some of the best Crème de Cassis and Crème de Framboise in Burgundy.

Trenel is one of the top-quality *négociants* working the Beaujolais/Mâconnais area. Their Mâcon-Villages and Pouilly-Fuissé are textbook examples, and have wonderfully fresh, fruity aromas, and good body and length on the palate. Among their Beaujolais, they consistently produce excellent wines from Fleurie, Moulin-à-Vent La Rochelle, Morgon Le Py, Chiroubles, Saint-Amour, and Juliénas. In comparison to the best-known wines of Beaujolais, those of Georges Duboeuf and Pierre Ferraud, the Trenel wines tend to be less elegant and a bit more tannic and muscular. However, they are still immensely satisfying, and are fuller flavored and slightly more alcoholic. Their Crème de Cassis and Crème de Framboise are a treat, and among the finest produced in Burgundy. They can be found in virtually all the top three-star restaurants in the Burgundy region.

DOMAINE MICHEL TRIBOLET (FLEURIE)**

> Wines Produced: Fleurie, Moulin-à-Vent.

This estate makes solid, reliable, fruity wines. Much of the production is sold to Beaujolais *négociants*.

DOMAINE GEORGES TRICHARD (LA CHAPELLE DE GUINCHAY)***

> Wines Produced: Beaujolais-Villages, Chénas, Saint-Amour, Saint-Amour Les Pierres.

I have had consistently good luck with Georges Trichard's wines. He ages them for six months in oak *foudres* before bottling. The wines age well, have intense blackberry, plummy fruit and are among the most highly regarded in Beaujolais. While he is best known for his Saint-Amour, insiders will tell you (and I would concur) that his Chénas is even better. Trichard has 17.9 acres in his estate.

DOMAINE J. TRUCHOT-MARTIN
(MOREY ST.-DENIS)****

Wines Produced: Bourgogne Rouge, Chambolle-Musigny, Chambolle-Musigny Premier Cru, Charmes-Chambertin, Clos de la Roche, Gevrey-Chambertin, Morey St.-Denis, Morey St.-Denis-Clos Sorbès.

Jacky Truchot runs this 15.2-acre domaine, spread throughout three separate appellations, Gevrey-Chambertin, Morey St.-Denis, and Chambolle-Musigny. He has tiny parcels, each representing just over an acre in Grands Crus such as Clos de la Roche and Charmes-Chambertin. They are complemented by a 3.13-acre parcel of Morey St.-Denis-Clos Sorbès and portions of Chambolle-Musigny, Gevrey-Chambertin, and Morey St.-Denis. The Truchot-Martin wines are aged in approximately one-third new oak casks (more are employed for the Grands Crus) for 18–24 months. This is a very traditional, serious cellar that produces long-lived, authentic wines that are excellent, sometimes outstanding. They are neither overly manipulated or processed. The domaine's name is not well known, but the wines from vintages such as 1985, 1987, and 1988 would be a good addition to anyone's cellar.

DOMAINE JEAN VACHET (SAINT-VALLERIN)***

Wines Produced: Bourgogne Rouge, Bourgogne Rouge Les Jardins, Montagny, Montagny Les Coeres.

Jean Vachet comes from a family with a long history of winemaking. This particular domaine was established in 1640 by members of his family. Vachet's specialties are his white wines, which are wonderfully round and bottled with a very light filtration to preserve the flavor. His Montagny Les Coeres is one of the top white wines of the appellation, along with the Château de la Saule wines and Louis Latour's Montagny. Vachet's red wines tend to be a little rustic and coarse, but local cognoscenti will tell you to search only for Vachet's white wines. These wines should be drunk within 3–4 years of the vintage.

DOMAINE G. VACHET-ROUSSEAU (GEVREY-CHAMBERTIN)**

Wines Produced: Gevrey-Chambertin, Gevrey-Chambertin Lavaux St.-Jacques, Mazis-Chambertin.

I have only followed the wines of this small 14-acre domaine since the early 1980s. While I was impressed with several of Vachet-Rousseau's efforts in the early eighties, his recent wines have displayed a light, diluted quality and feeble color. Vachet-Rousseau's most important holding is his 11.3 acres of Gevrey-Chambertin, but he also has a parcel of 1.3 acres of the excellent Premier Cru, Lavaux St.-Jacques, as well as 1.3 acres in the Grand Cru Mazis-Chambertin. At present, these are not wines that I can recommend.

DOMAINE VALLS-LABOUREAU (COUCHES)**

Wines Produced: Bourgogne Aligoté, Bourgogne Passe-Tout-Grains, Bourgogne Rouge, Côte de Beaune-Villages.

The Valls-Laboureau family owns 11.9 acres and makes four separate wines. They are proud of their Côte de Beaune-Villages, which comes from a vineyard near Cheilly-Lès-Maranges. The red wines see 20% new oak and are bottled after 12 months. The white wines see 12.5% new oak and are bottled after 6 months. These are wines to be consumed when they are young.

DOMAINE DES VAROILLES (GEVREY-CHAMBERTIN)***

Wines Produced: Bonnes Mares, Charmes-Chambertin, Clos Vougeot, Gevrey-Chambertin, Gevrey-Chambertin Champonet, Gevrey-Chambertin-Clos du Couvent, Gevrey-Chambertin-Clos du Meix des Ouches, Gevrey-Chambertin Clos Prieur, Gevrey-Chambertin-Clos des Varoilles, Gevrey-Chambertin La Romanée.

This wealthy domaine of 32.8 acres keeps a surprisingly low profile, mirroring the personality of its coproprietor, Jean-Pierre Naigeon. The wines are distributed throughout the world by the company of Naigeon-Chauveau et Fils, which also produces and sells wine under its own label. The wines of the Domaine des Varoilles have a considerable reputation, and while I have had some very good bottles, the style requires a great deal of patience on the part of the consumer. These wines are made in a lean, tannic, reserved style and possess high acidity, which takes 7, sometimes even 10–12 years to melt away and reveal the wine's depth and ripeness of fruit. At present, a lot of stems are used in the making of the wine. Between one-fourth and one-third new oak is used, although a higher percentage is used with the Grands Crus in riper, fuller vintages. The wines for export spend 18–22 months in oak casks and are then given a light filtration prior to bottling.

This large estate is the exclusive owner of the 14.9-acre Clos des Varoilles, a vineyard that sits high on the hillside behind the village of Gevrey-Chambertin, just to the south of the famous Premier Cru vineyard Clos St.-Jacques. Interestingly, it is one of the few vineyards in the Côte de Nuits to have a more southerly exposure, giving it the extra benefit of additional sunshine. The estate's other important holdings include Premiers Crus such as the 2.61-acre parcel of La Romanée and 2.59-acre parcel of Clos du Meix des Ouches, which sits further down the slope nearer the village. In many vintages there is a *cuvée* of Vieilles Vignes from this latter vineyard made from vines planted in 1902. The 1978 was a stunning example. Their holdings also include 1.92 acres of Grand Cru vineyard in Charmes-Chambertin and a 5.08-acre parcel in Clos Vougeot. There are smaller holdings in the Grand Cru Bonnes Mares and less than a hectare in Gevrey-Chambertin Clos du Couvent, Gevrey-Chambertin Clos Prieur, Gevrey-Chambertin, and Gevrey-Chambertin Champonet. However, the glories of this house remain the Charmes-Chambertin, the Gevrey-Chambertin-Clos des Varoilles, and Gevrey-Chambertin Clos du Meix des Ouches. Be forewarned, as the wines of the Domaine des Varoilles will take a long time (usually a decade) to reach maturity.

DOMAINE BERNARD VAUDOISEY-MUTIN (VOLNAY)***

Wines Produced: Bourgogne Rouge, Meursault Les Vireuils, Pommard, Volnay Les Beauregards, Volnay Les Caillerets.

Bernard Vaudoisey is reputed to be a very traditional winemaker, dedicated to producing robust, tannic, intense, ageworthy wines from vineyards with extremely low yields. He has a high percentage of old vines, and believes in using no more than 25% new oak casks for aging his wines for 14–18 months. Vaudoisey owns nearly 25 acres, with the bulk of his production in generic Bourgogne. His best reds are his Volnay

Les Beauregards (from a vineyard not entitled to Premier Cru status, but located just above the famous vineyard of Taillepieds) and his Volnay Les Caillerets.

DOMAINE DE VAUROUX (CHABLIS)***–****

Wines Produced: Chablis, Chablis Bougros, Chablis Montée de Tonnerre, Chablis Montmains.

Jean-Pierre Tricon and his brother Claude produce a Chablis that is midway between the two schools of thought prevalent in Chablis. The Tricons built their winery in 1979 with state-of-the-art steel fermentation vats that can be temperature controlled, as they believe in the importance of fermenting the wine in stainless-steel or enamel-lined concrete vats. However, they also believe that a limited amount of aging of the top Premier Cru and Grand Cru wines in oak casks adds a dimension of flavor and complexity. Consequently the Premiers Crus and their Grand Cru Bougros (2.4 acres still in young vines) are aged for 3–4 months in oak casks. The wines that result are not as obviously toasty and rich as those of producers such as René and Vincent Dauvissat, but have more character and complexity than the pure stainless-steel style wines from producers such as Jean Moreau. At present this modern, impeccably run estate produces very good Chablis that just misses being considered among the very best of the appellation. Most of this estate's 53.92 acres are in generic Chablis. In addition to their holdings in Bougros, they have a 2.47-acre parcel in Chablis Montée de Tonnerre and a slightly larger parcel in Chablis Montmains.

DOMAINE DES VELANGES (DAVAYÉ)**

Wines Produced: Saint-Véran.

This tiny estate of 8.4 acres produces a decent but standard-quality Saint-Véran, which the owner, Michel Paquet, feels should be drunk within 2–3 years of the vintage.

DOMAINE ALAIN VERDET (ARCENANT)***

Wines Produced: Bourgogne Aligoté, Bourgogne Hautes-Côtes de Nuits Blanc, Bourgogne Hautes-Côtes de Nuits Rouge, Crémant de Bourgogne Blanc, Crémant de Bourgogne Rosé.

Alain Verdet is a producer who believes in totally organically made wines. Consequently, he does not use any insecticides or fertilizers in his vineyard, and he follows the strict vinification and bottling rules required of organically made wines. There is no fining or filtration. The red wines spend up to 2 years in cask prior to bottling and the white wines up to 15 months. The wines often need a good 30–45 minutes of decanting or breathing to throw off some funky aromas, but they have excellent fruit, and are complex wines. The reds have earthy, tarry, spicy scents and the whites have crisp, rich flavors. They are bold expressions of winemaking and clearly not for everybody, but one has to admire both Monsieur Verdet's intentions and the wines he produces from his 19.76-acre domaine.

DOMAINE LUCIEN ET ROBERT VERGER
(SAINT-LAGER) ✼✼✼

> Wines Produced: Côte de Brouilly.

There is no doubt that Lucien Verger and his son Robert make the best wine in Côte de Brouilly. The Vergers own 19.76 acres, all in this Beaujolais cru, and their wines have a vividly rich, intense fruitiness, medium to full body, and plenty of heady alcohol. They are perfumed, delicious, and all that a Beaujolais should be. Verger's wines are bottled after six months aging in oak *foudres*.

DOMAINE VEUVE-STEINMAIER ET FILS
(MONTAGNY) ✼✼✼

> Wines Produced: Bourgogne Aligoté, Bourgogne Passe-Tout-Grains, Givry-Clos de la Baraude Blanc, Givry-Clos de la Baraude Rouge, Montagny, Montagny Mont Cuchot, Montagny Premier Cru.

Madame Steinmaier and her son Jean are great enthusiasts for the wines of Montagny, and produce wines to very high standards. Their very best wine, their Montagny Mont Cuchot, is one of the best red wines of its appellation. Consumers should also keep an eye out for their Givry Clos de la Baraude Blanc, which can be very good in vintages such as 1985, but tends to be a bit austere and severe in lighter years.

DOMAINE DES VIGNES DES DEMOISELLES (NOLAY)**

> Wines Produced: Bourgogne Hautes-Côtes de Beaune Rouge, Bour-
> gogne Passe-Tout-Grains, Côte de Beaune-Vil-
> lages, Santenay-Clos Rousseau.

Over half of proprietor Jean-Luc Demangeot's production is sold to
négociants in Beaune. The domaine's best wine is the Santenay-Clos
Rousseau, which spends 18 months in old, small oak casks and is
bottled after a light filtration. Demangeot's other wines tend to be
straightforward and a bit too tannic and compact for my taste.

DOMAINE THIERRY VIGOT
(HAUTES-CÔTES DE NUITS)***

> Wines Produced: Echézeaux, Hautes-Côtes de Nuits, Nuits St.-
> Georges, Vosne-Romanée Les Gaudichots.

Thierry Vigot has just begun to estate-bottle wine from his 5-acre estate. He has also begun to expand his vineyard holdings in the Hautes-
Côtes de Nuits. In the future, his wines from those vineyards will represent the bulk of his production. His best wines are his Echézeaux and
superb Vosne-Romanée Les Gaudichots, the latter from the great Premier Cru vineyard adjacent to the famous Grand Cru La Tâche. Other
than the Forcy family, Vigot is the only producer who makes a wine
from this Premier Cru vineyard. Vigot's 1988s exhibited excellent ripe
fruit, good structure and tannin, and impeccable winemaking. This
would appear to be an estate that merits significant interest. My star
rating may prove to be unduly conservative.

DOMAINE A. P. DE VILLAINE (BOUZERON)****

> Wines Produced: Bourgogne Aligoté de Bouzeron, Bourgogne Blanc
> Les Clous, Bourgogne Rouge La Digoine.

The famous Aubert de Villaine, the coproprietor of the Domaine de la
Romanée-Conti, and his wife Pamela, look after the production of the
wines from the Domaine A. P. De Villaine. This estate is considered by
many to be the best in Bouzeron. It is ironic that one of the proprietors
of the Domaine de la Romanée-Conti, which makes the most expensive
wines in Burgundy if not in France, also produces some of the best
values in Burgundy from his three vineyards in the Bouzeron region.

The Bourgogne Blanc Les Clous (9.8 acres) is aged in 20% new oak and is bottled after 9 months. It is one of the very best generic white burgundies made, and in vintages such as 1985, 1986, and 1987, it is almost akin to a village Chassagne-Montrachet or a Premier Cru. This domaine illustrates what highly talented winemaking and attention to detail can achieve. The Bourgogne Aligoté de Bouzeron (12.35 acres) made by Monsieur Villaine is perhaps the finest Aligoté made in France. It has a richness and fragrance that is simply shocking for Aligoté, a grape that normally tends to produce acidic and neutral wines. Like the Bourgogne Blanc, this wine sees 20% new oak and is bottled after 8–9 months. Lastly, the Bourgogne Rouge, called La Digoine (14.82 acres), sees 15 months of cask aging of which 25% is new oak. It is bottled unfiltered and is certainly one of the top three or four generic red burgundies made in the region.

This is an outstanding domaine, which produces excellent wines that represent good bargains.

DOMAINE HENRI DE VILLAMONT (SAVIGNY-LÈS-BEAUNE)**–***

Domaine Wines Produced: Chambolle-Musigny, Corton-Charlemagne, Gevrey-Chambertin Clos du Chapitre, Mercurey, Meursault Les Charmes, Puligny-Montrachet Clos du Cailleret, Savigny-Lès-Beaune Clos des Guettes, Savigny-Lès-Beaune La Village.

Note: Additionally, many wines are sold by this firm in its role as a *négociant*.

This estate is owned by the Schenk firm from Switzerland and consists of 25 acres, primarily in Savigny-Lès-Beaune. It produces wines that have a reputation for standard quality. Yet, in tastings I have felt these wines are slightly above average in quality and quite representative of their appellations. Their estate-bottled wines and some of their *négociant* wines appear under the name Henri de Villamont, but Villamont also makes wines that appear under the name Arthur Barolet, François Martenot, Étienne Vergy, Mesnard Père et Fils, Brocard et Fils, Louis Serrignon, and Cave de Valclair. Henri de Villamont was one of the first Burgundy wine firms to recognize the potential for good quality, reasonably priced wines from the Hautes-Côtes de Beaune and Hautes-Côtes de Nuits.

DOMAINE RENÉ VIRELY-ARCELAIN (POMMARD)***

> Wines Produced: Beaune, Bourgogne Rouge, Pommard, Pommard-
> Clos des Arvelets, Pommard Les Pézerolles.

René Virely has quite a reputation for his Pommard-Clos des Arvelets.
The wine is made from old vines situated on a 2.47-acre parcel. I have
tasted an equally impressive Pommard Les Pezerolles from this estate.
Virely sells off one-third of his estate's production to *négociants* and
estate-bottles the rest. Very little new oak is used and the wines are
bottled after 18–24 months of cask aging. It is a tiny estate, but based
on several vintages of the Pommard-Clos des Arvelets and Pommard
Les Pézerolles I have tasted, it merits greater recognition.

DOMAINE BERNARD VIRELY-ROUGEOT (POMMARD)***

> Wines Produced: Beaune-Clos de l'Ermitage St.-Désiré, Bourgogne
> Rouge, Meursault, Meursault Les Charmes, Pom-
> mard, Pommard-Clos des Arvelets, Pommard Pre-
> mier Cru.

This is a good, solid domaine that produces clean, competent, occasionally tasty and inspired wines from its 21.1 acres of vineyards. The best
wines include an excellent Pommard-Clos des Arvelets from a 2.4-acre
parcel, and a tasty Meursault Les Charmes from a minuscule .39 of an
acre parcel. The red wines see 17% new oak casks, and are bottled
after 18–24 months. The white wines see slightly less new oak and are
bottled after 12–14 months. The wines here are made in a style that
suggests they are best drunk young.

DOMAINE L. VITTEAU-ALBERTI (RULLY)***

> Wines Produced: Crémant de Bourgogne Blanc, Crémant de Bour-
> gogne Rosé.

This 11.1-acre domaine is dedicated to making sparkling wines prized
by French wine drinkers. These wines now grace the wine list of the
three-star Lameloise in Chagny and Taillevent in Paris. The domaine
was created in 1951 by the father of the current proprietor, Gérard
Vitteau. The wines are the product of an extremely modern cellar with
air-conditioning and state-of-the-art technology.

DOMAINE ÉMILE VOARICK
(SAINT-MARTIN-SOUS-MONTAIGU) **

> **Wines Produced:** Beaune Montée Rouge, Bourgogne Aligoté, Bourgogne Blanc, Bourgogne Passe-Tout-Grains, Bourgogne Rouge, Corton-Clos des Fiètres, Givry Rouge, Mercurey Blanc, Mercurey Rouge.

Pierre Voarick runs this sizeable domaine of 123.5 acres. Nearly half of the production is in generic Bourgogne Rouge. The winemaking is very traditional; the reds spend 12–18 months in cask and are bottled with very little fining or filtration. The small quantities of white wine (only 15% of the total production) see 6–8 months in vats and small old casks before bottling. No new oak is employed at this estate, and all the vineyards are harvested by machine. The rustic and straightforward wines have good body, and plenty of tannin. They lack finesse and sometimes taste simple, but they are solid, reliable wines that tend to be consistent from vintage to vintage. The entire production is estate-bottled. Émile Voarick sells most of his wine in Switzerland, the United Kingdom, Germany, and Belgium.

DOMAINE MICHEL VOARICK (ALOXE-CORTON) ****

> **Wines Produced:** Aloxe-Corton, Corton Les Bressandes, Corton-Charlemagne, Corton-Clos du Roi, Corton Les Languettes, Corton Les Rénardes, Pernand-Vergelesses, Romanée St.-Vivant.

There is no doubting that Michel Voarick is a serious winemaker. His cellars, right next to the lovely, tranquil Hôtel Clarion in Aloxe-Corton, are among the dampest and coolest in Burgundy. The wines are very traditionally made. There is no destemming, no new oak barrels (Voarick is totally against the use of new oak), and no filtration (except when the wines are intended for the American market). His red wines tend to be among the slowest to mature. They are the most structured Burgundies of the village of Aloxe-Corton, and usually need a good 5–7 years to show well. Additionally, his wines last for 10–15 or more years.

The estate includes 31.13 acres, and Voarick will tell you that the secret to high quality is limiting the yield to 25–35 hectolitres per acre. This is a domaine with some spectacular vineyards, including a holding of 1.63 acres in Romanée St.-Vivant, which should produce his best wine but does not. The top wines here are the Corton-Clos du Roi (from

1.23 acres of old vines), Corton Les Bressandes (from a 1.08-acre parcel that consistently produces sumptuous, fat, deep wines), and Corton Les Languettes (from a 3.45-acre parcel that produces wines that often need a decade of aging to reach their peak). Additionally, Voarick makes tiny quantities of a staggering Corton-Charlemagne, but I have never seen this wine in commercial channels. Most of it is sold to Voarick's private clients. The estate also produces a good Pernand-Vergelesses and Aloxe-Corton. Michel Voarick is responsible for cultivating the 4.94-acre parcel of the famous Corton-Cuvée Docteur Peste owned by the Hospices de Beaune. This is one of the best estates in Burgundy, but their wines should be purchased only by consumers who have the patience to wait for them to mature.

DOMAINE ROBERT VOCORET ET FILS (CHABLIS)****

> Wines Produced: Chablis, Chablis Blanchot, Chablis Les Clos, Chablis Le Forêt, Chablis Montée de Tonnerre, Chablis Les Vaillons.

Patrice, Michel, and Claude Vocoret are among the handful of producers in Chablis who continue to ferment their wines in large oak *foudres*. Once the initial fermentation is over, the wines are transferred to stainless-steel vats for their malolactic fermentation and aging up to 12 months. The results are wines that have both the fullness and richness of oak fermentation, and the cleanliness and precise definition to their flavor and character of aging in stainless steel. The Vocorets own a number of top vineyards (78.6 acres), including important parcels in two Grands Crus, Blanchot (4.79 acres) and Les Clos (4 acres), and significant holdings in Premiers Crus like Le Forêt (13.58 acres), Vaillons (11.5 acres), and Montée de Tonnerre (2.8 acres). The rest is in generic Chablis. This is a very high-quality source for excellent Chablis, which I would rank just below the top three or four domaines. Vocoret's wines age extremely well, and it is not unusual to find 10- to 12-year-old bottles of his Premier Cru or Grand Cru Chablis in superb drinking condition.

DOMAINE ALAIN VOEGELI (GEVREY-CHAMBERTIN)**

> Wines Produced: Gevrey-Chambertin.

Alain Voegeli inherited the 7-acre estate of the Domaine Étienne Gray. Only a rustic, lean, hard, and charmless Gevrey-Chambertin Villages is produced. I remember vintages from Gray showing more character and charm, but the first efforts from Monsieur Voegeli do not inspire great enthusiasm.

DOMAINE COMTE GEORGES DE VOGÜÉ (CHAMBOLLE-MUSIGNY)***

Wines Produced: Bonnes Mares, Chambolle-Musigny, Chambolle-Musigny Les Amoureuses, Musigny, Musigny Blanc, Musigny Vieilles Vignes.

The Domaine Comte de Vogüé is the most significant estate in Chambolle-Musigny because of its important vineyard holdings. The estate consists of 31 acres of vineyards, with 18 in Le Musigny (70% of that Grand Cru's acreage), 6.6 acres in Bonnes Mares, 1.5 in Les Amoureuses, and 4.5 in Chambolle-Musigny. The Domaine even has a tiny plot of Chardonnay vines, planted at the request of the late Comtesse de Vogüé, that produces 1,500–2,000 bottles of Musigny Blanc. The estate also holds an important place in the history of Burgundy, as it was established in the Middle Ages and provided many generations of nobility with *grand vin* from Chambolle-Musigny. Vogüé family records date from 1776. Some of the greatest bottles of red burgundy I have ever drunk have been Musigny Vieilles Vignes from the Comte de Vogüé. The 1945, 1947, 1966, 1969, and 1972 jump from the pages of my tasting notes. I remember these remarkable wines so vividly, I can seemingly still taste them today. However, since the mid-seventies the quality of the wines from the Domaine Comte de Vogüé has deteriorated. The 1972 was the last great vintage for their famed Musigny Vieilles Vignes, although later vintages still fetch exceptional prices from the trade. It is difficult to know exactly what transpired, but the domaine used to sell as much as one-third of its crop to *négociants* after selecting the best *cuvées* for its estate-bottled wines. Today, virtually the entire vintage is estate-bottled every year. Second, the estate began to filter its wine in the mid-seventies. Unfortunately, this practice has stripped the wine of much of its great fragrance and intense flavors. The *régisseur*, Alain Roumier, claimed he had to change his winemaking to satisfy Americans' obsession with brilliant, clear wines. Filtration can be a matter of degree, and many superb wines have been filtered. Perhaps the Domaine Comte de Vogüé employs an excessive degree of filtration, unnecessary for maintaining the quality of the wine.

Presently, the wine continues to be fermented in oak vats, put in small barrels for 18 months, fined with egg whites, and filtered at bottling. The wines are still quite good, with the best recent vintages being 1978, 1985, and 1988. But the breadth of flavor, the splendid complex bouquets, and the potential to evolve and improve in the bottle for 20–30 years is no longer evident. The estate has gone through some tragic times, with the illnesses and deaths of several winemakers, but I would like to see it again producing a wine that rivals the best half-dozen red wines of Burgundy. Alain Roumier has retired, and today, an oenologist, Monsieur Millet, produces the wines.

DOMAINE JOSEPH VOILLOT (VOLNAY)***–****

Wines Produced: Bourgogne Rouge, Meursault Premier Cru, Pommard, Pommard-Clos Michault, Pommard Les Epenots, Pommard Les Pézerolles, Pommard Les Rugiens, Volnay, Volnay Champans, Volnay Fremiets.

Joseph Voillot sells as much as three-fourths of his production from his 26.67-acre vineyard to *négociants*. Nevertheless, he does make some chunky, tannic, robust wines from his array of fine Premier Cru vineyards in Pommard and Volnay. This is an estate that could produce some fine wines with the helpful advice from an oenologist, and a more elevated use of new oak. At present, the estate-bottled wines see 25%–33% new oak and are bottled after 14–16 months. They tend to be robust, muscular wines that require cellaring.

DOMAINE LENI VOLPATO (CHAMBOLLE-MUSIGNY)***

Wines Produced: Bourgogne Passe-Tout-Grains, Chambolle-Musigny.

This 12-acre estate produces only two wines, but the Bourgogne Passe-Tout-Grains is the best wine of this type I have ever tasted. Volpato, an understated, middle-aged man, produces his wine primarily from a very old vineyard of Pinot Noir. He does not incorporate a percentage of Gamay into his wine, even though he is legally entitled to do so. His Bourgogne Passe-Tout-Grains would embarrass many of the more prestigious wines from the village of Chambolle-Musigny in a blind tasting, given its uncommonly rich color, intense spicy, peppery bouquet, and concentrated, old-vine flavors. It is a stunningly good wine for drinking in its first 5–6 years of life. Quite surprisingly, one would expect Volpato's Chambolle-Musigny to be even better, but that is not the case.

Volpato is such a superb winemaker, it is sad that he owns no Premier Cru or Grand Cru vineyards. I wonder what he could do if he were put in charge of making the wines for the classic underachiever of the village, the Domaine de Comte de Vogüé? This is a producer whose Bourgogne Passe-Tout-Grains may well represent the finest value in all of Burgundy.

DOMAINE DE VURIL (CHARENTAY)**

Wines Produced: Brouilly.

This tiny estate makes round, fruity, average-quality wines from its 20.99-acre vineyard. The wines are matured in vats prior to bottling.

ANDRÉ ZILTENER PÈRE ET FILS (GEVREY-CHAMBERTIN)**

Wines Produced: Bourgogne Rouge, Chambolle-Musigny, Clos Vougeot, Corton-Charlemagne, Corton Les Rénardes.

Most of the wine from this *négociant* in Gevrey-Chambertin is sold in Switzerland to private clients. The wines tend to be correct, but are not usually thrilling or dramatic.

PART II

THE VILLAGES
AND
APPELLATIONS
OF BURGUNDY

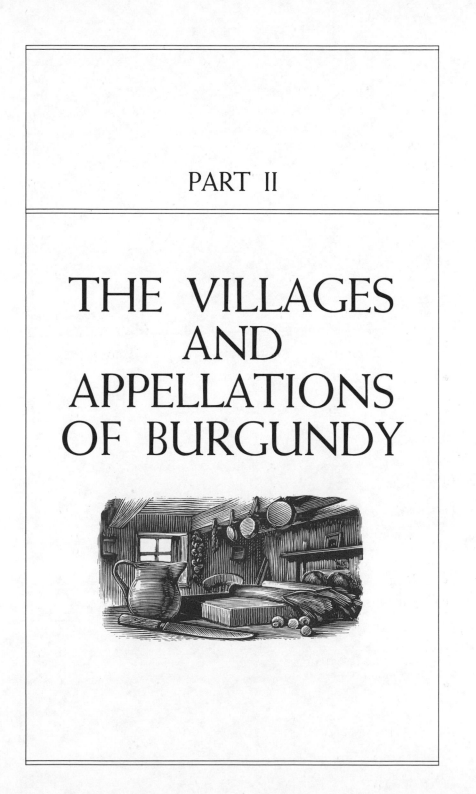

CHABLIS

An Overview

Location: Situated only 111 miles from Paris, the tiny town of Chablis sits in a valley midway between Auxerre, which is dominated by its splendid cathedral, and Tonnerre, which boasts the remarkable nearby Château de Tanlay. Chablis is a mere 2 hour trip from Paris on the famous Autoroute A 6, but it can also be reached by taking N 965 east from Auxerre, or via the more pastoral and tranquil D 91 that runs south from Migennes (6 miles south of Joigny). Chablis is referred to as Burgundy's "Golden Gate," and encompasses a vineyard area 10 miles long and 4 miles wide.

Acres under vine: 5,500 acres; 100% Chardonnay
       Grands Crus: 246 acres
     Premiers Crus: 1,482 acres
     Villages Wines: 3,772 acres

Grands Crus: A total of 7
      Blanchot, Les Clos, Les Preuses, Vaudésir, Valmur, Grenouilles, Bougros, and La Moutonne (not officially a Grand Cru, but it is located within both Vaudésir and Grenouilles, and has a de facto, quasi Grand Cru status).

Principal Premiers Crus: There are 22 principal Premiers Crus, 9 situated on the right bank of the Serein and 13 on the left bank. Those Premiers Crus shown with an asterisk (*) consistently produce higher quality wine than the others.

RIGHT BANK OF SEREIN
Chapelot*, Côte de Fontenys, Vaupulent, Fourchaume*, Mont de Milieu*, Montée de Tonnerre*, Pied d'Aloup*, Vaucoupin, Vaulorent*

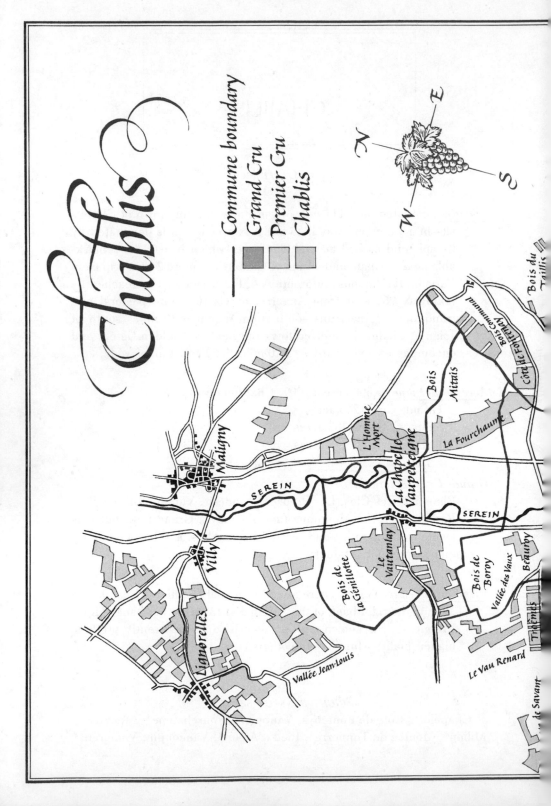

Chablis

Commune boundary
Grand Cru
Premier Cru
Chablis

Maligny

Villy

Lignorelles

SEREIN

L'Homme Mort

La Chapelle-Vaupelteigne

Bois Mitais

La Fourchaume

Côte de Fontenay

Bois du Taillis

Bois Communal

SEREIN

Bois de la Génillotte

Le Vautamlay

Bois de Boroy

Vallée des Vaux

Béauroy

THÉMES

Vallée Jean-Louis

Le Vau Renard

... de Savant

Les Vallées

Les Fourneaux

Flys

Plaine des Serres

Vaucoupin

Vaudecorce

Chichée

Vallée de Vaubarousse

Mont de Milieu

Pied d'Aloue

Chapelots

Fyé

Montée de Tonnerre

Vallée de Bréchain

SEREIN

Vaugiraud

Vallée de Vaudon

Plateau des Terrasses

Vauloroit

Bougros

Les Preuses

Vaudésir

Grenouilles

Valmur

Les Clos

Blanchots

La Maladière

SEREIN

Fbg. St-Pierre

Vosgros

Paradis

Vallée de Paradis

Chablis

Poinchy

Milly

Vauchaumot

Priault

Vaux Ragon

Bois de Milly

Bois de Léchet

Côte de Léchet

Bois des Lys

Les Lys

Les Épinottes

Vaillons

Séche

Châtains

Beugnons

Roncières

Mélinots

Butteaux

Montmains

Les Fôrets

Vallée de Chef des Prés

Grande Vallée

Courgis

Beauroy*, Beugnons, Butteaux*, Châtains, Côte de Léchet, Les
Forêts*, Les Lys*, Mélinots, Montmains*, Sécher Troesmes,
Vaillons*, Vosgros

Price levels: $25–$60 for Grands Crus; $20–$45 for Premiers Crus; $10–
$20 for Chablis; and $8–$12 for Petit-Chablis

General wine characteristics: There is immense diversity to the styles
of Chablis available, so the following comments should be con-
strued in the broadest possible context. Only white wine is made
exclusively from the Chardonnay grape, which frequently struggles to ripen in this cool, marginal area that is closer to Champagne's vineyards (17 miles away) than to the Côte d'Or (62 miles
away). The wines rarely have the fullness, tropical fruit ripeness,
or expansive, lush palate of the finest white burgundies from the
Côte d'Or. They are more acidic and austere, and taste drier, with
a characteristic steely, stony, mineral content that gives the best
examples a distinctive perfume and precision to their flavors.
However, the use of oak barrels for fermentation or aging, the
crop yields, and the degree to which the wine is highly processed
all greatly influence the individual styles of wine.

The most overrated producers: J. Moreau et Fils, Lamblin et Fils, Simonnet-Febvre et Fils

The best producers and their wines:

Grands Crus

Jean Collet: Chablis Valmur
Jean Dauvissat: Chablis Les Preuses
René Dauvissat: Chablis Les Clos, Chablis Les Preuses
Joseph Drouhin: Chablis Les Preuses, Chablis Les Clos,
Chablis Vaudésir
Château Grenouilles: Chablis Grenouilles
Domaine Laroche: Chablis Les Clos, Chablis Blanchot Vieilles
Vignes
Long-Depaquit (Bichot): Chablis Blanchot, Chablis Les Clos,
Chablis Vaudésir, Chablis La Moutonne
Domaine de la Maladière: Chablis Les Clos, Chablis Valmur, Chablis
Grenouilles, Chablis Les Preuses

Louis Michel: Chablis Grenouilles, Chablis Vaudésir,
Chablis Les Clos
Louis Pinson: Chablis Les Clos
François Raveneau: Chablis Blanchot, Chablis Les Clos,
Chablis Valmur
Guy Robin: Chablis Valmur, Chablis Blanchot
R. Vocoret: Chablis Blanchot, Chablis Les Clos

Premiers Crus

Jean Collet: Chablis Montmains, Chablis Mont de
Milieu, Chablis Butteaux
Jean Dauvissat: Chablis Mont de Milieu
René Dauvissat: Chablis Vaillons, Chablis Fourchaume,
Chablis Les Forêts
Daniel Defaix: Chablis Beugnons
Domaine de L'Eglantière: Chablis Fourchaume, Chablis Montée de
Tonnerre, Chablis Montmains
Alain Geoffroy: Chablis Beauroy, Chablis Fourchaume
Domaine Laroche: Chablis Fourchaume, Chablis Les Vaillons,
Chablis Montmains
Maladière: Chablis Chapelot, Chablis Vaillons, Chablis
Montée de Tonnerre, Chablis Les Lys
Louis Michel: Chablis Montmains, Chablis Montée de
Tonnerre, Chablis Vaillons, Chablis Les
Forêts, Chablis Fourchaumes
André Philippon: Chablis Mont de Milieu
Louis Pinson: Chablis Les Forêts, Chablis Mont de
Milieu, Chablis Montmains
François Raveneau: Chablis Montée de Tonnerre, Chablis
Chapelot, Chablis Les Vaillons
Guy Robin: Chablis Chapelot
Robert Vocoret: Chablis Les Forêts, Chablis Les Vaillons

Some important observations:
1. In addition to the Grands Crus and Premiers Crus, there is also an ocean of Villages Chablis produced, as well as the unappealing Petit-Chablis. The rule with straight Chablis and Petit-Chablis is caveat emptor. Most of it is watery, too acidic, and too frequently nasty and green. Muscadet, at one-third the price (from the Nantes area of the Loire), provides much more quality for your money.
2. Consumers need to identify what style of Chablis they prefer. The finest exponent of the school of Chablis that ferments and ages its

wines in stainless steel is Louis Michel. His wines are wonderful and precise. In contrast, the two best examples of the barrel-fermented and oak-aged style of Chablis are René Dauvissat and François Raveneau. Any lessons in quality Chablis should begin and end with the wines of these producers.

3. The Premier Cru area in Chablis has been expanded greatly and many of the new vineyards are dubious entries. The following Premiers Crus do not, in my opinion, merit their lofty titles—Chaume de Talvat, Côte de Cuissy, Les Beauregards, Les Landes et Verjuts, Vau-de-Vey, Vaugiraut, Vau Ligneau, Vaux Ragons, and Vosgros. All of these parcels lack the exposure to produce wines of true Premier Cru quality, and until recently were only entitled to a "Chablis Appellation" name.

4. Most Chablis, no matter the quality, is overpriced for the wine one gets in the bottle.

Where are the values? I do not think that any values exist in Chablis. Most of the wine below the Grand Cru and Premier Cru levels is vapid, denuded, and acidic with less flavor than Muscadet, but at twice the price. The top Premiers Crus and Grands Crus can be stunning, but are they worth their steep prices? Chablis has an image problem in terms of rapport in quality and price.

Most successful recent vintages: 1989, 1986, 1985, 1983, 1978

Aging potential: Grands Crus—5 to 15 years; Premiers Crus—4 to 8 years; Chablis—2 to 4 years; Petit-Chablis—1 to 2 years.

CHABLIS

(Les Miserables?)

Chablis seems to have just about everything going against it. Why, for example, would anyone trying to make a profit from the vine decide to plant in a marginal area where potential disaster is confronted nearly every year, from the deep freezes of winter, to spring forests, to summer weather that leaves the grapes unripe? Why would someone produce a wine from a region whose very name has been bastardized in America, Australia, New Zealand, and even South America, where any number of different grape varieties constituting wines ranging from innocuously dry to cloyingly sweet are called Chablis. Furthermore,

Chablis, among all of France's renowned wine regions, has never fully recovered from the great devastator, the late nineteenth-century phylloxera parasite that destroyed all the vines of France, including the nearly 100,000 acres in Chablis' Yonne department. Even taking into account the recent expansion in Chablis as a result of the worldwide thirst for Chardonnay, Chablis' current acreage of 5,500 is only 5% of what it was a hundred years ago. Perhaps all of this helps explain why England's Serena Sutcliffe calls the local residents of Chablis "contentious people."

Certainly, the prephylloxera history of Chablis is very distinguished. We know there were vineyards in this area during the Roman occupation of what was then known as Gaul. It is also established that the great Cistercian Abbey of Pontigny, a short distance from the village of Chablis, had extensive vineyard holdings during medieval times, and was responsible for the introduction of the Chardonnay grape to the Portlandian and Kimmeridgian limestone soil in which most of the best Chablis vineyards are planted. Chablis' development following its early exploitation by the monks was linked to the growing economic power and importance of Paris. Wines could easily be shipped there, first via France's system of inland waterways and later by rail.

The village of Chablis seems decidedly low-key considering that it is the hub of one of France's most significant viticultural areas. While the old stone houses differ little from those in many other French villages, visitors will no doubt observe that the center of the town is more modern. A stray bomb landed there in 1941, and downtown Chablis had to be rebuilt. Perhaps the only time the village comes to life is during the harvest, and on Sundays, when the morning market seems to draw most of the 2,400 residents.

THE VINEYARDS OF CHABLIS

Most Chablis villagers do not respond terribly well to the comment that Chablis is the best-known white wine in the world. In countries other than France, Chablis is synonymous with something made from French Colombard, Thompson's Seedless, or some unusual blend of grapes from Australia's Hunter Valley. Yet there is a great deal of authentic Chablis made. The recent expansion of the vineyards in this area brings the total acreage to just over 5,500 acres, all planted with Chardonnay. That is a lot of vines, but there are only 246 acres of Grand Cru Chablis, and 1,482 acres of Premier Cru, not all of it meriting Premier Cru status.

GRANDS CRUS VINEYARDS

There are only 7 Grands Crus, and they sit on what is the filet mignon
of the Chablis region. All these vineyards lie on slopes that are directly
north and east of the village, on the north bank of the Serein River,
which wends its way through the region. Two hundred forty-six acres
may sound like a lot of property, but there are a number of single
Bordeaux châteaux that possess as much acreage. The production from
these sloping hillside vineyards should and frequently does turn out the
very finest wines, largely because all of them sit on the richest Kimmeridgian limestone soil, which is intermixed with some marl. In alpha-
betic order, these vineyards are:

Blanchot (30.1 acres)—Situated southeast of the other Grands Crus,
Blanchot produces wines that are among the most delicate, perfumed,
and stylish of all the Grands Crus. But in principle, a Blanchot should
never have quite the power or richness of a Les Clos. The best producers of Blanchot have consistently been François Raveneau and the
Domaine Long-Depaquit, owned by the huge Bichot firm in Beaune.
Less consistent, but making wines that occasionally reach the heights
one would associate with a Grand Cru, are the Domaine Laroche's
Cuvée Vieilles Vignes, Guy Robin, and the Blanchot from the Vorcoret
family.

Bougros (35.3 acres)—At the very northwestern end of the loin of
Grands Crus is Bougros. This is probably the least well known of Chablis' Grands Crus. The locals claim it produces wines with less finesse
and elegance, and more power and robustness than might be preferred.
There is no superb producer of Bougros that I have tasted, but the
Domaine Auffray, Joseph Drouhin, the Domaine de la Maladière, and
the Domaine Laroche are the four most important landholders.

Grenouilles (23.1 acres)—One of the smallest Grands Crus, Grenouilles
sits right in the middle of the Grand Cru slope of Chablis. I would agree
with those observers and local experts who claim that top-quality Grenouilles always has the most penetrating and intense perfume of Chablis.
Certainly the Château Grenouilles, Louis Michel, and Testut Frères
make textbook examples.

Les Clos (61.1 acres)—This vineyard, undoubtedly the most famous
Grand Cru of Chablis, is superbly situated between Blanchot and Valmur. The top examples of Les Clos from the likes of François Raveneau, Louis Pinson, Louis Michel, Long-Depaquit, Domaine de la
Maladière, Joseph Drouhin, and René Dauvissat define what Chablis
can offer at its very best. There is an intrinsic strength to these wines
that suggests wet stones and minerals intertwined with flavors of apples

and lemons. Les Clos frequently has excellent acidity, superb depth, power, and richness, but it is the stony, mineral-like precision to its flavors that sets it apart from one of the Côte d'Or's top white burgundies. The great examples of Les Clos, too few indeed, often seem immortal. In fact, they are capable of lasting 15–20 years.

Les Preuses (28.9 acres)—Les Preuses sits at the very top of the hillside. It is occasionally criticized by fastidious Chablis aficionados for being too easy to drink. Undoubtedly they are referring to the fact that Les Preuses, in comparison with Les Clos or Blanchot, drinks the way Meursault does in comparison to Puligny-Montrachet. It gives the impression of more roundness, lushness, and fat on the palate without quite the precision and clarity that some of the other Grands Crus possess. However, this is not meant in a pejorative context because the locals will point out that Les Preuses has the best exposition of any of the Grands Crus on the côte, being higher up the hillside with even better drainage than its neighbors. It also receives more hours of sunshine than any other Grand Cru. Superb wines from Les Preuses are made by René Dauvissat, Jean Dauvissat, Domaine Long-Depaquit, and Domaine de la Maladière.

Valmur (29.4 acres)—Valmur is situated between Les Clos and Les Grenouilles at the bottom of the slope, and Vaudésir at the top of the slope. It is considered to have the potential to age as well as Les Clos in top years, and to produce wines that have the body and richness of Les Clos yet the penetrating perfume of Grenouilles. The very best wine I have ever tasted was the 1985 Valmur from Jean Collet (not a consistent producer, but when he gets it right, his wines can be some of the most profound and compelling of the appellation). The Raveneau family can also turn out stunning wines from this Grand Cru.

Vaudésir (31.8 acres)—The Grand Cru of Vaudésir includes the micro-vineyard of La Moutonne (5.8 acres), which has never received separate recognition as a Grand Cru, but straddles both the Grands Crus of Vaudésir and Les Preuses. The wines are recognized for their great clarity and precision of flavors, but are generally considered to have less body and power than Les Preuses, Valmur, Les Clos, or Blanchot. Louis Michel produces an excellent stainless-steel-fermented Vaudésir. Other excellent wines are also made by the Joseph Drouhin firm, and Long-Depaquit.

PREMIERS CRUS VINEYARDS

There are 40 Premiers Crus vineyards, but in practice a much smaller number of names are in use. The confusing Chablis regulations permit the Premiers Crus to be sold either with the name of the individual vineyard, or as one of the major groups of vineyards that has a better known Premier Cru name. As I have mentioned, there has been significant expansion of the acreage entitled to Premier Cru status since 1967, when there were 11 names that might include wines from as many as 27 different vineyards. For example, a grower who had a parcel of Montmains, Forêts, and Butteaux could vinify each wine separately and sell the wine under each of those names, or he could blend them together and call them Montmains. However, if they were blended together, he could not call his Chablis Premier Cru either Forêts or Butteaux. Very complicated indeed.

The following are today's 12 major Premier Cru names, together with the subparcels that can be included in the principal name or vinified separately and sold under their own name.

FOURCHAUME: Fourchaume, Vaupulent, Côte de Fontenay, Vaulorent, l'Homme Mort
MONTÉE DE TONNERRE: Monté de Tonnerre, Chapelot, Pied d'Aloup
MONT DE MILIEU
VAULCOUPIN
LES FOURNEAUX : Les Fourneaux, Morein, Côtes de Près-Girots
BEAUROY: Beauroy, Troesmes
CÔTE DE LÉCHET
VAILLONS: Vaillons, Châtains, Séchet, Beugnon, Les Lys
MELINOTS: Melinots, Roncières, Les Epinottes
MONTMAINS: Montmains, Forêts, Butteaux
VOSGROS: Vosgros, Vaugiraut
VAU-DE-VEY

For over a decade, the producers of Chablis have engaged in a controversial debate regarding the nature of Chablis. The purists, led by William Fèvre of the Domaine de la Maladière, believe that great Chablis can only be produced on the Kimmeridge soil, which is that mixture of clay and chalk with a quantity of fossilized oyster shells. In opposition is a group, led by the Domaine de l'Eglantière and headed by its founder Jean Durup. They argue that while soil is important, of more importance are the microclimates. Of course, the bottom line is that Jean Durup's group of expansionists have prevailed as the acreage under vine has increased significantly, although it is nowhere near what it was in the nineteenth century prior to the phylloxera scourge.

However, with the Premiers Crus, many are considered less worthy than others, and tasting some of the wines from Premiers Crus parcels clearly indicates that there is a great discrepancy in quality between the top Premiers Crus parcels such as Chapelot, Fourchaume, Mont de Milieu, Montée de Tonnerre, Pied d'Aloup, Vaulorent, Beauroy, Butteaux, Montmains, Vaillons and the other Premiers Crus vineyards. A close examination of a map of Chablis will show that these vineyards are spread out all over both banks of the river Serein and therefore have varying exposures, which accounts for the different times of ripening, as well as divergent soil types.

Some Chablis residents argue quite convincingly that several Premiers Crus probably should be Grands Crus. These include Chapelot, a 49-acre parcel that is extremely well situated at the bottom of the hillside on the right bank of the river. Among the winemakers, Raveneau and Guy Robin, vociferously state Chapelot should be elevated to Grand Cru status. Being vineyard owners, they are hardly disinterested parties.

Another Premier Cru many feel should be elevated to Grand Cru status is Fourchaume, a relatively large 84-acre parcel that sits just to the north of the hillside containing all the Grands Crus. Most top Fourchaumes from the best producers, such as the Domaine Laroche, have a striking power and elegance that can be quite exceptional. Still another Premier Cru that rivals the Grands Crus is the 84-acre Mont de Milieu, which is oriented toward the southeast, and has a microclimate that gives it an elevated amount of sunshine and slightly warmer temperatures than other Premiers Crus. Outstanding wines from Mont de Milieu are made by Jean Collet, Jean Dauvissat, Joseph Drouhin, André Philippon, Louis Pinson, and from time to time by the Vocoret family.

The same high quality is also often produced from the tiny, nearly 15-acre parcel of Montée de Tonnerre. In blind tastings, this microparcel is often judged to be a Grand Cru. It is regrettable that its reputation is not better known, but the tiny quantities of wine produced from it ensure that it will always remain an insider's wine. The Raveneau family makes a brilliant Montée de Tonnerre.

Another highly renowned parcel that François Raveneau claims is capable of producing wines of Grand Cru quality is Pied d'Aloup (17.29 acres). Guy Robin and Roger Vocoret agree.

Many who follow Chablis argue that these Premiers Crus should all be given Grands Crus status. The real danger is that while the authorities have allowed no changes to the number or size of the Grands Crus, there has been increasing pressure to continue to increase the number of Premiers Crus vineyards and acreage. The fact that some seem capable of producing Grand Cru quality while others are incapable of producing even Premier Cru quality raises serious questions about the credibility and rationale of those legislators who have established the appellation controls for Chablis.

OTHER WINES OF CHABLIS

The discussion of the Grands Crus and Premiers Crus takes into account only a very small percentage of the wine produced in this historic viticultural region. The increase in acreage of areas that were once entitled to be called only Petit-Chablis is also of concern, as many of these areas have been upgraded to Appellation Chablis Contrôlée status. This has undeniably precipitated a loss of confidence in the quality of generic Chablis because much of it is entirely too acidic, almost neutral in flavor, with little character.

Large crop yields are often a major problem for generic Chablis. We can blame not only overly enthusiastic and greedy growers who know no shame when fertilizing their vineyards, but also modern technology, which has invented machines that have virtually eliminated the danger of frost, Mother Nature's cruel but effective way of pruning back the size of the crop in Chablis.

Nevertheless, the producers who do not overproduce can make what is a delicious, zesty, almost zingy wine with great clarity and freshness. But for every good example one is lucky enough to find, there are 20 to 30 that are mediocre and vapid wines.

As for Petit-Chablis, I do not understand its merits. Perhaps twenty years ago there were some values, but today, most Petit-Chablis is green, nasty, severe wine that is rarely capable of producing pleasure.

VISITING THE VILLAGE OF CHABLIS
AND ITS PRODUCERS

The tiny, quiet village of Chablis is interesting, but hardly worthy of a detour. Still, its vineyards, particularly the Grands Crus, are an impressive sight. A more interesting place to visit is Auxerre, only 12 miles to the west. Auxerre is dotted with wonderful churches, including the Cathedral of St.-Étienne, built between the thirteenth and sixteenth centuries, and a number of old, half-timbered houses in the middle of the old part of the city. Auxerre has a number of fine hotels, including Le Maxime and Normandie, neither of which has a restaurant. One can find superb cooking in town at the Jardin Gourmand. Just outside of Auxerre, in the direction of Vaux on D 163, is the excellent La Petite Auberge. In the direction of Chevannes on D 1 about five miles outside of Auxerre is La Chamaille, another superb country restaurant owned by the Siri family.

In Chablis itself, one of my great discoveries was L'Étoile, a typically pleasant country hotel with regional cooking. Their wine list was once incredible and had many old vintages. In the mid-eighties, I remember first encountering an old Raveneau from the 1964 vintage that was in fabulous condition. Unfortunately, the old vintages have disappeared, but the wine list remains impressive, and the cooking is quite competent, if somewhat uninspired. Also in Chablis is the excellent Hostellerie des Clos, a hotel/restaurant with perhaps the highest quality and most innovative cooking south of the great La Côte St.-Jacques (a Michelin 3-star as well as an extravagantly appointed hotel/restaurant owned by the Lorain family in nearby Joigny). L'Abbaye St.-Michel, another luxurious hotel that boasts fine cuisine, is located about 10 miles from Chablis in the direction of Tonnerre. I've also had a good meal in Le St.-Bris, in the town by the same name about 11 miles from Chablis. It is easy to forget that this is a viticultural area based not on Chardonnay but the Sauvignon Blanc of the Loire Valley. For inexpensive, crisp, herbaceous Sauvignon as well as some Bourgogne Aligoté, St.-Bris le Vineux may be worth a stop.

The most interesting producers to visit in Chablis are François and Jean-Marie Raveneau. Their cellars are a must for any pilgrim in search of traditional Chablis. To experience a totally opposite but no less brilliant style, where wines are never exposed to oak casks, a visit to Louis Michel can be inspirational. Some of the more famous estates that may roll out the red carpet for you would include the Domaine de la Maladière of William Fèvre, and the merchant, J. Moreau et Fils, who makes huge quantities of Chablis. If you are willing to travel to Maligny, only a few miles away, I would recommend visiting one of Chablis' most powerful and influential citizens, Jean Durup, at his Domaine de L'Eglantière.

THE VILLAGES AND APPELLATIONS OF THE CÔTE DE NUITS

Marsannay and Fixin
Gevrey-Chambertin
Morey St.-Denis
Chambolle-Musigny
Vougeot
Vosne-Romanée and Flagey-Echézeaux
Nuits St.-Georges

MARSANNAY AND FIXIN

An Overview

Location: Marsannay is a quaint village of almost 6,000 people that sits a stone's throw from the end of Dijon's suburban sprawl. It is several miles north of Gevrey-Chambertin. Fixin, just over a mile to the south, is an even smaller village of 883 inhabitants. These towns are the two northernmost villages of Burgundy's Côte d'Or.

Acres under vine: Marsannay—100 acres out of a potential vineyard area of just over 1,000 acres; 770 acres are permitted for Pinot Noir, with the rest entitled for white and rosé wines.

Grands Crus: Marsannay—none

Principal Premiers Crus: Marsannay—none

Acres under vine: Fixin—320 acres, another 766 acres are entitled to Côte de Nuits-Villages

Grands Crus: Fixin—none

Principal Premiers Crus: Fixin—55 acres, a total of 7 Premiers Crus: Le Meix Bas, Clos Napoléon, Clos du Chapitre, Clos de la Perrière, Queue de Hareng, Les Arvelets, Les Hervelets

Price levels: Most Marsannays are reasonably priced, selling for $10–$15 a bottle. The Premiers Crus of Fixin, once bargains, have soared in price in recent years and now cost $20–$30 a bottle. The Villages wines of Fixin still sell at prices in the mid-teens.

General wine characteristics: Both the red and white wines of Marsannay are compact and straightforward. When well made they are no better than a Côte de Nuits-Villages. The rosés, especially those of Bruno Clair, are indeed among France's half-dozen best dry rosé wines. Fixin tends to produce sturdy, robust, muscular wines that often lack charm and elegance, but age well and can resemble a good Premier Cru from Gevrey-Chambertin.

The most overrated producers: Charles Quillardet, Derey Frères

The best producers and their wines:
    André Bart: Fixin Les Hervelets
    Denis Berthaut: Fixin Les Arvelets, Fixin Les Crais, Fixin Les Clos
    Marc Brocot: Marsannay Rouge
    Régis Bouvier: Marsannay Clos du Roy, Marsannay Vieilles Vignes
    Bruno Clair: Rosé de Marsannay, Fixin, Marsannay, Marsannay Les Longerois, Vaudenelles
    Faiveley: Fixin

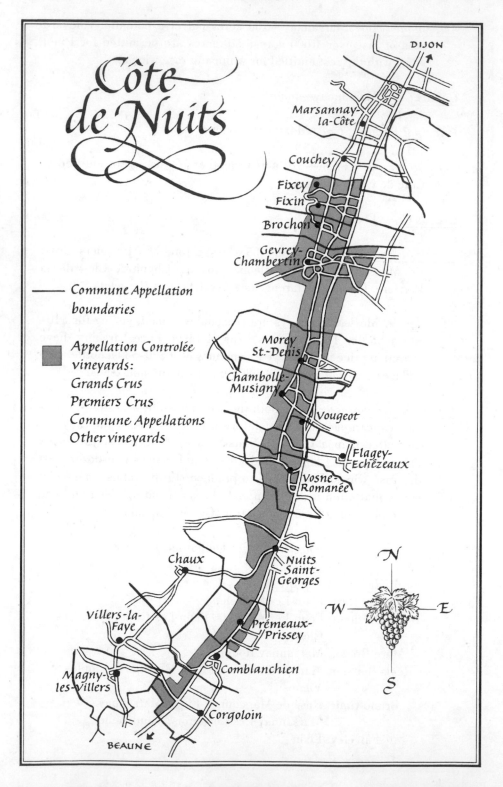

Côte
de Nuits

DIJON

Marsannay-
la-Côte

Couchey

Fixey
Fixin

Brochon

Gevrey-
Chambertin

—— Commune Appellation
boundaries

Appellation Controlée
vineyards:
Grands Crus
Premiers Crus
Commune Appellations
Other vineyards

Morey
St.-Denis

Chambolle-
Musigny

Vougeot

Flagey-
Echézeaux

Vosne-
Romanée

Chaux

Nuits
Saint-
Georges

Villers-la-
Faye

Prémeaux-
Prissey

Magny-
les-Villers

Comblanchien

Corgoloin

BEAUNE

N
W E
S

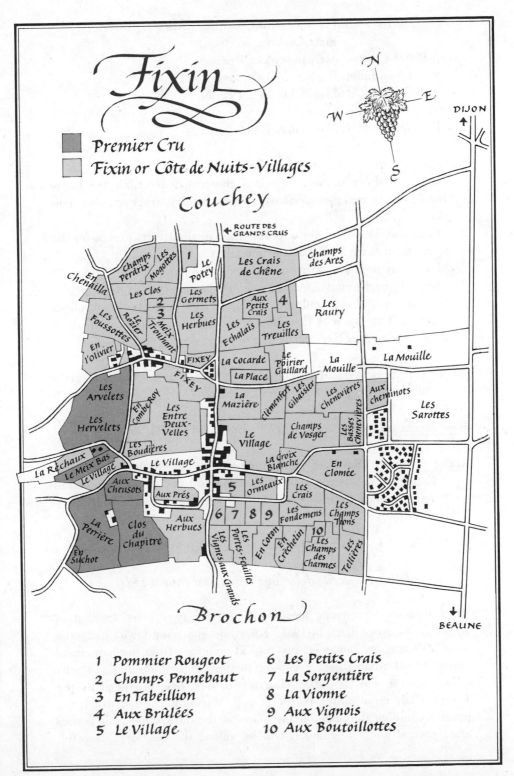

Fixin

Premier Cru

Fixin or Côte de Nuits-Villages

DIJON

Couchey

← ROUTE DES GRANDS CRUS

En Chenailla
Champs Perdrix
Les Mogottes
1
Le Potey
Les Crais de Chêne
Champs des Ares

Les Clos
Les Germets
Aux Petits Crais
4
Les Raury

Les Foussottes
Le Rozier
3
Meix Trouhant
2
Les Herbues
Les Echalais
Les Treuilles

En l'Olivier
FIXEY
La Cocarde
La Place
Le Poirier Gaillard
La Mouille
La Mouille

Les Arvelets
FIXEY
La Mazière
Clémenrot
Les Gibassier
Les Chenevières
Aux Cheminots
Les Sarottes

En Combe Roy
Les Entre Deux-Velles
Le Village
Champs de Vosger
Les Basses Chenevières

Les Hervelets
Les Boudières
La Croix Blanche
En Clomée

La Réchaux
Le Meix Bas
Le Village
Le Village
Les Ormeaux
Les Crais

Aux Cheusots
Aux Prés
5
Les Crais
Les Champs Tions

La Perrière
Clos du Chapitre
Aux Herbues
6 7 8 9
Les Fondemens
Les Champs des Charmes
10

En Suchot
Les Vignes aux Grands
Les Portes-Féuilles
En Coton
En Créchelin
Les Tellières

Brochon

BEAUNE

1	Pommier Rougeot	6	Les Petits Crais
2	Champs Pennebaut	7	La Sorgentière
3	En Tabeillion	8	La Vionne
4	Aux Brûlées	9	Aux Vignois
5	Le Village	10	Aux Boutoillottes

Pierre Gelin: Fixin-Clos du Chapitre, Fixin Les Hervelets,
Fixin Clos Napoléon
Jean-Pierre Guyard: Marsannay Les Recilles
Louis Jadot: Rosé de Marsannay
Philippe Joliet: Fixin-Clos de la Perrière
Mongeard-Mugneret: Fixin
Philippe Naddef: Marsannay Rouge

Some important observations:
1. The rosés of Marsannay, especially those of Bruno Clair and Louis
   Jadot, are to be taken seriously. They are dry, fragrant, and delicious.
2. Marsannay rouge has yet to prove itself qualitatively, except for the
   wines from Marc Brocot and Bruno Clair.
3. Marsannay produces a tiny quantity of uninteresting white wine.
4. Fixin, although small in acreage, should be on anyone's list of potential bargains. Prices will only go higher, particularly for excellent
   Premiers Crus such as Clos Napoléon, Clos du Chapitre, Clos de la
   Perrière, and Les Hervelets.

Where are the values? Marsannay Rosé and any of the wines of Fixin
   still qualify as good buys from Burgundy.

Most successful recent vintages: 1989, 1988, 1987, 1985, 1980, 1978

Aging potential: Rosé de Marsannay—6 to 18 months; Marsannay
   Rouge—2 to 5 years; Marsannay Blanc—1 to 2 years; Fixin—5 to
   7 years; Fixin Premier Cru—5 to 12 years

MARSANNAY AND FIXIN

(Value-priced, delicious rosés and robust reds)

After decades of economic depression, Marsannay received appellation
status as its own village in 1987. This tiny, charming town sits to the
west of Route Nationale 74, just as one emerges from the haphazard
sprawl of suburban Dijon. For much of this century, the village's only
claim to fame was its outstanding rosé wines, first produced by the
Joseph Clair family after World War I. Marsannay rosés, which are
made by pulling the juice off the skins of the dark Pinot Noir grapes
after several hours of contact, can be among the best dry, flavorful,

full-bodied rosés of France. Today, the best rosé of Marsannay is made by a direct descendant of Joseph Clair, Bruno Clair.

The red wines of Marsannay are equivalent, qualitatively, to a Côte de Nuits-Villages. The wines are too narrowly framed and often less distinguished than the best Côte de Nuits-Villages from some of the other viticultural areas in the Côte d'Or. Two producers, Marc Brocot and Bruno Clair, would appear to make the best red Marsannays, but the quantities of wine from their very old vines are limited. While Marsannay has no Premiers Crus, the local growers consider the following vineyards (increasingly listed on the wine's label) as their finest *terroirs:* Les Longeroies, Les Monchenevoy, Les Finottes, La Montagne, Les Echézeaux, Les Etalles, Les Recilles, Les Vaudenelles, Les Petits Puits, Le Rosey, Le Boivin, Le Clos de Jeu, Les Favières, Les Champs Salomon, Les Genelières, La Poulotte, Les Champs Perdrix, and Le Desert. This village will no doubt be exploited now that it has its own appellation status, and I suspect *négociants* will be offering greater selections of Marsannay rouge and rosé. Be sure to taste before you buy.

If Marsannay has yet to prove its potential for either white or red wine, Fixin has just emerged from a long period when the quality of its wines was underestimated. For much of this century most of the wines of Fixin were simply blended with those of Gevrey-Chambertin or called Côte de Nuits-Villages. With the growing appreciation of Fixin's Premiers Crus in the last two decades, there is now an increasing demand for the top wines of the appellation, and even the Villages wines are often presented to the consumer under the Appellation Fixin rather than Côte de Nuits-Villages.

Located a few miles north of Gevrey-Chambertin, Fixin has no Grands Crus, but its Premiers Crus are impressively situated high above the village on the relatively steep slopes of the same Bajocian limestone that Gevrey-Chambertin's best vineyards enjoy.

Everyone seems to agree that these Premiers Crus, when made by the likes of Bruno Clair, Denis Berthaut, Philippe Joliet, or Pierre Gelin, can be more similar than dissimilar to a good Premier Cru from Gevrey-Chambertin. However, they are not wines for those who lack patience, as most Premier Cru Fixins from top vintages need at least 5 to as many as 8 years to shed their considerable tannic clout. Nevertheless, the wines of Fixin have become quite popular. It is the solidity and robust, muscular nature of Fixin that gives these wines great appeal in the cold, wet, northern European countries such as Sweden, Belgium, Denmark, and West Germany. For other countries, it is no doubt the still realistic prices that have value-conscious connoisseurs of burgundy clamoring to lay away some of the best vintages of Fixin.

The soil that accounts for these hefty, deep-colored tannic wines is essentially a mixture of rich brown limestone and gravel. It is most notably in evidence at Clos de la Perrière and Clos du Chapitre, which have much more limestone, whereas Les Hervelets and Les Arvelets have more sand and thinner top soil, resulting in slightly lighter wines than those of Clos de la Perrière and Clos du Chapitre. Most of the Fixin Premiers Crus will age extremely well, if never quite developing the finesse and fragrance of a great wine from the more renowned Côte de Nuits appellations. I have had numerous bottles of 20- and 25-year old Fixins from Pierre Gelin, and while I would never say these wines were charming or full of finesse, they retained a robust, chunky fruitiness that was certainly agreeable.

VISITING THE VILLAGES OF MARSANNAY AND FIXIN AND THEIR PRODUCERS

Marsannay has an excellent restaurant, Les Gourmets, which serves some of the most innovative food of the area. The Perreaut family runs this tiny establishment, and has put together a top-notch wine list. For lodging, the modern Novotel is located directly on N 74, and offers spacious, modern rooms at $60–$70 a night.

Fixin has no hotels and only a small café. Fortunately, the village of Fixin has resisted the temptation to become another suburb of Dijon, and as a consequence has retained its charm. Many tourists who visit Fixin do so only to make the pilgrimage to a 15-acre park created by one of Emperor Napoleon's commanders, Claude Noisot. This park contains one of Burgundy's most famous bronze statues, "Napoleon Awakening" by sculptor François Rude. It is a controversial statue, for not everyone admires the depiction of Napoleon, who looks as if he has consumed one too many *menu dégustations*, and appears to be more of a gourmand than a shrewd commander.

Lastly, the most interesting cellars to visit would include those of Bruno Clair in Marsannay and those of both Pierre Gelin and Philippe Joliet in Fixin.

GEVREY-
CHAMBERTIN

An Overview

Location: Six miles south of Dijon on Route Nationale 74, Gevrey-Chambertin, with its population of 2,600, is the most northern Grand Cru village on Burgundy's famous Côte d'Or. Beaune is eighteen miles to the south.

Acres under vine: Approximately 1,462, all of which is Pinot Noir
     Grands Crus: 251 acres
     Premiers Crus: 212 acres
     Villages Wines: 889 acres with the balance entitled to be called
                 Côte de Nuits-Villages

Grands Crus: A total of 9
     Chambertin, Chambertin-Clos de Bèze, Chapelle-Chambertin, Charmes-Chambertin, Griotte-Chambertin, Latricières-Chambertin, Mazis-Chambertin, Mazoyères-Chambertin, Ruchottes-Chambertin

Principal Premiers Crus: A total of 28
     La Bossière, La Romanée, Poissenot, Etournelles, Estournelles (Clos des Varoilles), Les Verroilles (Clos des Varoilles), Lavaux (Lavaux St.-Jacques), Clos du Chapitre, Le Clos St.-Jacques, Les Cazetiers, Petits Cazetiers, Champeaux, Combe aux Moines, Les Goulots, Aux Combottes, Bel-Air, Cherbaudes, Champitenois, ou Petite Chapelle (Petite Chapelle), En Ergot, Clos Prieur-Haut (Clos Prieur), La Perrière, Au Closeau, Plantigone (Issarts), Les Corbeaux, Craipillot, Fontenys, Champonnet

Price levels: $50–$150 and up for Grands Crus; $25–$65 for Premiers Crus; $15–$35 for Appellation Gevrey-Chambertin Contrôlée (Villages wines)

General wine characteristics: There is greater variation in quality and style in Gevrey-Chambertin than in any other Burgundy appella-

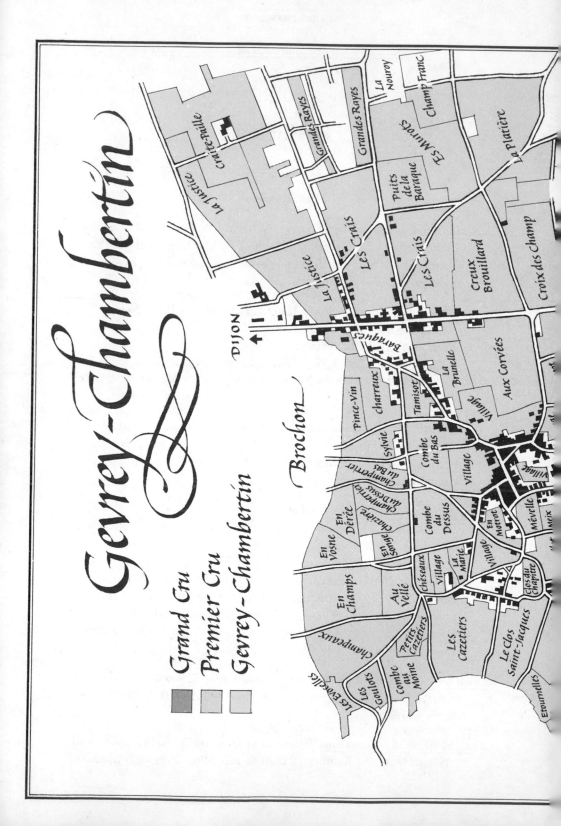

Gevrey-Chambertin

Grand Cru

Premier Cru

Gevrey-Chambertin

Brochon

DIJON

La Justice
Craite-Paille
Grandes Rayes
Grandes Rayes
La Nouroy
Champ Franc
Les Crais
Puits de la Baraque
Es Jouins
La Platière
La Justice
Les Crais
Les Crais
Creux Brouillard
Croix des Champ
Baraques
Pince-Vin
charreux
Tamisot
La Brunelle
Aux Corvées
Village
Sylvie
Combe du Bas
Village
En Dérée
Champerrier du Bas
Champerrier du Bas
Chaziere
En Songe
Combe du Dessus
En Motrot
Méxelle
Village
En Vosne
Chêsseaux
Village
La Marie
Village
Clos du Chapitre
En Champs
Au Vellé
Petits Cazetiers
Champeaux
Les Cazetiers
Le Clos Saint-Jacques
Les Evocelles
Les Goulots
Combe au Moine
Etournelles

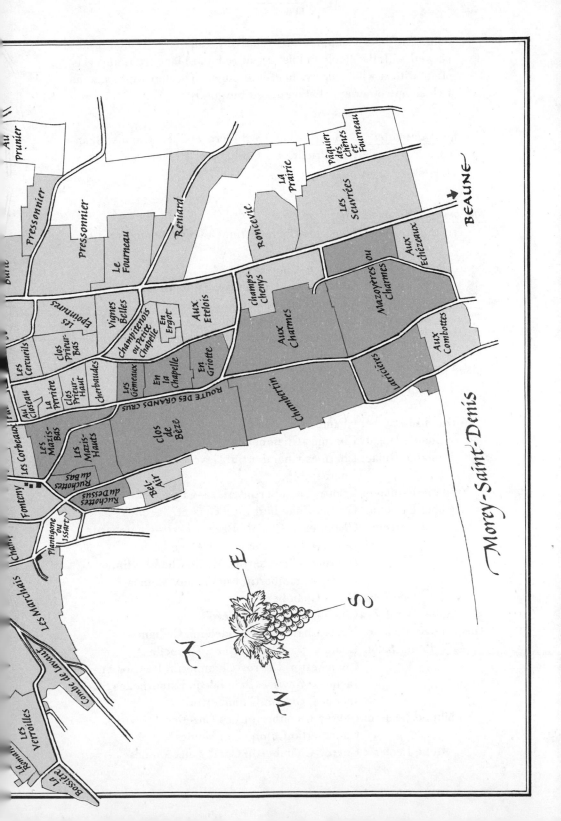

Morey-Saint-Denis

BEAUNE

tion. The best examples are relatively full, large-scaled wines packed with the smell and flavors of red and black fruit, and very often with a wild, earthy, beef-like smell. The top wines age as well as any other appellation of red burgundy.

The most overrated producers: Bouchard Père et Fils, Camus, Jean-Claude Fourrier, J. Prieur, C. Quillardet, Rebourseau, Remy, Trapet

The best producers and their wines:

Pierre Amiot: Charmes-Chambertin, Gevrey-Chambertin Les Combottes

Denis Bachelet: Charmes-Chambertin

Bourée: Chambertin, Charmes-Chambertin, Gevrey-Chambertin Clos de la Justice

Bruno Clair: Chambertin-Clos de Bèze, Gevrey-Chambertin Les Cazetiers, Gevrey-Chambertin-Clos St.-Jacques

Clos Frantin (Bichot): Chambertin

Joseph Drouhin: Chambertin-Clos de Bèze, Charmes-Chambertin, Griotte-Chambertin

Drouhin-Larose: Chambertin-Clos de Bèze

Claude Dugat: Charmes-Chambertin

Domaine Dujac: Charmes-Chambertin, Gevrey-Chambertin aux Combottes

Frédéric Esmonin: Griotte-Chambertin, Mazis-Chambertin

Michel Esmonin: Gevrey-Chambertin Le Clos St.-Jacques

Faiveley: Chambertin-Clos de Bèze, Gevrey-Chambertin Les Cazetiers, Latricières-Chambertin, Charmes-Chambertin, Mazis-Chambertin, Gevrey-Chambertin Combe aux Moines

Geoffrey: Mazis-Chambertin

Robert Groffier: Chambertin-Clos de Bèze

Hospices de Beaune: Mazis-Chambertin Madeleine Collignon

Louis Jadot: Chambertin-Clos de Bèze, Chapelle-Chambertin, Gevrey-Chambertin Le Clos St.-Jacques, Gevrey-Chambertin Estournelles St.-Jacques, Griotte-Chambertin

Philippe Leclerc: Gevrey-Chambertin Les Cazetiers, Gevrey-Chambertin Combe aux Moines

René Leclerc: Gevrey-Chambertin Combe aux Moines

Leroy: Chambertin, Mazis-Chambertin, Latricières-
     Chambertin
Hubert Lignier: Charmes-Chambertin
J. P. Marchand: Charmes-Chambertin, Griotte-Chambertin,
     Gevrey-Chambertin aux Combottes
Maume: Charmes-Chambertin, Mazis-Chambertin
Charles Mortet: Chambertin, Gevrey-Chambertin Champeaux
Georges Mugneret: Ruchottes-Chambertin
Philippe Naddef: Mazis-Chambertin, Gevrey-Chambertin Les
     Cazetiers, Gevrey-Chambertin Les Champeaux
Ponsot: Chambertin, Griotte-Chambertin, Latricières-
     Chambertin
Joseph Roty: Charmes-Chambertin, Griotte-Chambertin,
     Mazis-Chambertin
Roumier: Ruchottes-Chambertin, Charmes-Chambertin
Rousseau: Chambertin, Chambertin-Clos de Bèze, Gevrey-
     Chambertin Le Clos St.-Jacques
Christian Serafin: Charmes-Chambertin, Gevrey-Chambertin Les
     Cazetiers
Tortochot: Chambertin, Charmes-Chambertin
Truchot-Martin: Charmes-Chambertin
Vadey-Castagnier: Charmes-Chambertin

Some important observations:
1. Wine from the Grand Cru vineyard Clos de Bèze legally can be called Chambertin.
2. Wine from the Grand Cru vineyard Mazoyères is legally entitled to be (and usually is) called Charmes-Chambertin.
3. Chambertin, the most famous vineyard of the village and one of the magical names of Burgundy, is usually a disappointment unless it is from Rousseau or Leroy.
4. Among the Grands Crus, the most consistent high quality usually comes from Charmes-Chambertin and Griotte-Chambertin.
5. Among the Premiers Crus, Le Clos St.-Jacques, Les Cazetiers, Combe aux Moines, Lavaut St.-Jacques, Estournelles, and Aux Combottes often equal the Grands Crus in quality if not in prestige or price.
6. The overall quality level, among the worst of all Burgundy's villages in the sixties and seventies, is clearly on the rise. However, there are still numerous and conspicuous underachievers with great vineyard holdings in Gevrey-Chambertin.

Where are the values? Villages wines from the likes of Alain Burguet, P. Rossignol, Christian Serafin, and Bourée are the most likely candidates.

Most successful recent vintages: 1989, 1988, 1987, 1985, 1980, 1978

Aging Potential: Grands Crus—8 to 20 years; Premiers Crus—5 to 12 years; Villages wines—4 to 9 years

GEVREY-CHAMBERTIN
(Still the king?)

Of all the villages of Burgundy's Côte d'Or, none evokes more magic and prestige than does Gevrey-Chambertin. The village, one of the largest of the Côte d'Or, gets its name from its most famous vineyard, the Grand Cru Chambertin. Among the surrounding 1,400-plus acres of vineyards there are more Grands Crus than in any other village of Burgundy. Gevrey-Chambertin is located just a short 6 miles south of the bustling city of Dijon on the very northernmost border of the Côte d'Or. Bisected by the famous Route Nationale 74, it is a sprawling village that stretches up the hillside toward the forest at the top that provides an excellent windbreak. Virtually everyone in the village is involved in the production and sale of wine, and it is hard to believe that such an agriculturally oriented, seemingly primitive village could be so close to the sophisticated city of Dijon.

As in other Burgundy villages, the history of winemaking in Gevrey-Chambertin is largely a result of the efforts of the monastic orders that planted the original vineyards hundreds of years ago. At one time the most famous vineyard was that named after the Abbey of Bèze. This vineyard, cultivated by monks and later known as Chambertin-Clos de Bèze, was in existence prior to the Chambertin vineyard from which the village takes its name. The Chambertin vineyard was apparently named after a peasant named Bertin, who owned land next to the Clos de Bèze vineyard. His vineyard was known as Le Champ de Bertin (the field of Bertin). Hundreds of years later, the bastardized pronunciation of Bertin's fields became Chambertin. The reputation of these vineyards grew not only because of their close proximity to the major commercial center of Dijon, but also because the Emperor Napoleon made no secret of his admiration for the wines of Chambertin. Lamentably, he was no connoisseur, as he is alleged to have had his Chambertin not only chilled, but watered down so it would not upset his sensitive digestive system. Napoleon's love of Chambertin has no doubt been embellished by writers over the last 200 years. Many claim his defeat at the Battle of Waterloo was due to the fact that he did not have Chambertin with his dinner the night before. It is also said that after he was ostracized and imprisoned on the island of St.-Hélèna, his death was hastened by the fact that he was forced to drink Bordeaux rather than his favorite Chambertin (Bordeaux being easier to ship to St.-Hélèna than Burgundy).

As the legend of Chambertin's greatness grew, it became known as the wine of kings. Today it would be hard to justify that title given the diluted, often insipid quality of many wines bearing the Chambertin name. Yet, the name Chambertin has retained extraordinary significance and historical symbolism, and this appellation, which produces wines of enormous differences in quality, has actually become in the last 5 to 10 years one of the most promising places for young producers to make wine.

THE VINEYARDS OF GEVREY-CHAMBERTIN

In addition to the famous Grands Crus of Chambertin and Chambertin-Clos de Bèze, Gevrey-Chambertin has 7 other Grands Crus for a total of 9, more than any other Burgundy village. The surface area of the vineyards forms the shape of an irregular "T" turned on its right side, with the top forming the northern sector to the east and west of the village, and the stem of the "T" forming what would be the most prized section of the appellation with all the Grands Crus spread out on a hillside south of the village running in the direction of Morey St.-Denis.

All the Grands Crus vineyards sit at an altitude of approximately 1,000 feet, and are planted in soil bases that are Bajocian limestone. The topsoil is a chalky brown color with variable amounts of gravel and clay. It is interesting that certain Grands Crus such as Ruchottes and Latricières have much more limestone, whereas Griottes and Chapelle are on much thinner soil with occasional rock formations bursting through the top soil.

The majority of the best Premiers Crus of Gevrey-Chambertin sit just to the west of the village near the crown of the hill and are well protected by the forest situated at the top of the rise. Such outstanding vineyards as Lavaux St.-Jacques, Le Clos St.-Jacques, Les Cazetiers, Combe aux Moines, Champeaux, and Clos Les Varoilles have ideal exposures, but being at a higher and cooler altitude their grapes mature more slowly. Consequently, these vineyards are often the last in the village to be harvested. In the hands of a good producer these Premiers Crus can produce wine that approaches the quality of most of the Grands Crus. All of these vineyards are contiguous on the hillside above the village, north of the Grands Crus that are closer to Morey St.-Denis.

There are two Premiers Crus that might appear somewhat out of place. One is Les Combottes, which sits to the west of the Grand Cru Charmes and is south and adjacent to Latricières. It also borders Morey St.-Denis and to its south is the outstanding Grand Cru vineyard of Morey St.-Denis, Clos la Roche. One might argue that in the hands of a great grower such as Jacques Seysses of the Domaine Dujac, Combottes is truly a Grand Cru in quality if not in name. The other Premier Cru that seems slightly out of place is Bel-Air, which sits farther up the hill, just north of the Grand Cru Clos de Bèze. Inexplicably, it renders wine that never approaches the quality of the best Premiers Crus.

As for the Villages wines, they are all located farther down the hill, with many extending onto the flat plain to the east of the Route Nationale. The land here is flat and drainage is significantly inferior to that on the hillsides. For that reason, most of the Villages wines of Gevrey-Chambertin tend to be much lower in quality than those from neighboring Morey St.-Denis or even Chambolle-Musigny farther south. The one notable exception is the excellent, sometimes outstanding Clos de la Justice of the Bourée firm. This excellent wine, made from 4 separate vineyards all on the "wrong" side of N 74, has consistently proven to be of the quality of a Premier Cru, even though it is only a generic Gevrey-Chambertin.

What follows is a more detailed look at each of the top vineyards and a survey of those producers who seem to extract the most interesting wine from their land.

GRANDS CRUS VINEYARDS

Chambertin—The fields of the seventh-century peasant, Monsieur Bertin, produce this appellation's most famous wine. Yet, a close look at this Grand Cru, which fetches astronomical prices, would quickly cause one to suspect any claim to connoisseurship by its champions, such as Emperor Napoleon and the famous French poet Gaston Roupnel, who eloquently stated, "It blends grace and vigor. It unites firmness and power, finesse and delicious differing qualities that compress together an admirable synthesis of unique generosity and complete value." One wonders what he must have tasted given the fact that there are now 23 different proprietors of Chambertin's 32-acre vineyard, and only a handful of them seem committed to producing extraordinary wine.

The vineyard itself is announced with great fanfare (the billboard says *"Ici commence Chambertin"*) as one heads south on the Route des Grands Crus in the direction of Morey St.-Denis. The Chambertin vineyard is sandwiched between its two Grands Crus neighbors, Latricières to the south and Clos de Bèze to the north. On the eastern side of the road is the Grand Cru Charmes-Chambertin.

I have had some Chambertins that have lived up to the words of Gaston Roupnel. The 1969s of Trapet and Rousseau, as well as the 1949, 1955, 1959, and 1962 vintages of Leroy's Chambertin have justified the high prices and illustrious fame this Grand Cru vineyard has received over the centuries. I have also had some marvelous bottles from the Bichot-owned Clos Frantin parcel of Chambertin. In more recent vintages, both Ponsot and Bourée have turned out stunning Chambertin. But once past these wines, the best chance today's consumers have to find the real thing is to invest in a bottle from the Domaine Rousseau, Maison Leroy, Ponsot, or Bourée. One taste of a Chambertin from the likes of Camus, Bouchard Père et Fils, Jaboulet-Vercherre, Jacques Prieur, Domaine Quillardet, Domaine Rebourseau, Domaine Louis Remy, or recent insipid efforts from the Domaine Trapet will reveal Chambertins that are apparently the product of vineyards that have been stretched to their maximum production, and wines that lack concentration, character, and complexity. For wine enthusiasts, it is a tragedy, given the important holdings and wealth of such estates as Trapet (which has not made a great Chambertin since their 1969), Remy, Rebourseau, Jacques Prieur, Camus, and Pierre Damoy. Chambertin is probably the most disappointing wine, not only among the Grands Crus of Gevrey-Chambertin, but in Burgundy's Côte d'Or.

There does not appear to be any one standard for what great Chambertin should taste like. The finest producers of Chambertin are Rousseau, Leroy, and Ponsot. The Rousseau and Ponsot style offers velvety wines of great fragrance and richness, with an abundance of red and black fruits, and an elegance and finesse that would not qualify them as blockbuster, overly intense, or powerful wines. There is plenty of toasty new oak in the Rousseau wines, but none in the wines of Ponsot. Both these Chambertins have the cunning ability to age for decades. The Maison Leroy style, on the other hand, produces a wine that is clearly deeper in color with little evidence of new oak and more emphasis on body, tannin, and great concentration of berry and black fruits. The Leroy wine is monumental in every sense, and can last for 30–40 years. It is one of the great ironies of this appellation that there are other Grands Crus, as well as some top Premiers Crus, whose vineyard owners/winemakers are much more consistent and motivated, and who frequently produce wine from less prestigious sites that is markedly superior to Chambertin itself.

Chambertin-Clos de Bèze—The history of this vineyard dates from 630 A.D., when it was acquired by the monks of the Abbey of Bèze. They sold it 7 centuries later to the cathedral at Langres. It remained under church ownership until the French Revolution, at which time it was split up among the peasants. The 38-acre Grand Cru vineyard Clos de Bèze is slightly larger than Chambertin, and sits just to the north of that vineyard. The two Grands Crus are separated by a tiny road and have a similar soil base.

There are 18 proprietors of Chambertin-Clos de Bèze's 38 acres. The winemaking is clearly of a higher quality, more interesting, and more consistent than that from Chambertin. One must ask then, what are the differences between Chambertin and Clos de Bèze? My tasting experiences suggest that the best wines from Clos de Bèze are slightly fuller, deeper, more concentrated, and perhaps less fragrant than those of Chambertin.

The best producers of Clos de Bèze include the Maison Faiveley, the famous vineyard owner and *négociant* in Nuits St.-Georges, as well as the excellent *négociant* and vineyard owner in Beaune, Joseph Drouhin. The Domaine Robert Groffier in Morey St.-Denis also produces superb Chambertin-Clos de Bèze, as does the wealthy estate of Domaine Drouhin-Larose in Gevrey-Chambertin. Again, one cannot go wrong with the wines from the Domaine Rousseau, whose Chambertin-Clos de Bèze represents the quintessentially elegant style of wine from this Grand Cru vineyard. I have also had superb Clos de Bèze from Bruno Clair and the Maison Louis Jadot. I have had some great older bottles, the 1970 and 1966, from the Domaine Clair-Dau (sold and divided between the Maison Louis Jadot and Bruno Clair in the early eighties).

Not surprisingly, the underachievers from Chambertin-Clos de Bèze are the Domaine Pierre Damoy (the largest holder of Clos de Bèze), Jacques Prieur, and Henri Rebourseau.

Today, a Chambertin-Clos de Bèze gives the consumer a better chance to drink an extraordinary red burgundy than a bottle from Chambertin.

Latricières-Chambertin—The 18.2-acre Grand Cru vineyard Latricières sits immediately to the south of Chambertin. It produces a wine that is relatively light for a Grand Cru but one that does have certain characteristics in common with Chambertin. The vineyard has 12 proprietors, and the best wine is made by the Maison Faiveley in Nuits St.-Georges. The history of the vineyard suggests that it began to be cultivated in the sixteenth century. Its name means "small miracle," an appropriate

name for this Grand Cru vineyard, which is surpassed in quality by a
number of better Premiers Crus such as Les Cazetiers, Combe aux
Moines, and Clos St.-Jacques. Perhaps it is the soil composition, which
tends to be slightly harder and less well drained than the neighboring
Chambertin or Clos de Bèze, that is responsible for these wines, which
are a bit lighter and sometimes seem to be missing the finesse, concentration, and character one would expect from not only a Grand Cru, but
from a wine priced so dearly.

While the two famous domaines of Trapet and Camus are the largest
vineyard holders, neither seems to be capable at the moment of producing a great wine, or for that matter even a very good one from this
renowned field. Both have the resources and the wealth, but they lack
motivation. The same can be said for the Domaine Louis Remy and the
American-owned Domaine Newman, both of which produce relatively
light, insignificant wines that do not do justice to this Grand Cru vineyard. The message would appear to be that unless one restricts his
purchase to the Latricières of Ponsot, Faiveley, or the wines of the
Domaine Leroy (which recently acquired Remy's parcel of Latricières),
the results are disappointing.

Mazis-Chambertin—Mazis-Chambertin's 22.4 acres are encountered
immediately as one leaves the village of Gevrey-Chambertin on the
Route des Grands Crus. The quality of winemaking from this vineyard
is extremely high, as there are a number of magnificent wines emerging
from this tiny parcel. This is not to say everyone makes good wines, as
there are 30 different proprietors, but a good Mazis tends to be among
the darkest and deepest colored Grands Crus Chambertins with considerable body, richness, and plenty of tannin and concentration. The
finest Mazis-Chambertins come from the Hospices de Beaune's tiny
parcel called Cuvée Madeleine Collignon, the Domaine Maume, Joseph
Roty, the Maison Leroy, the Maison Faiveley, and to a lesser extent
from the Domaine Rousseau, and the Domaine Tortochot. I have had
disappointing wines from the Domaine Camus, Domaine Vachet-Rousseau, and of course, from the notorious underachiever, Domaine Rebourseau.

A good Mazis-Chambertin (which can also be spelled Mazy-
Chambertin) can easily last for 15 to 25 years, and might well be the
longest lived wine of the appellation of Gevrey-Chambertin.

Ruchottes-Chambertin—This is the second smallest of the Grands Crus
in Gevrey-Chambertin, consisting of only 8.1 acres. Even in abundant
years, less than 1,000 cases of wine are made from this tiny parcel of
vines situated just north of Mazis-Chambertin, contiguous with both
Mazis and the northwestern corner of Clos de Bèze. The vineyard has

extremely thin soil and is excessively rocky, making cultivation quite difficult. It is a cliché to say that the harder it is to cultivate the vineyard the better the wine, but it might explain why I have tasted so many great wines from this Grand Cru vineyard. The best wines have consistently come from the Domaine Georges Mugneret in Vosne-Romanée, Domaine Rousseau in Gevrey-Chambertin, the Maison Leroy, and the Domaine Roumier in Chambolle-Musigny. It is rare to find a *négociant* who has produced a Ruchottes-Chambertin. The only one I have seen has been the extraordinary wine selected by Lalou Bize-Leroy for her firm in Auxey-Duresses. I have had numerous profound wines from the late Georges Mugneret, particularly his 1955, 1969, and 1978. It is a shame such tiny quantities of this wine are produced, for in many ways it is the consummate Grand Cru of Gevrey-Chambertin, displaying astonishing richness, length, flavor intensity, and aging potential. The sole criticism of Ruchottes-Chambertin is that its wines possess less finesse than a great Chambertin-Clos de Bèze.

Griotte-Chambertin—Griotte-Chambertin (it can also be spelled Griottes), a minuscule jewel of a vineyard, consists of 6.7 acres located on the other side of the Route des Grands Crus from Clos de Bèze. Though Griotte-Chambertin produces less than 800 cases of wine in an abundant vintage, it does indeed produce some of the most extraordinary wines of Gevrey-Chambertin. The name of the vineyard itself is believed by some to have come from a French word for cherry tree, although Joseph Roty argues that the name is a bastardization of the word "grillottes," which has nothing to do with cherry trees.

The Griotte-Chambertin vineyard provides wines with all the richness and intensity of Clos de Bèze, but with an extra measure of perfume and complexity. I have had great wines from Joseph Roty, whose holding amounts to no more than several rows of vines, the Maison Joseph Drouhin in Beaune, and some spectacular Griottes from both Frédéric Esmonin and the Domaine Ponsot, which farms a parcel of Griotte-Chambertin owned by Monsieur Mercier. In the vintages of the eighties, the important Domaine Marchand in Gevrey-Chambertin and Louis Jadot have also begun to produce excellent wines from this superbly situated Grand Cru vineyard.

In contrast to the wines from Clos de Bèze, Ruchottes-Chambertin, or Mazis-Chambertin, most of the wines of Griotte tend to mature at a slightly earlier age.

Chapelle-Chambertin—The Grand Cru Chapelle-Chambertin sits just to the north of Griotte and across the road from Clos de Bèze. From its 13.5 acres of vineyards, it produces the lightest and most delicate wine of all the Grands Crus of Chambertin. The name originated from a small chapel built by the monks of the Abbey of Bèze, which was destroyed during the French Revolution.

The best wines from this Grand Cru, which has 8 separate proprietors, have consistently been those of the Domaine Clair-Dau and Domaine Drouhin-Larose. Of course, the Domaine Clair-Dau was sold and their parcel of Chapelle-Chambertin is now owned by Louis Jadot in Beaune. The 1985, 1987, and 1988 Chapelle-Chambertin from Louis Jadot were indeed excellent, so Jadot appears to be heir apparent to Clair-Dau as the best producer of this Grand Cru vineyard. The Domaine Drouhin-Larose was capable of turning out excellent wines, but their performance over recent vintages has been less consistent than in the seventies and sixties. Again, the two famous domaines of Pierre Damoy and Louis Trapet, who own relatively large parcels, continue to produce wines that do not merit significant consumer interest.

Charmes-Chambertin—Charmes-Chambertin is clearly the best known of all the Grands Crus in Gevrey-Chambertin. It is the largest Grand Cru vineyard, consisting of a total of 78 acres when one takes into account that most of the wine from Mazoyères is entitled to be called Charmes-Chambertin. There are a number of superb producers making Charmes-Chambertin, so the wine in many bottles so labeled usually merits its reputation.

The very best wines from this Grand Cru vineyard are produced by the small domaines of Joseph Roty, Christian Serafin, Domaine Dujac, Hubert Lignier, Bourée, Vadey-Castagnier, Domaine Maume, Claude Dugat, Bernard Bachelet, Pierre Amiot, and Faiveley. I have also had some superb bottles from the Domaine Charlopin (the 1980 was extraordinary), as well as the *négociant* Joseph Drouhin. The wines from the Domaines Camus and Rebourseau tend to be disappointing. The famous Domaine Rousseau, noted for their extraordinary Chambertin, Chambertin-Clos de Bèze, and Ruchottes-Chambertin, produces a lighter-styled, elegant Charmes-Chambertin but it is not one of the top wines of their domaine. Two other estates that have been making higher and higher quality wines in the 1980s include Jean-Claude Marchand and Jean Raphet.

A good Charmes-Chambertin, which curiously enough is not named after the French word for "charm" but rather after a type of tree common in this area called "chaume," tends to be among the more supple and easily appreciated wines of Gevrey-Chambertin. When made from old vines and a reduced crop size, its strength is its silky, supple, velvety richness. When overproduced, the wine can taste dull and insipid.

Mazoyères-Chambertin—Most of the producers who have plots in Mazoyères label their wines Charmes-Chambertin, but Mazoyères is the southernmost Grand Cru of Gevrey-Chambertin, adjacent to Charmes-Chambertin and across the Route des Grands Crus from Latricières-Chambertin. Two of the domaines that actually have the courage to sell their Mazoyères-Chambertin under its own name rather than using the more readily identifiable name of Charmes-Chambertin are the Domaine Camus and the Domaine Richard.

PREMIERS CRUS VINEYARDS

While there is slightly less Premier Cru Gevrey-Chambertin acreage than Grand Cru, the 212 acres of Premiers Crus still provide a great deal of wine of varying degrees of quality. However, the top Premiers Crus, such as Le Clos St.-Jacques, Les Cazetiers, Combe aux Moines, Champeaux, Lavaux St.-Jacques, Clos de Varoilles, and Aux Combottes, have producers who frequently make wines as good as those owners of Grands Crus parcels. There is no doubt that a Le Clos St.-Jacques from the Domaine Rousseau, Bruno Clair, Michel Esmonin, or Louis Jadot is of Grand Cru quality. The same can be said for the Estournelles St.-Jacques or Lavaux St.-Jacques of the Maison Leroy, the Aux Combottes of the Domaine Dujac, Les Cazetiers from Christian Serafin, Bruno Clair, Philippe Leclerc, Philippe Naddef, and Maison Faiveley, the Combe aux Moines from Philippe Leclerc, René Leclerc, and Maison Faiveley, and the Champeaux from Charles Mortet. All of these producers make Premiers Crus that are often significantly better than the majority of the wines entitled to the name Chambertin. They are wines to be sought out for their richness and breadth of flavor and complexity. Interestingly, most of the top Premiers Crus, with the exception of Aux Combottes, are located in the northwestern corner of the hillside above the village. If there is ever a reclassification of the Grands Crus and Premiers Crus vineyards, many will be in favor of elevating Clos St.-Jacques, as well as Les Cazetiers and Combe aux Moines, to Grand Cru status.

OTHER WINES OF GEVREY-CHAMBERTIN

Gevrey-Chambertin produces an immense quantity of ordinary wine under the Villages appellation. As I mentioned earlier, one of the very best wines made in all of Gevrey-Chambertin is entitled to only a Villages appellation: the Clos de la Justice, which comes from a parcel owned by the Bourée firm on the very northern edge of the Gevrey-Chambertin appellation, on the southeastern side of Route Nationale

74. Other excellent Villages wines come from committed, high-quality growers such as Alain Burguet, Philippe Rossignol, Christian Serafin, and Denis Bachelet. Even so, the consumer who randomly searches for a generic Gevrey-Chambertin will, more often than not, find an over-priced, diluted, simple wine that is of little interest.

VISITING THE VILLAGE OF GEVREY-CHAMBERTIN AND ITS PRODUCERS

If necessary one can easily stay in downtown Dijon and drive to Gevrey-Chambertin within 20 minutes, even during rush-hour traffic. However, Gevrey-Chambertin is not without its own fine hotels. Les Terroirs, located right on the Route Nationale 74, has 23 spacious and often beautiful rooms that cost roughly $50–$75 a night. If you plan to stay there, be sure to ask for a room in the back, as the well-travelled main road between Dijon and Nuits St.-Georges can occasionally be quite noisy. Les Terroirs is owned and managed by Madame René Leclerc. She knows all the wine producers and through her influence one can gain entrance into some of the cellars. The other hotel, Les Grands Crus, has 24 modest rooms ranging in price between $40 and $60 a night. Situated in the rear of the village among the vineyards, it is very tranquil and quiet, although its rooms are small.

Gevrey-Chambertin has fine restaurants as well. No visitor should miss the superb Les Millesimes, whose wine list is one of the greatest in France. The tiny restaurant, run by the Sangoy family, is located in an old wine cellar and offers extraordinary ambiance. On the other side of the village is La Rôtisserie du Chambertin. Located in a vaulted wine cellar much like Les Millesimes, this restaurant has a winemaking museum inhabited by numerous odd wax figures. The wine list is distressing, as only wines vinified by the Trapet firm are served. Nevertheless, the ambiance is superb and the food is certainly good.

Growers such as Philippe Leclerc regularly sell their wines directly to consumers and are available for visits whenever they are open. However, most producers expect visitors to make an appointment. Among the more interesting producers to visit would be the Domaine Rousseau, whose family, one of the first to begin estate-bottling burgundies, has been making great wines for over half a century. Other interesting growers include the wealthy estate of Drouhin-Larose, the Domaine des Varoilles, as well as the best *négociant* in Gevrey-Chambertin, Bourée. If you have patience, and an adventurous spirit, one grower not to be missed is Joseph Roty, whose enthusiasm and loquaciousness is unmatched in Burgundy.

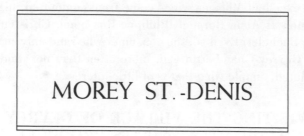

MOREY ST.-DENIS

An Overview

Location: A tiny village (654 residents) situated immediately to the south of Gevrey-Chambertin on the northern half of Burgundy's Côte d'Or.

Acres under vine: A total of 674, which, except for several microplots of Chardonnay and Pinot Blanc, is virtually all Pinot Noir.

    Grands Crus: 97.3 acres (the majority of which is within the appellation of neighboring Chambolle-Musigny), plus 3.7 acres of Bonnes Mares

  Premiers Crus: 109 acres

  Villages Wines: 464 acres

Grands Crus: A total of 5

    Bonnes Mares, Clos St.-Denis, Clos des Lambrays, Clos de la Roche, Clos de Tart

Principal Premiers Crus: A total of 20

    Les Genevrières, Monts Luisants, Les Chaffots, Clos Baulet, Les Blanchards, Les Gruenchers, Les Millandes, Les Fauconnières, Les Charrières, Clos des Ormes, Aux Charmes, Aux Cheseaux, Les Chenevery, Les Sorbès, Clos Sorbès, La Bussière, Les Ruchots, Le Village, Côte Rôtie, La Riotte

Price levels: $55–$125 for Grands Crus; $35–$75 for Premiers Crus; $20–$30 for Appellation Morey St.-Denis Contrôlée (Villages wines)

General wine characteristics: The best examples are firm, rich, fragrant, very ageworthy wines redolent with aromas of red and black fruits. The wines are often better balanced than those of Morey

St.-Denis's prestigious northern neighbor, Gevrey-Chambertin, having more depth and concentration and slightly less tannin.

The most overrated producers: Louis Remy and the Domaine des Lambrays

The best producers and their wines:
     Pierre Amiot: Clos de la Roche
     Bourée: Clos de la Roche
   Georges Bryczek: Morey St.-Denis Cuvée du Pape
   Joseph Drouhin: Bonnes Mares
   Drouhin-Larose: Bonnes Mares
   Domaine Dujac: Bonnes Mares, Clos de la Roche, Clos St.-Denis
      Faiveley: Clos de la Roche, Morey St.-Denis-Clos des
          Ormes
   Robert Groffier: Bonnes Mares
    Louis Jadot: Bonnes Mares
  Georges Lignier: Bonnes Mares, Clos de la Roche, Clos St.-Denis,
          Morey St.-Denis-Clos des Ormes
   Hubert Lignier: Clos de la Roche, Morey St.-Denis Premier Cru
  J. P. Marchand: Clos de la Roche
    Mommessin: Clos de Tart (since 1985)
   Pernin-Rossin: Morey St.-Denis Mont Luisants, Clos de la Roche
      Ponsot: Clos St.-Denis, Clos de la Roche-Cuvée Vieilles
          Vignes
     Roumier: Bonnes Mares, Bonnes Mares-Cuvée Vieilles
          Vignes, Morey St.-Denis-Clos de la Bussière
Domaine Rousseau: Clos de la Roche
  Bernard Serveau: Morey St.-Denis Les Sorbès
  Truchot-Martin: Clos de la Roche, Morey St.-Denis-Clos Sorbès
Vadey-Castagnier: Clos St.-Denis

Some important observations:
1. The wines, winemaking, and top vineyards are perhaps the most underrated of all the great villages of Burgundy's Côte d'Or. Burgundy insiders seek out these wines.
2. Three of the Grands Crus, Clos de la Roche, Clos St.-Denis, and Bonnes Mares, produce some of the greatest red burgundies made, yet rarely fetch the same price as the Grands Crus in neighboring Gevrey-Chambertin (to the north) or Chambolle-Musigny and Vosne-Romanée (to the south).

3. Three of the Premiers Crus, La Bussière, Clos des Ormes, and Monts Luisants, are close in quality to the Grands Crus.
4. Most of the production of Morey St.-Denis is estate-bottled, as Burgundy's *négociants* do little buying from this appellation.

Where are the values? Good to very good wines at realistic prices exist at the Villages and Premiers Crus levels. The top producers all produce fine generic Morey St.-Denis wines in good years.

Most successful recent vintages: 1989, 1988, 1987, 1985, 1983, 1982, 1980, 1978

Aging potential: Grands Crus—6 to 18 years; Premiers Crus—5 to 12 years; Villages wines—4 to 8 years

MOREY ST.-DENIS

(To be ignored no longer)

Given the present-day quality and potential of the 5 Grands Crus of Morey St.-Denis, it is surprising that this village has always lived in the shadows of both its northern and southern neighbors, Gevrey-Chambertin and Chambolle-Musigny. Today, there are no Burgundy Grands Crus better than Clos de la Roche, Bonnes Mares, or Clos St.-Denis. What's more, with the revival of the extraordinary Clos de Tart estate and the long anticipated renaissance of the other famous Grand Cru estate, Clos des Lambrays, Morey St.-Denis appears poised to enjoy a far greater reputation than it has in the past. Of course, one should not assume that the wines of Morey St.-Denis are undiscovered, because that could not be said about any red wines from the Côte d'Or.

The hamlet of Morey St.-Denis once belonged to the powerful Abbey of Cîteaux. The name Morey apparently derives from the Latin word *moriacum*, which meant a Moorish estate. The village was burned to the ground in the late seventeenth century, and afterwards suffered from plagues and from its reputation as a haven for misfits and beggars. It was not until after World War II that the village began to experience a degree of prosperity and become fully populated.

THE VINEYARDS OF MOREY ST.-DENIS

If one continues south on the Route des Grands Crus that traverses the hillside south of the village of Gevrey-Chambertin, past the Grands

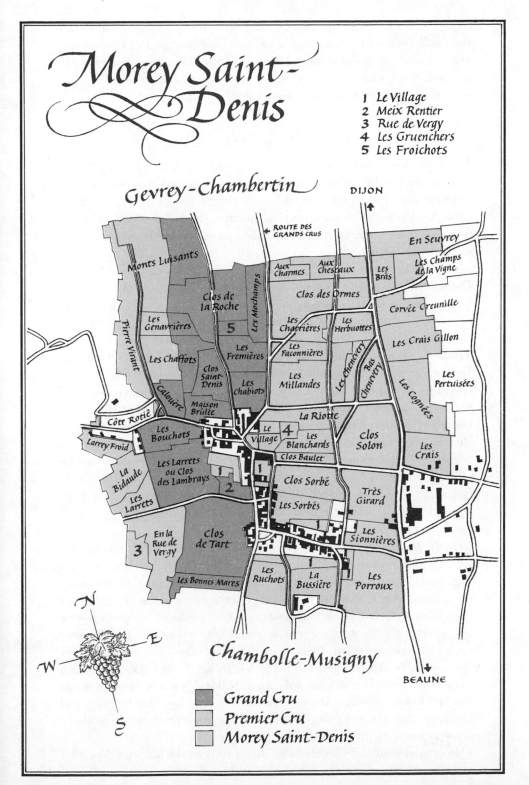

Morey Saint-Denis

1 Le Village
2 Meix Rentier
3 Rue de Vergy
4 Les Gruenchers
5 Les Froichots

Gevrey-Chambertin

DIJON

← ROUTE DES
GRANDS CRUS

Monts Luisants

En Seuvrey

Aux
Charmes

Aux
Chescaux

Les
Bras

Les Champs
de la Vigne

Clos de
la Roche

Clos des Ormes

Corvée Creunille

Pierre Virant

Les
Genavrières

Les Mochamps

Les
Chatrières

Les
Herbuottes

Les Crais Gillon

5

Les Chaffots

Les
Fremières

Les
Faconnières

Les Chenevery

Bas
Chanevery

Les Cognées

Les
Pertuisées

Clos
Saint-
Denis

Les
Chabiots

Les
Millandes

Calouère

Maison
Brûlée

La Riotte

Côte Rôtie

Les
Bouchots

Le
Village

4

Les
Blanchards

Clos
Solon

Les
Crais

Larrey Froid

Clos Baulet

1

La
Bidaude

Les Larrets
ou Clos
des Lambrays

Clos Sorbé

Très
Girard

2

Les
Larrets

Les Sorbés

Les
Sionnières

3

En la
Rue de
Vergy

Clos
de Tart

Les
Ruchots

La
Bussière

Les
Porroux

Les Bonnes Mares

Chambolle-Musigny

BEAUNE ↓

N
E
W
S

Grand Cru
Premier Cru
Morey Saint-Denis

Crus vineyards of Clos de Bèze, Chambertin, and Latricières, and past the small Premier Cru vineyard of Gevrey-Chambertin, Les Combottes, one will find the appellation of Morey St.-Denis. The top vineyards are planted in soil that is identical to that of Gevrey-Chambertin, Bajocian limestone intermixed with gravel and iron.

GRANDS CRUS VINEYARDS

Clos de la Roche—This 41-acre vineyard with its extraordinarily rocky, well-drained soil frequently produces some of the greatest wines in all of Burgundy. The wines from Clos de la Roche and its nearby neighbor Clos St.-Denis, the two Grands Crus north of the village, tend to be the deepest, most concentrated and robust wines among the Grands Crus of Morey St.-Denis.

Clos de la Roche is fortunate to boast superb owners, including the Domaine Ponsot, which makes an excellent regular *cuvée* of Clos de la Roche, and in great years produces a Cuvée Vieilles Vignes that is one of the top candidates for the wine of the vintage. Additionally, the Domaine Dujac, Bourée, Domaine Vadey-Castagnier, Domaine Truchot, Hubert Lignier, Georges Lignier, Pierre Amiot, Domaine Rousseau, and Jean-Claude Marchand all produce exemplary wines from this Grand Cru vineyard. While Ponsot, Bourée, and Hubert Lignier's wines tend to represent the most concentrated and rich, full-bodied style, for pure silky elegance those of the Domaine Dujac or Pierre Amiot are quintessentially elegant, suave wines. Among the *négociants*, I have consistently been impressed by the Clos de la Roche offered by the Maison Faiveley and that made by Joseph Drouhin in Beaune. I have not enjoyed the Clos de la Roche made by Bouchard Père et Fils. It neither reflects the appellation nor does it possess a great deal of character or individuality.

Clos St.-Denis—It is Clos St.-Denis, like Chambertin in the village of Gevrey-Chambertin and Musigny in the village of Chambolle-Musigny, that lends its name to that of its village. In 1927, the inhabitants chose the name of this Grand Cru to be added to the name of the village rather than Clos de la Roche. While most would argue that Clos de la Roche has greater significance since it is much larger than the tiny 16-acre Clos St.-Denis vineyard, there is no doubting that the wines from this spectacularly situated site, just to the northwest of the village and south of the Clos de la Roche vineyard, are unbelievably exciting when made by the likes of Domaine Dujac, Ponsot, Domaine Georges Lignier, and Domaine Vadey-Castagnier. There are other good producers, but these growers consistently turn out the finest wines.

In comparison to a Clos de la Roche, a Clos St.-Denis often has a bit more plum and berry-like fruit, less body, and a more silky, stylish personality. Three of the greatest red burgundies I have ever tasted are the 1978 Clos St.-Denis from Domaine Dujac, the 1985 Clos St.-Denis from Georges Lignier, and the 1985 Clos St.-Denis from Ponsot.

Clos des Lambrays—In 1981, this Premier Cru vineyard received the unique honor of being elevated to Grand Cru status in the Burgundy firmament. Virtually the entire parcel of 21.7 acres is owned by the brothers Fabien and Louis Saier. They purchased the property in 1979 and began an extensive replanting of the vineyard in 1980. Several rows of vines remain under the ownership of several other growers, including the Raphet and Magnien families, but their production is so tiny that the wine they produce is blended in with their other wines from Morey St.-Denis.

Legendary wines from Clos des Lambrays were made in the thirties and forties, at which time the wines were prized for their tremendous body, richness, and aging potential. I have had extraordinary wines made under the previous owners, the Cosson family, in vintages such as 1937, 1945, 1947, 1948, and 1949. Now that the vineyard has been torn up and replanted, the production in the eighties has been typical of a young, immature vineyard. The wines have lacked concentration and depth, and have been relatively light and one-dimensional. It is anticipated that this will change as the vineyard gets older, but thus far one has to be disappointed by the quality of wine that the owner, the Saier family, has produced from its new Grand Cru vineyard.

Clos de Tart—This 18.6 acre Grand Cru vineyard sits adjacent to and south of Clos des Lambrays. It was owned by Cistercian monks from the twelfth century until the French Revolution, when it was sold to a private individual. In 1932, the famous *négociant* from the Mâconnais region, Mommessin, acquired the estate, and for over 50 years this firm was content to live off the former reputation of Clos de Tart, producing a wine that was frequently thin and uninteresting. Presumably the production was pushed to the maximum and there was no selection process or commitment to producing the best this vineyard was capable of doing. Since 1985 the wine of Clos de Tart has clearly justified its exalted reputation. It is now one of the silkiest, richest, and most seductive red wines from the Côte de Nuits. Even given the renaissance of quality occurring at Clos de Tart, this wine will never have the body, power, or color depth of Clos de la Roche or Clos St.-Denis. However, it should have a greater fragrance and elegance than either of those two Grand Cru vineyards. It remains one of the handful of Grands Crus solely under the control of one owner and, therefore, is called a *monopole*.

Bonnes Mares—Most of the Grand Cru Bonnes Mares vineyard is located in Chambolle-Musigny rather than Morey St.-Denis. The biggest holding that officially sits within the Morey St.-Denis appellation was owned by the Domaine Clair-Dau and sold in the eighties to the Maison Louis Jadot in Beaune. The famous Morey St.-Denis estate of Georges Roumier continues to vinify two separate *cuvées* of Bonnes Mares, supposedly representing Bonnes Mares from the Chambolle-Musigny side and Morey St.-Denis side, but I doubt anyone can discern a difference, as the soils are identical.

PREMIERS CRUS VINEYARDS

One of the very best Premiers Crus of Morey St.-Denis is the Clos des Ormes. Situated north of the village, it produces extremely rich, full wines that can often approach Grand Cru quality when made by a top grower such as Georges Lignier, particularly in a vintage such as 1985. I have also had superb Clos des Ormes from the Maison Faiveley in Nuits St.-Georges (made from purchased grapes). Another outstanding Premier Cru located to the north of the village of Morey St.-Denis is Les Monts Luisants, which also produces Morey St.-Denis' only white wine, made primarily from Chardonnay (there is also some Pinot Blanc). The two most famous white wines of Morey St.-Denis, the Monts Luisants of the Domaine Ponsot and that of the young Bruno Clair, located in Marsannay, come from this rocky, pebble-strewn vineyard that sits further up the hill from the two Grands Crus, Clos St.-Denis and Clos de la Roche.

Among the other Premiers Crus are the excellent Les Millandes, just northeast of the village, and La Bussière, south of the village. The latter vineyard is solely owned by the Domaine Georges Roumier, and the resulting wine is rich and fragrant. It also represents one of the best values from this appellation.

It is interesting to note that it has been the common practice of many producers simply to blend their production from several different Premiers Crus and label the resulting wine Morey St.-Denis Premier Cru. This reflects their attitude that the Premiers Crus of Morey St.-Denis are significantly less well known than those of Chambolle-Musigny or Gevrey-Chambertin. I anticipate that this will change during the decade of the nineties.

VISITING THE VILLAGE OF MOREY ST.-DENIS AND ITS PRODUCERS

Morey St.-Denis is blessed with one of the most comfortable and tranquil hotels in all the Côte de Nuits, the Auberge le Castel de Très Girard. Located right at the entrance to the village, this charming inn also serves good, hearty Burgundian cuisine at modest prices. The rooms are small but comfortable, so if one has business to take care of anywhere in the Côte de Nuits, this is an excellent place in which to eat or spend the night.

Producers well worth seeing include Jean-Marie Ponsot, the longtime mayor of Morey St.-Denis. His performance in mediocre years such as 1982, 1984, and 1986 often leaves much to be desired, but in the great vintages this extraordinary estate excels. No one should visit Morey St.-Denis without stopping to see the Domaine Dujac, run with impeccable care and often unwavering brilliance by Jacques Seysses. Seysses has become a leader of a new generation of Burgundy growers committed to quality, and tasting in his cellars is both educational and enjoyable. Other interesting cellars worth a visit include those of Georges Lignier, Hubert Lignier, Pierre Amiot, and Bernard Serveau, whose cellars you will find adjacent to each other on the main road into the village after leaving Route Nationale 74.

Every Burgundy village seems to have its resident character. Joseph Roty or Philippe Leclerc would qualify as two of the most interesting personalities of Gevrey-Chambertin, and Georges Bryczek, a Polish sculptor, would take that honor in Morey St.-Denis. A visit with Bryczek is well worth your time. And finally, the famous *monopole* Grands Crus vineyards of Clos des Lambrays and Clos de Tart are worth a visit, more for their historical significance than for their contemporary record of quality.

CHAMBOLLE-MUSIGNY

An Overview

Location: Bordered on the north by the village of Morey St.-Denis and on the south by Vougeot, Chambolle-Musigny is a tiny village of 364 inhabitants (Les Chambollois).

Acres under vine: 550 acres; virtually all of it Pinot Noir, except for a tiny .75-acre plot of Chardonnay planted in the Grand Cru vineyard, Musigny.

   Grands Crus: 64 acres
Premiers Crus: 150 acres
Villages Wines: 283 acres

Grands Crus: A total of 2
Bonnes Mares, Musigny

Principal Premiers Crus: A total of 24
Les Sentièrs, Les Baudes, Les Noirots, Les Lavrottes, Les Fuées, Aux Beaux Bruns, Aux Échanges, Les Charmes, Les Plantes, Aux Combottes, Les Combottes, Derrière la Grange, Les Gruenchers, Les Groseilles, Les Chatelots, Les Grands Murs, Les Feusse-lottes, Les Cras, Les Carrières, Les Chabiots, Les Borniques, Les Amoureuses, Les Hauts Doix, La Combe d'Orveau

Price Levels: $50–$90 for Grands Crus: $25–$55 for Premiers Crus; $20–$30 for Appellation Chambolle-Musigny Contrôlée (Villages wines).

General wine characteristics: The wines of Chambolle-Musigny are frequently considered to be the lightest and most delicate red wines of the Côte de Nuits. This is attributable to the limestone soil and to the fact that centuries ago there were plantings of Pinot Blanc intermixed with the Pinot Noir. Today, there is no longer any Pinot Blanc, but the wines of Chambolle-Musigny are clearly less sturdy and full bodied than those of Morey St.-Denis or Gevrey-Chambertin. In the top examples, they seem to have a superb fragrance of red fruits and flowers.

The most overrated producers: Hervé Roumier, Grivelet

The best producers and their wines:
Bernard Amiot: Chambolle-Musigny Les Charmes
Barthod-Noellat: Chambolle-Musigny Les Charmes, Chambolle-Musigny Les Cras
Pierre Bertheau: Bonnes Mares, Chambolle-Musigny Les Amoureuses, Chambolle-Musigny Les Charmes
Joseph Drouhin: Bonnes Mares, Musigny
Drouhin-Larose: Bonnes Mares
Domaine Dujac: Bonnes Mares, Chambolle-Musigny Premier Cru
Faiveley: Musigny
Robert Groffier: Bonnes Mares, Chambolle-Musigny Les Sentièrs
Hudelot-Noëllat: Chambolle-Musigny Les Chabiots, Chambolle-Musigny Les Charmes

Louis Jadot: Bonnes Mares, Chambolle-Musigny Les
Amoureuses, Musigny
Leroy: Musigny
Georges Lignier: Bonnes Mares
Moine-Hudelot: Bonnes Mares, Chambolle-Musigny Les
Amoureuses, Chambolle-Musigny Les
Charmes, Musigny
Georges Mugneret: Chambolle-Musigny Les Feusselottes
Jacques-Frederic Mugnier: Bonnes Mares, Musigny
Ponsot: Chambolle-Musigny Les Charmes
Georges Roumier: Bonnes Mares, Bonnes Mares-Cuvée
Vieilles Vignes, Chambolle-Musigny Les
Amoureuses, Musigny
Bernard Serveau: Chambolle-Musigny Les Amoureuses
Servelle-Tachot: Chambolle-Musigny Les Amoureuses,
Chambolle-Musigny Les Charmes
Comte de Vogüé: Bonnes Mares, Chambolle-Musigny Les
Amoureuses, Musigny
Leni Volpato: Bourgogne Passe-Toute-Grains,
Chambolle-Musigny

Some important observations:
1. Two of Burgundy's greatest domaines are located in this village,
   Georges Roumier and the Comte de Vogüé. The Roumier estate
   continues to be among the finest in the Côte d'Or. The Comte de
   Vogüé estate, known for its brilliant wines in the forties, fifties, and
   sixties, slumped badly after the 1972 vintage and is now trying to
   regain its preeminence.
2. Musigny and Bonnes Mares are indeed two great Grands Crus, but
   top examples of the Premier Cru, Les Amoureuses, are almost as
   profound.
3. The most underrated Premier Cru vineyard of Chambolle-Musigny
   is Les Charmes.
4. The microquantities of Musigny Blanc that are produced are grossly
   overpriced, although the wine is certainly good.

Where are the values? The villages wines are notoriously mediocre as
are many of the Premiers Crus, but do look for wines from excellent vineyards such as Les Sentièrs, Les Cras, Les Feusselottes,
and Les Chabiots, as they represent good values.

Most successful recent vintages: 1989, 1988, 1987, 1985, 1980

Aging Potential: Grands Crus—7 to 15 years; Premiers Crus—4 to 10 years; Villages wines—2 to 7 years

CHAMBOLLE-MUSIGNY

(Too many underachievers)

Except for the tiny one-horse hamlet of Vougeot, the village of Chambolle-Musigny is the smallest of the famed appellations of the Côte de Nuits. As the Dutchman Hubrecht Duijker, in his excellent book _The Great Wines of Burgundy_, and the Englishman Anthony Hanson, in _Burgundy_, both point out, the village name comes from _Campus Ebulliens_, a reference to the ferociousness of the local tributary, which has had a tendency to overflow its banks and flood the village, as it did most recently in 1944 and 1965. Duijker also points out that at one time deformed Burgundians were often referred to as being as ugly as "the good Lord of Chambolle," a reference to the deformed Christ that appears on the front door of the church of Chambolle-Musigny.

The wine of Chambolle-Musigny has had a long history of staunch advocates, including the famed French poet Gaston Roupnel, who claimed that a Chambolle-Musigny was above all "a wine of silk and lace; supremely delicate with no hint of violence yet much hidden strength." Even allowing for embellishment, the best examples of a Grand Cru Musigny or Bonnes Mares, or the Premier Cru Chambolle-Musigny Les Amoureuses, should be the antithesis of the sturdy, full-bodied wines from Morey St.-Denis or Gevrey-Chambertin.

The soil of Chambolle-Musigny is predominantly limestone, rather than a limestone and clay mixture as is found in Morey St.-Denis and Gevrey-Chambertin. The resulting wines rely more on their fragrant perfume and silkiness than their strength, body, and robustness.

THE VINEYARDS OF CHAMBOLLE-MUSIGNY

GRANDS CRUS VINEYARDS

Musigny—The Musigny vineyard, all 26.4 acres of it, is squeezed in at the top of a hill like a tightly fitting crown on top of another Grand Cru, the great neighboring vineyard of Clos de Vougeot. There are 17 differ-

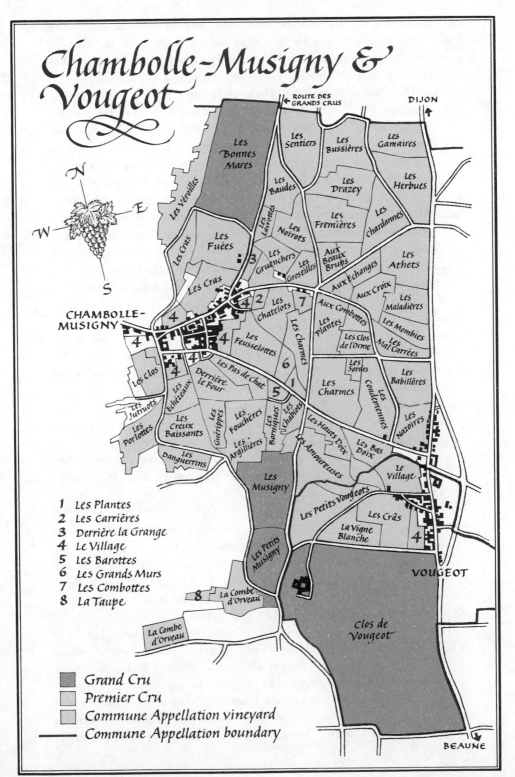

Chambolle-Musigny & Vougeot

ROUTE DES GRANDS CRUS

DIJON

N
E
W
S

Les Bonnes Mares

Les Sentiers
Les Bussières
Les Gamaires

Les Véroilles
Les Baudes
Les Drazey
Les Herbues

Les Cras
Les Fuées
Les Larrivées
Les Noirots
Les Fremières
Les Chardannes

3
Les Gruenchers
Les Groseilles
Aux Beaux Bruns
Les Athets

Les Cras
4
2
Les Chatelots
7
Aux Échanges
Aux Croix
Les Maladières
Les Mombies

CHAMBOLLE-MUSIGNY
4
Aux Combottes
Les Plantes
Les Mal Carrées

4
4
Les Feusselottes
6
Les Charmes
Les Clos de l'Orme
Les Sordes
Les Babillères

4
Les Clos
4
Les Échezeaux
Derrière Le Four
Les Pas de Chat
1
Les Charmes
Les Condemennes

Les Jutruots
Les Porlottes
Les Creux Baissants
Les Guerippes
Les Fouchères
Les Bornifques
Les Chabiots
5
Les Hauts Doix
Les Bas Doix
Les Nazoires

Les Danguerrins
Les Argillières
Les Amoureuses

Les Musigny
Le Village
Les Petits Vougeots
Les Crâs

1 Les Plantes
2 Les Carrières
3 Derrière la Grange
4 Le Village
5 Les Barottes
6 Les Grands Murs
7 Les Combottes
8 La Taupe

La Vigne Blanche
4
VOUGEOT

Les Petits Musigny

8
La Combe d'Orveau

La Combe d'Orveau

Clos de Vougeot

Grand Cru
Premier Cru
Commune Appellation vineyard
Commune Appellation boundary

BEAUNE

ent proprietors of this hallowed vineyard, and by most accounts the finest wine should always be that of its largest landholder, the 18-acre parcel of the Domaine Comte de Vogüé. For much of this century that has been the case, with such legendary Musignys as the 1945, 1947, 1948, 1949, 1959, 1964, 1966, 1969, 1971, and 1972 all taking their places among the most distinguished and extraordinary red burgundies of those vintages. However, after 1972 the quality slipped badly, and the domaine has only now begun to right itself. Even so, as good as recent vintages have been, they have not yet recaptured the glory of vintages such as 1972 and its predecessors. Perhaps the best Musigny at the moment is made by Madame Lalou Bize-Leroy, who produces incredibly long-lived, stylish, elegant wine that reflects this Grand Cru's reputation for wines of extraordinary fragrance and femininity. Other top Musigny is made by the Maison Faiveley, Joseph Drouhin, and the extraordinary estate of Georges Roumier in Chambolle-Musigny.

I have consistently been disappointed by the Musignys from other producers, particularly that of Jacques Prieur, who has an important 2-acre parcel of this Grand Cru.

Most Musignys can be drunk at a surprisingly young age, but in the top vintages they should be held for at least 5 or 6 years. They are capable of lasting for 10 to 15 years. All of the aforementioned great older vintages of the Comte de Vogüé are still remarkable wines, assuming they have been stored correctly.

The Comte de Vogüé also produces a tiny quantity of Musigny Blanc from Chardonnay grapes, a rare wine that commands outrageously high prices of nearly $100 a bottle. It is very good, sometimes excellent, but it is terribly overpriced, as one is paying for prestige and rarity rather than profoundness.

Bonnes Mares—Whereas the Grand Cru Musigny vineyard sits at the southernmost point of the appellation of Chambolle-Musigny, adjacent to the Clos de Vougeot, the other Grand Cru of the village, Bonnes Mares, sits at the northern border of the appellation adjacent to Morey St.-Denis. In fact, among the 37 acres in this Grand Cru, 3.7 of them are actually within the Morey St.-Denis appellation and the balance, 33.3, within the Chambolle-Musigny appellation.

The style of wine made by the best producers of Bonnes Mares is totally different from Musigny. Less fragrant, fuller-bodied, more tannic, and needing longer to reach maturity, Bonnes Mares has more in common with the other Grands Crus of the neighboring village of Morey St.-Denis than it does with Chambolle-Musigny's other famed Grand Cru. Nevertheless, Bonnes Mares can be excellent when made by producers such as the Domaine Dujac, Domaine Georges Roumier,

Domaine Georges Lignier, Domaine Bertheau, Domaine Hudelot-Noël-lat, Joseph Drouhin, Domaine Robert Groffier, Louis Jadot, Drouhin-Larose, Domaine Jean-Frédéric Mugnier, and on occasion, the Domaine Arlaud. Disappointments have usually come from the Domaine Newman and the Beaune *négociants*. The wines of the Comte de Vogüé, quite variable between 1973 and 1986, have improved immensely. Given the quality of most Grands Crus, one has an especially good chance of finding a great wine when buying a Bonnes Mares because of the quality producers who make it.

PREMIERS CRUS VINEYARDS

Among the 24 Premiers Crus of Chambolle-Musigny, most are not well known. However, there are 7 Premiers Crus that consistently produce better wines than the other 17. At the northern end of the appellation, surrounding the Grand Cru Bonnes Mares, are such excellent Premiers Crus as Les Sentièrs (Robert Groffier makes excellent wine from this vineyard), Les Baudes, Les Fuées, and Les Cras. The wines from these parcels, located north of the village, tend to be fuller and less fragrant than the 3 excellent Premiers Crus south and east of the village, Les Amoureuses, Les Charmes, and Les Chabiots, which produce slightly lighter, more elegant wines. When well made, these latter three are the epitome of delicate red burgundies.

OTHER WINES OF CHAMBOLLE-MUSIGNY

With respect to the Villages wines of Chambolle-Musigny, most of the better growers produce competent examples, but they lack the breadth of flavor and complexity of the best Villages wines of Morey St.-Denis. However, they are slightly more consistent as Villages wines than those of Gevrey-Chambertin. For those lucky enough to find any, the Villages wines from the tiny grower Leni Volpato, who owns no Premiers Crus or Grands Crus in Chambolle-Musigny, are the finest of their type. This committed, high-quality grower also produces an extraordinary Bourgogne Passe-Tout-Grains made primarily of Pinot Noir.

VISITING THE VILLAGE OF CHAMBOLLE-MUSIGNY AND ITS PRODUCERS

Chambolle-Musigny has managed to retain its ancient agricultural personality. Consequently, there are no restaurants or hotels here.

The most important estate that merits a visit is the Domaine Comte de Vogüé, with its impressive holdings in Bonnes Mares, Musigny Les Amoureuses, and, of course, Chambolle-Musigny. I hope it regains its potential to produce one of the greatest wines of Burgundy. The other great estate in Chambolle-Musigny is the Domaine Georges Roumier, with its impressive underground cellars and, of course, its extraordinary range of quality wines. This has long been one of the leading domaines of Burgundy, regardless of who has been in control, and the wines are benchmarks of quality for their respective appellations. A visit with its gregarious proprietor, Jean-Marie, or his son Christophe, is required for any student of fine burgundy.

While the Comte de Vogüé and Georges Roumier estates are the two most important in the village, some small growers worth visiting include the Domaine Bertheau, Domaine Daniel Moine-Hudelot, Domaine Hudelot-Noëllat, and the Domaine de Château du Chambolle-Musigny of Jacques-Frédéric Mugnier.

As for the resident character of Chambolle-Musigny, there is no one here to match a Georges Bryczek of Morey St.-Denis, or a Joseph Roty or Philippe Leclerc in Gevrey-Chambertin. However, there is no doubting the pixie-like, infectious enthusiasm of Jean-Marie Roumier of the Domaine Georges Roumier. A visit with this diminutive fireball is fun enough, and when one considers the extraordinary wines from that domaine that one can taste, it makes for an unforgettable rendezvous.

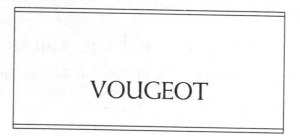

VOUGEOT

An Overview

Location: The dominant walled vineyard enclosing 124 acres sits one mile south of Chambolle-Musigny. The impressive château of Clos Vougeot sits on the hillside and can be seen for miles in all directions.

Acres under vine: 163 acres; mostly Pinot Noir, except for 7.41 acres of Chardonnay planted in the Premier Cru vineyard Le Clos Blanc.
    Grands Crus: 124 acres
   Premiers Crus: 28 acres
   Villages Wines: 11 acres

Grands Crus: Only 1
Clos de Vougeot

Principal Premiers Crus: A total of 4
Les Cras, La Vigne Blanche (Le Clos Blanc), Les Petits Vougeots,
Les Petits Vougeots (Clos de la Perrière)

Price levels: $45–$60 for the Grands Crus; $25–$40 for the Premiers
Crus

General wine characteristics: Naturally, all of the attention is devoted
to the Grand Cru, Clos de Vougeot, which is itself a perfect example of the complicated, morselated, frustrating world of modern-day Burgundy. Its 124 acres share 77 different proprietors,
and what true Clos de Vougeot should taste like remains the subject of intense debate. Nevertheless, the top examples share an
exquisitely pure, velvety, berry fruitiness in addition to their intense concentration of pure red fruits. The finest wines have neither the tannins nor muscle of a Grand Cru from Gevrey-
Chambertin or Morey St.-Denis, nor the fragrance and perfume
of a Grand Cru from Chambolle-Musigny. Yet, they are just as
impressive because of their purity of berry fruit (predominantly
raspberries, black cherries, and currants). The great examples of
Clos Vougeot can age extremely well despite its precocious
charm.

The most overrated producers: Château de la Tour (before 1985), Du-
Fouleur, François Lamarche, l'Heritier-Guyot, Pierre Ponnelle,
Jacques Prieur, Henri Rebourseau, Château de Bligny, Ropiteau-
Mignon, La Reine Pedauque

The best producers: The following classification of quality is offered as
a guide to understanding this Grand Cru vineyard.

RATING THE PRINCIPAL PRODUCERS OF
CLOS DE VOUGEOT

Outstanding

Chopin-Groffier	Méo-Camuzet
J. Confuron-Contidot	Mongeard-Mugneret
Gros Frère et Soeur	Georges Mugneret
Jean Gros	Georges Roumier
Haegelen-Jayer	Jean Tardy
Leroy	

Very Good to Excellent

Robert Arnoux

Cathiard-Molinier

Clos Frantin (Bichot)

Jean-Jacques Confuron

Joseph Drouhin

Drouhin-Larose

René Engel

Faiveley

Jean Grivot

Noël Hudelot

Hudelot-Noëllat

Louis Jadot

Jaffelin

Labouré-Roi (Lescure)

Thomas Moillard

Moine-Hudelot

Charles Mortet

Michel Noëllat

Jean Raphet

Bernard Rion

Daniel Rion

Roubaix-Indelli

Servelle-Tachot

Tortochot

Château de la Tour (since 1985)

Vadey-Castagnier

Average

Pierre André

Bertagna

Capitain-Gagnerot

Champy Père

Henri Clerc

Guy Coquard

Dufouleur

Francois Gerbet

Francois Gros

l'Heritier-Guyot

François Lamarche

Leymarie-Coste

Pierre-Yves Masson

Denis Mugnier

Pierre Ponnelle

Jacques Prieur

Henri Rebourseau

Ropiteau-Mignon

Hervé Roumier

Some important observations:

1. Much has been made of the fact that the Clos de Vougeot has three types of soil, with the best vineyards all situated on the higher ground, which is composed of a brown-colored calcareous clay/gravel soil. Not surprisingly, those growers I rated as outstanding, except for Chopin-Groffier and Leroy, have parcels at the very top of the hill.

2. The lowest part of the Clos de Vougeot, consisting of alluvial deposits that drain poorly, is not considered to be of Grand Cru quality. Yet, producers such as Leroy, Louis Jadot, Jean Grivot, Faiveley, Bichot's Clos Frantin, and Moine-Hudelot produce excellent wines from this undistinguished soil at the bottom of the Clos de Vougeot slope. What does that signify?

3. At its best, a great Clos Vougeot is one of Burgundy's most hedonistic wines, yet rarely does it fetch the price of Burgundy's other
Grands Crus. The perception of irregular quality has kept the price
of great Clos de Vougeot more affordable than other Grands Crus.
4. The Blanc de Clos Vougeot, the white wine made exclusively by
l'Heritier-Guyot, is the finest white wine made in the Côte de Nuits,
surpassing the Musigny Blanc of the Comte de Vogüé, the Monts
Luisants of the Domaine Ponsot in Morey St.-Denis, and even the
rare white Nuits St.-Georges La Perrière of Henri Gouges.

Where are the values? Chosen meticulously, a great Clos de Vougeot
from a vintage such as 1985, 1987, or 1988 is, relatively speaking,
a good value in the scheme of Grands Crus Burgundy prices.

Most successful recent vintages: 1989, 1988, 1987, 1985, 1983, 1980,
1978

Aging Potential: Clos de Vougeot—5 to 15 years; Vougeot Premier Cru
—5–8 years; Clos Blanc de Vougeot—5 to 10 years; Vougeot—3
to 8 years

CLOS DE VOUGEOT
(The top to bottom of the chaotic Clos)

It might come as a surprise to many followers of Burgundy that there is
actually a village just to the north of the famous walled vineyard of Clos
de Vougeot. It is the smallest village of the Côte de Nuits, with a
population of just under 200. As one might expect, almost everyone in
the village is involved in some aspect of the winemaking business.

Vougeot is probably Burgundy's most notorious appellation, and in
itself serves as a valuable illustration of why Burgundy's system of wine
production remains so excruciatingly complex and elusive. The huge
Clos de Vougeot, with its impressive château situated on the upper
slope, possesses 124 acres divided among 77 different proprietors.
Imagine, if you can, 77 different growers/producers of Château Pétrus
or Mouton-Rothschild! Clos de Vougeot is a microcosm of Burgundy,
infinitely confusing, distressingly frustrating, yet at its best, capable of
producing majestic wines.

To make matters even more baffling, there are three different soil
types within the vineyard. Additionally, the location of individual hold-

ings within the vineyard itself can heavily influence the ultimate quality of the wines, although perhaps not to the extent that many Burgundy commentators have suggested. There is no question that the very top of the Clos de Vougeot slope that forms the boundary with Musigny to the northwest and Grands Echézeaux to the southwest does indeed have the soil to produce the most complex and profound wines. The soil here is a clay/gravel, chalky brown-colored mixture, resting on bathonian limestone. It changes gradually as one proceeds downhill so that at the very bottom of the slope, contiguous to the famous Route Nationale 74, the soil is largely thick clay and alluvial deposits that have washed down from the upper slopes. The drainage here is terrible. It is obvious that after a rainfall the upper slope dries out much faster than the lower slope, which can remain damp for as long as a week or more after the upper slopes have shed their excess moisture. In his book on Burgundy, Anthony Hanson claims to have heard more than one Burgundian say that the land would be better used for "beet root cultivation" than for vineyards. I suspect such quotes can be attributed to those who have never tasted the superb Clos de Vougeots made by Leroy, Louis Jadot, Jean Grivot, Faiveley, Bichot's Clos Frantin, or the Domaine Moine-Hudelot, all proprietors of vineyards on the lower slopes. I won't deny that there is some merit to the naysayer's position, but it seems today that modern viticultural practices, yield of grapes per acre, and careful vinification go a long way in compensating for poor soils. Paradoxically, but not surprisingly, there are producers in Clos de Vougeot with superbly located, top-of-the-slope parcels, who are making insipid, over-cropped, watery wines. Does this mean that competence, or incompetence, in the wine cellar is more important than soil?

It was the Cistercian monks, during the thirteenth and fourteenth centuries, who originally planted the Clos de Vougeot vineyard and erected the high wall that encloses its 124 acres. The vineyard size has remained unchanged ever since. During the French Revolution the entire estate was confiscated from the Abbey of Cîteaux and sold at public auction. This divestiture from the church, combined with French inheritance law, has brought about today's chaotic situation of crazy quilt ownership by nearly 80 individuals.

It is important to know who the holders of the different parcels of Clos de Vougeot are and precisely where their parcels are located. What I have done is simply indicate whether the parcel is from the upper third of the slope, the middle third, or the bottom third of the slope. Readers should keep in mind that some of these producers sell their production to Burgundy *négociants* and never estate-bottle their own production. Others have farmed out their property under the

French *métayage* arrangements and their production may appear under the name of a nonowner.

Pierre André: 2.7-acre parcel located at the top of the slope at the southern end

Robert Arnoux: a 1-acre parcel located in the very middle of the upper slope, contiguous to the Grand Cru Grands Echézeaux

M. Bertagna: a .5-acre parcel located in the middle third of the slope on the northern side below the château

Capitain-Gagnerot: a .41-acre parcel of young vines (planted in 1975) located on the upper slope, contiguous to the Grand Cru Grands Echézeaux

Maison Champy: a 5.6-acre parcel located in the bottom third, near the southern end of the Clos adjacent to the N 74 and extending halfway up the slope. This vineyard was acquired by Louis Jadot in December, 1989.

Chantal Lescure: a .79-acre parcel located on the mid-slope between the Château of the Clos de Vougeot and the Château de la Tour. The wine is sold exclusively by the *négociant* Labouré-Roi in Nuits St.-Georges.

Chopin-Groffier: Daniel Chopin's superb Clos de Vougeot comes from a .98-acre parcel on the lower slope of Clos de Vougeot situated adjacent to the Chemin de la Grande Montagne and just south of the Château de la Tour of the Labet/Dechelette families.

Henri Clerc: .83 acre located at the very lowest part of the Clos de Vougeot

Felix Clerget: .83 acre located at the very top of the southern end of the Clos de Vougeot slope

Clos Frantin (Bichot): 4 parcels totaling 2.7 acres with nearly half of the acreage located on the lower part of the slope, but with approximately one-third of their vineyards located on the upper slope of the Clos de Vougeot. This particular wine is as good an example of a blend from the lower, middle, and upper slopes as one is likely to find.

Christian Confuron: .83 acre located at the very top of the Clos de Vougeot slope

Jacques Confuron: .61 acre located at the very bottom of the Clos de Vougeot slope

Jean-Jacques Confuron: 1.25 acres consisting of two parcels at the very top of the Clos, just to the south of the superbly situated parcel owned by Méo-Camuzet

Guy Coquard: .54 acre, a tiny strip of vines running from N 74 midway up the Clos

Coquard-Loison-Fleurot: .51 acre located in the lower third of the Clos

Joseph Drouhin: 2 parcels totaling 2.24 acres with the smaller parcel being at the very bottom of the southern end of the Clos de Vougeot slope, and the larger parcel situated on the mid-slope just above the large parcel owned by Château de la Tour. The vines were planted in 1973, 1981, and 1983, so these parcels are essentially planted in young vines.

Drouhin-Larose: A 3.2-acre parcel superbly located at the very top of the Clos de Vougeot

Dufouleur Frères: .51 acre located at the very top of the Clos in the direction of the southern boundary

René Engel: a 3.4-acre parcel that is extremely well placed at the very top of the Clos de Vougeot

Maison Joseph Faiveley: 3 separate parcels totaling 3.1 acres, with the 2 largest parcels located at the bottom of the slope and the smallest parcel (with vines having been planted in 1940) at the very top of the slope

Francis Gerbet: .76 acre located at the very bottom of the slope

Jean Grivot: a 4.6-acre parcel located at the very bottom of the slope. Perhaps the excellence of this wine can be explained by the fact that the planting dates of the different parcels within the vineyard were 1920, 1949, 1962, 1966, and 1970. Consequently, the entire vineyard is in relatively old vines.

Gros Frère et Soeur: If one grower were considered to have the very finest parcel of the Clos de Vougeot, it would be Bernard Gros, who has 3.95 acres high on the hillside in the very northwestern corner of Clos de Vougeot, immediately across from the Grand Cru Musigny vineyard. In addition, the vines here are relatively old, having been planted in 1953.

François Gros: 2.29 acres located at the very top of the Clos de Vougeot near the southern boundary

Jean Gros: .51 acre at the very top of the Clos, but completely torn out and replanted in the mid-eighties, so it will be a number of years before the outstanding potential of this parcel can again be realized

Alfred Haegelen-Jayer: 2 parcels totaling .86 acre, both located at the very top of the Clos de Vougeot slope. The larger parcel is at the very southern boundary and was planted in 1973 and 1974, whereas the smaller parcel is located adjacent to the Grand Cru Grands Echézeaux at the very top of the Clos de Vougeot and was planted in 1956. Not surprisingly, this is an extraordinary source of Clos de Vougeot, to the extent that one is able to find the wines.

l'Heritier-Guyot: 3.7 acres located on the very upper part of the slope

Noël Hudelot: a 1.06-acre parcel located on the upper slope

Alain Hudelot-Noëllat: 3 parcels totaling 1.06 acres. The parcels, all approximately equal in size, consist of 2 at the very top of the slope, planted in 1947, and 1 at the very bottom of the slope, planted less than a decade ago.

Louis Jadot: .79 acre located on the bottom third of the slope. Note that Jadot acquired Champy Père's parcel in 1989.

Jaffelin: 1.53 acres located on the mid-slope, near the northern boundary of the Clos de Vougeot, just above the Château de la Tour

François Lamarche: This famous domaine's four parcels total 3.45 acres. Three of the parcels are well situated on the upper slope, with the other parcel situated at the very bottom of the slope.

Lejay-Lagoute: a .44-acre parcel located at the very top of the slope, contiguous to the Grand Cru Grands Echézaux

Leroy: 3 parcels, 2 of which extend from the bottom of the slope midway up the slope. The third parcel is at the very top of the Clos de Vougeot, just to the south of the château itself. The total holdings now encompass 4.68 acres since the Domaine Leroy acquired the Domaine Noëllat's 4.17-acre holdings.

Leymarie-Coste: 1.2 acres located at top of the very southern end of the Clos de Vougeot slope

Liger-Belair: 1.8 acres located on the mid-slope at the southern border of the Clos de Vougeot. The wine is exploited under a *métayage* arrangement by Denis Mugneret in Vosne-Romanée, and the wines appear under his name.

Gérard Loichet: 2 acres on the mid-slope that are exploited by the family Servelle-Tachot of Chambolle-Musigny. Consequently, the wines appear under that family's name.

Comtesse M. de Loisy: 1.58 acres located between the bottom of the Clos de Vougeot and the mid-slope

Pierre-Yves Masson: 1.03 acres at the very bottom of the slope

Méo-Camuzet: one of the most important holdings of the Clos de Vougeot is the Méo family's 8.1-acre parcel on the very top of the slope, adjacent to the famed château itself

Paul Misset: 2 parcels totaling 5.1 acres located on the bottom third of the slope. The wines are exploited by both the Domaine des Varoilles in Gevrey-Chambertin and by Daniel Rion in Nuits St.-Georges. Consequently, under France's *métayage* arrangement, the wines can appear under the name of these two domaines.

Daniel Moine-Hudelot: a .34-acre parcel at the very bottom of the slope would seemingly suggest a mediocre Clos de Vougeot, but that is not the case as the average age of the vines exceeds 40 years

Mongeard-Mugneret: 2 parcels totaling 2.47 acres, both situated on the upper slope of Clos de Vougeot. The vines are old, having been planted in 1961.

G.A.E.C. Charles Mortet: a .76-acre parcel of vines planted in 1960 and 1985, located at the very bottom of the slope

Georges Mugneret: a .83-acre parcel planted in 1954, superbly located at the very top of the Clos de Vougeot, adjacent to the entrance to the château

Jean Nourissat: a superbly located .39-acre parcel that for years was vinified by the Domaine Charles Noëllat. This tiny parcel on the upper third of the slope should render exquisite wine as it is adjacent to that of Gros Frère et Soeur.

Pierre Ponnelle: a .83-acre parcel located at the bottom of Clos de Vougeot slope is owned by this firm. The vines were planted in 1981 and 1986, so the production is still from extremely young vineyards. Ponnelle is now owned and controlled by the huge *négociant*, Jean-Claude Boisset.

Jacques Prieur: 3.08 acres located on the northerly lower slope of Clos de Vougeot

Bernard Raphet: a .56-acre parcel is located at the very bottom of the slope

Jean Raphet: 2.32 acres, divided into 2 parcels, both located on the very bottom of the slope adjacent to the Route Nationale 74

Henri Rebourseau: 11.8 acres in Clos de Vougeot with the bulk of it in the mid-slope section. There is a healthy percentage of old vines from a planting in 1927, others in 1968, 1973, and the most recent planting in 1977. The potential here for excellent, even outstanding Clos de Vougeot is quite apparent, but has not yet been effectuated due to laissez-faire management of the property.

A. Ropiteau-Mignon: a .54-acre bottom-slope parcel located at the very southerly border of Clos de Vougeot, adjacent to the Route Nationale 74

Madame de Roubaix: 1-acre parcel at the southerly end of the Clos de Vougeot appellation, extending from midway up the slope down to the Route Nationale 74

Georges Roumier: 2 parcels, totaling 2 acres. One parcel was planted in 1954 and the other in 1974. The larger of the 2 parcels, which has the older vines, is located at the very top of the Clos de Vougeot. The other parcel runs from the middle of the slope down to Route Nationale 74.

Thomas-Moillard: a 1.45-acre parcel on the mid-slope

G.F.A. Domaine Tortochot: a .49-acre parcel extending from N 74 about halfway up the Clos de Vougeot slope

Château de la Tour: the Labet and Dechelette families are the largest single landholders in Clos de Vougeot, with 13.3 acres. They have 5 separate parcels with the bulk of the vineyard holdings being in the mid-slope area. They also have 2 tiny parcels on the lower slope that in the total blend represent a very small percentage of their Clos de Vougeot. This producer boasts one of the best situated parcels of all in the very upper slope, just to the south of the château of Clos de Vougeot.

Robert Tourlière: 1.58 acres located between N 74 and the mid-portion of the Clos de Vougeot slope. The entire production is sold to the Beaune *négociant*, Louis Jadot.

Marie-Annick Tremblay: a superbly situated .51-acre parcel of very old vines (planted in 1922) located on the upper slope of the Clos de Vougeot, adjacent to the well-situated parcel of René Engel. The production is exploited and commercialized by Michel Noëllat in Vosne-Romanée.

Gilbert Vadet: 1.23 acres of superbly situated vines at the very southern border of the Clos de Vougeot on the upper slope. The vineyard is still very young, having been planted in 1983 and 1987. The wines appear under the name of Guy Castagnier-Vadey.

André Wilhelm-Lecrivain: a .83-acre parcel on the upper slopes of Clos de Vougeot. The parcel has old vines planted in both 1946 and 1950. The entire production is sold to *négociants*.

THE CONFRÉRIE DES CHEVALIERS DU TASTEVIN

While the wines of Clos de Vougeot remain the favorite whipping boy of the anti-Burgundy wine press—unfairly, given the present-day level of quality—there is no doubting the importance of a group of Burgundians called the Confrérie des Chevaliers du Tastevin. By most accounts, this energetic group constitutes the most famous wine order in the world. The Confrérie was founded in November, 1934, in order to promote the wines of Burgundy, and to draw attention to that region. The association grew so quickly that in 1944 they purchased the Château of Clos de Vougeot and began a serious restoration program of this hallowed edifice and its grounds. Today there are chapters of the Confrérie throughout the world, with many located in the United States. The Confrérie is also responsible for the extraordinary black tie dinners that are held at the Château of Clos de Vougeot numerous times each year. These sit-down dinners, accommodating 500–600 guests, are a true burgundian gastronomic event with multiple courses, multiple wines, a great deal of good natured joking, and, of course, plenty of drinking and singing.

In their efforts to promote only the highest quality burgundy, the Confrérie instituted a wine competition in 1950 wherein the very best wines would be entitled to carry a very distinctive label called Tastevin. This elaborate, colorful label is supposed to be given only to those wines that reflect their appellations and are irrefutably of high quality. This procedure has been maligned, but I am unpersuaded that it is not just simple jealousy or ignorance that has caused the criticism, as virtually every wine I have ever tasted with the Tastevin label has been at least good. In most cases, the wines are very good to excellent. No doubt the Confrérie, given their power, high profile, and promotion-oriented philosophy, are easy targets for criticism. However, the fact remains that they have served an extremely valuable purpose in seeing that their Tastevin labels are only bestowed on good examples of Burgundy wines. One further point to consider is that many producers do not submit wines, so the fact that a wine does not have a Tastevin label does not mean that the wine is not of high quality.

VISITING THE VILLAGE OF VOUGEOT
AND ITS PRODUCERS

While the village of Vougeot itself lacks interest, it is worth a visit to the appellation to see the Château of Clos de Vougeot and the extraordinary walled vineyard that encloses the Clos. The château is one of Burgundy's most important buildings and no visit to the region is complete without a stop there. If you are lucky enough to extract an invitation to one of their Confrérie des Chevaliers du Tastevin dinners, then so much the better, as you will come away with an even greater understanding and appreciation of what this building represents to Burgundy.

Most of the wines from Clos de Vougeot are made by growers in surrounding villages rather than in Vougeot itself. However, there are two producers worth visiting in Vougeot, the Château de la Tour, particularly as they have significantly improved the quality of their wines since 1985, and the Domaine Bertagna.

This is not a good village for finding either lodging or culinary discoveries. There are no hotels in Vougeot, and the local restaurants are mediocre. One is well advised to stay and eat in either Gevrey-Chambertin or Nuits St.-Georges, although there is a decent restaurant in Vosne-Romanée called La Petite Auberge, which is only a 5-minute drive from Vougeot. The Auberge de Castel de Très Girard, located 5 minutes to the north in Morey St.-Denis, is also very good.

VOSNE-ROMANÉE AND FLAGEY-ECHÉZEAUX

An Overview

Location: Less than 3 miles north of the bustling town of Nuits St.-Georges on the west side of the Route Nationale 74 is the village of Vosne-Romanée. Most of the renowned Grands Crus sit on the high slope directly behind the village. In contrast to the lively village of Vosne-Romanée, the drab, solemn hamlet of Flagey-Echézeaux sits on the east side of N 74. There is little reason (except for the excellent bistro in the center of the village) to visit Flagey-Echézeaux as its two famous vineyards, Echézeaux and Grands Echézeaux, sit to the north of Vosne-Romanée, adjacent and above the walled Grand Cru vineyard of Clos de Vougeot.

Acres under vine: Flagey-Echézeaux—115.8 acres; Vosne-Romanée—449 acres

Grands Crus: A total of 7
Echézeaux, Grands Echézeaux, La Romanée, Romanée-Conti, Romanée St.-Vivant, Richebourg, La Tâche

Principal Premiers Crus: A total of 14
Les Beaux Monts, Les Rouges, En Orveaux, Aux Brûlées, Les Suchots, La Croix Rameau, Clos des Réas, La Grande Rue, Les Gaudichots, Les Chaumes, Aux Malconsorts, Cros Parantoux, Aux Reignots, Les Petits Monts

Price levels: This is Burgundy's most expensive red wine appellation. Most Grands Crus start at $50–$60 and go up to $300 a bottle or more for the wines of the Domaine de la Romanée-Conti. Premiers Crus sell for $35–$75 a bottle, and Villages wines for $20–$40.

General wine characteristics: At the top levels, great Vosne-Romanée offers Burgundy's most sumptuous and celestial wines—rich, fat, expansive, and staggeringly perfumed. The best examples epitomize wine at its most decadent and hedonistic richness. Today, the wines at the Premiers Crus and Grands Crus levels are consistently well made. However, the generic Vosne-Romanées, which benefit from the demand for their illustrious and prestigious cousins, the Premiers Crus and Grands Crus, are among the most overpriced and disappointing Villages wines of the Côte d'Or.

The most overrated producers: Domaine Lamarche, Domaine Charles Noëllat (prior to 1988, hence before its acquisition by the Maison Leroy)

The best producers and their wines:

Robert Arnoux: Romanée St.-Vivant, Vosne-Romanée Les Suchots, Vosne-Romanée Les Chaumes

Bouchard Père et Fils: La Romanée

Jacques Cacheux: Vosne-Romanée Les Suchots, Echézeaux

Cathiard-Molinier: Vosne-Romanée Les Malconsorts, Romanée St.-Vivant

Georges Clerget: Echézeaux

Clos Frantin (Bichot): Echézeaux, Grands Echézeaux, Vosne-Romanée Les Malconsorts

J. Confuron-Cotetidot: Vosne-Romanée Les Suchots, Echézeaux

Joseph Drouhin: Echézeaux, Grands Echézeaux

Domaine Dujac: Echézeaux

René Engel: Grands Echézeaux, Echézeaux

Faiveley: Echézeaux

Forey Père: Vosne-Romanée Les Gaudichots, Echézeaux

Jean Grivot: Richebourg, Vosne-Romanée Les Beaux Monts, Vosne-Romanée Les

Brûlées, Vosne-Romanée Clos des Réas

Jean Gros: Richebourg, Vosne-Romanée-Clos des Réas

Gros Frère et Soeur: Richebourg, Grands Echézeaux

Haegelen-Jayer: Echézeaux

Hudelot-Noëllat: Vosne-Romanée Les Malconsorts, Richebourg, Romanée St.-Vivant

Henri Jayer: Richebourg, Echézeaux, Vosne-Romanée Cros Parantoux, Vosne-Romanée Les Beaux Monts, Vosne-Romanée Les Brûlées

Jacqueline Jayer: Echézeaux, Vosne-Romanée Les Rouges

Lucien Jayer: Vosne-Romanée Les Suchots

Jayer-Gilles: Echézeaux

Labouré-Roi: Vosne-Romanée Les Suchots

Louis Latour: Romanée St.-Vivant

Leroy: Richebourg, Romanée St.-Vivant, Vosne-Romanée Les Beaux Monts, Vosne-Romanée Les Brûlées, Vosne-Romanée

Méo-Camuzet: Richebourg, Vosne-Romanée Les Brûlées, Vosne-Romanée Cros Parantoux

Moillard: Echézeaux, Romanée St.-Vivant

Mongeard-Mugneret: Grands Echézeaux, Echézeaux, Richebourg, Vosne-Romanée Les Suchots

Georges Mugneret: Echézeaux

Pernin-Rossin: Vosne-Romanée Les Beaux Monts

Bernard Rion: Vosne-Romanée Les Chaumes

Daniel Rion: Vosne-Romanée Les Beaux Monts, Vosne-Romanée Les Chaumes

Domaine de la Romanée-Conti: Romanée-Conti, La Tâche, Richebourg, Grands Echézeaux, Romanée St.-Vivant, Echézeaux

Robert Siruge: Grands Echézeaux, Vosne-Romanée Les Petits Monts

Jean Tardy: Vosne-Romanée Les Charmes

Michael Voarick: Romanée St.-Vivant

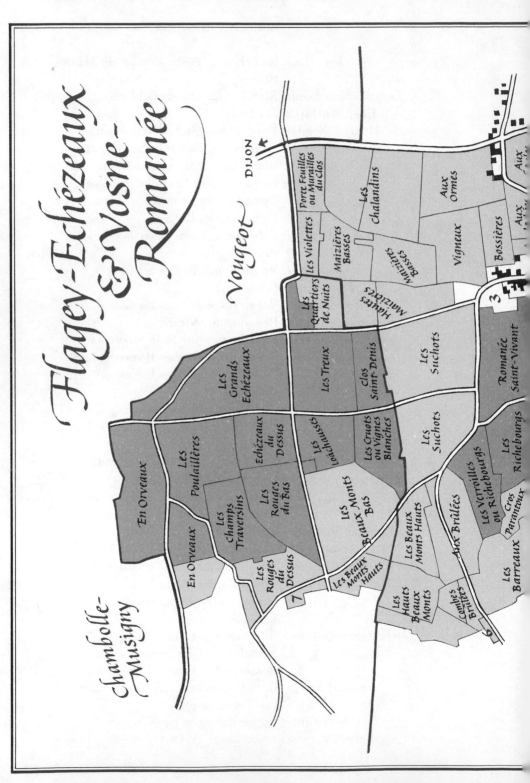

Flagey-Echézeaux & Vosne-Romanée

Chambolle-Musigny

Vougeot

DIJON

Porte Feuilles ou Murailles du Clos

Les Chalandins

Aux Ormes

Aux Violettes

Maizières Basses

Vigneux

Bossières

Aux

Maizières Basses

Hautes Maizières

Les Quartiers de Nuits

Les Suchots

Romanée Saint-Vivant

Les Grands Echézeaux

Les Treux

Clos Saint-Denis

En Orveaux

Les Poulaillères

Echézeaux du Dessus

Les Loächausses

Les Cruots ou Vignes Blanches

Les Suchots

Les Richebourgs

En Orveaux

Les Champs Traversins

Les Rouges du Bas

Les Beaux Monts Bas

Les Verroilles ou Richebourgs

Cros Parantoux

Les Rouges du Dessus

Les Beaux Monts Hauts

Aux Brûlées

Les Barreaux

Les Beaux Monts Hauts

Les Hauts Beaux Monts

Combes Brûlées

7

3

6

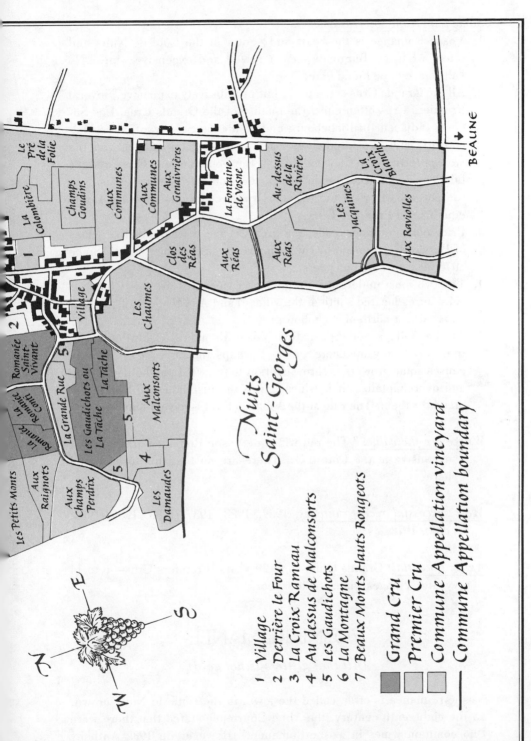

Nuits Saint-Georges

BEAUNE →

Le Pré de la Folie
La Colombière
Champs Goudins
Aux Communes
Aux Communes
Aux Genaivrières
La Fontaine de Vosne
Au-dessus de la Rivière
La Croix Blanche
Les Jacquines
Aux Raviolles
Clos des Réas
Aux Réas
Aux Réas
Les Chaumes
Village
Romanée Saint-Vivant
La Romanée
La Romanée Conti
La Grande Rue
Les Gaudichots ou La Tâche
La Tâche
Aux Malconsorts
Aux Champs Perdrix
Aux Raignots
Les Petits Monts
Les Damaudes

1 Village
2 Derrière le Four
3 La Croix Rameau
4 Au dessus de Malconsorts
5 Les Gaudichots
6 La Montagne
7 Beaux Monts Hauts Rougeots

Grand Cru
Premier Cru
Commune Appellation vineyard
Commune Appellation boundary

Some important observations:

1. Vosne-Romanée is the heart and center of the Côte de Nuits and offers what are Burgundy's most prized and expensive wines. No values are to be found here.

2. All the Grands Crus are superb, but prohibitively expensive. Several Premiers Crus often equal the quality of the Grands Crus. Les Suchots (adjacent to Richebourg and Romanée St.-Vivant), Les Malconsorts and Les Gaudichots (each bordering La Tâche), and the *monopole* vineyard Clos des Réas of the Domaine Jean Gros produce fabulous wines. La Grande Rue of the Domaine Lamarche also has the potential to rival the Grands Crus, yet its quality today rarely equals most Premiers Crus.

3. Price considerations aside, the greatest and most distinctive wines of Burgundy are made by the Domaine de la Romanée-Conti. Since 1978 they have had no peers.

4. The two most underrated Premier Cru vineyards are Les Chaumes (14.4 acres located south of the village) and Aux Brûlées (9.28 acres situated just north of Richebourg).

5. At the Villages or Appellation Vosne-Romanée Contrôlée level, there are many mediocre wines. Perhaps the fame of this village causes some growers to throw caution to the wind and both overcrop and overchaptalize their wines, given the insatiable worldwide demand for them. The rule at the Villages level is caveat emptor.

Where are the values? The red wines of Vosne-Romanée are the most expensive in the Côte d'Or. There are no bargains to be found here.

Most successful recent vintages: 1989, 1988, 1987, 1986, 1985, 1983, 1980, 1978

Aging Potential: Grands Crus—8 to 20 years; Premiers Crus—8 to 14 years; Villages wines—2 to 5 years

VOSNE-ROMANÉE

(All that glitters is not gold)

Vosne-Romanée is often called the jewel in the Côte de Nuits crown. In the eighteenth century, the Abbé Courtépée stated that there were "no common wines in Vosne-Romanée." However, in 1982 Anthony

Hanson lamented that this was now "a ridiculous statement." Neither declaration seems quite accurate today. Much has changed since Anthony Hanson decried the lack of quality in Vosne-Romanée.

First, the decade of the eighties was immensely successful for the wines of Vosne-Romanée, with the highly prized vintages of 1985, 1987, 1988, and 1989 making a strong case for the growers of that region. Additionally, whether because of Hanson's criticism or in response to an apathetic marketplace, the quality of many wines from Vosne-Romanée has improved appreciably since the early eighties.

Of course, no one doubts that the fame of Vosne-Romanée is a result of its seven illustrious Grands Crus that sell at stratospheric prices. Whether it is Romanée-Conti, Richebourg, La Tâche, Romanée St.-Vivant, La Romanée, Grands Echézeaux or Echézeaux, each one of these Grands Crus has an almost mystical name and worldwide reputation for quality. Today, it is hard to take issue with the quality of most of the wines from these Grands Crus, particularly when you consider that each of them produces wines vastly superior to any of the 9 Grands Crus of Gevrey-Chambertin. Yes, there is the occasional Chambertin or Chambertin-Clos de Bèze that is superb, but in 1990 it is hard to find a poorly made Grand Cru from Vosne-Romanée.

There is little to report about the history of Vosne-Romanée that is unrelated to wine. The village was known as Vaona in the seventh century, and apparently was a favorite hunting ground for the Ducs of Burgundy, who maintained a lodge in the present-day village. The architecture leaves much to be desired since most of the village was destroyed in the Franco-Prussian war of 1870. There is not a single one of the village's 530 inhabitants who does not make his living from the production of wine.

THE VINEYARDS OF VOSNE-ROMANÉE AND FLAGEY-ECHÉZEAUX

GRANDS CRUS VINEYARDS

Romanée-Conti—There is no better known vineyard or wine produced in Burgundy than Romanée-Conti, a tiny 4.32-acre vineyard owned exclusively by the Domaine de la Romanée-Conti. Prior to 1978 the vineyard had a tendency to produce wines that left one less than starry-eyed, but since the 1978 vintage the domaine's two extraordinary owners, Monsieur Aubert de Villaine and Madame Lalou Bize-Leroy, have simply let nothing go awry in the production of this legendary wine.

The vineyard itself is well marked and can be found by hiking or driving behind the village of Vosne-Romanée on what appears to be the steepest slope. On the north side of Romanée-Conti is Richebourg, on its west side La Romanée, and to its south the Premier Cru La Grande Rue.

Of course, there is really no secret as to why the wines of Romanée-Conti, as well as the other wines of the Domaine de la Romanée-Conti, are so superb. In 1990, the average age of the vines was 42 years. The domaine, a notoriously late harvester, intends to pick only fully mature grapes, with even an element of *sur maturité* apparently desired. And there are incredibly small yields of 20–25 hectoliters per hectare, which is about half of what other Grand Cru holders routinely obtain.

Prices for Romanée-Conti (assuming one can even find any) have been escalating to the point where a new vintage commands close to $4,000 a case. The wine of millionaires has become destined to be drunk only by billionaires. We can only hope they have the requisite appreciation of fine wine to realize just how extraordinary this perfumed, exotic, expansively flavored wine can be.

La Tâche—The 14.4-acre La Tâche vineyard, again owned exclusively by the Domaine de la Romanée-Conti, is much larger than Romanée-Conti. However, this has only been true since 1932, when the French government permitted the original La Tâche vineyard, which consisted of 3.5 acres, to be augmented by absorbing 11 acres of the neighboring vineyard called Les Gaudichots. There is still a tiny section of Les Gaudichots left that is, perplexingly, only entitled to Premier Cru status. However, those lucky enough to run across the wines of the Domaine Forey, who have their cellars adjacent to those of the Domaine de la Romanée-Conti, can taste the wine from the remaining parcel of the Les Gaudichots vineyard. I'm sure they won't be disappointed.

Much has been made about the differences between La Tâche and Romanée-Conti, but I feel both of them are often among the top 3 or 4 red wines of Burgundy. Romanée-Conti is usually lighter in color, more perfumed, more elegant, and slightly less intense and concentrated, whereas La Tâche seems to have a deeper color, more body, muscle, and concentration. This is really splitting hairs, as both wines retain the multidimensional, profound, oriental spice in their bouquets, and highly extracted, exotic flavors that characterize these two titans from the Domaine de la Romanée-Conti. Perhaps the greatest red burgundies I have ever tasted have been the 1959, 1962, 1966, 1978, 1980, and 1985 vintages of La Tâche. It is a wine that seems to drink well young but continues to improve for several decades. Its price is almost as high as that of Romanée-Conti. In 1990 it is selling for $2,500–$3,500 a case.

Richebourg—I am always surprised by the fact that many dedicated collectors claim a greater fondness for Richebourg than La Tâche or Romanée-Conti. Perhaps the price of these latter two wines makes Richebourg appear to be a relative bargain. Richebourg is indeed one of the greatest red wines of the Côte d'Or. In contrast to the other Grands Crus in Vosne-Romanée, I find it to be the richest and most concentrated, with a remarkable abundance and generosity of fruit that even wines such as La Tâche, Romanée-Conti, or Echézeaux cannot match.

Additionally, there is extraordinary competition among those growers who share a parcel of this hallowed 19.8-acre vineyard. Like La Tâche, Richebourg was expanded in size in the 1930s from 12.3 acres to 19.8 acres with the inclusion of a large parcel of the Premier Cru Les Varoilles. This apparently has had no effect on the quality of this sensual, fragrant, remarkably concentrated wine. Of course, the most famous Richebourg is made by the Domaine de la Romanée-Conti, and there are those followers of the domaine who claim it is their best wine. Certainly my memories of the 1966 and 1978 Richebourgs from the Domaine de la Romanée-Conti would support their findings. However, extraordinary Richebourgs are also made by the Domaine Jean Gros, Domaine Gros Frère et Soeur, Domaine Leroy, Domaine Méo-Camuzet, and of course, the Domaine Clos Frantin (owned by the Beaune *négociant* Bichot). Outstanding Richebourgs also come from Jean Grivot, Hudelot-Noëllat, and the great, now retired master winemaker, Henri Jayer. In addition, the Domaine Mongeard-Mugneret acquired a tiny parcel of this vineyard in the mid-eighties. Given the oustanding quality of this firm's Grands Echézeaux, Echézeaux, and Clos de Vougeot, this should be another estate from which one can expect high-quality Richebourg.

Most of the great wines of Richebourg are less seductive in their youth than those of La Tâche or Romanée-Conti. Therefore, a Richebourg from a top vintage should be given a good 4 or 5 years of bottle age before it is consumed.

Romanée St.-Vivant—The 23.5-acre Grand Cru vineyard of Romanée St.-Vivant is situated just to the west of the village, bounded by the Premier Cru Les Suchots on the north and the Grand Cru Richebourg to the west. It has never been my favorite Grand Cru of Vosne-Romanée, but its admirers are fond of its spicy, perfumed, cinnamon, and earthy bouquet that relies more on spices than red or black fruits for its appeal. It will never have the concentration or power of Richebourg, or the exotic complexity of La Tâche or Romanée-Conti.

There are only a handful of producers making Romanée St.-Vivant and the best is clearly the Domaine de la Romanée-Conti, which had leased this vineyard from the Marey-Monge family since 1966 until they were able to purchase it in 1988. The Domaine Leroy is now producing a Romanée St.-Vivant that should rival, perhaps even surpass that made by the Domaine de la Romanée-Conti. Other excellent Romanée St.-Vivants are made by Louis Latour, who has 2.5 acres of this Grand Cru vineyard, Moillard (1.75 acres), Hudelot-Noëllat, and Robert Arnoux.

Most of the wines of Romanée St.-Vivant mature very quickly, and should be consumed well before the Grands Crus of La Tâche, Richebourg, and Romanée-Conti.

La Romanée—La Romanée is the tiniest of the Grands Crus of Burgundy, being only 2.5 acres in size. The vineyard itself sits just above La Romanée-Conti and is bounded on the north by Richebourg and on the south by the outstanding Premier Cru La Grande Rue. The property is owned exclusively by the Liger-Belair family, but the wine itself is made by the Forey family in cellars adjacent to those of the Domaine de la Romanée-Conti. It is then sold in cask to the immense Beaune *négociant*, Bouchard Père et Fils, who have had the exclusive right to commercialize the wine since 1976. The wine is matured in 100% new oak casks, and since the early eighties has been impeccably made. The only responsibility of the Bouchards is simply to bring it up in the cellars, and one hopes their high-tech philosophy of filtration for all their burgundies is not applied too severely to La Romanée.

Recent vintages I have tasted included a stunning 1985 and an excellent 1987. In style, the wine seems to have more in common with Richebourg than either Romanée-Conti or La Tâche. It is a deeply colored, rich, concentrated wine with a great deal of fruit, body, and tannin. The wines from La Romanée would seemingly be capable of matching most of the Grands Crus in quality, but so little of it is made it is virtually impossible to taste a range of vintages of this rare treasure.

Grands Echézeaux—If one were to be so bold as to suggest that any Grand Cru of Vosné-Romanée could actually represent good value, it would be the wines from the 22.7-acre parcel of Grands Echézeaux, located on the northern side of the stone wall enclosing the upper slope of the Clos de Vougeot. The Grands Echézeaux wines from the Domaine de la Romanée-Conti have been quite extraordinary over the last 12 to 15 years and, of course, sell at a fraction of the price of the more famous La Tâche and Romanée-Conti. For those who are unable to afford such expensive luxuries, a bottle of Grands Echézeaux is as good an introduction to the style of Domaine de la Romanée-Conti as one is likely to find. Other superb wines from the Grands Echézeaux vineyard are made by René Engel, whose wines have been particularly strong since 1985, Domaine Mongeard-Mugneret, Leroy, Clos Frantin, Joseph Drouhin, Gros Frère et Soeur, and Robert Siruge.

A good Grands Echézeaux can easily last for up to 15 years in vintages such as 1983, 1985, and 1988.

Echézeaux—The large 93-acre vineyard of Echézeaux is located higher up the slope, above both Clos de Vougeot and Grands Echézeaux. The soil is lighter, and the resulting wines much more variable in quality than any other Grand Cru from Vosne-Romanée. This is not to suggest that some excellent wines are not produced from Echézeaux, as anyone can attest who has tasted the Echézeaux of the Domaine de la Romanée-Conti, Jacques Cacheux, Jacky Confuron, René Engel, Forey Père, Henri Jayer, Jacqueline Jayer, Mongeard-Mugneret, Georges Mugneret, Joseph Drouhin, Domaine Dujac, Faiveley, Jayer-Gilles, or Haegelen-Jayer. Year in and year out these producers make the finest wines from this Grand Cru vineyard. Yet there are still a number of wines with the Echézeaux name, mostly from *négociants*, that simply do not merit Grand Cru status as a result of their light, watery, shallow flavors and lack of intensity. No Echézeaux will have the color, power, intensity, or flavor expansion and depth of a Grands Echézeaux. The best place for one to see the vivid differences between these two Grands Crus would be those cellars that produce both an Echézeaux and a Grands Echézeaux, such as Mongeard-Mugneret, Domaine de la Romanée-Conti, and the Bichot-owned Clos Frantin. As good as their Echézeaux can be, their Grands Echézeaux is simply superior from both an aromatic and flavor perspective.

Most of the wines from the Echézeaux vineyard reach maturity very quickly, and should be consumed within 10 to 12 years of the vintage, much sooner if it was not a top-quality vintage.

PREMIERS CRUS VINEYARDS

Vosne-Romanée is blessed with a number of outstanding Premiers Crus. Most observers would no doubt agree that one taste from a Vosne-Romanée-Les Suchots (a vineyard situated just north of Richebourg and Romanée St.-Vivant) from the likes of Jacky Confuron, Robert Arnoux, Jacques Cacheux, Jean Grivot, or Lucien Jayer would make one wonder why this vineyard is not rated a Grand Cru. The same can be said for a Vosne-Romanée Les Malconsorts from Clos Frantin or Hudelot-Noëllat. Other outstanding Premiers Crus would certainly include the *monopole* vineyard of Clos des Réas of the Domaine Jean Gros, the superbly situated Premier Cru Les Gaudichots of Forey Père et Fils (located between La Tâche and La Grande Rue), and of course, La Grande Rue itself, which owes much of its fame to the Lamarche family, who for years made the wine here, often selling it at Grand Cru prices. This 3.75-acre parcel has dazzling potential but neither the late Henri Lamarche nor his son have been able to recapture the magic this vineyard was capable of achieving in the thirties, forties, and fifties. Recent vintages have shown improvement, but La Grande Rue remains a wine that is still not as good as its vineyard's potential.

In addition to those I have listed, Vosne-Romanée is rich with other outstanding Premiers Crus. I have had superb wines from Premiers Crus such as Les Beaux Monts, Les Rouges, Aux Brûlées (with a real smoky, toasty character that clearly indicates how the vineyard got its name), Les Chaumes, and of course, the extraordinary Cros Parantoux from the likes of Henri Jayer and Méo-Camuzet.

Vosne-Romanée has many Premiers Crus, and except for a handful of perennial underachievers the level of quality today is extremely high. Certainly the difference in price between the inconsistent, irregular-quality Villages wines of Vosne-Romanée and those from the Premiers Crus would suggest to an astute consumer that it is well worth it to spend the extra money for a top Premier Cru where one is likely to get something of true pleasure and quality.

VISITING THE VILLAGE OF VOSNE-ROMANÉE AND ITS PRODUCERS

There are no hotels in Vosne-Romanée, but this should hardly be a problem, as Nuits St.-Georges, only a 5-minute drive to the south, has a number of excellent places to stay and eat. These would include the Hostellerie Gentilhommière, one of the hotels from the Ibis chain, which offers straightforward, simple, modern rooms, and the Hotel St.-Georges located right off the Autoroute.

With respect to restaurants, there is the tiny and appropriately named La Petite Auberge, located just in front of the cellars of Robert Arnoux, directly on the Route Nationale 74, which offers competent, straightforward Burgundy cooking. In Nuits St.-Georges there are many excellent restaurant choices listed in the next chapter. The best place for dining is in the drab village of Flagey-Echézeaux. The restaurant is not marked, but it sets across from the small church next to a public telephone booth. It is run by the Robert Losset family and serves up bountiful plates of regional cooking at bargain prices. It is always packed, there is no menu, just whatever Madame Losset chooses to cook. Given this restaurant's popularity, it is best to telephone before going. Their number is 80-62-88-10.

NUITS ST.-GEORGES

An Overview

Location: With a population of 5,461, Nuits St.-Georges is the largest town between Beaune and Dijon. Located nearly halfway between these two towns (Beaune is 12 miles to the south and Dijon 15 miles to the north), Nuits St.-Georges is the jumping-off point for the northern half of Burgundy's Côte d'Or, the Côte de Nuits. After Beaune, this is the most important commercial center of Burgundy.

Acres under vine: A total of 785.7
    Grands Crus: none
    Premiers Crus: 352.7 acres
    Villages Wines: 433 acres

Grands Crus: None

Principal Premiers Crus: A total of 40
    Aux Champs Perdrix, En La Perrière Noblot, Les Damodes, Aux Boudots, Aux Cras, La Richemone, Aux Murgers, Aux Vigne-rondes, Aux Chaignots, Aux Torey, Aux Argillas, Aux Bousselots, Les Crots (Château Gris), Les Crots, Rue de Chaux, Les Hauts Pruliers, Les Procès (Les Pruliers), Les Pruliers, Roncière, Les Saint-Georges, Les Cailles, Les Poirets (Porets St.-Georges), Les Poirets (Clos des Porets St.-Georges), Les Valle-rots, Les Pou-lettes, Les Perrières, Les Chaboeufs, Les Vaucrains, Chaines Carteaux, Les Grandes Vignes (Clos des Grandes Vignes), Clos de la Maréchale, Clos Arlot, Les Didiers, Les Forêts (Clos de Forêts St.-Georges), Aux Perdrix, Aux Corvées (Clos des Cor-vées), Aux Corvées (Clos des Corvées Pagets), Aux Corvées (Clos St.-Marc), Les Argillières, Les Argillières (Clos des Argillières)

Price levels: Most of the best Premiers Crus of Nuits St.-Georges are less expensive than Premiers Crus of Vosne-Romanée, Chambolle-Musigny, Morey St.-Denis, and Gevrey-Chambertin, averaging $25–$40 a bottle.

General wine characteristics: There is as much diversity in wine quality and styles of wine in Nuits St.-Georges as there is in Gevrey-Chambertin due to numerous factors that have a significant impact on the wines of Nuits St.-Georges. The Meuzin Valley splits the appellation in half. The northern half of the vineyards, running from the town itself north to Vosne-Romanée, lies on higher slopes and thus at a higher altitude. To the south of Nuits St.-Georges, the vineyards are located very close to the Route Nationale 74, and are planted in richer, heavier soils with more clay and less stone. Consequently, they produce fuller, more robust and powerful wines. More than any other Côte de Nuits red burgundy, a top Nuits St.-Georges tends to be smoky, earthy, and robust, with a more marked *gout de terroir.*

The most overrated producers: Henri Gouges, Guy Dufouleur, Charles Vienot, Jean-Claude Boisset, F. Chauvenet, Geisweiler et Fils, Robert Dubois

The best producers and their wines:
Domaine de l'Arlot: Nuits St.-Georges-Clos de l'Arlot, Nuits St.-Georges-Clos des Forêts St.-Georges, Nuits St.-Georges-Clos de l'Arlot Blanc
Cathiard-Molinier: Nuits St.-Georges Les Murgers
Jean Chauvenet: Nuits St.-Georges Les Vaucrains, Nuits St.-Georges Les Bousselots
Robert Chevillon: Nuits St.-Georges Les Saint-Georges, Nuits St.-Georges Les Vaucrains, Nuits St.-Georges Les Perrières, Nuits St.-Georges Les Cailles
Georges Chicotot: Nuits St.-Georges Les Pruliers, Nuits St.-Georges Les Vaucrains, Nuits St.-Georges Les Saint-Georges
Chopin-Groffier: Nuits St.-Georges Les Chaignots
Faiveley: Nuits St.-Georges Les Saint-Georges, Nuits St.-Georges Clos de la Maréchale, and the different Hospices de Nuits wines
Henri Gouges: Nuits St.-Georges Les Perrières Blanc
Machard de Gramont: Nuits St.-Georges Les Damodes, Nuits St.-Georges Les Hauts Pruliers, Nuits St.-Georges en La Perrière Noblot

Jean Grivot: Nuits St.-Georges Les Pruliers, Nuits St.-Georges Les Boudots

Louis Jadot: Nuits St.-Georges Clos des Corvées

Henri Jayer: Nuits St.-Georges Les Murgers

Leroy: Nuits St.-Georges Les Boudots, Nuits St.-Georges Les Lavières, Nuits St.-Georges La Richemone, Nuits St.-Georges Les Vignes Rondes

Manière-Noirot: Nuits St.-Georges Les Damodes, Nuits St.-Georges Les Boudots

Méo-Camuzet: Nuits St.-Georges aux Boudots, Nuits St.-Georges Les Murgers

Alain Michelot: Nuits St.-Georges Les Vaucrains, Nuits St.-Georges Les Cailles, Nuits St.-Georges Les Forêts, Nuits St.-Georges Les Chaignots, Nuits St.-Georges La Richemone, Nuits St.-Georges Les Champs Perdrix

Moillard: Nuits St.-Georges La Richemone, Nuits St.-Georges Clos de Torey

Mongeard-Mugneret: Nuits St.-Georges Les Boudots

Georges Mugneret: Nuits St.-Georges Les Chaignots

Pernin-Rossin: Nuits St.-Georges La Richemone

Henri Remoriquet: Nuits St.-Georges Les Damodes, Nuits St.-Georges Les Bousselots

Bernard Rion: Nuits St.-Georges Les Murgers

Daniel Rion: Nuits St.-Georges Hauts Pruliers, Nuits St.-Georges Les Vignes Rondes

Jean Tardy: Nuits St.-Georges Les Boudots

Some important observations:

1. While there are no Grands Crus, the very best Premiers Crus, Les Vaucrains and Les Saint-Georges (both located south of town), and Les Damodes, La Richemone, and Aux Boudots (adjacent to the appellation of Vosne-Romanée), are close in quality to Grand Cru level.

2. The Burgundian saying, "the larger the production of the village, the more attention one must pay to the wine," is clearly justified in Nuits St.-Georges. There are many mediocre wines from this appellation, especially from some famous names (i.e. Domaine Henri Gouges).

3. Nuits St.-Georges has its own charity auction, the Hospices de Nuits. Less renowned and less publicized than Beaune's auction,

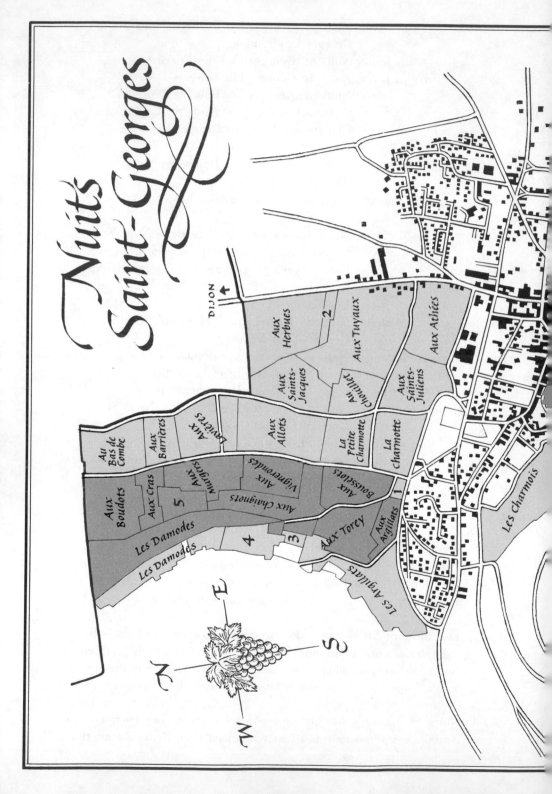

Nuits Saint-Georges

DIJON

Aux Herbues

2

Aux Tuyaux

Aux Saints-Jacques

Chaliot

Aux Saints-Juliens

Aux Athées

Au Bas de Combe

Aux Barrières

Aux Poirets

Aux Allots

La Petite Charmotte

La charmotte

Aux Boudots

Aux Cras

5

Aux Murgers

Aux Vignerondes

Aux Chaignots

Aux Bousselots

Les Charmois

Les Damodes

Les Damodes

4

3

Aux Torey

Aux Argillats

1

Les Argillats

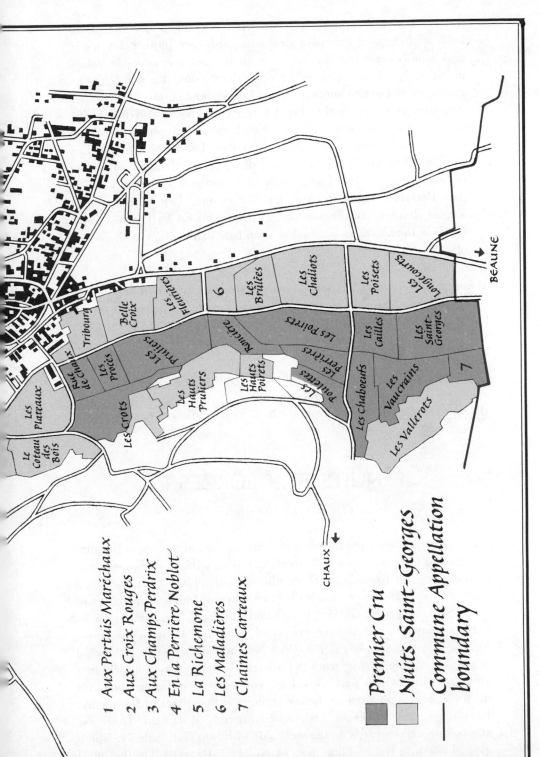

CHAUX

BÉAUNE

Le Coteau des Bois

Les Plateaux

Rue de Chaux

Tribourg

Les Procès

Les Crots

Les Pruliers

Belle Croix

Les Fleurières

6

Les Brûlées

Les Chaliots

Les Poisets

Longécourts

Roncière

Les Poirets

Les Perrières

Les Cailles

Les Saint-Georges

Les Hauts Pruliers

Les Hauts Poirets

Les Poulettes

Les Chaboeufs

Les Vaucrains

Les Vallerots

7

1 Aux Pertuis Maréchaux
2 Aux Croix Rouges
3 Aux Champs Perdrix
4 En la Perrière Noblot
5 La Richemone
6 Les Maladières
7 Chaînes Carteaux

Premier Cru

Nuits Saint-Georges

Commune Appellation boundary

the wines of the Hospices de Nuits (there are 15 separate *cuvées*, all from well-situated Premiers Crus vineyards) are impeccably made and usually represent not only top quality but a reasonable value, particularly when compared to the prices asked for wines at the Hospices de Beaune auction. Smart buyers take note!

4. Accepted doctrine is that the finest Premiers Crus of Nuits St.-Georges are those south of the town, Les Saint-Georges, Les Vaucrains, Les Pruliers, Les Cailles, Roncière, Les Perrières, and Les Poirets, to name the best known. I disagree, particularly when one considers the quality of wine from such northern Premiers Crus as Aux Boudots, Les Damodes, La Richemone, Les Murgers, Aux Vignes Rondes, Aux Bousselots, Perdrix, and En La Perrière Noblot. It is time to abandon such a simplistic explanation of the wines of Nuits St.-Georges.

Where are the values? Lesser known Premiers Crus such as Clos de Corvées, Clos de Torey, Aux Champs Perdrix, Chaines Carteaux, and Les Procès offer excellent rapport in quality and price when compared to other Premiers Crus from Vosne-Romanée.

Most successful recent vintages: 1989, 1988, 1987, 1985, 1980, 1978

Aging Potential: Premiers Crus—5 to 12 years; Villages wines—5 to 8 years

NUITS ST.-GEORGES

(Tender are the nights)

As one heads north from the town of Beaune, the entrance into Burgundy's famed Côte de Nuits is distressingly well marked at the entrance to the village of Corgoloin, the number-one candidate for Burgundy's ugliest village. However, this is the starting point for the appellation of Nuits St.-Georges. In addition to this honor, Corgoloin is famous for its marble quarries, which have produced stone for many of the finest buildings in this part of France. On a hot, humid day when little wind is blowing, a film of dust from the quarries covers everything within a 10-mile radius. Once past Corgoloin, you must pass through another drab village, Comblanchien, before arriving at the village of Prémeaux. Here the scenery takes on the look of Burgundy at its best. There are steep, sloping vineyards on the west side of Route Nationale 74, which extend north to the bustling town of Nuits St.-Georges. On the other side of Nuits St.-Georges the vineyards continue on slightly higher slopes and run for several kilometers north of the village, until the appellation of Nuits St.-Georges ends and that of Vosne-Romanée begins. While Nuits St.-Georges is not the largest of the Côte de Nuits appellations, it is the longest, encompassing over 4 miles of vineyards.

Nuits St.-Georges suffers in comparison with Beaune as a wine center. Nevertheless, its importance is considerable, and it is the home of a number of major *négociants* and cellars of Burgundy. The entire appellation of Nuits St.-Georges, which includes 785.7 acres, has no Grands Crus, but there are 40 principal Premiers Crus covering 352.7 acres. The Premiers Crus are located both north and south of the village. Most commentators have shown a preference for the Premiers Crus that lie south of Nuits St.-Georges, in the direction of Prémeaux. The soils here are richer and heavier, and if quality is to be based solely on weight and muscle, there is no doubting that Premiers Crus such as Les Vaucrains and Les Saint-Georges, the two most famous Premiers Crus of Nuits St.-Georges, make everybody's top list. In fact, one can argue that these two particular vineyards produce wines that often rival Grands Crus from other villages. However, because Les Saint-Georges and Les Vaucrains garner much of the praise, there has been a tendency to overlook the Premiers Crus vineyards to the north of the village that abut the commune of Vosne-Romanée and have lighter, more stony soils. While the greatness of Les Saint-Georges and Les Vaucrains can be easily witnessed in the wines from producers such as Robert Chevillon, Jean Chauvenet, Alain Michelot, and Georges Chicotot, there is no question that in the hands of producers such as Jean Tardy, Mongeard-Mugneret, Méo-Camuzet, Pernin-Rossin, Leroy, Alain Michelot, and Machard de Gramont, northern Premiers Crus vineyards in Nuits St.-Georges such as Les Damodes, Aux Boudots, and Aux Murgers can produce wines every bit as stunningly complex, fragrant, and rich as their neighbors to the south. Nevertheless, it is the wine from Les Saint Georges and Les Vaucrains that will fetch the highest price. Nuits St.-Georges is no different from any other appellation of Burgundy, where the quality of winemaking is dictated by the individual who is responsible for producing the wine.

All these vineyards produce exceptional Pinot Noir, the best of which rivals the finest Premiers Crus from anywhere in the Côte de Nuits. Unfortunately, the production from these vineyards is small, with Les Damodes being only 21.4 acres, Aux Boudots 15.5 acres, La Richemone 4.94 acres, Aux Murgers 12.35 acres, Les Saint-Georges 18.5 acres, and Les Vaucrains 15.3 acres. It is just a sad fact of Burgundy that so many top vineyards are under 20 acres in size.

Of course, the best values of Nuits St.-Georges at the Premier Cru level come from vineyards that are less well known. The largest Premier Cru vineyard is that of the Clos de la Maréchale, which is the southernmost Premier Cru of Nuits St.-Georges. It is leased entirely to the famous high-quality firm of Faiveley in Nuits St.-Georges, and is comprised of 23.6 acres. The wine is the lightest of the Premiers Crus, but the Faiveley firm extracts as much character and quality out of it as I suspect is possible. In addition, they sell it at the most reasonable price of all the Nuits St.-Georges Premiers Crus.

Other excellent Premiers Crus south of Nuits St.-Georges that consistently make top wine are Les Pruliers, Les Cailles, Les Perrières, La Roncière, and Chaînes Carteaux. This last vineyard is situated just to the south of the more famous and prestigious Les Vaucrains.

To the north of Nuits St.-Georges several smaller vineyards such as Aux Champs Perdrix, Aux Torey, Aux Bousselots, and Aux Vignes Rondes produce excellent wines that remain less well known than those northern Premiers Crus already mentioned.

When examining the wines of Nuits St.-Georges closely I have been disappointed by the quality from several of the largest producers. Certainly, there is the famous firm of Faiveley, whose standards of winemaking are as high as anyone's in Burgundy. Additionally, the firm of Labouré-Roi has consistently upgraded the quality of its wines in the decade of the eighties. But the appellation's most famous domaine of all, that of Henri Gouges, has just completed 20 years of mediocrity. I remember well my first visit to this estate in 1975, when I tasted the different Premiers Crus from the 1966 and 1969 vintages. This was an extraordinary lesson in how great red burgundy can be. However, this famous domaine, which did so much in the thirties, forties, fifties, and sixties to draw attention to the appellation of Nuits St.-Georges, and whose low-yielding clones of Pinot Noir were considered to be some of the best in Burgundy, began a sad decline in 1970 with a number of disappointing vintages. It has been trying to break out of its slump throughout the eighties, but to date the wines lack the dimension of flavor and concentration of the top wines of the appellation. Several other large firms, such as Jean-Claude Boisset, Charles Vienot, Geisweiler et Fils, and Guy Dufouleur, all with cellars in Nuits St.-Georges, appear content to produce mediocre wines.

Despite the fact that there are so many underachievers in Nuits St.-Georges, there remain many high-quality, very famous producers. However, skepticism about the wines of Nuits St.-Georges abounds, particularly in the English market, which was badly damaged in the sixties by the fraudulent labeling and sale of generic burgundy as Nuits St.-Georges. This practice is not permitted under the Appellation Contrôlée laws of France, yet the wines of Nuits St.-Georges are still tainted in the minds of many. Even the notable charity auction of the Hospices de Nuits, which owns 23 acres of top Premiers Crus vineyards and produces wines every bit as good as those of the Hospices de Beaune, rarely gets the accolades it deserves. These cuvées, which are sold largely to *négociants*, include some extraordinary wines from Premiers Crus vineyards such as Aux Murgers, Les Boudots, Les Poirets, Les Didiers, Les Corvées-Pagets, and Les Saint-Georges. Certainly, consumers interested in good quality should be more aware of how excellent these wines can be. Of course, one should also be aware that if they are purchased by an incompetent *négociant* who does not look after its upbringing in the cellars, the wine can be ruined. However, I have rarely seen this happen to recent vintages.

I would be remiss in not mentioning the small quantity of white wine produced in Nuits St.-Georges. Less than several hundred cases of white wine are produced, primarily by the Domaine Henri Gouges from a tiny parcel of the Premier Cru Les Perrières vineyard. There is also some splendid white wine produced from the Premier Cru Clos Arlot. Both of these whites tend to be quite powerful, rich, very perfumed wines that are a treat to drink. They are expensive, given their rarity, but well worth trying. Little is exported, and the best place to try a bottle is probably at the world renowned Paris restaurant of Taillevent, which for decades has been the largest purchaser of Henri Gouges' white Nuits St.-Georges.

VISITING THE VILLAGE OF NUITS ST.-GEORGES AND ITS PRODUCERS

The small back streets in Nuits St.-Georges conceal many of the top small growers, several of which are well worth visiting. Some of the most interesting proprietors to visit would include Daniel Chopin-Groffier, hidden on the back streets of Prémeaux, the Machard de Gramont, also in Prémeaux, as well as Jean Chauvenet, Georges Chicotot, Robert Chevillon, and of course, Alain Michelot. Perhaps the most pleasant way to learn about the differences among the top Premiers Crus vineyards in Nuits St.-Georges would be to visit Chevillon and Michelot. Both men produce a bevy of wines that are faithful to their respective vineyards, and representative of the highest quality wines from this appellation.

The firm of Joseph Faiveley is also located in Nuits St.-Georges. If one is able to get an appointment, this is an extraordinary place to taste not only a range of superb wines from Nuits St.-Georges, but from the

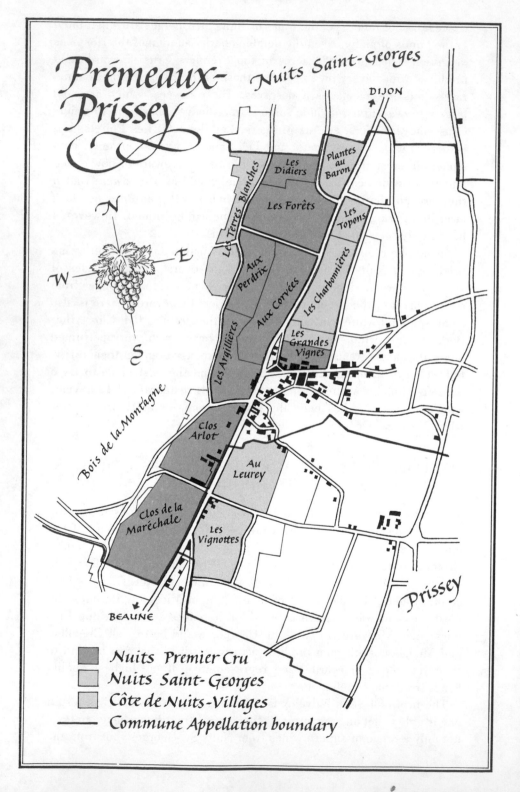

Prémeaux-Prissey

Nuits Saint-Georges

DIJON

Les Didiers

Plantes au Baron

Les Terres Blanches

Les Forêts

Les Topons

Aux Perdrix

Aux Corvées

Les Charbonnières

Les Argillières

Les Grandes Vignes

Bois de la Montagne

Clos Arlot

Au Leurey

Clos de la Maréchale

Les Vignottes

BEAUNE

Prissey

Nuits Premier Cru

Nuits Saint-Georges

Côte de Nuits-Villages

Commune Appellation boundary

entire Côte de Nuits and Côte Chalonnaise, since the Faiveley firm is one of today's greatest producers of authentic, handcrafted, usually unfiltered red and white burgundy. Two other important firms that have cellars in Nuits St. Georges are Moillard and Labouré-Roi. Both merit a visit.

Nuits St.-Georges makes a convenient stopover point for visiting the Côte de Nuits. There is easy access to the autoroute to the Côte de Beaune and farther south, and the northernmost villages of the Côte de Nuits, Fixin and Marsannay are only a 10-minute drive. There are several good hotels in Nuits St.-Georges, including the Hostellerie Gentilhommière, and the Hôtel Ibis, a sort of budget Novotel with clean, spartan rooms. Next to the autoroute at the Nuits St.-Georges exit is the Hôtel St.-Georges, which has reasonable prices and clean, no-nonsense lodging. The best restaurant in the town is the Côte d'Or, but I find it overpriced and inconsistent.

Lastly, a visit to Nuits St.-Georges should certainly include a look at the church of St.-Symphorien, a Romanesque building erected at the end of the thirteenth century. It is certainly the most impressive church between Dijon and Beaune. Another site worth visiting is the Roman archaeological ruins in the Bolards Vineyard. Artisans' homes, workshops, and a great many artifacts from ancient times have been unearthed at this site.

THE VILLAGES AND APPELLATIONS OF THE CÔTE DE BEAUNE

Ladoix-Serrigny
Aloxe-Corton
Pernand-Vergelesses
Savigny-Lès-Beaune
Chorey-Lès-Beaune
Beaune
Pommard
Volnay
Monthélie
Auxey-Duresses
Saint-Romain
Meursault
Puligny-Montrachet
Chassagne-Montrachet
Saint-Aubin
Santenay

LADOIX-SERRIGNY

An Overview

<u>*Location:*</u> Many visitors have only stopped in Ladoix, the most northern of the Côte de Beaune villages, thanks to the long arm of the law —caught in the frequent radar traps set up by the French police to catch those speeding on Route Nationale 74 as it cascades

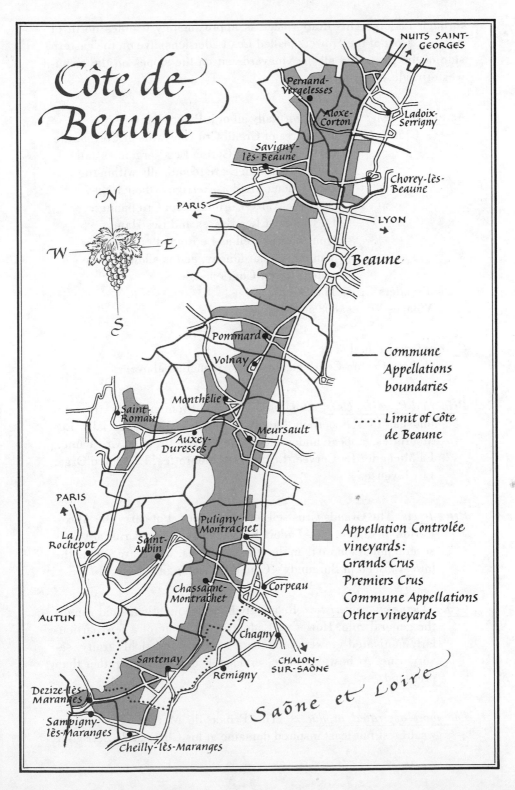

Côte de Beaune

NUITS SAINT-GEORGES

Pernand-Vergelesses

Aloxe-Corton

Ladoix-Serrigny

Savigny-lès-Beaune

Chorey-lès-Beaune

PARIS

LYON

Beaune

Pommard

Volnay

Monthélie

Saint-Romain

Auxey-Duresses

Meursault

—— Commune Appellations boundaries

.... Limit of Côte de Beaune

PARIS

La Rochepot

Saint-Aubin

Puligny-Montrachet

Chassagne-Montrachet

Corpeau

Appellation Contrôlée vineyards:
Grands Crus
Premiers Crus
Commune Appellations
Other vineyards

AUTUN

Chagny

CHALON-SUR-SAÔNE

Santenay

Remigny

Dezize-lès-Maranges

Sampigny-lès-Maranges

Cheilly-lès-Maranges

Saône et Loire

through Ladoix. This drab village is approximately 6 miles north of Beaune. Most of the growers (called Les Ladoisiens) live on the eastern side of the road, and all the vineyards sit on the slopes on the north-western side.

Acres under vine: 904 acres, virtually all of it Pinot Noir
          Grands Crus: 45.4 acres of Grand Cru vineyards of Corton, the best known being Corton Les Vergennes and Corton Le Rognet, are technically within the appellation of Ladoix-Serrigny, though they carry the Aloxe-Corton Grand Cru banner. 14.8 acres of Les Basses and Les Hautes Mourottes as well as Le Rognet en Corton is planted in Chardonnay, and is allowed to be called Corton-Charlemagne
     Premiers Crus: 35.5 acres
     Villages Wines: 808 acres

Grands Crus: a total of 2
     Corton, Corton-Charlemagne (see explanation above)

Principal Premiers Crus: a total of 5 principal Premiers Crus. (It is not unusual to see certain Ladoix Premiers Crus, especially Les Mourottes, appear under the Aloxe-Corton Premier Cru name.) La Micaude, La Corvée, Les Hautes Mourottes, Le Clou d'Orge, Les Joyeuses

Price levels: The Grands Crus sell for bold prices, but carry the Aloxe-Corton pedigree, not Ladoix-Serrigny. Premiers Crus are only several dollars more than the Villages wines, which are among the lowest priced in Burgundy's Côte d'Or, selling for $8 to $15.

General wine characteristics: Relatively light, frequently insipid wine is the general rule. However, Ladoix is the home of a few particularly motivated growers/producers who turn out richly fruity, savory wine. At best, it will be serviceable and pleasant rather than profound.

The most overrated producers: The Prince de Merode. He has the wealthiest but least inspired domaine at his Château de Serrigny.

The best producers and their wines:
> Capitain-Gagnerot: Ladoix, Ladoix Les Micaudes, Ladoix Les
> Grechons (white)
> Chevalier Père et Fils: Ladoix-Premier Cru
> Edmond Cornu: Ladoix
> Michel Mallard: Ladoix Les Joyeuses
> Prince Merode: Ladoix Les Hautes Mourottes (white)
> André Nudant: Ladoix Premier Cru
> Gaston et Pierre Ravaut: Ladoix Les Corvées

Some important observations:
1. Ladoix is Burgundy's least known appellation, making it an attractive place to shop for serviceable wines (largely red) that are inexpensive. Most cost less than California and Oregon Pinot Noir.
2. It is a curiosity of geography, and no doubt politics, that Ladoix-Serrigny's best vineyards—those sitting on the east face of the Bois de Corton—are permitted to carry the title of Corton for the red wines and Corton-Charlemagne for the white wines. It is odd that Ladoix does not have the political clout necessary to have the wines from its vineyards affiliated with its name rather then neighboring Aloxe-Corton.
3. Avoid *négociant*-bottled Ladoix, as it frequently tastes coarse and listless. Because this is so, many *négociants* have begun to blend it with other wine from the Côte de Beaune-Villages.

Where are the values? Consider Capitain-Gagnerot's wines, as Monsieur Capitain is Ladoix's most enthusiastic cheerleader as well as its finest wine producer.

Most successful recent vintages: 1989, 1988, 1985

Aging Potential: Premiers Crus—3 to 7 years; Villages wines—1 to 4 years

LADOIX-SERRIGNY

(The forgotten appellation of the Côte de Beaune)

The dull village of Ladoix-Serrigny, which sits on both sides of the famous Route Nationale 74, is the northernmost of the Côte de Beaune appellations. Like Rodney Dangerfield, it gets little respect. Its best vineyard sites are located on the slopes of the massive hill of Corton

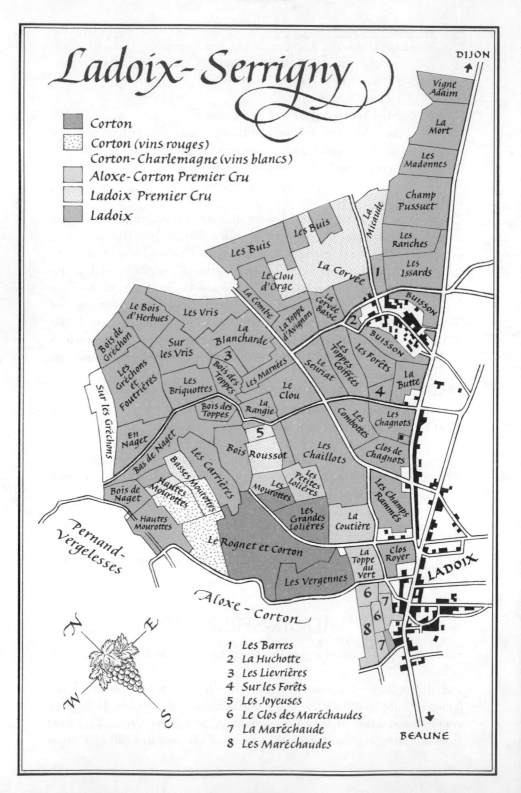

Ladoix-Serrigny

Corton
Corton (vins rouges)
Corton-Charlemagne (vins blancs)
Aloxe-Corton Premier Cru
Ladoix Premier Cru
Ladoix

DIJON

Vigne Adam

La Mort

Les Madonnes

Champ Pussuet

Les Ranches

Les Issards

La Micaude

La Corvée

Les Buis

Les Buis

Les Buis

Le Clou d'Orge

La Combe

La Toppe d'Avignon

La Corvée Basse

BUISSON

BUISSON

Le Bois d'Herbues

Les Vris

Bois de Grèchon

Sur les Vris

La Blancharde

Bois des Toppes

Les Marnées

Le Séuriat

Les Toppes Coiffées

Les Forêts

La Butte

Les Grèchons et Foutrières

Les Briquottes

Le Clou

Sur les Grèchons

Bois des Toppes

La Rangie

En Naget

Bas de Naget

Bois Roussot

Les Chaillots

Les Combottes

Les Chagnots

Clos de Chagnots

Les Champs Rammés

Basses Mourottes

Les Carrières

Hautes Mourottes

Les Mourottes

Les Petites Loliéres

Bois de Naget

Hautes Mourottes

Le Rognet et Corton

Les Grandes Loliéres

La Coutière

La Toppe au Vert

Clos Royer

LADOIX

Pernand-Vergelesses

Les Vergennes

Aloxe-Corton

BEAUNE

1 Les Barres
2 La Huchotte
3 Les Lievrières
4 Sur les Forêts
5 Les Joyeuses
6 Le Clos des Maréchaudes
7 La Maréchaude
8 Les Maréchaudes

N E W S

and are entitled to be called Aloxe-Corton Premier Cru, or Corton-Charlemagne if planted in Chardonnay, and Corton or Le Rognet en Corton if planted with Pinot Noir. This is ironic, since Ladoix no doubt would have a more visible reputation in the wine world if its name were Ladoix-Corton, rather than Ladoix-Serrigny. For years, many producers refused to sell their wine under the name Ladoix, preferring simply to call it Côte de Beaune-Villages. Many *négociants* still prefer this practice rather than trying to market an essentially anonymous appellation.

The wines are usually sound and quaffable, but rarely exciting. No doubt part of the problem for Ladoix is that too many of its neighbors produce better wine. In places like Chorey-Lès-Beaune, better as well as less expensive wine is made. Consequently, Ladoix is caught in a difficult marketing situation. Nevertheless, there are some fine domaines making not only Ladoix, but wines from neighboring appellations as well. With more modern vinification techniques finally being used to shed some of the roughness of these wines, the potential for good, fragrant, and easy to drink young wines from Ladoix does exist.

THE VINEYARDS OF LADOIX-SERRIGNY

All of the vineyards of Ladoix-Serrigny sit on what is the eastern extension of the appellation of Aloxe-Corton, on the northwestern side of Route Nationale 74. It is difficult to believe that a stone's throw away are the prestigious Grands Crus of Aloxe-Corton: Corton Les Maréchaudes, Corton Les Bressandes, Corton Les Rénardes, and Corton-Clos du Roi. These are four of the most prestigious Grands Crus in the entire Côte d'Or, yet their soils are not terribly unlike those found in the vineyards of Ladoix-Serrigny, particularly those vineyards that are legally permitted to adopt the name of Aloxe-Corton, such as Les Vergennes, Le Rognet en Corton, and Les Mourottes. Perhaps no one thinks that wines as good as these should be associated with Ladoix, so therefore they are permitted to carry the flag of Aloxe-Corton.

The problem Ladoix faces is that little of its wine appears as a Premier Cru under the Ladoix-Serrigny appellation, and much of the Villages wine is relatively tough, severe, and ungenerous. This situation lends credibility to the view that perhaps Chardonnay might do better here than Pinot Noir. Or should it be Gamay? The *négociants* are also at fault because they have now decided en masse to give up trying to market Ladoix as a separate entity, and simply blend their purchases from Ladoix-Serrigny with their Côte de Beaune-Villages selections.

While politics and image are not yet in favor of Ladoix, things are beginning to improve. Some growers are beginning to behave a bit more chauvinistically about their wines, and are willing to spend a few dollars to promote what can be undervalued and well-made red wines. No one is any more promotion- or quality-conscious when it comes to Ladoix than the tall, intense, loquacious Roger Capitain, whose ability to extol the virtues of Ladoix knows no shame or bounds. He makes several cuvées of Ladoix that will make converts of those who are fortunate enough to taste his supple, seductive wines. However, despite his allegiance to Ladoix, I note that his Premier Cru Les Mourottes, which he could legally call Ladoix, is labeled Aloxe-Corton Les Mourottes.

The best wines I have drunk from the Premiers Crus of Ladoix have come from those that are listed among the recommended producers. I have found that the wines can possess a deep ruby color, a chunky, compact texture, significant body and tannin, as well as keeping qualities for up to a decade of cellaring. What they usually lack is charm, suppleness, and complexity.

VISITING THE VILLAGE OF LADOIX-SERRIGNY AND ITS PRODUCERS

There are several hotels and restaurants in Ladoix-Serrigny. Given all the truck traffic that winds its way over Route Nationale 74 to Dijon or Beaune, I cannot imagine that these hotels, Les Paulands, La Gremelle, and Donno, are as quiet as one might desire. The best restaurant of this area is Le Coquinage. The cooking is excellent.

As far as I am aware, there are no buildings or landmarks of special architectural interest to visit in Ladoix-Serrigny.

ALOXE-CORTON

An Overview

Location: Twenty miles south of Dijon and 4 miles north of Beaune is the delightful village of Aloxe-Corton. Situated at the foot of the Montagne de Corton, a vast hill covered with vineyards, Aloxe-

Corton has three legitimate châteaux—Corton-André, Corton-Grancey, and Aloxe-Corton. The towers and colorful tiled roofs of these châteaux offer a memorable and photogenic view.

Acres under vine: A total of 605.15 acres
    Grands Crus: 396* acres in red wine; 177 acres in Corton-
              Charlemagne
  Premiers Crus: 92.9* acres
  Villages Wines: 221.5* acres

Grands Crus: A total of 22 (21 red wines and 1 white wine)
There is one Grand Cru, Corton, to which the names of single vineyards are frequently added. They are Le Corton, Corton Les Pougets, Corton Les Languettes, Corton Les Rénardes, Corton Les Chaumes, Corton Les Perrières, Corton Les Grèves, Corton Le Clos du Roi, Corton Les Bressandes, Corton Les Paulands, Corton Les Maréchaudes, Corton Les Fiètres, Corton-Clos des Meix, Corton Les Combes, Corton La Vigne au Saint, Corton Les Carrières, Corton La Toppe au Vert, Corton Les Vergennes, Corton Les Grandes Lolières, Corton Les Moutottes, Corton Le Rognet, Corton Les Mourottes, and the white wine Grand Cru: Corton-Charlemagne

Principal Premiers Crus: A total of 12
Aloxe-Corton Les Chaillots, Aloxe-Corton Les Fournières, Aloxe-Corton Les Meix, Aloxe-Corton Les Guérets, Aloxe-Corton Les Vercots, Aloxe-Corton Les Valozières, Aloxe-Corton Lés Paulands, Aloxe-Corton Les Maréchaudes, Aloxe-Corton La Toppe au Vert, Aloxe-Corton Les Petites Lolières, Aloxe-Corton Les Mourottes, Aloxe-Corton La Coutière

Price levels: $35–$60 for Corton Grand Cru red wine; $50–$80 for Corton-Charlemagne. The Premiers Crus and Villages wines are much more reasonably priced, selling for $20–$30 and $15–$25 a bottle, respectively.

General wine characteristics: Red wine: The red wines have a pronounced, earthy, intense, spicy, burnt cherry *gout de terroir* character that is unique. Perhaps a useful comparison are the very

---

* These figures include acreage within the neighboring appellations of Ladoix-Serrigny and Pernand-Vergelesses.

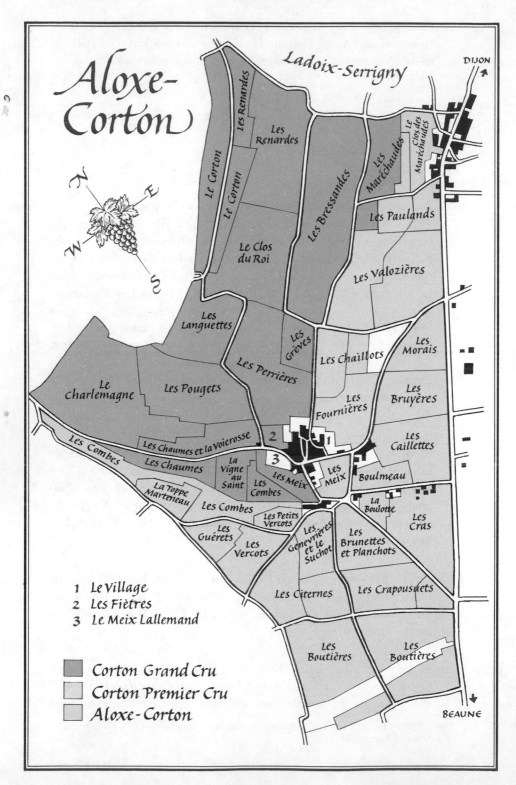

Aloxe-Corton

Ladoix-Serrigny

DIJON

Les Renardes
Les Renardes
Le Corton
Le Corton
Les Bressandes
Les Maréchaudes
Le Clos des Maréchaudes
Les Paulands
Le Clos du Roi
Les Valozières
Les Languettes
Les Grèves
Les Chaillots
Les Morais
Les Perrières
Le Charlemagne
Les Pougets
Les Fournières
Les Bruyères
Les Chaumes et la Voierosse
Les Combes
Les Chaumes
La Vigne au Saint
Les Combes
Les Meix
Les Meix
Boulmeau
Les Caillettes
La Toppe Marteneau
Les Combes
Les Petits Vercots
La Boulotte
Les Cras
Les Guérets
Les Vercots
Les Genevrières et le Suchot
Les Brunettes et Planchots
Les Citernes
Les Crapousuets
Les Boutières
Les Boutières
BEAUNE

1 Le Village
2 Les Fiètres
3 Le Meix Lallemand

Corton Grand Cru
Corton Premier Cru
Aloxe-Corton

mineral, tobacco-scented and flavored wines of the Graves appellation of Bordeaux. Red Corton, because of its earthy, often dusty, tannic character, is more difficult to appreciate when young. The best examples can age as well, perhaps even longer, than the top wines from the Côte de Nuits.

White Wine: Corton-Charlemagne is truly one of the world's most compelling expressions of the Chardonnay grape. It is a big, forceful, powerful wine that usually needs 4 to 5 years to open up. There are many great producers of Corton-Charlemagne, and it is one Grand Cru that usually lives up to its reputation, provided you have the patience to wait.

The most overrated producers: Prince de Merode, La Reine Pedauque, Bouchard Père et Fils, Max Quenot

The best producers and their wines:

Adrien Belland: Corton-Charlemagne, Corton Les Grèves
Besancenot-Mathouillet: Corton-Charlemagne
Bonneau de Martray: Corton-Charlemagne
Capitain-Gagnerot: Corton-Charlemagne, Corton Les Rénardes
Chandon de Briailles: Corton Les Bressandes, Corton-Clos du Roi, Corton Les Maréchaudes, Corton Blanc
Maurice Chapuis: Corton-Charlemagne
Clos Frantin (Bichot): Corton
J. F. Coche-Dury: Corton-Charlemagne
Edmond Cornu: Corton Les Bressandes
Marius Delarche: Corton-Charlemagne, Corton Les Rénardes
Doudet-Naudin: Corton, Corton Les Maréchaudes
Dubreuil-Fontaine: Corton-Charlemagne, Corton-Clos du Roi, Corton Les Bressandes
Faiveley: Corton-Charlemagne, Corton-Clos des Cortons
Hospices de Beaune: Corton-Charlemagne-Cuvée François de Salins, Corton-Cuvée Dr. Peste, Corton-Cuvée Charlotte Dumay
Louis Jadot: Corton-Charlemagne, Corton Les Pougets
Laleure-Piot: Corton-Charlemagne
Louis Latour: Corton-Charlemagne, Corton-Grancey, Corton-Clos de la Vigne au Saint
Mallard: Corton, Corton Les Rénardes
Moillard: Corton-Clos du Roi
André Nudant: Corton-Charlemagne, Corton Les Bressandes

Domaine Pavelot: Corton-Charlemagne
Domaine Rapet: Corton, Corton-Charlemagne
Remoissenet: Corton-Charlemagne
Georges Roumier: Corton-Charlemagne
Daniel Senard: Corton-Clos du Roi, Corton Les Bressandes,
    Corton-Clos des Meix, Corton
Tollot-Beaut: Corton-Charlemagne, Corton, Corton Les
    Bressandes
Michel Voarick: Corton-Clos du Roi, Corton Les Rénardes,
    Corton Les Bressandes, Corton-Charlemagne

Some important observations:
1. I have always been baffled by the high proportion of this appellation's acreage that is entitled to Grand Cru status for red wine. The
   only vineyards that consistently produce wine at a true Grand Cru
   level are Les Bressandes, Le Clos du Roi, Les Rénardes, and Le
   Corton. On occasion, Les Pougets and La Vigne au Saint are top
   drawer.
2. At the top of the Corton hill, on stony limestone soil, just below the
   forest that crowns the crest, is the Corton-Charlemagne vineyard.
   There seems no doubt that this splendidly situated slope facing the
   southeast is one of the world's greatest spots for the Chardonnay
   grape.
3. At the top levels, both the red and white wines from this appellation
   justify their reputation for impressive longevity.
4. Great Grand Cru red Corton is, I think, the least flattering red burgundy to drink young. The high tannin levels and coarse earthiness
   smooth out with age, but are forbidding in their youth.

Where are the values? Interestingly, those growers who live and have
   their primary vineyards in Ladoix or Pernand-Vergelesses, with
   only small parcels in Aloxe-Corton, frequently charge less for
   their wines than those growers located in Aloxe-Corton. For example, look for Premiers Crus and Villages wines from Edmond
   Cornu, André Nudant, Gaston and Pierre Ravaut, Capitain-
   Gagnerot, Rapet, Dubreuil-Fontaine, and Michel Mallard.

Most successful recent vintages: 1989, 1988, 1985, 1982, 1979, 1978

Aging Potential: Corton-Charlemagne—5 to 20 years; Grands Crus
   (red)—7 to 15 years; Premiers Crus—5 to 10 years; Villages wines
   —3 to 10 years

ALOXE-CORTON

(Awesome white wines and overrated reds)

The Côte d'Or's most prominent landmark is the domed hill, immodestly called the Montagne de Corton, that rises subtly from the landscape just a few miles north of Beaune. This impressive hillside, with a forest crowning its crest, is similar to the huge, granite hill of Hermitage in the Rhône Valley that makes that appellation so distinctive. However, it is not Marsanne or Syrah that are planted on the hill at Corton, but rather Chardonnay, Pinot Noir, and tiny quantities of both Pinot Blanc and Pinot Gris. The tiny village at the foot of the hill, Aloxe-Corton, is one of the prettiest places in all of Burgundy, with its trio of splendid châteaux and their colorful, remarkably patterned roofs, much like the famous Hôtel Dieu in Beaune. The village boasts a population of just under 300, mostly farmers and growers, and perhaps half that many cats.

Aloxe-Corton has almost as much history as that of Beaune. The ruins found here prove the existence of human settlement all the way back to the days of the Roman Empire. The famous Grand Cru white wine, Corton-Charlemagne, took its name from Emperor Charlemagne, who not only owned land in the village, but made it known that this was one of his favorite wines. In the eighth century, Charlemagne made a gift of some of the best situated vineyards to the Abbey of Saulieu. One suspects little has changed in Aloxe-Corton over the subsequent centuries. The suburban sprawl that has made the southern, eastern, and western borders of Beaune look like any growing town has never moved in the direction of Aloxe-Corton. The village therefore seems like a precious, small museum left to itself, with little to mark the passage of time.

THE VINEYARDS OF ALOXE-CORTON

The entire appellation is quite large, consisting of 605 acres. Most of this acreage is situated on the huge slopes that wrap around the Montagne de Corton. The Chardonnay of the Grand Cru Corton-Charlemagne is planted at the very top of the slope, just below the woods where the composition of the soil is light, stony limestone. As one proceeds down the slope, the soils become deeper, and have at the very bottom a great deal of alluvial sand and gravel. Pinot Noir is planted on the lower slopes, which contain mostly Grands Crus vineyards. There is no other appellation of Burgundy that has so much of its acreage devoted to a Grand Cru. However, after tasting all the wines of Corton sporting a Grand Cru label, I do wonder why the term Grand Cru is applied so liberally in Aloxe-Corton, yet barred in Aloxe-Corton's most famous neighbor to the north, Nuits St.-Georges. After researching this area for over a decade, I have no doubt that the top red wines from such Corton Grands Crus vineyards as Les Bressandes, Les Rénardes, Le Clos du Roi, and Le Corton clearly justify their Grand Cru status, but I have seldom tasted a red wine from the other Grands Crus vineyards that has the magical perfume and profound concentration of flavor that are required of Grands Crus from Burgundy's other appellations. How odd it is that Burgundy commentators normally vent their anger at the Grand Cru vineyard Clos de Vougeot, when the greatest embarrassment to the system of Grands Crus are the wines from Aloxe-Corton that are entitled to Burgundy's highest pedigree yet in actuality taste like generic wines.

The root of the problem in this appellation is that there are three conspicuous underachievers who have significant vineyard holdings and who also actively promote their wines. The first is the Domaine of the Prince de Merode, a famous name and a producer of some great wines in the sixties and early seventies. Unfortunately, an obsession with high technology and filtration seems to have eviscerated this domaine's wines of much of their flavor. They are now relatively straightforward, monolithic, commercial examples of their appellations. The same charge can be leveled at the second underachiever, the enormously wealthy, vast empire of Bouchard Père et Fils. Two of the greatest Cortons I have ever drunk were the 1947 and 1959 Cortons from this very famous Burgundy *négociant* and vineyard holder. To suggest they are making wines today that remotely resemble the 1959 or 1947 would be absurd. The third notorious underachiever is La Reine Pedauque, which has one of the most beautiful châteaux in Aloxe-Corton, as well as a tasting room that does a thriving business. Their wines tend to be insipid rather than inspired.

What should a great Grand Cru from Corton taste like? This is one appellation whose wines should not be drunk young, for they often have plenty of tannin and an earthy, rustic character that melts away with age, revealing remarkable red fruit flavors and an equally majestic perfume. Anyone who has tasted some of the mature examples from cellars such as Tollot-Beaut, Domaine Chandon de Briailles, Dubreuil-Fontaine, Daniel Senard, Michel Voarick, Faiveley, Louis Jadot, Louis Latour, or the two famous Hospices de Beaune cuvées, Cuvée Dr. Peste and Cuvée Charlotte Dumay, knows these are wines that clearly justify not only their Grand Cru status, but also their reputation for being majestic and long lived.

The Corton-Charlemagne vineyard is large by Burgundy standards, consisting of nearly 177 acres situated high on the south side of the Corton hill, sloping gently in the direction of the sleepy village of Pernand-Vergelesses. Legends about Charlemagne and his love for this particular wine have no doubt been embellished over the years, but most growers continue to claim that Charlemagne's wife felt the emperor's insatiable thirst for red wine did not go well with his sloppy drinking habits, leaving his white beard too frequently stained with red wine. As the growers say, after years of persuasion she finally convinced Charlemagne that if he drank only white wine he would have the noble, stain-free appearance of an emperor. Of course, the actual truth is not known, but if the emperor did indeed appreciate this wine, his taste was impeccable.

No one is foolish enough to raise questions about the pedigree, aging potential, or ultimate pleasure that a great Corton-Charlemagne is capable of providing. The grapes from this sun-drenched, hilltop vineyard produce what I consider to be the greatest white burgundy after Montrachet and Chevalier-Montrachet. Corton-Charlemagne is a wine of extraordinary richness and aging potential. Furthermore, most of the people who own its vineyards exploit them to their full potential. Corton-Charlemagne is not as forbidding to drink young as some of the great red Grands Crus of Corton. In fact, given the present day's rush to gratify one's needs, most Corton-Charlemagnes are probably consumed within several hours of their purchase. However, they can last for 10 to 20 years when made by producers such as Louis Jadot, Louis Latour, Bonneau de Martray, Marius Delarche, and Tollot-Beaut. Two of the most sublime Corton-Charlemagnes, although both are very hard to find, are those from Faiveley (less than 300 cases are made each year), and the splendid grower in Meursault, Jean-François Coche-Dury. There is also the Hospices de Beaune Corton-Charlemagne Cuvée François de Salins, that sells at preposterously high prices of $150 and $200 a bottle. This wine takes as long to develop as any of the great Corton-Charlemagnes, and I have had 20-year-old bottles of it that have indeed been splendid.

The most famous producer of Corton-Charlemagne is the Beaune *négociant*, Louis Latour. Latour has extensive vineyard holdings, as well as his remarkable Château Grancey. Many people consider the Corton-Charlemagne made by Latour to be the reference point for the other wines of the vintage. It is usually a compelling wine, frequently reaching 13.5%–14% alcohol naturally—not the sort of Chardonnay to sip with crackers by the side of a swimming pool. This is full-throttle, intense, highly concentrated wine that begs for lobster or salmon. While Louis Latour has the most significant parcel of the Corton-Charlemagne vineyard (over 23 acres), another outstanding Corton-Charlemagne is made by the Maison Louis Jadot in Beaune. Equally unctuous and powerful, it may not have quite the longevity of the Corton-Charlemagne from Louis Latour, but it is still a thrilling bottle of Chardonnay. I have already mentioned those small growers who make excellent to outstanding wines from Corton-Charlemagne, but the problem is that availability is extremely limited, and the wines are difficult to find in the marketplace. Nevertheless, with the exception of a few disappointments, such as the Corton-Charlemagne from Bouchard Père et Fils, this is one Grand Cru appellation for white wine where the general level of winemaking does justice to its Grand Cru status.

VISITING THE VILLAGE OF ALOXE-CORTON AND ITS PRODUCERS

A visit to the village of Aloxe-Corton and a look at its steep vineyards is a must for anyone travelling through Burgundy. The small yet impeccably run and furnished Hôtel Clarion opened in the mid-eighties, good news for those visitors who want to spend the night. This tiny hotel (reservations are essential) does not have a restaurant, but meals can easily be had in Beaune (at most a 10-minute drive by car), or in one of the local restaurants along the Route Nationale 74.

The most impressive domaine in Aloxe-Corton is that of Louis Latour. A visit to his Château Corton Grancey, is highly warranted, not just because of the splendid facility, but also because of the exquisite Corton-Charlemagne Latour produces. A visit to the cellars of Daniel Senard, or those of the chain-smoking Michel Voarick (adjacent to the Hôtel Clarion), are also highly recommended, as both men are among the great characters of Burgundy. Most of the other producers who make top wines from this appellation are located in neighboring Ladoix or Pernand-Vergelesses.

PERNAND-VERGELESSES

An Overview

Location: The 334 residents of Pernand-Vergelesses (they are called Les Pernandais) reside in the shadow of the huge Montagne de Corton and that appellation's more renowned village, Aloxe-Corton. The pretty village of Pernand is situated on a hillside and is only several minutes from both Savigny-Lès-Beaune and Aloxe-Corton. Beaune is only 10 minutes away.

Acres under vine: 869 acres, which includes Pinot Noir, Chardonnay, and Aligoté
    Grands Crus: 42.6 acres
    Premiers Crus: 139.5 acres
    Villages Wines: 339.8 acres, the balance entitled to the Côtes de
              Beaune-Villages appellation

Grands Crus: 42.6 acres of the great white wine Grand Cru, Corton-Charlemagne (total acreage is 177 acres), is technically within the Pernand-Vergelesses appellation

Principal Premiers Crus: A total of 4
    En Caradeux, Les Fichots, Île des Vergelesses, Les Vergelesses

Price levels: Wines of Pernand-Vergelesses are relatively obscure and therefore fairly priced. The Premiers Crus sell for $15–$25 a bottle. The great Grand Cru Corton-Charlemagne is priced similarly to other renowned white burgundy Grands Crus, and it is rare to find a bottle for less than $50.

General wine characteristics: Approximately 25% of the production of Pernand-Vergelesses is white wine. The portion of the appellation that is entitled to Grand Cru status, Corton-Charlemagne, produces very long-lived, steely, concentrated wines that can last for 10–20 years. The other white wines have generally been tough,

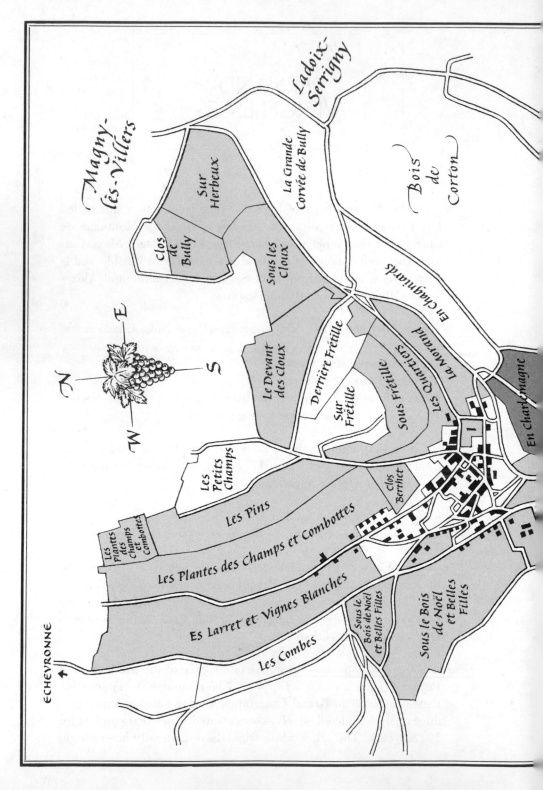

Magny-
lès-Villers

Ladoix-
Serrigny

Sur
Herbeux

La Grande
Corvée de Bully

Bois
de
Corton

Clos
de
Bully

Sous les
Cloux

En Chaignards

Le Devant
des Cloux

Derrière Frétille

Sous Frétille

La Morand

Les Quartiers

Sur
Frétille

En Charlemagne

Les Petits
Champs

Clos
Berthet

Les Pins

Les Plantes
des
Champs
et
Combottes

Les Plantes des Champs et Combottes

Es Larret et Vignes Blanches

Sous le
Bois de Noël
et Belles Filles

Sous le Bois
de Noël
et Belles Filles

Les Combes

ÉCHEVRONNE

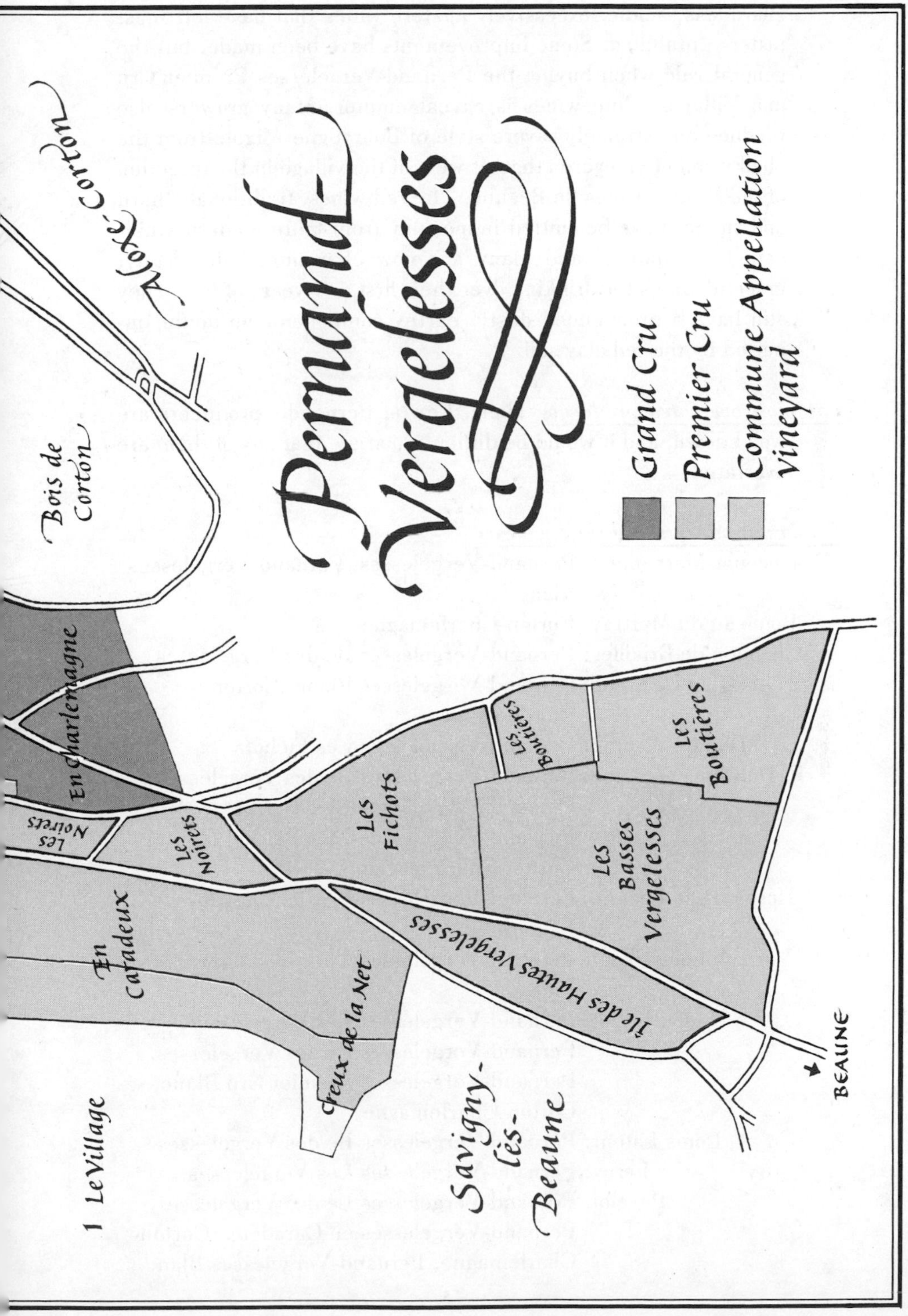

Pernand-Vergelesses

Grand Cru
Premier Cru
Commune Appellation vineyard

Aloxe-Corton

Bois de Corton

En Charlemagne

Les Noirets

Les Noirets

En Caradeux

Le Village

Creux de la Net

Les Fichots

Ile des Hautes Vergelesses

Les Bas Boutières

Les Boutières

Les Basses Vergelesses

Savigny-lès-Beaune

BEAUNE

1 Le Village

charmless, acidic, excessively austere wines that have left most
tasters unfulfilled. Some improvements have been made, but the
general rule when buying the Pernand-Vergelesses Premier Cru
and Villages white wines is caveat emptor. Many growers also
produce an extremely severe style of Bourgogne Aligoté from the
chalky soil of vineyards that sit west of the village in the direction
of the Hautes-Côtes de Beaune. The red wines, traditionally hard
and rustic, have benefitted immensely from more modern vinification techniques, and many are now charming, light, fruity,
graceful wines for drinking over their first 6–7 years of life. They
still have a pronounced dusty, earthy component, no doubt im-
parted by the red clay soil.

The most overrated producers: None. Few of Pernand's producers are
well known, and it would be difficult to argue that any of them are
overrated.

The best producers and their wines:
Besancenot-Mathouillet: Pernand-Vergelesses, Pernand-Vergelesses
Blanc
Bonneau du Martray: Corton-Charlemagne
Chandon de Briailles: Pernand-Vergelesses Île des Vergelesses
Marius Delarche: Pernand-Vergelesses Blanc, Corton-
Charlemagne
Doudet-Naudin: Pernand-Vergelesses Les Fichots
P. Dubreuil-Fontaine: Pernand-Vergelesses Île des Vergelesses,
Pernand-Vergelesses-Clos Berthet (red),
Pernand-Vergelesses-Clos Berthet (white),
Corton-Charlemagne
Hospices de Beaune: Pernand-Vergelesses-Cuvée Rameau-
Lamarosse
Louis Jadot: Pernand-Vergelesses-Clos de la Croix
Pierre
Laleure-Piot: Pernand-Vergelesses Les Vergelesses,
Pernand-Vergelesses Île des Vergelesses,
Pernand-Vergelesses Premier Cru Blanc,
Corton-Charlemagne
Louis Latour: Pernand-Vergelesses Île des Vergelesses
Leroy: Pernand-Vergelesses Les Vergelesses
Pavelot: Pernand-Vergelesses Île des Vergelesses,
Pernand-Vergelesses en Caradeux, Corton-
Charlemagne, Pernand-Vergelesses Blanc

Rapet Père et Fils: Pernand-Vergelesses Les Vergelesses,
                        Pernand-Vergelesses Sous la Vierge Blanc,
                        Corton-Charlemagne
M. Rollin Père et Fils: Pernand-Vergelesses Île des Vergelesses

Some important observations:
1. Pernand-Vergelesses is the home of a handful of very fine growers and winemakers who extract as much character and charm from their less favorably situated and renowned vineyards as the many growers who are blessed with more promising vineyards. Dubreuil-Fontaine, Laleure-Piot, Régis Pavelot, and Roland Rapet are highly motivated producers doing the best they can with the raw materials that nature provides.
2. The northeasterly exposure of their best vineyards, such as Île des Vergelesses, Les Vergelesses, and Les Fichots, is not ideal, but the red clay and iron-like soils of these three vineyards do produce a red wine that has staying power.
3. Some producers in Pernand-Vergelesses prefer to sell their wines under the name Côte de Beaune-Villages because they feel that name has greater market recognition than the obscure Pernand-Vergelesses, which is also considered difficult to pronounce by foreigners.
4. A surprising quantity of highly acidic Bourgogne Aligoté emanates from Pernand's producers. Most of it needs a healthy dosage of cassis to soften its sharp edges. It is highly promoted, but not nearly as good as the Aligoté that comes from the Bouzeron area, near the town of Chagny, in southern Burgundy.

Where are the values? Good red Premier Cru Pernand-Vergelesses is undoubtedly a value because it has never been in fashion. However, this is an appellation where one must stick to the top producers, and only then in the best years. The less-than-perfect exposure of most of Pernand's vineyards often results in grapes that never attain full maturity.

Most successful recent vintages: 1989, 1988, 1985

Aging Potential: Corton-Charlemagne (Grand Cru)—5 to 20+ years; Premiers Crus (red)—5 to 12 years; Premiers Crus (white)—3 to 8 years; Villages wines—3 to 5 years; Bourgogne Aligoté—1 to 3 years

PERNAND-VERGELESSES

(An improving yet unfashionable appellation)

Pernand-Vergelesses is close to Beaune, but it could just as well be far away when one realizes how few Burgundy wine enthusiasts make the short trek to this charming village hidden in the valley by the great Montagne de Corton. This is a shame because there are some highly competent, extremely motivated producers in Pernand, whose only problem is that their vineyards simply cannot produce the superb fruit that is available from some of the better exposed appellations of the Côte d'Or. Nevertheless, Pernand-Vergelesses can claim nearly 25% of the Grand Cru Corton-Charlemagne, and there is no doubting that when yields are kept conservative a number of realistically priced wines emerge from this appellation. However, many growers in Pernand-Vergelesses continue to downgrade their wines and sell them under the name of Côte de Beaune-Villages because of this appellation's obscurity and unmarketable name.

THE VINEYARDS OF PERNAND-VERGELESSES

Three-fourths of the production of Pernand-Vergelesses is in red wine, primarily from the top 4 Premiers Crus. Most notable are the Île des Vergelesses (24 acres) with its clay and iron-like soil, Les Vergelesses (44 acres), Les Fichots (27.7 acres), and En Caradeux (35.5 acres). The best of the Premiers Crus, in my opinion, is Île des Vergelesses. Perhaps this is because it sits a little higher on the slope and has the benefit of more sunshine than the other two Premier Crus that sit below it, Les Vergelesses and Les Fichots. The problem with these vineyards is that they have a northeasterly exposure, which causes the grapes to ripen late. Burgundy has notoriously unstable weather in late September and early October, with the potential for heavy and devastating rainstorms. The clay soil of this area does not afford the drainage that the more gravelly soil does in other appellations, and the results are waterlogged vines and, consequently, diluted grapes. Nevertheless, in good vintages a top Premier Cru Pernand-Vergelesses will be a relatively rich, rustic, concentrated wine that is often compared to that of its nearby neighbor. Savigny-Lès-Beaune. In actuality the wine will be less elegant, with more aging potential, and a more muscular, fuller-bodied character, but one is unlikely to be disappointed with the quality of the wines from the best vintages made by the recommended growers listed in the Overview.

For the most traditional, rustic, and longest-lived Pernand-Vergelesses of all, do not hesitate to try the Pernand-Vergelesses Les Fichots
from Doudet-Naudin, the vineyard owner and *négociant* in Savigny-
Lès-Beaune. This is a wine that can easily last 20 or more years in top
vintages.

Many producers have made good progress in taming the rough tannins that the soil tends to bequeath the red wines of Pernand-Vergelesses. Modern presses and techniques such as total destemming are
more helpful with a wine from Pernand than with examples from some
of the other appellations. The results have been some surprisingly
charming wines from producers such as Dubreuil-Fontaine, Laleure-
Piot, Domaine Chandon de Briailles, Louis Jadot, Leroy, Besancenot-
Mathouillet, Louis Latour, and of course, the Hospices de Beaune.

White wine is also produced in Pernand-Vergelesses. Except for Corton-Charlemagne, it is not impressive, although I have had consistently
good examples of Pernand-Vergelesses white from Laleure-Piot, Dubreuil-Fontaine, Régis Pavelot, and Rapet Père et Fils. Virtually every
producer in Pernand-Vergelesses also produces a small quantity of
Aligoté from vineyards that sit behind the village in the direction of the
Hautes-Côtes de Beaune. While there is clearly a need for a reasonably
priced Bourgogne Aligoté, most Aligotés from Pernand's producers are
extremely acidic and rarely can be served on its own merits without a
helpful addition of crème de cassis.

Lastly, Corton-Charlemagne is made in Pernand-Vergelesses and
sold under the Corton-Charlemagne name. The vineyards within the
Pernand appellation are considered to be slightly less desirable parcels
of the Grand Cru Corton-Charlemagne than those that are a part of the
Aloxe-Corton appellation. Nevertheless, producers such as Laleure-
Piot, Dubreuil-Fontaine, and one of the most famous producers of
Corton-Charlemagne, Bonneau du Martray, have succeeded in making
outstanding wines from their parcels of Corton-Charlemagne.

VISITING THE VILLAGE OF PERNAND-VERGELESSES AND ITS PRODUCERS

Rest assured that if you get stuck in Pernand-Vergelesses with an
empty stomach there will be no problem filling it. The local restaurant,
called Le Charlemagne, is surprisingly good, serving hefty portions of
delicious food at reasonable prices. I know of no suitable lodging in the
tiny village. Unfortunately, Pernand-Vergelesses, while charmingly situated on the hillside and valley floor, lacks the character and beauty of
its nearby neighbor, Savigny-Lès-Beaune, and even the mosaic rooftops

of its easterly neighbor, Aloxe-Corton. Nevertheless, there is the attractive Chapel of Nôtre Dame de Bonne Espérance, built in 1854. Its bell tower dominates the small, pretty village.

The growers with the most forceful personalities, and who also provide the best tastings, would certainly include the ebullient Dubreuil family, whose cellars (which are always full of their clients) are carved into the hillside, the Domaine Laleure-Piot, and if you can get an appointment, the one cellar most first-time visitors should visit, Domaine Bonneau du Martray, a significant landholder in Corton-Charlemagne and highly reputed as one of the finest producers of this rare yet highly prized, expensive white wine. If you have an opportunity to visit Bonneau du Martray, the finest barrels and equipment will be evident. For a dramatic contrast, just walk across the street and visit the family-operated cellars of Marius Delarche. This is a spotty producer, but he is capable of turning out excellent wines in good years. What I really like about Delarche is the total family involvement, and the artisanal winemaking style that is a radical departure from what one encounters in the cellars of Bonneau du Martray.

SAVIGNY-LÈS-BEAUNE

An Overview

Location: Aside from Beaune, most of the villages of the Côte d'Or are simple functional villages inhabited by growers, with little of architectural interest or notable historical value. Savigny-Lès-Beaune is one of Burgundy's most beautiful exceptions. Located three miles to the north of Beaune, Savigny-Lès-Beaune sits between two hillsides at the entrance to a pastoral valley called Combe de Fontaine-Froide. The immensely charming village has 1,405 inhabitants (Les Savigniens) according to the latest census.

Acres under vine: 1,343 acres, of which 97% is planted with Pinot Noir and the balance with Chardonnay
   Grands Crus: none
   Premiers Crus: 356 acres
   Villages Wines: 987 acres

Grands Crus: None

Principal Premiers Crus: A total of 11
> Aux Vergelesses (north bank), Les Lavières (north bank), Aux Serpentières (north bank), Aux Clous (north bank), Aux Guettes (north bank), Les Narbantons (south bank), La Dominode (also called Les Jarrons) (south bank), Les Jarrons (south bank), Les Hauts Jarrons (south bank), Les Marconnets (south bank), and Les Peuillets (south bank).

Price levels: The Premiers Crus sell for $15–$25 a bottle. Appellation Savigny-Lès-Beaune contrôlée sells for $10–$15 a bottle.

General wine characteristics: Savigny-Lès-Beaune's general reputation is for light, berry-scented (primarily cherry) wines that often have a rustic, earthy undertone to them. There are significant differences between those wines produced on the village's opposing hillsides, however. The southern hillsides have a less-than-ideal north/northeasterly exposure, and lighter, more gravelly and sandy soils. The resulting wines tend to be ready to drink when released, are lighter bodied and less alcoholic. The northern hillsides, which overlook the Rhoin River that cuts this appellation in half, have heartier soils representing an amalgam of iron, clay, and limestone. These vineyards produce Savigny's finest, richest, most intense and ageworthy wines, not only because of the better soil, but because of the ideal southerly exposure that allows the grapes to ripen 5–7 days earlier than on the southern border.

The most overrated producers: Henri Villamont, Antonin Guyon

The best producers and their wines:

Red Wines
> Simon Bize: Savigny-Lès-Beaune aux Vergelesses, Savigny-Lès-Beaune aux Guettes, Savigny-Lès-Beaune Premier Cru (a blend)
> Bonnot-Lamblot: Savigny-Lès-Beaune Les Dominodes
> Capron-Manieux: Savigny-Lès-Beaune Les Lavières
> Champy Père: Savigny-Lès-Beaune Les Dominodes

Chandon de Briailles: Savigny-Lès-Beaune Les Lavières
Chanson: Savigny-Lès-Beaune Les Dominodes
Bruno Clair: Savigny-Lès-Beaune Les Dominodes
Doudet-Naudin: Savigny-Lès-Beaune Les Guettes
Joseph Drouhin: Savigny-Lès-Beaune Premier Cru (a blend)
Maurice Ecard: Savigny-Lès-Beaune Les Serpentières,
Savigny-Lès-Beaune Les Narbantons
J. M. Giboulot: Savigny-Lès-Beaune Les Serpentières
Machard de Gramont: Savigny-Lès-Beaune Les Guettes
Pierre Guillemot: Savigny-Lès-Beaune Les Serpentières,
Savigny-Lès-Beaune Les Jarrons
Hospices de Beaune: Savigny-Lès-Beaune-Cuvée Arthur Girard,
Savigny-Lès-Beaune-Cuvée Fouquerand,
Savigny-Lès-Beaune-Cuvée Forneret
Mongeard-Mugneret: Savigny-Lès-Beaune
Albert Morot: Savigny-Lès-Beaune Les Vergelesses-Clos la
Bataillère
Pavelot-Glantenay: Savigny-Lès-Beaune Les Dominodes, Savigny-
Lès-Beaune Les Guettes
Jean Pichenot: Savigny-Lès-Beaune
Tollot-Beaut: Savigny-Lès-Beaune Les Lavières

White Wines

Capron Manieux: Savigny-Lès-Beaune
Doudet-Naudin: Savigny-Lès-Beaune Redrescul
Maurice Ecard: Savigny-Lès-Beaune Les Hauts Jarrons
Pierre Gillemot: Savigny-Lès-Beaune
Machard de Gramont: Savigny-Lès-Beaune Les Vergelesses
Pierre Labet: Savigny-Lès-Beaune Les Vergelesses

Some important observations:

1. If you believe that all red and white burgundies are too expensive,
consider the best examples from Savigny-Lès-Beaune. Yes, it is true
these wines lack the body and big, dramatic flavors of top Côte de
Nuits or the seductive, velvety, berry fruitiness of Volnay or Pommard. However, the top wines are usually ready to drink young and
are very fruity and stylish—commodities hard to find in Pinot Noir
for under $20 a bottle. Selection is critical, as some Savignys are
often coarse, hard, and lacking fruit.

2. The finest Premiers Crus all seem to come from the north bank, in

the direction of Pernand-Vergelesses. No official classification other than for Premiers Crus has been done, but the finest wines consistently come from Aux Serpentières, Aux Guettes, and Les Lavières. The only southern hillside vineyard that rivals these is La Dominode, which sits midway up the slope in the direction of Beaune. The very best wines of the appellation are the Hospices de Beaune-Cuvée Arthur Girard, Bruno Clair's Savigny-Lès-Beaune La Dominode, Simon Bize's Savigny-Lès-Beaune aux Guettes, and Machard de Gramont's Savigny-Lès-Beaune Les Guettes. Ironically, these wines, with the exception of Bize's, are made by producers outside Savigny.

3. The white wine from Savigny, constituting only 4,000–4,500 cases (less than 5% of the total output), can be surprisingly good, contrary to its poor reputation. Pierre Labet, the proprietor of Château de la Tour in Vougeot, produces 150 cases of splendidly rich, barrel-fermented Chardonnay that shares much in common with Corton-Charlemagne. The same can be said for the white Savigny from Machard de Gramont. Maurice Ecard produces a barrel-fermented, delicious white Savigny from 100% Pinot Blanc.

Where are the values? Virtually any of the recommended producers' wines sell for under $25 a bottle, making them a notable bargain for Pinot Noir. Doudet-Naudin white Savigny from the Redrescul vineyard is reported to be capable of 10–15 years of evolution.

Most successful recent vintages: 1989, 1988, 1987, 1985, 1980

Aging Potential: Premiers Crus—4 to 10 years; White wines—3 to 7 years; Villages wines—2 to 5 years

SAVIGNY-LÈS-BEAUNE

(Where pleasure is more important than prestige)

If one takes the famed A-6 superhighway south from Paris past Chablis, the first great vista one has of Burgundy is a full view of Savigny-Lès-Beaune sitting in a valley, dwarfed by the two hillsides that loom over it. While the village is far down the hierarchy in terms of reputation, it does make very competent wines, and the top growers produce wines that offer good value. Additionally, the village itself makes a worthy detour for anyone visiting the region.

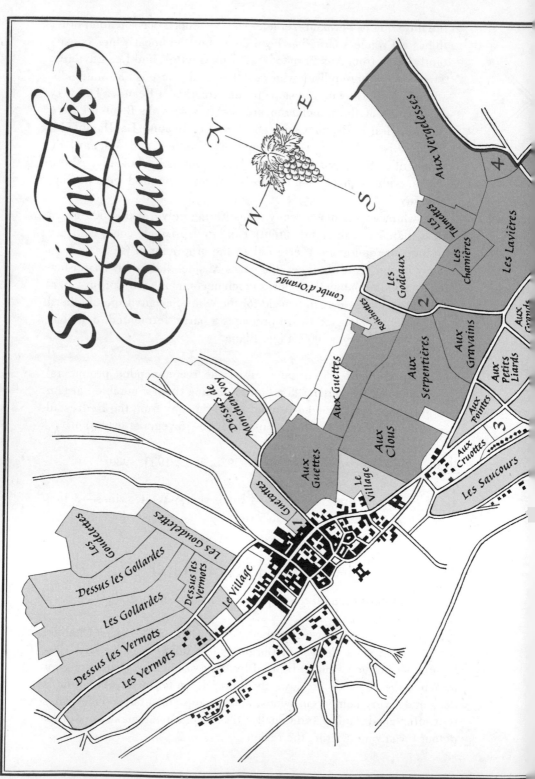

Savigny-lès-Beaune

Aux Vergelesses

Les Talmettes

Les Chamières

Les Lavières

Aux Grands

Aux Petits Liards

Aux Pointes

Les Godeaux

Aux Gravains

Aux Serpentières

Combe d'Orange

Rotchottes

Aux Guettes

Aux Clous

Aux Cruottes

Les Saucours

Dessus de Montchenevoy

Aux Guettes

Le Village

Guettotes

Les Goudelettes

Les Goulettes

Dessus les Vermots

Le Village

Les Gollardes

Dessus les Gollardes

Dessus les Vermots

Les Vermots

1

2

3

4

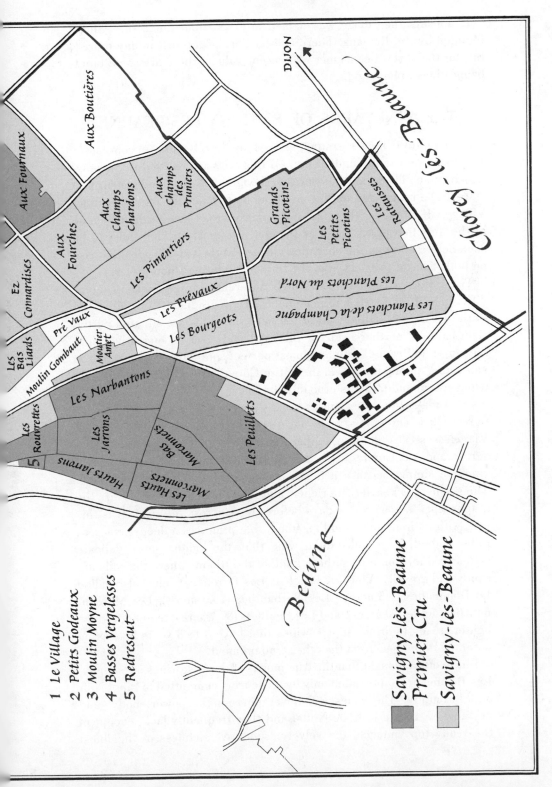

DIJON

Chorey-lès-Beaune

Aux Boutières

Aux Fournaux

Aux Champs des Pruniers

Aux Champs Chardons

Aux Fourches

Les Pimentiers

Grands Picotins

Les Petits Picotins

Les Ratausses

Ez Connardises

Les Prévaux

Les Planchots du Nord

Pré Vaux

Les Bourgeots

Les Planchots de la Champagne

Les Bas Liards

Moulin Gombaut

Moutier Amet

Les Narbantons

Les Rouvrettes

Les Jarrons

Bas Marconnets

Les Peuillets

Hauts Jarrons

Les Hauts Marconnets

Beaune

1 Le Village
2 Petits Godeaux
3 Moulin Moyne
4 Basses Vergelesses
5 Redrescut

Savigny-lès-Beaune
Premier Cru

Savigny-lès-Beaune

It appears the village was named after Saviniacum, a tiny village founded by the Romans. There is a lot here of interest to any tourist, but for the shrewd consumer looking for values, there are some tantalizing wines to be found.

THE VINEYARDS OF SAVIGNY-LÈS-BEAUNE

The viticultural area surrounding Savigny Les Beaune encompasses 1,343 acres currently under vine. Of this, 589 are entitled to Savigny-Lès-Beaune villages and 356 acres to Savigny-Lès-Beaune Premier Cru status. The remainder are Savigny-Côte de Beaune or Côte de Beaune-Villages. If one takes the small, well-marked road just north of Beaune in the direction of Savigny-Lès-Beaune, the most striking thing to be seen before entering the charming village are the two hillsides that rise on both sides of the road from the tiny, meandering Rhoin River.

These vineyards produce strikingly different wines, even allowing for differences in the style and personality of the producer. As I indicated in the Overview, virtually all of the best vineyards are situated on the right-hand or northern side of the road and river as one drives into Savigny-Lès-Beaune, with an almost perfect southern exposure. These vineyards, among the few in the entire Côte d'Or that have a southerly exposure, include what is probably the finest parcel (or are the producers that make the wine from its grapes simply the best?), Aux Serpentières (30.4 acres), as well as Aux Vergelesses (37 acres), Aux Vergelesses-Clos de la Bataillère (4.47 acres), Les Lavières (43.4 acres), and Aux Guettes (34.6. acres), the latter perhaps the best known vineyard simply because it is the closest Premier Cru to the village. The soil here is heavier and richer, and with the southerly exposure the grapes ripen a good 5 to 7 days before those across the road. It is this soil, with its iron, clay, and limestone, that produces a deeper colored, fuller bodied, more substantial wine than the lighter, more delicate styles produced on the southern bank of the Rhoin, where the soils are sandy and gravelly. Vineyards such as Les Jarrons, which is also called La Dominode (19.5 acres), Les Narbantons (25.5 acres), Les Marconnets (just under 20 acres), and Les Peuillets (39.7 acres) tend to produce lighter, ready-to-drink, supple wines that have 3 to 5 years less aging potential than those from the other embankment.

I have often thought that the true merits of the best wines of Savigny-Lès-Beaune are appreciated only by those truly committed to Pinot Noir and Burgundy. The wines will never possess the power, body, and perfume of the top Côte de Nuits, and they frequently lack, except in the really top vintages, the velvety, seductive richness of the finest wines of Beaune, Volnay, or even Pommard. They are always lighter, no doubt because the Premiers Crus all have probably the worst expositions of any Premier Cru vineyard in the Côte d'Or. This situation gives rise to speculation that Savigny-Lès-Beaune may not really merit any Premiers Crus, but certainly a taste of the Hospices de Beaune-Cuvée Arthur Girard, or some of the other top Savigny-Lès-Beaune, refutes this assessment.

The wines of Savigny-Lès-Beaune are favorites of those Burgundy insiders who consider value and pleasure to be more important than prestige. Most producers in Savigny simply cannot fetch top dollar for their wines, and the smarter producers have realized that the charm of a well-made Savigny is its up-front, precocious perfume of strawberry and berry fruit with a nice touch of oak, and an easy-to-understand, easy-to-appreciate palate.

Few producers have been able to pack enough flavor and body into the wines to allow them to age more than 10 years with grace, character, and charm. Those that have include the famous old-line *négociant* making wines for those with nineteenth-century taste (wines that should be tried by any serious connoisseur of Burgundy), Doudet-Naudin, whose cellars are in Savigny; the Hospices de Beaune-Cuvée Arthur Girard; and the cuvée of extremely old vines of Savigny-Lès-Dominaudes from the famous producer in the Côte de Nuits, Bruno Clair of Marsannay.

One wine that seems more akin to generic red burgundy and at its best is no better than Côte de Beaune-Villages is that from Savigny-Lès-Beaune entitled to the Villages appellation. Virtually all of these vineyards are on the flat plains between the Route du Vin and the village. As soon as one starts up the road leading to Savigny, the vineyards are all Premiers Crus. A walk through the vineyards in the flatlands shows extremely rich, deep soil that easily retains moisture. The yields from these vineyards are often too excessive to obtain concentration and character in the wines.

There is a tiny quantity of high-quality white wine made in Savigny-Lès-Beaune. The best I have tasted comes from the barrel-fermented Chardonnay of Pierre Labet, more renowned as the proprietor of the famous Château de la Tour in Clos Vougeot. If you want a white burgundy that will last for 20 or more years you should try Doudet-Naudin's Savigny-Lès-Beaune Redrescul, a remarkable wine that has a timeless quality to it. It is hard to believe how well this wine ages and fills out. It has never become very fashionable, so shrewd consumers should take note—it always sells at a reasonable price but it will most likely last for several decades.

In conclusion, it is probably best to think of Savigny-Lès-Beaune as a wine that fills an important void—one that offers decent red or white burgundy for a fair price. Let no one tell you that Savigny is compelling or profound, but be equally suspicious of those who claim that it has little merit.

VISITING THE VILLAGE OF SAVIGNY-LÈS-BEAUNE AND ITS PRODUCERS

I doubt that anyone will be disappointed making the 5-minute car ride from Beaune to Savigny. There are a number of interesting buildings, including several châteaux. The most interesting one dates from the fourteenth century. A smaller one is referred to by the locals as *le petit château*. There is also a Romanesque clock tower, and the charming church of St.-Cassien.

There are a number of interesting producers located in Savigny that are associated with other appellations as well. For those who believe that burgundy should not have to be drunk within its first decade of life, an obligatory stop must certainly be the cellars of Doudet-Naudin. Monsieur Doudet, who speaks impeccable English, will lead any visitor on a fascinating tour through his incredible cellars, and no doubt recount the story of the library cellar, which was walled up during the German occupation and never discovered by the Nazis. It contains bottles that are over 100 years old, and resembles a smaller-sized version of the famous library of Mouton-Rothschild in Bordeaux. Another interesting place to visit because of the impressive manor house (or is it a château?) and grounds is the Domaine Chandon de Briailles. This estate is probably better known for its excellent wines from Aloxe-Corton, but they are located in downtown Savigny-Lès-Beaune and are well worth a visit. One might try to buy some of their rare Corton Blanc, a splendidly concentrated, barrel-fermented Chardonnay that is rarely seen in the export markets.

There are also several growers worth visiting. Monsieur Ecard is located in town, and makes some of the best examples of textbook Savigny, both red and white (although his white is made from Pinot Blanc, not Chardonnay). There is also Simon Bize, who has always been one of the benchmark producers for Savigny-Lès-Beaune, as well as Pierre Guillemot, whose Savigny Les Serpentières is clearly one of the standard-bearers for the appellation.

As for dining and lodging, only one place can be recommended, the 22-room l'Ouvrée on the road to Bouilland. This modestly equipped hotel serves competent, sometimes very good food at reasonable prices.

It has one additional virtue. Its proprietor is also a vineyard owner, and he serves his own Savigny-Lès-Beaune at modest prices. Another virtue of staying in Savigny-Lès-Beaune is its close proximity to Beaune. At night this is one of the quietest villages in all the Côte d'Or.

For exceptional cuisine as well as comfortable lodging, I highly recommend the Hostellerie du Vieux Moulin, located in Bouilland, a quiet village of 136 farmers, 7 miles farther west. The cooking of Monsieur Silva, the young chef, is as inspired as it is brilliant. This is one of my favorite restaurants in Burgundy. The wine list is also breathtaking. The attached hotel has 11 rooms, costing $70–$120 per night.

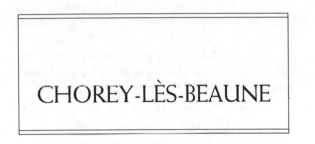

CHOREY-LÈS-BEAUNE

An Overview

Location: The largely forgotten village of Chorey-Lès-Beaune (503 inhabitants) is several minutes by car from Beaune, bounded on the south by the high-speed Paris/Lyon Autoroute A6, and by Ladoix-Serrigny to the north. The vineyards, generally spread over a flat, sandy, stony soil east of N 74 with a few parcels on the preferred, or western side of the road, are the source for some pleasant, straightforward red wines that are attractively priced.

Acres under vine: 320 acres, but this is subject to expansion as there has never been an official delineation of the appellation borders.
   Grands Crus: none
   Premiers Crus: none
   Villages Wines: 320 acres

Grands Crus: None

Premiers Crus: None

Price levels: $8–$16. Only La Maison Leroy has the courage to charge more for a bottle.

General wine characteristics: At their best these are soft, fruity, light
   wines filled with scents and flavors of strawberries and cherries.
   These are wines to drink young when they are fresh and exuberant.

The most overrated producers: None

The best producers and their wines:
                    Domaine Arnoux: Chorey-Lès-Beaune
              Capitain-Gagnerot: Chorey-Lès-Beaune
                   Edmond Cornu: Chorey-Lès-Beaune
                       Gay Père: Chorey-Lès-Beaune
      Domaine Jacques Germain: Chorey-Lès-Beaune-Château de
                                Chorey
                          Leroy: Chorey-Lès-Beaune
        Machard de Gramont: Chorey-Lès-Beaune Les Beaumonts
   Domaine Maillard Père et Fils: Chorey-Lès-Beaune
                  André Nudant: Chorey-Lès-Beaune
                  Daniel Senard: Chorey-Lès-Beaune
                   Tollot-Beaut: Chorey-Lès-Beaune

Some important observations:
1. The wines from the above producers in a top year such as 1989,
   1988, or 1985 are truly fine bargains.
2. While there are no Grands Crus or Premiers Crus in Chorey-Lès-
   Beaune, there are some respected *lieux-dits* (place names) that produce the best wines. Some of these *lieux-dits* are frequently indicated on the label. On the southern, Beaune side of Chorey-Lès-
   Beaune, there are Aux Clous and Les Crais, on the northern border
   with Ladoix there are Les Bons Ores and Les Champs Longs, and
   on the western side of Route Nationale 74 there is Les Beaumonts.
3. Drink your Chorey-Lès-Beaune within 3–4 years of the vintage.

Where are the values? All the wines from the recommended producers
   in good years are irrefutable bargains.

Most successful recent vintages: 1989, 1988, 1985

Aging Potential: Villages wines—2 to 4 years, seldom longer

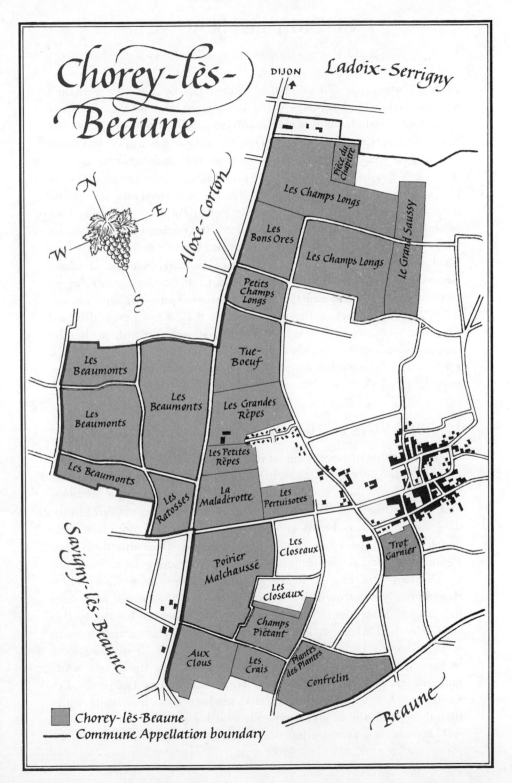

Chorey-lès-Beaune

DIJON

Ladoix-Serrigny

Aloxe-Corton

Pièce du Chapitre

Les Champs Longs

Le Grand Saussy

Les Bons Ores

Les Champs Longs

Petits Champs Longs

Tue-Boeuf

Les Beaumonts

Les Beaumonts

Les Beaumonts

Les Grandes Rêpes

Les Beaumonts

Les Petites Rêpes

Les Ratosses

La Maladerotte

Les Pertuisotes

Savigny-lès-Beaune

Les Closeaux

Trot Garnier

Poirier Malchaussé

Les Closeaux

Champs Piétant

Aux Clous

Les Crais

Plantes des Plantes

Confrelin

Beaune

Chorey-lès-Beaune
Commune Appellation boundary

CHOREY-LÈS-BEAUNE

(The appellation for good values)

At first glance it would seem that Chorey-Lès-Beaune has a distinct and impossible disadvantage. This tiny village and its vineyards are located on very flat, sandy, gravelly soil east of Burgundy's famous wine road, the Route du Vin, or N 74. Traditional logic has always indicated that no fine wines are likely to be made on the eastern, or wrong side of N 74. Nevertheless, we should be grateful that there are a number of high-quality growers in Chorey-Lès-Beaune that recognize the limitations under which they work, and do not attempt to make anything more than what Mother Nature provides. By keeping their yields relatively conservative and trying to make unabashedly fruity, straightforward Pinot Noir, producers such as Domaine Arnoux, Jacques Germain, Domaine Maillard, Tollot-Beaut, Capitain-Gagnerot, Edmond Cornu, André Nudant and the Maison Leroy all succeed, in an intentionally low-brow way, in turning out a wine that, if not a great drinking experience, is, nevertheless, a pleasant, straightforward, authentic-tasting Pinot Noir for which one does not have to hock the family jewels. Furthermore, since it has no pretentions, it can be gulped with pleasure in its first 2–3 years of life.

THE VINEYARDS OF CHOREY-LÈS-BEAUNE

There is nothing distinctive about the vineyards of Chorey-Lès-Beaune. It is one of the only appellations in the Côte d'Or to possess no Premiers Crus. There are three general zones of soil that exert a major influence on the resulting wines. The vineyards that lie to the west of N 74 in the direction of Savigny-Lès-Beaune are on soil that has more limestone and iron in it. The wines from the most famous *lieux-dits* there, Les Beaumonts, tend to be sterner, with more body and colors. Since one usually looks for charm, lightness, and freshness in a Chorey-Lès-Beaune the wines from this section are atypical. For wines with more flattering characteristics, the best come from the sandy, stony, thin soils near the Ladoix-Serrigny border. This area includes the *lieux-dits* of Les Champs Longs and Les Bons Ores. South of Chorey, adjacent to France's famed A6 autoroute between Paris and Lyon, is a white marl and gravel subsoil with several *lieux-dits*, such as Aux Clous, Les Crais, and Les Champs Pietant, that produce lean, less fruity wines than those from the sandy, stony soils near Ladoix.

There are two famous domaines with their cellars in Chorey-Lès-

Beaune. One is Tollot-Beaut, one of the first small producers to estate-bottle their wines. Americans first became aware of this domaine when it was discovered by the late Frank Schoonmaker. The other is the Domaine Jacques Germain, which produces extremely stylish wines from not only Chorey-Lès-Beaune but also from the surrounding appellations of Beaune and Ladoix.

VISITING THE VILLAGE OF CHOREY-LÈS-BEAUNE AND ITS PRODUCERS

Given Chorey-Lès-Beaune's close proximity to N 74 and the fact that it is only several minutes from downtown Beaune, this is an easy village to visit. Usually the only purpose one has in visiting here is to see Jacques Germain, Tollot-Beaut, or some of the other growers whose wines may have interested you.

For architectural buffs there is a seventeenth-century château with several towers that are of interest, as well as the ruins of an old fortress. The locals claim there have been a number of excavations revealing Gallo-Roman artifacts, suggesting this was once a thriving hamlet during the Roman occupation of what was then known as Gaul.

Most people who visit Chorey-Lès-Beaune probably stay in Beaune, but right on N 74 there is the lavish, somewhat oppressively decorated Ermitage de Corton of André Parra. One can be assured of eating sumptuously and expansively, but the decor reminds me of a bad nightmare. Nevertheless, the food is to be taken seriously, and from what I have been told, the 5 rooms and 5 apartments are splendidly decorated and quite comfortable. However, they are very expensive. Another restaurant in the village is the Bareuzai. Despite its mention in the Guide Michelin, I have had nothing but unsuccessful meals there.

BEAUNE

An Overview

Location: Beaune, the capital and heart of Burgundy, is 192 miles south of Paris, only 26 miles south of Dijon, and the gateway to the Côte d'Or. It is a fascinating walled city that houses 21,127 people (Les Beaunois), most of them in the wine or tourism business. Filled with historic buildings, excellent restaurants, hotels, and wine shops, Beaune is one of France's most visited and admired small medieval cities.

Acres under vine: 1,617 acres, of which 95% is planted in Pinot Noir and the balance in Chardonnay
   Grands Crus: None
   Premiers Crus: 795 acres
   Villages Wines: 310 acres of Appellation Beaune, the balance
                 being entitled to the Côte de Beaune-Villages
                 appellation

Grands Crus: None

Principal Premiers Crus: A total of 28 principal Premiers Crus
   Les Boucherottes, Les Chouacheux, Les Epenottes, Le Clos des Mouches, Les Montrevenots, Les Vignes Franches, Pertuisots, Les Aigrots, Les Sizies, Clos Landry, Les Avaux, Champs Pimont, Le Clos de la Mousse, Les Reversées, Blanche Fleur, Clos du Roi, Les Fèvres, Les Cents Vignes, Les Bressandes, Les Toussaints, Les Marconnets, En Genêt, Les Perrières, Les Grèves, Aux Coucherias, Les Teurons, Montée Rouge, La Mignotte

Price levels: Most Beaune Premiers Crus sell for $20–$40 a bottle, making them among the most reasonably priced Premiers Crus of Burgundy. The Villages wines sell for $18–$30 a bottle.

General wine characteristics: The red wines, which account for well
over 95% of this appellation's production, are less earthy, spicy,
and meaty than those from the Côte de Nuits. Their primary
traits, when well made and from the best vintages, are an intense
bouquet of berry fruit, principally black cherries and strawberries. The wines are rarely massive or large scaled, relying more
on their smooth, silky, berry fruitiness and harmony to seduce
tasters than on pure power and bulk. The tiny production of white
wine is more difficult to describe, but the best example, Drouhin's
Clos des Mouches, is not unlike a rich, nutty, buttery Meursault.

The most overrated producers: Albert Bichot, Bouchard Père et Fils,
Patriarche Père et Fils

The best producers and their wines:

Robert Ampeau: Beaune-Clos du Roi
Besancenot-Mathouillet: Beaune-Clos du Roi, Beaune Les Cents
Vignes, Beaune Les Teurons, Beaune Les
Grèves, Beaune Les Bressandes
Bouchard Père et Fils: Beaune-Clos de la Mousse, Beaune Les
Grèves (l'Enfant Jésus)
Jean-Marc Bouley: Beaune Les Reversées
Bourée: Beaune Les Epenottes
Champy Père: Beaune Les Avaux, Beaune-Clos des
Mouches
Chanson: Beaune-Clos des Fèves, Beaune-Clos des
Marconnets, Beaune-Clos du Roi
Joseph Drouhin: Beaune-Clos des Mouches, Beaune Les
Grèves
Faiveley: Beaune Les Champs Pimont
Bernard Fevre: Beaune Les Epenottes, Beaune Les
Montremenots
Jacques Germain: Beaune Les Boucherottes, Beaune Les
Teurons, Beaune Les Vignes-Franches
Machard de Gramont: Beaune Les Chouacheux, Beaune Les
Epenottes
Hospices de Beaune: Beaune-Cuvée Nicholas Rolin, Beaune-
Cuvée Maurice Drouhin, Beaune-Cuvée Clos
des Avaux, Beaune-Guigone de Salins,
Beaune-Cuvée Brunet, Beaune-Cuvée
Hughes et Louis Bétault, Beaune-Cuvée
Dames Hospitalières, Beaune Rousseau
Deslandes

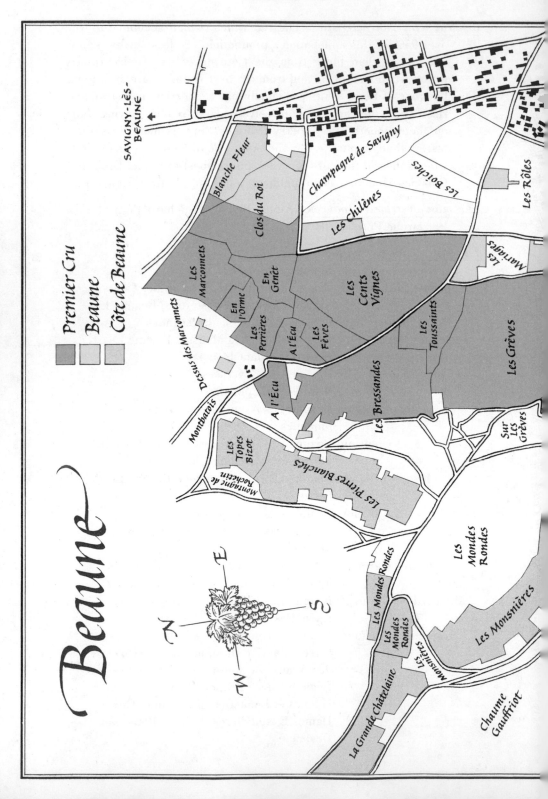

Beaune

Premier Cru
Beaune
Côte de Beaune

SAVIGNY-LÈS-BEAUNE

Blanche Fleur
Clos du Roi
Champagne de Savigny
Les Chilènes
Les Botches
Les Rôles
Les Marconnets
En Genêt
Les Mariages
Les Cents Vignes
Dessus des Marconnets
En l'Orme
Les Perrières
A l'Écu
Les Fèves
Les Toussaints
Les Grèves
Montbatois
A l'Écu
Les Bressandes
Sur Les Grèves
Les Topes Bizot
Montagne de Rochetin
Les Pierres Blanches
Les Mondes Rondes
Les Mondes Rondes
Les Mondes Rondes
Monsnières
Les Monsnières
La Grande Châtelaine
Chaume Gaufriot

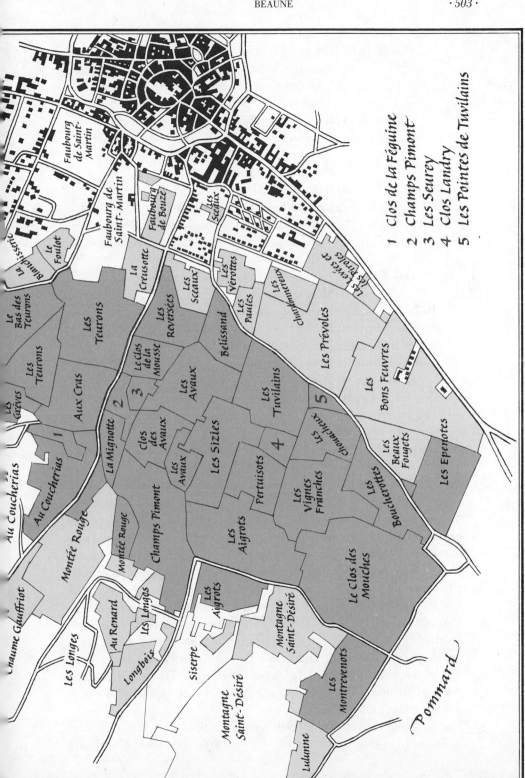

1 Clos de la Féguine
2 Champs Pimont
3 Les Seurey
4 Clos Landry
5 Les Pointes de Tuvilains

Jaboulet-Verchere: Beaune-Clos de l'Écu

Louis Jadot: Beaune-Clos des Ursules, Beaune Les
Teurons, Beaune Les Boucherottes, Beaune-
Clos des Couchereaux, Beaune Les Cents
Vignes

Louis Latour: Beaune Les Vignes-Franches

Leroy: Beaune Les Grèves, Beaune Les Coucherias,
Beaune La Mignotte, Beaune Les Perrières,
Beaune Les Sizies

Domaine Maillard: Beaune Les Grèves

Albert Morot: Beaune Les Marconnets, Beaune Les Cents
Vignes, Beaune Les Bressandes, Beaune Les
Toussaints, Beaune Les Grèves, Beaune Les
Teurons

André Mussy: Beaune Les Epenottes, Beaune Les
Montremenots

Domaine Parent: Beaune Les Epenottes

Pothier-Rieusset: Beaune Les Boucherottes

Prieur-Brunet: Beaune Clos du Roi

Michel Prunier: Beaune Les Sizies

Remoissenet: Beaune Les Marconnets

Tollot-Beaut: Beaune Les Grèves

Some important observations:

1. For reasons that escape me, the finest Premiers Crus of Beaune
   have never engendered the same degree of enthusiasm from consumers that other Côte d'Or appellations enjoy. This state of affairs
   can be put to the consumer's advantage, as there are numerous top-
   quality wines made from Beaune's best vineyards, and they are
   priced below the Premiers Crus of Beaune's nearby neighbors, Pommard and Volnay.

2. Much of the Beaune wine trade is dominated by the large *négociants*
   who have their cellars spread out below the city. Some *négociants*
   are open to tourists and actively promote their wines. Firms such as
   Patriarche and La Reine Pedauque produce indifferent wines, but
   are highly visible in Beaune. Distinguished houses such as Louis
   Jadot, Joseph Drouhin, and Louis Latour are all in Beaune, their
   cellars marked only by small plaques on the wall. They each produce
   some of Beaune's most notable red wines, yet they maintain a surprisingly low profile.

3. For the longest-lived Premiers Crus of Beaune, the wines of Mademoiselle Choppin, who trades under the name of Albert Morot, are

worthy of any conscientiously stocked cellar. Her wines frequently
need 5–6 years of age. When many other Beaune Premiers Crus are
beginning to fade, hers blossom and seem timeless, often lasting for
2 to 3 decades.

4. Beaune has no Grands Crus, but such vineyards as Les Epenottes
and Le Clos des Mouches (both adjacent to the Premiers Crus of
Pommard), Les Grèves, Les Bressandes, Les Cents Vignes, Clos du
Roi, and Les Marconnets (all behind and to the northwest of
Beaune), and finally Les Avaux and Les Sizies (southwest of the
town) are consistently top sources for excellent red wine.

5. The cuvées made from the holdings of the Hospices de Beaune are
uniformly excellent to outstanding, but lamentably sell at prices 2 to
4 times higher than the other Premiers Crus. They are also much
more marked by new oak, as the Hospices de Beaune believes in the
use of 100% new oak casks.

Where are the values? Consider the wines of Albert Morot, Besancenot-
   Mathouillet, Louis Jadot, Tollot-Beaut, Machard de Gramont, and
   Michel Prunier.

Most successful recent vintages: 1989, 1988, 1985, 1982, 1978

Aging Potential: Premiers Crus—4 to 10 years; Villages wines—2 to 6
   years

BEAUNE

(The heart and soul of Burgundy's Côte d'Or)

The medieval town of Beaune, which is encircled by ramparts, is best
approached from the north via N 74, the famous Route du Vin that runs
from Beaune to Dijon. The urban sprawl that has afflicted Beaune over
the last decade is less pronounced to the north, and the view of the
ramparts is spectacular. What's more, Port St.-Nicolas is the most
impressive gate of arrival into this hallowed city.

Even if Beaune were not the capital of Burgundy and the heart of the
Côte d'Or, it would be a mecca for tourists given its charm, quaint
streets, and excellent hotels and restaurants. The town itself was once
a Roman encampment and dates from 52 B.C. There is some conflict as
to where the actual name of Beaune came from, but Dutchman Hubrecht Duijker suggests that the name came from the word "Belen,"

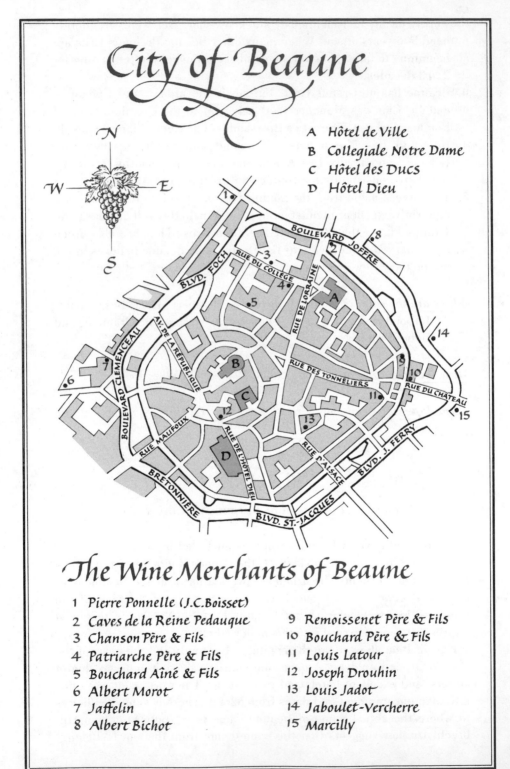

City of Beaune

A Hôtel de Ville
B Collegiale Notre Dame
C Hôtel des Ducs
D Hôtel Dieu

The Wine Merchants of Beaune

1 Pierre Ponnelle (J.C.Boisset)
2 Caves de la Reine Pedauque
3 Chanson Père & Fils
4 Patriarche Père & Fils
5 Bouchard Aîné & Fils
6 Albert Morot
7 Jaffelin
8 Albert Bichot

9 Remoissenet Père & Fils
10 Bouchard Père & Fils
11 Louis Latour
12 Joseph Drouhin
13 Louis Jadot
14 Jaboulet-Vercherre
15 Marcilly

the god of the Gauls, or that it is a debasement of the word "Belisana," a name for the goddess Minerva, or from the word "Belna," meaning a small villa. However, it was the ducs of Burgundy who brought Beaune its riches and fame: It became their favorite residence and obtained a position of strategic importance in the numerous power struggles that afflicted Europe during the Middle Ages.

Today, no one can visit Beaune without acquiring a bit of knowledge about the wines of the region. The city itself sits on an underground network of catacombed passages and wine cellars owned by the most influential of Burgundy's *négociants*. Many of them have also constructed large, modern bottling operations in one of Beaune's suburbs. A casual walk through the streets of Beaune will reveal the businesses of Albert Bichot, Bouchard Aîné, Bouchard Père et Fils, Champy Père (now owned by Louis Jadot), Chanson Père, Joseph Drouhin, Jaboulet-Vercherre, Louis Jadot, Jaffelin, Louis Latour, Coron, P. De Marcilly Frères, Patriarche Père et Fils, Pierre Ponnelle (owned by Jean-Claude Boisset), La Reine Pedauque, and Remoissenet Père et Fils. The gentlemen who run these prestigious firms are the principal movers and shakers of Burgundy. They are as responsible as anyone for controlling the marketplace as well as Burgundy's image today.

Beaune's biggest annual event (some would say it is even more important than the harvest itself) is the 3-day festival held the third weekend of November. It is called Trois Glorieuses. During this weekend no motorized traffic is allowed within the city walls. The population of Beaune triples as tourists, journalists, and wine buyers descend on the city to taste the new vintage and to partake in an array of feasts and festivities that would have made Rabelais proud. The festivities begin with a 6-hour eating and drinking marathon, held at the Château of Clos Vougeot by the Confrérie des Chevaliers du Tastevin de Clos Vougeot, and concludes on Monday with the famous luncheon called the Paulée, in Meursault. A healthy stomach and liver are necessary to survive the entire weekend. The weekend's most significant event is the world's most famous wine auction, Sunday's Hospices de Beaune sale. This sale raises money for local hospitals by offering the various cuvées of wine that are made from those vineyards owned by the Hospices de Beaune. Buyers from all over the world participate, and the prices fetched for the Hospices de Beaune *cuvées* frequently serve as a valid barometer for the pricing to be established for the newest vintage. The entire sale, which normally requires 6–7 hours to complete, is a huge media event in France, covered by all that country's television stations. While regular participants may have a tendency to become blasé about this extraordinary weekend, from my perspective, the Trois Glorieuses is the greatest drinking and eating experience on the face of this planet.

Between 15,000 and 17,000 cases of wine are sold at the Hospices de Beaune, but it is the other vineyards of Beaune, producing over 220,000 cases of wine in an abundant vintage, that most consumers are more likely to encounter. Over 95% of the wine production from Beaune is red, with only a tiny quantity of white wine being produced. The best white wine has always been Joseph Drouhin's Beaune-Clos des Mouches.

THE VINEYARDS OF BEAUNE

Perhaps the best way to take in the panoramic view of the vineyards of Beaune, which sit to the west behind the town, spread over several hillsides, is to take a car ride in the direction of Montagne de Beaune and Bouze Les Beaune. From the high ground, a look backward at the ocean of vines is spectacular. Impressively, nearly half of the vineyards surrounding the village of Beaune are entitled to Premier Cru status. While one might lament the fact that there are no Grands Crus, this is an impressive percentage of high-quality vineyard land. Consequently, there is a significant amount of wine emerging from the nearly 800 acres of Premier Cru vineyards.

Conventional wisdom has it that the Premier Cru vineyards to the south of Beaune, touching the border of Pommard, are primarily planted on lighter, thinner soil, and produce quick-maturing, softer, more elegant and graceful wines. The top vineyards that sit to the northwest of the city, in the direction of Savigny-Lès-Beaune, produce the appellation's firmest, fullest, deepest-colored, and richest wines. While this generalization is viable, the fact remains that the style of an individual producer or grower can frequently shape the personality of the wine more than the actual *terroir* of the vineyard.

Not surprisingly, most of the Premier Cru vineyards of Beaune are controlled by *négociants*. This has caused some to suggest that Beaune wines lack the great individuality and character of those wines from appellations that have a higher number of growers willing to estate-bottle their wines. I do not agree with this, although there is no doubting there is a lot of Beaune Premier Cru on the market from famous names that is unexciting, overproduced wine. However, taste a top Premier Cru from the likes of Louis Jadot, Joseph Drouhin, or Leroy, and you are likely to be getting a Beaune that is filled with individual character, and is as well made as the finest wines from the top growers who estate-bottle.

All the best Premier Cru vineyards are on argillo-calcareous soil and generally sit near the top of the slopes west of the town. The most

significant vineyards in the north, near Savigny-Lès-Beaune, include
Les Cents Vignes (58 acres), which offers one of Beaune's most forceful, concentrated and richest wines, and Les Grèves (77 acres), producing at its best a supple, explosively cherry-scented, luscious wine that
usually must be drunk within a decade of the vintage. Two other highly
renowned vineyards are Les Bressandes (39.52 acres), tucked away on
one of the higher slopes to the north of the village, and Les Clos des
Mouches (62 acres), primarily owned by Joseph Drouhin, which is recognized as the source for not only wonderfully light, delicate, graceful
red wines, but Beaune's finest white wine. Other producers have small
parcels in the Clos des Mouches, including Chanson, Giradin, and
Louis Jadot, who recently acquired the parcel formerly owned by
Champy Père et Fils. To the south of the village, near Clos des
Mouches, lies the excellent Les Sizies (19.76 acres), and slightly further
up the hill, adjacent to Les Sizies, sits Les Champs Pimonts (43 acres).
Two of my favorite vineyards, both adjacent to the appellation of Pommard, are Les Boucherottes (19.76 acres) and Les Epenottes (19 acres),
each capable of producing gloriously fragrant, supple, easy-to-drink
Beaune wines.

The appellation of Beaune is renowned for tiny parcels called *clos*, or
walled vineyards, which are often part of a larger vineyard. Perhaps
the most famous is the Clos des Ursules, which is entirely owned by
the famous house of Louis Jadot. This 6.17-acre parcel, located within
the larger Premier Cru of Les Vignes-Franches, is situated near both
Les Boucherottes and Le Clos des Mouches. It produces stunningly
graceful, flavor-filled wines that drink well young, yet have the cunning
ability to age well for up to two decades, and sometimes longer. In
addition to the Clos des Ursules, there is the Clos des Marconnets, a
9.2-acre parcel owned entirely by Chanson, producing one of that firm's
fullest-bodied and most interesting wines. Another famous clos is the
Clos du Roi, located in the very northern section of the Beaune appellation in the direction of Savigny-Lès-Beaune and bordered on the west
by Les Marconnets. This is a beautifully situated 34.5-acre parcel and
domaines such as Tollot-Beaut, Robert Ampeau, and Prieur Brunet
produce excellent wines from their holdings. There is also the Clos des
Couchereaux, a tiny 5-acre parcel primarily owned by Louis Jadot. The
famous and wealthy firm of Bouchard Père et Fils produces one of their
few interesting and exciting wines, Beaune Clos de la Mousse, from an
8.3-acre parcel situated right in the middle of the Beaune appellation.
One of the most famous cuvées is the Clos des Avaux, the nearly 5-acre
parcel owned by the Hospices de Beaune that produces a wine with
splendid concentration and often magnificent perfume.

The other clos among the Premiers Crus of Beaune are the Clos de la Féguine, a 4.9-acre parcel that frequently renders one of the best wines from the Domaine Prieur in Meursault, and the Clos des Fèvres, a 9.2-acre parcel exclusively owned by Chanson that produces one of their best wines.

VISITING THE VILLAGE OF BEAUNE AND ITS PRODUCERS

Every visitor to France should try to spend at least a day, preferably several days, in the elegant, medieval town of Beaune. If you are reluctant to make the 3- to 4-hour drive from Paris, France's high-speed train, called the TGV (which runs almost hourly from the Gare de Lyon), can put you in Beaune in less than 2 hours. The real city of Beaune starts inside the ring of ramparts. It is exhilarating just to walk on Beaune's cobblestone streets with their narrow, dignified buildings that give one the feeling that not much has changed since Beaune's most famous resident, Nicholas Rolin, passed away in 1443. It was Rolin who decreed that all his possessions be sold to build a hospital to provide for the impoverished residents of Beaune. That hospital, the Hôtel Dieu, was completed in 1451.

The Hôtel Dieu is Beaune's most magnificent building and the top tourist attraction of the city. It is situated adjacent to Beaune's most famous square, the Place Carnot. A guided tour of the now defunct hospital takes about an hour, but it is well worth it for observing the medieval facilities, the pharmacy, the kitchen, and of course, the Flemish painter Van der Weyden's "Last Judgment."

Other significant tourist sites include the Hôtel de Ville, at one time an Ursuline convent, the Church of Nôtre Dame, a beautiful Romanesque building, and the fourteenth-century bell tower. Of course, just walking around the ramparts and the medieval streets gives one the feeling that Beaune has always been a remarkably wealthy city patronized by those who appreciated the finest in art, architecture, and wine.

Once you have done the obligatory touring it is time to visit your favorite producer/négociant. Many négociants are open to the public, but those such as Joseph Drouhin, Remoissenet, Louis Jadot, Louis Latour, and Bouchard Père et Fils require an appointment. Whichever négociant you visit, be sure to request a subterranean tour of the remarkable caves beneath the streets of Beaune.

Beaune is filled with some of the most satisfying hotels and restaurants in Burgundy, and makes a great touring base provided you can find a parking spot for your car. If you plan to stay in Beaune, I would highly recommend the Hôtel de la Poste, located on the so-called belt-way, or *périphérique*, that encircles Beaune just adjacent to the road leading out of Beaune to Pommard and Meursault. There is also the newly renovated, outstanding Le Cep, with its excellent restaurant called Bernard Morillon. In addition, there are a handful of hotels just outside the ramparts that offer less difficulty with respect to automobile parking. The new Henry II is located on the road to Dijon, just outside the ramparts, facing the Port St.-Nicolas. On the road to Pommard are the Samôtel and La Closerie. Both have good parking facilities, and the Samôtel has the added advantage of abutting Beaune's vineyards.

With respect to dining, I have already mentioned the outstanding cuisine of Bernard Morillon of the Auberge Le Cep. I have also had consistently excellent meals at Relais de Saulx, the Rôtisserie La Paix, and l'Ecusson. Two places where I have had disappointing meals more than once are Auberge St.-Vincent and Jacques Lainé. For value, you cannot beat the excellent food available at the Central Hôtel, which houses a small restaurant just adjacent to the Place Carnot. If you want to throw caution to the wind and spend plenty of money, but be re-warded with superb cuisine and the most lavish setting in the Côte d'Or, then make the 4-mile trip to Levernois (in the direction of the autoroute) for a meal at Jean Crotet's Hostellerie de Levernois. Long-time visitors to Burgundy will remember that he was the chef and inspiration behind the excellent restaurant, Le Côte d'Or, in Nuits St.-Georges.

Just to the north of Beaune in the direction of Dijon (about 10 minutes outside of town) is the Ermitage de Corton. Monsieur Parra runs this garish, ostentatious restaurant that looks more like a French house of ill repute. Don't underestimate the rather heavy yet rich, well-prepared cooking, however, which is classic and satisfying.

Beaune is to Burgundy what the city of Bordeaux is to that region—the heart and soul, as well as the capital of one of the world's most renowned winemaking regions. While there is no doubting the appeal of visiting your favorite growers or *négociants*, do not neglect the city itself. You will never regret it.

POMMARD

An Overview

Location: Several miles south of Beaune (be sure to take the right-hand fork of N 73, marked Autun) is the bustling village of Pommard, with a population of 626.

Acres under vine: A total of 1,655 acres—all of it Pinot Noir
    Grands Crus: none
  Premiers Crus: 309.2 acres
  Villages Wines: 528 acres of Appellation Pommard; the balance
             is Côte de Beaune-Villages

Grands Crus: None

Principal Premiers Crus: A total of 27
    La Chanière, Les Charmots, La Platière, Les Arvelets, Les Saussilles, Les Pézerolles, En Largillière, Les Grands Epenots, Clos des Epeneaux, Les Petits Epenots, Les Boucherottes, Clos Micot, Les Combes-Dessus, La Refène, Clos de la Verger, Clos de la Commaraine, Clos Blanc, Village, Derrière St.-Jean, Les Chaponnières, Les Croix Noires, Les Poutures, Les Bertins, Les Fremièrs, Les Jarolières, Les Rugiens, Les Chanlins

Price levels: $25–$45 for Pommard Premiers Crus, $20–$30 for Pommard Villages wines.

General wine characteristics: Pommard at its best is the fullest wine made in the Côte de Beaune. Less tannic but fatter than Corton, it is soft as well as concentrated, with a big, heady perfume. It could not be more different from its elegant, charming, suave neighbor to the south, Volnay, or the pretty, feminine, soft Beaune red wines to the north. While maligned in many circles as too coarse, too alcoholic and obvious, Pommard from the finest grow-

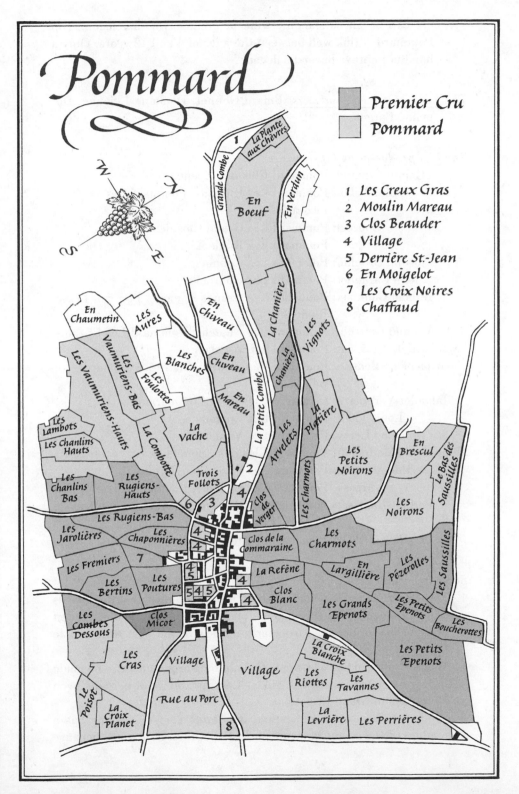

Pommard

Premier Cru
Pommard

1 Les Creux Gras
2 Moulin Mareau
3 Clos Beauder
4 Village
5 Derrière St.-Jean
6 En Moigelot
7 Les Croix Noires
8 Chaffaud

La Plante aux Chèvres
Grande Combe
En Boeuf
En Verdun
La Chanière
Les Vignots
En Chaumetin
Les Aures
En Chiveau
En Chiveau
Les Blanches
Les Foulottes
La Chanière
La Pl.tière
Les Vaumuriens-Bas
Les Vaumuriens-Hauts
En Mareau
La Petite Combe
Les Arvelets
Les Lambots
La Vache
La Combotte
Les Chanlins Hauts
Trois Follots
Les Petits Noirons
En Brescul
Le Bas des Saussilles
Les Chanlins Bas
Les Rugiens-Hauts
Les Charmots
Les Noirons
Les Rugiens-Bas
Clos de Verger
Les Jarolières
Les Chaponnières
Clos de la Commaraine
Les Charmots
Les Saussilles
Les Fremiers
En Largillière
Les Pézerolles
Les Bertins
La Refène
Les Poutures
Clos Blanc
Les Petits Epenots
Les Boucherottes
Les Combes Dessous
Clos Micot
Les Grands Epenots
Les Cras
Village
La Croix Blanche
Les Petits Epenots
Le Poisot
Village
Les Riottes
Les Tavannes
La Croix Planet
Rue au Porc
La Levrière
Les Perrières

ers can be an outstanding wine of great flavor dimension. Top Pommards drink well between the ages of 4 and 12 years. Only a handful improve beyond a decade.

The most overrated producers: Billard-Gonnet, Domaine Lejeune, Domaine Parent

The best producers and their wines:
Comte Armand: Pommard-Clos des Epeneaux
Ballot-Millot: Pommard Les Rugiens, Pommard Les Pézerolles
Courcel: Pommard Les Grand Clos des Epenots, Pommard Les Rugiens
Joseph Drouhin: Pommard Les Epenots
Jean Garaudet: Pommard Les Charmots
Michel Gaunoux: Pommard Les Grands Epenots, Pommard Les Rugiens
Armand Girardin: Pommard Les Rugiens, Pommard Les Epenots
Machard de Gramont: Pommard le Clos Blanc
Hospices de Beaune: Pommard Dames de la Charité, Pommard Billardet
Jaboulet-Vercherre: Pommard-Clos de la Commaraine
Louis Jadot: Pommard Les Epenots
Domaine Leroy: Pommard Les Vignots
Château de Meursault: Pommard-Clos des Epenots
Hubert de Montille: Pommard Les Pézerolles, Pommard Rugiens
Mussy: Pommard Les Epenots, Pommard Premier Cru
Pothier-Rieusset: Pommard Les Rugiens, Pommard-Clos des Vergers, Pommard Les Epenots
Pousse d'Or: Pommard Les Jarolièrers

Some important observations:
1. For the size of the appellation, there are far too few great Pommards being produced. Yet, this appellation still receives an undue amount of malicious criticism, particularly in view of the best wines made there.
2. While Pommard has no Grands Crus, strong arguments can be made in favor of elevating Les Rugiens, Les Epenots, and perhaps even Pézerolles to Grand Cru status.
3. While it is an oversimplification, it is often said that if one has a fondness for a good Châteauneuf-du-Pape, then Pommard, because

of its strength, ripeness, and expansive, broad flavors, should be that person's favorite Côte de Beaune.

4. As a general rule, most of the Pommards bottled by Beaune's *négociants* are to be avoided, as they rarely reflect the quality that the top estates are capable of achieving.

5. The Domaine Parent's Pommards, which were for this author a benchmark for quality in the decade of the sixties, are still good, but not nearly as profound and complex as they once were.

Where are the values? Some of the better-situated, less prestigious Premiers Crus offer considerable value. Look for the wines from the following Premier Cru vineyards: Les Boucherottes (bounded on the west by Beaune's Clos des Mouches), Clos de Verger (just north of the village), Les Charmots (situated farther up the slope above Les Grands Epenots), and Le Clos Blanc (the vineyard immediately north of the village on the right side of the road from Beaune).

Most successful recent vintages: 1989, 1988, 1987, 1985, 1980, 1979, 1978

Aging Potential: Premiers Crus—7 to 12 years; Villages wines—3 to 8 years

POMMARD

(The Côte de Beaune's most hedonistic red wine)

It is easy for the first-time visitor to the Côte de Beaune to miss the road to Pommard. Leaving Beaune, heading south on Route Nationale 74, just past the Samotel on the right, one comes to a fork in the road. The village of Pommard is a short 5-minute drive along the right hand fork, N 73, in the direction of Autun. Pommard is a sleepy, small wine village that takes its name from a Roman temple dedicated to Pomona, a goddess of fruits and gardens. There is some interesting architecture, including the famous Château de Pommard, a legitimate as well as elegant château that sits on the left just before the entrance to the village. Additionally, visitors should not miss the unusual belfry in the fifteenth-century church built in the middle of the village. But, of course, the real reason to go to Pommard is for its wines, which have always enjoyed a great deal of popularity all over the world, no doubt in part because of the easily pronounced name and the generous and heady qualities of the wine itself.

The appellation of Pommard is very large, covering over 1,600 acres. Less than 20% of that is in Premiers Crus. There are those who advise uneducated consumers simply to stay away from any bottle called Appellation Pommard Contrôlée. I believe there are some good straightforward Villages wines from a handful of conscientious producers, but in general, the odds are indeed stacked against the consumer who simply buys a bottle of Pommard at random. Most of these wines are too harsh, alcoholic, and lacking in character and finesse.

Nevertheless, at the Premier Cru level there are some outstanding wines to be found. In fact, my comprehensive tastings of all the wines of Pommard over the last decade have convinced me that the list of top growers is only half as long as it should be. Certainly there are a handful of growers ready to enter the top class, particularly when one considers such thrill-a-sip wines as Coucel's Pommard Les Rugiens, Michel Gaunoux's Pommard Les Rugiens, Mussy's Pommard Les Epenots, or a 15-year-old Pommard Les Rugiens or Pommard Les Pézerolles from the famous Hubert de Montille.

THE VINEYARDS OF POMMARD

The vineyards of Pommard are sandwiched between those of Beaune on the north and Volnay to the south. Yet, the wines from Pommard could not be more different from those of its two neighbors. If you are looking for a red wine from the Côte de Beaune that expresses elegance, lightness, and delicacy, then Pommard is not the place to go. The top Pommards are full-bodied, chunky, muscular, fleshy wines that impress one more for their power and expansive, mouthfilling texture than for pure finesse. The entire appellation sits to the west of Route Nationale 74, with many of the Villages vineyards located between N 74 and N 73, which runs right through the village. To the west of N 73 and up the slope are all the Premiers Crus, the most famous of which are Les Epenots and Les Rugiens. This hillside is composed of clay/limestone soil. It is believed that the red clay gives these wines their full body and muscular, fleshy texture.

Les Rugiens, which is divided into two sections called Hauts (high) and Bas (low), is located to the south of the village near the border of the Volnay appellation. One of the greatest red burgundies I have ever tasted was the 1949 Pommard Les Rugiens from the Domaine Pothier-Rieusset. Most of the Rugiens have a rich, robust, intense taste, and often display a pronounced peppery, spicy *gout de terroir* (earthy, soil-like taste). There are some outstanding producers of Pommard les Rugiens, including the aforementioned Pothier-Rieusset, as well as Hubert de Montille, Michel Gaunoux, and the Domaine Courcel. If Pommard ever obtains Grand Cru status for one of its vineyards, it should be Les Rugiens.

The other famous Premiers Crus vineyards that are often ranked in quality with Les Rugiens are Les Grands Epenots and Les Petits Epenots, both located on the Beaune side of the village of Pommard. These wines are slightly lighter than a Rugiens, but are by no means wimpish. There are some superbly rich, flavorful, spicy and intense wines from the Epenots vineyards made by the likes of Pommard's mayor, Armand Girardin, as well as by Joseph Drouhin, Pothier-Rieusset, Michel Gaunoux, and Domaine Courcel. Perhaps the best two wines I have ever tasted from Epenots are the Domaine Mussy Pommard Les Epenots, and the Domaine Comte Armand, whose Epenots comes from an exclusively owned clos within the Epenots vineyard called Clos des Epeneaux.

While most of the very best wines of this appellation emanate from these vineyards, some extraordinary Pommards come from the small Les Pézerolles vineyard, which sits slightly further up the slope from Epenots, just to the south of the famous Premier Cru from the Beaune appellation called Clos des Mouches. Whether I have been very fortunate or not I do not know, but I have had stunning Pommards from here made by both the Domaine Hubert de Montille and Ballot-Millot.

Other Premiers Crus vineyards to look for include the Clos Blanc, situated just north of the village to the west of Route Nationale 73. In the hands of producers such as the Machard de Gramont, wines from this vineyard can be quite stunning. Also, look for wines from the Clos de la Commaraine, a superbly situated, potentially outstanding vineyard rendering good, sometimes very good wines from the firm of Jaboulet-Vercherre. This extraordinary vineyard of 9.23 acres is a *monopole* (or solely owned) vineyard of Jaboulet-Vercherre, and is clearly the crown jewel in this firm's rather undistinguished lineup of wines. One should look for the wines from the Premiers Crus of Les Boucherottes and Clos de la Verger, made by Pothier-Rieusset, and the Pommard Les Vignots from the Domaine Leroy. This last vineyard, not a Premier Cru but a Villages wine, is located well to the north of the village. In the hands of a conscientious producer such as Madame Lalou Bize-Leroy, this vineyard has proven it can produce magnificent wine. The 1988 is simply stunning. Another excellent wine is the Domaine de Pousse d'Or Pommard Les Jarolières. While most people think of the Domaine de Pousse d'Or as one of the leading private domaines of

Volnay, their Pommard Les Jarolières, the only wine they make from this appellation, was superb in 1985 and 1978.

The most impressive estate of the entire appellation of Pommard does not produce a Premier Cru, but makes an interesting, well-structured wine for long aging. The Château de Pommard, owned by Jean-Louis Laplanche, has an entirely walled vineyard of nearly 50 acres sitting to the south of Route Nationale 73, immediately before the entrance of the village on the road from Beaune. This impressive château produces wine that, while not quite at the level of the best Premiers Crus, is clearly well above the level of a Villages wine. In fact, it is the only Villages wine that can be recommended without hesitation. Aged in 100% new oak casks, the wine is muscular and tannic. While skeptics point out that the soil on this lower, flat area of the Pommard appellation has poor drainage, there is no doubting Professor Laplanche's commitment to quality, and his ability to extract as much as he can from his vineyard.

Pommard does have numerous underachievers. As mentioned in the Overview at the beginning of this section, I cut my teeth on some extraordinarily great Pommards from the Epenots and Rugiens vineyards from the Domaine Parent in the 1960s. I remember the 1962, 1964, and 1966, which were some of the greatest burgundies I had drunk in the early seventies. Yet, this famous domaine, with its wealth of vineyards and requisite ability to make something splendid from the appellation, is now producing wines that are clearly more commercial in orientation, consequently lacking the compelling richness and profound character of their vintages in the sixties. The wines are still good, but given this domaine's historical position, and its traditional leadership of the appellation, they are not up to the quality of the top wines from Pommard's best producers. Two other domaines that produce mediocre wines are the Domaine Billard-Gonnet and the Domaine Lejeune. There is no question that the Billard-Gonnet wines have a certain following, but they are lean, hard, and charmless. Those from Lejeune are merely straightforward and simple. In addition, there are many *négociant* bottlings from the big firms in Beaune that rarely offer high quality. Two major exceptions are those wines from the *négociants* Joseph Drouhin and Louis Jadot. Drouhin has a small holding in Pommard Les Epenots and can usually be counted on to make one of the best wines from the appellation.

Those critics of the appellation of Pommard, and there are many, lament the fact that the wines rarely hold up with cellaring. But, having had the opportunity to taste well-aged bottles from the cellars of Pothier-Rieusset, Hubert de Montille, and Michel Gaunoux, I have no doubt that a top Pommard Les Rugiens or Les Epenots can last 20 years or more. I have already mentioned that one of the greatest bottles of red burgundy I have ever tasted from either the Côte de Beaune or the Côte de Nuits was the 1949 Pothier-Rieusset Pommard Les Rugiens. Nearly as good were the 1962 Pommard Les Rugiens from Michel Gaunoux, and the 1962 Pommard Les Rugiens from Madame Courcel. Old bottles from Hubert de Montille have also exhibited remarkable life and longevity. If one is buying top-quality Pommard to drink in 10 or 15 years, these 3 estates merit serious consideration. I would be a bit more careful with the Pothier-Rieusset wines since the quality after 1985 appears to have declined. It remains to be seen whether this domaine, which made so many extraordinarily rich wines in the post–World War II era, can rebound.

VISITING THE VILLAGE OF POMMARD AND ITS PRODUCERS

There are no suitable lodgings in Pommard, so most visitors stay at one of the hotels in the suburbs of Beaune, or in Beaune itself, which is only a 10-minute drive away, even when Route Nationale 74 is highly congested. You also could easily stay in Puligny-Montrachet, at a hotel such as Le Montrachet, only 6 miles from Pommard, or in Chagny, at the luxurious hotel and restaurant Lameloise, which is only a 15-minute drive from Pommard.

If you intend to visit the producers of Pommard, I highly recommend a stop at the Château de Pommard. It is a magnificent building with extraordinary underground cellars. The wine, while not of the same quality as the top Premiers Crus, is still the best Villages wine made in the appellation, and the tour run by the proprietor is informative and interesting. Two small growers that match most people's perception of a burgundy grower would be Virgil Pothier and André Mussy. Both have made many great wines over their long careers, and it is a joy to visit them and listen as they explain the differences between a Rugiens and an Epenots. Other estates well worth a visit would include the Comte Armand, who owns the *monopole* vineyard Clos des Epeneaux, the Domaine Courcel, and Hubert de Montille, the hard-to-reach lawyer from Dijon. At Hubert de Montille's estate you will witness winemaking in its most natural, unfiltered, unmanipulated style.

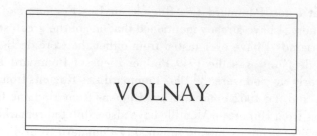

VOLNAY

An Overview

Location: Immediately south of Pommard is the appellation and village of Volnay. Smaller than Pommard (population 461 Volnaisiens), Volnay is nestled on a hillside with the majority of its vineyards spread out below the village. The view from the fourteenth-century church, or one of the other higher spots in the village, affords a beautiful vista of Volnay's vineyards to the east. On a clear day, the growers claim Mont Blanc can be seen.

Acres under vine: A total of 904 acres, all of it Pinot Noir
  Grands Crus: none
  Premiers Crus: 284 acres
  Villages Wines: 243 acres are in the Volnay appellation; the
      balance is Côte de Beaune-Villages

Grands Crus: None

Principal Premiers Crus: A total of 35
  Chanlin, Pitures, Lassolle, Clos des Ducs, Le Village (Clos de la Cave des Ducs), Le Village (Clos du Château des Ducs), Le Village (Clos de l'Audignac), Le Village (Clos de la Chapelle), Le Village, La Barre, Bousse d'Or, Le Village (Clos de la Bousse d'Or), Les Brouillards, Les Mitans, En l'Ormeau, Les Angles, Pointes d'Angles, Fremiets, Fremiets (Fremiets-Clos de la Rougeotte), Le Village (Clos de la Rougeotte), La Gigotte, Les Grands Champs, Les Lurets, Robardelle, Carelle sous la Chapelle, Carelles, Le Ronceret, Les Aussy, Les Champans, Les Caillerets, Clos des 60 Ouvrées, En Chevret, Taillepieds, En Verseuil, Clos des Chênes

Price levels: Appellation Volnay Contrôlée and Volnay Premier Cru are reasonably priced given the general cost of fine red burgundy. Villages wines cost $18–$25 a bottle and Premiers Crus $20–$45.

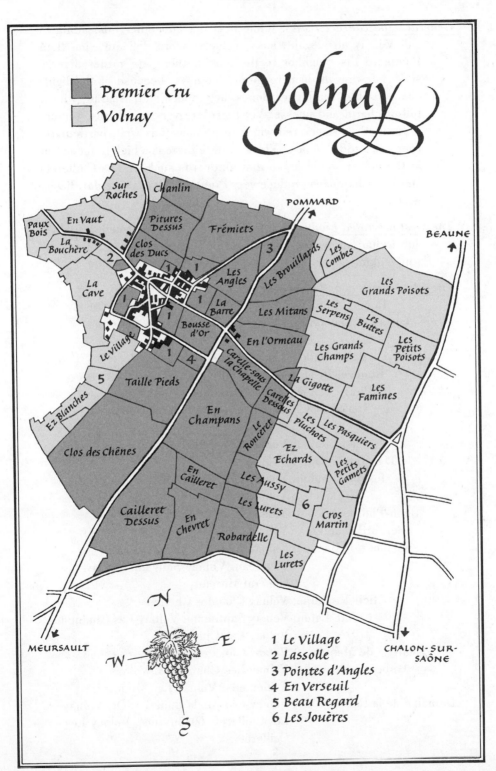

Premier Cru
Volnay

Volnay

Sur Roches
Chanlin
Paux Bois
En Vaut
Pitures Dessus
Frémiets
POMMARD
BEAUNE
La Bouchère
2
Clos des Ducs
1
1
Les Angles
Les Brouillards
Les Combes
3
La Cave
1
1
La Barre
Les Mitans
Les Serpens
Les Buttes
Les Grands Poisots
Le Village
1
Bousse d'Or
En l'Ormeau
Les Grands Champs
Les Petits Poisots
4
Carelle-sous la Chapelle
La Gigotte
Les Famines
5
Taille Pieds
Carelles Dessus
Ez Blanches
En Champans
Le Ronceret
Les Pluchots
Les Pasquiers
Clos des Chênes
Ez Echards
Les Petits Gamets
En Cailleret
Les Aussy
6
Cailleret Dessus
En Chevret
Les Lurets
Cros Martin
Robardelle
Les Lurets

N
E
W
S

1 Le Village
2 Lassolle
3 Pointes d'Angles
4 En Verseuil
5 Beau Regard
6 Les Jouères

MEURSAULT

CHALON-SUR-SAÔNE

General wine characteristics: While it is not altogether misleading to
call Volnay an elegant, silky, velvety, more delicate wine than
Pommard (its neighbor to the north), there are rather diverse
styles of wine made here. Many Volnays, because of the light,
chalky soil on the higher slopes, are indeed soft, fragrant wines,
full of charm and finesse. Yet there are very ageworthy, tannic,
fuller-bodied, structured wines from Volnay as well, particularly
from the middle slope of Volnay where there is a high iron content
in the soil. I would argue that vineyards such as Les Caillerets
and Les Champans produce very Pommard-like, muscular, fleshy
wines.

The most overrated producers: Bouchard Père et Fils, though it is difficult to find an overrated producer of Volnay as the quality of the
winemaking is very high.

The best producers and their wines:

Robert Ampeau: Volnay Santenots
Marquis d'Angerville: Volnay-Clos des Ducs, Volnay Les
Champans
Ballot-Millot: Volnay Taillepieds
Bitouzet-Prieur: Volnay Taillepieds
Pierre Boillot: Volnay Santenots
J. M. Bouley: Volnay Clos des Chênes, Volnay Les
Caillerets
Jean Clerget: Volnay Les Caillerets
J. F. Coche-Dury: Volnay
Joseph Drouhin: Volnay Clos des Chênes
Faiveley: Volnay Les Champans
Jean-Philippe Fichet: Volnay Les Champans
Bernard Glanteney: Volnay Clos des Chênes
Hospices de Beaune: Volnay-Jehan de Massol, Volnay-
Blondeau, Volnay-Sauvain, Volnay-
General Muteau
Michel Lafarge: Volnay Clos des Chênes
Comte Lafon: Volnay Santenots, Volnay Les Champans
Leroy: Volnay Les Champans
Château de Meursault: Volnay Clos des Chênes
Hubert de Montille: Volnay Les Champans, Volnay
Taillepieds, Volnay Les Mitans
Domaine de la Pousse d'Or: Volnay-Clos de la Bousse d'Or, Volnay
Les Caillerets 60 Ouvrées, Volnay Les
Caillerets

Michel Prunier: Volnay Les Caillerets
Michel Rossignol: Volnay Les Pitures

Some important observations:
1. Volnay, much like Morey St.-Denis in the Côte de Nuits, has a high-quality level of winemaking. Consequently, the consumer is likely to get an authentic, interesting bottle of wine from this appellation.
2. The top Volnays possess an immense, seductive fruitiness and lushness, particularly from vineyards such as Clos des Chênes, Taille-pieds, Bousse d'Or, Clos des Ducs, and Les Pitures.
3. Volnay's most structured, tannic wines come from Les Caillerets and Les Champans.
4. Volnay has no Grands Crus, but Clos des Chênes can often produce wines of Grand Cru quality. Volnay has a number of excellent Premiers Crus vineyards, but Clos des Chênes is its finest.
5. Most Volnays drink exceptionally well young, giving the deceptive impression that they do not age well. However, the best do, lasting and improving for 8 to 12 years or longer.

Where are the values? Most Villages appellation contrôlée wines from Burgundy are not worth the price. Many are disappointing. Volnay is one appellation where you will find many good Villages wines, but consumers should seek out only those from the best producers. Among the Premiers Crus, look for less renowned names such as Les Pitures, Les Fremiets, Les Mitans, and Les Brouil-lards, all located north of the village near the border of the Pommard appellation.

Most successful recent vintages: 1989, 1988, 1987, 1985, 1980, 1978

Aging Potential: Premiers Crus—4 to 12 years; Villages wines—4 to 8 years

VOLNAY

(The Queen of the Côte de Beaune)

Leaving Pommard, the small, two-lane Route Nationale 73 climbs up the slope for several miles to the tiny village of Volnay, nestled on the hillside with an expansive view of all its vineyards to the east. It is the only famous Burgundy village that sits above its vineyards. Volnay was a favorite vacation spot for the Dukes of Burgundy, who built a large château that, regrettably, was destroyed in the eighteenth century. It also marks the end of the major red winemaking appellations of the Côte d'Or. After Volnay, white wine from the Chardonnay grape takes priority until one reaches the southern end of the Côte d'Or, at the casino town of Santenay. Although some of the Premiers Crus vineyards of Volnay, such as Les Caillerets and Les Champans, tend to make relatively structured, more muscular wine, it is the finesse, feminine grace, and delicacy that make the wines of Volnay in the Côte de Beaune the equivalent of those of Chambolle-Musigny in the Côte de Nuits. These are clearly wines of fragrance, delicacy, and charm that should never be heavy, overly alcoholic, or muscular.

THE VINEYARDS OF VOLNAY

Volnay's vineyards are all located to the west of Route Nationale 74, with most of the Villages wines sandwiched between N 74 and N 73. The Premiers Crus generally sit to the west of N 73 and extend up the relatively steep slopes of Volnay. There are three basic soil types that highly influence the quality and character of the wines. On the higher slopes, most of the best Premiers Crus are located on Argovian limestone. The soil is extremely chalky and light, giving these Volnays their extraordinary delicate character and less fleshy, muscular texture. Well-known vineyards such as Bousse d'Or, Clos des Ducs, and Taillepieds are located in this soil band. Moving down the slope, the second band of soil, which includes some of the Premiers Crus east of N 73, is richer with a more rocky base of Bathonian limestone, and a relatively reddish-brown color. The Volnays from the Premiers Crus vineyards located here, such as Les Caillerets and Les Champans, tend to be more tannic, fuller-bodied, and altogether bigger wines, more akin to an elegantly styled Pommard than a Volnay. At the bottom of the slope where the Premiers Crus end and the Villages wines begin, the soil is deeper with more gravel, and, of course, the drainage is significantly diminished. Here the wines vary greatly in quality. While some good wines do come from these parcels, their quality owes more to the competence of the winemaker than the soil itself.

One of the most often heard comments about the winemaking in Volnay is that the overall quality there is significantly higher than in many other of the famous Burgundy wine villages. I would agree, and I suspect there are two reasons for this. First, the growers themselves are quite conscientious and competitive; second, Volnay is the home of Jacques d'Angerville. For much of this century d'Angerville's family has fought to have only low-yielding, high-quality clones planted in the best Burgundy vineyards, and has fought for purity in the wines of Burgundy. D'Angerville's wines tend to be among the lightest and most elegant of the appellation, yet have a cunning ability to age well in spite of their light colors, seemingly low tannins, and less than overwhelming concentration. I still wonder why d'Angerville, who is as committed to quality as anyone, believes in filtering his wines; this process, in my opinion, robs Pinot Noir of a great deal of its finesse and character. D'Angerville's most famous holding is the Clos des Ducs, a tiny *monopole* vineyard his family has owned for years. This vineyard is tucked high up on the slope adjacent to the village, and produces one of the lightest of all the Volnays. Perhaps better than this wine is d'Angerville's Champans, which has a bit more body and flavor.

For much of the sixties and seventies the very finest winemaker in Volnay was the Domaine de la Pousse d'Or. This extraordinarily beautiful domaine, which sits right in the village with a fabulous vista of the vineyards from its terrace, has been run with impeccable care by the articulate and scholarly Gérard Potel. I do not believe it is unfair to say that the greatest Volnays I have ever tasted have come from this domaine, particularly the estate's 1964s, 1976s, and 1978s. The two stars are the Volnay-Clos de la Bousse d'Or, situated directly in front of the domaine's cellars, and the Volnay Les Caillerets Clos des 60 Ouvrées. Whereas the Bousse d'Or is all silky, velvety elegance, typical of Volnay at its very apogee of quality, the Les Caillerets from the Domaine de la Pousse d'Or is a structured, fuller-bodied, richer, more muscular wine that ages unbelievably well. Potel's great success in Volnay has diminished somewhat since 1979, when he began to filter his wines. Perhaps he will recognize how much flavor and character have been eviscerated from his wines since his last great vintage, 1978, and will return to the time-proven methods that made him famous in the sixties and seventies.

As I have already indicated, the best vineyard, and the only Premier Cru vineyard in Volnay that could well be a Grand Cru, is the Clos des Chênes, located south of the village. This particular vineyard produces some staggering wines that exhibit exceptional richness and ripeness without any loss of elegance and finesse. No one makes a greater Clos des Chênes than Michel Lafarge from his Domaine Lafarge, or Jean-Marc Bouley from his estate of the same name. Both wines express the utter richness and velvety quality of this splendid vineyard. Beaune *négociant* Joseph Drouhin often purchases grapes from Clos des Chênes and produces an excellent wine that is faithful to both the appellation of Volnay and this particular Premier Cru vineyard.

Another excellent Premier Cru that can sometimes be almost as good as Clos des Chênes is Les Taillepieds, which is just to the south and east of the village, bounded by Clos des Chênes to the south and just a stone's throw from the superb Bousse d'Or vineyard to the north. Excellent wines from the Les Taillepieds vineyard are made by the Domaine Bitouzet-Prieur, Hubert de Montille (the master of classic, long-lived Pommard as well), and the excellent domaine based in Meursault called Ballot-Millot. The wines from Taillepieds often share the same characteristics as Clos des Chênes—perhaps not quite as velvety or as concentrated, but still an elegant, classic example of Volnay wine at its best.

One other fabulous source for excellent Volnay since 1978 has been the Hospices de Beaune, which offer four separate cuvées of Volnay. The two best year in and year out are the Volnay-Cuvée Jehan de Massol, which comes entirely from the Premier Cru Santenots vineyard, and the Volnay-Cuvée Blondeau, which comes primarily from the Champans and Taillepieds vineyards. This is an absolutely voluptuous, stunningly rich cuvée of Volnay that in vintages such as 1985 and 1988 has certainly had the potential to be one of the top wines of the appellation. As with all wines from the Hospices de Beaune, their care and handling subsequent to purchase at the auction is critical as to whether their ultimate potential is realized in the bottle. The Hospices de Beaune's other two cuvées of Volnay, Cuvée General Muteau and Cuvée Gauvain, are certainly very good, but rarely approach the Cuvée Jehan de Massol or Cuvée Blondeau.

There are also a number of fine Volnays made by growers in the nearby white wine producing village of Meursault. It is interesting to note that the elegance and finesse of the Volnays from the lighter soils of this appellation seemingly signify that one is about to leave a primarily red wine producing area and move into a white-wine area. Curiously, within the appellation of Meursault there is a vineyard entitled to Premier Cru red-wine status for Volnay called Volnay Santenots. White wines from this parcel are entitled only to a Meursault Villages appellation. Such is the confusing, often complicated nature of Burgundy. In Meursault, however, some outstanding Volnay Santenots are made by Robert Ampeau and Pierre Boillot. Another excellent Volnay Villages is made by the outstanding Meursault producer Jean-François Coche-Dury.

Most of the *négociants* who offer selections of Volnay can usually be counted on to provide excellent wine. I have already mentioned the excellent Volnay-Clos des Chênes of Joseph Drouhin. Superb Volnays from the Champans vineyard are frequently offered by Faiveley in Nuits

St. Georges and Leroy in Auxey-Duresses. I remember the 1986 Volnay-Champans from Faiveley as being one of the stars from this half of the Côte d'Or. Leroy has also made some superb wine from the Champans vineyard in the top vintages. Neither of these two *négociants* has domaines in Volnay, but the famous, wealthy house of Bouchard Père et Fils does have holdings in Volnay Les Caillerets and Volnay Fremiets-Clos de la Rougeotte. While this wine empire has made significant progress in the quality of its wines since 1986, they are still not producing examples of Volnay that can compete with the wines from the best producers listed in the introduction to this chapter.

It seems that excessive fining and filtration strips the wines of Volnay even more than the wines of Vosne-Romanée or Gevrey-Chambertin, as the very best wines from this appellation are most often those that are lightly fined and unfiltered. Perhaps the decline in quality of the wines of the Domaine de la Pousse d'Or can be traced to nothing more than their decision to begin filtering in 1979.

VISITING THE VILLAGE OF VOLNAY AND ITS PRODUCERS

Volnay is an easy village to visit simply because it is so small: most of the growers' cellars are within a 5- to 10-minute walk of the square in front of the village's fourteenth-century church. Inside the church visitors will find an interesting statue of St.-George wrestling with a wicked dragon. The village itself is one of the oldest in the Côte d'Or and most of the growers will readily admit that wine was apparently being made here even before the Romans occupied the region. A good base for exploring Volnay would be either one of the aforementioned small hotels in Puligny-Montrachet or in Chagny, or of course, any one of the number of establishments in Beaune, only a 15-minute drive to the north. Volnay has two restaurants, Le Cellier Volnaysien and Auberge des Vignes, both of which offer reasonably priced, straightforward Burgundian specialties that will hardly be confused with the haute cuisine of the nearby luxury restaurant of Lameloise in Chagny. I have had better luck at the Auberge des Vignes.

If you would like to pay a visit to an interesting grower, I highly recommend Gérard Potel of the Domaine de la Pousse d'Or, or Michel Lafarge. Both have a broad view of what is going on in Burgundy, and are extremely well-informed, helpful gentlemen. An appointment with the Marquis d'Angerville should not be missed, particularly in view of his remarkable knowledge and commitment to unadulterated, pure burgundy.

MONTHÉLIE

An Overview

Location: The 198 inhabitants of Monthélie, known as Monthéliens, have mixed emotions about the scant number of tourists who visit their village. A tiny, ancient town only 2 minutes west from Volnay, this naturally sheltered, hilltop village apparently still looks as it did in the sixteenth century.

Acres under vine: 450 acres, 97% planted in Pinot Noir, the balance in Chardonnay
　　Grands Crus: none
　　Premiers Crus: 77 acres
　　Villages Wines: 269 acres are entitled to the Monthélie
　　　　　　　　appellation; the balance is Côte de Beaune-
　　　　　　　　Villages

Grands Crus: None

Principal Premiers Crus: A total of 9
　　Sur La Velle, Les Champs Fulliot, Les Duresses, Les Vignes Rondes, Les Riottes, Le Meix Bataille, Le Clos Gauthey, Le Cas Rougeot, La Taupine

Price levels: $15–$20 for Premiers Crus, several dollars less for the Villages wines

General wine characteristics: Most of the red wines from Monthélie are sturdy and imbued with a great deal of tannin and body, but not much finesse or charm, at least when they are young. However, the contributions of such superb winemakers as Jean Garaudet, the Comte Lafon, and André Pernin of Domaine Pernin-Rossin may lead to the production of more aromatic, graceful, elegant wines. The finest red wines usually come from Le Côteau de

Volnay, a hillside of limestone and red clay-like soil that sits between the village and Volnay.

The most overrated producers: Denis Boussey, Domaine Monthélie-
Douhairet

The best producers and their wines:
Eric Boussey: Monthélie
J. F. Coche-Dury: Monthélie
Louis Deschamps: Monthélie Les Mandenes
Gérard Doreau: Monthélie Les Champs Fulliot
Jean Garaudet: Monthélie
Hospices de Beaune: Monthélie-Cuvée Lebelin
Louis Jadot: Monthélie
Jehan-Changarnier: Monthélie
Comte Lafon: Monthélie
Pernin-Rossin: Monthélie
Henri Potinet-Ampeau: Monthélie
Eric de Suremain: Monthélie-Château de Monthélie, Monthélie-
Sur la Velle

Some important observations:
1. This tiny appellation could be an up-and-coming source for high-
quality red burgundy that sells at a modest price. The vineyards
adjacent to the Volnay border are on high ground, and are reputed
to get more sunshine than any other spot in the Côte d'Or.
2. Les Champs Fulliot Premier Cru vineyard is adjacent to the superb
Premier Cru of Volnay Les Caillerets, yet the wine is not comparable in quality. Is it the winemaking?
3. To date, the quality of the white wines from Monthélie has been
suspect. They tend to be hard, charmless wines that are rustic and
unpleasant.
4. Few *négociants* bottle Monthélie because of the problem with name
recognition. Most of the production is estate-bottled or produced by
the local cooperative.

Where are the values? The best Premiers Crus merit buying, as do the
Villages wines from Jean Garaudet, Comte Lafon, and Pernin-
Rossin, the three newest stars of the appellation.

Most successful recent vintages: 1989, 1988, 1985

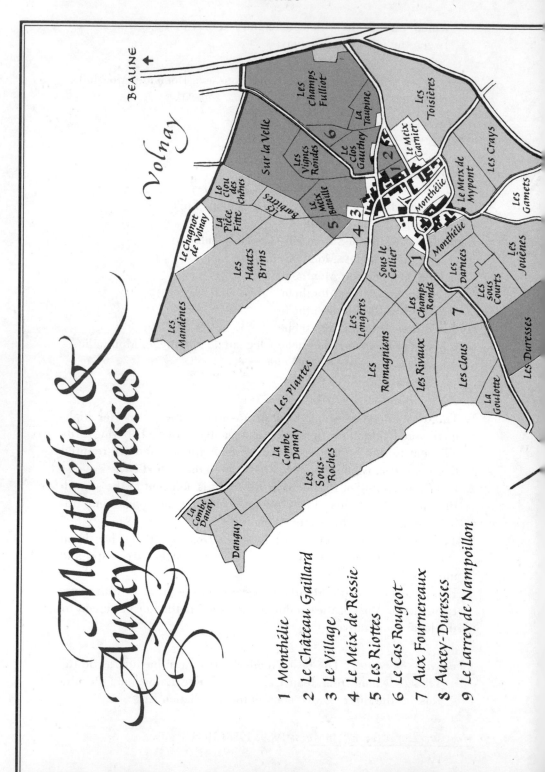

Monthélie & Auxey-Duresses

1 Monthélie
2 Le Château Gaillard
3 Le Village
4 Le Meix de Ressie
5 Les Riottes
6 Le Cas Rougeot
7 Aux Fournereaux
8 Auxey-Duresses
9 Le Larrey de Nampoillon

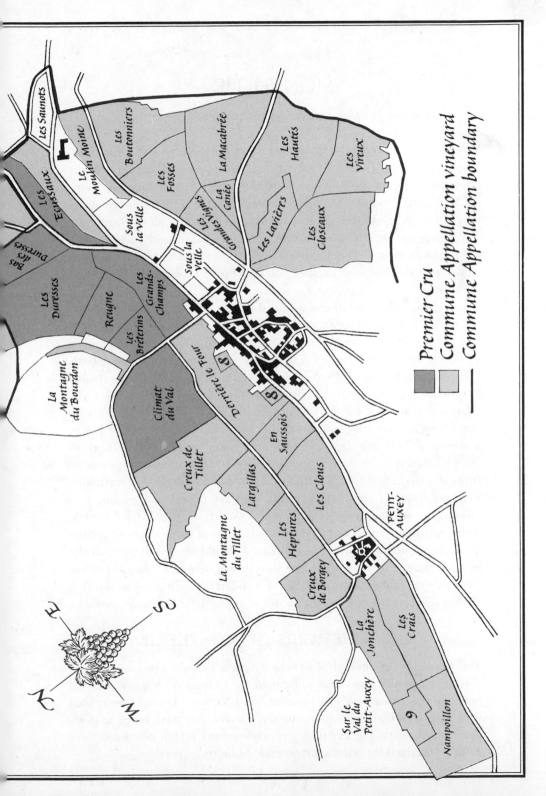

Premier Cru

Commune Appellation vineyard

Commune Appellation boundary

Les Saunots
Le Moulin Moine
Les Boutonniers
Les Fosses
Les Hautés
La Macabrée
La Canée
Les Vireux
Les Écussaux
Sous la velle
Lès Vignes
Les Grandes-Champs
Les Lavières
Les Closeaux
Bas des Duresses
Les Duresses
Reugne
Sous la velle
Les Bréterins
La Montagne du Bourdon
Les Grands-Champs
Derrière le Four
Climat du Val
Creux de Tillet
Largillas
En Saussois
Les Clous
La Montagne du Tillet
Les Heptures
Creux de Borgey
PETIT-AUXEY
La Jonchère
Les Crais
Sur le Val du Petit-Auxey
Nampoillon

Aging Potential: Premiers Crus—4 to 8 years; Villages wines—4 to 6 years

MONTHÉLIE

(Wines for those with nineteenth-century tastes?)

Monthélie is a worthy stop on any Burgundy enthusiast's itinerary. However, I must confess I only stumbled into this village by mistake after making a wrong turn on the road leading from Volnay to Meursault. Thank goodness for my poor navigational skills! I ended up in one of the most charming and photogenic villages in all of Burgundy. The village sits on a hill overlooking Volnay and Meursault, and according to the renowned Dutch wine writer, Hubrecht Duijker, it takes its name from the Celtic expression *"Mont-Oloye,"* meaning a high point in the road.

Until 1937, when Monthélie received its Appellation Contrôlée status, virtually all the production not consumed by the growers themselves was sold as Volnay or Pommard. Why has Monthélie never enjoyed anywhere near the reputation of its two most prominent neighbors, Meursault and Volnay? Perhaps because the winemakers here tended to produce a relatively rustic, brawny, coarse wine lacking finesse and charm, one often imbued with entirely too much tannin for those with other than nineteenth-century palates. Positive change is taking place, however. Whether it is the influence of such superb winemakers as Jean Garaudet, who makes the best wine of the village, emphasizing fruit, elegance, and charm rather than power and tannin, or Dominique Lafon of Comte Lafon, whose young vineyard is just now coming into production, or the famous vigneron of Vosne-Romanée, André Perrin, is difficult to say. There is no doubting that these three talented gentlemen will shape the future of Monthélie. I should also point out that the brilliant maker of Meursault and Corton-Charlemagne, Jean-François Coche-Dury, makes tiny quantities of wonderfully rich, supple Monthélie that has much in common with the wines of neighboring Volnay.

THE VINEYARDS OF MONTHÉLIE

The top vineyard sites of Monthélie sit on a hillside composed of red clay and gravelly limestone soil called Le Côteau de Volnay, located between the village and the appellation of Volnay. There is no reason why these vineyards should not produce wines that have much in common with Volnay, but the primitive winemaking techniques used have simply obscured the wine's charm and character.

The vineyard everyone claims is the most promising of the appellation, Les Champs Fulliot, is located adjacent to the famous Volnay Les Caillerets. This is a splendidly situated 20-acre parcel with a fabulous exposure that is clearly capable of making better wine than what has heretofore emerged. There is also Sur la Velle, a 14.82-acre parcel adjacent to Les Champs Fulliot. Behind these two vineyards, abutting the village itself, are the smaller Premiers Crus such as La Taupine (3.7 acres), Le Clos Gauthey (4.4 acres), Le Cas Rougeot (1.38 acres), and Le Meix Bataille (5.6 acres). Probably the best-known Premier Cru is Les Duresses (16.6 acres). It is the only one in Monthélie that sits in what is referred to as La Valley d'Auxey-Duresses. The soil here, which is primarily limestone, varies significantly from that of the other Premiers Crus. It also has more of an eastern exposure—less ideal than those of the other Premiers Crus. This is the same Premier Cru Les Duresses that extends into the appellation of Auxey-Duresses. There is one excellent wine from Les Duresses. The Hospices de Beaune, which owns 2.5 acres of that Premier Cru vineyard, consistently produces an excellent Monthélie sold under the name Cuvée Lebelin, after the benefactor who donated the property to the Hospices de Beaune.

As the producers in Monthélie become more aware of just how much potential they have to produce top-quality wine, one can expect the above mentioned Premiers Crus to find their way onto the labels of the wines produced here. Many producers have often just blended them together and called them Monthélie Premier Cru.

There is a sizeable cooperative in the village, Les Caves de Monthélie, that boasts 26 producers who own over 240 acres. An appointment can be arranged to taste and purchase these wines. At this time, the cooperative's wines are nowhere near the quality of the top wines from the growers recommended at the beginning of this chapter.

While all the world seems to agree that Monthélie has nowhere near the class and character of Volnay, it is an appellation on the brink of realizing its potential. The white wine production of Monthélie remains negligible, and the wines generally poor in quality, but the red wines may begin to take a more prominent place in conscientiously stocked cellars of collectors and restaurants looking for quality and value.

VISITING THE VILLAGE OF MONTHÉLIE AND ITS PRODUCERS

As I have already mentioned, Monthélie is one of the prettiest villages of the entire Côte d'Or. There is an attractive twelfth-century Romanesque church, and an eighteenth-century château that boasts an impressive fortified tower.

There are no hotels in Monthélie, but there are a number of excellent ones in the neighboring villages.

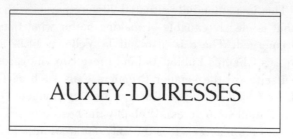

AUXEY-DURESSES

An Overview

Location: West of the renowned village of Meursault, in the direction of Saint-Romain, flanking both sides of N 73, is Auxey-Duresses. Situated at the entrance to a gorge, with Mont Melian, a formidable hillside, looming over the village, Auxey-Duresses has a population of 345 people. The finest vineyards, including the two finest Premiers Crus, Les Duresses and Clos du Val, sit on the northerly slopes of La Montagne du Bourdon, immediately to the right as you enter the village from the direction of Meursault or Monthélie.

Acres under vine: A total of 1,235 acres, of which 70% is in Pinot Noir and 30% in Chardonnay
    Grands Crus: none
   Premiers Crus: 78.2 acres
   Villages Wines: 341 acres are entitled to the Auxey-Duresses appellation; the balance is Côte de Beaune-Villages

Grands Crus: None

Principal Premiers Crus: A total of 6
    Clos du Val, Les Duresses, Les Grands Champs, Les Bréterins, Les Ecussaux, Reugne

Price levels: On the whole, prices are very reasonable, as Auxey-Duresses has never enjoyed its day in the sun. Villages wines sell for $12–$20 and Premiers Crus for $15–$25 a bottle.

General wine characteristics: While many have described Auxey-Duresses as being similar to neighboring Monthélie, or a "poor man's Volnay," such comments are pejorative. Good Auxey-Duresses red wine from top producers is a wine with surprising character and depth, with a robust, spicy, black-cherry, dusty fruitiness and good aging potential. The white wines are mixed, but when well made they share the nutty, creamy-style characteristic of Meursault whites. They are higher in acidity, however, since the Chardonnay rarely attains the super-ripeness and sugar levels (because of its less well-exposed vineyards) of Meursault.

The most overrated producers: There are few even known outside the Côte de Beaune, so no one could possibly be said to be overrated.

The best producers and their wines:
Robert Ampeau: Auxey-Duresses Ecussaux
Jean-Pierre Diconne: Auxey-Duresses, Auxey-Duresses (white)
Hospices de Beaune: Auxey-Duresses-Cuvée Boillot
Domaine Jessiaume: Auxey-Duresses Ecussaux
Domaine Lafouge: Auxey-Duresses La Chapelle, Auxey-Duresses (white)
Leroy: Auxey-Duresses, Auxey-Duresses (white)
Duc de Magenta (Jadot): Auxey-Duresses, Auxey Duresses (white)
Maroslavic-Leger: Auxey-Duresses Les Bréterins
Pernin-Rossin: Auxey-Duresses
Michel Prunier: Auxey-Duresses-Clos du Val
Roy Frères: Auxey-Duresses-Le Val
René Thevenin: Auxey-Duresses-Clos du Moulin aux Moines

Some important observations:
1. Auxey-Duresses is best known as the headquarters of the Leroy empire, which is run with extraordinary energy and enthusiasm by Madame Lalou Bize-Leroy.
2. Prospective buyers at the Hospices de Beaune should consider the Cuvée Boillot, made from a choice parcel of 1.35 acres of the best Premier Cru, Les Duresses. It usually sells for significantly less than the more fashionable cuvées from Beaune, Pommard, and Volnay. The quality is consistently excellent.
3. Until recently, many producers sold their wine under the label of Côte de Beaune-Villages because of the lack of consumer recognition for Auxey-Duresses.

Where are the values? Virtually all the best wines of Auxey-Duresses
sell for no more than top Pinot Noirs or Chardonnays from California and Oregon.

Most successful recent vintages: 1989, 1988, 1985, 1982, 1978

Aging Potential: Premiers Crus (red)—5 to 15 years; Villages wines
(white)—3 to 8 years; Villages wines (red)—3 to 8 years

AUXEY-DURESSES

(Underrated wines from an unfashionable appellation)

Auxey-Duresses, a short 3- or 4-minute car ride from Meursault and
Monthélie, is an old wine producing village that sits in a narrow valley
between two mountains, Mont Melian (on the southern side, where the
white wine vineyards are located) and La Montagne du Bourdon (on the
north side, where the top red wine Premiers Crus vineyards are located). Once through the tiny village, one cannot help but notice the
gorge of Mont Melian, and further up the road the even more charming
village of Saint-Romain.

   Auxey-Duresses produces approximately 70% red and 30% white
wine, which increasingly appears on the market under the name of
Auxey-Duresses. Previously, given the low prestige and lack of consumer recognition of the name Auxey-Duresses, the wines were often
sold under the more widely known and marketable name of Côte de
Beaune-Villages.

THE VINEYARDS OF AUXEY-DURESSES

There are no Grands Crus in Auxey-Duresses, and a handful of skeptics
maintain there should not be any Premiers Crus. However, out of the
slightly more than 1,200 acres under vine, only 78.2 acres are dedicated
to Premiers Crus, all of them located on the slopes of La Montagne du
Bourdon. The soil is extremely thin and stony here, with a high limestone content. The best Premier Cru without question is Les Duresses,
a 25-acre parcel with a less than perfect eastern exposition. Of the 25
acres, approximately 10 make up what is referred to as the Bas de
Duresses, which is considered a less successful plot, though it is still
entitled to Premier Cru status. To confuse consumers even more, the
wine from Bas de Duresses can take the name of Les Duresses.

Another excellent Premier Cru is the Clos du Val (22.7 acres), which
has a southerly exposition. There seems to be more ripeness in many
of the wines from Clos du Val, with less tannin and muscular robustness, and a more velvety, intense berry fruitiness, suggesting the
grapes attain greater maturity than those from Les Duresses. Other
Premiers Crus include Les Ecussaux, a tiny 7.6-acre parcel sitting at
the very bottom of the hillside of the Montagne du Bourdon, and Les
Bréterins, a 4.4-acre parcel with a tiny subplot called La Chapelle.

There has always been a tendency to dismiss both the red and white
wines from Auxey-Duresses. This seems unfair, given the best examples from the famous house of Leroy, which has its impressive cellars
and business office in Auxey-Duresses. Very good wines are also produced by Michel Prunier, the Duc de Magenta (whose wines are now
impeccably made and marketed by the Maison Louis Jadot in Beaune),
and the splendid Cuvée Boillot from the Hospices de Beaune. The good
red wines have plenty of depth, a spicy, robust, leathery character, and
in the top vintages more than sufficient fruit. Consumers can maximize
the odds in their favor by buying Auxey-Duresses only in vintages where
there is superb ripeness in Burgundy (i.e., 1989, 1988, and 1985). However, many fine 1987s were also produced in Auxey-Duresses. In cold,
wet, less-than-ideal years, the wines of Auxey-Duresses, much like
those from other lesser Burgundy appellations that sit inland, should
probably be avoided.

VISITING THE VILLAGE OF AUXEY-DURESSES
AND ITS PRODUCERS

Most people who have made the pilgrimage to Auxey-Duresses do so to
meet and taste with the formidable Madame Lalou Bize-Leroy. For
those who appreciate the very best in Burgundy and who have unlimited
financial resources, a tasting with Lalou Bize is incredibly instructive.
There is no one in Burgundy who is more committed to authenticity and
top quality. Getting an appointment if you are not an important buyer
may be a problem, but if you can manage it, don't pass up the opportunity. She is one of the great personalities and moving forces of the
region, and she will continue to shape the future of Burgundy—for the
better.

Another interesting producer who merits a visit is Michel Prunier,
whose cellars are directly across from the excellent restaurant called
La Cremaillère, one of my favorite country restaurants in Burgundy.
The food is surprisingly good and their wine list is packed with selections from the local growers.

For archaeological buffs, Auxey-Duresses boasts the remains of an old fortress. Several of the towers of the fortress are still in remarkably good condition. There is also a fourteenth-century church with an impressive clock tower, an old water mill, and several charming chapels.

SAINT-ROMAIN

An Overview

Location: Several miles west of Auxey-Duresses on N 73 in the direction of Autun is the quaint, rather unknown hamlet of Saint-Romain. The vineyards here have the highest altitude in the Côte d'Or. Saint-Romain actually encompasses two tiny villages—the picturesque Saint-Romain Le Haut, sitting atop a rocky ledge, and Saint-Romain Le Bas, further down the hillside in the valley.

Acres under vine: The total acreage of the appellation is 1,573 acres, but only 345 acres are planted with vines. 55% is planted with Chardonnay and 45% with Pinot Noir.

Grands Crus: None

Premiers Crus: None

Important Lieux-dits:　Le Dos d'Ane, Sous le Château, Sous la Velle, Sous Roche

Price levels: $15 will purchase any producer's Saint-Romain white or red wine

General wine characteristics: Chardonnay fares better than Pinot Noir in this appellation. The stony, Argillo-calcareous soil and high, cool altitude allow Chardonnay to ripen more evenly than Pinot Noir. The white wines are fresh, crisp, light, and tasty. The red

wines are light, early maturers that smell and taste of strawberries.

The most overrated producers: None

The best producers and their wines:
      Bernard Fèvre: Saint-Romain (red)
      Jean Germain: Saint-Romain Sous le Château (white)
      Alain Gras: Saint-Romain (white and red)
      Louis Latour: Saint-Romain (white)
  Taupenot Père et Fils: Saint-Romain (white and red)
      René Thévenin: Monthélie Saint-Romain (white and red)

Some important observations:
1. This village is better known as the home of the famous barrel makers, François Frères (who sell their barrels throughout the world),
   than for its crisp, light white and red wines.
2. There appears to be far greater potential for Chardonnay than Pinot
   Noir in the stony, windswept soils of this area.
3. This is one of only two Côte de Beaune appellations to have no
   Premiers Crus (the other is Chory-Lès-Beaune).

Where are the values? When well made, both the red and white wines
    represent very good values, particularly the white wines.

Most successful recent vintages: 1989, 1988

Aging Potential: Villages wines (red)—2 to 4 years; Villages wines
    (white)—1 to 3 years

SAINT-ROMAIN

(The Côte d'Or's best source for inexpensive Chardonnays)

This quaint village (actually two villages when one considers the upper
and lower towns as separate entities) is somewhat off the beaten track,
but it is still only a 10-minute drive from Meursault or Volnay. Most
visitors to Saint-Romain are looking to purchase barrels from one of
France's most famous and successful *tonneleries*, François Frères, who
sells his barrels to top wine producers all over the world. The huge
success of François Frères tends to overshadow what are some delight-

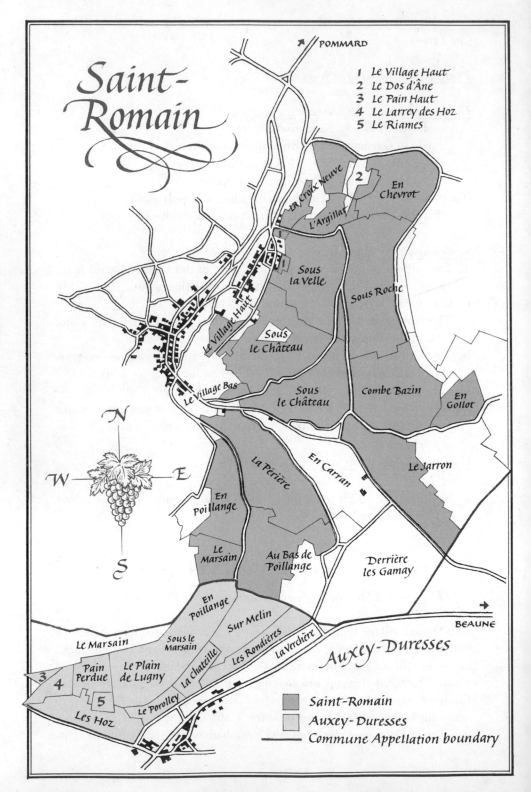

Saint-Romain

1 Le Village Haut
2 Le Dos d'Âne
3 Le Pain Haut
4 Le Larrey des Hoz
5 Le Riames

POMMARD

En Croix Neuve
L'Argillat
En Chevrot
Sous la Velle
Sous Roche
Sous le Château
Sous le Château
Combe Bazin
En Gollot
La Périère
En Carran
Le Jarron
En Poillange
Le Marsain
Au Bas de Poillange
Derrière les Gamay
En Poillange
Sur Melin
Le Marsain
Sous le Marsain
Les Rondières
La Verchère
BEAUNE
Pain Perdue
Le Plain de Lugny
La Chateille
Auxey-Duresses
Les Hoz
Le Porolley

N
W   E
S

Saint-Romain
Auxey-Duresses
Commune Appellation boundary

fully fresh, exuberant wines made from the Chardonnay, and some less interesting, light, cherry- and strawberry-scented red wines.

The appellation itself was founded in 1947, and its limited success in commercial circles is due mainly to the Thévenin family, who have long promoted and supported the appellation.

THE VINEYARDS OF SAINT-ROMAIN

The appellation of Saint-Romain is much larger than the current acreage under vine would suggest. Just over 20% of the total acreage is planted. This is not hard to believe when one surveys the windswept, stony, rugged terrain, which is more reminiscent of the Hautes-Côtes de Beaune than the Côte d'Or.

While there are no Premiers Crus, everyone agrees that the best vineyards lie just to the north of the road leading into the village from Auxey-Duresses. These vineyards, called *lieux-dits*, include Sous le Château (60 acres) and Sous la Velle (29 acres). These parcels are considered to make the best red and white wines from Saint-Romain, and are the two leading candidates for Premiers Crus if this village is ever awarded any.

The Chardonnay grape seems to do very well in the rugged, stony, windswept *terroir* of Saint-Romain. While no wines can be called profound, they do have a fresh, lemony, apple-like fruitiness that makes them ideal for drinking in their first several years of life. Probably because of the argillo-calcareous, stony soil, Pinot Noir has fared less well, although there have been good examples made by such producers as Bernard Fèvre, René Thévenin, and Alain Gras. However, many Saint-Romain red wines tend to have an underlying medicinal bitterness that can only be attributed to the soil. Yet, given the reasonable prices that Saint-Romain sells for, this is not a village that should be cavalierly dismissed.

VISITING THE VILLAGE OF SAINT-ROMAIN AND ITS PRODUCERS

If you have some spare time, Saint-Romain is well worth a visit, if only to take the short, steep walk up to the panoramic lookout on top of the mountain that looms over Saint-Romain Le Bas. On a clear day the vista is quite stunning. Saint-Romain is also well known for its grottos, wherein many significant archaelogical finds, such as Gallo-Roman jewelry, coins, and pottery, have been made. Ongoing digs suggest that the history of winemaking here cannot be traced back to the Gallo-Roman period. However, Saint-Romain was part of some sort of fortification or line of defense used during that period. Before leaving the village one should also visit the twelfth-century church with its Romanesque bell tower.

As far as visiting the growers, the best white wine I have tasted is that of Jean Germain, but his cellars are located in Meursault, not Saint-Romain. In Saint-Romain itself I would suggest a visit with Bernard Fèvre, who is making a number of fine wines from surrounding appellations, Alain Gras, and the Domaine René Thévenin.

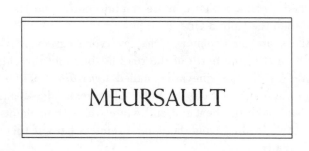

MEURSAULT

An Overview

Location: Five miles south of Beaune and 28 miles south of Dijon is the sprawling village of Meursault. Its immediate neighbor to the north is Volnay, to the south, Puligny-Montrachet. The most celebrated vineyards sit to the south of the village. All these hallowed sites are on the gentle slopes of a hillside. Meursault is not a large village (there are 1,646 residents called Les Murisaltiens), but its streets seem to have no rhyme or reason, and this maze is difficult for the first-time visitor to navigate.

Acres under vine: A total of 2,482
      Grands Crus: none
     Premiers Crus: 325.8 acres
    Villages Wines: 753 acres are entitled to appellation Meursault;
                   the balance is Côte de Beaune-Villages
Note: There are also 58 acres in Meursault-Blagny, 24 acres in Blagny, 109.6 acres in Blagny Premier Cru, and 72 acres in Volnay-Santenots. The latter is a curiosity. It is the northernmost vineyard of Meursault and is planted with Pinot Noir. The red wine is permitted to be called Volnay-Santenots, and the rare white wine from this parcel is called Meursault-Santenots.

Grands Crus: None

Principal Premiers Crus: A total of 13

Les Cras, Les Caillerets, Les Santenots, Les Charmes, Les Perrières, Les Genevières, Le Poruzot, Les Bouchères, Les Gouttes d'Or, La Jeunelotte, La Pièce Sous le Bois, Sous Le Dos d'Ane, Sous Blagny

Price levels: Meursault has never been an unfashionable appellation. While prices are generally below the top Premiers Crus and Grands Crus of its southern neighbors, Puligny-Montrachet and Chassagne-Montrachet, several of the finest growers in Meursault are able to fetch astronomical amounts for their wines (i.e., J. F. Coche-Dury and Comte Lafon). Generally, Meursault Villages sells for $20–$30 a bottle and Premiers Crus for $25–$50 a bottle. The finest Meursault Les Perrières or one of the Meursault *cuvées* from the Hospices de Beaune may sell for twice that.

General Wine Characteristics: The Premiers Crus, as well as the finest Villages Meursaults from the top vineyards, are among the easiest drinking white burgundies in the world. Why? High-quality Meursault is opulent, almost unctuous, with a fatness and a juicy, succulent, buttery, hazelnut and apple, peach-like fruitiness that often roars from the glass. Of course, this is assuming the growers do not let their yields get out of control, a lamentable tendency given the immense worldwide popularity of this appellation's wines. For every exhilarating Meursault there are a half-dozen dull, diluted examples.

The most overrated producers: Bouchard Père et Fils, Chartron et Trébuchet, Guy Bocard, René Monnier, H. Bouzereau-Gruère, Jacques Prieur

The best producers and their wines:

Robert Ampeau: Meursault Les Perrières, Meursault Les Charmes

Ballot-Millot: Meursault Les Charmes, Meursault Les Perrières

Bitouzet-Prieur: Meursault Les Perrières, Meursault-Clos du Cromin

Pierre Boillot: Meursault Les Charmes

Coche-Debord: Meursault Les Gouttes d'Or, Meursault Les Charmes, Meursault Les Chevalières

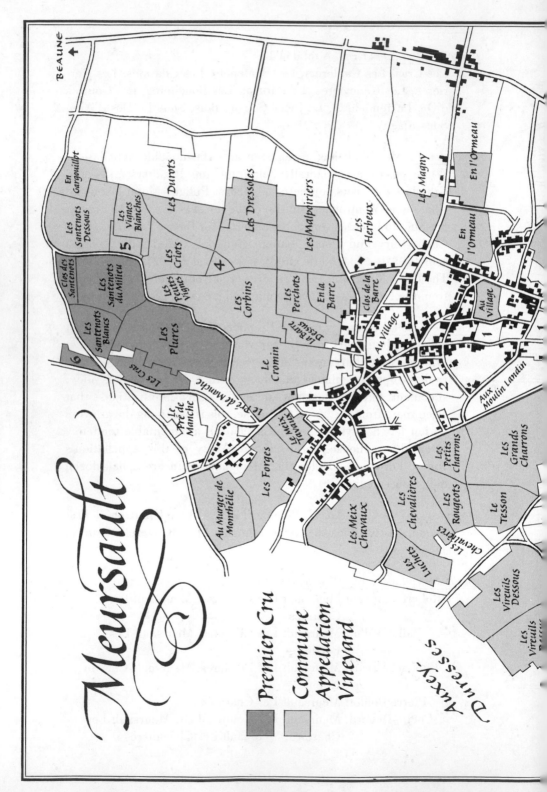

Meursault

Auxey-Duresses

BEAUNE ↑

Premier Cru

Commune
Appellation
Vineyard

En Gargouillot
Les Santenots Dessous
Les Vignes Blanches
Les Durots
5
Clos des Santenots
Les Santenots du Milieu
Les Petits Vignes
Les Criots
4
Les Dressoles
Les Malpiriers
Les Herbeux
Les Magny
En l'Ormeau
En l'Ormeau
Les Santenots Blancs
Les Plures
Les Corbins
Les Perchots
En la Barre
La Barre Dessus
Clos de la Barre
Au Village
Au Village
1
Le Cromin
Au Village
1
1
2
Les Cras
Le Pré de Manche
Le Pré de Manche
1
1
Aux Moulin Landin
Le Pré de Manche
Le Meix Tavaux
1
3
Au Murger de Monthélie
Les Forges
Les Meix Chavaux
Les Chevalières
Les Chevalières
Les Rougeots
Les Petits Charrons
Les Grands Charrons
Le Tesson
Les Luchets
Les Vireuils Dessous
Les Vireuils Dessus

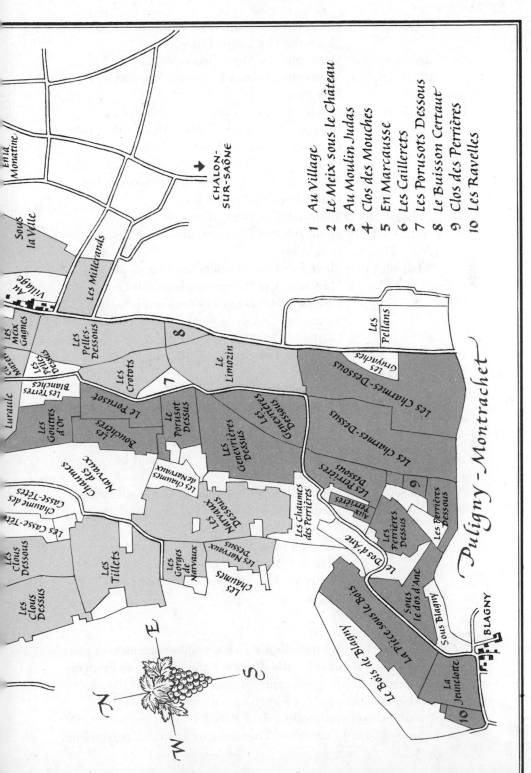

CHALON-SUR-SAÔNE

1 Au Village
2 Le Meix sous le Château
3 Au Moulin Judas
4 Clos des Mouches
5 En Marcausse
6 Les Caillerets
7 Les Porusots Dessous
8 Le Buisson Certaut
9 Clos des Perrières
10 Les Ravelles

En la Monatine

Sous la Velle

Les Millerands

Au Village

Les Meix Gagnes

Les Pelles Dessus

Luraule

Les Terres Blanches

Les Pelles-Dessous

Les Gouttes d'Or

Les Bouchères

Le Porusot

Les Crotots

Le Porusot Dessus

Le Limozin

Les Genevrières Dessus

Genevrières Dessous

Les Charmes-Dessus

Les Charmes-Dessous

Les Gruyaches

Les Pellans

Chaumes des Narvaux

Les Chaumes de Narvaux

Les Narvaux Dessous

Les Perrières Dessous

Aux Perrières

Les Perrières Dessus

Les Perrières Dessous

Chaume des Casse-Têtes

Les Casse-Têt

Les Clous Dessous

Les Tillets

Les Gorges de Narvaux

Les Narvaux Dessus

Les Chaumes

Les Chaumes des Perrières

Le Dos d'Âne

Sous le dos d'Âne

Sous Blagny

Les Clous Dessus

La Pièce sous le Bois

Le Bois de Blagny

La Jeunelotte

BLAGNY

Puligny-Montrachet

J. F. Coche-Dury: Meursault Les Perrières, Meursault-Rougeot, Meursault Les Casse Têtes

Jean Germain: Meursault Les Meix Chavaux

Albert Grivault: Meursault-Clos des Perrières, Meursault Les Perrières

Hospices de Beaune: Meursault-Cuvée Loppin, Meursault Les Charmes Bahezre de Lanlay, Meursault-Cuvée Goureau, Meursault Les Genevrières Cuvée Baudot, Meursault-Jehan Humblot, Meursault Les Charmes Albert Grivault, Meursault Les Genevrières Philippe le Bon

Louis Jadot: Meursault Les Genevrières

François Jobard: Meursault Les Charmes, Meursault Les Genevrières

Labouré-Roi: Meursault-Clos des Bouches Chères-Manuel

Comte Lafon: Meursault Les Perrières, Meursault Les Charmes, Meursault Les Genevrières, Meursault-Clos de la Barre, Meursault Les Gouttes d'Or

Leroy: Meursault Les Perrières, Meursault-Les Narvaux

Château de Meursault: Meursault

Michelot-Buisson: Meursault Les Charmes, Meursault Les Genevrières, Meursault Les Perrières, Meursault Les Narvaux, Meursault Les Tillets

Perrin-Ponsot: Meursault Les Perrières, Meursault Les Charmes

Pitoiset-Urena: Meursault Les Genevrières, Meursault Le Poruzot

Rougeot: Meursault Les Charmes

Guy Roulot: Meursault Les Perrières, Meursault Les Charmes, Meursault Les Meix Chavaux, Meursault Les Tessons, Meursault Les Luchets

Some important observations:

1. Two of Burgundy's and the world's greatest white winemakers possess cellars in Meursault—the Comte Lafon and Jean-François Coche-Dury. Both are proponents of intensely flavored (thanks to low yields), unmanipulated, compelling, unfiltered Meursaults.

2. Les Perrières, while officially only a Premier Cru, produces white burgundies of Grand Cru status. The wines are splendid, resembling

more than anything else those from the renowned vineyard, Le Montrachet.

3. With the exception of Leroy, Louis Jadot, and, when he produces them, Faiveley, the Meursaults from the large *négociants* lack character and concentration. While I do not subscribe to the theory that estate-bottled burgundies are always better than those from the *négociants*, I do believe that when buying Meursault you must search out the finest growers.

4. There are some exceptional vineyards not entitled to Premier Cru status that qualitatively rival many of the Premiers Crus. Consider such vineyards, or *lieux-dits*, as Les Tessons (Roulot), Le Cromin (Bitouzet-Prieur), Clos de la Barre (Lafon), Les Meix Chavaux (Roulot), Les Chevalières (Coche-Debord), Les Rougeots (Coche-Dury), Les Tillets (Roulot), Les Narvaux (Leroy), and Les Casse Têtes (Coche-Dury).

5. There is plenty of Meursault produced (approximately 160,000 cases), but the quality is variable, particularly those wines from *négociants* and those produced as Villages or Meursault appellation wines.

Where are the values? Search out the best *lieux-dits* or vineyard-designated Meursault (not Premiers Crus) from producers such as Guy Roulot and Bitouzet-Prieur. The Clos du Château-Bourgogne Blanc from the Château de Meursault, made from vines just outside the appellation, is as good as many producers' Meursaults.

Most successful recent vintages: 1989, 1986, 1985, 1982, 1979

Aging potential: Premiers Crus—4 to 8 years, except for Les Perrières, which can last and improve for 15–20 years in certain vintages (i.e., 1969, 1978, 1985, and 1986); Villages wines—3 to 7 years

MEURSAULT

(Burgundy's most hedonistic and user-friendly white wines)

Meursault, just a 10-minute drive south from Beaune, is a large appellation, rivaling the nearby villages of Beaune and Gevrey-Chambertin for the greatest number of growers and quantity of wine produced. The village, which dwarfs its two famous neighbors to the south, Chassagne-Montrachet and Puligny-Montrachet, has remained a sleepy, quiet town, even though it always seems to be teeming with visiting tourists. The locals are proud to point out that it is the Côte d'Or's most visited village after Beaune. The reason must be the number of fine cellars where wine can be tasted and bought directly, as well as the ample pleasures that a good bottle of Meursault provides. Certainly there is little of great architectural interest in the village. It sports an attractive but hardly inspiring church. The most interesting structure of the village is the seventeenth-century Château de Meursault. The Château is owned by the immensely successful Beaune *négociant*, Patriarche, and is run with great flair by André Boisseaux. Most of the excitement in the town centers around three events—the political elections in early spring, the harvest in late September or early October, and the famous feast called the Paulée de Meursault, celebrated on the Monday after the Hospices de Beaune sale in November.

As soon as you pass through the southern edge of the Volnay appellation, past one of its most famous Premier Cru vineyards, Clos des Chênes, you enter Meursault. The northern, smaller half of the appellation possesses some attractively sloped vineyards, such as Les Santenots, Les Plures, and Les Cras, nestled up against the appellation of Volnay. Both red and white Premier Cru wines are permitted to be made here. Curiously, the Pinot Noir planted in the Santenots vineyard in Meursault is allowed to be called Volnay-Santenots, and the Chardonnay is called Meursault Les Santenots. It is rare to see much Meursault Les Santenots, but some of the best is made by the Domaine Bitouzet-Prieur in Volnay.

The soil in the area near Volnay is a brownish-red limestone containing both gravel and clay, more suitable for the production of red rather than white wine. As one proceeds south of the village, the soil becomes lighter in color, more gravelly, even rocky in certain places. It is here that the best vineyards of Meursault are located on a classic base of Jurassic limestone. It is this soil that helps produce wines of such obvious richness and comprehensibility that they are in demand the world over. They are less austere and backward than Puligny-Montrachet and are splendidly drinkable, whether from the cask or bottle, whether they are 1, 2, or 5 years old.

THE VINEYARDS OF MEURSAULT

PREMIERS CRUS VINEYARDS

The wealth and fame of Meursault is in large part based on its Premiers Crus vineyards, of which the most famous are Les Perrières (31.36

acres), Les Genevrières (16.1 acres), and the largest Premier Cru vineyard, Les Charmes (78 acres). All three are located to the south of the
village. Both Les Charmes and Les Perrières, which is located adjacent
to Les Charmes but further up the slope, are nestled next to the appellation of Puligny-Montrachet. Les Genevrières abuts both Les Perrières, and Les Charmes to the north in the direction of the village.
These three vineyards produce the greatest wines from Meursault, yet
while they share Meursault's general signature with regard to opulence
and a fragrant, ripe apple, peach-like, hazelnut fruitiness, when tasted
side by side it is easy to distinguish one from another.

I have no doubt that Les Perrières is the greatest of the three vineyards. It makes the most backward and compelling of the Meursaults,
often needing 2–3 years longer in the bottle than either Les Charmes
or Les Genevrières to display its remarkable complexity and perfume.
I am not alone in feeling it should be promoted to a Grand Cru. It
produces a wine with great similarity to the most famous white burgundy of all, Le Montrachet. Those producers of Meursault Perrières
don't dispute the comparison. They often quote the famous Frenchman,
Dr. Lavalle, who in 1855 stated, *"apres le vrai Montrachet, je ne connais
aucun vin blanc plus exquis."*

The Perrières vineyard has much lighter, thinner, more stony soil
than that of its neighbor situated just down the slope, Les Charmes,
which produces the quintessential, textbook example of Meursault. It
is often lower in acidity, fatter, and initially a more amply endowed
wine than Les Perrières, and it frequently gives off the *sur maturité*
aroma of peaches and apricots that Chardonnay takes on when it is
extremely ripe. In the hands of the best producers, Les Charmes is
always a full, round, seductively pleasing, and frequently exhilarating
wine. However, don't expect it to have the aging potential of Les Perrières. Les Charmes is the largest of the Premiers Crus, with 78 acres
under vine. This has no doubt led to its international following, since
Charmes yields nearly two and a half times more wine than Perrières.

The other famous Premier Cru, which fetches the highest prices, is
Les Genevrières. It produces wines that are midway between the more
profound and compelling style of Les Perrières and the more obvious,
forward style of Les Charmes. The best expression of a Meursault Les
Genevrières is often from the cellars of Comte Lafon or François Jobard. They infuse a leanness and restraint in their Les Genevrières that
is not apparent in their Les Charmes. In many respects, the Les Genevrières vineyard, which sits on the northern edge of both Les
Charmes and Les Perrières on the mid-slope leading north to the village
of Meursault, produces wines that seem more identifiable with Puligny-
Montrachet than with Meursault.

While no one doubts the renown of these three vineyards, there are two less-known Premiers Crus that are often priced significantly lower, and can be as good as most wines from Les Charmes and Les Genevrières when made by the top producers. Le Poruzot, a 17.29-acre vineyard located adjacent to and just north of Les Genevrières, is an outstanding source for top-quality Meursault. Poruzot tends to produce wines not unlike that of Genevrières, perhaps a bit riper and richer with less elegance, but extremely attractive, ample wines. Another sleeper Premier Cru vineyard is Les Gouttes d'Or, a 13.1-acre vineyard that lives up to its translated name of "drops of gold." Les Gouttes d'Or is the first Premier Cru vineyard found upon leaving the village in the direction of Puligny-Montrachet. It is situated high up on the slope with an elevation similar to that of Les Perrières and the very best parcels of Les Charmes. Les Gouttes d'Or, particularly that from Comte Lafon or Coche-Debord, can be a superb wine. It is classic Meursault, with a flamboyant, nutty, obviously rich, plump bouquet, and a superabundance of fruit.

Of all the Premiers Crus listed in the introduction to this chapter, these are the ones that consistently produce the finest wines.

OTHER WINES OF MEURSAULT

Customers have often been confused by the many Meursaults that have been made in the last twenty years with their vineyard, or as the French say, *lieux-dits* or *climat*, listed on the label. Many consumers have mistakenly assumed these were Premiers Crus when, in fact, they were simply Meursault Villages wines from specific vineyards. This is not to denigrate the best of them, for they offer excellent quality at prices 20%–50% below those of the top Premiers Crus. The best of these vineyards are located south of the village and include Les Tessons, Les Meix Chavaux, and Les Tillets, all wines sold under their name by the excellent Meursault producer Guy Roulot. Les Narvaux also produces top-quality Meursault, the best usually from the Maison Leroy. Les Casse Têtes of Coche-Dury is marvelous, as is his Les Chevalières and Les Rougeots. Clos de la Barre is the exclusive, wall-enclosed vineyard owned by the Comte Lafon. The quality of its wines is outstanding. Le Cromin is another excellent vineyard, and the best examples always seem to come from the small cellar of Vincent Bitouzet-Prieur in Volnay.

In most cases, none of these wines can be expected to last as long as a great Les Perrières, Les Charmes, or Les Genevrières, but in the hands of the top producers such as Coche-Dury, Coche-Debord, or the

Maison Leroy, they can prove to be surprisingly long lived. A good rule
of thumb suggests that these Meursaults should be drunk within their
first 5–6 years.

VISITING THE VILLAGE OF MEURSAULT AND ITS PRODUCERS

As previously mentioned, it is hard to grasp the layout of this village
since there does not appear to be any coherent pattern to the streets.
Most of the 1,600-plus inhabitants seem to derive their livings from the
production of wine. Perhaps the best strategy when visiting Meursault
is to simply park your car near the church and meander about the
village.

The personality of the village is no doubt a reflection of that of Bernard Michelot, whose cellars are located on the outskirts of town on the
road leading to Puligny-Montrachet. A visit with the affable, enthusiastic, often flamboyant Michelot offers an education regarding the different soils and vineyards of Meursault. Michelot, who recently made a
remarkable recovery from open-heart surgery, seems to prefer a lot of
oakiness in his flamboyant, rich Meursault, but some skeptics have
claimed they do not last as long as they should.

The historic and beautiful Château de Meursault merits a visit if you
are travelling through the village. This property, which markets its
Meursault as a Villages wine at extremely high prices, makes its Meursault from a blend of its holdings in Les Charmes and Les Perrières
vineyards. The wine is superb. It is put in a heavy, hard-to-bin bottle,
but the wine is frequently one of the best of the vintage, and certainly
the best domaine wine produced by the huge Beaune *négociant*, Patriarche Père et Fils. The Château and surrounding grounds are the tourists' preferred place to taste and purchase wines.

For the serious connoisseur of white burgundy, a visit to Meursault
must include a stop at the cellars of the Comte Lafon. This family sets
the benchmarks for what great white burgundy is all about. In the
1920s, the grandfather of the current generation, Comte Jules Lafon,
decided to expand the famous weekend of eating and drinking held by
the Confrérie des Chevaliers du Tastevin at Clos Vougeot. Monsieur
Lafon decided to hold a huge banquet and feast in Meursault on the
Monday after the traditional Hospices de Beaune sale. At this festive
event all the producers of Meursault bring their best bottles and the
invited guests (more than 600) spend the day drinking and eating. It is
the least formal, and perhaps most enjoyable event of the hedonistic
trois glorieuses weekend. While this event has done much to promote

the wines of Meursault and to encourage comradeship among the growers, it is Lafon's wines, which have been brilliantly and uncompromisingly made for decades that are Meursault's greatest glory. Dominique Lafon and his brother produce splendidly rich, complex, fragrant, long-lived Meursaults in one of the dampest and coldest cellars in Burgundy. A visiting oenologist might be horrified by the fact that the wines are not racked but kept on their lees for almost 2 years prior to bottling, which takes place with no filtration. Yet the results in the bottle are splendid.

Another practitioner of the unfiltered school of white burgundies is Jean-François Coche-Dury. His tiny production is significantly less than that of Comte Lafon, and it is all spoken for well in advance of its release. Additionally, Coche-Dury's prices are even higher than those of Comte Lafon.

Another outstanding cellar to visit is that of Guy Roulot, located immediately in front of the eastern entrance into the village. Roulot passed away in the early eighties, and the winemaking is now in the capable hands of his wife and Franck Greux. Both have continued the tradition of making outstanding Meursault from this domaine's holdings. It is a treat to taste through their different *cuvées*.

Perhaps the best lodging available near Meursault is at the Motel Au Soleil Levant, located on the main road between Volnay and Beaune. They have 35 spartan rooms available at reasonable prices. Other places to stay include the two hotels in the village, the Hôtel du Centre and Hôtel les Arts, which have 7 and 16 tiny, no-frill rooms.

As far as eating in Meursault, there is only one place where I have had consistently good but simple food—the Relais de la Diligence. This restaurant sits adjacent to the railroad station, and one can get a respectable and filling meal for $10–$20 per person.

PULIGNY-MONTRACHET

An Overview

<u>Location:</u> Situated slightly more than six miles south of Beaune, bordered by Meursault on the north and Chassagne-Montrachet to the south, is the tiny hamlet of Puligny-Montrachet. Just over 500

people reside in Puligny, most of them involved in some aspect of
the production of wine. Aside from the wealth of wine riches
tucked away in the underground cellars that lie beneath the village, there is not much at Puligny-Montrachet that could be described as scenic. There is a decent thirteenth-century church
that will hardly inspire architectural buffs, and a Napoleonic museum located in the airy, formal park in the village's center.

Acres under vine: A total of 1,259
> Grands Crus: 76.26 acres
> Premiers Crus: 247 acres
> Villages Wines: 285 acres are entitled to the Puligny-Montrachet
> > appellation; the balance is Côte de Beaune-
> > Villages

Grands Crus: A total of 4
> Montrachet, Chevalier-Montrachet, Bâtard-Montrachet, Bien-
> venues-Bâtard-Montrachet

Premiers Crus: A total of 14
> Les Chalumaux, Champ Canet, Clos de la Garenne, La Garenne,
> Hameau de Blagny, La Truffière, Champ Gain, Les Folatières, Le
> Cailleret (Les Demoiselles), Les Pucelles, Clavaillon, Les Per-
> rières, Les Referts, Les Combettes

Price levels: This is the realm for millionaires, superstar athletes, and
> successful actors and actresses, as prices for the Premiers Crus
> and Grands Crus of Puligny-Montrachet will drain the average
> consumer's bank account. Premiers Crus sell for $40–$65 a bot-
> tle, and Grands Crus soar to prices between $60 and $400 and up
> for the rare Montrachet. Insatiable worldwide demand ensures
> that even a copious year's production of 100,000 cases is snapped
> up immediately.

General wine characteristics: There is enormous variation between the
> styles of growers and the personality of the wines from the differ-
> ent vineyards, so the following is a broad summary. At the Pre-
> mier Cru level, Puligny-Montrachet is less alcoholic, less opulent,
> and usually higher in acidity than the Premiers Crus of Meursault
> or Chassagne-Montrachet. There are, however, exceptions, like
> Les Combettes, a superb vineyard adjacent to Meursault's famed
> Les Charmes. For me, Les Pucelles, Les Folatières and Le Cail-
> leret are quintessential, stylish, graceful, well-balanced, elegant

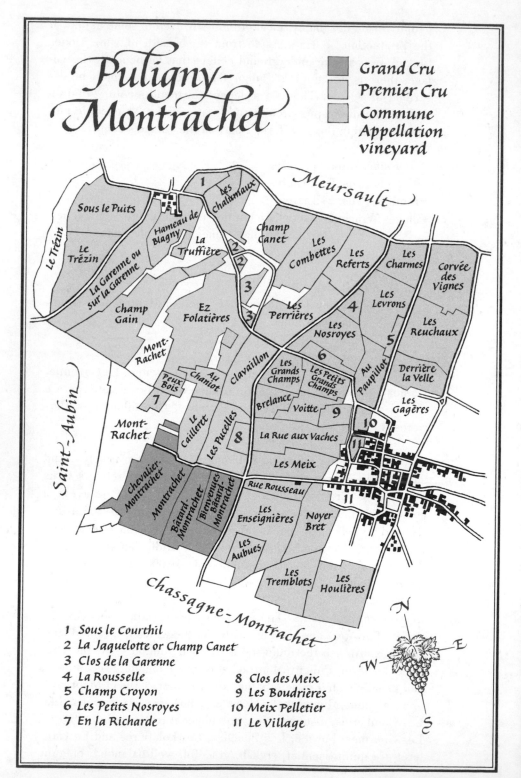

Puligny-Montrachet

Grand Cru
Premier Cru
Commune Appellation vineyard

Meursault

Sous le Puits

Le Trézin

Le Trézin

La Garenne ou Sur la Garenne

Hameau de Blagny

La Truffière

Les Chalumaux

Champ Canet

Les Combettes

Les Referts

Les Charmes

Corvée des Vignes

Champ Gain

Ez Folatières

Les Perrières

Les Levrons

Les Reuchaux

Les Nosroyes

Mont-Rachet

Clavaillon

Les Grands Champs

Les Petits Grands Champs

Au Paupillot

Derrière la Velle

Peux Bois

Au Chaniot

Brelance

Voitte

Les Gagères

Saint-Aubin

Mont-Rachet

Le Cailleret

Les Pucelles

La Rue aux Vaches

Les Meix

Chevalier-Montrachet

Montrachet

Bâtard-Montrachet

Bienvenues Bâtard-Montrachet

Rue Rousseau

Les Enseignières

Noyer Bret

Les Aubues

Chassagne-Montrachet

Les Tremblots

Les Houlières

1 Sous le Courthil
2 La Jaquelotte or Champ Canet
3 Clos de la Garenne
4 La Rousselle
5 Champ Croyon
6 Les Petits Nosroyes
7 En la Richarde
8 Clos des Meix
9 Les Boudrières
10 Meix Pelletier
11 Le Village

N
E
W
S

Puligny-Montrachets. Among the Grands Crus, Chevalier-Montrachet is the most opulent and precocious, Montrachet and Bâtard-Montrachet the most backward and longest lived. Perhaps I have had bad luck, but Bienvenues-Bâtard-Montrachet seems to be no better than the best Premiers Crus, except for the Bienvenue from the Domaine Ramonet. Top-class Puligny-Montrachet will keep for 7–20 years. Look for aromas of butter, apples, herbs, and oranges in a top Puligny-Montrachet Premier Cru or Grand Cru wine. The flavors are rich yet steely, buttressed nicely by acidity. They expand with both airing and aging. The Villages wines of Puligny are often gambles because too many producers fail to restrict production yields, and rarely make a serious selection.

The most overrated producers: Bouchard Père et Fils, Olivier Leflaive, Charton et Trébuchet (only their line of *négociant* wines), Henri Clerc, Henri Moroni, Blondeau-Danne, Jacques Prieur

The best producers and their wines:

Amiot-Bonfils:	Le Montrachet, Puligny-Montrachet Champ Gain, Puligny-Montrachet Le Cailleret, Puligny-Montrachet Les Demoiselles
Robert Ampeau:	Puligny-Montrachet Les Combettes
Bachelet-Ramonet:	Bâtard-Montrachet
Charles Bavard:	Bâtard-Montrachet
Roger Caillot:	Bâtard-Montrachet
Louis Carillon:	Puligny-Montrachet Les Combettes, Puligny-Montrachet Champ Canet, Puligny-Montrachet Les Perrières, Puligny-Montrachet Champ Gain
Jean Chartron:	Chevalier-Montrachet, Puligny-Montrachet-Clos de la Pucelle
Chavy:	Bâtard-Montrachet
Fernand Coffinet:	Bâtard-Montrachet
Marc Colin:	Montrachet
Georges Deleger:	Chevalier-Montrachet
Robert Deleger:	Chevalier-Montrachet
Joseph Drouhin:	Montrachet (Laguiche), Bâtard-Montrachet, Puligny-Montrachet Les Pucelles, Puligny-Montrachet Les Folatières, Puligny-Montrachet-Clos du Cailleret

Jean-Noël Gagnard: Bâtard-Montrachet
Gagnard-Delagrange: Bâtard-Montrachet
Louis Jadot: Chevalier-Montrachet, Montrachet
Comte Lafon: Montrachet
Louis Latour: Chevalier-Montrachet
Domaine Leflaive: Bâtard-Montrachet, Bienvenues-
Bâtard-Montrachet, Chevalier-
Montrachet, Puligny-Montrachet Les
Pucelles, Puligny-Montrachet Les
Combettes
Lequin-Roussot: Bâtard-Montrachet
Bernard Morey: Bâtard-Montrachet
Marc Morey: Bâtard-Montrachet
Michel Niellon: Chevalier-Montrachet, Bâtard-
Montrachet
Paul Pernot: Bâtard-Montrachet, Puligny-
Montrachet Les Folatières, Puligny-
Montrachet Les Pucelles
Domaine de la Romanée-Conti: Montrachet
Domaine Ramonet: Montrachet, Bienvenues-Bâtard-
Montrachet, Bâtard-Montrachet
Étienne Sauzet: Batard-Montrachet, Puligny-
Montrachet Les Combettes, Puligny-
Montrachet La Truffière, Puligny-
Montrachet Champ Canet, Puligny-
Montrachet Les Referts

Some important observations:

1. Puligny-Montrachet is the ranking white wine aristocrat of Burgundy's famed Côte d'Or. Greatness is taken for granted here, so the growers are unlikely to flinch if knowledgeable observers claim the *overall* quality of winemaking may actually be better at nearby Chassagne-Montrachet.

2. There are two domaines in Puligny-Montrachet that irrefutably merit the worldwide fame they have garnered—Domaine Leflaive and Domaine Sauzet. They should be on the shopping list of anyone who wants to experience just what heights the Chardonnay grape can attain.

3. Is Montrachet worth its current price of $200–$500 plus per bottle? The production from this 19.76-acre parcel has recently ballooned to nearly 6,000 cases, so rarity may not be quite the determining factor the producers would have you believe. Most Montrachets are

forbiddingly backward and would likely prove disappointing if drunk in their first 6 to 7 years of life. The offerings from Ramonet, Drouhin, and the Domaine de la Romanée-Conti would appear to be the most exhilarating examples. I have never tasted a Comte Lafon Montrachet that was even close to maturity. Other examples, except for those of Louis Jadot and Louis Latour (although I prefer each firm's Chevalier-Montrachet), have left me less than moved.

4. Prices aside, the most sumptuous and richest white burgundies, usually with at least a decade of life, are from Chevalier-Montrachet, the 18.1-acre parcel further up the slope above Le Montrachet. Perhaps it is because so many fine producers make outstanding Chevalier-Montrachet. Who could ignore the sumptuous, heady, splendidly concentrated Chevalier-Montrachets of Domaine Leflaive, Michel Niellon, Louis Jadot, Louis Latour, Domaine Jean Chartron, and Georges Deleger.

5. The most glamorous Premiers Crus, often rivaling the Grands Crus, are Les Combettes (adjacent to Meursault Les Charmes), Les Folatières (high on the slope behind the village), Le Cailleret (just north of Montrachet, and Les Pucelles (next to both Bâtard and Bienvenues-Bâtard-Montrachet).

6. It is usually best to avoid the straight Villages wines called Puligny-Montrachet. They are too frequently the result of excessive yields.

Where are the values? None exist in Puligny-Montrachet

Most successful recent vintages: 1989, 1986, 1985, 1983, 1979, 1978

Aging Potential: Grands Crus—Le Montrachet—8 to 20 years; Chevalier-Montrachet—5 to 12 years; Bâtard-Montrachet—7 to 15 years; Bienvenues-Bâtard-Montrachet—3 to 8 years; Premiers Crus—3 to 10 years; Villages wines—1 to 4 years

PULIGNY-MONTRACHET

(Home of the world's most expensive and sometimes greatest dry white wine)

Puligny-Montrachet is the crown jewel of white burgundy, with a reputation for producing the most profound and noble expressions of Chardonnay in the world.

The village itself offers little interest. Its spacious layout, however, does contrast sharply with the neighboring villages of Pommard, Volnay, and Meursault, where so many of the growers' homes seem to be built virtually on top of each other. In Puligny there is a large park and square, but the only significant building of architectural interest is the Château de Puligny-Montrachet. History indicates that the name Puligny came from a Gallo-Roman encampment named Puliniacus.

The production of Puligny-Montrachet is not as significant as that of Meursault, but in several of the superabundant vintages in the decade of the eighties it has soared past 100,000 cases. Virtually all of the production has been in white wine. However, there are tiny quantities of red wine produced that are somewhat of a collector's item given their rarity.

Despite the acclaim Puligny-Montrachet receives, the Villages wine, the Appellation Puligny-Montrachet Contrôlée, often leaves much to be desired. The yields are excessive and the wine too frequently light and watery. It is the Premier Cru and Grand Cru vineyards that have made this village a symbol of excellence, and are the reason why the wine world beats a path to the doors of the best cellars in search of extraordinary Chardonnays.

THE VINEYARDS OF PULIGNY-MONTRACHET

GRANDS CRUS VINEYARDS

Le Montrachet—It is one of those quirks of fate that the great Grand Cru vineyard of Le Montrachet is nearly always associated with the village of Puligny rather than that of Chassagne, even though a look at the map reveals that just a little more than half of Montrachet's 19.76 acres lies within the appellation of Puligny-Montrachet. Whatever the reason, the village of Chassagne has never quite been able to garner the reputation that Puligny has. Montrachet derives its name from the poor, rock-based hillside it sits on called Mont Rachat, literally translated to mean bare or bald mountain. There is no doubting this is a magical site with a superbly situated south to southeast exposure that basks the vineyard with maximum sunlight from dawn until midway through the evening.

Then, of course, there is the soil. It is mainly calcareous, permitting superb drainage and allowing the Chardonnay vines to firmly entrench their roots in the hard, limestone subsoil. Much has been made of the government's decision when building the famous superhighway, A-6, to spend significant amounts of money to divert the highway away from

Le Montrachet rather than jeopardize the integrity of this vineyard (I suspect only in France would this occur). Visitors will have no trouble finding the vineyard on a visit to the village. It is high up on the slope just to the south and west of the town, in the direction of Chassagne. The vineyard is well marked by a large gate with some formidable looking iron bars, suggesting that only growers are welcome (of course, only until the wine is ready to be sold).

Le Montrachet was entirely owned by one family, the Clermonde-Montoizons, until the French Revolution ensured that most of the privately owned or church-held Burgundy vineyards were divided among the peasants. Today, the three largest holders include Bouchard Père et Fils, the Domaine de Baron Thenard (the wine is commercialized by the Beaune *négociant* Remoissenet), and the Domaine Marquis de Laguiche (this wine is both produced and marketed exclusively by the Beaune firm of Joseph Drouhin). None of these producers makes the most admirable Montrachet, although Drouhin's Montrachet from the Marquis de Laguiche has begun to resemble what one might expect from a $200 bottle of Chardonnay. The progression in quality started with the 1979 vintage, and soared to star-like proportions in 1985, 1986, and 1988. The Montrachet from the Domaine de Baron Thenard is very good, but in a blind tasting with some of the top Premiers Crus, most objective tasters would walk away shaking their heads about its lackluster performance. Lastly, I have had enough experience with the Montrachets from Bouchard Père et Fils to recognize that these have never fulfilled one's expectations of what Montrachet should taste like.

This is not to suggest there are not some extraordinary Montrachets being made. One taste from a bottle of the 50 to 75 cases made each year by the Domaine Ramonet from vintages such as 1978, 1979, 1982, 1983, 1985, 1986, and even 1987 is enough to restore one's faith in the legendary prestige and acclaim everyone from Dr. Lavalle to Voltaire has extended to Montrachet. Ramonet's Montrachet is true nectar, with an opulence and intensity of flavor that is the essence of Chardonnay. Its clarity and precision, all the more difficult to achieve because of its awesome concentration, frequently produce a hauntingly perfect wine. It makes me wish that other producers would seek to attain such levels of quality.

If it is pure power and unctuous richness you desire, $500 will buy a bottle (provided you are able to find one) of the Domaine de la Romanée-Conti's Montrachet. This is an utterly mind-blowing Montrachet, but I should note that several British critics consider it overblown, too alcoholic, and perhaps too much of a good thing. Their production is between 7 and 14 barrels, and their yield per hectare is by far the most conservative of the appellation, ranging from a low of 15 hectolitres per hectare in 1981 to a very modest 31 hectolitres per hectare in the superabundant vintage of 1982. It makes a perfect present for billionaires.

Both of the Beaune *négociants*, Louis Latour and Louis Jadot, often produce an outstanding Montrachet that, though not quite up to the compelling level of quality of these wines made by the Domaine Ramonet or Domaine de la Romanée-Conti, are clearly wines that warrant their reputations. Another small grower who has a microparcel of Montrachet is Marc Colin. He produces 25 cases or less of an outstanding Montrachet, as does the Domaine Amiot-Bonfils. The problem with both Marc Colin and Guy Amiot is that their production is usually only one barrel, so very few people ever get a chance to taste their wines. One Montrachet that I am sure ages to perfection must be that of Comtes Lafon, but since I have never come close to seeing the wine near maturity, it is hard really to speculate how wonderful Lafon's Montrachet might be. Based on tastings young, it never quite seems to have the sheer style and complexity of their Meursault Les Perrières, or the concentration of their Meursault Les Charmes, but that might just be my inability to see through a wine that will not be ready to drink for 10 or 15 years.

The bottom line is that most people who buy Montrachet probably don't really care about its price. Rumors continue to circulate that the biggest markets for Montrachet are in Miami, where merchants often suspect that drug kingpins are this wine's most loyal customers. No doubt they lack the patience, given their short life expectancy, of waiting for a bottle of Montrachet to age properly.

Chevalier-Montrachet—If you have the requisite financial resources to spend $70 or $80 rather than $200-plus, my advice is to buy Chevalier-Montrachet. While the great Montrachets from Ramonet and Domaine de la Romanée-Conti are clearly better than any Chevalier-Montrachet I have ever tasted, most Chevalier-Montrachets are significantly superior to everybody else's Montrachets.

The vineyard, 18.1 acres in size, sits adjacent to Montrachet, but further up the hillside. It is entirely within the boundaries of Puligny-Montrachet. It is often pejoratively referred to as the chief pretender, but excluding the wines of Ramonet and the Domaine de la Romanée-Conti, a blind tasting might well prove that this pretender wears the crown. The slope of Chevalier-Montrachet is steeper, the soil thinner, and a walk through the vineyards reveals that the vines literally grow from a rocky, limestone base with hardly any topsoil.

The reason I am enthralled with so many of the wines from Chevalier-

Montrachet is because the producers who make this wine all seem to have such high aspirations. Perhaps the only exception is Bouchard Père et Fils. When compared to Montrachet, Chevalier-Montrachet seems more opulent, more honeyed, faster to age, and no doubt lacking the great longevity of a Montrachet from Ramonet or the Domaine de la Romanée-Conti. It ages magnificently for 10–12 years, which I suspect is more than sufficient for most readers.

The two most important vineyard holders are Bouchard Père et Fils (nearly 6 acres) and the Domaine Leflaive (nearly 5 acres). Their combined acreage is over half of this entire tiny vineyard. The Chevalier-Montrachet from Bouchard Père et Fils is an austere, often meagerly endowed wine that rarely blossoms forth into maturity. On the other hand, the Chevalier-Montrachet of Domaine Leflaive is a brilliant example of what decadent, hedonistic, opulent Chardonnay is all about.

Other superb Chevalier-Montrachets are made by the Domaine Jean Chartron, Louis Jadot, Louis Latour, Michel Niellon, and Georges Deleger. All these wines share an extraordinary concentration of flavor and richness, and I doubt any one of them will ever disappoint you.

Bâtard-Montrachet—Bâtard-Montrachet, like Le Montrachet, has its vineyards almost evenly split between the appellations of Puligny-Montrachet and Chassagne-Montrachet, yet it seems to be more properly associated with Puligny-Montrachet. The entire vineyard of 29.3 acres, of which 14.8 are in the appellation of Puligny, routinely produces over 5,000 cases of generally exceptional Chardonnay. It is rare to find a Bâtard-Montrachet with the same stunning concentration and richness as a Chevalier-Montrachet, but they do exist, particularly from producers such as Michel Niellon, Fernand Coffinet, Blain-Gagnard, Domaine Ramonet, Domaine Lequin-Roussot, Domaine Leflaive, and Domaine Bavard, who sell their exquisite wine to the *négociant* Antonin Rodet.

Situated just to the east of Le Montrachet, the soil of Bâtard-Montrachet is slightly richer and deeper, with the limestone outbreaks well covered by top soil. With the exception of the aforementioned producers' Bâtards, when I have a choice between a Bâtard-Montrachet and a Chevalier-Montrachet, I will usually pick the Chevalier because the difference in price between the two is negligible. But, since Bâtard is a larger vineyard and much more of it is available in the marketplace, consumers are more likely to encounter Bâtard, the bastard of Montrachet, as its name implies.

Bienvenues-Bâtard-Montrachet—Bienvenues-Bâtard-Montrachet is a tiny enclave surrounded on two sides by the Bâtard-Montrachet vineyard and on one side by the outstanding Premier Cru, Les Pucelles. It is the smallest of the Grands Crus, comprising only 9.1 acres. While the wines from the Domaine Ramonet, and on occasion those from the Domaine Leflaive and Robert Carillon, frequently justify their Grand Cru status, I have often thought this vineyard produces wines that are more legitimately Premiers Crus than Grands Crus. Perhaps that is because the wines from Bienvenues-Bâtard-Montrachet rarely ever seem to have the compelling richness and honeyed complexity of the other Grands Crus.

PREMIERS CRUS VINEYARDS

Puligny-Montrachet is blessed with 247 acres of superbly situated Premiers Crus that are located on the same slope as Bâtard-Montrachet, Le Montrachet, and Chevalier-Montrachet. The styles of the wines from the Premiers Crus vineyards obviously vary with the respective producers and vineyard locations, but for pure hedonistic richness and sumptuous flavors—and perhaps for what one might call the poor man's Chevalier-Montrachet—I have always been enamored with the Puligny-Montrachet Les Combettes. This vineyard is located next to the commune of Meursault and the outstanding Premier Cru vineyard of that appellation, Les Charmes. Les Combettes is one of the great secrets of the Domaine Leflaive, and is equally outstanding from the Domaine Sauzet and Robert Ampeau.

No other Premier Cru seems to equal Les Combettes for pure sumptuousness, richness, and power. But for the sheer elegance and finessse of great Chardonnay, Puligny-Montrachet has at least three vineyards capable of producing wines close to the quality of a Grand Cru. In order of quality they include Les Folatières, a large Premier Cru of nearly 42 acres that sits well behind the village, high up on the slope with an altitude and soil base not unlike that of Chevalier-Montrachet. Outstanding Puligny-Montrachet Les Folatières is produced by Paul Pernot, Joseph Drouhin, and Louis Jadot. Les Folatières seems to combine an extraordinary apple, buttery, mineral-scented elegance with graceful, stylish, wonderfully precise flavors that are never as opulent as Les Combettes or Chevalier-Montrachet, but never lacking for flavor or character.

Another superb Premier Cru vineyard is Les Pucelles, a 17-acre parcel adjacent to and just north of Bâtard-Montrachet and Bienvenues-Bâtard-Montrachet. An absolutely brilliant wine is made from this vineyard by both the Domaine Leflaive and Paul Pernot. In fact, I would argue that the Domaine Leflaive's Puligny-Montrachet Les Pucelles is often better than many producers' Bienvenues-Bâtard-Montrachets.

Another superb Premier Cru making the most structured and perhaps the longest-lived wines among the Premiers Crus of Puligny-Montrachet is Le Cailleret. This vineyard, not surprisingly, is on the upper slope, immediately adjacent to Le Montrachet. It is just under 10 acres in size, including a tiny 1.4-acre morsel called Les Demoiselles. Joseph Drouhin and Guy Amiot-Bonfils make exhilarating wines from Le Cailleret, as does Domaine Jean Chartron.

One of my favorite Premier Cru wines from Puligny-Montrachet (which I can usually only find on wine lists in French restaurants) is the outstanding Puligny-Montrachet La Truffière (6.12 acres) from the Domaine Étienne Sauzet. The tiny parcel of La Truffière is located up the slope, behind the village, near those sections of Puligny-Montrachet that can produce red wine. La Truffière is not the only excellent vineyard in this area of the appellation. Excellent wines are also made at Champ Gain and Les Chalumaux. It is in this area, which borders Blagny, where nearly 4,000 cases of Pinot Noir are made, called Puligny-Montrachet. It is quite rare, and not considered to be highly marketable, but for searchers of rare wines as well as curiosity seekers, a red Puligny-Montrachet is a prize to be desired. One producer who consistently makes a sound red Puligny-Montrachet is Henri Clerc.

In short, there are really not any disappointing Premiers Crus from Puligny-Montrachet as long as you restrict your purchases to the best producers.

VISITING THE VILLAGE OF PULIGNY-MONTRACHET AND ITS PRODUCERS

I do not find Puligny-Montrachet the most interesting village in Burgundy. That is not to suggest it does not make a pleasant place to visit and stay briefly. There is an excellent hotel and restaurant (Le Montrachet) situated right on the large, formal park in the middle of the village called Place de Maronnières. It has over 20 rooms and the cooking is top class. As one might expect, the wine list is loaded with treasures from the village. The fact that night life is nonexistent in the village means one will usually have a restful, tranquil night of sleep.

I do not see how any serious wine enthusiast could leave Puligny-Montrachet without visiting the Domaine Leflaive. It not only produces some of the greatest wines, but is also the home of Vincent Leflaive, one of the great personalities in all of Burgundy. His flamboyant style often is so captivating that one is tempted to ignore his wines, which are consistently great benchmarks for white burgundy. They are all elegance and style. Another superb domaine is that of Étienne Sauzet, which produces wines that are slightly fuller and richer, but of superlative quality.

CHASSAGNE-MONTRACHET

An Overview

Location: The drab, one-horse village of Chassagne-Montrachet (454 inhabitants) is even duller than Puligny-Montrachet. There is no park, little of architectural interest except for the attractive Château de la Maltroye, and no decent restaurants or hotels. Chassagne, located immediately south of Puligny-Montrachet, is the last and most southern of the three great white winemaking appellations of Meursault, Puligny-Montrachet, and Chassagne-Montrachet. A rarely discussed fact is that half of this village's production is in red wine.

Acres under vine: 1,109 acres

       Grands Crus: 28.17 acres, which includes 9.8 acres of Le Montrachet, 14.5 acres of Bâtard-Montrachet, and 3.9 acres of Criots-Bâtard-Montrachet that are located within the Chassagne appellation

      Premiers Crus: 392.2 acres

      Villages Wines: 443.6 acres are entitled to the Chassagne-Montrachet appellation; the balance is Côte de Beaune-Villages

Grands Crus: A total of 3

      Le Montrachet, Bâtard-Montrachet, Criots-Bâtard-Montrachet

Principal Premiers Crus: A total of 16

      Clos St.-Jean, Cailleret, Les Chaumées, Les Vergers, Les Chenevottes, La Maltroie, La Chapelle, Vigne Blanche, Morgeot, La Boudriotte, Les Embrazées, Les Baudines, La Romanée, Les Grandes Ruchottes, Champ Gain, Les Fairendes

Price levels: $50–$200 and up for Grands Crus; $25–$50 for Premiers Crus; $20–$30 for Villages wines

General wine characteristics: Just over half of this village's production is red wine, and these moderately priced, frequently overlooked red burgundies should not be ignored. The top red Chassagne-Montrachets are velvety, soft, light- to medium-bodied with a pronounced bing cherry fruitiness. The white wines tend to be fatter, more opulent, alcoholic, and dominated more by tropical fruit aromas and flavors such as pineapples, coconuts, and oranges than the more austere and restrained wines of Puligny-Montrachet. The overall quality of winemaking in Chassagne is excellent, higher than that of Puligny-Montrachet, although only the Domaine Ramonet is as internationally renowned as Leflaive and Sauzet are in Puligny.

The most overrated producers: René Lamy, Bernard Moreau

The best producers and their wines:

Red Wine

Jean-Noël Gagnard: Chassagne-Montrachet-Clos de la Maltroie, Chassagne-Montrachet-Clos St.-Jean

Duc de Magenta (Louis Jadot): Chassagne-Montrachet-Clos de la Chapelle

Château de la Maltroye: Chassagne-Montrachet-Clos du Château, Chassagne-Montrachet-Clos St.-Jean, Chassagne-Montrachet-Clos de la Boudriotte

Paul Pillot: Chassagne-Montrachet-Clos St.-Jean

Domaine Ramonet: Chassagne-Montrachet-Clos de la Boudriotte

Domaine Roux: Chassagne-Montrachet-Clos St.-Jean

White Wines

Bachelet-Ramonet: Chassagne-Montrachet La Romanée, Chassagne-Montrachet Les Caillerets, Chassagne-Montrachet Les Ruchottes

Blain Gagnard: Criots-Bâtard-Montrachet, Chassagne-Montrachet Les Caillerets, Bâtard-Montrachet

Marc Colin: Chassagne-Montrachet Les Caillerets, Chassagne-Montrachet Champ Gain

Georges Deleger: Chassagne-Montrachet Morgeot, Chassagne-Montrachet Les Vergers

Jean-Noël Gagnard: Bâtard-Montrachet, Chassagne-Montrachet Morgeot, Chassagne-Montrachet Les Caillerets

Gagnard-Delagrange: Bâtard-Montrachet, Chassagne-Montrachet Morgeot, Chassagne-Montrachet La Boudriotte

Lequin Roussot: Chassagne-Montrachet Les Caillerets, Bâtard-Montrachet, Chassagne-Montrachet Morgeot

Duc de Magenta (Louis Jadot): Chassagne-Montrachet-Clos de la Garenne, Chassagne-Montrachet-Clos de la Chapelle

Château de la Maltroye: Bâtard-Montrachet, Chassagne-Montrachet La Vigne Blanche, Chassagne-Montrachet Les Grandes Ruchottes, Chassagne-Montrachet La Romanée, Chassagne-Montrachet-Clos du Château

Bernard Morey: Chassagne-Montrachet Les Embrazées, Chassagne-Montrachet Morgeot, Chassagne-Montrachet Les Baudines, Chassagne-Montrachet Les Caillerets

Jean-Marc Morey: Chassagne-Montrachet Les Caillerets, Chassagne-Montrachet Les Chaumées

Marc Morey: Bâtard-Montrachet, Chassagne-Montrachet Les Chenevottes

Michel Niellon: Bâtard-Montrachet, Chassagne-Montrachet Les Vergers, Chassagne-Montrachet-Clos de la Maltroie

Paul Pillot: Chassagne-Montrachet La Romanée, Chassagne-Montrachet Les Caillerets

Domaine Ramonet: Bâtard-Montrachet, Chassagne-Montrachet Les Ruchottes,

Chassagne-Montrachet Les
Caillerets, Chassagne-Montrachet
Morgeot

Some important observations:

1. Currently, Chassagne-Montrachet is not as fashionable as its more sexy neighbors, Puligny-Montrachet and Meursault. That can be to the consumer's advantage, for not only is the overall quality of wine-making better than in Puligny, but prices are generally 15% to 25% lower for Chassagne's top Premiers Crus when compared to those of Puligny. White wine enthusiasts who prefer rich, lusty, heady, toasty, nutty Chardonnays with gobs of flavor will no doubt prefer Chassagne to Puligny.

2. There are 4 Premier Cru vineyards that can often rival the top Grands Crus. These are Les Embrazées (24.6 acres), Les Ruchottes (5.26 acres), and Les Caillerets (26.3 acres), all located south of the village, and Les Vergers (23.2 acres), north of the village.

3. Most *négociants* tend to buy much more wine from Meursault and Puligny-Montrachet than from Chassagne. Therefore, most of the production is estate-bottled. Outstanding small producers include the Domaine Ramonet, Michel Niellon, the various Moreys and Gagnards, Paul Pillot, Marc Colin, Georges Deleger, and the beautiful Château de la Maltroye.

4. While the image of Chassagne-Montrachet is of a white wine village, the significant production of good, sound red burgundy should be given consideration by cost-conscious consumers.

5. The straight Villages wines, entitled merely to the name of Chassagne-Montrachet, are significantly better than the Villages wines of Meursault and Puligny-Montrachet. Since Chassagne is not chic or à la mode, the growers tend to have more conservative yields and resist the temptation to stretch their vineyards.

Where are the values? Few white burgundies could ever be called "values," but if one compares prices, top Premiers Crus of Chassagne-Montrachet and the Villages wines are reasonably priced vis-à-vis their neighbors. In addition, several producers have very realistic pricing policies. Look for the white wines from Lequin-Roussot, Marc Colin, Paul Pillot, and the Château de la Maltroye. Red Chassagne-Montrachet is one of the Côte d'Or's most pleasingly priced wines. Any one of the red wine producers recommended above is a relatively good bargain.

Most successful recent vintages: 1989, 1988, 1987, 1986, 1985

Aging Potential: Grands Crus—7 to 15 years; Premiers Crus—3 to 10
    years; Villages wines—2 to 5 years

CHASSAGNE-MONTRACHET

(The most underrated village of Burgundy's Côte d'Or)

Three things come to mind when I think of Chassagne-Montrachet. One
—this village supposedly known for white wine actually produces more
red; two—nearly half of its vineyard area is entitled to be designated
as Premier Cru, an exceptionally high proportion that is rarely equaled
by any other appellation in the Côte d'Or; and three—I know of no
other village in France that has no restaurant, hotel, or bar. In fact,
several observers have argued that it is perhaps the lack of a bar (where
the producers and their clients could argue the merits of Chassagne-
Montrachet) that is the real reason why this village's wines have never
attained the reputation and following of those of its more prominent
neighbors, Puligny-Montrachet and Meursault. Chassagne-Montrachet
is the most underrated appellation of Burgundy, producing glorious
white wines, and a surprising number of delicious red wines.

Chassagne-Montrachet's winemaking history can be traced to the
third century, when vineyards were cultivated by local monastic orders.
Much of the history thereafter is unknown, save the destruction of the
village in the fifteenth century by Louis XI. While Chassagne's fame
today rests primarily on its white burgundy, there are some important
stone quarries in the hills behind the village that produce a pink marble-
like stone that is highly prized in the Côte de Beaune. But it is grapes,
not stones, that keep the tiny population of just over 500 content with
life.

THE VINEYARDS OF CHASSAGNE-MONTRACHET

GRANDS CRUS VINEYARDS

As I have mentioned, both the famed Grand Cru vineyards of Le Montrachet and Bâtard-Montrachet lie in both Puligny-Montrachet and
Chassagne-Montrachet. If one were to ask the general public what
appellation these two famous Grands Crus were most associated with,

no doubt the majority would say Puligny-Montrachet. However, the truth of the matter is that nearly half of each of these Grands Crus is situated in Chassagne-Montrachet. This little known fact says a lot about this appellation's lack of fame. Chassagne-Montrachet does have one Grand Cru that it does not share with Puligny-Montrachet, namely Criots-Bâtard-Montrachet.

Criots-Bâtard-Montrachet—This is the smallest of the Grands Crus in either Puligny-Montrachet or Chassagne-Montrachet, boasting only 3.87 acres. A look at the map of the commune shows that Criots resembles an unwanted appendage of Bâtard-Montrachet. What is also lamentable is that the growers who own parcels here, other than the Gagnard family—producers such as the Domaine Blondeau-Danne, Charles Bonnefoy, André Perrot, and René Renner—simply do not aspire to produce true Grand Cru Chardonnay from this vineyard. Perhaps the lackluster performance of the only Grand Cru that Chassagne can truly call its own has kept the popularity and recognition of this village's wines to a minimum.

PREMIERS CRUS VINEYARDS

Chassagne-Montrachet is a treasure trove for outstanding Premier Cru vineyards. In fact, certain Premiers Crus such as Les Caillerets, Les Ruchottes (also called Les Grandes Ruchottes), Les Vergers, and Les Embrazées are superlative vineyards producing wines from committed growers that often achieve Grand Cru status in quality if not in name. These are not the only excellent Premiers Crus, but they are the four that consistently stand out above the rest. There are also Les Baudines, which sits just to the north of Les Embrazées; La Romanée, which sits just south of Les Ruchottes; Les Chaumées, which sits just above and further up the hillside from Les Vergers; and other very good Premiers Crus such as Morgeot, Vigne Blanche, and La Maltroie. All of these vineyards are dedicated to the production of Chardonnay, which in Chassagne tends to have an opulent, toasty, smoky voluptuous texture, and intense perfume. If there is any criticism of this wine it is that rarely does Chassagne live as long in the bottle as a great Puligny-Montrachet. But since most white burgundies are drunk within several hours of purchase, I doubt this is a critical concern for many buyers.

Chassagne-Montrachet does produce some very good red wine, but it has been largely ignored by just about everyone but the local restaurants of the region. Most of the best wine comes from the Clos St.-Jean, La Boudriotte, or La Maltroie, all recognized as the best Premiers Crus vineyards for red wine. While in the past I often remarked that

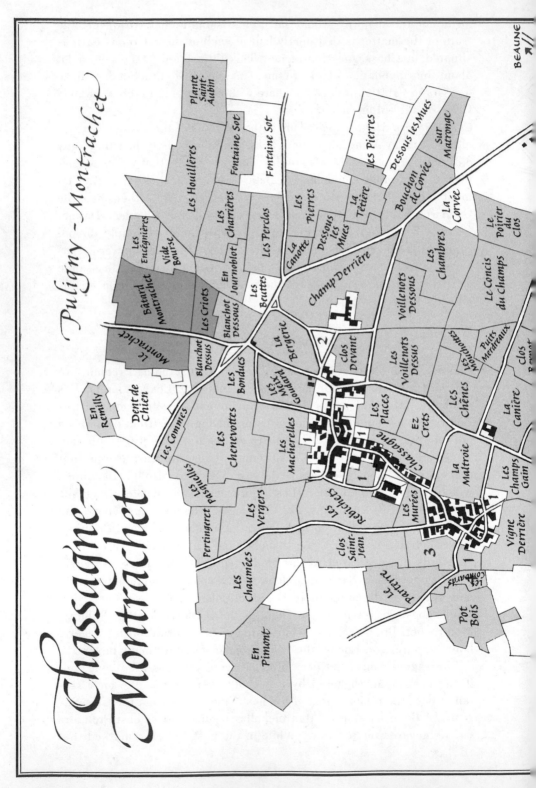

BEAUNE

Chassagne-Montrachet

Puligny-Montrachet

Plante Saint-Aubin

Fontaine Sot

Fontaine Sot

Les Houillières

Les Charrières

Les Pierres

Dessous les Mues

Sur Matronge

Les Perclos

Les Pierres

La Tétière

Bouchon de Corvée

La Corvée

Les Enseignères

Vide Bourse

La Canotte

Dessous les Mues

Les Chambres

Le Poirier du Clos

Bâtard Montrachet

Les Criots

En Journoblot

Blanchot Dessous

Les Beuttes

Champ Derrière

Voillenots Dessous

Le Concis du Champs

Le Montrachet

Blanchot Dessus

Les Bondues

La Bergerie

Clos Devant

Les Voillenots Dessus

Les Choinottes

Puits Merdreaux

Clos Pasout

En Remilly

Dent de Chien

Les Mexil Goudard

Les Chênes

La Canière

Les Commes

Les Macherelles

Les Places

Ez Crets

Les Champs Gain

Les Chenevottes

Chassagne

La Maltroie

Les Pasquelles

Pertingeret

Les Vergers

Les Rebichets

Les Murées

Vigne Derrière

Les Chaumées

Clos Saint-Jean

Le Parterre

Les Combards

En Pimont

Pot Bois

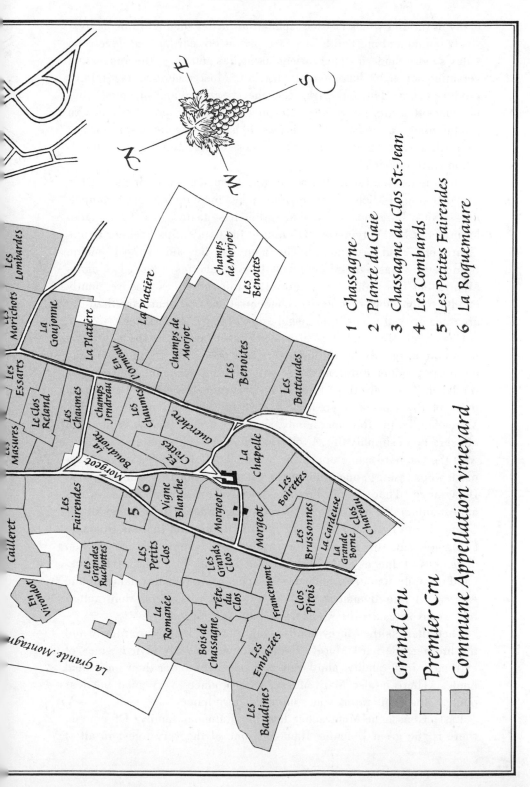

1 Chassagne
2 Plante du Gaie
3 Chassagne du Clos St.-Jean
4 Les Combards
5 Les Petites Fairendes
6 La Roquemaure

Grand Cru
Premier Cru
Commune Appellation vineyard

many of the red wines of Chassagne-Montrachet seemed to be aggressively tannic and marked by a very pronounced, earthy *gout de terroir*,
today's more modern style of winemaking has enhanced the appeal and
versatility of red Chassagne-Montrachet. Most recent vintages have
produced some deliciously fragrant, cherry-scented and -flavored, supple wines that are, given the stratospheric prices for most Premier Cru
red burgundy, quite fairly priced. I would have to say the best red wines
from Chassagne-Montrachet are even more underrated than that appellation's white wines.

Chassagne-Montrachet has some superb small growers, including the
tiny domaine of Michel Niellon, who makes outstanding, even compelling white burgundies. Anyone who has tasted his Chassagne-
Montrachet Les Vergers realizes that in his hands, this Premier Cru is
clearly of Grand Cru quality. The same can be said of the Domaine
Ramonet's Chassagne-Montrachet Les Ruchottes and Chassagne-
Montrachet Les Caillerets, two utterly profound wines that frequently
exhibit much more complexity, concentration, and character than the
great majority of wines from neighboring Puligny-Montrachet.

Chassagne-Montrachet is also a perfect example of the confusing
nature of Burgundy, of the problems that occur when multiple family
members produce different wines with the same surname appearing on
the label. There are three families in Chassagne-Montrachet that have
undoubtedly caused a great deal of confusion for consumers—the
Morey family, the Ramonet family, and the Gagnard family. While I am
not sure I can simplify this, I will try. There are four separate domaines
with the Gagnard name appearing on the label. There is Jacques Gagnard, whose wines appear under the estate name of Domaine Gagnard-
Delagrange. There is his brother, Jean-Noël Gagnard, whose wines
appear under his own name. There is a separate estate called Blain-
Gagnard, run by Jean-Marc and Claudine Blain. And there is Domaine
Fontaine-Gagnard. These latter two estates came into being when
daughters of Jacques Gagnard married into other families. The husband's family name, in both cases, appears first in the name of the
estate. All four domaines produce excellent Chassagne-Montrachet,
but my favorites are the wines from Jean-Noël Gagnard.

Then there is the Morey family, comprised of Jean-Marc Morey and
his brother, Bernard Morey. Both produce similarly styled wines of
extremely high quality, and bottle and sell them under their individual
names. There is also Marc Morey, who produces very good but less
opulent and exhilarating wines under his own name.

Last, Chassagne-Montrachet has the Ramonet family. Of course,
there is the great Domaine Ramonet, one of the very finest in all of

winedom. Run by the father, André, with his two sons, Noël and Jean-Claude, who have assumed increasing control, the Domaine Ramonet is the beginning and end of the search for profound Chardonnay for many Burgundy wine lovers. But there are other Ramonets, in particular, Pierre, the brother of André, who makes the wines of the Domaine Ramonet-Prudhon, which can be very good but are inconsistent. Even at their best they are never of the same class of those of the Domaine Ramonet. And there is the Domaine Bachelet-Ramonet, managed by Jean Bachelet, who married one of the Ramonet women. It is horrifying for the neophyte to be confronted with all these different labels, and it is one of the reasons for the great confusion and complications of buying red and white burgundy today.

VISITING THE VILLAGE OF CHASSAGNE-MONTRACHET AND ITS PRODUCERS

You had better bring along a camper or be prepared to sleep under the stars if you want to spend a night in Chassagne-Montrachet, as there is no hotel in the village. The best place to use as a base for visiting the growers in Chassagne-Montrachet is probably Puligny-Montrachet. There is no better hotel and restaurant close by than Le Montrachet in Puligny. Of course one could throw caution to the wind and stay at the luxurious three-star restaurant and hotel complex of Lameloise, in the industrial village of Chagny, only several miles further south.

There are a lot of interesting growers to visit in Chassagne, but be prepared to speak French as most of them are used to seeing only people from the trade. If you are able to arrange a visit, the Domaine Ramonet is a required stop on anyone's itinerary. Other superb estates to visit include either Jean-Marc or Bernard Morey, Michel Niellon, and the most beautiful château in the village, the Château de la Maltroye. Fortunately, their wines, which were somewhat spotty in the late seventies, have been increasingly well made during the decade of the eighties.

SAINT-AUBIN

An Overview

Location: Several miles west of Chassagne-Montrachet, adjacent to Autoroute 6, in a valley flanked by several steep slopes, is Saint-Aubin and the nearby hamlet of Gamay. Saint-Aubin borders the appellations of both Puligny-Montrachet and Chassagne-Montrachet. The population of this tiny village consists of 281 Saint-Aubinois.

Acres under vine: 584 acres out of a total plantable appellation area of 1,588 acres, 70% planted in Pinor Noir and 30% in Chardonnay
   Grands Crus: None
  Premiers Crus: 386.5 acres
  Villages Wines: 198 acres

Grands Crus: None

Principal Premiers Crus: A total of 10
   Le Charmois, En Remilly, Les Murgers des Dents de Chien, Les Frionnes, Sur le Sentier du Clou, Es Champs, Les Castets, Le Village, La Chatenière, Sous Roche Dumay

Price levels: Price levels are on the rise, as consumers and members of the wine trade increasingly recognize the potential for high quality red and white wines from this appellation. Villages wines still sell for $12–$16 a bottle, but the Premiers Crus now range in price from $12–$20.

General wine characteristics: The red wines from the better producers who own old vines can be surprisingly robust, full, concentrated, and chewy. They represent true discoveries. The white wines are often excellent, exhibiting a stony, hazelnut-scented fruitiness and good depth—a poor man's Puligny-Montrachet!

The most overrated producers: Lamy-Pillot

The best producers and their wines:

Jean-Claude Bachelet: Saint-Aubin Les Champlots (white), Saint-Aubin Derrière la Tour (red)

Raoul Clerget: Saint-Aubin Charmois (white), Saint-Aubin Les Frionnes (red)

Charton et Trébuchet: Saint-Aubin (white), Saint-Aubin La Chatenière (white)

Marc Colin: Saint-Aubin La Chatenière (white), Saint-Aubin (red)

Langoureau (Gilles Bouton): Saint-Aubin en Remilly (red)

Bernard Moreau: Saint-Aubin en Remilly (white)

Bernard Morey: Saint-Aubin (white)

Jean-Marc Morey: Saint-Aubin Le Charmois (white)

Henri Prudhon: Saint-Aubin Sentiers de Clou (red), Saint-Aubin Les Frionnes (red), Saint-Aubin (white)

Domaine Roux Père et Fils: Saint-Aubin La Pucelle (white), Saint-Aubin La Chatenière (white), Saint-Aubin (red)

Gérard Thomas: Saint-Aubin Les Murgers des Dents de Chien (white), Saint Aubin les Frionnes (red)

Some important observations:

1. This appellation will come under increasing scrutiny given the generally high level of quality of its wines and its fair prices.

2. Saint-Aubin houses some very talented, highly motivated winemakers, such as Jean-Claude Bachelet, Marc Colin, Gérard Thomas, Henri Prudhon, Gilles Bouton, and the Domaine Roux Père et Fils.

3. The appellation has two distinct sectors. One is near the hamlet of Gamay. The finest white wines are from the Premiers Crus in this area, because these vineyards have excellent exposure and a limestone soil. La Chatenière, Le Charmois, and Sous Roche Dumay are located on this slope. Many of the best red wines come from the Montagne du Ban, a stretch of rocky soil that runs south from Gamay to the village of Saint-Aubin. Les Frionnes and Sur le Sentier du Clou are located there.

4. French authorities have seen fit to bestow Premier Cru status on 67% of the current acreage under vine—impressive credentials for a largely unknown appellation.

Where are the values? They are everywhere, but move quickly, as reputations and prices of the wines of many of these young, ambitious growers can only go up.

Most successful recent vintages: 1989, 1988, 1986, 1985

Aging potential: Premiers Crus (red)—3 to 7 years; Premiers Crus (white)—2 to 4 years; Villages wines (red)—2 to 4 years; Villages wines (white)—1 to 3 years

SAINT-AUBIN

(A star of the 1990s?)

Not every appellation in Burgundy produces overpriced, over exposed, over glamorous wines that require you to take out a second mortgage on your home to purchase them. Saint-Aubin is a burgundy wine lover's paradise. It is filled with young, talented, aggressive, and ambitious growers, and possesses some excellent vineyards poised to produce both top-quality red and white Burgundy. Like Saint-Romain, Saint-Aubin sits behind the more famous appellations of the Côte d'Or, nestled in a valley several minutes away from Puligny-Montrachet and Chassagne-Montrachet. The appellation takes its name from the village of Saint-Aubin, but there is also the neighboring hamlet of Gamay. The grape varietal used to produce Beaujolais was named after this village. However, the Gamay that was once planted here proved to be too plebian for the tastes of the local elite and was banned by the Ducs of Burgundy. Today this is a good fertile area for Chardonnay and Pinot Noir.

THE VINEYARDS OF SAINT-AUBIN

Two-thirds of the current acreage under vine in Saint-Aubin is entitled to Premier Cru status, an impressive statistic that reflects confidence that this is an up-and-coming appellation. The vineyards themselves begin just north of the appellation border of Puligny-Montrachet and Chassagne-Montrachet, winding their way up the hillside of the Roche Dumay to the little village of Gamay. There they turn west and south, running along the Montagne du Ban to the village of Saint-Aubin and beyond. All the best Premiers Crus for Chardonnay tend to be, not surprisingly, on the Chassagne and Puligny border. Here are excellent vineyards, such as Le Charmois (37 acres), En Remilly (70 acres), La

Chatenière (17.5 acres), Les Murgers des Dents de Chien (39.5 acres), and Sous Roche Dumay (5.5 acres). While some very tasty cherry-scented and -flavored, elegant red wines are produced from this limestone soil mixed with gravel and brown clay, it is the Chardonnay that seems to excel here. Most observers and producers feel this is where the future for the finest Chardonnay from Saint-Aubin lies.

The other band of *terroir* is also characterized by a great deal of limestone and rocky soil, but has a more easterly as opposed to south-easterly exposure. Pinot Noir seems to do better than Chardonnay in such excellent Premier Cru vineyards here as Les Frionnes (29.6 acres) and Sentier du Clou (27 acres). To the southwest of the village of Saint-Aubin is the last Premier Cru, Les Castets. The rest of this area under vine is entitled only to Villages wines status. I have tasted some attractive, lighter-styled white burgundies from the very northwestern end of the appellation of Saint-Aubin called Les Pucelles.

For whatever reason, the *négociants* of Beaune have essentially let the growers of Saint-Aubin alone. The result has been a highly competitive but friendly effort to attract the public's attention to the wines of Saint-Aubin. It is interesting that Saint-Aubin probably has as many up-and-coming young, inspired growers as the internationally known village of Gevrey-Chambertin in the northern Côte de Nuits. For example, who could discount the talents and the wines made to date by Jean-Claude Bachelet, Marc Colin, Gérard Thomas, Henri Prudhon, Gilles Bouton, and Bernard and Jean-Marc Morey, who, of course, are much more associated with their brilliant wines from Chassagne-Montrachet, but who also make excellent Saint-Aubin. The only *négociant* who seems to have recognized the potential for high-quality wines from Saint-Aubin is Charton et Trébuchet, located in neighboring Puligny-Montrachet. I predict this lack of attention will change. On my last several visits I have noticed a definite increase in the number of members of the wine trade—as well as private clients—knocking on the doors of Saint-Aubin's producers.

VISITING THE VILLAGE OF SAINT-AUBIN AND ITS PRODUCERS

In the hamlet of Gamay there is the striking Château de Gamay, which is well worth a visit, as well as a Romanesque church. There are no restaurants or hotels, but Saint-Aubin is less than 10 minutes by car from Puligny-Montrachet and Meursault. The narrow streets and old stone homes make walking around this quaint, old winemaking village quite rewarding.

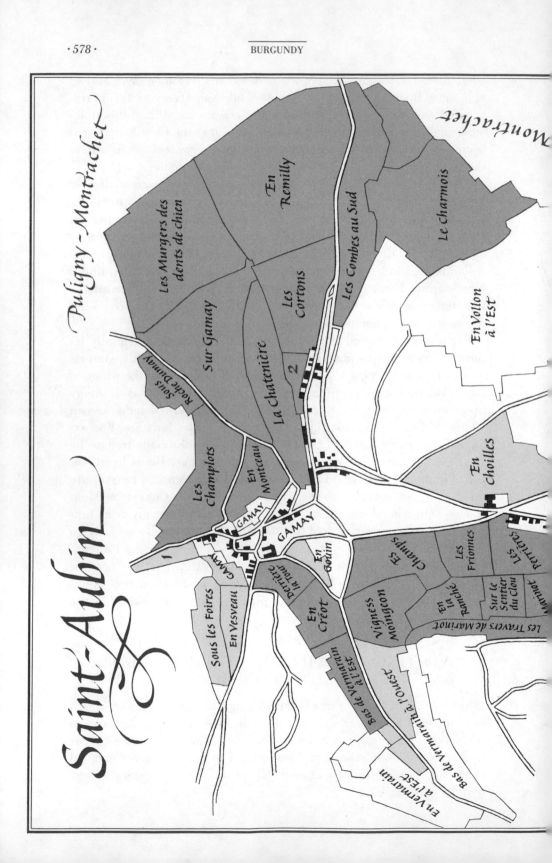

Saint-Aubin

Puligny-Montrachet

Montrachet

Les Murgers des dents de chien

En Remilly

Le Charmois

Les Cortons

Les Combes au Sud

En Vollon à l'Est

Sur Gamay

La Chatenière

2

Sous Roche Dumay

En Choilles

Les Champlots

En Monteceau

GAMAY

GAMAY

Les Frionnes

Les Perrières

1

CAVAY

Derrière la Tour

En Gollin

Es Champs

En la Ranché

Marinot

Sous les Foires

En Vesveau

En Créot

Vignes Moingeon

Sur le Sentier du Clou

Les Travers de Marinot

Bas de Vermarain à l'Est

Bas de Vermarain à l'ouest

En Vermarain à l'Est

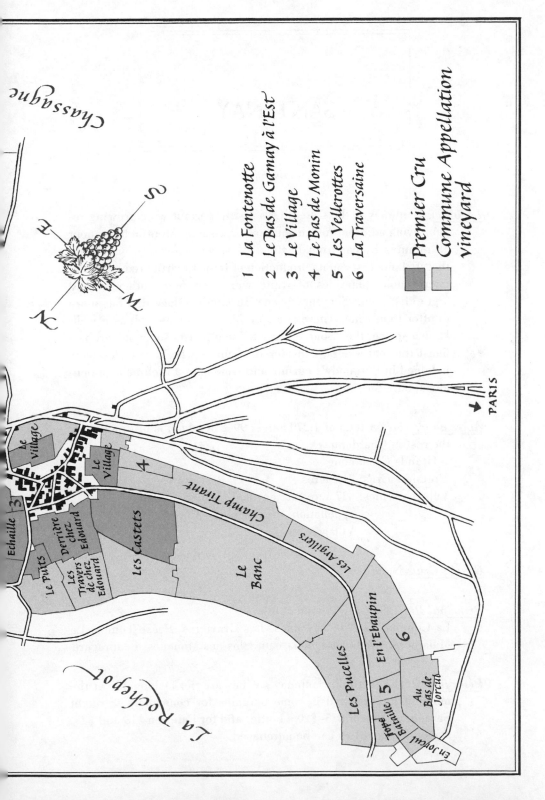

Chassagne

La Rochepot

Chassagne

1 La Fontenotte
2 Le Bas de Gamay à l'Est
3 Le Village
4 Le Bas de Monin
5 Les Vellerottes
6 La Traversaine

Premier Cru
Commune Appellation vineyard

PARIS

Le Village
Le Village
Echaille
Le Puits
Les Travers de chez Edouard
Derrière chez Edouard
Les Castets
Champ Tirant
Les Argillers
Le Banc
Les Pucelles
En l'Ebaupin
Au Bas de Jorcul
Sous Bataille
En Jocul

SANTENAY

An Overview

Location: Santenay is the Côte d'Or's last important wine growing region, lying adjacent to and south of Chassagne-Montrachet, about 15 minutes by car from Beaune. Most wine lovers would claim that its fame rests on its production of robust, earthy red wine and microscopic quantities of white wine, but many others would argue that point. Santenay is one Burgundy village that has more to offer than wine. There is a gambling casino as well as a well-known spring, the "Source Carnot," that boasts some of Europe's finest thermal waters, considered by many who have excessively indulged in Burgundy's cuisine and wine over a lifetime as a beneficial cure for gout.

Acres under vine: A total of 1,270 acres, 99% of which is in Pinot Noir, the rest in Chardonnay
    Grands Crus: none
   Premiers Crus: 319 acres
   Villages Wines: 627 acres are entitled to the Santenay appellation; the balance is Côte de Beaune-Villages

Grands Crus: None

Principal Premiers Crus: A total of 8
    La Comme, Clos de Tavannes, Les Gravières, Passe Temps, La Maladière, Grand Clos Rousseau, Clos des Mouches, Beauregard

Price levels: The fact that Santenay's wines are not fashionable at the moment has resulted in some bargains for consumers. Straight Santenay sells for $15–$20 a bottle; and for between $18 and $25, a good Premier Cru can be purchased.

General wine characteristics: Undoubtedly there are far too many Santenays that are excessively tannic, hollow, and pleasureless
wines, but the good examples tend to possess more than adequate
strawberry and cherry fruit, have a pronounced mineral-like,
stony, earthy character along with the scent of almonds, and good
body. Furthermore, the best examples exhibit surprising aging
potential.

The most overrated producers: No producers or growers here can boast
an inflated reputation.

The best producers and their wines:
          Bernard Bachelet: Santenay
          Adrien Belland: Santenay-Clos des Gravières, Santenay
                 La Comme
          Marc Colin: Santenay
          Joseph Drouhin: Santenay
          Jean-Noël Gagnard: Santenay-Clos de Tavannes
          Jean Girardin: Santenay-Clos Rousseau, Santenay La
                 Maladière, Santenay La Comme
          Jessiaume Père: Santenay Gravières (red), Santenay Les
                 Gravières (white)
          Lequin-Roussot: Santenay Premier Cru (white)
          Leroy: Santenay
          Château de La Maltroye: Santenay (white), Santenay La Comme,
                 Santenay Les Gravières
          Bernard Morey: Santenay-Grand Clos Rousseau
          Jean-Marc Morey: Santenay-Grand Clos Rousseau
          Domaine de la Pousse d'Or: Santenay-Clos Tavannes
          Prieur-Brunet: Santenay La Maladière, Santenay La
                 Comme, Santenay-Clos Rousseau (white),
                 Santenay Les Gravières
          Prosper-Maufoux: Santenay-Domaine St.-Michel, Santenay-
                 Clos des Gravières (white)
          Remoissenet: Santenay-Clos de Tavannes, Santenay
                 Les Gravières

Some important observations:
1. Santenay is an elongated appellation spreading out over an area that
   includes three villages—Santenay Le Haut (where the casino and
   springs are), Santenay Le Bas, where many of the growers have their
   cellars, and Saint-Jean, a tiny village with a charming Romanesque

church. The best vineyards run from Santenay Le Bas north to the border of the appellation of Chassagne-Montrachet. In this sector lie Les Gravières, La Comme, Clos de Tavannes, and Passe Temps, irrefutably the four best red wine vineyards of Santenay.

2. As fashionable as Santenay's spa may be with Burgundy's middle class, the wines have never been à la mode. This has kept supplies adequate and prices reasonable. However, even the best examples of Santenay are hardly mindblowing red or white burgundies. At best, good Santenay fills a void, and represents an earthy, spicy style of affordable Pinot Noir. The best red wines from the top growers do repay keeping for upwards of ten years, so they cannot be criticized for their lack of longevity.

3. Santenay is the home of one major *négociant*, Prosper Maufoux, which produces sound rather than exhilarating wines from many different appellations. Their best wines are, not surprisingly, their Santenays.

4. From a viticultural perspective, Santenay is a curiosity, as the choice of pruning methods is different from most other Burgundy appellations. In Santenay (as well as Chassagne-Montrachet) the Cordon de Royat system is preferred over the more commonly seen Guyot pruning method. This is of importance because the soil is richer than in other appellations of the Côte d'Or, and seems to tire out the vines at a much younger age. Consequently, a drive through the vineyards of Santenay always reveals much younger-looking vines than in other appellations. Santenay's growers claim this method causes more-even ripening and is effective against the early spring frosts that tend to plague Santenay more than other appellations. Critics argue that it results in excessive yields.

Where are the values? Stick to the best producers and, in general, their Premiers Crus in the top vintages. You can then be assured of getting a well-made, fairly priced bottle of wine.

Most successful recent vintages: 1989, 1988, 1985

Aging Potential: Premiers Crus (red)—5 to 12 years; Premiers Crus (white)—3 to 7 years; Villages wines (red)—3 to 7 years

SANTENAY

(Overcoming the image as the "last" of the
Côte d'Or appellations)

Santenay, with its population of just over 1,000 people, is either at the beginning or the end of Burgundy's Côte d'Or—depending on from which direction you arrive. It must be the only appellation in Burgundy that can boast three villages. It encompasses a serpentine stretch of vineyards that totals approximately 1,270 acres.

The wines of Santenay, which are 99% red, have always had an image problem. Many people would rather spend their money in Santenay's gambling casino or taking the cure with the village's therapeutic waters than on a bottle of the village's wine. One noted British wine merchant even went on record as saying, "Life's too short to drink Santenay." All of this seems a bit unfair, particularly if you take the time to search out the best wines from this appellation. Times have changed, and the winemaking is now better than when many casually dismissed the wines of Santenay as if they were an afterthought or an unmerited appendage to the rest of Burgundy's Côte d'Or.

There are some surprisingly good white wines made in Santenay, although the quantities produced are so tiny that their commercial viability and visibility are limited. However, the red wines offer good value, and the best examples have an attractive strawberry, cherry fruitiness often intermixed with the intense smell of almonds. There does seem to be a pronounced earthiness in many wines of Santenay, a characteristic shared by the red wines of its northern neighbor, Chassagne-Montrachet, as well.

Santenay, called Sentennacum in Roman times, deserves a more cherished place in the heart of the wine consumer. Perhaps importers need to be more aggressive in promoting the wines of Santenay so consumers have the best selection available.

THE VINEYARDS OF SANTENAY

Traditional logic has always held (and I agree) that the very best wines of Santenay come from the border of Chassagne-Montrachet, particularly from vineyards such as La Comme (53.3 acres), Les Gravières (56.8 acres), the smaller Clos de Tavannes (14 acres), actually considered to be part of Les Gravières, and Le Passe Temps (28.3 acres). These vineyards, which have more of a gravelly, limestone/marl-based soil, produce wines with more structure, richness, and tannin. All these

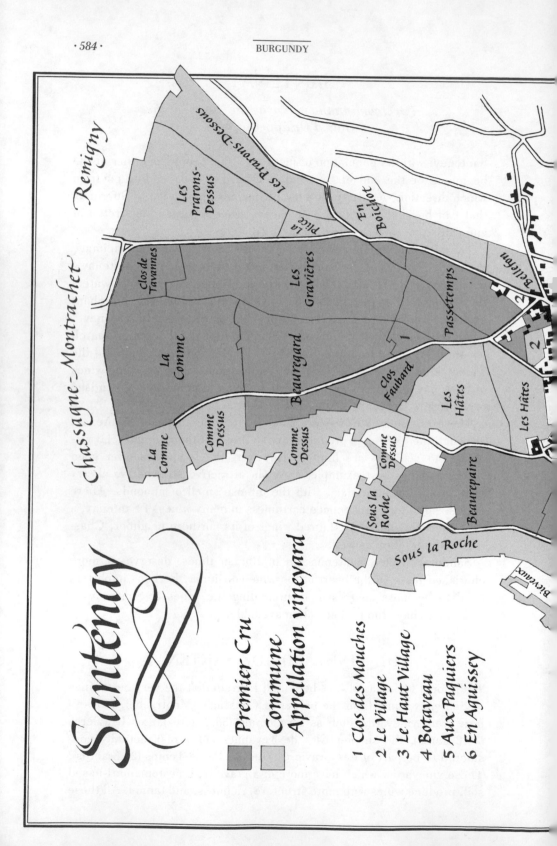

Santenay

Premier Cru
Commune
Appellation vineyard

1 Clos des Mouches
2 Le Village
3 Le Haut Village
4 Botaveau
5 Aux Paquiers
6 En Aguissey

Remigny

Chassagne-Montrachet

Les Prarons-Dessus

Les Prarons-Dessus

En Boichot

La Plice

Clos de Tavannes

Les Gravières

Passetemps

Belefon

La Comme

Beauregard

Clos Fauband

Les Hâtes

Les Hâtes

La Comme

Comme Dessus

Comme Dessus

Comme Dessus

Beaurepaire

Sous la Roche

Sous la Roche

Bievaux

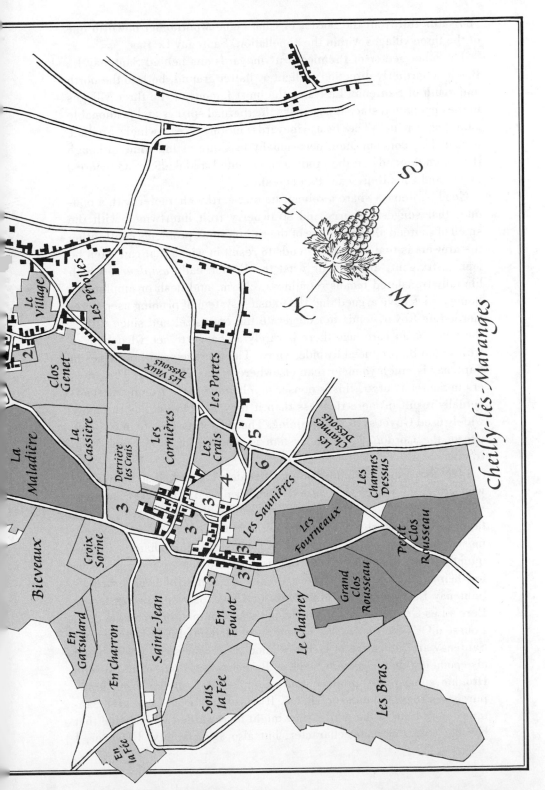

Cheilly-lès-Maranges

Le Village
Les Pérolles
Clos Genet
Les Vaux Dessous
Les Potets
La Maladière
La Cassière
Derrière les Crais
Les Cornières
Les Crais
Les Charmes Dessous
Bicveaux
Croix Sorine
Les Saunières
Les Fourneaux
Petit Clos Rousseau
En Gatsulard
En Charron
Saint-Jean
En Foulot
Le Chainey
Grand Clos Rousseau
Sous la Fée
Les Bras
En la Fée

vineyards run from the border of Chassagne-Montrachet down to one of the three villages within the appellation, Santenay Le Bas.

The other sector of Premier Cru vineyards sits behind Santenay Le Bas in a northerly direction on lighter, flatter ground, both to the north and south of Santenay Le Haut, the most famous of the three villages in the appellation since it possesses the thermal springs and fashionable gambling casino. The best vineyards in this area, which produce lighter, less concentrated, occasionally less interesting wine (although that often depends on the producer), include La Maladière (33.6 acres) and Grand Clos Rousseau (19.4 acres).

Good Santenays share a robust, tannic, earthy character with a bouquet that suggests cherry and strawberry fruit intertwined with the smell of sautéed almonds. One of the troublesome problems confronting the growers is that the *terroir* tends to result in wines that can often be lean, astringent, and lacking what the French call *"ampleur,"* which liberally translated means roundness, charm, and flesh or ampleness. Some critics have argued that the unusual system of pruning used here, Cordon de Royat, tends to exaggerate the crop size, and since it tires the vines at an early age there is rarely a chance to see what kind of fruit would be produced by older vines. The average age of the vines in Santenay is much younger than elsewhere in the Côte d'Or. The growers in Santenay argue this is nonsense, claiming their pruning methods actually result in more ripeness than if they were to employ the more widely used Guyot system of pruning. The only other area to make wide use of the Cordon de Royat system is neighboring Chassagne-Montrachet.

I feel that I must defend Santenay because I have had so many good wines from the village that were reasonably priced. The best Santenays need some time to mellow and shed some of their astringent, coarse tannins, but because the wines are not terribly expensive or renowned, most consumers tend to want to pull their corks immediately. Consequently, they often find a wine that is a bit too coarse and aggressive for their tastes. Certainly a 5- to 10-year-old example of Jean Girardin's Santenay La Comme, La Maladière, or Clos Rousseau, or Jessiaume Père's Les Gravières, or Prieur-Brunet's La Comme, or Domaine de la Pousse d'Or's Santenay-Clos Tavannes, or Madame Lalou Bize-Leroy's Santenay are indicative of just how good these wines can be. I should also point out that *négociants* such as Remoissenet, Bourée, and Joseph Drouhin consistently produce fine examples of Santenay from grape purchases they make in the village. If consumers would just give Santenay more time in the bottle, they might be rewarded with a wine that has not only surprising character, but also aging ability. However, I

would caution that this is not an appellation to buy in rainy, damp years.
It is best to restrict your purchases to years where there is super ripeness, such as 1989, 1988, and 1985. The vineyards drain less well in
Santenay than those further north in the Côte d'Or. Consequently,
given the younger vines and their seemingly unquenchable thirst, a
rainy harvest is often anathema to the quality of Santenay.

VISITING THE VILLAGE OF SANTENAY AND ITS PRODUCERS

For some inexplicable reason Santenay was snubbed in the 1990 edition
of France's Guide Michelin, which of course only serves to encourage
the lack of respect that this village's growers must endure. Perhaps
Santenay's biggest problem is that unlike every other village in the Côte
d'Or, there is not one truly compelling producer consistently turning
out great wines who would serve as a magnet or drawing card for the
wine trade and tourists. Certainly the therapeutic springs and gambling
casino bring plenty of visitors to the village, but Santenay has yet to
discover the formula for promoting its own wines. The growers themselves are partially to blame as they are fiercely independent and individualistic. This is the only appellation that seems to lack an espirit de
corps among its growers. They have never been able to reach an agreement as to how to promote their wines.

Nevertheless, there are some great characters in Santenay for adventurous wine travelers to meet. Brothers René and Louis Lequin of the
Domaine Lequin-Roussot make splendid white wines from the vineyards in Chassagne, and in 1988 began a highly motivated program to
improve the quality of their red wines. This may well be the domaine
to emerge in the nineties for both top-quality red and white wine. This
Mutt-and-Jeff duo is an engaging twosome, and a visit to their cellars is
highly recommended. If you can persuade them to open a bottle of their
Bâtard-Montrachet or Chassagne-Montrachet Les Vergers you are in
for one of the best white wine drinking experiences in all of Burgundy.

Another cellar clearly worth visiting, although I find the wines less
interesting than the producer, is that of Philippe, Gérard, Michel, and
Gilbert Mestre. They certainly have enough commitment, but their
wines often seem too rustic and earthy. Of course, the most famous
estate in all of Santenay is that of the large *négociant*, Prosper-Maufoux, who owns the Domaine St.-Michel in Santenay. As I have already
stated, their wines are sound, but rarely inspirational.

The casino in Santenay is closed in the winter, and since I have never
partaken of the cure, I cannot speak with any experience regarding the

alleged beneficial effects of the spa, where the water is so high in lithium it is considered to be a wonderful cure for anxiety. Wine seems to do the same thing for me. Traveling around the hillsides of Santenay one is likely to encounter some windmills, which are somewhat unusual for this particular region. Windmills are much more in evidence further south in the Mâconnais and Beaujolais areas. Additionally, there is a superb church in the little hamlet of Saint-Jean (just adjacent to Santenay Le Haut) that is renowned for its stunning statues. In fact, the Église St.-Jean is clearly the most interesting architectual building of Santenay, although less visited than the nearby casino.

Should you be inclined to spend the night in Santenay, the Hôtel Santana on the Avenue des Sources, with its 60-plus rooms, is good. While I have never eaten in the restaurant, it enjoys a fine reputation.

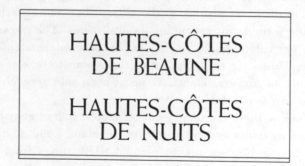

HAUTES-CÔTES DE BEAUNE
HAUTES-CÔTES DE NUITS

An Overview

<u>Location</u>: *Hautes-Côtes de Beaune*—The Hautes-Côtes de Beaune consists of three viticultural areas located to the west of the Côte de Beaune. The smallest, about 4 miles long and 1 mile wide, is northwest of Aloxe-Corton on both sides of D 18. A second area is traversed by D 23 out of Monthélie, and is situated behind the renowned appellations of Volnay, Pommard, and Beaune. The largest sector is approximately 9 miles long and 6 miles wide. It begins in the north behind Saint-Romain and ends in the south well west of the town of Chagny and the three Côte de Beaune villages of Dezize-Lès-Maranges, Sampigny-Lès-Maranges, and Cheilly-Lès-Maranges. It is best reached by taking N 6 from Saint-Aubin in the direction of Nolay, or by following the signs in Saint-Aubin for La Rochepot.

Hautes-Côtes de Nuits—The entire appellation, about 6 miles wide and 9 miles long, sits on the hillsides and plateaus west of the Côte de Nuits. The villages of Corgoloin and Chambolle-Musigny mark the southern and northern borders, respectively. The area is best reached by taking D 115 west from Corgoloin, or D 25 west from Nuits St.-Georges.

Acres under vine:
Hautes-Côtes de Beaune: 617 acres; 36% Pinot Noir, 64% Chardonnay
   Hautes-Côtes de Nuits: 494 acres; 97% Pinot Noir, 3% Chardonnay

Grands Crus:
Hautes-Côtes de Beaune: none
   Hautes-Côtes de Nuits: none

Premiers Crus:
Hautes-Côtes de Beaune: none
   Hautes-Côtes de Nuits: none

Communes having the right to the Hautes-Côtes de Beaune appellation:
   Baubigny, Bouze-Lès-Beaune, Cirey-Lès-Nolay, Cornot, Echevronne, La Rochepot, Mavilly-Mandelot, Meloisey, Nantoux, Nolay, Vauchignon, Change, Creot, Epertully, Paris l'Hôpital, and part of the communes of Cheilly-Lès-Maranges, Dezize-Lès-Maranges, and Sampigny-Lès-Maranges

Communes having the right to the Hautes-Côtes de Nuits appellation:
   Arcenant, Bevy, Chaux, Chevannes, Collonges les Bevy, Curtil-Vergy, L'Etang-Vergy, Magny les Villers, Messanges, Marey les Fussey, Reulle-Vergy, Segrois, Villars-Fontaine, Villers-la-Faye, Meuilley

Price levels: Inexpensive to moderate. Most of these wines sell for $8–$15 a bottle.

General wine characteristics: As befitting appellations with an extremely high percentage of young vines, the wines are light, but there are several superb producers who magically attain levels of quality that are stunning. As a general rule, the white wines are fresher and more consistent than the reds. In addition to Chardonnay, there is also some Pinot Gris, Pinot Blanc, and Aligoté planted in the Hautes-Côtes.

The most overrated producers: None

The best producers and their wines:

Hautes-Côtes de Beaune

Denis Caré: Bourgogne Hautes-Côtes de Beaune (red)

François Charles: Bourgogne Hautes-Côtes de Beaune (red)

Doudet-Naudin: Bourgogne Hautes-Côtes de Beaune (red)

Jean Féry: Bourgogne Hautes-Côtes de Beaune (red)

Guillemard Dupont: Bourgogne Hautes-Côtes de Beaune (red), Bourgogne Hautes-Côtes de Beaune (white, mostly Pinot Gris)

Lucien Jacob: Bourgogne Hautes-Côtes de Beaune (red)

Robert Jayer-Gilles: Bourgogne Hautes-Côtes de Beaune (red and white)

Jean Joliot: Bourgogne Hautes-Côtes de Beaune (red)

Mazilly Père et Fils: Bourgogne Hautes-Côtes de Beaune (red)

Parigot Père et Fils: Bourgogne Hautes-Côtes de Beaune (red)

Domaine des Vignes des Demoiselles: Bourgogne Hautes-Côtes de Beaune (red)

Hautes-Côtes de Nuits

Yves Chaley: Bourgogne Hautes-Côtes de Nuits (red and white)

Claude Cornu: Bourgogne Hautes-Côtes de Nuits (red)

Doudet-Naudin: Bourgogne Hautes-Côtes de Nuits (red)

Marcel et Bernard Fribourg: Bourgogne Hautes-Côtes de Nuits (red and white)

Jean Gros: Bourgogne Hautes-Côtes de Nuits (red)

Bernard Hudelot-Verdel: Bourgogne Hautes-Côtes de Nuits (red and white)

Robert Jayer-Gilles: Bourgogne Hautes-Côtes de Nuits (red
and white)
Henri Naudin-Ferrand: Bourgogne Hautes-Côtes de Nuits (white)
Simon Fils: Bourgogne Hautes-Côtes de Nuits (red)
Domaine Thevenot-Le Brun: Bourgogne Hautes-Côtes de Nuits-Clos
du Vignon (white and red), Bourgogne
Hautes-Côtes de Nuits (white Pinot
Blanc)
Alain Verdet: Bourgogne Hautes-Côtes de Nuits (red
and white)

Most successful recent vintages: 1989, 1988

Aging Potential: White wines—1 to 3 years; Red wines—3 to 5 years

HAUTES-CÔTES DE BEAUNE
HAUTES-CÔTES DE NUITS

(The backwoods of Burgundy)

The vineyards of the Hautes-Côtes de Beaune and Hautes-Côtes de
Nuits should take on increasing importance for consumers and the wine
trade as the vines get older and as more people begin to recognize that
there is an entire viticultural area in Burgundy distinct from the one
that exists along the famed Côte d'Or. Neither the Hautes-Côtes de
Beaune nor the Hautes-Côtes de Nuits is more than a 10-minute drive
from the Côte d'Or, but each is obscured both literally and metaphori-
cally by the hillside that is the "golden" slope.

Grape growing and wine production is nothing new in these valleys
and hills to the west of the Côte d'Or. Both were firmly entrenched here
as early as the seventeenth century. According to historians, there were
nearly 11,000 acres under cultivation when the devastating phylloxera
scourge attacked France's vineyards in the late nineteenth century. The
vineyards in the Hautes-Côtes de Beaune and Hautes-Côtes de Nuits,
like those throughout the country, were destroyed. It was not until the
early 1960s that people began to hear about these areas again, as increasing numbers of growers, forced out of the Côte d'Or due to that
area's stratospheric prices for real estate, moved back to the tiny valleys, forests, meadows, and hills west of the Côte de Nuits and Côte de
Beaune. In 1961, both areas received Appellation Contrôlée status from
the French government.

THE VINEYARDS OF HAUTES-CÔTES DE BEAUNE AND HAUTES-CÔTES DE NUITS

There are no Premiers Crus in either of these areas, and don't gamble on any being established. While good, sometimes even excellent wines can certainly be made, the problem for most of this area is the high altitude (between 1,000 and 1,500 feet), and the relatively cool climate. These factors, combined with the less-than-ideal exposure of many of the vineyards, often results in less than fully ripe grapes. This is true in most vintages, except in the super-ripe, superb, sun-drenched years such as 1985 and 1989.

Controversial viticultural methods are practiced in the Hautes-Côtes. The vines are trained on much higher poles, with the foliage spread out in order to expose the grapes to as much sun as possible. Additionally, the number of vines planted per acre is significantly less dense than elsewhere in the Côte d'Or. The yields also tend to be relatively high, unless a conscientious grower prunes vigorously and keeps fertilization to a minimum. This, combined with the less-than-perfect maturity of the grapes, often results in relatively light yet straightforward, serviceable wines.

Much of the wine produced here is still controlled by the local cooperative, Les Caves des Hautes-Côtes, which has more than 100 members owning over two-thirds of the acreage in Hautes-Côtes de Beaune and Hautes-Côtes de Nuits. While efforts have been made to increase the quality of their wines, most produced by the cooperative is still relatively light, straightforward, and lacking distinction and charm. Visitors to Burgundy interested in tasting the selections of the cooperative will find them on display at the cooperative's cellars located just three miles south of Beaune on the Route de Pommard.

Observers who continue to complain that no fine wines have yet emerged from Hautes-Côtes de Beaune or Hautes-Côtes de Nuits must certainly never have tasted those from the superb Robert Jayer-Gilles, who makes stunning white and red wines from both areas. Jayer's wines often surpass Premiers Crus from the Côte de Nuits and Côte de Beaune in blind tastings. He is a producer who keeps yields to a minimum, utilizes a great deal of new oak, and despite a climate and altitude that stacks the odds against great wine being made, does indeed turn out wines that are benchmarks for Hautes-Côtes de Beaune and Hautes-Côtes de Nuits. The same can also be said for the superb Vosne-Romanée grower-producer, Madame Jean Gros, who makes outstanding, supple, delicious Bourgogne Hautes-Côtes de Nuits. The other recommended producers make less profound wines, but they are serviceable,

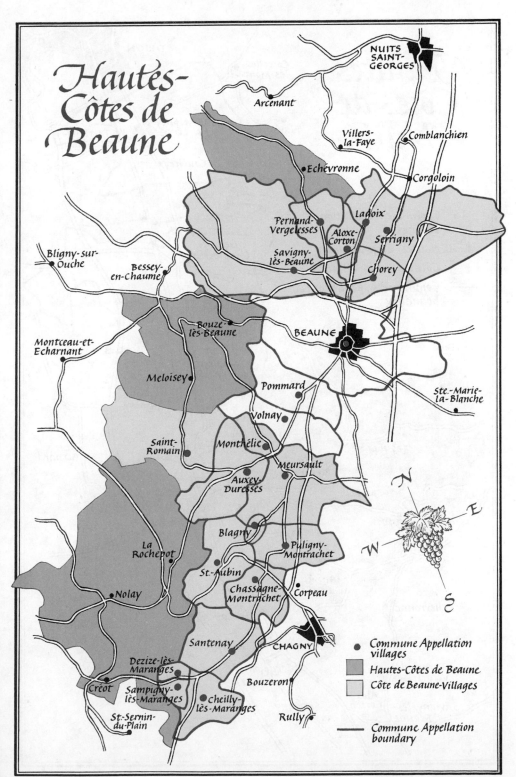

Hautes-Côtes de Beaune

NUITS SAINT-GEORGES

Arcenant

Villers-la-Faye

Comblanchien

Echevronne

Corgoloin

Pernand-Vergelesses

Ladoix

Aloxe-Corton

Serrigny

Bligny-sur-Ouche

Bessey-en-Chaume

Savigny-lès-Beaune

Chorey

Bouze-lès-Beaune

BEAUNE

Montceau-et-Echarnant

Meloisey

Pommard

Ste.-Marie-la-Blanche

Volnay

Saint-Romain

Monthélie

Meursault

Auxey-Duresses

Blagny

La Rochepot

Puligny-Montrachet

St-Aubin

Nolay

Chassagne-Montrachet

Corpeau

Santenay

CHAGNY

Dezize-lès-Maranges

Créot

Bouzeron

Sampigny-lès-Maranges

Cheilly-lès-Maranges

St-Sernin-du-Plain

Rully

Commune Appellation villages

Hautes-Côtes de Beaune

Côte de Beaune-Villages

Commune Appellation boundary

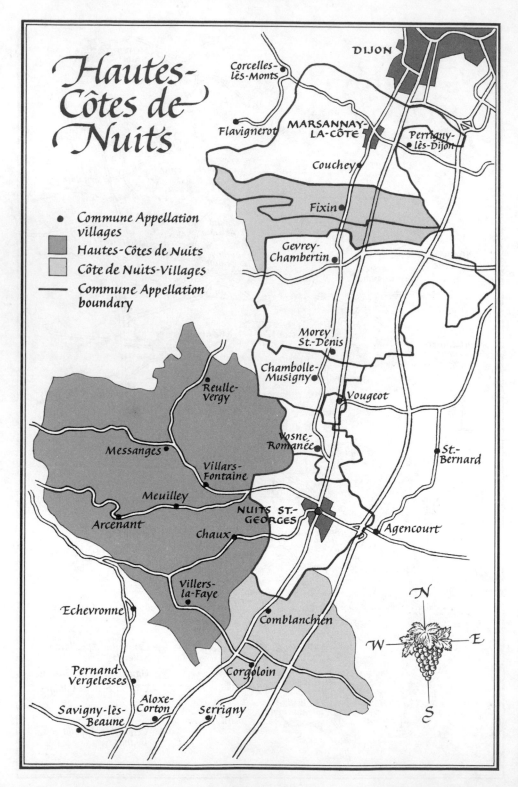

Hautes-
Côtes de
Nuits

- Commune Appellation villages
- ▮ Hautes-Côtes de Nuits
- ▮ Côte de Nuits-Villages
- —— Commune Appellation boundary

DIJON

Corcelles-lès-Monts

Flavignerot

MARSANNAY-LA-CÔTE

Perrigny-lès-Dijon

Couchey

Fixin

Gevrey-Chambertin

Morey St.-Denis

Chambolle-Musigny

Vougeot

Reulle-Vergy

Vosne-Romanée

St.-Bernard

Messanges

Villars-Fontaine

Meuilley

Nuits St.-Georges

Arcenant

Chaux

Agencourt

Villers-la-Faye

Echevronne

Comblanchien

Pernand-Vergelesses

Corgoloin

Aloxe-Corton

Savigny-lès-Beaune

Serrigny

N
W   E
S

interesting wines that do constitute decent values. I would be sure to restrict my purchases to only the top years, such as 1989 and 1988, because most of the vineyards in the Hautes-Côtes simply do not ripen as well in years where there is less sunshine and heat.

VISITING THE HAUTES-CÔTES DE NUITS AND HAUTES-CÔTES DE BEAUNE AND THEIR PRODUCERS

One of the favorite destinations of travelers to the backwater area of Burgundy called Hautes-Côtes de Nuits is the little hamlet of Marey les Fussey, where La Maison des Hautes-Côtes is located. This is a promotional center and restaurant featuring deliciously authentic local specialties such as *coq au vin bourguignon* and escargots, along with wines from Hautes-Côte de Nuits producers. This tiny village also has an attractive twelfth-century Cistercian abbey. In addition, one of the best domaines in the Hautes-Côtes de Nuits is located there, the Domaine Thevenot Le Brun. Nearby is Villers-la-Faye, which boasts a sixteenth-century church and thirteenth-century château. Another tiny village worth visiting, Magny les Villiers, is situated on several hillsides and boasts a twelfth-century Romanesque church. It is also the home of the remarkable cellars of Robert Jayer-Gilles. Not only does Robert Jayer make some of Burgundy's most expressive and brilliant wines, he also produces the finest red and white wines from the Hautes-Côtes de Nuits and Hautes-Côtes de Beaune. His underground cellar is visually stunning and functionally impeccable. A visit with this extraordinary winemaker is highly recommended.

When making forays into the Hautes-Côtes de Beaune, it is probably best to make your base either in Beaune itself, Puligny-Montrachet, or Chagny. This puts you within ten minutes of the major viticultural areas of the Hautes-Côtes de Beaune. I find the Hautes-Côtes de Beaune landscape generally less attractive, but still pastoral and bucolic.

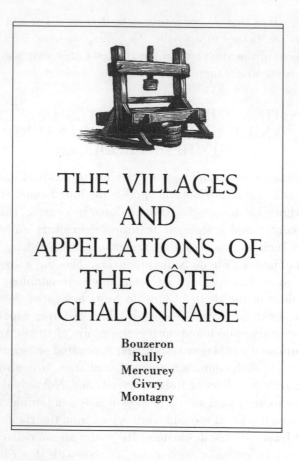

THE VILLAGES AND APPELLATIONS OF THE CÔTE CHALONNAISE

Bouzeron
Rully
Mercurey
Givry
Montagny

BOUZERON

An Overview

<u>Location:</u> Bouzeron is less than two miles from Chagny and is surrounded on three sides by the appellation of Rully.

<u>Acres under vine:</u> 65 acres
    Grands Crus: none
    Premiers Crus: none
    Villages Wines: 50 acres

Grands crus: None

Premiers Crus: None

Price levels: $8–$12 should buy the best Bourgogne Aligoté or Bourgogne Rouge from the likes of this appellation's very finest producer, Aubert and Pamela de Villaine

General wine characteristics: The village of Bouzeron is of little significance, but in 1979 it became the only viticultural region in France to receive appellation status for the Aligoté grape, a varietal that somehow reaches heights in the soils of Bouzeron that it is unable to attain anywhere else. The Aligoté from Bouzeron has flavor and a creamy texture that is missing from Aligotés from other appellations, which are frequently excessively acidic and austere. This is also a source for some light, straightforward, innocuous red and white burgundy.

The most overrated producers: none

The best producers and their wines:
Bouchard Père et Fils: Bourgogne Aligoté
Chanzy Frères: Bourgogne Aligoté-Clos de la Fortune
Michel Goubard: Bourgogne Rouge Mont Avril, Bourgogne Blanc
A. & P. de Villaine: Bourgogne Blanc Les Clous, Bourgogne Aligoté
de Bouzeron, Bourgogne Rouge La Digoine

Most successful recent vintages: 1989, 1988

Aging Potential: Bourgogne Blanc—1 to 2 years; Bourgogne Rouge—2 to 5 years; Bourgogne Aligoté—1 year

BOUZERON

(If it's Bouzeron, it must be Aligoté)

I suspect if it were not for the fact that one of Burgundy's great gentlemen and famous proprietors, Aubert de Villaine, and his family live in Bouzeron, there would be little reason to pass through this tiny village just southwest of Chagny. However, thanks to Villaine, who makes France's and the world's finest Bourgogne Aligoté, as well as two of the very best generic white and red burgundies one is likely to find, Les Clous (white) and La Digoine (red), many people are beginning to recognize just what high quality and reasonably priced wine Bouzeron is capable of producing.

There are several other good producers here as well, including the firms of Bouchard Père et Fils, Émile Chandesais, Chanzy-Frères, and Michel Goubard. All of these producers turn out good Bourgogne Aligoté.

RULLY

An Overview

Location: Rully is the first major village of the Côte Chalonnaise, situated only a few minutes from the town of Chagny along D 981. It has a population of 1,550. A stop in this charming village, with its impressive Château de Rully, built in the twelfth century as one of the leading fortifications of the area, is well worth the time.

Acres under vine: 494 acres, of which 47% is planted in Chardonnay and 53% in Pinot Noir

Grands Crus: none

Principal Premiers Crus: A total of 19
Margoté, Grésigny, Vauvry, Mont-Palais, Meix-Caillet, Les Pierres, La Bressande, Champs Cloux, La Rénarde, Pillot, Cloux, Raclot, Rabourcé, Ecloseaux, Marissou, La Fosse, Chapitré, Préau, Molesme

Price levels: $10–$20 will buy virtually any bottle of Rully.

General wine characteristics: The red wines from Rully seem less successful than the whites. Most of the reds tend to be extremely light, with an almost fleeting bouquet of cherries and strawberries intertwined in less ripe years with the scent of green herbs. The wines can be sharp and malnourished, something I rarely find to be a problem with Rully's Chardonnays, the wines that should propel this appellation into the nineties. The white wines are not long lived, but are extremely fresh and lively with good, clean, applelike Chardonnay fruit. Some of the more ambitious growers who barrel ferment their wines have turned out surprisingly complex, interesting wines that could easily be mistaken in a blind tasting for a Premier Cru white burgundy from Puligny-Montrachet.

The most overrated producers: None

The best producers and their wines:

Michel Briday: Rully-Grésigny (white), Rully La Pucelle (white)

Émile Chandesais: Rully (white)

Domaine du Chapitré: Rully Les Cloux

Charton et Trébuchet: Rully La Chaume (white)

Joseph Drouhin: Rully (white)

Domaine G. Duvernay: Rully en Rabourcé (white)

Faiveley: Rully (white)

Domaine de la Folie: Rully-Clos St.-Jacques (white), Rully Les St.-Jacques (white), Rully (white), Rully-Clos Roche (white), Rully-Clos de Bellecroix (white), Rully-Clos de Bellecroix (red)

H. & P. Jacqueson: Rully Les Cloux (red), Rully Les Chaponnières (red), Rully-Grésigny (white)

Moillard: Rully (red)

Domaine de la Rénarde: Rully Premier Cru (red)

Antonin Rodet: Rully (white), Rully (red), Rully Les Thivaux (white)

Château de Rully: Rully La Bressande de Château (white), Rully Molesme (red)

Domaine de Rully St.-Michel: Rully Les Cloux (white), Rully Rabourcé (white), Rully Les Champs Cloux (red), Rully-Clos de Pelleret (red)

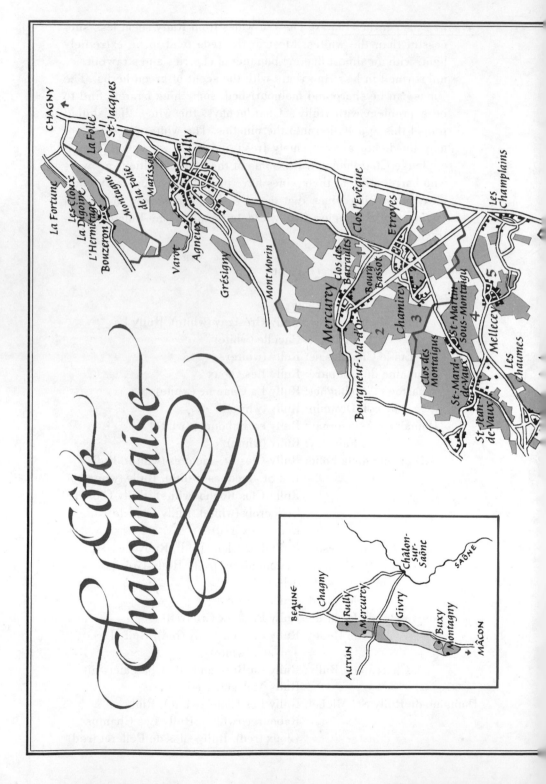

Côte chalonnaise

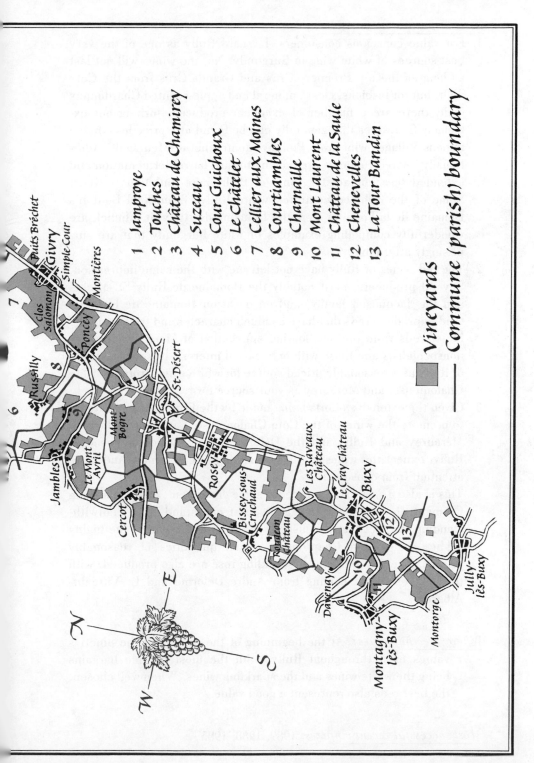

Vineyards

Commune (parish) boundary

1 Jamproye
2 Touches
3 Château de Chamirey
4 Suzeau
5 Cour Guichoux
6 Le Châtelet
7 Cellier aux Moines
8 Courtiambles
9 Charnaille
10 Mont Laurent
11 Château de la Saule
12 Chenevelles
13 La Tour Bandin

Puits Bréchet
Givry
Simple Cour
Clos Salomon
Poncey
Montières
Rusilly
St-Désert
Mont Bogre
Jambles
Le Mont Avril
Cercot
Rosey
Bissey-sous-Cruchaud
Rouleon Château
Les Raveaux Château
Le Cray Château
Buxy
Davenay
Montorge
Montagny-lès-Buxy
Jully-lès-Buxy

Some important observations:

1. For value conscious consumers, I regard Rully as one of the very best sources of white wine in Burgundy. No, the wines will not last as long as the top Premiers Crus and Grands Crus from the Côte d'Or, but for luscious, clean, mineral and apple-scented Chardonnay fruit, there are a number of excellent producers turning out extremely fine wines that generally can be found at a price less than a famous Villages wine from Puligny-Montrachet or Meursault. Additionally, more producers are moving toward barrel fermentation and extended lees contact for some of their more ambitious cuvées. Some of the rich, concentrated white Rullys from Noël Bouton's Domaine de la Folie, or from the Domaine de Rully St.-Michel, are wonderfully compelling examples of white burgundy that are surprisingly affordable.

2. The red wines of Rully have not left me with the same impression. Several producers, most notably the Domaine de Rully St.-Michel and the Jacqueson family, and on occasion Domaine de la Folie, tend to produce reds that have as much character and fruit as do the better reds from the neighboring appellation of Mercurey. But for nonspecialists and those with only casual interest, it is best to think of Rully as a reasonably priced source for white wines from the Côte Chalonnaise, and Mercurey as your source for red wines.

3. Given the extensive efforts being made by the firm of Antonin Rodet to promote the wines of the Côte Chalonnaise, particularly those of Mercurey and Rully, and the Delorme family, which is based in Rully, expect the wines of this appellation to catch more and more attention from consumers.

4. This is also a surprising source for some competent, crisp, sparkling Crémant de Bourgogne that at its best can stand alone, notwithstanding the fact that it is usually made from a blend of the highly acidic Aligoté and Chardonnay. Small quantities of reasonably priced, generally well-made, sparkling rosé are also produced, with the best examples coming from André Delorme and L. Vitteaut-Alberti.

Where are the values? At the beginning of the decade of the nineties values exist throughout Rully, with the most notable bargains being the white wines and the sparkling wines. When well chosen, the best reds also represent a good value.

Most successful recent vintages: 1989, 1988, 1985

Aging Potential: Premiers Crus (red)—2 to 5 years; Premiers Crus (white)—1 to 3 years; Villages wines (red and white)—1 to 4 years

RULLY
(An excellent, frequently overlooked white wine appellation)

Rully is a rapidly expanding appellation and town that apparently derived its name from a Roman village called Rubilia Vicus. Its wines have become much more visible, and are even promoted in some circles due to the public's fascination with both white and sparkling wine. The reputation of Rully has long been for a tradition of sparkling wine and excellent, value-priced white wine, with the red wine being considered at best mediocre. This historical reputation seems to be borne out in tasting the wines from the top producers, although today there are more red wines of higher quality than in the past.

However, it is still the white wines, with their wonderfully fresh, apple, hazelnut flavors, that draw most of the compliments. The production of white wine has not yet reached 50%, but in the decade of the nineties it can be expected to surpass the red wine production as more vineyards are planted with Chardonnay.

THE VINEYARDS OF RULLY

The trend in recent years has been to identify the Premier Cru on the label, so consumers wanting to learn more about the wines of Rully should know at least some of the better Premiers Crus that show up in the market, such as Champs Clou, Raclot, Grésigny, and La Rénarde. However, as with Mercurey, the Premiers Crus vineyards are probably not as important as the quality and commitment of the producer. For example, offerings from Noël Bouton's Domaine de Folie, including such superb wines as the Clos St.-Jacques Blanc and Clos de Bellecroix Blanc, are not Premiers Crus. The finest red wines come from H. & P. Jacqueson, whose delicious Rully Les Cloux and Rully Les Chaponnières rival even the best red wines made in nearby Mercurey. Ironically, Jacqueson, who also produces several wines from the appellation of Mercurey, makes better wines from Rully. So much for the theory that the red wines of Mercurey are vastly superior to the red wines from Rully. Other excellent reds are made by the Domaine de Rully St.-Michel, which gets my nod as the most consistent and best producer of the entire appellation, followed closely by Domaine de la Folie and H. & P. Jacqueson.

The two largest vineyard holders in Rully are André Delorme and Antonin Rodet. Both produce extremely good white wines and competent red wines.

VISITING THE VILLAGE OF RULLY
AND ITS PRODUCERS

This village is not used to having tourists or wine writers visiting the cellars, so appointments, which are suggested for any meetings with wine producers, are especially recommended here.

The old section of Rully is dotted with ancient homes. In addition there is the twelfth-century Château de Rully, which has commanding views and is a superb example of a fortified feudal château. There is a fourteenth-century church, and there are two sound hotel/restaurants, Le Rully and Le Commerce.

The most interesting producers to visit would certainly include the Château de Rully, now managed by Antonin Rodet. The firm of Rodet has a lease on this property through the year 2020, and it could well become the benchmark estate of Rully given the investment and commitment to quality evidenced by this firm. I also recommend Domaine de la Folie, which has been for many years one of the leading estates of the Côte Chalonnaise, as well as the Domaine de Rully St.-Michel. The latter two estates have their wines on most of the top restaurant wine lists of France, and are professionally run. If you want to visit some of the other growers, the firm of Henri and Paul Jacqueson have their cellars in Rully, as does Michel Briday. If you are in the mood for sparkling wine, a tour of the cellars of André Delorme is highly recommended.

Most of the growers, because they do not receive many tourists, are more than happy to make the effort to acquaint you with the wines of Rully as this village has yet to enjoy the renown of many of its more famous neighbors.

MERCUREY

An Overview

Location: Mercurey, the village and the appellation, is approximately
10 miles from Beaune, and only 6.5 miles from Chagny. This
makes it a short 10-minute drive for anyone staying at the luxury
hotel and restaurant, Lameloise. The vineyards are spread out
over an area approximately 3 miles wide and 3 miles long, encompassing the villages of Mercurey, Saint-Martin-Sous Montaigu,
and Bourgneuf Val d'Or. Mercurey is best reached by taking D
978 west from the commercial city of Chalon-sur-Sâone, or D 981
from Chagny. The more adventurous traveller can follow the
Route du Vin from Chagny through Bouzeron and Rully.

Acres under vine: 1,482 acres of which 95% is Pinot Noir and 5% Chardonnay

Grands Crus: None

Principal Premiers Crus: A total of 6
Clos du Roi, Clos Voyen, Clos Marcilly, Clos des Fourneaux, Clos
des Montaigus, Clos des Barraults
Note: Curiously, some of the best parcels in Mercurey are not yet
Premiers Crus. In particular, there is the excellent Clos des Myg-
lands, owned entirely by the Faiveley firm of Nuits St.-Georges,
as well as their white wine producing parcel in Mercurey, called
Clos Rochette. Other excellent vineyards that are not Premiers
Crus include Clos l'Évêque, Les Champs Martins, Les Nauges,
Les Veleys, and Clos du Château de Montaigu.

Price levels: Prices for the red wines of Mercurey seem to be on the
rise given the high level of quality that has consistently emerged
from the appellation in recent years. While the wines used to be
priced at the same level as a Côte de Beaune-Villages, now most

wines of Mercurey from the top producers sell for between $12 and $20 a bottle, putting them dangerously close to the price of a top Villages wines from the Côte d'Or. In many cases they are better wines, but consumers often balk at paying such high prices for a wine from the Côte Chalonnaise. On the other hand, the white wines of Mercurey seem to be underpriced, and no doubt will eventually catch up with the red wines. There are some excellent white wine values to be found in Mercurey, selling for $10 to $15 a bottle.

General wine characteristics: The best white wines have plenty of stony, mineral scents, a buttery, applelike fruitiness, good crisp acidity, and plenty of character. They are meant for drinking within their first several years of life and are not candidates for aging. The red wines vary significantly, from relatively light, somewhat diluted, vapid and vaguely strawberry-scented wines, to wines with a great deal of ripeness, character, and rich strawberry and cherry fruit. The producer is more important in Mercurey than any of the Premier Cru vineyard sites or notable *lieux-dits.*

The most overrated producers: None

The best producers and their wines:
> Château de Chamirey: Mercurey (red), Mercurey (white)
> Charton et Trébuchet: Mercurey-Clos des Hayes (red)
> Faiveley: Mercurey-Clos du Roi (red),
> Mercurey-Clos des Myglands (red),
> Mercurey-Clos Rochette (white)
> Jeannin-Naltet Père et Fils: Mercurey-Clos des Grands Voyens (red)
> Michel Juillot: Mercurey-Clos des Barraults (red),
> Mercurey-Clos Tonnerre (red),
> Mercurey (white)
> Domaine de Meix Foulot: Mercurey Les Veleys (red), Mercurey-Clos du Château de Montaigu (red)
> Domaine de la Monette: Mercurey (red)
> Domaine Fabian et Louis Saier: Mercurey Les Champs Martins (red)
> Domaine de Suremain: Mercurey-Clos Voyen (red),
> Mercurey-Clos l'Évêque (red)
> Émile Voarick: Mercurey (red), Mercurey-Clos du Roi

Some important observations:
1. Mercurey is the most important winemaking village of the Côte Chalonnaise, and there is currently a great deal of vineyard expansion

taking place. Mercurey has tripled in size in the last 35 years. The
two biggest movers and shakers are the firm of Antonin Rodet,
whose home is nearby, and the famous Nuits St.-Georges vineyard
owner and *négociant*, Faiveley, who has built a new state-of-the-art
winemaking facility and continues to aggressively produce and market high-quality wines from Mercurey.

2. The reputation of Mercurey is for its red wine, and that is indeed
justified when tasting the best examples, but one taste of a white
Mercurey from Faiveley, Rodet, or Michel Juillot will certainly make
a strong case that Chardonnay can do extremely well in the limestone, clay, and sand soil of the appellation. Some parcels in Mercurey are enriched with significant iron deposits, whereas others
have much more limestone intertwined with iron-enriched marl.

3. Mercurey has its own brotherhood, called La Confrérie Saint-Vin-
cent et des Disciples de la Chante Fluté. Founded in 1972, this
organization sponsors an annual tasting to select the best wines
made in the appellation. Those wines that are selected by the jury
are entitled to bear a special label called Chante Fluté. This process,
which is similar to the Tastevinage awards and labels given out by
La Confrérie des Chevaliers du Tastevins of Clos Vougeot, has resulted in high-quality wines, but has not helped promote the wines
of Mercurey as much as the growers who began this practice thought
it would.

4. There has never been a realistic and accurate appraisal of the different vineyards in Mercurey. Many of the best vineyard sites would
appear to be on the slopes, but there is plenty of vineyard land
planted on the flat areas, where the soil is richer and the drainage
less ideal.

Where are the values? Mercurey is in the process of being discovered
internationally. The values that exist now are not likely to remain,
as both consumers and the wine trade recognize how good the
best Mercureys can be. Already firms such as Rodet, Faiveley,
and Michel Juillot are selling their entire offering of wines almost
immediately. Expect the prices for red Mercurey to continue to
rise slowly, and prices for white wines to escalate considerably.

Most successful recent vintages: 1989, 1988, 1986, 1985

Aging Potential: Premiers Crus (red)—3 to 7 years; Premiers Crus
(white)—1 to 3 years; Villages wines (red)—2 to 4 years; Villages
wines (white)—1 to 3 years

MERCUREY

(The appellation of the future in the Côte Chalonnaise)

Mercurey is the most important and largest wine-producing village of the Côte Chalonnaise. Given appellation status in 1936, it has long been an insider's favorite choice, particularly in view of the number of good producers who make wines there. Furthermore, prices asked for Mercurey are a fraction of what is paid for wines from Burgundy's more hallowed Côte d'Or. Mercurey has always had a high profile in commercial markets, largely because of the appellation's nearly 1,500 acres, which continue to be expanded as the full potential of this area becomes more apparent. It produces nearly a quarter of a million cases of red wine and a tiny percentage of surprisingly good, even excellent white wine. About half of the vineyard acreage in Mercurey is owned by major merchants from the Côte d'Or, including Faiveley, Bouchard Aîné, Protheau, and Mercurey's own favorite son, the house of Antonin Rodet. This has ensured that the wines are represented and promoted in foreign markets. There is even a movement underway to rename the Côte Chalonnaise the Région de Mercurey, in deference to the political clout of these firms, and because the Mercurey appellation dwarfs its fellow Chalonnaise neighbors of Montagny, Givry, and Rully in size.

Mercurey does indeed have the political clout, boasting a population that approaches one person per acre of vineyard (1,500). The town itself is an attractive and functional one that apparently derived its name from that of the mythical god of speed, Mercury.

THE VINEYARDS OF MERCUREY

Most people who know Burgundy agree that the very best examples of Mercurey, whether it be the tiny quantities of white wine, or the huge amounts of red wine, represent the best rapport of quality and price in Burgundy today. There is hope that some of the other emerging villages of the Côte d'Or, such as Saint-Aubin and Saint-Romain, and perhaps even Auxey-Duresses, may challenge Mercurey's inside position. But there is doubting that once you have tasted a top Mercurey from the likes of Michel Juillot, Yves Launay's Domaine de Meix-Foulot, Faiveley, or Rodet's Château de Chamirey, you can only be impressed by the delicious cherry fruitiness of these wines intertwined with a touch of spicy oak, and on occasion, the scent of sautéed almonds.

As mentioned in the introduction to this chapter, even though there are Premiers Crus located in Mercurey, it is the producer's commitment to quality that is everything. Some producers with less renowned vineyards make better wine than those who own Premiers Crus. As is so often the case, those producers who are conservative with respect to their yields tend to produce wines with more concentration and character. The soils of Mercurey are not unlike that of southern Côte de Beaune-Villages, such as Chassagne-Montrachet. In Mercurey, however, there are many vineyards planted on flat, poorly drained parcels of property. The best vineyards are hillside locations with an easterly or southeasterly exposure. The best soils of Mercurey are those with a clay/sand topsoil and a limestone base. There are some parcels with deposits of iron-enriched marble, which add a more mineral-like character to the wine.

Even allowing for these slight differences, one must not underestimate the impact that the firms of Faiveley and Rodet, both committed to high quality, have had on this appellation. The Faiveley firm often produces three or four separate *cuvées* of Mercurey, including their top two wines, the Mercurey-Clos du Roi and Mercurey-Clos des Myglands. They have invested in a new winemaking installation in Mercurey, and the young, enthusiastic François Faiveley has long promoted the potential for this appellation. The same is true of the firm of Antonin Rodet, which has made significant strides in quality over the last few years. Rodet is now producing some of the very best wines of the Chalonnaise region.

Most of the wines of Mercurey should be drunk young, the white wine within several years, and the reds within 5–7 years of the vintage.

VISITING THE VILLAGE OF MERCUREY
AND ITS PRODUCERS

When visiting Mercurey, it is best to get off the main road through the middle of Mercurey as quickly as possible. The side streets and quiet village lanes going up the hillsides are more interesting and scenic. Mercurey has one excellent hotel/restaurant, Le Val d'Or, run by the Cogny family. The hotel has eleven attractive rooms and the restaurant produces excellent regional Burgundy cooking that I have enjoyed immensely, particularly their salad of frog's legs, scallops with saffron, and their wonderful, seasonal rabbit fricassee. This establishment makes a good base for exploring the whole Chalonnaise area. Rully, Bouzeron, Givry, and the southern Côte de Beaune are within a 10-minute drive. There are also at least a half dozen privately owned châteaux, in the surrounding area that merit a visit.

Lastly, if you want a quick and inexpensive taste of what straightforward Mercurey is all about, be sure to visit Mercurey's cooperative, Les Vignerons du Caveau de Mercurey, which produces not only decent examples of red and white Mercurey, but also an especially good marc, the high-spirited alcohol made from grape skins. The co-op has 182 members who own over 300 acres of vineyards.

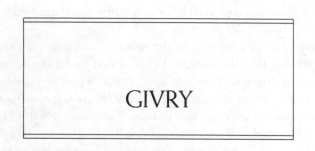

GIVRY

An Overview

Location: About 2 miles west of the bustling Chalon-sur-Sâone is the appellation of Givry. The appellation itself is 4 miles wide and 2 miles long, and is easily reached by either N 80 south from Chalon-sur Sâone, or D 69. It can also be reached by driving south on D 981 from Rully and Mercurey.

Acres under vine: 250 acres, of which 90% is planted with Pinot Noir and the remainder in Chardonnay

Grands Crus: None

Premiers Crus: None

Best-known Vineyards: Clos Salomon, Clos Saint-Pierre, Clos Saint-Paul, Cellier-aux-Moines

Price levels: Most of the best red wines of Givry sell for $10–$20 a bottle, and the whites for $10–$15.

General wine characteristics: Givry, which received appellation contrôlée status in 1946, is reputed to have a sharp, bitter taste, but I have not found that to be the case. Perhaps when winemaking was less consistent and there was less attention to detail this may have been true, but today Givry is another underrated appellation of burgundy, in this case for excellent red wines. Most of the best wines of Givry now see cask aging and show a character not unlike a good red from the Côte de Beaune. There is an earthy, cherry, sometimes raspberry fruitiness, good body, and enough acidity and tannin to insure 5 to 7 years of longevity. The white wines are infrequently encountered. However, they tend to be competent, if a little sharp and austere. Certainly the whites of Mercurey, Rully, and Montagny are significantly more enjoyable and consistent than those of Givry.

The most overrated producers: None

The best producers and their wines:
> René Bourgeon: Givry
> Jean Chofflet: Givry
> Gardin-Clos Salomon: Givry
> Jean-François Delorme: Givry-Clos du Cellier-aux-Moines
> Domaine Joblot: Givry-Clos du Cellier-aux-Moines, Givry-Clos du Bois Chevaux, Givry-Clos de la Servoisine
> Louis Latour: Givry
> Gérard Mouton: Givry
> Domaine Veuve Steinmaier: Givry (white), Givry-Clos de la Baraude
> Domaine Thenard: Givry-Clos Saint-Pierre, Givry-Cellier-aux-Moines, Givry Les Bois Chevaux
> Thierry Lespinasse: Givry en Choué
> Émile Voarick: Givry

Most successful recent vintages: 1989, 1988, 1985

Aging Potential: Single vineyard wines (red)—3 to 7 years; Villages wines (red)—2 to 5 years; Villages wines (white)—1 to 2 years

GIVRY
(A source for delicious red wine values)

Givry once had a superb reputation for its red wines, which many felt could rival the best from the Côte de Beaune. However, phylloxera and two world wars proved to be Givry's undoing. Subsequently, many parcels of land perfect for growing Pinot Noir were sold off to real estate developers from the ever-expanding city of Chalon-sur-Sâone. Appellation status, which was granted in 1946, no doubt helped give the local growers a bit of pride and identity. Prior to 1946, much of the wine was sold off as Mercurey or sold in bulk to *négociants* in Beaune for blending.

THE VINEYARDS OF GIVRY

There are no Premiers Crus in Givry, although everyone agrees that the best parcels are those of Cellier-aux-Moines, Clos Saint-Paul, Clos Saint-Pierre, and Clos Salomon. The soil of Givry tends to produce wines with good firmness, a plummy, berry fruitiness, and perhaps a bit more acidity than in nearby Mercurey or Rully. This gives the wines a slight bite and angular texture when young, but this seems to fall off in one to two years, revealing a more interesting, earthy, often peppery, spicy, surprisingly large-scaled wine.

There are a number of excellent producers in Givry. Two of the best, and the youngest, are the up-and-coming stars of Domaine Joblot and Domaine Thierry Lespinasse. Both of these domaines are beginning to experiment with new oak casks, and keeping their yields small, and have a great deal of pride in what their wines can offer. Givry's best-known estate is that of the Domaine Thenard. Thenard's wines are commercialized through the famous Beaune *négociant*, Remoissenet. The Clos Salomon of the Gardin family can be very good, but is inconsistent, and represents an old style of red winemaking with its rustic, dry tannins. Rather surprisingly, few *négociants* offer a selection from Givry. The best of those that do is the Givry from Louis Latour, a wine that exhibits an attractive earthy, spicy character.

VISITING THE VILLAGE OF GIVRY
AND ITS PRODUCERS

Givry, a fortified town in the Middle Ages, is now a quaint village with a less hectic pace than that of Mercurey. The Hôtel de la Halle, which offers good meals at realistic prices, also has ten serviceable no-non-sense rooms available. If you visit Givry, be sure not to miss the large marketplace, and what the locals call the Monk Cellar.

MONTAGNY

An Overview

Location: Montagny is the southernmost appellation of the Côte Cha-lonnaise. It is the only appellation of the Chalonnaise that is restricted to growing only one varietal—Chardonnay. The appellation runs about 3.5 miles from north to south and is about 6 miles wide. It encompasses the villages of Buxy, Montagny-Les-Buxy, St.-Vallerin, and Jully-Les-Buxy. Montagny is easily reached by car from Chalon-sur-Sâone via D 977, or from Givry via D 981.

Acres under vine: 741 acres planted exclusively with Chardonnay

Grands Crus: None

Premiers Crus: Rather amazingly, any wine that reaches the minimum 11.5% alcohol level within the appellation of Montagny can be called a Premier Cru, a situation that exists in no other appellation in France.

Price levels: Given the world's insatiable demand for Chardonnay and white burgundy, it is not surprising that the prices of Montagny are on the rise. While many producers' wines could be found for under $10 five years ago, as we start the decade of the nineties it looks as though most Montagnys are going to sell for $15 and $20 a bottle.

General wine characteristics: Some skeptics have called Montagny wines overpriced and glorified northern Mâcons, but I think they miss the point. The best wines from top producers such as Château de la Saule, Jean Vachet, and Antonin Rodet have a delicious buttery, nutty, applelike Chardonnay fruitiness, crisp acidity, and a style not unlike a well-made generic Chassagne-Montrachet.

The most overrated producers: None

The best producers and their wines:
Caves des Vignerons de Buxy: Montagny Cuvée Speciale, Montagny Premier Cru
Louis Latour: Montagny
Bernard Michel: Montagny Les Coeres
Domaine Millet: Montagny Premier Cru
Moillard: Montagny Premier Cru
Picard Père et Fils: Montagny Premier Cru-Château de Davenay
Antonin Rodet: Montagny
Alain Roy: Montagny Premier Cru
Château de la Saule: Montagny Premier Cru, Montagny
Domaine Veuve Steinmaier: Montagny Les Mont Cuchot
Jean Vachet: Montagny Les Coeres

Most successful recent vintages: 1989, 1988, 1986

Aging Potential: Montagny and Montagny Premier Cru—1 to 2 years.

MONTAGNY

(Elegant, stylish, and reasonably priced white wines)

The tiny artisanal village (population 220) of Montagny-Les-Buxy derives its name from the word Montanum, a name apparently given to a village in this area by the Romans. Montagny seems to be in the sleepiest part of Burgundy. Few tourists and even fewer members of the wine trade make the pilgrimage looking for straightforward, inexpensive yet eminently quaffable, useful white burgundy. Why more *négociants* have not seen the virtues of Montagny remains a mystery. Louis Latour in Beaune and Moillard in Nuits St.-Georges have certainly established an excellent name for Montagny thanks to their aggressive wine purchases from this appellation.

At the top levels the wines are very well made, and in addition, the local cooperative, the Caves des Vignerons de Buxy, is one of the most respected grower cooperatives in France.

THE VINEYARDS OF MONTAGNY

As noted in the introduction to this chapter, every parcel capable of producing wine that reaches a minimum 11.5% alcohol level is entitled to Premier Cru status under Montagny's rather unique regulations. However, certain Premiers Crus are more equal than others. Some of the best vineyard names that frequently show up on labels include Les Coeres, L'Épaule, Clos Chaudron, Les Bouchots, and Les Bassets. Some producers just label their wines Montagny, apparently unaware that the word Premier Cru has great significance to the world at large. According to the local syndicate, there are at least fifty vineyards that have official names and are entitled to Premier Cru status if they reach the minimum of 11.5% alcohol.

VISITING THE VILLAGE OF MONTAGNY
AND ITS PRODUCERS

There are several fifteenth-century châteaux near Montagny that are worth a visit. So is the Caves de Vignerons de Buxy cooperative, which turns out surprisingly competent, well-made wines.

The most interesting domaines include the Château de la Saule, owned by Alain Roy-Thevenin, and the other producer who many consider to produce wines rivaling those of Thevenin, Jean Vachet, whose cellars are in Saint-Vallerin.

THE VILLAGES AND APPELLATIONS OF THE MÂCONNAIS

MÂCONNAIS

An Overview

Location: Approximately 6 miles north of the historic town of Tournus (population 6,704), which is dominated by its huge, ancient, Romanesque abbey and Église St.-Philibert, is the northern border of the Mâconnais region. The district extends southward for 30 miles, past the city of Mâcon and overlaps the northern edge of Beaujolais, specifically the commune of La Chapelle de Guinchay at Saint-Amour. At its widest, the Mâconnais region is less than 18 miles. To reach the northern village called Chardonnay, take D 56 south from Tournus for 5 miles. To reach the picturesque villages of Fuissé, Loché, or Solutré in the southern sector of Mâconnais, take D 169 south from Mâcon and then D 172 west to Loché and Fuissé.

The Appellations	Percentage of Total Region's Output
Mâcon	less than one-tenth of 1%
Mâcon-Supérieur	4%
Mâcon-Villages	59%
Saint-Véran	12%
Pouilly-Fuissé	20%
Pouilly-Loché	less than one-tenth of 1%
Pouilly-Vinzelles	1%
Beaujolais Blanc	4%

Note: While the Mâconnais is considered a white wine (Chardonnay) district, one-fourth of the acreage is planted with Gamay, and about 7% with Pinot Noir. The red wine resulting from these two grapes is usually of dubious quality.

Price levels:

Mâcon: $4 to $8
Mâcon-Supérior: $4 to $8
Mâcon-Villages: $5 to $9
Saint-Véran: $7 to $10
Pouilly-Fuissé: $10 to $40*
Pouilly-Loché and Pouilly-Vinzelles: $8 to $12
Beaujolais Blanc: $7 to $9

General wine characteristics: The great majority of the pale white wines are made for gulping down uncritically. They offer fresh scents and flavors of apples and lemony fruit. Major cooperatives dominate the area and their goal is to produce clean, fresh, straightforward wines that can be bottled early and drunk immediately. In general, the wines from Saint-Véran and Pouilly-Fuissé exhibit more ripeness and fullness.

---

* A handful of the barrel-fermented and cask-aged wines can cost as much as $30 a bottle.

The best producers and their wines:

The Domaine-bottled wines—Mâcon-Villages

Auvigue-Burrier-Revel

André Bonhomme

Domain Chenevière (represented
    by Georges Duboeuf)

Domaine de Chervin (Albert
    Goyard)

Domaine des Granges (J.F.
    Cognard); also represented by
    Georges Duboeuf

Domaine de la Greffière (Henri
    Greuzard)

Domaine Guffens-Heynen

Domaine du Lys (Thorin)

Domaine Manciat-Poncet

Domaine René Michel

Domaine de Montbellet

Domaine du Prieuré (Pierre Janny)

Domaine de Roally (Henri Goyard)

Domaine Talmard

Domaine Jean Thévenet or
    Domaine de Bongrand

The Domaine-bottled wines—Saint-Véran

Château de Beauregard

André Besson

Domaine Corsin

Château Fuissé

Henry-Lucius Grégoire

Thierry Guérin

Roger Lasserat

Bernard Léger-Plumet

Roger Luquet

Domaine de la Maison (Georges
    Chagny)

Maurice Martin

Domaine des Pierres Rouge

Domaine Saint-Martine

Jacques Sumaize

The Domaine-bottled wines—Pouilly-Fuissé

Château de Beauregard

Domaine Corsin

Louis Curveux

J. A. Ferret

André Forest—Cuvée Vieilles
    Vignes

Château Fuissé—both their
    regular bottling and spectacular
    Cuvée Vieilles Vignes

Guffens-Heynen
Thierry Guérin—Clos de France
Domaine Edmond Laneyrie
Roger Lasserat
Bernard Léger-Plumet
Jean-Jacques Litaud
Roger Luquet
Manciat-Poncet
Domaine Mathias
Gilles Noblet
Roger Sumaize

The Best Cooperatives

Mâcon-Clessé: Cooperative Clessé
Mâcon-Igé: Cooperative Igé
Mâcon-Lugny: Cooperative Lugny
Mâcon-Prissé: Cooperative Prissé
Mâcon-Viré: Cooperative Viré

The Best Négociants

Joseph Drouhin: Mâcon-Villages-La Forêt
Georges Duboeuf: Mâcon-Villages, Saint-Véran, Beaujolais Blanc
Louis Jadot: Mâcon-Villages, Pouilly-Fuissé, Beaujolais Blanc
Louis Latour: Mâcon-Lugny-Les Genevrières, Pouilly-Fuissé
Loron et Fils: Mâcon-Villages
Trenel Fils: Mâcon-Villages, Pouilly-Fuissé

Some important observations:
1. The great majority of the wines of Pouilly-Fuissé are overpriced. However, several wines from this appellation can compete with the finest white wines of the Côte d'Or. Look for the Pouilly-Fuissés from J. A. Ferret, Thierry Guérin, Château Fuissé (the cuvée Vieilles-Vignes is of Grand Cru quality), and Guffens-Heynen. These wines are very expensive (over $30 a bottle), but are superb expressions of Chardonnay.
2. The most underrated and undervalued wines of the Mâconnais are from Saint-Véran. Most Saint-Vérans are significantly better than most Pouilly-Fuissés, and cost half the price.
3. The least-known delicious white wine from the Mâconnais is Beaujolais Blanc. However, most growers are discontinuing it because it

is difficult to sell. This is a shame given the general overall quality of this white wine made from the Gamay grape.

4. The worldwide obsession with the Chardonnay grape has caused most Mâcon-Villages growers to overproduce, stretching their crops to the maximum. The cooperatives that dominate this region's production have encouraged this lamentable trend, which has resulted in thinner and less interesting wine.

5. There are 42 villages entitled to the Mâcon-Villages appellation. Eight of them overlap the Beaujolais region. The quality of wine from these villages varies widely. The finest wines are from Mâcon-Charnay, Mâcon-Clessé, Mâcon-Fuissé, Mâcon-Igé, Mâcon-Loché, Mâcon-Lugny, Mâcon-Prissé, Mâcon-La Roche Vineuse, and Mâcon-Viré.

6. The red wines of the Mâconnais are generally vapid, sharp, and of little interest. The only exceptions are those from Guffens-Heynen and Jean-Claude Thévenet.

Most successful recent vintages: 1989, 1988, 1986

Aging Potential: Mâcon-Villages—1 to 3 years; Saint-Véran—2 to 4 years; Pouilly-Fuissé—3 to 10+ years*; Mâcon (red wine)—2 to 5 years

MÂCONNAIS

(A whiter shade of pale)

South of the Chalonnais region you are unlikely to notice any significant differences in the landscape, which remains a pastoral, agricultural area sprinkled with farms and grazing herds of France's famed Charolais beef. However, if you are travelling south on Autoroute 6, the first hint that Burgundy will soon be coming to an end are the ridges that rise to the west, and the increasing number of orange-tiled rooftops that announce Provence is not far away. The vast Mâconnais area begins 6 miles north of the ancient town of Tournus, with its southern border overlapping Beaujolais 30 miles farther south. While the Mâconnais is largely associated with the production of an ocean of pale white wine, more than one-fourth of the acreage is still planted with red wine grapes, principally the Gamay, which has trouble ripening in the lime-

* Only the Pouilly-Fuissé of Madame J. A. Ferret and Château Fuissé's Cuvée Vieilles Vignes can age well past a decade.

stone-based soil of this area. There is also a little Pinot Noir planted that has even greater difficulty reaching maturity.

The Mâconnais region has been providing wines to thirsty markets since the seventeenth century. It was then that a man of great wealth and influence by the name of Claude Brosse decided to promote the wines of Mâcon. His wines caught the fancy of the King of France, Louis XIV. At that time, much of the Mâcon wine was red rather than white, but today, over 75% of the production is in white wine. Some growers who have planted Gamay make a delicious, underrated Beaujolais Blanc from their Gamay. The production of white wine in Mâconnais is over 3 times that made from the rest of the entire region of Burgundy. For much of the last several decades, this wine has been enthusiastically drunk, and looked upon as representing one of France's greatest white wine values.

However, things are not all rosy at the moment, despite sales that suggest otherwise. The region's cooperatives, which control 85% of the Mâconnais production, have recklessly encouraged overproduction and high yields. The results have been wines that no longer represent the value they once did. A good Mâcon-Villages should be fresh and fruity, with almost a creamy, applelike character. Above all, it should be easy to drink. What has emerged in recent years are diluted, watered-down versions, the products of simple greed—too much wine from the vineyard. These wines have only a vague resemblance to Chardonnay. There are high-quality cooperatives and committed growers, however, and they are listed in the introduction to this chapter.

While the 42 villages of Mâcon account for nearly 60% of the region's production, there is much more to the wines of Mâconnais than just Mâcon-Villages. Anyone who visits the region will see that the Route du Vin, which can be picked up just south of Tournus via D 56, is a wonderful way to spend a tranquil weekend touring the tiny villages that sit among the enchanted hillsides of the Mâconnais region. The area as a whole does not match the stunning beauty of Beaujolais, but it is a highly desirable tourist route.

In addition to Mâcon-Villages, there are some minor appellations such as generic Mâcon and Mâcon-Supérieur that turn out the mediocre red wine. Red Mâcon is one of France's dinosaurs, and is increasingly being made into a white wine and called Beaujolais Blanc, or a good rosé. There are also tiny quantities of wine made from Pouilly-Vinzelles and Pouilly-Loché. Both of these villages lie between the famous village of Fuissé (which gives Pouilly-Fuissé its name), and produce minuscule quantities of good wine that is rarely encountered outside the local growing area.

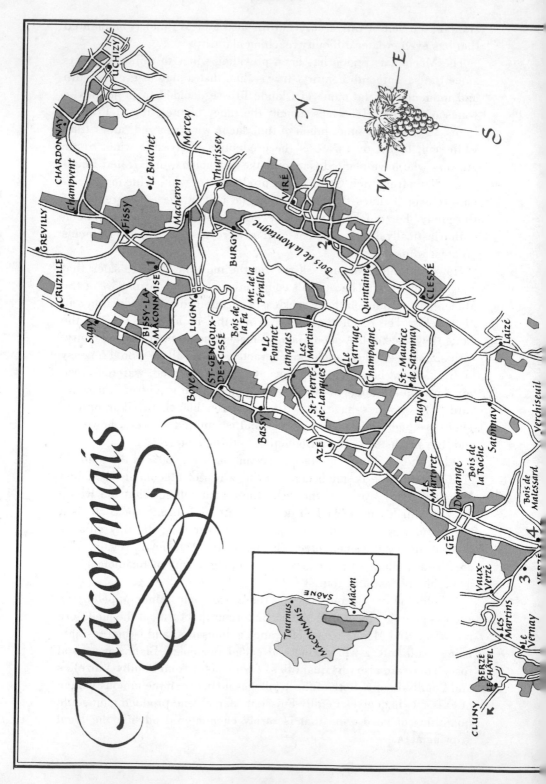

Mâconnais

CLUNY

BERZÉ-LE-CHÂTEL

Le Vernay

LES Martins

VAUX-VERZÉ

VERZÉ

3

IGÉ

Le Marbret

Domange

Bois de la Roche

Bois de Malessard

Verchiseuil

4

Satonay

Bugy

St-Maurice de Satonay

Champagne

Le Carruge

Quintaine

CLESSÉ

Laizé

AZÉ

BASSY

St-Pierre-de-Lanques

Les Martins

Le Fournet Lanques

Bois de la Fu

Mt. de la Peralle

Bois de la Montagne

BURGY

2

VIRÉ

Boye

ST-GENGOUX-DE-SCISSÉ

LUGNY

BUSSY-LA-MACONNAISE

1

Saÿy

CRUZILLE

GREVILLY

FISSY

Champvent

CHARDONNAY

Le Bouchet

Macheron

Mercey

Thurissey

SAÔNE

Mâcon

MÂCONNAIS

Tournus

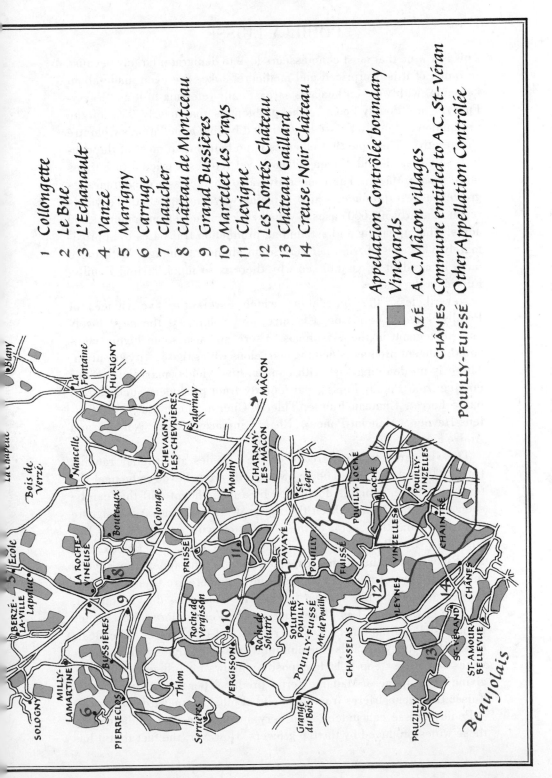

1 Collongette
2 Le Bue
3 L'Echanault
4 Vanzé
5 Marigny
6 Carruge
7 Chaucher
8 Château de Montceau
9 Grand Bussières
10 Martelet les Crays
11 Chevigne
12 Les Rontés Château
13 Château Gaillard
14 Creuse-Noir Château

Appellation Contrôlée boundary
Vineyards
A.C. Mâcon villages
Commune entitled to A.C. St-Véran
Other Appellation Contrôlée

AZÉ
CHÂNES
POUILLY-FUISSÉ

POUILLY-FUISSÉ

This is a wine that most connoisseurs love to denigrate, largely because so much of it is overpriced and mediocre. Jokes are even made about its name, with wine enthusiasts sarcastically referring to it as "Pussy-Fussy," or "Pouilly-Fools." The problem is that nearly 95% of the production of Pouilly-Fuissé is controlled by that appellation's Chaintré Cooperative. The wine that emerges is no better than most of the neutral, soulless, diluted Mâcon-Villages, yet fetches a price 3 to 5 times more than a Mâcon. The cooperative also shamelessly encourages its growers to overproduce, which explains why this appellation's yields result in nearly 500,000 cases of wine being produced from a mere 1,500 acres. That appalling and astounding production translates to approximately 333 cases of wine per acre in an abundant vintage. With these facts in mind, it is easy to see why there is so much insipid Pouilly-Fuissé on the market.

Nevertheless, the appellation, which covers the five villages of Pouilly, Fuissé, Vergisson, Chaintré, and Solutré, is the most lovely and photogenic in the Mâconnais. There are also some highly motivated, diligent producers making marvelous wines that justify attention. There is no doubting that with conservative yields, marvelous wines emerge from Pouilly-Fuissé, particularly from producers such as Madame Ferret, Château Fuissé, Thierry Guérin, Roger Lasserat, Guffens-Heynen, Manciat-Poncet, Roger Sumaize, Gilles Noblet, and André Forest.

The vineyards are scattered over the hillsides at altitudes ranging from 1,000 to 1,300 feet. The best vineyards are believed to be near the town of Solutré, which is dominated by a magnificent cliff that can be seen for miles around. Often the top growers will vineyard designate the wines from this sector of the appellation with names such as Les Chailloux, Les Boutières, Les Chanrues, Les Pras, Les Peloux, and Les Rinces. The other highly respected sector of the appellation adjoins the quaint town of Fuissé. The best vineyards here are Château Fuissé (owned entirely by the Vincent family), Le Clos, Clos de Varambond, Clos de la Chapelle, Les Menestrières, Les Versarmières, Les Vignes Blanches, Les Chantenets, Les Perrières, and Les Brûlées. The locals claim that the vineyards surrounding Fuissé produce richer, fuller wines since the steep hillside exposition allows for full sunshine, thus giving more ripeness. Madame Ferret produces her sumptuous Pouilly-Fuissé Les Menestrières from this band of hillside vineyards.

Pouilly-Fuissé can indeed be a very special wine, as evidenced by those wines produced by the top growers. However, the fact that it has attained a great international following has resulted in overproduction and higher prices. The cooperative at Chaintré and several of the *négociants* are fully responsible for this. But so is the consumer, who rarely balks at paying high prices for such mediocrity.

SAINT-VÉRAN

Saint-Véran, oddly enough, takes its name from the village called Saint-Vérand (the "d" is inexplicably dropped), which is actually within the appellation of Saint-Amour in Beaujolais. Perhaps this is why Saint-Véran has always been given second-class treatment as the understudy for Pouilly-Fuissé. It received appellation status in 1971, when the government recognized that the Chardonnay produced in the chalky hillsides seemed to have nearly as much character as Pouilly-Fuissé itself. The fact remains that Saint-Véran has really never caught on, except with a small group of wine enthusiasts who recognize that the best Saint-Vérans are far superior to the majority of Pouilly-Fuissés produced. Is it because the growers and *négociants* have higher standards for their Saint-Vérans than they do for their Pouilly-Fuissés, or is it that the world demand is so lukewarm toward Saint-Véran that no one is encouraged to overproduce, and therefore they do not make watery, diluted wines? Whatever the reasons, the consumer should clearly take advantage of the current quality and pricing of Saint-Véran. It is probably the best wine for your dollar from the Mâconnais region.

A good Saint-Véran is a more concentrated, richer, riper wine than the best wines from Mâcon-Villages. In many respects it is a Pouilly-Fuissé lookalike. It can have a creamy, soft, apple-buttery fruitiness that is altogether seductive and enjoyable.

While several top producers in Pouilly-Fuissé are now fermenting in oak barrels, and producing luxury cuvées of vieilles vignes, the best producers of Saint-Véran generally are unable to fetch a high enough price to afford such indulgences. One producer who does make a *cuvée* of vieilles vignes of Saint-Véran is Roger Lasserat. It is better wine than his Pouilly-Fuissé. All the other good producers of Saint-Véran seem content to ferment and age the wine in stainless steel, and bottle it as early as possible. Nevertheless, the results are impressive and enjoyable wines.

The appellation of Saint-Véran is cut completely in two by that of Pouilly-Fuissé. There is a northern sector, which includes the villages of Prissé and Davayé, and a southern sector, which overlaps into Beaujolais and includes the villages of Saint-Amour-Bellevue (one of the ten crus of Beaujolais), Saint-Vérand (the village from which the appellation takes its name), and the two tiny one-horse villages of Leynes and Chasselas. Of all the villages, the most interesting is Saint-Vérand. It has some impressive medieval buildings and fortifications, making it well worth the winding, often dangerously curving, 10-minute drive down from Pouilly-Fuissé.

Although appellation status came to Saint-Véran only two decades ago, it was largely due to the efforts of Louis Dailly. To honor him, there is the Coupe Dailly, the prize given to the best Saint-Véran made in a given vintage. That wine is normally purchased by Georges Duboeuf and marketed under his name, with a special label recognizing the Coupe Dailly award.

VISITING THE MÂCONNAIS AND ITS PRODUCERS

If you are coming from Paris or the Côte d'Or, the best way to tour the Mâconnais is to exit at Tournus, pick up D 56, and follow it until you arrive at the village of Chardonnay—the village that gave this world-famous grape variety its name. It is then just a matter of following the Route du Vin signs.

There are a number of stunning hilltop villages that compete very favorably with the bucolic beauty of neighboring Beaujolais. The magnificent cliffs of Solutré and Vergisson, which seem to jump up from the rolling pastoral hillsides, are not to be missed. Other places of interest include large, medieval fortifications at Berzé-le-Chatel; the extraordinary abbey in nearby Cluny, which was founded in 910 A.D. and was the power center for monks developing and exploiting the vineyards of the Mâconnais and Beaujolais area; the eleventh-century church in Clessé; the twelfth-century church in the quaint little town of Fuissé; Château de Montceau in Prissé; and the Museum of Prehistoric History in the village of Solutré. I would also recommend seeing the village of Saint-Vérand, with its Romanesque church and medieval fortifications.

The Mâconnais is not far from Lyons, so it is not surprising that food is given a high priority here. My favorite mecca for extraordinary classic French cooking is the sensational restaurant, Greuze, run by Monsieur Ducloux and his wife in the historic town of Tournus. Attached to the restaurant is a very attractive, 21-room hotel. I make a pilgrimage to Greuze on my trips to Burgundy simply to eat what are the finest quenelles of pike I have ever tasted. Another specialty of the house is an extraordinary Pâté en Croute Alexandre Dumaine, which is bursting with foie gras and black truffles, and served in a *périgourdine* sauce. I have had these dishes numerous times, washing the pâté down with the exceptional Morgon of Jean Descombes, which is always on the wine list, and the quenelles with the Cuvée Vieilles Vignes from Château Fuissé. There are few restaurants in the world where I have enjoyed my meals more than at Greuze. But a word of warning: Be sure you are hungry when you go there. Another outstanding hotel and restaurant in Tournus is Le Rempart, a 5-minute walk from Greuze.

Tournus makes a wonderful jumping-off point for visiting the Mâconnais area. If you do not mind the 30-minute drive, it can also be used as a base for touring Beaujolais.

Within the Mâconnais area itself, there is the excellent Château d'Igé in Igé, a small thirteenth-century castle with excellent rooms and rather expensive, somewhat pretentious cooking. Another possibility, and excellent base for touring both Mâconnais and Beaujolais, is the bustling city of Mâcon. There are two good hotels in Mâcon, the Altéa-Mâcon on the Rue de Coubertin, and the Hôtel de Genève. Restaurants where I have enjoyed particularly good meals include the Caveau St.-Pierre in Lugny, which has a wonderful view of the surrounding vineyards and simple, straightforward food, and the Auberge Bressane in Mâcon. If you do not mind making the 14-mile drive from Mâcon to Cluny, a fabulous ancient city with outstanding tourist appeal because of the sheer number of impressive buildings, and particularly the ancient Abbey, there is the excellent restaurant/hotel called Bourgogne, run by the Gosse family.

For the true gourmet/gourmand, I would be remiss in not recommending one of the world's greatest and most sublime eating experiences. You must be willing to make the grueling, one-hour drive from the Mâconnais to Roanne, but believe me, it is worth it. There you will find the Hotel des Frères Troisgros, whose 20 rooms are not a bargain, but are by no means exorbitant. However, the real reason to make the pilgrimage to this drab city is to taste the cooking of Pierre Troisgros and his son. For me, they run one of the two or three best restaurants in France. If you are touring the Mâconnais or Beaujolais, why not go ahead and splurge?

THE VILLAGES AND APPELLATIONS OF BEAUJOLAIS

Saint-Amour
Juliénas
Chénas
Moulin-à-Vent
Fleurie
Chiroubles
Morgon
Régnié
Brouilly
Côte de Brouilly
Côteaux de Lyonnais

BEAUJOLAIS

What is the most successful and lucrative wine produced in Burgundy? The answer is Beaujolais. This wine is made from vineyards strung across a number of enchanted mountainsides that mark the beginning of what is known as France's *Massif Central*. The region of Beaujolais is 34 miles long from north to south, and 7 to 9 miles wide. The granite mountainsides range in height from 2,300 feet to more than 3,400 feet, and provide a backdrop for what is one of France's two most beautiful viticultural regions (the other being Alsace). There are nearly 4,000 growers making a living in this idyllic area. Some of them sell tiny portions of their crops locally, but most prefer to sell to one of the large firms that dominate the business.

The only grapes permitted by law to be used in making Beaujolais are the Gamay, or Gamay Noir à Jus Blanc, to use its official name. It seems to thrive in the stony, schistous soils of the region. Most red wine grapes have trouble producing high-quality crops in granite-based soils, but Gamay seems to be a natural. The compelling characteristic of Gamay wine is its youthful, fresh, exuberant, crunchy fruit, which the vignerons of Beaujolais have learned to maximize by producing it by an unusual method called carbonic maceration. In this style of vinification, the grapes are not pressed, but are simply dumped unceremoniously into a vat in full bunches. Grapes at the very bottom of the vat burst because of the weight on top of them. That juice begins to ferment, warming up the vat and causing fermentation in the unbroken grapes to begin inside their skins. The advantage of this technique is that a wine's perfume and fruity intensity is largely related to what is inside the grape skin. The acid and tannin are largely extracted from the breaking and pressing of the skins.

This interesting fermentation method results in fruity, exuberant, intensely perfumed wines that are ideal when chilled and drunk in the so-called nouveau style. Today this nouveau style is a phenomenon in the export markets, but it only started in the late seventies. Nouveau Beaujolais, which can be released only on the third Thursday in November, accounts for nearly half of the enormous production of this region. It is one of France's most successful export items since the insatiable thirst for this wine results in hundreds of thousands of cases being airfreighted to such far-flung locations as Sydney, Tokyo, Hong Kong, Seoul, San Fràncisco, New York, Stockholm, London, and of course, Paris.

The Nouveau hysteria and the incredible profits taken by the wine trade from the sales of Nouveau have resulted in a school of thought that has attempted to disparage not only the wine, but those who consume it. This is all nonsense, because there is no doubting that in top vintages such as 1989 and even 1988, delicious, zesty, exuberant, fresh, vibrantly fruity Beaujolais Nouveau is made. The only limitation is that it should be drunk within 3–4 months of its release. Beaujolais Nouveau has become a useful wine for introducing people to the glories of red wine. It has also weaned people off some of the sugary, sweet, white zinfandels and cloying liebfraumilchs that have long dominated the

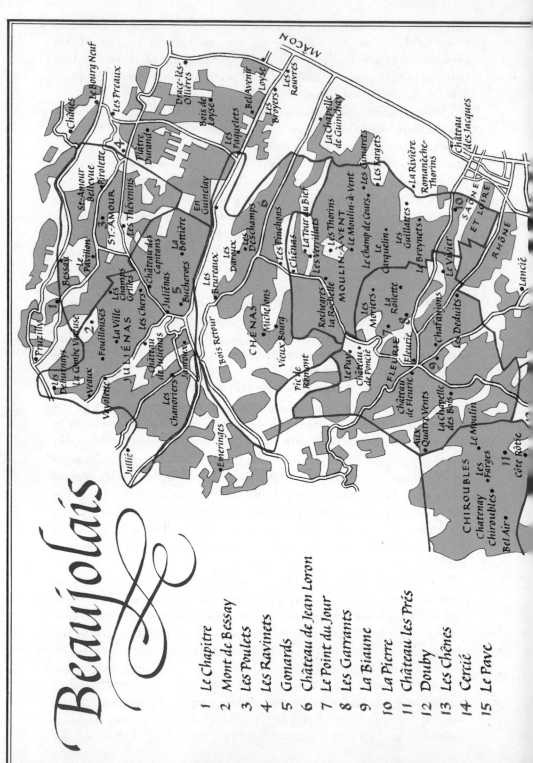

Beaujolais

1 Le Chapitre
2 Mont de Bessay
3 Les Poulets
4 Les Ravinets
5 Gonards
6 Château de Jean Loron
7 Le Point du Jour
8 Les Garrants
9 La Biaune
10 La Pierre
11 Château les Prés
12 Douby
13 Les Chênes
14 Cercié
15 Le Pavé

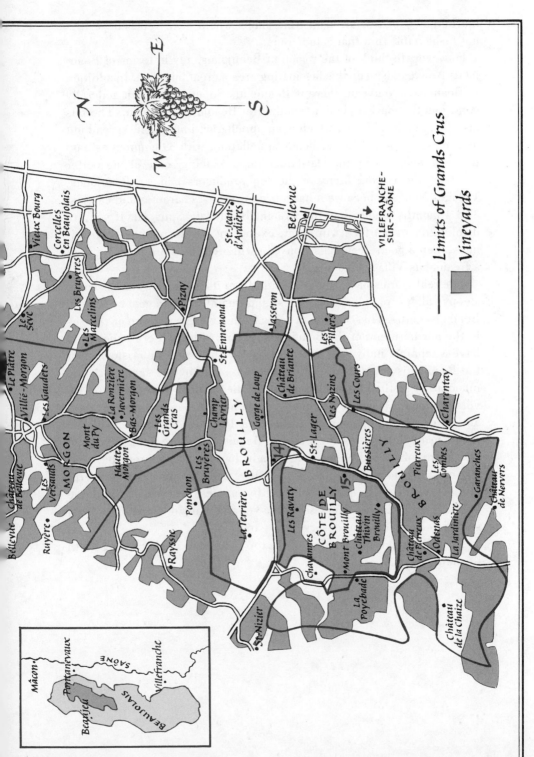

Limits of Grands Crus
Vineyards

VILLEFRANCHE-SUR-SAÔNE

Bellevue
St-Jean d'Ardières
Jasseron
Les Pillers
Corcelles en Beaujolais
Vieux Bourg
Le Piâtre
Les Bruyères
Les Marcelins
Pizay
St-Ennemond
Château de Briante
Les Cours
Les Nizins
Charentay
Le Sève
Les Gaudets
Villié-Morgon
La Ronzière
Javernière
Bas-Morgon
Les Grands Cras
Gorge de Loup
Champ Livrier
St-Lager
Château de Bellevue
Bellevue
Ruyère
Les Versauds
MORGON
Mont du Py
Hautte Morgon
Les Bruyères
BROUILLY
14
Bussières
Pierreux
Les Combes
Garanches
Château de Nervers
Ponchon
La Terrière
Les Ravaty
CÔTE DE BROUILLY
15
Mont Brouilly
Château Thivin
Brouilly
Château de Pierreux
Odenas
La Jardinière
Rayssie
Chavannes
La Foyebade
Château de la Chaize
St-Nizier

Mâcon
Pontanevaux
SAÔNE
Villefranche
Beaujeu
BEAUJOLAIS

marketplace. A few arrogant wine snobs would have you believe it is not fashionable, but that is ludicrous.

However, to think of the region of Beaujolais only in terms of Beaujolais Nouveau is to do this fascinating area a great injustice. In addition to Beaujolais Nouveau, there is Beaujolais Supérieur, which generally comes on the market about a month after Beaujolais Nouveau. There is also Beaujolais-Villages, which is an appellation unto itself, spread out over most of the entire Beaujolais appellation, with 39 communes having been selected by the legislature for producing some of the better wines of the region. Many of the top producers make a Beaujolais-Villages Nouveau because it has a firmer, robust character and can last 3 to 4 months longer than the straight Beaujolais Nouveau. If you are drinking Nouveau for its up-front, exuberant, fresh, unabashed fruitiness, then a good Beaujolais Nouveau will often be more pleasing than a Beaujolais-Villages Nouveau.

The real glories of Beaujolais, aside from its narrow, winding roads, sleepy valleys, photogenic hillsides, and quaint, old villages, are the 10 Beaujolais crus. These wines all come from a village or group of villages in the northern end of the Beaujolais region, with each cru believed to have a separate individual style of its own. These are the aristocrats of the Beaujolais appellation. While they are made by the same carbonic maceration method as other Beaujolais, the best cru wines from the 10 villages should be more perfumed, more luscious, more concentrated, and altogether more complete and enjoyable wines. Of course, with the major firms dominating the trade in Beaujolais, there is an argument that many of the differences that might have been apparent between the most southern cru, Côte de Brouilly, and the most northern cru, Saint-Amour, are frequently blurred by careless *négociants* and large firms. But all of these wines should have, and many do have, individual specific characters that deserve to be amplified.

The following is an overview of the top Beaujolais crus, running north to south.

SAINT-AMOUR

Location: Saint-Amour is the most northern of the 10 Beaujolais crus. It is also one of the 3 smallest, the other 2 being its neighbors, Juliénas and Chénas. The entire appellation consists of only 692 acres. Saint-Amour is located just a few miles to the southwest of the bustling city of Mâcon.

Acres under vine: 692 acres

Price levels: $8 to $14 a bottle

General wine characteristics: Most of the Gamay in Saint-Amour is planted on mountainsides facing east and southeast, with granite and slate soil intermixed with stones that sometimes appear to be smaller versions of those that make up the soil in Châteauneuf-du-Pape. Given the exposition of the vineyards, Saint-Amour often needs great ripeness to achieve its highest level of quality. For that reason, vintages such as 1985 and 1989 are preferred to vintages such as 1986 and 1987. A good Saint-Amour has fine color, but often is lacking in body and length. In the top vintages (I remember some wonderful 1985s), this commune seems to shine. The wines produced have good blackberry, raspberry fruitiness, medium body, and soft textures.

The best producers: Domaine du Clos du Fief (Michel Tête), Domaine Dufour, Domaine Janin, Domaine du Paradis (frequently represented by Georges Duboeuf), Domaine Jean Patissier, Domaine des Ducs, Francis Saillant, Georges Trichard, Domaine des Pins

Most successful recent vintages: 1989

Aging potential: 1 to 3 years

SAINT-AMOUR

Saint-Amour would appear to be one of the easiest of the 10 Beaujolais crus to forget. Perhaps it is because it is the most northern, and is the only Beaujolais cru to be entirely in the Sâone-et-Loire départment. In fact, it often seems that the vineyards are simply an extension of the Mâconnais region. Several of the finest wines of Pouilly-Fuissé come from a field only a stone's throw from Saint-Amour. Perhaps the reputations of the villages of Vinzelles, Fuissé, and Loché, all no more than 5 minutes away, overwhelm the reputation of Saint-Amour. Saint-Amour also suffers because the white wine made within the appellation is entitled to be called Saint-Véran (the delicious, underrated Chardonnay from the Mâconnais region).

The village of Saint-Amour-Bellevue is the hub for the growers of Saint-Amour. It is best reached from Mâcon by taking D 169 south to D 469 out of Vinzelles and Chaintré. The population is listed as 550, all of whom seem to be wine growers. The history of Saint-Amour leaves much in doubt. Appellation status was not granted until 1946, largely because of the efforts of Saint-Amour's most famous and persistent proponent, Louis Dailly. The derivation of the name of Saint-Amour has various historical explanations. One has it that a Roman soldier fell in love with a local girl, was converted to Christianity, married her, and later was martyred at the site of the village. The soldier's name was Amore.

Serena Sutcliffe facetiously claims that Saint-Amour is the wine for St. Valentine's Day, but I might add that it should be purchased only in the very best vintages, given the fact that it often seems a bit thin and lean when the grapes do not fully ripen, as in 1986 and 1987.

Today, over 180,000 cases of Saint-Amour are produced in an abundant year. That includes a small production of white wine, a rarity from the village.

If you are travelling through the village of Saint-Amour, the lovely sixteenth-century Château de Saint-Amour merits a visit, and there are several restaurants, including Auberge du Paradis and Chez Jean-Pierre Ducote. Both offer straightforward French country cuisine, which frequently seems at its very best in the mountains of Beaujolais.

Those producers worth visiting would include the Domaine du Paradis, whose wines are sold under its own name but also are bottled and represented by the famous King of Beaujolais, Georges Duboeuf. In addition, the two outstanding domaines of Janin, located in Saint-

Amour, and Georges Trichard in La Chapelle-de-Guinchay, should not be missed.

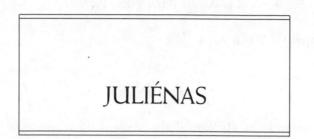

JULIÉNAS

Location: Juliénas, twice the size of its northern neighbor, Saint-Amour, is spread out over some incredibly steep mountainsides composed of granite and schist. The best vineyards of Juliénas usually have a southerly exposure. They can easily be reached by taking D 17 west from Pontanevaux, or by continuing on D 486 through Saint-Amour-Bellevue in the direction of Juliénas on Beaujolais' Route du Vin.

Acres under vine: 1,433 acres

Price levels: $8 to $14 a bottle

General wine characteristics: Juliénas is one of my favorite crus of Beaujolais. It produces some of the sturdiest, fullest, and richest wines from that appellation. Juliénas enjoys an excellent location with steep vineyards, the best of which have the benefit of full sunshine. Additionally, the producers in Juliénas are highly competitive, and turn out wines that are among the highest in quality in Beaujolais. The finest examples display the exuberant, rich, fresh fruitiness of Beaujolais, backed up by plenty of body, intensity, and a heady alcohol content. A good Juliénas should be at its prime between 2 and 4 years after the vintage, yet can last up to 5 years.

The best producers: Ernest Aujas, Domaine de Boischampt, Domaine de la Boittière, Domaine du Clos du Fief (Michel Tête), Domaine Gonon, Claude and Michel Joubert, Château de Juliénas (François Condemine), Domaine des Mouilles (represented and commercialized by Georges Duboeuf), Domaine André Pelletier, Domaine de la Seigneurie de Juliénas (represented and commercialized by

Georges Duboeuf), Raymond and Michel Tete, Château des Vignes (represented and commercialized by Georges Duboeuf).

Most successful recent vintages: 1989, 1988, 1985

Aging Potential: 2 to 5 years

JULIÉNAS

Juliénas is undoubtedly one of the stars of Beaujolais. It is both a bustling village with a population of 650, and a viticultural area that is of significant historical interest. It is claimed that the vines of Juliénas were the first planted in Beaujolais. Some also believe the claim that the name of Juliénas was derived from Julius Caesar.

The best vineyards of Juliénas must be totally cultivated, manicured, and harvested by hand, for the slopes are so steep that no machines or tractors can safely work in them. The southerly exposure of the best hillsides of Juliénas is no doubt the reason so many of the wines have a power and richness that is usually only exceeded by the wines of Moulin-à-Vent, and on occasion, by those of Morgon. In an abundant year, 210,000 cases of Juliénas are produced.

While Juliénas is not the most quaint of the mountaintop Beaujolais villages, it does have several good restaurants, including Madame Boucaud's Chez La Rose, and Le Coq au Vin. Both are known for their generous portions and hearty, country-style cooking. There are also adjoining hotels that offer serviceable, if spartan, accommodations.

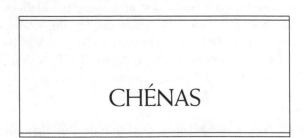

CHÉNAS

Location: Chénas, the smallest cru of Beaujolais, is just over a mile southeast of Juliénas. It is actually a subviticultural region, bordered on the south by Moulin-à-Vent, and almost seems a part of that more famous appellation. Surprisingly, the wines from a large portion of Chénas can be called Moulin-à-Vent should their producers so desire.

Acres under vine: 642 acres

Price levels: $8 to $14 a bottle

General wine characteristics: As one might expect, the wines of Chénas share a similarity to those of Moulin-à-Vent. A good Chénas, and there are some superb producers in this appellation, has a deep, robust, intense color, and a muscular, rich, concentrated style. It is fuller and more chunky than a Juliénas, yet seems to lack that appellation's perfume and elegance. For some reason, it never seems to age as well as a Juliénas, always having a more rustic quality 4 or 5 years after the vintage than some of the better wines from its neighbor to the northwest. Nevertheless, these are attractive, fleshy wines that should be better known, particularly those from the top producers.

The best producers: Château Bonnet (Pierre Perrachon), Domaine Guy Braillon, Domaine des Brureaux (Daniel Robin), Domaine Louis Champagnon, Château des Chénas, Domaine de la Combe-Remont (represented and commercialized by Georges Duboeuf), Gérard Lapierre, Hubert Lapierre, Manoir des Journets (represented and commercialized by Georges Duboeuf), Jean-Louis Santé, Domaine Remont (represented and commercialized by Pierre Ferraud).

Most successful recent vintages: 1989, 1988

Aging Potential: 2 to 4 years

CHÉNAS

Chénas should enjoy a better reputation. Certainly, the fact that it is the smallest of the crus of Beaujolais has meant that its wines are not as widely available in the export markets. What's more, much of the production of Chénas is sold as Moulin-à-Vent rather than as Chénas, because the growers attempt to capitalize on the fame and higher prices fetched by Moulin-à-Vent.

The village and the wines take their name from the old oak trees

(chênes) that once stood on the hillsides. These have now been replaced
by vineyards. At one time there was even talk that the growers of
Moulin-à-Vent would like to see the smaller cru of Chénas absorbed
within Moulin-à-Vent, but that has now ceased as the producers of
Chénas, particularly Louis Champagnon, Guy Braillon, and Daniel
Robin from the Domaine des Brureaux, have successfully proved that
a top Chénas can be as good a Beaujolais as one is likely to find. In
fact, in the top vintages, Daniel Robin's Domaine des Brureaux is one
of the 10 best wines in Beaujolais. Coincidentally, Robin is the owner
of one of the finest restaurants in the entire Beaujolais region. Called
Le Relais des Grandes Crus, the restaurant is in the village of Chénas.
If you visit it on a nice day, ask to be seated on the shady terrace.

Chénas itself is not among the more interesting of the Beaujolais
villages, but just east of it is La Chapelle de Guinchay, with its growing
population of just over 2,000 people. La Chapelle de Guinchay, which
sits at the threshold of two crus, Chénas and Moulin-à-Vent, is well
worth a visit as there are at least a half dozen fourteenth- and fifteenth-
century châteaux within 5 minutes of this bustling small town.

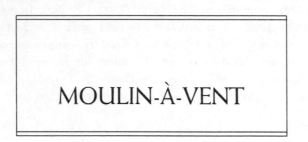

MOULIN-À-VENT

Location: Due west of the bustling Romanèche-Thorins is Moulin-à-
Vent, which takes its name from the only windmill still in existence in Beaujolais. The windmill, which stands to the northwest
of Romanèche-Thorins, is at least 300 years old and has been
declared an historic monument by the French government. It is
perched on a hill overlooking the vineyards of Moulin-à-Vent.

Acres under vine: 1,605 acres

Price levels: $10 to $15 a bottle

General wine characteristics: Moulin-à-Vent produces the most powerful, concentrated, and ageworthy wine of Beaujolais. It is highly

prized, and the most expensive wine of the region. In size and texture, Moulin-à-Vent frequently resembles a red wine from the Côte d'Or rather than a Beaujolais.

The best producers: M. Gabriel Aligne, Domaine René Berrod, Domaine de la Bruyère (Raymond Siffert), Domaine des Caves (represented and commercialized by Georges Duboeuf), Domaine Louis Champagnon, Domaine Chauvet (represented and commercialized by Georges Duboeuf), Domaine Diochon, Domaine des Héritiers-Tagent (represented and commercialized by Georges Duboeuf), Château des Jacques, Domaine Jacky Janodet, Domaine Lémonon (represented and commercialized by Loron et Fils), Château de Moulin-à-Vent (Jean-Pierre Bloud), Domaine de la Teppe (represented by Chanut Frères), Domaine de la Tour du Bief (represented and commercialized by Georges Duboeuf).

Most successful recent vintages: 1989, 1988, 1987, 1986, 1985, 1983

Aging Potential: 4 to 10+ years

MOULIN-À-VENT

Moulin-à-Vent is often referred to as the King of Beaujolais. This is something of a misnomer, as far as I am concerned, since Moulin-à-Vent is the least typical wine of the entire Beaujolais region. There is no doubt, however, that the best Moulin-à-Vents are the richest, fullest, and most ageworthy wines produced in Beaujolais. A 7- or 10-year-old example from one of the best producers will often have more in common with a Pinot Noir from the Côte de Beaune than anything produced from the Gamay grape. The advent of more producers fermenting and aging their Moulin-à-Vents in new oak casks has subdued and altered the intensely fruity character of the Gamay grape even more, and the results are wines that seem unlike either Beaujolais or red burgundy, but are a synthesis of both.

Moulin-à-Vent is the only cru of Beaujolais to take its name not from a village, but from a windmill. The main commerical center for Moulin-à-Vent is Romanèche-Thorins, the home of the undisputed King of Beaujolais, Georges Duboeuf.

The production of Moulin-à-Vent, which is now creeping up toward

400,000 cases annually, has no shortage of buyers willing to pay one of the highest prices asked for any of the crus of Beaujolais (although those of Fleurie and Morgon are catching up). Many attribute the underlying richness and structure of Moulin-à-Vent, which produces larger-scaled, more muscular wines, to the fact that the granite-based soil is rich in minerals such as manganese. This provides a greater depth of color and flavor than Gamay is capable of achieving from the granite soils of the other crus. What makes Moulin-à-Vent somewhat deceptive is that most people approach Beaujolais as if it should be drunk immediately, but many of the best Moulin-à-Vents from the likes of Jean-Pierre Bloud's Château de Moulin-à-Vent, or the Domaine Jacky Janodet, or Georges Duboeuf's Domaine de Héritiers-Tagent, need a good 2 or 3 years in the bottle to reveal their character. I would be remiss in not pointing out that the Château des Jacques, which again seems to be making wines worthy of its lofty reputation, provided me with some of the greatest Moulin-à-Vents I have ever tasted. When I was in college, I remember buying cases of the 1969 and 1970 Château des Jacques Moulin-à-Vent Clos de Carquelin. I drank my last bottle of it in the early eighties, when the wine was just over 10 years old. I preferred them young, but even at 10 years there was still fruit left, and they reminded me more of wines from farther north in the Côte d'Or than any Beaujolais I had ever tasted. These wines do deserve the reputation they have for outlasting anything else in Beaujolais.

Romanèche-Thorins, which is one of the exits off France's famed Autoroute A6 between Paris and Lyons, makes a very convenient base for visiting the entire Beaujolais region. I highly recommend the hotel/restaurant Les Maritonnes, where I have enjoyed many superb meals. I can also recommend their warm and comfortable rooms. The wine list is superb, particularly if you are looking for some of the best wines from the Mâconnais and Beaujolais regions.

As far as sightseeing, no visit to Romanèche-Thorins would be complete without a stop at Georges Duboeuf's vast enterprise. During the third week of November, as the Nouveau is about to be released, the entire town is closed to traffic and only container trucks are allowed in. This creates quite an impressive sight, with hundreds and hundreds of trucks parked and waiting to take their precious cargo of Beaujolais Nouveau all over Europe and to destinations abroad. Romanèche-Thorins itself is a relatively drab and boring town, but to the west is the photogenic windmill from which Moulin-à-Vent takes its name. Additionally, there are a number of châteaux around Romanèche-Thorins that, while not open to the public, are visually pleasing and add to the beauty of the enchanted Beaujolais landscape.

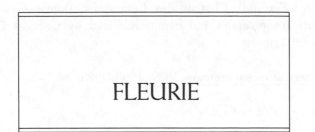

FLEURIE

Location: About 5 to 10 minutes west of Romanèche-Thorins is the quaint, charming village of Fleurie, situated right in the heart of the Beaujolais hills. It is 250 miles from Paris, 12 miles from Mâcon, and 36 miles from Lyons. Fleurie, with its extraordinary location and undeniable charm, is one of the most visited villages of the entire Beaujolais region. It is also the home of the finest restaurant in the entire Beaujolais region, the Auberge du Cep, owned by Monsieur Cortembert.

Acres under vine: 1,976 acres

Price levels: $8 to $15 a bottle

General wine characteristics: The same people who call Moulin-à-Vent King of Beaujolais often refer to Fleurie as its Queen. This designation has apparently met with the approval of the wealthy Swiss, who are perhaps Fleurie's greatest admirers. They buy much of the crop and drive the price up to levels that sometimes surpass even that of Moulin-à-Vent. Prior to World War II, much of the wine of Fleurie was sold as Moulin-à-Vent, but now, with Fleurie arguably the most popular wine of the Beaujolais region, its growers are content to sell their nearly 500,000 cases of wine to merchants around the world, all by themselves. What makes Fleurie so tasty is that it has the richness and headiness of a top Moulin-à-Vent without the weight or tannin. At its best, it is a pure, lush, silky fruity wine that is seductive and disarming.

The best producers: Domaine Bachelard (represented and commercialized by George Duboeuf), René Berrod-Les Roches du Vivier, Michel Chignard-les-Moriers, Château des Deduits (represented and commercialized by Georges Duboeuf), Guy Depardon, Domaine de la Grand Cour (Jean Dutraive), Domaine de la Grand Cru, Château de Grand Pré (represented and commercialized by

Pierre Ferraud), Château des Labourons, Domaine des Quatre Vents (represented and commercialized by Georges Duboeuf), Michel Tribolet.

Most successful recent vintages: 1989, 1988, 1985

Aging Potential: 2 to 4 years

FLEURIE

At the moment, Fleurie seems to have everything going for it—a charming village, the finest restaurant in the region (Auberge du Cep), and an insatiable worldwide demand for its incredibly aromatic, seductive, lush wines. Tourists almost ignore Moulin-à-Vent on their way to visit one of the cellars in Fleurie, which also has a very important cooperative formed in 1927 and now claims 322 members who own over 900 acres of vineyards. Its wine is a competent example of Fleurie, but does not reach the level of the best domaine Fleuries, or those represented by Georges Duboeuf or Pierre Ferraud.

Most Fleuries will not last as long as Moulin-à-Vent, but I doubt if most people care since most wines from Fleurie are normally consumed within several hours of purchase.

Fleurie is a lovely hilltop town, but unfortunately, the exquisite Auberge du Cep restaurant offers no lodging. Instead, there is the Hôtel des Grands Vins, a good hotel with 20 rooms, located just outside Fleurie on D 119.

CHIROUBLES

Location: Chiroubles sits just to the west of Fleurie. Its vineyards, located at an altitude of over 1,500 feet, make it the highest-situated cru in the Beaujolais region. Chiroubles is in the most gorgeous area of Beaujolais, with its village perched on a hilltop (at 2,500 feet) overlooking the vast plain created by the river

Sâone. A drive up the nearby Fut d'Avenas on a clear day will offer a view of Mont Blanc and its shiny glaciers.

Acres under vine: 865 acres

Price levels: $8 to $12 a bottle

General wine characteristics: Considered the most ethereal and fragrant of the Beaujolais crus, Chiroubles derives much of its character from its penetrating, pervasive fragrance. It matures rapidly, and must be drunk within 2 years of the vintage.

The best producers: Domaine Bouillard, Georges Boulon, Domaine Desmeures (represented and commercialized by Georges Duboeuf), Château de Javernand (represented and commercialized by Georges Duboeuf), Bernard Meziat, Giles Meziat, Georges Passot, Château de Raousset (part of the crop is represented and commercialized by Georges Duboeuf), René Savoye, Domaine de la Source.

Most successful recent vintages: 1989, 1988

Aging Potential: 1 to 2 years

CHIROUBLES

If you are searching for the most aromatic Beaujolais, and are willing to sacrifice body, power, and intense fruit, then search out the wines of Chiroubles.

The production of over 200,000 cases seems to have no shortage of admirers, even though in years when there are less-than-perfect growing conditions a Chiroubles can often be thin, watery, and unripe. Some skeptics have called Chiroubles too light hearted and precocious to rank as a Beaujolais cru, but then, I suspect they have never tried the best bottles from producers such as Georges Duboeuf's Domaine Desmeures, Château de Javernand, or Château de Raousset. A grower such as René Savoye also produces a textbook Chiroubles that provides an extraordinary, explosive perfume of red fruits, with bananas and raspberries sometimes in evidence in the top years. Because of its lightness and aromatic freshness, Chiroubles should be consumed in its first year or two of life.

Chiroubles, which is the most remote of the Beaujolais crus, offers breathtaking views of the vineyards. Anyone who visits there will no doubt be seduced by the pure beauty of its spectacular location and become a Chiroubles advocate for life. I do not remember seeing any hotel in the village, but there are two restaurants, Monsieur Gonin's La Terrasse de Beaujolais, and Lallement. I especially recommend the former. There is also a cooperative called La Maison des Vignerons, founded in 1929, with over 90 members farming 400-plus acres. It offers free tastings and the option to purchase their wines. There is a statue of Monsieur Pulliat in the town that is of importance because he was the man who first planted a grafted Gamay on American root stock in Beaujolais after the dreaded phylloxera epidemic had devastated the vineyards in the late nineteenth century.

MORGON

Location: The teeming town of Morgon is located 2 miles southeast of Chiroubles, and is one of the two largest of the Beaujolais crus. There are actually two villages, the more significant one being Villié-Morgon, and the other Bas-Morgon. They are separated by the extraordinary Mont du Py, the big, granite hillside from which the most interesting vineyards and compelling wines of Morgon emerge. Villié-Morgon is about a 5-minute drive south from Romanèche-Thorins.

Acres under vine: 2,717 acres

Price levels: $8 to $14 a bottle

General wine characteristics: There are actually two styles of Morgon, depending on where the vineyard in question is located. Some are located on the Côte de Py, a slope of brownish, decomposed slate soil that the locals claim provides both a special *gout de terroir* as well as the weight and richness that has given Morgon a reputation for being one of the most robust and ageworthy of the Beaujolais crus. The vineyards that lie on the flat land of Morgon produce a much lighter wine that should be drunk within several years after bottling. Some producers have blended the wines from the two areas, feeling that the wines from the Côte de Py are on occasion too full and rich, lacking the precocious charm that most modern-day consumers expect of Beaujolais. The actual location of the Côte de Py is between the two villages of Morgon and Villié-Morgon. The decomposing slate soil, or as the French say, *roche-pourrie* (rotten rock), is to be found here.

The best producers: Georges Brun, Domaine de la Chanaise (Dominique Piron), Domaine Jean Descombes (represented and commercialized by Georges Duboeuf), Claude Desvignes, Sylvain Fessy-Cuvée André Gauthier, Georges Passot, Domaine des Pillets, Domaine de Pizay, Domaine de la Princess Lieven (represented and commercialized by Georges Duboeuf), Domaine Savoye, Domaine Jacques Trichard, Domaine des Versaudes (represented and commercialized by Georges Duboeuf).

Most successful recent vintages: 1989, 1988, 1985

Aging Potential: 2 to 5 years

MORGON

Morgon has always been one of my favorite villages, not only because the bustling town of Villié-Morgon is an enticingly chaotic place both at the time of the harvest and when the Beaujolais Nouveau is released, but also because my favorite Beaujolais producer of all, the flamboyant Jean Descombes, has his cellars here. The wine of Morgon can be among the best of Beaujolais, although for overall consistency it can not rival Fleurie, Moulin-à-Vent, or Juliénas. Nevertheless, Morgon, perhaps because it is easy to pronounce and also because there is so much of it made (nearly 650,000 cases in an abundant year), is easily found in all the major export markets.

The fullest and richest wines tend to come from the ridge of decomposed slate soil on the Côte de Py. An area adjacent to Côte de Py called Les Charmes is also highly reputed for producing the heady, rich, almost sumptuous style of Beaujolais that makes Morgon famous.

In fact, there is perhaps no other village in Beaujolais where I detect in a ripe year the exotic flavors of overripe cherries, peaches, and apricots. Some commentators have even compared the smell and taste to that of kirsch, which is not surprising.

Morgon tends to reach great ripeness because of the perfect exposure of many of its vineyards, particularly those on the Côte de Py, which reaches an altitude of 1,150 feet. The alcohol content of Morgon can also be relatively high, approaching 14% in vintages such as 1985, and more than 14% in a year such as 1989.

While the locals claim the wines of Morgon can last for 8 to 10 years, I have found that even the most brilliant wines made by Jean Descombes should be consumed by the time they are 5 or 6 years old.

This cru of Beaujolais is well stocked with hotels. In Villié-Morgon is the Hotel de Parc, an attractive, highly regarded hotel, as well as the Hotel du Col de Truges. There are also a number of restaurants, including Le Morgon, Le Relais des Caveaux, and Cellier d'Anclachais. My favorite is Le Relais des Caveaux.

If one can arrange it, a visit to see the ebullient Jean Descombes is most rewarding. His cellars, which seem to be with American eyes a contradictory homage to both pornography and his Lord, are quite extraordinary, matched in flamboyance and exotic qualities only by his remarkable wine.

RÉGNIÉ

Location: Régnié is shaped like a triangle, sandwiched between Morgon to its east and north, and a section entitled to Beaujolais-Villages status to its west. To the south is Brouilly and the Côte de Brouilly. Régnié is located just over 12 miles from Villefranche to the southeast, and only 3.5 miles from Beaujeu, the village in the Beaujolais-Villages appellation from which the entire region took its name. Régnié takes its name from the village called Régnié-Durette.

Acres under vine: 1,606 acres

Price levels: $7 to $10 a bottle

General wine characteristics: Those observers who have followed the upgrading of Régnié to cru status in 1989 from its simple Beaujolais-Villages status agree there are three general styles of Régnié. In the northeast section of Régnié, in the *lieux-dits* called La Haute la Basse-Ronze, La Grange Barjot, Les Chastys, and Les Grandes Bruyères, all of which are very close to Villié-Morgon, the style of wine is one of more robustness and generosity marked by aromas of cherries, kirsch, raspberries, and sometimes bananas. These wines might be called the Morgon style of Régnié, and can last 3 to 5 years in the bottle. In the southern part of Régnié, the largest section, between Cercié, Lantignié, and Quincié, the wines are more floral with more cassis in their bouquet. The sandy soil there creates wines that are slightly higher in acidity and much lighter in color, without the generosity that one finds in the northeastern sector of the appellation. These wines are closer to Brouilly in style. Admirers of Régnié claim that the most original and perhaps the most typical Régnié comes from the western sector of the appellation. These wines have an intense smell of cassis and raspberries, and seem to represent what Régnié should be, a synthesis of Brouilly and Morgon. The best *lieux-dits* in this section include La Plaigne, Vernus, Les Forchets, and La Tour Bourdon.

The best producers: M. Gabriel Aligne, Paul Cinquin, Deplace Frères-Domaine du Crêt des Bruyères, Georges Duboeuf,* Jean Durand, Domaine de la Gerarde, Pierre Ferraud,* Alain Pierre, Domaine du Potet (represented and commercialized by Georges Duboeuf), Michel and Jean-Paul Rampon, Joel Rochette, Jean-Paul Ruet, Claude and Bernard Roux, René and Bernard Vassot

Most successful recent vintages: 1989

Aging Potential: 2 to 4 years

* The *cuvées* of Pierre Ferraud and Georges Duboeuf are an assemblage of different purchases, but given the quality of these wines in 1988 and 1989, they would certainly compete with the best estate-bottled, grower-produced Régniés.

RÉGNIÉ

For some time the wines of Régnié have sold at slightly higher prices than the other Beaujolais-Villages, and because of this there was a movement to upgrade Régnié to its own cru status. This was granted in 1989. The appellation now forms a triangle, abutted on the east by Morgon, on the west by the Beaujolais-Villages, and on the south by Brouilly. Many people compare the wines of Régnié to the wines of Brouilly. Based on my tastings of the 1989s, I thought the Régniés were significantly higher in quality than the Brouillys. The domaines and a number of *négociants* who offer Régnié selections seem to be putting both feet forward in their efforts to showcase these wines which seem to have more character in their bouquets, as well as more flavor depth, than many of the Brouillys. While some people complain that the creation of this 10th cru of Beaujolais was unjustified, based on the 1989s I tasted that would not appear to be true. Régnié clearly produces as interesting and as pleasurable Beaujolais as Brouilly and Côte de Brouilly. Not surprisingly, the huge *négociant*, Georges Duboeuf, has led the charge with a bevy of alluring selections from Régnié.

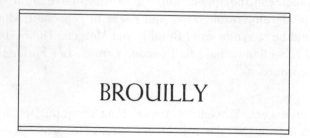

BROUILLY

Location: The viticultural area of Brouilly surrounds the smaller appellation of Côte de Brouilly on 3 sides. Brouilly can be easily reached by taking the Belleville exit off the autoroute and proceeding west on D 37 for about 10 minutes, or 5 miles, until reaching the village of Cercié. Cercié sits at the foot of Mont Brouilly and marks the northern boundary of the appellation of Brouilly.

Acres under vine: 2,964 acres

Price levels: $8 to $12 a bottle

General wine characteristics: There are huge quantities of Brouilly made, and much of it is quite mediocre. Many enthusiasts of the crus of Beaujolais turn their glass upside down when a bottle of Brouilly is brought out. That is unfortunate, because there are some excellent examples of Brouilly. The top producers make a relatively light, aromatic, fruity wine that at its best can combine the charm of an excellent Chiroubles with the lush fruit and substance of Régnié. The best vineyards in Brouilly are located in the six communes of Quincié, Cercié, Charentay, St.-Étienne-la-Varenne, St.-Lager, and Odenas.

The best producers: Antoine Beroujon, Château de Bluizard (represented and commercialized by Georges Duboeuf), Robert Condemine, Pierre Cotton, Domaine de la Grand Cour (Jean Dutraive), Marcel Joubert, Château de la Chaize, Domaine de Lavant (Robert Farjat), Château de Nervers (represented and commercialized by Georges Duboeuf), Domaine du Prieuré (represented and commercialized by Georges Duboeuf), Domaine de la Roche (represented and commercialized by Georges Duboeuf), Domaine André Ronzière, Jean-Paul Ruet, Château des Tours.

Most successful recent vintages: 1989

Aging Potential: 1 to 3 years

BROUILLY

Brouilly's whopping 2,964 acres ensures its presence on many restaurant wine lists and on the sales sheets of the world's wine merchants. The fact that this Beaujolais cru produces more wine than any other cru has engendered a degree of criticism, some of it justified. But certainly the best examples show the frank, straightforward, exuberant fruitiness that one expects in a good wine from one of Beaujolais' 10 crus.

The entire appellation is dominated by an extinct volcano, the 1,585-foot-high Mont Brouilly. The word Brouilly is derived from the word *brûlé*, meaning burnt.

The appellation produces over 800,000 cases of wine, and many accuse the growers of needing no encouragement to permit their yields to soar beyond the maximum allowed by law. It also can be difficult for the growers, who claim their wines do not fetch the same prices as some of the other crus of Beaujolais.

Brouilly can claim, however, one of the most magnificent châteaux of the region, the Château de la Chaize. It is open to the public, although an appointment must be made for a tour of this magnificent estate. For years the wine of Château de la Chaize was light and quite mediocre, but recently it has begun to show considerable improvement. It is probably the most recognizable and best-known Brouilly, mainly because its 237 acres of vineyards represent the appellation's largest parcel of land. It is owned by the Marquise Nicole de Roussy, a director of the famous House of Christian Dior.

One of the more amusing legends of Burgundy comes from the appellation of Brouilly, which has a vineyard called Pisse-Vieille. The growers are all in agreement as to the history behind the unusual name of this vineyard. It is believed that a woman by the name of Mariette, who was slightly deaf, attended confession one day and was told by the priest, who was new to the village, "*Allez. Et ne pechez plus.*" The priest was attempting to tell Mariette to leave and not to sin again. What Mariette believed she heard in the local dialect was "go and do not piss again." According to the legend, Mariette, a committed Catholic, did exactly what she was told. After several days, she was, not unexpectedly, in great pain, and her husband, recognizing something was wrong, went to see the priest. The husband quickly realized that her slight deafness may have led her to misinterpret the priest's advice. As he was rushing home he began yelling, "*pisse-vieille,*" meaning, piss, old woman! There are several wines made today that can be found with the words Brouilly-Pisse-Vieille on them. Joel Rochette and the Hospices de Beaujeu produce wines with this amusing name.

I know of no local restaurants or hotels I can recommend within the appellation of Brouilly, but close by in Belleville is the excellent restaurant, Le Beaujolais, on the Rue Maréchal-Foch, which serves authentic regional specialities. A restaurant within Brouilly that is recommended by the growers is Le Relais Beaujolais in Cercié.

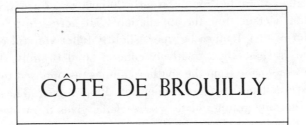

CÔTE DE BROUILLY

Location: Côte de Brouilly is a viticultural area encompassing the hill-sides of the Mont de Brouilly. It is encircled on 3 sides by Brouilly and impossible to miss if you are in the area since Mont de Brouilly can be seen from quite a distance. It was once an active volcano but is now extinct.

Acres under vine: 716 acres

Price levels: $7 to $12 a bottle

General wine characteristics: In general, Côte de Brouilly is a bit richer and riper, and has more character than most wines from Brouilly. This is because the vineyards are up on the slopes of Mont de Brouilly with much better exposure. The grapes mature more easily and consequently have higher sugar levels than those from Brouilly. Appellation regulations therefore require a Côte de Brouilly to have a higher minimum alcohol content (10.5%) than Brouilly, which is only required to have 10%. Like Brouilly, Côte de Brouilly should be drunk within the first 2 to 3 years of life.

The best producers: L. Bassy, Alain Bernillon, Guy Cotton, Domaine André Large, Domaine Pavillon de Chavannes, Domaine du Petit Pressoir, Château Thivin, Lucien and Robert Verger.

Most successful recent vintages: 1989, 1988

Aging Potential: 1 to 3 years

CÔTE DE BROUILLY

Created in 1935 as a separate appellation, the Côte de Brouilly vineyards are all situated on the steep, blue granite sides of the extinct volcano called Mont de Brouilly. Nearly 200,000 cases are now made in an abundant vintage from the appellation's 716 acres. In principle and often in form, they tend to be riper, slightly fuller yet still exuberant, fresh wines resembling a relatively concentrated Brouilly. The locals claim the wine made from the southern slopes, as opposed to the western or eastern slopes, is more concentrated and robust. They also suggest that the blue granite, or the *tierre bleue*, gives the wines an extra degree of finesse not shared by the wines of Brouilly. I am not sure if this is the reason that most Côte de Brouilly is better than Brouilly. The yields of the former tend to be slightly lower, and I would insist that Côte de Brouilly is a more intense and concentrated wine largely because of its vineyards' exposure. Certainly in the hot years, such as 1989, 1985, and 1983, many of the Côte de Brouilly wines can reach and surpass 14% natural alcohol because of the vineyards' exposures. They are much bigger wines from an alcoholic standpoint than their neighbors in Brouilly.

A NOTE ON THE *NÉGOCIANTS* OF BEAUJOLAIS

Much of what I have written about Beaujolais has dealt with the different vineyards or appellations, and the best producers. However, it must be stated that the *négociants* dominate the real market for Beaujolais, buying much of the growers' production, making blends, and then selling the wines internationally. Georges Duboeuf's name has appeared with great regularity because he is simply the best at what he does. He is also the largest and most successful of the *négociants*, and his remarkable publicity skills have as much if not more to do with the success of Beaujolais Nouveau than all of the other gimmicks associated with the release of this exuberant wine the third week in November. Duboeuf was also the first to recognize the importance of colorful labels and early bottling of his wines. Duboeuf's "flower labels" have revolutionized wine labels throughout the world. His emphasis on early bottling to preserve a wine's freshness and fruit has met with worldwide acclaim. The quality of his Beaujolais usually represents the finest the region can provide.

However, there are other *négociants* who believe in bottling authentic, fresh, and representative Beaujolais from the different crus. Experience has taught me the two firms that come closest to rivaling the selections of Georges Duboeuf are Pierre Ferraud in Belleville and Trenel Fils in Charnay-Les-Mâcon. I have written more about them in the producers section of this book, but I felt they should be mentioned here too. The Ferraud wines tend to be more traditional Beaujolais, rather sturdy yet still fresh, tasty wines, whereas Trenel seems to emphasize rich, ripe, intense fruit.

Other *négociants* have had more mixed success. These include Sylvain Fessy (Vins Dessalle in Belleville). I remember being highly impressed with some of Fessy's selections in the early eighties, but more recent vintages have shown some inconsistency. However, he can be a producer whose wines merit attention.

Another producer whose wines do well in blind tastings is Chanut Frères in Romanèche-Thorins. Unfortunately, Chanut Frères live in the gigantic shadow cast by Georges Duboeuf, and as a result, this firm does not get the recognition it deserves.

AN APPELLATION FOR THE FUTURE

I would be remiss in not saying a few words about a new appellation that was created in 1984. It is called the Côteaux du Lyonnais, and constitutes a vast area that was a vibrant viticultural region at the turn of the century. But two world wars and a growing fascination with the fresh, fruity reds of Beaujolais led most of the growers there to seek other professions. The wines, which are inexpensive, are starting to draw the attention of many people, including Georges Duboeuf. They are not as fruity as Beaujolais, and are more sturdy and robust, but for the time being they are extremely good values, and generally are soundly made. It will be interesting to see what the growers are able to do in this, as of now, totally untapped source for inexpensive red wines.

PART III

THE VINTAGES
(1945–1989)

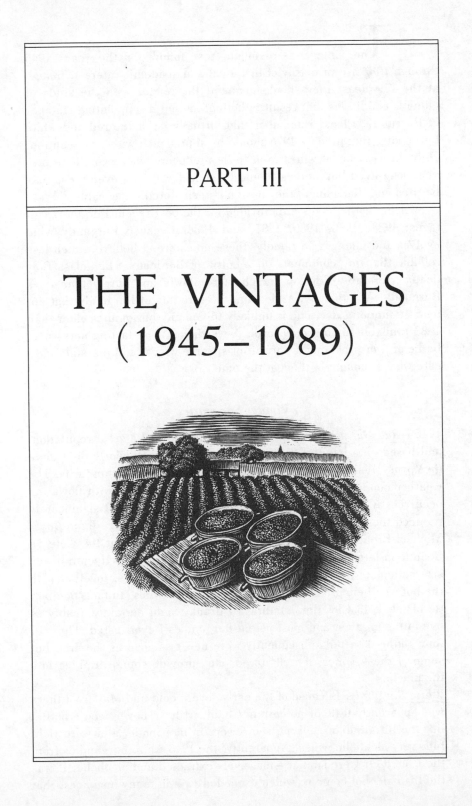

The vintage assessments that follow for the years 1945 through 1982 are primarily of historical and academic interest, though at the very least they should acquaint the reader with the kinds of climatic conditions that result in both great and disappointing vintages of Burgundy. Please remember that virtually all of the red and white burgundies that predate 1976 should be approached with great caution. Only the very finest wines from those producers whose goal is to produce long-lived burgundies should be considered, and even these may be tired and in decline if they have not been stored impeccably.

Specific tasting notes are provided for the best recent Burgundy vintages: 1983, 1985, 1986, 1987, and 1988. Because Burgundy wine evolves and changes so rapidly, these notes are, I believe, much less reliable than my comments on a bottle of Bordeaux. High-class Bordeaux irrefutably develops much more slowly and surely than does Burgundy. Additionally, aside from the rare lots of Burgundy that appear at auction sales, one is unlikely to find any burgundies older than 1983 available at the retail level. Nevertheless, the tasting notes may be helpful in providing a portrait of specific wines, and certainly indicate what I thought of them at the time.

Vintage Summaries

1945—*Red Burgundy*. This vintage has always had a great reputation, and based on a handful of wines I have tasted, particularly the Comte de Vogüé-Musigny and Clos des Lambrays, I can understand why. The weather conditions were apparently quite remarkable, with flowering occurring at the end of May after a severe frost on May 1 significantly reduced the potential crop size. In his *The Great Vintage Wine Book*, Michael Broadbent reported that a ferocious cyclone hit the Côte de Beaune in late June, further reducing the crop to one-sixteenth of the size anticipated. These extremely minuscule quantities, together with the hot weather, produced highly concentrated wines. In fact, one bottle of the 1945 Clos des Lambrays I drank would certainly qualify as one of the greatest and most potent burgundies I ever tasted. Three or four bottles I tasted subsequently were never as good as the first, but some of these wines, if well stored, may provide sound drinking into the nineties.

White Burgundy. Because of the early severe cold and May frost there was apparently little or no crop in Chablis. I have never seen a bottle, but the Burgundians tell me some were in fact made, and were rich, full, very alcoholic wines. Apparently, the 1945 white burgundies from the Côte d'Or were similar—massively extracted and alcoholic. It was the high alcohol content, which exceeded 15% in many instances, that allowed some of these wines to last for 20 or 30 years. I doubt very much if any are still drinking well today, unless they come from the cellars of Madame Lalou Bize-Leroy.

1946—I have no tasting notes on any wine from the 1946 vintage in Burgundy or Chablis. The reports are that it was a moderately sized crop that ripened well despite the cool, rainy weather experienced before the harvest. The wines have a reputation of being extremely supple, and they evolved rapidly and were better than most people expected. The 1946s have been mainly forgotten since connoisseurs prefer the 1945s and 1947s.

1947—*Red Burgundy*. Since this is my birth year, I have had the chance to taste a number of 1947s. It was a vintage of extremely opulent, alcoholic, very concentrated, no doubt low-acid wines. The best 1947s I tasted, which were still drinking beautifully in 1987 and 1988, were Pothier-Rieusset's Pommard Les Rugiens and Ponsot's Clos de la Roche. These two wines gave me a sense of eternal youth, and are timeless monuments that could age well for another 10–20 years. Another outstanding 1947 I have had a chance to try is the Corton from Bouchard Père et Fils, which was splendidly mature but still possessed all its fleshy, luscious fruit. A number of wines from the Côte de Nuits, however, particularly a Chambertin from Damoy and one from Faiveley, had all seen better days when tasted in 1988. The year 1947 produced a relatively small crop, and in its day was considered a great vintage. *White Burgundy*. This was a vintage much like 1945, but with an even hotter summer, where the wines allegedly approached 15%–16% alcohol (which no doubt would horrify many of today's oenologists). There were many cases of stuck fermentations because the grapes were so full of sugar. Given that combination, I doubt many have aged gracefully after their first 20 or 30 years in the bottle. In Chablis, the growers still talk about 1947 as one of the greatest vintages of the century, but no one ever seems to have a bottle they are willing to share.

1948—*Red Burgundy*. 1948 was the most abundant vintage for Burgundy's Côte d'Or after 1944. The weather was characterized by a relatively cool and wet summer, but dry weather arrived in the autumn. The result was large quantities of some surprisingly good wines. *White Burgundy*. While I have never tasted any 1948 red burgundies, I have had several whites that seemed to justify their excellent reputation. A Bâtard-Montrachet from Lequin-Roussot drunk in 1987 was monumental, still fresh and loaded with fruit. A Chablis Les Clos I found in a Baltimore restaurant's wine cellar, with the shipper's name illegible because of mold, was pure perfection. It is very frustrating not to know whom to credit for its production.

1949—*Red Burgundy*. This was probably the best of the post-World

War II vintages before 1959. After early rains resulted in a poor flowering in June, the summer was hot and extremely dry. Just before the harvest, when growers were fearful that the drought-like conditions would cause the vines to shut down, thus halting the maturation process, the rains came to the rescue. The welcome precipitation also prevented the wines from being overly tannic. Yields were very low, but in excess of those in 1945. The wines turned out with better acidities and slightly lower alcohol levels than the richer, fuller, initially more dramatic 1947s. The truly compelling 1949 red burgundies I have tasted included an absolutely celestial Pommard-Rugiens from Pothier-Rieusset, and a great Musigny-Vieilles Vignes from the Comte de Vogüé. Another surreal wine was Leroy's 1949 Chambertin, which I would rate slightly behind the first two, but it is still a monumental, profound bottle of burgundy.

White Burgundy. The Chablis producers have always proclaimed that 1947 was better than 1949. Since I have never tasted any 1949 Chablis, I can only trust their judgment. In the Côte d'Or, 1949 was considered slightly less stupendous for the whites than for the reds, but certainly it was an excellent year, offering well-balanced, rich, concentrated wines from relatively low yields.

1950—A wet, rainy summer followed by a sunny fall resulted in the most abundant vintage in Burgundy between 1945 and 1970. Nearly 60 hectoliters per hectare were routinely produced, both in Chablis and the Côte d'Or. The wines were quite variable, owing no doubt to a less than rigorous selection process, and the fact that the growers knew nothing about the modern-day technique of _saigner_ (increasing the ratio of skins to juice by bleeding off the excess juice). I have never tasted any 1950s, red or white, so I do not have any personal impressions to convey. But since they were apparently light, low-acid, diluted wines, it is hard to believe any could have held up this long.

1951—As in Bordeaux, this was a terrible vintage throughout France. A spring frost, which decimated the crops, was followed by a dismal, wet, cold summer that prevented the vines from ripening. I have never seen any 1951s, but apparently they were unsuccessful wines across the board and were either sold off in bulk by many of the domaines or downgraded to generic or regional appellation wines.

1952—_Red Burgundy_. 1952 was a relatively small crop, even by the standards of the fifties, with a production of half that of 1950's record-setting year. Dry, hot summer weather kept the yields low. September was cooler than normal, and the harvest occurred with only moderate rainfall. The results were excellent wines that were well structured, rich in fruit, and quite tannic.

White Burgundy. While the reputation for the wines of Chablis is one of an average quality and quantity vintage, the whites from the Côte d'Or were reputed to be elegant, flavorful wines, lacking the great depth and richness of 1949, 1947, or 1945, but lighter, less alcoholic, and well balanced. I would be surprised if any have lasted into the nineties.

1953—*Red Burgundy*. The 1953 red burgundies had much the same style and character as the 1953 clarets from Bordeaux. Soft, supple, easy to drink and understand, the wines were delicious when released in 1955 and continued to drink well through the mid-sixties. However, unlike the clarets, most of the 1953 red burgundies began to decline quite rapidly in the late sixties according to André Gagey of the Beaune firm of Louis Jadot. Some of the first truly magnificent red burgundies I ever encountered were from this vintage. They included the Domaine de la Romanée-Conti's Grands Echézeaux and Romanée-Conti, and George Mugneret's Clos Vougeot.

White Burgundy. Ripe, soft, honeyed, precocious wines were produced in 1953 that were ideal for drinking in their first 5–10 years of life. In Chablis, the size of the crop was greatly reduced because of hail. The quality was deemed to be good to very good by the producers, although I have met no one from Chablis who could even remember tasting a bottle of a 1953.

1954—*Red Burgundy*. A generally rainy summer followed by a hot autumn resulted in a moderately large crop ranging from mediocre to very good in quality. The wines were extremely soft and drinkable at an early age.

White Burgundy. Reputedly a good vintage in Chablis, but those who remember the wines say they were meant to be consumed within 5–6 years of the vintage. I have never tasted a white 1954 from the Côte d'Or, but the growers harvested early, producing relatively lean wines, extremely high in acidity, that never blossomed.

1955—*Red Burgundy*. 1955 was the second largest crop of the decade, behind 1950. It produced generally medium-bodied, pleasant wines that rarely have stood the test of time. One major exception is the wines of the Leroy firm. Madame Lalou Bize-Leroy's 1955s are still at their glorious plateaus of perfection. The vintage has a sound reputation, but old-timers claim it was surpassed in quality by 1959, 1953, and even by 1957.

White Burgundy. Because an Indian summer provided excellent harvest conditions resulting in full maturity in the vineyards, the white burgundies were considered more successful than the red wines. They were, however, relatively soft and opulent, so I would be suspicious if any were still alive today. The most-prized white burgundies of 1955 were from Corton-Charlemagne, where many of the wines reached 15% or more natural alcohol.

1956—1956 was the year of the big chill all over Europe. Many vineyards were totally destroyed because of the unusually cold winter. The entire Grand Cru harvest in Chablis was declassified because of unacceptable quality, and many of the Premiers Crus were never bottled. What was made was deemed poor to mediocre. Even the summer was cold with long periods of rain. While some sun and heat arrived in September, it was far too late to save the tiny crop. I have never seen a bottle of 1956 red or white burgundy, and most commentators agree it was the worst vintage of the fifties.

1957—*Red Burgundy*. This might be one of the oldest vintages that is still well worth purchasing today. Their reputation has never been high, but the general level of quality of the red 1957s I have tasted would seemingly indicate otherwise. Because the vintage tended to produce wines that were concentrated yet high in acidity, many 1957s have aged quite slowly. If they have been well stored, they could still be in excellent condition. In some ways the 1957s remind me of the 1972 vintage for red burgundy—a vintage maligned at first because of high acidity, that has matured gracefully and impressively. I have had a number of fine 1957s, particularly from the Hospices de Beaune, which were tasted in the mid-eighties and were quite impressive. They were deeply colored, rich, meaty, flavorful red burgundies that were neither shy nor malnourished.

White Burgundy. The white burgundies also had extremely high acidity in 1957, but also excellent ripeness, a rare combination, particularly today. I have never tasted a 1957 white burgundy, but given their constitution I would not be surprised if some of these wines have admirably stood the test of time. In Chablis, there was horrific frost damage that reduced the size of the crop and little wine was actually made. I have never seen a bottle, so I have no idea what the quality was actually like, but most of the producers claimed it was a sad year.

1958—*Red Burgundy*. An abundant year that was until 1970 surpassed only by 1950 and 1955, 1958 produced extremely light, soft, quick-to-mature and quick-to-fade wines. A lot of rain in August and early September seriously diluted the wines and lowered acids, making the 1958s somewhat lightweight, commercial examples, destined to be consumed immediately.

White Burgundy. The heavy rains of late summer and early September washed out the chance for a good vintage in the Côte d'Or. Chablis' undoing was not only rain, but significant rot caused by the dampness and humidity. While 1958 is not nearly as bad as 1956, it is considered to be one of the worst vintages in the last four decades.

1959—*Red Burgundy*. Michael Broadbent considered this vintage one of the "last classic heavyweights" that Burgundy produced. I would tend to agree with him, although certainly some of the 1964s and 1985s should rival even the richest and fullest of the 1959s. The weather conditions in Burgundy were not much different from those in Bordeaux. There was an excellent flowering that guaranteed a large crop, followed by hot, dry weather for much of the summer. Some rain in early September was beneficial, and the harvest commenced under ideal conditions. The red burgundies I have tasted from this vintage have been splendidly full, rich, and intense. I have had truly profound bottles from the Domaine de la Romanée-Conti, such as Grands Echézeaux and Romanée-Conti. Also, a Bouchard Père et Fils Corton was quite remarkable and in superb condition when tasted in 1987. The wines drank beautifully from their inception, although I would suspect now most are beginning to show the decay of age. Nevertheless, this is a vintage well worth a serious look if you can find the very best examples that have been well stored.

White Burgundy. Many of the successful producers of white burgundy in the incredibly hot year of 1983 compared their 1983s to their 1959s. The 1959s were irregular, ranging from flabby, overly alcoholic, low-acid behemoths, to extraordinary full, rich, concentrated wines that took excess to the limit. I wonder how many have stood the test of time. I also have heard that the 1989s resemble the 1959s. Chablis produced much better-balanced wines because they possessed higher natural acidities than the wines from the Côte d'Or.

1960—*Red Burgundy*. 1960 was a poor vintage, largely because of a cool July and very wet August and September, which caused rot as well as a lack of maturity in the grapes. As a result, even the successful wines were light.

White Burgundy. Considered to be just barely better than the 1960 reds, the white wines were thin and light but high in acidity, which gave them a degree of longevity, but they never possessed much flavor. In Chablis, a devastating frost once again reduced the crop size dramatically, and rain watered down the quality.

1961—*Red Burgundy*. If red burgundy can suffer in years such as 1957, 1972, and 1980 because of the fortunes of the Bordeaux vintage, it can also benefit in years where it has a good rather than great vintage, but Bordeaux has an extraordinary vintage. This was the case in 1961. I have never tasted a great 1961 red burgundy. Ones I have had recently all seemed tired and undistinguished. The crop size was small; the year was hot and dry. The wines, for whatever reason, lacked the flavor and intensity of the 1959s and 1947s, which they were initially believed to resemble. But because of Bordeaux's great success in 1961, the demand for burgundy was insatiable and prices were high. This vintage has probably always been tremendously overvalued and overpriced in Burgundy. It should be avoided now as the wines have both feet in the grave.

White Burgundy. The white burgundies also benefited from the great reputation Bordeaux enjoyed in 1961. Those I have tasted seemed to be good, but unexciting. They were certainly surpassed by the great 1962s, which turned out to be one of the four or five best white burgundy vintages in the last thirty years. If there were any great white burgundies made it was in Chablis, which had a small crop that produced extremely concentrated, well-balanced wines.

1962—*Red Burgundy*. A late harvest, because of rain in September, caused doubts about what had otherwise been a fine growing season. The wines turned out to be delicious, but it has been years since I have seen a 1962, and so I have no idea of how they have matured. It was a memorable year for the Domaine de la Romanée-Conti. Their wines lived up to their celestial reputation, producing truly monumental wines from their vineyards in Grands Echézeaux, Richebourg, La Tâche, and Romanée-Conti. It was also a superb vintage for Henri Gouges, and for the Comte de Vogüé's Bonnes Mares and Musigny-Vieilles Vignes. The house of Roumier in Chambolle-Musigny also turned out delicious 1962s, as did a number of Pommard's finest producers, such as Michel Gaunoux and Madame Courcel. But since I have tasted none of these wines recently, I wonder how they have matured.

White Burgundy. Looking back, the greatest vintages for white burgundy have been 1962, 1966, 1969, 1973, 1985, 1986, and probably 1989. Few of the modern-day vintages will last as long as the 1962s have. I remember a tasting in 1987 where I was served blind the 1962 Corton-Charlemagne of Louis Latour. It was pure perfection, still fresh yet incredibly rich, unctuous, opulent, and bursting with fruit. Apparently, this was not a fluke, as old-timers in Chassagne, Puligny, and Meursault speak with awe about the 1962s. I am not sure what my advice would be should any of the great 1962 Grands Crus from the Côte d'Or appear on the auction block, but if you are interested in taking a chance on purchasing a rare old bottle of white burgundy, they may well be worth the gamble. While the reputation for the whites of Chablis was surpassed by 1961, many of the growers claim their 1962s have outlasted their 1961s.

1963—*Red Burgundy*. The most memorable aspect of 1963 was the fact that the harvest was the latest on record, with some growers not bringing in their grapes until early November. The reason for this was an extremely rainy August and a cold, wet September, followed by a sunny, Indian summer in October. However, it was too late to make up for what summer could not provide. While there was a tendency by some of the French commentators to call this a miracle year, the wines turned out to be acidic, pale, thin, and vapid.

White Burgundy. The star of white burgundy in 1963 was the Comte Lafon. He produced the best wines, but many white burgundies appeared not to have suffered as much from the poor weather conditions and resulting late harvest as did the reds. I had a 1963 Meursault Les Perrières from Comte Lafon in 1986 which was still concentrated and full. It did not strike me as particularly well balanced, but it was a delicious wine to drink. In Chablis, the quantity of the crop was surprisingly large, but the quality was deemed dismal to disastrous. Many of the most conscientious growers declassified their entire crop or sold it in bulk.

1964—*Red Burgundy.* Burgundy, unlike Bordeaux, was able to get most of its crop in before the heavy rains began to fall. At the time, 1964 was considered a truly magnificent vintage for burgundy, producing high-alcohol, rich, intense, full-bodied, potentially long-lived wines. The summer had been extremely hot with just enough rain to keep the maturity process going. It was a great vintage for Lalou Bize-Leroy, and all her 1964s from the Côte de Nuits are still magnificent. They are about as rich, full, and ageworthy red burgundies as anyone is likely to find. It was also a great vintage for the Domaines Rousseau and Trapet in Gevrey-Chambertin, one which clearly showed the differences in style between these two producers. Rousseau's Chambertin and Chambertin-Clos de Bèze were pure power, richness and fullness; Trapet's Chambertin was delicate yet compellingly fragrant and complex. The famous Domaine Roumier in Chambolle-Musigny also turned out a number of stunning wines, including a great Bonnes Mares and a Chambolle-Musigny Les Amoureuses. The wines from the Domaine de la Romanée-Conti were excellent, although with the exception of the Richebourg, I did not think they were as superb as the domaine's 1962s or 1966s. Henri Gouges, who was then in his prime, made splendid wines in Nuits St.-Georges, as did Jean-Marie Ponsot in Morey St.-Denis. This is a vintage that has certainly stood the test of time, but I would not buy a bottle unless I was sure it had been kept in perfect cellar conditions.

White Burgundy. I have never seen a bottle of 1964 white burgundy, which is unfortunate, because from what I have read they sound like the style of wine I find quite appealing. They were relatively full, luscious, and drank well at an early age, which is probably the reason why none are to be found today. In Chablis, a freak rainstorm of awesome proportions struck just as the harvest got underway. It damaged the grapes, caused acidities and sugar levels to fall, and given the very humid conditions of the harvest, fostered the growth of rot, causing a serious decline in the quality of what could have been a truly great vintage in Chablis. Nevertheless, some producers did prevail. In the mid-eighties I remember tasting a 1964 Raveneau Les Clos at the Hôtel L'Étoile in Chablis that was glorious.

1965—*Red Burgundy*. 1965 was a very poor year, a result of the summer that never was. June, July, and August were unbelievably cold, overcast, and rainy. While the harvest was delayed until mid-October, the weather never warmed up sufficiently for the grapes to ripen. As a result, even with excessive chaptalization, thin, diluted, pale wines with little depth or richness were produced. It is a vintage that should be approached with the greatest apprehension.

White Burgundy. White burgundy was even more disastrous than the red burgundy because of the incessant rain and cold weather. It was also a catastrophic vintage for Chablis.

1966—*Red Burgundy*. This was the first of what I call the modern-day burgundy vintages. It combined relatively high quantity with high quality, and made many friends for burgundy in the late sixties and early seventies. The early summer weather did not suggest the good things that were to come. In fact, by the end of August many growers were anticipating a poor vintage of unripe grapes. But September was hot and dry and the Pinot Noir matured marvelously under textbook conditions. When first released, the red wines seemed less impressive than the larger-scaled, top-line 1964s, but they were still more elegant and sometimes better balanced. There were a lot of fine wines made in this vintage, including absolutely splendid wines from Henri Gouges in Nuits St.-Georges, the Domaine Roumier in Chambolle-Musigny, the Domaines Rousseau and Drouhin-Larose in Gevrey-Chambertin, and the Domaines Georges Mugneret and Jean Gros in Vosne-Romanée. Sensational wines were made at the Domaine de la Romanée-Conti, which were not to be surpassed in quality until 1978. Even the *négociants* turned in superlative performances. The Maison Faiveley made stunning 1966s, as did Louis Jadot, and the ubiquitous Madame Lalou Bize-Leroy. Sadly, the magnificence of these 1966s is now fading. Often they are just shadows of what they were five or ten years ago. Even the wines of the Domaine de la Romanée-Conti, which were probably the finest made in the vintage, seem to be turning the corner and heading downward. Buying 1966s now is fraught with risk, but I suspect if you can find wines from the top producers that have been stored in extremely cold cellars, they may offer tremendously rewarding drinking.

White Burgundy. This was also an exciting vintage for white burgundy producers. Several of the greatest white burgundies I have ever tasted were produced in 1966. I remember an absolutely monumental Le Montrachet from the Domaine de la Romanée-Conti, and a nearly as profound Bâtard-Montrachet from the little-known domaine of Charles Bavard. It was also a superb vintage for the wines of the Comte Lafon and Louis Latour. I have been told that the Domaine Leflaive's wines were superb, but I have never seen a bottle. In Chablis, for the first time in the modern era, production hit and surpassed 100 hectoliters per hectare, which was perhaps an ominous sign of things to come. The quality, if not great, was sound. The wines were fruity, pleasant, and easy to drink.

1967—*Red Burgundy*. Like so many other vintages, 1967 could have been great, but after a wonderfully sunny, hot July and August, several weeks of rain in September unleashed rot in the vineyards. The result was a mixed bag, with relatively light, sometimes rot-tainted red burgundies that fell apart quickly. I've never had a wine from this vintage that I thought was excellent, and I would think that buying a 1967 red burgundy today would be foolish.

White Burgundy. Reputedly better than the reds, the handful of white burgundies I tasted years ago left me unconvinced. Given the harvest conditions, most of the Chardonnay from the Côte d'Or had to have been harvested in the rain, but perhaps some of the early pickers had enough ripeness to make good wines. The best wine I remember tasting from this vintage was the Corton-Charlemagne from Louis Latour. Chablis fared much better given the fact that frost cut back the quantity, and there was less troublesome rain in Chablis than in the Côte d'Or.

1968—Whether it was red burgundy, white burgundy or Chablis, the results were catastrophically dismal. Rain, cool weather, and rot were the undoing of this vintage. It had no chance after an extremely hot June. I have never seen a bottle of a 1968 burgundy, and everyone has told me I would have no desire to taste one if I did. Some commentators have claimed that the whites were better than the reds.

1969—*Red Burgundy*. 1969 produced an excellent, sometimes outstanding vintage of classic, long-lived wines. At the time, many felt they would not turn out to be as good as the 1966s. The 1969s have now outlasted the 1966s, and the best examples should continue to drink well for another decade, making them rare birds by modern-day burgundy standards. The weather did not suggest this would turn out to be a top-notch vintage. Although July and August were hot, wet and cool weather continued through September, delaying the harvest until early

October. However, the crop size was small and the skins thick as a result of the heat during the summer. What resulted was concentrated, beautifully structured wines built for the long haul. They had excellent bouquets and balance. This is a memorable vintage for a number of Burgundy's best domaines, including Trapet in Gevrey-Chambertin, Domaine Rousseau, who produced absolutely thrilling 1969s, Domaine Clair-Dau in Marsannay, Domaine Ponsot in Morey St.-Denis, Domaine Dujac in Morey St.-Denis, Domaine Jean Gros (the wines were sold by Alexis Lichine), Domaines Georges Mugneret and Mongeard-Mugneret in Vosne-Romanée, Domaine Roumier in Chambolle-Musigny, the Comte de Vogüé in Chambolle-Musigny, Henri Gouges in Nuits St.-Georges, Tollot-Beaut in Chorey-Lès-Beaune, Domaine Pothier-Rieusset in Pommard, Domaine Courcel in Pommard, Domaine de la Pousse d'Or in Volnay, and the Marquis d'Angerville in Volnay. It was also an excellent vintage for the *négociants*, with outstanding efforts turned in by Faiveley in Nuits St.-Georges, Louis Jadot in Beaune, and the firm of Leroy in Auxey-Duresses. Interestingly, the Domaine de la Romanée-Conti, which made the finest wines of the vintage in 1966, seemed to be going through a somewhat shaky period, and while their wines were very good, they have aged rapidly, and may have suffered from being too alcoholic and overly chaptalized. I would approach the Domaine de la Romanée-Conti's wines in 1969 with a degree of caution.

White Burgundy. Initially, the reputation of the white burgundies was overshadowed by that of the reds, but truly spectacular wines have emerged from the underrated 1969 vintage. This was the first vintage from which I was able to taste the wines from the Domaine Leflaive in Puligny-Montrachet. They were absolutely spectacular as late as the early eighties, but I have not seen a bottle since. Perhaps the greatest wine, and one of the most magnificent white burgundies I have ever tasted, was the Meursault Les Perrières from Leroy. This wine, tasted as recently as January 1990, was absolutely profound, a magnificent white burgundy, bursting with complexity, concentration, and fruit. The Comte Lafon again turned in an excellent performance in 1969, as did Raveneau in Chablis. In fact, there seem to have been a number of superb Chablis produced from a vintage that perhaps has never been given its full credit. It may have only been surpassed in quality since by the 1978 vintage.

1970—*Red Burgundy*. This was a record-setting crop that exceeded even the huge yields of 1950. The flowering in June went well and the summer was hot in July, cool in August, and warm again in September and October. The harvest occurred under generally sound conditions. The resulting red wines were very good. In fact, some examples, such as those from the Domaine Clair-Dau, the Domaine Clos-Frantin, and the Domaine Drouhin-Larose, were positively brilliant. But the wines aged very rapidly, demonstrating their lack of grip and concentration, and began showing a certain dilution and lack of flavor. This is a vintage that I would avoid today, given how rapidly the wines fell apart.

White Burgundy. Some outstanding white wines were apparently produced in 1970, but those I have notes on all seem to have been good rather than exciting. I doubt that any of them have stood the test of time. Chablis had tremendous overproduction, resulting in light, quick-maturing, low-acid wines that fell apart by the mid-seventies.

1971—*Red Burgundy*. A cold, wet June resulted in a poor flowering and tiny harvest. The size of the crop was further diminished, at least on the Côte de Beaune, by a serious hailstorm late in the summer. However, after June the weather was virtually perfect with a hot July, a torrid, stormy August, and a superb, sunny September. The result was wine that today might be maligned, much like the 1983s were, because of a certain taste of rot. But with the 1971s, this rot seemed to age out, giving way to an earthy, raunchy character that only seemed to add to the wines appeal and complexity. However, most 1971s lacked acidity, and have not held up as well as their supporters would have one believe. I don't mean to shortchange the vintage, as there were many gorgeous wines produced. Excellent wines were made by Domaine Roumier in Chambolle-Musigny, Leroy in Auxey-Duresses, Drouhin-Larose in Gevrey-Chambertin, and by Louis Jadot in Beaune. However, in what could have been a more consistent vintage, 1971 marked what was the beginning of a serious decline in quality of the wines from the Domaine Henri Gouges and Domaine Clair-Dau. It was also not a terribly successful year for the Domaine de la Romanée-Conti.

White Burgundy. The firms of Leflaive and Louis Latour made exceptional white burgundies in this vintage, as did most of the top domaines and producers in Chablis. Prices for the 1971s (both red and white) have always been high because the crop size was small. I would envision more disappointments than surprises should anyone purchase these wines now. Exact knowledge of a bottle's storage conditions is probably the most critical factor in determining whether or not one should buy a 1971.

1972—*Red Burgundy*. Initially maligned, probably because of the terrible reputation of the 1972 red Bordeaux, the 1972 red burgundies have turned out to be one of the great surprises of the last two decades. Although the summer was cool, it was also dry. However, there was some heat in September, which allowed the grapes to mature. The results, from what turned out to be a small crop, were wines that were concentrated, but extremely high in acidity because of the cool summer. Most early tasters dismissed the vintage, saying it was too green, ignoring the sensationally dark colors and concentration. However, when compared to the opulent, forward, dramatic 1971s, the 1972 vintage would, I am sure, have appeared to be lean and mean. Nevertheless, the wines matured slowly but steadily, and today, in my opinion, this may well be the best vintage of the seventies not only to buy cheaply, but to buy well, since most 1971s have fallen apart, and most 1978s are exorbitantly priced. While the Domaine de la Romanée-Conti's performance was acceptable, its wines were uninspiring. Domaine Dujac did admirably, although it is not a great vintage. The Comte de Vogüé produced their last great vintage in 1972. Ponsot made a splendid wine; Drouhin-Larose and Domaine Rousseau made super wines from their holdings in Gevrey-Chambertin; and *négociants* such as Faiveley, Leroy, Louis Jadot, and Joseph Drouhin turned in excellent efforts. Representatives of this vintage may well appear on the auction block since many of them were literally undrinkable for their first decade of life, and have only recently begun to exhibit their impressive concentration and depth. They may also be underpriced given the dismal reputation of 1972 wines in Europe.

White Burgundy. The Chardonnay in the Chablis region simply never ripened, and it was a catastrophic vintage. In the Côte d'Or, some growers chaptalized so much that the wines actually tasted sweet and soupy. Overall it was a disappointing vintage for the whites.

1973—*Red Burgundy*. 1973 was another record-setting crop, just barely eclipsing the huge production of 1970. However, not unlike 1970, there was significant rainfall from mid-summer through the harvest, resulting in an overabundance of bloated grapes. The red wines lacked acidity and were diluted. They were either consumed immediately for their lightness and charm, or long ago died an ignominious death.

White Burgundy. Highly applauded and acclaimed at its inception, primarily by the *négociants*, this vintage did indeed produce some stunning wine, particularly from Louis Latour and Louis Jadot. It was also a great success for the Domaine Leflaive in Puligny-Montrachet. It has been at least five years since I have tasted a 1973 white burgundy, but given their lusciousness and early charm, I would be doubtful that any could survive into the nineties. In Chablis, the crop size was also large, but nowhere near the record crop of 1970. The wines displayed more structure and generally aged well for about a decade.

1974—*Red Burgundy*. An excellent summer was undone by bitterly cold weather and torrential rains in September, which diluted the grapes and made harvesting unbearably brutal work. I never met a 1969

Bordeaux I did not dislike, and I think the same might be said about the 1974 red burgundies. They were dismal, green, acidic, and should be forgotten.

White Burgundy. Often, as in 1974, the Chardonnay is harvested before the Pinot Noir, and thus is not ruined by subsequent bad weather. The whites turned out to be light, but at least possessed a bit of fruit, which was not the case with the red wines. I actually tasted several excellent 1974s from the Domaine Ampeau in Meursault that were still drinking beautifully in the late eighties, no doubt because of their unduly high acidities. In Chablis, the harvest occurred under torrential rain, which diluted the grapes as well as the acidity.

1975—*Red Burgundy*. It was hard for the growers to believe, but 1975 was even worse than 1974. With stormy weather from mid-August through the harvest, rot proved to be unstoppable, and was eventually the undoing of the wines. Many domaines who estate-bottled their wines (probably because they had not made any 1974s) later regretted it because the wines were hollow, moldy tasting, and they fell apart after several years in the bottle.

White Burgundy. In the Côte d'Or, the Chardonnay suffered from the same problems as the Pinot Noir, producing light, insipid wines of no great charm or flavor. Yet, one of the anomalies of this vintage is that it turned out to be exceptional in Chablis. It was perhaps not of the same quality as 1978 or 1969, but it was the third best year of the decade. The vagaries of the weather allowed Chablis to escape the torrential rains that buffeted the Côte d'Or from mid-August on, and the Chablis turned out to be classic, concentrated, powerful wines with good acidity. I have not seen any examples of 1975 Chablis for some time, but I would not be surprised if many of them are still drinking well as we enter the decade of the nineties.

1976—*Red Burgundy*. Initially it was believed this would be a great vintage, but the second-guessers and revisionists were taking shots at the 1976s by the end of that decade. Because of the extraordinary heat and drought France endured during the summer of 1976, it was one of the earliest harvests of the century. The wines were difficult to vinify, given the thick skins and relatively low yields. Initially, the best wines were believed to be bigger, richer, and longer-lived examples than the best wines from Burgundy's most classic vintages—1947, 1949, 1959, and 1964. However, too few of the wines had what would be considered good balance between their fruit and their tannins. Even the wines of the Domaine de la Romanée-Conti tasted sweet and fragile, although large-scaled and full in the mouth. The best 1976s I have had came from Domaine Courcel in Pommard, Domaine de la Pousse d'Or in

Volnay, Louis Jadot in Beaune, Moillard in Nuits St.-Georges, and the Domaine Roumier in Chambolle-Musigny. There are some surprising disappointments from some big names such as Rousseau, Henri Gouges, and Bouchard Père et Fils. 1976 is a vintage to approach with a great deal of caution, but if you know your red wines in this vintage, some remarkably long-lived, great wines may await you in another four or five years.

White Burgundy. Most white burgundies in 1976, including those from Chablis, were extremely high in alcohol, often approaching 14.5%. As strange as it may seem, some growers, attempting to harvest before the grapes became too saturated with sugar, picked green grapes and made relatively lean, thin wines as a result. Those that waited made full, low-acid, hefty wines that lacked finesse, and aged very quickly. Even the 1976s from Louis Latour seemed to be tiring by the mid-eighties.

1977—*Red Burgundy*. A wet summer was followed by a good September and a pleasant October. The Pinot Noir, however, never fully ripened, and the results were light, somewhat green wines that have held up better than expected. Most should have been consumed by now.

White Burgundy. The white wines fared much better than the reds. While tasters initially maligned the whites for their extremely high acidity, they had changed their tunes by the early eighties when the acidity was accompanied by the presence of fuller, richer, honeyed Chardonnay fruit. In fact, some of the Leflaive wines turned out to be absolutely delicious. However, I have not had them in over five years and they probably should have been consumed by now. Nevertheless, this minor, lightweight year should be remembered for some attractive whites and poor to mediocre reds.

1978—*Red Burgundy*. 1978 was dubbed "the miracle year" by the famous peripatetic English wine writer, Harry Waugh, referring to the sensational Indian summer that saved the Bordeaux wines from disaster. Similar good fortune also befell Burgundy. Spring and early summer were miserably cold and wet, causing poor flowering and a relatively small crop. In fact, the Burgundians claim the weather did not begin to improve until the very end of August, at which time the vineyards were nearly three weeks behind schedule—always an ominous sign. However, in one of the most unusual turnarounds in decades, fine weather moved in at the end of the third week in August and did not leave until the end of October. The crop size was small, but the sunshine and heat of September and October allowed the Pinot Noir to ripen beautifully. The red wines have never had the tannins or pure power of the 1976s, but they displayed from their birth elegance, balance, aromatic purity, and beautiful, rich red and black berry fruits. The wines drank well young, and there are few that are not now in full maturity. The only question is how much longer they will last. Before you invest significant amounts of money in any of the producer's wines recommended below, be sure they have been properly stored. My best guess is that most of the 1978s should be consumed before 1995, with only those wines from the houses of Faiveley, Leroy, Louis Jadot, Bourée, and the Domaine de la Romanée-Conti capable of surviving the turn of the century.

RECOMMENDED PRODUCERS

Robert Arnoux	Leroy
Bichot's Clos Frantin	Georges Lignier
Bourée Père et Fils	Hubert Lignier
Domaine Courcel	Alain Michelot
Joseph Drouhin	Hubert de Montille
Drouhin-Larose	Georges Mugneret
Domaine Dujac	Mongeard-Mugneret
Joseph Faiveley	André Mussy
Michel Gaunoux	Pernot-Fourrier
Machard de Gramont	Domaine des Perrières
Jean Gros	Domaine Ponsot

Hospices de Beaune (the various *cuvées*, 1978 marked the first vintage that the brilliant André Porcheret had outstanding raw materials with which to produce superb wine)

Louis Jadot	Domaine de la Pousse d'Or
Henri Jayer	Domaine de la Romanée-Conti
Robert Jayer	Joseph Roty
Jayer-Gilles	Georges Roumier
Michel Lafarge	Domaine des Varoilles

White Burgundy. The 1978 crop was small, due largely to the cold spring weather and wet, chilly period during flowering, but it gave rise to what has long been considered a great and classic vintage for white burgundy. However, the wines have been stubborn, and extremely slow to evolve, giving rise to the question of whether they will ever be as good as their early supporters claimed. Of course, there were some superb successes, such as the big, rich Côte d'Or whites from André Ramonet, Leflaive, Sauzet, Comte Lafon, and Robert Ampeau. *Négociants* such as Joseph Drouhin, Louis Jadot, and Remoissenet also produced excellent 1978s. While none of the 1978s have fully blossomed, neither do they show signs of going over the hill. This could be one of those rare white wine vintages, such as 1962, that at the top levels, lasts for twenty or more years. When these wines infrequently appear at the auctions, prices are extremely high. I cannot stress enough the importance of cellaring conditions. There is no doubt that the wines of Chablis turned out to be sensational. I drank many in the eighties that were as concentrated and rich as any Chablis I have ever tasted. Some of the producers of Chablis liken the 1978s to the 1929s and 1921s, calling it one of the three greatest vintages of this century. No doubt the best producers of 1978 Chablis Grands Crus and a handful of the Premiers Crus will probably last another decade or more.

1979—*Red Burgundy*. As in most of France, the spring and summer of 1979 were unseasonably cool, but whereas most cool summers in France also tend to be wet, 1979 was surprisingly dry. There was a successful flowering that set the stage for an enormous crop, and though July did have some rain, the overall precipitation was below average. The vineyards of Nuits St.-Georges and southern Vosne-Romanée were devastated by hailstorms. The huge crop that emerged for red burgundy tended to produce wines that were light, lacking grip, body, and tannin. In the worst-case scenarios, they showed the effects of rot and hail damage. Save for a handful of wines, this would not be a vintage I would buy. Most of the 1979 red wines have fallen apart. There were major disappointments from some great names in this vintage, including the wines from Armand Rousseau, Domaine Roumier, Mongeard-Mugneret, Joseph Drouhin, Faiveley, Louis Trapet, Comte de Vogüé, and Robert Arnoux.

RECOMMENDED PRODUCERS

Domaine Dujac	Leroy
Machard de Gramant	Albert Morot
Jean Gros	André Mussy
Hospices de Beaune Cuvées	Pothier-Rieusset
Henri Jayer	Domaine de la Romanée-Conti
Philippe Leclerc	Tollot-Beaut

White Burgundy. An excellent year despite a prolific crop size. The wines were soft, generously flavored, and surprisingly rich, and have generally performed better than the closed, tightly knit 1978s. However, most 1979s reached full maturity by the late eighties, and existing stocks should be consumed.

RECOMMENDED PRODUCERS

Robert Ampeau   Louis Latour
Jean-Noël Gagnard   Domaine Leflaive
Albert Grivault   Leroy
Hospices de Beaune Cuvées   Domaine Ramonet
Louis Jadot   Domaine Sauzet
Comte Lafon

1980—*Red Burgundy*. 1980 has proven to be one of the most underrated and pleasing red wine vintages from Burgundy during the decades of the eighties. All of the wines are fully mature, and the best are capable of lasting another five to six years, but no longer. Despite the initial bad press, 1980 produced, particularly from the Côte de Nuits, surprisingly concentrated, deeply colored wines that exhibited great aromatic dimension, and pure, intense flavors. In many ways 1987 resembles 1980, with a number of underpriced, underrated, surprisingly fine wines. Nothing about the weather suggested that so many good wines would result. The spring was cold, the flowering took place under difficult, cool, windy, chilly weather. The result was a small crop. The weather remained wet and generally frosty until the end of July. It then improved until immediately prior to the harvest, which began in early October. Most of the successful domaines spread out their harvesting dates until the third week of October. I remember tasting the wines early and finding them somewhat skinny and lacking concentration. But they seemed to grow and expand in the barrel, which is one of the tricky things about judging red burgundy. There are a number of wonderful wines from this vintage which I would highly recommend, assuming they have been well stored, particularly if you are looking for immediately drinkable, somewhat underpriced, delicious Pinot Noir. The best wines of the vintage were produced by the Domaine de la Romanée-Conti, whose great 1980s are surpassed only by their extraordinary 1985s, 1988s, and 1989s.

RECOMMENDED PRODUCERS

Robert Arnoux   Philippe Leclerc
Bichot's Clos Frantin   Hubert Lignier
Bourée Père et Fils   Domaine Maume
Robert Chevillon   Hubert de Montille
Domaine Dujac   Georges Mugneret
Faiveley   Domaine Ponsot
Hospices de Beaune Cuvées   Domaine de la Pousse d'Or
Louis Jadot   Domaine de la Romanée-Conti
Henri Jayer   Armand Rousseau

White Burgundy. As surprisingly good as the red wines are, the white wines lacked flavor, body, and never had much charm or character. Most should have been drunk by now. Chablis fared no better than the Côte d'Or and produced simple, straightforward, malnourished wines that were at their best years ago. This was a disappointing vintage.

1981—*Red Burgundy*. Bad weather seemed to come at all the wrong times for Pinot Noir in 1981. There was early promise as a result of an unseasonably hot spring, which started the flowering off on a good note. However, July turned cold and pessimism began to set in. August and the first half of September were gloriously hot and dry, and the growers began to think that an excellent vintage could be produced. However, heavy rainstorms, including severe hailstorms, hit the northern half of the Côte de Nuits as well as Mercurey in the Chalonnaise, and not only damaged the grapes, but continued throughout the harvest. The grapes were diluted and rot became rampant. There is not a single 1981 that I have found good enough to recommend, and I have tasted all the best estates' wines. There are some competent, decently made, pleasant wines, but they should have been consumed by now.

White Burgundy. White burgundies fared considerably better than did the reds in 1981. The initial impression was that it was a small crop of concentrated, tightly knit, firmly structured wines built for the long haul. As the decade ended many of the 1981 whites had yet to blossom, and some appear now to be losing fruit, revealing only a skeleton of acid, wood, and alcohol. I tend to be pessimistic about the future of this vintage for white burgundy. Some surprisingly good wines were made by André Ramonet, Michel Niellon, the Moreys, and François Jobard. Perhaps the best whites of the vintage are the Meursaults from Coche-Dury. However, these wines should have been drunk up by 1990.

1982—*Red Burgundy*. Wonderful spring and early summer weather provided all the ingredients for superb flowering and the setting for a large crop. June and July were extremely hot and sunny, and optimism was the rule of the day by early August. However, rain moved in later in August and destroyed the hopes for a great vintage. In fact, the rain further bloated what was already a massive crop. The good weather returned in September, and the harvest began during the third week under excellent conditions. Unfortunately, if the growers had pruned back their vines and not fertilized as much in an effort to reduce yields, this might still have been a great vintage. Very few did, and the results were a gigantic, record-breaking crop with diluted flavors. At my first tastings out of barrel, most of the Pinot Noir looked like California white Zinfandels and had very little flavor depth. The best ones did develop more character and richness as they evolved, and I have been surprised recently by how well some of the best 1982s have turned out. The best producers made delicious wines, which should be consumed over the next 3–4 years as they will not make "old bones."

RECOMMENDED PRODUCERS

Robert Chevillon	Philippe Leclerc
Domaine Dujac	Hubert Lignier
Faiveley	Domaine Maume
Hospices de Beaune Cuvées	Domaine de la Romanée-Conti
Louis Jadot	

White Burgundy. The wonderful summer and huge crop that resulted caused many people to dismiss the wines prematurely, claiming it was impossible to obtain good concentration. But surprises abounded in what turned out to be a deliciously forward, precocious vintage of charming, and in a number of cases, surprisingly concentrated, rich white burgundies. Superb wines were made by Jean-François Coche-Dury, Albert Grivault, and the Comte Lafon in Meursault. The firm of Leroy in Auxey-Duresses also made outstanding wines not only from Meursault, but from other white wine appellations such as Auxey-Duresses. The Domaine Ramonet in Chassagne-Montrachet made hauntingly perfect wines, particularly their Montrachet, which is one of the single greatest and most concentrated white burgundies I have ever tasted. *Négociants* such as Louis Jadot and Joseph Drouhin turned in beautiful efforts with their white wines, as did a handful of other small growers such as Georges Deleger and Gagnard-Delagrange. While they were not disappointing, the two most famous domaines in Puligny-Montrachet, Domaine Leflaive and Domaine Sauzet, turned in good rather than spectacular efforts in this overly abundant vintage. Most 1982 white burgundies should be consumed over the next 3–5 years, with the exception of those from the Domaine Ramonet and the Comte Lafon. In Chablis, the gigantic production rendered wines that were extremely low in acidity, relatively diluted, too soft to be classy, and often sorely lacking in concentration. The best wines of the vintage were those from the Domaine Raveneau. They alone among all the Chablis have continued to drink well into the nineties, but they should be consumed before the middle of the decade.

1983 RED BURGUNDY

A knowledgeable oenologist once asked me, "Is 1983 really a great vintage, or the Burgundy sham of the century?" It is hard to judge any vintage in black-and-white terms because of the innumerable variables that affect quality, but I have always felt that only a small fraction of the wines that I've tasted from the 1983 vintage had the potential, concentration, and overall balance to be considered great. The severe hailstorms that hit the Côte de Nuits in July and the rampant rot in the vineyards from the tropical heat and rain in August and early September created significant problems.

Many wine journalists who do not look very closely at all the facts or laboriously taste across the field of play obviously read that the hot dry weather in late September and October caused sugar readings to soar in the grapes and the harvest to occur under textbook conditions. So they concluded that it must surely be a great vintage, and like their counterparts, prophets of doom, who also talk and write before tasting, the optimists reported that this was truly a great vintage. One crucial detail was forgotten—it is difficult to make wine from unhealthy grapes, and in 1983, there were plenty of rot-infested and scarred grapes on the vine.

The key to making great burgundy in 1983, therefore, was to separate the rotten grapes from the healthy ones. This had to be done at the time of picking. It was extremely time-consuming work, but absolutely essential in order to produce a clean, well-balanced wine. There were, of course, other factors that would have a significant effect on the outcome. Because the grape skins were extremely thick and ripe, extreme care had to be taken with the vinification so as not to extract an excess of tannin. Some growers pulled the wine off the skins too fast for fear of obtaining a taste of rot and getting too much tannin. Their wines tend to be lighter in color and much more precocious in style. Other growers went for maximum extract and produced wines so tannic that the 1976 burgundies, known for their tannic ferocity, look almost supple in comparison. Some growers used too much new wood in an attempt to mask the smell of rot. Others did not use enough new wood. Some growers fined their wines excessively, hoping the egg-white fining would help cut the harsh tannins. These intense finings worked, but all too well in some cases, because both color and flavor were also taken out. And of course, some growers over-zealously filtered and/or pasteurized their wine to destroy any taste or smell that would identify its place of origin.

So with the red burgundies of 1983, you will find many abrasive, harsh, tannic, dry wines with a *goût de sec* and *goût de moisi*. There are also wines that have lost significant color because of the rot. Unlike the terribly underrated 1980 burgundy vintage, in which the wines seemed to deepen in color and flavor concentration as they aged in the cask, the 1983s have lightened up considerably in color, with some examples taking on orange, brownish edges, a particularly ominous sign. If you do not like the 1976 red burgundies because of their hard tannins and unyielding firmness, these wines will be no more pleasing.

Does all of this sound very pessimistic? You bet it does, but enough small quantities of very good to superb wines were produced in 1983 to permit connoisseurs of burgundy to replenish their cellar stocks. Of course, they will not be cheap, but many of the very best burgundies were made in exceptionally small quantities because the grower ruthlessly discarded any tainted grapes. For a few growers, 1983 is truly a great vintage. For the rest, the vintage is a mixed bag of high-alcohol, harsh, rather imbalanced wines, many of which even taste a little bizarre. For those lucky enough to get a hold of any of the greatest wines, they are undoubtedly in possession of real treasures. However, everyone should remember that these wines are quite tannic and most of the best wines will not be ready to drink before 1993. 1983 is an extremely irregular and overrated vintage. Only the very best wines are worth the high price.

Note: All of these 1983 Burgundies were first tasted from the barrel in the summer of 1984 and again in spring 1985. From the bottle, the wines were tasted during the summer and fall of 1985 and retasted in fall, 1987, and again in fall, 1989.

PIERRE AMIOT (MOREY ST.-DENIS)

1983 CLOS DE LA ROCHE	87
1983 GEVREY-CHAMBERTIN AUX COMBOTTES	86
1983 MOREY ST.-DENIS AUX CHARMES	86
1983 MOREY ST.-DENIS LES BAUDES	86
1983 MOREY ST.-DENIS MILLANDES	85
1983 MOREY ST.-DENIS VILLAGES	84

Amiot bottled all of his 1983s late. As the scores indicate, the wines are quite consistently successful, if not at the very highest level of quality. In general, Amiot's 1983s typify the Michel Broadbent expression, "an iron fist in a velvet glove." They have a good measure of tannin but also have more supple, lush, voluptuous fruit than one usually sees in the 1983s. Most of Amiot's 1983s should be cellared until 1990–1991, but they are clearly much more accessible, fragrant, and precocious than other 1983s. Comparing them, the Clos de la Roche has the most class, and slightly more concentration and complexity, but both the Morey

St.-Denis Les Baudes and Morey St.-Denis aux Charmes are delicious, rich and fruity wines with broad, authentic Pinot Noir flavors. The Les Baudes is slightly more tannic and darker in color and will evolve less quickly. The Gevrey-Chambertin aux Combottes is perhaps the biggest wine Amiot made in 1983, rather substantial and alcoholic with ripe, earthy flavors. It clearly begs for cellaring until 1990–1991. The Morey St.-Denis Villages has lovely, open-knit, broad, round, fruity flavors and at a young age was the most easily drunk wine of Amiot. In contrast, the Morey St.-Denis Millandes is Amiot's darkest colored as well as his most backwardly tannic wine. It needs cellaring until around 1993.

DOMAINE ARLAUD (NUITS ST.-GEORGES)

1983 CHAMBOLLE-MUSIGNY	85
1983 CHARMES-CHAMBERTIN	84

These two 1983s from Arlaud have all the tannic toughness of the vintage but also show the apparent house style, in that they are rather fat, alcoholic, jammy, and richly fruity. There is quite a lot of Pinot Noir flavor and a pleasing lushness. No doubt both should be drunk by 1992. The Chambolle-Musigny is much the better value.

ROBERT ARNOUX (VOSNE-ROMANÉE)

1983 CLOS VOUGEOT	87
1983 NUITS ST.-GEORGES LES CORVÉES-PAGET	76
1983 NUITS ST.-GEORGES LES POISETS	78
1983 VOSNE-ROMANÉE	78
1983 VOSNE-ROMANÉE LES CHAUMES	85
1983 VOSNE-ROMANÉE PREMIER CRU	78
1983 VOSNE-ROMANÉE LES SUCHOTS	85

Interestingly, Arnoux bottled his 1983s very early, in late winter of 1985. He employed 30 new oak barrels for the 1983 vintage. As the above scores indicate, Arnoux made good 1983s, but given a choice I would opt for his lineup of 1980s and 1978s over these wines. My main criticism of the Arnoux 1983s, with the possible exception of the Clos Vougeot, Vosne-Romanée Les Suchots and Les Chaumes, is that they are extremely tannic, perhaps even excessively so. From cask and from bottle the Clos Vougeot looks to be the best. It has the deepest color of Arnoux's wines, with an exotic bouquet of toasty oak, licorice, and black currants. Full bodied, tannic but balanced, it needs 8–10 years of cellaring. Next best, and usually the top wine from Arnoux, the Vosne-Romanée Les Suchots shows less complexity than the 1980 and 1978 did at a similar stage, but has a deep color, hard tannin, plenty of power and fruit, and a dry finish. It needs 7–8 years. Les Chaumes is also very good, but lacks the dimension in flavor and depth compared to both the Clos Vougeot and Les Suchots. Arnoux's two selections from Nuits St.-Georges are good, but, given the reputation of Arnoux and the vintage, not terribly exciting wines. Les Poisets is deeper and more attractive with a spicy black-currant fruitiness. The Les Corvées-Paget has less color, and is rather light with an excess of tannin in the finish. Both the Vosne-Romanée and Vosne-Romanée Premier Cru share adequate color, body, and depth, but are extremely hard and astringent. I doubt seriously that the fruit can outlast the tannin.

BERNARD BACHELET (CHASSAGNE-MONTRACHET)

1983 CHASSAGNE-MONTRACHET	74
1983 CÔTE DE BEAUNE-VILLAGES	78
1983 SANTENAY	82

These three wines exhibit the irregularity one finds in the 1983 vintage. The Côte de Beaune-Villages is quite alcoholic and big with an aggressive finish. The Chassagne-Montrachet has very fine color, but suffers from an excessively high level of hard tannins, although the underdeveloped bouquet of leather and berry fruits hints at finer things. My favorite is the Santenay, a dark, rather tannic but full-bodied, rich, deep wine that possesses the concentration of fruit to outlast the tannins. It needs 4 years.

BARTHOD-NOËLLAT (CHAMBOLLE-MUSIGNY)

1983 CHAMBOLLE-MUSIGNY	84
1983 CHAMBOLLE-MUSIGNY LES CHARMES	86

Barthod's 1983s are full of charm and elegance without the excess of tannin one so often finds in the wines of this vintage. He is also another *viticulteur* who succeeded admirably in overcoming the problems of both the 1982 and 1984 vintages to make good wine. Barthod's style of winemaking produces rather lightly colored wines that are much more flavorful and rich than their color suggests. Not surprisingly, both these wines were rather light in color, particularly for 1983s, but one whiff of the rather rich, complex, fruity, smokey, spicy bouquet leaves no doubt that some serious wine is in the glass. They are rather ripe, fat, fleshy wines with surprisingly soft tannins. The Les Charmes has more aroma and flavor to recommend it. Though somewhat hard to resist right now, 4–6 years will reveal additional pleasures.

ADRIAN BELLAND (SANTENAY)

1983 CHAMBERTIN	84
1983 CORTON-CLOS DE LA CENT VIGNES	87
1983 CORTON-GRÈVES	?
1983 SANTENAY	83
1983 SANTENAY LES GRAVIÈRES	85

In 1983 Belland's best wines are deeply colored, tannic, quite concentrated and full-bodied, and if they have a flaw at all, it is a lack of finesse. Nevertheless, these are burgundies with flavor. The near classic in this group is the lovely Corton Clos de La Cent Vignes, which is a very rich, beautifully concentrated, full-bodied wine with an impressive, leathery, rich, plummy bouquet and a very long finish. The Santenay Les Gravières is also very good and quite a fine value given its quality. It has a big, toasty, spicy, rather full-blown bouquet, ripe, rich flavors, deep color, and a clean, moderately tannic finish. Neither of the aforementioned wines will be at their peak before 1990. The Santenay is big and alcoholic but tannic, and while I have scored it well, I am concerned about the fruit/tannin balance. The Corton-Grèves is his lightest offering, and while there is plenty to like in its leathery, spicy aroma and rich, alcoholic flavors, I believe there is an excess of tannin and a touch of rot in the taste that has also caused the color to lighten. Belland makes some Chambertin, and the 1983 is quite good, smokey, rather light in color, but rich and powerful with plenty of alcohol.

DOMAINE GUY BERTHAUT (FIXIN)

1983 FIXIN LES ARVELETS	77
1983 FIXIN LES CLOS	75

1983 FIXIN LES CRAIX	72
1983 GEVREY-CHAMBERTIN	76

Berthaut's wines are robustly styled, big, and rather forceful. He is an honest winemaker and willing to discuss problems he has had in a particular year. Interestingly, his 1983s tasted severe, terribly tannic, and dry, with traces of the ominous *goût de sec*. With the exception of Les Arvelets, I just could not find enough fruit to balance out the tannins. Perhaps 10 years of cellaring will prove these opinions wrong, but I think Berthaut's 1983s are real gambles.

DOMAINE MATHOUILLET-BESANCENOT (BEAUNE)

1983 BEAUNE LES CENT VIGNES	86
1983 BEAUNE CLOS DU ROI	85

This small, well-run domaine right outside the walls of Beaune makes very elegant, fragrant, supple, silky, easy-to-enjoy wines from vineyards in the Côte de Beaune. In the years 1979 and 1980, the wines tasted fully mature when released, but the 1983 Besancenots needed 4–5 years to reach their peak. The two top 1983s tasted were very, very fine, exhibiting no signs of rot and showing excellent balance. Both of these wines were impressive, showing rich, concentrated cherry fruit, spicy, fragrant bouquets, long, lush textures and moderately ripe, round tannins. They had a good measure of alcohol, 13%–13.5%, as do most 1983s, but were impeccably clean and well-made wines for drinking over the near term.

DOMAINE BILLARD-GONNET (POMMARD)

1983 BEAUNE LA LUNE MONTREVENOTS	70
1983 POMMARD	77
1983 POMMARD LES CHAPONNIÈRES	80
1983 POMMARD LES RUGIENS	81

My experience with Billard-Gonnet's wines has been limited to very young vintages, which have always tasted rather tough, closed, and backward. Not surprisingly, his 1983s are reserved and restrained wines obviously made for long-term cellaring. His Pommards looked to be the best, but you must be willing to wait a minimum of 5–7 years before drinking them. The Beaune is very light in color, has a pleasant bouquet, but tastes weak and simple on the palate. The Pommard is certainly a good run-of-the-mill wine, but lacks excitement and personality. The Pommard Chaponnières has considerably more personality, a ruby color, a chocolate and spice-box aroma, long, ripe, sufficiently deep flavors, but hard, rather dry tannins. It has the balance, but one must wait until 1993. The Pommard Rugiens is an even bigger, more alcoholic wine with depth, flavor and mouthsearing tannins. It may be ready by 1995.

PIERRE BOURÉE (GEVREY-CHAMBERTIN)

Côte de Beaune

1983 BEAUNE PREMIER CRU	84
1983 CHASSAGNE-MONTRACHET	80
1983 CORTON	87
1983 PERNAND-VERGELESSES	80
1983 SANTENAY LES GRAVIÈRES	87
1983 VOLNAY	79

Côte de Nuits

1983 BONNES MARES	86
1983 CHAMBERTIN	85
1983 CHAMBOLLE-MUSIGNY	74
1983 CHARMES-CHAMBERTIN	84
1983 CLOS VOUGEOT	87
1983 CÔTE DE NUITS-VILLAGES	83
1983 ECHÉZEAUX	87
1983 GEVREY-CHAMBERTIN-CLOS DE LA JUSTICE	88
1983 GEVREY-CHAMBERTIN PREMIER CRU	86
1983 LATRICIÈRES-CHAMBERTIN	84
1983 MOREY ST.-DENIS	84
1983 NUITS ST.-GEORGES	78
1983 VOSNE-ROMANÉE	78

This has always been an intriguing *négociant* to follow. There is no Pierre Bourée, but rather a shy, yet very professional Monsieur Vallet who runs the operation. The 1983s were bottled directly from the barrel (no assemblage to avoid barrel-to-barrel differences) and, thankfully, no flavor-stripping filtration was done. The firm claims their 1983s are better than the 1978s. There are quite a few wines produced here, and while I tasted no great 1983s, I tasted some good to very good wines. As the above scores reflect, there is a greater range in quality in Bourée's Côte de Beaune wines than those from the Côte de Nuits, where of course the firm is based. However, nothing produced here is flawed or just bland. The two stars from the Côte de Beaune are the wonderful Santenay Les Gravières and the powerful Corton. The Santenay Les Gravières may ultimately merit a higher score. It was among the very finest Santenays I tasted and could clearly hold its own against many Grand Cru red burgundies. Fleshy, deeply colored with rich, ripe, concentrated fruit, it should prove to be a real eye opener between 1995–2000. The Corton is equally impressive, perhaps a trifle more rustic, alcoholic, and powerful, but very, very fine, and again having enough fruit to outlast the tannins. Like the Santenay, 1990–2000 should be this wine's glory years.

The Bourée firm produces an extensive range of red burgundies from the Côte de Nuits as well. In 1983, the quality here is quite consistently good rather than great. The Villages or commune wines like Morey St.-Denis, Vosne-Romanée, Nuits St.-Georges, and Chambolle-Musigny are what one expects. The Morey is much better than the others, the Chambolle-Musigny too dry and severe and perhaps affected by the hail that hit this commune. Certainly the Gevrey-Chambertin-Clos de la Justice, always one of Bourée's best wines, is especially rich, tannic, full bodied and concentrated in 1983. Its smokey, plummy, earthy bouquet and big, rich flavors beg for 5–7 years of cellaring. The Gevrey-Chambertin Premier Cru is almost as good, more supple, but rich, savory, fat, and quite forward tasting. It should be at its best in 4–5 years. Curiously, the Grand Cru Latricières-Chambertin is less rich than the Clos de la Justice or the Premier Cru. Nevertheless, it is quite flavorful, robust, and in need of 3–6 years of cellaring. The Clos Vougeot is excellent, with a rich bouquet of berry fruit, some toasty, vanillin oakiness, long, deep, rich flavors, immense body, and very good length. It will be excellent in 1990–1995. Both the Echézeaux and Bonnes Mares are atypical 1983s in that they are surprisingly light in color, very lush and accessible, and should be ready to drink soon, say in 3–4 years. Both are lovely wines, with the bouquet of the Echézeaux particularly fine. The Charmes-Chambertin looked and felt promising but was quite closed, and the Chambertin was alcoholic, fat, spicy, long in the finish but rather forward. I suspect it will be ready by 1990–1992. Last, don't overlook Bourée's Côte de Nuits-Villages, which in 1983 is like previous renditions of this wine, always a good value and one of the better wines of its type. It should be drunk over the next 3–4 years.

L. J. BRUCK (NUITS ST.-GEORGES)

1983 CHAMBOLLE-MUSIGNY	68
1983 CÔTE DE NUITS-VILLAGES	77
1983 ECHÉZEAUX	79
1983 GEVREY-CHAMBERTIN	76
1983 GEVREY-CHAMBERTIN LAVAUX ST.-JACQUES	85
1983 HAUTES-CÔTES DE NUITS	78
1983 NUITS ST.-GEORGES-CORVÉES-PAGETS	82

A medium-sized *négociant* in Nuits St.-Georges (and now owned by Jean-Claude Boisset), this firm produces wines that are generally well colored, tannic, and firm, but dull. The wines from vineyards in Nuits St.-Georges and Gevrey-Chambertin are the best in my opinion. One sees the house style in all of these burgundies, from the lower-priced Hautes-Côtes de Nuits to the Echézeaux. The wines have good color, full body, some tough tannin, but monolithic personalities. The Nuits St.-Georges-Corvées-Pagets, aged in 100% new oak barrels, is a big, forceful, rich, ripe wine with plenty of concentration and a big, alcoholic finish. It certainly was the classiest of the red wines I tasted from Bruck. The Gevrey-Chambertin Lavaux St.-Jacques also stood out for having the requisite richness of fruit to balance out the hard tannins of the 1983 vintage. The expensive Echézeaux is well made, perhaps a little too alcoholic, but tasty and rather precociously styled.

ALAIN BURGUET (GEVREY-CHAMBERTIN)

1983 GEVREY-CHAMBERTIN	75

This small grower only makes a Gevrey-Chambertin, but it is usually quite concentrated and powerful and for a straight Villages appellation wine, perhaps the best one can find. The highly touted 1983 vintage has produced a wine that is well colored, but abrasively tannic. Ten years of cellaring is the bare minimum, but I doubt the fruit will hold.

CHAMPY PÈRE (BEAUNE)

1983 BEAUNE LES AVAUX	83
1983 CLOS VOUGEOT	65
1983 SAVIGNY-LÈS-BEAUNE LA DOMINODE	80

Champy Père was the oldest *négociant* in all of Burgundy, dating from 1720. The firm and its vineyards were purchased by Louis Jadot in 1989. The 1983s I tasted were not that impressive, but were for the most part acceptable, even though they did seem to be made in a old, heavy style. Unfortunately, I did not have a chance to try a second bottle of the Clos Vougeot. While the first had a dark color, the aroma and flavors were flawed by a filthy barnyard smell. Considering how very successful the wines of Clos Vougeot were in 1983, I was surprised by the lack of quality apparent in this bottle. The Savigny La Dominode is robust and beefy and a solid, rather heavy, rustic sort of wine that should be at its best in 1990. The Beaune Les Avaux was the best of these Champy wines. It had a vivid bouquet of cherry fruit and oak, a full-bodied texture, and 12 years of evolution ahead of it.

DOMAINE DE LA CHARRIÈRE (SANTENAY)

1983 SANTENAY LA COMBE	84
1983 SANTENAY LA MALADIÈRE	85

The wines from this estate offer another example of why consumers should take more notice of the good values that emanate from Santenay. Monsieur Girardin makes solid wines that are chunky, robust, deeply fruity and ageworthy. Both of these wines are quite robust, well colored, fleshy, ripe wines that should age well for up to a decade. The Maladière has a more interesting aroma and flavor. it is hard to find burgundies of this quality for this price.

JEAN CHAUVENET (NUITS ST.-GEORGES)

1983 NUITS ST.-GEORGES	83
1983 NUITS ST.-GEORGES LA PERRIÈRE	83

1983 NUITS ST.-GEORGES LES VAUCRAINS	85
1983 VOSNE-ROMANÉE	81

Chauvenet does not filter his wines. His best wine is consistently the Les Vaucrains, the Premier Cru Nuits St.-Georges. Chauvenet's Vosne-Romanée and Nuits St.-Georges are rather understated but graceful wines, rather typical of his winemaking style. They should drink well within the first 4 years of availability, but will not age well over the long term. The Nuits St.-Georges La Perrière has more weight and richness but is still on the charming lighter side for a 1983. The Nuits St.-Georges Les Vaucrains has the broadest and most expansive flavors, shows very good winemaking, some subtle, smokey notes, and mild but firm tannins. Drink these wines up by 1992.

ROBERT CHEVILLON (NUITS ST.-GEORGES)

1983 NUITS ST.-GEORGES	81
1983 NUITS ST.-GEORGES LES CAILLES	86
1983 NUITS ST.-GEORGES LA PERRIÈRE	87
1983 NUITS ST.-GEORGES LES SAINT-GEORGES	90
1983 NUITS ST.-GEORGES LES VAUCRAINS	88

Since 1978, Robert Chevillon has unquestionably established his domaine as one of the very finest in the Côte d'Or. If one were to judge the entire 1983 vintage on the basis of his wines, then all the hoopla and hype would have been justified. His 1983s are excellent, and among the very finest and best-balanced wines of this notoriously overrated vintage. The wines from La Perrière, Les Vaucrains, and Les Saint-Georges are rich and intense, pure and clean, and show no evidence of rot or hail damage. The colors are dark, the bouquets explosive, and the length and balance truly superb. They are bigger and much more full bodied than most 1983s, with a powerful alcoholic clout. Expect these three wines to be at their best between 1992–2000. The Les Saint-Georges is one of the great wines of this vintage. As for the other 1983s, Les Cailles is slightly tougher and tannic, and I have less confidence that it will hit the heights of Chevillon's other wines. The Villages wine is good, a little stern and unyielding, but well made.

BRUNO CLAIR (MARSANNAY)

1983 BOURGOGNE	82
1983 FIXIN LA COLLE BLANCHE	84

1983 MOREY ST.-DENIS	81
1983 SAVIGNY-LÈS-BEAUNE LA DOMINODE	88

One look at the score for the Savigny La Dominode might cause some to think there has been a typographical error. Yes, the darkly colored wine does merit the score. It is an extremely powerful, dense, rich, full-bodied wine with plenty of tannin and a great finish. Clair told me it was made from 80-year-old vines. Based on my last tasting of it in September, 1989, it will need cellaring until 1993–1995. The Fixin La Colle Blanche may suffer in comparison, but it is a rich, beefy, ripe, very well-made wine that should be ready to drink by 1990. The Morey St.-Denis is above average, but a little tough and perhaps excessively tannic. The generic Bourgogne is one of the best of its type, fruity, fat, clean, and very attractive for drinking now.

DOMAINE CLAIR-DAU (MARSANNAY)

1983 BONNES MARES	88
1983 BOURGOGNE	83
1983 CHAMBERTIN-CLOS DE BÈZE	89
1985 CHAMBOLLE-MUSIGNY LES ARMOUREUSES	88
1983 CHAPELLE-CHAMBERTIN	86
1983 CLOS VOUGEOT	87
1983 GEVREY-CHAMBERTIN LES CAZETIERS	88
1983 GEVREY-CHAMBERTIN CLOS DE FONTENY	86
1983 GEVREY-CHAMBERTIN CLOS ST.-JACQUES	85
1983 VOSNE-ROMANÉE CHAMPS PERDRIX	85

It is easy to start with superlatives concerning the 1983 Clair-Dau wines, certainly this domaine's best vintage since 1970. Between 1971 and 1980 this estate produced quite mediocre wines that in no way merited the price they commanded or reflected the excellent reputation this very important domaine had in the sixties. However, the 1983s were among the finest red burgundies I sampled. Rich in color and extract, there was no evidence of the *goût de sec* or *goût de moisi* (dryness or musty flavors) that taints many 1983 red burgundies. All of the wines had excellent color and clean, ripe Pinot Noir aromas. They all possess various degrees of rich, fat character, good, ripe tannins and very good to great depth. Most of the 1983 Clair-Dau wines should reach maturity between 1990 and 1995. For value, the Bourgogne is very good. At the top level, the Bonnes Mares was dense, ripe, rich and close to being spectacular. It had a hauntingly great perfume. The Chambertin-Clos de Bèze and Gevrey-Chambertin Les Cazetiers both merit serious consideration. Both are strong, robust, alcoholic, rich wines with powerful bouquets, deep colors, layers of Pinot Noir fruit and a total absence of any taste or smell of rot. The Chamboille-Musigny Les Amoureuses is notable for its sheer elegance and lush seductiveness—it is named appropriately in 1983. The Clos Vougeot is a very big wine, perhaps a little rustic and overblown in size and weight, but if it obtains some finesse with bottle aging, it could well prove to be outstanding. Of all these wines, the Chapelle-Chambertin and Clos St.-Jacques had the lightest color and could appear to be the two wines here (except for the Bourgogne) that should mature fully before 1990. Both were packed with fruit but were simply more precocious and forward than the others. The Clair-Dau 1983s were extremely exciting wines to taste, and mark this domaine's return as one of the leaders in Burgundy.

DOMAINE CLERGET (CHAMBOLLE-MUSIGNY)

1983 BOURGOGNE	75
1983 CHAMBOLLE-MUSIGNY	74
1983 CHAMBOLLE-MUSIGNY LES CHARMES	77
1983 ECHÉZEAUX	82
1983 VOSNE-ROMANÉE LA VIOLETTE	80

All of these wines have surprisingly ruby/amber colors and increasingly exhibit the bitter, harsh, dry, dusty tannins that frequently show up in this vintage. The simple Bourgogne offers robust, coarse fruit. It should have been drunk up by 1988. I liked it as much as the Chambolle-Musigny, which is a solid, chunky, dry, astringent wine, but for its appellation it lacks a little complexity. The Vosne-Romanée La Violette is a rather rich, fat, moderately tannic wine with good concentration, clean, pure Pinot Noir flavors and should be drunk by 1990–1991. The Chambolle-Musigny Les Charmes is concentrated, chewy, and rich with full body and a deep, dark color but some musty, earthy, rot flavors appear to be emerging. The other, the Echézeaux, a dark ruby-colored wine, has cassis and plumlike fruit, medium to full body and a lingering finish.

DOMAINE EDMOND CORNU (LADOIX)

1983 ALOXE-CORTON	83
1983 ALOXE-CORTON LES MOUTOTTES	76
1983 CHOREY-LÈS-BEAUNE	83
1983 CORTON LES BRESSANDES	87
1983 LADOIX	84
1983 SAVIGNY-LÈS-BEAUNE	75

Cornu did not produce great 1983s, but he did make very attractive wines. The obvious star is the Corton Les Bressandes. It is a powerful wine, rich in color and extract, with layers of ripe fruit and good, firm, but not astringent tannins. However, it will need cellaring until 1993–1995. Those who cannot defer their gratification would be better advised to try the less expensive Chorey-Lès-Beaune with its bouquet of leather and cherries, medium body and good, clean fruit, or the spicy, cherry-scented, medium-bodied Ladoix. Two tough, tannic customers are the Savigny-Lès-Beaune, which, although it seems to have ample fruit, may turn out to be too tannic for its own good, and the Aloxe-Corton Les Moutottes, a leathery, spicy yet hard, *très dur* wine, as the French say. The Aloxe-Corton, in contrast to these two wines, is almost jammy with rather deep, alcoholic, rich flavors. It needs until 1990–1993 to mature.

ALBERT DEREY (MARSANNAY)

1983 BOURGOGNE COTEAUX DE COUCHEY	76
1983 BOURGOGNE LES VIGNES MARIE	75
1983 FIXIN	?

The Les Vignes Marie is a good medium-bodied, robust, earthy wine for drinking by 1990. The Coteaux de Couchey has supple, ripe, rather broad Pinot Noir flavors, shows good depth, and possesses an alcoholic punch with only a slight touch of rot in its flavors. The Fixin had an orange rim and a smell of rot. It is a real risk.

JOSEPH DROUHIN (BEAUNE)

1983 BEAUNE CLOS DES MOUCHES	86
1983 CHAMBOLLE-MUSIGNY	72

1982 CHAMBOLLE-MUSIGNY LES AMOUREUSES	?
1983 CLOS VOUGEOT	87
1983 GRIOTTE-CHAMBERTIN	72
1983 SANTENAY	81
1983 VOSNE-ROMANÉE LES SUCHOTS	76

The Drouhin 1983s were given an intense filtration, no doubt because many of them are placed on American restaurant wine lists, where one is unlikely to find many who understand the virtues of sediment. I found the Santenay a spicy, fruity, medium-weight wine with a good finish but little excitement. It should have been at its best by 1988. The red Beaune Clos des Mouches, always one of this firm's best wines, has a moderate deep color, a lovely ripe cherry and spicy oak bouquet, good flavor concentration, and moderate tannins. It should be at its best between 1988–1995. The Chambolle-Musigny has some real dusty, astringent tannins and a dry finish. It has plenty of fruit, but I sensed a touch of rot. The Clos Vougeot, absurdly costly, was clearly the star although it is not a great wine—only priced that way. It had a dark ruby color, excellent fat, sweet fruit, full body, and a rich, long finish. It should peak between 1990–2000. The Vosne-Romanée Les Suchots lacked balance, seemed awkward, and its color seemed light and the tannins very hard and severe. The Chambolle-Musigny Les Amoureuses was somewhat perplexing to evaluate. It had very good color, ripe, rich fruitiness, and good body, but once again, very astringent, almost bitter tannins. I liked it, but one will have to wait until 1992–1993 for it to mature. the Griotte-Chambertin seems to have a *goût de sec,* and was very severe, very astringent in the finish without sufficient underlying fruit.

DROUHIN-LAROSE (GEVREY-CHAMBERTIN)

1983 BONNES MARES	75
1983 CHAMBERTIN-CLOS DE BÈZE	85
1983 CHAPELLE-CHAMBERTIN	85
1983 CLOS VOUGEOT	85
1983 GEVREY-CHAMBERTIN	76

The style of wine here is hardly classic, but rather one that produces rich, alcoholic, fat, hedonistic wines with plenty of fragrance, body, sweetness, and color. Unfortunately, Bernard Drouhin began to filter the wines he sends to America because it is "the safe thing to do." By his own admission, the 1983 vintage is "great because the journalists said it was." Outspoken Drouhin prefers his 1980s and 1978s. With the exception of the Clos Vougeot and Chambertin-Clos de Bèze, the 1983s from Drouhin-Larose were light in color but exhibited broad, dusty, earthy flavors. The Gevrey-Chambertin is mediocre. The Chapelle-Chambertin has plenty of supple, ripe berry fruitiness, an attractive, oaky, herbal note in the bouquet and a long, sweet finish. It should be ready by 1990. The Clos Vougeot is darker in color with an intense perfume of vanillin oak and raspberries. Long, rich, deep, and moderately tannic, it should be ready by 1990–1992. The Bonnes Mares had a slight taste of rot and dry bitterness in the finish. Light in color with dusty tannins, it shows all the warning signs of having been afflicted by both rot and hail. The Chambertin-Clos de Bèze, *la fleur de la cave* of Drouhin-Larose, is a wonderful wine, long, ripe, succulent, rich and fruity with excellent depth and a great finish. It should be ready by 1990–1992.

DOMAINE DUJAC (MOREY ST.-DENIS)

1983 BONNES MARES	88
1983 CLOS DE LA ROCHE	86
1983 CLOS ST.-DENIS	87
1983 GEVREY-CHAMBERTIN LES COMBOTTES	83
1983 MOREY ST.-DENIS	78

It is no secret that this estate did not have the success in 1983 that one might have expected. Jacques Seysses was apprehensive about the rampant rot in the vineyards and pulled the skins off the macerating grape juice very quickly in order to avoid the taste of rot in his wines. Consequently, the wines are less deeply colored than other 1983s. They are, however, certainly very good. No doubt the Bonnes Mares, the best of Dujac's 1983s, will be impossible to obtain, for only two barrels, or 50 cases, were produced. It is a very fragrant, richly perfumed wine with only a medium ruby color, but long, spicy flavors suggestive of berry fruit and cinnamon. Some firm tannins are present, so expect the Bonnes Mares to be at its peak by 1992–1995. The same can be said for the very fine Clos St.-Denis and Gevrey-Chambertin Les Combottes. The Clos St.-Denis is Dujac's darkest-colored 1983, has a rich, ripe, deep, fruity texture, medium to full body, and long finish. The Gevrey-Chambertin Les Combottes is extremely spicy and earthy on the nose (I detect some rot), with big, rich, alcoholic, flabby flavors, and a powerful finish. The Morey St.-Denis tasted much less complex and serious than the other wines and appeared to be losing its color. It should have been drunk by 1988. The Clos de la Roche is undoubtedly very good, but rather closed, quite tannic, and unyielding. It should be given until 1990–1992.

DOMAINE RENÉ ENGEL (VOSNE-ROMANÉE)

1983 CLOS VOUGEOT	85
1983 ECHÉZEAUX	74
198E GRANDS ECHÉZEAUX	78
1983 VOSNE-ROMANÉE	62
1983 VOSNE-ROMANÉE LES BRÛLÉES	65

The 1983s are good rather than exciting. However, the Clos Vougeot is certainly very fine, with a rich, sweet texture, very good depth, a spicy, leathery, jammy bouquet, and aging potential until 1990–1993. Both the Grands Echézeaux and Echézeaux had a lovely, rich, sweet fruitiness, medium body, and lush texture, but also a trace of hard, dry, astringent tannins that come from the rot. They have plenty of appeal and character, but they are not sure bets. The Vosne-Romanée Les Brûlées has even more noticeable rot in its flavors. As for the straight Vosne-Romanée, it is supple and fruity but the aroma of rot is disturbing. It should be drunk by 1990.

FAIVELEY (NUITS ST.-GEORGES)

1983 CHAMBERTIN-CLOS DE BÈZE	90
1983 CLOS VOUGEOT	88
1983 CORTON-CLOS DES CORTONS	87
1983 GEVREY-CHAMBERTIN LES CAZETIERS	87
1983 GEVREY-CHAMBERTIN COMBE AUX MOINES	88
1983 MAZIS-CHAMBERTIN	88
1983 NUITS ST.-GEORGES-CLOS DE LA MARÉCHALE	85

The 1983s from Faiveley turned out to be very good. None of the Faiveley 1983s show signs of the astringent, dry tannin, or the moldy flavors caused by rot. They are very powerful, rich, deep, tannic wines that ideally need 8–10 years of cellaring. The firm regards them very highly. The Gevrey-Chambertin Les Cazetiers and Combe aux Moines are very brawny, fleshy, rich and tannic, full-bodied wines, but have excellent underlying sweetness and length. The colors are dark, but the Combe aux Moines is the darker of the two. These two wines may deserve a higher score in 1995 when they reach maturity. The Nuits St.-Georges-Clos de la Maréchale has plenty of rich, meaty fruitiness, a heady alcoholic content, wonderful texture, and firm tannins. One must wait until 1990–1992. The Corton was very closed on the nose, but dark in color, with a very big framework; it will need plenty of time as well. The Clos Vougeot is one of the richest and biggest wines of Faiveley's 1983s. With great depth of flavor and length, it has plenty of alcohol, rich round tannins, and an exceptional finish. It needs a decade of cellaring. The Mazis-Chambertin has a bouquet of leather and berry fruit, great density, an explosive fruitiness, and superb length. The Chambertin-Clos de Bèze has even more. Huge, powerful, dense, and rich, it is truly a great red burgundy from the 1983 vintage. These wines are among the very finest produced in 1983.

DOMAINE HENRI GOUGES (NUITS ST.-GEORGES)

1983 NUITS ST.-GEORGES	72
1983 NUITS ST.-GEORGES LES CHAIGNOTS	75
1983 NUITS ST.-GEORGES LES PORETS	75
1983 NUITS ST.-GEORGES LES PRULIERS	76
1983 NUITS ST.-GEORGES LES SAINT-GEORGES	82
1983 NUITS ST.-GEORGES LES VAUCRAINS	82

This famous and important estate historically has produced some of the finest red burgundies in the Côte d'Or. However, the wines in the seventies slipped considerably in quality, and in good vintages like 1971, 1976, and 1978, the wines have looked strikingly pale and tasted meagerly endowed when compared with their peers. I know Michel Gouges and his son Christian well, having visited with them on many occasions. It is therefore all the more difficult to say that I do not believe their wines are nearly as concentrated and as rich as they should be. The 1983s are very light in color and, except for the Les

Saint-Georges, seem also lacking in concentration. Gouges filters his wines, perhaps too aggressively. The only wines of interest here are Les Vaucrains and Les Saint-Georges. The other four wines have the color of most 1982s, and lack richness and concentration. The Les Vaucrains is good, has medium ruby color, and should be at its peak by 1992. The Les Saint-Georges is deep ruby in color, has a concentrated richness to it, and it is clearly the best wine Gouges made in 1983. Expect it to be fully mature by 1992.

MACHARD DE GRAMONT (NUITS ST.-GEORGES)

1983 NUITS ST.-GEORGES LES DAMODES	85
1983 NUITS ST.-GEORGES LES HAUTS PRULIERS	84
1983 NUITS ST.-GEORGES LA PERRIÈRE NOBLOT	84
1983 POMMARD-CLOS BLANC	86

The 1983s are good, deeply colored, richly fruity yet harshly tannic wines. If none of these wines can be called outstanding, they can certainly be considered very good. Dark in color with no trace of rot or hail damage, these plummy, rather chunky wines have good tannins and fleshy textures. The Pommard-Clos Blanc is the richest and deepest and suggests that it needs 5–6 years to reach its prime. The Nuits St.-Georges Les Damodes is similarly styled, a little more lush, and less tannic. Both the Nuits St.-Georges La Perrière Noblot and Les Hauts Pruliers have the same house style, but are slightly less elegant and complex.

DOMAINE JEAN GROS (VOSNE-ROMANÉE)

1983 HAUTES-CÔTES DE NUITS	81
1983 RICHEBOURG	89
1983 VOSNE-ROMANÉE	79
1983 VOSNE-ROMANÉE-CLOS DES RÉAS	88

Madame Gros is the mayor of Vosne-Romanée as well as the proprietor of this highly respected domaine. The 1983s here have very fine color, a silky, lush richness wrapped in a firm velvet glove. As my notes indicate, two of the Gros wines are very special. The Hautes-Côtes de Nuits is a pleasant, soft, very agreeable wine with good fruit and some

complexity. The Vosne-Romanée had supple, sweet, plummy fruitiness, medium body, good length, but has faded in the last several years.
The Vosne-Romanée-Clos des Réas is excellent, possibly outstanding.
Dark ruby with an explosive blackberry, earthy bouquet complemented
by vanillin oak and scents of licorice, rich and full bodied with very fine
extract, this is a wine to drink between 1990 and 2000. It is not as good
as the Richebourg, which has a more complex bouquet, layers of fruit,
medium to full body, and firm tannins. It should be at its best between
1992 and 2000.

DOMAINE GROS SOEUR ET FRÈRE (VOSNE-ROMANÉE)

1983 CLOS VOUGEOT	92
1983 RICHEBOURG	83
1983 VOSNE-ROMANÉE	83

The 1983 Clos Vougeot is fabulous, one of the single greatest red burgundies I tasted from this vintage. The other wines are inconsistent.
Inexplicably, neither the Richebourg, which was extremely tannic and
dry, nor the Vosne-Romanée, which was spicy but simple, approach
the Clos Vougeot. The 1983 Clos Vougeot has exceptional color, a huge
bouquet of intense berry fruit, coconut, ripe oranges, and spices. Enormous on the palate with layers of ripe, very concentrated fruit, this
moderately tannic wine will be a real treasure for those lucky to find a
bottle or two.

DOMAINE JACQUESON (RULLY)

1983 MERCUREY LES NAUGUES	82
1983 RULLY LES CHAPONNIÈRES	84
1983 RULLY LES CLOUDS	84

The wines from Domaine Jacqueson generally offer good value, and are
cleanly made with rather vivid and rich, chewy flavors. This is definitely
a domaine to seek out when it comes to good values. All three of these
wines are similar. They have deep, bright ruby colors, moderately intense bouquets of black cherries, a lovely, silky, ripe concentration of
fruit, and light tannin. The Les Clouds is a very seductive, medium-
weight, lush wine. The Chaponnières has a very attractive Pinot fragrance, and the Mercurey Les Naugues soft, spicy, chewy flavors.

LOUIS JADOT (BEAUNE)

1983 BEAUNE LES BOUCHEROTTES	85
1983 BEAUNE-CLOS DES URSULES	85
1983 CHAMBERTIN-CLOS DE BÈZE	88
1983 CLOS VOUGEOT	90
1983 CORTON LES POUGETS	88
1983 CÔTE DE BEAUNE-VILLAGES	83
1983 NUITS ST.-GEORGES-CLOS DES CORVÉES	86
1983 PERNAND-VERGELESSES-CLOS DES VERGELESSES	85

André Gagey and his enthusiastic cellarmaster, Jacques Lardière, succeeded in 1983, but admitted that it was a tough year with frequent failures elsewhere in the Côte d'Or. The Pernand-Vergelesses tastes like many producers' Corton—ripe, rich, rustic, big and full, and in need of 7–8 years of cellaring. Jadot's Beaune Les Boucherottes and Clos des Ursules already exhibit big, complex bouquets of black cherries and vanillin oak. The Boucherottes has richer and riper fruit; the Clos de Ursules has more body and is more marked by oak. Both should be *en pleine forme* in 5–6 years. The Nuits St.-Georges-Clos des Corvées is smokey, robust, quite aromatic, full-bodied, and tannic. Drink it over the next 7–8 years. The Corton Les Pougets should make a delicious bottle of savory, ripe, broadly flavored wine. It is already extremely impressive, with excellent concentration, super ripeness, a long finish, and moderate tannins. Drink it in 1990–1995. The Clos Vougeot is outstanding. With great color, great fragrance, great richness, this wine has the texture and intensity of a top 1982 Bordeaux. Last tasted in April, 1990, it will need until 1994 to develop fully. Last, the Chambertin-Clos de Bèze is surprisingly forward and accessible, with a voluptuous, seductive richness, long, deep flavors, and ripe tannins. The secret to Jadot's success in 1983 was to avoid the hail damage and rot. After severe selections were made, the wines were fermented at very hot temperatures for a short period. It obviously worked.

DOMAINE HENRI JAYER (VOSNE-ROMANÉE)

1983 ECHÉZEAUX	88
1983 VOSNE-ROMANÉE	84

1983 VOSNE-ROMANÉE LES BEAUX MONTS	87
1983 VOSNE-ROMANÉE LES BRÛLÉES	85
1983 VOSNE-ROMANÉE-CROS PARANTOUX	89
1983 NUITS ST.-GEORGES LES MURGERS	86
1983 RICHEBOURG	92

Several brokers in Burgundy have suggested that Henri Jayer's 1983s were not as good as they should have been. Perhaps this is true. Jayer did lose a significant portion of his crop because of hail and rot. However, I found his 1983s to be sumptuous wines. There's no question that Jayer's Richebourg is his finest wine in 1983, but he only made 25 cases of it, so the chances of getting any are nil. There are 175 cases of Vosne-Romanée-Cros Parantoux, which is extremely elegant with broad, deep flavors tinged with spicy oak. It has the best length of all Jayer's Vosne-Romanées. It should be ready to drink by 1992. The Vosne-Romanée-Les Brûlées is a more spicy, more expressive wine with harder tannins, a very good color, full body, but less concentration. The Vosne-Romanée Les Beaux Monts is a fat yet tannic wine with dark ruby color, clean flavors of ripe, sweet Pinot Noir, and a long finish. It has more concentration than the Les Brûlées. The Nuits St.-Georges Les Murgers is quite good, with fat, fleshy flavors, rather supple for a 1983, and will probably be mature by 1990. The Echézeaux is excellent, elegant, complex, highly aromatic, with seductive, round, rich flavors wrapped in a glove of tannin. Jayer's straight Vosne-Romanée is good, but will no doubt be rather expensive.

DOMAINE JACQUELINE JAYER (VOSNE-ROMANÉE)

1983 ECHÉZEAUX	78
1983 NUITS ST.-GEORGES LES LAVIÈRES	72
1983 VOSNE-ROMANÉE	59
1983 VOSNE-ROMANÉE LES ROUGES	65

The 1983s from Jacqueline Jayer (a relative of both Henri and Lucien) were so abrasively tannic and astringent and seemed so devoid of fruit. I will be shocked if there is enough fruit here to outlive the excessive tannin levels.

DOMAINE MICHEL LAFARGE (VOLNAY)

1983 BEAUNE LES GRÈVES	84
1983 VOLNAY	82
1983 VOLNAY CLOS DES CHÊNES	85
1983 VOLNAY PREMIER CRU	84

All of these wines now have a ruby/amber color, and a seductive, velvety, black cherry fruitiness interlaced with smells of vanillin oakiness, leather, and decaying leaves. The tannins are obvious and harsh. The Beaune Les Grèves is more open-knit and has a lighter color with a strong alcoholic finish. It should be ready by 1990. The Volnay has very harmonious flavors, a smoky, ripe berry fruit bouquet, and long finish. The Volnay Premier Cru is slightly deeper, with layers of rich fruit and 5–8 years of further evolution. The Volnay Clos des Chênes is the richest, the most aromatic, the deepest and most complete of all these wines. It should be at its peak by 1990–1995.

DOMAINE COMTE LAFON (MEURSAULT)

1983 VOLNAY CHAMPANS	83
1983 VOLNAY SANTENOTS	86

These two 1983s show no signs of rot or astringent bitterness. The Champans is a velvety, yet big, fruity wine that will mature by 1990. The Santenots is bigger-framed, quite ripe, rich, fat, and alcoholic with a good, firm edge and tannins for support. It should be mature between 1990–1995. Neither wine was filtered.

DOMAINE CLOS DES LAMBRAYS (MOREY ST.-DENIS)

1983 CLOS DES LAMBRAYS	72
1983 MERCUREY LES CHEVELOTS	73
1983 MOREY ST.-DENIS	65

This famous estate, now under the new ownership of Louis and Fabien Saier, is making numerous changes in an effort to modernize the style of wine produced at the Clos des Lambrays. The wine is now aged in one-third new oak barrels and bottled after 18–22 months. The 1983s were filtered prior to bottling, perhaps excessively so. The Clos des Lambrays is shockingly light and exhibits an aroma and flavor of decaying vegetation and old meat. It has good concentration but harsh tannins in the finish. The Morey St.-Denis is medium weight and flavored by rot and excessive tannins.

DOMAINE LAMY-PILLOT (CHASSAGNE-MONTRACHET)

1983 BLAGNY-LA PIÈCE SOUS LE BOIS	76
1983 CHASSAGNE-MONTRACHET-CLOS SAINT-JEAN	69
1983 SAINT-AUBIN LES CASTETS	65
1983 SANTENAY LES CHARRONS	59

René Lamy's 1983s did not fare well. The prices are reasonable, but with the exception of the Blagny, which has some tobacco scents, and decent berry ripeness, the wines had very vegetal, bizarre aromas. Unless you get excited over the smell of rotten vegetables interlaced with the scent of manure, there is nothing much to like about these wines.

PHILIPPE LECLERC (GEVREY-CHAMBERTIN)

1983 GEVREY-CHAMBERTIN	84
1983 GEVREY-CHAMBERTIN LES CAZETIERS	86
1983 GEVREY-CHAMBERTIN LES CHAMPEAUX	84
1983 GEVREY-CHAMBERTIN COMBE AUX MOINES	87

Not surprisingly, all of these wines are powerful, deeply scented wines that show no trace of rot or bitter tannins. The Gevrey-Chambertin is alcoholic, well colored, rich, and in need of 1–3 years cellaring. The Les Champeaux is also rather soft and surprisingly accessible but has broad, spicy, ripe flavors. One of the two stars here is Les Cazetiers, a powerful, rich, substantial wine with layers of sweet Pinor Noir fruit. It is a full-bodied, big, alcoholic wine that will be close to full maturity by 1990–1992. The top wine is Combe aux Moines, which has an intense flavor of old wines, a rich, chewy, lush texture, moderate rather than excessive tannins, and a huge finish. It should be superb between 1990– 1995.

RENÉ LECLERC (GEVREY-CHAMBERTIN)

1983 GEVREY-CHAMBERTIN CLOS PRIEUR	85
1983 GEVREY-CHAMBERTIN COMBE AUX MOINES	90
1983 GEVREY-CHAMBERTIN LAVAUX ST.-JACQUES	89

All three of these wines are rich, robust, darkly colored, full-bodied wines with excellent extract and potential. I could have rated the Clos Prieur a little higher because it is rich, long, typically alcoholic, but it is also extremely tannic. It will need 5–6 more years. The Lavaux St.-Jacques is a dense, very fat, rich, immense wine with 5–8 years of positive evolution ahead of it. The layers of flavors are very impressive. The Combe aux Moines is clearly one of the great wines of this vintage. It is very concentrated, dense, and powerful, and has a huge finish. Drink it between 1991 and 1996.

DOMAINE LEQUIN ROUSSOT (SANTENAY)

1983 CHASSAGNE-MONTRACHET MORGEOT	78
1983 CORTON	85
1983 POMMARD	55
1983 SANTENAY	75
1983 SANTENAY-CLOS DES HAUTS VILLAGES	70
1983 SANTENAY LA COMBE	73

The 1983s from Lequin Roussot were aged in 50% new wood and have plenty of character, but are excessively hard and tannic. The Pommard was so hard, tough, and tannic that I am quite concerned it will never be balanced. Lequin Roussot produced a decent, spicy, full-bodied Santenay for drinking in 1990, but a harsh, tannic Chassagne-Montrachet Morgeot and Santenay-Clos des Hauts Villages. The Santenay La Combe exhibits riper, more plummy fruit, a meaty, leathery bouquet, ruby/amber color, and a long finish. Equally good is the Corton, which has a healthy, deep color, full body, very good depth and is also very tannic. It will need 5–6 years of cellaring.

DOMAINE HUBERT LIGNIER (MOREY ST.-DENIS)

1983 CLOS DE LA ROCHE	90
1983 MOREY ST.-DENIS	85

To **DAVID SCHWARZ**

Date **03/07/95** Time **6:11 PM**

WHILE YOU WERE OUT

M **ANDREW MCKINLEY**

of _____

Phone **310 455-9891**

Area Code		Number	Extension
TELEPHONED	✓	PLEASE CALL	X
CALLED TO SEE YOU		WILL CALL AGAIN	
WANTS TO SEE YOU		URGENT	
RETURNED YOUR CALL			

Message _____
_____
_____
_____
_____

Operator

Lignier's Morey St.-Denis is quite attractive, rich, and supple, yet powerful and firm. It has dark color, a lovely bouquet, yet it still needs 4–6 years to develop fully. His Clos de la Roche is truly superb. Deep, ripe with the scent of plums and violets, it is remarkably fruity and complex but needs 6–8 years to shed the moderate tannins that are present.

CHÂTEAU DE LA MALTROYE (CHASSAGNE-MONTRACHET)

1983 CHASSAGNE-MONTRACHET-CLOS DE LA MALTROYE	85
1983 CHASSAGNE-MONTRACHET-CLOS SAINT-JEAN	85
1983 SANTENAY LA COMME	84

The Château de la Maltroye's 1983s were all quite good. All three wines have moderately intense bouquets of leather, spice, and ripe cherry fruit. Rather elegant for 1983s, but still powerful and fuller bodied than one might normally expect, these wines are fully mature. The Clos Saint-Jean is slightly more forward than the others, the Clos de la Maltroye more tannic and tough, and the Santenay La Comme the lightest.

DOMAINE MAUME (GEVREY-CHAMBERTIN)

1983 GEVREY-CHAMBERTIN	83
1983 GEVREY-CHAMBERTIN LAVAUX ST.-JACQUES	87
1983 MAZIS-CHAMBERTIN	89

The Villages Gevrey-Chambertin has plenty of good, ripe fruit, but its score is kept low by some hard tannins in the finish. Both the Lavaux St.-Jacques and Mazis-Chambertin are powerfully built wines meant to mature slowly. Neither should be mature until 1993–1995. The Mazis-Chambertin has a huge aroma of violets, leather, and ripe plums. It is dense and rather huge on the palate, with full body and outstanding length. The Lavaux St.-Jacques is almost identically styled, perhaps more tannic, but equally as rich and full proportioned.

DOMAINE MÉO-CAMUZET (VOSNE-ROMANÉE)

1983 CORTON ROGNET	87
1983 NUITS ST.-GEORGES AUX BOUDOTS	88

1983 NUITS ST.-GEORGES LES MURGERS	?
1983 RICHEBOURG	86
1983 VOSNE-ROMANÉE LES BRÛLÉES	85

This appears to be a domaine that succeeded admirably in the difficult 1983 vintage. Not great burgundies, the wines of Jean Méo are about as good as the 1983s can be. They are not tainted by rot, although the Nuits St.-Georges Les Murgers was clearly bizarre and unusual when I tasted it. The Nuits-St.-Georges aux Boudots is quite excellent, potentially outstanding. Deep ruby in color with a full-intensity bouquet of spicy new oak, plums, truffles, and licorice, this rich, concentrated wine will make a fine bottle in 1990–1995. The Corton Rognet and Richebourg had similarly dark colors, excellent extract, clean, well-delineated Pinot Noir flavors, with a pure, ripe character. The Richebourg tasted slightly less tannic. Give both wines a full 5–6 years of cellaring. The Vosne-Romanée Les Brûlées had the same style, only by comparison showed less depth and fragrance.

PRINCE FLORENT DE MERODE (LADOIX-SERRIGNY)

1983 ALOXE-CORTON	82
1983 CORTON LES BRESSANDES	86
1983 CORTON-CLOS DU ROI	85
1983 CORTON LES MARÉCHAUDES	83
1983 CORTON LES RÉNARDES	84
1983 POMMARD-CLOS DE LA PLATIÈRE	84

The 1983s are surprisingly light and less powerful than most wines from this vintage. They are also totally free of any traces of rot. The Aloxe-Corton and Corton Les Maréchaudes have good fruit, a light to medium ruby color, spicy, vanillin aromas intermixed with cherry fruit and short finishes. They are clean, elegant, understated wines. The Pommard-Clos de la Platière is a more serious wine with ripe, round, forward, cherry fruit, better color, some depth, and weight. It can be drunk now or aged for 4–5 years. The Corton Les Rénardes' bouquet is all cherry and vanillin. On the palate, it is a medium-bodied, pleasant, elegant wine that will be ready to drink soon. The star of the Merode 1983s is the Corton Les Bressandes. It is by far the richest and deepest of these wines, fragrant, loaded with ripe, cherry fruit complemented by spicy new oak. Fuller, richer, and more complex than the others, the Bressandes should be fully mature by 1990–1992. The Corton-Clos du Roi is almost as good, but its toughness and dryness kept it from scoring higher. It does seem to have the concentration of fruit to outlast the tannins. It will need 6–8 years.

MOILLARD (NUITS ST.-GEORGES)

1983 AUXEY DURESSES	75
1983 BEAUNE	73
1983 BEAUNE LES GRÈVES	80
1983 BONNES MARES	85
1983 BOURGOGNE HAUTES-CÔTES DE NUITS	80
1983 CHAMBERTIN-CLOS DE BÈZE	87
1983 CLOS VOUGEOT	83
1983 CORTON-CLOS DU ROI	83
1983 CORTON-CLOS DES VERGENNES	85
1983 CÔTE DE NUITS-VILLAGES-DOMAINE CHEVILLON	82
1983 FIXIN	78
1983 FIXIN-CLOS DE LA PERRIÈRE	80
1983 NUITS ST.-GEORGES-CLOS DES TOREY	86
1983 NUITS ST.-GEORGES LA RICHEMONE	86
1983 ROMANÉE ST.-VIVANT	86
1983 VOLNAY CLOS DES CHÊNES	85
1983 VOSNE-ROMANÉE LES MALCONSORTS	83
1983 VOSNE-ROMANÉE LES BEAUX MONTS	83

The 1983s I tasted from Moillard showed several things. First, this firm produces consistently above-average wines; there were no bad wines tasted. Second, while the wines are not great, there are some very fine, fleshy, rich, dense, chunky selections that offer plenty of palate pleasure. The best two values are the Côte de Nuits-Villages and Bourgogne Hautes-Côtes de Nuits. The Romanée St.-Vivant and Bonnes Mares have the most complexity and reflected their appellations the best. The

Chambertin-Clos de Bèze was the biggest and most concentrated with another 10 years of drinkability ahead of it. The two wines from Moillard's home base of Nuits St.-Georges, the Richemone and Clos des Torey, are both big, thick, jammy, almost opaque wines. Both were rather atypical Pinot Noirs, but offered dense, smokey, very rich fruit and full body. The Volnay Clos des Chênes has aromas and flavors of black cherries, is alcoholic and rich; the Corton-Clos des Vergennes was quite good, spicy, deep, fat, rich, and long. Both wines should be cellared for 5 years. As for the other wines, it was difficult to tell them apart.

DOMAINE MOINE-HUDELOT (CHAMBOLLE-MUSIGNY)

1983 CHAMBOLLE-MUSIGNY	70
1983 CHAMBOLLE-MUSIGNY LES AMOUREUSES	81

This tiny estate is run by Daniel Moine-Hudelot, the mayor of Chambolle-Musigny. He is a philosophical chap who explains quite succinctly why burgundy is so expensive and irregular in quality—too much demand, not enough quantity, and too much illegal stretching. Moine-Hudelot is a serious winemaker, but he makes so little wine that only tiny quantities are exported. Both of his 1983s have a ruby/orange color and a pronounced leathery, herbaceous, raspberry-like bouquet. The Chambolle-Musigny is a little dry and astringent in the finish, the Chambolle-Musigny Les Amoureuses ripe, full bodied, alcoholic, rich, but simple. Both wines are fully mature.

DOMAINE MONGEARD-MUGNERET (VOSNE-ROMANÉE)

1983 CLOS VOUGEOT	90
1983 ECHÉZEAUX	88
1983 FIXIN	82
1983 GRANDS ECHÉZEAUX	92
1983 VOSNE-ROMANÉE	85

Mongeard's wines were great successes in 1983. All have excellent color and clean, ripe, deeply scented bouquets. His Fixin offers a lighter-weight and light-density version of his more serious wines. Broad, ripe, alcoholic flavors are complex and soft in this medium-bodied wine. It is mature. The Vosne-Romanée has excellent color and the depth and richness of most growers' Premiers Crus. Deep flavored, full bodied, high in alcohol with moderate tannins, this delicious wine is ready to drink. The Echézeaux, Clos Vougeot, and great Grands Echézeaux are wines to lay away until 1993–1995. The Echézeaux is wonderfully fruity, chewy, fleshy and so, so concentrated. Its bouquet is one of vanillin, violets, and ripe berry fruit. It is potentially outstanding, but next to the spectacular Clos Vougeot and Grands Echézeaux, it is overwhelmed. Mongeard's Clos Vougeot has remarkable intensity, great depth of flavor, super richness and is altogether a great young wine. Drink it between 1990 and 1996. The Grands Echézeaux is, along with several of the Domaine de la Romanée-Conti 1983s and Ponsot's Clos de la Roche Vieilles Vignes, among the greatest red burgundies of the vintage. The bouquet is filled with complex scents of flowers, plums, oaks, and exotic spices. Incredibly rich and concentrated with layers of fruit, this is a great wine that should be at its best between 1990–2000.

DOMAINE ALBERT MOROT (BEAUNE)

1983 BEAUNE LES BRESSANDES	86
1983 BEAUNE LES CENT VIGNES	87
1983 BEAUNE LES GRÈVES	86
1983 BEAUNE LES MARCONNETS	86
1983 BEAUNE LES TEURONS	85
1983 BEAUNE LES TOUSSAINTS	84
1983 SAVIGNY LES VERGELESSES	85

The 1983s included an impressive array of Beaune wines. For elegance and drinking in 4–5 years, the Savigny Les Vergelesses and Beaune Les Toussaints would be my choices. The most backward wine at the moment is the Beaune Les Teurons, which is dark ruby, medium to full-bodied, but very tannic. Don't touch it before 1993. The Beaune Les Marconnets needs 5–8 years, but has excellent color, a big, tarry, berry-scented bouquet, long, ripe flavors and firm tannins. The Beaune Les Bressandes is very similar, perhaps slightly more fruity, but deep and broad, particularly for a Beaune. The Beaune Les Cent Vignes tastes the richest and most concentrated, with just something extra in the bouquet and flavor. Again, it would be a shame to drink this wine before 1993. The Beaune Les Grèves is excellent, with deep color, no trace of rot or hail damage, firm tannin, and rich, jammy fruit, and medium to full body. Looking for some unadultered Pinot Noir to drink over the next decade at a reasonable price? Then consider these very fine offerings from Albert Morot.

DOMAINE GEORGES MUGNERET (VOSNE-ROMANÉE)

1983 CLOS VOUGEOT	89
1983 ECHÉZEAUX	86
1983 NUITS ST.-GEORGES LES CHAIGNOTS	85
1983 NUITS ST.-GEORGES LES VIGNES RONDES	78
1983 RUCHOTTES-CHAMBERTIN	86
1983 VOSNE-ROMANÉE	76

I was afraid that the late Dr. Georges Mugneret's use of 100% new oak barrels for the 1983s might have been a mistake. The wines were already very tannic and they hardly needed any additional wood tannins. Happily, the wines have turned out to be very good, with the Clos Vougeot potentially outstanding. The Vosne-Romanée has a roasted, ripe, spicy bouquet, very good concentration, a trace of astringence, but it should age well for 5–8 years. The Nuits St.-Georges Les Vignes Rondes tasted less concentrated, a little too hard and dry. It has good, ripe fruit, but I worry about it drying out before it matures. On the other hand, the Nuits St.-Georges Les Chaignots, despite the presence of very aggressive tannins, has a ripe, roasted character, deep color, and a long finish. It must have 10 years of cellaring. The Echézeaux, another wine that requires patience before drinking, is dark ruby, very spicy, quite robust and concentrated, but very, very tannic. The 1983 Ruchottes-Chambertin has less charm than the lovely, seductive 1982, but is a very big wine, dark in color, and potentially better than the rating, but it is so, so tannic. The Clos Vougeot gets my nod as Mugneret's best. It is very intense and powerful with mouth-searing tannins, but also oodles of ripe, plummy fruit. It should be sublime between 1995–2005. These wines were retasted with Dr. Mungeret's daughter in 1989 and confirmed his success in this vintage.

DOMAINE GÉRARD MUGNERET (VOSNE-ROMANÉE)

1983 NUITS ST.-GEORGES LES BOUDOTS	84
1983 VOSNE-ROMANÉE	78
1983 VOSNE-ROMANÉE LES SUCHOTS	86

Gérard Mugneret's 1983s are stylish, elegant, and well-balanced wines. They all have a strong vanillin-scented character from new barrels, but also lean, ripe, graceful Pinot aromas. They do not have the size, weight, and aggressiveness one sees in other 1983 wines, but they are very cleanly made, attractive wines that should mature quite rapidly and be ready by 1990.

NAIGEON-CHAUVEAU (GEVREY-CHAMBERTIN) DOMAINE DES VAROILLES

Naigeon-Chauveau

1983 CHASSAGNE-MONTRACHET	78
1983 CÔTE DE BEAUNE-VILLAGES	73
1983 CÔTE DE NUITS-VILLAGES	?
1983 NUITS ST.-GEORGES	70
1983 NUITS ST.-GEORGES LES DAMODES	75
1983 NUITS ST.-GEORGES LES PRULIERS	78
1983 SANTENAY LE PASSE TEMPS	74

These 1983s are sound, very tannic, deeply colored, true *vins de garde*. None of these wines is bad, but none of them is particularly interesting. The Nuits St.-Georges Les Pruliers had the most color and concentration, but was somewhat dull and overly tannic. The others are quite aggressively tannic, raising serious questions about whether they will dry out before the tannins subside. The wines under the Domaine des Variolles label are vastly superior to those under the *négociant label*, Naigeon-Chauveau.

Domaine des Varoilles

1983 BONNES MARES	82
1983 CHARMES-CHAMBERTIN	82
1983 CLOS VOUGEOT	84
1983 GEVREY-CHAMBERTIN	75
1983 GEVREY-CHAMBERTIN CHAMPONNET	85
1983 GEVREY-CHAMBERTIN-CLOS DE COUVENT	82
1983 GEVREY-CHAMBERTIN-CLOS DES MEIX OUCHES VIEILLES VIGNES	86

1983. GEVREY-CHAMBERTIN-CLOS DE PRIEUR	79
1983 GEVREY CHAMBERTIN-CLOS DES VAROILLES	85
1983 GEVREY-CHAMBERTIN-CLOS DES VAROILLES VIEILLES VIGNES	86
1983 VOSNE-ROMANÉE LA ROMANÉE	82

These are very tannic, backward wines. I would guess that it will be 1995 or beyond before these wines are mature. Even the lower-level wines, such as the Gevrey-Chambertin, are 5–6 years away from maturity. The Gevrey-Chambertin-Clos de Prieur seemed to lack richness and color, and the Vosne-Romanée La Romanée was light, particularly for a 1983. The Gevrey-Chambertin-Clos de Couvent, made from 40-year-old vines, had decent color, with good body and rich fruit to balance out its considerable tannic clout. The Gevrey-Chambertin Champonnet may need 10 years, but it has the requisite concentration to outlast the tannins, and is nearly as good as the Clos des Meix Ouches Vieilles Vignes, which has plenty of ripe, sweet Pinot Noir fruit, a spicy, rich leathery bouquet, and tough tannins. The Clos des Varoilles Vieilles Vignes is not as good as the excellent 1978, but is more powerful and tannic. It will need 10–15 years, but it has excellent concentration and makes a powerful albeit rustic impression on the palate. The regular cuvée of the Clos des Varoilles is not as rich nor as tannic; it may be ready by 1995. As for the Grands Crus, the Charmes-Chambertin is a typically coarse, hard 1983, big and rich, but also tough and tannic. The Bonnes Mares has tons of tannin, but deeper fruit and better color than the Charmes-Chambertin. The Clos Vougeot is the most precocious of this latter trio, has excellent ripeness, full body, and a long finish.

DOMAINE PERNOT-FOURRIER (GEVREY-CHAMBERTIN)

1983 GEVREY-CHAMBERTIN	?
1983 GEVREY-CHAMBERTIN-CLOS ST.-JACQUES	87
1983 GEVREY-CHAMBERTIN COMBE AUX MOINES	86
1983 GEVREY-CHAMBERTIN PREMIER CRU	?
1983 GRIOTTE-CHAMBERTIN	?
1983 VOUGEOT PREMIER CRU	85

The 1983s from this domaine are extremely tannic, macho wines. In fact, several may be far too tannic ever to develop properly. The Gevrey-Chambertin tastes severe and astringent. I will pass on judging it for the time being. The Gevrey-Chambertin Premier Cru is even more abrasively tannic and its future is suspect. The Griotte-Chambertin has plenty of ripe, rich, sweet fruit, but the musty taste of rot is present. That is a shame, because the wine has a lot of power and richness. Some growers claim that with extended aeration this smell blows off. Perhaps you are willing to take that chance. . . . I am not. As for the rest, the Vougeot is very tannic and full bodied, but also has a lot of rich, ripe, deep fruit. It should peak in 8–10 years. The Combe aux Moines is another tannic titan, but it has very fine concentration, some lush, sweet fruit, and 5–6 years of evolution ahead of it. The Clos St.-Jacques is the best of the bunch, a big, alcoholic, rich, deep, and tannic wine that has balance and depth. However, it begs for 8–10 years of cellaring.

DOMAINE PONSOT (MOREY ST.-DENIS)

1983 CHAMBERTIN	85
1983 CLOS DE LA ROCHE	86
1983 CLOS DE LA ROCHE VIEILLES VIGNES	92
1983 CLOS ST.-DENIS VIEILLES VIGNES	90
1983 GRIOTTE-CHAMBERTIN	87
1983 LATRICIÈRES-CHAMBERTIN	88

The wines of Ponsot can be truly great. The 1980 Clos de la Roche Vieilles Vignes is one of the greatest young burgundies I have ever tasted. Jean-Marie Ponsot and his son argue that 1983 is "an extraordinary year," the best since 1947 and 1949. For several of their wines, they might be right. Some of their 1983s are unbelievably concentrated and powerful. In addition to their superb Clos de la Roche, the Latricières-Chambertin and Clos St.-Denis are the top 1983s from this estate, which never filters its wines. These wines are all very good, even spectacular in quality, but they do differ considerably in style and will be ready to drink at different times. The Griotte-Chambertin is fairly precocious, with oodles of supple, yet soft, ripe tannins. It is so rich it is almost jammy. Drink it between 1990–1995. The Chambertin, a greater name but not greater wine, is rather light in color, especially for a Ponsot wine, has soft, classy, complex flavors, and ready to drink. It is extremely long in the mouth, but is very elegant for a Chambertin. The regular Clos de la Roche (250 cases produced) is very dark in color, with a huge aroma of black cherries, apricots, and spicy oak. Quite full bodied, deep, and concentrated, this excellent wine should be at its best between 1990–1998. The Latricières-Chambertin is similar. Dense, dark, almost jammy, with full body, a long, rich, deep texture, excellent concentration, it is more exotic and fragrant than the Clos de la Roche. It should peak between 1992–2000. The sensational Clos St.-Denis (75 cases produced) combines power with finesse, has a voluptuous, deeply concentrated, long taste, is highly aromatic and superbly flavored. It can be drunk now, but promises to be extraordinary in 5–7 years. Last but far from least is the Clos de la Roche Vieilles Vignes (200 cases produced). It is in the same class as the staggering 1980, only the wine is more powerful (the alcohol is 14.5%) and denser. It simply must be tasted to be believed. This is an old heavyweight style of red burgundy that no one but Ponsot produces anymore. It should be mature by 1995 and last at least another decade.

DOMAINE POTHIER-RIEUSSET (POMMARD)

1983 BEAUNE LES BOUCHEROTTES	80
1983 BOURGOGNE	75
1983 BOURGOGNE GRAND ORDINAIRE	74
1983 POMMARD	82
1983 POMMARD-CLOS DES VERGERS	82
1983 POMMARD LES EPENOTS	84
1983 POMMARD LES RUGIENS	84

The basic Bourgogne Grand Ordinaire, which is made from Gamay, not Pinot Noir, is a pleasant, rather simple but fruity wine. The Bourgogne is a step up in quality and interest. Pothier's Bourgognes generally have been excellent values (his 1979 and 1980 are very nice). The 1983 is spicy and fruity with good body and length. The Beaune Les Boucherottes is, of course, a more serious wine. Ready to drink, it has a lovely, earthy Pinot fragrance, good, ripe, round, spicy fruit, medium body and soft, moderate tannins. The real specialities of this house are the Pommards, and all of them, while stunning from the cask, are less impressive from the bottle—no doubt because Pothier was persuaded to filter his 1983s. The Pommard has sweet fruit, a long, alcoholic finish, and hard tannins. It should be at its best between 1989–1996. The Pommard Les Epenots has a ripe, exotic, leathery, vegetal aroma, broad but coarse flavors of raspberries tinged with vanillin oakiness and sharp tannins. It should be delicious by 1990 and hold for a decade. The Clos des Vergers is a very structured wine with 13.5% alcohol. Its staggering perfume of cedarwood, truffles, flowers, ripe berry fruit, and decaying vegetation is not for everyone. Full-bodied, but still closed and hard, it should not be drunk until 1993–1995. The Rugiens is, by comparison, a more exotic, fleshy wine, but is still very hard and impenetrable. It had stupendous richness from the cask, but is now dominated by its harsh, astringent tannins. Pothier thinks it is the best Rugiens since his 1949, which is a legendary wine. Don't drink it until 1995.

GÉRARD POTEL—DOMAINE DE LA POUSSE D'OR (VOLNAY)

1983 POMMARD LES JAROLIÈRES	67
1983 SANTENAY-CLOS D'AUDIGNAC	72
1983 SANTENAY-CLOS TAVANNES	75
1983 VOLNAY-CLOS DE LA BOUSSE D'OR	80
1983 VOLNAY LES CAILLERETS	80
1983 VOLNAY LES CAILLERETS 60 OUVRÉES	83

In general, these wines are medium ruby/orange in color, quite hard and tannic, and several, notably the Pommard Les Jarolières, are just too severe and unpleasant. Neither Santenay greatly impressed me. They both had light color and a dry *sec* finish. The Volnay Les Caillerets has more obvious depth and fruit, but needs 5–6 more years of cellaring. Certainly the Volnay-Clos de la Bousse d'Or and Volnay Les Caillerets 60 Ouvrées show richer and greater fruit, more depth and richness, and long finishes, but they are coarse and taste harsh, particularly for wines from this estate. Will they develop more charm?

DOMAINE CHARLES QUILLARDET (MARSANNAY)

1983 BOURGOGNE LES GRANDS VIGNES	72
1983 BOURGOGNE-MONTRE CUL	67
1983 CHAMBERTIN	83
1983 FIXIN	75
1983 GEVREY-CHAMBERTIN	72

1983 GEVREY-CHAMBERTIN LE BEL AIR	75
1983 GEVREY-CHAMBERTIN CHAMPEAUX	78

This estate makes wines that I find clumsy, dull, and very Rhône-like. They are dark in color, chewy, but there is sometimes a bit too much of the barnyard in the aroma, and rarely do I find textbook Pinot Noir flavors. Nevertheless, the wines have a certain following and are fairly priced, save for the Chambertin, which is always overpriced, regardless of who produces it. The 1983s are mediocre wines. The problem is that all the wines from Gevrey-Chambertin taste alike. The prices are different, but I see little or no difference between the Villages Gevrey-Chambertin and Chambertin. I would also like to know how Quillardet gets Pinot Noir grapes to produce the wines with this color and such a chunky, dense, heavy character. The Montre Cul, with its juvenile label displaying a woman's derrière and its heavy, coarse flavors, gives new meaning to the notion of poor taste. Would you believe me if I said it also had a fecal aroma?

DOMAINE HENRI RÉBOURSEAU
(GEVREY-CHAMBERTIN)

1983 CHAMBERTIN	55
1983 CHARMES-CHAMBERTIN	52
1983 CLOS VOUGEOT	60
1983 GEVREY-CHAMBERTIN	65
1983 MAZIS-CHAMBERTIN	55

This is an historic old property made famous by the now ancient Général Rébourseau. The late Frank Schoonmaker claimed the 1929s from Rébourseau were among the greatest burgundies he had drunk. Now the younger Rébourseau runs the show, and the wines are certainly less rich and full bodied than in the past. The 1983s are terribly flawed. They are suspiciously light in color, but do make a powerful, heady, alcoholic impact on the palate. However, after 20–30 minutes in the glass, moldy smells of rot emerge and after an hour these smells have overtaken everything in the glass. I went to the trouble and expense of tasting these wines three separate times to be sure I was right. My conclusion is that they are badly affected by rot. The Mazis and Clos Vougeot are less afflicted, the Charmes totally flawed. Some tasters may not object to this character. It resembles the smell and taste of a "corked" bottle.

REMOISSENET (BEAUNE)

Côte de Beaune

1983 BEAUNE LES GRÈVES	85
1983 BEAUNE LES MARCONNETS	87
1983 BEAUNE LES TOUSSAINTS	84
1983 BOURGOGNE PASSE-TOUT-GRAINS	74
1983 CORTON-CLOS DU ROI	86
1983 GIVRY-BARON THENARD	83
1983 MERCUREY-CLOS FOURTOUL	75
1983 POMMARD	76
1983 LA RENOMMÉE	72
1983 SANTENAY LES GRAVIÈRES	75
1983 VOLNAY	80

This is unquestionably one of the wealthiest domaines in Burgundy. Roland Remoissenet is the gregarious genius behind this empire. The quality of wines here has always been quite good, perhaps not as exciting as the prices charged for the wines suggests, but nevertheless ripe, round Pinot Noir–flavored wines. In tasting through the line of Remoissenet wines, I got the impression that Roland Remoissenet thinks 1983 is a good vintage, but no more. The quality level in 1983 at Remoissenet is good, but I found no great red burgundies, adding evidence to my feeling that 1983 is by no means a super vintage. Remoissenet bottled his 1983s late as he wanted to soften the tannins as much as possible. The range of Remoissenet wines from the Côte de Beaune was surprisingly mediocre. Only five wines stood out. The 1983 Givry from Baron Thenard, always a good value from Remoissenet, is robust, fruity, substantial on the palate and interesting. Look for it to be fully mature between 1990–1994. The Beaune Les Toussaints has a lovely black cherry bouquet, spicy, rather hard, tannic flavors, medium body, and at least 5–8 years of positive evolution ahead of it. The Beaune Les Marconnets was my favorite Côte de Beaune wine from Remoissenet. Rich, ripe cherry and spicy oak aromas inundate the nose. On the palate, the wine is dense and concentrated, moderately tannic, and simply longer and deeper in flavor than these other wines. Give it 6–8 years of cellaring. The Beaune Les Grèves has broad flavors, but not the length or complexity of the Beaune Les Marconnets. The Corton-Clos du Roi is the biggest and most alcoholic of these wines. Deep, fat but also hard and tough in the finish, it should make a fine bottle in 8 or so years.

Côte de Nuits

1983 CHARMES-CHAMBERTIN	69
1983 CLOS VOUGEOT	86
1983 GEVREY-CHAMBERTIN	70
1983 GEVREY-CHAMBERTIN AUX COMBOTTES	87
1983 GEVREY-CHAMBERTIN-CLOS ST.-JACQUES	87
1983 GRANDS ECHÉZEAUX	84
1983 MAZIS-CHAMBERTIN	83
1983 NUITS ST.-GEORGES	84
1983 NUITS ST.-GEORGES LES PERDRIX	86
1983 RICHEBOURG	?
1983 VOSNE-ROMANÉE LES BEAUX MONTS	70

Remoissenet's wines from the Côte de Nuits reveal higher quality than their wines from the Côte de Beaune. That is not to say there are no disappointments. The Gevrey-Chambertin is thin and hard, the Charmes-Chambertin totally one-dimensional and musty in flavor. The Vosne-Romanée Les Beaux Monts smelled herbaceous and stemmy. Lastly, the Richebourg tasted uncommonly harsh and astringent. As for the good news, the Nuits St.-Georges exhibited a smoky, earthy richness, deep color, good body, and 6–8 years of life ahead of it. The Nuits St.-Georges Les Perdrix is even better, rich, smoky, dark in color, full bodied, tannic, and powerful. Give it 8–10 years. The Gevrey-Chambertin-Clos St.-Jacques is a definite winner—deeply colored, full-bodied, ripe, intense, rich, and quite loaded with fruit. I liked the Gevrey-Chambertin aux Combottes equally as much for its spicy, rich, very complex bouquet, ripe, dense, alcoholic, powerful flavors and excellent finish. It is a big "impact" wine that needs 7–10 years of cellaring. The Grands Echézeaux is delicious, but rather light and not as concentrated as one might expect. The Clos Vougeot, while very tannic and in need of 10 years of cellaring, is rich in extract, spicy, full-bodied with a long, deep finish.

DOMAINE DANIEL RION (NUITS ST.-GEORGES)

1983 CLOS VOUGEOT	85
1983 CÔTE DE NUITS-VILLAGES	78
1983 NUITS ST. GEORGES LES HAUTS PRULIERS	84
1983 VOSNE-ROMANÉE	82
1983 VOSNE-ROMANÉE LES BEAUX MONTS	82

Rion's wines generally are not long lived. A tasting recently of the 1978s showed them to be drying out. The 1983 Côte de Nuits Villages is a solid, chunky, straightforward wine with moderate tannins and some elegant Pinot Noir character. The Vosne-Romanée is a lively, medium-bodied wine with a suppleness and pleasing lushness that give it appeal now. It should be drunk over the next 1–2 years. Curiously, the Vosne-Romanée Les Beaux Monts has a similar character and, while more tannic, seems too close in style and quality to the Vosne-Romanée to merit the additional price. I liked both the Nuits St.-Georges Les Hauts Pruliers and Clos Vougeot considerably more than the other Rion wines. The Nuits St.-Georges Les Hauts Pruliers has a lot of spicy oak in its bouquet as well as some ripe plums. On the palate it is deep and relatively rich with very good length and depth. The Clos Vougeot is even better, with a dense-looking, dark ruby color, a very fragrant plum and oak bouquet, fat, rich fruit, full body, and moderate rounded tannins. Drink them up.

DOMAINE DE LA ROMANÉE-CONTI (VOSNE-ROMANÉE)

1983 ECHÉZEAUX	85
1983 GRANDS ECHÉZEAUX	90
1983 RICHEBOURG	90
1983 ROMANÉE-CONTI	92
1983 ROMANÉE-ST.-VIVANT	88
1983 LA TÂCHE	92

The 1983 vintage for Domaine de la Romanée-Conti was a very tough year. First there was hail, then the advent of rot in August thanks to the tropical heat and humidity. When the harvest occurred, the domaine instructed its pickers to pick the grapes, not the grape bunches, by hand and to discard all of the rotten grapes. The results are splendidly concentrated, rich wines, but wines that are extremely expensive and need at least a decade of cellaring. At the summit of quality are the Romanée-Conti and La Tâche, two sensational wines with rich yet youthful fragrances, long, deep flavors, and plenty of body. The Richebourg is closed, the Grands Echézeaux the most velvety and forward, and given its quality, also the best value for a Domaine de la Romanée-Conti wine. The Romanée-St.-Vivant is very spicy, a little rustic, but tannic and big. The Echézeaux is the lightest, and while good, not terribly exciting. It is the only wine that suggests the moldy taste of rot. With the exception of the Echézeaux, these wines should reach their apogee between 1993 and 2000.

DOMAINE ARMAND ROUSSEAU
(GEVREY-CHAMBERTIN)

1983 CHAMBERTIN	88
1983 CHAMBERTIN-CLOS DE BÈZE	90
1983 CHARMES-CHAMBERTIN	82
1983 CLOS DE LA ROCHE	78
1983 GEVREY-CHAMBERTIN	76
1983 GEVREY-CHAMBERTIN LES CAZETIERS	85
1983 GEVREY-CHAMBERTIN-CLOS ST.-JACQUES	90
1983 MAZIS-CHAMBERTIN	85
1983 RUCHOTTES-CHAMBERTIN	88

Many of Rousseau's 1983s are exceptional, but they are very tannic indeed. With the exception of the Gevrey-Chambertin, which may be mature by 1990, all of these wines require a minimum of another 5 years of cellaring. The tannins are ripe and hard rather than the dry and astringent tannins caused by rot. All the wines are deep in color, the deepest being the Clos de Bèze, Clos St.-Jacques, and Ruchottes. The most forward wine is the Clos de la Roche, but it still needs 4–5 years. The most backward wine is the Chambertin. If I had just one of these excellent wines to buy, it would be the Clos St.-Jacques, which has layers of sweet fruit and will be significantly less expensive than the Clos de Bèze or Chambertin. If you have a good cellar and plenty of discretionary income, the Clos de Bèze and Chambertin will be superb in 10–15 years.

DOMAINE ROUMIER (CHAMBOLLE-MUSIGNY)

1983 BONNES MARES	92
1983 CHAMBOLLE-MUSIGNY	84
1983 CHAMBOLLE-MUSIGNY LES AMOUREUSES	88
1983 CLOS VOUGEOT	90
1983 MOREY ST.-DENIS-CLOS DE LA BUSSIÈRE	87
1983 MUSIGNY	90
1983 RUCHOTTES-CHAMBERTIN	93

The 1983s from Roumier are among the very best of the vintage. Roumier always makes top-quality burgundy, but his 1983s are among the best I have ever tasted, including the sensational wines he produced in 1969, 1976, and 1988. His 1983s have an opulence and richness to go along with their power and firm tannins. They are not likely to be fully mature until 1992–2000. These are truly great red burgundies—it is well worth a careful search of the marketplace to find them. The Morey St.-Denis-Clos de la Bussière is an excellent red burgundy by any standards, but when tasting it alongside the other top wines here it gets lost. It has a dark ruby color, an intense, sweet fruitiness, medium to full body, and firm tannins. It should be ready by 1992. The Chambolle-Musigny is a bit more tough and tannic, and while the color and concentration are excellent, the wine has some dry, astringent tannins in the finish that suggest hail or rot problems. It is the only Roumier wine where I noticed this. The Chambolle-Musigny Les Amoureuses (only 200 cases made) is rather powerful, alcoholic, but extremely deep and concentrated. Give it 10 years. The four great wines produced by Roumier include a staggeringly rich Clos Vougeot, so packed with ripe Pinot Noir fruit and so complex and aromatic that this powerful, rather massive red burgundy will not be fully mature until 1993–1995. Roumier's Musigny is also a great wine, more sensual and elegant, but extremely ripe and rich, dark in color with an intense, supple lushness to its fruit. It has great balance and should drink beautifully between 1992–2000. Two of the very greatest wines are the Bonnes Mares and Ruchottes-Chambertin. I truly don't think one can taste better burgundy. The Bonnes Mares tastes denser and richer than the Musigny.

The Ruchottes-Chambertin is a monument, a prodigious and magnificent wine of incredible power, richness and depth. All of these wines are beginning to drink well but can last for 10–15 more years.

DANIEL SENARD (ALOXE-CORTON)

1983 CORTON	?
1983 CORTON LES BRESSANDES	86
1983 CORTON-CLOS DU MEIX	85
1983 CORTON-CLOS DU ROI	87

Senard's red 1983s are rather typical wines for the vintage—big, backward, tannic, and undeveloped. Patience is required here, a lot of it. With the exception of the Corton, which I found impossible to judge because of the mouthsearing tannins and apparent absence of ripe fruit, the other three Cortons, while tannic and hard, seem to have the concentration of fruit to balance out the tannins. The Corton-Clos du Roi is the most impressive. It has a fine deep color and density of fruit with a promising bouquet of vanillin oak and ripe cherries. Give it 10 years of storage. The Corton Les Bressandes is a more supple, fragrant, ripe, medium- to full-bodied wine that also needs 10 years of cellaring. The Corton-Clos du Meix is similarly styled, yet very tannic and really in need of 5–8 years of aging. It does have plenty of ripe fruit and a rustic, alcoholic punch to it, but it is so, so backward.

BERNARD SERVEAU (MOREY ST.-DENIS)

1983 CHAMBOLLE-MUSIGNY LES AMOUREUSES	88
1983 CHAMBOLLE-MUSIGNY LES SABIOTS	80
1983 MOREY ST.-DENIS LES SORBÈS	78

The Morey St.-Denis Les Sorbès has lost some color, but still retains a pleasing ripeness and sweetness of Pinot Noir fruit. It is a delicate rather than powerful 1983, and should be drunk now. The Chambolle-Musigny Les Sabiots has a trifle more concentration, surprising suppleness for a 1983, and very good ripeness. It is ready to drink. The Chambolle-Musigny Les Amoureuses should prove to be a winner. Dark in color, with an expansively fragrant, ripe bouquet of flowers and plums, this silky, medium-bodied wine has very good concentration and moderate, rather gentle tannins. It should be at its peak between 1990–1995.

ROBERT SIRUGE (VOSNE-ROMANÉE)

1983 GRANDS ECHÉZEAUX	90
1983 VOSNE-ROMANÉE	80
1983 VOSNE-ROMANÉE LES PETITS MONTS	84

This small grower in Vosne-Romanée produces elegant, supple wines that generally mature quite quickly. His 1983s are above-average to good wines, with the exception of the Grands Echézeaux, which is outstanding. The Villages Vosne-Romanée is light to medium ruby in color, has a pleasing oaky, spicy bouquet, a strong lashing of tannin and some powerful alcoholic punch to it. It needs 5–6 years of cellaring. The Vosne-Romanée Les Petits Monts is darker in color, ripe, and alcoholic, but finishes hard and dry with a touch of the *goût de moisi*. It is certainly a good wine, but its development must be watched. The Grands Echézeaux is quite outstanding, dark ruby in color, with a really superb, intense bouquet of very ripe fruit and spicy oak. It is quite concentrated, very deep and rich with good tannins that add firmness rather than astringence. It should be at its best between 1992–2000.

DOMAINE GABRIEL TORTOCHET (GEVREY-CHAMBERTIN)

1983 CHAMBERTIN	89
1983 CLOS VOUGEOT	84
1983 GEVREY-CHAMBERTIN LAVAUX ST.-JACQUES	83
1983 MAZIS-CHAMBERTIN	88

Tortochet's 1983s are very big, full-bodied wines with an almost roasted ripeness to them. Both the Gevrey-Chambertin Lavaux St.-Jacques and Clos Vougeot tasted closed and tough, but had good concentration and some underlying suppleness. They showed no signs of rot damage, and definitely need 1–4 years of cellaring. The Mazis-Chambertin and Chambertin are very old-style wines, thick, rich, full-throttle burgundies with roasted, spicy, intense bouquets, rich, sweet, almost creamy flavors, full body, and ripe, round tannins. They are approachable now, but you should cellar them 2–3 years to realize their full potential.

DOMAINE LOUIS TRAPET (GEVREY-CHAMBERTIN)

1983 CHAMBERTIN	74
1983 CHAMBERTIN-CUVÉE VIEILLES VIGNES	84
1983 CHAPELLE-CHAMBERTIN	79
1983 LATRICIÈRES-CHAMBERTIN	77

I have not always been pleased with the Trapet wines. They certainly have an excellent reputation, but in some vintages, they have turned out too light, and show a tendency to turn brown in color at an early age. Jean Trapet, the current Trapet in charge, is a short, affable man. He aged the 1983s 15–18 months in oak barrels, one-third of which are new. His 1983s were bottled after a slight filtration. Trapet used the new "Bouteille Bourgogne" for his 1983s, an ugly, cheap-looking bottle that resembles that used for the generic Côtes du Rhône wines. The style of wine produced here is generally lighter than that made at such domaines as Leclerc, Rousseau, Clair-Dau and Varoilles. The 1983s from Trapet, which tasted very good from the cask, appear to be totally different wines from the bottle. All of them have an orange/brownish color, suggesting they are 20–25 years old. They also exhibited intense, musty, decaying smells of rot to go along with their broad, ripe, smokey, sweet Pinot flavors. Firm tannins are present, but these wines are much more accessible and forward than most 1983s. The Chapelle-Chambertin is quite rich, round, and fruity, with a bizarre bouquet of rotting cardboard, smoke, and vegetal fruit. Yet the flavors are lush and intense. Drink it up. The Latricières-Chambertin is less evolved and more obviously tannic, yet as it develops in the glass it reveals scents of rotten meat, toffee, caramel, and hickory. It has a velvety texture and very long finish. It should be drunk over the next 2–3 years. The Chambertin is the most closed and tannic of these four wines. It is spicy and rich, but for the moment not revealing the same depth and complexity of flavor as the other wines. The Chambertin-Cuvée Vieilles Vignes, produced from 80-year-old vines and made on an average of only once every decade (there were 100 cases in 1983), is a decadently rich and opulent Pinot Noir. However, the strong smell of rotting vegetables, aged beef, and the local barnyard may prove too much for many people. Sweet, ripe, long, and very expansive on the palate, this medium- to full-bodied wine should be drunk over the next 2–3 years.

COMTE DE VOGÜÉ (CHAMBOLLE-MUSIGNY)

1983 BONNES MARES	84
1983 CHAMBOLLE-MUSIGNY	75
1983 CHAMBOLLE-MUSIGNY LES AMOUREUSES	83
1983 MUSIGNY	85

The 1983s are better than many of the wines made by Comte de Vogüé in the dismal 1973–1982 period, but they are not even close to being considered among the best in this variable vintage. For fear of tainting the macerating grape juice with the *goût de moisi* from rot- and hail-scarred grapes, the decision was made to pull the skins off after only a week. Several other producers made similar decisions and the results were rather lightly colored, elegant, fruity wines that lacked depth and concentration. The Villages Chambolle-Musigny is very light, but clean and pleasant. The Chambolle-Musigny Les Amoureuses has considerably more fruit and flavor, decent body, some attractive vanillin oakiness, and a good, lush finish. It should be at its best by 1990. The Bonnes Mares is very precocious tasting, has medium body, good concentration, an underlying pleasing suppleness, and 4–6 years of evolution ahead of it. The Musigny is darker in color with more tannin and slightly more concentration. Its tannins are soft, the bouquet dominated by the smell of new oak and cherries. The Musigny should reach full maturity between 1990–1994.

1983 WHITE BURGUNDY

The 1983 white burgundies are among the most enormous white wines I have ever tasted from the region. Ranging from 14%–16% alcohol, they are extremely alcoholic, heavy, clumsy wines that will have your head spinning. Some can be magnificent if the balancing acidity is present, but many are rather oafish wines that will please while young but fall apart by 1992 as the fruit fades and the ugly level of alcohol becomes dominant. The two *négociants* Louis Jadot and Louis Latour were splendidly successful, as was the Domaine Leflaive.

RECOMMENDED PRODUCERS

Bonneau du Martray   J. A. Ferret
Domaine Coche-Dury   Château Fuissé

Domaine Jean-Noël Gagnard
Louis Jadot
Louis Latour
Domaine Leflaive
Domaine Long-Depaquit
  (Bichot)

Château de Meursault
Bernard Morey
Michel Niellon
Domaine Ramonet
Domaine Raveneau
Étienne Sauzet

1984—*Red Burgundy*. This was another extremely difficult year for burgundy. Cold, wet weather plagued the growers during the summer, but at least modern-day sprays prevented the onset of rot, which had been the undoing of so many previous vintages. However, when the grapes were harvested, the natural sugar content would have produced wines with an alcohol content of only 9%–10%, so chaptalization was widely employed, sometimes excessively so. As we head into the decade of the nineties, most 1984s are showing a disturbing tendency to turn brown. The best examples should all be consumed. These would include the wines from the Domaine de la Romanée-Conti, Domaine Jean Gros, Philippe Leclerc, Georges Mugneret, Armand Rousseau, Trapet, Robert Chevillon, Faiveley, and Georges Roumier. Perhaps the nicest thing I have heard about this vintage came from Jancis Robinson, who called the wines "appealing, if not desperately serious" when she was tasting one of Louis Jadot's Beaune Premiers Crus, the Clos des Ursules.

White Burgundy. The rain diluted the grapes, and the coldness kept maturity well below the desired levels. The result was thin wines high in acidity, lean, and generally unattractive. They may last, but they will never be interesting or charming wines, even in a lighter sense. Chablis was even worse than the Côte d'Or, with very green, malnourished, light wines produced.

1985 RED BURGUNDY

I am hardly the first to tell you how great the red 1985 burgundies are. The hype has droned on since the wines were conceived—yet it is true. When I first saw the wines in 1986, many seemed to be too soft and to lack the structure needed to be considered exceptional. Needless to say, they have put on weight, length, and structure, and I have no hesitation in saying that they are the deepest, richest, most seductive and delicious red burgundies I have ever tasted. This is not to say everyone made great wine. Some producers made good instead of exceptional wines, but as the ratings attest, no viticultural area has produced so many great wines since Bordeaux in 1982. Why are the 1985s so exceptional? The growing season was ideal, quite hot, but more importantly hail and rot free. As a general rule, the wines are the deepest-colored burgundies I have seen. The wines explode with pure Pinot Noir fruit, are lush and full-bodied, quite concentrated, and moderately tannic. Because of the exceptional ripeness and opulent textures of the wines, the acids are not high. But neither are they too low. This great ripeness and richness, combined with the low but adequate acids, give these wines a stunning appeal and accessibility today. However, the best wines will not reach their plateau of maturity until 1990–1993, and last 5–10 years therafter if properly stored in a cool, humid area.

Note: The 1985s were first tasted from the barrel in both the summer and the fall of 1986. From the bottle, they have been closely monitored in peer group tastings in fall, 1988, and the spring and fall of 1989.

BERNARD AMIOT (CHAMBOLLE-MUSIGNY)

1985 CHAMBOLLE-MUSIGNY	85
1985 CHAMBOLLE-MUSIGNY LES CHARMES	85

These two wines are both very forward, ripe, richly scented, lush burgundies that have plenty of fat and soft tannins. The Villages Chambolle-Musigny seemed every bit as good as the Premier Cru Les Charmes. The latter tasted slightly more alcoholic and marginally more tannic. Anticipated maturity: 1990–1992.

PIERRE AMIOT (MOREY ST.-DENIS)

1985 CLOS DE LA ROCHE	90
1985 GEVREY-CHAMBERTIN AUX COMBOTTES	87
1985 MOREY ST.-DENIS	83
1985 MOREY ST.-DENIS LES BAUDES	85
1985 MOREY ST.-DENIS AUX CHARMES	87
1985 MOREY ST.-DENIS LES MILLANDES	85

Pierre Amiot's 1985s are his best wines since 1978. They are very fruity, supple, precocious wines that are undeniably charming and will drink well for 5 to 7 years after the vintage. Both the Morey St.-Denis and Morey St.-Denis Millandes are well-colored, richly fruity, soft wines that are drinking well now. The Aux Charmes has more depth and gives a broader, more expansive, almost sweet impression. In comparison, the Les Baudes is more tannic and firmer structured, but promising. The Gevrey-Chambertin Aux Combottes combines a bit more power and tannin with the opulent, ripe fruit of the vintage, offering a bigger, more robust style of wine. The Clos de la Roche is outstanding. Rich, sweet, and quite concentrated with a penetrating bouquet of berry fruit, oriental spices, and layers of soft fruit, it should age well for 4 to 5 more years. Anticipated maturity: 1990–1994.

MARQUIS D'ANGERVILLE (VOLNAY)

1985 VOLNAY CHAMPANS	84
1985 VOLNAY-CLOS DES DUCS	86

The 1985s here are very stylish, lighter-weight examples of the vintage, with light to medium ruby color, a touch of vanillin from aging in 25% new oak barrels, and elegantly wrought cherry fruit flavors. The Champans should be at its peak around 1990–1991 and keep for 5 to 6 years thereafter. The Clos des Ducs is richer and deeper, with plenty of ripe cherry fruit as well as a denser color.

COMTE ARMAND (POMMARD)

1985 POMMARD-CLOS DES EPENEAUX	88

As Serena Sutcliffe says in her excellent *Pocket Guide to the Wines of Burgundy,* this wine "is for those who say that present burgundy is too light." The 1985 has a dense, rich, ruby/purple color, a big, oaky, plummy, intense bouquet, significant flavor interest, and considerable body. Anticipated maturity: 1992–1998.

ROBERT ARNOUX (VOSNE-ROMANÉE)

1985 CLOS VOUGEOT	86
1985 NUITS ST.-GEORGES CORVÉES DES PAGETS	87
1985 NUITS ST.-GEORGES LES POISETS	86
1985 NUITS ST.-GEORGES LES PROCÈS	86
1985 ROMANÉE ST.-VIVANT	88
1985 VOSNE-ROMANÉE LES CHAUMES	87

1985 VOSNE-ROMANÉE LES MAZIERS	84
1985 VOSNE-ROMANÉE LES SUCHOTS	90

Arnoux's 1985s are his best vintage since the marvelous 1978s. The Vosne-Romanée Les Maziers is fruity, but straightforward and simple. The Nuits St.-Georges Les Poisets is a bigger, richer, deeper-colored wine with more length and depth. The Les Procès shows an equally concentrated quality, but has more new wood aromas, tannin and structure. The Corvées des Pagets is rich, creamy, fat, and loaded with fruit. More supple than the other two wines from Nuits St.-Georges, it is a joy to drink right now. Two Arnoux vineyards that always do well are Les Chaumes and Les Suchots, both from Vosne-Romanée. The 1985 Les Chaumes is characteristically a more open-knit, fruitier, softer version of the Les Suchots. Already quite round and expansive on the palate, the Les Chaumes is well colored, fat yet elegant, ripe, and full bodied. The Les Suchots is exceptionally concentrated, seductive, very deep in color, quite aromatic, and has 3 to 7 years further aging potential. The Clos Vougeot was closed when I tasted it and seemed tough, more akin to a 1983 than 1985 in terms of personality. It has a dark color and a promising level of concentration, but is extremely tight. The Romanée St.-Vivant is the second best wine from Arnoux in 1985. Rich and alcoholic, supple, expansive, and very complex in the nose (raspberries, new oak, and flowers), this wine should age nicely for a decade, yet I can hardly blame those who want to drink it now.

BERNARD BACHELET (CHASSAGNE-MONTRACHET)

1985 CHASSAGNE-MONTRACHET	84
1985 CÔTE DE BEAUNE-VILLAGES	85
1985 SANTENAY	85

These are three good examples of richly fruity, pure Pinot Noir. The Chassagne-Montrachet has less complexity, more tannin, and may just need more time to show all its attributes. The 1985 Côte de Beaune-Villages and Santenay are deeply colored, chewy, ripe wines that have silky textures, oodles of clean Pinot fruit, medium to full body, and a seductive sweetness and lushness. Anticipated maturity: 1990–1993.

GASTON BARTHOD-NOËLLAT (CHAMBOLLE-MUSIGNY)

1985 BOURGOGNE	83
1985 CHAMBOLLE-MUSIGNY AUX BEAUX BRUNS	86
1985 CHAMBOLLE-MUSIGNY LES CHARMES	87
1985 CHAMBOLLE-MUSIGNY LES CRAS	87

According to Barthod, the 1985s are the best wines made at this estate since the 1959s and 1978s. He also said something similar about his 1988s. The generic Bourgogne is deep in color, plummy, and should provide pleasant drinking until around 1992. The Les Charmes has very good color, a rich, spicy, pure bouquet bursting with Pinot fruit, medium to full body, and plenty of length. It will be at its best between 1990–1995. The Les Cras, a Premier Cru vineyard near Bonnes Mares, is less seductive, but richer, more tannic, and loaded with ripe fruit. It should reach full maturity between 1990–1996. Last, the style of Beaux Bruns seems to fall somewhere between the silky, voluptuous finesse and fruitiness of Les Charmes, and the fuller-bodied, more tannic Les Cras.

ADRIEN BELLAND (SANTENAY)

1985 CHAMBERTIN	86
1985 CORTON CLOS DE LA VIGNE SAINT	85
1985 CORTON LES GRÈVES	87
1985 CORTON LES PERRIÈRES	85
1985 SANTENAY LES GRAVIÈRES	85
1985 SANTENAY CLOS GENÊT	85
1985 SANTENAY LA COMME	86

Belland's 1985s, if not exceptional, are full-bodied, rich, flavorful, dark ruby-colored wines with plenty of palate presence. Given the ratings, which are all approximately the same, the best values are his Santenays. The Clos Genêt, from a less publicized vineyard, has broad, fat, creamy flavors, gobs of fruit, plenty of color, and a full-bodied, lengthy finish. It should last until at least 1995. The La Comme has a similar texture, but tasted slightly more concentrated. The Gravières has a spicy note to its bouquet, and a more dusty, tannic texture. Among the three Cortons, the Grèves, made from 25-year-old vines, has loads of rich black cherry fruit, impressive length and depth, and should easily age well until 1995. By comparison, the Perrières tasted fat but less complex. The Clos de la Vigne Saint, certainly the most famous of the three Cortons, has very high acidity and an austere, tart personality, but plenty of underlying fruit and depth. It is the only wine here that requires 5 to 7 years of cellaring before drinking. The Chambertin is quite good, but hardly lives up to its name. The sweet, ripe bouquet offers plenty of appeal, but the wine seems to lack concentration and has a soupy texture. Anticipated maturity: 1990–1995, except for the slow-to-develop Clos de la Vigne Saint.

DENIS BERTHAUT (FIXIN)

1985 FIXIN	81
1985 FIXIN LES ARVELETS	86
1985 FIXIN LE CLOS	85
1985 FIXIN LES CRAIS	83
1985 GEVREY-CHAMBERTIN	84

You will not find great wine here, but you will find good, forceful burgundy with excellent aging qualities. Berthaut's 1985s are softer and more openly fruity than usual, with medium to full body, good tannins for 2 to 6 years of cellaring, and clear, pure Pinot Noir flavors. The Les Crais is distinguished by a minty, very spicy bouquet. The Le Clos is rich, berry scented, and lush, and the Les Arvelets is the most concentrated and the best wine of the Berthaut stable. Anticipated maturity: 1990–1993.

DOMAINE BERTHEAU (CHAMBOLLE-MUSIGNY)

1985 BONNES MARES	88
1985 CHAMBOLLE-MUSIGNY	85
1985 CHAMBOLLE-MUSIGNY LES AMOUREUSES	87

Bertheau's 1985s look very good. Supple, richly fruity, almost jammy, with loads of sweet, smoky, raspberry fruit, they are unfiltered and have a small sandy sediment. The Villages wine, the Chambolle-Musigny, will have to be drunk by 1991–1992, but given its round, generous, ripe flavors and velvety texture, no one will object. The Les Amoureuses is fuller and deeper, and utterly delicious—rich, sweet, round, fat, and bursting with fruit. It is surpassed only by the Bonnes Mares, a dark ruby-colored, opulent, abundantly fruity wine with excellent ripeness and length. It has the potential to cellar well until 1992–1995.

DOMAINE BILLARD-GONNET (POMMARD)

1985 BEAUNE LES MONTREVENOTS	83
1985 POMMARD	83
1985 POMMARD LES CHAPONNIÈRES	?
1985 POMMARD CLOS DE VERGER	85
1985 POMMARD LES RUGIENS	87

Billard-Gonnet produces tannic, lean, classic wines that are slow to develop. His wines are usually among the least impressive burgundies when young. Most vintages need a good 4 to 5 years to shed their cloaks of tannin. Even the 1985s, a precocious, flattering vintage to taste young, are firm and introverted. The Beaune Les Montrevenots has a well-developed, moderately intense, cherry fruitiness, a nice touch of toasty oak, and a soft texture. The Pommard is firm and well structured, but tannic and closed. There is a noticeable leap in quality starting with the Clos de Verger, which has a lovely oaky, black cherry–scented bouquet, rich, long flavors, and enough tannin to merit cellaring for 4 to 5 years before drinking. The Les Chaponnières is very tannic and quite closed, though the color is deep. I found the wine very difficult to judge. The top wine here is the Rugiens, a deeply colored, full-bodied, rich, concentrated wine that has plenty of extract and quite a finish. It should be ready to drink by 1991–1992.

BITOUZET-PRIEUR (VOLNAY)

1985 VOLNAY	83
1985 VOLNAY LES AUSSY	85
1985 VOLNAY CLOS DES CHÊNES	88
1985 VOLNAY PITURES	86
1985 VOLNAY TAILLEPIEDS	90

The village of Volnay has many well-known and good, reliable wine-makers. Yet one of the best and surprisingly least known is Vincent Bitouzet. His 1985s are the finest wines I have tasted from him. A believer in hot fermentations (35° C) to extract color, tannin, and fruit, Bitouzet's 1985s are all rich, deeply colored, quite concentrated wines that exhibit considerable flavor purity. All were filtered with the Kissel-guhr System prior to bottling, except for the splendid Taillepieds. The Volnay is a lively, well-colored, solid wine with a chunky, fleshy fruiti-ness. It should provide pleasant drinking until 1990–1991. The Volnay Les Aussy is fat, richly fruity, concentrated and expansive on the palate with plenty of raspberry fruit. The Volnay Pitures, on the other hand, is tannic, burly, rich, and robust with a good deal of body. It leans toward Pommard in its style. The Volnay Clos des Chênes, normally the best wine as the vineyard is one of the best in Volnay, is a gorgeous wine with layers of rich cherry and raspberry fruit, full body, and a sublime elegance and finesse. It should be at its best in the decade of the nineties. However, the star of the 1985 vintage is the Volnay Tail-lepieds, a majestic, rich, deep, layered wine with superb extract, and a wonderfully pure, balanced feel on the palate. The wine is a near-perfect Volnay, and while quite accessible now, should drink well until at least 1999.

LUCIEN BOILLOT (GEVREY-CHAMBERTIN)

1985 CÔTES DE NUITS-VILLAGES	84
1985 GEVREY-CHAMBERTIN	78
1985 GEVREY-CHAMBERTIN LES CHERBAUDES	85
1985 GEVREY-CHAMBERTIN LES CORBEAUX	83
1985 NUITS ST.-GEORGES LES PRULIERS	85
1985 POMMARD LES CROIX NOIRES	83
1985 VOLNAY-CRU DES ANGLES	84

These are respectable 1985s, but Lucien Boillot is not one of my favorite growers in Burgundy. The 1985s are cleanly made in an ancient style. Tannic, aged in old barrels, they all lean toward coarseness. Perhaps with 4 to 5 years of cellaring they will reveal more charm and grace. The Côte de Nuits-Villages is almost as good as the other wines. Robust, spicy, and deeply colored, it has plenty of presence on the palate. The Gevrey-Chambertin is especially hard and austere for a 1985. The

Les Cherbaudes shows much more fruit and plenty of tannin, yet has better balance and more concentration than the closed, tough Les Corbeaux. I had similar problems with both the lean, sinewy Volnay and angular Pommard. Potentially the best wine, the Nuits St.-Georges Les Pruliers offers enough rich, black cherry fruit to match the fierce tannins.

BOURÉE PÈRE ET FILS (GEVREY-CHAMBERTIN)

1985 BEAUNE PREMIER CRU	86
1985 BONNES MARES	86
1985 CHAMBERTIN	90
1985 CHAMBOLLE-MUSIGNY	82
1985 CHAMBOLLE-MUSIGNY LES AMOUREUSES	90
1985 CHAMBOLLE-MUSIGNY LES CHARMES	87
1985 CHARMES-CHAMBERTIN	91
1985 CLOS DE LA ROCHE	96
1985 CÔTE DE BEAUNE-VILLAGES	80
1985 CÔTE DE NUITS-VILLAGES	84
1985 GEVREY-CHAMBERTIN LES CAZETIERS	87
1985 GEVREY-CHAMBERTIN CLOS DE LA JUSTICE	90
1985 GEVREY-CHAMBERTIN LAVAUX ST.-JACQUES	90
1985 MOREY ST.-DENIS	83
1985 NUITS ST.-GEORGES	80
1985 NUITS ST.-GEORGES LES VAUCRAINS	89
1985 VOSNE-ROMANÉE	80

The Bourée firm is a small *négociant* located right on the main thoroughfare in Gevrey-Chambertin. For some years this quality enterprise has been run by M. Vallet, the nephew of the late Pierre Bourée. The wines are made in what is clearly the *ancienne méthode*, meaning there is no destemming here, an extremely long *cuvaison* of 21–26 days, a high temperature fermentation, the least possible racking, never any filtration, and bottling of the wine by barrel. One wishes there were more people like Vallet in Burgundy. Vallet thinks his 1985s are the best wines made by the firm since the 1949s. In general, I found the 1985s to be richly colored, very structured wines with the best of them quite special. At the lower level of the burgundy hierarchy, the Beaune Premier Cru showed surprising depth, richness, and structure. It should cellar well for 5 to 10 years after the vintage. The Côte de Nuits-Villages was deeply colored, tannic, and quite big. Among the Villages wines from the Côte de Nuits, while the Vosne-Romanée was boring and one dimensional, the Morey St.-Denis had plenty of power, depth, structure, and character, as did the softer, more seductive and perfumed Chambolle-Musigny. The Nuits St.-Georges was extremely tannic, closed, and not at all easy to evaluate.

However, the real stars of the Bourée house in 1985 are the Premiers Crus and Grands Crus. Of course, Clos de la Justice in Gevrey-Chambertin is not a Premier Cru, but Vallet owns this property and makes what is certainly the finest red burgundy from the "wrong" or eastern side of the Route Nationale 74 that runs through Burgundy's famed Côte d'Or. I thought the 1985 Clos de la Justice the finest example I have ever tasted of this wine. Deep ruby with a super bouquet of ripe plummy fruit and hickory smoke, this full-bodied wine is quite concentrated and very long. It should be at its peak between 1990–2005. I marginally preferred it to the Chambolle-Musigny Les Charmes, which has layers of velvety ripe fruit but seemed less complex and concentrated. The Les Amoureuses has great extract of flavor, a rich, supple texture, quite an expansive feel on the palate, and good tannins. The Bonnes Mares inexplicably tasted much lighter, and while certainly very good, lacked the breadth of the Les Amoureuses. The Nuits St.-Georges Les Vaucrains tasted enormous, but also broodingly backward and tannic. It will need at least 6 to 10 years after the vintage until it is ready to drink. Vallet's selections from the Gevrey-Chambertin appellation are usually the top wines from this *négociant*. The two Premier Cru vineyards, Lavaux St.-Jacques and Les Cazetiers, are real insiders' wines, not only here but from other producers as well. Both vineyards have a beautiful exposure and often approach Grand Cru quality. The difference between the two wines at Bourée is that the Lavaux is more fleshy, supple, and open-knit, but has super fruit and length. In contrast, the Cazetiers is more tannic and savage, yet even deeper and richer; it will take more time to reach maturity. I would estimate the Lavaux peaking between 1989 and 1996, the Cazetiers between 1992–2005. For pure elegance and oodles of plump, succulent, berry fruit, the Charmes-Chambertin offers a truly hedonistic drinking experience. It is round, generous, and explosively fruity. The Chambertin is tannic, a trifle too oaky, and less impressive. Vallet's greatest wine in 1985, and one of the superstars of the vintage, is his Clos de la Roche. One hundred cases (4 barrels) were produced of this wine, which is almost black in color and possesses the type of flavor intensity and exceptional length and richness that I have rarely seen in red burgundy. It is a staggeringly great red burgundy that will drink superbly for the rest of this century.

CHÂTEAU DE CHAMBOLLE-MUSIGNY (CHAMBOLLE-MUSIGNY)

1985 BONNES MARES	86
1985 CHAMBOLLE-MUSIGNY LES AMOUREUSES	85
1985 LE MUSIGNY	87
1985 LE MUSIGNY VIEILLES VIGNES	90

This highly reputed domaine produces elegant, rather delicate wines that get a mighty dosage of aging in new oak barrels—too much so in my view. That being said, the 1985s are very fragrant, aromatic wines with a great deal of toasty vanillin aroma. The colors of these wines are deceptively light, but they have plenty of graceful, silky, smooth berry fruit flavors, especially the splendid cuvée of old vines from the Grand Cru vineyard of Musigny. These are wisest drunk within 5–7 years of the vintage.

DOMAINE DE LA CHARRIÈRE (SANTENAY)

1985 SANTENAY LA COMME	87
1985 SANTENAY LA MALADIÈRE	85

Both these 1985s are deep ruby in color, full bodied, rich in flavor, and have the potential to age until 1993–1997. The Maladière is more accessible. In fact, it is delicious right now—round, supple and elegant, with plenty of berry fruit character and Pinot Noir well displayed. The Santenay La Comme is a serious wine. It is dense, ripe, full bodied, very concentrated, and surprisingly long, and the tannin level suggests it will keep until the mid- to late nineties.

F. CHAUVENET (NUITS ST.-GEORGES)

1985 BEAUNE LES TEURONS	78
1985 CHARMES-CHAMBERTIN	87

1985 CLOS ST.-DENIS	87
1985 CORTON	85
1985 CÔTE DE BEAUNE-VILLAGES	82
1985 ECHÉZEAUX	85
1985 NUITS ST.-GEORGES LES PERRIÈRES	80
1985 POMMARD LES EPENOTS	84
1985 SANTENAY	78

This *négociant* has recently turned out some good red wines. All the wines are "correct," well-colored, very fruity, soft burgundies that miss being special because they lack personality and individuality. Nevertheless, they are tasty wines. The top two wines are the fat, rich, velvety, succulent Charmes-Chambertin, and the more classically rendered Clos St.-Denis. Both wines are hard to resist because of their voluptuous fruit and soft tannins, and both should age nicely until 1992–1994. After these two wines, the lighter, but still effusively fruity, darkly colored Corton, and the elegant, fragrant Echézeaux looked good. As for the other wines, they all have very fine deep ruby color and good ripe fruit, but several are straightforward and one dimensional.

J. CHAUVENET (NUITS ST.-GEORGES)

1985 NUITS ST.-GEORGES	85
1985 NUITS ST.-GEORGES LES BOUSSELOTS	90
1985 NUITS ST.-GEORGES LES VAUCRAINS	90
1985 VOSNE-ROMANÉE	87

Jean Chauvenet, a small grower, should not be confused with the *négociant* reviewed above. They are not related. His 1985s are the finest wines he has yet made and were bottled without any fining or filtration. The Villages Vosne-Romanée has a deep color, a lush, rich, blackberry fruitiness, and makes a sweet impression on the palate from the great ripeness attained in the 1985 vintage. The Villages Nuits St.-Georges is much more tannic and closed, although it should drink well by 1992. Chauvenet made two great wines in 1985. His Les Vaucrains, almost black in color, is a wine of enormous richness, has expansive, pure

Pinot Noir flavors, and awesome length. Expect it to peak between 1990–2000. The Les Bousselots should turn out to be every bit as good. It is also virtually black in color, extremely rich, full bodied, long, and packed with flavor, but also much more tannic. It should reach its plateau of maturity between 1992–2005.

ROBERT CHEVILLON (NUITS ST.-GEORGES)

1985 NUITS ST.-GEORGES	85
1985 NUITS ST.-GEORGES LES CAILLES	90
1985 NUITS ST.-GEORGES LES PERRIÈRES	87
1985 NUITS ST.-GEORGES LES RONCIÈRES	89
1985 NUITS ST.-GEORGES LES SAINT-GEORGES	?
1985 NUITS ST.-GEORGES LES VAUCRAINS	92

The 1985s are much more flattering to the taste than Chevillon's large-scaled, massive 1983s. The Nuits St.-Georges is deliciously ripe, fruity, well colored, and well endowed for a Villages wine. It should be drunk by 1992–1993. The Perrières is similarly precocious, opulently fruity, soft, broadly flavored, and ideal for consuming between 1992–1994. With Chevillon's Roncières, one not only sees sumptuous levels of Pinot fruit, but also more structure, body, and tannin, no doubt from an elevated use of new oak. The Roncières should offer ideal drinking until at least 1994. Two splendid wines made by Chevillon in 1985 are Les Cailles and Les Vaucrains. Les Cailles, a rich, decadent, explosively fruity wine, comes from a field where the vines average 50 years of age. It is very deep and profound, and can be drunk now or cellared until 1995–1997. The enormous bouquet of smoky oak and stupendous fruit of the Les Vaucrains left me searching for new adjectives. Absolutely gorgeous and bursting at the seams with fruit, this hedonistic wine will be impossible to resist drinking now, but it has the balance and structure to last until 1995–1997. Chevillon had some problems with his Les Saint-Georges, and he hopes, with a longer time in cask, the wine will come together.

BRUNO CLAIR (MARSANNAY)

1985 CÔTE DE NUITS-VILLAGES	83
1985 FIXIN LA CROIX BLANCHE	83

1985 MARSANNAY	82
1985 SAVIGNY LES DOMINODES	85

Clair's 1985 Marsannay is good, but simple and uncomplicated. The Côte de Nuits-Villages is round, well colored, but lacking a bit in body. Perhaps it has been over-filtered. The Fixin La Croix Blanche seems to have the same absence of mid-range. His Savigny Les Dominodes, made from old vines, had a very deep color, seemed rich but was also dry and very tannic in the finish. Normally this wine is a real heart stopper. At the insistence of his agent, Tim Marshall, Bruno Clair has begun to use the tricky Kisselguhr System to filter and fine his red wines. Could this be the reason these wines tasted less impressive than I had hoped?

CLOS FRANTIN (BEAUNE)

1985 BICHOT BEAUNE MONTÉE ROUGE	55
1985 BICHOT CHÂTEAU DE DRACY	65
1985 BICHOT POMMARD LES RUGIENS	72
1985 CLOS DE VOUGEOT CLOS FRANTIN	90
1985 ECHÉZEAUX CLOS FRANTIN	87
1985 GEVREY-CHAMBERTIN CLOS FRANTIN	78
1985 GRANDS ECHÉZEAUX CLOS FRANTIN	90
1985 NUITS ST.-GEORGES CLOS FRANTIN	76
1985 VOSNE-ROMANÉE LES MALCONSORTS CLOS FRANTIN	92

This gigantic *négociant* produces an ocean of insipid, dull wine under the name Bichot and several *sous-noms*, or second labels, which I find overpriced and not at all representative of Burgundy. Yet, the wines from their own Clos Frantin vineyards in the Cote de Nuits and their Chablis estate, Long-Depaquit, rank with the finest made in Burgundy. The ratings above are indicative of the huge dichotomy of wine styles from Bichot. The Bichot offerings taste cooked, dull, and are of no interest. The Clos Frantin wines range from standard quality to absolutely superb in the case of the rich, deep, powerful Clos Vougeot, the silky, seductive Echézeaux, the profound Grands Echézeaux, and the astonishingly rich, deep, sublime Vosne-Romanée Les Malconsorts. I did not taste them but there are usually an outstanding Clos Frantin

Richebourg and Corton as well. However, only tiny quantities of these
are produced.

CLOS DES LAMBRAYS (MOREY ST.-DENIS)

1985 CLOS DES LAMBRAYS	87
1985 MOREY ST.-DENIS	85

The Morey St.-Denis admirably exhibits the personality traits that make
the 1985 vintage for red burgundy so seductive and appealing. Deep in
color with a bouquet full of red fruit, the palate impression is one of
generosity and velvety flavors. It will drink well until 1992–1993. On
the other hand, the famous Clos des Lambrays is more tannic and
closed. It has plenty of ripe fruit and underlying depth, but needs
several years to shed its cloak of tannin.

EDMOND CORNU (LADOIX)

1985 ALOXE-CORTON	85
1985 ALOXE-CORTON LES MOUTOTTES	86
1985 CHOREY-LÈS-BEAUNE LES BONS ORES	82
1985 CORTON LES BRESSANDES	93
1985 LADOIX	84
1985 SAVIGNY-LÈS-BEAUNE	84

For those who say all burgundy is expensive, Cornu's prices are hard
to beat, particularly in view of the quality of his 1985s, which were
bottled unfined and unfiltered at the insistence of his American importer, Neal Rosenthal. The Chorey-Lès-Beaune has a straightforward
raspberry fruitiness, an elegant framework, and should age well until
1991–1993. The Ladoix is a big, rich, creamy textured wine with some
scents of new oak, great color, and a long, lush finish. The Savigny-
Lès-Beaune tasted much bigger still, exhibited plenty of tannin, full
body, and has excellent concentration. It should peak around 1991–
1993. Cornu really excels with his wines from Aloxe-Corton. The 1985
Aloxe-Corton is rich, fat, very plump and succulent with layers of fruit,
but also plenty of tannin and structure. The Aloxe-Corton Les Moutottes
offers more concentration, plenty of rich, plummy, ripe fruit, a nice
touch of toasty oak, and a powerful, long finish. It should make an

excellent bottle between 1991–1998. The Corton Les Bressandes is an astonishingly rich wine with sensational depth and length, a huge bouquet of raspberry fruit, toasty new oak, and flowery scents. It has outstanding balance and seems to explode on the palate because of its concentration. It comes from an old 1.3-acre vineyard with many of the vines planted in 1920. Do not miss it!

ALBERT DEREY (FIXIN)

1985 FIXIN	82
1985 FIXIN LES HERVELETS	85
1985 MARSANNAY-CHANTE PERDRIX	81

Here are some wines that offer uncomplicated Pinot Noir flavors at decent prices. The Marsannay is a little rough at the edge and by no means delicate, but it is fruity and ripe. The Fixin has an earthy, cherry-scented bouquet, rather light to medium body, and a clean, fresh finish. It should be drunk up by 1992. The Fixin Les Hervelets, from one of the three best vineyards of this appellation, is a seductive, ripe, rich, soft, lush wine that should drink well until at least 1993.

JOSEPH DROUHIN (BEAUNE)

1985 ALOXE-CORTON	85
1985 BEAUNE CHAMP PIMONT	83
1985 BEAUNE CLOS DES MOUCHES	87
1985 BONNES MARES	87
1985 CHAMBERTIN	87
1985 CHAMBOLLE-MUSIGNY	82
1985 CHAMBOLLE-MUSIGNY PREMIER CRU	85
1985 CHARMES-CHAMBERTIN	92
1985 CHASSAGNE-MONTRACHET	83
1985 CHOREY-LÈS-BEAUNE	78
1985 CLOS DE LA ROCHE	86
1985 CLOS VOUGEOT	88
1985 CORTON LES BRESSANDES	86

1985 CÔTE DE BEAUNE-VILLAGES	78
1985 ECHÉZEAUX	90
1985 GEVREY-CHAMBERTIN	81
1985 GEVREY-CHAMBERTIN LAVAUX ST.-JACQUES	87
1985 GRANDS ECHÉZEAUX	88
1985 GRIOTTE-CHAMBERTIN	88
1985 MONTHÉLIE	82
1985 MOREY ST.-DENIS	83
1985 MUSIGNY	87
1985 NUITS ST.-GEORGES	78
1985 NUITS ST.-GEORGES LES RONCIÈRES	85
1985 POMMARD	84
1985 POMMARD LES EPENOTS	87
1985 SANTENAY	84
1985 SAVIGNY-LÈS-BEAUNE	83
1985 VOLNAY	84
1985 VOLNAY CLOS DES CHÊNES	87
1985 VOSNE-ROMANÉE	75
1985 VOSNE-ROMANÉE LES BEAUX MONTS	86
1985 VOSNE-ROMANÉE LES SUCHOTS	87

The 1985s from this famous firm are all impeccably clean, correct, well-made wines. Drouhin has managed to preserve the individual identity of each appellation as the wines do not taste alike. There is of course a house style, but that can be said of the wines from a small grower as well.

With respect to the Côte de Beaune wines, the majority of them tasted like ideal restaurant wines—richly fruity, easy to drink and understand, and totally correct for their appellations, but not filled with a great measure of character. However, there are several notable exceptions. The Beaune Clos des Mouches is a deeply colored, broadly flavored wine bursting with ripe cherry fruit. It will drink well until 1991–1992. The Volnay Clos des Chênes has more of a supple, rich raspberry fruitiness married nicely with a touch of new oak. It should keep well until 1992–1997. The most impressive of the Côte de Beaune red wines is the Pommard Les Epenots. Surprisingly big, bold, and forceful with plenty of underlying depth and body, this concentrated, alcoholic, tannic wine should age well until the late nineties. The Corton Les Bressandes is even more powerful, but I thought I detected a touch of overripeness in the bouquet. It is a fleshy, rich, high-alcohol wine that seems a bit out of step with Robert Drouhin's winemaking philosophy.

When one tastes all the Côte de Nuits offerings, once past the bland Villages of Nuits St.-Georges, Chambolle-Musigny, Morey St.-Denis, Vosne-Romanée, and Gevrey-Chambertin, the quality takes a quantum leap. There is more color, substance, and richness to both the Nuits St.-Georges Les Roncières and Chambolle-Musigny Premier Cru. Both should keep well for upwards of a decade. Among the two Vosne-Romanées, the Les Suchots looks especially good, with an intense spicy, cinnamon-scented bouquet. It is a full-bodied wine with excellent color and depth. Even more robust, ageworthy, and tannic, yet concentrated and balanced, is the Lavaux St.-Jacques, a big, chewy wine to put away until 1995–1997.

At the Grands Crus level, all the wines are excellent, except for the Echézeaux and Charmes-Chambertin, which are superb. The Echézeaux has a haunting and heady bouquet of violets, crushed berry fruit, and new oak. Extremely elegant, supple, rich, and concentrated, it is enticing to drink now and should be even better over the next two to four years. The Charmes-Chambertin is a great wine, filled with layers of ripe, rich fruit, a complex, full-intensity bouquet of toasty new oak, and a supple, velvety texture, but enough tannins to ensure a decade of longevity. As for the other Grands Crus, the Clos Vougeot is an effusively fruity wine, yet it is quite powerful and full-bodied. Its low acidity suggests current drinkability, but there is plenty of tannin lurking beneath the surface. The Clos de la Roche is very good but herbaceous. On the palate, it is robust and rich, and should be at its best between 1991–1995. The Grands Echézeaux has a sweet, ripe, broad, plummy fruitiness, medium to full body, super ripeness and length, but less complexity and sheer class than the aforementioned Echézeaux. I suspect the Bonnes Mares will ultimately merit a higher score as it is opulent, quite tannic, but deep, well colored, and very long. The Musigny is more open, more perfumed, and easier to evaluate. It is not a big wine, but is harmonious, well balanced, and richly fruity. Few Chambertins live up to the majesty that the name and price tag certainly suggest. Drouhin's Chambertin is dark ruby, has plenty of extract, is ripe and concentrated as well as tannic, but does not seem profound or special. It should be cellared until about 1992, but will keep for ten years after that. Last, the Griotte-Chambertin is oozing with berry fruit, has a super bouquet of toasty oak and jammy fruit, full body, a velvety texture, and excellent length. It will peak between 1989–1996.

DOMAINE DUJAC-JACQUES SEYSSES
(MOREY ST.-DENIS)

1985 BONNES MARES	97
1985 CHARMES-CHAMBERTIN	94
1985 CLOS DE LA ROCHE	96
1985 CLOS ST.-DENIS	92
1985 ECHÉZEAUX	90
1985 GEVREY-CHAMBERTIN AUX COMBOTTES	89
1985 MOREY ST.-DENIS	86

This is one of the finest estates in Burgundy. Unfortunately, not everyone in America understands these wines, particularly those restaurants and lazy merchants who are at a loss to explain the positive quality of wines with sandy sediment in the bottle. Seysses will not filter his wines, and after six months to several years, depending on the vintage, a fine sediment will form—a natural occurrence in handmade wines. Such wines are also very vulnerable to heat prostration because they are alive. Perhaps America's fanatical obsession with squeaky-clean, crystal-clear bottles of wines that have had much of their flavor eviscerated by numerous sterile filtrations is why Seysses now only sells 20% of his crop to America. What a tragedy! His 1985s are the finest wines he has made in an already illustrious career, greater even than his glorious 1978s. The Villages Morey St.-Denis is good, fragrant, complex, deep, and lush. It should drink well until 1993–1995. His Gevrey-Chambertin aux Combottes has a full intensity, very spicy, rich, multidimensional bouquet, and deep, rich, flowing flavors that last and last. It will keep well until the end of this decade. Among the Grands Crus, all aged in 100% new oak, there are enough splendid wines to satisfy the most demanding palate. Ascending the ladder of quality, one starts with the lightest and most elegant, the Echézeaux, a great wine, particularly in view of the fact that the vines were only 5 years old at the time of this vintage. Ripe, rich aromas of strawberry and cherry fruit jump from the glass. Medium bodied with super finesse, this is the earliest maturing wine of the Dujac stable. The Clos St.-Denis has a very deep color, an intense, ripe, spicy, very fragrant, penetrating bouquet. Full bodied and rather tannic, it explodes at the finish. It should peak between 1990–2000. The Charmes-Chambertin is loaded with seductive qualities. An open-knit, fabulous bouquet of toasty oak, flowers, berry fruit, and oriental spices is followed by a wine that is very concentrated, long, lush, and exciting. The last two are superstars that offer everything one could really ever want in a burgundy. The Clos de la Roche is the most powerful and concentrated wine the domaine made in 1985. A blockbuster wine that should evolve until 1997–2002, it has great color, and a remarkably opulent, expansive texture on the palate. The Bonnes Mares tasted slightly more concentrated and less tannic, and I was not surprised that my original tasting notes contained the words "great" three times and "extraordinary" twice. One can make no mistake with Dujac's 1985s, provided the importers ship them properly. The trek to the West Coast through the Panama Canal offers great danger for unfiltered wines unless the importers use temperature controlled "reefer" containers.

RENÉ ENGEL (VOSNE-ROMANÉE)

1985 CLOS VOUGEOT	89
1985 ECHÉZEAUX	85
1985 GRANDS ECHÉZEAUX	90
1985 VOSNE-ROMANÉE	83
1985 VOSNE-ROMANÉE LES BRÛLÉES	?

Engel thinks the 1985s are the finest wines made at the estate since 1959 and 1964. The Vosne-Romanée tasted alcoholic, but there is enough fruit and color for drinking until 1990–1991. While the Echézeaux tasted surprisingly light, the color is dark and the wine exhibits good ripeness. I thought the Vosne-Romanée Les Brûlées had excellent flavors and depth, but unfortunately there is a real barnyard aroma that is quite bothersome. Certainly no one will complain about the Grands Echézeaux, a wine that is rich, deep ruby in color, long, with a savory, lush fruitiness. It should age well until 1995–1997. The same can be said for the Clos Vougeot. The 1985 is opulent, deep, expansive on the palate, has the most concentration of all the Engel wines, and 13.5% natural alcohol.

J. FAIVELEY (NUITS ST.-GEORGES)

1985 BEAUNE LES CHAMPS PIMONTS	86
1985 CHAMBERTIN-CLOS DE BÈZE	94
1985 CHARMES-CHAMBERTIN	98
1985 CLOS DE LA ROCHE	92
1985 CORTON CLOS DES CORTONS	93
1985 ECHÉZEAUX	89
1985 FIXIN	78
1985 LATRICIÈRES-CHAMBERTIN	96
1985 MERCUREY CLOS DES MYGLANDS	86
1985 MERCUREY CLOS DU ROI	87
1985 MERCUREY LES MAUVARENNES	84
1985 MOREY ST.-DENIS CLOS DES ORMES	94
1985 NUITS ST.-GEORGES	85
1985 NUITS ST.-GEORGES CLOS DE LA MARÉCHALE	87
1985 NUITS ST.-GEORGES LES DAMODES	88
1985 NUITS ST.-GEORGES LES SAINT-GEORGES	91

The Faiveleys are important vineyard holders in Mercurey, and their three offerings were the best Mercureys I tasted except for those of Yves de Launay. The Les Mauvarennes is not terribly distinguished, but offers a soft, ripe, sweet, round texture and good fruit, and will be delightful to drink until at least 1992. The Clos des Myglands, a wine I used to drink cases of (the 1971 and 1970) in law school, is excellent in 1985. It is quite a ripe, rich, generous wine with a cascade of berry fruit. Even better is the Clos du Roi, a very rich, creamy textured, smoky wine oozing with sweet layers of fruit. The Fixin is a decent wine, but I could not get excited by it. The Nuits St.-Georges has a rich, perfumed bouquet of red fruit, a concentrated, full-bodied feel on the palate, and lovely finish.

The three Premiers Crus from Nuits St.-Georges range from excellent to outstanding. The Clos de la Maréchale is surprisingly deep, rich, long, and ripe with layers of velvety fruit; it should age well until 1992–1995. The Les Damodes is even deeper, more tannic, with a splendid bouquet of red fruits, full body, and plenty of length. It will keep until

1992–1998. The Les Saint-Georges, of which there are only 100 cases, is a fabulously rich, multidimensional wine that is extremely concentrated and has super length. It should be at its best between 1990–2000. The Beaune Les Champs Pimonts is a fat, plump, seductive wine that offers immediate gratification. The Morey St.-Denis Clos des Ormes is another very special wine (only 95 cases were produced). The explosive bouquet of ripe plums, cherries, toasty oak and violets is followed by a very rich, long, velvety, full-bodied wine that has enough tannin to ensure cellaring until 1997.

The Faiveley Grands Crus are all exceptional. The Echézeaux, full of finesse and elegance as well as an amazing level of fruit, will offer good drinking until the late nineties. The Clos de la Roche tastes more robust, has great length, a fabulous "presence" on the palate, and amazing length. It will peak between 1990–2000. Shockingly, the Latricières-Chambertin was even better; my notes said "staggering depth." Like all these wines, it has very deep color, more tannin than others, and unbelievable concentration. While the Chambertin-Clos de Bèze and Corton Clos des Cortons were the most backward, and will not approach maturity until 1993, each is enormously concentrated, loaded with fruit extract, tannin, and potential. One of the greatest wines of the vintage is the Charmes-Chambertin (125 cases produced). What can I say about it? I remember it as if I had a glass in my hand as I write this. Virtually perfect, this marvelously concentrated wine has a bouquet that is unbelievable, super depth, layers of fruit, and a finish that persists and persists. It should age well until the turn of the century.

DOMAINE FOREY PÈRE ET FILS (VOSNE-ROMANÉE)

1985 ECHÉZEAUX	86
1985 NUITS ST.-GEORGES LES PERRIÈRES	84
1985 VOSNE-ROMANÉE	83
1985 VOSNE-ROMANÉE LES GAUDICHOTS	87

Their Vosne-Romanée is good, quite fruity, and charming. The Nuits St.-Georges Les Perrières is medium bodied, supple, somewhat alcoholic, but good. The Vosne-Romanée Les Gaudichots did not taste like La Tâche, but is certainly very good with long, velvety flavors and a very fine color. The Echézeaux has a deep color and plenty of substance, but tasted closed yet promising.

DOMAINE GELIN-MOLIN (FIXIN)

1985 CHAMBERTIN-CLOS DE BÈZE	86
1985 FIXIN CLOS DU CHAPITRE	84
1985 GEVREY-CHAMBERTIN	85

This firm has provided me with some notable values over the years, particularly their Premier Cru Fixins, which are never especially elegant, but robust and hearty. That being said, I had hoped that the 1985s would be better. They are good, and for value the chewy, chocolatey, deep, spicy, powerful Gevrey-Chambertin will be hard to beat. I preferred it to the Fixin Clos du Chapitre, which tasted compact, lean, and a little too dry and hard edged. Last, the Chambertin-Clos de Bèze has oodles of very ripe, unctuous Pinot Noir fruit. I am a little concerned that it is too ripe, but it does offer a huge mouthful of wine and will last until 1995–1997.

GEOFFREY PÈRE ET FILS (GEVREY-CHAMBERTIN)

1985 GEVREY-CHAMBERTIN	83
1985 GEVREY-CHAMBERTIN CLOS PRIEUR	86
1985 GEVREY-CHAMBERTIN PREMIER CRU	85
1985 MAZIS-CHAMBERTIN	88

I have had no previous experience with this estate, but several friends in France told me the quality was on the upswing so I paid a visit to their cellars.

There is a very fine Gevrey-Chambertin Clos Prieur, and a ruby/purple, intensely oaky, powerful Mazis-Chambertin. These are not what I call classical red burgundies, but they are intensely colored, very oaky, satisfying wines.

ARMAND GIRARDIN (POMMARD)

1985 POMMARD LES CHARMES	87
1985 POMMARD LES EPENOTS	90
1985 POMMARD LES RUGIENS	90

The wines of Armand Girardin, the Mayor of Pommard, are among the blackest-colored Pinot Noirs I have seen. The Charmes is fat, succulent, sweet, unctuous, and chocolatey; it should offer a lot of pleasure until at least 1995. The Epenots, with its black/ruby color, astonishing bouquet of toasty, smoky oak and ripe fruit, super concentrated flavors, full body, and sledgehammer finish, made quite an impression. It should last until 1995–1997. Not surprisingly, the Rugiens is even better, more complex, again incredibly concentrated, pure, and long.

DOMAINE HENRI GOUGES (NUITS ST.-GEORGES)

1985 NUITS ST.-GEORGES	81
1985 NUITS ST.-GEORGES LES CHAIGNOTS	83
1985 NUITS ST.-GEORGES CLOS DES PORRETS	84
1985 NUITS ST.-GEORGES LES PRULIERS	86
1985 NUITS ST.-GEORGES LES SAINT-GEORGES	87
1985 NUITS ST.-GEORGES LES VAUCRAINS	86

The straight Nuits St.-Georges has good color, not much character or depth, but offers uncomplicated drinking for the early nineties. The Les Chaignots has a pronounced earthy, spicy character and cellaring potential until 1991–1992. The Clos des Porrets is somewhat light, but it has the most exotic and exciting bouquet, although it tails off in the finish. The Les Pruliers is a denser, richer wine with good color, an earthy, intense bouquet, lush, deep flavors, and some muscle in the finish. It should keep until 1993–1995. The Les Vaucrains should ultimately prove to be even better, as it is more tannic, richer, deeper, and longer lived. It should be at its best between 1990–2000. The Les Saint-Georges raises the level of tannins still further, has broad, expansive flavors, full body, and may prove to be the finest Gouges wine made since his legendary 1969s.

BERTRAND DE GRAMONT (NUITS ST.-GEORGES)

1985 NUITS ST.-GEORGES LES ALLOTS	86
1985 NUITS ST.-GEORGES LES HAUTS PRULIERS	90

This relatively new domaine, the result of a family dispute, is very tiny, with only 7.6 acres of vineyard, nearly half of which are in Les Hauts Pruliers. The wines are vinified and raised in the cellars, much like those of the other Gramont, only less new oak is present here. The Les Allots is a smooth, easy-to-drink wine exhibiting the hallmark of the 1985 vintage, an opulence of pure fruit well displayed. It will be at its best between 1991–1992. The Les Hauts Pruliers is, as the French say, "extra." Dense in color and extract, the super-ripe, sweet, almost jammy intensity of Pinot Noir fruit is a marvel to behold. It should be drunk between 1992–1994.

MARCHARD DE GRAMONT (NUITS ST.-GEORGES)

1985 ALOXE-CORTON LES MORAIS	87
1985 BOURGOGNE LA VIERGE ROMAINE	84
1985 CHOREY-LÈS-BEAUNE LES BEAUMONTS	86
1985 NUITS ST.-GEORGES LES DAMODES	90
1985 NUITS ST.-GEORGES LES HAUTS POIRETS	88
1985 NUITS ST.-GEORGES LA PERRIÈRE NOBLOT	87
1985 POMMARD LE CLOS BLANC	92

I was enchanted with the quality of the 1985s made here. They have wonderful deep colors, are bursting with supple, rich fruit, and yet also have the requisite structure to age through the decade of the nineties. Gramont keeps 50% of the stems in the fermentation and uses 30% new oak. Even the generic Bourgogne La Vierge Romaine is surprisingly ripe, fat, and filled with flavor. Another fine value is the Chorey-Lès-Beaune Les Beaumonts, a dark, ruby-colored wine that has amazing flavor purity and intensity for its appellation. Its ripe, precocious, opulent character made it difficult to resist drinking young. The Aloxe-Corton Les Morais is similarly styled, only slightly deeper, longer, and has a long, sweet, lush finish that is altogether captivating. All three Premiers Crus from Nuits St.-Georges have very dark colors, sumptuous flavors of ripe berry fruit, and expansive and multidimensional textures. The Damodes is a wine of breathtaking richness, power, and balance. All three wines should keep until the late nineties. At the summit of quality is Gramont's Pommard Le Clos Blanc, which produces a wine from a well-placed Premier Cru vineyard next to the famous Les Grands Epenots. The 1985, produced from vines that are between 50 and 70 years old, is packed with ripe cherry fruit, and has a magnificent bouquet of toasty oak and grilled almonds. Sensationally concentrated on the palate, this unctuous, deep wine is a privilege to drink. It should be at its best between now and 1995.

JEAN GRIVOT (VOSNE-ROMANÉE)

1985 CLOS VOUGEOT	88
1985 NUITS ST.-GEORGES LES BOUDOTS	86
1985 VOSNE-ROMANÉE	83

The young Étienne Grivot, who now runs this estate in addition to making the wines of the Domaine Jacqueline Jayer, is one of Burgundy's most promising talents. The emphasis here is on pure, elegant, finely etched Pinot Noir fruit. These wines are never too alcoholic or tannic, but rather are prototypes for the delicate style of Pinot. The Villages Vosne-Romanée, while light in color, offers moderately intense strawberry-scented fruit and a soft texture. The Nuits St.-Georges Les Boudots exhibits the same silky, strawberry, cherry fruitiness, a touch of toasty new oak, and plenty of depth underneath some good tannins. The Clos Vougeot should be cellared until 1990–1992, when it will fully open. It has exceptionally pure Pinot fruit, medium to full body, fine depth, and plenty of tannin.

ROBERT GROFFIER (MOREY ST.-DENIS)

1985 BONNES MARES	84
1985 CHAMBOLLE-MUSIGNY LES AMOUREUSES	83
1985 CHAMBOLLE-MUSIGNY LES SENTIERS	80

For reasons that Robert Groffier himself cannot explain, his 1985s are less successful than his 1986s. None of the three 1985s I tasted is as concentrated as his 1986s. They seem very soft and soupy, and lack definition. They are pleasing wines, but given the outstanding vineyards that Groffier owns, the investment made in 100% new oak, and Groffier's considerable talent, they should be much better than they are. Drink them up by 1991–1992.

JEAN GROS (VOSNE-ROMANÉE)

1985 RICHEBOURG	93
1985 VOSNE-ROMANÉE	85
1985 VOSNE-ROMANÉE CLOS DES RÉAS	89

There is not a more elegant woman in all of Burgundy than Madame Gros. And not surprisingly, her wines are usually impeccably made. Madame Gros thinks 1985 is her best vintage since 1978. The Vosne-Romanée has a deep color, plenty of ripeness and tannin, and needs to be cellared at least until 1990. The *monopole* Vosne-Romanée Clos des Réas is rich and perfumed in 1985, has a dark ruby color, makes a very broad impression on the palate, and should be ideal for drinking between 1990 and 2000. Of course, the Richebourg is extra special. The complex aromas of ripe fruit, flowers, and new oak (it is aged in 100% new casks) are altogether exciting. On the palate, the wine has outstanding richness, and plenty of body and tannin that will ensure greatness until at least the year 2000.

GROS FRÈRE ET SOEUR (VOSNE-ROMANÉE)

1985 CLOS VOUGEOT	89
1985 RICHEBOURG	90
1985 VOSNE-ROMANÉE	85

Bernard Gros makes an interesting wine that is usually very sweet and perfumed, smelling almost too much of cherry and cassis. The Vosne-Romanée reeked of apricot and cherries, as if someone had dumped several liters of eau-de-vie in the barrel. Rich, fat, and precocious, it is, however, a joy to drink. The Clos Vougeot, normally a real superstar as the vineyard is next to Musigny, has an amazing level of jammy fruit, but also a very elevated level of alcohol. In the finish, there is plenty of tannin. It is a very exotic wine that should keep well until 1995–1997. The Richebourg tastes highly chaptalized. It is quite sweet, but the level of fruit extract in the wine is amazing. The cherry and cassis flavors are remarkably vivid, as is the concentration of the wine.

ANTONIN GUYON (SAVIGNY-LÈS-BEAUNE)

1985 ALOXE-CORTON LES VERCOTS	83
1985 BOURGOGNE HAUTES-CÔTES DE NUITS	83
1985 CORTON CLOS DU ROI	87
1985 PERNAND-VERGELESSES	83

The Bourgogne Hautes-Côtes de Nuits has good color and a compact yet fruity taste, but it is one dimensional. The Pernand-Vergelesses shows some new oak in its bouquet, clean, ripe fruit, and a fleshy finish. The Aloxe-Corton Les Vercots has more depth, a rather rough texture, and is easily the most tannic of the Guyon wines. The best wine I tasted from Guyon was the Corton Clos du Roi, a wine with huge body, deep, long, chewy flavors, a boatload of tannin, and good acidity. It should round out by 1992–1993.

A. HUDELOT-NOËLLAT (VOSNE-ROMANÉE)

1985 CHAMBOLLE-MUSIGNY	85
1985 CLOS VOUGEOT	?
1985 VOSNE-ROMANÉE	78
1985 VOSNE-ROMANÉE LES MALCONSORTS	89

The wines of Hudelot-Noëllat are usually models of consistent excellence and elegance. Consequently, I was a little perplexed by the so-so showing of the Vosne-Romanée, and the odd, vegetal, peppery qualities of the Clos Vougeot. Perhaps they were just in an awkward stage when I tasted them. Certainly there is nothing wrong with the showing of the Chambolle-Musigny, which is full of berry fruit, has considerable charm, and a smooth, silky texture. It should be drunk between 1992–1995. The nearly outstanding Vosne-Romanée Les Malconsorts has very deep color, excellent depth of fruit, moderate tannins, full body, and a powerful, long finish.

LOUIS JADOT (BEAUNE)

1985 BEAUNE LES BOUCHEROTTES	85
1985 BEAUNE CLOS DES COUCHEREAUX	87
1985 BEAUNE CLOS DES URSULES	88
1985 BONNES MARES	92
1985 BOURGOGNE	84
1985 CHAMBERTIN-CLOS DE BÈZE	93
1985 CHAMBOLLE-MUSIGNY	83
1985 CHAMBOLLE-MUSIGNY LES AMOUREUSES	90
1985 CHAPELLE-CHAMBERTIN	92
1985 CHASSAGNE-MONTRACHET MORGEOT CLOS DE LA CHAPELLE (MAGENTA)	86

1985 CLOS VOUGEOT	91
1985 CORTON LES POUGETS	88
1985 CÔTE DE BEAUNE-VILLAGES	85
1985 GEVREY-CHAMBERTIN	82
1985 GEVREY-CHAMBERTIN CLOS ST.-JACQUES	91
1985 GEVREY-CHAMBERTIN ESTOURNELLES ST.-JACQUES	90
1985 HOSPICES DE BEAUNE CUVÉE HOSPITALIÈRES	87
1985 HOSPICES DE BEAUNE CUVÉE NICOLAS ROLIN	90
1985 MUSIGNY	87
1985 NUITS ST.-GEORGES	85
1985 NUITS ST.-GEORGES LES BOUDOTS	89
1985 NUITS ST.-GEORGES CLOS DES CORVÉES	90
1985 PERNAND-VERGELESSES	?
1985 VOSNE-ROMANÉE	74

Jadot's 1985s are loaded with aromas and flavors of red fruits, are judiciously complemented by one-third new oak barrels, and have super color, thanks in part to a very high fermentation temperature of 35°–36° C.

With respect to the red wines from the Côte de Beaune, even the generic Bourgogne exhibits character. The Beaune Les Boucherottes is fat, tasty, quite round, and generously fruity, and capable of lasting until 1996–1998. The Beaune Clos des Ursules tastes even more rich, full, and well structured, yet has the wonderful opulence that marks this very special vintage. The Corton Pougets tastes similar, although my notes read "explosive cherry fruit." Between the two Hospices de Beaune wines, the Cuvée Nicolas Rolin had super richness, a haunting perfume of red fruits and flowers, as well as great length. It will keep well until 1997–2000. The Cuvée Hospitalières has less complexity, but is very amply endowed with layers of fruit. The Pernand-Vergelesses was totally closed, hard, and impossible to evaluate.

Among the selections from the Côte de Nuits, the Villages wines are of standard quality except for the surprisingly rich, voluptuous Nuits St.-Georges. The Nuits St.-Georges Les Boudots jumped up a big notch in quality. Dark ruby, this wine is very rich, spicy, full bodied, plummy, and quite long. It should be gorgeous between 1989 and 1996. The Nuits

St.-Georges Clos des Corvées is a great burgundy, offering exceptional depth, length, as well as the telltale opulent fruitiness of this vintage, but also structure and harmony.

Both of the Premiers Crus of Gevrey-Chambertin, the Estournelles St.-Jacques and Clos St.-Jacques, are new offerings from the old Clair-Dau estate. Both are rich, broadly flavored, amazingly deep, pure wines with power adroitly balanced by elegance. I thought the Clos St.-Jacques had just a bit more length, but at this level I'm just splitting hairs. Jadot always makes a fine Clos Vougeot and in 1985 it is top flight, bursting at the seams with juicy, succulent fruit, but full bodied and deceptively tannic in the finish. The Chambolle-Musigny Les Amoureuses is appropriately named in 1985—you will love it for its flashy depth of fruit, elegance, and charm. It is slightly lighter than the Clos Vougeot, but no less seductive. I thought the Chapelle-Chambertin, made from 40-year-old vines, was one of the three best wines from Jadot in 1985, but I must admit its cascade of unctuous, berry fruit, toasty oakiness, and remarkable precociousness argue that this wine should be drunk young, by 1992–1995. The Bonnes Mares tasted vastly superior to the elegant but polite, understated Musigny. Perhaps the latter wine was overwhelmed by the sheer power and decadent level of fruit extract in the Bonnes Mares. Last, the Chambertin-Clos de Bèze, from the Clair-Dau estate vineyards, is the most enormous and structured of the 1985 Jadot red burgundies. It is also admirably concentrated, long, and impeccable. Most of these wines will drink exceptionally well young, but where well stored should last and evolve until 1995–2002.

HENRI JAYER (VOSNE-ROMANÉE)

1985 ECHÉZEAUX	93
1985 NUITS ST.-GEORGES LES MURGERS	90
1985 RICHEBOURG	96
1985 VOSNE-ROMANÉE LES BRÛLÉES	91
1985 VOSNE-ROMANÉE CROS PARANTOUX	91

When asked why his wines are so consistently great, Jayer simply responds, "I make the kind of wine I like." His wines are aged in 100% new oak, are never filtered, and are bottled directly from the barrel. The excellent color and well-delineated, intense Pinot Noir fruit he gets could well come from his special "cold maceration," which involves totally destemming the grapes after picking and putting them in tanks where they stay before the fermentation starts. Modern oenologists would no doubt be horrified at such a process as the risk of oxidation is high, but never, ever have I tasted a volatile or oxidized bottle of wine from Jayer. As he says, to make great wine, one must assume certain risks. Jayer feels his finest vintages are 1978, 1985, 1980, and 1986. The 1985s are all quite profound, deeply colored, and packed with fruit. They should last and improve until at least 1997–2003. They are more tannic than many other 1985s. The Nuits St.-Georges Les Murgers is rich, tannic, deep, and backward, but oh so pure. The two Vosne-Romanées, the Cros Parantoux and Les Brûlées, are very different. The Cros Parantoux has a voluptuous raspberry fruitiness, the Les Brûlées is softer, smoky, and exceptionally concentrated, no doubt because it comes from 55-year-old vines. The Echézeaux is what one expects of Grand Cru burgundy but rarely gets—an explosively rich yet elegant wine that titillates the palate with exotic flavors. The Riche-bourg should reach its full potential around 1994–1995, and the staggering concentration of fruit, tight structure, and smashing length of this wine are the sorts of things that make great burgundy legendary.

DOMAINE JACQUELINE JAYER (VOSNE-ROMANÉE)

1985 ECHÉZEAUX	89
1985 NUITS ST.-GEORGES LES LAVIÈRES	87
1985 VOSNE-ROMANÉE	85
1985 VOSNE-ROMANÉE LES ROUGES	87

As one might expect when the winemaker is Étienne Grivot, one of Burgundy's most talented young wine producers, the style of these wines emphasizes an opulent purity of cherry and raspberry fruit, supple textures, and impeccable balance. All four of the above wines show a delicious, tasty, rich fruitiness, medium to full body, soft tannins, and just the right amount of spicy oak. The Echézeaux is obviously the class wine of this quartet; all can be drunk now but promise to be even better if cellared for several more years.

JAYER-GILLES (HAUTES-CÔTES DE NUITS)

1985 CÔTE DE NUITS-VILLAGES	85
1985 ECHÉZEAUX	93

1985 HAUTES-CÔTES DE BEAUNE	85
1985 HAUTES-CÔTES DE NUITS	85

I suspect no one makes better Hautes-Côtes de Beaune and Nuits red wines than Robert Jayer. Dark in color, ripe with good sweetness and flesh, these are tasty wines that sell at reasonable prices. They should be drunk by 1991–1992. The Côte de Nuits-Villages is a more burly wine, but no better in terms of quality. The Echézeaux challenges that of his cousin Henri in quality, and should last until at least the turn of the century. Deep ruby/purple with super concentration and length, this medium- to full-bodied wine is impeccably made and balanced.

DOMAINE JOBLOT (GIVRY)

1985 GIVRY CLOS DU CELLIER AUX MOINES	86

Vinified and aged totally in new oak, this savory, fat, supple wine has a nice marriage of concentrated berry fruit and spicy new oak, and represents a good value for red burgundy. Drink it up by 1991–1992.

MICHEL LAFARGE (VOLNAY)

1985 BEAUNE LES GRÈVES	86
1985 BOURGOGNE	78
1985 VOLNAY	82
1985 VOLNAY CLOS DES CHÊNES	86
1985 VOLNAY PREMIER CRU	85

Lafarge's 1985s, while attractively fruity and soft, lacked some definition and tasted a little soupy. The Bourgogne is pleasant but too mild mannered, the Volnay light, fruity, and simple. The Volnay Premier Cru exhibits more flavor dimension, a ripe, juicy fruitiness, and should be drinkable until 1992–1993. The Volnay Clos des Chênes has the most guts and power of this group, but for whatever reason seemed to lack the great depth this wine is capable of attaining. The Beaune Les Grèves was in full form. Oozing with ripe cherry fruit, it has a rich, creamy texture, and gorgeously lush finish. I would drink it between 1992–1994.

HENRI LAMARCHE (VOSNE-ROMANÉE)

1985 CLOS VOUGEOT	85
1985 VOSNE-ROMANÉE LA GRANDE RUE	85
1985 VOSNE-ROMANÉE LES MALCONSORTS	83

A very famous estate with superbly situated vineyards, the Domaine Lamarche is beginning once again to make good, not great, wine after a decade of spotty performances. While the wines should still be better, particularly in view of the vineyards owned, they are soft and fruity, not terribly concentrated, but round and immediately accessible. As for the 1985s, the Vosne-Romanée La Grande Rue has slightly more depth than the other two, but all of these wines should be drunk over the next 3–4 years.

LOUIS LATOUR (BEAUNE)

1985 ALOXE-CORTON CHAILLOTS	84
1985 BEAUNE LES VIGNES-FRANCHES	85
1985 CORTON DOMAINE LATOUR	87
1985 CORTON GRANCEY	90
1985 ECHÉZEAUX	85
1985 GIVRY	84
1985 MERCUREY	75
1985 NUITS ST.-GEORGES LES ARGILLIÈRES	84
1985 SANTENAY	83
1985 SAVIGNY-LÈS-BEAUNE LES GRAVAINS	84
1985 VOSNE-ROMANÉE LES BEAUX MONTS	85

The Louis Latour firm is one of the most important houses in Burgundy. While everyone agrees their white wines are top flight, the red wines have been viewed skeptically ever since Anthony Hanson's book on Burgundy reported that they were pasteurized. This technique, which I have reservations about as well, has been used for almost a century at Louis Latour, and involves heating the wine to 70° C for 7 seconds, then cooling it immediately. There is ample evidence that the Burgundian monks used similar techniques 500 years ago. In any event, the red wines here in 1985 were above average in quality. Their flagship wine, the Corton Grancey from the gorgeous estate of the same name, has exceptional quality. What one does notice when tasting across the line of red wines is a certain sameness of character and taste. Is this a result of the flash pasteurization or just a house style of Latour? I do not know. Certainly the red wines are big, tannic, alcoholic, and age-worthy, but aside from the 1985 Corton Grancey they do not represent the most complex style of red burgundy. Among the Côte de Beaune reds, the Beaune Les Vignes-Franches has excellent color, plenty of power and muscle, some spicy new oak, and fine length. The tannic, backward, broodingly deep Vosne-Romanée Les Beaux Monts is also quite good, well colored, and ageworthy. The Echézeaux is good, but hardly exciting for a Grand Cru. Latour does very well with his Cortons and the Corton Domaine Latour had a very deep color, layers of rich, ripe fruit, and showed a much more individualistic character that the other red wines. The Corton Grancey exhibits plenty of new oak in its bouquet, super concentration and length, firm tannins, and an opulent, long finish. It should make a great bottle of wine between 1995–2000.

YVES DE LAUNAY (MERCUREY)

1985 MERCUREY CLOS DU CHÂTEAU DE MONTAIGNU	88
1985 MERCUREY MEIX FOULOT	85
1985 MERCUREY LES VELEYS	86

These unfiltered 1985 wines from Mercurey are exceptional. The Meix Foulot is dark ruby with tons of ripe, fleshy fruit, full body, and 13.5% natural alcohol. It should drink well until 1992–1994. The Les Veleys is a more powerful, full-bodied wine with considerably more tannin, but again, significant depth and length for a wine from Mercurey. The Château de Montaignu, aged in 33% new oak, is simply the finest Mercurey I have ever tasted. Oozing with raspberry fruit and toasty oak, this serious wine has astonishing concentration, and will no doubt age well until 1993–1994.

PHILIPPE LECLERC (GEVREY-CHAMBERTIN)

1985 GEVREY-CHAMBERTIN LES CAZETIERS	93
1985 GEVREY-CHAMBERTIN COMBE AUX MOINES	96
1985 GEVREY-CHAMBERTIN LA PLATIÈRE	86

The 1985s are the best Philippe Leclerc has ever made. Not a Premier Cru, the La Platière is explosively fat, fruity, long, and will be a joy to drink between 1991–1992. The Les Cazetiers, from one of the great vineyards of this appellation, is extravagantly rich and luxurious, loaded with layers of sumptuous fruit, and has mind-boggling length. The Combe aux Moines is close to perfection, a magnificent, broad-flavored wine of seemingly endless depth and breadth. Both these latter wines are undeniably delicious young, but will age well until 1997–2000.

RENÉ LECLERC (GEVREY-CHAMBERTIN)

1985 GEVREY-CHAMBERTIN	84
1985 GEVREY-CHAMBERTIN CLOS PRIEUR	84
1985 GEVREY-CHAMBERTIN COMBE AUX MOINES	90
1985 GEVREY-CHAMBERTIN LAVAUX ST.-JACQUES	86

Like his brother, Philippe, René Leclerc neither fines nor filters his wines. His villages Gevrey-Chambertin had a spicy, ground beef aroma, broad flavors, and soft texture. The Clos Prieur tasted a little diluted and slightly weedy despite some appealing jammy fruit. The Lavaux St.-Jacques leaps up in quality. Deep ruby with a full intensity bouquet, velvety yet structured flavors, and plenty of body, it will need to be cellared until 1991–1992. The top wine from René Leclerc is his Combe aux Moines, made from 50-year-old vines. Deep ruby with a fascinating bouquet of plummy fruit, this dense, unctuous, full-bodied wine has considerable appeal.

LEROY (AUXEY-DURESSES)

1985 AUXEY-DURESSES	87
1985 BEAUNE	87
1985 BEAUNE LES GRÈVES	92
1985 BEAUNE MIGNOTTE	90
1985 BEAUNE LES PERRIÈRES	83
1985 BEAUNE LES PERTUISOTS	88
1985 BEAUNE LES SIZIES	86
1985 BOURGOGNE D'AUVENAY	86
1985 CHAMBERTIN	96

1985	CHAMBOLLE-MUSIGNY	74
1985	CHARMES-CHAMBERTIN	87
1985	CHASSAGNE-MONTRACHET	82
1985	CHOREY-LÈS-BEAUNE	84
1985	CLOS VOUGEOT	92
1985	CÔTE DE BEAUNE-VILLAGES	86
1985	GEVREY-CHAMBERTIN	86
1985	GEVREY-CHAMBERTIN LES CHAMPEAUX	89
1985	GEVREY-CHAMBERTIN CORBEAUX	84
1985	GEVREY-CHAMBERTIN ESTOURNELLES ST.-JACQUES	90
1985	GEVREY-CHAMBERTIN LAVAUX ST.-JACQUES	94
1985	HOSPICES DE BEAUNE CUVÉE BOILLOT	86
1985	HOSPICES DE BEAUNE CUVÉE MADELEINE COLLIGNON	100
1985	MAZIS-CHAMBERTIN	93
1985	MERCUREY	86
1985	MONTHÉLIE	75
1985	MUSIGNY	87
1985	NUITS ST.-GEORGES	82
1985	NUITS ST.-GEORGES LES ARGILLIÈRES	90
1985	NUITS ST.-GEORGES CLOS DES CORVÉES	92
1985	NUITS ST.-GEORGES LES PERDRIX	92
1985	NUITS ST.-GEORGES LA RICHEMONE	94
1985	POMMARD	86
1985	POMMARD LES VIGNOTS	88
1985	RUCHOTTES-CHAMBERTIN	94
1985	SANTENAY	87
1985	SAVIGNY-LÈS-BEAUNE	85
1985	SAVIGNY LES MARCONNETS	90
1985	SAVIGNY LES SERPENTIÈRES	92
1985	VOLNAY	87
1985	VOLNAY BROUILLARDS	87

1985 VOLNAY CLOS DES CHÊNES	88
1985 VOLNAY LASSOLLE	87
1985 VOLNAY PREMIER CRU	87
1985 VOLNAY TAILLEPIEDS	90

Much has been written about the dynamic Madame Lalou Bize-Leroy. Some of it has been malicious and motivated strictly by insidious jealousy. From time to time I have complained of her pricing structure. Yet there should never be any criticism of her philosophy of what burgundy should be. Her wines are among the noblest and purest expressions of Pinot Noir in Burgundy. They are treated with the care of a pampered child, never filtered, and bottled barrel by barrel. I have tasted many great wines, but I shall never forget spending most of the day tasting the above wines in her cellars. Many of them are what dream wines are all about. Given the size of her wines and their power and structure, in a cool damp cellar they will last 20 to 25 years. Bize-Leroy thinks 1985 is one of the two best burgundy vintages in the last twenty years, the other being 1978. Given the range of wines I tasted, 44 in all, 16 were exceptional, 21 very good to excellent. Thirty-seven very good to exceptional wines out of 44 is an amazingly high percentage, and I would be proud to own any of them.

Côte de Beaune

I doubt there has ever been another vintage like 1985, where so many generic red burgundies tasted so good. Take Leroy's Bourgogne d'Auvenay, for example. The 1985 is even better than the 1978 was, powerful, rich, intense, and loaded with fruit. The Mercurey is a big, tannic, fleshy wine that will keep well until 1997. The Côte de Beaune-Villages possesses plenty of ripe raspberry fruit, has surprising depth for a wine of its class, and is ideal for drinking between 1991–1995. Both the Santenay and Auxey-Duresses are also quite powerful, expressive wines filled with great fruit, body, and concentration. The lineup of Volnays is very impressive, and certainly no small grower, not even Gérard Potel of Pousse d'Or, can claim such a high level of success. The most open-knit and accessible wine is the Villages Volnay, a fat, ripe, yet elegant wine that shows plenty of raspberry fruit. The Volnay-Lassolle is more tannic yet powerful and deep. The Volnay Premier Cru also tasted muscular, tannic, and capable of long cellaring. The most elegant of this set of wines was the Volnay Brouillards. The cascade of lush raspberry fruit and the supple, seductive texture give it more near-term appeal. For the more patient, the rewards of cellaring the Volnay Clos des Chênes and Volnay Taillepieds are obvious. The Taillepieds is an especially distinguished wine with fabulous length and depth. It will age well until 1997–2000. The Clos des Chênes is every bit as concentrated, but more tannic and very backward. It should be cellared until about 1995–1997. The Pommard is rich and full bodied, but the Pommard Les Vignots has outstanding concentration, and is a tightly structured, tannic wine that could prove to be exceptional if one is willing to wait until 1993–1997. Madame Bize-Leroy made several stunning wines from Beaune in 1985. The Beaune Les Pertuisots has an aromatic bouquet of berry fruit, a velvety texture, and considerable style and class. It does not, however, compete with the exquisite Beaune Les Grèves, which is fabulously rich and so long that it is hard to believe it is a Beaune. It will drink well into the next century. The Beaune Mignotte has the same superb depth and concentration, but is more structured and tannic. I suspect no one pays much attention to Savigny-Lès-Beaune, a terribly underrated appellation near Aloxe-Corton. Bize-Leroy's two superstars are from opposite hillsides, the Marconnets and the Serpentières, closer to the village of Savigny. I remember several great bottles of the Hospices de Beaune's Savigny-Lès-Beaune Cuvée Arthur Girard, but these two are the most remarkable bottles of Savigny I have ever tasted. As special and marvelous as the Marconnets is, the Serpentières, with its awesome concentration, heady perfume of berry fruit and spices, and significant size, should still be going strong at the turn of the century.

Côte de Nuits

Forgetting the above-average quality but unexciting Nuits St.-Georges and bland Chambolle-Musigny, which will prove to Madame Bize-Leroy's critics that she is not infallible, the other wines range from very good to exceptional, and in the case of one wine, sheer perfection. I was blown away by her Nuits St.-Georges Premiers Crus. The most supple and easy to drink is the unctuous Les Argillières, a sexy, flashy, voluptuous wine that has layers of fruit. The Clos des Corvées is more structured and ageworthy, but once again, mightily constructed with exciting levels of fruit and complexity. How can one chose between it and the Les Perdrix, another magical, exotic wine that is dark ruby in color, and quite unforgettable? Believe it or not, La Richemone, a Premier Cru near the Vosne-Romanée border, is even more sublime. It is a wine for toasting the twenty-first century. While more closed than the others, this wine explodes on the palate with enough balanced power and finesse to please anyone. There are several superb Premiers Crus from Gevrey-Chambertin. Both the fabulous Lavaux St.-Jacques and the fragrant, more forward Estournelles St.-Jacques made the very good Corbeaux and Champeaux look like undernourished children. All of these wines will last 20 years.

The selection of Grands Crus will no doubt cost plenty. I enjoyed both the Musigny and Charmes-Chambertin, but in the company of the other wines they did nothing to suggest they were great. The huge fruit and structure of the Clos Vougeot will fool no one; it is a majestic wine. The Ruchottes-Chambertin is a real powerhouse of a burgundy with huge extract, sensational intensity, and enough tannin and depth to carry it 25 or more years. The Mazis-Chambertin is savage and wild, with tremendous sweetness of jammy Pinot fruit, but also a boatload of tannins. It was tasted next to the Mazis-Chambertin Hospices de Beaune Madeleine Collignon, a perfect wine. Perfect wines are exceedingly rare, and until that day in Madame Bize-Leroy's cellars I had never tasted what I thought to be the quintessential red burgundy. Many of the 1985s are near misses, but I tasted two perfect red burgundies from this vintage—will this ever happen again? I have no doubt about this wine: It has everything, and when I smelled it, I knew that it was something beyond reason, beyond previous tasting parameters. How does one describe it? It is rich, long, powerful, and deep in color, but the magical perfume, the symphony of flavors, the constant intrigue to its nuances of aromas and flavors just went on and on. I suspect it will peak between 1992–2010.

Last, how often does a Chambertin live up to the grandeur of its name? This one does, for, believe me, it was tasted after a perfect wine and I was still shocked by the wealth of luxurious fruit counterbalanced against its power and tannin.

These are sensational red burgundies. I wish they were cheaper, but America is the smallest market for Leroy's wines. Most of her wine is sold to top French restaurants and collectors in Switzerland and Belgium. She knows full well what she has produced, and she also knows there will be no shortage of wealthy customers willing to pay for this rare level of quality. Her wines are what great Burgundy is all about, and it is a tragedy that there are not more people in Burgundy who share a comparable commitment to quality.

GEORGES LIGNIER (MOREY ST.-DENIS)

1985 BONNES MARES	91

1985 CHAMBOLLE-MUSIGNY	86

1985 CLOS DE LA ROCHE	95
1985 CLOS ST.-DENIS	90
1985 GEVREY-CHAMBERTIN	84
1985 GEVREY-CHAMBERTIN AUX COMBOTTES	88
1985 MOREY ST.-DENIS	84
1985 MOREY ST.-DENIS CLOS DES ORMES	87

On the main road leading into Morey St.-Denis from Route Nationale 74, the major artery between Dijon and Beaune, are the wine cellars of some outstanding small growers. On the left is Dujac, on the right are Hubert Lignier, Pierre Amiot, Bernard Serveau, and Georges Lignier. All of them produce totally different styles of wine. Serveau and Amiot move mostly in the direction of precocious, elegant, delicate wines. Hubert Lignier and Dujac balance power with finesse, and Georges Lignier leans more toward unbridled richness and muscle. The young Georges Lignier, who must work in one of the dampest, moldiest cellars in Burgundy, is not as consistent a winemaker as some of his peers, but his 1985s are in full form. The 32 acres of vineyards that make up this domaine read like a Who's Who. Unfortunately, at the insistence of his agent, Tim Marshall, Lignier has begun to filter for fear that bad storage or shipment of the wines would cause them to spoil. This is sad. The quantities of great wine made here are so small. They should not be sold to firms that will not take the precautions to protect them. While the Morey St.-Denis and Gevrey-Chambertin are good, fruity wines with plenty of substance, it is the Chambolle-Musigny that first grabbed my attention. Quite forward and developed, it has a gorgeous bouquet of ripe fruit, round, generous flavors, and a soft finish. The Morey St.-Denis Clos des Ormes has excellent color, a spicy, peppery bouquet, quite a bit of power and body, and will keep until 1993–1994. Lignier made 125 cases of Gevrey-Chambertin aux Combottes, which in 1985 is almost as exquisite as the same wine made at Domaine Dujac. Quite rich and broadly flavored, it has an expansive, long finish and super sweetness to the Pinot fruit. It will drink well until 1993–1995. Among the three Grands Crus, there is a very powerful Bonnes Mares (14% natural alcohol), which has great depth and richness, and oodles of fruit, but plenty of tannin in the finish. It will keep until 1997–2000. The Clos St.-Denis tasted more supple, even jammy, with a wealth of berry fruit and velvety texture. There are 500 cases of it for the world. The very summit in the Lignier cellar in 1985 is the Clos de la Roche, a densely colored, tremendously powerful wine with 14% natural alcohol that was aged in 100% new oak barrels. Lignier made 250 cases of this majestic wine. It will be a revelation for those who say modern burgundy is too light.

HUBERT LIGNIER (MOREY ST.-DENIS)

1985 CLOS DE LA ROCHE	94
1985 MOREY ST.-DENIS PREMIER CRU	85

Hubert Lignier's Morey St.-Denis Premier Cru is deeply colored, rich in fruit, has no harsh edges, and is quite concentrated. It will offer ideal drinking until 1994. The Clos de la Roche is impeccable, much fatter, richer, and softer than the firmly structured, tannic 1983, and more concentrated than the compelling 1978. Like the great majority of 1985 red burgundies, it has a savory, forward opulence, super color, and a cascade of plummy fruit. Neither wine is fined or filtered. A treat to drink now, this wine should be even greater if cellared until 1992–1993.

CHÂTEAU DE LA MALTROYE
(CHASSAGNE-MONTRACHET)

1985 CHASSAGNE-MONTRACHET CLOS DE LA MALTROYE	85
1985 CHASSAGNE-MONTRACHET CLOS SAINT-JEAN	85

This estate is much better known for its bevy of white burgundies, but good red wines are also made here. They are typical of the southern Côte de Beaune style—round, soft, medium bodied, and dominated by the scent and taste of bing cherries. Both 1985s are soft, seductive, round, fleshy wines that are a pleasure to drink now, but should keep well for 4–6 years.

J. P. MARCHAND (GEVREY-CHAMBERTIN)

1985 CHARMES-CHAMBERTIN	87
1985 GEVREY-CHAMBERTIN AUX COMBOTTES	86
1985 GRIOTTE-CHAMBERTIN	89

I predict that the young Jean-Philippe Marchand—whose domaine owns an impressive 25 acres of Grands Crus such as Griotte-Chambertin, Charmes-Chambertin, and Clos de la Roche, as well as Premiers Crus such as Combottes—is on the threshold of stardom. His 1985s are excellent, but do have that brilliant, polished look that comes from too intense a filtration. If Marchand's American importer, Neal Rosenthal, can persuade him to filter less or not at all, there is no telling what he can attain, since the other aspects of the vinification and élevage for his red wines are impeccable. The Combottes is very supple, lush, fat, and ideal for drinking until about 1992–1993. The Charmes-Chambertin may not approach the quality of Charmes made by Dujac or Faiveley in 1985, but it is still an excellent wine with plenty of concentrated berry fruit, medium to full body, and a precocious, lush texture. The Griottes-Chambertin is a decadently intense, rich mouthful of wine. There are good tannins submerged behind the fruit, but this is clearly a wine to consume by 1994–1995.

JOSEPH MATROT (MEURSAULT)

1985 BLAGNY-LA PIÈCE SOUS LE BOIS	88
1985 VOLNAY SANTENOTS	86

I suspect Matrot is better known for his white wines than his reds, which tend to be overlooked. However, they are often quite good. The Blagny, from a vineyard situated just northwest of the Meursault-Charmes vineyard, is a very silky, intense, richly fruity wine that offers a resounding blast of cherry fruit, toasty oak, and full body. It should be drunk by 1993. The Volnay Santenots is similar in style, only more restrained. It too should be drunk by 1993.

DOMAINE JEAN MÉO-CAMUZET (VOSNE-ROMANÉE)

1985 CLOS VOUGEOT	91
1985 NUITS ST.-GEORGES LES BOUDOTS	87
1985 NUITS ST.-GEORGES LES MURGERS	88
1985 RICHEBOURG	93
1985 VOSNE-ROMANÉE LES BRÛLÉES	86

In the 1985 legendary winemaker, Henri Jayer, was brought on as a consultant here, so this historic domaine, with some of the best-situated vineyards in Burgundy, can be expected to produce greater and greater wines. Certainly there is no problem with the 1985s, which are unbelievably seductive, exotic, smoky, rich wines that can be drunk with extraordinary pleasure today. Whether it is the bacon fat–scented, opulent Clos Vougeot, or the unreal Richebourg, any of these wines is well worth having, even in the most conscientiously stocked wine cellar. Jayer, who believes in no filtration and 100% new oak, has left his fingerprints all over the 1985s. This is certainly an up-and-coming superstar estate in the Côte d'Or.

PRINCE DE MÉRODE (LADOIX-SERRIGNY)

1985 ALOXE-CORTON PREMIER CRU	84
1985 CORTON LES BRESSANDES	88
1985 CORTON-CLOS DU ROI	90
1985 CORTON LES MARÉCHAUDES	86
1985 CORTON LES RÉNARDES	87
1985 LADOIX	83
1985 POMMARD-CLOS DE LA PLATIÈRE	85

This important domaine has made its best wines since 1978. Yet I suspect they could even be better with less filtration. The Ladoix is light ruby, has a pleasant strawberry, supple fruitiness, and should drink well until about 1990. The Aloxe-Corton delivers more cherry fruit, is very easy to taste and appreciate, and should keep until 1991–1992. The quality of Cortons in 1985 from Mérode is quite impressive. The Maréchaudes, usually the lightest offering, has good body, plenty of velvety, supple, cherry fruit, a good lashing of tannin in the finish, and should be drinkable until at least 1997. The Rénardes exhibits more stuffing, an elevated percentage of new oak, and a lovely, expansive, long finish. It is drinkable now, and should keep until 1997. The Bressandes, made from 40-year-old vines, has a dark ruby color, is seriously concentrated, shows a complex cherry-like and sweet oaky taste, and is full bodied. It should be mature between 1990–1996. There is no doubt that the Clos du Roi is the fullest, deepest, most powerful and concentrated wine Mérode produced in 1985. It combines intensity with finesse. Give it until about 1994 to develop fully. Last, the Pommard-Clos de la Platière has an earthy, super-ripe character, exudes gobs of cherry jam and oak, and is very tasty.

MOILLARD (NUITS ST.-GEORGES)

1985 BEAUNE LES GRÈVES	87
1985 BOURGOGNE	82
1985 BOURGOGNE HAUTES-CÔTES DE NUITS	78
1985 CLOS VOUGEOT	90
1985 CORTON-CLOS DU ROI	92
1985 CÔTE DE NUITS-VILLAGES	83
1985 ECHÉZEAUX	91
1985 GEVREY-CHAMBERTIN	84
1985 MERCUREY	89
1985 NUITS ST.-GEORGES CLOS DE TOREY	89
1985 SANTENAY	85
1985 VOSNE-ROMANÉE LES MALCONSORTS	88

The Thomas family, which owns Moillard, says consumers "like supple, round, velvety, dark-colored wines," and that is what Moillard delivers. I should also note that prices for Moillard's wines are not unreasonable, so given the high quality of their 1985s, this is a source for some very fine, even exceptional red burgundy, provided you like their big, meaty, fleshy, deeply colored style of wine.

The Santenay is a rather powerful, chunky, rich wine with a good dosage of alcohol and fruit. It will keep until 1997. The Nuits St.-Georges Clos de Torey has a very dense color, great extract, a huge, tarry, plummy bouquet, broad flavors, and a solid lashing of tannin. It should last until 1998–2000. The Clos Vougeot is exceptional. It oozes with a cascade of ripe bing cherry fruit, exhibits plenty of toasty new oak in its aroma, and has sensational concentration and length. It will last until 1997–2002. The Beaune Les Grèves is typical of many top 1985 red burgundies. Opulent, even explosively fruity, this succulent, sensual wine gives enormous pleasure and should last until 1992–1997. I thought the Corton-Clos du Roi was the best of the Moillard 1985 red burgundies. Aged in 100% new oak, it has an extraordinary bouquet of exotic spices, and super-concentrated fruit. Deep, rich, full bodied, tannic, and exceptionally long, this wine should provide grand drinking until 1999–2004. The Vosne-Romanée Les Malconsorts has less power and substance, but is still very concentrated, supple, and long. The big, penetrating, persistent aroma of the Echézeaux offers nothing but joyous ripeness and complex Pinot Noir smells. Less full bodied and tannic than either the Corton-Clos du Roi and Nuits St.-Georges Clos de Torey, it is a wine full of elegance and finesse, and should be drunk by 1997.

MONGEARD-MUGNERET (VOSNE-ROMANÉE)

1985 CLOS VOUGEOT	92
1985 ECHÉZEAUX	90
1985 FIXIN	85
1985 GRANDS ECHÉZEAUX	96
1985 RICHEBOURG	90
1985 VOSNE-ROMANÉE	87
1985 VOSNE-ROMANÉE LES ORVEAUX	86
1985 VOSNE-ROMANÉE LES SUCHOTS	88

Mongeard's Fixin has a delicious fruity quality, deep ruby color, a soft texture, and a good finish. The Villages Vosne-Romanée is excellent, and inexplicably tastes better than the Les Orveaux, a more expensive wine. The Vosne-Romanée has deep, silky fruit, a sweet, plummy richness, and considerable length. It should drink well until 1994–1995. The Les Orveaux is quite tannic and closed. As for the Vosne-Romanée Les Suchots, it is especially rich, expansively flavored, full bodied, packed with fruit, and should age well until at least 1997. The Echézeaux is outstanding with a perfumed, sweet, flowery, fruity nose, an expansive palate, and cellaring potential until 1995–1996. I thought the Clos Vougeot tasted even better, with more depth, power, greater intensity of fruit, plus more tannin and structure. It should keep until 1997–2002. As fine as the elegant, velvety, aromatic Richebourg is, it is not as exceptional as the profound Grands Echézeaux. The latter wine, usually one of the superstars of Burgundy, has an extraordinary bouquet of cassis fruit, violets, and chocolate. Stunningly rich, full bodied, and long, it should be at its best between 1990 and 1998.

ALBERT MOROT (BEAUNE)

1985 BEAUNE LES BRESSANDES	88
1985 BEAUNE LES CENT VIGNES	86
1985 BEAUNE LES GRÈVES	86

1985 BEAUNE LES MARCONNETS	87
1985 BEAUNE LES TEURONS	87
1985 BEAUNE LES TOUSSAINTS	83
1985 SAVIGNY LES VERGELESSES	85

While Albert Morot is a *négociant*, the wines above are all from their own vineyards. All the 1985s are dark, expressive wines that have the telltale personality characteristics of the vintage—a fat, opulent fruitiness, plenty of soft tannins, and adequate but low acidities. The three top wines of 1985 from Morot are the Beaune Les Bressandes, Beaune Les Marconnets, and Beaune Les Teurons, although the differences are largely negligible. The Beaune Les Bressandes has super color and an intense richness marked by smells of blackcurrants and licorice. It is a very big wine for a Beaune. The Beaune Les Marconnets is a bit more tannic and structured, but has the same impressive power and richness on the palate. The Beaune Les Teurons is the least open and most tannic, but the underlying depth is impressive. All three of these wines should age well until at least 1997.

DENIS MORTET (GEVREY-CHAMBERTIN)

1985 BOURGOGNE	84
1985 CHAMBERTIN	87
1985 CLOS VOUGEOT	88
1985 GEVREY-CHAMBERTIN	84
1985 GEVREY-CHAMBERTIN CHAMPEAUX	87
1985 GEVREY-CHAMBERTIN CLOS PRIEUR	85

In 1985, Mortet made a good, attractive, easy-to-understand Bourgogne that I found to be just as good as his Gevrey-Chambertin. A specialty here is the Gevrey-Chambertin Champeaux, made from 60-year-old vines. It is a big, rich, dense, yet tannic and full-bodied wine that will keep until 1997–2000. The Gevrey-Chambertin Clos Prieur tastes less concentrated, but round, supple, elegant, and fruity. I thought Mortet's Clos Vougeot richer, more concentrated, and altogether a more serious *vin de garde* than his famous Chambertin. The latter wine is fruity, elegant, and tasty, but for the money, the Clos Vougeot and Champeaux are superior wines at lower prices.

GEORGES MUGNERET (VOSNE-ROMANÉE)

1985 BOURGOGNE	88
1985 CLOS VOUGEOT	96
1985 ECHÉZEAUX	91
1985 NUITS ST.-GEORGES LES CHAIGNOTS	91
1985 RUCHOTTES-CHAMBERTIN	95
1985 VOSNE-ROMANÉE	85

The Vosne-Romanée reminded me immensely of the lovely, elegant 1984 Saintsbury Pinot Noir from California. Impeccably clean, fruity, and pure, it is a delight to drink. The surprising wine is the generic Bourgogne. Aged in 100% new oak, it has immense fruit and a sumptuous texture. I have never drunk an ordinary Bourgogne this special. The lineup of great wines starts with the Nuits St.-Georges Les Chaignots. Deep in color, profound in aroma, it has a broad, deep, rich intensity. This wine should improve until 1997–2000. How many times does someone tell you an Echézeaux should smell of violets? This Echézeaux does, but it has more than just pretty floral aromas. It is a gorgeous wine with the opulence of the 1985 vintage well displayed. The problem, however, is that the Ruchottes-Chambertin is out and out great stuff. The superb purity of fruit, the remarkable delineation of flavors, the structure and length suggest that it will last and perhaps even improve until at least the year 2000. If that is not enough, the Clos Vougeot is nearly perfect. A truly magical wine, a gustatory tour de force, it will last until 2000–2005. Dr. Georges Mugneret made great wines in 1953, 1966, and 1978, but his 1985s are indeed special.

PHILIPPE NADDEF (COUCHEY)

1985 GEVREY-CHAMBERTIN	82
1985 GEVREY-CHAMBERTIN LES CAZETIERS	87
1985 MAZIS-CHAMBERTIN	89

Young Philippe Naddef is short on winemaking experience (he is only in his twenties), but he is quickly making a name for himself. One hundred percent new oak is used and the wines have excellent color, ripeness, and plenty of toasty oak. They are bold, ageworthy wines that should last 8–10 years.

DOMAINE PARENT (POMMARD)

1985 CORTON LES RÉNARDES	85
1985 POMMARD CLOS MICAULT	82
1985 POMMARD LES EPENOTS	84
1985 POMMARD LES RUGIENS	85

This famous firm, founded in 1650, has one of the highest reputations in Burgundy. It produced a bevy of 1964s and 1966s that I cut my teeth on when discovering Burgundy in the late sixties. Today, the style of the wine is less impressive and more commercial, with the emphasis on turning out soft, alcoholic, somewhat diffuse wines from over 60 acres of vineyards (mostly in Pommard) that all have similar tastes and personality. While the wines are estate-bottled, the current generation at Domaine Parent has a *négociant* mentality. These are wines to drink over the next 4–5 years.

PERNIN-ROSSIN (VOSNE-ROMANÉE)

1985 MOREY ST.-DENIS MONTS LUISANTS	85
1985 NUITS ST.-GEORGES LA RICHEMONE	92

Some consumers might approach Pernin-Rossin's wines with a degree of skepticism. They have a density of color and level of fruit extract that seem unbelievable for a Burgundy, but they taste of Pinot Noir, so I do not think he is pulling any tricks. The two 1985s I tasted included very alcoholic, very fruity, soft, lush Morey St.-Denis Monts Luisants that delivers immediate gratification. Simply extraordinary is the Nuits St.-Georges La Richemone. It has a sweetness of fruit and such an unbelievable aroma and flavor of cassis that one is amazed. It also has a good measure of tannin and body, which should allow it to age well until 1992–1996.

PERNOT-FOURRIER (GEVREY-CHAMBERTIN)

(In 1985 this estate's name became Domaine Jean-Claude Fourrier)

1985 CHAMBOLLE-MUSIGNY	75
1985 GEVREY-CHAMBERTIN	72
1985 GEVREY-CHAMBERTIN CLOS ST.-JACQUES	82

1985 GEVREY-CHAMBERTIN COMBE AUX MOINES	82
1985 GEVREY-CHAMBERTIN PREMIER CRU	76
1985 GRIOTTES-CHAMBERTIN	84
1985 MOREY ST.-DENIS	70
1985 VOUGEOT PREMIER CRU	76

This famous estate turned out fabulous wines in 1978, 1976, and 1969. However, the current proprietor, Jean-Claude Fourrier, has not equaled the success of his predecessors. The 1985s are too alcoholic and only average in color, and should have been bottled months before they actually were. All of the wines are tasty, ripe, and supple, but they are dangerously low in acidity, have a soupy texture, and lack definition. They had to be drunk young in order to be enjoyed.

JEAN PICHENET (SAVIGNY-LÈS-BEAUNE)

| 1985 SAVIGNY-LÈS-BEAUNE | 85 |

This is a pretty wine, redolent with the scent of ripe strawberry fruit. It has a creamy texture and plum fatness that will give it appeal until around 1991–1992.

CHÂTEAU DE POMMARD (POMMARD)

| 1985 POMMARD | 86 |

The wine here is aged in 100% new oak casks and put in very heavy and expensive bottles. Much has been made of the fact that the location of this vineyard is not ideal, but Laplanche's meticulous attention to the wine results in a chunky, long-lived, deeply colored, firm, and tannic wine that can last for 15 or more years. The 1985 is all of these things, and certainly the best wine made here since 1978.

PONSOT (MOREY ST.-DENIS)

1985 CHAMBERTIN	99
1985 CHAMBOLLE-MUSIGNY LES CHARMES	90
1985 CLOS DE LA ROCHE VIEILLES VIGNES	96

1985 CLOS ST.-DENIS VIEILLES VIGNES	92
1985 GRIOTTE-CHAMBERTIN VIEILLES VIGNES	96
1985 LATRICIÈRES-CHAMBERTIN	96

I think the 1985s here are stupendous, but both the Ponsots feel their 1983s will outlive the 1985s by 10 to 15 years. All of the above wines will drink well and last until 1995–2000. Some of these wines also appear under the label Domaine des Chezeaux; this is not a second label as the wines are identical.

The Chambolle-Musigny Les Charmes smells of sweet, ripe apples and flowers, has a luscious creamy texture, super color, and soft tannins. The Griotte-Chambertin (spelled without an "s" here) is a dazzling wine made from 65-year-old vines. Dark ruby with an intense raspberry fruitiness, extraordinary concentration and depth on the palate, this mind-boggling wine should drink well until 1997. I thought the Chambertin to be nearly perfect. My virgin tasting notes contained all of the following words—awesome, unbelievable, staggering, sensational, and frightening. It is what legends are made of. Unfortunately, only 25 cases came to America. The Latricières-Chambertin may well be as good. It also had a level of concentration more akin to vintage port or 1982 red Bordeaux than burgundy. It is wilder and more structured and tannic than the Chambertin. Sadly, the Clos St.-Denis is merely an exceptional wine. In the company of such treasures as the Chambertin and Latricières-Chambertin, all I could muster in my tasting notes was "dark ruby, great wine, explosive richness, heady, and splendid." The vines for Clos St.-Denis were planted in 1925, making it a true cuvée Vieilles Vignes. The Clos de la Roche Vieilles Vignes (there were a whopping 120 cases shipped to America) has the misfortune of being merely a great wine, but not Ponsot's greatest wine in 1985. It is much more forward than either the backward 1983 or slowly developing 1980. If you have access to it, and have a fat bank account, do not dare pass it up.

V. POTHIER-RIEUSSET (POMMARD)

1985 BEAUNE LES BOUCHEROTTES	83
1985 BOURGOGNE	75
1985 POMMARD LES CHARMOTS	85
1985 POMMARD-CLOS DES VERGERS	86

1985 POMMARD LES EPENOTS	89
1985 POMMARD LES RUGIENS	89

Pothier's 1969s and 1972s are just now opening up. His 1985s are considerably softer than his tannic 1983s, but still they are among the most structured 1985s I have tasted. His generic Bourgogne tastes surprisingly lean and tannic. As for the Beaune Les Boucherottes, it is deep in color, quite full bodied and tannic, and concentrated as well. It should last until 1993–1999. The Pommard-Clos des Vergers has very good acidity for a 1985, is quite deep in color, very backward, yet dense and promising. It needs cellaring until at least 1993–1995. The Pommard Les Charmots is dense, chunky, and softer in style than the Vergers. Normally, the Pommard Rugiens is Pothier's top wine, and it is almost great in 1985—very dark ruby, rich in extract, full bodied, and tannic. But his best cuvée is the Pommard Les Epenots. It is splendid—fabulously concentrated, quite profound in aroma, and should drink well until 1997–2002. Pothier compares his 1985s to his 1969s.

POUSSE D'OR (VOLNAY)

1985 POMMARD LES JAROLIÈRES	89
1985 SANTENAY-CLOS TAVANNES	84
1985 VOLNAY LA BOUSSE D'OR	90
1985 VOLNEY LES CAILLERETS	87
1985 VOLNAY LES CAILLERETS 60 OUVRÉES	88

Gérard Potel prefers his 1978s to his 1985s, saying the style of the 1985s falls somewhere between that of years such as 1966 and 1978. The Santenay-Clos Tavannes is quite drinkable, as it is supple, smooth, very fruity, and ripe. This medium-bodied wine should drink well until 1991–1992. The Volnay Les Caillerets is a wonderfully elegant wine, round, supple, yet firm enough to keep until 1997–2000. The Volnay Les Caillerets 60 Ouvrées is even deeper and darker in color, more intense and more tannic, with a very seductive, gorgeous bouquet of cherry fruit and toasty oak. It should last from 1997–2000. The Pommard Les Jarolières has great richness of fruit, a succulent, juicy character, full body, and plenty of ripe tannins in the fruit. Potel's best wine, however, is the Volnay La Bousse d'Or, a gloriously ripe, fruity, unctuous wine with layers of berry fruit wrapped gently in a veil of smoky, toasty oak. It will last into the next century. However, there are only 750 cases of this nectar for the entire world.

MICHEL PRUNIER (AUXEY-DURESSES)

1985 AUXEY-DURESSES CLOS DU VAL	87
1985 AUXEY-DURESSES PREMIER CRU	85
1985 BEAUNE LES SIZIES	86
1985 VOLNAY LES CAILLERETS	86

Prunier's 1985s are the best wines I have ever tasted from him. From the soft, lovely, effusively fruity Auxey-Duresses Premier Cru to the intense, velvety, seductive Beaune Les Sizies and the fat but structured Volnay Les Caillerets, there is something for everyone. These wines are cleanly made, ripe, rich in fruit, deeply colored, and quite tasty. The star is the Auxey-Duresses Clos du Val, the most tannic, concentrated, and promising wine, with cellaring potential until 1995–1997.

CHARLES QUILLARDET (GEVREY-CHAMBERTIN)

1985 GEVREY-CHAMBERTIN	?
1985 GEVREY-CHAMBERTIN LE BEL-AIR	85
1985 MARSANNAY	83

Charles Quillardet, a big, playful man, is a well-known producer located right on the main route through Gevrey-Chambertin. I often find his wines perplexing to evaluate and generally not to my liking. He makes a controversial generic burgundy called Monte Cul—controversial because the label contains an uncensored view of a woman's buttocks as she bends over to pick grapes. He did not show me the 1985 version of this wine, perhaps because I've written that the 1983 had a fecal aroma. His Gevrey-Chambertin has a defective bouquet (probably mercaptans), but on the palate, the wine is certainly fruity. The Marsannay exhibits good clean berry fruit, medium body, and a soft texture. The best wine is the Gevrey-Chambertin Le Bel-Air, a densely colored, big, thick wine with considerable tannin. It needs until 1993–1994 to fully develop.

REMOISSENET (BEAUNE)

1985 ALOXE-CORTON	75
1985 BEAUNE LES GRÈVES	86
1985 BEAUNE LES MARCONNETS	87

1985 BONNES MARES	82
1985 BOURGOGNE ROUGE	78
1985 CHAMBOLLE-MUSIGNY LES CHARMES	86
1985 CHARMES-CHAMBERTIN	83
1985 CLOS VOUGEOT	86
1985 GEVREY-CHAMBERTIN	78
1985 GIVRY	85
1985 GRANDS ECHÉZEAUX	87
1985 MERCUREY-CLOS FOURTOUL	80
1985 NUITS ST.-GEORGES	79
1985 NUITS ST.-GEORGES LES ARGILLIÈRES	85
1985 NUITS ST.-GEORGES LES BOUDOTS HOSPICES DE NUITS	89
1985 POMMARD LES EPENOTS	86
1985 RICHEBOURG	84
1985 SANTENAY-CLOS DE TAVANNES	85
1985 SANTENAY LA COMME	86
1985 SANTENAY LES GRAVIÈRES	84
1985 SAVIGNY-LÈS-BEAUNE	80
1985 SAVIGNY-LÈS-BEAUNE LES GRAVAINS	84
1985 SAVIGNY-LÈS-BEAUNE LES GUETTES	82
1985 SAVIGNY-LÈS-BEAUNE LES MARCONNETS	84
1985 SAVIGNY-LÈS-BEAUNE LES SERPENTIÈRES	82
1985 VOLNAY	80
1985 VOSNE-ROMANÉE	77
1985 VOSNE-ROMANÉE LES CHAUMES	87
1985 VOSNE-ROMANÉE LES SUCHOTS	87

The 1985 reds are all soundly made, correct wines, but only 13 out of 29 had enough personality and character befitting their appellations to get a recommendation. The 1985s have more tart acidity at Remoissenet than elsewhere, as well as more noticeable alcohol levels and tannins. They are, like virtually all 1985s, well colored. Many seemed to resemble one another. For value, the spicy, fleshy Givry is quite good. While the selection of Savignys is not inspiring, the Santenays are quite good, full-bodied, fleshy, rich, well-made wines that will handsomely repay cellaring until 1998–2000. Both the Beaune Les Grèves and Beaune Les Marconnets (the latter wine is always top rank here) are lovely, broadly flavored, deep wines with concentrated, rich, cherry-scented personalities. I also thought the Pommard Les Epenots to be a very fine, powerful, deep, rich, lovely, and full-bodied wine.

Among the Côte de Nuits wines the top offering is clearly the extremely rich, concentrated, long Nuits St.-Georges Les Boudots, which is oozing with ripe berry fruit, and is quite complex. Certainly, the fat, alcoholic, but super-concentrated Grands Echézeaux, and the elegant, stylish Chambolle-Musigny Les Charmes are both lush, rich, full-bodied, and concentrated wines that can age well. The Vosne-Romanée Les Suchots and Vosne-Romanée Les Chaumes also stood above the pack. The Clos Vougeot and Nuits St.-Georges Les Argillières are also good. None of these wines is exceptional, but all are sturdy, reliable, chunky, fleshy wines that will last.

RION PÈRE ET FILS (NUITS ST.-GEORGES)

1985 CLOS VOUGEOT	86
1985 CHAMBOLLE-MUSIGNY LES ECHÉZEAUX	78
1985 NUITS ST.-GEORGES LES MURGERS	84
1985 VOSNE-ROMANÉE LES CHAUMES	87

This Rion should not be confused with Daniel Rion. The wines made here are very old style, dense, tannic, and full bodied. Where the fruit is adequate, they will last until the year 2000 or later. The Vosne-Romanée Les Chaumes has an excellent level of fruit extract, so the balance is correct. Do not drink it before 1993–1994. The Clos Vougeot is clearly the winner in 1985 for Rion.

MAURICE ROLLAND (PERNAND-VERGELESSES)

1985 PERNAND-ÎLE DE VERGELESSES	86+
1985 PERNAND-VERGELESSES	86
1985 SAVIGNY-LÈS-BEAUNE	86

These wines are notably good values. They are fruity, deep in color, and quite concentrated, and will keep until 1992–1995. The Savigny is especially voluptuous; the Île de Vergelesses more powerful, tannic, and long lived. All three are unfiltered.

DOMAINE DE LA ROMANÉE-CONTI (VOSNE-ROMANÉE)

1985 ECHÉZEAUX	92
1985 GRANDS ECHÉZEAUX	95
1985 ROMANÉE-CONTI	100
1985 ROMANÉE ST.-VIVANT	94
1985 RICHEBOURG	96
1985 LA TÂCHE	98

This fabled estate has had a brilliant track record since 1978. Lalou Bize-Leroy and Aubert de Villaine seem to have everything tightly within their grasps, so it is unlikely that some of the lapses in quality control that occurred previously will resurface. I am sure they still cannot understand why their estate is so frequently singled out for malicious attacks, but no one should have any trouble appreciating the domaine's 1985s, which are their best wines in decades, even surpassing their sensational 1978s. The problem is coming up with the cash to finance them. The wines, aged in 100% new oak, are never filtered. The Echézeaux, normally the lightest and least distinguished of their wines, is the best I have tasted from them. Deep ruby, with a fragrant, rich, complex bouquet of violets and spicy oak, this full-bodied wine is quite long, velvety, and will keep until 1995–2000. The Grands Echézeaux is opulent, deep in color, fatter, and more alcoholic than the lovely 1980, and less tannic than the 1983. Its huge fruit, sweetness, and length are terrific. Drink it between now and 2000. The Romanée St.-Vivant is much more tannic, has the telltale iron-like scent, cinnamon, and *goût de terroir* that, for me, make it the most unique wine of the Domaine de la Romanée-Conti stable. It is quite tannic and needs cellaring until 1993–1994. The Richebourg is enormous in an old, heavyweight style. It is a tannic, relatively closed wine, with a broodingly deep color, and sensational depth and length. It would be a crime to drink it before 1992–1995, and it will last two decades. The La Tâche offers surreal and celestial aromas of oriental spices and flowers, masses of ripe fruit, scents of truffles, dazzling concentration, tremendous breadth of flavor, exquisite length, and 20 or more years of cellaring potential. The Romanée-Conti is utterly mind blowing. The heady, intoxicating bouquet delivered penetrating and sublime aromas that were even more intense than those from the La Tâche. On the palate, there is a veritable smorgasbord of earthly and heavenly delights. Needless to say, it is very rich, very opulent, and very concentrated. Red burgundy and red wine do not get any better than this. My guess is that it will peak between 1990 and 2005, as it is a bit more forward than either the La Tâche or Richebourg.

PHILIPPE ROSSIGNOL (GEVREY-CHAMBERTIN)

1985 BOURGOGNE	86
1985 CÔTE DE NUITS-VILLAGES	84
1985 GEVREY-CHAMBERTIN	86

There is no doubt that the generic Bourgogne is a lovely, rich, unfiltered, intense wine with gobs of sweet oak in the bouquet as well as surprising depth. Drink it between 1992–1994. Surprisingly, I liked it better than the Côte de Nuits-Villages, which is quite tannic. The Gevrey-Chambertin is smoky, ripe, full bodied, and shows fine depth and length. It will age well until 1992–1995.

JOSEPH ROTY (GEVREY-CHAMBERTIN)

1985 CHARMES-CHAMBERTIN	98
1985 GEVREY-CHAMBERTIN LES CHAMPCHENYS	88
1985 GEVREY-CHAMBERTIN LES FONTENYS	90
1985 MAZIS-CHAMBERTIN	94
1985 PINOT NOIR LES PRESSONIÈRES	84

The extremely hyperactive and talkative Joseph Roty is a fabulous winemaker. While he has been "discovered" numerous times, I doubt Roty has ever made better wines than these 1985s. The generic Bourgogne has a dark ruby color, an intense, spicy nose, and at least 5 to 6 years of life. The specialties here are his wines from his own backyard, Gevrey-Chambertin. The Les Champchenys, not a Premier Cru, but a good vineyard near Charmes-Chambertin, is amazing for a Villages wine from Gevrey. Ruby/purple in color with a penetrating bouquet of toasty oak, this full-bodied wine is very rich, long, concentrated, and will last until 1997–2002. The Premier Cru Les Fontenys is even more loaded. A broodingly rich, smoky, intense, power-laden wine, it has the requisite concentration, length, and tannin to carry it 20 years. While Roty's Mazis-Chambertin is undoubtedly a great wine, with its astonishing black-purple color, huge, oaky, intense bouquet of cassis, and dazzling power and depth, the Charmes-Chambertin is simply awesome. From the bouquet of violets, intense cherry fruit, and toasty new oak, to the staggering level of extract and purity of Pinot Noir fruit, this full-bodied yet sensual and elegant Charmes-Chambertin is one of the most impressive bottles of young burgundy I have ever tasted. It should keep until 2000–2005.

EMANUEL ROUGET (NUITS ST.-GEORGES)

1985 ECHÉZEAUX	89
1985 NUITS ST.-GEORGES	85

The young Emanuel Rouget, nephew of Henri Jayer, began making the wines of Jayer in 1987. He also has several small parcels himself, from which he produces the above wines. They are not filtered and are bottled directly from the barrel. The Nuits St.-Georges has a good color, a charming, elegant berry fruitiness, medium body, and cellaring potential until 1991–1995. The Echézeaux has exceptional purity of raspberry fruit, deep color, a long, flowing fruitiness, medium to full body, and should age well until 1997.

GEORGES ROUMIER (CHAMBOLLE-MUSIGNY)

1985 BONNES MARES	88
1985 CHAMBOLLE-MUSIGNY	85
1985 CHAMBOLLE-MUSIGNY LES AMOUREUSES	90
1985 CLOS VOUGEOT	87
1985 MOREY ST.-DENIS CLOS DE LA BUSSIÈRE	87

The Villages Chambolle-Musigny has good length, a supple, charming ripeness and berry fruitiness, and should age well until 1991–1992. The Clos de la Bussière has a deep color, a broad, sweet, smoky, cherry-scented bouquet, velvety texture, full body, and should age well until 1994–1995. The Bonnes Mares may turn out to be a great wine. It is quite dark in color, is closed and tannic, but swells in the glass and appears to have significant depth and richness on the palate. Drink it between 1990 and 2000. The Clos Vougeot is similarly tight and closed, but has an impressive color and possibly great potential, as it possesses oodles of fruit extract, plenty of body, and length. On the other hand, the Les Amoureuses gushes from the glass with explosive richness, intense aromas of sweet vanillin oak, ripe cherries, and spring flowers. Full bodied, with extravagant fruit, this wine will drink well until 1997–2000.

HERVÉ ROUMIER (CHAMBOLLE-MUSIGNY)

1985 BONNES MARES	85
1985 BOURGOGNE	75
1985 CHAMBOLLE-MUSIGNY	79
1985 CHAMBOLLE-MUSIGNY LES AMOUREUSES	86

The 1985s ranged from average to quite good. Both the Bourgogne and Chambolle-Musigny are simple, rather undistinguished wines. The Les Amoureuses has a dark ruby color, soft, supple, concentrated fruitiness, medium to full body, and good aging potential until 1991–1992. The Bonnes Mares tastes good, but is not special or particularly concentrated given the vintage. Nevertheless, the wine has plenty of appeal because of its pure, velvety Pinot Noir fruitiness.

ARMAND ROUSSEAU (GEVREY-CHAMBERTIN)

1985 CHAMBERTIN	91
1985 CHAMBERTIN-CLOS DE BÈZE	90
1985 CHARMES-CHAMBERTIN	87
1985 CLOS DE LA ROCHE	87
1985 CLOS DES RUCHOTTES	88
1985 GEVREY-CHAMBERTIN	83
1985 GEVREY-CHAMBERTIN LES CAZETIERS	85
1985 GEVREY-CHAMBERTIN CLOS ST.-JACQUES	89
1985 MAZIS-CHAMBERTIN	86

If Rousseau's 1985s are not spectacular, they are consistently very good to excellent. Two of the wines, the Les Cazetiers and Mazis-

Chambertin, tasted too supple and lacked some definition. The Charmes-Chambertin is very seductive and expansive, but can be drunk young. The Clos de la Roche is similarly styled but, surprisingly, not rich or tannic enough to be great. The Clos St.-Jacques, made from 61-year-old vines, has oodles of black cherry fruit, a deep color, and layer upon layer of extract. It needs until 1990–1991 to develop fully, but will keep for 10 to 15 years. The Clos des Ruchottes is similar, but even more structured. The two great wines are the Chambertin-Clos de Bèze and the Chambertin. Both wines will age well until the year 2000, have deep color, powerful, rich, intense flavors, plenty of spicy, new oak, and gobs of tannin, as well as impeccable length.

SAIER (MERCUREY)

1985 MERCUREY CHAMPS MARTIN	86
1985 MERCUREY LES CHENELOTS	84

The Saier family, which also owns the famous Clos des Lambrays in Morey St.-Denis, has vineyards in Mercurey. The quality of their two 1985 Mercureys is good to very good. The Les Chenelots is soft, ripe, attractively fruity, and offers plenty of soft berry fruit. The Champs Martin, said by some to be the best vineyard in Mercurey, is a much richer wine, exhibits toasty, plummy scents and flavors, has medium to full body and a velvety finish. Both wines should drink well until 1992–1993.

DANIEL SENARD (ALOXE-CORTON)

1985 CORTON	89
1985 CORTON LES BRESSANDES	87
1985 CORTON-CLOS DU MEIX	85
1985 CORTON-CLOS DU ROI	87

Daniel Senard, one of Aloxe-Corton's most visible proprietors, made delicious 1985s that possess vibrant, well-focused black cherry fruit married handsomely with toasty vanillin oak. On the palate all the wines show the personality characteristics of the 1985 vintage—soft, lush fruit, medium to full body, and very soft, light tannins. My three favorites included the outstanding Corton, Corton Les Bressandes, and Corton-Clos du Roi. All these wines can be drunk now—the wonderful dilemma with most 1985 burgundies—or can be cellared for 5–10 years.

G. SERAFIN (GEVREY-CHAMBERTIN)

1985 GEVREY-CHAMBERTIN LES CAZETIERS	88

Aged in 100% new oak, this impressive wine exhibits exceptional finesse, a long, deep, supple fruitiness, and nearly great character and concentration. It should age well until 1992–1994.

BERNARD SERVEAU (MOREY ST.-DENIS)

1985 BOURGOGNE	86
1985 CHAMBOLLE-MUSIGNY LES AMOUREUSES	90
1985 CHAMBOLLE-MUSIGNY LES CHABIOTS	86
1985 MOREY ST.-DENIS LES SORBÈS	87

These wines are always graceful examples of red burgundy—supple enough to be drunk young, yet structured and concentrated enough to age 7 to 10 years. The surprise here is the ripe, juicy, round, sweet, aromatic Bourgogne, which has excellent depth and loads of fruit. In the high-priced world of burgundy, it is a real bargain. Serveau's Morey St.-Denis Les Sorbès is pure elegance—ripe, seductive, well structured, and loaded with scents and flavors of raspberry fruit and new oak. It should evolve well until 1994–1995. The Chabiots is effusively fruity, but less deep and structured, and so should be drunk before 1993. Serveau is glorious Chambolle-Musigny Les Amoureuses has a dazzling level of fruit extract, a wonderful purity, elegance, balance, and sensational length. It should be at its best between 1990 and 1996.

ROBERT SIRUGUE (VOSNE-ROMANÉE)

1985 GRANDS ECHÉZEAUX	90
1985 VOSNE-ROMANÉE	86
1985 VOSNE-ROMANÉE LES PETITS MONTS	86

The tan, animated, friendly, and very commercially oriented grower Robert Sirugue, smiles broadly when asked to talk about his 1985s. The Villages Vosne-Romanée is sweet and round with lovely fruit; it should age well until 1991–1992. The well-situated Vosne-Romanée Les Petits Monts (the vineyard touches Romanée-Conti and Richebourg) tasted less rich and complex than I had hoped, but in all fairness, I tasted it only one month after bottling. It had very good color, ripe, fruity, supple flavors, and seemed nearly ready to drink then. The Grands Echézeaux was deep ruby in color with a ripe, rich, perfumed bouquet of berry fruit, spicy new oak, and flowers. It is a rich, well-structured, and delineated wine that makes a considerable impression on the palate. It should be fully mature around 1991–1992, but will keep 5 to 7 years thereafter.

TOLLOT-BEAUT (CHOREY-LÈS-BEAUNE)

1985 BEAUNE CLOS DU ROI	89
1985 CORTON LES BRESSANDES	90
1985 CÔTE DE BEAUNE-VILLAGES	84
1985 SAVIGNY LES LAVIÈRES	85

This very special property has quite a traditional approach to winemaking—wood fermenters, plenty of punching down, high fermentation temperatures, no finings, and only minimal filtration. The 1985s are very good to exceptional in quality. The Côte de Beaune-Villages has a moderately intense bouquet of clear cherry fruit, some appealing fatness, and fine length. It should be drunk by 1991–1992. The Savigny Les Lavières is a big, rather tannic wine with considerable fruit, but it also possesses a firm, very well-structured character. It should be drunk between 1990–1995. The great bouquet, the super rich, ripe fruit, the powerful, deep, full-bodied character, and the explosive nature of the Beaune Clos du Roi suggest that this big wine should be drunk between 1992 and 2000. The Corton Les Bressandes is even more stupendous. A huge wine of exceptional concentration, full body, very ripe fruit, spicy oak, and amazing finish, it will be a real keeper. Drink it between 1992 and 2005.

LOUIS TRAPET (GEVREY-CHAMBERTIN)

1985 CHAMBERTIN	87
1985 CHAMBERTIN-VIEILLES VIGNES	88
1985 CHAPELLE-CHAMBERTIN	85
1985 GEVREY-CHAMBERTIN	85

1985 GEVREY-CHAMBERTIN PREMIER CRU	84
1985 LATRICIÈRES-CHAMBERTIN	87

Trapet says his 1985s are the finest overall vintage here in the last three decades, even better than his superb 1969s. His 1985s have an elegance and rich berry fruitiness that give them a precocious appeal and charm now, but they should last for at least a decade. The Gevrey-Chambertin has a rich, earthy, berry-scented bouquet, good color, smoky, plummy fruit, medium body, and a long, lush finish. I preferred it to the Gevrey-Chambertin Premier Cru, which tasted slightly less rich and multidimensional. The Chapelle-Chambertin, while it has a good structure, is all silky elegance with a big, penetrating, toasty, earthy bouquet, concentrated, supple fruitiness, and a long finish. It should be drinkable until 1993–1996. The Latricières-Chambertin is richer, more full bodied and tannic than the Chapelle. It may turn out to be Trapet's best wine in 1985. Quite rich, smoky, and earthy with super length and ripeness, this is an atypically "big" wine for Trapet. The Chambertin is long, ripe, rich, and less full bodied than the Latricières, more elegant and fruity, and aged in 50% new oak barrels. It will drink well young and should age until 1994–1996. The Chambertin-Vieilles Vignes has gobs of sweet, ripe berry fruit, a well-structured palate impression, medium to full body, broad, expansive flavors, and a long finish. It is much better colored and more flattering to drink than the not-afflicted 1983 version of this wine.

VADEY-CASTAGNIER (MOREY ST.-DENIS)

1985 CHAMBOLLE-MUSIGNY	86
1985 CHARMES-CHAMBERTIN	88
1985 CLOS DE LA ROCHE	88
1985 CLOS VOUGEOT	87
1985 GEVREY-CHAMBERTIN	86

While I did not find any of the 1985s to be exceptional, they are all very good to excellent red burgundies, bursting with ripe aromas and flavors. The Chambolle-Musigny is full of charm and finesse, and has a super, jammy personality and round fruit. It should be drunk by 1990–1992. The Gevrey-Chambertin is more smoky and fat with layers of succulent

Pinot Noir fruit. It is quite an excellent Villages wine and should be drunk over the next 5–6 years. The Clos Vougeot is also very forward and precocious, but more concentrated, full bodied, and longer. It is loaded with sweet, ripe, pure Pinot fruit. It should drink well until 1992–1995. The two best wines from Castagnier are the Clos de la Roche and Charmes-Chambertin. The Clos de la Roche is bigger, more robust, and potentially the longest-lived wine from Castagnier, but packed with velvety, deep, rich fruit, and has a penetrating sweet, roasted aroma. Drink it between 1995–1997. The Charmes-Chambertin has the identical texture and level of sweet, ripe fruit, but is less robust and more elegant. All of these wines have plenty of hedonistic appeal.

MICHEL VOARICK (ALOXE-CORTON)

1985 ALOXE-CORTON	83
1985 CORTON LES BRESSANDES	87
1985 CORTON-CLOS DU ROI	90
1985 CORTON LES LANGUETTES	85
1985 PERNAND-VERGELESSES	85
1985 ROMANÉE ST.-VIVANT	86

Michel Voarick's 1985s are very tannic, densely colored wines that he compares to the 1964s and 1959s, and not to the 1978s, which he says are lighter and less powerful. The Pernand-Vergelesses should be cellared until 1992–1995. Powerful and rich, but too closed and tannic, it is quite a sizeable wine for its appellation. The Aloxe-Corton has an unusual tar-like smell, and despite its chewy, dense style tasted too tannic. I liked the Corton Les Languettes, and although it should be cellared until 1992–1993, I thought it suffered in comparison with the other Voarick wines. The Corton Les Bressandes is sumptuous, fat, very rich and deep, and should evolve until 1992–1999. It is quite full bodied and tannic. The Corton-Clos du Roi is even better. A huge, intense, rich, concentrated wine of extremely generous proportions, it oozes with scents and flavors of cherries. It needs until 1992–1996 to develop. The Romanée St.-Vivant, while quite elegant and tasty, does not live up to its price or reputation. It is stylish, but a slight dilution in its mid-range keeps its score lower than a wine of its pedigree should merit.

1985 WHITE BURGUNDY

Production was significantly below the bumper crop of 1986. Paradoxically, some wines appeared to lack complexity and depth. The grapes were so healthy and free of mold and rot that some growers claimed the wines are too clean and perfect. At the top levels, the wines are fat and rich, but low in acidity. Yet, there are numerous splendid wines for drinking between 1990 and 1995. Overall, the quality is much more variable than the vintage's "great" reputation would suggest. For example, some wines from Mâcon and Pouilly Fuissé are diffuse and too light. There were great successes in Chablis, as well as Meursault and Chassagne-Montrachet. In comparison with the higher-acid, lighter-bodied 1986s, the 1985s exhibit more power and are richer, yet not always more complex. Prices are extremely high, owing to the acclaim surrounding this vintage. 1985 is undoubtedly one of the finest white burgundy vintages in the last several decades, but is it a great year?

RECOMMENDED PRODUCERS

Pierre Bitouzet
Bitouzet-Prieur
Roger Caillot
Louis Chapuis
Coche-Debord
J. F. Coche-Dury
Fernand Coffinet
Comte Lafon
René Dauvissat
Georges Deleger
Joseph Drouhin
J. A. Ferret
Château Fuissé
Jean-Noël Gagnard

Albert Grivault
Louis Jadot
Domaine Leflaive
Lequin-Roussot
Château de Meursault
Louis Michel
Michelot-Buisson
Moillard
Bernard Morey
Pierre Morey
Michel Niellon
Domaine Ramonet
Guy Roulot
Étienne Sauzet

1986 RED BURGUNDY

1986 is not a bad vintage, but rather one of great irregularity and inconsistency thanks to overproduction and rot. Those producers who eliminated rotten grapes and who kept their yield per hectare to reasonable limits have made very acceptable, fruity, albeit slightly dry and tannic wines. Those producers who are motivated by greed, who do not uphold the highest winemaking standards, or are just incompetent, have made hard, skinny wines with washed-out flavors. The best wines are clearly from the northern half of Burgundy, the Côte de Nuits. The value of the good 1986s is that they are more reasonably priced than the 1985s or the 1988s. Selection is always the most important factor when buying burgundy regardless of a vintage's reputation. In 1986, as in all burgundy vintages, you must stick to the most committed and consistent growers who have usually done well. All things considered, 1986 red burgundies are vastly superior to 1984, 1982, 1981, and 1979.

Note: The 1986s were tasted from the barrel during the summer of 1987 and have been evaluated from the bottle in the spring and fall of 1988.

PIERRE AMIOT (MOREY ST.-DENIS)

1986 CLOS DE LA ROCHE	84
1986 GEVREY-CHAMBERTIN AUX COMBOTTES	78
1986 MOREY ST.-DENIS	75
1986 MOREY ST.-DENIS AUX CHARMES	83
1986 MOREY ST.-DENIS LES RUCHOTTES	82

Pierre Amiot's 1986s are light, may have an excess of tannin for the amount of fruit they possess, but are still pleasant, pure, and stylish. The Les Ruchottes, a Premier Cru vineyard located below the famous Clos de Tart estate, is open, fragrant, and already easy to drink. The Gevrey-Chambertin aux Combottes has more extract but also more tannin. It should be better with another year of bottle age. The Morey St.-Denis tasted slightly diluted and one dimensional. The wine I liked best was the tannic, medium-bodied, spicy, coffee-and-leather–scented Clos de la Roche, but I wonder if its fragile balance of fruit and tannin will endure beyond 1991 or 1992. The Morey St.-Denis aux Charmes seemed slightly less tannic, more fruity, but not as deep as the Clos de la Roche. Overall, Amiot's 1986s are acceptable but unexciting wines.

MARQUIS D'ANGERVILLE (VOLNAY)

1986 VOLNAY CHAMPANS	79
1986 VOLNAY-CLOS DES DUCS	82

This highly respected domaine always leaves me perplexed. I never judge burgundy by its color, but certain wines have such a pale hue I cannot help but be apprehensive. For most of the vintages of the 1980s, d'Angerville's Volnays have tasted too light, over-cropped, or over-filtered. His 1986s are very light with soft, but adequate strawberry fruit in evidence. I am sure some writer might suggest that these wines will age into something sublime, but older vintages of d'Angerville's wines have rarely left me completely satisfied. The Clos des Ducs has more depth and fruit than the Champans, and should last until 1992–1993. Both wines could be more inspiring.

COMTE ARMAND (POMMARD)

1986 POMMARD-CLOS DES EPÉNEAUX	87

This is a very successful wine. However, don't expect a classically proportioned burgundy. Deep in color, very full bodied, jammy, and quite oaky, this is a super-concentrated, surprisingly large-scaled 1986 that should be at its best between 1990 and 1995.

ROBERT ARNOUX (VOSNE-ROMANÉE)

1986 CLOS VOUGEOT	85
1986 NUITS ST.-GEORGES LES CORVÉES PAGET	82
1986 NUITS ST.-GEORGES LES POISETS	80
1986 NUITS ST.-GEORGES LES PROCÈS	81
1986 ROMANÉE ST.-VIVANT	86
1986 VOSNE-ROMANÉE	81
1986 VOSNE-ROMANÉE LES CHAUMES	84
1986 VOSNE-ROMANÉE LES SUCHOTS	86

Arnoux's 1986s are most reminiscent of his 1982s. They are lighter wines than he normally makes, somewhat fragile, but scented, clean, pleasant, and, while not very concentrated, tasty and harmonious. The three best wines are the medium-bodied, spicy, berry-scented Clos Vougeot, the deeper, more seductive, ripe, and complex Vosne-Romanée Les Suchots (for my money Arnoux's best and most consistent wine year in and year out), and his more powerful, fragrant Romanée St.-Vivant. All three of these wines should drink well until 1994–1995. As for the other Arnoux wines, they are soft, not very deep, but round, elegant, lightish wines that should be drunk between 1992–1993.

BERNARD BACHELET (CHASSAGNE-MONTRACHET)

1986 CHASSAGNE-MONTRACHET	78
1986 CÔTE DE BEAUNE-VILLAGES	82
1986 POMMARD LES CHANLINS	84
1986 SANTENAY	?

To varying degrees all of these wines showed some of the dilution caused by the super-abundant crop of 1986. While the Santenay was, I hope, an off bottle, the Chassagne-Montrachet tasted as if it had too much tannin for its meager fruit. I preferred the Côte de Beaune-Villages, which tasted of supple cherries and spicy oak; it should be drunk now. The best wine is Bachelet's Pommard Les Chanlins—his first vintage for this wine. It is supple, fruity, and very attractive for drinking between 1991–1992.

DOMAINE DENIS BACHELET (GEVREY-CHAMBERTIN)

1986 CHARMES-CHAMBERTIN	88
1986 GEVREY-CHAMBERTIN LES CORBEAUX VIEILLES VIGNES	85
1986 GEVREY-CHAMBERTIN VIEILLES VIGNES	86

Denis Bachelet's 1986s are excellent. The Gevrey-Chambertin Vieilles Vignes is a smooth, intensely fruity, supple wine that can be drunk between now and 1994–1995. The Gevrey-Chambertin Les Corbeaux again had a lovely rich fruitiness suggestive of ripe plums and cherries. On the palate it is a medium-bodied wine with excellent length, but I would still want to drink it between 1992–1993. My notes on the Charmes-Chambertin said, "quintessentially elegant," so surely I was blown away by its bouquet. It is loaded with fruit, it is very soft, sweet, expansive, and has a creamy texture. It admirably demonstrates what one could do in 1986 when the yields were restrained and the wines not over-oaked.

BARTHOD NOËLLAT (CHAMBOLLE-MUSIGNY)

1986 CHAMBOLLE-MUSIGNY AUX BEAUX BRUNS	84
1986 CHAMBOLLE-MUSIGNY LES CHARMES	82
1986 CHAMBOLLE-MUSIGNY LES CRAS	80

Gaston Barthod's 1986s are certainly successful. All of these wines are Premiers Crus from Chambolle-Musigny. Beaux Bruns appears to be the best, with a good ruby color, a cherry, spicy bouquet, and pleasant, medium-bodied flavors. Les Charmes is an attractively fruity wine made in a lighter style. Les Cras is quite light but does have clean cherry and strawberry fruit. All three wines should be drunk between 1991–1993.

DOMAINE DENIS BERTHAUT (FIXIN)

1986 FIXIN	75
1986 FIXIN LES ARVELETS	82
1986 FIXIN LES CLOS	82
1986 FIXIN LES CRAIS	82
1986 GEVREY-CHAMBERTIN CLOS CHÉSEAUX	84

Denis Berthaut produces robust, spicy, attractively full, yet tannic wines that tend to age well. I often wish they had more forward fruit, but his style is oriented toward muscle and body. His 1986s are all decent wines, although the Fixin is too light as well as too hard. I thought all the Premiers Crus Fixin to be similar in quality, and they should age well until 1992–1994. Berthaut's best wine in 1986 is the ripe, woody, well-colored Gevrey-Chambertin Clos Chéseaux. It is a very good wine for the price.

DOMAINE BERTHEAU (CHAMBOLLE-MUSIGNY)

1986 BONNES MARES	90
1986 CHAMBOLLE-MUSIGNY	85
1986 CHAMBOLLE-MUSIGNY LES AMOUREUSES	89
1986 CHAMBOLLE-MUSIGNY LES CHARMES	88

Bertheau's 1986s tasted more like 1985s. All were impressively rich, deep, concentrated wines with plenty of class and charm. For those lucky enough to find it, the Bonnes Mares exhibits super concentration, great color and length, moderate tannins, and has that intense old-vine taste that one can always sense but not describe very well. The Bonnes Mares should be at its best between 1991 and 2000. The Chambolle-Musigny is especially impressive for a Villages wine. Deep in color, ripe, and richly fruity, sporting a bouquet filled with scents of flowers and berries, it will drink nicely until 1994–1995. Perhaps the finest wine of this group for consuming by 1995 is the Chambolle-Musigny Les Amoureuses. Very fragrant, intense, ripe, and complex, this seductive, hedonistic wine has layers of flavor, and is a top success for this variable vintage. Last, the Chambolle-Musigny Les Charmes is also top notch, leaving a velvety, deep, expansive impression on the palate, with gobs of berry fruit, and excellent length. These impressive 1986s are wines that should be sought out.

DOMAINE BESANCENOT-MATHOUILLET (BEAUNE)

1986 BEAUNE LES CENT VIGNES	83
1986 BEAUNE CLOS DU ROI	83

This serious estate has its cellar immediately outside the gates of Beaune. While his 1986s are not my favorites (his 1978s, 1980s, and 1985s are the finest I have tasted), they are light, elegant wines that will require drinking by 1993. They are clean, smell of berries and strawberries, but show the dilution of the gigantic crop in 1986.

DOMAINE BILLARD-GONNET (POMMARD)

1986 BEAUNE LES MONTREVENOTS	?
1986 POMMARD	74
1986 POMMARD CLOS DE VERGERS	74
1986 POMMARD LES RUGIENS	84

I have never fully understood this man's wines. I have been told that they age extremely well, but I wonder how much true pleasure they ever provide! The Beaune Les Montrevenots is unforgivably hard, lean, and tough, and is still years away from drinkability. Frankly, I don't ever see it coming into balance. The Pommard is also very lean, sinewy, and short on fruit and charm. The Pommard Clos de Vergers is riper and has more substance, but finishes with a considerable tannic clout. It should be put away until at least 1993–1994. The Pommard Les Rugiens is medium to full bodied, has a good raspberry fruitiness, plenty of spicy new oak, and a hard, tannic finish. All of these wines are very typical of the Billard-Gonnet style, but I wish they had more fruit and fat. Those who prefer very lean, highly structured wines will like these better than I did.

BITOUZET-PRIEUR (VOLNAY)

1986 VOLNAY	72
1986 VOLNAY LES AUSSY	73
1986 VOLNAY CLOS DES CHÊNES	75
1986 VOLNAY PITURES	78
1986 VOLNAY TAILLEPIEDS	82

Vincent Bitouzet, one of only a handful of producers who seem equally adroit making red and white burgundy, has not done well in 1986. For whatever reason (probably the enormous crop size), the wines have turned out light and diluted, in shocking contrast to his smashing 1985s. The Volnay is very thin, even watery, and the Volnay Les Aussy seems insipid and dull. The Volnay Clos des Chênes is rather hard, lean, and charmless, and while the Volnay Pitures is better and does show some decent cherry flavors, there is not much of a finish. The Volnay Taille-pieds, usually the top wine of Bitouzet, has some solid cherry fruit, is spicy, medium bodied, and should age well until 1992–1993.

BOUCHARD PÈRE ET FILS (BEAUNE)

1986 ALOXE-CORTON	82
1986 BEAUNE LE CHÂTEAU	84
1986 BEAUNE CLOS DE LA MOUSSE	85
1986 BEAUNE LES GRÈVES L'ENFANT JÉSUS	85
1986 BEAUNE LES TEURONS	81
1986 CHAMBOLLE-MUSIGNY	82
1986 LE CORTON	89
1986 NUITS ST.-GEORGES CLOS ST.-MARC	86
1986 POMMARD PREMIER CRU	82
1986 VOLNAY LES CAILLERETS	86
1986 VOLNAY FREMIETS CLOS DE LA ROUGEOTTE	84

1986 VOLNAY TAILLEPIEDS	86
1986 VOSNE-ROMANÉE AUX REIGNOTS	82

In the past I have found both the white and red wines of Bouchard lacking in spark and individuality. They seem always to have been made in a very safe, middle-of-the-road manner. With the installation of a new winemaking facility, inaugurated with the 1986 crop, the wines appear to be taking on more flavor and a bit more character. Given the enormous resources of this firm, they could certainly do anything they desired. The 1986s are good at Bouchard, but the 1987s are better, and the 1988s I saw are potentially the finest wines this firm has produced since the late fifties. The style here is one aimed at moderately structured, compact wines of medium body. The wines spend 15–18 months in oak casks, and depending on the wine, the percentage of new oak varies from 30% to 100%. I think a little less filtration might result in more aromatic, less sculptured wines. As for the 1986s, my favorites included a supple, floral, and berry-scented, concentrated Beaune Clos de la Mousse, a more tannic yet still deep and spicy Beaune Les Grèves L'Enfant Jésus, a rich, tannic, full-bodied, very structured Volnay Taillepieds, a similarly backward yet deep, well-scented Volnay Les Caillerets, an excellent, expansive, broad-shouldered, oaky, rich Le Corton, and a fragrant, supple, well-colored, medium-bodied, somewhat oaky Nuits St.-Georges Clos St.-Marc. All of these wines will need 4–5 years of cellaring after the vintage, with Le Corton requiring a good 6–7 years of aging prior to consumption. Virtually all the Bouchard 1986s possess a fairly hefty tannin content. As for the other 1986s from Bouchard, they were all well-made, clean, structured red burgundies. They will not excite anyone, but are soundly made examples of red burgundy for the less adventurous.

JEAN-MARC BOULEY (VOLNAY)

1986 POMMARD LES PÉZEROLLES	84
1986 POMMARD LES RUGIENS	85
1986 VOLNAY CLOS DES CHÊNES	85

As for the 1986s, they are firmer, harder, more tannic wines than Bouley's 1987s. All three of the above wines have very good color for the vintage, no signs of dilution as a result of the huge crop, good tannins that are not astringent or harsh, and good aging potential until 1993–1996. The Volnay Clos des Chênes and Pommard Les Rugiens both had a more aromatic character than the Pommard Les Pézerolles, hence the slightly higher ratings.

DOMAINE MARC BROCOT (MARSANNAY)

1986 GEVREY-CHAMBERTIN	76
1986 MARSANNAY	85

The Marsannay, made from 30-year-old vines, is one of the finest red wines I have tasted from this new Burgundy appellation. Deep, rich, full bodied, intense, even a little too powerful for its own good, this big wine will easily age well until 1995–1996. The Gevrey-Chambertin should be better, but it is a hard, tannic, lean wine that does not appear to possess enough fruit.

ALAIN BURGUET (GEVREY-CHAMBERTIN)

1986 GEVREY-CHAMBERTIN VIEILLES VIGNES	89

What a shame this man does not own any Premier Cru or Grand Cru vineyards. His 1986 Gevrey-Chambertin Vieilles Vignes is quite amazing stuff. Packed with fruit, deep in color, rich, long, very fragrant, and intense, this sensational wine drinks well now but should last until 1996–1997.

DOMAINE CAMUS (GEVREY-CHAMBERTIN)

1986 CHAMBERTIN	84
1986 CHARMES-CHAMBERTIN	82
1986 GEVREY-CHAMBERTIN	75
1986 LATRICIÈRES-CHAMBERTIN	77
1986 MAZOYÈRES-CHAMBERTIN	81

The Gevrey-Chambertin is a one-dimensional, spicy, medium-bodied wine that is light but adequate. The Charmes-Chambertin has an attractive nose of berry fruit and spicy oak, but an astringent, tannic finish. The Mazoyères-Chambertin has the same dry, harsh finish that keeps my marks down. The Latricières-Chambertin is the most severe in style, exhibiting a hardness and toughness that seem far too excessive for the amount of fruit. The wine I did find well balanced is the Chambertin. It not only had the deepest color, but also had some depth and a rich, smoky, game-like, exotic Pinot character. It finished dry and hard but seemed to have enough fruit to stand up to the tannins. All in all, the 1986s of Camus are not nearly as good as this domaine's 1985s.

GUY CASTAGNIER (MOREY ST.-DENIS)

1986 BONNES MARES	88
1986 CHAMBOLLE-MUSIGNY	84
1986 CLOS DE LA ROCHE	87
1986 CLOS ST.-DENIS	89

These wines also appear under the label of Vadey-Castagnier. I thought the domaine was quite successful in 1986. The Villages Chambolle-Musigny is very well done. The moderately intense bouquet of spicy oak and berry fruit is attractive. On the palate the wine is fruity and soft, and should be drunk between 1991–1992. The Bonnes Mares is excellent, with sweet, ripe fruit, an opulent, generous texture, and loads of length and flavor. It should be drinkable until 1993–1994. The Clos de la Roche is more tannic but shares the same open-knit, generously fruity, plump, round style that seems to characterize Castagnier's 1986s. The best wine, in terms of pure pleasure, is the Clos St.-Denis. The bouquet shows a super perfume and on the palate the wine is medium bodied, rich in flavor, spicy, and finishes with a heady alcoholic punch. It, too, should be enjoyed until 1993–1994.

DOMAINE CECI (VOUGEOT)

1986 CHAMBOLLE-MUSIGNY LES ÉCHANGES	84
1986 CLOS VOUGEOT	84

This tiny estate seems quite committed to turning out very fine wines, judging by those I tasted on my first visit to their cellars. The domaine owns 10 acres, and the wines are aged in entirely new oak. The Chambolle-Musigny Les Échanges is quite oaky, but there is a lovely, supple, juicy, succulent berry fruitiness. The wine is very forward and should be drunk by 1991. The Clos Vougeot is similarly styled with a great deal

of strawberry and cherry fruit, gobs of spicy new oak, and a charmingly
seductive texture and taste. It should be drunk young.

CHÂTEAU DE CHAMBOLLE-MUSIGNY (CHAMBOLLE-MUSIGNY)

1986 BONNES MARES	85
1986 CHAMBOLLE-MUSIGNY LES FUÉES	86
1986 LE MUSIGNY VIEILLES VIGNES	90

Proprietor Jacques-Frédéric Mugnier loves spicy, toasty, new oak almost to an extreme. I thought his 1985s were a bit too woody, but the
1986s I tasted seemed to marry the toasty character of new oak with
plenty of seductive berry fruit. The Bonnes Mares is a little light, but
seductive, creamy, ripe, and smooth. Drink it by 1994–1996. The
Chambolle-Musigny Les Fuées is a fat wine with excellent color, a big,
bold, oaky, aromatic bouquet, soft, lush flavors, and a smooth finish. It
should be drunk by 1993–1994. The Musigny Vieilles Vignes is remarkably seductive, intense, complex, and even profound. Gobs of sweet,
toasty fruit are present in this medium- to full-bodied wine. It drinks
extremely well now, but should keep until 1993–1994. These are surprisingly concentrated wines for the vintage.

CHAMPY PÈRE (BEAUNE)

1986 BEAUNE LES AVAUX	86
1986 CLOS VOUGEOT	87
1986 POMMARD	85
1986 SAVIGNY-LÈS-BEAUNE LES DOMINAUDES	86

I thought the 1986s were very successful at Champy. The Beaune Les
Avaux had a deep color, a robust, forceful texture, plenty of oaky,
cherry fruit, and very good length. The Clos Vougeot is excellent—
deep, full bodied, rich, tannic, yet well balanced. Don't drink it before
1992. The Villages Pommard could easily surpass many of the Premiers
Crus of that village. It is a fat, hedonistic, deep wine with plenty of
extract and flavor. Drink it by 1994. Last, the Savigny-Lès-Beaune Les
Dominaudes is a powerful, intense, full-bodied, tannic wine loaded with
black cherry fruit. It will drink well for the next decade. All in all, the
1986s from Champy are reliable wines.

DOMAINE CHANDON DE BRIAILLES
(SAVIGNY-LÈS-BEAUNE)

1986 CORTON LES BRESSANDES	87
1986 CORTON-CLOS DU ROI	89
1986 CORTON LES MARÉCHAUDES	84
1986 PERNAND-VERGELESSES ÎLE DES VERGELESSES	85
1986 SAVIGNY-LÈS-BEAUNE LES LAVIÈRES	82

The 1986 Savigny-Lès-Beaune Les Laviéres has good color, a spicy, ripe-cherry, oak-scented bouquet, firm, taut flavors, and medium body. It needs until about 1991 to round out. A step up in quality is the Pernand-Île des Vergelesses, a rich, spicy, relatively deep wine with plenty of red fruit. It has both power and elegance and should be ready between 1992 and 1996. The estate has a fine range of wines from Aloxe-Corton that showed especially well in 1986. The Corton Les Bressandes exhibits a toasty, new oaky character with gobs of bing cherry fruit in the background, a full body, and plenty of fat and length. Drink it between 1993 and 1998. The Corton Les Maréchaudes seemed good, but I rated it a bit lower because of its rather tough, excessively hard style, which obscured some of the fruit. Much better was the Corton-Clos du Roi. Aged in 100% new oak, this is a deeply colored, rather old-style, heavyweight red burgundy with a great deal of size, concentration, and potential. Drink it between 1995 and 2003.

CHANZY FRÈRES (BEAUNE)

1986 BOURGOGNE CLOS DU LA FORTUNE	80
1986 MERCUREY CLOS DU ROI	82
1986 RULLY	75

I found the 1986s from Chanzy Frères to be adequate, but hardly inspiring. The Bourgogne is straightforward, clean, fresh, medium bodied, and ideal for drinking between 1990–1991. The Mercurey Clos du Roi, from one of that appellation's finest vineyards, is a firmly structured, deep, ruby-colored wine with nice depth and balance. Drink it between now and 1993. The Rully is too hard, very tannic, and ungenerous.

DOMAINE DE LA CHARRIÈRE (SANTENAY)

1986 SANTENAY CLOS ROUSSEAU	75
1986 SANTENAY LA COMME	78

The 1986s from the Domaine de la Charrière are mediocre, owing their character to the excessively large-sized crop. The La Comme has a good deep color, is tough, very tannic, and in need of cellaring until 1992–1993. The Clos Rousseau is lighter in color, has a decent cherry-scented bouquet, medium body, but some of the same toughness in the finish.

F. CHAUVENET (NUITS ST.-GEORGES)

1986 BEAUNE CLOS DES MOUCHES	72
1986 BEAUNE LES GRÈVES	73
1986 CLOS ST.-DENIS	81
1986 CLOS VOUGEOT	77

This up-and-coming *négociant* has recently been turning out some very pleasant, fruity wines. Unfortunately, this cannot be said for the 1986s, which are short, very light, lean, and generally charmless. If you must try only one wine, make it the Clos St.-Denis. These wines should all be drunk by 1991.

J. CHAUVENET (NUITS ST.-GEORGES)

1986 NUITS ST.-GEORGES	80
1986 NUITS ST.-GEORGES LES BOUSSELOTS	83
1986 NUITS ST.-GEORGES LES VAUCRAINS	85

Chauvenet's 1986s do not compare to his 1985s, but they are light, stylish, well-made wines that accurately reflect the 1986 vintage. The Nuits St.-Georges has good color, is spicy, attractively fruity in a picnic-light style, and has a soft finish. It will require consumption by 1991. The Premier Cru Les Bousselots shows slightly more fruit, is light to medium bodied with clean, correct flavors, but not much of a finish. The best wine from Jean Chauvenet in 1986 is Les Vaucrains, which has much more red fruit in its spicy, subtly oaky bouquet. On the palate the wine is medium bodied, somewhat light, but charming. Drink it between 1991–1992.

ROBERT CHEVILLON (NUITS ST.-GEORGES)

1986 NUITS ST.-GEORGES	81
1986 NUITS ST.-GEORGES LES CAILLES	85
1986 NUITS ST.-GEORGES LES PERRIÈRES	85
1986 NUITS ST.-GEORGES LES RONCIÈRES	81
1986 NUITS ST.-GEORGES LES SAINT-GEORGES	87
1986 NUITS ST.-GEORGES LES VAUCRAINS	87

Chevillon has again made fine wines in 1986. They are not spectacular, but reliably good. His Villages Nuits St.-Georges is soft, fruity, supple, and ready to drink—ideal for restaurants. His Les Cailles shows good color, fine depth, medium body, some tannin, and adequate length. I would drink it between 1990 and 1995. Les Perrières is more tannic and even richer, I believe, with a lovely spicy, berry-scented nose. It should drink well until at least 1999. Les Roncières seemed more tight and closed, and while I liked it, I worried about whether the fruit would fade prior to the tannin. The two stars of the Chevillon stable are Les Vaucrains and Les Saint-Georges. Both have the greatest depth of fruit and length of Chevillon's 1986s. The Saint-Georges, while quite tannic, is rich, long, complete, and should be at its best between 1994–2000. In comparison, Les Vaucrains has a smoky, berry-scented bouquet, rich, medium- to full-bodied flavors, good tannins, excellent balance, and aging potential until 1993–2001. Chevillon also made very high-quality 1987s, but his production in that vintage is tiny because of hail damage in June. Here is a Burgundy producer whose wines can be bought with great confidence.

DOMAINE CHOPIN-GROFFIER (PRÉMEAUX)

1986 CHAMBOLLE-MUSIGNY	87
1986 CLOS VOUGEOT	90
1986 CÔTE DE NUITS-VILLAGES	83
1986 NUITS ST.-GEORGES	86

1986 NUITS ST.-GEORGES LES CHAIGNOTS	90
1986 VOUGEOT	89

It was hard to make better 1986s than these wines. For starters, there is a well-made, ruby-colored Côte de Nuits-Villages that should provide pleasurable drinking until 1992. The Villages Nuits St.-Georges is surprisingly deep, richly fruity, ripe, and long. It should keep until 1995–1996. Immensely seductive and full of finesse and elegance is the Chambolle-Musigny. It has excellent fruit and could have easily been mistaken for a Premier Cru. The Vougeot borders on being fabulous. It has outstanding depth, a full-bodied, expansive feel in the mouth, oodles of succulent berry fruit, and just the right amount of oak. It should drink well until 1993–1995. The Nuits St.-Georges Les Chaignots is less flattering and more tightly structured, but has amazing depth of fruit and richness for a 1986. It should be at its best between 1991 and 1996. The Clos Vougeot, made from 50- to 60-year-old vines, has sensational extract and richness, full body, a perfumed bouquet that is a head turner, and an opulent, very long finish. It is delicious and should keep until 1994–1996.

BRUNO CLAIR (MARSANNAY)

1986 CHAMBERTIN-CLOS DE BÈZE	84
1986 CÔTE DE NUITS-VILLAGES	75
1986 GEVREY-CHAMBERTIN LES CAZETIERS	88
1986 GEVREY-CHAMBERTIN CLOS ST.-JACQUES	87
1986 GEVREY-CHAMBERTIN LE FONTENY	86
1986 SAVIGNY-LÈS-BEAUNE LES DOMINODES	82

Incidentally, before I give you my impressions of the red wines, I have to recommend Clair's delicious, vibrant Rosé of Marsannay. Don't hesitate to try it, as it is the finest dry rosé made in Burgundy but be sure to always purchase the newest vintage as its aging potential rarely exceeds 1–2 years. With respect to the red wines, I was disappointed with the thin, somewhat hollow Côte de Nuits-Villages, and I thought the Savigny-Lès-Beaune Les Dominodes should have shown better, given the fact that it is made from very old vines. Perhaps it was in an awkward stage. However, Clair's other wines showed extremely well. The Fontenys exhibited a great deal of elegance, medium ruby color, and plenty of berry fruit with a long, supple finish. It should drink well

until 1993–1996. Les Cazetiers received my highest marks. Deep ruby
with a smoky, intense, fruity bouquet complemented nicely by spicy
oak, it is clearly the deepest and richest of Clair's wines in 1986. This
wine should evolve and drink nicely until 1995–1999. It is one of the
top successes from this cave in 1986. Virtually every bit as good is the
Clos St.-Jacques. Deep ruby with plenty of perfume and depth plus a
bit more tannin than the other wines, this medium- to full-bodied wine
should be at its best between 1992 and 1998. Last, the Chambertin-
Clos de Bèze is closed and tannic, and though less powerful and weighty
than the Les Cazetiers and Clos St.-Jacques, may have too much tannin
for the depth of fruit. When tasted in 1989, I found it hard to judge and,
if you buy it, be sure to leave it in your cellar until 1992–1993.

DOMAINE CLOS DES LAMBRAYS (MOREY ST.-DENIS)

1986 CLOS DES LAMBRAYS 71

The 1986, even allowing for the dilution caused by the prodigious crop,
is a watery, woody, insipid wine that is preposterously overpriced. It
should have been declassified to a Bourgogne Rouge.

DOMAINE EDMOND CORNU (LADOIX)

1986 ALOXE-CORTON 67

1986 ALOXE-CORTON LES MOUTOTTES 72

1986 CHOREY-LÈS-BEAUNE LES BONS ORES 69

1986 CORTON LES BRESSANDES 82

1986 SAVIGNY-LÈS-BEAUNE 75

After the great success this producer enjoyed in 1985, these wines were
quite disappointing. The single exception was the light, medium-
bodied, somewhat tannic Corton Les Bressandes. Perhaps the other
wines were in a bad stage, but to varying degrees they all exhibited
dried out, hard, harsh flavors marred by excessive tannins.

DELARCHE PÈRE ET FILS (PERNAND-VERGELESSES)

1986 CORTON LES RÉNARDES 86

1986 PERNAND-VERGELESSES ÎLE DES VERGELESSES 83

1986 PERNAND-VERGELESSES LES VERGELESSES 72

The 1986s from this domaine, while not exhilarating, are very competent wines. The Corton Les Rénardes exhibited plenty of rich, ripe berry fruit, and judicious use of oak, full body, and fine length. Drink it between 1990 and 1997. The Pernand-Vergelesses Île des Vergelesses is hardly a glamorous wine in the States, but it has plenty of power plus a mouthful of excruciating tannin. My virgin notes read "too tough for me." The Pernand-Vergelesses Les Vergelesses had a very earthy nose, slightly cooked flavors, and a hard finish.

ALBERT DEREY (MARSANNAY)

1986 FIXIN	72
1986 FIXIN LES HERVELETS	75

Both of these wines are straightforward, light bodied, somewhat coarse and charmless, with an excess of tannin for their fruit. Pass them by.

JOSEPH DROUHIN (BEAUNE)

1986 ALOXE-CORTON	77
1986 BEAUNE CLOS DES MOUCHES	80
1986 CHAMBOLLE-MUSIGNY	72
1986 CHARMES-CHAMBERTIN	86
1986 CLOS DE LA ROCHE	83
1986 CLOS VOUGEOT	85
1986 ECHÉZEAUX	82
1986 GEVREY-CHAMBERTIN	78
1986 GRANDS ECHÉZEAUX	87
1986 GRIOTTE-CHAMBERTIN	87
1986 MUSIGNY	84
1986 VOSNE-ROMANÉE LES BEAUX MONTS	84

Drouhin's 1986s are well made, although they are nowhere near as stunning as his 1985s, or as the 1987s and 1988s are likely to be. Drouhin ignored much of the Côte de Beaune crop in 1986 because he was not satisfied with the quality. The selections he did make include a straightforward Aloxe-Corton that should be drunk immediately, and a more lively and vibrant yet foursquare Beaune Clos de Mouches. Among the wines from the Côte de Nuits, the Chambolle-Musigny is thin and watery, and the Clos de la Roche is charming and pleasant, though it could use more flesh and power. The Clos Vougeot is appealing, displaying better color, more ripeness, and an attractive raspberry, spicy fruitiness. It should drink well until 1994–1995. I found both the Echézeaux and Gevrey-Chambertin to be relatively innocuous wines, but the Grands Echézeaux, Charmes-Chambertin, Griotte-Chambertin and Vosne-Romanée Les Beaux Monts all had fine depth, velvety, richly fruity textures, elegance, and some real length on the palate. These latter four wines should be drunk between 1990 and 1996. The Griotte-Chambertin and Grands Echézeaux would be my two favorites.

DOMAINE DUJAC (MOREY ST.-DENIS)

1986 BONNES MARES	88
1986 CHAMBOLLE MUSIGNY PREMIER CRU	85
1986 CHARMES-CHAMBERTIN	85
1986 CLOS DE LA ROCHE	87
1986 CLOS ST.-DENIS	88
1986 ECHÉZEAUX	84
1986 GEVREY-CHAMBERTIN AUX COMBOTTES	87
1986 MOREY ST.-DENIS	80

Jacques Seysses' top wine in 1986 is the Bonnes Mares, which has a deep, complex, plummy, spicy bouquet, as well as excellent concentration and depth. Still, a slight bitterness to the tannins kept my score down. Drink it between 1992 and 2000. The Charmes-Chambertin is good, well colored, powerful, and big, but the dry, astringent tannins in the finish concerned me. It will certainly become good, possibly excellent, but don't dare drink it until 1992–1993. The Clos de la Roche is Dujac's most powerful 1986. Very dry, hard tannins cover a rather full-bodied, rich, well-constituted wine. It has length and ripe fruit, but when will the tannins melt away—1994? Certainly the Clos St.-Denis has much more current and near-term charm. It has a lovely, ripe, aromatic bouquet, gobs of velvety berry, coffee, vanillin-scented fruit, medium to full body, and excellent balance between its fruit and tannins. Drink it between 1990 and 2000. The Echézeaux is light, elegant, understated, pleasant, and fruity, though it finishes a bit short and reminds me of many 1982 red burgundies. Dujac's Gevrey-Chambertin aux Combottes has a subdued nose, but exhibits an attractive sweetness and fatness on the palate with its round, delicious, smoky, plump Pinot flavors. In terms of value, this should be the best buy of the Dujac stable in 1986. Last, the Morey St.-Denis tasted light but adequate, and the Chambolle-Musigny Premier Cru velvety, expansive, supple, and well balanced. The latter two wines should be drunk by 1994–1995.

DOMAINE RENÉ ENGEL (VOSNE-ROMANÉE)

1986 CLOS VOUGEOT	85
1986 ECHÉZEAUX	84
1986 GRANDS ECHÉZEAUX	88
1986 VOSNE-ROMANÉE	70
1986 VOSNE-ROMANÉE LES BRÛLÉES	78

The Vosne-Romanée is spicy, shows a bit of moldy rot, and finishes with some decent fruit. There is entirely too much tannin in the Vosne-Romanée Les Brûlées for the amount of fruit present, and as a result the wine is hard and out of balance. The Echézeaux is light, but has a lovely perfume of berry fruit and spicy oak, light to medium body, and an adequate finish. The Clos Vougeot is richer and riper with medium body, good depth, some fatness of fruit as well as charm and an attractive finish. Drink it by 1993–1994. The top wine of Philippe Engel in 1986 is the Grands Echézeaux. It has a richness and extract that must certainly come from old vines, a deep ruby color, a complex, aromatic bouquet and excellent length. It is a top 1986 and should keep until 2000.

DOMAINE MICHEL ESMONIN (GEVREY-CHAMBERTIN)

1986 GEVREY-CHAMBERTIN CLOS ST.-JACQUES	86

This new estate was quite a discovery. The proprietor, who has about 3½ acres of the tiny Clos St.-Jacques Vineyard, has previously supplied his grapes to Lalou Bize-Leroy. He now estate-bottles, using 50% new oak, and goes for plenty of flavor and finesse. I tasted a mind-boggling 1985 Clos St.-Jacques and a great 1988, as well as a very good 1987. The 1986 is the lightest of these three wines, but it still has oodles of rich cherry fruit married nicely with spicy oak. It should drink well until 1994–1996. Keep an eye out for this producer.

FAIVELEY (NUITS ST.-GEORGES)

1986 AUXEY-DURESSES	84
1986 BONNES MARES	92
1986 BOURGOGNE JOSEPH FAIVELEY	84
1986 BOURGOGNE PASSE-TOUT-GRAINS	81
1986 CHAMBERTIN-CLOS DE BÈZE	90
1986 CLOS DE LA ROCHE	87
1986 CÔTE DE BEAUNE-VILLAGES	84
1986 CÔTE DE NUITS-VILLAGES	82
1986 FIXIN	85
1986 GEVREY-CHAMBERTIN COMBE AUX MOINES	86
1986 LATRICIÈRES-CHAMBERTIN	87
1986 MAZIS-CHAMBERTIN	89
1986 MERCUREY CLOS DU ROI	86
1986 MERCUREY LA FRAMBOISIÈRE	86
1986 MOREY ST.-DENIS CLOS DES ORMES	86
1986 NUITS ST.-GEORGES LES DAMODES	86
1986 NUITS ST.-GEORGES LES DIDIERS CUVÉE CABET	91
1986 NUITS ST.-GEORGES LES SAINT-GEORGES	92
1986 NUITS ST.-GEORGES LES SAINT-GEORGES CUVÉE GEORGES FAIVELEY	91
1986 POMMARD	81
1986 VOLNAY	85
1986 VOLNAY CHAMPANS	96
1986 VOSNE-ROMANÉE	75

There can be little doubt that this firm, which has always made very good wine, has, under the leadership of the young François Faiveley, leaped to the forefront in quality among Burgundy producers this decade. The excellent 1983s (rot and hail-free wines here) were followed by some of the finest 1984s, some truly sensational 1985s, and superlative 1986s. The latter wines, as I've mentioned, were made in a year when the skill of the winemaker meant everything. François Faiveley has become convinced of the need of cold maceration prior to fermentation and has steadfastly maintained that his top cuvées of red burgundy should not be filtered. I don't ever remember tasting a Bourgogne Passe-Tout-Grains from Faiveley, but this 1986 is light, fruity, soft, and would make a pleasant restaurant wine. Insiders in France always look for this firm's generic wine called Bourgogne Cuvée Joseph Faiveley. Americans have never realized its value. The 1986 has an excellent color, is elegant, fruity, and ripe with good balance and length. Drink it before 1993–1995. The Faiveley firm exploits a number of the best vineyards in Mercurey, an appellation that can offer very fine values from the top producers. Perhaps it is the name, but I certainly thought I smelled and tasted raspberries in the Mercurey la Framboisière. Very perfumed, soft and supple, this velvety wine will make ideal drinking until about 1994. In comparison, the Mercurey Clos du Roi, aged in 20% new oak, is a fuller, bigger, more structured wine. I enjoyed it almost as much as the effusively, fruity, complex 1985. It should age nicely until 1992–1996. Two other wines of notable value and current drinkability are the soft, medium-bodied, berry-scented Côte de Beaune-Villages and the fuller, more earthy Auxey-Duresses. Both should be consumed by 1993–1994. I thought the Côte de Nuits-Villages to be much tougher, but it was still well made. The Fixin tasted spicy, had a lovely fruitiness, excellent ripeness, and good length. It turned out to be more successful than the 1985 and should drink until 1992–1995. The Volnay is more elegant and supple, as well as very lush and charming with very good depth, but I would advise drinking it soon. The Pommard seemed atypical—minty, ripe, and hard, almost as if it were a Pinot Noir from Napa Valley. As for the other villages wines, the Vosne-Romanée tasted lean and short but the Morey St.-Denis was round, fruity, well colored and quite attractive. At the Premier Cru level, Faiveley's 1986s were led by the sensational Volnay Champans. An explosively rich, concentrated wine that is bursting with raspberry and strawberry fruit, this incredibly concentrated, elegant wine is about as remarkable as red burgundy gets. Only 50 cases were made and they should be drunk over the decade of the nineties. The Morey St.-Denis Clos des Ormes is not as sublime as the 1985, yet it is a very well made, medium-bodied, moderately tannic wine with fine definition and length. I thought the Gevrey-Chambertin Combe aux Moines was similarly styled, a bit more spicy and earthy but of medium weight and ideal for drinking between 1992–1996. Among the wines from Gevrey-Chambertin, the Mazis-Chambertin needs several years to shed its tannins. It is a promising, full-bodied wine with excellent flavor depth and should evolve until 1992–1999. The Latricières-Chambertin is much lighter, earthy, fruity, and very fine, but nowhere near the super 1985. The Chambertin-Clos de Bèze is probably Faiveley's most backward 1986 and should last 15 years or more after the vintage, though it will be drinkable around 1994. It is a big, deep, rich, full-bodied, spicy wine with excellent length and depth. Faiveley always seems to turn out super Clos de Bèze and the 1986 is no exception. I hesitate to write about them given the fact that less than 100 cases of each were made, but if you can find any, the trio of remarkable unfiltered, explosively rich, intense wines from Nuits St.-Georges Les Didiers, Les Saint-Georges, and Les Saint-Georges Cuvée Georges Faiveley are about as hedonistic and as complex as red burgundy can get. All three should drink well until 1999–2004. All in all, these are very impressive wines from one of the most conscientious firms in all of Burgundy.

DOMAINE JEAN-PHILIPPE FICHET (VOLNAY)

1986 VOLNAY	84
1986 VOLNAY CHAMPANS	86

The Villages Volnay has a good nose, is ripe, fruity, spicy and well balanced. I would drink it by 1992–1993. The Volnay Champans is an intense, deep, concentrated wine bursting with cherry and plummy fruit. Medium to full bodied, it is cleanly made and long. I thought it should drink well until 1994–1995.

GEOFFREY PÈRE ET FILS (GEVREY-CHAMBERTIN)

1986 GEVREY-CHAMBERTIN CLOS PRIEUR	85
1986 GEVREY-CHAMBERTIN PREMIER CRU	77
1986 MAZIS-CHAMBERTIN	85

The style of winemaking here is to use nearly 100% new oak, extract plenty of color, body, and fruit, and give the wine a lengthy sojourn in the barrel. The results are a bit controversial. The wines are very deeply pigmented, are overtly oaky, taste much alike, and have plenty of alcohol. That being said, these chunky wines are pleasing because of their gush of uncomplicated blackberry fruitiness and heavy reliance on smoky, vanilla scents of oak. I thought the Gevrey-Chambertin Premier Cru to be too tannic as well as too oaky. The Clos Prieur had the lush, ripe fruit to match the lavish amount of oak. It is not complex but full bodied, fat, and tasty. The Mazis-Chambertin tasted very similar, is deep ruby/purple in color, with gobs of smoky oak and a full-bodied, uncomplicated fruitiness. I have no idea how well these wines will age, but my guess would be until 1994–1995.

DOMAINE JACQUES GERMAIN (BEAUNE)

1986 BEAUNE LES BOUCHEROTTES	84
1986 BEAUNE LES TEURONS	86
1986 BEAUNE LES VIGNES-FRANCHES	85
1986 CHÂTEAU DE CHOREY-LÈS-BEAUNE	84

The Côte de Beaune suffered more from the rain and rot in 1986 than the Côte de Nuits, so it is good to see stylish, fruity wines such as these. The Chorey-Lès-Beaune is light and fragrant with a delicious spicy oakiness and soft cherry fruit. The Beaune Les Boucherottes is spicy and oaky with a plump, round, berry fruitiness. Drink it by 1991–1992. The Beaune Les Vignes-Franches is a deeper wine with intense, ripe cherry fruit, medium body, plenty of spicy new oak, and a good finish. It is a seductive wine for drinking between 1992–1993. Perhaps the best wine of the group is the Beaune Les Teurons. It has a big, spicy, oaky nose, excellent definition, medium body, a creamy texture, and a lush finish. It is drinkable now and should continue to drink well until 1993–1994.

DOMAINE HENRI GOUGES (NUITS ST.-GEORGES)

1986 NUITS ST.-GEORGES	72
1986 NUITS ST. GEORGES LES CHAIGNOTS	74
1896 NUITS ST.-GEORGES CLOS DES PORETS	76
1986 NUITS ST.-GEORGES LES PRULIERS	80
1986 NUITS ST.-GEORGES LES SAINT-GEORGES	81
1986 NUITS ST.-GEORGES LES VAUCRAINS	79

The overproduction in 1986 left its watery fingerprints on these wines. The shallow, insipid Nuits St.-Georges has no substance or finish. The

Les Chaignots is simple, soft, light, and diluted. The Clos des Porets has more evidence of some strawberry fruitiness, is cleanly made, but fades away on the palate. Les Pruliers has a real *goût de terroir*, with the mineral and earthy character that a wine from this vineyard should have. I only wish it had more depth and length. It should be drunk between 1991–1992. Les Saint-Georges has the best nose, the deepest color (only a medium-light ruby), and the most fruit, but I would want to drink it by 1990. Last, Les Vaucrains is a light-bodied, thin wine with most of its appeal being its attractive smoky, berry-scented bouquet. As an epilogue, let me say that while I abhor giving this sort of review, there have been too many excuses and too much false praise for the "progress" this domaine is making. By any standard of measurement, these are mediocre wines selling at outrageously high prices. After performances such as these for 20 years (and this vintage is better than many from Henri Gouges), I think it's time someone finally cried foul.

MACHARD DE GRAMONT (NUITS ST.-GEORGES)

Wine	Score
1986 ALOXE-CORTON LES MORAIS	81
1986 BOURGOGNE LA VIERGE ROMAINE	73
1986 CHOREY-LÈS-BEAUNE LES BEAUMONTS	77
1986 NUITS ST.-GEORGES LES DAMODES	83
1986 NUITS ST.-GEORGES LES HAUTS POIRETS	79
1986 NUITS ST.-GEORGES LA PERRIÈRE NOBLOT	85
1986 POMMARD LE CLOS BLANC	84
1986 SAVIGNY-LÈS-BEAUNE LES GUETTES	65

The Aloxe-Corton Les Morais has good color, but is hard and tannic with no more than adequate fruit. It is a well-structured wine, but will the fruit last? As for the wines from Nuits St.-Georges, which are usually among the firm's best, the star of the class is the Nuits St.-Georges La Perrière Noblot. It has a generosity and ampleness not seen in Gramont's other 1986s. There is a balance between the fruit and the tannins, and the fragrant bouquet suggests that this wine will age nicely until 1993–1995. Both the Hauts-Poirets and Les Damodes have decent fruit, but seem unyielding and will not be drinkable until 1991–1992. I would not want to gamble on them. A better bet is the Pommard le Clos

Blanc, which was superb in 1985 and 1987 as well. The 1986 is a richly fruity, velvety wine that because of its suppleness should be drunk by 1993–1995. One wine that appears entirely too tannic ever to come into balance is the Savigny-Lès-Beaune Les Guettes. Extremely dry, astringent, and coarse, this wine has a very dubious future.

JEAN GRIVOT (VOSNE-ROMANÉE)

1986 CLOS VOUGEOT	87
1986 NUITS ST.-GEORGES LES BOUDOTS	87
1986 NUITS ST.-GEORGES PREMIER CRU	84
1986 RICHEBOURG	87

I found it odd that I rated three of these wines the same score because they are all different. The lightest, though it is still fruity and soft, is the Nuits St.-Georges Premier Cru. It should be drunk between 1991–1992. The Clos Vougeot is lovely, with a velvety, berry fruitiness, plenty of spicy oak, medium body, excellent fragrance, and balance. Drink it between 1992–1993. The Nuits St.-Georges Les Boudots has black fruits in the nose and tastes of plums, has plenty of toasty, vanilla-scented new oak, and a less alcoholic feel than the Clos Vougeot. Last, the Richebourg is backward, concentrated, and long, but in need of cellaring until 1992–1993. It may ultimately merit a much higher score.

ROBERT GROFFIER (MOREY ST.-DENIS)

1986 BONNES MARES	86
1986 CHAMBERTIN-CLOS DE BÈZE	88
1986 CHAMBOLLE-MUSIGNY LES AMOUREUSES	89
1986 CHAMBOLLE-MUSIGNY LES SENTIERS	83
1986 GEVREY-CHAMBERTIN	74

Few producers in Burgundy made better 1986s than 1985s, bu Groffier is one of them. For whatever reason his 1986s are vastly superior, as are his 1987s. Groffier used 100% new oak in 1986 for his top wines and did a serious *saigner*, a bleeding out of the excess juice. The excess was sold to several *négociants* in Beaune! While all these wines will require drinking by 1994–1995, I doubt that anyone will complain. However, do avoid the thin, innocuous Gevrey-Chambertin and the good, but hard Chambolle-Musigny Les Sentiers, and go after the rich, sweet, ripe, fat, heady, and perfumed Bonnes Mares, the even better, richer, oaky, splendidly perfumed, expansive Chambolle-Musigny les Amoureuses, or the delectable, broadly flavored, sumptuous, profoundly fruity, smooth Chambertin-Clos de Bèze. These last three wines are very aromatic and loaded with fruit. They are an absolute joy to drink.

DOMAINE JEAN GROS (VOSNE-ROMANÉE)

1986 BOURGOGNE HAUTES-CÔTES DE NUITS	84
1986 NUITS ST.-GEORGES	76
1986 RICHEBOURG	89
1986 VOSNE-ROMANÉE	84
1986 VOSNE-ROMANÉE CLOS DES RÉAS	86

This domaine's Hautes-Côtes de Nuits is always a fine value. The 1986 is a straightforward, spicy, fruity wine of medium body. The Nuits St.-Georges displays high acidity and finishes short, whereas the Vosne-Romanée, while light, has elegance, character, and immediate appeal. However, neither of these two wines is in a class with the supple, berry-scented, spicy, seductive Vosne-Romanée Clos de Réas. While the 1986 cannot compare to the 1985, 1983, or 1987, it is a fragrant, textbook Vosne-Romanée with a bouquet of plums, spicy oak, vanilla, and minerals. Medium bodied, soft, and fruity, this wine should be drunk between 1992–1994. The Richebourg is more complex and has a marvelous bouquet that beautifully integrates the intense fruit of this vineyard with 100% new oak. Medium to full bodied, soft and ready to drink, this seductive, layered wine will provide great pleasure until 1994.

DOMAINE GROS SOEUR ET FRÈRE (VOSNE-ROMANÉE)

1986 CLOS VOUGEOT	90
1986 RICHEBOURG	92
1986 VOSNE-ROMANÉE	82

The 1986s from Gros might be even better than his exotic 1985s. The Clos Vougeot is rich and sweet, hardly classic, but staggeringly exotic; it is hard to believe it is a 1986. The Richebourg's bouquet of oranges, raspberries, and apricots can fill a room. It is fabulously deep, rich,

round, and expansive on the palate, and is sure to provoke many a
comment at a tasting or dinner party. The Vosne-Romanée is good but
suffers in comparison with the other two wines. As I have said
before, I have never tasted Pinot Noir like that made by Bernard
Gros. Both the Clos Vougeot and Richebourg should drink well until
1995–1997.

JEAN GUITTON (BEAUNE)

1986 ALOXE-CORTON	85
1986 BEAUNE LES SIZIES	86
1986 LADOIX CÔTE DE BEAUNE	86
1986 SAVIGNY HAUTS GARRONS	86
1986 SAVIGNY HAUTS PRULIERS	85

This estate is run with wisdom and care by the young Jean Guitton, who
worked in the vineyards before taking over the family's cellar. This
domaine was quite a find. The wines are delicious, richly fruity red
burgundies aged in 60% new oak and sold at reasonable prices. The
Aloxe-Corton has a complex bouquet of smoky tobacco, plenty of
plump, expansive, sweet fruit, a pleasing roundness and charm, and
should drink well until 1994–1995. The Beaune Les Sizies is a much
bigger, more tannic wine with a good deal of depth, ripe cherry fruit,
and fine length. Drink it between 1991 and 1996. I know Ladoix is not
a glamorous appellation, but for shrewd, cost-conscious consumers this
can be a source of fine, richly fruity, solid wine. Guitton's Ladoix is a
fleshy, chewy wine that is short on finesse but big on flavor. It is deep
ruby with good aging potential until 1995–1996. Guitton also does some
nice things from another underrated appellation, Savigny-Lès-Beaune.
The Savigny Hauts Pruliers is a good wine, with plenty of berry fruit
interwoven nicely with spicy oak. The Savigny Hauts Garrons is even
deeper with plenty of spicy oak, deep fruit, full body, and excellent
length. The youthful Jean Guitton seems well on his way to establishing
a glowing reputation for both fine wine and good value.

HAEGELEN-JAYER (VOSNE-ROMANÉE)

1986 CHAMBOLLE-MUSIGNY	84
1986 CLOS VOUGEOT	88
1986 ECHÉZEAUX	86

The Chambolle-Musigny from Haegelan-Jayer is soft, fragrant, not very concentrated, but ripe, round, fruity, and ideal for drinking between 1992–1993. The Clos Vougeot is extremely good. Medium-dark ruby with a penetrating bouquet of rich berry fruit, flowers, and spices, this medium- to full-bodied wine shows depth, harmony, and soft tannins. Drink it between 1995–1996. The Echézeaux is lighter, as one would expect, very delicate, soft, supple, and quite tasty. It should be consumed between 1993–1994. These are excellent wines for the vintage and they will provide fine drinking between 1993–1995.

DOMAINE S. HERESZTYN (GEVREY-CHAMBERTIN)

1986 GEVREY-CHAMBERTIN	83
1986 GEVREY-CHAMBERTIN LES GOULOTS	85

The two 1986s I tasted from this domaine (the rest were already sold out) included an elegant, stylish, light- to medium-bodied, ready-to-drink Gevrey-Chambertin, and a slightly richer, deeper, more perfumed Gevrey-Chambertin Les Goulots. The winemaking style here seems to emphasize plenty of up-front fruit and charm.

A. HUDELOT-NOËLLAT (VOSNE-ROMANÉE)

1986 CLOS VOUGEOT	87
1986 RICHEBOURG	88
1986 ROMANÉE ST.-VIVANT	?
1986 VOSNE-ROMANÉE	78
1986 VOSNE-ROMANÉE LES MALCONSORTS	85
1986 VOSNE-ROMANÉE LES SUCHOTS	82

This estate can produce immensely seductive wine with a super fragrance and lush, velvety textures. M. Hudelot prefers his 1987s and 1988s, but he has made several very fine 1986s that will require consumption by 1992–1993. The Clos Vougeot shows a classy bouquet of sweet black fruit, some spicy new oak, a lush, supple texture, and low acidity. I would not resist drinking it now. The villages Vosne-Romanée tastes a bit too chaptalized and not very concentrated, resulting in a rather cloying wine. The Vosne-Romanée Les Malconsorts has an overripe smell of oranges and peaches, is extremely soft and loosely knit, but is quite a tasty mouthful. Drink it by 1991. Similarly styled but less concentrated is the Vosne-Romanée Les Suchots, which is soft, ripe, and ready to be consumed. I detected a musty *sec* character in the Romanée St.-Vivant that suggested rot. Perhaps I had a bad bottle. The Richebourg had no problems whatsoever. Its exotic, intense nose of berry fruit and apricot jam, married generously with spicy new oak, is quite captivating. On the palate the wine is round, fat, concentrated, and a total joy to drink. Consume it by 1991–1992.

LOUIS JADOT (BEAUNE)

1986 BEAUNE LES BOUCHEROTTES	82
1986 BEAUNE CLOS DES COUCHEREAUX	85
1986 BEAUNE CLOS DES URSULES	87
1986 BONNES MARES	86
1986 BOURGOGNE	78
1986 CHAMBERTIN-CLOS DE BÈZE	86
1986 CHAMBOLLE-MUSIGNY	79
1986 CHAPELLE-CHAMBERTIN	84
1986 CHASSAGNE-MONTRACHET MORGEOT CLOS DE LA CHAPELLE (MAGENTA)	85
1986 CLOS VOUGEOT	84
1986 CORTON LES POUGETS	84
1986 GEVREY-CHAMBERTIN	75
1986 GEVREY-CHAMBERTIN CLOS ST.-JACQUES	85
1986 GRIOTTE-CHAMBERTIN	84
1986 MAZIS-CHAMBERTIN	85
1986 MUSIGNY	83
1986 NUITS ST.-GEORGES	81
1986 NUITS ST.-GEORGES CLOS DES CORVÉES	87
1986 PERNAND-VERGELESSES CLOS DE LA CROIX DE PIERRE	85
1986 POMMARD	82
1986 RUCHOTTES-CHAMBERTIN	87
1986 VOSNE-ROMANÉE	78

The generic Bourgogne is a straightforward, clean, fruity, lighter-styled wine for drinking by 1991–1992. The Chassagne-Montrachet Morgeot from Magenta has excellent color, plenty of body and tannin, and needs until 1994–1995 to round out. The Pernand-Vergelesses Clos de la Croix de Pierre has even more extract as well as tannin, but must be cellared until 1993–1994 because of its sturdy, tough character. Jadot's selection of Beaune Premiers Crus is usually very fine. As one might expect, the Beaune Clos de Couchereaux and Beaune Clos des Ursules were both well made. The Couchereaux, with a vivid, ripe, plump, sweet fruitiness backed up by spicy oak and moderate tannins, should be ready by 1992–1993. The Ursules was one of my favorite wines from Jadot's stable in 1986 and a noteworthy success for a 1986 red burgundy. It has an opulent ripeness, length, and plenty of charm. Drink it between 1990 and 1994. I found the Corton Les Pougets rather lean and tough; I wish it had more fruit. As for Jadot's Villages wines, the Pommard tastes plump and attractive, the Nuits St.-Georges straight-forward and fuller, but somewhat charmless, the Gevrey-Chambertin lean, rather skinny, and showing too much of the dilution of the 1986 vintage, and the Vosne-Romanée another bare-bones wine of no great distinction. The Chambolle-Musigny is clearly the finest of the villages wines. Full of finesse and charming fruit, it should be drunk by 1992–1993. As one shifts to the bigger, more structured Côte de Nuits wines from Jadot, there is more color, more depth, and frequently more character. The Nuits St.-Georges Clos des Corvées shows a lot of new oak, has gobs of blackberry fruit, a pleasing suppleness, and aging potential until 1992–1994. I thought the Clos Vougeot to be good but light, especially when you compare it to Jadot's 1983, 1985, and 1987 Clos Vougeots. I felt the Musigny also showed a bit of dilution in its pleasant yet rather dry, hard finish. As for the Premiers Crus and Grands Crus of Gevrey-Chambertin, the Griotte-Chambertin is soft, has a pleasing berry fruitiness, medium body, and is ideal for drinking between now and 1994. The Chapelle-Chambertin shows more power and depth, has more body, but less charm. It should drink well from 1992–1997. The Mazis-Chambertin is rough, hard, even savage, with a high level of tannins for the amount of fruit. I have three favorite wines from Jadot in 1986. The Ruchottes-Chambertin is excellent, a big, deep, robust, concentrated wine with a great deal of character, length, and intensity. Drink it between 1992 and 2000. The Chambertin Clos de Bèze is similarly constructed, but is more delicate in the bouquet and slightly less powerful on the palate. It, too, should be consumed between 1992 and 2000. The Bonnes Mares (Jadot is now the largest maker of Bonnes Mares), which benefitted from a long 26-day *cuvaison*, is a deep, rich, full wine that is closed yet promising. It should be drunk between 1993 and 2003.

DOMAINE HENRI JAYER (VOSNE-ROMANÉE)

1986 ECHÉZEAUX	92
1986 NUITS ST.-GEORGES LES MURGERS	89
1986 RICHEBOURG	94
1986 VOSNE-ROMANÉE CROS PARANTOUX	90
1986 VOSNE-ROMANÉE LES BRÛLÉES	90

Henri Jayer's 1986s have a purity of fruit, a richness and character that is exceptional. The Echézeaux is fabulous. Its deep ruby color and extraordinary perfume of subtle oak, violets, and raspberries are breathtaking. On the palate the wine is rich, supple, and should drink and evolve well until 1996–1997. The Nuits St.-Georges Les Murgers is more backward—the result of a 24-day *cuvaison*—and has an exotic, smoky, plummy bouquet, full body, dense, tannic flavors, and considerable aging potential. Jayer says that it should not be drunk before 1995. The Richebourg (75 cases produced for the entire world) is the richest and deepest of Jayer's 1986 red burgundies. It is a generous, sumptuous wine bursting with flavor and character. Every time I taste it I somehow feel I should bow my head. It will drink especially well between 1992 and 2000. The Vosne-Romanée Cros Parantoux, which had a 26-day *cuvaison*, is made from 35-year-old vines. Jayer thinks it could well be his longest-lived 1986, lasting "25 years." It is still quite tannic, but reveals intense fruit, none of the watery mid-ranges found in lesser 1986s, excellent length and richness, and surprising size and girth for a 1986. The Vosne-Romanée Les Brûlées has the correct name: Its bouquet displays a very intense, smoky aroma of black fruit (plums!). It is a well-structured, concentrated wine of exceptional length and aging potential. Made from 50-year-old vines, it should be at its best between 1993 and 2003. Anyone who loves or makes Pinot Noir should study Jayer's wines, for they serve as a modern-day reference point for those desiring to produce the best possible wines from this fickle grape variety.

DOMAINE JACQUELINE JAYER (VOSNE-ROMANÉE)

1986 ECHÉZEAUX	87
1986 VOSNE-ROMANÉE LES ROUGES	84

It is hard to find anything less than good wine produced by the various Jayers of the Côte de Nuits. At last count there was Henri Jayer, Lucien

Jayer, Robert Jayer, and, of course, Jacqueline Jayer. Her Echézeaux has an elegant, sweet nose of vinnalin and berry fruit. It is smooth, velvety, and ready to drink. It should keep well until 1993–1994. The Vosne-Romanéee Les Rouges is lighter but delicate, fruity, medium bodied and quite stylish. It should be drunk by 1993–1994. Jayer's wines are made by Étienne Grivot, one of the most innovative as well as most competent of the younger generation of Burgundy winemakers.

JAYER-GILLES (HAUTES-CÔTES DE NUITS)

1986 CÔTE DE NUITS-VILLAGES	85
1986 ECHÉZEAUX	91
1986 HAUTES-CÔTES DE NUITS	85

Proprietor Robert Jayer uses 100% new oak and the quality of his wines is impeccable. As one might expect, Jayer's wines have plenty of toasty, smoky oak in them, but he extracts enough fruit to stand up to the wood. His Côte de Nuits-Villages has a large measure of oak but also plenty of black-fruit flavors, good definition, and depth. It should drink well until 1993–1994. The Echézeaux is something special. Always big boned, backward, and deeply concentrated, the 1986 has astonishing length and depth for the vintage, plenty of tannin, and heaps of fruit. My notes suggest 8–20 years of aging potential. There is no dilution in this wine. I know the Hautes-Côtes de Nuits is not a fashionable appellation, but at this domaine this wine is seriously rich, deep in flavor, and capable of aging until 1995–1996. Unfortunately, this is a small, very expensive cave, but no one leaves this cellar without an appreciation of the high quality to which Robert Jayer aspires.

DOMAINE JOBLOT (GIVRY)

1986 GIVRY CLOS DU CELLIER AUX MOINES	82

This is a serious estate in Givry that made an impressive 1985 and 1987, and a light but adequately fruity 1986. Eighty percent new oak has been employed in recent vintages, which has given the wine more structure and character. The 1986 is light, oaky, spicy, and should be drunk by 1991.

DOMAINE MICHEL LAFARGE (VOLNAY)

1986 VOLNAY	78
1986 VOLNAY CLOS DU CHÂTEAU DES DUCS	84
1986 VOLNAY CLOS DES CHÊNES	84
1986 VOLNAY PREMIER CRU	77

The silver-haired, handsome Michel Lafarge has shown a propensity to make his best wines in years that prove troublesome for other growers as he did in 1981. For that reason I had expected his 1986s to be a bit better. The Volnay is spicy and pleasant, but light and simple. The Volnay Clos du Château des Ducs has much better depth and fruit, plenty of spicy oak, a bit of dilution, or *un peu liquide*, as the French say, and should be drunk between 1991–1993. The Volnay Clos des Chênes is elegant, stylish, medium bodied and soft, and has fruit that impresses one more for its delicate charm than intrinsic depth and concentration. The Volnay Premier Cru is lean, spicy, and light, but clean and adequate. All of these wines should be drunk while they are young and fresh as their aging potential is suspect.

HENRI LAMARCHE (VOSNE-ROMANÉE)

1986 CLOS VOUGEOT	82
1986 ECHÉZEAUX	84
1986 VOSNE-ROMANÉE LA GRANDE RUE	86
1986 VOSNE-ROMANÉE LES MALCONSORTS	84
1986 VOSNE-ROMANÉE LES SUCHOTS	82

All of the 1986s here are reminiscent of the 1982s and 1979s. They are light, quite perfumed, clean, fruity, soft, and ideal for drinking by 1992–1993. They will not be keepers. The 1986 Clos Vougeot is delicate, soft, pleasant, and light bodied. It will keep until 1993–1994. The Vosne-Romanée la Grande Rue is the most perfumed of all the Lamarche 1986s. While light in color, it has plenty of fruit and charm, but must be drunk soon. The Vosne-Romanée Les Malconsorts is slightly richer and fuller than the light, soft Vosne-Romanée Les Suchots. The Echézeaux is more tannic and oaky, but I wondered if the fruit would outlast the tannins.

YVES DE LAUNAY (MERCUREY)

1986 MERCUREY CLOS DU CHÂTEAU DE MONTAIGNU	83
1986 MERCUREY CUVÉE SPÉCIALE	85
1986 MERCUREY MEIX FOULOT	77
1986 MERCUREY LES VELEYS	77

The house of Faiveley and Yves de Launay are, at the moment, the top wine producers of Mercurey, although the firm of A. Rodet is beginning to make some attractive wines. I thought Launay's 1986s, while certainly sound, tasted a trifle too lean and hard. The sole exception was the Cuvée Spéciale, which is a deep, rich, fuller wine that could benefit from cellaring until 1991–1992. The Cuvée Spéciale and the Clos du Château de Montaignu would be the best bets in 1986, but if you can still find his 1985s or his 1987s, do so, as those two vintages are undoubtedly superior to his 1986s. De Launay began to utilize 25% new oak in 1987, and he rarely filters his wines, which is always the sign of a committed winemaker.

PHILIPPE LECLERC (GEVREY-CHAMBERTIN)

1986 GEVREY-CHAMBERTIN LES CAZETIERS	86
1986 GEVREY-CHAMBERTIN COMBE AUX MOINES	88
1986 GEVREY-CHAMBERTIN LES PLATIÈRES	81

While Leclerc's 1986s are not up to the quality of his spectacular 1985s, they are notable successes. The Gevrey-Chambertin Les Cazetiers has oodles of rich, super-ripe red fruit and oak in its bouquet, a sweet, expansive palate, medium to full body, and a soft, lightly tannic finish. It should drink well between 1990 and 1996. The Gevrey-Chambertin Combe aux Moines is fatter, deeper, and more seductive, quite concentrated and fleshy, aromatic and surprisingly long. It should drink well until 1997–1998. I am less enthusiastic about the Gevrey-Chambertin Les Platières, a soft, pleasant but essentially foursquare wine that should be drunk by 1992–1993.

RENÉ LECLERC (GEVREY-CHAMBERTIN)

1986 GEVREY-CHAMBERTIN	77
1986 GEVREY-CHAMBERTIN CLOS PRIEUR	81

| 1986 GEVREY-CHAMBERTIN COMBE AUX MOINES | 84 |
| 1986 GEVREY-CHAMBERTIN LAVAUX ST.-JACQUES | 82? |

René Leclerc is one of the well-known Leclerc brothers of Gevrey-Chambertin, and can usually be counted on to produce very good to excellent wines. Therefore, I was somewhat surprised that his 1986s did not show better in my tastings. The Gevrey-Chambertin has a light color and soft, spicy, cherry fruit, but some bitterness and astringence in the finish. The Clos Prieur is slightly bigger in stature, cleanly made, and pleasant, but tasted essentially simple and one dimensional. The Combe aux Moines, often a blockbuster here, had the deepest color and best depth of fruit, but the tannins seemed elevated for such a medium-bodied wine. It needs until 1991–1996 to round out and appears to be the best wine René Leclerc made in 1986. The Lavaux St.-Jacques, usually excellent as well, tasted entirely too tannic and hard for the amount of fruit I found in it.

DOMAINE LEQUIN-ROUSSOT (SANTENAY)

1986 CHASSAGNE-MONTRACHET MORGEOT	76
1986 SANTENAY	72
1986 SANTENAY LE PASSE TEMPS	74

René and Louis Lequin make superb white burgundies and can, in very ripe, trouble-free vintages such as 1985 and 1988, produce elegant, attractive red wines. However, their 1986s left me unexcited. All three wines are very light in color and body, and finish short with some astringence. They were obviously hurt by the rains. But don't miss Lequin-Roussot's 1986 white burgundies, especially their Premiers Crus from Chassagne-Montrachet and their Bâtard-Montrachet. These are indeed splendid, very long-lived white wines.

LEROY (AUXEY-DURESSES)

1986 AUXEY-DURESSES	86
1986 BEAUNE LES GRÈVES	88
1986 BEAUNE LES MIGNOTTES	85
1986 BEAUNE LES PERRIÈRES	88

1986	BEAUNE LES PERTUISOTS	85
1986	BEAUNE LES SIZIES	89
1986	BOURGOGNE D'AUVENAY	86
1986	CHAMBOLLE-MUSIGNY	86
1986	CHARMES-CHAMBERTIN	90
1986	CHOREY-LÈS-BEAUNE	85
1986	CLOS VOUGEOT	88
1986	GEVREY-CHAMBERTIN	85
1986	GEVREY-CHAMBERTIN CLOS ST.-JACQUES	90
1986	GEVREY-CHAMBERTIN LES CORBEAUX	90
1986	GEVREY-CHAMBERTIN ESTOURNELLES ST.-JACQUES	87
1986	MAZIS-CHAMBERTIN	92
1986	MOREY ST.-DENIS CLOS DES ORMES	90
1986	NUITS ST.-GEORGES	84
1986	POMMARD LES VIGNOTS	89
1986	RUCHOTTES-CHAMBERTIN	90
1986	VOLNAY CHAMPANS	87

In 1986 the formidable Madame Lalou Bize-Leroy was considerably less aggressive in her purchase of wines than she was in 1985. Therefore she has less wine to sell. As I have stated before, she is a perfectionist, with no time to waste on fools and idiots. Not surprisingly, her 1986s are among the very finest red wines in Burgundy. Lalou is based in Auxey-Duresses, and her wines from this unheralded appellation are always good. Her 1986 needs until 1993–1994, but is a meaty, full-bodied, spicy, well-balanced wine that represents good value. While everyone is usually shocked by this firm's high prices, Leroy's Bourgogne D'Auvenay is, along with the Cuvée Joseph Faiveley made by the Faiveley firm, one of the two best generic red burgundies made. The 1986 is full, rich, deep in color, loaded with fruit, and will keep until 1996–2001. No one exploits the potential of the Premiers Crus of Beaune better than Leroy, and her best wines in 1986 are her Beaune Les Sizies, Beaune Les Grèves and Beaune Les Perrières, followed closely by the Beaune Les Mignottes and Beaune Les Pertuisots. All of these tannic, full-bodied wines should be at their best between 1993 and 2005. It is hard choosing between the Sizies and Grèves, as both are loaded with rich plummy fruit, are full bodied, deep in color, and very tannic. I thought the Sizies had slightly more depth. The Perrières has a lovely perfume, perhaps not the sheer depth of the Sizies or Grèves, but it is still a beauty. Both the Mignottes and Pertuisots are very good, but neither showed as much depth of fruit as Leroy's other three Beaunes. Moving north, the Chambolle-Musigny is full of elegance and finesse, is lighter than the Beaunes, but is a charming wine for drinking until 1994–1995. I was especially impressed by the exquisite Charmes-Chambertin, a wine that is not tannic or structured, but has gorgeous layers of soft, velvety fruit, and a huge fragrance of exotic spices and berry fruit. It should evolve until 1994–1999. The Clos Vougeot is similarly styled, not a blockbuster or an overly structured wine, but rather an elegant, richly fruity, ripe, deep wine that should drink well for 10–12 years after the vintage. Leroy's wines from Gevrey-Chambertin were among the very best produced in 1986. In addition to the outstanding Charmes-Chambertin, she has made superlative wines from Gevrey-Chambertin Les Corbeaux, Gevrey-Chambertin Clos St.-Jacques, Ruchottes-Chambertin, and Mazis-Chambertin. Les Corbeaux is super supple, fat, ripe, and gushing with berry fruit and spicy oak. It is seductive now but should age well for a decade. The Clos St.-Jacques is less precocious, more tannic, fuller bodied, yet has a wonderful purity and depth of fruit that lingers on the palate. Drink it between 1993 and 2006. Similarly tannic and backward but very rich and full is the impressive Ruchottes-Chambertin. This is a powerful, backward wine that will not be ready before 1996 and should easily last a decade. As one might expect, the Mazis-Chambertin is Leroy's finest 1986 red burgundy, splendidly concentrated with a huge bouquet of deep, spicy, oaky, berry fruit, full body, wonderful layers of extract, and a finish that lasts for several minutes. Drink it between 1997 and 2010. There is a very good Villages wine from Gevrey-Chambertin that is ripe, supple, spicy, and ready for near-term consumption. I found the Estournelles St.-Jacques to be backward and hard, but it did show excellent depth and richness beneath the tannins. As for Leroy's other 1986s, there is a hard, spicy, good yet not special Nuits St.-Georges, a super-ripe, seductive, gloriously fragrant, intense, hedonistic Morey St.-Denis Clos des Ormes that will provide luxurious drinking until the end of the century, a very earthy, spicy, chunky but intense, heady Pommard Les Vignots, and a lovely, well-balanced, elegant, expansive, and seductive Volany Champans. In summary, Leroy's 1986s are certainly among the stars of the vintage. Most will be at their drinking plateau between 1993 and 2007.

GEORGES LIGNIER (MOREY ST.-DENIS)

1986 BONNES MARES	86
1986 CHAMBOLLE-MUSIGNY	78
1986 CLOS DE LA ROCHE	86
1986 CLOS ST.-DENIS	87
1986 GEVREY-CHAMBERTIN	79
1986 MOREY ST.-DENIS	77
1986 MOREY ST.-DENIS CLOS DES ORMES	85

I found all the Villages wines—the Chambolle-Musigny, Morey St.-Denis, and Gevrey-Chambertin—to be soft and agreeable, but they were too light and revealed the effects of the huge crop size in 1986. Lignier's other wines showed greater flavor dimension and character. The Morey St.-Denis Clos des Ormes is a ripe, tasty, smooth, perfumed wine that is medium bodied and perfect for drinking by 1993–1994. Both the Bonnes Mares and Clos de la Roche have a medium-bodied weight, good depth, precocious, ripe, perfumed fruit, a certain elegance and appeal, as well as aging potential until 1993–1994. They are not big wines but they do have merit. I thought the finest wine of the Lignier stable to be the Clos St.-Denis. Certainly the complex bouquet of grilled nuts, berry fruit, and toasty oak would catch anybody's attention. Quite soft yet ripe and fleshy, this velvety, seductive wine should drink well until at least 1994.

DOMAINE HUBERT LIGNIER (MOREY ST.-DENIS)

1986 CLOS DE LA ROCHE	87
1986 MOREY ST.-DENIS PREMIER CRU	83

Hubert Lignier is a sure-handed winemaker who not only hits the peaks in the great vintages, but also makes very good wines in the mediocre years. His 1986s are better than mediocre so one would expect Lignier's much renowned Clos de la Roche to be excellent. It is. Deep ruby with a fragrant, ripe, aromatic bouquet filled with the scent of raspberries, it is a deliciously supple, lush wine to drink between 1995–2000. The Morey St.-Denis is less concentrated but elegant, understated, well balanced, and ideal for consuming between 1992–1993. While his wines are hard to find, this is a small grower to search out.

J. P. MARCHAND (GEVREY-CHAMBERTIN)

1986 CHARMES-CHAMBERTIN	87
1986 GEVREY-CHAMBERTIN	78
1986 GEVREY-CHAMBERTIN AUX COMBOTTES	85
1986 MOREY ST.-DENIS	84
1986 MOREY ST.-DENIS CLOS DES ORMES	87
1986 MOREY ST.-DENIS PREMIER CRU	84

Marchand made very good 1986s. In fact, I predict he will soon be recognized as one of the up-and-coming stars of Burgundy. There has been no filtration done at the Marchand estate since 1985. The Charmes-Chambertin, aged in 100% new oak, is a rich, tannic, full-bodied wine that requires cellaring until 1993. The Gevrey-Chambertin aux Combottes is spicy, earthy, has very good fruit, more immediate suppleness than the Charmes-Chambertin, and can be drunk until 1994–1995. The Gevrey-Chambertin is tannic and hard without enough underlying fruit, and is entirely too tough. As for the Morey St.-Denis, it shows much better fruit, a certain degree of lushness and plentitude, and good length. Drink it between 1991–1992. The Morey St.-Denis Premier Cru is similarly styled, ripe, fruity and spicy without the excess of hard tannins often found in this vintage. The Morey St.-Denis Clos des Ormes is much more impressive with a deep, berry-scented bouquet, medium to full body, loads of fruit, plenty of depth, and surprising length. Drink it by 1993–1994.

JOSEPH MATROT (MEURSAULT)

1986 BLAGNY-LA PIÈCE SOUS LE BOIS	84

Matrot is better known for his white than red wine, but he has consistently turned out a highly scented, rich, creamy Pinot Noir from this vineyard adjacent to Meursault. It always has a huge dollop of oak, but the velvety fruit is there to carry it along. The 1986 is no 1985 or 1987, but for drinking between now and 1992, it provides some pleasure.

DOMAINE MAUME (GEVREY-CHAMBERTIN)

1986 CHARMES-CHAMBERTIN	73?
1986 GEVREY-CHAMBERTIN	83

1986 GEVREY-CHAMBERTIN LAVAUX ST.-JACQUES	79
1986 GEVREY-CHAMBERTIN EN PALUD	75
1986 MAZIS-CHAMBERTIN	83

I was surprised to see the 1986s of Domaine Maume perform so unin-spiringly. Inexplicably, the Villages Gevrey-Chambertin performed as well as any of the other wines. It had an earthy, spicy, ripe berry-scented nose and a good, supple fruitiness. The Lavaux St.-Jacques, from an excellent vineyard, already has some amber at the edge, a tough, leathery, sinewy texture, and decent fruit. The Mazis-Chamber-tin, usually the best wine of Maume, did have more size and depth, but the astringent tannins left me worrying about its future balance. The Charmes-Chambertin was even harder to penetrate and the tannins entirely too harsh for the moderate amount of fruit. I cannot see it ever coming into balance. Last, the Gevrey-Chambertin en Palud has a very earthy, spicy taste, but I thought I also detected evidence of rot. As a group, these Maume wines lacked charm and finesse.

DOMAINE MÉO-CAMUZET (VOSNE-ROMANÉE)

1986 CLOS VOUGEOT	84
1986 NUITS ST.-GEORGES BOUDOTS	85
1986 NUITS ST.-GEORGES LES MURGERS	80
1986 RICHEBOURG	87
1986 VOSNE-ROMANÉE	72
1986 VOSNE-ROMANÉE LES BRÛLÉES	87
1986 VOSNE-ROMANÉE LES CHAUMES	77

The 1986s are variable. Whereas the Vosne-Romanée, Vosne-Romanée Les Chaumes, and Nuits St.-Georges Les Murgers show the effect of the gigantic yields of juice in their light ruby, rather washed-out colors and light-bodied flavors, the Clos Vougeot is elegant, fruity, and supple, and the Nuits St.-Georges Boudots is smoky, more structured, and shows finer depth. Even better is the Vosne-Romanée Les Brûlées, which has a big, spicy, roasted nose, an exotic, plummy fruitiness, and lush, expansive finish. It should be drunk by 1993–1994. The Riche-bourg offers up classic blackberry and cherry Pinot Noir flavors and aromas with plenty of toasty new oak mixed in for complexity. It, too, should be drunk by 1993–1994. Méo-Camuzet is not one of the best known domaines, but since they began to estate-bottle in 1983 (before that all the wine was sold in bulk), the quality has been consistently promising.

PRINCE FLORENT DE MÉRODE (LADOIX-SERRIGNY)

1986 CORTON LES BRESSANDES	80
1986 CORTON-CLOS DU ROI	76
1986 CORTON LES MARÉCHAUDES	76
1986 LADOIX LES CHAILLOTS	73
1986 POMMARD CLOS DE LA PLATIÈRE	84

The 1986s from Prince Florent de Mérode resemble some of our country's fitness freaks—they are hard, they are lean, they are skinny, but they are boring. In short, most wines here have an excess of tannins for their meager fruit. The Corton Les Bressandes has a pretty bouquet of new oak and cherries and the best color of this lot, but is hard and ungracious. The Corton-Clos du Roi is even harder and more charmless. Ditto for the Corton Les Maréchaudes and Ladoix Les Chaillots. The only wine of charm and some character is the Pommard Clos de la Platière, a wine of spicy oak, some ripe fruit, and hard but not excessive or astringent tannins.

ALAIN MICHELOT (NUITS ST.-GEORGES)

1986 NUITS ST.-GEORGES	84
1986 NUITS ST.-GEORGES LES CAILLES	85
1986 NUITS ST.-GEORGES LES CHAIGNOTS	86
1986 NUITS ST.-GEORGES LES CHAMPS PERDRIX	88
1986 NUITS ST.-GEORGES LES PORRETS SAINT-GEORGES	75
1986 NUITS ST.-GEORGES LA RICHEMONE	87
1986 NUITS ST.-GEORGES LES VAUCRAINS	85

Quite fragrant to smell, supple and fruity, Michelot's 1986s had none of the dry, hard tannins that have plagued other wines from this vintage. The Les Cailles is a spicy, plummy wine with plenty of fruit and depth that should keep nicely until 1993–1994. The Les Chaignots is marginally deeper, has firm fruit, length, the big, penetrating, intense bouquet that Michelot often obtains, and should drink nicely until 1994–1996. The finest wine for Michelot in 1986 is Les Champs Perdrix, a wine that has gobs of blackberry and cherry fruit, excellent definition, length, and full body. It is a very impressive wine for drinking until 1996–1997. The Porrets St.-Georges, made from young vines, is short, very tannic, and lean—a wine I did not care for. The Richemone has a fabulous nose of berry fruit, subtle oak and flowers, as well as licorice. On the palate it is deep, expansive, and rich—more akin to a 1985 than 1986. Last, Les Vaucrains is very forward, has the trademark roasted, smoky nose of the vineyard, and finishes with a smoothness that suggests it should be drunk sooner rather than later. Little of Michelot's wine is sent to America, which is a shame, for he is a top-rank producer.

DOMAINE MOILLARD (NUITS ST.-GEORGES)

1986 BEAUNE LES GRÈVES	75
1986 BONNES MARES	?
1986 CHAMBERTIN	86
1986 CLOS VOUGEOT	78
1986 CORTON-CLOS DU ROI	77
1986 FIXIN CLOS DE LA PERRIÈRE	65
1986 NUITS ST.-GEORGES CLOS DES CORVÉES	75
1986 NUITS ST.-GEORGES CLOS DE TOREY	73
1986 VOSNE-ROMANÉE LES MALCONSORTS	75

The poor showing of these wines out of bottle made me wonder if they had been severely damaged in transit. Yet, none of the bottles showed any signs of heat damage (pushed out corks, sticky residue of wine on the outside of the bottle, or stained labels). Whatever the reason, the wines all looked light, overly oaked (the woody taste in some wines obliterated most of the fruit), and had short, alcoholic finishes. Only the oaky, rich, spicy Chambertin possessed depth and complexity. The Bonnes Mares, tasted twice, was thin, light, and excessive oaky one time and rich, much deeper in color, and quite excellent the other time. Since my notes show that Moillard only made 300 cases of this wine, what can account for such great bottle discrepancy?

MOMMESSIN (MÂCON)

1986 CLOS DE TART	79

The 1986 Clos de Tart from Mommessin is light, a bit astringent and hard, without a great deal of depth or charm. It is doubtful whether there is more fruit hiding behind the dry tannins.

DOMAINE MONGEARD-MUGNERET (VOSNE-ROMANÉE)

1986 CLOS VOUGEOT	88
1986 ECHÉZEAUX VIEILLES VIGNES	87
1986 FIXIN	81
1986 GRANDS ECHÉZEAUX	86
1986 NUITS ST.-GEORGES LES BOUDOTS	85
1986 RICHEBOURG	88
1986 VOSNE-ROMANÉE	75
1986 VOSNE-ROMANÉE LES SUCHOTS	83

Some of Mongeard's 1986s are excellent—well worth buying and drinking. For example, his Clos Vougeot is an exotic, smoky, intense wine with a super bouquet, plenty of new oak in evidence, and lush, rich, deep fruit on the palate. Virtually as fine as the Echézeaux Vieilles Vignes, which has a big, smoky, bacon-fat sort of bouquet intertwined with oodles of damson plum fruit. Medium to full bodied, quite rich and long, this fine wine should drink well until 1994–1996. The Fixin is light but tasty, though in an uncomplicated sense. The Grands Echézeaux, usually a blockbuster here (ah, the 1985, 1983, and 1980 were something special . . . !), has to take a back seat to the Clos Vougeot and Echézeaux in 1986. Perhaps it was going through a dumb stage, but it was quite tannic, closed, and hard to evaluate when I tasted it. That was not the case with Mongeard's Richebourg, which has a sensational bouquet of smoky, exotic, plum and raspberry fruit wrapped in a glove of toasty new oak. On the palate, it is forward, soft, and ripe, and should drink well until 1992–1996. I thought both the Vosne-Romanée and Vosne-Romanée Les Suchots to be much less successful than their 1985 counterparts. The Vosne-Romanée tasted slightly overripe and oaky, the Suchots rather clumsy and straightforward. Lastly, the Nuits St.-Georges Les Boudots showed quite well, displaying an exotic, smoky, richly fruity bouquet and soft, supple, ready-to-drink flavors.

DOMAINE MONTHÉLIE-DOUHAIRET (MONTHÉLIE)

1986 MONTHÉLIE	72
1986 MONTHÉLIE PREMIER CRU	77
1986 POMMARD LES CHANLINS	85
1986 VOLNAY CHAMPANS	?

The Monthélie has a cheesy, musty nose, big, deep flavors, and enough tannin to last until 1994 or later. The Monthélie Premier Cru has a smell of damp chestnuts, is very ripe and full, but aggressively tannic and hard. The Volnay Champans has a bizarre nose that smells fecal in origin. It is also extremely tannic and tough. The Pommard Les Chanlins is the estate's best wine in 1986, displaying plump, spicy, rich fruit, plenty of body, and well-integrated tannins. It should drink well until 1994–1995.

DOMAINE ALBERT MOROT (BEAUNE)

1986 BEAUNE LES BRESSANDES	84
1986 BEAUNE LES MARCONNETS	83
1986 SAVIGNY LA BATAILLIÈRE	83

I did not sample the entire range of 1986s after bottling, but given the difficulties in Beaune in 1986, the Domaine Albert Morot has managed to produce some spicy and robust—though slightly too dry and tannic —wines that need until 1991–1992 to round out. They are medium bodied and have good color, but like many 1986s they're a little short on charm and plump fruit. My favorite here is the 1986 Beaune Les Bressandes, which is made from 50-year-old vines. It has a deep color, rich, penetrating bouquet of cherry fruit and oak, as well as plenty of tough tannins. Drink it between 1992 and 1997.

DENIS MORTET (GEVREY-CHAMBERTIN)

1986 BOURGOGNE	82
1986 CHAMBERTIN	84
1986 CLOS VOUGEOT	87
1986 GEVREY-CHAMBERTIN	84

1986 GEVREY-CHAMBERTIN CHAMPEAUX	86
1986 GEVREY-CHAMBERTIN CLOS PRIEUR	85

Mortet's Bourgogne is soft, fruity, round, and pleasant—as it should be. The Villages Gevrey-Chambertin is quite attractive. It has a lovely berry-scented bouquet, medium ruby color, good depth, and should drink well until 1994–1995. I was impressed by the Gevrey-Chambertin Champeaux, a deep, rich, broad-shouldered wine with excellent flavor definition, full body, and fine length. Drink it between 1992 and 1999. The Gevrey-Chambertin Clos Prieur is also well made, though it is more tannic and powerful and has less fruit and charm than the Champeaux. The top wine of the Mortet cellar in 1986 is the Clos Vougeot, which is bursting with plenty of red fruits, has excellent depth and length, full body, moderate tannins, and should be drinkable until 1995–1997. The Chambertin should have been exceptional, but like so many wines with this great name, it is disappointingly light, somewhat diluted, medium bodied, and potentially short lived. I thought it no better than the Villages Gevrey-Chambertin.

DOMAINE GEORGES MUGNERET (VOSNE-ROMANÉE)

1986 CHAMBOLLE-MUSIGNY FEUSSELOTTES	82
1986 CLOS VOUGEOT	88
1986 ECHÉZEAUX	86
1986 NUITS ST.-GEORGES LES CHAIGNOTS	76
1986 RUCHOTTES-CHAMBERTIN	85
1986 VOSNE-ROMANÉE	73

The late Dr. Mugneret's 1986s are not as rich and seductive as his 1985s, but once past the straightforward, somewhat shallow Vosne-Romanée and the hard, austere, spicy but tough Nuits St.-Georges Les Chaignots, there are some attractive wines. The Chambolle-Musigny Feusselottes is elegant, well made, and fruity, but finishes a little short. The Ruchottes-Chambertin is good, medium bodied, elegant, richly fruity, spicy, complex, and ideal for drinking until 1993–1994. The Echézeaux has a deceptively light color yet is very flavorful, shows quite a bit of new oak, is round and expansive on the palate as well as stylish and seductive. It should be drunk by 1993–1994. The top wine from this cellar in 1986 is the Clos Vougeot, which tastes more like a 1985.

Its sweet, expansive flavors of cherries and vanilla are top notch. Very soft, ripe, and supple, this delicious wine should be drunk between now and 1995.

DOMAINE MUSSY (POMMARD)

1986 BEAUNE LES EPENOTTES	86
1986 BEAUNE LES MONTREVENOTS	87
1986 POMMARD LES EPENOTS	90
1986 POMMARD PREMIER CRU	88

The ebullient Monsieur Mussy harvested late in 1986. The results are wines that taste like 1985s, not 1986s. In fact, it is hard to imagine that anybody made better wines from the Côte de Beaune than André Mussy. For starters, there is the Beaune Les Montrevenots, a wine with a gorgeously seductive bouquet of rich berry fruit. On the palate the wine is lavishly lush, deep, fat, even opulent. Drink it before 1994–1995. The Beaune Les Epenottes is less evolved and seems less concentrated, but it is a deep, expansive, ripe, sweet wine that will be a joy to drink between now and 1995. The Pommard Premier Cru shows some new oak and loads of rich, lavish, plum-like fruit. This medium-to full-bodied wine makes a fine case for the late harvesters in 1986. Absolutely astounding in 1986 is the Pommard Les Epenots, a multidimensional wine with a penetrating bouquet of toasty oak, super-ripe fruit, and spices. On the palate the wine is explosively rich and deep with layers of concentrated Pinot fruit. Made from 62-year-old vines, this beauty should drink well until 1996–1997. I wish there were more growers like André Mussy.

PHILIPPE NADDEF (COUCHEY)

1986 BOURGOGNE	83
1986 GEVREY-CHAMBERTIN	84
1986 GEVREY-CHAMBERTIN LES CAZETIERS	86
1986 MARSANNAY	81
1986 MAZIS-CHAMBERTIN	87

Naddef seems to think his 1986s are as good as his 1987s, only much more tannic. The wines are fruity, pure, and well balanced. For a decent value there is the Bourgogne, a solid, medium-bodied wine that smells of bing cherries. The Marsannay is very similar, but much harder and leaner. As for the other wines, the Gevrey-Chambertin shows a great deal of new oak, good color, rich fruit, and medium body. It has surprising class for a Villages wine. The Gevrey-Chambertin Les Cazetiers is fuller, richer, more complex and complete, and should be at its best between 1992 and 1998. The Mazis-Chambertin is perfumed with abundant scents of black plums and toasty new oak. On the palate it is not as powerful as one might expect, but it is filled with finesse and elegance. Drink it between 1991 and 1997. Philippe Naddef is certainly a name to watch.

DOMAINE PARENT (POMMARD)

1986 POMMARD LES CHAPONNIÈRES	82
1986 POMMARD CLOS MICAULT	78
1986 POMMARD LES EPENOTS	83
1986 POMMARD LES RUGIENS	85

All of the 1986s tasted soft, fat, and quite similar. The Pommard Les Chaponnières is chunky and solid but seems too straightforward to merit high marks. The Pommard Clos Micault is light, one dimensional, and fruity. The Pommard Les Epenots is deeper, more alcoholic, and substantial in size, but I found myself wanting a bit more complexity. The Pommard Les Rugiens appears to have more depth and interest, with a smoky, oaky nose, and great richness and dimension to its flavors. Parent's 1986s will probably be at their best between 1991 and 1998.

DOMAINE JEAN-MARC PAVELOT
(SAVIGNY-LÈS-BEAUNE)

1986 SAVIGNY-LÈS-BEAUNE	84
1986 SAVIGNY-LÈS-BEAUNE LES DOMINODES	87
1986 SAVIGNY-LÈS-BEAUNE AUX GUETTES	85

These wines are quite successful for 1986s. The Savigny-Lès-Beaune is a lighter-styled, fruity, pleasant wine with ample fruit and soft tannins. The Aux Guettes has excellent color, a ripe, rich nose, medium body, and surprising flavor length and depth. It should drink nicely until 1993–1994. The Dominodes smells of violets, is fragrant, long, and rich

—a winemaking tour de force for a wine from this appellation. It should drink extremely well until 1994–1995.

PERNIN-ROSSIN (VOSNE-ROMANÉE)

1986 MOREY ST.-DENIS MONTS LUISANTS	88
1986 NUITS ST.-GEORGES LA RICHEMONE	90

Every time I taste this grower's wines I am unsure how to judge them, or if they are really capable of evolving in the bottle. They are not typical burgundies: They have a rather purple hue to their color; intense, almost Côte Rôtie–like bouquets of sweet raspberry fruit; and voluptuous, expansive, lush flavors. My friend Michel Bettane, an extraordinarily gifted taster and a writer for the *Revue du Vin de France*, considers these wines top class. Certainly Monsieur Pernin's prefermentation cold maceration of the grapes is the new rage in Burgundy— it results in wines with an incredible up-front perfume and glorious fruitiness. But, will they keep? Who really knows? However, the disciples of this practice are not only Burgundy's new wine guru/oenologist, Guy Accad, but his growing list of clients: Étienne Grivot, Jackie Confuron, Daniel Senard, Château de La Tour, and to a lesser degree, François Faiveley. (It should be noted that Accad's belief in 5 to as many as 10 days of cold maceration of the grapes prior to fermentation was pioneered—although not quite to this extreme—by Henri Jayer. For the record, Jayer's wines do age beautifully.) In any event, a taste of these two hedonistic 1986s displays plentiful raspberry fruit, and plenty of the same fat and depth that seem to gush forth from wines made in this style. For 1986s, these wines are marvelously deep, scented, and a joy to drink. I only wonder how they will age.

DOMAINE PERNOT-FOURRIER (GEVREY-CHAMBERTIN)

1986 CHAMBOLLE-MUSIGNY	76
1986 GEVREY-CHAMBERTIN	73
1986 GEVREY-CHAMBERTIN-CLOS ST.-JACQUES	82
1986 GEVREY-CHAMBERTIN COMBE AUX MOINES	83
1986 GEVREY-CHAMBERTIN PREMIER CRU	76
1986 GRIOTTE-CHAMBERTIN	75

1986 MOREY ST.-DENIS	65
1986 VOUGEOT PREMIER CRU	72

This estate is now called Jean-Claude Fourrier after the current proprietor. This domaine has excellent vineyards, yet the inflexibility, even
ineptitude that M. Fourrier brings to his efforts to produce the maximum amount of wine from his vineyard has resulted in mediocre 1985s
and 1986s that are formless and diluted. Ironically, if M. Fourrier had
done some crop thinning or a *saigner* (bleeding the vat of excess juice
in order to increase the proportion of the remaining juice to skins), both
his 1985s and 1986s would have been greatly improved. All of this is
rather sad for in the sixties and early seventies this estate made superlative red burgundies. In 1986, as in most recent vintages, his two best
wines are the Clos St.-Jacques and Combe aux Moines from Gevrey-
Chambertin.

DOMAINE LES PERRIÈRES (GEVREY-CHAMBERTIN)

1986 GEVREY-CHAMBERTIN	72
1986 GEVREY-CHAMBERTIN CHAMPERRIER	80
1986 GEVREY-CHAMBERTIN PETITES CHAPELLES	84

This is another of those small, rather unheralded estates in Burgundy
that can on occasion produce some fine wine at realistic prices. The
1978 and 1980 Petites Chapelles, for example, would place well in many
a blind tasting of the wines from those two fine vintages. As for the
1986s, they are somewhat foursquare, chunky wines—dense, even substantial on the palate but without complexity. The Villages Gevrey-
Chambertin is thin and washed out, the Champerrier robust and one
dimensional. Only in the Petites Chapelles (always this domaine's best
wine) does one see some interest and focus to go along with the full-
bodied, chewy texture of these wines. Drink them by 1993–1996.

JEAN PICHENET (SAVIGNY-LÈS-BEAUNE)

1986 SAVIGNY-LÈS-BEAUNE	84

I suppose it is easy to bypass a wine with the appellation Savigny-Lès-
Beaune, but Jean Pichenet's offerings are consistently elegant, fruity,
soft, graceful wines that offer charm and plenty of up-front tasty fruit.
His 1986 will not make you forget his 1985, but if you want a nice red

burgundy to consume over the next several years, this is a meritorious choice.

CHÂTEAU DE POMMARD (POMMARD)

1986 POMMARD	83

The 1986 Pommard is not as fragrant and tasty as the 1985, but it is still a burly, spicy, oaky, medium-bodied wine that will not shed its tannins until 1992–1993. It is good, but just not exciting. Drink it between 1992 and 1997.

DOMAINE PONSOT (MOREY ST.-DENIS)

1986 CHAMBERTIN	72
1986 CHAMBOLLE-MUSIGNY LES CHARMES	76
1986 CLOS DE LA ROCHE VIEILLES VIGNES	79
1986 CLOS ST.-DENIS VIEILLES VIGNES	80
1986 GRIOTTE-CHAMBERTIN VIEILLES VIGNES	77
1986 LATRICIÈRES-CHAMBERTIN	69

I tasted all of these wines four separate times after bottling, the last time in the cellars of Ponsot, and was disappointed each time. By 1990 the wines were already revealing an amber/orange rim, which is an unhealthy sign in a 2.5-year-old wine, and washed-out colors and flavors. The Latricières-Chambertin is thin, diluted, and very pale in color with little flavor depth. The Chambolle-Musigny Les Charmes tastes like a simple generic Bourgogne. The Clos de la Roche Vieilles Vignes (sometimes one of the 5 or 6 greatest wines of Burgundy) has an excellent spicy, ripe nose but alarmingly light, shallow flavors—my rating may be too generous. The Clos St.-Denis Vieilles Vignes is the best of this mediocre lot. It has good medium ruby color, a moderately intense bouquet of berry fruit, some attractive vanillin scents and good flavor depth. Drink it by 1993–1994. The Griotte-Chambertin Vieilles Vignes is light in color, medium bodied with soft, watery flavors and not much of a finish. Last, the Chambertin would make Napoleon turn over in his grave. It is overly woody, thin, and lacking fruit and length. From one of my favorite wine producers in Burgundy (and one who charges a high tariff for his products), these wines are inexcusable.

DOMAINE POTHIER-RIEUSSET (POMMARD)

1986 BEAUNE LES BOUCHEROTTES	74
1986 POMMARD LES CHARMOTS	75
1986 POMMARD CLOS DES VERGERS	75
1986 POMMARD LES EPENOTS	73
1986 POMMARD LES RUGIENS	79

Virgile Pothier's 1986s look watery and light, as if overproduction is the culprit. This is rather sad, for here is a man who built quite a reputation that, as he nears retirement, appears to be in serious jeopardy. To various degrees, all of the 1986s are inexcusably light and diluted with hollow, tannic flavors. Only the Pommard Les Rugiens has decent amounts of smoky, cherry-scented fruit. These wines will age very fast. What a pity!

POUSSE D'OR (VOLNAY)

1986 POMMARD LES JAROLIÈRES	85
1986 SANTENAY CLOS TAVANNES	77
1986 VOLNAY BOUSSE D'OR	83
1986 VOLNAY LES CAILLERETS	79
1986 VOLNAY LES CAILLERETS 60 OUVRÉES	79

The huge yield, Potel's use of filtration prior to bottling (something he never did before 1979), and the rain in September of 1986 have all combined to render light-weight, shallow wines. The top wine in 1986 is the Pommard Les Jarolières, as it has the best fruit, a good measure of spicy oak, medium body, and some length and charm. Drink it between 1990 and 1994. The Santenay Clos Tavannes shows some pleasant Pinot ripeness in the nose, but the dry, astringent tannins are disquieting. The Volnay Bousse d'Or, usually my favorite, is also hard, ungenerous, stiff, and unyielding. The Volnay Caillerets suffers from the same leanness and one must ask—where's the fruit? The tannins and charmlessness of the Volnay Caillerets 60 Ouvrées also bothered me. Except for the Pommard Les Jarolières, these are mediocre wines, proving that even highly competent winemaking can have its shortcomings.

MICHEL PRUNIER (AUXEY-DURESSES)

1986 AUXEY-DURESSES CLOS DU VAL	86
1986 AUXEY-DURESSES PREMIER CRU	85
1986 BEAUNE LES SIZIES	86
1986 VOLNAY LES CAILLERETS	78

Prunier's 1986s will make ideal drinking until 1992–1994. The Auxey-Duresses Clos du Val, from 50-year-old vines, is wonderfully fragrant, supple, and round with tremendous elegance and a long, velvety finish. I thought I was tasting a 1985. The Auxey-Duresses Premier Cru offers up plenty of spicy oak and raspberries, is soft and silky, medium bodied, and delicious. The Beaune Les Sizies, from 70-year-old vines, is full bodied, dense, powerful, and has the potential to improve until 1994–1999. As Prunier half jokingly says, "It's a Beaune, but tastes like a Vosne!" The only wine I felt to be less than good was the Volnay Les Caillerets. It showed a diluted, watery character and low-intensity flavors. I sure wish we would see more of this man's wines in America.

DOMAINE CHARLES QUILLARDET (MARSANNAY)

1986 GEVREY-CHAMBERTIN	73
1986 GEVREY-CHAMBERTIN LE BEL-AIR	74
1986 MARSANNAY	69

I have never been a great fan of this producer's wines, which tend to be burly, charmless, too tannic, and hard. The 1986s lack concentration, seem out of balance (in favor of their tannins), and would appear dubious bets to improve with aging.

HENRI REMORIQUET (NUITS ST.-GEORGES)

1986 NUITS ST.-GEORGES	77
1986 NUITS ST.-GEORGES LES ALLOTS	81
1986 NUITS ST.-GEORGES LES BOUSSELOTS	83
1986 NUITS ST.-GEORGES LES DAMODES	87

Remoriquet's 1986s tended to be chunky, robust, tannic wines that I found lacking a bit in fruit and charm. The pick of the litter here is the

Nuits St.-Georges Les Damodes, which is a big, dense, chewy wine with a lot of concentration and tannin. Drink it between 1992 and 1999.

DOMAINE HENRI RICHARD (GEVREY-CHAMBERTIN)

1986 CHARMES-CHAMBERTIN	86
1986 GEVREY-CHAMBERTIN	82
1986 GEVREY-CHAMBERTIN MAZOYÈRES	85

The 1986 Gevrey-Chambertin is a dusty, woody, very spicy, muscular wine with character and charm. I would drink it by 1992–1993. The Gevrey-Chambertin Mazoyères has a good dosage of spicy oak, some nice sweet, ripe fruit, and some surprising power and depth for a 1986. The Charmes-Chambertin is more tannic, shows good ripeness and depth, has a lot of body, and is quite long. It should be at its best between 1990 and 1995.

RION PÈRE ET FILS (NUITS ST.-GEORGES)

1986 CLOS VOUGEOT	77
1986 NUITS ST.-GEORGES LES MURGERS	80
1986 VOSNE-ROMANÉE LES CHAUMES	80

Bernard Rion's 1986s are light and show a certain feebleness. The Clos Vougeot is tight and tannic and I doubt it has the fruit to cover the tannins. The Nuits St.-Georges Les Murgers and Vosne-Romanée Les Chaumes are similarly styled wines with barely enough fruit. I would advise seeking out Rion's 1987s or those 1985s that are still available.

DOMAINE DANIEL RION (NUITS ST.-GEORGES)

1986 CHAMBOLLE-MUSIGNY AUX BEAUX BRUNS	85
1986 NUITS ST.-GEORGES CLOS DES ARGILLIÈRES	86
1986 NUITS ST.-GEORGES LES HAUTS PRULIERS	88
1986 NUITS ST.-GEORGES LES VIGNES RONDES	85
1986 VOSNE-ROMANÉE LES BEAUX MONTS	86
1986 VOSNE-ROMANÉE LES CHAUMES	90

These were very impressive wines from an estate that is going from strength to strength. There is nothing here that I would not be proud to own and drink. The quantities of gorgeous, sumptuous fruit in these wines are breathtaking. The Nuits St.-Georges wines all showed well. For example, the Les Vignes Rondes is a supple, expansive, ripe, medium- to full-bodied wine that should offer fine drinking until 1992. The Clos des Argillières shows more new oak, has plenty of sweet, tasty, berry fruit, medium body, and a smooth, velvety finish. The Les Hauts Pruliers is even richer and deeper. Quite full bodied, loaded with plummy fruit and sweet oak, this lush, hedonistic wine has all the seductive power that great Burgundy can provide. I thought the Chambolle-Musigny aux Beaux Bruns to be less impressive, although certainly good. It has a lighter color, plenty of spicy oak, an attractive finish, and immediate appeal. The Vosne-Romanée Les Chaumes is a great wine with a profoundly complex bouquet of ripe plums, black cherries, vanilla, and smoky oak. Full bodied, well colored, smooth and velvety, with gobs of sweet fruit, this wine will make grand drinking until 1992–1994. The Vosne-Romanée Les Beaux Monts is merely good, juicy, succulent Pinot Noir without the extra depth and dimension of the Les Chaumes. Patrice Rion, the talented winemaker here, is clearly on a hot streak.

MAURICE ROLLIN (PERNAND-VERGELESSES)

1986 PERNAND-VERGELESSES	72
1986 PERNAND-VERGELESSES ÎLE DES VERGELESSES	?
1986 SAVIGNY-LÈS-BEAUNE	76

These wines all tasted light, had astringent tannins, and tough textures. I also thought I detected some rot in the Pernand-Vergelesses Île de Vergelesses.

DOMAINE DE LA ROMANÉE-CONTI (VOSNE-ROMANÉE)

1986 ECHÉZEAUX	90
1986 GRANDS ECHÉZEAUX	92
1986 RICHEBOURG	94
1986 ROMANÉE-CONTI	94
1986 ROMANÉE ST.-VIVANT	89
1986 LA TÂCHE	93

Except for their prices, it seems impossible to find fault with the wines
from the Domaine de la Romanée-Conti. Many of the best wines of the
1986 vintage are once again produced at this estate. The 1986s are
much more tannic and structured wines than the 1987s, and they are
less flattering to taste than the 1985s were at a similar stage of their
development. However, if you are able to defer your gratification until
1994–1995, then I think these wines should be taken quite seriously.
Certainly, the Echézeaux is one of the best examples of this wine the
domaine has made recently. Deep in color (darker actually than the
1985), this wine has an exotic, intense bouquet of plums, oriental
spices, oak, and berry fruit. It is, as one would expect, the most forward
of their wines, but I would still not opt for opening it until 1993–1994.
The Grands Echézeaux also has super color, a great nose of intense,
smoky, exotic Pinot Noir fruit, full body, and plenty of extract as well
as tannins. Not as forward as either the 1985 or 1987, the 1986 Grands
Echézeaux should be at its best between 1994 and 2008. Even more
spectacular is the Richebourg, which has a stunning nose, is more full
bodied and powerful than usual, very long, but also quite tannic. I
tasted it twice and my estimate on peak drinkability was between 1996
and 2012. It should be a real ager. The Romanée-Conti is very backward in 1986. The fabulous nose of oriental spices, new oak, and ripe
fruit is amply displayed, but on the palate the wine is tight, hard, and
very rich but still mostly inaccessible. It has a smashingly long finish
and should be drinkable between 1993 and 2010. I thought the 1987
Romanée St.-Vivant superior to the 1986, which has a very earthy,
tannic, hard texture, excellent color and length, but a persistent hardness and toughness. It may well merit a higher score in 5 more years,
but I would have liked to have seen a bit more fruit. La Tâche, made
from 35-year-old vines, is another brooding infant. Splendidly perfumed
(a trait shared by all their 1986 wines), it, too, showed great depth and
richness but plenty of mouthsearing tannins that suggest it needs until
1995–1996. It is quite a big, bold, dramatic red burgundy (as all this
domaine's wines tend to be), but it would be a shame to drink it before
1995. All in all, these are among the few superstars of this vintage, but
the 1986s are not for drinking soon—patience is most definitely required.

PHILIPPE ROSSIGNOL (GEVREY-CHAMBERTIN)

1986 BOURGOGNE	72
1986 CÔTE DE NUITS-VILLAGES	77
1986 GEVREY-CHAMBERTIN	80

Phillippe Rossignol, one of the many Rossignols making wine in Burgundy, is located in Gevrey-Chambertin, and while he has no Premiers Crus or Grands Crus in his estate, he often produces wines that are among the best of their types. All three of his 1986s smelled complex, rich, and interesting, but once on the palate they seemed rather tart, lean, and narrowly focused. Given how attractive the bouquets were, I wonder if I may have caught these wines in an awkward stage of development? For now, they suggest good fruit and character in the nose, but fall short on the palate.

JOSEPH ROTY (GEVREY-CHAMBERTIN)

1986 CHARMES-CHAMBERTIN	85
1986 GEVREY-CHAMBERTIN LES CHAMPCHENYS	81
1986 GEVREY-CHAMBERTIN CLOS PRIEUR	82
1986 PINOT NOIR LES PRESSONIÈRES	67

The loquacious Joseph Roty made ethereal wines in 1985, and although his 1986s are sound, even good, they are not as striking as I expected, given his enormous talents. The 1986 Charmes-Chambertin is the stand-out wine, but the light color suggests a problem of over-dilution. It is a spicy, fruity, medium-bodied wine that is extremely tannic. Whether enough of the tannins melt away for this wine to come into balance remains questionable. As for the other wines, the Les Champchenys appear to have excessive tannins for the amount of fruit, yet it should be cellared until 1991–1992. The Clos Prieur also seems excessively hard and tough, and I seriously wonder if there is enough fruit covering its bones. Lastly, the Pinot Noir Les Pressonières showed a trace of rot and tasted very hard. Roty's 1986s are all gambles. Caveat emptor.

GEORGES ROUMIER (CHAMBOLLE-MUSIGNY)

1986 BONNES MARES	89
1986 CHAMBOLLE-MUSIGNY	84
1986 CHAMBOLLE-MUSIGNY LES AMOUREUSES	89
1986 MOREY ST.-DENIS CLOS DE LA BUSSIÈRE	87

Jean-Marie Roumier and Christophe, his son, have one of the most important and respected cellars in Burgundy's Côte d'Or. From their infant days in the cask, the 1986s have had the reputation of being some of the finest 1986s made. I concur. The Bonnes Mares is a very structured, medium- to full-bodied wine with a great deal of depth and intensity, a scented nose of subtle oak and ripe berry fruit. There is plenty of length and at least a decade's worth of aging potential. Drink it between 1993 and 2002. The Chambolle-Musigny is quite elegant, exhibiting plenty of fruit and spice in the nose and, while very good, finishes a little too short to get high marks. The Chambolle-Musigny Les Amoureuses resembles a 1985 more than a 1986. It is quite seductive, fragrant, medium to full bodied, deep, and quite long on the palate. It will be ready before the Bonnes Mares. Drink it between now and 1998. Last, the Morey St.-Denis Clos de la Bussière is a meaty, fleshy, red burgundy made to last for a decade or more. It was somewhat closed but clearly dense, concentrated, and well balanced. Drink it between 1993 and 2000.

HERVÉ ROUMIER (VOSNE-ROMANÉE)

1986 BOURGOGNE	78
1986 CHAMBOLLE-MUSIGNY	80
1986 CLOS VOUGEOT	84

I was not overwhelmed by this producer's 1985s or 1986s. The 1986 Bourgogne has a sweet, ripe nose, soft, light-bodied, fruity flavor, and a decent finish. Drink it by 1990. The Chambolle-Musigny is made to emphasize a very dry, floral, berry-scented character, has light to medium body and offers clean, undramatic flavors that are correct. The Clos Vougeot has more depth and weight, a good dosage of alcohol, and a supple, pleasing fruitiness. It should be drunk by 1991–1992.

DOMAINE ARMAND ROUSSEAU
(GEVREY-CHAMBERTIN)

1986 CHAMBERTIN	90
1986 CHAMBERTIN-CLOS DE BÈZE	90
1986 CHARMES-CHAMBERTIN	86
1986 CLOS DE LA ROCHE	86
1986 CLOS DES RUCHOTTES	83

1986 GEVREY-CHAMBERTIN	81
1986 GEVREY-CHAMBERTIN CLOS ST.-JACQUES	87
1986 MAZIS-CHAMBERTIN	85

Charles Rousseau, the meticulous proprietor of this famous estate, has produced excellent 1986s. The top wine, as one might reasonably expect, is the Chambertin. It has a good ruby color, a full-intensity bouquet of spicy new oak, and lush berry fruit, with layers of flavor, superb definition and depth, and none of the dry, astringent tannins that plague some 1986s. It is less developed than the Chambertin-Clos de Bèze, which has a wonderfully forward, sweet, smoky, perfumed, fruity nose with plenty of new oak in evidence. The Chambertin should be at its best between 1992 and 2002, the Clos de Bèze between 1990 and 1998. Both wines are stars of the 1986 vintage. The Charmes-Chambertin is soft and supple, very good rather than special. It has a tannic bite that suggests aging until 1991–1992 is warranted. The Clos de la Roche is very open knit, forward, deliciously fruity, and soft. I would advise drinking it by 1993–1994. I found the Clos des Ruchottes very rustic, a touch too tannic, and hard to merit high marks. Perhaps it will show more fruit and charm with aging. The Gevrey-Chambertin is straightforward and pleasant, but essentially one-dimensional. The Mazis-Chambertin is quite closed and, while certainly very good, will appeal to those consumers who prefer a leaner, drier, more structured style of red burgundy. It should be at its best between 1991 and 1998.

SAIER (MERCUREY)

1986 MERCUREY CHAMPS MARTIN	74
1986 MERCUREY LES CHENELOTS	72

These wines simply lack depth and character. Both are rather thin, insipid examples from two of Mercurey's best vineyards. Overproduction would appear to be the culprit.

DANIEL SENARD (ALOXE-CORTON)

1986 ALOXE-CORTON	72
1986 CORTON LES BRESSANDES	78
1986 CORTON-CLOS DU ROI	77

All three wines I tasted from Philippe Senard exhibited the effects of the overly abundant 1986 crop. To put it mildly, they were light and rather straightforward, not without charm, but just did not have enough fruit and depth to hold my interest. However, the 1987s are knockouts. Interestingly, this is another estate that has come under the spell of the oenologist Guy Accad, whose style aims for deeply colored, very intensely fruity, rich wines that drink well young. Look for the 1987s and 1988s from Senard.

G. SERAFIN (GEVREY-CHAMBERTIN)

1986 CHARMES-CHAMBERTIN	90
1986 GEVREY-CHAMBERTIN LES CAZETIERS	92

I was knocked over by Serafin's 1986s, which are among the very finest wines produced in Burgundy. The Charmes-Chambertin is a wine filled with finesse, gorgeous amounts of berry fruit, a lush, titillating texture, and superb length. It was showing so well that you would want to drink it by 1993–1994. The Les Cazetiers (from 35-year-old vines) was even more sensational. Tasting more like a 1985 or 1988 than a 1986, this powerful, very concentrated yet supple wine will make great drinking until 1995–1997.

BERNARD SERVEAU (MOREY ST.-DENIS)

1986 CHAMBOLLE-MUSIGNY LES AMOUREUSES	85
1986 CHAMBOLLE-MUSIGNY LES CHABIOTS	83
1986 MOREY ST.-DENIS LES SORBÈS	82
1986 NUITS ST.-GEORGES CHAÎNES-CARTEAUX	78

Very light, fragrant, somewhat fragile wines were made by M. Serveau in 1986. All of these wines should be drunk by 1991–1992 as I do not expect them to last. The top wine is, as one might expect, the Chambolle-Musigny Les Amoureuses, which has the best color (medium ruby), plenty of velvety, sweet red fruits, an elegant, spicy bouquet, and moderately soft tannins. Les Chabiots and Les Sorbès are soft, a trifle light and diluted, but fresh, clean, and ideal for straightforward, near-term drinking. The Nuits-St. Georges Chaînes-Carteaux lacks depth and tastes too simple to merit a higher rating.

JEAN TARDY (VOSNE-ROMANÉE)

1986 CLOS VOUGEOT	87
1986 NUITS ST.-GEORGES BOUDOTS	86
1986 VOSNE-ROMANÉE LES CHARMES	82?

The 1986 Clos Vougeot is Tardy's top wine. It has a deep color for a 1986 and a rich, open-knit bouquet of raspberry fruit and smoky new oak. Medium to full bodied, rather powerful and closed, it will need until 1992–1993 to round out. The Nuits St.-Georges Boudots is also very good, deep in color, spicy, rich but quite tannic; however, the fruit is sufficient to balance out the tannins. The Vosne-Romanée Les Charmes is much lighter and has quite a bit of tannin for the fruit. I doubt that it will age well.

DOMAINE DE LA TASSÉE (CHAMBOLLE-MUSIGNY)

1986 CHAMBOLLE-MUSIGNY LES BAUDES	81
1986 CHAMBOLLE-MUSIGNY LES CHARMES	83

I have only seen this producer's wines over three vintages, 1984, 1985, and 1986. The wines have tended to be sound rather than exciting. The Les Baudes smells of bing cherries, is ripe, tasty, a little heavy-handed and alcoholic, but certainly pleasant. The Les Charmes exhibits good ripeness but less alcoholic punch and more finesse and elegance in its medium-bodied, berry fruit flavors. Drink both of these wines by 1993–1995.

CHÂTEAU DE LA TOUR (VOUGEOT)

1986 CLOS VOUGEOT	84

Its offerings in 1987 and 1988 suggest that this is one of the up-and-coming stars of Burgundy. Over the last decade, however, this fabulous property, which has one of the largest sections of Clos Vougeot, made a group of undistinguished, light, relatively innocuous wines that lacked depth and character. The 1985 is not up to the standards of that wonderful vintage, yet the 1986, while light with narrowly focused flavors and medium body, is typical of the majority of 1986s. I would skip the 1986 and go for the 1987 or 1988 instead.

BRENTANO'S

```
        5007   102   4065   06-05-93
        REL   2.9A    44   11:18:43

01 0671633783                        39.95
PREF NO. 400105417  EXP 12/93
PREF DISC     39.95 10% OFF          4.00-
              SUBTOTAL              35.95
CALIFORNIA 8.25% TA                  2.97
              TOTAL                 38.92
5416215281683939 M C               38.92
              PV# 0024065
```

BOOKS MAKE THE GREATEST

CUSTOMER COPY

38.92   5416215281683939 M C

PREF NO. 400105417 EXP 12/93

SALE   5007 102 4065 06-05-92
REL   2.94   44 11:18:43

IMPORTANT: RETAIN THIS COPY FOR YOUR RECORDS.

5416 2152 8168 3939

1621 SDFCU 11/94
DAVID A SCHWARZ

BRENTANOS
5007
LOS ANGELES CA
5044305217

0.0593

AUTHORIZATION
064853

CUSTOMER SIGNATURE
X

MANAGEMENT SIGNATURE - FOR CREDIT ONLY
X

DOMAINE LOUIS TRAPET (GEVREY-CHAMBERTIN)

1986 CHAMBERTIN	79
1986 CHAPELLE-CHAMBERTIN	77
1986 GEVREY-CHAMBERTIN	67
1986 LATRICIÈRES-CHAMBERTIN	79

It is tragic that the three largest holders of choice Premier Cru and Grand Cru vineyards of Gevrey-Chambertin—Camus, Damoy, and Trapet—hardly set the highest standards for quality in the appellation. Jean Trapet, a delightful, gregarious, extremely hospitable man, has for the fourth straight year turned out wines that taste distinctly inferior to what he showed me out of cask. I have always thought that he has a heavy hand when it comes to fining and filtration, thus stripping his wines of much of their fruit and bouquet. The 1986s, which showed much better out of cask in 1987, are very light, washed-out wines with an excess of tannin for the meager fruitiness. The Chambertin is too oaky, shallow, and diluted. The Chapelle-Chambertin is again a little wine, narrowly constructed, oaky, and lacking depth and fat. The Gevrey-Chambertin is all water, tannin, and wood. The Latricières-Chambertin has some power and weight, but again the wood and tannins dominate the fruit. This is a famous domaine with the vineyards and cellar to produce exceptional wine if Jean Trapet would limit his yields and go back to the traditional techniques (no filtration) of his father, Louis.

COMTE DE VOGÜÉ (CHAMBOLLE-MUSIGNY)

1986 BONNES MARES	84
1986 CHAMBOLLE-MUSIGNY LES AMOUREUSES	84
1986 MUSIGNY	86

As usual, good rather than exhilarating wines were made at this famous estate in Chambolle-Musigny. Despite reports that quality here has returned to the form of the 1972 and prior vintages, I remain convinced that this property is producing entirely too much wine to obtain the concentration necessary. What's more, its decision to filter its wines a decade ago has stripped many of the wines of at least 30% of their potential bouquet and flavor. These are light, fruity, elegant, somewhat charming wines, but they are grossly overpriced and must be drunk by 1993–1994 before their fragile fruit fades away.

LENI VOLPATO (CHAMBOLLE-MUSIGNY)

1986 BOURGOGNE PASSE-TOUT-GRAINS	84
1986 CHAMBOLLE-MUSIGNY	82

This estate produces only two wines, but I have to say that the Bourgogne Passe-Tout-Grains is the best one I have tasted. Leni Volpato, an understated, middle-aged man, produces this wine from mostly Pinot Noir. It has a big color, a peppery, spicy bouquet, an attractive suppleness, and nice length. For drinking between now and 1992 it is excellent. Volpato's Chambolle-Musigny, excellent in 1985 and 1987, is a little hard and lean in 1986, with an excess of tannin.

1986 WHITE BURGUNDY

The growers and *négociants* are comparing 1986, a huge, bountiful crop, with the good, abundant year of 1979. The wines range from very good to superb. There is plenty of fresh acidity, and the extract levels, while quite variable, have provided wines ranging from diluted to those that are wonderfully concentrated. I hear comments that the 1986s are more "classic" than the fatter 1985s. Certainly, there is some additional complexity in the 1986s as a result of the botrytis, or noble rot, that attacked some of the Chardonnay. In my tastings, the wines performed extremely well, with the strongest wines appearing to be in the appellations of Corton-Charlemagne, Chassagne-Montrachet, Puligny-Montrachet, and Pouilly-Fuissé. The wines, because of their good acidity, should age well for 5–10 years. Prices are lower for the 1986s than the 1985s. The wine press has generally declared 1986 to be a better year than 1985, but interestingly, producers such as Leflaive, Jadot, Comte Lafon, and Sauzet claim time will prove the 1985s superior.

RECOMMENDED PRODUCERS

Amiot-Bonfils

Robert Ampeau

Pierre Bitouzet

Bonneau de Martray

Roger Caillot

J. F. Coche-Dury

Fernand Coffinet
Jean Collet
René Dauvissat
Georges Deleger
Faiveley
J. A. Ferret
Fontaine-Gagnard
Château Fuissé
Jean-Noël Gagnard
Albert Grivault
Louis Jadot
Comte Lafon
Louis Latour

Domaine Leflaive
Leroy
Long-Depaquit (Bichot)
Louis Michel
Bernard Morey
Jean-Marc Morey
Michel Niellon
Paul Pernot
Perrin-Ponsot
Domaine Ramonet
Domaine Raveneau
Guy Roulot
Étienne Sauzet

1987 RED BURGUNDY

This is the sleeper vintage of the eighties decade. The summer was warm and dry enough to give the wines concentration and ripeness, but a succession of weather depressions hit Burgundy in September prior to and during the early days of the harvest. These rains caused much of the wine media to dismiss the vintage prematurely as disappointing. These early impressions ignored the sound overall health of the grapes and the small yields. However, the tastings of the 1987s at the Hospices de Beaune sale in late November, 1987, seemed to confirm the fact that 1987 was a disappointing year. The wines were in full malolactic fermentation at the time of the tasting, making proper evaluation impossible even for the most skilled of tasters. When I did my first tasting of the 1987s in the spring of 1988, I was impressed by their aromatic purity and perfume, good color, crisp acidity, and overall sense of balance and harmony. They were not sumptuous, opulent blockbusters in the mold of the top 1985s, nor were they as impressively deep in color as the top 1988s. However, most producers made wines that are significantly better than the dry, astringent, somewhat hollow 1986s, and are clearly more consistent in quality than the sometimes awful, sometimes spectacular 1983s. In November, 1988, and September, 1989, I had the chance to do comprehensive tastings of the 1987s from the bottle. Based on them, I am convinced that 1987 is a very good vintage that merits serious consideration. Furthermore, prices are well below those of 1988, and will probably be below those of 1989 as well. Some producers have even made better 1987s than 1988s (i.e., Jean Gros, Gros Frère et Soeur, Bernard Rion, Robert Arnoux). Other producers have made

1987s nearly as good as their 1988s. However, do not expect the 1987 red burgundies to be long lived. They do not have a high tannin level, a great deal of body, or elevated alcohol contents. They are well colored, pure, aromatic, and perfumed, with a very good acidity (better acidity than 1985 or 1988). Most 1987s should be consumed by 1996–1997. There will, however, be some very long-lived wines capable of lasting until 2002–2010, most notably those of the Domaine de la Romanée-Conti.

Note: The 1987s were tasted from the barrel in the spring and the fall of 1988, and from the bottle in fall, 1989, and early in winter, 1990.

BERTRAND AMBROISE (PRÉMEAUX)

1987 CÔTE DE NUITS-VILLAGES	85

Bertrand Ambroise's Côte de Nuits-Villages is excellent, showing a deep ruby color, a big, fragrant, ripe, berry-scented bouquet, and long, lush, velvety flavors. It is ideal for drinking between now and 1993–1994.

BERNARD AMIOT (CHAMBOLLE-MUSIGNY)

1987 CHAMBOLLE-MUSIGNY LES CHARMES	86
1987 CHAMBOLLE-MUSIGNY CHATELOTS	84

This domaine is a very reliable, consistent source of lighter-styled, immediately drinkable, short-lived, yet very pleasant-tasting, authentic wines from the village of Chambolle-Musigny. Amiot's Chambolle-Musigny Chatelots is tasty, soft, light, but elegant and perfumed. Even better is his Chambolle-Musigny Les Charmes. It offers more richness and depth with a lovely, fragrant, jammy perfume and soft, flowing, silky flavors. Both wines should be consumed by 1992–1993. Amiot, a great believer in filtration, has finally been convinced by his importer not to filter those wines that are exported to America.

DOMAINE DE L'ARLOT (PRÉMEAUX)

1987 CÔTE DE NUITS-VILLAGES CLOS DU CHAPEAU	84
1987 NUITS ST.-GEORGES-CLOS DE L'ARLOT	87
1987 NUITS ST.-GEORGES-CLOS DES FORÊTS ST.-GEORGES	89

The results of the first two vintages (1987 and 1988) from Jean-Pierre de Smet's 31.2-acre estate have been stunning. No wonder. There is no destemming; a prefermentation cold maceration of 3 to 5 days is followed by a long maceration. The wines are aged in 50% new oak casks, there is minimal racking, and no filtration. The Côtes de Nuits-Villages is elegant, light, supple, and ready to drink, displaying a fragrant, authentic Pinot bouquet and soft, pleasant flavors. The Clos de l'Arlot exhibits a rich, penetrating bouquet of berry fruit, herbs, vanillin-scented, spicy oak, and supple, expansive, rich flavors that typify the elegant, perfumed style of burgundy. Even better is the Clos des Forêts St.-Georges, which has an exceptional bouquet of berry fruit, spices, and herbs, long, supple, velvety flavors, and a hedonistic, heady finish. These latter two wines are drinking beautifully now and should be consumed by 1994–1996. I should also point out that the colorful, very modern label has unsettled the traditionalists in Burgundy. This is an up-and-coming star to consider, and the 1987s are beauties.

DOMAINE DU COMTE ARMAND (POMMARD)

1987 POMMARD CLOS DES EPENEAUX	85

The 1987 from this excellent estate is medium bodied with a light ruby color, good ripe cherry fruit, and a nice touch of spicy oak, but it lacks the concentration and charm of the best wines of the vintage. It should be drunk over the next 2 to 4 years.

ROBERT ARNOUX (VOSNE-ROMANÉE)

1987 NUITS ST.-GEORGES LES CORVÉES PAGET	85
1987 NUITS ST.-GEORGES LES PROCÈS	82
1987 ROMANÉE ST.-VIVANT	87
1987 VOSNE-ROMANÉE	77
1987 VOSNE-ROMANÉE LES CHAUMES	85
1987 VOSNE-ROMANÉE LES SUCHOTS	86

I think admirers of Robert Arnoux's wines will find his 1987s to be good to very good, and only a notch below the quality of his excellent 1985s. They are vastly superior to his somewhat fragile, light, overcropped 1986s. All his 1987s share in common a suppleness, velvety texture, and forward, ripe, precocious personality. There is not a wine in his stable that I would not consume between now and 1994–1995. The best wine of Arnoux is usually his Vosne-Romanée Les Suchots, and the 1987 shows excellent ripeness, a spicy, berry, herbaceous-scented fruitiness, smooth texture, and light tannins in the finish. The Vosne-Romanée Les Chaumes does not have the concentration to match the Les Suchots. Fortunately, the Romanée St.-Vivant offers more complexity in the nose and the same degree of ripeness and richness on the palate as the Les Suchots. I felt the Vosne-Romanée and the Nuits St.-Georges Les Procès to be light and simple. However, the Nuits St.-Georges Les Corvées Paget was spicy, with good ripe berry fruit and a soft texture, giving it an overall impression of elegance and character.

DOMAINE DENIS BACHELET (GEVREY-CHAMBERTIN)

1987 GEVREY-CHAMBERTIN LES CORBEAUX	83
1987 GEVREY-CHAMBERTIN VIELLES VIGNES	78

The top wine from Bachelet is always the Grand Cru, Charmes-Chambertin. Unfortunately, I did not see the 1987. Of the two wines I did taste, the Gevrey-Chambertin Vieilles Vignes is much lighter than I would have suspected, and fell off on the palate. There was a lack of concentration and a surprisingly innocuous personality to the wine. The Premier Cru Les Corbeaux was not much better, although it did have more ripeness and concentration. Perhaps these bottles were in an awkward stage of development, because Denis Bachelet's wines have consistently been well above the rank and file of the Gevrey-Chambertin producers.

DOMAINE DE BAPTAULT (BEAUNE)

1987 BEAUNE-CLOS DES AVAUX	76
1987 BEAUNE LES AVAUX	74
1987 BEAUNE LES CHAMPS PIMONTS	69
1987 BEAUNE AUX CRAS	74
1987 BEAUNE LES GRÈVES	79
1987 BOURGOGNE-CUVÉE LA CHAPELLE DE BAPTAULT	72

These were uninspiring wines from a Swiss-owned domaine outside Beaune. I do not have any experience with prior vintages, but the wines were diluted, shallow, and seemed clearly the product of a domaine that had produced entirely too much wine, rather than keeping yields down and looking for some concentration and character. All these wines should be consumed by 1991–1992. It is hard to muster enthusiasm for any of them, but the best of this mediocre group was the Beaune Les Grèves, as it showed more fruit.

ANDRÉ BART (MARSANNAY)

1987 BONNES MARES	84
1987 CHAMBERTIN-CLOS DE BÈZE	84
1987 CHAMBOLLE-MUSIGNY	82
1987 CÔTE DE NUITS-VILLAGES	80
1987 FIXIN LES HERVELETS	73
1987 MARSANNAY	74
1987 SANTENAY EN BIEVAU	70

A visit to the cellars of André Bart and his son Martin left me disappointed. The wines from Marsannay, Côte de Nuits-Villages, Santenay, and Fixin Les Hervelets were only of average quality. Additionally, I expected more from the Grands Crus vineyards such as Bonnes Mares and Chambertin-Clos de Bèze. The cellars are certainly well kept and the use of 35%–40% new oak for the top wines seems appropriate. Yet the Bonnes Mares tastes dull, is medium bodied, and lacks the depth and richness one would expect from this great Grand Cru vineyard. The same can be said for the Chambertin-Clos de Bèze, which showed a lot of spicy new oak, adequate flavor concentration, but not a great deal of complexity. The 1988s were slightly better, but still uninspiring examples of Burgundy winemaking.

BARTHOD-NOËLLAT (CHAMBOLLE-MUSIGNY)

1987 BOURGOGNE ROUGE	74
1987 CHAMBOLLE-MUSIGNY	82
1987 CHAMBOLLE-MUSIGNY AUX BEAUX BRUNS	85
1987 CHAMBOLLE-MUSIGNY LES CHARMES	86
1987 CHAMBOLLE-MUSIGNY LES CRAS	86
1987 CHAMBOLLE-MUSIGNY LES VAROILLES	87

The Bourgogne Rouge is light, acidic, and tough-textured. It may be reasonably priced, but it provided me with little pleasure. Much better is the Chambolle-Musigny. Light, supple, and medium bodied, it is ideal for drinking now. Certainly the four Premiers Crus offered by Barthod are completely different in style and texture. The Chambolle-Musigny aux Beaux Bruns has good acidity, light to medium body, wonderful freshness and purity, and plenty of attractive ripeness. The Chambolle-Musigny Les Cras is much more tannic, has good acidity, and shows more ripeness and body than the lighter and more zesty Beaux Bruns. Concentration and opulence characterize the Chambolle-Musigny Les Charmes, probably Barthod's most elegant Premier Cru in 1987. It should drink nicely until 1995–1996. In 1987 he has also produced a Chambolle-Musigny Les Varoilles. This Premier Cru vineyard sits above the Grand Cru Bonnes Mares. It has the deepest color of all his wines, with a very leathery, ground beef, earthy character. It is deep, rich, and the most concentrated and largest-scaled wine produced by Barthod in 1987. It needs a good 2 to 3 years in the cellar to round out.

BILLARD-GONNET (POMMARD)

1987 POMMARD	84
1987 POMMARD LES CHAPONIÈRES	79
1987 POMMARD LES CHARMOTS	77
1987 POMMARD LES PÉZEROLLES	84
1987 POMMARD LES RUGIENS	86

A handful of Billard's 1987s appear to represent a new direction for the estate, as there is more fruit and less tannin and acidity. Perhaps this domaine, which has excellent vineyards in Pommard, has decided to produce more flattering, graceful wines. The Pommard showed good, tasty, berry fruit nicely wrapped in spicy oak. I preferred it to the rather light, medium-bodied, somewhat hard Pommard Les Chaponières and the high-acid, lean, tough Pommard Les Charmots. Both recalled the sort of wines Billard has been making for much of the last several decades. Nevertheless, while the Pommard Les Pézerolles showed a slightly tart character, it still had attractive fruit, a good, spicy, ripe bouquet, and good length on the palate. It should be drunk by 1994–1995. The best wine of Billard-Gonnet in 1987 is their Pommard Les Rugiens. This wine revealed excellent depth and ripeness, and a smooth, velvety, chocolatey, plummy character with plenty of fruit and depth.

DOMAINE JEAN-MARC BOILLOT (POMMARD)

1987 BEAUNE LES MONTREVENOTS	84
1987 POMMARD	72
1987 POMMARD LES SAUSSILLES	69

Jean-Marc Boillot, son of André Boillot, the winemaker for Olivier Leflaive, made an attractively light, elegant, medium-bodied, cherry-scented Beaune Les Montrevenots, but his Pommard and Pommard Les Sausscilles both seemed overcropped, light, thin, meagerly endowed wines destined to be consumed immediately before they lose what little charm they possess.

JEAN-CLAUDE BOISSET (BEAUNE)

1987 ALOXE-CORTON	64
1987 BONNES MARES-CLAUDINE DESCHAMPS	78
1987 CHAMBOLLE-MUSIGNY	74
1987 CHARMES-CHAMBERTIN-DOMAINE CHARLES VIENOT	79
1987 ECHÉZEAUX	69
1987 GEVREY-CHAMBERTIN-CLAUDINE DESCHAMPS	75
1987 GEVREY-CHAMBERTIN LAVAUX ST.-JACQUES	79
1987 NUITS ST.-GEORGES	66
1987 POMMARD	71
1987 SANTENAY	71
1987 SAVIGNY-LÈS-BEAUNE LES LAVIÈRES	76
1987 VOSNE-ROMANÉE LES SUCHOTS	72

Jean-Claude Boisset is one of the largest producers of Burgundy. His numerous firms produce an entire range of generic as well as Premier Cru and Grand Cru burgundies. Despite the success this firm has in many export markets, I have never been impressed with the quality. Most of the 1987s are seriously lacking in character. Furthermore, they rarely reflect their appellations. Far too many wines were not only watery, thin, and sharp, but possessed cooked, almost pasteurized sorts of flavors and eviscerated personalities suggesting they had been overly processed. Wines such as the thin, sharp Nuits St.-Georges, the cooked Aloxe-Corton and Pommard, as well as the Vosne-Romanée Les Suchots make me wonder what really transpired during the fermentation and upbringing of the wines. Also, how could the Echézeaux taste so woody, stemmy, green, and thin? The best wines were some of the domaine wines from the Domaine Claudine Deschamps and Domaine Charles Vienot, but even these high-priced Grands Crus are no better than many other producers' generic burgundies. This is a regrettable situation, to be sure.

BOUCHARD PÈRE ET FILS (BEAUNE)

1987 ALOXE-CORTON	82
1987 BEAUNE LE CHÂTEAU PREMIER CRU	82
1987 BEAUNE-CLOS DE LA MOUSSE	82
1987 CHAMBOLLE-MUSIGNY	82
1987 CHAPELLE-CHAMBERTIN	?
1987 CORTON	85
1987 NUITS ST.-GEORGES-CLOS ST.-MARC	82
1987 POMMARD PREMIER CRU	78
1987 VOLNAY PREMIER CRU	82

This extraordinary empire is the largest vineyard holder in the Côte d'Or, with the majority of its holdings in the Côte de Beaune. Until 1986, this firm was not exploiting the fullest potential of its vineyards or utilizing its immense wealth to produce the highest quality wines. Since 1986 there has been some improvement in quality, though the wines remain relatively compact, straightforward, and somewhat clipped. It is hard to get enthusiastic about them. Their philosophy of winemaking aims for safety, security, and consistency, at the expense of risk-taking—a terrible shame because the Bouchard Père et Fils vintages from the forties and fifties can be remarkable. I misguidedly purchased red wines from the 1978 vintage and whites from the 1981 vintage, including their Chevalier-Montrachet and Montrachet, which were in impeccable condition when purchased and have been stored properly. Today these wines are remarkable only for their disappointingly thin, neutral flavors. The firm's suggestion that their wines need bottle age is, in my opinion, invalid. Although I did not taste the full range of 1987s, they do not appear to be as good as the 1986s, and the 1988s I tasted out of cask appeared to be good rather than inspiring examples of red and white burgundy. As for the 1987s, there is a certain similarity to all the wines.

In my opinion, this would be a wonderful place to send in an adventurous winemaker, fire all the oenologists, and throw out all the filters. Perhaps then some amazing products might emerge from the Bouchard's excellent vineyards. The 1987 Aloxe-Corton is straightforward, compact, has good color, but offers little satisfaction. One of my favorites among their 1987s is their Beaune Le Château Premier Cru, a blend of a number of Premiers Crus vineyards. It has a good, solid, cherry nose, some spicy oak, and depth, but like most of the other Bouchard wines, does not inspire a great deal of enthusiasm. The Beaune-Clos de la Mousse is identical. The 1987 Volnay Premier Cru (the bulk of the blend is from the excellent Premier Cru vineyard Taillepieds) has a great deal of tannin, is a spicy, decent wine, but again lacks spark, complexity, and flavor dimension. The same can be said for the fuller-bodied, rather shy, understated Pommard Premier Cru.

Among the other 1987s, the Chapelle-Chambertin had so much tannin and leanness that it was impossible to find the fruit. It does not appear to have the depth one would expect from a Grand Cru. The Nuits St.-Georges-Clos St.-Marc is an attractive wine, fruity, soft, and spicy, has a deep color, and should drink nicely until 1994–1995. The same can be said for the Chambolle-Musigny, which represents a more fleshy style Chambolle-Musigny. It displays some ripeness, elegance, and a style that sets it apart from the other reds from Bouchard Père et Fils. The best wine I tasted in 1987 from Bouchard is their Corton, one of the house specialties. It shows some spicy new oak, has ripeness as well as depth and length. It should prove to be one of the longer-lived 1987s, reaching full maturity between 7 and 15 years of age.

JEAN-MARC BOULEY (VOLNAY)

1987 BEAUNE LES REVERSÉES	86
1987 BOURGOGNE	76
1987 POMMARD	79

1987 POMMARD LES FREMIÈRES	85
1987 POMMARD LES PÉZEROLLES	87
1987 POMMARD LES RUGIENS	90
1987 VOLNAY	75
1987 VOLNAY LES CAILLERETS	88
1987 VOLNAY LES CARELLES	85
1987 VOLNAY CLOS DES CHÊNES	89

Bouley's 1987s are among the very best wines of the Côte de Beaune. His 1987 Bourgogne Rouge is adequate, light, and clean. Much better is the Beaune Les Reversées, which shows rich, supple, black cherry fruit, a judicious touch of spicy, vanilla-scented new oak, and medium body. It is a wine that should be drunk young. His Volnay seemed a little angular, high in acidity, and was lacking charm. However, Bouley made two sensational 1987s from the Premier Cru vineyards of Volnay Les Caillerets and Volnay Clos des Chênes. Both wines may well merit outstanding ratings in another year or two. The Les Caillerets is a powerful, intense, rich, gorgeously perfumed, velvety wine with layers of luscious berry fruit wrapped smartly in toasty, smoky oak. It should drink beautifully until 1995–1996. The Volnay Clos des Chênes is more tannic and structured than the Les Caillerets, but every bit as concentrated and just oozing with ripe berry fruit. Again, there are two examples of wines from a so-called off-year vintage that have more in common with a vintage such as 1985 or 1988. The Volnay Les Carelles is marked by an abundant use of oak, and is an elegant, perfumed wine without the length or richness of either the Les Caillerets or the Clos des Chênes. His Pommard is tannic, somewhat one-dimensional, but ripe and chunky. Bouley's Pommard Les Fremières is better; it has good solid, fleshy fruit, a chocolatey, plummy character to its flavors, and 7 to 8 years of good drinking ahead of it. Even better is the Pommard Les Pézerolles, a lavishly rich, medium-bodied, velvety wine with a wonderful fruit purity to its personality. It should drink nicely until 1995–1996. An exceptional wine is the Pommard Les Rugiens, which should last for at least 10 years. It has a fabulous roasted bouquet of black fruits and spicy oak, full body, layers of extract, and a finish that lasted for well over a minute. Very exotic, rich, and profound, this is a wine to search out. All of Bouley's wines are reasonably priced for their quality.

BOURÉE (GEVREY-CHAMBERTIN)

1987 BEAUNE LES EPENOTTES	87
1987 BOURGOGNE ROUGE	83
1987 CHAMBERTIN	93
1987 CHAMBOLLE-MUSIGNY	85
1987 CHAMBOLLE-MUSIGNY LES CHARMES	87
1987 CHARMES-CHAMBERTIN	90
1987 CLOS DE LA ROCHE	87
1987 GEVREY-CHAMBERTIN LES CAZETIERS	86
1987 GEVREY-CHAMBERTIN-CLOS DE LA JUSTICE	86
1987 GEVREY-CHAMBERTIN-CLOS ST.-JACQUES	90
1987 MOREY ST.-DENIS	82
1987 VOSNE-ROMANÉE	84

Among Bourée's 1987s, there is a good, straightforward Bourgogne Rouge, but I think one of the wines to seek out in 1987 will be their Beaune Les Epenottes, which shows gobs of rich, velvety, ripe berry fruit, medium body, and a soft, velvety texture. I also thought their 1987 Gevrey-Chambertin-Clos de la Justice was excellent, with a big, spicy, cinnamon-scented, earthy, almost truffle-like bouquet, plenty of deep berry fruit, and excellent length and body. This is a wine that ages extremely well, as the average age of the vines is 40 years. I wonder how such high quality can come from a vineyard that is not endowed with the finest soil, but somehow the Vallet family gets tremendous extract and character out of the vineyard. Bourée's best wines in 1987 are from the Côte de Nuits, and particularly from the village of Gevrey-Chambertin, where their cellars are located. They always make a big, spicy, robust Gevrey-Chambertin Les Cazetiers, and the 1987 is no exception. It may be ready to drink in 3 to 4 years. The Gevrey-Chambertin-Clos St.-Jacques (100 cases were produced) is potentially outstanding. It is a rich, full-bodied, amazingly concentrated wine with 10 to 15 years of excellent aging potential. Their 1987 Charmes-Chambertin is another unqualified success, with great depth, richness, and ripeness, and the potential to last for another 10 to 15 years. I did not think the Clos de la Roche was as profound as their Charmes-Chambertin, but it did exhibit a wonderfully sweet, ripe, expansive fruitiness, full body, and a dusty texture. Their Chambolle-Musigny Les Charmes exhibited a very forward, precocious, fruity style with good acidity but light tannins. The greatest wine made by this firm in 1987 is their Chambertin. This is what Chambertin is all about—wonderfully perfumed, extraordinarily concentrated, rich and full, and profound in every sense. It is a wine that should be at its best around 1993–1994 and last until 2002–2005. It is a strong candidate for one of the great wines of the 1987 vintage. For those who lament the fact that burgundy does not taste the way it used to, Bourée will change your mind.

MARC BROCOT (MARSANNAY)

1987 GEVREY-CHAMBERTIN	82
1987 MARSANNAY	84

Brocot's 1987 Marsannay is not quite as intense as his 1986, but is still a well-made, reasonably priced, good bargain in red burgundy. It should drink nicely until 1993–1994. There is no fining, but there is a light filtration prior to bottling.

DOMAINE ALAIN BURGUET (GEVREY-CHAMBERTIN)

1987 GEVREY-CHAMBERTIN VIELLES VIGNES	86

Burguet has no Premiers Crus or Grands Crus vineyards and is resigned to the fact that he can only produce a Gevrey-Chambertin Cuvée Vieilles Vignes. But what a generic Gevrey-Chambertin! His 1987 is less muscular and slightly less concentrated than his profound 1986, but it is supple, ripe, shows excellent spicy, animal-like, berry fruit with a smell of ground beef as well as red and black berries. The wine needs a good 1 to 2 years in the bottle, but should last for at least a decade.

JACQUES CACHEUX-BLÉE (VOSNE-ROMANÉE)

1987 ECHÉZEAUX	87
1987 VOSNE-ROMANÉE	84
1987 VOSNE-ROMANÉE LES SUCHOTS	87

Cacheux thinks his 1987s are better than his 1979s and 1982s. His 1987 Vosne-Romanée was extremely pure, supple, elegant, and very fruity

—a delightful wine for drinking between now and 1992–1993. His Premier Cru Vosne-Romanée Les Suchots was excellent in 1987, showing an opulence and lushness to its berry fruitiness, a nice touch of smoky, toasty new oak, and a long, smooth finish. It is impossible to resist drinking now, yet should last until 1994–1996. I thought Cacheux's 1987 Echézeaux, which was tannic and more closed, needed another 1 or 2 years in the bottle to round into form. Although I rated it the same as the Les Suchots, I suspect with further aging it will probably show more aromatic complexity. It is an excellent wine, medium to full bodied, and concentrated. Jacques Cacheux is an excellent winemaker. He deserves far greater recognition and attention.

CAPITAIN-GAGNEROT (LADOIX)

1987 ALOXE-CORTON LES MOUTOTTES	85
1987 CORTON LES RÉNARDES	86
1987 LADOIX	79
1987 LADOIX LES MICAUDES	85

Roger Capitain's 1987s, which he compares with the 1971 vintage in Burgundy, include a rather straightforward, simple Ladoix, and an excellent Ladoix Les Micaudes. It is richly fruity, round, and bursting with aromas of black cherries and strawberries. It is supple, silky, and smooth, and should be consumed by 1994–1995. Their Aloxe-Corton Les Moutottes has excellent rich, ripe fruit, more alcohol and headiness than the Ladoix Les Micaudes; it is quite appealing. The 1987 Corton-Rénardes exhibits supple, broad flavors, relatively high alcohol, and is immensely enjoyable to drink young. All of the 1987s here are best drunk by 1992–1993.

GUY CASTAGNIER (MOREY ST.-DENIS)

1987 BONNES MARES	87
1987 CHAMBOLLE-MUSIGNY	78
1987 CLOS DE LA ROCHE	86
1987 CLOS ST.-DENIS	87
1987 LATRICIÈRES-CHAMBERTIN	86

In a vintage such as 1987, where the gentle personality of the wines mandates that they be drunk young, Castagnier has done extremely well. While the Villages Chambolle-Musigny seems a bit too light and lacking depth, the rest of his wines from his Grands Crus will provide attractive drinking until 1994–1995. The Clos St.-Denis is smooth and velvety with gobs of berry fruit wrapped nicely in toasty, smoky oak. It is low in acidity, but is absolutely delicious for drinking over the near term. A bit more structured and tannic is the 1987 Clos de la Roche, which has more body, but less color than the Clos St.-Denis. Wait at least until late 1990 before opening it. The Latricières-Chambertin, with its bouquet of wild flowers, damp earth, and berry fruit, is a more complex and interesting wine to smell, yet it does not quite seem to have the depth and opulence of the Clos St.-Denis. It should be consumed by 1994–1996. The Bonnes Mares may be Castagnier's best wine in 1987. It is certainly the most concentrated and intense, with layers of supple berry fruit, some attractive spicy oak, and a heady, alcoholic finish. My notes indicated it would be best between 1990–1996.

SYLVAIN CATHIARD (VOSNE-ROMANÉE)

1987 VOSNE-ROMANÉE LES MALCONSORTS	87
1987 VOSNE-ROMANÉE EN ORVEAUX	85

I was very impressed with these two wines from the 1987 vintage produced by Sylvain Cathiard. Both the Vosne-Romanée en Orveaux and the Vosne-Romanée Les Malconsorts had a style that was very similar to the wines of the better-known Robert Arnoux. The Vosne-Romanée En Orveaux is a classic, supple, fragrant wine with a great deal of fruit, spicy oak, round, ripe, generous flavors, and is ideal for drinking by 1995–1996. The Vosne-Romanée Les Malconsorts is deeper, showed a bit more tannin, has excellent concentration, and very pure, classic Pinot Noir fruitiness. It should drink beautifully for the next decade.

CHAMPY PÈRE ET FILS (BEAUNE)

1987 BEAUNE LES AVAUX	86
1987 BEAUNE-CLOS DES MOUCHES	86
1987 BOURGOGNE ROUGE	85
1987 CLOS VOUGEOT	85
1987 SAVIGNY-LÈS-BEAUNE LES DOMINAUDES	84

This old-line, traditional *négociant* believes in making deeply colored, robust, muscular wines that age extremely well. Their 1987 Bourgogne Rouge should be sought by anyone looking for an excellent red burgundy at a realistic price. It is a fleshy, chewy wine with a deep color as well as plenty of depth and ripeness. It is one of the most successful generic red wines I tasted on my recent trip to Burgundy. The 1987 Savigny-Lès-Beaune Les Dominaudes should have shown better, but I suspect it is going through a tough, tannic, closed stage, as wines from this vineyard have a tendency to do. There is good acidity, excellent color, and an impression of weight and ripeness on the palate, but the wine was impenetrable and difficult to assess. I am sure the wine is better than I have rated it, but I would not want to open a bottle until 1992–1993; it should keep for at least 10 to 12 years. One of the specialties of Champy Père et Fils is their Beaune Les Avaux. The 1987 is excellent. It is a deep ruby-colored wine with fine depth of fruit, a big, plummy, spicy, almost chocolatey bouquet, plenty of concentration, and a robust character. I would drink it over the next 6 to 7 years. I was also impressed with this firm's 1987 Beaune-Clos des Mouches. This wine had an almost Pommard-like, fat, chunky, brawny constitution, showed excellent concentration, superb color, and plenty of length. It is not elegant, but for those who like their burgundy big and burly, it is an ideal choice for drinking over the next decade. The Clos Vougeot had a rather tar-like, toasty, ripe, plummy bouquet that resembled the Beaune-Clos des Mouches. It should be drunk over the next 7 to 8 years.

DOMAINE CHANDON DE BRIAILLES
(SAVIGNY-LÈS-BEAUNE)

1987 CORTON LES BRESSANDES	87
1987 CORTON-CLOS DU ROI	87
1987 CORTON LES MARÉCHAUDES	85
1987 PERNAND-VERGELESSES ÎLE DES VERGELESSES	85
1987 SAVIGNY-LÈS-BEAUNE	82
1987 SAVIGNY-LÈS-BEAUNE LES LAVIÈRES	78

This beautiful domaine located in Savigny-Lès-Beaune is making better and better wines. I found both the 1987 Savigny-Lès-Beaune and Savigny-Lès-Beaune Les Lavières a bit tough, rather hard, tannic, and lacking the concentration and ripeness of fruit to balance the considerable tannins. This may have been a case where destemming was merited. There is an excellent Pernand-Vergelesses Île des Vergelesses. While every bit as tannic as the Savigny-Lès-Beaune, the Pernand-Vergelesses has much more ripeness and depth. It needs two years to shed its tannins, but it shows fine complexity and is a top success for a wine from this appellation. Of course, the glories of this house are its holdings in Corton. The Corton Les Maréchaudes shows plenty of spicy, new oak, is a backward, tannic, potentially long-lived wine that has excellent ripeness, depth, and good color. I found it closed, but displaying potential. Among the best wines of Domaine Chandon de Briailles is the Corton Les Bressandes. It has tremendous depth and ripeness, in addition to having more fruit than tannin—always a good sign. It is bursting with the smell of ripe cherries, spicy oak, and should last until the turn of the century, although it will be drinkable by 1991–1992. I thought the Corton-Clos du Roi was very similar in style, perhaps slightly deeper colored and more supple in texture, but exhibiting the same rich, spicy, cherry fruitiness, medium body, and excellent ripeness and depth.

CHARTRON ET TRÉBUCHET (PULIGNY-MONTRACHET)

1987 BOURGOGNE HAUTES-CÔTES DE NUITS LES DAMES HUGUETTES	82
1987 BOURGOGNE-PINOT NOIR L'ORME	84
1987 CHASSAGNE-MONTRACHET MORGEOTS	84
1987 MERCUREY-CLOS DES HAYES	85
1987 NUITS ST.-GEORGES-HOSPICES DE NUITS SOEURS HOSPITALIÈRES	88
1987 POMMARD-HOSPICES DE BEAUNE CUVÉE CYROT CHAUDRON	86
1987 PULIGNY-MONTRACHET-CLOS DU CAILLERET	85

This *négociant* in Puligny-Montrachet continues to expand its rather extensive portfolio of offerings. The Bourgogne-Pinot Noir l'Orme is fruity, soft, and shows a very nicely etched Pinot Noir character in a light- to medium-bodied, smooth, velvety format. It is a wine to drink over the next several years. Similarly styled, but more elegant, is the Mercurey-Clos des Hayes. One of their best red wines is a rare offering from the Premier Cru vineyard Clos du Cailleret in Puligny-

Montrachet. It shows excellent ripeness, deep, spicy, cherry fruitiness, a nice touch of oak as well as the potential to drink well until 1993–1994. Both the Hospices wines performed well in my tastings. The Pommard-Hospices de Beaune Cuvée Cyrot Chaudron exhibits abundant quantities of spicy, toasty, vanillin-scented new oak, ripe berry fruitiness, light tannins, and medium body. Those tasters who eschew a lot of new oak in their wine may find it less attractive than I did. As for the Nuits St.-Georges-Hospices de Nuits Soeurs Hospitalières, it is probably the best wine I tasted from Chartron et Trébuchet in 1987. It had a gorgeous bouquet, excellent, deep richness to its earthy, smoky, berry fruit, light, soft tannins, and a luscious texture. The wine is clearly drinkable now, but should be even better by 1991–1992.

JEAN CHAUVENET (NUITS ST.-GEORGES)

1987 NUITS ST.-GEORGES	86
1987 NUITS ST.-GEORGES PREMIER CRU	87

In 1987 Chauvenet's crop size was so small he blended together his two Premiers Crus, Les Bousselots and Les Vaucrains, to produce his Nuits St.-Georges Premier Cru. It has a rich, lush, exotic nose of berry fruit and spicy oak that complements the long, deep, velvety flavors. It should reach full maturity by 1990–1991 and drink well for 7 or 8 years. As good as that is, the real bargain here is the Nuits St.-Georges, a wine displaying excellent ripeness, an intense ruby color, a supple, round, generous, berry fruitiness, medium body, and excellent balance. It should drink nicely over the next 6 to 7 years. Chauvenet's wines are unfiltered.

GEORGES CHICOTOT (NUITS ST.-GEORGES)

1987 NUITS ST.-GEORGES	85
1987 NUITS ST.-GEORGES LES PRULIERS	88
1987 NUITS ST.-GEORGES LES SAINT-GEORGES	89
1987 NUITS ST.-GEORGES LES VAUCRAINS	90

Chicotot's Nuits St.-Georges exhibited a wonderfully smooth, supple, elegant fruitiness, excellent deep, dark color (a characteristic of the Accad wines), and plenty of length. It should drink well until 1995. His three Premiers Crus in 1987 are all brilliant wines. It takes no genius to see that his policy of no fining, no filtration, a month-long *cuvaison* and cold maceration prior to fermentation has resulted in wines that are nearly black in color and extraordinarily concentrated. The Nuits St.-Georges Les Pruliers displays an alluring tarry, rich, peppery, plummy fruitiness, medium to full body, great depth and ripeness, and plenty of soft tannins in the finish. Although it is drinkable now, it should last until at least 1996–1997. The Nuits St.-Georges Les Saint-Georges is even more impressive (yet more tannic with slightly higher acidity). It is a 1987 to put away in your cellar until about 1994–1995 as it does not have the precocious, flattering, up-front fruit of many wines from this vintage. This is an atypically big, tannic, powerful wine with plenty of muscle and promise. Chicotot's best 1987 wine is his Nuits St.-Georges Les Vaucrains. A sensational bouquet of plums, spices, and roasted fruit is followed by a wine that has exceptional depth and richness, gobs of soft tannins, and a massive, long, intense finish. It should be at its best between 1991 and 2003.

DOMAINE CHOPIN-GROFFIER (PRÉMEAUX)

1987 CHAMBOLLE-MUSIGNY	86
1987 CLOS VOUGEOT	90
1987 NUITS ST.-GEORGES	85
1987 NUITS ST.-GEORGES LES CHAIGNOTS	88
1987 VOUGEOT PREMIER CRU	85

It would be difficult to find a better generic wine than the 1987 Chambolle-Musigny. It has great finesse in addition to a huge, beautifully evolved bouquet of berry fruit, spices, and flowers. It is as smooth as silk on the palate and therefore should be consumed by 1992–1993. It is not a blockbuster, but for pure charm and lovely, balanced fruit it is hard to beat. The Nuits St.-Georges is also round, supple, and soft yet slightly less perfumed than the Chambolle-Musigny. It makes for a delicious, hedonistic mouthful of wine. It, too, should be consumed by 1992–1993. The Vougeot Premier Cru shows good ripe fruit, has a bit more tannin to it, and while drinkable now should continue to hold until 1993–1994. One of the two top wines from this excellent domaine is its Nuits St.-Georges Les Chaignots. The 1987 displays superb ripeness and depth, a precocious, forward personality, wonderful purity of fruit, and a long, expansive finish. As good as it is, it cannot approach the Clos Vougeot of Daniel Chopin, made from a parcel of 50- to 60-year-old vines. Deep ruby in color with a rich, ripe, concentrated nose of red currants, this harmonious wine has an expansive, sweet, opulent texture, a long finish, soft tannins, and the potential to continue to provide enjoyment until at least 1996–1997. It is one of the great successes of the 1987 vintage.

BRUNO CLAIR (MARSANNAY)

1987 CHAMBERTIN-CLOS DE BÈZE	88
1987 FIXIN LA CROIX BLANCHE	85
1987 GEVREY-CHAMBERTIN LES CAZETIERS	87
1987 GEVREY-CHAMBERTIN-CLOS DE FONTENY	86
1987 GEVREY-CHAMBERTIN-CLOS ST.-JACQUES	87
1987 MARSANNAY	80
1987 MOREY ST.-DENIS	84
1987 SAVIGNY-LÈS-BEAUNE LES DOMINAUDES	87
1987 VOSNE-ROMANÉE LES CHAMPS PERDRIX	86

Clair's small crop of 1987s are not blockbusters, but they are impressive wines. The 1987 Marsannay is a light, pleasant, straightforward wine with more character to its bouquet than its monolithic flavors. His 1987 Fixin La Croix Blanche, made from 50-year-old vines, is good. It is a larger-scaled wine with plenty of tannin, muscle, and depth. It is not ready to drink, but it should represent an excellent bargain in quality red burgundy for drinking between 1991–1998. I thought the Morey St.-Denis was supple, fruity, soft, slightly one-dimensional, and a good effort for a generic wine. In Vosne-Romanée, Bruno Clair makes an attractive wine from the excellent Premier Cru vineyard Les Champs Perdrix. The 1987 is ripe and supple with a fragrant bouquet of berry fruit, toasty oak, and minerals. It is not a powerful wine, but is elegant, stylish, and graceful. Clair's Savigny Les Beaune Dominaudes, made from extremely old vines, is always a success, but prospective purchasers should know that this is Clair's slowest maturing wine. It has a deep, rich color, plenty of tannins, medium to full body, and excellent depth and richness. Patience is definitely required. Clair's strengths are his wines from Gevrey-Chambertin. In 1987 there is an expansive, succulent, medium-bodied, round, and very flattering Gevrey-Chambertin-Clos de Fonteny. It should be drunk over the next 4 to 6 years. If you like a more savage, brutal Gevrey-Chambertin, I suggest you try

Clair's Gevrey-Chambertin Les Cazetiers. This vineyard always produces robust, rich, concentrated, brawny wines with a great deal of muscle. Yet they also have a wild berry fruitiness, a hint of exotic oriental spices, and the smell of ground beef. Clair's offering from this vineyard is no exception; it is a wine to drink from the early 1990s through the year 2000. Clair also produces an excellent Gevrey-Chambertin-Clos St.-Jacques. It is not superior to the Les Cazetiers, but is a tamer wine, relying on its pure, straightforward, rich, lush, berry fruitiness. Last, the Chambertin-Clos de Bèze is rich, full bodied, deep, and should prove to be Clair's longest-lived wine from the 1987 vintage. I would not think of drinking it before 1993; it should keep for 10 years.

JACKY CONFURON-CONTIDOT (VOSNE-ROMANÉE)

1987 CHAMBOLLE-MUSIGNY	86
1987 ECHÉZEAUX	90
1987 VOSNE-ROMANÉE LES SUCHOTS	87–90?

Confuron's Chambolle-Musigny, made from 40-year-old vines, was a concentrated, rich mouthful of wine, showing a plummy, herbaceous fragrance, ripe, supple fruit, and a long finish. It seemed totally different from his Vosne-Romanée Les Suchots. I had two separate bottles of this wine—one from the cellar of Confuron that I rated a 90, and one in a blind tasting that I rated 87. Both had sensational color, a great perfume of black fruits as well as exotic spices and herbs. Both tasted typical of Vosne-Romanée. The wine I rated slightly lower had more of an herbaceous character, and made me wonder whether Confuron bottles barrel by barrel or does an assemblage. However, he was not an easy man to deal with and was reluctant to answer questions. The Vosne-Romanée Les Suchots had plenty of rich, ripe tannins in the finish and is a candidate to last until 1999. His Echézeaux was another outstanding wine with fabulous color, a rich, expansive, sweet taste of black fruits, a Côte Rôtie-like intensity, medium to full body, and a long, supple, explosively rich and powerful finish. You can expect it to drink well for a decade.

DOMAINE CLAUDE CORNU (HAUTES CÔTES)

1987 CORTON	83
1987 HAUTES-CÔTES DE BEAUNE	72
1987 HAUTES-CÔTES DE NUITS	78

I have had some luck with Claude Cornu's wines in the past. However, in 1987, the Hautes-Côtes de Beaune showed some oxidation in its nose, and had unattractive, lean, hard, tough flavors with an excess of tannin. The Hautes-Côtes de Nuits was slightly better, but was still a very attenuated, sinewy, charmless wine lacking fruit and character. The Corton was more concentrated, but given its price, it is no value. The wine did possess more ripeness, plenty of spicy oak, but lacked depth and richness.

EDMOND CORNU (LADOIX)

1987 ALOXE-CORTON LES MOUTOTTES	84
1987 CORTON LES BRESSANDES	86
1987 LADOIX	78

Cornu is an unheralded yet excellent winemaker. If his top wine is frequently his Corton-Bressandes, his best bargain is his Aloxe-Corton Les Moutottes. His 1987 Ladoix is rather angular, showing decent acidity, a pleasant strawberry-like fruitiness, and an adequate finish. His Aloxe-Corton Les Moutottes shows a spicy, ripe fruitiness, medium body, and a smooth, soft finish. It is ideal for drinking now. For more ripeness, body, and intensity try the Corton Les Bressandes. It will not make anyone forget the phenomenal 1985, but it is pleasant, tasty, and well made. It should drink nicely until 1995–1996.

MARIUS DELARCHE (PERNAND-VERGELESSES)

1987 CORTON LES RÉNARDES	83
1987 PERNAND-VERGELESSES	72
1987 PERNAND-VERGELESSES LES VERGELESSES	74
1987 PERNAND-VERGELESSES ÎLE DES VERGELESSES	77

Delarche's 1987 red wines were not impressive. The light, tea-scented Pernand-Vergelesses lacked concentration, the stemmy Pernand-Vergelesses Les Vergelesses was somewhat thin, and the more serious Pernard-Vergelesses Île des Vergelesses was undernourished. All these wines lacked color, concentration, and charm. Certainly Delarche's best red wine in 1987 is his Corton Les Rénardes (if you happen to see any of the extraordinary 1985 around, do not hesitate to buy a bottle— it's sublime). The 1987 Rénardes has more fruit to it, but for a Grand Cru Corton it is light and thin, making me wonder what went awry.

DOUDET-NAUDIN (SAVIGNY-LÈS-BEAUNE)

1987 ALOXE-CORTON PREMIER CRU	85
1987 BEAUNE-CLOS DU ROI	85
1987 CORTON LES MARÉCHAUDES	86
1987 PERNAND-VERGELESSES LES FICHOTS	83
1987 SAVIGNY-LÈS-BEAUNE LES GUETTES	85

In tasting the 1987s, one could easily see that these wines are impenetrable when young, very hard, very tannic, yet concentrated, full and rich. These wines are not meant to be seductive young, so I asked if it would be possible to taste some of the older vintages from both mediocre and good years. The results were impressive. Judging by the old vintages, these are wines that keep for a long time. Of course, they are not for everybody, and those who want to drink their burgundy within the first decade of the vintage might as well stop reading this section. I am sure Doudet-Naudin considers it to be infanticide to open one of their wines before it is at least 10 years old. It seems the only compromise made to modern technology by this firm is their decision to filter. This does not make any sense, given the rest of the vinification process. Nevertheless, they do filter, although they still seem to get plenty of extract and character in the wines. Most of this firm's small production is sold in England and Switzerland. Their 1987 specialties are wines from the Côte de Beaune. If you are willing to wait 10 to 15 years, you cannot go wrong with their Savigny-Lès-Beaune Les Guettes, Beaune-Clos du Roi, or Corton Les Maréchaudes. I am sure my scores will be perceived as conservative should anyone read them in 15 years.

JOSEPH DROUHIN (BEAUNE)

1987 BEAUNE-CLOS DES MOUCHES	85
1987 BEAUNE-HOSPICES DE BEAUNE- CUVÉE MAURICE DROUHIN	87
1987 BONNES MARES	87
1987 CHASSAGNE-MONTRACHET LES BAUDES	84
1987 CHASSAGNE-MONTRACHET MORGEOT	78
1987 CLOS DE LA ROCHE	87
1987 CLOS VOUGEOT	87

1987 CORTON LES BRESSANDES	86
1987 GRANDS ECHÉZEAUX	90
1987 GRIOTTE-CHAMBERTIN	89
1987 LADOIX	83
1987 MOREY ST.-DENIS LES MONTS LUISANTS	74
1987 MUSIGNY	90
1987 POMMARD LES BOUCHEROTTES	79
1987 SAVIGNY-LÈS-BEAUNE	78
1987 SANTENAY PREMIER CRU	84
1987 VOLNAY CLOS DES CHÊNES	84
1987 VOSNE-ROMANÉE LES BEAUX MONTS	87

Robert Drouhin has made very good 1987 red wines that should prove to be among his better wines of the 1980s. The 1987 reds have ample charm and a supple, pure red-fruit character. For example, there is a fruity, straightforward, pleasant Ladoix and a rather tart, high acid, lean, sinewy Savigny-Lès-Beaune and Chassagne-Montrachet Morgeot. The latter two wines lacked charm and fruit, and came across on the palate as a bit attenuated and sharp. Drouhin's Santenay Premier Cru, however, was excellent, and showed some of the dusty tannins common in the red wines of Santenay. It also had good ripeness, a bing cherry-flavored sort of fruitiness, and the potential to last until 1994–1995. The Beaune-Clos des Mouches was more elegant and revealed the smell of cherries, almonds, and spicy oak. This deliciously supple, hedonistic wine will make an excellent bottle of red burgundy for drinking between now and 1993–1994. Even better is the Hospices de Beaune-Cuvée Maurice Drouhin. Like most of the wines from the Hospices, it showed abundant quantities of vanillin-scented, toasty new oak, and excellent ripe, round, rich cherry fruit with a soft, lush finish. It is ideal for drinking now and until 1995–1996. Drouhin's Volnay-Clos des Chênes lacks elegance as well as the round, ripe berry fruit of a good Volnay. The Pommard Les Boucherottes and the Morey St.-Denis Les Monts Luisants seemed too tart, lean, and malnourished to deserve high marks. The latter wine was hard, tough, and graceless. On the other hand, the Chambolle-Musigny Les Baudes displayed an impressive deep ruby color, a big, spicy, plummy bouquet, good crisp acidity, well-delineated flavors, and some tannin in the finish. It needs until

1991 to round out, but it should keep for 7 or 8 years thereafter. The Corton Les Bressandes had a captivating bouquet of lush, intense, berry fruit, spicy oak, and flowers. Again, it had fine crisp acidity and is Drouhin's most concentrated wine from the Côte de Beaune in 1987.

In the Côte de Nuits, Drouhin's Vosne-Romanée Les Beaux Monts is rich, medium to full bodied with ripe, long, spicy, black-fruit flavors, and some spicy yet soft tannins in the finish. It should drink nicely through the next decade. The Clos de la Roche was somewhat lighter, but showed an interesting, fragrant, cinnamon, gingery sort of nose, and ripe, lush, soft flavors with enough tannin to suggest that 5 to 6 years of cellaring is possible. The Griotte-Chambertin from Drouhin's own parcel of this great Grand Cru vineyard is nearly as outstanding. Lavishly rich, soft, voluptuous, even opulent, this delectably rich, silky wine, redolent with the scent and flavors of cherries and spicy oak, will be an absolute joy to drink over the next 5 to 6 years. In contrast, Drouhin's Bonnes Mares is extremely backward and tannic. It shows an elevated use of new oak, but has good flavor definition and depth; it will need at least until 1992–1993 to shed its tannins, and should prove to be one of Drouhin's longest-lived wines from the 1987 vintage. The Musigny is magnificent, with a well-developed, intense bouquet of flowers, spices, and ripe Pinot fruit. This wine is seductive and expansive on the palate; it has no hard edges, and everything seems to be in complete harmony. I would drink it over the next 5 to 6 years. I rated the 1987 Clos Vougeot slightly below the Musigny, but it is an excellent wine revealing a deep ruby color, zesty acidity, and the potential to last until 1996–1997. Drouhin made another outstanding wine from his parcel of the Grand Cru vineyard Grands Echézeaux. It is very rich, full bodied and deep, with impressive length and ripeness. It has the fat and concentration reminiscent of the 1985 vintage, and should drink well until 1996–1997. As with most of the top 1987s, these are wines that should be drunk young.

DOMAINE DUJAC (MOREY ST.-DENIS)

1987 BONNES MARES	88
1987 CHARMES-CHAMBERTIN	90
1987 CLOS DE LA ROCHE	90
1987 CLOS ST.-DENIS	92
1987 ECHÉZEAUX	88

1987 GEVREY-CHAMBERTIN LES COMBOTTES	89
1987 MOREY ST.-DENIS	85

The Domaine Dujac's wines in 1987 should turn out to be Dujac's third or fourth best vintage of the decade. The year 1985 was potentially one of the all-time great burgundy vintages, but his 1987s will not rival the ultimate quality or longevity of those wines. They are just slightly behind the quality of his 1988s. Nevertheless, they are extremely successful wines and will make delicious drinking in their first decade of life. His soft, ripe Morey St.-Denis exhibits a fragrant, intense perfume of berry fruit, herbs, and spicy new oak. I would drink the 1987 by 1993–1994. Dujac also has a small parcel of the outstanding Premier Cru vineyard in Gevrey-Chambertin known as Les Combottes. His Les Combottes is pure, silky elegance, and offers a hedonistic, generously flavored, fragrant bottle of wine. Its perfume of spicy oak, leather, cedar, and ripe black fruits is captivating. This is a supple yet concentrated wine that displays excellent ripeness and the potential to last until 2000, although it is difficult to resist drinking it now. Not surprisingly the Charmes-Chambertin is very similar to the Les Combottes. Les Charmes is a Grand Cru vineyard that sits adjacent to Les Combottes and often exhibits a similar spicy, fragrant, richly fruity bouquet with a suggestion of cedar and exotic spices. However, it is deeper and more concentrated than the Les Combottes. It should be at its best between 1990 and 2000. I thought Jacques Seysses' best wine in 1987 was his superb Clos St.-Denis. Most people would take this wine for a 1985 rather than a 1987. Its fabulous bouquet of plums, ground beef, soy sauce, exotic spices, and new oak makes for a superb impression. This is followed by explosively fruity, ripe, rich wine with long flavors and a finish that seems to last for several minutes. Typical for a 1987, it is supple and shows good acidity, but not much tannin. It should be at its best between now and the turn of the century. The Clos de la Roche is more closed, but exhibits fine depth, a blossoming bouquet of earthy, plummy fruit, and some firm tannins in the finish. It is an outstanding wine but needs until 1990–1991. Dujac's Echézeaux is usually his lightest and most delicate wine, and it never possesses the depth or profound complexity of his Clos St.-Denis, Charmes-Chambertin, Clos de la Roche, or Gevrey-Chambertin Les Combottes. It does show a beautiful ripe berry fruitiness, a light- to medium-bodied texture, and a soft, velvety finish. I would opt for drinking it by 1993–1996. The Bonnes Mares is a complex, lovely wine that is round, fruity, and ideal for drinking over the next 6 to 7 years.

MAURICE ECARD (SAVIGNY-LÈS-BEAUNE)

1987 SAVIGNY-LÈS-BEAUNE LES JARRONS	84
1987 SAVIGNY-LÈS-BEAUNE LES NARBANTONS	85
1987 SAVIGNY-LÈS-BEAUNE LES SERPENTIÈRES	85

Ecard's 1987s are ready to drink and are light, richly fruity, seductive red burgundies ideal for consumption between now and 1994–1995. Ecard's two best wines are generally his superb Les Serpentières and Les Narbantons. The Les Serpentières is usually more concentrated and more explosively fruity than the structured and tannic Les Narbantons. The excellent fresh, pure fruitiness in all of Ecard's wines is impressive.

PHILIPPE ENGEL (VOSNE-ROMANÉE)

1987 CLOS VOUGEOT	86
1987 ECHÉZEAUX	88
1987 GRANDS ECHÉZEAUX	89
1987 VOSNE-ROMANÉE	82
1987 VOSNE-ROMANÉE LES BRÛLÉES	84

Engel has certainly made successful wines in 1987. His Vosne-Romanée is round and fruity yet it is a bit simple and lacks spark and zip. It is a competently made, decent bottle of burgundy, that should be drunk between now and 1991–1992. I have always felt his Vosne-Romanée les Brûlées should be better, particularly when I taste wine from this same vineyard from producers like Méo-Camuzet or Henri Jayer. But Engel claims his parcel of this Premier Cru vineyard is in young vines. His 1987 is light, but fruity and well balanced; it will make an attractive, rather than sublime, bottle of wine ready for drinking by 1994–1995. Engel's Echézeaux is excellent and has a very perfumed, aromatic, intense bouquet of red fruits and spicy oak. On the palate it is quintessentially elegant, medium bodied, and shows a great deal of charm and ripe fruit. It finishes without a rough edge or an excessive amount of alcohol. The Clos Vougeot is richly fruity, ripe, supple, smooth, and impossible to resist now. It should continue to drink well until 1994–1995. It lacks the stature and complexity of his 1988, but is a very appealing, medium-weight burgundy that should be ready for drinking

between now and 1994–1995. Engel's best wine is his Grands Echézeaux. It is a fatter, more concentrated, expansively flavored, more
complex wine than the Echézeaux. There are copious amounts of rich
berry fruit wrapped intelligently in spicy oak. The wine shows excellent
balance, soft tannins, yet good, zesty acidity. This wine should drink
well until 1996–1997.

DOMAINE MICHEL ESMONIN (GEVREY-CHAMBERTIN)

1987 GEVREY-CHAMBERTIN	83
1987 GEVREY-CHAMBERTIN-CLOS ST.-JACQUES	90

Esmonin's 1987 Gevrey-Chambertin is ripe and elegant, but slightly
light. While sufficient, it finishes a bit too short on the palate to get high
marks. On the other hand, his Gevrey-Chambertin-Clos St.-Jacques is
exceptional, displaying a fabulous bouquet of rich, intense berry fruit,
spicy new oak, and long, supple, expansive flavors. It can be drunk
now, but should continue to age beautifully until 1997–2000. If you
missed out on the 1987s, get your reservations in for Esmonin's sublime
1988s.

FAIVELEY (NUITS ST.-GEORGES)

1987 BEAUNE LES CHAMPS PIMONTS	87
1987 BONNES MARES	88
1987 BOURGOGNE-PINOT NOIR	80
1987 CHAMBERTIN-CLOS DE BÈZE	90
1987 CHAMBOLLE-MUSIGNY	84
1987 CHARMES-CHAMBERTIN	89
1987 CLOS DE LA ROCHE	88
1987 CLOS VOUGEOT	90
1987 CORTON-CLOS DES CORTON	92
1987 CÔTE DE BEAUNE-VILLAGES	72
1987 CÔTE DE NUITS-VILLAGES	84
1987 ECHÉZEAUX	90
1987 GEVREY-CHAMBERTIN	85
1987 GEVREY-CHAMBERTIN LES CAZETIERS	87

1987 GEVREY-CHAMBERTIN LA COMBE AUX MOINES	88
1987 LATRICIÈRES-CHAMBERTIN	89
1987 MAZIS-CHAMBERTIN	90
1987 MERCUREY-CLOS DU ROI	83
1987 MOREY ST.-DENIS	84
1987 MOREY ST.-DENIS CLOS DES ORMES	86
1987 NUITS ST.-GEORGES	74
1987 NUITS ST.-GEORGES-CLOS DE LA MARÉCHALE	85
1987 NUITS ST.-GEORGES LES DAMODES	90
1987 NUITS ST.-GEORGES-HOSPICES DE NUITS LES SAINT-GEORGES (GEORGES FAIVELEY)	91
1987 NUITS ST.-GEORGES LES PORETS SAINT-GEORGES	87
1987 NUITS ST.-GEORGES LES SAINT-GEORGES	90
1987 POMMARD LES CHAPONNIÈRES	88
1987 RULLY LES VILLERANGES	78
1987 SAVIGNY-LÈS-BEAUNE	83
1987 VOLNAY-CLOS DES CHÊNES	88
1987 VOSNE-ROMANÉE	82

I am happy to report Faiveley's 1987s are very successful. The Bourgogne-Pinot Noir offers a good value with its light, fruity, ripe nose, medium body, and soft, pleasant texture. Among the other lower-priced wines is a straightforward, adequate Rully Les Villeranges, and a good Mercurey-Clos du Roi. Faiveley has invested significantly in vineyards in Mercurey, and the wines from this appellation have become one of their specialties. The 1987 Clos du Roi, while not up to the quality of the 1985, is a strawberry and cherry–scented wine that shows a nice touch of new oak, light to medium body, and soft yet ripe fruit flavors. I was unimpressed with the tart, thin, and lean Côte de Beaune-Villages, but Faiveley's Côte de Nuits-Villages is a well-made, richly fruity, spicy, earthy wine with good body and 5 to 6 years of drinkability. The Savigny-Lès-Beaune also showed abundant red fruit, and a supple, smooth, and velvety texture; it should be consumed by 1992–1993. Faiveley's other Villages wines from the Côte de Nuits include a rather short, high-acid, tart, lean Nuits St.-Georges, a more interesting, fruity, supple, easy-to-drink Vosne-Romanée, and a rich, concentrated, ripe, and generously flavored Chambolle-Musigny. Faiveley's Morey St.-Denis offers good depth, ripeness, and a spicy, berry bouquet. However, it has a bigger framework and more tannin than the elegant, seductive Chambolle-Musigny. As for the Gevrey-Chambertin, it delivers a ground beef and leather–scented, robust character typical of the best wines from this appellation. It is spicy with a peppery bouquet and rustic texture. Among the Premiers Crus from the Côte de Beaune, there is a stylish Beaune Les Champs Pimonts. This wine provides wonderfully rich, vanilla-scented, ripe, black cherry fruit, a supple, velvety texture, good concentration and ripeness, just enough acidity for balance, and plenty of length in the finish. It is drinkable now and should last until 1996–1997. Faiveley aged this wine in 50% new oak casks. Faiveley's Volnay-Clos des Chênes is another excellent Premier Cru from the Côte de Beaune. This unfiltered red burgundy is even richer, fuller, and deeper colored than the excellent Beaune Les Champs Pimonts. It has less up-front charm and precociousness than the Beaune yet more tannin, muscle, and body. It should last until the turn of the century. Faiveley also produced an unfiltered Pommard Les Chaponnières. This supple wine has a smoky, toasty, plummy bouquet, with excellent depth and richness. This attractive, fleshy wine should drink well until 1998–2000. While Faiveley clearly can make excellent wines from the Côte de Beaune, the firm has some of its most important vineyard holdings in the Côte de Nuits. All the Nuits St.-Georges *cuvées* produced in 1987 are unfiltered, except for the Nuits St.-Georges-Clos de la Maréchale. This wine is normally made in a style that offers a supple, creamy texture, an elegant, perfumed, earthy, peppery, plum-like bouquet, and easy-to-drink, soft fruit flavors. The 1987 shares these characteristics, and is an ideal wine for consumers or restaurants desiring a complex, tasty, medium-bodied burgundy ready for drinking by 1994–1995. Faiveley's Nuits St.-Georges Les Porets Saint-Georges is an excellent wine, and shows a rich, full-bodied character, excellent color and depth, a soft, concentrated texture, and at least another 8 to 10 years of drinkability. Like most of the 1987s, it is approachable but promises to improve with a few years of bottle age. The great wines from Nuits St.-Georges that Faiveley produced in 1987 include Les Damodes, which has a huge bouquet of cassis fruit and smoky oak. On the palate, the wine has crisp acidity and rich, well-structured, deep flavors. It is a serious candidate for extended cellaring. I would not drink it before 1992. The unfiltered Nuits St.-Georges Les Saint-Georges, made from the domaine's vineyard, and Nuits St.-Georges Les Saint-Georges Cuvée Georges Faiveley, purchased by the Faiveley firm from the Hospices de Nuits, make an interesting comparison. When I tasted these wines with François Faiveley and his staff, they preferred the wine from their own vineyard. It exhibited a deep ruby color, fresh acidity, long, full body, plummy, earthy flavors, and a nice subtle touch of oak. I preferred the Hospices de Nuits Cuvée, which seemed to have a more vibrant, even more explosive bouquet of rich, bing cherries, and smoky, toasty oak. The acidity of the Hospices de Nuits Cuvée is lower, but both of these wines should last for a decade. The Faiveley firm has been making an excellent Morey St.-Denis-Clos des Ormes since 1985. The 1987, while not up to the quality of the surreal 1985, is a wonderfully ripe, long, lovely, richly perfumed wine that offers a velvety texture, zesty acidity, and adequate tannin and concentration of fruit to last until 1996–1997. The firm's Gevrey-Chambertin Les Cazetiers has an intense bouquet of ripe raspberries, cherries, and toasty oak. It is made from some of Faiveley's oldest vines, and is a big, well-structured, medium- to full-bodied wine that ideally needs 2 to 3 years, perhaps even longer in the bottle to resolve its tannins. It is one of the larger-scaled wines from Faiveley in 1987. It may be one of the few wines from this vintage that can age well for 10 to 15 years. In contrast, I felt the Gevrey-Chambertin La Combe aux Moines, from a slightly higher-placed vineyard on the hills behind Gevrey-Chambertin, tasted richer, riper, and more concentrated. It is more seductive and appealing than the Les Cazetiers, and should probably be drunk within its first 7 to 8 years of life. Their Clos Vougeot has an explosive, rich bouquet of red fruits, and a very soft, lush, velvety texture that exhibits excellent concentration. It should probably be drunk by 1995–1996. As for the Echézeaux, it has a very complex nose of subtle herbs, rich, plum-like fruit, an elegant, soft texture, and an ethereal, graceful, silky fruitiness that give it immense appeal. It will not be one of the longest-lived wines, but it offers tremendous appeal for drinking over the next 5 to 6 years. The Bonnes Mares has less complexity than the Echézeaux but it is deeper and fatter on the palate and has excellent depth of fruit and ripeness. It should drink nicely until 1996–1997. The Clos de la Roche, which is aged in 70% new oak casks (as are all the Grands Crus from Faiveley), showed the cinnamon-like, earthy, mineral and blackberry fruitiness typical of this great Grand Cru vineyard. Very long on the palate with the well-delineated, crisp flavors, medium to full body, and good tannins in the finish, this wine may well merit an outstanding rating in 2 to 3 years. It should certainly last for another 10 years. Faiveley's Mazis-Chambertin has an exotic melange of aromas that run the gamut from soy sauce and ground beef to hoisin sauce. There is also plenty of toasty new oak and ripe plum-like fruit. On the palate, the wine is full bodied, deep, rich, concentrated, and in need of 3 to 4 years of cellaring. It should last for 12 to 14 years—a surprisingly long time for a 1987 red burgundy. Faiveley believes the Latricières-Chambertin is every bit as good as their outstanding 1985. I would not rate it quite that high, but it is certainly more forward and seductive than the Mazis-Chambertin or the Clos de la Roche. It is supple with pungent herb-tinged berry fruit backed up nicely by smoky oak. There is a sort of roasted ripeness to the wine that gives it great appeal. I think that this wine should be drunk by 1996–1997. The Charmes-Chambertin displays a gorgeous ripeness and velvety, supple texture. It has nice fresh acidity for balance and not much tannin, but good length and wonderful precision to its flavors. Perhaps the two longest-lived wines from Faiveley in 1987 are their Chambertin-Clos de Bèze and their Corton-Clos des Corton. Both these unfiltered wines have magnificent color. The Faiveleys have almost 8 acres of this Grand Cru Corton and produced 45 barrels (1,125 cases) in 1987. This wine is backward, yet is potentially one of the greatest wines of the vintage. The deep ruby/purple color, the strong bouquet of cassis fruit, and the intense concentration backed up by plenty of powerful tannins suggest this wine needs a decade of cellaring. It is a winemaking tour de force in 1987. The Chambertin-Clos de Bèze, which is normally Faiveley's best wine, has to take a back seat to the extraordinary Clos des Corton in 1987. The Clos de Bèze has a beautifully rich, spicy, fragrant, intense bouquet of berry fruit, toasty oak, as well as the smell of new saddle leather. On the palate the wine shows excellent, even outstanding depth, wonderful elegance, ripeness, and moderate tannins; it should be every bit as good as the beautiful 1980. I cannot say that the Chambertin-Clos de Bèze is as superb as their 1988 or 1985, but it is a beautifully made wine that should be at its best in about 4 to 5 years and should last 12 to 15 years.

JEAN FAUROIS (VOSNE-ROMANÉE)

1987 CLOS VOUGEOT	90
1987 VOSNE-ROMANÉE LES CHAUMES	87

Jean Faurois' 1987s are lovely wines, and his Clos Vougeot is one of the top wines of the vintage. It has a beautifully deep, rich color, and an explosively full, intense, fragrant bouquet of ripe berry fruit, minerals, and spicy oak. On the palate, it shows superb depth, excellent balance, an old vine intensity, and a rich, full finish. In a blind tasting this wine would surely be picked by most tasters to be a 1985. It should drink beautifully until 1996–1997. The Vosne-Romanée Les Chaumes exhibits a rich, intense berry fruit to its nose, a nice cedary, herbaceous spiciness, medium to full body, and a smooth finish. While fully drinkable now, it will develop more nuances with another 2 to 3 years of bottle age; it should last for 7 to 8 years. The wines of Jean Faurois are unfined and unfiltered.

BERNARD FEVRE (SAINT-ROMAIN)

1987 AUXEY-DURESSES	85
1987 BEAUNE LES EPENOTTES	87
1987 BEAUNE LES MONTREVENOTS	86
1987 SAINT-ROMAIN	84

Bernard Fevre is another young *viticulteur* who is fast acquiring an excellent reputation. Through 1988 his wines were vinified by André Mussy of the Domaine Mussy in Pommard. The only difference between the wines of Fevre and those of Mussy is that Fevre bottles his wines 3 to 4 months sooner than Mussy. Fevre makes a very good, reasonably priced Saint-Romain. It is not terribly complex, but does exhibit a bouquet of ripe red fruits, spicy oak, and flavors reminiscent of cherries. It is a wine to drink over the next 3 to 4 years. If you have the patience, invest in a few bottles of Fevre's Auxey-Duresses, made from 80-year-old vines. There is an amazing amount of muscle to this robust, tannic, true *vin de garde*. It is a big, sturdy, long-lived wine that should not be drunk before the mid-nineties. The Beaune Les Montrevenots is a deliciously supple, round, velvety wine that is elegant, soft, and ideal for drinking between now and 1994–1995. The Beaune Les Epenottes does indeed taste identical to the wine from Mussy (it is the same wine), but Fevre's earlier bottling seems to have given more penetration and focus to the wine's intense berry-scented bouquet and more lift and focus to its concentrated, lush, silky flavors. It is a delicious wine.

FOREY PÈRE ET FILS (VOSNE-ROMANÉE)

1987 ECHÉZEAUX	87
1987 NUITS ST.-GEORGES LES PERRIÈRES	85
1987 VOSNE-ROMANÉE	83
1987 VOSNE-ROMANÉE LES GAUDICHOTS	86

The Vosne-Romanée displays a nice touch of spicy oak, good berry-scented fruit, medium body, and light tannins. It should be drunk by 1993–1994. The Nuits St.-Georges Les Perrières shows more depth, ripeness, and tannin. Nevertheless, it is a wine to drink after several years in the bottle. It is very spicy, with an underlying truffle earthiness to accompany its plummy fruit. The Vosne-Romanée Les Gaudichots is one of the domaine's best wines. It has a fine color, a moderately intense, ripe, somewhat exotic bouquet of oriental spices and ripe fruit, medium body, good depth, fresh acidity, and enough tannin and balance to last until 1994–1997. The tiny parcel of Les Gaudichots, which sits adjacent to La Tâche, is planted with true "vieilles vignes" (the average age of the vines is 60 years). The other top wine from this domaine is their Echézeaux. It is extremely elegant, with a well-evolved and penetrating bouquet of berry fruit and spicy new oak. Medium bodied, soft, concentrated, and well balanced, this complex, seductive wine should drink nicely until 1996–1997.

DOMAINE JEAN GARAUDET (POMMARD)

1987 MONTHÉLIE	86
1987 POMMARD	85
1987 POMMARD LES CHARMOTS	88

Made from 70-year-old vines, the 1987 Pommard is a fat, ripe, concentrated wine that is totally ready to drink, but should age well until 1993–1994. Most generic Pommards are relatively dull and alcoholic, but this Pommard has real class and style. The Monthélie may be the best wine I have ever tasted from an appellation that usually turns out rugged, brawny, frequently coarse wines. Aged in small barrels, the 1987 is supple, deliciously fruity, and has charm (a characteristic uncommon for Monthélies). The top wine is the Pommard Les Charmots, made from a vineyard planted in 1902. Garaudet produces less than 100 cases of this hedonistic Pommard every year. The 1987 is bursting with berry fruit and toasty, vanilla-scented new oak. Supple, ripe, generously fruity and velvety in the mouth, with a lavish opulence to its texture, this dazzling wine should drink well for another 5 to 7 years.

LUCIEN GEOFFROY (GEVREY-CHAMBERTIN)

1987 GEVREY-CHAMBERTIN LES CHAMPEAUX	85
1987 GEVREY-CHAMBERTIN-CLOS PRIEUR	86
1987 GEVREY-CHAMBERTIN LES ESCORVÉES	80

1987 GEVREY-CHAMBERTIN LES PERRIÈRES	84
1987 MAZIS-CHAMBERTIN	86

Geoffroy's 1987s are definitely better than the 1986s. The Les Escor-vées was simple, straightforward, round, and tasty, but lacked com-plexity and finesse. The Les Champeaux showed a ton of spicy new oak in the bouquet, had a color that looked more like Côte Rôtie or Bor-deaux than Burgundy, and exhibited expansive, rich, sweet, ripe, plummy, black fruit flavors. It is an attractive and flavorful wine that should be drunk by 1995–1996. Even more impressive was the Clos Prieur. It showed toasty, smoky new oak, amazing concentration, plenty of muscle, and surprising power and depth. It is not a classic burgundy, but there is no doubting its appeal, concentration, and in-tense flavors. I was less impressed with the Les Perrières, which tasted overwhelmingly of oak and tannin. Perhaps I caught it in an awkward stage of its development. Lastly, Geoffroy's Mazis-Chambertin offered a big, stemmy, earthy, spicy, herbaceous bouquet, and intense, rich flavors. It is a potentially excellent wine that seems to have a great deal of tannin, and evidence of new oak. Perhaps it will deserve a higher score in a few years. For now, it is a gawky, concentrated, formidable wine that appears to need 2 to 3 years of bottle age.

DOMAINE JACQUES GERMAIN (BEAUNE)

1987 BEAUNE LES BOUCHEROTTES	82
1987 BEAUNE LES TEURONS	83
1987 BEAUNE LES VIGNES-FRANCHES	83
1987 CHÂTEAU DE CHOREY-LÈS-BEAUNE	74

I was less impressed with Germain's 1987s than with his 1986s. I sus-pect the wines were aged for too long a period in cask. As a result, their fragile fruitiness has been obliterated by the smell and taste of new oak barrels. The tannin content appears high relative to the concentration of fruit. Nevertheless, there is good cherry and strawberry fruitiness in the Premiers Crus. The raw materials appear to have been available, but given the light, delicate style of Pinot Noir in this vintage, it is curious that the wines were not bottled earlier. These wines should all be consumed by 1992–1993.

DOMAINE ARMAND GIRARDIN (POMMARD)

1987 POMMARD LES CHARMOTS	87
1987 POMMARD LES EPENOTS	89
1987 POMMARD LES RUGIENS	90

This estate has very old vines (all three parcels average between 50 and 60 years old), practices an extended maceration, and uses plenty of new oak. The results, while not subtle, are highly concentrated wines that may be the most powerful and intense Pommards of the appellation. Les Charmots, aged in 25% new wood casks, exhibits plenty of toasty oak, chocolate, herbs, and rich berry fruit in its bouquet. It is supple with excellent depth and ripeness, and medium to full body. While approachable now, it should be at its best between 1991–2002. Les Epenots is even deeper and denser, with a huge chocolaty, berry-like aroma, an amazing opulence of fruit, a chewy texture, full body, and at least 5 to 12 more years of aging potential. It is not easy to find Pommards this highly extracted, but then, Monsieur Girardin's yields are conservative. Lastly, the Les Rugiens is an exceptional wine from this vintage with fabulous depth and a sweet, expansive, broad-flavored palate oozing with flavors of berry fruit, toasty new oak, chocolate, and plums. On the palate, it is slightly softer than the more tannic Epenots. All of these wines are unfiltered.

MACHARD DE GRAMONT (NUITS ST.-GEORGES)

1987 ALOXE-CORTON LES MORAIS	75
1987 BEAUNE-CHOUACHEUX	84
1987 BEAUNE LES EPENOTTES	86
1987 CHAMBOLLE-MUSIGNY	84
1987 CHOREY-LÈS-BEAUNE LES BEAUMONTS	84
1987 NUITS ST.-GEORGES LES DAMODES	86
1987 NUITS ST.-GEORGES LES HAUTS POIRETS	84
1987 NUITS ST.-GEORGES EN LA PERRIÈRE NOBLOT	84
1987 NUITS ST.-GEORGES VALLEROTS	85
1987 POMMARD	83
1987 POMMARD LE CLOS BLANC	86

1987 SAVIGNY-LÈS-BEAUNE	78
1987 SAVIGNY-LÈS-BEAUNE LES GUETTES	86

The Chambolle-Musigny is representative of Chambolle. It is fragrant, supple, light, but fruity and ready to drink. The Savigny-Lès-Beaune is straightforward, a little dry and hard, but adequate. The Chorey-Lès-Beaune Les Beaumonts is a good value, and exhibits attractively round, smooth, supple fruit, medium body, good color, and an engaging precociousness; it should be consumed over the next 3 to 4 years. The Beaune-Chouacheux is also supple, ripe, fruity, and pleasant. The Beaune Les Epenottes and Savigny-Lès-Beaune Les Guettes are more structured, concentrated, and serious. Gramont is especially fond of his wine from Les Guettes, since it is made from some of his oldest vines. The 1987 Les Guettes is excellent. It has deep ruby color, is spicy and tannic, medium to full bodied, and capable of lasting until 1994–1996. I was less impressed with his Aloxe-Corton Les Morais. In most vintages I found it to be rather lean, tannic, and hard—correct but never inspiring. On the other hand, this is an excellent house for Premiers Crus from Nuits St.-Georges. The Hauts Poirets is well made with good fruit, medium body, and an attractive plummy, earthy fruitiness. The Nuits St.-Georges en La Perrière Noblot is an excellently placed vineyard. The 1987 is supple, straightforward, and well made. It is not terribly concentrated, but is charming and light. It should be drunk by 1992–1993. Gramont's Nuits St.-Georges Les Vallerots is more serious. It shows an earthy, truffle-like spiciness, good, ripe berry fruit, and a soft, smooth finish. Gramont's best 1987 Nuits St.-Georges is his Les Damodes. In addition to the peppery, earthy, ripe berry fruit in the nose, the wine's floral component provides an extra measure of complexity. It is a round, seductive, velvety wine with abundant fruit, and is difficult to resist drinking. I would not expect any of these wines to age beyond 1993–1994. The Pommard shows some fatness but not a great deal of complexity. However, one of Gramont's best wines year in and year out is the Pommard Le Clos Blanc. I have wonderful memories of the 1978, 1979, and 1985. The 1987 shows excellent rich, ripe fruit, a nice spicy, vanilla-scented oakiness, plenty of body, and surprising power for a 1987. It is drinkable now but will certainly last until 1995–1996.

MARCHAND GRILLOT (GEVREY-CHAMBERTIN)

1987 CHAMBOLLE-MUSIGNY	78
1987 GEVREY-CHAMBERTIN	75

1987 GEVREY-CHAMBERTIN LA PETITE CHAPELLE	85
1987 MOREY ST.-DENIS	82
1987 RUCHOTTES-CHAMBERTIN	87

While both the 1987 Gevrey-Chambertin and Chambolle-Musigny were
light and thin, the Morey St.-Denis showed some attractive berry, floral
fruitiness, and a nice touch of new oak. It could have had a longer
finish. One of the top two wines in Gevrey-Chambertin from this grower
is the stylish, supple Gevrey-Chambertin La Petite Chapelle. It should
be drunk by 1993–1994. It offers a generous, round, berry fruitiness,
some spicy, toasty new oak, medium body, light tannins, and a good
finish. The Ruchottes-Chambertin is a bigger, more structured and
powerful wine. It has a smoky, game-like bouquet, big, plummy, black
fruit flavors, medium to full body, and some soft tannins in the finish.
It can be drunk now or cellared until 1994–1995.

JEAN GRIVOT (VOSNE-ROMANÉE)

1987 ECHÉZEAUX	90
1987 NUITS ST.-GEORGES LES BOUDOTS	87
1987 VOSNE-ROMANÉE LES BEAUX MONTS	86

Grivot is the most famous domaine to follow the winemaking philosophy
of the Nuits St.-Georges oenologist, Guy Accad. In 1987, a cold maceration prior to fermentation was practiced for the first time. It is difficult
to tell whether or not these wines will lose their color, as have some of
Accad's wines. The Vosne-Romanée Les Beaux Monts, with its deep,
dark ruby color, big, rich, jammy bouquet, medium to full body, and
lush, silky finish is certainly of high quality. Even more impressive is
the Nuits St.-Georges Les Boudots, which has an almost black/ruby
color, long deep, jammy, black fruit flavors, medium to full body,
and a smooth finish. Both of these Premiers Crus should drink well
until 1995–1996. The Echézeaux was superb in 1987, but I could not
help noticing it smelled like Syrah rather than Pinot Noir. Skeptics
of the Guy Accad style of winemaking will say the wine does not
taste like Echézeaux. However, it is a great wine, impressively colored,
rich, and full. This is a wine to drink by 1996–1997 and appreciate
for its wonderfully pure, hedonistic, seductive fruit and voluptuous
texture.

ROBERT GROFFIER (MOREY ST.-DENIS)

1987 BONNES MARES	90
1987 CHAMBERTIN-CLOS DE BÈZE	88
1987 CHAMBOLLE-MUSIGNY LES AMOUREUSES	88
1987 CHAMBOLLE-MUSIGNY LES HAUTS DOIX	78
1987 CHAMBOLLE-MUSIGNY LES SENTIERS	86

This seems to be a domaine that, after a period of inconsistency, has gotten things sorted out. In 1987, while the Chambolle-Musigny Les Hauts Doix is a bit light, tart, and short, the rest of Groffier's portfolio is quite impressive. For example, the Chambolle-Musigny Les Sentiers is wonderfully rich, fragrant, pure, elegant, and simply a dazzling and beautiful burgundy to drink between now and 1994–1995. I would not count on it lasting because it is so well developed, and is indeed a delicious, wonderfully expansive, perfumed, heady wine. The Chambolle-Musigny Les Amoureuses is slightly richer and more expansive. The Chambertin-Clos de Bèze shares the same wonderfully fragrant, toasty, roasted, ripe berry-scented bouquet, lovely, lush, even opulent flavors, and a soft, silky texture. However, there is more tannin in the finish, suggesting that this may be Groffier's only wine capable of aging past 1996–1997. My favorite wine from this excellent producer in 1987 is his Bonnes Mares. It had a fabulous bouquet of ripe, plummy fruit combined with smoky, toasty, vanillin scents and the scent of raw ground beef and Worcestershire sauce. Once past the gorgeous bouquet, one finds a superbly rendered, rich, velvety, dazzling wine with layers of berry fruit oozing from the glass. This is an exquisite 1987, but there is one caveat—it must be drunk by 1994–1995.

DOMAINE JEAN GROS (VOSNE-ROMANÉE)

1987 BOURGOGNE HAUTES-CÔTES DE NUITS	84
1987 RICHEBOURG	95
1987 VOSNE-ROMANÉE	86
1987 VOSNE-ROMANÉE-CLOS DES RÉAS	90

Madame Gros, long-time mayor of Vosne-Romanée, and her son Michel continue to be among the standard-bearers for high-quality wine-making. Their Bourgogne Hautes-Côtes de Nuits is an elegant, ripe, richly fruity wine that should last for the next 4 to 5 years. I especially liked their Vosne-Romanée, which revealed a nice toasty, oaky component, deep, ripe berry fruit, medium body, and a smooth, velvety finish. It should be consumed by 1994. The Gros have not made any Clos Vougeot since they ripped up the vineyards on their superb parcel several years ago. However, they hope to make small quantities in 1990. Their Clos des Réas should give the wonderful 1985 and brilliant 1983 some competition. It has a fabulously complex nose of oriental spices, black fruits, spicy oak, and plums. On the palate, the wine shows great length and concentration, superb richness, and is another superlative example of just how delicious the 1987s can be. Drinkable now, it should last until 1997–2000. The Richebourg is simply celestial, and is one of the candidates for the wine of the vintage in Burgundy. I have had it on three different occasions and have been knocked over by it each time. It could even be greater than the 1985 and 1983 Richebourgs produced by Madame Gros. Explosively rich and concentrated, it seemed to resemble one of the great Richebourgs from the Domaine de la Romanée-Conti. Extraordinarily complex, profoundly concentrated, long, and rich, it is soft enough to be drunk now, but should continue to fill out and develop more nuances to its bouquet between now and 1996–1997. This is clearly a winemaking tour de force.

DOMAINE GROS FRÈRE ET SOEUR (VOSNE-ROMANÉE)

1987 BOURGOGNE ROUGE	85
1987 CLOS VOUGEOT	90
1987 GRANDS ECHÉZEAUX	89
1987 RICHEBOURG	92
1987 VOSNE-ROMANÉE	86

Long-time readers know of my admiration for the remarkable character that Bernard Gros seems to get consistently in his red burgundies. They are perhaps the most staggeringly exotic wines made in Burgundy. I found his 1987s to be outstanding wines, but less exotic than previous vintages. His delicious Bourgogne Rouge will make many friends for Burgundy. It is a round, ripe, expansively flavored wine that shows the suppleness of the 1987 vintage as well as the ripe, pure fruit common in this year of low yields. The Vosne-Romanée was a bit more tannic and less oaky than that of Bernard's mother, Madame Jean Gros, but was still richly fruity, medium bodied, and ideal for drinking until 1993–

1994. The Clos Vougeot at this estate comes from the only parcel of the Clos Vougeot vineyard that is contiguous to the Grand Cru of Musigny. Those consumers lucky enough to purchase a bottle of the Gros Frère et Soeur Clos Vougeot will notice that in small print the word "Musigny" does appear on the label under the larger printed name of Clos Vougeot. The Clos Vougeot, aged in 50% new oak, is a rich, intense, flamboyant wine with a bouquet of raspberries, apricots, spicy, vanillin-scented oak, and long, flowing, exotic flavors. It is full bodied for the vintage, and should drink well for at least a decade. I thought the Grands Echézeaux were just as concentrated yet more closed and less exotic than the Clos Vougeot. It will probably be an outstanding wine in several years, but for now it is excellent, quite rich, highly extracted, and another top success for the 1987 vintage. As for the Richebourg, while it may not have the sublime, rather surreal quality of Madame Jean Gros's Richebourg (possibly the wine of the vintage), it is an outstanding wine. Deep ruby in color with an emerging bouquet of black raspberries, spicy oak, minerals, and spring flowers, this full-bodied, rich, concentrated yet tannic wine should be at its best by 1991–1992 and last for a good decade. It would appear that the entire Gros family has done something special in the 1987 vintage. The 1987s of this cellar are essentially equal in quality to the more highly applauded 1988s.

JEAN GUITTON (BEAUNE)

1987 ALOXE-CORTON	78
1987 BEAUNE LES SIZIES	85
1987 LADOIX LA CORVÉE	75
1987 SAVIGNY-LÈS-BEAUNE	?
1987 SAVIGNY-LÈS-BEAUNE LES HAUT JARRONS	77
1987 SAVIGNY-LÈS-BEAUNE LES PEUILLETS	83

I remember liking Guitton's 1987s when I tasted them out of the cask, but I was disappointed when I tasted them from the bottle. They had been in the bottle for some time, so there was no reason to suspect bottle sickness. All the wines from Guitton seemed to be too herbaceous, green, and the product of young vines. The only exception was the Beaune Les Sizies, which shared none of the vegetal character plaguing the other wines. It had a rich, ripe, supple fruitiness and was a tasty, smooth wine for drinking between now and 1993–1994.

STANISLAS HERESZTYN (GEVREY-CHAMBERTIN)

1987 CLOS ST.-DENIS	85
1987 GEVREY-CHAMBERTIN	83
1987 GEVREY-CHAMBERTIN LES CHAMPONNETS	87
1987 GEVREY-CHAMBERTIN LES CORBEAUX	87
1987 GEVREY-CHAMBERTIN LES GOULOTS	84
1987 GEVREY-CHAMBERTIN LA PERRIÈRE	85

The 1987s were much more impressive from the cask. While they have turned out to be good wines, intense filtration has clearly stripped the wines of the extra dimension of flavor and aromatic complexity they possessed in barrel. This is a shame because there is no doubt this producer knows how to make fine wine. If the Heresztyn family would cut back or completely eliminate filtration, everyone would see the full potential of this underrated producer. The 1987 Gevrey-Chambertin shows a nice soft, supple, curranty fruitiness and some attractive spices. It should be drunk by 1993–1994. Their Gevrey-Chambertin Les Goulots, which was absolutely outstanding from cask, is now lighter and less intense, but is still a very good, ready to drink, plummy, earthy, richly fruity wine that will provide pleasing drinking until 1994–1995. Another wine, the Gevrey-Chambertin Les Champonnets, was also outstanding. After tasting this wine from cask my notes contained unbridled enthusiasm, but out of bottle it has a polished look that can come only from intense filtration; it seems to have had at least 4 to 5 points in its flavor and bouquet knocked out. It is still a fine wine with good to excellent depth, a brilliant deep ruby color, fine ripeness, and a smooth, silky finish. It should be drunk by 1993–1994. As for the other wines from Heresztyn, I had extremely impressive notes from the cask on both the Gevrey-Chambertin La Perrière, and Gevrey-Chambertin Les Corbeaux. While both have turned out to be very good wines, when I compare my notes on them out of the bottle with those from cask, it is apparent that the wines now have less intense and less complex bouquets, less color, and seemingly less flavor dimension and concentration. Both wines are still attractive, well-made 1987s with a good sweetness and plumpness of fruit, but it is a shame to see such wonderful raw materials and talented winemaking go to waste because of an oenologist's obsession with security and stability in the bottle. Last, the Grand Cru Clos St.-Denis seems to be less impressive than many of the Premiers Crus from this estate. I wonder if their Grand

Cru is planted in young vines, resulting in a lighter-styled wine that does not have the depth of their top Premiers Crus.

ALAIN HUDELOT-NOËLLAT (VOSNE-ROMANÉE)

1987 CLOS VOUGEOT	86
1987 NUITS ST.-GEORGES LES MURGERS	83
1987 RICHEBOURG	87
1987 ROMANÉE ST.-VIVANT	87
1987 VOSNE-ROMANÉE	84
1987 VOSNE-ROMANÉE LES SUCHOTS	84
1987 VOUGEOT PREMIER CRU	68

Alain Hudelot is a serious winemaker, but again, he falls victim to the practice of filtering his wines too vigorously at the time of bottling. He has made very good 1987s, but one suspects these scores would be from 2 to 5 points higher had there not been such a traumatic filtration. The Vosne-Romanée is a good Villages wine, ripe, relatively full sized, tannic, and spicy. It should last for 7 to 8 years. Something was wrong with his Vougeot Premier Cru, as it tasted vegetal, had extremely pale color, and seemed to be the product of very young vines; it should have been sold off to a *négociant* or declassified rather than bottled under Hudelot's name. The Vosne-Romanée Les Suchots, from one of the great Premier Cru vineyards of Vosne-Romanée, should also have been better. It has plenty of tannin and good acidity, but it lacks the depth and concentration of the top 1987s. The same can be said for the Nuits St.-Georges Les Murgers (another superb Premier Cru vineyard near the border of Vosne-Romanée). It has excellent color, but again lacks concentration, is lean and excessively high in acidity. The Clos Vougeot is one of Hudelot's best three wines in 1987. It has a deep ruby color, excellent ripeness, a muscular, medium- to full-bodied, tannic struc-ture, and plenty of length; it should drink nicely between 1990–1998. The Richebourg is very tannic, still relatively closed and hard, but has good intensity, shows excellent ripeness and fine color. It should be cellared until at least 1991–1992 but has the potential to last for at least a decade. Hudelot's top wine in 1987 is the Romanée St.-Vivant. Still closed, with high acidity, this wine exhibited plenty of excellent rich-ness and ripeness. However, it is not close to being ready to drink and is another candidate for laying away for 2 to 3 years until its tannins soften.

H. & P. JACQUESON (RULLY)

1987 MERCUREY	84
1987 MERCUREY LES NAUGUES	78
1987 RULLY LES CHAMPONNIÈRES	86
1987 RULLY LES CLOUDS	85

Jacqueson is a well-known name and makes reliably excellent wines from Rully. In addition, the wines sell for reasonable prices. Both 1987s are worthy additions to the cellars of any shrewd consumers looking for value in red burgundy. The Rully Les Clouds showed a wonderfully vibrant, exuberant bouquet of bing cherries and some spicy oak followed by supple, delicious fruitiness, medium body, and soft texture. It should drink beautifully until 1991–1993. The Rully Les Champonnières is a bit more serious. It exhibits a more elevated use of toasty new oak, and is a deeper, more structured wine with excellent concentration, and 5 to 7 years of aging potential. It is a serious Rully that should be cellared for a few years while you are enjoying the Rully Les Clouds. As for the two Mercureys, the Mercurey is elegant and ripe with a bouquet of leather, berries, and spicy oak. I did not think it had quite the charm and fruit of either of the Rullys. The Mercurey Les Naugues was lean, tart, tough edged, and not as charming and appealing as the other three wines from Jacqueson.

LOUIS JADOT (BEAUNE)

1987 AUXEY-DURESSES DUC DE MAGENTA	85
1987 BEAUNE LES BOUCHEROTTES	87
1987 BEAUNE-CLOS DES URSULES	87
1987 BEAUNE-TRADITION	87
1987 BONNES MARES	90
1987 BOURGOGNE ROUGE-PINOT NOIR	83
1987 CHAMBERTIN-CLOS DE BÈZE	89
1987 CHAMBOLLE-MUSIGNY	84
1987 CHAPELLE-CHAMBERTIN	88
1987 CHASSAGNE-MONTRACHET MORGEOT-CLOS DE LA CHAPELLE (DUC DE MAGENTA)	85

1987 CLOS VOUGEOT	87
1987 CORTON LES POUGETS	87
1987 GEVREY-CHAMBERTIN	81
1987 GEVREY-CHAMBERTIN-CLOS ST.-JACQUES	88
1987 GEVREY-CHAMBERTIN ESTOURNELLES ST.-JACQUES	86
1987 GRIOTTE-CHAMBERTIN	88
1987 MARSANNAY	72
1987 MAZIS-CHAMBERTIN	90
1987 MUSIGNY	87
1987 NUITS ST.-GEORGES	84
1987 NUITS ST.-GEORGES LES BOUDOTS	87
1987 NUITS ST.-GEORGES-CLOS DES CORVÉES	88
1987 PERNAND-VERGELESSES-CLOS DE LA CROIX PIERRE	85
1987 POMMARD	85
1987 POMMARD LES EPENOTS	88
1987 RUCHOTTES-CHAMBERTIN	87
1987 VOSNE-ROMANÉE	85

Overall, Jadot's 1987 red wines are riper, fuller, and more interesting wines to taste than the lean, hard, more tannic 1986s. Jadot also made superb 1988s that will rival the quality of his wines in 1985. In short, a lot of good wine will be emerging from this excellent Beaune *négociant* and vineyard owner. This firm pays as much attention to the lower appellations as it does to the glamorous wines from world-renowned appellations. They feel, with justification, that most consumers are more likely to taste their Bourgogne Rouge or Pouilly-Fuissé than their Chambertin-Clos de Bèze or Corton-Charlemagne. This is evidenced by their excellent Bourgogne Rouge-Pinot Noir, 40% of which was aged in small casks. It is a fruity, ripe, round, soft, pleasing wine ready for drinking over the next 2 to 4 years. Their Marsannay Rouge is a bit thin, acidic, and tough, so I would opt for the Bourgogne when looking for a reasonably priced Pinot Noir from Burgundy. Their Auxey-Duresses from the Duc de Magenta estate (where Jadot has the exclusive rights to make and market the wine) is excellent. It is an unfiltered, rich, spicy, medium-bodied wine with good tannins, plenty of depth, and is an excellent example of how the best wines from Auxey-Duresses are often underrated. Equally good is the Pernand-Vergelesses-Clos de la Croix Pierre, which, for a 1987, showed surprising power, muscle, and body. I would ideally give it until 1991–1992 before contemplating its consumption. Another Duc de Magenta wine, the Chassagne-Montrachet Morgeot-Clos de la Chapelle exhibited beautifully rich, spicy, cherry fruit married intelligently with toasty oak. Among the Villages wines from the Côte de Nuits, I found the Chambolle-Musigny to be seductive, tender, soft, and ideal for drinking over the next several years. The Gevrey-Chambertin was also soft, but lacked charm because of its high tannin content and its more rustic style. The Nuits St.-Georges was more concentrated than the prior two wines, but was also tannic, making me wonder whether it possessed the requisite balance of fruit. My favorite among the generic Villages wines from the Côte de Nuits was the 1987 Vosne-Romanée. It showed a beautiful, well developed, penetrating bouquet of berry fruit, spices, herbs, and leather. Supple and ripe, it is an excellent example of a Villages wine. I also do not want to forget the excellent Pommard made by Louis Jadot. Most generic Pommards tend to be too rustic, too coarse, and overly alcoholic, and lacking fruit. Not so with this wine, which was bottled unfiltered. It shows wonderful ripeness and a plump, chocolatey, berry fruit character. It should drink beautifully until 1995–1996.

Jadot employed an extremely long maceration for his Premiers Crus in 1987 to extract as much fruit and concentration as possible. Most of the wines were macerated for over 3 weeks, many for almost a month. This is evident in wines like the Beaune Les Boucherottes. It has an intense aroma of red fruits and spicy oak, is supple, deep, concentrated, with enough tannin to age well for at least a decade. It is quite a sturdy wine for a 1987 Beaune. The Beaune-Clos des Ursules shows more new oak and exotic spices. The 1987 has gobs of rich, jammy, berry fruit, spicy, vanillin oak, and medium to full body. It is very approachable now, but another 2 to 3 years in the bottle should make it even more appealing. It should keep until 2000. In 1987 Jadot blended wine from several Premiers Crus to make a Beaune Tradition (there are 500 cases). It competes very favorably with the Beaune-Clos des Ursules. It is an excellent wine, richly fruity, lush, even opulent, with clean berry fruit, good acidity, and light tannins. I would certainly drink it by 1993–1994. Louis Jadot's Pommard Les Epenots is one of his outstanding 1987s (it is also astonishing in 1988). The 1987 shows a captivating bouquet of toasty, smoky, vanillin oak, rich, berry fruit, a whiff of herbs, and long, flowing, deeply concentrated, silky flavors. It is too good to resist now, but should keep until 1995–1996. The Jadot

Corton Les Pougets is almost as good, more structured and tannic; I would not want to touch it before 1992.

In the Côte de Nuits, Jadot produces several excellent wines from Nuits St.-Georges including a smoky, ripe, roasted, somewhat exotic Nuits St.-Georges Les Boudots that should drink beautifully until 1995–1996. There is little tannin to it so I see no reason not to drink it young. The Nuits St.-Georges-Clos des Corvées needs more time in the bottle to resolve its tannins. The Jadot firm controls 80% of the production of this well-placed Premier Cru in Nuits St.-Georges, and their 1987 shows excellent ripeness and color, but patience is required. This wine should not peak until 1991–1992. Jadot now has important holdings in the appellation of Gevrey-Chambertin since he bought a large portion of the famous Clair-Dau estate in the mid-eighties. Their wines in 1987 from Gevrey-Chambertin are all very good to excellent. Several are potentially outstanding. The Gevrey-Chambertin Estournelles St.-Jacques is the lightest of the wines, displaying a less profound color than the other wines from Gevrey, but a forward, soft, game-like, berry-scented bouquet, plenty of ripe fruit, and a silky, smooth finish. I would be sure to drink it over the next 5 to 6 years. The Gevrey-Chambertin-Clos St.-Jacques is more tannic and actually needs several years in the bottle to reach maturity. It is a full-bodied wine for a 1987 with excellent rich berry fruitiness backed up by some spicy oak. Jadot's Griotte-Chambertin is another supple, hedonistic style of wine from Gevrey-Chambertin. This is a silky smooth, wonderfully perfumed wine that is a treat to drink. The Ruchottes-Chambertin is much more tannic and *sauvage*, as the French say (meaning rustic and wild). It is a full-bodied, broad-shouldered, deep wine with very good concentration but plenty of tannin to resolve. Whether it will ever have the pure elegance of the Griotte-Chambertin or Clos St.-Jacques is debatable. The Chapelle-Chambertin, made from 50-year-old vines, is excellent. Unfortunately only 150 cases of this wine were made. It is a chewy, rich, opulently fruity, lush, seductive wine that should age beautifully until 1996–1997. The Mazis-Chambertin is one of the two most concentrated wines from Jadot in the 1987 vintage. It has an intense, deep ruby color, a spicy, earthy, rich, plummy bouquet, and gobs of fruit and tannin. This suggests that it will be at its best between 1993–2005. It is an impressive 1987 with more of a kinship to a 1985 than 1987. Among the other Grands Crus from Jadot in 1987 is the excellent Chambertin Clos de Bèze. While not as sublime as the 1985, it is not far behind in quality. It is long, medium to full bodied, very deep, has good tannins, and a fabulous nose of spicy new oak and berry fruit. The Bonnes Mares is well worth searching out as it is truly great, and one of the very top wines of the vintage. It has a gorgeous, complete bouquet of herbs, rich berry fruits, spicy new oak, and exotic spices. Rich with a chewy, fleshy texture, and fresh acidity, it has one of the longest finishes of any wine I have tasted from this vintage. Drinkable now, this wine should get better over the next 5 or 6 years and last for a decade thereafter. Jadot's Musigny is much lighter but extremely elegant. One is unlikely to see this wine in the marketplace as only 75 cases were made. It is a smooth, supple wine for drinking over the next 7 to 8 years. Last, there is Jadot's Clos Vougeot, which has an explosive bouquet of red fruits and spicy oak. It is ripe, round, and velvety—quite typical of the 1987 vintage. In quality, it is only a shade behind the superb 1985 and 1983 made by this impeccably run, brilliant supplier of red burgundy.

JAFFELIN (BEAUNE)

1987 MONTHÉLIE	79
1987 SANTENAY LA MALADIÈRE	85
1987 VOLNAY	83

This négociant in Beaune (owned by the firm of Joseph Drouhin) produces very reliable, sound wines. While they are somewhat commercial, they are usually straightforward, satisfying, and unpretentious. The firm makes many more wines than those I listed, but I only had an opportunity to taste these three. My favorite was the Santenay La Maladière, which showed an attractive, moderately intense, spicy, cherry-scented bouquet, medium body, a soft texture, and light tannins in the finish. It is ideal for drinking now. The Monthélie, from an appellation with more potential than actual quality at the moment, is cleanly made, avoids the coarseness and astringent tannins typical of many wines from this appellation, and offers straightforward, simple, red fruit flavors with some spicy, dusty tannins in the finish. The Volnay admirably reflects its appellation with its soft, elegant, berry fruitiness, light to medium body, and smooth, supple finish. It should be consumed by 1992–1993.

HENRI JAYER (VOSNE-ROMANÉE)

1987 ECHÉZEAUX	93
1987 NUITS ST.-GEORGES LES MURGERS	89
1987 RICHEBOURG	95

1987 VOSNE-ROMANÉE	85
1987 VOSNE-ROMANÉE LES BEAUX MONTS	90
1987 VOSNE-ROMANÉE AUX BRÛLÉES	92
1987 VOSNE-ROMANÉE CROS PARANTOUX	91

Among Jayer's 1987s, there is a good, fruity, perfumed, supple, ready-to-drink Vosne-Romanée, an elegant, spicy, plum and licorice–scented Nuits St.-Georges Les Murgers, and a fat, supple, velvety, ready-to-drink Vosne-Romanée Les Beaux Monts. None of these three wines is likely to make "old bones," as the English say, but for drinking before 1994–1995, they are sure to please. The Vosne-Romanée Cros Parantoux has more body and tannin, a deep ruby color, fabulous extract, good, fresh acidity, and ripe, dense, long, berry fruit. It is drinkable now, but it should be at its best between 1991 and 1997. Jayer's Vosne-Romanée Les Brûlées is even richer and deeper. It is made from 50-year-old vines and reveals the intense, penetrating fragrance and ripeness that low yields and impeccable winemaking can give to sensational grapes harvested from well-placed vineyard. Like many of the top 1987s, it is fragrant and richly fruity with little tannin. At the very top level are Jayer's two Grands Crus. His Echézeaux (125 cases were produced in 1987) might not have quite the size or richness of the Vosne-Romanée Les Brûlées or Vosne-Romanée Cros Parantoux, but it is a wonderfully stylish, elegantly wrought wine with a bouquet that seems to jump from the glass. The ripe, lush, yet relatively lightweight berry flavors do not go unnoticed. It is a beautiful wine to admire for its sublety rather than strength. Few winemakers seem capable of pairing richness with subtlety as well as Henri Jayer. Lastly, the Richebourg (all 25 cases of it) could easily be confused with a 1985. It has a deep, dark ruby color, a fabulous bouquet of raspberry fruit, vanilla, and toast, and a long, velvety, rich finish. It has plenty of soft tannins to help it last, but it will be difficult not to drink this wine before 1994–1996 as it tastes so good.

ROBERT JAYER-GILLES (HAUTES-CÔTES DE NUITS)

1987 CÔTE DE NUITS-VILLAGES	87
1987 ECHÉZEAUX	91
1987 HAUTES-CÔTES DE NUITS	87
1987 NUITS ST.-GEORGES LES DAMODES	91

When I last visited Robert Jayer in late 1989 he had just completed
what is certainly the most spectacular underground cellar in Burgundy's Côte d'Or. There is no one who makes better wines from the
Hautes-Côtes de Beaune and Hautes-Côtes de Nuits than Jayer. He is
a believer in obtaining exceptional extract and using a great deal of new
oak for his wines. In 1987, Jayer produced some wines of exceptional
quality from lower appellations. For example, there is his Hautes-Côtes
de Nuits. After tasting Jayer's wine from the Hautes-Côtes de Nuits,
you have to wonder why other producers cannot attain such a remarkable level of quality. The 1987 has an amazingly deep, rich color, a big,
spicy, plum and licorice–scented bouquet, ripe, savory fruit, and
enough ripe tannins as well as balance to age nicely until 1992-2000.
His Côte de Nuits-Villages is every bit as good, slightly softer than the
Hautes-Côtes de Nuits, but supple, rich, and flavorful. In a blind tasting, it could easily be mistaken for a top-notch Premier Cru from the
Côte de Nuits. It is a beautiful wine for drinking in the nineties. One of
Robert Jayer's great wines from the 1987 vintage is his sensational
Nuits St.-Georges Les Damodes. Unfortunately, only two barrels (or 50
cases) of this wine were produced. Much of it is allocated to one of
Jayer's most fervent admirers, the superb restaurateur in Paris, Jean-
Claude Vrinat, owner of the Taillevent restaurant. The Les Damodes
1987 has explosive richness and a profound, concentrated, broad palate
that oozes with aromas of black fruits, flowers, and exotic spices. The
wine is approachable now, but will easily last for up to a decade. In
texture and character, it reminded me of some of the wines of the
brilliant Vosne-Romanée winemaker, Henri Jayer, from another branch
of the Jayer family. Last, the 1987 Echézeaux, usually the top wine of
Robert Jayer, is not superior to his remarkable Nuits St.-Georges Les
Damodes. Deep ruby in color, with a very perfumed, aromatic bouquet
suggesting violets, plums, blackberries, and spicy oak, the Echézeaux
has exceptional depth, and is rounder and more supple than the outstanding 1986. It should be consumed now or aged until 1997-2001. I
have heard complaints that Robert Jayer charges too much money for
some of his wines. This may be true, but he has very few peers in
Burgundy.

DOMAINE JOBLOT (GIVRY)

1987 GIVRY-CLOS DU CELLIER AUX MOINES   86

This is another excellent producer who makes wines from Givry that
can compete with some of the better Premiers Crus from the Côte d'Or.

However, they sell at modest prices. Joblot, who made some marvelous 1988s, also made a supple, spicy, delicious 1987, which should certainly last until 1996–1997. It shows an exuberant, ripe berry fruitiness, a good dosage of spicy new oak, and a long, smooth finish. It is hard to find burgundy of this quality at this price.

LABOURÉ-ROI (NUITS ST.-GEORGES)

1987 BEAUNE PREMIER CRU	77
1987 BOURGOGNE-PINOT NOIR	80
1987 CHAMBOLLE-MUSIGNY-DOMAINE MODOT	78
1987 CLOS VOUGEOT	86
1987 CÔTE DE BEAUNE-VILLAGES	82
1987 CÔTE DE NUITS-VILLAGES-BELLE MARGUERITE	84
1987 ECHÉZEAUX	85
1987 GEVREY-CHAMBERTIN-DOMAINE JACQUESON	85
1987 NUITS ST.-GEORGES LES DAMODES-CHANTAL LESCURE	87
1987 POMMARD LES BERTINS	84
1987 VOLNAY	77

There are some bargains at this estate's lower price levels. The Côte de Nuits-Villages-Belle Marguerite is excellent, and a very good bargain. It is a relatively full-bodied, spicy, muscular wine with a good deal of fruit and character. I also enjoyed the excellent Gevrey-Chambertin-Domaine Jacqueson. It could easily have been a Premier Cru given its excellent depth, rich, robust berry fruitiness, and interesting, complex bouquet. One of the firm's top 1987 red wines was their Nuits St.-Georges Les Damodes-Domaine Chantal Lescure, which displayed a big, earthy, spicy, smoky bouquet, medium- to full-bodied flavors, and adequate acidity and tannin. It can be drunk young or aged until 1996–1997. The Echézeaux was more tannic and oaky. While good, it did not have the depth of the Nuits St.-Georges Les Damodes. Their Clos Vougeot seemed richer and more concentrated than the Echézeaux, but it is also quite backward, spicy, and tannic. While this *négociant* does not produce wine of the same quality as Faiveley, or of Louis Jadot or Joseph Drouhin in Beaune, it is a reliable, sound house that makes a good range of wines.

DOMAINE HENRI LAMARCHE (VOSNE-ROMANÉE)

1987 CLOS VOUGEOT	83
1987 ECHÉZEAUX	85
1987 GRANDS ECHÉZEAUX	86
1987 VOSNE-ROMANÉE	82
1987 VOSNE-ROMANÉE LES CHAUMES	83
1987 VOSNE-ROMANÉE LA GRANDE RUE	86
1987 VOSNE-ROMANÉE LES MALCONSORTS	84
1987 VOSNE-ROMANÉE LES SUCHOTS	86

Lamarche's 1987s are good, relatively light in color, pure, elegant, fruity, soft wines that should be drunk over the next 5 or 6 years. The only question one might ask is, given the domaine's extraordinary vineyards, could the wines have been better? Perhaps lower yields and/or a longer maceration and/or less filtration at bottling should be considered here. The Vosne-Romanée is plump, soft, fruity, straightforward, and ideal for drinking over the next several years. The same can be said for the Vosne-Romanée Les Chaumes and Vosne-Romanée Les Malconsorts. The Les Chaumes vineyard is certainly capable of producing wines with greater richness and fullness. Les Malconsorts is an exceptional vineyard that can often produce wines of Grand Cru quality, yet Lamarche's Malconsorts tastes light. The vines could be young or the production too excessive. I did think the Vosne-Romanée Les Suchots was among the most concentrated of the Premiers Crus from this domaine. It had much deeper color and more richness, ripeness, and length than any of the other wines from Vosne-Romanée, except for the Vosne-Romanée La Grande Rue. The La Grande Rue from Lamarche has intense fruit, a fragrant bouquet of red berry fruit and spicy new oak. It is soft, ripe, round, and should be drunk by 1995–1996. As for this estate's Grands Crus, the Echézeaux has an excellent bouquet, supple, expansive flavors, light to medium body, and is ideal for drinking by 1993–1994. The Grands-Echézeaux is a bit darker in color and is not as dense as I might have anticipated, but it is soft, elegant, and easy to understand and drink. As for the Clos Vougeot, it is velvety, medium-bodied, very light, and not immensely impressive for a Grand Cru. It should be drunk by 1992–1993. Fortunately, the Clos Vougeot from Lamarche showed significantly more concentration and intensity. Although the light wines could be a result of this estate's style, I would guess they are caused by excessive yields. These are relatively light, stylish, graceful wines that are very cleanly made and quite tasty. They should be consumed young.

YVES DE LAUNAY (MERCUREY)

1987 MERCUREY-CLOS DU CHÂTEAU DE MONTAIGNU	85
1987 MERCUREY-MEIX FOULOT	82
1987 MERCUREY LES VELEYS	85

Yves de Launay is one of Mercurey's better small growers. There are three separate cuvées of red wine made, including the Mercurey-Meix Foulot. In 1987 it shows fresh acidity, a soft ripe berry fruitiness, and light to medium body. I would drink it over the next 4 to 5 years. The Mercurey Les Veleys is a bigger, more tannic wine with a lot of spicy, robust berry fruit, medium body, in need of 1 to 2 years of cellaring before it is ready to drink. Normally the most concentrated wine here is the Clos du Château de Montaignu. In 1987 it has fine color, a big, rich, spicy bouquet, medium body, and the potential to last for 7 to 10 years. These are wines that age extremely well.

PHILIPPE LECLERC (GEVREY-CHAMBERTIN)

1987 BOURGOGNE ROUGE	86
1987 GEVREY-CHAMBERTIN LES CAZETIERS	91
1987 GEVREY-CHAMBERTIN COMBE AUX MOINES	92
1987 GEVREY-CHAMBERTIN LES PLATIÈRES	85

There is no doubting that Leclerc's 1987s are significantly better than his 1986s, 1984s, 1982s, and 1981s, and every bit as good as his outstanding 1980s. His Bourgogne Rouge displays excellent ripeness and richness with a brooding sort of fatness and depth. I fully expect it to be every bit as good as my conservative score. It may be one of Burgundy's few Bourgogne Rouges that is neither fined nor filtered. The Gevrey-Chambertin from the vineyard called Les Platières seemed to be no better than his Bourgogne Rouge. It showed excellent ripeness, a broad-shouldered, lush fruitiness, some attractive spicy oak, and a soft texture. It will clearly be a wine to drink young. As for his top two wines, the Gevrey-Chambertin Les Cazetiers and Gevrey-Chambertin Combe aux Moines, the Les Cazetiers is excellent. It exhibits a deep ruby color, exceptional ripeness, a big, spicy, chocolaty, plummy bouquet, large quantities of fruit, full body, and a very long finish. After tasting both the Les Cazetiers and the exceptional 1987 Combe aux Moines, I wonder how the 1987 vintage received so much criticism in the press. As impressive as the Les Cazetiers is, the Combe aux Moines seems to have a greater dimension of flavor and a more penetrating bouquet reminiscent of beef blood, chocolate, ripe berry fruit, and oriental spices. On the palate, the wine is very fleshy and concentrated with soft tannins and an amazing finish. These wines are of extremely high quality, but probably will not age as long as many of his vintages. These two top 1987s should be fully drinkable by the early 1990s and should last for at least 10 to 12 years thereafter.

LEQUIN-ROUSSOT (SANTENAY)

1987 CHASSAGNE-MONTRACHET MORGEOT	82
1987 POMMARD	70
1987 SANTENAY	76
1987 SANTENAY LA COMBE	82

The Lequin brothers, an engaging, humorous team of serious winemakers, continue to excel with their white wines and struggle with their red wines. However, their 1988 red wines look to be their best, so perhaps improvements have been made. The red wines made in 1987 tend to be lean with dusty, rather rough tannins. In short, they lack charm as well as depth of fruit. Certainly the Santenay La Combe and Chassagne-Montrachet Morgeot are their best two reds in 1987. The Pommard is entirely too astringent and hard.

LEROY (AUXEY-DURESSES)

1987 ALOXE-CORTON	85
1987 AUXEY-DURESSES-HOSPICES DE BEAUNE-CUVÉE BOILLOT	87
1987 BEAUNE BLANCHE FLEUR	85
1987 BEAUNE-COUCHERIAS	88
1987 BEAUNE LES GRÈVES	87
1987 BEAUNE-MIGNOTTE	87
1987 BEAUNE LES PERRIÈRES	87

1987 BEAUNE LES PERTUISOTS	85
1987 BEAUNE LES SIZIES	85
1987 CHAMBERTIN	94
1987 CHAMBOLLE-MUSIGNY	83
1987 CHOREY-LÈS-BEAUNE	86
1987 CORTON-HOSPICES DE BEAUNE-CHARLOTTE DUMAY	94
1987 GEVREY-CHAMBERTIN	83
1987 GEVREY-CHAMBERTIN LEX CHAMPEAUX	87
1987 MAZIS-CHAMBERTIN	94
1987 MAZIS-CHAMBERTIN-HOSPICES DE BEAUNE-MADELEINE COLLIGNON	92
1987 MUSIGNY	90
1987 NUITS ST.-GEORGES	87
1987 PERNAND-VERGELESSES LES VERGELESSES	86
1987 POMMARD LES VIGNOTS	90
1987 SANTENAY	86
1987 VOLNAY CHAMPANS	89
1987 VOLNAY CLOS DES CHÊNES	88
1987 VOLNAY PREMIER CRU	86

The red wines from Leroy in 1987 typify the vintage, with their good, fresh acidity, wonderful pure, evolved, aromatic complexity, and fine depth. What many observers fail to recognize when comparing the 1987 and 1988 vintages is that the production yields in Burgundy in 1987 were much smaller. In 1988, many producers made too much wine to get the concentration necessary for greatness. At the lower level of the Leroy hierarchy there are some good wines ready for drinking before 1996–1997. The Santenay has good ripeness and suppleness as well as firm tannins and crisp acidity. It is surprisingly deep for a Villages wine from Santenay. A bit lighter but nevertheless quite fruity, ripe, and attractive is the Chorey-Lès-Beaune. It should be ideal for drinking over the next 7 or 8 years. The Pernand-Vergelesses Les Vergelesses has a broad, expansive, bing cherry fruitiness, medium to full body, and none of the hard, rustic, coarse tannins that often afflict the red wines from this appellation. The Auxey-Duresses is a bit closed and tannic, which is typical for many of the wines from this appellation, but it offers concentration and a good finish. For more immediate drinking one should take a look at Leroy's Auxey-Duresses Cuvée Boillot, purchased from the Hospices de Beaune. Like most wines from the Hospices, the wines have more noticeable toasty, smoky, vanillin oak because of the new barrels used by the Hospices to vinify and age their wines. The wine is soft, supple, and delicious on the palate. I would suggest drinking it between now and 1995–1996. Bize-Leroy always offers an array of wines from Volnay and Beaune, and in 1987 all her Volnays merit attention. The Volnay Premier Cru (a blend of small lots from several Premiers Crus vineyards) is soft, ready to drink, and shows an elegant, richly fruity, ripe character and soft tannins. I would certainly recommend drinking it between now and 1995–1996. Leroy's other two Volnays in 1987 are fuller, more structured, broader-scaled wines that show excellent concentration. The Volnay Clos des Chênes has a fabulous nose. Here the ripeness and exotic complexity of this wine have more in common with a 1985 than a 1987, a vintage with an underrated reputation. It is rich, long, and has a wonderfully opulent texture. Drinkable now, it should last until at least 2000. The Volnay Champans is every bit the equal of the Clos des Chênes, but is more structured and tannic. While the Clos des Chênes can be drunk now, I would advise waiting until 1991–1992 for the Champans, after which I would fully expect it to last for another 10 to 12 years. It is an impressive, rich, berry-scented wine. Leroy's Pommard Les Vignots deserves greater recognition. The 1987 is indeed a great wine in this vintage. It appears she knows how to extract flavor and character from this vineyard. The 1987 has a deep ruby, almost opaque color, exceptional concentration of chocolaty, plummy, cherry fruit, a spicy character, and ample tannins in the finish. It should reach full maturity by 1991–1992.

There is an extensive selection of Premiers Crus from Beaune in 1987. The Beaune Blanche Fleur is the lightest and easiest to drink at the moment. Leroy's Beaune-Coucherias shows superb depth, medium body, and is an elegant bottle of wine. Her Beaune Les Grèves is a wine she often prefers (it was exceptional in 1985). In 1987 it is less impressive, and more tannic and closed than some of her other selections. It possesses a spicy, mineral-scented fruitiness, and has plenty of muscle, but it needs several years to reveal its full character. The Beaune-Mignotte was drinking beautifully when I tasted it. It exhibited a gorgeously smooth, silky texture as well as excellent length. Leroy's Beaune Les Sizies was somewhat tannic and closed, much like the Beaune Les Grèves. I found the Beaune Les Pertuisots to be lacking the complexity and richness of some of their other top Premiers Crus.

It is a good wine, but at these prices one should go for the best. Last, the Beaune Les Perrières is one of her top Premiers Crus from Beaune in 1987. A rich, intense, complex bouquet was followed by a wine that is very concentrated and ripe with just enough tannin to ensure a sound evolution until 1996–1997. The other two selections from the Côte de Beaune included a straightforward, meaty, fleshy Aloxe-Corton, and a celestial Corton-Charlotte Dumay, the latter purchased from the Hospices de Beaune. This wine had a bouquet that literally seemed to fill the room with a stunning display of opulent blackcherry fruit, toasty, spicy oak, and exotic spices. Fortunately, it also had the concentration, depth, and power to match its profound bouquet. It is an absolutely extraordinary, seductive burgundy for drinking over the next decade. Given the low prices at the Hospices de Beaune in 1987, this would have been one cuvée to have purchased in quantity.

Moving to the Côte de Nuits, Madame Leroy's Nuits St.-Georges is one of the best Villages wines I tasted from this appellation in 1987. Her other Villages wines seemed slightly less impressive. They include a delicate yet well-made, attractive Chambolle-Musigny and a tannic, tough, hard-edged Gevrey-Chambertin. Bize-Leroy clearly likes the wines and believes in the potential of the top vineyards of Gevrey-Chambertin. In vintages such as 1987 and 1985 she has a number of top selections from this appellation. Her Gevrey-Chambertin Les Champeaux showed broad, expansive, rich, sweet, pure, robust, berry fruit, and surprising power for a 1987. It should drink well until 1999–2001. In 1987, as in 1985, she offered two wines from the Grand Cru vineyard of Mazis-Chambertin. In 1987 the better of the two wines is the Mazis-Chambertin with its fabulous color, rich, powerful, intense bouquet, superb depth, length, and enough concentration, body, and tannin to last until 1999–2004. It may well turn out to be one of the longest-lived wines from what should be a relatively short-lived burgundy vintage. The Mazis-Chambertin Hospices de Beaune Cuvée Madeleine Collignon is also a stunning wine, but when tasting the two wines side by side, Leroy's regular Mazis-Chambertin has more concentration and length. Nevertheless, this selection from the Hospices is a great wine, but much more flattering, oaky, and evolved than the other Mazis. It is rich and concentrated, smooth, silky, and ideal for drinking through the nineties. Leroy produced two other Grands Crus in 1987: 25 cases of Chambertin and a similar amount of Musigny. The Chambertin is extraordinary, perhaps without the great depth and profound concentration of her 1987 Mazis-Chambertin, but with more complexity—at least from an aromatic perspective. The bouquet is filled with aromas of ground beef, herbs, black fruits, minerals, and flowers.

On the palate, the wine is wonderfully supple, smooth, full-bodied, and makes for a glorious mouthful of wine. It is drinking extremely well now, but it should last for a decade. Last, the Musigny is a classic example of what this Grand Cru vineyard can produce. It does not have nearly the weight of Leroy's wines from Chambertin, but its appeal is its ethereal bouquet of flowers, rich berry fruit, and spices, as well as its light yet amazingly penetrating, lush, broad flavors. Texturally, the wine does not possess the weight or full palate impression of the Chambertin or Mazis-Chambertin. This excellent wine articulates beautifully what makes a Musigny great. It should drink well until 2000.

In conclusion, the 1987s of Lalou Bize-Leroy are often just a notch below her phenomenal 1985s. They provide additional convincing evidence that the 1987 vintage is probably the most underrated Burgundy vintage (along with 1980) in the last 20 years.

GEORGES LIGNIER (MOREY ST.-DENIS)

1987 BONNES MARES	88
1987 CHAMBOLLE-MUSIGNY	80
1987 CLOS DE LA ROCHE	87
1987 CLOS ST.-DENIS	87
1987 GEVREY-CHAMBERTIN	82
1987 GEVREY-CHAMBERTIN LES COMBOTTES	79
1987 MOREY ST.-DENIS	79
1987 MOREY ST.-DENIS-CLOS DES ORMES	77

The 1987 Villages wines from Morey St.-Denis, Gevrey-Chambertin, and Chambolle-Musigny are all representative of their respective appellations. The Morey St.-Denis is relatively light, spicy, and earthy, the Gevrey-Chambertin is deeper colored and firmer, with a bit more muscle and depth to it, and the Chambolle-Musigny is the most fragrant and feminine of this trio. Among the Premiers Crus, the Gevrey-Chambertin Les Combottes is a Premier Cru vineyard that could easily be a Grand Cru, as it is sandwiched between Charmes-Chambertin to the north and Clos de la Roche to the south. However, the Les Combottes from Lignier seems a bit lean, high in acidity, and too tannic for its concentration of fruit. It is not bad, and perhaps more fruit will emerge as the wine ages, but it seems to be a gamble. As for the excellent Premier Cru Morey St.-Denis-Clos des Ormes, I found considerable discrepancy in my tasting notes. One bottle was excellent—deep, fragrant, supple, and quite seductive—whereas the other, tasted in the cellar with Lignier in September, was thin, too acidic, and lacking ripeness and concentration. Lignier's Grands Crus are all very good to excellent in 1987. The Clos de la Roche is a classic example of a wine from this underrated Grand Cru vineyard. It is rich, full bodied, and deep, with an earthy, mineral character to its plummy fruit. It needs a few years in the cellar to round out and reach maturity, and then should last until the turn of the century. If you want a more seductive wine, the Clos St.-Denis is velvety, deep in color, richly fruity, and offers a generous, lush mouthful of hedonistic burgundy. The excellent Bonnes Mares, which is Lignier's best wine in 1987, seems to be the synthesis of both the more rustic, tannic Clos de la Roche and the more flattering and precocious-tasting Clos St.-Denis. Bonnes Mares is medium to full bodied, concentrated, and rich with an expansive Pinot fruitiness and a long finish. It will be ideal to drink between 1991–2000.

HUBERT LIGNIER (MOREY ST.-DENIS)

1987 CHARMES-CHAMBERTIN	87
1987 CLOS DE LA ROCHE	89
1987 MOREY ST.-DENIS PREMIER CRU	85

Hubert Lignier's 1987s are excellent. His Morey St.-Denis Premier Cru shows the wonderful color typical of his vineyards, a big, plummy, berry-scented bouquet, good acidity, medium body, and a fine, well-balanced finish. Ideally, the wine needs another 1 to 2 years in the bottle to develop more nuances, but it should last until 1996–1997. Lignier is now producing tiny quantities of Charmes-Chambertin (he proudly told me that he had acquired a whopping one-tenth of a hectare, about one-fourth of an acre). His Charmes-Chambertin has a deep ruby color and a rich, sweet, expansive palate. It shows a glorious opulence for the vintage and has a seductive, lush finish. It is medium to full bodied, has surprising concentration, and should drink beautifully until 1996–1997. It is a charming mouthful of wine. Even better is his fabulous Clos de la Roche, which just misses being outstanding. Slightly less profound in color than the Charmes-Chambertin, it shows a great bouquet of plummy fruit combined with exotic spices and toasty new oak. On the palate, the wine offers super ripeness, splendid richness, medium to full body, and a long finish. It is ideal for drinking over the next decade. All of Lignier's wines are bottled unfined and unfiltered.

HENRI MAGNIEN ET FILS (GEVREY-CHAMBERTIN)

1987 GEVREY-CHAMBERTIN	78
1987 GEVREY-CHAMBERTIN LES CAZETIERS	77
1987 GEVREY-CHAMBERTIN PREMIER CRU	80

This estate produces light, elegant wines. However, tastings of the 1987s and 1988s suggest that the Magnien family are simply overproducing their vineyards with little care for selection or the ultimate quality of the wine. There is no reason these wines should be light, watery, and insipid. Unfortunately, the 1988s look to be even worse—thin, diluted, and inexcusable given the quality of the vintage. At a time when most of the underachievers in Burgundy are beginning to make better wine, particularly in view of the potentially high prices and demand for quality burgundy, it is a shame that the Domaine Henri Magnien, with such excellent holdings, continues to live in the past.

DOMAINE MALDANT (CHOREY-LÈS-BEAUNE)

1987 ALOXE-CORTON PREMIER CRU	83
1987 CHOREY-LÈS-BEAUNE	83
1987 CORTON LES RÉNARDES	86

In 1987 this estate produced a decently fruity, straightforward Chorey-Lès-Beaune, an elegant, pretty, pleasant, light- to medium-bodied Aloxe-Corton Premier Cru, and an excellent Corton Les Rénardes. The latter wine shows real depth, structure, and intensity. It is capable of lasting until 1994–1996.

CHÂTEAU DE MALTROYE (CHASSAGNE-MONTRACHET)

1987 CHASSAGNE-MONTRACHET BOUDRIOTTES	84
1987 CHASSAGNE-MONTRACHET- CLOS DE CHÂTEAU MALTROYE	86
1987 CHASSAGNE-MONTRACHET-CLOS ST.-JEAN	85

This beautiful estate in Chassagne-Montrachet is renowned for its excellent white wines. They have been consistently good since the early eighties. The quality of the red wines is often overlooked. The 1987 red wines are certainly among the better reds from the village of Chassagne-Montrachet. There is an elegant, cherry-scented, fresh, charming Chassagne-Montrachet Boudriottes, which is ideal for drinking before 1992–1993. A bit richer, riper, and fuller is the more tannic and structured Chassagne-Montrachet-Clos St.-Jean. However, my favorite Château de Maltroye red wine in 1987 is their Chassagne-Montrachet-Clos de Château Maltroye. It has an impressive deep color, a beautifully perfumed bouquet of spicy new oak, bing cherries, and flowers. On the palate the wine is supple, expansive, offers good depth and ripeness, and should drink beautifully until 1993–1995.

JEAN-PHILIPPE MARCHAND (GEVREY-CHAMBERTIN)

1987 CHARMES-CHAMBERTIN	89
1987 GEVREY-CHAMBERTIN	83
1987 GEVREY-CHAMBERTIN LES CHERBAUDES	80
1987 GEVREY-CHAMBERTIN LES COMBOTTES	88
1987 MOREY ST.-DENIS	82
1987 MOREY ST.-DENIS-CLOS DES ORMES	87

In the 1980s, young Jean-Philippe Marchand made considerable progress in his winemaking, and his new vintages increasingly demonstrate class, complexity, and style. He has even stopped filtering his wines. This is an important domaine with impressive vineyard holdings. The Morey St.-Denis is a straightforward, fruity, medium-bodied wine that is well made and pleasant, but is lacking in complexity. It is ideal for drinking now. The Morey St.-Denis-Clos des Ormes displays an excellent use of spicy new oak, has a big, ripe, plummy, exotic bouquet, concentrated, fleshy, Pinot fruit, and a long finish. It will be delicious for drinking over the next decade. Marchand's wines from his own village, Gevrey-Chambertin, include a rather high-acid, lean, angular, and taut Gevrey-Chambertin, and a Gevrey-Chambertin Les Cherbaudes that tastes hard edged and tough. Marchand's 1987 Gevrey-Chambertin Les Combottes is a beautiful wine. It offers a voluptuous texture and a rich, aromatic, complex bouquet of plums, exotic spices, and toasty new oak. Rich, velvety, and hedonistic, it is a seductive burgundy. The Charmes-Chambertin has an expansive palate, slightly deeper color, and a very penetrating perfume of red and black fruits, spicy new oak, and exotic spices. This amply endowed, lush, concentrated wine should drink beautifully between 1992–1999.

DOMAINE MAUME (GEVREY-CHAMBERTIN)

1987 GEVREY-CHAMBERTIN	80
1987 GEVREY-CHAMBERTIN LAVAUX ST.-JACQUES	83
1987 MAZIS-CHAMBERTIN	88

I did not get to see the whole range of 1987s from Domaine Maume, but those I did taste included a straightforward, simple, compact but well-colored, ripe, fruity Gevrey-Chambertin, a fuller-scaled, spicy, meaty, robust, leathery Gevrey-Chambertin Lavaux St.-Jacques, and an excellent rich, ripe, concentrated, surprisingly muscular and tannic Mazis-Chambertin. This wine could well prove to be one of the longer-lived wines of the vintage. I would not touch either of the latter two wines until at least 1993–1994; they should last for a decade thereafter.

DOMAINE MÉO-CAMUZET (VOSNE-ROMANÉE)

1987 CLOS VOUGEOT	88
1987 CORTON	87
1987 NUITS ST.-GEORGES	87
1987 NUITS ST.-GEORGES LES BOUDOTS	?
1987 NUITS ST.-GEORGES LES MURGERS	90
1987 RICHEBOURG	90
1987 VOSNE-ROMANÉE	85
1987 VOSNE-ROMANÉE AUX BRÛLÉES	90
1987 VOSNE-ROMANÉE LES CHAUMES	79
1987 VOSNE-ROMANÉE CROS PARANTOUX	87

The Domaine Méo-Camuzet used to practice a light polishing filtration prior to bottling. Monsieur Méo, the proprietor, stopped this practice in 1988 as he decided that filtration was damaging the wines' bouquets and flavor intensity. This superb estate turned out excellent wines in 1987 that are significantly better than their 1986s, and not far off the mark of their glorious 1988s. They are just another example of how delicious, clean, ripe, and tasty the 1987s have turned out to be in many of Burgundy's best cellars. The Vosne-Romanée is straightforward, soft, and light, yet lacks the flavor dimension and complexity of most of the other wines. If you want to see just how good a Villages wine can be, I highly recommend the Nuits St.-Georges, which shows wonderful ripeness, a sweet, expansive, round palate, and amazing complexity and length for a wine of its class. I cannot recall ever tasting a generic Nuits St.-Georges this seductive and rich. Both of these wines should be consumed between now and 1993–1994. As for the Premiers Crus from Méo-Camuzet, the Vosne-Romanée Les Chaumes (made from Méo's youngest parcel of vines) is a pretty wine with light, elegant flavors, but little concentration. It also falls off on the palate. The Vosne-Romanée aux Brûlées is exceptional. I have tasted it three times since it was bottled, twice rating it a 90 and once an 88. This is a wine of surprising power, richness, length, and concentration. After tasting this wine, no one would ever believe that 1987 is a so-called off year for red burgundy. It should drink well for over a decade, and displays a rich, smoky, roasted, ripe berry-scented bouquet and long, velvety, rich flavors. In comparison, the Vosne-Romanée Cros Parantoux is more tannic, but still shares the same ripeness and richness of fruit, very good color, and the potential to age well until 1994–1998. Méo has some outstanding Premier Cru vineyards in Nuits St.-Georges, and his Nuits St.-Georges Les Murgers is the most exotic wine in the Méo stable. An intense bouquet of smoky, roasted, rich, black cherry fruit is married beautifully with lush, ripe, heady flavors, medium to full body, and soft smooth tannins. These all combine for a totally hedonistic red burgundy drinking experience. It is a gorgeous wine to drink now, and while I am tempted to say it will not keep, wines like this often have the cunning ability to age for 6 to 7 years. It is curious, but the 1987 Nuits St.-Georges Les Murgers reminds me somewhat of the 1985 Clos Vougeot from this domaine. As for the Nuits St.-Georges Les Boudots, my tasting notes were a bit inconsistent both from the cask and after the wine was bottled. My highest rating was 87 points, but even then I noted it had some relatively hard, tough tannins in the finish that could prove problematic if the fruit fades. Out of the bottle, the wine does seem to be the lightest among the Premiers Crus from Méo-Camuzet, and I wonder if the fruit is there to balance out the tannins and high acids. Given the great success Méo had with his other wines in 1987, perhaps my impression is misleadingly conservative. Among the Grands Crus, the Corton is a big, deep, hard wine. It needs at least 5 years in the bottle to round out, but shows impressive color and plenty of muscle and depth. At present, I prefer the more hedonistic, velvety, rich, complex Richebourg, which has a big, oaky, vanillin-scented bouquet, and deep, round, supple, intense flavors. It is all that a Richebourg should be, although in the competition for the top wines from this fabulous Grand Cru vineyard in the Côte de Nuits, Méo's Richebourg will have to take a back seat to the outstanding Richebourgs made by Jean Gros, the Domaine de la Romanée-Conti, and Gros Frère et Soeur.

ALAIN MICHELOT (NUITS ST.-GEORGES)

1987 NUITS ST.-GEORGES	78
1987 NUITS ST.-GEORGES LES CAILLES	85
1987 NUITS ST.-GEORGES LES CHAIGNOTS	88
1987 NUITS ST.-GEORGES LES CHAMPS PERDRIX	87
1987 NUITS ST.-GEORGES LES PORRETS ST.-GEORGES	85
1987 NUITS ST.-GEORGES LA RICHEMONE	82
1987 NUITS ST.-GEORGES LES SAINT-GEORGES	87
1987 NUITS ST.-GEORGES LES VAUCRAINS	84

Michelot's 1987s are extremely elegant, flavorful, supple wines that are representative, not only of the vintage, but also of the different vineyards in Nuits St.-Georges. His 1987 Nuits St.-Georges is a correct, simple, monolithic wine with no great character or dimension, adequate for uncritical quaffing. There are some great wines from the Premier Cru La Richemone vineyard, but Michelot's 1987 seems light, although elegant, fruity, and totally mature. His wines give the impression that his parcel of La Richemone is in young vines. Perhaps that also explains why his Les Vaucrains is not better. The 1987 Les Vaucrains is a bit deeper than La Richemone, but it still comes across as a relatively light, medium-bodied, soft, forward wine that should be drunk by 1992–1993. Michelot's Les Cailles is more tannic and slightly spicier and deeper. Ideally it needs another 1 to 2 years in the bottle. It should certainly last for 7 to 10 years. The other wines are a bit richer and fuller, including a well-balanced, stylish, medium-bodied Les Porrets St.-Georges, and an extremely rich, intense, complex, even profound Les Champs Perdrix. Not surprisingly, this wine comes from some of the oldest vines Michelot owns. Unfortunately, he only produces 100 cases of this sensational wine. His Nuits St.-Georges Les Saint-Georges has the most expansive palate of all his 1987s with broad, supple, sweet, plummy fruit, a very fragrant, perfumed character, and a lush, opulent finish. It is ideal for drinking before 1994–1995. The earthy, spicy, peppery Nuits St.-Georges Les Chaignots is similarly impressive and quite concentrated, but is a bit more tannic and marked by the scent of truffles. It is a large-scaled wine with more body and tannin than any of the other Michelot wines. Ideally, I would drink it between 1991–2000.

DOMAINE MOILLARD (NUITS ST.-GEORGES)

1987 DOMAINE THOMAS-MOILLARD NUITS ST.-GEORGES-CLOS DE TOREY	87
1987 DOMAINE THOMAS-MOILLARD VOSNE-ROMANÉE LES MALCONSORTS	85
1987 GEVREY-CHAMBERTIN	69
1987 MOILLARD-FIXIN-CLOS DE LA PERRIÈRE	78

I did not taste the entire line of Moillard's 1987s, but this huge *négociant* should be taken seriously, particularly with respect to their domaine-bottled wines, now carrying the label of Domaine Thomas-Moillard. The Gevrey-Chambertin has a stemmy, vegetal nose that made it unappealing and disappointing. The Fixin-Clos de la Perrière smelled of peanut butter, had rather hard flavors, and intrusive quantities of new oak. One of this firm's top wines, from the Domaine Thomas-Moillard, was a very spicy, oaky, round, ripe, and fruity Vosne-Romanée Les Malconsorts. It does not compare to their great 1985, but it is certainly good, and ideal for drinking over the next 5 to 6 years. The best wine is the Nuits St.-Georges-Clos de Torey. It offers rich, rather massive black fruit flavors, tons of toasty new oak, and plenty of alcohol in the finish. What it lacked in finesse it makes up for in power and intensity. I would drink this rather large-scaled red burgundy by 1996–1997.

MOINE-HUDELOT (CHAMBOLLE-MUSIGNY)

1987 BONNES MARES	85
1987 CHAMBOLLE-MUSIGNY	77
1987 CHAMBOLLE-MUSIGNY LES AMOUREUSES	85
1987 CHAMBOLLE-MUSIGNY LES CHARMES	83
1987 CHAMBOLLE-MUSIGNY PREMIER CRU	82
1987 MUSIGNY	86

I am not against filtration, as it is sometimes necessary. In many vintages where the wines fail to fall brilliant naturally, they cannot be put in the bottle cloudy, and therefore must be filtered. Excessive filtration, however, troubles me greatly. Pinot Noir, given its fragility and intrinsic delicacy, cannot tolerate a vigorous filtration. Daniel Moine's 1987s showed much more depth and ripeness from cask. While he has turned out good to very good wines in 1987, all of them taste as if they have been overfiltered. His Chambolle-Musigny is light and falls off on the palate. The Chambolle-Musigny Premier Cru is similar, but has more middle depth and length. The Chambolle-Musigny Les Charmes has slightly more depth yet is still relatively light, soft, supple, and elegant. The Chambolle-Musigny Les Amoureuses exhibits a soft, supple, smooth fruitiness that is attractive and appealing, but one wishes there were more depth and length. The Bonnes Mares would be very good if it were judged as a Premier Cru, but it is one of the great Grands Crus of Burgundy and should have more complexity and flavor dimension. The wine has moderate ripeness and a soft finish. The Grand Cru Musigny is Daniel Moine's best wine in 1987. Very light and medium bodied, its appeal is in its lovely, aromatic, berry-scented, spicy, floral bouquet. The flavors exhibit light tannins and adequate acidity; the wine should provide excellent drinking if consumed before 1991–1992. In fact, all of Moine-Hudelot's 1987s should be consumed immediately. Someone needs to give Monsieur Moine a heart-to-heart talk about the dangers of excessive filtration.

DOMAINE MONGEARD-MUGNERET (VOSNE-ROMANÉE)

1987 CLOS VOUGEOT	88
1987 ECHÉZEAUX VIEILLES VIGNES	90
1987 FIXIN	83
1987 GRANDS ECHÉZEAUX	90
1987 RICHEBOURG	89
1987 SAVIGNY-LÈS-BEAUNE	82
1987 VOSNE-ROMANÉE	82
1987 VOSNE-ROMANÉE LES SUCHOTS	87

When I saw Monsieur Mongeard in September, 1989, he was hesitant about showing his 1987s. He explained that they had just been bottled and he was concerned they would not show well. I felt the wines at the top end were superb, and if they get any better he will have a vintage that is probably every bit as good as 1985. In 1987, he added Savigny-

Lès-Beaune to his portfolio, and it is a light yet smooth, supple, berry-scented wine with good flavor and ripeness. It should be consumed by 1991–1993. I thought his 1987 Fixin had a more muscular personality and deeper color. As for the 1987 Vosne-Romanée, it is a pleasant, straightforward, tasty wine, but is light and ready to drink. There is a quantum leap in quality with the Vosne-Romanée Les Suchots. It displays a gorgeous, toasty, roasted bouquet of plummy fruit, fleshy, opulent flavors, and a smooth, silky finish. It is ideal for drinking between now and 1994–1995. The Echézeaux Vieilles Vignes is outstanding, and has the additional virtue of being ready to drink. It should last for a decade, but it is difficult to resist immediate consumption of this immensely seductive, fragrant, velvety, medium- to full-bodied wine with layers of red and black fruits. The Grands Echézeaux is similarly superb, a bit more structured, and in need of 1 to 2 more years in the bottle to reach its full potential. Rich and full with layers of ripe, concentrated, berry fruit, it has a lot of tannin and structure for a 1987. I agree with Monsieur Mongeard that the Grands Echézeaux is frequently his very best wine. In contrast, the Clos Vougeot is silky smooth, totally ready to drink, but capable of lasting until 1994–1996 given its excellent depth, ripeness, and richness. Once again, it is hard to resist because of its explosive bouquet of berry and plum-like fruit, toasty vanillin oak, and flavors that match the gorgeous nose. The Richebourg is slightly less concentrated than the Grands Echézeaux, and seems less complex than the Echézeaux. Nevertheless, it is a rich, ripe, full-bodied wine with excellent color, layers of extract, and the potential to drink well until 1996–1997.

DOMAINE RENÉ MONNIER (MEURSAULT)

1987 BEAUNE LES TOUSSAINTS	77
1987 CÔTE DE BEAUNE LES FUSSIÈRES	77
1987 POMMARD LES VIGNOTS	77
1987 VOLNAY CLOS DES CHÊNES	82

Monnier has a very good reputation in Burgundy, but as my scores attest I was unimpressed with his red wines from the 1987 vintage. They were generally light, agreeably supple, but lacking fruit and charm. Both the Beaune Les Toussaints and Pommard Les Vignots were entirely too tannic, tough textured, and hard for their meager concentration and light framework.

DOMAINE MONTHÉLIE-DOUHAIRET (MONTHÉLIE)

1987 MONTHÉLIE	83
1987 MONTHÉLIE LES DURESSES	83
1987 POMMARD LES CHANLINS	85
1987 VOLNAY CHAMPANS	84

The wines made at this domaine by the octogenarian, Madame Douhairet, tend to be rather old-style, rustic, chunky wines with a great deal of tannin and body. Although the wines often have aromas that are not terribly clean, the 1987s do not seem to have that problem. The Monthélie is soft, displays good, clean, tarry, berry fruit, and should be consumed by 1993–1994. The Premier Cru, the Monthélie Les Duresses, has a great deal more tannin to it, a certain toughness and hardness, and while it will no doubt last longer than the Monthélie, I do not find it any better. As for the Volnay Champans, it is an extremely tannic, robust, old-style wine that seems to have as much tannin as any 1987 wine I tasted from the Côte d'Or. It is well made, and should ideally be consumed between 1992–1997. However, it is possible that the tannins are excessive for the amount of fruit. Madame Douhairet's best wine in 1987 is the Pommard Les Chanlins. Ripe with a robust, exuberant personality, this old-style wine had plenty of depth, tannin, and body; it should easily last for up to a decade.

DOMAINE ALBERT MOROT (BEAUNE)

1987 BEAUNE LES BRESSANDES	85
1987 BEAUNE LES MARCONNETS	85
1987 BEAUNE LES TEURONS	86
1987 SAVIGNY-VERGELESSES LA BATAILLIÈRE	85

As Mademoiselle Choppin poetically puts it, "my Beaunes drink like Vosnes." Her 1987s are certainly better than her rather lean, tannic 1986s, but I doubt they will equal the quality of her superb 1988s. In any event, these wines remain very reasonably priced, particularly given their aging potential. The Savigny-Vergelesses La Bataillière has a big, spicy, ripe, oaky, berry-scented bouquet, excellent depth, good, crisp acidity, medium body, and the potential to last for 10 to 12 years. The Beaune Les Bressandes showed spectacularly well from the cask, but seems to have disappeared since it was bottled. I suspect my score will be considered conservative in about 5 to 6 years' time. Currently, the wine shows plenty of depth and ripeness but high acidity and a rather closed, tough, almost impenetrable style. I would not touch it before 1993 or 1994. The Beaune Les Marconnets is clearly richer, deeper, and more flattering. It has surprising body and muscle for a 1987. Very deep in color, it shows a good lashing of toasty, smoky oak, plenty of pure black cherry flavors, and a long, tannic finish. It should be at its best between 1995–2005. Mademoiselle Chopin's Beaune Les Teurons is by far the biggest wine she made in 1987. It reveals plenty of oak, a great deal of body, excellent concentration and depth, as well as enough tannin to preclude enjoyable drinking until at least 1992–1993. If you are looking for old-style, impeccably made, extremely age-worthy Premiers Crus from the Côte de Beaune, look no further than this superbly run domaine.

DOMAINE GEORGES MUGNERET (VOSNE-ROMANÉE)

1987 CHAMBOLLE-MUSIGNY LES FEUSSELOTTES	88
1987 CLOS VOUGEOT	90
1987 ECHÉZEAUX	89
1987 NUITS ST.-GEORGES LES CHAIGNOTS	86
1987 RUCHOTTES-CHAMBERTIN	90
1987 VOSNE-ROMANÉE	84

The 1987s from Georges Mugneret are brilliant examples of the full potential of this vintage. The Chambolle-Musigny Les Feusselottes is a rich, ripe, round, velvety, medium-bodied wine bursting with red fruits, and a smooth, supple finish. It shows a lovely touch of toasty new oak (50%–60% new oak barrels are used at this domaine), soft tannins, and plenty of ripe, pure Pinot fruit. The Clos Vougeot is quite outstanding and could easily be confused with a 1985. It further supports the view that 1987 is probably the most underrated vintage of red burgundy this decade. It has a deep ruby color, an expansive, penetrating bouquet of intense berry fruit and spicy oak. In the mouth, the wine has a lavish richness, medium body, and layers of supple Pinot Noir fruit. Like the Chambolle-Musigny, it is certainly drinkable now, but it has a bit more structure, body, and tannin, and could easily last until 1996–1997. As for the Echézeaux, it is slightly lighter in color (although it still possesses a good medium-ruby hue). In both its bouquet and flavors, my notes suggested that this is the quintessentially elegant, complex, Grand Cru red burgundy. It has broad, expansive, supple flavors, soft, moderate tannins, and just enough toasty vanillin oak to give it com-

plexity without overwhelming the delicate fruit. It is drinking beautifully now, but it should last until 1994–1996. The Nuits St.-Georges Les
Chaignots has a more earthy, spicy character with less fragrance than
the Echézeaux and Clos Vougeot, as well as less of their pure, intense,
red berry character. It is medium bodied, and has slightly tougher and
harder-edged tannins. For that reason, I would cellar it until 1990–1991
before consuming it; it has the potential to last until 1996–1997. The
Ruchottes-Chambertin is again superb in 1987; it is certainly the biggest wine among Mugneret's 1987s. It has quite a bit of tannin, and a
big, projected bouquet of leather, spices, and black fruits. There is also
a real *terroir* character to the wine that the French would no doubt call
sauvage (meaning savage). This is not meant in a pejorative sense. The
Ruchottes-Chambertin is usually one of the great wines from this domaine, and the 1987 is a close rival to the sublime, otherworldly 1985.
It should be the Mugnerets' best 1987 candidate for extended cellaring.
It will reach its peak somewhere between 1993 and 2002. Last, the 1987
Vosne-Romanée has straightforward, ripe Pinot fruit, light to medium
body, and soft tannins. It is a good example of a Villages wine. The
1987s from the Domaine Georges Mugneret are high-class wines and
should be sought out by any connoisseur and lover of red burgundy.

GÉRARD MUGNERET (VOSNE-ROMANÉE)

1987 ECHÉZEAUX	87
1987 NUITS ST.-GEORGES LES BOUDOTS	85

Gérard Mugneret, the nephew of the late Dr. Georges Mugneret, tends
to produce relatively tannic, full-bodied burgundies that need some
time to show their full character. I tasted two of his 1987s and both
were atypically backward and filled with tannin. The Nuits-St.-Georges
Les Boudots was more supple and forward with excellent fruit, moderate tannins, and the potential to age until 1994–1997. The Echézeaux
was extremely tannic but was also concentrated and long. These are
relatively muscular, old-style, intense wines that surprised me because
of their tannic ferocity. I would not drink them before 1993–1994.

DOMAINE J. F. MUGNIER-CHÂTEAU DE CHAMBOLLE-MUSIGNY (CHAMBOLLE-MUSIGNY)

1987 CHAMBOLLE-MUSIGNY	85
1987 CHAMBOLLE-MUSIGNY LES AMOUREUSES	89
1987 CHAMBOLLE-MUSIGNY LES FUÉES	87
1987 LE MUSIGNY	89

Monsieur Mugnier of the Château de Chambolle-Musigny produces relatively light, soft, velvety wines that are marked by obvious aromas and
flavors of toasty, smoky new oak. I have noted that some tasters find
the oakiness intrusive. While I would agree that there is a great deal of
oak to these wines, I do not think it detracts from the overall appeal
and quality of this estate's excellent wines. Nevertheless, I note it
because some consumers prefer less oak. The Chambolle-Musigny offers a wonderfully elegant, berry-scented bouquet bursting with fruit
and spicy, toasty oak. The wine is fully mature and should be consumed
by 1991–1992. It is not a blockbuster, but it expresses the silky elegance of Pinot Noir very well. The Premier Cru Chambolle-Musigny
Les Fuées is more seductive with an opulence to its fruit, medium body,
excellent ripeness, and a silky, smooth texture that seems to be a
hallmark of the wines from this domaine. It will not last past 1995–
1996, but for drinking over the near term it is difficult to surpass. The
Chambolle-Musigny Les Amoureuses is a bit more structured and has
slightly more stuffing and length than the previous two wines. Again, it
is marked by a very noticeable sojourn in toasty new oak barrels, has a
ripe berry, smoky bouquet, gorgeous layers of fruit, and a silky finish.
It should be consumed by 1994–1996. The Musigny is a larger-framed
wine. Ultimately, it may not turn out to be better than the Les Amoureuses, but it is certainly a wine that could eventually be outstanding.
There is an abundance of lavishly rich, ripe berry fruit, medium body,
good fresh acidity (another characteristic of the 1987s), and plenty of
length. The wine, at least from an aromatic and textural standpoint,
shows less precociousness and openness than Mugnier's two Premiers
Crus. These are wines to buy only if you intend to drink them over the
near term, as their aging potential is limited.

ANDRÉ MUSSY (POMMARD)

1987 BEAUNE LES EPENOTTES	86
1987 BEAUNE LES MONTREVENOTS	86
1987 POMMARD	80
1987 POMMARD LES EPENOTS	87
1987 POMMARD PREMIER CRU	85
1987 VOLNAY	85

André Mussy's 1987s are less fat and concentrated than his excellent
1986s (probably the best wines made in the Côte de Beaune in that

difficult vintage). His 1987 Beaune Les Epenottes shows a gorgeously fragrant, ripe cherry-scented bouquet, has tasty, supple, silky flavors, medium body, and should be consumed by 1993–1994. The Beaune Les Montrevenots shares much of the same velvety character and lush fruitiness, but has a bit more tannin to it. While drinkable now, it should outlast the Epenottes by several years. I felt the Pommard was a bit light and lacking some concentration, but it is certainly an adequate, competent example of a generic wine from this appellation. The Pommard Premier Cru was fat, ripe, and tasty with excellent fruit, medium body, and soft tannins in the finish—clearly a wine to drink between now and 1993–1994. Mussy's Volnay is his most rustic and coarsely styled wine. Although it had plenty of fruit and depth, it did seem to be a different style of wine. His best wine in 1987 is no surprise. The Pommard Les Epenots is the most structured as well as the most tannic wine of the Mussy stable; it has excellent rich, ripe fruit, plenty of depth, a good deal of soft tannins, and plenty of length. It is another excellent effort from this superb small domaine in Pommard.

PHILIPPE NADDEF (COUCHEY)

1987 BOURGOGNE ROUGE	82
1987 GEVREY-CHAMBERTIN	83
1987 GEVREY-CHAMBERTIN LES CAZETIERS	87
1987 GEVREY-CHAMBERTIN LES CHAMPEAUX	85
1987 MARSANNAY	83
1987 MAZIS-CHAMBERTIN	87

Young Philippe Naddef has an increasing following for his wines, particularly his top three wines, the Gevrey-Chambertin Les Champeaux, Gevrey-Chambertin Les Cazetiers, and his Mazis-Chambertin. He is a serious winemaker. His 1987 Bourgogne Rouge is light yet elegant, pleasant, and straightforward. The Marsannay is similarly styled, perhaps more compact, but cleanly made and adequate for current drinking. The Gevrey-Chambertin displays attractive, elegant fruit, nice spice, a soft texture, and 2 to 3 years of further drinkability. Among the Premiers Crus, the Gevrey-Chambertin Les Champeaux offers greater ripeness, more length and fullness, some attractive flesh and berry fruit, and a smooth finish. It should be drunk by 1992–1993. In many vintages (1987 and 1988 for example) Naddef's Gevrey-Chambertin Les Cazetiers is as good as his Mazis-Chambertin. In fact, in 1988 I would argue that his Les Cazetiers is better than his Mazis-Chambertin. In 1987, the two are similarly styled wines revealing excellent color, fragrant bouquets, excellent depth of ripe Pinot fruit, plenty of spicy new oak, and medium to full body. The Mazis has more tannin, but for the difference in price I would buy the Les Cazetiers. Both should drink well until 1995–1996.

DOMAINE PARIGOT (HAUTES CÔTES)

1987 BEAUNE LES GRÈVES	82
1987 POMMARD LES CHARMOTS	72?

This domaine has adequate raw materials to make sound, even delicious ripe, fruity, red burgundy. Yet, the producer is enamored by new oak. His excessive use of new oak has resulted in wines that taste coarse, too oaky, and have a texture in the mouth not unlike sawdust. While the wines have plenty of ripeness and density, they are simply overwhelmed by their aging in oak casks.

JEAN-MARC PAVELOT (SAVIGNY-LÈS-BEAUNE)

1987 SAVIGNY-LÈS-BEAUNE	82
1987 SAVIGNY-LÈS-BEAUNE LES GUETTES	84

Jean-Marc Pavelot is one of the best producers from the underrated and often ignored appellation of Savigny-Lès-Beaune. He is not, however, in the same class as Maurice Ecard or Patrick Bize. His wines are light yet stylish and elegantly crafted, displaying a strawberry and cherry fruitiness, supple textures, and enough tannin to age for 5 to 8 years. The 1987s, while light and high in acidity, are, nevertheless, well made, fresh, clean examples of good wines. Both of these wines should be drunk between now and 1991–1994.

PERNIN-ROSSIN (VOSNE-ROMANÉE)

1987 NUITS ST.-GEORGES LA RICHEMONE	87
1987 VOSNE-ROMANÉE LES BEAUX MONTS	87

Pernin is another disciple of the well-known oenologist Guy Accad. While several of Accad's clients such as Georges Chicotot and Jacky

Confuron have proved their wines can stand the test of time, I have serious doubts about the aging potential of Pernin's wines. Although I have rated Pernin's wines highly in the past, I have seen far too many examples from the 1982, 1983, and 1985 vintages where they lost their color and collapsed in the bottle for no apparent reason. Perhaps the 1982 and 1983 vintages could explain the premature demise of Pernin's wines in those vintages, but 1985 is different. I thought these two 1987s were impressively colored, rich, ripe, concentrated wines, but I hope they do not follow the pattern of their predecessors. The Vosne-Romanée Les Beaux Monts has the typical Accad dark ruby/purple color, with an intense, rich, rather straightforward, monolithic bouquet of very jammy berry fruit. On the palate the wine is ripe, deep, and concentrated, but I cannot tell if it will age well. The Nuits St.-Georges La Richemone is similar to the Vosne-Romanée Les Beaux Monts. It is ruby/purple, almost black, with superb ripeness bordering on jamminess, medium to full body, and a long, lush finish. It shows no sign of falling apart. Perhaps Pernin's problems with color and losing fruit are totally unrelated to following Guy Accad's method of cold maceration prior to the fermentation. It is too soon to know, but it is something to keep in mind if you are going to invest in these wines.

DOMAINE DE LA POUSSE D'OR (VOLNAY)

1987 POMMARD LES JAROLIÈRES	77
1987 SANTENAY-CLOS TAVANNES	78
1987 VOLNAY LES CAILLERETS	79
1987 VOLNAY LES CAILLERETS-CLOS DES 60 OUVRÉES	80
1987 VOLNAY-CLOS DE LA BOUSSE D'OR	81

As in other recent vintages, the 1987s from the Domaine de la Pousse d'Or taste stripped and eviscerated. There is no doubt that proprietor Gérald Potel's decision to filter his wines in 1979 has had some effect on the quality, but I suspect the problem may be more than just filtration. He may also have excessive yields although Potel steadfastly denies this. The 1987s are similar to the 1986s. They are lean and hard with high acidity, and lack charm and grace. One should not criticize burgundy for its light color, because often Pinot Noir does not render deeply colored wines, but these wines possess a suspiciously shallow color, and the tannins are excessively elevated considering the concentration of fruit. Great vineyards such as the Volnay-Clos de la Bousse d'Or and Volnay Les Caillerets-Clos des 60 Ouvrées are capable of producing wines with greater ripeness, richness and character.

MICHEL PRUNIER (AUXEY-DURESSES)

1987 AUXEY-DURESSES-CLOS DU VAL	84
1987 AUXEY-DURESSES PREMIER CRU	82
1987 BEAUNE LES SIZIES	77
1987 VOLNAY LES CAILLERETS	85

Prunier's 1987s were not as successful as expected. In 1987, his best wine is the Volnay Les Caillerets. It has ripe, long, rustic tannins, and a rich, berry fruitiness. Ideally, it needs several years in the bottle to round out, but it should last until 1996–1997. I found his other 1987s to be a bit attenuated, lean, and hard. For example, his Beaune Les Sizies, normally a winner here, seemed to possess too much tannin for its meager fruitiness. Both his Premiers Crus from Auxey-Duresses, including his excellent Clos du Val, were rather tannic and hard, but had some fruit.

BERNARD RION PÈRE ET FILS (VOSNE-ROMANÉE)

1987 BOURGOGNE ROUGE	79
1987 CHAMBOLLE-MUSIGNY LES ECHÉZEAUX	86
1987 CLOS VOUGEOT	90
1987 NUITS ST.-GEORGES	83
1987 NUITS ST.-GEORGES LES MURGERS	90
1987 VOSNE-ROMANÉE LES CHAUMES	89

Bernard Rion made outstanding 1987s. He considers them to be the finest wines he has ever produced. His yields were very small so he increased the percentage of new oak. The results are splendidly concentrated wines, even in comparison with the very best 1985s. His top 1987s are rich, tannic, and potentially long lived. Bernard Rion's style is totally different from that of the other famous Rions, Daniel and Patrice. Daniel and Patrice Rion's style delivers pure, clean, very forward, precocious fruit to wines that are easy to understand and flattering to drink young. Bernard Rion's wines are much more muscular and concentrated. While the Bourgogne Rouge is straightforward, it has excellent acidity and deep color. It may actually improve in the bottle with several years of aging. The Nuits St.-Georges is a big, spicy, deeply colored wine with excellent fruit, a robust texture, and plenty of tannin in the finish. It ideally needs another 1 to 2 years in the bottle to shed its tannins. The Chambolle-Musigny Les Echézeaux exhibits excellent depth, richness, surprisingly deep ruby color, medium to full body, and a long, powerful, muscular finish. This wine should be at its best between 1993 and 2002. The Vosne-Romanée-Les Chaumes is an impressively deep-colored, full-bodied wine with plenty of spicy, toasty new oak and black plums. On the palate it is a well-endowed, massive wine that may merit an outstanding rating in 2 or 3 years. It is a wine that should last until 1997–2000. Bernard Rion's great 1987s include his Nuits St.-Georges Les Murgers, which is a bit softer and more exotic than the Vosne-Romanée Les Chaumes. It is velvety and opulent on the palate with fabulous richness and length, medium to full body, and has a silky, smooth finish. Ideal to drink now, it should last until 1996–1997. Rion's Clos Vougeot is a classic example of how the best wines from the Grand Cru vineyard have the potential for longevity. It has an intense, even explosive berry fruitiness and is one of the darkest-colored wines I saw from the 1987 vintage. It is a tannic, full-bodied, powerful, rich, compelling wine that is atypically massive and intense for a 1987.

DOMAINE DANIEL ET PATRICE RION
(NUITS ST.-GEORGES)

1987 CHAMBOLLE-MUSIGNY AUX BEAUX BRUNS	87
1987 CLOS VOUGEOT	88
1987 CÔTE DE NUITS-VILLAGES	85
1987 NUITS ST.-GEORGES CLOS DES ARGILLIÈRES	86
1987 NUITS ST.-GEORGES LES GRANDS VIGNES	87
1987 NUITS ST.-GEORGES LES HAUTS PRULIERS	90
1987 NUITS ST.-GEORGES LES VIGNES RONDES	89
1987 VOSNE-ROMANÉE	74
1987 VOSNE-ROMANÉE LES BEAUX MONTS	86
1987 VOSNE-ROMANÉE LES CHAUMES	89

There are many growers in the Côte de Nuits who applaud the accomplishments of Patrice Rion. His wines are appreciated by both connoisseurs and inexperienced wine consumers. Rion's wines display a vivid, rich, ripe, pure, berry fruitiness, and just enough toasty oak (no more than 30% new oak barrels) to provide a measure of complexity and structure. All the 1987s share supple, seductive textures that provide great appeal. This estate made excellent 1985s, wonderful 1986s (a vintage where many producers failed), and has again turned out succulent, juicy, charming, and hedonistic 1987s. Even wines such as the generic Côte de Nuits-Villages offer round, generous, ripe berry flavors, and a smooth texture. The Nuits St.-Georges Les Grands Vignes is ripe with sweet, expansive, rich flavors, and is ideal for drinking over the next 6 to 7 years. Equally lush, supple, and elegant is the fragrant and perfumed Chambolle-Musigny aux Beaux Bruns. Many keen observers feel this Premier Cru vineyard merits Grand Cru status. My only disappointment was the rather stern, tannic, lean, undernourished Vosne-Romanée. Among the other Premiers Crus there is nothing but rich, ripe, lavish amounts of berry fruit, a good lashing of toasty oak, and textures that are sure to please the great majority of Burgundy enthusiasts. For example, the Vosne-Romanée Les Beaux Monts is ready to drink, shows excellent ripeness and depth, and should be consumed over the next 5 to 7 years. The Vosne-Romanée Les Chaumes is again a star in 1987. It is opulent, rich, and loaded with immensely satisfying berry flavors and spicy oak. It is drinkable now, but should last until 1996–1997. The Nuits St.-Georges Clos des Argillières displays more oak and is tougher textured. It has all the depth and ripeness of wines such as the Les Chaumes and Les Beaux Monts from Vosne-Romanée, so my score may be conservative. The Nuits St.-Georges Les Vignes Rondes, a specialty of this house, possesses excellent deep ruby color, a velvety texture, ripe fruit, and plenty of spicy oak. One of the two top wines of Patrice and Daniel Rion in 1987 is the Nuits St.-Georges Les Hauts Pruliers. Full bodied for a 1987, it has gobs of blackberry and plummy fruit, a strong lashing of vanilla-scented, toasty, smoky new oak, and long, rich, deep flavors with dazzling flavor depth and length. It is seductively smooth and approachable now. As for the Clos Vougeot, the only Grand Cru in the Rion stable, it is excellent with plenty of color, ripeness, and richness. However, it possesses more tannin and is clearly more closed and ageworthy than the other wines from Patrice and Daniel Rion. While some might criticize these wines as being too obvious and charming, most growers in Burgundy would love to be able to turn out wines with such immediate appeal. These wines have the depth and richness to age for 7 to 8 more years. They will not last for a decade, but for near-term consumption, these wines offer immense appeal.

DOMAINE DE LA ROMANÉE-CONTI (VOSNE-ROMANÉE)

1987 ECHÉZEAUX	90
1987 GRANDS ECHÉZEAUX	92
1987 RICHEBOURG	93
1987 ROMANÉE-CONTI	95
1987 ROMANÉE ST.-VIVANT	87
1987 LA TÂCHE	93

While both Aubert de Villaine and Lalou Bize-Leroy (the co-owners) believe their 1986s are slightly superior to their 1987s, I think it is really a matter of taste. Unquestionably the 1986s are more tannic, structured, and muscular wines than the 1987s. While the 1987s have a purity of fruit not dissimilar to the 1985s, they do not have the weight and concentration of the 1985s. They also have much less tannin than the 1986s, but slightly higher acidity. It will be interesting to see how all these wines evolve in the aging process. There can be no doubt that their 1987s are great wines with one possible exception—the Romanée St.-Vivant. It may turn out to be entirely too tannic for its own good, but time will tell. With respect to the other wines, the Echézeaux is as exciting as the 1986. More flattering and precocious in style, it shows excellent color, a lovely rich bouquet of plum-like fruit, plenty of spicy oak, relatively full body, and a long, crisp finish. It will be the first to mature among the domaine's wines, and should be ready by 1992–1993; it will age well for 15 or more years. In most vintages, the Grands Echézeaux is superior in quality to the Echézeaux. However, I am not sure that is true in 1987. When one compares the quality and price, the Grands Echézeaux is probably the good buy (if such a thing is appropriate to say) of the Domaine de la Romanée-Conti portfolio. In 1987 the Grands Echézeaux is slightly richer and fuller than the Echézeaux, but it is not appreciably superior. Deep dark ruby in color, with that exotic, penetrating, perfumed bouquet that only this domaine seems to attain, this full-bodied, rich, concentrated wine needs a good 4 to 5 years in the bottle to round into form. It should last for 15 or more years. It shows superb ripeness and richness for the vintage. I have already alluded to the fact that I feel that the Romanée St.-Vivant is too tannic and tastes extremely hard, tough, and lean. Admittedly I tasted it within 2 months of being bottled so perhaps it was in an awkward stage as a result of recent bottling. However, my notes on the wine out of cask also raised the same specter of the wine's being too tannic and hard for the amount of fruit. At the present time, this seems to be the only wine from the Domaine de la Romanée-Conti that is not profound or potentially superb. As for the Richebourg, it has large quantities of tannin, but it has the stuffing and huge concentration of fruit and ripeness to match. It is a very full-bodied, rich, super-concentrated wine that should last for several decades. I would not dare open a bottle until 1994–1995. It will be interesting to see how it evolves when compared with the superb 1986 they produced. Certainly both their 1986 and 1987 Richebourgs are not as profound as either the 1985 or 1988. As for the two titans of this domaine, La Tâche is again an extraordinary wine with a magical complexity and celestial quality that is difficult to articulate. I expect it will need to be cellared for at least 6 to 8 years—perhaps longer—to resolve all its tannins; it remains a fabulously concentrated, rich, full-bodied wine with good acidity, plenty of tannin, and remarkable length. It has the potential to last for 20 to 25 years. In many vintages it is difficult to say that the Romanée-Conti is the best wine produced at the Domaine de la Romanée-Conti, but in 1987 it is utterly compelling. My notes indicate that it is more evolved and precocious than either La Tâche, Richebourg, or Grands Echézeaux. Extremely concentrated, exotic, and sensationally perfumed, with its telltale bouquet of oriental spices, toasty vanillin oak, berry fruit, and plums, this wine had fabulous gingery, cinnamon flavors as well as astonishing length. It is one of the most unique tasting experiences in the world. It is all pleasure, finesse, complexity and richness, and my feeling is that it is clearly the best wine this domaine has made in 1987. There are 225 cases to be allocated throughout the world.

JACQUES ROSSIGNOL (VOLNAY)

1987 BEAUNE LES TEURONS   87

This is an excellent Beaune, and I am sure in a blind tasting with some of the top 1985s it could easily hold its own. Deep ruby in color, it has a well-developed, intense bouquet of jammy, berry fruit and spicy oak. On the palate the wine is broad, expansive, and velvety with a medium to full body and a long finish. The tannins are soft, suggesting that this wine can be drunk now, although I am sure additional nuances will emerge with another 1 to 2 years of aging.

JOSEPH ROTY (GEVREY-CHAMBERTIN)

1987 CHARMES-CHAMBERTIN   ?

1987 GEVREY-CHAMBERTIN LES CHAMPCHENYS   84

1987 GEVREY-CHAMBERTIN-CLOS PRIEUR	85
1987 GEVREY-CHAMBERTIN LES FONTENYS	86
1987 MARSANNAY	69
1987 MAZIS-CHAMBERTIN	?
1987 PINOT NOIR LES PRESSONIÈRES	75

When presented with fully mature, ripe grapes, Roty is as successful as any producer in Burgundy. When his grapes do not have as much ripeness, and the tannins or acidity need to be watched, the wines are often not as good as could be expected given his brilliance in the great years. Roty's 1987s, while clearly superior to his 1986s, are all marked by excessive amounts of new oak (100% new oak casks are frequently used). In vintages such as 1985, such high quantities of new oak can be employed, but in years such as 1987, where the fruit is more fragile, too much oak overwhelms a wine's subtleties. Roty's Pinot Noir Les Pressonières was vegetal and herbaceous, although soft and drinkable. The Marsannay was thin, high in acidity, and unappealing. The glories of the Domaine Joseph Roty are the wines from Gevrey-Chambertin. Les Champchenys showed ripeness and depth, and a smooth finish. Roty did not over-oak it in 1987, making it a wine that should be drunk by 1995–1996. The Gevrey-Chambertin-Clos Prieur offers generous amounts of toasty, smoky, vanillin oak, good, deep, ripe fruit, medium body, and a spicy, soft finish. It is ideal for drinking now and over the next 5 to 6 years. The Gevrey-Chambertin Les Fontenys is extremely oaky but has plenty of ripeness and richness. I have given it a good score, but if you do not like a lot of new toasty oak, this wine may not be as pleasing as my rating suggests. Last, the two Grands Crus, the Charmes-Chambertin and Mazis-Chambertin, may merit ratings in the mid-eighties, but I gave them question marks because I thought both of them had excruciatingly painful tannin levels, as well as intrusive quantities of oak. Together, these two characteristics obliterated my ability to find any fruit. Both had excellent color, ripeness, and depth. My experience with wines that are this tannic and oaky suggests that the fruit rarely ever emerges.

EMANUEL ROUGET (NUITS ST.-GEORGES)

1987 ECHÉZEAUX	87
1987 NUITS ST.-GEORGES	75

1987 VOSNE-ROMANÉE	78
1987 VOSNE-ROMANÉE LES BEAUX MONTS	84

Emanuel Rouget, the young nephew of Henri Jayer, has the greatest teacher in Burgundy. He should be able to improve upon his efforts in 1987. His two Villages wines, the Nuits St.-Georges and Vosne-Romanée, are relatively light, simple, straightforward wines with decent fruit, but little character or depth. The Vosne-Romanée Les Beaux Monts has more depth and ripeness, medium body, good fruit, and should be drunk by 1992–1993. Rouget's best wine in 1987 is his Echézeaux. It shows a ripe, berry-scented bouquet, medium to full body, good acidity, and fine length. Drink it between 1990 and 1995.

DOMAINE GEORGES ROUMIER
(CHAMBOLLE-MUSIGNY)

1987 BONNES MARES	89
1987 CHAMBOLLE-MUSIGNY	85
1987 CHAMBOLLE-MUSIGNY LES AMOUREUSES	87
1987 MOREY ST.-DENIS CLOS DE LA BUSSIÈRE	78
1987 RUCHOTTES-CHAMBERTIN	88

In addition to being one of my very favorite cellars to visit, this remains one of the top estates of the entire Côte d'Or. Its historical significance is not to be discounted either. Domaine Roumier was one of the benchmark estates of the late Frank Schoonmaker, a man who did more than any other American to expose consumers in this country to the glories of estate-bottled burgundies. It is unfortunate for Americans that only 10% of Roumier's production is sold in this country, but the demand in Europe is insatiable. Switzerland, England, and France account for 50% of the sales. The meticulous winemaking is increasingly handled by the young Christophe Roumier who has been well trained by his father, Jean-Marie. This is an estate that often excels in off years and is positively brilliant in the great vintages. For example, consider 1983. The Domaine Roumier made some of the very finest wines of the Côte d'Or. None of their wines display any taste of rot or hail damage, and their 1983s are capable of lasting well into the twenty-first century. As for the 1987s, I was a little disappointed with the Morey St.-Denis Clos de la Bussière. It was elegant but seemed a bit lean and attenuated on the palate. Perhaps it had too much tannin for its concentration of fruit.

It is a good wine, but a little bit more ripeness and charm would have resulted in a higher mark. The Chambolle-Musigny is excellent, displaying a wonderfully fragrant, aromatic bouquet, medium body, and lovely, supple, smooth, berry flavors married nicely with spicy oak. The Chambolle-Musigny Les Amoureuses is higher in quality with greater length, richness, and ripeness as well as a wonderfully evolved penetrating bouquet of spicy oak, berry fruit, and oriental spices. It is hard to resist drinking given its smooth, opulent texture, yet I have no doubt it should last until 1996–2000. One of the best-kept secrets of this domaine is the Ruchottes-Chambertin, normally the largest-scaled wine the Roumiers produce. In 1987 it has a profound earthy, cedary, cinnamon, ground beef and berry-scented bouquet. In the mouth, the wine is full bodied, very ripe, deep, and concentrated; it should be ready to drink by 1991–1992. It will not be long lived, but will certainly keep until 1999–2001. The Bonnes Mares is potentially outstanding given the wine's remarkable depth, ripeness, richness, excellent color, and smooth, harmonious, velvety texture. It has layers of fruit and is just one of a number of superb examples from the 1987 vintage.

ARMAND ROUSSEAU (GEVREY-CHAMBERTIN)

1987 CHAMBERTIN	88
1987 CHAMBERTIN-CLOS DE BÈZE	88
1987 CHARMES-CHAMBERTIN	86
1987 CLOS DE LA ROCHE	86
1987 GEVREY-CHAMBERTIN	77
1987 GEVREY-CHAMBERTIN LES CAZETIERS	84
1987 GEVREY-CHAMBERTIN-CLOS ST.-JACQUES	87
1987 GEVREY-CHAMBERTIN LAVAUX ST.-JACQUES	86
1987 MAZIS-CHAMBERTIN	83
1987 RUCHOTTES-CHAMBERTIN-CLOS DES RUCHOTTES	85

The wines produced by this estate in the eighties, while not as intense, powerful, and rich as vintages in the sixties, are still excellent. I would like to see Rousseau abandon his policy of filtering the wines prior to bottling, but that is unlikely given his problems with bacterial spoilage in the late seventies. Charles Rousseau believes 1983 is his best vintage in the eighties, although he has high hopes that 1989 will be one of the great vintages of his lifetime. The 1987s are slightly below the quality of his 1986s (his 1986s turned out to be some of the better wines of that vintage). They are soft and supple, which is not what Rousseau desires in his wines. He would prefer them to be relatively full bodied, powerful, tannic, and extremely long lived (hence his adoration of his 1983s). The 1987s should all be consumed by 1997; I do not see any of them lasting longer. His Gevrey-Chambertin is forward, cleanly made, soft, and correct. The Gevrey-Chambertin Les Cazetiers is not one of the best examples from this excellent Premier Cru vineyard. It is ripe and tasty, but lacks a little substance, as well as the wild and savage character that many of the wines from this well-placed Premier Cru vineyard frequently possess. I was impressed with his Lavaux St.-Jacques, as it exhibited deeper, richer fruit, more body, and the suppleness and aromatic complexity that the 1987 vintage offers. The Charmes-Chambertin is similar in style with a velvety, smooth palate and good depth of fruit; it is ideal for drinking between now and 1994–1996. Rousseau's Mazis-Chambertin was very tough and tannic; the tannins may actually be excessive for the wine's amount of fruit. The Clos de la Roche was deeper yet quite developed for a wine from this great Grand Cru vineyard. It had a nice, spicy, earthy plumminess, medium body, and soft tannins. One of Rousseau's top wines in 1987 was his excellent Gevrey-Chambertin-Clos St.-Jacques. It is not quite up to the quality of the 1986 or 1985, but is still a very good, opulently fruity wine with expansive, sweet, smoky, Pinot Noir fruit on the palate, good spicy oak, and a moderately long finish. It should last until 1998–2000. The Ruchottes-Chambertin-Clos des Ruchottes tastes light. It shows a spicy, bing-cherry fruitiness, medium body, attractive suppleness, and some pleasant but soft tannins in the finish. It seemed atypically soft and tame for a wine from Ruchottes-Chambertin. It should drink nicely until 1994–1996. The Chambertin-Clos de Bèze and Chambertin are of equal quality in 1987. I thought the Chambertin had more of a sweet, vanilla oakiness than the explosively ripe fruity Clos de Bèze. The Clos de Bèze was admirably backed up by a velvety, even voluptuous texture and a soft finish. It is extremely seductive, yet should continue to drink well until 1996–1997. The Chambertin tastes more tannic and exhibits excellent depth, ripeness, and a long finish. I would expect it to be at its best between 1992–2000.

DANIEL SENARD (ALOXE-CORTON)

1987 ALOXE-CORTON	85
1987 CORTON	89
1987 CORTON-CLOS DU ROI	87

Daniel and Philippe Senard have come under the spell of the Nuits St.-Georges oenologist, Guy Accad. However, there is no doubting their 1987s are the best wines this estate has produced in many years. They have all the Accad trademarks, a fabulously deep, dark ruby almost purple/black color, tremendous fruit and muscle, and plenty of length. The Aloxe-Corton has a beautifully expansive, sweet, ripe fruitiness, supple texture, and a smooth finish. It should be drunk by 1993–1994. The Corton-Clos du Roi is quite a mouthful of wine with a penetrating bouquet of black fruits and toasty, smoky, vanillin oak. On the palate it is full bodied, rich, fat, and long. Its soft tannins are concealed by a cascade of rich fruit. I would opt for drinking this wine between 1990–2000. The top wine, which may well merit an outstanding rating in another year or so, is the Corton. It is explosively rich with layers of intense black cherry and raspberry fruit, full body, a lush texture, and a very long finish that conceals significant tannins. This wine should drink beautifully until 1996–1997, as it has a lower acidity level than many 1987s.

CHRISTIAN SERAFIN (GEVREY-CHAMBERTIN)

1987 CHARMES-CHAMBERTIN	90
1987 GEVREY-CHAMBERTIN	85
1987 GEVREY-CHAMBERTIN LES CAZETIERS	91
1987 GEVREY-CHAMBERTIN LE FONTENY	85
1987 GEVREY-CHAMBERTIN VIEILLES VIGNES	87

The tiny 10-acre domaine of Serafin is quite famous in Swiss wine-drinking circles, but unfortunately is relatively unknown in America. In fact, this is one of the very finest producers in Gevrey-Chambertin. Since the 1985 vintage, my tastings have revealed that Mr. Serafin knows how to make great wine. Even his Gevrey-Chambertin has a wonderfully pure blackberry fruitiness, a good touch of spicy new oak, and ripe, savory, velvety flavors. It should be drunk by 1993–1994. For something quite special, look for Serafin's Gevrey-Chambertin Vieilles Vignes, made from three parcels of vines that average 30, 40, and 60 years in age. This wine is better than many producers' Premiers Crus, and is significantly superior to the Grands Crus from underachievers like Rebourseau, Trapet, Camus, and Remy. These producers' Grands Crus would get blown away in a blind tasting with Serafin's generic Gevrey-Chambertin made from old vines. The 1987 has a wonderfully deep ruby color and a big, penetrating, spicy, berry-scented bouquet with just enough new oak to give it character. On the palate, it shows excellent depth, ripeness, and a lush, seductive texture. I would recommend drinking it by 1994–1995. The Gevrey-Chambertin Le Fonteny, which showed so impressively well from cask, is certainly very good, but it lacks the extra dimension of flavor and complexity that I thought it possessed from the barrel. Serafin made a stunning Gevrey-Chambertin Les Cazetiers. I think it is superior to his Charmes-Chambertin, even though Les Cazetiers is only a Premier Cru and Charmes is one of Gevrey-Chambertin's most famous Grands Crus. Aged in 100% new oak, this spectacularly rich, deep, profound wine has great concentration and a velvety texture. Drinkable now, it also has the depth and balance to last for a decade. It is an exhilarating, concentrated, impressive wine and another poignant example of just how impressive the top 1987s can be. The Charmes-Chambertin is actually softer and less structured than the Les Cazetiers. It shows a beautifully rich, velvety, seductive, and opulent texture, medium to full body, splendid concentration, and a long finish. It is actually more forward than Les Cazetiers, but should last. Unfortunately, the wines of Serafin are quite limited in availability, but they are well worth seeking out.

BERNARD SERVEAU (MOREY ST.-DENIS)

1987 CHAMBOLLE-MUSIGNY LES AMOUREUSES	87
1987 CHAMBOLLE-MUSIGNY LES CHABIOTS	87
1987 CHAMBOLLE-MUSIGNY LES SENTIERS	86
1987 MOREY ST.-DENIS-CLOS DES SORBÈS	83
1987 NUITS ST.-GEORGES LES CHAÎNES-CARTEAUX	84

Never that deep in color, and always avoiding excesses in alcohol and body, these wines clearly represent the elegant, graceful, stylish school of winemaking in Burgundy. Serveau's 1987 wines are probably not as deep as his 1985s or 1988s, but they are still successful and are probably his third best vintage (not including, of course, 1989) of this decade. The Morey St.-Denis-Clos des Sorbès tends to be among his most robust wines. It usually lacks the charm and delicacy of his Premiers Crus from Chambolle-Musigny. The 1987 has good fruit in a rather straightforward, spicy style, and is ideal for drinking over the next 6 to 7 years. Among the three Premiers Crus of Chambolle-Musigny, the

1987 Les Sentiers is excellent with a well-developed, ripe, rich, berry and floral-scented bouquet, medium body, plenty of juicy, succulent fruit, and a smooth, velvety finish. In comparison, Les Chabiots shares much of the same elegant, stylish framework, has as much concentration, but more tannin in the finish. While Les Amoureuses is the lightest in color, it is the broadest and most concentrated in flavor. It is also Serveau's only wine to see a small percentage of new oak barrels for aging. It is appealingly seductive in 1987, extremely fragrant, and displays excellent ripeness and balance. Like the other Premiers Crus from Chambolle-Musigny, it should be drunk over the next 5 to 6 years. The Nuits St.-Georges Les Chaînes-Carteaux is an earthy, peppery, spicy wine that tastes completely different from the other wines in the Serveau lineup. It is soft, but is much more marked by the *terroir* and soils of Nuits St.-Georges. Like the other Serveau wines, it should be consumed over the near term.

SERVELLE-TACHOT (CHAMBOLLE-MUSIGNY)

1987 CHAMBOLLE-MUSIGNY	78
1987 CHAMBOLLE-MUSIGNY LES CHARMES	84
1987 CLOS VOUGEOT	86

My experience with the wines of Servelle has shown them to be very light, perfumed, stylish wines that are never terribly concentrated or meant for long aging. Given their polished, brilliant color, I think that a less vigorous filtration would increase the wines' stuffing and aging ability. In 1987 the Chambolle-Musigny is light and pretty, but simple. The Chambolle-Musigny Les Charmes offers riper fruit, some oaky scents, and a moderately intense, velvety texture. It should be drunk by 1991–1992. The best wine is the Clos Vougeot, which has more body, some interesting ripeness, and moderate length. It should drink well until 1994–1995.

JEAN TARDY (VOSNE-ROMANÉE)

1987 CHAMBOLLE-MUSIGNY	85
1987 CLOS VOUGEOT	88
1987 NUITS ST.-GEORGES LES BOUDOTS	89
1987 VOSNE-ROMANÉE LES CHAUMES	86

In 1987, Jean Tardy has had a great deal of success with an excellent, serious, intense, richly fruity, round, and elegant Chambolle-Musigny. It is almost as good as his Vosne-Romanée Les Chaumes. This wine shows the precociousness of the vintage, and has a spicy, somewhat cedary, plummy bouquet, and round, soft flavors. It should be drunk by 1994–1995. However, the two top wines from Tardy in 1987 are his two traditional stars. The Nuits St.-Georges Les Boudots has a gigantic, exotic, intense bouquet of smoky, roasted fruit, plums, toasty new oak, and magnificently rich, long, ripe, intense flavors. It is light in tannin but has good acidity and should last until 1996–1997. The Clos Vougeot from Tardy (he owns a well-placed parcel high up the slope of the Clos) is more tannic and closed, and actually needs 2 to 3 years of bottle age. It should last for a decade, perhaps longer, making it a candidate for one of the longer-lived wines from this vintage. The bouquet now exhibits a great deal of ripe, intense red fruits, spicy new oak, and shows medium to full body, excellent, possibly outstanding concentration, and a very long finish on the palate. I would not be surprised if this wine merited an outstanding score in a few more years.

JEAN TAUPENOT-MERME (MOREY ST.-DENIS)

1987 CHAMBOLLE-MUSIGNY	85
1987 CHARMES-CHAMBERTIN	86
1987 GEVREY-CHAMBERTIN	73
1987 MOREY ST.-DENIS	85

I have had little experience with the domaine of Jean Taupenot, but his wines are aged in 50% new oak barrels and half the grapes are destemmed prior to the fermentation. Based on the last several vintages, the wines tend to be very peppery, slightly herbaceous with a lot of ripe berry fruit. They also exhibit a great deal of texture and soft tannins in the finish. The 1987s, save for another rather hard, lean, tough, charmless Gevrey-Chambertin, are very flavorful wines with a great deal of alcohol and generosity. Critics might argue that the 1987 Chambolle-Musigny is too alcoholic to be a textbook example of the appellation, but it has excellent ripeness and a seductive plumpness. It should be drunk by 1992–1993. The Morey St.-Denis is tannic and spicy and has excellent color and surprising length and depth for a generic wine. I would cellar it until 1990–1991. Taupenot's best wine is the Charmes-Chambertin, but given the differential in price and the fact that it is a Grand Cru, it is not significantly better than the other wines. It is very spicy, has a good, ripe, round, rich fruitiness, medium to full body, some firm tannins in the finish, and excellent ruby/purple color. Drink it between 1990 and 1996.

DOMAINE THIERRY-LESPINASSE (GIVRY)

1987 GIVRY EN CHOUÉ	86

The Domaine Thierry-Lespinasse's Givry en Choué is an excellent value from the Côte Chalonnaise. I tasted this same wine from the 1986 vintage too late to get it into my comprehensive report on that vintage in issue 61, but the 1987 is even more impressive. The wines spend six months in new oak casks after fermentation and are then moved to older and larger oak *foudres* to await bottling. This is a superb wine for the appellation of Givry. It shows a rich, smoky, intense, berry-scented bouquet, long, velvety flavors, and makes an ideal and inepxensive choice for those who want to drink serious red burgundy.

TOLLOT-BEAUT (CHOREY-LÈS-BEAUNE)

1987 BEAUNE LES GRÈVES	80
1987 CHOREY-LÈS-BEAUNE	69
1987 CORTON LES BRESSANDES	84
1987 SAVIGNY-LÈS-BEAUNE LES LAVIÈRES	75

Tollot-Beaut's 1987s were compact and thin, and appeared to lack the charm and fat that one frequently sees in the best vintages. For example, the Chorey-Lès-Beaune had too much tannin for its fruit. Buyers would be wiser to seek out the 1985 or wait for the excellent 1988. The Savigny-Lès-Beaune Les Lavières displayed better balance, but on the palate came across as a relatively light, lean wine that should be consumed by 1992–1993. Although the Beaune Les Grèves had more fruit, I would have liked to see more intensity; it should be consumed by 1991–1992. The best 1987 wine from Tollot-Beaut is their Corton Les Bressandes, which exhibited excellent ripe cherry fruit, some spicy tannins, medium body, and an attractive, spicy, pit fruit character. It should be drunk by 1993–1994.

CHÂTEAU DE LA TOUR (VOUGEOT)

1987 BEAUNE PREMIER CRU (DOMAINE PIERRE LABET)	86
1987 CLOS VOUGEOT	89

Château de la Tour is the largest vineyard holder of the famous Grand Cru vineyard of Clos Vougeot. For years the wines were mediocre, but in the mid-eighties this estate fell under the influence of the controversial oenologist from Nuits St.-Georges, Guy Accad. His belief in an extensive cold maceration of the grapes prior to fermentation is cautiously followed at this estate, as they allow the grapes to sit for only 6 to 7 days. However, this practice has resulted in an impressive, nearly superb 1987 Clos Vougeot and another top wine in 1988. The 1987 Clos Vougeot shows a stunningly deep ruby color and a big, explosively rich, berry-scented bouquet backed up with plenty of toasty new oak. There is excellent depth, ripeness, and considerable length on the palate. The wine displays the suppleness of the 1987 vintage, but has some good tannins in the finish. Ideally it should be drunk between 1992–2000. For those lucky enough to find any, Chateau de La Tour also makes tiny quantities of a Cuvée Vieilles Vignes Clos Vougeot. The wine is nearly impossible to find in commercial markets. The other wines produced are sold by Pierre Labet under his own label. The 1987s include an excellent Beaune Premier Cru that shows the Accad style with its fabulously profound, deep ruby color and large quantities of rich berry fruit. It has a heady alcoholic finish, but it is delicious.

DOMAINE DU COMTE DE VOGÜÉ
(CHAMBOLLE-MUSIGNY)

1987 BONNES MARES	84
1987 CHAMBOLLE-MUSIGNY	82
1987 MUSIGNY-VIEILLES VIGNES	86

This is an extremely important domaine. In the forties, fifites, and sixties, it made wines that were considered as great as those of the Domaine de la Romanée-Conti. Many an old-timer in Burgundy has told me that in the forties and fifties the greatest wines in Burgundy were the Musigny-Vieilles Vignes from Comte de Vogüé and the La Tâche, Richebourg, and Romanée-Conti from the Domaine de la Romanée-Conti. I have written much about the fact that since the 1972 vintage, this estate has not produced any great wine. At present an oenologist is in charge of the winemaking. I found it very difficult to get answers to any of the questions I asked on my past visit. The quality of the 1987s is good. The domaine has apparently chosen to take a very safe, sterile, no-risk philosophy when it comes to making wine. Stability and security are at the expense of extracting the maximum from their vineyards.

This is unfortunate as the Domaine du Comte de Vogüé owns 70% of the vineyard of Musigny as well as important parcels in Bonnes Mares and Chambolle-Musigny Les Amoureuses. They also own over an acre of Chardonnay, from which they make their Musigny-Blanc. In 1987, the Chambolle-Musigny is light, lacking a bit in concentration and character, but straightforward and fruity. The Bonnes Mares represents a stylized, risk-free sort of wine with good ripeness, nice firm tannins, and the potential to last for 5 to 10 years. As for the Musigny-Vieilles Vignes, it is very fine, delicate, complex, and will certainly keep for 10 to 15 years. It is not as concentrated as I had expected, but it is, nevertheless, a very good wine. If someone like Christophe Roumier was making these wines, I think they could be even better. I have to believe that more extract, complexity, and character could be obtained if it was so desired. The 1987s are good, but they probably could have been thrilling.

LENI VOLPATO-COSTAILLE (CHAMBOLLE-MUSIGNY)

1987 BOURGOGNE PASSE-TOUT-GRAINS	85
1987 CHAMBOLLE-MUSIGNY	85

I have never tasted a better Bourgogne Passe-Tout-Grains than Leni Volpato-Costaille's. This excellent grower is located on the back streets of the village of Chambolle-Musigny. Volpato is a superb winemaker and it is sad that he owns no Premier Cru or Grand Cru vineyards. It would be interesting to see what he could produce from the vineyards of the classic underachiever of the village, the Domaine du Comte de Vogüé. In 1987, his Bourgogne Passe-Tout-Grains is as good as his Chambolle-Musigny. The huge, deep ruby color, ripe, intense, berry fruit, excellent perfume, and soft tannins suggest this wine is ideal for drinking over the next 5 to 6 years; it may even last longer. The wine is a result of a 24-day maceration and no destemming. This is a wonderful burgundy for under $10 a bottle. There are very few Pinot Noirs from California or Oregon that could touch it in quality. The Chambolle-Musigny smells of ripe tomatoes and herbs. It is lusciously fruity, spicy, and ideal for drinking over the next 5 to 6 years.

1987 WHITE BURGUNDY

The 1987 harvest of the Chardonnay grapes took place under miserable weather conditions, and my tastings suggest a mediocre year similar to

1984. Surprisingly, some of the wines have filled out. While they will be short lived and should be drunk up by 1993, there were some fine, fleshy white 1987s that are significantly better than I would ever have believed. There are even a handful of superstar wines from the likes of the Domaine Leflaive and André Ramonet.

RECOMMENDED PRODUCERS

Faiveley
François Jobard
Comte Lafon

Domaine Leflaive
Michel Niellon
Domaine Ramonet

1988 RED BURGUNDY

This is a very good, sometimes excellent year for the red wines. All of the vintage charts and commentators will probably place 1988 on a much higher plateau of quality than 1987, as it is a better overall vintage. Yet the difference in quality between these two vintages is not as significant as one might be led to believe. The 1988s have a deeper, richer color than the 1987s and are fuller bodied and more tannic, but the huge yields of 1988 (in many places twice the size of 1987) have resulted in many wines that are not appreciably better than the 1987s. Furthermore, prices for the 1988s are significantly higher than for the underrated 1987s. Ignoring the exciting possibilities of 1989, 1988 looks as if it will be the best vintage of this decade after 1985 for red burgundies. This is particularly true with the wines from the Côte de Nuits, as the 1985s have more depth, richness, and opulence than the 1988s. There are, of course, 1988s from the Côte de Nuits that are superior to the 1985s. I am thinking primarily of the extraordinary red wines of the new Domaine Leroy (formerly Charles Noëllat) in Vosne-Romanée, the Château de la Tour, Jacky Confuron-Cotidot, Bruno Clair, Robert Groffier, and Georges Roumier. In those cellars, the 1988s surpass their 1985s. Where 1988 may prove superior to 1985 is in the three Côte de Beaune-Villages of Volnay, Pommard, and Santenay. Many of the 1988s from these top producers looked more impressive than their 1985s.

Note: All the 1988s have been given a rating and descriptive note based on barrel tastings done in November 1988, spring 1989, and fall 1989.

BERTRAND AMBROISE (PRÉMEAUX)

1988 CORTON ROGNET	90
1988 NUITS ST.-GEORGES	86

1988 NUITS ST.-GEORGES RUE DE CHAUX	90
1988 NUITS ST.-GEORGES LES VAUCRAINS	89

If Bertrand Ambroise, now in his mid-thirties, continues to produce wines like his 1987s and 1988s, he should prove to be one of the names to remember in the nineties. He believes in 100% destemming, aging his wines for 18 months in oak casks, and intervening minimally when possible. He uses barrels made from the Cîteaux oak, and made his finest wines in 1988. Even his Villages Nuits St.-Georges shows a wonderful purity and ripeness, good harmony among its elements, and a long, smooth finish. It should be consumed over the next 4–5 years. His Nuits St.-Georges Les Vaucrains should be better than his Nuits St.-Georges Rue de Chaux, but that is not the case. Although the Les Vaucrains is an excellent wine, full bodied, ripe, concentrated, with a deep, smoky, plum-like fruitiness, and 5–10 years of longevity, it is his Nuits St.-Georges Rue de Chaux that is fabulous. It displays deep ruby/ purple color, a huge bouquet of smoky, berry fruit, minerals and licorice, and long, splendidly deep, supple, fruit flavors. I would drink it over the next 7–8 years. Not surprisingly, his Corton, while displaying all the purity and ripeness of the other wines, is more backward, has more tannin, and needs 3–4 years to shed its tough texture and develop nuances and complexity.

BERNARD AMIOT (CHAMBOLLE-MUSIGNY)

1988 CHAMBOLLE-MUSIGNY	78
1988 CHAMBOLLE-MUSIGNY LES CHARMES	82
1988 CHAMBOLLE-MUSIGNY LES CHATELOTS	80

Amiot certainly has the potential to make very good wines, but his yields are too high. A stricter selection process would result in more concentrated and ageworthy wines. All his 1988s are fully mature, soft, show some dilution in character and fruit, and should be consumed over the next 2–3 years. The best of this trio of wines is his Les Charmes. It has more fruit and character than the other wines, which tail off in the finish and evidence the effects of an overly abundant crop.

DOMAINE COMTE ARMAND (POMMARD)

1988 POMMARD-CLOS DES EPENEAUX	90

This is the best wine the Comte Armand has produced since the beautiful 1985. It is intensely colored with a huge bouquet of red and black fruits, spicy new oak, and an intriguing earthy, *terroir* character. In the mouth, it is splendidly concentrated and full bodied with good acidity. There is plenty of tannin in the finish. This is a large-scaled, yet graceful and well-balanced, Pommard that can be drunk over the next 10–12 years.

ANDRÉ BART (MARSANNAY)

1988 BONNES MARES	86
1988 CHAMBERTIN-CLOS DE BÈZE	86
1988 CHAMBOLLE-MUSIGNY	82
1988 CÔTE DE NUITS-VILLAGES	75
1988 FIXIN LES HERVELETS	75
1988 MARSANNAY	78

The overall quality of the 1988 wines from André Bart appears unimpressive. The Fixin, Marsannay, and Côte de Nuits-Villages are all too tannic, lean, high in acidity, and lack charm and finesse. There were some redeeming features to the Chambolle-Musigny: It exhibited good color, a pleasurable spicy, berry fruitiness, and medium body. The best two wines are the Grands Crus, the Bonnes Mares and Chambertin-Clos de Bèze. I would expect them to be even better given the prices they fetch. The 1988 Bonnes Mares is a very good wine, tannic, medium to full bodied with a spicy, earthy, plum-like fruitiness, a nice touch of new oak and some firmness and acidity in the finish. It should have 2–3 years in the cellar before it is consumed. The Chambertin-Clos de Bèze is excellent, but I expect profound wine at these prices, particularly in a fine vintage such as 1988. It is moderately concentrated and medium bodied with a big, chocolatey, herb-scented bouquet, oaky, berry flavors, and a fine finish. It should be at its best between 1991 and 2000.

BARTHOD-NOËLLAT (CHAMBOLLE-MUSIGNY)

1988 CHAMBOLLE-MUSIGNY	84
1988 CHAMBOLLE-MUSIGNY AUX BEAUX BRUNS	86
1988 CHAMBOLLE-MUSIGNY LES CHARMES	86
1988 CHAMBOLLE-MUSIGNY LES CRAS	89

Gaston Barthod made some of his best wines of the eighties in 1988. His Villages Chambolle-Musigny exhibits supple, tasty, medium-bodied fruitiness, soft texture, and is ideal for drinking over the next 1–2 years. Among his Premiers Crus, the most precocious is the Chambolle-Musigny aux Beaux Bruns. It is forward with excellent color, large amounts of red fruits, and spicy new oak. It should age gracefully for 4–8 years. If you have the patience to wait 2 or 3 years, the Chambolle-Musigny Les Cras, from the superb Premier Cru vineyard next to the Grand Cru Bonnes Mares, is intense, full bodied, and deep, with gorgeous levels of fruit. However, it needs time to shed its tannins. Of the 1988s, it is by far Barthod's most powerful wine. His Chambolle-Musigny Les Charmes is a bit leaner, displays a good, spicy, fresh, fruity nose, is medium-bodied, and extremely well-balanced. It should be cellared for several years before being consumed, and should keep for 7–8 years.

JEAN-MARC BOULEY (VOLNAY)

1988 POMMARD	85
1988 POMMARD LES RUGIENS	90
1988 VOLNAY	85
1988 VOLNAY LES CAILLERETS	90
1988 VOLNAY-CLOS DES CHÊNES	88

The young Jean-Marc Bouley continues to demonstrate a talent that could easily make him one of the Côte de Beaune superstars of the nineties. He has followed his superb 1987s with another top-notch effort in 1988. His Volnay is spicy, ripe, lush, and has a lot of flavor and character; it should be consumed over the next 5–7 years. I thought his aromatic Pommard was a more tannic and larger-scaled wine. It does not possess the charm or elegance of the Volnay. However, contrasting the elegance of the Volnay and the power of the Pommard is like comparing apples and oranges. As for his Premiers Crus, the Volnay-Clos des Chênes is a beautifully made, concentrated, deep, flavorful wine displaying loads of tannin, spicy new oak, and layers of rich fruit. It is precocious, but gives every indication of lasting for 7–12 years. The compelling Volnay Les Caillerets is an even deeper, richer, and more structured wine. This intensely flavored, medium- to full-bodied, impressively made wine shows layers of fruit, good acidity, and soft yet considerable tannins in its finish. While approachable now, it will not be fully mature for 3–4 years, and should last for a decade thereafter. Bouley's best wine in 1988 is his Pommard Les Rugiens (it was also superb in 1987). He has produced a gorgeous wine with layers upon layers of deep berry fruit, a healthy lashing of toasty new oak, and excellent ripeness and length. It should be at its best between 1993 and 2005.

BOURÉE PÈRE ET FILS (GEVREY-CHAMBERTIN)

1988 BEAUNE LES EPENOTTES	88
1988 CHAMBERTIN	86
1988 CHAPELLE-CHAMBERTIN	92
1988 CHARMES-CHAMBERTIN	91
1988 CLOS DE LA ROCHE	90
1988 CÔTE DE NUITS-VILLAGES	83
1988 FIXIN LES HERVELETS	83
1988 GEVREY-CHAMBERTIN LES CAZETIERS-CUVÉE RÉSERVE	91
1988 GEVREY-CHAMBERTIN-CLOS DE LA JUSTICE	88
1988 GEVREY-CHAMBERTIN-CLOS ST.-JACQUES	90
1988 MOREY ST.-DENIS	82

While I am rarely ever enthralled by Bouree Père et Fils' white wines, the red wines are of extremely high quality, particularly in the top vintages. They are very traditional burgundies that are vatted for over three weeks, kept in old oak barrels (although I did spot them using a few new barrels for their Chambertin), and bottled unfiltered. In fact, the Bourée Père et Fils may be the last firm in the Côte d'Or to bottle their burgundies in a top vintage. This firm maintains a surprisingly low profile and its prices are extremely reasonable considering the quality of their wines. Burgundy lovers should search out some of their excellent 1988s. At the bottom level of the quality hierarchy is a rustic, spicy, peppery, plum and herb–scented Côte de Nuits-Villages, which should drink nicely for 5–7 years (Bourée's wines last as well as just about anybody's in Burgundy) and a rustic, coarse-textured, substantial Fixin Les Hervelets. One of the newest entries in the Bourée stable is their excellent Premier Cru Beaune Les Epenottes, of which the Vallet family now owns one-fourth a hectare of old vines. The 1988 is deliciously supple and smooth, and crammed with black cherry and raspberry fruit. It also exhibits a touch of toasty new oak, unusual for a Bourée wine. The Gevrey-Chambertin-Clos de la Justice is produced from a parcel of vines that everyone says is "on the wrong side" of N 74. Yet this wine continues to defy all of the experts. The Bourées have long shown that the combination of old vines, careful viticultural practices, and minimal intervention when making and cellaring the wine, can produce higher-quality wines from this parcel than from many of Gevrey-Chambertin's Premiers Crus. The 1988 is spicy, earthy, and rich with deeply etched flavors, and plenty of tannin and body. It should last for 10–15 years, perhaps longer. The other Premier Cru from Gevrey-Chambertin, the Clos St.-Jacques, will fetch a much higher price, and is deliciously fruity, soft, much more supple, and less ageworthy than the Gevrey-Chambertin-Clos de la Justice. The only disappointing 1988 I tasted from Bourée (or was allowed to taste) was a simple, straightforward Morey St.-Denis.

Among the Grands Crus, the Charmes-Chambertin is usually superb, as it is from one of this firm's own vineyards. In 1988 it shows a huge bouquet of plummy, spicy fruit, smooth, rich, velvety flavors, full body, and plenty of length. I liked it nearly as much as the Chappelle-Chambertin, which was expansive, gorgeously sweet and intense, with astounding length and a dazzling level of fruit extract. Both of these wines were better than the Clos de la Roche, which was extremely concentrated, but hard, closed, and tannic. It is a promising candidate for at least 7–12 years of cellaring. I was a little disappointed in the Chambertin, but I may have seen it when it was too closed. Despite the fact that it was aged in new oak, something new for the Bourée firm, it seemed less impressive than their outstanding 1987.

Last, be sure and look for their Gevrey-Chambertin Les Cazetiers-Cuvée Réserve. It represents a special parcel of very old vines from the superbly situated Premier Cru vineyard of Les Cazetiers. It is a decadently rich, full-bodied wine with an almost wild, exotic character. It should last for another 10–15 years. These are all high quality wines from one of Burgundy's perennial overachievers.

JACQUES CACHEUX-BLÉE (VOSNE-ROMANÉE)

1988 BOURGOGNE ROUGE	82
1988 ECHÉZEAUX	91
1988 NUITS ST.-GEORGES	83

1988 VOSNE-ROMANÉE	84
1988 VOSNE-ROMANÉE LES SUCHOTS	89

This is a very serious domaine that deserves to be far better known. Unfortunately, the gracious Monsieur Cacheux does not produce a lot of wine. What he does make is neither fined nor filtered, and is the product of relatively low yields. In 1988, a year he claims is not nearly as good as 1976, 1978, 1985, or 1989, he produced two excellent to outstanding wines and three competent examples of their appellations. The Bourgogne Rouge shows a pleasant ripeness, is straightforward, fruity, and destined to be drunk over the next 2–3 years. The Nuits St.-Georges has an excellent spicy, smoky, earthy nose, attractive berry fruit, but a relatively short finish. I thought the Vosne-Romanée Villages had a longer finish, and at the same time a complex, richly fruity, spicy, toasty bouquet. Like the Nuits St.-Georges, it should be drunk over the next 3–4 years. Cacheux's top wines are consistently his Vosne-Romanée Les Suchots and Echézeaux. In 1988, the Vosne-Romanée Les Suchots is splendidly supple, hedonistic, very drinkable, and loaded with berry fruit and toasty oak. It should be drunk over the next 5–6 years. Made from vines planted in 1934 and 1945, the Echézeaux is outstanding. It is a shame Cacheux only produces 225 cases of this gloriously fragrant, sublime wine. Deep ruby in color with a spectacular bouquet of violets, plums, minerals, and new oak, this medium- to full-bodied wine is silky smooth, concentrated, and has a long finish.

CAPITAIN-GAGNEROT (LADOIX)

1988 ALOXE-CORTON LES MOUTOTTES	85
1988 BOURGOGNE ROUGE	78
1988 CLOS VOUGEOT	84
1988 CORTON LES RÉNARDES	90
1988 LADOIX LES MICAUDES	87
1988 PERNAND-VERGELESSES LES VERGELESSES	84

I found Roger Capitain's 1988s all delicious to drink. His wines tend to be relatively heady, supple, and deliciously fruity. The Bourgogne Rouge seemed light and straightforward, but the Pernand-Vergelesses Les Vergelesses had real fat and quality to it. It is certainly a worthy effort from an appellation that often produces red wines that are too rustic and tough. One of the best values of the Capitain portfolio is their Ladoix Les Micaudes, made from 35-year-old vines. It displays excellent ripeness, medium body, and oodles of black cherry fruit. The Aloxe-Corton les Moutottes is slightly lighter and perhaps not as structured or as ageworthy. Light ruby in color with a bouquet redolent of cherries and raspberries, this luscious, soft wine should be consumed over the next 3–4 years. Capitain's one great 1988 wine is his Corton-Rénardes. He produced only 175 cases of this wine from a vineyard that has an average vine age of 35 years. It is superb with a fabulous bouquet of black fruits and spicy oak, explosively rich, full-bodied flavors, and a long, supple finish. Its great fruit extract actually seemed to be concealing moderate tannins. As for the Clos Vougeot, I did not think it compared at all with the Corton Les Rénardes, and Roger Capitain agreed. he said it was largely the product of a vineyard where the vines average 15 years in age. The Clos Vougeot is ready to drink and should be consumed over the next 3–4 years for its direct, straightforward fruit and charm.

DOMAINE CHANDON DE BRIAILLES
(SAVIGNY-LÈS-BEAUNE)

1988 CORTON-CLOS DU ROI	91
1988 CORTON LES BRESSANDES	89
1988 CORTON LES MARÉCHAUDES	88
1988 PERNAND-VERGELESSES	70
1988 PERNAND-VERGELESSES-ÎLE DES VERGELESSES	85
1988 SAVIGNY-LÈS-BEAUNE	79
1988 SAVIGNY-LÈS-BEAUNE LES LAVIÈRES	86

I suspect that the 1988s from the Domaine Chandon de Briailles will turn out to be even better than their 1985s. Collectively, the 1988s seem to be the finest wines this famous domaine has produced in a long time. While the straight Savigny-Lès-Beaune has a tannic, hard finish that overwhelms its elegant, light-bodied flavors, the Savigny-Lès-Beaune Les Lavières is excellent, with deep, medium-bodied, tannic yet concentrated flavors. It should possess excellent aging potential. It has fine color, is built for the long haul, and should last 12–15 years. I thought the Pernand-Vergelesses was excessively hard, rustic, and tannic for the amount of fruit to be found. However, the domaine's Pernand-

Vergelesses-Île des Vergelesses has lots of rich raspberry and blackberry fruit, married beautifully with the toasty, spicy oak. Medium bodied, well structured with good acidity and tannin, this wine should also last for up to 10–12 years.

At the Grand Cru level there are three excellent wines. The Corton Les Maréchaudes is the most precocious and supple wine, displaying a dazzling level of rich, raspberry fruit, toasty vanillin oak, excellent color, and the potential to last for 7–10 years. It is soft enough to drink early, but should have even more nuances after several years in the cellar. The 1988 Corton Les Bressandes is a much more tannic and harder wine, but at the same time is more concentrated and powerful, with perhaps 5–15 years of aging potential. It has the longest finish, but the high level of tannins precludes drinking for at least 3–5 years. Last, the Corton-Clos du Roi, of which there are only 150 cases, is truly superb, displaying a profound bouquet of minerals, black fruits, and spicy oak intertwined with the subtle scent of herbs. In the mouth, it is extremely deep, rich, and powerful, with a stunning finish. Given its relatively aggressive tannins, I would wait at least 2–3 years before drinking this excellent wine.

JEAN CHAUVENET (NUITS ST.-GEORGES)

1988 NUITS ST.-GEORGES	85
1988 NUITS ST.-GEORGES LES BOUSSELOTS	90
1988 NUITS ST.-GEORGES LES VAUCRAINS	91

Chauvenet remains one of the best kept secrets in Nuits St.-Georges. His production is tiny, and in most vintages he only produces three wines, all from his hometown appellation. These are unfiltered, wonderfully expressive, rich, intense red burgundies. In 1988 he made the best wines he has produced since the superb 1985 vintage. His Nuits St.-Georges Villages is loaded with cassis and raspberry fruit, shows a nice touch of oak, is soft, lush, medium-bodied, and should be drunk over the next 4–5 years. The Nuits St.-Georges Les Bousselots is an outstanding red burgundy with a huge bouquet of cassis, spicy oak, and licorice. In the mouth, it shows excellent concentration, impeccable balance, and has a soft, concentrated, long finish. It should be at its best between 1992–2000. Last, the Nuits St.-Georges Les Vaucrains is a textbook example of this superb Premier Cru vineyard. Its expansive bouquet of smoke, jammy raspberry fruit, minerals and herbs is compelling. Superbly concentrated, extremely long, deep, and medium bodied, this is a magnificent example of Premier Cru Nuits St.-Georges. It should be drunk over the next 10–12 years.

GEORGES CHICOTOT (NUITS ST.-GEORGES)

1988 NUITS ST.-GEORGES LES PRULIERS	87
1988 NUITS ST.-GEORGES LES SAINT-GEORGES	90
1988 NUITS ST.-GEORGES LES VAUCRAINS	88

Chicotot, a follower of the cold maceration technique, does not fine or filter his wines. As a result, he produces some of the most chewy, enormous, dense, highly concentrated wines from the Côte d'Or. His 1988s are all extremely tannic and muscular wines possessing superb depth. Unlike many 1988s, they need at least 5–6 years in the bottle to shed their tannins and develop more harmony and complexity. The Nuits St.-Georges Les Pruliers, the product of vines averaging between 25–55 years old, had an impressive black/ruby color, full body, a lot of tannin, and a closed and almost impenetrable taste. I would wait at least 5 years before drinking it. The Nuits St.-Georges Les Vaucrains was similar, but its bouquet had a more compelling, earthy, smoky, exotic character. Although this black/ruby-colored wine displayed great depth and richness on the palate. It had excruciatingly high tannin levels. I think it should age for at least 10–12 years so that its component parts can come into full balance. The most forward of Chicotot's 1988s was the 1988 Nuits St.-Georges Les Saint-Georges, which had a fabulous bouquet of black, plum-like fruit, smoky oak, and licorice. In the mouth, it has exceptional ripeness, full body, awesome extract, and a firm, tannic, hard finish. I would advise 4 to 5 years of cellaring, given the construction of Chicotot's wines.

DOMAINE CHOPIN-GROFFIER (PREMEAUX)

1988 CLOS VOUGEOT	91
1988 NUITS ST.-GEORGES	85
1988 NUITS ST.-GEORGES LES CHAIGNOTS	87
1988 VOUGEOT	86

Chopin's gorgeously elegant, graceful, ready-to-drink style of wine-making has produced some lovely wines in 1988. The villages wines of Nuits St.-Georges and Vougeot are wonderfully supple, smooth, and destined to be drunk over the next 3–4 years. Their purity and grace make them charming and full of finesse. The Nuits St.-Georges Les Chaignots has a big, earthy, plum-like bouquet and round, soft, fruity flavors. Although it may not have the concentration of the 1987, it is a delicious wine for drinking over the next 4–5 years. The Clos Vougeot is always Chopin's best wine, and the 1988 is stuffed with jammy, berry fruit. It shows a judicious use of toasty, smoky, new oak, is medium bodied, ripe, long, and displays marvelous concentration and excellent length. While drinkable now, it should last for up to a decade.

BRUNO CLAIR (MARSANNAY)

1988 CHAMBERTIN-CLOS DE BÈZE	90
1988 CÔTE DE NUITS-VILLAGES	85
1988 FIXIN LA CROIX BLANCHE	86
1988 GEVREY-CHAMBERTIN LES CAZETIERS	90
1988 GEVREY-CHAMBERTIN-CLOS DE FONTENY	87
1988 GEVREY-CHAMBERTIN-CLOS ST.-JACQUES	88
1988 MARSANNAY	84
1988 MARSANNAY LA CASSE TÊTE	86
1988 MARSANNAY-LONGEROIS	87
1988 MOREY ST.-DENIS	87
1988 SAVIGNY-LÈS-BEAUNE LES DOMINAUDES	90
1988 VOSNE-ROMANÉE LES CHAMPS PERDRIX	87

Bruno Clair's 1988s are the best he has yet made. Visiting him is comparable to spending time at a California winery because he makes so many different wines—a bevy of whites, one rosé, and his famous red wines. His Rosé de Marsannay is the best rosé in Burgundy—wonderfully fresh and lively. However, you should buy the 1989, or the most recent vintage. Clair has not made one mistake with respect to this excellent, dry, immensely flavorful rosé. I recommend it highly. The 1988 Marsannay, made from very rocky, stony soil, is supple, even fat, with gobs of berry fruit, but not much complexity. It still remains an excellent choice for drinking over the next 4–5 years. The 1988 Marsannay La Casse Tête, from 30-year-old vines, is a much more serious wine with an iron-like, black cherry–scented bouquet, medium to full

body, and some tannins in the finish. It is a wine that can be drunk now
or aged for another 4–5 years. Clair's best Marsannay, however, is the
Marsannay-Longerois. It has greater concentration than his other Marsannays, a deep, brooding, smoky, berry-like fruitiness, good acidity,
soft tannins in the finish, and plenty of body and length. It is one of the
finest red Marsannays I have ever tasted and demonstrates the promising potential for this appellation just outside Dijon. The Côte de Nuits-
Villages is a nice, chunky, rich, berry-scented wine with medium to full
body. It is not complex, but is nicely structured, and shows fine depth
and ripeness. I did not think Clair's Fixin La Croix Blanche was any
better, although I suspect it will last longer, and probably blossom with
aging more than the Côte de Nuits-Villages. It has a similar deep ruby
color, is spicy and long, but does not have the extra measure of complexity and finesse to merit higher marks. Clair's parcel of Vosne-
Romanée Les Champs Perdrix is in very old vines. The 1988 has excellent levels of rich red and black berry-scented fruit with an underlying
aroma of Provençal herbs. Medium bodied, stylish, and soft, this wine
should be consumed over the next 6–7 years. One of the specialties of
this house is its Savigny-Lès-Beaune Les Dominaudes from extremely
old vines. It is always the deepest colored wine in the Clair portfolio
and the 1988 is no exception. It exhibits a black/ruby color, an intense,
exotic, spicy, tar and black fruit-scented bouquet, rich, full-bodied flavors, plenty of tannin, and great length. It is a wine that should not be
approached for 3–4 years, and should drink well for up to 15 years. In
Clair's cellars, the Savigny-Lès-Beaune is of Grand Cru quality! Most
people who buy this estate's red wines want to get as many of Clair's
Gevrey-Chambertins as possible. His Clos de Fonteny is quite elegant,
stylish, and medium-bodied with light tannins and an attractive berry
fragrance as well as taste. It should be drunk over the next 5–7 years.
In contrast, the Gevrey-Chambertin Les Cazetiers is a much more ani-
mal-scented, rather savage (or as the French say *sauvage*) wine with a
wild berry, game-like character. It is richer and fuller on the palate
with a great deal more muscle, tannin, and body. It needs a few years
to shed some of its toughness, but should drink well for the rest of this
century. The Gevrey-Chambertin-Clos St.-Jacques possessed gobs of
sweet berry fruit and a nice touch of spicy oak, but did not seem to
have quite the potential or complexity of the Les Cazetiers. It is a
delicious wine for drinking over the next 7–8 years. Another extremely
impressive wine from Bruno Clair in 1988 is his Chambertin-Clos de
Bèze. It is his most backward wine and is even less developed than the
Savigny-Lès-Beaune Les Dominaudes. With coaxing, a rich, berry-
scented, spicy, intense bouquet of Pinot fruit emerges. On the palate,

one can see its excellent, even outstanding depth, impressive structure, and long finish. This wine should not be consumed before the mid-nineties, and it should last through the first decade of the twenty-first century.

JACKY CONFURON-COTETIDOT (VOSNE-ROMANÉE)

1988 BOURGOGNE ROUGE	87
1988 CHAMBOLLE-MUSIGNY	88
1988 CLOS VOUGEOT	96
1988 ECHÉZEAUX	92
1988 GEVREY-CHAMBERTIN	90
1988 NUITS ST.-GEORGES	88
1988 NUITS ST.-GEORGES PREMIER CRU	90
1988 VOSNE-ROMANÉE LES SUCHOTS	93

The diminutive Jacky Confuron and his son, Jean-Pierre, practice the controversial cold maceration prior to fermentation counseled by the Nuits St.-Georges oenologist Guy Accad. Confuron goes to the extreme, giving his Pinot Noir a cold maceration for 7–10 days before starting the fermentation. The maceration temperature is never allowed to go higher than 25° C. A full 30-day *cuvaison* is employed prior to putting the wine in barrels (20% are new). The 1988s here are positively celestial. I think that some of the irresponsible criticism leveled at Confuron should cease, at least with regard to what he has done in 1988. His Villages wines are as good as you can find. The secret, of course, is very low yields and extremely old vines. Before trying one of the Villages wines, do not miss Confuron's Bourgogne Rouge. It is as intense, rich, and concentrated a Bourgogne Rouge as I have tasted. Bursting with spicy, herbaceous, berry fruit, it is a medium-bodied wine, and should be consumed over the next 5–6 years. As for the Villages wines, it is hard to choose the best. There is the exceptionally concentrated, highly extracted, deep, profound, spicy, smoky Nuits St.-Georges, made from 70-year-old vines, and the Chambolle-Musigny, which is slightly lighter, but still remarkably dense, concentrated, and aromatic. It is made from 40-year-old vines. Last, there is the Gevrey-Chambertin, made from a parcel of 80-year-old vines situated near the Grand Cru Charmes-Chambertin. It is a truly awesome wine with a black/ruby color, splendid layers of damson plum fruit, medium to full body, and an underlying supple, silky texture that suggests this wine should be drunk within its first 8–10 years of life. These Villages wines taste better than many producer's Premiers Crus. Confuron also produces a Nuits St.-Georges Premier Cru from a blend of the two Premiers Crus vineyards of Les Vignes Rondes and Les Murgers. The 1988 is smoky, deep in color, rich, full, and represents the essence of Pinot Noir. It is a massive wine for a Nuits St.-Georges Premier Cru, but should last for 10 years or more.

Of course, Confuron's three greatest wines are his Vosne-Romanée Les Suchots, Echézeaux, and Clos Vougeot. Unfortunately, he only makes a small amount of these wines. The 1988 Vosne-Romanée Les Suchots is extraordinary; it displayed magnificent concentration, an incredible perfume of herbs, black fruits, minerals, and vanilla-tinged, smoky oak. Extremely concentrated, medium to full bodied yet still supple, this stunningly made wine should drink well between 1995–2010. The Echézeaux is a sweeter, more supple, and flattering wine to drink. It displays remarkable color as a result of Confuron's cold maceration technique. It has a fabulous bouquet of violets, herbs, and wet stones as well as long, concentrated, almost jammy, raspberry fruit flavors. There is good underlying acidity that suggests this wine should last 10–15 years. The Clos Vougeot was mind-blowing, and I lament the fact that only 75 cases are available for the entire world. It was one of the most concentrated, dramatic red burgundies I tasted from the 1988 vintage, and textually, resembled to the port-like Bordeaux produced in 1947. Extremely velvety, supple, but oozing with cassis and raspberry-like fruit, this intensely concentrated, fascinating wine with its dazzling bouquet and flavors should last for at least two decades. All of Confuron's wines are bottled unfiltered.

DOMAINE COURCEL (POMMARD)

1988 POMMARD LES FREMIÈRS	85
1988 POMMARD-GRAND CLOS DES EPENOTS	90
1988 POMMARD LES RUGIENS	88

Madame Courcel produced some rich, concentrated, intense wines in 1988, as this vintage should prove to be her most successful vintage since 1985. The Pommard Les Fremièrs is forward, spicy, rustic, flavorful, and ideal for drinking over the next 4–5 years. There is a huge leap in quality with the Pommard Les Rugiens, which has an intensely spicy, almost peppery, plum-like fruitiness, a judicious use of toasty new oak, a big, heady, alcoholic finish, and the potential to last for another decade. The Pommard-Grand Clos des Epenots is extremely concentrated with a dazzling bouquet of plums, chocolate, cedar, and spicy new oak. On the palate, the wine exhibits superb concentration, an old-vine intensity, and plenty of alcohol and tannin in the finish. Approachable now, one suspects this wine will merit an even higher score with 3–4 years of aging. It has the potential to last for 10–15 years.

MARIUS DELARCHE (PERNAND-VERGELESSES)

1988 CORTON LES RÉNARDES	86
1988 PERNAND-VERGELESSES-ÎLE DES VERGELESSES	82

After Delarche's disappointing performance in 1987, it is nice to see this high-quality, motivated producer return to form. His Pernand-Vergelesses-Île des Vergelesses is light in color, but shows a vigorous, spicy, stemmy, rustic personality, medium body, and some tough-textured tannins in the finish. I would recommend drinking it in about two years so as to savor its exuberant character. The Corton Les Rénardes is very good in 1988, but is nowhere near the quality of the sensational 1985. It is ripe and spicy with a lovely concoction of rich berry fruit and toasty new oak. It should drink nicely for the next 7–8 years, but will not prove to be long lived.

JOSEPH DROUHIN (BEAUNE)

1988 BEAUNE-CLOS DES MOUCHES	87
1988 CHAMBOLLE-MUSIGNY	81
1988 CHAMBOLLE-MUSIGNY LES SENTIERS	88
1988 CHASSAGNE-MONTRACHET	84
1988 CLOS DE LA ROCHE	85
1988 CLOS VOUGEOT	88
1988 ECHÉZEAUX	87
1988 GEVREY-CHAMBERTIN	81
1988 GRANDS ECHÉZEAUX	90
1988 GRIOTTE-CHAMBERTIN	91
1988 MUSIGNY	90

1988 POMMARD	85
1988 SANTENAY	85
1988 VOLNAY	82
1988 VOSNE-ROMANÉE LES BEAUX MONTS	87

Joseph Drouhin's 1988 red wines are extremely good. They fall just short of being dazzling because of his reluctance to take any great risks when making them. However, there is a consistency and respect for appellations evident in these wines that is available only from a handful of other *négociants*. All his reds from the Côte de Beaune are attractive wines. For value, he makes a fine generic Santenay, which is stylish, supple, and ready to drink; a good Chassagne-Montrachet, which is bursting with cherry fruit; a slightly light Volnay; a chunky, more muscular Pommard; and a gorgeous Beaune-Clos des Mouches with a big bouquet of plums, black cherries, and spicy oak, and a soft, silky texture that is disarmingly seductive. All these wines should be consumed over the next 5–6 years. I also liked his top-notch Chambolle-Musigny Les Sentiers, which exhibited wonderfully deep, rich flavors, a heady, almost intoxicating bouquet of plums and smoky oak, and a suave, supple, gorgeous texture. It would be hard to keep my hands off a bottle of this wine, and I suspect it should be drunk over the next 5–6 years. Another fine Premier Cru from the Côte de Nuits is Drouhin's Vosne-Romanée Les Beaux Monts. Exhibiting a heady degree of alcohol, and ripe, earthy, plummy flavors, this supple, full-bodied wine is relatively big by Drouhin's standards, and should be drunk over the next 5–6 years. The Clos de la Roche is tannic and closed with very spicy, earthy flavors. Its toughness gave me some concern about its overall harmony, and the tannins may prove to be excessive for the amount of fruit. The Echézeaux is characterized by pure charm and finesse. It is much lighter than the Clos de la Roche, but much more tasty, perfumed, and attractive. It is a lovely wine, but again, it should be drunk soon.

Drouhin produced some outstanding Grand Crus in 1988. For example, his Clos Vougeot has a superb bouquet of red fruits and spicy oak, is relatively alcoholic, and deep, round, and generous with a beautiful finish. Among Drouhin's other Grands Crus, I thought his Griotte-Chambertin was top notch. It had explosive black cherry fruit, good, spicy, toasty, new oak, medium to full body, and a lush texture. The Musigny is slightly lighter, but nevertheless filled with finesse. It provides an expansive, savory, generous mouthful of wine. The compelling Grands Echézeaux is deep, full, and one of the more backward wines in Drouhin's stable in 1988. It is extremely concentrated and full bodied with a bouquet of seductive black fruits, flowers, minerals, and spicy new oak. Drouhin's oenologist told me the tannin and acidity levels of the wines were higher in 1988 than in 1985, but my tastings made me think otherwise. Perhaps as these wines recover from bottle shock they will show more structure and acidity, and will be more worthy candidates for long-term aging. However, for the most part, I would drink Drouhin's 1988s within their first decade of life.

DOMAINE DUJAC (MOREY ST.-DENIS)

1988 BONNES MARES	88
1988 CHARMES-CHAMBERTIN	90
1988 CLOS DE LA ROCHE	90
1988 CLOS ST.-DENIS	92
1988 ECHÉZEAUX	87
1988 GEVREY-CHAMBERTIN LES COMBOTTES	87
1988 MOREY ST.-DENIS	84

Jacques Seysses is one of Burgundy's most influential winemakers and is a guiding light to a younger generation of winemakers committed to making quality wines. His 1988s, by his own admission, are very good, but he still claims the best vintages he has produced in his 20-year tenure as the proprietor of the Domaine Dujac are 1985, 1983, 1978, 1976, and 1969. He feels almost all the 1988s are wines to be consumed within their first decade of life, with the exception of a handful of the most structured and concentrated ones. For example, his 1988 Morey St.-Denis is an elegant, soft, ready-to-drink wine, redolent with aromas of red fruits and spicy new oak. It has light ruby color and is smooth in the finish. I would suggest drinking it over the next 4–5 years. His Gevrey-Chambertin Les Combottes always has a more exotic, spicy component. The 1988 is also extremely smooth and velvety, but lacks the concentration needed to be top class. It is very aromatic, displaying its meaty, cinnamon-like, berry-scented bouquet with soft, medium-bodied flavors. I would drink it over the next 6–7 years. Among the Grands Crus, the Echézeaux is the lightest and most perfumed of the Domaine Dujac wines. It is made from a relatively young vineyard, and never seems to have quite the intensity and length of the other Grands Crus. I applaud the 1988's rich, aromatic, berry-scented nose, and soft, supple flavors, but I would want to drink it over the next 5–6 years. The Bonnes Mares was perhaps not up to the quality level of Seysses's super 1985, but it still boasted a gorgeous, even decadent bouquet of earthy, animal-like, plum-scented fruit, lush, rich, concentrated flavors, medium to full body, and some light tannins in the finish. It should drink nicely for 7–8 years. The 1988 Charmes-Chambertin was even more seductive, somewhat lighter, but silky smooth. This has to be one of Dujac's most consistent Grands Crus, yet it is often overlooked. It is excellent in 1988, although when tasted side by side with the 1987, I could not rate one vintage higher than the other. The 1988 shows ripe, nearly opulent berry-flavored fruit, a generous lashing of toasty new oak, a heady perfume of leather, cedar, and plums, and a soft finish. It should be drunk over the next 7–8 years. The two biggest and best-structured wines from the Domaine Dujac in 1988 were the Clos St.-Denis and Clos de la Roche. I think that the Clos St.-Denis actually might be the top wine from this domaine. The 1988 resembled the 1985 with its extraordinary rich, sweet, expansive bouquet of flowers, plum-like fruit, and smoky, toasty oak. In the mouth, it is fabulously concentrated, gorgeously rich and long, and altogether a superb glass of red burgundy. There are some tannins in the finish, and while drinkable now, this wine should be cellared for another 1–2 years in order to round out. It should last for at least a decade. The Clos de la Roche is similarly structured, but it did not seem to have the extra dimension, complexity, and depth of the Clos St.-Denis. I do not mean to criticize the Clos de la Roche, because it is an outstanding red burgundy— spicy, earthy, rich, and perhaps the fullest and most muscular of the Domaine Dujac wines in 1988. It needs a good 2 years in the cellar before consuming it, and I would expect it to last for at least 10–12 more years. All of the Domaine Dujac wines are bottled unfiltered.

MAURICE ECARD (SAVIGNY-LÈS-BEAUNE)

1988 SAVIGNY-LÈS-BEAUNE LES CLOUS	87
1988 SAVIGNY-LÈS-BEAUNE LES JARRONS	85
1988 SAVIGNY-LÈS-BEAUNE LES NARBANTONS	86
1988 SAVIGNY-LÈS-BEAUNE LES PEUILLETS	87
1988 SAVIGNY-LÈS-BEAUNE LES SERPENTIÈRES	86

Ecard is one of the top producers in Savigny-Lès-Beaune. He seems to consistently produce wines of great elegance and delicious fruit. It is unlikely that they will age past 7–8 years, but for drinking in the near future, they are full of charm, finesse, and character. His 1988s are quite successful, and are slightly more concentrated and fuller than his very fine 1987s. The Savigny-Lès-Beaune Les Jarrons is soft and stylish, ready to drink, and makes an overall elegant, pleasing impression. The 1988 Savigny-Lès-Beaune Les Serpentières has a very supple, smooth, velvety, deep, bing cherry fruitiness as well as a nice touch of spicy oak intertwined with a whiff of herbs. It is perhaps slightly fuller than Les Jarrons, but just as soft, and should also be consumed over the next 4–6 years. The Savigny-Lès-Beaune Les Narbantons is a more structured wine. While it is no better than Les Jarrons or Les Serpentières, it is less precocious, more charming, and requires more aging. It has more body and slightly more acidity. I would age it in the bottle for about a year, and then drink it over the next 4 or 5. One of Ecard's richest, deepest wines in 1988 was the Savigny-Lès-Beaune Les Clous. It is admirably concentrated, fuller-bodied, and has long, well-delineated, berry fruit flavors married nicely with toasty oak. It can be drunk now or aged for 7–8 years. The biggest, but not necessarily the best of all the Ecard wines in 1988 is the Savigny-Lès-Beaune Les Peuillets, from a vineyard near the excellent Beaune Premier Cru, Les Marconnets. It is robustly concentrated, fruity, and ripe, but not terribly complex.

RENÉ ENGEL (VOSNE-ROMANÉE)

1988 CLOS VOUGEOT	88
1988 ECHÉZEAUX	89
1988 GRANDS ECHÉZEAUX	90
1988 VOSNE-ROMANÉE	83
1988 VOSNE-ROMANÉE LES BRÛLÉES	83

René Engel, a very serious and extremely honest winemaker, makes no bones about saying that his 1988s generally lack the character of his richer, more compelling 1985s. Nevertheless, he had great success in 1988. His Vosne-Romanée is straightforward, compact, and pleasant, but the Vosne-Romanée Les Brûlées is disappointing given that it comes from such a superb vineyard. His three Grands Crus in 1988 are excellent to outstanding. He uses 30%–35% new oak for the Grands Crus, and his 1988 Echézeaux displayed beautiful toasty new oak which only seemed to accentuate the wine's perfumed, flowery character.

Elegant, medium bodied with a lovely berry fruitiness, the wine, while precocious and drinkable now, should last for 7–8 more years. Engel's Clos Vougeot, from vines that average 25–35 years of age, possesses a deep, jammy, berry fruitiness, some attractive smoky, toasty oak, and an inner strength and richness. It may well merit a higher score when it reaches full maturity in several years. The most concentrated, deepest, and most profound wine from Engel's cellar in 1988 is the Grands Echézeaux. It has a wonderful sweetness and intensity of flavor, long, concentrated flavors, spicy new oak, and soft acids and tannins. It should drink well for another 5 to 7 years. Engel admits that when his 1985s were conceived, he was not as talented a winemaker; his wines suffered as a result. From a technical point of view, his 1988s are the best wines he has produced.

DOMAINE MICHEL ESMONIN (GEVREY-CHAMBERTIN)

1988 GEVREY-CHAMBERTIN	84
1988 GEVREY-CHAMBERTIN-CLOS ST. JACQUES	90

Esmonin's 1988 Gevrey-Chambertin displays an attractive stylish, cherry-scented fruitiness, and a nice touch of oak, but lacks the depth and nuances to merit higher marks. However, his Gevrey-Chambertin-Clos St.-Jacques is concentrated, and reveals a dazzling array of aromas such as plums, cassis, dried herbs, and toasty new oak. It is altogether enthralling. In the mouth, the wine is harmonious and surprisingly soft, but there is tannin in the finish. This rich, relatively large-scaled wine should age gracefully for another 7–8 years, but it can be consumed earlier.

FAIVELEY (NUITS ST.-GEORGES)

1988 CLOS DE LA ROCHE	87
1988 CLOS VOUGEOT	92
1988 CHAMBERTIN-CLOS DE BÈZE	90
1988 CORTON-CLOS DE CORTON	91
1988 GEVREY-CHAMBERTIN LES CAZETIERS	86
1988 GEVREY-CHAMBERTIN LA COMBE AUX MOINES	87
1988 LATRICIÈRES-CHAMBERTIN	90
1988 MAZIS-CHAMBERTIN	88

The Faiveley firm produced good wines in 1988, but the margin of success was less than might have been expected, given the firm's excellent 1987s. No one will compare Faiveley's 1988s with his brilliant and sublime 1985s. Even François Faiveley admits his 1988s are less concentrated and less well structured for aging than the 1985s. Nevertheless, there are still many fine wines to choose from, including a very supple, cherry-scented, smooth and silky Nuits St.-Georges-Clos de la Maréchale. This is always an excellent choice for consumers in search of wines that should be drunk in their first 5–7 years of life, or restaurants looking for ready-to-drink burgundy. The 1988 should last for 5–7 years. There is also an outstanding, rich, peppery, earthy, slightly oaky but plum-flavored Nuits St.-Georges Les Damodes, and an even fuller, riper Nuits St.-Georges Les St.-Georges. Les Damodes can be drunk over the next 7–8 years while waiting for the firmer, fuller-bodied, more ambitious Les Saint-Georges to reach maturity.

As for Faiveley's two Premiers Crus from Gevrey-Chambertin, it is always hard to pick a favorite. I find La Combe aux Moines slightly more classic with richer, riper berry fruit, and more graceful elegance, whereas Les Cazetiers seems more oaky and a bit more rustic with berry flavors intertwined with scents of ground beef, leather, and exotic spices. Both wines, while drinkable young, should last up to a decade.

With respect to the Grands Crus, the Clos de la Roche has a wonderful forward, soft, supple texture and smooth finish. It is amazingly easy to drink now, and for that reason it should be drunk over the next 6–7 years. Faiveley made a great Latricières-Chambertin in 1988 that rivals the superb 1985 he produced. He thinks it may be even better than his 1985. There is no doubting its awesome concentration, profound, spicy, leathery, ground beef, exotic sort of aroma, and concentrated, medium- to full-bodied texture. It is soft, but has good, firm tannins in the finish. Drinkable early on, this wine should easily benefit from 2–3 years of bottle age and should last for up to a decade. Faiveley also made a stunning Clos Vougeot in 1988, which is oozing with the smell of red currants and toasty oak. In the mouth, it is pure velvet, jammy, berry fruit, and has a long, heady, alcoholic finish. It is a big wine by the standards of 1988, and while I did not see a great deal of tannin in it, the wine's sheer size suggests it will last for up to a decade. The 1988 Chambertin-Clos de Bèze may not be as profound as the 1985, but it is still another top-notch effort from Faiveley. It is softer and more approachable than usual, without the structure and depth typical of this wine. In comparison to most of the wines Faiveley produced from this vineyard, it is destined to be relatively short lived, lasting only for 8–12 years. It has a big, beefy, chocolate and berry-scented bouquet, and soft, smooth flavors. Last, Faiveley made another sensational wine from the firm's exclusively owned Corton-Clos de Corton *monopole* vineyard. It is the most backward and tannic of all the Faiveley 1988s, and has a dense ruby/purple color, a sensational bouquet of raspberries that reminded me more of Côte Rôtie than Burgundy, fabulous length and richness, good acidity, and an elevated level of tannins in the finish. This wine should be one of the few 1988s from Faiveley to last 20 or more years.

JEAN FAUROIS (VOSNE-ROMANÉE)

1988 CLOS VOUGEOT	90
1988 VOSNE-ROMANÉE LES CHAUMES	88

If you are fortunate enough to find the wines of Jean Faurois, you will rarely be disappointed, as this man is a meticulous craftsman whose handcrafted wines provide extraordinary pleasure. His 1988 Vosne-Romanée Les Chaumes has wonderfully deep, rich, luscious, berry fruit intertwined with the scent of herbs and spicy oak. He bottles his wines unfined and unfiltered, so there is no chance of losing any flavor between the barrel and bottle. Full bodied, intense, and silky, this beautiful wine should drink extremely well for the next 7–8 years. Unfortunately, only 100 cases were made—for the world. His Clos Vougeot, from a parcel of 70-year-old vines located next to the Château de Clos Vougeot, is also superb. The wine is concentrated and intense, bursting with highly extracted, jammy, red fruits yet buttressed nicely by the use of toasty new oak; it should drink well for 7–8 years. Faurois is a great winemaker, and has been remarkably consistent in recent vintages.

BERNARD FEVRE (SAINT-ROMAIN)

1988 AUXEY-DURESSES	87
1988 BEAUNE LES EPENOTTES	90
1988 BEAUNE LES TEURONS	87

1988 POMMARD LES EPENOTS	87
1988 SAINT-ROMAIN	84

All of these wines brilliantly display pure cherry and cassis fruit. The fullest and most muscular wine of the group is the Auxey-Duresses; it is robust, intense, and a true *vin de garde*. It is concentrated and should last for at least a decade. If you desire immediate gratification, look for the gorgeously scented, supple, fat, plump Beaune Les Epenottes, or the heady, very round, delicious Beaune Les Teurons. Both of these wines should drink well for the next 6–7 years, but deliver their charms immediately. The 1988 Pommard Les Epenots is almost as structured, full bodied, and tannic as the Auxey-Duresses. However, it does have a more precocious personality than the Auxey-Duresses, and should be drunk in its first 8–9 years of life. It shows excellent concentration, good spicy, cherry fruitiness, and a long, harmonious finish.

FOREY PÈRE ET FILS (VOSNE-ROMANÉE)

1988 ECHÉZEAUX	88
1988 NUITS ST.-GEORGES LES PERRIÈRES	86
1988 VOSNE-ROMANÉE	84
1988 VOSNE-ROMANÉE LES GAUDICHOTS	90

This small producer located on the back streets of Vosne-Romanée near the cellars of the Domaine de la Romanée-Conti, is probably best known for its famous La Romanée. They produce this wine for the Belair family and then turn it over to the huge Beaune *négociant*, Bouchard Père et Fils. Their own wines include an elegant, stylish Vosne-Romanée. In 1988 it is smooth and supple, and should be consumed over its first 4–5 years. They make a Premier Cru from Nuits St.-Georges called Les Perrières, which is a spicy, robust, moderately tannic wine that needs a few years in the cellar to round into form. In 1988, it is good rather than dazzling. The Foreys own a tiny portion of the Vosne-Romanée Les Gaudichots vineyard, the vineyard from which the great Grand Cru La Tâche was carved. The 1988 Les Gaudichots from Forey is superb, possessing an exotic, rich, intense, berry- and spice-scented bouquet, fabulously deep velvety flavors with layers and layers of fruit, and moderate tannins in the finish. This is quite a splendid wine made from vines planted in 1929. Unfortunately, only 50 cases were made. Last, their Grand Cru, the 1988 Echézeaux, seemed very successful, but exhibited no greater concentration than their 1987 Echézeaux. It has a lot of spicy new oak in the nose, and the scent of cassis and berries. It should drink well early on, and represents a graceful, stylish, elegant effort from this vineyard.

JEAN GARAUDET (POMMARD)

1988 BEAUNE-CLOS DES MOUCHES	87
1988 MONTHÉLIE	86
1988 POMMARD	87
1988 POMMARD LES CHARMOTS	92

Garaudet is a terrific but generally unknown source for superb wines. He is a great believer in low yields, which accounts for the striking concentration and purity to his wines. His youngest vineyard (15-year-old vines) is the Beaune-Clos des Mouches. In 1988 he made an excellent wine. It has an explosion of red fruit in the nose and is soft, supple, and absolutely delicious to drink now. I would not want to hold it more than another 4–5 years, given its low acidity and undeniable charm. His Monthélie, which may be the best example from this appellation, has none of the rustic, coarse tannins that so often plague the wines from this village. In 1988 he made only 625 cases, and the wine has wonderful ripeness, a hedonistic black cherry fruitiness, medium body, excellent balance, and a long, heady, alcoholic finish. The tannins are soft, and the wine should be consumed over the next 5–7 years. Garaudet is famous for his two Pommards. His generic Pommard, made primarily from 70-year-old vines, is aged in 50% new oak casks for 18 months, and is a gloriously decadent, rich, lush wine bursting with pure berry fruit and spicy new oak. It is so delicious to drink now, I am tempted to say it will not age, but I suspect if consumed over the next 5–6 years, it will provide a great deal of pleasure. Garaudet's Pommard Les Charmots is absolutely dazzling in 1988, and is certainly one of the top wines of the vintage. Aged in 100% new oak and made from a vineyard planted in 1902, it is irrefutably great Pinot Noir. With its fabulous heady, intoxicating bouquet of black fruits, spicy oak, and minerals, this full-bodied, awesomely rich, concentrated wine is as sensational as Pinot Noir can get. I would drink it over the next 7–8 years, and not worry about deferring my gratification.

LUCIEN GEOFFROY (GEVREY-CHAMBERTIN)

1988 GEVREY-CHAMBERTIN LES CHAMPEAUX	85
1988 GEVREY-CHAMBERTIN-CLOS PRIEUR	88
1988 GEVREY-CHAMBERTIN LES ESCORVÉES	87
1988 MAZIS-CHAMBERTIN	90

I have stated many times that I am sometimes at a loss to fully understand Geoffroy's wines. They are remarkably deep in color, but are often excessively oaked and impossible to characterize as Gevrey-Chambertins. I thought his 1988s were his most successful wines, as they not only expressed their appellation, but also the style of the vintage. They again showed the impressive deep color Geoffroy is able to obtain, and also revealed rich fruit and plenty of toasty new oak. In addition to a relatively light yet charming Les Champeaux, which borders on being overly oaked, Geoffroy produces a fine Gevrey-Chambertin Les Escorvées with a plummy, tarry-like bouquet, spicy new oak, and medium to full-bodied finish. One of Geoffroy's best wines is the Gevrey-Chambertin-Clos Prieur. It has generous amounts of smoky, toasty oak, gorgeous amounts of ripe, plummy fruit, medium to full body, good acidity, and the potential to last for 8–10 more years. Geoffroy's other top wine is the Mazis-Chambertin, which is superb, offering a glorious amalgam of scents including tar, Provençal herbs, black fruits, and spicy oak. In the mouth, it is long, rich, extremely concentrated, and should last for at least a decade or more.

DOMAINE ARMAND GIRARDIN (POMMARD)

1988 BEAUNE-CLOS DES MOUCHES	85
1988 POMMARD LES CHARMOTS	87
1988 POMMARD LES EPENOTS	90
1988 POMMARD LES RUGIENS	90

What Girardin's wines lack in finesse they more than compensate for in power, concentration, and a gutsy level of fruit that borders on the unreal. Low yields and old vines seem to be Girardin's magic formula. His 1988s are equal to, but no better than, his stunning 1987s. His Beaune-Clos des Mouches displays a deep ruby color, excellent ripeness as well as a lot of spice and hard tannins in the finish. It is uncharacteristically big and forceful for a Premier Cru from Beaune. I would age it for 3–4 years. Among the Pommards, the Les Charmots is always the lightest. It is deep and rich, quite spicy with a tar-like, chocolaty, raspberry, and herb-tinged flavor. Medium to full bodied with some moderate tannins to shed, I would not touch it for 2–3 years. However, it should be drunk within its first 12 years of life. The two top wines here are consistently the Pommard Les Epenots and Pommard Les Rugiens, because they both come from vineyards that are 80 years old. The Epenots is very rich and concentrated with the telltale chewy, chocolatey, berry fruit characteristic of Girardin's wines. Full bodied with plenty of alcohol and large amounts of tannin in the finish, it is a beefy, muscular wine that should be drunk between 1992–2005. The Rugiens is even riper and fuller with expansive, powerful flavors, plenty of toasty new oak, and once again, a chewy, chocolatey, plum-like fruitiness. It should last for 10–15 years, perhaps longer.

MACHARD DE GRAMONT (NUITS ST.-GEORGES)

1988 BEAUNE-CHOUACHEUX	89
1988 BEAUNE LES EPENOTTES	88
1988 CHAMBOLLE-MUSIGNY	85
1988 NUITS ST.-GEORGES LES DAMODES	90
1988 NUITS ST.-GEORGES LES HAUTS POIRETS	88
1988 POMMARD LE CLOS BLANC	90

Monsieur Gramont is one of my favorite producers in Burgundy. He never succumbs to overstating a vintage. He will not agree with those who claim the 1988 reds were better than the 1985s, arguing that if they are, it is because the producer did not know how to make wine in 1985. He claims his 1985s are the wines to cellar, while his 1988s should provide delicious drinking for their first 7–8 years of life. I couldn't agree more. This is an excellent domaine to consider. There are a lot of reds from which to choose, and they all share a certain suppleness and forward, generous, ripe berry character. The Chambolle-Musigny is pure charm and elegance, and should be consumed over the next 4–5 years. Among Gramont's Premiers Crus from the Côte de Beaune is the excellent Beaune Les Epenottes. It is a deep, quite concentrated, rich, long, and an altogether hedonistic, intensely flavorful wine that is undeniably appealing now and should only get better over the next 5–6 years. The Beaune-Chouacheux is more structured than the Epenots.

While it is not as charming at the moment, it shows deliciously intense, rich, ripe berry fruit, a nice touch of oak, and the potential to last for up to a decade. The Pommard Le Clos Blanc is usually one of Gramont's finest wines, and has been absolutely marvelous in vintages such as 1985, 1979, and 1978. The 1988 is another success revealing a heady, intoxicating perfume, spicy oak, plum and berry-like fruitiness, and rich, alcoholic, muscular flavors. It is soft and supple with low acidity and should be consumed over the next 7–8 years. Gramont has a number of vineyards in the Côte de Nuits. I did not see all of them, but I was extremely impressed with his Nuits St.-Georges Les Hauts Poirets, which is a great wine for the vintage as it possesses super ripeness, a big damson plum-like bouquet, deep color, oodles of fleshy fruit, low acidity, and a heady, alcoholic finish. His Nuits St.-Georges Les Damodes is even more impressive than Les Hauts Poirets. Explosively rich and ripe with a huge aroma of plum-like fruit, deep, earthy, berry-like flavors, and a gorgeous texture, this wine, although drinkable now, should be at its best in several years, and last about 8–10 years thereafter. Gramont's 1988s are clearly his most successful overall vintage since 1985.

ROBERT GROFFIER (MOREY ST.-DENIS)

1988 BONNES MARES	91
1988 BOURGOGNE ROUGE	84
1988 CHAMBERTIN-CLOS DE BÈZE	92
1988 CHAMBOLLE-MUSIGNY LES AMOUREUSES	90
1988 CHAMBOLLE-MUSIGNY LES HAUTS DOIX	85
1988 CHAMBOLLE-MUSIGNY LES SENTIERS	88
1988 GEVREY-CHAMBERTIN	84

Robert Groffier and his young, enthusiastic son, Serge, have put together three excellent vintages in a row for the first time since Groffier began estate-bottling his wines following the 1972 vintage. After producing relatively light, thin 1985s (an anomaly, given the superb quality of the raw materials that year), Groffier has been very successful, and the 1988s look to be the best he has yet made. For those wanting something to drink over the next 4–5 years at a reasonable price, Groffier's Bourgogne Rouge has crisp, lovely, cherry-like flavors, excellent ripeness, medium body, and a real sense of finesse and elegance. He makes this wine from a parcel of moderately old vines situated just outside the appellation of Clos Vougeot. I thought it was every bit as good as the Gevrey-Chambertin. Although the Gevrey-Chambertin is supple and pleasant, the young vineyard was just replanted in 1985. Groffier's Chambolle-Musigny Les Hauts Doix is all sweet, silky, supple, berry fruit wrapped intelligently in a glove of toasty oak. It is totally beguiling at present, and it could be consumed over the next 4–5 years. There is a significant jump in quality, extraction, and character with Groffier's Chambolle-Musigny Les Sentiers. An explosive bouquet of red fruits and toasty, smoky, new oak is followed by a wine with gorgeous amounts of extract, long, deep, supple flavors, medium body, soft tannins, and low acidity. Yet the requisite fruit and depth necessary to age well for 3–7 years is also present. Groffier routinely uses 50% new oak casks for his Premiers Crus, and 100% for his Grands Crus.

The best Premier Cru of the 1988 vintage is the staggeringly concentrated, dramatically scented, exotic Chambolle-Musigny Les Amoureuses (175 cases were produced). It has a fabulous bouquet of toasty new oak, and deep, rich, dark, plummy fruit. In the mouth, it is concentrated, medium to full bodied, quite soft and velvety, exotic, and altogether a hedonistic mouthful of burgundy. I would drink it over the next 5–6 years. The same can be said for Groffier's Bonnes Mares, although he only makes 175 cases. It is slightly deeper and more structured than Les Amoureuses, and shows a more smoky character because it is aged in 100% new oak (Les Amoureuses sees 50%). It has a long, deep, somewhat gamey character with sensational flavor extract and length. It is drinkable now, but should be at its best between 1991–2000. As wonderful as the Bonnes Mares is, Groffier's finest wine in 1988 is his Chambertin-Clos de Bèze. Produced from 45-year-old vines, he kept the yield in the relatively abundant year of 1988 to 25 hectoliters per hectare. Only 75 cases of this compelling wine were produced. It is powerful, but has a huge, smoky, almost bacon fat–scented bouquet with lots of rich, berry and plum-like fruit, full body, layers of extract, and a long, velvety, lush finish. My tendency is to suggest it should be drunk immediately, but there is tannin and good acidity, and one suspects this wine should last easily for 8–12 years.

JEAN GROS (VOSNE-ROMANÉE)

1988 BOURGOGNE HAUTES-CÔTES DE NUITS	84
1988 RICHEBOURG	90
1988 VOSNE-ROMANÉE	85
1988 VOSNE-ROMANÉE-CLOS DES RÉAS	88

This superb domaine has produced many compelling wines in the eighties. While the Madame Gros 1988s do not compare with her great 1985s, 1983s or even her stunning 1987s, they are excellent wines for the vintage. Madame Gros is a great believer in the Hautes-Côtes de Nuits potential for quality and value, and her 1988 is an extremely fruity, ripe, deliciously supple, attractive wine ready for drinking over the next 3–4 years. The Vosne-Romanée Villages seems to lack the complexity and precision of flavor of the 1987, but it is spicy, shows an attractive ripeness, and should be consumed over the next 4–5 years. The 1988 Vosne-Romanée-Clos des Réas seems to be slightly lighter than the 1987, 1985, or 1983, but it is elegant, shows its telltale bouquet of oriental spices, black fruits, spicy oak, and plums, and is soft and smooth in the finish. I would drink it over the next 5–7 years. The Richebourg, which was absolutely profound and one of the three or four greatest wines of the 1987 vintage, seems less concentrated, but is still full of black fruits, spicy oak, and a touch of minerals and flowers. It is more forward than the 1987, yet also seems to have more tannin in the finish. This seems contradictory, but it does not appear to have the exceptional harmony the 1987 possessed. It should be drunk over the next 7–8 years.

GROS FRÈRE ET SOEUR (VOSNE-ROMANÉE)

1988 BOURGOGNE ROUGE	83
1988 CLOS VOUGEOT	87
1988 GRANDS ECHÉZEAUX	87
1988 RICHEBOURG	88
1988 VOSNE-ROMANÉE	85

Bernard Gros, much like his mother, Madame Jean Gros, let his yields get a bit too high in 1988. This prevented him from producing truly profound wine. As a result, I tend to prefer the 1987s from both these producers. Bernard Gros' 1988s include a rather light, soft, straightforward, adequate Bourgogne Rouge, and a much more interesting, but still light, fruity, soft, ready-to-consume Vosne-Romanée. None of the Grands Crus exhibit the splendid concentration and exotic character of the great vintages from Bernard Gros, such as his 1987s, 1985s, and 1983s. His Clos Vougeot is an excellent wine by any standard, but lighter than usual with plenty of intense strawberry and bing cherry fruit, a nice touch of spicy oak, medium body, and a soft, low-acid finish. The Grands Echézeaux is precocious as well, showing less intensity and concentration than the 1987, a heady, alcoholic bouquet, ripe, berry-scented flavors, medium body, and a supple finish. The Richebourg has a great deal of tannin, and is a fuller-bodied, more structured wine. It was aged in 66% new oak casks in 1988. It is big and rich, but I did not think it had the overall character of Bernard Gros' splendid 1987.

LOUIS JADOT (BEAUNE)

1988 AUXEY-DURESSES-DUC DE MAGENTA	86
1988 BEAUNE LES BOUCHEROTTES	89
1988 BEAUNE-CLOS DES URSULES	90
1988 BEAUNE-HOSPICES DE BEAUNE-CUVÉE NICOLAS ROLIN	88
1988 BONNES MARES	85
1988 BOURGOGNE ROUGE	84
1988 CHAMBERTIN-CLOS DE BÈZE	92
1988 CHAMBOLLE-MUSIGNY	85
1988 CHAPELLE-CHAMBERTIN	94
1988 CHASSAGNE-MONTRACHET MORGEOT-CLOS DE LA CHAPELLE (DUC DE MAGENTA)	87
1988 CLOS VOUGEOT	90
1988 CORTON LES POUGETS	87
1988 GEVREY-CHAMBERTIN	84
1988 GEVREY-CHAMBERTIN-CLOS ST.-JACQUES	87
1988 GEVREY-CHAMBERTIN ESTOURNELLES ST.-JACQUES	85
1988 GEVREY-CHAMBERTIN LA PETITE CHAPELLE	90
1988 GRIOTTE-CHAMBERTIN	92
1988 MARSANNAY	84
1988 MAZIS-CHAMBERTIN	89
1988 MUSIGNY	89
1988 NUITS ST.-GEORGES	86
1988 NUITS ST.-GEORGES LES BOUDOTS	89
1988 NUITS ST.-GEORGES-CLOS DES CORVÉES	89

The outstanding firm of Louis Jadot is run by André Gagey, his son, Pierre-Henri, and oenologist Jacques Lardière. The 1988 was their second best vintage for red wines in the eighties. This firm has always enjoyed a sensational reputation for its white wines, but I continue to be amazed by the number of people who do not recognize the excellence of Jadot's traditional, old-style red wines. There are no gimmicks or modern-day techniques used in the vinification, simply a long *cuvaison* and warm fermentation. The results are wines that will last for many years in the bottle, and admirably represent their appellations. In 1988, Jadot produced a good Bourgogne Rouge (30,000 cases were made). Jadot's 1988 Bourgogne-Rouge should be consumed over its first 3 years of life. The 1988 Marsannay is tasty, straightforward, and simple, but shows less supple, berry fruit. The Duc de Magenta's holdings in Auxey-Duresses produce more serious wines, including a 1988 Auxey-Duresses-Duc de Magenta that revealed nice fatness, medium to full body, good, spicy, cherry fruitiness buttressed by crisp acidity and some robust tannins. Magenta's Chassagne-Montrachet Morgeot from his vineyard called Clos de la Chapelle was even deeper, with more elegance and another layer of ripe red fruits superimposed on a solid framework of toasty oak. It is hard to produce a good quality wine from Pernand-Vergelesses, but Jadot's Clos de la Croix Pierre exhibits a pleasing plumpness, a bouquet that suggests toasted almonds and bing cherries, medium body, and a soft, lush finish; it is ideal for drinking over the next 4–6 years.

Among the Villages wines from the Côte de Nuits, Jadot produced a light, seductive, tender yet agreeably fruity Chambolle-Musigny, a more tannic, tougher-textured, coarser yet still ripe and concentrated Gevrey-Chambertin, a smoky, earthy Nuits St.-Georges, and a lean, malnourished, disappointing Vosne-Romanée. Perhaps one of the best Villages wines made is Jadot's 1988 Pommard from the Côte de Beaune. In the end, the southern part of the Côte de Beaune may have had the greatest success in the 1988 vintage, and this Villages wine is truly wonderful. It is oozing with ripe red and black fruits, shows a deft touch of toasty new oak, and a lush, supple, concentrated texture with layers of super-ripe fruit in the finish. It should drink nicely for 5–6 years.

With regard to the other Premiers Crus and Grands Crus from the Côte de Beaune, Jadot normally specializes in the two Premiers Crus of Beaune Les Boucherottes and Beaune-Clos des Ursules. Both are top wines in 1988. The Beaune Les Boucherottes, which enjoyed nearly a month's *cuvaison* and is made from 60-year-old vines, is a deliciously rich, long, supple, intensely concentrated wine that should drink beautifully for at least a decade. The Beaune Clos des Ursules is even better, because it seems to have more elegance and every bit as much seductive power as the Boucherottes. It is aged in 40% new oak and displays a nice toasty, vanillin scent to go along with its jammy, intense, berry fruitiness. All these wines are a bit fuller bodied, bigger, and have slightly more tannin than Jadot's 1987s.

Jadot also purchased several cuvées from the Hospices de Beaune in 1988. His best is the Cuvée Nicolas Rolin, named after the founder of the Hospices de Beaune. It is a pure, silky, berry-scented wine exhibiting a generous touch of toasty new oak, and opulent, silky, smooth flavors. It is deceptively easy to drink now, but one suspects, given its weight and structure, that it will age nicely for 10 or more years.

I would be remiss if I did not tell everyone to get their orders in for Jadot's extraordinary Pommard Les Epenots in 1988. This cuvée, of which there were only 225 cases made, will rival the best wines from top-notch domaines such as the Comte Armand, Madame Courcel, and Pothier-Rieusset. It is a massive wine oozing with black cherry fruit. Full bodied, awesomely concentrated, even unctuous and opulent on the palate, this splendid, compelling wine should drink well for at least a decade. The Corton Les Pougets is slightly below the Pommard Les Epenots in quality. It has excellent ripeness, a mineral-scented black fruit character, medium body, but not nearly the weight of the Pommard Les Epenots.

Traditionally a house that operated generally within the confines of the Côte de Beaune, the firm of Jadot has continued to build its empire with the acquisition of prime vineyards in the Côte de Nuits. The addition of many of the vineyards from the famous old Clair-Dau estate, and more recently those of Champy Père et Fils (with holdings in Clos Vougeot), will help to make Jadot's name synonymous not only with outstanding red and white burgundies from the Côte de Beaune, but also with superlative reds from the Côte de Nuits. In 1988 the estate produced an excellent Nuits St.-Georges Les Boudots, which has a smoky, elegant, plum-scented bouquet, earthy, rich, medium-bodied flavors, excellent extract, and the potential to last for at least 10 years. Jadot's Nuits St.-Georges-Clos des Corvées is even fuller. Not surprisingly, this is a specialty of the house, as Jadot controls 80% of the production of this Premier Cru vineyard. It is more tannic and structured than Les Boudots, shows excellent ripeness, but needs several years in the bottle to round into form. It should drink well from the mid-nineties through the first decade of the next century.

Jadot rarely makes a Vosne-Romanée Les Suchots but in 1988 the firm produced a superlative example from this great Premier Cru vineyard. Quite concentrated and aromatic with plenty of muscle and richness, this stunningly proportioned, herbaceous, and black-cherry-scented wine should last for 10 or more years. Their Clos Vougeot is equally superb and has been a consistent winner for Jadot throughout the eighties. For example, one of the great 1983s was made from their holdings in Clos Vougeot, and another top wine was produced in 1985. The 1988 is intense, with a big, forceful, dramatic bouquet of red fruits and spicy oak, explosive richness on the palate, medium to full body, and a silky, luscious finish. Its precociousness suggests it should drink extremely well early on, and I would opt for consuming it over the next 7–8 years.

Gevrey-Chambertin has become one of Jadot's favorite appellations because of their acquisition of many of the vineyards of the Clair-Dau estate. In 1988 they made a relatively light, but elegant, pretty wine from Gevrey-Chambertin Estournelles St.-Jacques. It is delicious, stylish, not terribly concentrated, but ideal for drinking over the next 4–5 years. I also thought their Gevrey-Chambertin-Clos St.-Jacques did not compete favorably with the extraordinary Clos St.-Jacques made by the small grower Michel Esmonin. Jadot's is tannic, medium bodied, has good ripeness and fine length, but for the moment appears to be a very good rather than profound example from this superbly situated vineyard.

Jadot makes three outstanding wines from the Grands Crus Griotte-Chambertin, Ruchottes-Chambertin, and Chapelle-Chambertin. These should be on the shopping list of anyone with money to spend. The 1988 Griotte-Chambertin is a gorgeous wine. It displays a huge bouquet of roasted, ripe berry fruit, exhibits a nice touch of toasty, smoky oak, is full-bodied, lush, and opulent on the palate, and should drink well for the next 5–10 years. I do not expect it to be a long-lived brute like the Ruchottes-Chambertin, but it is pure, silky hedonism at the moment. Ruchottes-Chambertin, a big, powerful, muscular, structured, almost savage wine, is impressive because of its weight and intensity, but it needs some time to reveal all its charm and finesse. The 1988 is one of

Jadot's most backward wines from this vintage, and should prove to be very special if it is aged for the 6–8 years it requires to round into form; it should drink well through the first decade of the twenty-first century. Jadot's Chapelle-Chambertin, made from 50-year-old vines, is regrettably produced only in very small quantities (150 cases in 1988). It is a soft, silky, almost tender wine, and its appeal is its seductive perfume, and velvety, lush texture. I would drink it over the next 6–7 years while waiting for the Ruchottes to shed some of its tannic clout. The Mazis-Chambertin is excellent, but did not seem to have quite the complexity or concentration of the other three Grands Crus. It is deep and fat with a lot of rich, spicy, earthy, berry fruit, and needs a good 2–3 years in the cellar to reach its apogee. Not surprisingly, the Chambertin-Clos de Bèze, always a winner from this house, received 26 days of maceration in 1988. The result is a beautifully scented wine smelling of exotic spices, soy sauce, ground beef, and lots of ripe berry fruit. It is full bodied, very rich, but is not comparable to the celestial 1985. Nevertheless, it is an outstanding red burgundy from this vintage. I was a little disappointed in the 1988 Bonnes Mares, which was good, but tasted a little diluted. It lacked the length and concentration I would expect from one of the Côte de Nuits' most underrated Grand Cru vineyards. Last, the Musigny displayed slightly more concentration in 1988 than in 1987. It had the elegance one expects from this Grand Cru, a beautiful bouquet of berry fruit and toasty oak, and medium body on the palate. It should drink nicely for the next 7–8 years.

If it is available, you should not forget the Gevrey-Chambertin La Petite Chapelle. This is a great wine in 1988, somewhat low in acidity, but bursting with huge quantities of red and black fruits, spicy new oak, and the scent of spring flowers. It should provide excellent drinking for the next 5–7 years.

ROBERT JAYER-GILLES (MAGNY-LES-VILLERS)

1988 CÔTE DE NUITS-VILLAGES	90
1988 ECHÉZEAUX	96
1988 HAUTES-CÔTES DE BEAUNE	87
1988 HAUTES-CÔTES DE NUITS	88
1988 NUITS ST.-GEORGES LES DAMODES	91

Robert Jayer should prove to be one of the great stars of the nineties. He makes the finest wines from the Hautes-Côtes de Beaune and

Hautes-Côtes de Nuits that I have ever tasted. His wines often rival the finest Premiers Crus from the Côte d'Or, and while I have heard people complain that his prices are high, they never lament the quality of Jayer's wines. 1988 may well be his most successful overall vintage. His Hautes-Côtes de Beaune is a truly wonderful wine; It is loaded with black cherry fruit, has a medium to full body, is wrapped nicely in toasty new oak, and is smooth in the finish. It is a gorgeous wine for restaurants and should drink nicely for another 5–6 years. Shockingly, the 1988 Hautes-Côtes de Nuits is even richer and fuller, with a wonderful blackcurrant bouquet intertwined with the scent of herbs, toasty new oak, and exotic spices. It is a superb wine for the appellation. If other growers could produce as much character and quality in their Hautes-Côtes de Nuits, it would definitely be an appellation to search out for fine wines at great prices. Jayer also produced the finest Côte de Nuits-Villages wine I have *ever* tasted. When I first tasted it, I thought I was actually tasting one of his Premier Cru or Grand Cru. I was not. This is an astonishingly rich, full-bodied, fabulously concentrated, highly extracted wine that would embarrass many mediocre and good growers' Premiers Crus and Grands Crus from the Côte d'Or. You must try it in order to see what this man is capable of doing with a lowly appellation. One of the most renowned wines of Jayer's portfolio, is the Nuits St.-Georges Les Damodes, which in 1988 is extremely tannic, muscular, full bodied, bursting with extract, but in need of at least 4–5 years of cellaring. It is black/ruby in color, and a worthy successor to his excellent 1987, which was one of the very best wines of the vintage. Jayer's other renowned wine is his Echézeaux, and in 1988 it is mindboggling. It is a staggering wine that simply defines great Pinot Noir. From its marvelous multidimensional bouquet of violets, spicy new oak, red and black fruits, and minerals, to its astonishingly precise, welldelineated flavors, this rich yet superbly harmonious wine should drink beautifully for another 10–15 years. Bravo!

DOMAINE JOBLOT (GIVRY)

1988 GIVRY-CLOS DE BOIS CHEVAUX	86
1988 GIVRY-CLOS DES CELLIER AUX MOINES	87
1988 GIVRY-CLOS DE LA SERVOISINE	88

The Domaine Joblot's wines from Givry are impeccable examples of fine red burgundy that is still fairly priced. The young Joblot has increased the size of his domaine as well as the percentage of new oak, and the results are some deliciously supple, concentrated wines that prove him to be a motivated, talented winemaker. In 1988, there are three Givrys to choose from: a soft yet excellent, highly aromatic, but lighter-styled Clos de Bois Chevaux; a richer, deeper, more ageworthy, fuller Clos des Cellier aux Moines; and the biggest and richest of the trio, the Clos de la Servoisine, an extremely concentrated, spicy, highly extracted, and immensely impressive wine. It could be confused with some Premiers Crus or even some Grands Crus from the Côte de Nuits. These are excellent wines for drinking over the next 5–7 years.

LABOURÉ-ROI (NUITS ST.-GEORGES)

1988 CHAMBOLLE-MUSIGNY-DOMAINE MODOT PREMIER CRU	84
1988 CLOS VOUGEOT	77
1988 CÔTE DE NUITS-VILLAGES-BELLE MARGUERITE	84
1988 ECHÉZEAUX	85
1988 GEVREY-CHAMBERTIN-DOMAINE JACQUESON	84
1988 POMMARD LES BERTINS-DOMAINE CHANTAL LESCURE	86

This reliable mid-sized firm in Nuits St.-Georges produced sound rather than dazzling 1988s. One of their best values is their excellent Côte de Nuits-Villages called Belle Marguerite. In 1988 it is a big, beefy, spicy, almost peppery wine with a lot of fruit and character for its price. It should drink nicely for 4–5 years. Labouré-Roi represents a number of domaines, including the Domaine Modot in Chambolle-Musigny and the Domaine Jacqueson in Gevrey-Chambertin. The Chambolle-Musigny is an elegant, medium ruby-colored wine with good fruit and spice, in addition to some acidity and soft tannins in the finish. The Gevrey-Chambertin-Domaine Jacqueson is a bit riper and fuller and has more of an earthy character. Both wines should be consumed over the next 4–5 years. The Pommard Les Bertins is usually one of the top red wines made at Labouré-Roi, and the 1988 manifests a big, peppery, spicy, herb- and plum-scented bouquet, medium to full body, good structure and acidity, and a competent finish. It should drink well for the next 6–7 years. The Echézeaux is ripe, elegant, and medium bodied with an attractive raspberry-scented bouquet buttressed nicely by some toasty vanillin oak. In the mouth, it is medium bodied, has good acidity, and a decent finish. As for the Clos Vougeot, I found this wine entirely too tannic and tough textured. It also lacked the fruit necessary to back up the tannins.

DOMAINE LAMARCHE (VOSNE-ROMANÉE)

1988 CLOS VOUGEOT	87
1988 ECHÉZEAUX	85
1988 GRANDS ECHÉZEAUX	85
1988 VOSNE-ROMANÉE	80
1988 VOSNE-ROMANÉE LES CHAUMES	81
1988 VOSNE-ROMANÉE LA GRANDE RUE	87
1988 VOSNE-ROMANÉE LES MALCONSORTS	82

Here is an estate making good, commercial examples of their appellations. However, with lower yields and perhaps a more extended *cuvaison*, this domaine has the potential to produce positively brilliant wines. I do not think it is just that the domaine seeks to produce wines that are light and ready to drink when released. The 1988s are all soft, very forward, and lacking somewhat in concentration, but they are attractive and easy-to-drink wines. They should all be consumed within the first 6–7 years after the vintage. The Vosne-Romanée is spicy, soft, and straightforward. The Vosne-Romanée Les Chaumes is also light, and seems to be produced from relatively young vines, given the slight vegetal character in the nose. It has some tannin in the finish, but there is just not much fruit or substance on the palate. The same can be said for the Vosne-Romanée Les Malconsorts, which has an almost rosé color, a light perfume of red fruits and toasty oak, medium body, and a low-acid, soft, somewhat diluted finish. It is a pleasant, lighter-weight burgundy. However, this wine comes from one of the great Premier Cru vineyards of Vosne-Romanée, and tastes more like a generic Bourgogne-Rouge. Fortunately, there is an upward turn in quality with the Grands Crus. The Echézeaux is ripe, displays better color than the other wines, is medium bodied, soft, and should be consumed over the next 5–6 years. It is hardly profound, but is a good bottle of burgundy. The Grands Echézeaux exhibits a deeper color, a richer, more cassis-scented bouquet, a judicious use of toasty new oak, light to medium body, and 5–7 years of potential evolution. As for the Vosne-Romanée La Grande Rue, it is the pride and joy of this house, and has long been considered by outside observers to be capable of producing Grand Cru quality wine. However, as good as the 1988 is, it is no Grand Cru. It has good color, and is probably the best wine Lamarche has made from this vineyard in well over a decade, but it should have more depth and complexity. It is a medium-bodied, aromatic, stylish wine with attractive berry fruit and spicy new oak, but it lacks outstanding concentration and complexity. The Clos Vougeot should prove to be the best wine made by Lamarche in 1988. It is by far the most concentrated wine, exhibiting more body, tannin, and depth than his others. It also has an enthralling bouquet of intense berry fruit, and the potential to last up to a decade, a long period of time by Lamarche's standards.

PHILIPPE LECLERC (GEVREY-CHAMBERTIN)

1988 BOURGOGNE ROUGE	84
1988 GEVREY-CHAMBERTIN LES CAZETIERS	95
1988 GEVREY-CHAMBERTIN LES CHAMPEAUX	89
1988 GEVREY-CHAMBERTIN COMBE AUX MOINES	94
1988 GEVREY-CHAMBERTIN LES PLATIÈRES	87

Given the insatiable worldwide demand for Leclerc's wines, their extraordinary quality, and the increasingly high prices being asked for them, it is curious that other growers do not follow his lead. In 1988, Leclerc made staggeringly great wines, on a par with his 1985s. He likes them better than his 1985s, but then, it is rare to find a French winemaker who does not believe that his or her best wine is the one that is available for sale. In 1988, Leclerc extended his *cuvaison* to nearly one month, a practice almost unheard of in Burgundy. His wines are also never fined nor filtered. All of them spend nearly three years in 100% new oak casks prior to bottling. His 1988 Bourgogne Rouge is a straightforward, plump, chunky, wonderfully fruity, but essentially simple wine that will make ideal drinking over the next 3–4 years. His Gevrey-Chambertin Les Platières has a big, peppery, spicy, earthy bouquet, and powerful, deep flavors that border on being akin to something from the southern Rhône rather than Burgundy. It has excellent color and plenty of depth. It should drink well for 7–8 years. The Gevrey-Chambertin Les Champeaux tasted supple with expansive flavors of cassis and other herb-tinged, black fruits. It is full-bodied, rich, and seductive. It is a wine to drink over the next 6–7 years. Leclerc's greatest wines in 1988 should come as no surprise. In most years I have had a slight preference for the Combe aux Moines, but in 1988 I thought his Gevrey-Chambertin Les Cazetiers was on par with the great wines from the Domaine de la Romanée-Conti. The fabulously exotic, rich, multidimensional bouquet was followed by gorgeous layers of extract, layer upon layer of smoky, herb-tinged fruit flavors, soft tannins, a full body, and a finish that must last several minutes. It is a wine that can be drunk young, but will certainly last for a dozen or more years. The 1988 Gevrey-Chambertin Combe aux Moines is an equally compelling wine, although I did not think it had quite the extra measure of depth of Les Cazetiers. Perhaps it is simply more backward and the depth will emerge in time. It is truly a great expression of Gevrey-Chambertin, with its wild, savage, animal-like bouquet that exhibits exotic spices, sweet, toasty oak, and powerful, black cherry aromas. In the mouth, it is awesomely concentrated, full bodied, rich, and long with the potential to last for another 7–12 years. These last two wines will be among the great stars of the vintage in 1988.

FRANÇOIS LEGROS (NUITS ST.-GEORGES)

1988 BOURGOGNE ROUGE	78
1988 CHAMBOLLE-MUSIGNY LES NOIROTS	90
1988 MOREY ST.-DENIS-CLOS SORBÈS	82
1988 NUITS ST.-GEORGES LES BOUSSELOTS	85
1988 VOUGEOT LES CRAS	86

All of François Legros' 1988s were well-made wines, including a straightforward, tannic, peppery, spicy Bourgogne Rouge, which should last for 4–5 years. His Morey St.-Denis-Clos Sorbès, made from his youngest vines, exhibited a pure raspberry and strawberry-like character and good tannin, but showed a lack of depth and finish due to the youth of the vineyard. However, his other wines performed admirably. The Nuits St.-Georges Les Bousselots was an excellent wine with a big, aromatic bouquet of damson plum fruit, medium body, nice ripeness and richness, and soft tannins in the finish. It should drink well for 5–6 years. The Vougeot Les Cras was even better. Intensely perfumed with the smell of jammy strawberries and raspberries, this rich, ripe, medium- to full-bodied wine displayed plenty of depth and ripeness, and should last for up to a decade. Another of his top 1988s was his Chambolle-Musigny Les Noirots, which is made from very old vines, and is surprisingly concentrated, muscular, and deep for a wine from Chambolle-Musigny. Almost black in color with layers of fruit, this should prove to be one of the sleepers of the vintage. François Legros' other Premiers Crus from Nuits St.-Georges, La Roncière, La Perrière, and Rue de Chaux were sold off to *négociants* in 1988, but will be estate-bottled in 1989.

LEQUIN-ROUSSOT (SANTENAY)

1988 CHASSAGNE-MONTRACHET MORGEOT	85
1988 BOURGOGNE ROUGE	82
1988 POMMARD	86
1988 SANTENAY	84
1988 SANTENAY LA COMBE	85

I have long been an admirer of the superlative white wines produced by the Lequin brothers in Santenay. Lequin-Roussot remains one of the most underpublicized sources of top-notch white burgundy in the Côte d'Or. However, for years their red wines were another matter entirely —often thin, tannic, and lacking in charm and finesse. They have been making efforts to correct their faults and seem to have been successful in the 1988 vintage. An excellent year overall, 1988 favored the southern part of the Côte de Beaune. Their Bourgogne Rouge reveals good ripeness, an attractive strawberry and cherry fruitiness, medium body and soft tannins. It should be drunk within 2–3 years of the vintage. The Santenay has a more spicy, smoky *terroir* character, medium body, light tannins, and some good berry fruit in evidence. The Santenay La Combe is better yet; it increases the level of extract, has a richly fruity, smoky, medium-bodied texture, good length, harmony, and enough tannin and depth to last for 5–8 years. In fact, it might be worth aging this wine for a year or two so that the tannins will melt away a bit. The Chassagne-Montrachet Morgeot has an impressive, rich, jammy, cherry-scented nose, a touch of dried herbs, and a relatively full-bodied, tannic constitution. It is quite well made, but needs several years in the cellar to round out. It is a wine that should last easily for a decade. If you like rustic and earthy red burgundies, this is a good choice in 1988. Finally, the Pommard is excellent, probably the best red wine I have tasted from the Lequin brothers. Very intense and rich, with gobs of deep berry-scented fruit, and an almost chocolate-like, cedary character to it, this concentrated, full-framed wine is about as good a Villages Pommard as you will find. Drink it over the next 7–8 years.

DOMAINE LEROY (AUXEY-DURESSES)

1988 AUXEY-DURESSES	87
1988 CHAMBERTIN	96

1988 CLOS VOUGEOT	90
1988 MUSIGNY	90
1988 NUITS ST.-GEORGES LES ALLOTS	87
1988 NUITS ST.-GEORGES LES BOUDOTS	93
1988 NUITS ST.-GEORGES LES LAVIÈRES	87
1988 NUITS ST.-GEORGES LES VIGNES RONDES	88
1988 POMMARD LES VIGNOTS	92
1988 RICHEBOURG	98
1988 ROMANÉE ST.-VIVANT	98
1988 SAVIGNY-LÈS-BEAUNE LES NARBANTONS	88
1988 VOSNE-ROMANÉE	90
1988 VOSNE-ROMANÉE LES BEAUX MONTS	89
1988 VOSNE-ROMANÉE AUX BRÛLÉES	94

Most of these wines represent the first vintage for Madame Lalou Bize-Leroy's new domaine in Vosne-Romanée. Many of the vineyards she acquired were previously owned by the Domaine Noëllat. Her first, and perhaps best decision, was to hire the Hospices de Beaune's extraordinarily talented winemaker, André Porcheret. Madame Leroy's remarkable commitment to quality has resulted in sensational 1988s. The yields were kept to an ultraconservative 20–25 hectoliters per hectare, and in 1989 she began making the wines organically. Given the remarkable quality and Lalou Bize's unwavering, highly motivated commitment to quality, I expect the new Domaine Leroy to rival the Domaine de la Romanée-Conti. The 1988 Auxey-Duresses, which is part of her previous portfolio of holdings, but is now incorporated into the new Domaine Leroy, is ripe, round, delicious, and soft, showing none of the coarse tannins that often come from the red wines of Auxey-Duresses. It has plenty of length and richness, and I would expect it to be at its best over the next decade. Savigny-Lès-Beaune is a terribly underrated appellation. With a highly talented winemaker and low yields, the results are wines such as the Savigny-Lès-Beaune Les Narbantons. It has strikingly deep, rich, berry fruit in evidence, medium to full body, a soft, voluptuous texture, and a super finish. It should drink beautifully for 10–12 years. The 1988 Pommard Les Vignots is a wine to search out. It is absolutely fabulous, and in style and character seems to resemble the 1985 more than any other vintage. It has a dazzling rich, highly-scented bouquet of black and red fruits, spicy new oak, and minerals. In the mouth, the wine has awesome concentration and an extremely full body with stunning levels of fruit extract, all handsomely packaged in a medium- to full-bodied format. This gorgeous wine should drink well for up to two decades. In comparison, the Nuits St.-Georges Les Allots (one of four Premiers Crus that Bize-Leroy now makes wines from in Nuits St.-Georges) is ripe, with a smoky, deep, earthy fruitiness, medium body, and a soft, underlying texture. It is a very good rather than profound wine, ideal for drinking over the next 7–8 years. Les Lavières is another elegant wine from Nuits St.-Georges. It has a deep ruby red color, a round, medium-bodied texture, and excellent ripe fruit. The overall impression is one of lightness and elegance in a more delicate style than Les Allots. For pure, decadent, hedonistic levels of soft, silky, plum-like fruit, try the Nuits St.-Georges Les Vignes Rondes. This wine is already performing splendidly well, and given its precocious personality and charm, it should be consumed over the next 6–8 years. It is a delight to drink. However, the Domaine Leroy's greatest Nuits St.-Georges made in 1988 is the Nuits St.-Georges Les Boudots. The huge, roasted, plummy bouquet suggests sensational extract character and *sur maturité*. In the mouth, this wine has spectacular depth, richness, and layers of fruit. The acidity is sound, and the balance is virtually perfect. This rich, concentrated, lavishly endowed wine should drink beautifully over the next 15 or so years. I doubt that any of these wines will qualify as great bargains, but I have never tasted a better Vosne-Romanée Villages than that made by the Domaine Leroy. Only 125 cases of this spectacular Vosne-Romanée were made from a vineyard planted in 1902. It is clearly indicative of what old vines and low yields can extract from a parcel that is not as well placed as the Premiers Crus or Grands Crus of Vosne-Romanée. Astonishingly deep, rich, and concentrated with gorgeous amounts of red and black fruits, this wine should drink well for another 10–15 years. Do not pass it up because it is only a Villages wine.

Among the Premiers Crus from Vosne-Romanée, the Vosne-Romanée aux Brûlées is more concentrated, deeper, and compelling than the Vosne-Romanée Les Beaux Monts. While this latter wine is excellent, displaying fine ripeness, good tannins, sound acidity, and a concentrated, nicely textured feel on the palate, the Vosne-Romanée aux Brûlées is awesomely rich, packed with fruit, and full bodied, with a fabulously long finish. It has a roasted richness and ripeness that is usually found only in the great vintages.

As for the Grands Crus, there is a highly extracted, explosively scented, berry fruit flavored Clos Vougeot that is medium-bodied, supple, and lovely to drink. It is not profound by Lalou Bize-Leroy's standards, but it is an extremely concentrated, well-balanced bottle of wine that should evolve gracefully for 10–20 years. Lalou also produced a legendary Romanée St.-Vivant in 1988. A surreal wine that easily surpasses any wine I have ever tasted from this Grand Cru vineyard, it comes preciously close to perfection. It should drink well from the mid-nineties through the first two decades of the next century, perhaps even longer. It is a phenomenal bottle of wine, equalled only in 1988 by the Domaine Leroy's 1988 Richebourg. This wine has slightly less finesse and a less perfect bouquet than the Romanée St.-Vivant, but it is more muscular, fuller-framed, and a titan of a wine with its huge proportions and massive concentration and depth. These are monumental old-style burgundies that are meant to last for ages, and I am envious of anyone who is fortunate enough to put them in their cellars.

The Domaine Leroy also produces an elegant, ginger- and floral-scented Musigny that is quite aromatic, medium bodied, and all finesse and charm. I doubt that it will be that long lived, but it should certainly last 10–15 years. If it were not for the Romanée St.-Vivant and Richebourg, I would be ecstatic over the fabulous 25 cases of Chambertin that Lalou Bize-Leroy made in 1988. However, for now it must take a back seat to the other two wines. It is a big, rich, earthy, cinnamon, almost raunchy-scented wine, but is sensationally concentrated and full bodied, with fabulous balance and precision to its flavors. I would not touch a bottle before the mid-nineties, and I would fully expect it to mature beautifully for another 20 years thereafter.

The 1988 vintage attests to a remarkably auspicious start for the new Domaine Leroy in Vosne-Romanée.

GEORGES LIGNIER (MOREY ST.-DENIS)

1988 BONNES MARES	85
1988 CHAMBOLLE-MUSIGNY	77
1988 CLOS ST.-DENIS	85
1988 CLOS DE LA ROCHE	87
1988 GEVREY-CHAMBERTIN	81
1988 GEVREY-CHAMBERTIN LES COMBOTTES	83
1988 MOREY ST.-DENIS	79
1988 MOREY ST.-DENIS-CLOS DES ORMES	86

This is an estate with immense potential, given the extraordinary vineyards owned by Lignier. However, the tendency to let yields balloon upward to filter the wine, and the practice of bottling the wine a little too late often result in wines that are more impressive from cask than from bottle. Lignier has consistently maintained that he likes his 1988s better than his 1985s, but I disagree. He claims that the 1988s remind him of a hypothetical blend of 1978 and 1985. I found his 1988s to be a bit light and lacking concentration across the board. His Morey St.-Denis is straightforward, fruity, and soft; it should be drunk over the next several years. The same can be said for his Chambolle-Musigny in 1988, although it is even lighter and has more acidity. His Villages wine from Gevrey-Chambertin is better. It is spicy, ripe, round, and straight-forward, but it is concentrated and a good wine for drinking over the next several years. Georges Lignier is one of the fortunate few to have a parcel of the outstanding Premier Cru vineyard in Gevrey-Chambertin, Les Combottes. His 1988 is soft and round, slightly jammy and lacks a bit of grip and concentration. However, it is spicy, and ideal for drinking over the next 3–4 years. Lignier also owns one of the outstanding Premier Cru vineyards of Morey St.-Denis, the Clos des Ormes. His 1988 is aromatic, very elegant, and extremely soft, with loads of berry fruit. It should be drunk immediately, given its fragile structure. His Clos St.-Denis (Lignier is the largest vineyard holder of this great Grand Cru) displays more tannin than most of his other wines, but still has a ripe, velvety, berry fruitiness, a moderately long finish, and me-dium body. It is also marked by much more new oak. However, I do not share Lignier's belief that this wine is better than his profound 1985 from this vineyard. I thought Lignier's best 1988 was his Clos de la Roche, which had a great nose of berry fruit, spicy new oak, minerals, and flowers. In the mouth, it offered excellent concentration, medium body, wonderful harmony among all its elements, and a long finish. It is the most concentrated and longest-lived 1988, but I would still want to drink it within its first decade of life. Lignier's 1988 Bonnes Mares (only 100 cases were made) is soft and lacking a bit of structure, but it is fruity, very forward, and pleasant. All things considered, I suspect if the yields had been lower and Lignier had bottled his 1988s earlier, they would have been significantly better.

HUBERT LIGNIER (MOREY ST.-DENIS)

1988 CHAMBOLLE-MUSIGNY LES BAUDES	87
1988 CHARMES-CHAMBERTIN	96
1988 CLOS DE LA ROCHE	96
1988 MOREY ST.-DENIS PREMIER CRU	88

Hubert Lignier's 1988s should prove to be among the superstars of the vintage, particularly his two Grand Cru efforts, which are utterly mind-blowing. His 1988 Premiers Crus are also excellent wines. For example, his Chambolle Musigny Les Baudes is an extremely rich, concentrated, harmonious wine. It exhibits a stunning marriage of new oak and ripe, jammy, berry fruit. It is concentrated, but very precocious, and should be drunk over the next 6–8 years. The 1988 Morey St.-Denis Premier Cru is more concentrated, has more structure and tannin, and is also fuller bodied. Again, Lignier manifests his brilliant winemaking with a superb marriage of toasty new oak and fruit. This wine actually needs 1–3 years in the cellar to round out and shed some tannin; it could deserve an outstanding rating by 1992–1993, and should last for up to a decade. In 1988 Lignier produced his second vintage of Charmes-Chambertin. It is one of the most monumental wines produced in burgundy during the eighties. Phenomenally extracted with a dazzling black/ruby color, this wine, made from extremely old vines, exhibits sensational concentration and an unbelievable richness. Unfortunately, there will only be a handful of cases available for the export market. For the lucky few who find a bottle of this sublime and staggering red burgundy, it should make a fabulous glass of hedonistic wine between 1995–2005. Lignier's 1988 Clos de la Roche, of which there are 300 cases for the world, is every bit as good. It is not quite as black/ruby in color as the Charmes-Chambertin, but it too is awesomely concentrated with a fabulous, highly scented perfume of black fruits, exotic spices, and toasty new oak. In the mouth, the layers of fruit are astounding, and the finish lasts for at least two minutes. Lignier has made some spectacular wines in 1988. None of the wines are fined or filtered, and as a result, they will throw a heavy sediment in 2–3 years time.

HENRI MAGIEN ET FILS (GEVREY-CHAMBERTIN)

1988 GEVREY-CHAMBERTIN	69
1988 GEVREY-CHAMBERTIN LES CAZETIERS	72
1988 GEVREY-CHAMBERTIN PREMIER CRU	70

This domaine's 1988s were significantly inferior to its mediocre 1987s. All the wines were excessively high in acidity, and watery, as if the yields were too high. They also had entirely too much tannin and acidity for the meager amounts of fruit present. These wines cannot be recommended under any circumstances.

DOMAINE MALDANT (CHOREY-LÈS-BEAUNE)

1988 ALOXE-CORTON PREMIER CRU	75
1988 CHOREY-LÈS-BEAUNE	78

1988 CORTON-GRÈVES	73
1988 CORTON LES RÉNARDES	76

All of these wines lacked fruit, and tasted stripped, as if they had been excessively fined and/or filtered. When a Chorey-Lès-Beaune shows as much fruit and character as a Corton Grand Cru like the Rénardes, something is clearly amiss. Perhaps I saw bad bottles, or caught the wines in a very odd stage of development, but my conclusions are that the wines are light, simple, overly processed, and lacking depth and concentration.

JEAN-PHILIPPE MARCHAND (GEVREY-CHAMBERTIN)

1988 CHAMBOLLE-MUSIGNY LES SENTIERS	86
1988 CHARMES-CHAMBERTIN	89
1988 GEVREY-CHAMBERTIN	82
1988 GEVREY-CHAMBERTIN LES CHERBAUDES	86
1988 GEVREY-CHAMBERTIN LES COMBOTTES	88
1988 MOREY ST.-DENIS	82
1988 MOREY ST.-DENIS-CLOS DES ORMES	90
1988 MOREY ST.-DENIS LES FAUCONNIÈRES	74

Jean-Philippe Marchand could well be a name to watch in the nineties. He has continually demonstrated his commitment to high quality, and has had the courage to stop filtering his wines. He has also made other improvements, such as branding all his corks and using heavier bottles. All of these signs point to a domaine on the verge of stardom. Among the 1988s, there is a fruity, supple, soft Morey St.-Denis, a relatively lean, high-acid, shallow Morey St.-Denis Les Fauconnières, and a gloriously perfumed, heady, sumptuous Morey St.-Denis-Clos des Ormes. The Clos des Ormes, with its explosive red fruit character, should make a delicious wine for drinking over the next 7–8 years. The Chambolle-Musigny Les Sentiers shares the same good, crisp acidity as Marchand's other 1988s, plenty of depth and fruit, medium to full body, and an attractive, highly aromatic bouquet of toasty new oak and raspberry fruit. Marchand made a straightforward, firmly structured, well-colored Villages wine from Gevrey-Chambertin in 1988, a much richer, spicier, tannic, and tough-textured Gevrey-Chambertin Les Cherbaudes (it needs several years in the cellar to round out), and a fragrant,

deep, spicy, complex Gevrey-Chambertin Les Combottes. The latter
wine may be, along with Marchand's Charmes-Chambertin and Clos
des Ormes, his best wine of the vintage. Concentrated with deep, berry
and animal-like flavors, medium to full body, and a compelling and
penetrating bouquet, this wine should be drunk between 1992–2000. As
for the Charmes-Chambertin, it is softer and more flattering to taste
than some of his other wines. It has excellent color, very good ripeness,
attractive acidity (which gives precision and clarity to its flavors), medium body, and a long finish. It should age handsomely for up to a
decade.

DOMAINE MONGEARD-MUGNERET (VOSNE-ROMANÉE)

1988 CLOS VOUGEOT	91
1988 ECHÉZEAUX-CUVÉE VIEILLES VIGNES	90
1988 FIXIN	80
1988 GRANDS ECHÉZEAUX	92
1988 RICHEBOURG	93
1988 SAVIGNY-LÈS-BEAUNE LES NARBANTONS	87
1988 VOUGEOT PREMIER CRU	85
1988 VOSNE-ROMANÉE	83
1988 VOSNE-ROMANÉE ORVEAUX	86
1988 VOSNE-ROMANÉE LES SUCHOTS	87

Mongeard's great 1988s should equal the quality of his wonderful 1985s.
He has also added another vineyard to his growing empire, the excellent
Premier Cru, Les Narbantons in Savigny-Lès-Beaune. In 1988 the Villages wines were aged in 50% new oak and the Grands Crus in 70%.
Mongeard, like Jacques Seysses of the Domaine Dujac, believes in a
minimum 48-hour prefermentation cold maceration and no destemming. He differs significantly from the Domaine Dujac in that his wines
spend 20–24 months in oak casks. Mongeard's wines are generally
bottled with little or no filtration. The 1988 Fixin is soft, ripe, totally
ready to drink, and should be consumed over the next 4–5 years. It is
a decent value in the pricing scheme of Burgundy. 1988 marks the
release of Mongeard's first Savigny-Lès-Beaune Les Narbantons. The
wine clearly reflects the parcel's 50-year-old vines. It is very concentrated with a huge, intense, berry-scented bouquet, medium to full

body, plenty of structure, good acidity, and a long finish. It is a wine that can easily age for up to 10 years. The generic Vosne-Romanée is richly fruity, straightforward, supple, and ideal for restaurants and consumers desiring wine to consume over the next 3–4 years. The Vosne-Romanée Orveaux shows more depth, and a fragrant, raspberry and oak-dominated bouquet. It is medium bodied and lush, and should be drunk soon. Deeper still, and one of Mongeard's best Vosne-Romanées, is his 1988 Vosne-Romanée Les Suchots. Concentrated, full bodied, and exceptionally long in the mouth with a wonderful, silky, smooth texture, this seductive wine should make beautiful drinking for the next 7–8 years. The Vougeot Premier Cru is spicy, soft, easy to drink, and should be consumed over the next 4–5 years. The 1988 Clos Vougeot is a truly compelling wine. Its high quality is due in part to the fact that Mongeard's parcel is located high up on the slope. It is deep ruby in color with a huge bouquet of raspberry and blackberry–scented fruit judiciously backed up by the aroma of spicy new oak. It is crammed with fruit and tastes medium to full bodied, long and rich, making it a superb wine for drinking over the next decade. Mongeard's 1988 Echézeaux-Cuvée Vieilles Vignes is an excellent wine, but is not superior to his wonderful 1987. It is fuller bodied, and has more tannin to its personality, but the overall impression is one of great seductive power, black fruits, spicy new oak, and long, luscious flavors. The 1988 Grands Echézeaux, which I find to be Mongeard's best wine almost every year, has to take second place to his Richebourg. Perhaps it is because the Grands Echézeaux needs 2–3 years in the bottle to shed some of its tannin. It is a magnificent wine and is extremely concentrated and fabulously perfumed. It has excellent color and a very long, intense finish. In 4–5 years time it should rival the great wines Mongeard made from this Grand Cru in 1985 and 1983. Above all, I preferred the Richebourg. It was the most precocious of all the Grands Crus; an explosively rich, highly scented, celestial wine, it may not justify its exorbitant price tag, but it is still a profound bottle of great red burgundy. Drinkable now, it should last for up to a decade.

DOMAINE ALBERT MOROT (BEAUNE)

1988 BEAUNE LES BRESSANDES	88
1988 BEAUNE LES CENTS VIGNES	86
1988 BEAUNE LES MARCONNETS	88
1988 BEAUNE LES TEURONS	89
1988 SAVIGNY-LÈS-VERGELESSES-CLOS BATAILLIÈRE	86

For those readers who do not like to spend a lot of money for great red burgundy, the Domaine Morot offers some marvelous wines. It produces some of the longest-lived wines of the entire Côte d'Or at a fraction of the price of the wines from the famous vineyards and most renowned producers. The secret here is low yields, commitment to tradition, and the remarkable Madame Choppin. Her wines often need a good 7–8 years to reveal themselves but they can last up to 20 or more years. This aging potential is unheard of in today's world of soft-styled burgundies. Her 1988s should prove to be her best wines since the 1985s. There is an excellent Savigny-Lès-Vergelesses-Clos Bataillière. It exhibits tremendous extract, a spicy, earthy, berry fruitiness, medium body, good acidity, and some firm tannin in the finish. It needs several years to soften. Among the Premiers Crus in Beaune—the specialty of this house—there is a round, supple, charming, and delicious Beaune Les Cents Vignes, a richer, fuller, more expansively flavored, deeper Beaune Les Bressandes, a massive, medium- to full-bodied, tannic, backward, hugely impressive Beaune Les Marconnets, and a nearly outstanding, potentially long-lived, concentrated, spicy, toasty Beaune Les Teurons. With the exception of the Beaune Les Cents Vignes, I would give all of these wines at least 2–5 years in the cellar before drinking them. For example, the 1979s from this domaine are just beginning to drink beautifully, when many other producers' wines are starting to fall apart. The same can be said for the 1972s from Madam Choppin. Her wines from that vintage took nearly 15 years to reach maturity. This is a serious estate making very traditional, old-style red burgundies that merit more attention.

DENIS MORTET (GEVREY-CHAMBERTIN)

1988 BOURGOGNE ROUGE	84
1988 CHAMBERTIN	88
1988 CHAMBOLLE-MUSIGNY AUX BEAUX BRUNS	85
1988 GEVREY-CHAMBERTIN	81
1988 GEVREY-CHAMBERTIN LES CHAMPEAUX	88
1988 GEVREY-CHAMBERTIN-CLOS PRIEUR	85

Denis Mortet is one of the young, enthusiastic growers of Gevrey-Chambertin. His name will certainly become better known in the nineties. He uses 50% new oak and makes very stylish, elegant, fragrant wines with a lot of fruit. These wines do not have great aging potential, but for drinking within their first 7–8 years, they merit serious consideration. In 1988 Mortet made a fine generic Bourgogne Rouge with an attractive suppleness and soft, easy-going flavors. I liked it better than his straight Gevrey-Chambertin, which seemed somewhat diluted and too light. His Gevrey-Chambertin-Clos Prieur is a well-made, stylish, graceful wine. It is not a blockbuster, but is pretty, fruity, and easy to drink; I would consume it over the next 5–6 years. One of the secrets of this house is that Mortet's Gevrey-Chambertin Les Champeaux is better than his famed Grand Cru Chambertin. The 1988 is excellent with a sweet, expansive palate of black fruits, herbs, and new oak. It is luscious, seductive burgundy at its best, and should be consumed over the next 5–7 years. I also liked Mortet's Chambolle-Musigny aux Beaux Bruns, but it did not quite have the stature and complexity of the Les Champeaux. It is from an excellent Premier Cru vineyard that is not terribly well known. Lastly, the Chambertin shows plenty of toasty, smoky new oak, very good concentration, and is as good as the Gevrey-Chambertin Les Champeaux. It is lighter and more elegant. It has less concentration, but perhaps more complexity because of its multidimensional bouquet and soft, smooth finish. It should be drunk over the next 6–8 years.

GEORGES MUGNERET (VOSNE-ROMANÉE)

1988 CHAMBOLLE-MUSIGNY LES FEUSSELOTTES	89
1988 CLOS VOUGEOT	91
1988 ECHÉZEAUX	90
1988 NUITS ST.-GEORGES LES CHAIGNOTS	86
1988 RUCHOTTES-CHAMBERTIN	92
1988 VOSNE-ROMANÉE	84

The domaine of the late Georges Mugneret, now run by his beautiful daughter and niece, continues to turn out superlative expressions of Pinot Noir. Since the fifties this domaine, unlike most, has never experienced a slump in quality. It may not be obvious that the 1988s are better than the excellent 1987s (which were among the very best of that vintage). However, Mugneret's 1988s are fuller, more tannic, more ageworthy wines than his 1987s. The 1988 Vosne-Romanée exhibits excellent depth for a Villages wine. It has less complexity than the Premiers

Crus or Grands Crus, but has a vibrant, herb-tinged, berry fruitiness, medium body, good acidity, and the potential to drink well for another 5–6 years. The 1988 Nuits St.-Georges Les Chaignots tends to get overlooked, but it is an uncommonly elegant, smoky, well-made wine possessing a true Nuits St.-Georges *terroir*, earthy, roasted character. It tasted deceptively fruity, but I suspect it will last up to a decade. The Chambolle-Musigny Les Feusselottes is another wine that is often over-looked, but it certainly merits attention from any conscientious burgundy connoisseur. Made from moderately old vines averaging 25 years in age, the 1988 is a classic Chambolle-Musigny displaying a gorgeous bouquet of rich, ripe berry fruit, herbs, smoke, and flowers. In the mouth, it is velvety, silky, and should be consumed over the next 3–12 years. Mugneret's three Grands Crus are superlative expressions of wine—in nearly every vintage. The elegant, fragrant, and graceful Echézeaux possesses layers of berry fruit, a touch of violets, medium body, and an intense finish. Drinkable now, it should only get better over the next decade. The Ruchottes-Chambertin is consistently one of Mugneret's great wines. It is from an extraordinary Grand Cru vineyard that deserves a greater reputation than it has. The yields are kept conservatively low, 30–35 hectoliters per hectare, and the results are a compellingly concentrated, deep, rich, intense, full-bodied wine with a spicy, almost raunchy, game-like character, medium to full body, a lot of tannin, and layers of extract. The 1988 should ultimately rival his superb 1985 and 1978 Ruchottes-Chambertins. I would not drink it before the mid-nineties. The 1988 Clos Vougeot does not appear to have the outstanding concentration of Mugneret's 1985. In my tastings, I found that even the 1987 fared better than the 1988. However, the 1988 is an outstanding wine by any measure of burgundy. It is rich, full bodied, with good acidity, and an abundance of ripe berry fruit in the finish. It should drink well for another 10–12 years.

PHILIPPE NADDEF (COUCHEY)

1988 BOURGOGNE ROUGE	82
1988 FIXIN	80
1988 GEVREY-CHAMBERTIN	84
1988 GEVREY-CHAMBERTIN LES CAZETIERS	91
1988 GEVREY-CHAMBERTIN LES CHAMPEAUX	90
1988 MARSANNAY	84
1988 MAZIS-CHAMBERTIN	88

Philippe Naddef is capable of producing some truly fine wines from his impeccably managed cellar, particularly at the top level of the quality hierarchy in Burgundy. In 1988 his lower-level wines, like the Fixin, Bourgogne Rouge, Marsannay, and Gevrey-Chambertin, are all competent, straightforward wines exhibiting good ripeness, supple fruitiness, and balance. However, like most wines from those appellations, they are not dazzling. While Naddef's best wine should be the great Grand Cru Mazis-Chambertin, this is not true in 1988. His best two wines in this vintage are his Gevrey-Chambertin Les Champeaux and Gevrey-Chambertin Les Cazetiers. The Les Champeaux is made from 40-year-old vines, and displays a sensationally concentrated, intense palate, a glorious bouquet of black fruits and toasty new oak, and enough depth and balance to age for up to a decade. The Les Cazetiers is even better. It has greater depth, a more individualistic bouquet of ground beef, oriental spices, soy sauce, and gobs of black fruits. In the mouth, it is rich and concentrated, but more tannic than Les Champeaux. Both these wines seemed to overwhelm the shy, elegant, and graceful Mazis-Chambertin, an atypical wine for this Grand Cru vineyard. It was quite soft, fruity, medium-bodied, and seemingly ready to drink. However, I may have caught it at a bad period after it was bottled.

DOMAINE PONSOT (MOREY ST.-DENIS)

1988 CLOS DE LA ROCHE-CUVÉE VIEILLES VIGNES	95
1988 CLOS DE LA ROCHE-CUVÉE WILLIAM	92
1988 GRIOTTE-CHAMBERTIN	90
1988 LATRICIÈRES-CHAMBERTIN	88

It is a difficult and contradictory task for a buyer and critic to follow the fortunes of the Domaine Ponsot. The wines from this domaine can be absolutely staggering, as they were in vintages such as 1980, 1983 (which still needs another 5–10 years in the bottle), 1985, and now 1988. The inflexible philosophy of picking late, regardless of weather conditions, not chaptalizing, regardless of whether it is essential or not, never destemming, and never using sulfur dioxide can, when all the conditions are right, produce something quite compelling. When a little magic and the helpful addition of a few bags of sugar are essential, Ponsot's discipline is admirable, but his wines are less than mind-boggling. I did not have a chance to taste Ponsot's whole range of 1988s, but those I did see seemed stunning and the quality equivalent of their 1985s. However, they are more tannic and burly than the more suave, graceful 1985s. This domaine's Griotte-Chambertin always shows superb ripeness, a huge, herb-tinged, explosive, berry-scented bouquet, lush, sensual flavors, medium to full body, and a heady, alcoholic finish. The 1988 looks as if it will drink beautifully young, but I would not be surprised to see it last 15 more years. The Latricières-Chambertin was fat, full-bodied, ripe, and deep with an animal-like bouquet of ground beef, soy sauce, dried herbs, and overripe cherries. It is quite a hedonistic and sensual wine. It should provide provocative drinking for at least 12–15 years. In 1988, Ponsot decided to name one of the *cuvées* of Clos de la Roche, Cuvée William, after the founder of this estate. This wine would do the founder justice, as it is a truly magnificent concentrated wine with gobs of highly extracted fruit and an astounding multidimensional palate impression that seems to last for up to two minutes. It is a knockout wine, surpassed only by Ponsot's Clos de la Roche-Cuvée Vieilles Vignes. The latter wine is even richer, fuller, and deeper, made from vines averaging 35 years in age. When Ponsot is successful, he produces truly profound examples of old-style, highly extracted red burgundy that can last for two or more decades.

MICHEL PRUNIER (AUXEY-DURESSES)

1988 AUXEY-DURESSES-CLOS DU VAL	85
1988 AUXEY-DURESSES PREMIER CRU	84
1988 BEAUNE LES SIZIES	84
1988 VOLNAY LES CAILLERETS	87

It is unfortunate that Prunier's wines are largely unknown in the export markets because they represent surprisingly good values in vintages such as 1985 and 1988. His best wine is always his Volnay Les Caillerets. The 1988 is an impressive, rich, concentrated, well-structured wine redolent with the scents and flavors of red berry fruits, spicy oak, and with enough tannin to insure 6–8 years of longevity. His two wines from Auxey-Duresses also exhibit good winemaking. The Premier Cru is spicy with deep color, some rustic tannins, but plenty of ripeness, and 5–6 years of aging potential. The Auxey-Duresses-Clos du Val is a bit more elegant, and the tannins finer and less coarse. It is an attractive, medium-bodied, spicy, earthy wine, ideal for drinking over the next 5–

6 years. The Beaune Les Sizies is all fruit and charm with light to medium body, soft tannins, and a nice, heady, alcoholic finish. It is soft and delicious, and should be consumed over the next 2–3 years.

BERNARD RION PÈRE ET FILS (VOSNE-ROMANÉE)

1988 BOURGOGNE ROUGE	78
1988 CHAMBOLLE-MUSIGNY LES ECHÉZEAUX	88
1988 CHAMBOLLE-MUSIGNY LES GRUENCHERS	72
1988 CLOS VOUGEOT	92
1988 NUITS ST.-GEORGES	75
1988 NUITS ST.-GEORGES LES MURGERS	88
1988 VOSNE-ROMANÉE	80
1988 VOSNE-ROMANÉE LES CHAUMES	86

Bernard Rion made absolutely spectacular wines in 1987. They were better than his 1985s and his 1988s. The 1988s are sensationally concentrated at the top level, particularly the spectacular Clos Vougeot. This wine is so crammed with rich red and black fruits that it should turn out to be one of the great wines of the vintage when it reaches full maturity in 6–9 years. It is a splendid wine, and clearly something special. I hope consumers can find it. Some of the other wines were also impressive, if backward, high in acidity, and extremely tannic. One cannot deny the impressive color, richness, and structure of the Vosne-Romanée Les Chaumes and the Nuits St.-Georges Les Murgers. As impressive as both these wines are, I cannot help but point out their high acidity, excruciatingly high tannin levels, and pronounced oakiness. Perhaps everything will come together in another 3–4 years of aging. They appear to be very good, powerful, muscular wines that will take some patience to fully comprehend and appreciate. I thought the Chambolle-Musigny Les Echézeaux was better balanced, at least for near-term drinking, displaying a wonderfully ripe, plummy bouquet, excellent structure and length, and medium to full body. The other wines seemed slightly out of balance, in particular, a very lean, mean, acidic Chambolle-Musigny Les Gruenchers, an overly oaky yet dense Vosne-Romanée, and an excessively tannic Nuits St.-Georges. Rion's Bourgogne Rouge in 1988 should definitely be tried for its impressive color and power, but again, it is extremely oaky.

DOMAINE DE LA ROMANÉE-CONTI (VOSNE-ROMANÉE)

1988 ECHÉZEAUX	92
1988 GRANDS ECHÉZEAUX	95
1988 RICHEBOURG	96
1988 ROMANÉE-CONTI	97
1988 ROMANÉE ST.-VIVANT	90
1988 LA TÂCHE	97

The prices for the wines of the Domaine de la Romanée-Conti may be exorbitant but the quality of the wines produced in the eighties is truly remarkable. The 1988s are celestial wines selling at stratospheric prices. The 1988 production was twice what it was in 1987, but the same as in 1985. The 1988s are fuller-bodied, deeper, more concentrated wines than the superb 1987s, and will need some time in the cellar to shed their generous amounts of tannin. The only vintage they can be favorably compared with is the 1985 vintage, and the 1985s were a great deal more forward and flattering to taste when young. There is more depth in the 1988s than in the 1986s or even the superb 1980s (which turned out to be the finest wines made in that underrated vintage). Given 5–10 years of aging, the 1988s from the Domaine de la Romanée-Conti should prove to be dazzling wines. I do not think I have ever tasted a better example of Echézeaux, a wine that is usually their lightest and quickest to mature. In 1988, it is bursting with rich, concentrated, berry fruit, has the exotic, oriental spice character that often marks the wines from this domaine, and is sensationally long and full. Even though it is the most forward wine from the domaine, I would wait at least 5 years before drinking this beauty. I feel it has the requisite depth, concentration, power, and tannin to last two decades. I have been telling people for years that this domaine's "best buy," if such a label can be applied here, is the Grands Echézeaux. While it is not Romanée-Conti or La Tâche, it often comes very close to those two titans, at a fraction of the price. In 1988, it is fabulous. In fact, my unedited tasting notes had the words "fabulous" in them twice and "awesome" once. It is decadently rich and spicy with an extraordinary perfume of violets, gamey, plum-like fruit, toasty new oak, and a finish that must last several minutes. It, like the Echézeaux, should not be consumed for at least 5 years, and should easily last until 2010 or longer. I had a slight reservation about the Romanée St.-Vivant. As in 1987, I wondered whether the 1988 was excessively tannic and a gamble for the long run. There is no doubting its massive constitution, full body, and rich extract, but the tannins seemed extremely hard and tough, and this wine would appear to be at least a decade away from drinkability. Perhaps because one so rarely encounters this old-style, tannic type of burgundy, it is tempting to dismiss it as too hard and tough. Yet this wine might very well have the unheard-of aging potential of 30 or more years. As for the Richebourg, this was an explosive wine with an earthy, cinnamon, gingery, soy sauce aroma backed up with the intense smell of plums and toasty new oak. Extremely rich, full bodied, and awesomely proportioned, this heroic wine should be drunk from the late nineties through the first two decades of the twenty-first century. It seems bigger, fuller, and more powerful than even the celestial 1985. The two cornerstones of the Domaine de la Romanée-Conti are La Tâche and Romanée-Conti. The 1988 La Tâche has the monumental, telltale bouquet of overripe, gamey, exotic fruit, oriental spices, and flavors that simply overwhelm. It is clearly a fabulous wine with extraordinary concentration and presence on the palate and a mindblowing, utterly compelling finish. Fortunately, given the large production in 1988, there are 1,806 cases to be allocated around the world. My notes show an anticipated maturity date of 1995–2015. It is an incredible wine. Last, in 1988 there are 575 cases of Romanée-Conti. Consumers should be deliriously happy, considering there were only 225 cases in 1987. It is more backward than the 1987, 1986, or 1985, and is one of the fullest and most tannic examples of Romanée-Conti I have tasted this decade. It may even outlive the otherworldly 1985. It is staggeringly concentrated with a bouquet that almost defies articulation. There is no doubting what it is and who made it. It is a flashy, dramatic wine with astonishing length and mystique. I would not dare touch a bottle before the mid- to late nineties.

JOSEPH ROTY (GEVREY-CHAMBERTIN)

1988 CHARMES-CHAMBERTIN	92
1988 GEVREY-CHAMBERTIN LES CHAMPCHENYS	86
1988 GEVREY-CHAMBERTIN-CLOS PRIEUR	88
1988 GEVREY-CHAMBERTIN LES FONTENYS	88
1988 MARSANNAY	82
1988 MAZIS-CHAMBERTIN	90
1988 PINOT NOIR LES PRESSONIÈRES	84

Roty's use of 100% new oak and the bold personalities of his wines work best in years where the vintage rather than the winemaker shapes the wines. For example, he made positively brilliant 1985s, disappointing 1986s, adequate 1987s, and exceptional 1988s. Where the 1986s and 1987s lacked color, and seemed to be overwhelmed by Roty's insistence in using 100% new oak barrels, the 1988s represented the perfect foil for this style of winemaking. They are exotic, decadent wines, with the exception of the straightforward, lean Marsannay and soft, fruity Pinot Noir. Roty's other wines are stunning with deep, rich, concentrated, black fruit flavors, gobs of spicy new oak, and a style that someone will certainly say lacks subtlety and finesse. If that is true, these wines clearly compensate with a blast of rich berry fruit and oak. The best of the Premiers Crus is the Gevrey-Chambertin Les Fontenys. It has excellent concentration and depth, and could easily be confused for a Grand Cru. It should last for 10–12 years. I have always preferred the Charmes-Chambertin to Roty's Mazis-Chambertin. In 1988, the Charmes seems to be the better of the two wines, although they are strikingly similar. The Charmes has a softer texture and a flamboyant and dramatic, rich berry fruitiness backed up by spicy, new oak, full body, and plenty of soft tannin in the finish. It is cunningly and deceptively delicious to drink now, but given its depth and balance, it should last for 10–12 years, perhaps longer. The Mazis-Chambertin needs 2–3 years to shed its tannins and allow the wood to blend more with the black fruit character of the wine. It is rich, concentrated, and almost too much of a good thing, but for fans of this intense style, Roty is clearly on the mark in 1988.

DOMAINE GEORGES ROUMIER
(CHAMBOLLE-MUSIGNY)

1988 BONNES MARES	91
1988 BONNES MARES-CUVÉE VIEILLES VIGNES	96
1988 CHAMBOLLE-MUSIGNY	85
1988 CHAMBOLLE-MUSIGNY LES AMOUREUSES	90
1988 CHARMES-CHAMBERTIN	90
1988 CLOS VOUGEOT	87
1988 MOREY ST.-DENIS-CLOS DE LA BUSSIÈRE	87
1988 MUSIGNY	92
1988 RUCHOTTES-CHAMBERTIN	92

I have great admiration for Christophe Roumier and his father, Jean-Marie. While they have never really deviated from their philosophy of making long-lived, outstanding red burgundy, they have never been against modifications where it is necessary. Consequently, all their cellars were totally air-conditioned and humidified several years ago. After experimenting for much of the last several decades with a very light, gravity filtration, Christophe Roumier told me that the 1988s were bottled by hand with no filtration. I never thought the filtration stripped their wines, but it is encouraging to see they are always thinking of ways to improve them. This estate made great 1983s, a vintage that proved excessively difficult for many growers. While there have been some triumphant vintages for the Roumier family (1969, 1971, 1972, 1978, 1983, and 1985), the 1988s will certainly take their place with the best they have ever produced. Starting at the bottom of the hierarchy, there is an excellent, ripe, elegant, graceful Chambolle-Musigny that reflects the appellation and shows delicious cherry and raspberry fruit, medium body, and a soft texture. The Morey St.-Denis-Clos de la Bussière, which is aged in 25%–30% new oak, is a fleshy, elegant wine with an aromatic bouquet, medium to full body, and a spicy, earthy finish. It should drink nicely for 7–8 years. The 1988 Chambolle-Musigny Les Amoureuses is superb, with outstanding extract, a long, fleshy, seductive palate impression, and an excellent bouquet of red fruits and spicy new oak. It is delicious enough to drink young, but is capable of lasting for up to a decade. The Clos Vougeot, did not have the concentration of Les Amoureuses, but it was full bodied, redolent with the scent and flavors of black cherry fruit, and revealed a deft touch with new oak casks. The Charmes-Chambertin is impossible to find as the entire production is sold in Switzerland. They have only been making the wine since 1984, and the 1988, should anyone be lucky enough to find a bottle in Zurich or Geneva, is well worth buying. It is an outstanding wine—all finesse and velvety smoothness—and ideal for drinking over the next 6–7 years. In contrast; the Ruchottes-Chambertin is a muscular, full-bodied, highly extracted and flavorful wine with a great deal of character. In fact, some people feel it suffers from too much complexity. There is a sweet, leathery, almost ground beef and soy sauce aroma, and long, tannic, powerful, heady flavors. This wine should be laid away for at least 4–5 years and consumed over the following 15. It should prove to be one of the longest-lived wines of the vintage. In 1988 Roumier decided to make two cuvées of Bonnes Mares. The regular *cuvée* is an outstanding wine. It is supple, velvety, with gobs of rich berry fruit, a seductive finish, and an aging potential of 3–15 years. One hundred cases were made from a parcel of vines that averages 40 years in age. It is a staggering wine and is as concentrated as the finest Roumier wines I have ever tasted, hauntingly perfumed

with the scent of black fruits, spicy new oak, and minerals. It is unbelievably long and concentrated on the palate. It is tempting to say it is
drinkable now given its extraordinary fruit extract, but I suspect this
wine's apogee will be sometime between 1993 and 2010. Last, the Musigny displayed great fruit, elegance, and a tremendous aromatic penetration. It had nowhere near the weight of either the Bonnes Mares-
Cuvée Vieilles Vignes or Ruchottes-Chambertin, but made up for that
deficiency with its sheer velvety elegance and charm. It should drink
beautifully young, but will age gracefully for up to a decade.

CHRISTIAN SERAFIN (GEVREY-CHAMBERTIN)

1988 BOURGOGNE ROUGE	84
1988 CHARMES-CHAMBERTIN	90
1988 GEVREY-CHAMBERTIN	86
1988 GEVREY-CHAMBERTIN LES CAZETIERS	92
1988 GEVREY-CHAMBERTIN LE FONTENY	89
1988 GEVREY-CHAMBERTIN VIEILLES VIGNES	87

Christian Serafin has an admirable track record in off years such as
1986 and 1987, so one would expect him to excel in 1988. He is not the
best-known grower in Gevrey-Chambertin, but is certainly one of the
finest. People will hear his name more and more often in the nineties.
His traditionally conservative yields and increased usage of new oak
barrels seem to be the perfect marriage for the wonderfully rich, blackberry, cassis fruit he manages to routinely obtain from his vineyards.
His Bourgogne Rouge is a soft, straightforward, smooth wine that represents a good value, but do not buy it unless you plan to drink it over
the next several years. His generic Gevrey-Chambertin, aged in 100%
new oak, shows excellent ripeness and spicy, toasty oakiness. It is a
fine effort from an appellation where most of the Villages wines are
insipid and diluted. The Gevrey-Chambertin Vieilles Vignes has more
richness and ripeness, but the difference between the two in 1988 is not
as apparent today as it may be in 3–4 years' time. Wines like this,
which are backward and concentrated, often need several years to
mature fully. As for the other wines, Serafin made an absolutely wonderful Gevrey-Chambertin Le Fonteny. This is surprising given the
young age of his vineyard. It is deep ruby/purple in color with a huge
bouquet of cassis intertwined with the smell of herbs and toasty new

oak. It is ripe, medium to full bodied with layers of extract, and should drink well for the next 7–8 years. To me, Serafin's best wine, year in and year out is not his Grand Cru Charmes-Chambertin, but his Gevrey-Chambertin Les Cazetiers, a Premier Cru. In 1988 it is the most explosively rich, concentrated wine in his portfolio, and should be in any conscientiously stocked cellar in the world. It is bursting with black fruits and has an underlying licorice and exotic character that makes it even more riveting. It is awesomely concentrated and should be at its best between 1992 and 2002. As for the Charmes-Chambertin, it is slightly lighter, but all finesse, charm, roundness, and generosity. It does not have the wild, savage character of Les Cazetiers, but for pure elegance and finesse it is a superior wine.

BERNARD SERVEAU (MOREY ST.-DENIS)

1988 CHAMBOLLE-MUSIGNY LES AMOUREUSES	88
1988 CHAMBOLLE-MUSIGNY LES CHABIOTS	86
1988 CHAMBOLLE-MUSIGNY LES SENTIERS	86
1988 MOREY ST.-DENIS LES SORBÈS	85

Serveau's wines are among the most elegant expressions of Pinot Noir from the Côte d'Or. They are never deeply colored, robust, or muscular. Instead they are silky, light, aromatic, and designed to charm you into submission. The 1988 Morey St.-Denis Les Sorbès offers a lovely ripeness, very supple, smooth flavors, and a soft finish. It is hard to believe it will last beyond 5–6 years, but its balance is impeccable. The Chambolle-Musigny Les Sentiers seems to have a bit more focus and slightly longer, richer flavors, but it still carries the hallmark of this house in its velvety, soft, stylish personality. The Chambolle-Musigny Les Chabiots has an attractive, medium ruby color, a blossoming bouquet of flowers and red fruits, low acidity, good freshness and precision to its flavors, and a medium-bodied finish. The top wine from Serveau's portfolio in 1988 is no surprise: the Chambolle-Musigny Les Amoureuses. Although very little of this wine is made, it is always his ripest, richest, and most ageworthy wine. It shows more tannin and body than his other wines, but at the same time does not taste too hard or coarse to drink now. In fact, that is what is so appealing about Serveau's wines. They are cunningly delicious when released, and sometimes dismissed as being unworthy candidates for aging. However, their balance in good years is always a hallmark, and they can often last up to 10 years without losing their fruit and freshness.

JEAN TARDY (VOSNE-ROMANÉE)

1988 CHAMBOLLE-MUSIGNY	87
1988 CLOS VOUGEOT	92
1988 NUITS ST.-GEORGES LES BOUDOTS	90
1988 VOSNE-ROMANÉE LES CHAUMES	88

Tardy uses 100% new oak and is an exceptionally skilled winemaker. Fortunately, he decided to discontinue selling his production to Beaune *négociants* such as Louis Jadot and Joseph Drouhin and begin estate-bottling his wines. Tardy has a knack for turning out hedonistic, decadently rich, flavorful burgundies from his tiny vineyard holdings. The 1988s are his best wines since 1985. The Chambolle-Musigny displays superb ripeness, richness, a fragrant, aromatic bouquet, medium body, and a silky, smooth texture. The wine has tannin and some acidity, but its precociousness makes me think it should be drunk over the next 5–6 years. The Vosne-Romanée Les Chaumes has an explosive perfume of toasty vanillin oak and ripe, black cherry fruit. It is soft, but with superb length. It is richer, fuller, and more fragrant than the Chambolle-Musigny, and should last a few years longer. Tardy made two great wines in 1988, including his Nuits St.-Georges Les Boudots, which has a gigantic bouquet of overripe plums, smoky toast, and minerals. In the mouth, the wine is full bodied with layers of extract, and is rich and smooth in the finish. There is tannin, but like the 1985s, its pure, silky, fruitiness suggests it should be drunk within its first 7–8 years of life. Tardy has one of the best situated parcels in Clos Vougeot, and his 1988 is a mind-blowing wine. The overwhelming bouquet of red fruits and spicy oak is pure and intense. In the mouth, the purity and flavor extraction are awesome, and this gorgeously rich, full wine should drink well for another 8–9 years.

JEAN TAUPENOT-MERME (MOREY ST.-DENIS)

1988 CHARMES-CHAMBERTIN	86
1988 MOREY ST.-DENIS	85

The style of Taupenot's wines is a bit different from other producers', but there is something to be said for their heady, alcoholic, herbaceous aromas and soft, chaptalized, sweet, soupy structure. I would like to see more precision and delineation, but these clearly seem to be wines that are meant to be drunk young, in their lusty, direct state. Both these 1988s should be consumed over the next 3–4 years.

DOMAINE THIERRY-LESPINASSE (GIVRY)

1988 GIVRY EN CHOUÉ	86

This is an up-and-coming producer in the Côte Chalonnaise, making a ripe, berry-scented wine with good color, and surprising extract, charm, and fruit. It should drink well for the next 4–5 years. This is a producer to seek out in Givry for high quality at reasonable prices.

TOLLOT-BEAUT (CHOREY-LÈS-BEAUNE)

1988 BEAUNE-CLOS DU ROI	87
1988 BEAUNE LES GRÈVES	86
1988 CHOREY-LÈS-BEAUNE	84
1988 CORTON LES BRESSANDES	87
1988 CORTON LA COMBE	85
1988 SAVIGNY-LÈS-BEAUNE LES LAVIÈRES	85

This famous estate, discovered for the American market by the late Frank Schoonmaker, is a delicious source for supple, richly fruity, red wines in good vintages. The Tollots believe their 1988s are less tannic and concentrated than their outstanding 1985s. The 1988 Chorey-Lès-Beaune is a lighter-styled, but pleasantly fruity, soft, restaurant wine ideal for drinking over the next 3–4 years. The Savigny-Lès-Beaune Les Lavières has more depth and character to it with some delicious black cherry fruit, medium body, low acidity, and light tannins; I would drink it in the next 3–4 years. Monsieur Tollot makes some of the best Premiers Crus of Beaune. In 1988, he produced an excellent Beaune Les Grèves, which has a smooth, silky, seductive character with gorgeous levels of ripe berry fruit and toasty new oak. It is ideal for consuming over the next 4–5 years. Even better is his Beaune-Clos du Roi. It shows more structure than Les Grèves, a dazzling level of black cherry fruit, low acidity, and light to medium body. It is pure charm and finesse, provided it is consumed within the next 2–3 years. Among the bigger, more expensive wines from Tollot-Beaut is their Corton La

Combe, which I actually thought was less impressive than either of the Premier Cru Beaunes. It displayed a nice softness and ripeness, but did not seem to have the concentration I would expect from this vineyard. The Corton Les Bressandes, made from a 35-year-old parcel of vines, had more flesh and depth than any other red wine in the Tollot stable, but it is not as good as their smashing 1985. It is forward and precocious, and while there is no doubting its appeal, I would drink it over the next 4–5 years.

CHÂTEAU DE LA TOUR (VOUGEOT)

1988 BEAUNE	82
1988 BEAUNE-COUCHERIAS	86
1988 CLOS VOUGEOT	90
1988 CLOS VOUGEOT-CUVÉE VIEILLES VIGNES	93

Both the Beaune wines appear under the label Domaine Pierre Labet, the name of the proprietor of the Château de la Tour. They are actually made and cellared at the Château de la Tour and are available only in very small quantities. This house practices cold maceration. Since they began utilizing this technique with the 1987 vintage, the results have been impressive. The generic 1988 Beaune has excellent color, a broad, slightly soupy, but berry-flavored character, and low acidity. It should be consumed over the next 3–4 years. On the other hand, the Beaune-Coucherias exhibits better concentration, an impressive, deep ruby color, plenty of extract, and a long finish. The wine also reflects the spicy, new oak barrels in which it is aged. In 1988, Pierre Labet produced two cuvées of Clos Vougeot. The one you are most likely to encounter in the export markets, the Clos Vougeot, is made from a blend of 25- and 40-year-old vines. It has a splendid deep ruby color, a huge bouquet of jammy, raspberry, and cherry fruit, medium to full body, a judicious touch of toasty new oak, and a long finish. Drinkable now, it should continue to evolve and improve for another 7–10 years. The Cuvée Vieilles Vignes, made from a parcel of vines planted in 1910, is an absolutely astonishing wine with a rare opulence and concentration. It is bursting with berry fruit, and I thought it lacked acidity and tannin until I carefully inspected the wine's components. The wine is so obviously fruity and intense it is easy to overlook its good acidity and tannin levels. Unfortunately, Labet produces tiny amounts of the Cuvée Vieilles Vignes. This splendid wine should be drunk over the next decade.

DOMAINE COMTE DE VOGÜE (CHAMBOLLE-MUSIGNY)

1988 BONNES MARES	86
1988 CHAMBOLLE-MUSIGNY	77
1988 CHAMBOLLE-MUSIGNY LES AMOUREUSES	86
1988 MUSIGNY-VIEILLES VIGNES	88

1988 may turn out to be the Comte De Vogüé's best overall vintage since 1972. However, I suspect this estate's wines could be even greater, given the enormous potential of the vineyards. This firm used 45% new oak in 1988, and it almost overwhelmed the light, medium-bodied, pale-colored, tannic Chambolle-Musigny. I do not see how this wine will ever have the fruit to balance out its oak and acidity. There is a large increase in quality with the Chambolle-Musigny Les Amoureuses. It is much longer and riper with a lovely elegance and graceful, rich berry fruitiness married intelligently with toasty, smoky new oak. It should drink beautifully for 7–8 years. Although it is a Grand Cru, the Bonnes Mares failed to overwhelm the Chambolle-Musigny Les Amoureuses. It shared an elegant, graceful style, medium body, and attractive fruitiness, but seemed constrained. The overall impression was one of compactness; the quality seemed very good rather than exhilarating. The Musigny-Vieilles Vignes (1,405 cases were made in 1988) is an excellent wine, but I feel it would have deserved greater concentration and length to merit an outstanding rating. It is the best wine in the Comte de Vogüé's stable in 1988, and revealed an attractive medium ruby color, spicy, toasty oak, a fragrant, berry-scented bouquet, and supple, nicely balanced flavors. However, it did not seem exciting when compared to the finest wines of the vintage.

LENI VOLPATO (CHAMBOLLE-MUSIGNY)

1988 BOURGOGNE PASSE-TOUT-GRAINS	87
1988 CHAMBOLLE-MUSIGNY	85

Volpato is a wizard when it comes to making wine, and it is very unfortunate that he does not own any Premiers Crus or Grands Crus. Volpato's Bourgogne Passe-Tout-Grains is the most amazing wine I have ever tasted from this appellation. It exhibits a dazzling level of rich, red fruits, spicy herbs, and the scent of tomatoes, plums, and thyme. In the mouth, it is gloriously rich, soft, and ideal for drinking over the next

4–5 years. This wonderful wine is probably the single best value in all of Burgundy. Curiously, Volpato's Chambolle-Musigny, which is rich, long, and deep, appears to have less complexity than his Bourgogne Passe-Tout-Grains. Both these wines should be consumed over the next 4–5 years.

1988 WHITE BURGUNDY

If rain was the undoing of the 1987 white burgundies, overproduction is the reason why so many 1988 white burgundies lack depth and concentration. It is a good vintage by today's standards as the grapes were healthy. However, excessive yields make this a vintage that is not comparable to the white burgundies produced from the 1985 or 1986 vintages. The wines have surprisingly good acidity, but they all seem to lack the depth and complexity expected of top white burgundies.

There are some successes, not unexpectedly, from the Domaine Leflaive in Puligny-Montrachet, Lequin-Roussot, André Ramonet, Michel Niellon, Jean-Noël Gagnard, and the Château de la Maltroye.

In Meursault, the gigantic yields were too much for the producers to handle, and while there were a number of good wines, there were very few superb ones. Perhaps the best wines, although they were not yet bottled when I tasted them, will come from Jean-François Coche-Dury and the Comte Lafon. However, I doubt even their wines will approach the quality of vintages such as 1985 or 1986.

Among the *négociants*, I thought the white wines of Joseph Drouhin, Louis Latour, and Louis Jadot were adequately concentrated and well made in 1988. While not the rivals of their 1985s or 1986s, they will certainly be as good as the fine array of wines produced in 1982.

Most of the 1988 white burgundies should last for up to a decade because of their good acidity, but I suspect they will actually have to be drunk young because their fruit content is substantial. All things considered, 1988 is a good vintage that could have been excellent to outstanding if the growers had kept their yields at more conservative levels.

RECOMMENDED PRODUCERS

J. F. Coche-Dury
Joseph Drouhin
J. A. Ferret
Château Fuissé

Jean-Noël Gagnard
Albert Grivault
Louis Jadot
Comte Lafon

Louis Latour
Domaine Leflaive
Lequin-Roussot
Château de la Maltroye

Michel Niellon
Paul Pernot
Ramonet
Étienne Sauzet

1989—*Red Burgundy*. Most of the white wines from the 1989 vintage will not be released until 1991, and the reds late 1991 and early 1992. However, this vintage does have exciting potential. The whole cycle of maturity was early due to a very warm, balmy month of April. Blossoming began in the beginning of June, and the harvest officially commenced on September 13, the earliest date since 1976. Although the summer was unbelievably hot and dry, there was sufficient rain in Burgundy to maintain the maturity process and prevent the skins from becoming too thick (and the wines too tannic, as in 1976). The Pinot Noir was harvested in extraordinarily healthy condition (as in 1985), but with sugar readings that would produce remarkable wines of 12.2% to 14.2% natural alcohol. The yields were much higher than expected for Pinot Noir. Consequently, the quality should vary from very good to exceptional. Many growers and oenologists claim that the 1989 vintage may not only equal 1985 and 1988, but may actually surpass 1959, a vintage that produced massive wines with high levels of extract. The wines are low in acidity, but do have plenty of tannin, great color, and high alcohol contents. The reports of high yields are, however, a cause for concern.

White Burgundy. When the prices for white burgundy jumped by 97% at the famous Hospices de Beaune auction in November, 1989, it was an indication of the high expectations for the Chardonnay grape in 1989. Incredibly hot weather sent the Chardonnay's sugars soaring, producing wines with a natural alcohol content between 13%–14.5%. The crop size for Chardonnay was much lower than expected, particularly in Meursault where many producers claimed they produced the greatest wines in over 30 years. The wines are soft and very heady, with high glycerin levels. They are extremely full bodied, and low in acidity, but are exceptionally flavored and ideal for drinking within their first 7–8 years of life. 1989 should be the kind of vintage that will leave white burgundy enthusiasts in awe of the concentration and complexity of the wines. However, it is unlikely to be a vintage that will age gracefully past 10 years. The hysteria over the generally accepted belief that 1989 is the finest vintage for white burgundy since 1966 has caused prices to reach absurdly high levels.

STAR RATINGS OF
THE GROWERS
AND PRODUCERS

(*Note:* Where a producer has been assigned a range of stars in Part I, ***–**** for example, the lower rating has been used for placement in this hierarchy.)

*****(OUTSTANDING PRODUCERS)*

Domaine J. F. Coche-Dury (Meursault)
Domaine René et Vincent Dauvissat (Chablis)
Domaine Pierre Dugat (Gevrey-Chambertin)
Domaine Dujac (Morey St.-Denis)
Joseph Faiveley (Nuits St.-Georges)
Domaine J. A. Ferret (Fuissé)
Château Fuissé (Fuissé)
Domaine Jean Gros (Vosne-Romanée)
Domaine Henri Jayer (Vosne-Romanée)
Domaine Comte Lafon (Meursault)
Domaine Philippe Leclerc (Gevrey-Chambertin)

Domaine Leflaive (Puligny-Montrachet)
Domaine Leroy (Vosne-Romanée)
Hubert Lignier (Morey St.-Denis)
Domaine Mugneret-Gibourg (Vosne-Romanée)
Domaine Michel Niellon (Chassagne-Montrachet)
Domaine Ramonet (Chassagne-Montrachet)
Domaine François et Jean-Marie Raveneau (Chablis)
Domaine de la Romanée-Conti (Vosne-Romanée)
Domaine Georges Roumier (Chambolle-Musigny)
Domaine Étienne Sauzet (Puligny-Montrachet)

****(EXCELLENT PRODUCERS)

Domaine Bertrand Ambroise (Prémeaux)
Amiot-Bonfils (Chassagne-Montrachet)
Domaine Robert Ampeau (Meursault)
Domaine de l'Arlot (Prémeaux)
Domaine Comte Armand (Pommard)
Domaine Robert Arnoux (Vosne-Romanée)
Domaine Denis Bachelet (Gevrey-Chambertin)
Domaine Jean-Claude Bachelet (Saint-Aubin)
Domaine Ballot-Millot (Meursault)
Domaine Barthod-Noëllat (Chambolle-Musigny)
Domaine Charles et Paul Bavard (Puligny-Montrachet)
Domaine Adrien Belland (Santenay)
Domaine René Berrod-Les Roches du Vivier (Fleurie)
Domaine Pierre Bertheau (Chambolle-Musigny)
Domaine Besancenot-Mathouillet (Beaune)
Domaine Pierre Bitouzet (Savigny-Lès-Beaune)
Domaine Simon Bize et Fils (Savigny-Lès-Beaune)
Domaine Blain-Gagnard (Chassagne-Montrachet)
Domaine Pierre Boillot (Meursault)
Domaine André Bonhomme (Viré)
Domaine Bonneau du Martray (Pernand-Vergelesses)
Domaine Jean-Marc Bouley (Volnay)
Bourée Père et Fils (Gevrey-Chambertin)
Domaine Guy Braillon (Chénas)
Domaine des Brureaux (Chénas)
Domaine Georges Bryczek (Morey St.-Denis)
Alain Burguet (Gevrey-Chambertin)
Domaine Jacques Cacheux-Blée et Fils (Vosne-Romanée)
Roger Caillot et Fils (Meursault)

Domaine Guy Castagnier (Morey St.-Denis)
Domaine Cathiard-Molinier (Vosne-Romanée)
Château de Chambolle-Musigny (Chambolle-Musigny)
Domaine Champagnon (Chénas)
Domaine de la Chanaise (Villié-Morgon)
Domaine Chandon de Briailles (Savigny-Lès-Beaune)
Chanut Frères (Romanèche-Thorins)
Domaine Jean Chartron (Puligny-Montrachet)
Château de la Charrière (Santenay)
Domaine Jean Chauvenet (Nuits St.-Georges)
Domaine des Chazelles (Viré)
Domaine Georges et Michel Chevillon (Nuits St.-Georges)
Robert Chevillon (Nuits St.-Georges)
Domaine Georges Chicotot (Nuits St.-Georges)
Domaine Michel Chignard (Fleurie)
Domaine Daniel Chopin-Groffier (Prémeaux)
Domaine Bruno Clair (Marsannay)
Domaine Fernand Coffinet (Chassagne-Montrachet)
Domaine Marc Colin (Chassagne-Montrachet)
Domaine Michel Colin (Chassagne-Montrachet)
Domaine Jean Collet (Chablis)
Domaine J. Confuron-Cotetidot (Vosne-Romanée)
Domaine Dalicieux (Lavernette)
Domaine Georges Deléger (Chassagne-Montrachet)
Jacques Depagneux (Villefranche sur Sâone)
Domaine des Deux Roches (Davayé)
Domaine Diochon (Romanèche-Thorins)
Joseph Drouhin (Beaune)
Georges Duboeuf (Romanèche-Thorins)
Domaine P. Dubreuil-Fontaine et Fils (Pernand-Vergelesses)
Domaine Maurice Ecard et Fils (Savigny-Lès-Beaune)
Domaine René Engel (Vosne-Romanée)
Domaine M. Frédéric Esmonin (Gevrey-Chambertin)
Domaine Michel Esmonin (Gevrey-Chambertin)
Domaine Jean Faurois (Vosne-Romanée)
Pierre Ferraud et Fils (Belleville)
Domaine Fontaine-Gagnard (Chassagne-Montrachet)
Domaine Jean-Noël Gagnard (Chassagne-Montrachet)
Domaine Jean Garaudet (Pommard)
Domaine Michel Gaunoux (Pommard)
Domaine Pierre Gelin (Fixin)
Domaine Jacques Germain (Chorey-Lès-Beaune)

Domaine Armand Girardin (Pommard)

Domaine Bertrand de Gramont (Nuits St.-Georges)

Machard de Gramont (Nuits St.-Georges)

Château de la Greffière (La Roche Vineuse)

Domaine Albert Grivault (Meursault)

Domaine Jean Grivot (Vosne-Romanée)

Domaine Robert Groffier (Morey St.-Denis)

Domaine Gros Frère et Soeur (Vosne-Romanée)

Domaine Guffens-Heynen (Vergisson)

Domaine Haegelen-Jayer (Vosne-Romanée)

Domaine Hospices de Beaune (Beaune)

Domaine Hospices de Nuits (Nuits St.-Georges)

Louis Jadot (Beaune)

Domaine Jacky Janodet (Romanèche-Thorins)

Domaine Robert Jayer-Gilles (Magny-Les-Villers)

Domaine François Jobard (Meursault)

Domaine Joblot (Givry)

Domaine Philippe Joliet (Fixin)

Domaine Jean Lathuilière (Cercié)

Domaine René Leclerc (Gevrey-Chambertin)

Domaine François Legros (Nuits St.-Georges)

Leroy *(Négociant)* (Auxey-Duresses)

Domaine A. Long-Depaquit (Chablis)

Domaine du Duc de Magenta (Chassagne-Montrachet)

Château de la Maltroye (Chassagne-Montrachet)

Domaine Manciat-Poncet (Charnay-Lès-Mâcon)

Domaine Manière-Noirot (Vosne-Romanée)

Domaine Jean Marechal (Mercurey)

Domaine Maume (Gevrey-Chambertin)

Domaine Méo-Camuzet (Vosne-Romanée)

Domaine Louis Michel/Domaine de la Tour Vaubourg (Chablis)

Domaine René Michel (Clessé)

Domaine Alain Michelot (Nuits St.-Georges)

Domaine Michelot-Buisson (Meursault)

Domaine de la Monette (Mercurey)

Domaine Mongeard-Mugneret (Vosne-Romanée)

Domaine Jean Monnier et Fils (Meursault)

Domaine Jean-Pierre Monnot (Puligny-Montrachet)

Domaine Hubert de Montille (Volnay)

Domaine Bernard Morey (Chassagne-Montrachet)

Domaine Jean-Marc Morey (Chassagne-Montrachet)

Domaine Pierre Morey (Meursault)

Domaine Albert Morot (Beaune)
Château du Moulin-à-Vent (Romanèche-Thorins)
Domaine André Mussy (Pommard)
Domaine Gilles Noblet (Fuissé)
Domaine Alain Passot (Chiroubles)
Domaine Paul Pernot (Puligny-Montrachet)
Domaine Pernin-Rossin (Vosne-Romanée)
Domaine André Philippon (Fleys)
Domaine Pitoiset-Urena (Meursault)
Domaine Ponsot (Morey St.-Denis)
Domaine Pothier-Rieusset (Pommard)
Domaine de la Pousse d'Or (Volnay)
Domaine Prieur-Brunet (Santenay)
Domaine Bernard Rion Père et Fils (Vosne-Romanée)
Domaine Daniel Rion (Nuits St.-Georges)
Domaine Joseph Roty (Gevrey-Chambertin)
Domaine Guy Roulot (Meursault)
Domaine Armand Rousseau (Gevrey-Chambertin)
Domaine Ruet (Cercié)
Domaine de Rully Saint Michel (Rully)
Domaine Jean-Louis Santé (La Chapelle de Guinchay)
Château de la Saule (Montagny)
Domaine Savoye (Villié-Morgon)
Domaine Christian Serafin (Gevrey-Chambertin)
Domaine Jean Tardy (Vosne-Romanée)
Domaine Philippe Testut (Chablis)
Domaine Jean Thevenet (Quintaine-Clessé)
Domaine Tollot-Beaut et Fils (Chorey-Lès-Beaune)
Château de la Tour (Vougeot)
Domaine J. Truchot-Martin (Morey St.-Denis)
Domaine A. P. de Villaine (Bouzeron)
Domaine Michel Voarick (Aloxe-Corton)
Domaine Robert Vocoret et Fils (Chablis)

*** (GOOD PRODUCERS)

Pierre Amiot et Fils (Morey St.-Denis)
Domaine Pierre André (Aloxe-Corton)
Domaine Marquis d'Angerville (Volnay)
Auvigue-Burrier-Revel (Charnay-Lès-Mâcon)
Domaine L. Bassy (Odenas)
Château du Basty (Lantignié)

Paul Beaudet (Pontenevaux)
Château de Beauregard (Fuissé)
Domaine Joseph Belland (Santenay)
Domaine Gérard Berger (Cheilly-Lès-Maranges)
Domaine Bernard (Fleurie)
Domaine Pierre Bernollin (Jully-Lès-Buxy)
Domaine Bertagna (Vougeot)
Domaine Denis Berthaut (Fixin)
Domaine André Besson (Solutré-Pouilly)
Domaine Bitouzet-Prieur (Volnay)
Domaine Marcel Bocquenet (Nuits St.-Georges)
Domaine Henri Boillot (Pommard)
Domaine Lucien Boillot (Gevrey-Chambertin)
Domaine Boisson-Vadot (Meursault)
Domaine Bonnot-Lamblot (Savigny-Lès-Beaune)
Domaine Bordeaux-Montrieux (Mercurey)
Domaine Bouillard (Chiroubles)
Domaine Georges Boulon (Chiroubles)
Domaine Denis Boussey (Monthélie)
Domaine Boyer-Martenot (Meursault)
Domaine Jean-Claude Brelière (Rully)
Domaine Bressand (Pouilly-Fuissé)
Domaine Michel Briday (Rully)
Domaine A. Buisson-Battault (Meursault)
Domaine Camus (Gevrey-Chambertin)
Domaine Luc Camus (Savigny-Lès-Beaune)
Domaine Capitain-Gagnerot (Ladoix-Serrigny)
Domaine Capron-Manieux (Savigny-Lès-Beaune)
Domaine Louis Carillon (Puligny-Montrachet)
Domaine de la Cave Lamartine (Saint-Amour Bellevue)
Caves des Vignerons de Buxy (Buxy)
Domaine Ceci (Vougeot)
Domaine Yves Chaley (Curtil-Vergy)
Champy Père (Beaune)
Domaine Émile Chandesais (Fontaines)
Domaine Chanson Père et Fils (Beaune)
Domaine Maurice Chapuis (Aloxe-Corton)
Domaine François Charles (Nantoux)
Domaine Philippe Charlopin-Parizot (Marsannay)
Domaine Jean-Marc Charmet (Le Breuil)
Chartron et Trébuchet (Puligny-Montrachet)
Château de Chassagne-Montrachet (Chassagne-Montrachet)

F. Chauvenet (Nuits St.-Georges)
Domaine Anne-Marie Chavy (Puligny-Montrachet)
Domaine Paul Chevrot (Cheilly-Lès-Maranges)
Domaine Cheysson-Les-Fargues (Chiroubles)
Domaine Jean Chofflet (Russily)
Domaine André Chopin et Fils (Comblanchien)
Domaine Michel Clair (Santenay)
Domaine Henri Clerc et Fils (Puligny-Montrachet)
Domaine Georges Clerget (Vougeot)
Domaine Michel Clerget (Vougeot)
Domaine Yvon Clerget (Volnay)
Domaine Julien Coche-Debord (Meursault)
Domaine les Colombiers (Saint-Véran)
Domaine de la Combe au Loup (Chiroubles)
Domaine de la Condemine (Mâcon-Villages/Pierre Janny)
Domaine Jean-Jacques Confuron (Prémeaux)
Cooperative la Chablisienne (Chablis)
Cooperative Clessé-la-Vigne-Blanche (Clessé)
Cooperative Igé-les-Vignerons d'Igé (Igé)
Cooperative Lugny (Lugny)
Cooperative Prissé (Prissé)
Cooperative Viré (Viré)
Domaine Coquard-Loison-Fleurot (Flagey-Echézeaux)
Domaine Roger Cordier (Fuissé)
Château de Coreaux (Leynes)
Domaine Edmond Cornu (Ladoix-Serrigny)
Domaine Coron Père et Fils (Beaune)
Domaine Guy Cotton (Odenas)
Domaine Louis Curveux (Fuissé)
Domaine Jean Dauvissat (Chablis)
Domaine Jean Defaix (Milly)
Domaine Marius Delarche (Pernand-Vergelesses)
Domaine André Depardon (Leynes)
Domaine Louis-Claude Desvignes (Villié-Morgon)
Domaine Jean-Pierre Diconne (Auxey-Duresses)
Domaine Doudet-Naudin (Savigny-Lès-Beaune)
Domaine Paul Droin (Chablis)
Domaine Drouhin-Larose (Gevrey-Chambertin)
Domaine Roger Duboeuf et Fils (Chaintré)
Domaine Duchet (Beaune)
Domaine des Ducs (Saint-Amour-Bellevue)
Dufouleur Père et Fils (Nuits St.-Georges)

Domaine Duperon (Chasselas)

Domaine Raymond Dupuis (Coulanges la Vineuse)

Domaine Jean et Yves Durand (Régnié-Durette)

Domaine Dureuil-Janthial (Rully)

Domaine de l'Eglantière (Maligny)

Domaine Bernard Fèvre (Saint-Romain)

Domaine William Fèvre/Domaine de la Maladière/Ancien Domaine
    Auffray (Chablis)

Domaine Fichet (Volnay)

Domaine René Fleurot-Larose (Santenay)

Domaine de la Folie (Rully)

Domaine André Forest (Vergisson)

Domaine Forey Père et Fils (Vosne-Romanée)

Domaine G. A. E. C. de Chantemerle (La Chapelle-Vaupelteigne)

Domaine G. F. A. de Combiaty (Saint-Étienne la Varenne)

Domaine Gagnard-Delagrange (Chassagne-Montrachet)

Domaine Michel Gaidon (Romanèche-Thorins)

Domaine du Gardin-Clos Salomon (Givry)

Domaine Gay Père et Fils (Chorey-Lès-Beaune)

Domaine Geantet-Pansiot (Gevrey-Chambertin)

Château Génot Boulanger (Meursault)

Domaine Alain Geoffroy (Beines)

Domaine Lucien Geoffroy (Gevrey-Chambertin)

Domaine de la Gérarde (Régnié-Durette)

Domaine François Gerbet (Vosne-Romanée)

Domaine Henri Germain (Meursault)

Maison Jean Germain (Meursault)

Domaine Émilian Gillet (Mâcon)

Domaine Bernard Glantenay (Volnay)

Gobet (Blaceret)

Domaine Laurent Goillot (Bernollin)

Domaine René Gonon (Juliénas)

Domaine Michel Goubard (Saint-Desert)

Château du Grand Vernay (Charentay)

Domaine des Grandes Bruyères (Saint-Étienne-des-Oullières)

Domaine des Granges (Chaintré)

Domaine Alain Gras (Saint-Romain)

Domaine Henri-Lucius Gregoire (Davayé)

Groupement de Producteurs de Prissé (Prissé)

Domaine Pierre Guillemot (Savigny-Lès-Beaune)

Domaine Heresztyn (Gevrey-Chambertin)

Domaine Alain Hudelot-Noëllot (Vougeot)

Domaine Bernard Hudelot-Verdel (Villars-Fontaine)

Domaine Lucien Jacob (Echevronne)

Château des Jacques (Romanèche-Thorins)

Paul et Henri Jacqueson (Rully)

Jaffelin (Beaune)

Domaine Georges Jayer (Vosne-Romanée)

Domaine Jacqueline Jayer (Vosne-Romanée)

Domaine Jeannin-Naltet Père et Fils (Mercurey)

Domaine Georges Jobert (Mâcon)

Domaine Jean Joliot et Fils (Nantoux)

Domaine Michel Juillot (Mercurey)

Château de Juliénas (Juliénas)

Labouré-Roi (Nuits St.-Georges)

Domaine Michel Lafarge (Volnay)

Domaine Lafouge (Auxey-Duresses)

Domaine Laleure-Piot (Pernand-Vergelesses)

Domaine Lamarche (Vosne-Romanée)

Domaine Hubert Lamy (Saint-Aubin)

Domaine Edmund Laneyrie (Solutré)

Domaine Hubert Lapierre (La Chapelle de Guinchay)

Domaine Laroche (Chablis)

Domaine Roger Lassarat (Vergisson)

Louis Latour (Beaune)

Château de Latour-Bordon (Régnié-Durette)

Domaine Latour-Giraud (Meursault)

Domaine Roland Lavantureux (Lignorelles)

Olivier Leflaive Frères (Puligny-Montrachet)

Domaine Lejeune (Pommard)

Domaine Lequin-Roussot (Santenay)

Domaine Thierry Lespinasse (Givry)

Domaine Georges Lignier (Morey St.-Denis)

Loron et Fils (Pontanevaux)

Domaine Roger Luquet (Fuissé)

Lycée Agricole et Viticole (Beaune)

Domaine Michel Magnien (Morey St.-Denis)

Domaine Maillard Père et Fils (Chorey-Lès-Beaune)

Domaine la Maison (Leynes)

Domaine Michel Mallard et Fils (Ladoix-Serrigny)

Domaine Yves Marceau-Domaine de la Croix Gault (Mercurey)

Domaine Marchand-Grillot et Fils (Gevrey-Chambertin)

P. de Marcilly Frères (Beaune)

Domaine des Maronniers (Préhy)

Domaine Tim Marshall (Nuits St.-Georges)
Domaine Maurice Martin (Davayé)
Domaine René Martin (Cheilly-Lès-Maranges)
Les Vins Mathelin (Châtillon-d'Azergues)
Domaine Joseph Matrot (Meursault)
Domaine Meix Foulot (Mercurey)
Domaine Prince Florent de Mérode (Ladoix-Serrigny)
Château de Meursault (Meursault)
Domaine Bernard Meziat (Chiroubles)
Domaine Michel (Vosne-Romanée)
Domaine Bernard Michel (Saint-Vallerin)
Domaine Jean Michelot (Pommard)
Domaine Pierre Millot-Battault (Meursault)
Domaine René et Christian Miolane (Salles en Beaujolais)
Moillard (Nuits St.-Georges)
Domaine Daniel Moine-Hudelot (Chambolle-Musigny)
Château de Monthélie (Monthélie)
Domaine Marc Morey (Chassagne-Montrachet)
Domaine Denis Mortet (Gevrey-Chambertin)
Domaine Gerard Mouton (Poncey)
Domaine Gerard et René Mugneret (Vosne-Romanée)
Domaine Guy Mugnier-la-P'Tiote Cave (Chassey Le Camp)
Philippe Naddef (Couchey)
Domaine P. M. Ninot-Cellier-Meix-Guillaume (Rully)
Domaine André Nudant et Fils (Ladoix-Serrigny)
Domaine Parent (Pommard)
Domaine Parigot Père et Fils (Meloisey)
Domaine Pavelot-Glantenay (Savigny-Lès-Beaune)
Domaine André Pelletier (Juliénas)
Domaine des Perdrix (Prémeaux-Prissey)
Domaine les Perrières (Gevrey-Chambertin)
Domaine Perrin-Ponsot (Meursault)
Domaine des Pierres Blanches (Beaune)
Domaine des Pierres Rouges (Chasselas)
Domaine des Pillets (Villié-Morgon)
Domaine Paul Pillot (Chassagne-Montrachet)
Louis Pinson (Chablis)
Château de Pizay (Saint-Jean d'Ardières)
Domaine Jean Podor (Irancy)
Château de Pommard (Pommard)
Domaine de la Poulette (Corgoloin)
Domaine Maurice Prieur (Sampigny-Lès-Maranges)

Domaine du Prieuré (Lugny)
Domaine du Prieuré (Rully)
Prosper-Maufoux (Santenay)
Domaine Henri Prudhon (Saint-Aubin)
Domaine Michel Prunier (Auxey-Duresses)
Château de Raousset (Chiroubles)
Domaine Rapet Père et Fils (Pernand-Vergelesses)
Domaine Gaston et Pierre Ravaut (Ladoix-Serrigny)
Remoissenet Père et Fils (Beaune)
Domaine Henri Remoriquet (Nuits St.-Georges)
Domaine des Remparts (Saint-Bris le Vineux)
Domaine de la Rénarde (Rully)
Domaine Henri Richard (Gevrey-Chambertin)
Domaine de Roally (Viré)
Domaine Guy Robin (Chablis)
Domaine Joel Rochette (Régnié-Durette)
Antonin Rodet (Mercurey)
Ropiteau Frères (Meursault)
Domaine Michel Rossignol (Volnay)
Domaine Philippe Rossignol (Gevrey-Chambertin)
Domaine Régis Rossignol-Changarnier (Volnay)
Domaine Rougeot (Meursault)
Domaine Emmanuel Rouget (Nuits St.-Georges)
Domaine Roux Père et Fils (Saint-Aubin)
Château de Rully (Rully)
Domaine Francis Saillant (Saint-Amour)
Domaine Sainte-Claire (Prehy)
Robert Sarrau-Caves de l'Ardières (Belleville)
Domaine René Savoy (Chiroubles)
Domaine Daniel Senard (Aloxe-Corton)
Domaine Bernard Serveau (Morey St.-Denis)
Domaine Servelle-Tachot (Chambolle-Musigny)
Domaine Robert Sirugue (Vosne-Romanée)
Domaine Luc Sorin (Saint-Bris le Vineux)
Domaine Talmard (Uchizy)
Raymond et Michel Tête (Juliénas)
Domaine Thenard (Givry)
Domaine Thevenot-le-Brun et Fils (Marey-Lès-Fussey)
Domaine Gérard Tremblay-Domaine des Îles (Poinchy)
Trenel et Fils (Charnay-Lès-Mâcon)
Domaine Georges Trichard (La Chapelle de Guinchay)
Domaine Tortochot (Gevrey-Chambertin)

Domaine Jean Vachet (Saint-Vallerin)
Domaine des Varoilles (Gevrey-Chambertin)
Domaine Bernard Vaudoisey-Mutin (Volnay)
Domaine de Vauroux (Chablis)
Domaine Alain Verdet (Arcenant)
Domaine Lucien et Robert Verger (Saint-Lager)
Domaine Veuve-Steinmaier et Fils (Montagny)
Domaine Thierry Vigot (Hautes-Côtes de Nuits)
Domaine René Virely-Arcelain (Pommard)
Domaine Bernard Virely-Rougeot (Pommard)
Domaine L. Vitteau-Alberti (Rully)
Domaine Comte Georges de Vogüé (Chambolle-Musigny)
Domaine Joseph Voillot (Volnay)
Domaine Leni Volpato (Chambolle-Musigny)

**(AVERAGE PRODUCERS)

Bernard Amiot (Chambolle-Musigny)
Domaine Arlaud Père et Fils (Nuits St.-Georges)
Domaine Arnoux Père et Fils (Chorey-Lès-Beaune)
Domaine Bernard Bachelet et Fils (Dezize-Lès-Maranges)
Domaine Bachelet-Ramonet (Chassagne-Montrachet)
Château Bader-Mimeur (Chassagne-Montrachet)
Domaine André Bart (Marsannay)
Domaine Philippe Batacchi (Gevrey-Chambertin)
Domaine Alain Bernillon (Saint-Lager)
Domaine Bersan et Fils (Saint-Bris le Vineux)
Domaine Leon Bienvenu (Irancy)
Domaine Billard-Gonnet (Pommard)
Domaine Billaud-Simon (Chablis)
Domaine de Blagny (Blagny)
Domaine Blondeau-Danne (Meursault)
Domaine Guy Bocard (Meursault)
Jean-Marc Boillot (Pommard)
Domaine Lucien Boillot et Fils (Gevrey-Chambertin)
Domaine de Boischampt (Jullié)
Château de Boisfranc (Jarnioux)
Château de la Boittière (Juliénas)
Domaine René Borgeon (Jambles)
Bouchard-Aîné et Fils (Beaune)
Bouchard Père et Fils (Beaune)
Domaine Xavier Bouzerand (Monthélie)

Domaine Michel Bouzereau (Meursault)
Domaine Hubert Bouzereau-Gruère (Meursault)
Domaine Luc Brintet et Frédéric Charles (Mercurey)
Domaine Marc Brocot (Marsannay)
Domaine de la Bruyère (Romanèche-Thorins)
Château de Byonne (Charnay-Lès-Mâcon)
Domaine Lucien Camus-Bauchon (Savigny-Lès-Beaune)
Domaine Denis Carré (Meloisey)
Caves de Bailly (Saint-Bris le Vineux)
Cellier des Samsons (Quincié)
Château de la Chaize (Odenas)
Domaine du Château de Chamilly (Chamilly)
Domaine Bernard Champier (Odenas)
Domaine Chanzy Frères-Domaine de l'Hermitage (Bouzeron)
Domaine Maurice Charleux (Dezize-Lès-Maranges)
Château du Chassclas (Chasselas)
Domaine de Chervin (Burgy)
Domaine Chevalier Père et Fils (Buisson)
Domaine Thomas la Chevalière (Beaujeu)
Domaine Chouet-Clivet (Meursault)
Domaine Raoul Clerget (Saint-Aubin)
Domaine du Clos des Lambrays (Morey St.-Denis)
Domaine Michel Clunny et Fils (Brochon)
Domaine Robert Colinot (Irancy)
Domaine Evon et Chantal Contat-Grange (Cheilly-Lès-Maranges)
Cooperative Charnay-Lès-Mâcon (Charnay-Lès-Mâcon)
Cooperative Mancey (Mancey)
Château de Corcelles (Corcelles en Beaujolais)
Domaine Claude Cornu (Magny-Lès-Villers)
Domaine Corsin (Pouilly-Fuissé)
Domaine des Courtis (Milly)
Domaine Gérard Creusefond (Auxey-Duresses)
Domaine Pierre Damoy (Gevrey-Chambertin)
Domaine Darnat (Meursault)
Domaine David et Foillard (St.-Georges de Reneins)
Domaine Robert et Philippe Defrance (Saint-Bris le Vineux)
Domaine Amédée Degrange (Chénas)
Domaine Roger Delaloge (Irancy)
Domaine Denis Père et Fils (Pernand-Vergelesses)
Domaine Desplace Frère (Régnié-Durette)
Domaine Gérard Doreau (Monthélie)
Domaine Marcel Duplessis (Chablis)

Domaine Guillemard Dupont et Fils (Meloisey)

Domaine Michel Dupont-Fahn (Meursault)

Domaine Dupont-Tisserandot (Gevrey-Chambertin)

Domaine René Durand (Comblanchien)

Domaine Jacques Durand-Roblot (Fixin)

Domaine G. Duvernay (Rully)

Domaine Gabriel Fournier (Meursault)

Domaine Jean-Claude Fourrier (Gevrey-Chambertin)

Domaine Marcel et Bernard Fribourg (Villers la Faye)

Domaine G. A. E. C. du Colombier (Fontenay)

Domaine Paul Gauthier (Blacé)

Geisweiler et Fils (Nuits St.-Georges)

Domaine Louis Genillon (Villié-Morgon)

Domaine Maurice et Jean-Michel Giboulot (Savigny-Lès-Beaune)

Domaine Girard-Vollot et Fils (Savigny-Lès-Beaune)

Domaine Henri Gouges (Nuits St.-Georges)

Domaine de la Grand Cour (Fleurie)

Domaine Anne-Françoise Gros (Vosne-Romanée)

Domaine Claudius Guerin (Odenas)

Domaine René Guerin (Vergisson)

Domaine Guillot (Mâcon)

Domaine Jean Guitton (Bligny-Lès-Beaune)

Domaine Antonin Guyon (Savigny-Lès-Beaune)

Domaine Hubert Guyot-Veripot (Rully)

Château Philippe le Hardi (Santenay)

Domaine des Hautes-Cornières (Santenay)

Domaine André l'Heritier (Chagny)

Domaine l'Heritier-Guyot (Dijon)

Domaine Huguenot Père et Fils (Marsannay)

Domaine Frederick Humbert (Gevrey-Chambertin)

Jaboulet-Vercherre (Beaune)

Domaine Patrick Javillier (Meursault)

Domaine Jessiaume Père et Fils (Santenay)

Domaine Jean-Luc Joillot-Porcheray (Pommard)

Domaine Pierre Jomard (Fleurieux Sur l'Arbresle)

Château des Labourons (Fleurie)

Domaine André et Bernard Labry (Melin)

Château de Lacarelle (Saint-Étienne-des-Ouillières)

Domaine Henri Lafarge (Bray)

Domaine Lahaye Père et Fils (Pommard)

Lamblin et Fils (Maligny)

Domaine Lamy-Pillot (Santenay)

Domaine Larue (Saint-Aubin)

Domaine Henri Latour (Auxey-Duresses)

Domaine de Levant (Saint-Étienne-La Varenne)

Domaine Lumpp Frères (Givry)

Lupé-Cholet (Nuits St.-Georges)

Domaine Henri Magnien (Gevrey-Chambertin)

Domaine des Malandes (Chablis)

Domaine Maldant (Chorey-Lès-Beaune)

Domaine Maroslavac-Léger (Chassagne-Montrachet)

Domaine Mathias (Chaintré)

Domaine Mazilly Père et Fils (Meloisey)

Domaine Louis Menand Père et Fils (Mercurey)

Château de Mercey (Cheilly-Lès-Maranges)

Domaine Mestre Père et Fils (Santenay)

Domaine M. Millet (Montagny)

Domaine Raymond Millot et Fils (Meursault)

P. Misserey (Nuits St.-Georges)

Domaine René Monnier (Meursault)

Domaine de Montbellet (Lugny)

Domaine Monthélie-Douhairet (Monthélie)

Domaine Henri Morconi (Puligny-Montrachet)

Domaine Bernard Moreau (Chassagne-Montrachet)

Domaine Jean Moreau (Santenay)

J. Moreau et Fils (Chablis)

Domaine Jean Mortet (Romanèche-Thorins)

Domaine Mosnier-Sylvain (Chablis)

Domaine Gabriel Muskovac (Pernand-Vergelesses)

Domaine Henri Naudin-Ferrand (Magny-Lès-Villers)

Domaine Newman (Morey St.-Denis)

Domaine Jean Pascal et Fils (Puligny-Montrachet)

Pasquier-Desvignes (Saint-Lager)

Patriarche Père et Fils (Beaune)

Baron Patrick (Chablis)

Domaine Pavelot (Pernand-Vergelesses)

Domaine Pavillon de Chavannes (Quincié)

Domaine Joseph Pellerin (Saint-Georges de Reneins)

Domaine Noël Perrin (Culles Les Roches)

Domaine Henri Perrot-Minot (Morey St.-Denis)

Piat Père et Fils (La Chapelle de Guichay)

Château de Pierreux (Odenas)

Domaine Fernand Pillot (Chassagne-Montrachet)

Domaine Michel Pouhin-Seurre (Meursault)

Jacques Prieur (Meursault)
Domaine du Prieuré (Savigny-Lès-Beaune)
Domaine Propriete des Vignes (Poncey)
Domaine Maurice Protheau et Fils (Mercurey)
Domaine Roger Prunier (Auxey-Duresses)
Max Quenot Fils et Meuneveaux (Aloxe-Corton)
Domaine Charles Quillardet (Gevrey-Chambertin)
Quinson (Fleurie)
Domaine Ragot (Poncey)
Domaine Rebougeon-Muré (Pommard)
Domaine Henri Rebourseau (Gevrey-Chambertin)
A. Regnard et Fils (Chablis)
La Reine Pedauque (Aloxe-Corton)
Domaine Louis Remy (Gevrey-Chambertin)
Domaine Riger-Briset (Puligny-Montrachet)
Domaine de la Roche (Saint-Véran)
Domaine André la Rochette (Chanes)
Domaine Maurice Rollin Père et Fils (Pernand-Vergelesses)
Domaine Hervé Roumier (Chamboulle-Musigny)
Domaine Michel du Roure (Davayé)
Domaine Roy Frères (Auxey-Duresses)
Domaine Roy Père et Fils (Gevrey-Chambertin)
Domaine du Ruyère (Villié-Morgon)
Domaine Fabian et Louis Saier (Mercurey)
Paul Sapin (Lancié)
Domaine Maurice et Hervé Sigaut (Chambolle-Musigny)
Domaine Simon Fils (Marey-Lès-Fussey)
Simonnet-Febvre et Fils (Chablis)
Domaine de la Sorbière (Quincié)
Domaine Albert Sotheir (Saint-Etienne-la-Varenne)
Domaine Suremain (Mercurey)
Domaine Taupenot Père et Fils (Saint-Romain)
Domaine René Thevenin-Monthélie et Fils (Saint-Romain)
Château Thivin (Denas)
Domaine Gérard Thomas (Saint-Aubin)
Domaine Francis Tomatis et Fils (Chiroubles)
Domaine de la Tour Bajole (Saint-Maurice Les Couches)
Château des Tours (Saint-Étienne la Varenne)
Domaine Louis Trapet (Gevrey-Chambertin)
Domaine Michel Tribolet (Fleurie)
Domaine G. Vachet-Rousseau (Gevrey-Chambertin)
Domaine Valls-Laboureau (Couches)

Domaine des Velanges (Davayé)
Domaine des Vignes des Demoiselles (Nolay)
Domaine Henri de Villamont (Savigny-Lès-Beaune)
Vins Dessalle (Saint-Jean d'Ardières)
Vins Fessy (Saint-Jean d'Ardières)
Domaine Émile Voarick (Saint-Martin Sous Montaigu)
Domaine Alain Voegeli (Gevrey-Chambertin)
Domaine du Vuril (Charentay)
André Ziltener Père et Fils (Gevrey-Chambertin)

*(OTHER PRODUCERS)

Albert Bichot (Beaune)
Jean-Claude Boisset (Nuits St.-Georges)
Château Cambon (Saint-Jean d'Ardières)
Domaine Bernard Cantin (Irancy)
G. A. E. C. du Clos du Roi (Coulanges la Vineuse)

Some of the material in this book is based upon tastings and research done by Robert Parker in conjunction with the publishing of *The Wine Advocate,* an independent consumer's guide to fine wine that is issued six times a year. A one-year subscription to *The Wine Advocate* costs $35.00 for delivery in the continental United States, $40.00 for Canada, and $65.00 for air-mail delivery anywhere in the world. Subscriptions or a sample copy may be obtained by writing to The Wine Advocate, P.O. Box 311, Monkton, MD 21111, or by fax, 301-357-4504.

INDEX

(Page numbers in **boldface** refer to main entries in Growers and Producers section. Page numbers in *italic* refer to maps.)